AF654929

biztantra
Management for the Flat World!

HOUGHTON MIFFLIN

A Note for the Reader

Introducing the "GLOCAL" TEXT Editions from Biztantra, the next level of adaptation publishing for the student community

dia has been a beacon of progress and foreign investment in the recent years. We have been growing a rate of over 8% annually in our GDP estimates. With almost all of the Fortune 500 companies tting up operations in our country, the need and demand for management students is reaching an all-ne high. In order to meet this growing need, all leading management institutes are instilling the proach of "Glocal" education – i.e. Global + Local perspectives.

In 2004, Biztantra and Houghton Mifflin (HMCo) published India's first ever adaptation program vering the entire spectrum of management education. It is a matter of pride that over 75,000 anagement students have embraced our product line since its launch. It is also gratifying to know that e Indian Institutes of Management have also adopted these adaptations.

We have been researching the need for Indian content in foreign textbooks for over four years. We lieve that Indian students are now much more sophisticated, globally aware, and cognizant of the obal brands and companies, compared to just a few years ago. Equally important, these students are vare of the Indian companies which are making rapid strides on the global scene.

To meet the needs of these students, we at Biztantra and HMCo are now pleased to introduce the first er *Glocal Texts* range in India. This is another testament to Biztantra's innovative team and its strong artnership with Boston-based Houghton Mifflin Co. HMCo is a leader in academic publishing in the US ith revenues of over $1.3 US billion. The *Glocal Texts* are Indian adaptations of these HMCo textbooks ith the right blend of both Indian and International case studies. The *Glocal Texts* give Indian students e right mix of what needs to be learnt from Indian companies as well as imbibing the wisdom of global rporations. Hence, it will be a textbook range with a "Glocal Perspective".

It is a matter of pleasure that the works of world's leading academicians and celebrated authors such s A Parasuraman, Ricky Griffin, Charles Hill, Gareth Jones will be published under the *Glocal Texts* nge.

These titles will be adapted by a team of highly capable Indian professors taken from IIM Bangalore, dian Institute of Foreign Trade and International Management Institute to name a few. At the same me we have also recruited young and budding academicians who are from a select group of private BA institutes in order to bridge the gap between the top 10 and the upcoming institutions of tomorrow.

The first set of books will cover the areas of Strategic Management, Financial Accounting, Marketing esearch, OB, Consumer Behavior, Microeconomics, Global Marketing and International Management. ther areas too will shortly follow.

We sincerely hope that the *Glocal Texts* will touch a chord with Indian students and might redefine anagement learning. We would be happy to receive your comments and suggestions and ideas at ahul@dreamtechbt.com.

Best regards,

Rahul Gupta
CEO, Biztantra

Timothy J. Cullen
Manager (Rights & International Business)
Houghton Mifflin Company

Features that integrate **Hot Topics** and **Engage Students**

Interactive Annotations

Interactive annotations link the textbook and the Internet to create a dynamic, instructive, and interesting learning tool. They include contemporary anecdotes, quotations, self-assessment tools, and thought-provoking questions that give students opportunities to practice and sharpen their conceptual skills, self-management and teamwork skills, and administrative skills. Students can visit their textbook website for an interpretation of the annotations. **http://business.college.hmco.com/students/** (select Kreitner, *Management,* 10e)

the changing workplace

These chapter-opening cases focus on current real-world managers and organizations to draw students into many of the issues covered in the chapter.

- Can the 10-Day Sofa Save American Jobs? (Ch. 1)
- The Survivor (Ch. 2)
- Home Depot Goes Old School (Ch. 3)
- MTV's Passage to India (Ch. 4)
- Money and Morals at GE (Ch. 5)
- Plan B (and C and D and...) (Ch. 6)
- Starbucks Tries to Hum a New Strategic Tune (Ch. 7)
- The Stats Wonk Who Runs a Pro Sports Team (Ch. 8)
- Southwest Finds Trouble in the Air (Ch. 9)
- Business NOT as Usual at W. L. Gore: Part 1 (see the Closing Case in Chapter 15 for Part 2) (Ch. 10)
- Finding Workers Who Fit (Ch. 11)
- How to Start Turning Around a Behemoth (Ch. 12)
- Pat McGovern Motivates Through Respect (Ch. 13)
- Do Business and Friendship Mix in the Workplace? (Ch. 14)
- eBay's Secret Weapon (Ch. 15)
- What CEO Anne M. Mulcahy Learned From Turning Around Xerox (Ch. 16)
- Ronald Gets Back in Shape (Ch. 17)

THE GLOBAL MANAGER

Focusing on this crucial AACSB-mandated topic, these boxed inserts recognize that the world is shrinking rapidly and that students must understand the global nature of the business environment.

- Your Custom Car Is Ready (Ch. 2)
- Culture Affects How Planning and Control Are Perceived: Russian versus Western Views (Ch. 6)
- The Ultimate Fairly Inexpensive Driving Machine (Ch. 7)
- A Globe-Trotting Organizational Thinker Looks at the Future of Work Organizations (Ch. 10)
- Paying Employees to Go on a Global Search for Self-Actualization (Ch. 13)
- How Dell Survived a Global Supply Chain Crisis (Ch. 17)

MANAGEMENT ETHICS

Addressing another AACSB-mandated topic, these boxes focus on the importance of ethical decision making. Chapter 5 addresses the issues of ethics and social responsibility in detail.

- PNC Financial Services Recycles Its Old Building (Ch.1)
- MBAs Majoring in Morality (Ch. 5)
- Should We Admire Wal-Mart? (Ch. 9)
- Keeping Blogs in Check (Ch. 12)
- How Do You Feel About "Hard Ball" Organizational Politics? (Ch. 14)

MANAGING DIVERSITY

This third AACSB-mandated topic is covered thoroughly in Chapters 3 and 11 as well as being integrated throughout the text. These boxes also draw attention to the importance of valuing diversity in the contemporary workplace.

- Finally in the Director's Chair (Ch. 3)
- Dealing with Religion in the U.S. Workplace (Ch. 4)
- Are You a Biased Decision Maker? (Ch. 8)
- Diversity Goes Global (Ch. 11)
- A Native American's Vision for a Better Future (Ch. 15)
- Tempered Radicals As Everyday Leaders (Ch. 16)

SKILLS & TOOLS

This text puts a big emphasis on skill development and preparing students to be tomorrow's managers. This end-of-chapter feature is just one of many places students will find how-to tips and instructions.

- Career Tips for Today's and Tomorrow's Managers (Ch. 1)
- Recommended Periodicals for Staying Current in the Field of Management (Ch. 2)
- How Business Leaders Can Help Women Break the Glass Ceiling (Ch. 3)
- Competencies You Need to Develop to Work Effectively in a Foreign Culture (Ch. 4)
- An International Code of Ethics (Ch. 5)
- Ten Common Errors to Avoid When Writing a Plan for a New Business (Ch. 6)
- Reengineering (Ch. 7)
- How to Construct a Fishbone Diagram (Ch. 8)
- How to Build Your Organization's Learning Capability (Ch. 9)
- If You Want to Be Delegated Important Duties, Then Demonstrate a Lot of Initiative (Ch. 10)
- How to Handle the Job Interview Successfully (Ch. 11)
- How You Speak Shows How You Rank (Ch. 12)
- Stress Management 101 (Ch. 13)
- How to Use Cooperative Conflict to Avoid Groupthink (Ch. 14)
- Putting the Empowerment Puzzle Together (Ch. 15)
- How to Express Anger (Ch. 16)
- How to Avoid a Public Relations Nightmare in a Crisis (Ch. 17)

CLOSING CASE

Like The Changing Workplace feature at the beginning of each chapter, these concluding cases show students additional real-world examples as a context for solving problems.

- Sudhakar Ghate: An Enterpreneur by Choice (Ch. 1)
- Mr Soni (Ch. 2)
- Innovations at Wipro (Ch. 3)
- A Clash of Cultures (Ch. 4)
- Reviving Khadi in India (Ch. 5)
- Ford's Hybrid SUV Team Races to the Finish (Ch. 6)
- The Loyal Employee (Ch. 7)
- Hindustan Motors' Struggle for Survival (Ch. 8)
- Change Management @ ICICI (Ch. 9)
- A Virtually Great New Business for UPS (Ch. 10)
- Indian Airlines - HR Problems (Ch. 11)
- Communication Gap (Ch. 12)
- The Taj's People Philosophy and STAR System (Ch. 13)
- The Sales Girls (Ch. 14)
- Leadership Style (Ch. 15)
- Exit of Reddy (Ch. 16)
- Pristine International (Ch. 17)

TEST PREPPER

These short quizzes are found at the end of each chapter and include ten true-false and ten multiple-choice questions (with answers at the end of the book).

Management

About the Author

Robert ("Bob") Kreitner is Professor Emeritus of Management at Arizona State University (ASU). After a 26-y career at ASU, Bob was named to the University's W. P. Carey School of Business Faculty Hall of Fame. He recei bachelor's and master's degrees in business from the University of Nebraska, Omaha and a PhD in business fr the University of Nebraska-Lincoln. He has taught at UNO, UNL, Western Illinois University, Thunderbird, a ASU, as well as in Micronesia, Albania, and Switzerland. He is the author or co-author of six college textbooks t have been through a total of 23 editions and translated into Mandarin Chinese, Spanish, French, and Italian. E continues to pursue his passion for learning and teaching by working on new editions of his textbooks, conduct management development seminars, and guest lecturing at universities that use his textbooks. Among consulting and management development clients are American Express, Nazarene School of Large Chu Management, Ford Motor Company, SABRE Computer Services, Honeywell, Motorola, Salt River Project, Amda the Hopi Indian nation, State Farm Insurance, Goodyear Aerospace, Doubletree Hotels, Bank One-Arizo Caterpillar, and U.S. Steel.

About the Indian Adaptor

Mamata Mohapatra, Ph.D. (Personnel Management & Industrial Relations, Faculty Development Program (Indi Institute of Management, Ahmedabad - IIMA), Masters in Personnel Management & Industrial Relations, LI B.A.(Hons.) Economics. Dr Mohapatra is currently Assistant Professor and Program Director of PGPHRM International Management Institute (IMI), New Delhi. She has over 10 years of experience in teaching, traini and research in the field of Organizational Behavior, Human Resource Management, Industrial Relations as w as planning, coordinating and organizing higher level educational courses, national level training prograr workshops. Apart from IMI she has taught at Asia Pacific Institute of Management - New Delhi and Institute Integrated Learning in Management (IILM) - New Delhi. She has also been engaged in consultancy and Execut Development Programs. Her involvement in publications and research papers has also been extensive.

Management

2008 Edition (Glocal Text)

Robert Kreitner
Arizona State University

Indian Adaptor

Mamata Mohapatra
IMI, New Delhi

In this adaptation, materials have been changed, altered and/or deleted to suit the Indian environment.

biztantra
Management for the Flat World!
19-A, Ansari Road, Daryaganj, Delhi-110002

Houghton Mifflin Company Boston New York

This edition has been published by arrangement with the **Houghton Mifflin Co., USA** and published in India by **Biztantra, An Imprint of Dreamtech Press, 19-A, Ansari Road, Daryaganj, New Delhi-110002.**

ISBN (10): 81-7722-759-9
(13): 978-81-7722-759-8

Edition : 2008

Printed at: Himal Impressions, 168, Raja Garden, New Delhi.

Brief Contents

Contents

PART FIVE

Organizational Control Processes 421

Preface to the Original Edition

Today's managers face a complex web of difficult and exciting challenges. A global economy in which world-class quality is the ticket to ride, increased diversity in the work force, the proliferation of technology and e-business, and demands for more ethical conduct promise to keep things interesting. As trustees of society's precious human, material, financial, and informational resources, today's and tomorrow's managers hold the key to a better world. A solid grounding in management is essential to successfully guiding large or small, profit or nonprofit, organizations in the twenty-first century. *Management,* Tenth Edition, represents an important step toward managerial and personal success in an era of rapid change. It is a comprehensive, up-to-date, and highly readable introduction to management theory, research, and practice. This tenth edition is the culmination of my thirty-three years in management classrooms and management development seminars around the world. Its style and content have been shaped by interaction with literally thousands of students, instructors, reviewers, and managers. All have taught me valuable lessons about organizational life, management, and people in general. Organized along a time-tested functional/process framework, *Management,* Tenth Edition, integrates classical and modern concepts with a rich array of contemporary real-world examples, cases, and Interactive Annotations.

New Topics and Research Insights

Many changes have been made in response to feedback from students, colleagues, and managers who read the previous edition and reflecting the latest trends in management thinking. **There are 1,225 source material references throughout this new edition dated 2004 or 2005.**

Major Changes and Improvements

These significant improvements can be found in the Tenth Edition of *Management:*

- A built-in study guide in the form of a "Test Prepper" at the end of each chapter with 10 true-false and 10 multiple-choice items (with an answer key at the end of the book)
- Chapter 15 now titled "Influence, Power, and Leadership"
- More than 30 new topics (see below)
- All seventeen chapter-opening cases are new to this edition
- Five of the six Managing Diversity boxed features throughout the text are new
- Four of the six The Global Manager boxed features throughout the text are new
- Four of the five Management Ethics boxed features throughout the text are new
- Thirteen of the seventeen chapter-closing cases are new
- Fourteen new cartoons
- The Internet Exercises following each chapter have been completely updated and eight are new
- A more compact design has shortened this textbook

New Topics

Comprehensive revision of *Management,* Tenth Edition, is evidenced by these new topics:

- The "offshoring" of jobs controversy (Chapter 1)
- New data on the Internet (Chapter 1)
- New small business statistics (Chapter 1)

- Critique of "management by best seller" plus a table with capsule summaries of 14 best selling business/management books since 1981 (Chapter 2)
- New support for on-the-job remedial education (Chapter 3)
- New gender pay gap and glass ceiling data (Chapter 3)
- New immigrant data for U.S. (Chapter 3)
- New data on America's largest minority group: Hispanics/Latinos (Chapter 3)
- Why diversity needs a push today (Chapter 3)
- Seven new technologies to watch (Chapter 3)
- New key term: cultural intelligence (Chapter 4)
- Nine competencies for successful cross-cultural adaptation (Chapter 4)
- Carroll's new global corporate social responsibility pyramid (Chapter 5)
- Documentation of recent corporate misconduct (Chapter 5)
- New data on ethics training (Chapter 5)
- Six roles played by project managers (Chapter 6)
- Seven basic Internet business models (Chapter 7)
- Bias and decision making (Chapter 8)
- Ethical perspective of Wal-Mart's effectiveness (Chapter 9)
- American Indian storytelling traditions in corporations (Chapter 9)
- Linux as a virtual organization (Chapter 10)
- The employee selection process at Google (Chapter 11)
- The coming skilled-worker shortage in the U.S. (Chapter 11)
- The e-grapevine and Web logs—blogs (Chapter 12)
- Ethics of keeping blogs in check (Chapter 12)
- Exit interviews and knowledge management (Chapter 12)
- Five commandments of cell phone etiquette (Chapter 12)
- Four types of meetings (Chapter 12)
- New pointers for conducting successful meetings (Chapter 12)
- The power of on-the-spot incentives (Chapter 13)
- Six inspiring examples of family-friendly companies (Chapter 13)
- Drucker's 2004 leadership effectiveness criteria (Chapter 15)
- The leaders vs. managers debate: a middle ground (Chapter 15)
- Leadership and "practical intelligence" (Chapter 15)
- Rejection of the born leader notion (Chapter 15)
- Positive reinforcement as "bucket filling" (Chapter 15)
- Passive-aggressive organizational culture and resistance to change (Chapter 15)
- New examples of recent crisis-generating events (Chapter 17)
- How Dell survived a global supply chain crisis (Chapter 17)
- What *kaizen* means at Toyota (Chapter 17)

To make room for these new topics and the following research insights, outdated material and examples and unnecessary wording were studiously identified and eliminated. The net result is an efficient and very up-to-date introduction to the field of management.

New Coverage Based on Cutting-Edge Research

Management, Tenth Edition, draws useful insights from the following recently-reported research areas:

- New globalization statistics (Chapter 1)
- New survey data on perceived business ethics (Chapter 1)
- Clark L. Wilson's managerial skills profile based on 30 years of field research (Chapter 1)
- All new demographic data for U.S. workforce (Chapter 3)
- Cultural dimensions and leadership lessons from the GLOBE project (Chapter 4)
- New research evidence on why U.S. expatriates go home early (Chapter 4)

- Research findings on six ways people tend to rationalize unethical conduct (Chapter 5)
- Research evidence about downsizing survivors and increased cardiovascular deaths (Chapter 9)
- Data supporting rigorous background checks for job seekers (Chapter 11)
- New data on the content and delivery of today's training (Chapter 11)
- Recent data on upward communication (Chapter 12)
- New data on how employee wellness programs pay (Chapter 13)
- House's updated path-goal model of leadership (Chapter 15)
- New research showing why internal audits are necessary (Chapter 17)

Complete Harmony with AACSB International's Revised Accreditation Standards

AACSB International (The Association to Advance Collegiate Schools of Business), the leading accrediting organization for business, management, and accounting programs, recently revised its Standards for Business Accreditation. A major "conceptual change" took place: "curriculum standards have been replaced with standards requiring 'Assurance of Learning'. This is a shift of perspective from structural input to learning outcome. It asks for evidence, rather than intent." (*Source:* "Second Working Draft: Eligibility Procedures and Standards for Business Accreditation," **www.aacsb.edu**, March 22, 2002, p. 5.) **Learning objectives** at the beginning of each chapter, repeated at appropriate locations in the margin and answered in the chapter summary, make this entire textbook "**outcome-focused.**"

Moreover, topical coverage in *Management,* Tenth Edition, aligns very closely with AACSB International's list of "management-specific knowledge and skills:" creating value by producing goods and services; understanding the economic, political, legal, and global contexts of business; knowledge of individual and group dynamics in organizations; information management; the individual's responsibilities to the organization and society; and "Other management-specific knowledge and abilities as identified by the school." (*Source:* Ibid., p. 25.)

Major Themes

The study of management takes in a great deal of territory, both conceptually and geographically. Therefore, it is important for those being introduced to the field to have reliable guideposts to help them make sense of it all. Four major themes guiding our progress through the fascinating world of management are change, skill development, diversity, and ethics.

An Overriding Focus on Change

It may be a cliché to say "the only certainty today is change," but it is nonetheless true. The challenge for today's and especially tomorrow's managers is to be aware of *specific* changes, along with the factors contributing to them and their likely impact on the practice of management. Change has been woven into the fabric of this new edition in the following ways:

- Under the heading of "The Changing Workplace," each chapter-opening case introduces students to real-world managers and changes at large and small, domestic and foreign organizations (all 17 opening cases are new to this edition).
- Chapter 1 profiles the twenty-first-century managers and ten major changes in the practice of management.

- Chapter 1 provides an overview of the Internet and e-business revolution.
- Chapter 3 is entirely devoted to the changing social, political/legal, economic, and technological environment that management faces. Workplace demographics document the changing face of the work force.
- Chapter 4 discusses the growth of global and transnational corporations and how to adapt to cross-cultural situations.
- Chapter 6 covers project planning/management, underscoring the ad hoc nature of today's workplaces.
- Chapter 7 has a completely updated section titled E-business Strategies for the Internet, including seven basic Internet business models.
- Chapter 8 discusses knowledge management as a strategic tool for better decision making.
- Chapter 9 discusses learning organizations as well as how to detect and avoid organizational decline.
- Chapter 10 describes the new virtual organizations.
- Chapter 11 covers the concept of "human capital" and features Pfeffer's seven people-centered practices.
- Chapter 14 covers virtual teams and how to build them.
- Chapter 15 covers emotional intelligence, a vital trait for adaptable managers and leaders.
- Chapter 16 offers comprehensive treatment of change, resistance to change, and how to bring about unofficial grassroots change.
- Chapter 17 covers the timely topic of crisis management.
- Completely updated Internet Exercises at the end of each chapter help the reader stay in touch with recent changes in the world of management.

Emphasis on Skill Development

Managers tell us they want job applicants who know more than just management theory. They value people who can communicate well, solve problems, see the big picture, and work cooperatively in teams. Consequently, this edition has a very strong skills orientation.

- ***Skills & Tools*** sections at the end of each chapter teach students how to manage their career, stay current with management literature, help women break the glass ceiling, develop competencies to work effectively in foreign cultures, behave ethically around the world, write a new business plan, reengineer the organization, construct a fishbone diagram (for problem finding), build an organization's learning capability, demonstrate initiative, successfully handle a job interview, develop a more effective speaking style, manage stress, use cooperative conflict to avoid groupthink, empower employees, constructively express anger, and avoid public-relations problems in a crisis.
- ***How-to-do-it instructions*** are integrated into the text for the following skills and tasks: preparing employees for foreign assignments, examining the ethics of a business decision, using management by objectives (MBO), constructing flow charts and Gantt charts, building a PERT network, performing a break-even analysis, writing planning scenarios, making decisions, avoiding decision-making traps, managing creative people, avoiding layoffs, delegating, cellphone etiquette, interviewing, discouraging sexual harassment, communicating via e-mail, participating in a videoconference, listening, writing effectively, running a meeting, using rewards, making employee participation programs work, curbing organizational politics, preventing groupthink, building trust, modifying behavior, managing change, overcoming resistance to change, managing conflict, negotiating, using Deming's Plan-Do-Check-Act cycle, and improving product and service quality.

■ Emphasis on Diversity

Labor forces and customers around the globe, particularly in the United States, are becoming more diverse in terms of national origin, race, religion, gender, predominant age categories, and personal preferences. Managers are challenged to manage diversity effectively to tap the *full* potential of *every* individual's unique combination of abilities and traits. The following diversity coverage and themes can be found in this edition:

- Six boxed features (5 new) titled **Managing Diversity** throughout the text focus needed attention on networking among Black top executives, dealing with religion in the workplace, bias in decision making, the globalization of diversity, Native American empowerment, and how to change the organization's culture by being a "tempered radical."
- Women play important managerial roles in the chapter-opening cases for Chapters 2, 10, 15, and 16 and the chapter-closing cases for Chapters 5, 6, and 7.
- A diverse selection of individuals is featured in cases, boxes, examples, and photos.
- Chapter 1 describes the demand for multilingual and multicultural managers.
- Chapter 3 includes a section on managing diversity.
- Chapter 4 discusses managing across cultures and emphasizes the importance of learning foreign languages. Chapter 4 also describes the work goals and leadership styles in different cultures.
- Chapter 5 discusses different value systems.
- Chapter 8 describes different information-processing styles and how to manage creative individuals.
- Chapter 11 discusses moving from tolerance to appreciation when managing diversity. It also covers equal employment opportunity, affirmative action, and the Americans with Disabilities Act (ADA) and how to develop policies for sexual harassment and substance abuse.
- Chapter 13 discusses how to motivate a diverse work force and provides coverage of the U.S. Family and Medical Leave Act (FMLA).
- Chapter 14 includes major coverage of teamwork.
- Chapter 15 discusses women and the use of power as well as different leadership styles.
- Chapter 16 discusses *cooperative* conflict and describes different conflict resolution styles.

■ Emphasis on Ethics

Simply put, society wants managers to behave better. Ethical concerns are integrated throughout this edition, as well as featured in Chapter 5. Ethical coverage is evidenced by:

- Five (4 new) **Management Ethics** boxes throughout the text
- Offshoring of jobs controversy (Chapter 1)
- Discussion of management's ethical reawakening in Chapter 1
- Chapter 5, in Part One, entirely devoted to management's social and ethical responsibilities, providing an ethical context for the entire book
- Carroll's new global corporate social responsibility pyramid (Chapter 5)
- Research: how people rationalize unethical conduct (Chapter 5)
- New data on ethics training (Chapter 5)
- Ethical aspects of e-commerce (Chapter 7)
- Value judgments in decision making in Chapter 8
- Is Wal-Mart an ethical organization? (Chapter 9)
- Ethics of downsizing and layoffs in Chapter 9

- Blogs (Web logs) as an ethical issue (Chapter 12)
- Ethical implications of group norms and avoiding groupthink in Chapter 14
- Greenleaf's ethical "servant leader" in Chapter 15
- Covey's ethical win-win negotiating style in Chapter 16

An Interactive Textbook

Active rather than passive learning is the preferred way to go these days. As well it should be, because active learning is interesting and fun. This textbook employs two interactive-learning strategies: Web-linked interactive annotations and hands-on exercises.

Interactive Annotations

This feature, unique to *Management,* was introduced three editions ago. The idea was to link the textbook and the Internet to create a dynamic, instructive, and interesting learning tool. In short, to make the textbook come alive. This pedagogical experiment has been a great success. (In fact, students say they read the annotations first when turning to a new page.) Consequently, there are 149 interactive annotations in this tenth edition (110 are new and 5 have been updated) that integrate timely facts, provocative ideas, discussion questions, and back-to-the-opening-case questions into the flow of the book.

At the instructor's discretion, many of the annotations provide stimulating opportunities for cooperative learning. Valuable new insights are gained and interpersonal skills are developed when students work together in groups and teams.

Hands-On Exercises

There is one Hands-On Exercise at the end of each chapter. These exercises strive to heighten self-awareness and build essential managerial skills. The exercises can be completed alone or in cooperative-learning teams. Each exercise is followed by a set of questions for personal consideration and/or class discussion. The 17 Hands-On Exercises include: an entrepreneur's quiz, open-system thinking for dealing with global terrorism, rating the probability of futuristic predictions, a cultural-awareness survey, a personal values survey, how to write good objectives and plans, doing a strategic SWOT analysis, a creativity test, an organizational culture assessment, a field study on organization structure and design, writing behavioral interview questions, communicating in an awkward situation, a quality-of-worklife survey, a management teamwork survey, an emotional intelligence (EQ) test, managing a conflict, and measuring service quality.

Successful Pedagogical Structure for Students

As with the previous edition, pedagogical features of the text, make *Management,* Tenth Edition, a complete and valuable learning tool—one that will satisfy the needs of both students and professors. This is demonstrated by the following:

- Chapter objectives at the beginning of each chapter focus the reader's attention on key concepts.
- Chapter objectives are repeated at appropriate locations, in the text margin, to pace the reader's progress.

- Key terms are emphasized in bold, where first defined, repeated in marginal notes, and listed at the close of each chapter to reinforce important terminology and concepts.
- A stimulating photo/art program and an inviting, user-friendly layout make the material in this edition visually appealing, accessible, and interesting. Captioned color photographs of managers in action and organizational life enliven the text discussion.
- In-text examples and boxes with three different themes—The Global Manager, Management Ethics, and Managing Diversity—provide students with extensive, interesting real-world illustrations to demonstrate the application and relevance of topics important to today's managers.
- Clear, comprehensive chapter summaries refresh the reader's memory of important material.
- Cases at the beginning and end of each chapter provide a real-world context for handling management problems. **Thirty (88 percent) of the cases in this edition are new.**
- A Skills & Tools section follows each chapter to give today's and tomorrow's managers practical tools for the twenty-first-century workplace.
- A Hands-On-Exercise following every chapter to provide interactive and experiential learning.
- Internet exercises at the end of each chapter challenge the reader to learn more about relevant managerial topics and problems.
- A "Test Prepper" at the end of each chapter provides a handy self-quiz with 10 true-false and 10 multiple-choice items. An answer key is provided at the end of the book.
- Managers-in-Action Videos at the end of each part foster experiential learning by providing real-world exposure to key managerial functions and skills.
- A student Web site **http://business.college.hmco.com/students/** (select Kreitner, *Management*, 10e) provides comments on the text annotations, links to the sites discussed in the Internet exercises and any necessary updates to the exercises, links to the companies highlighted in each chapter's boxes and cases, a description of and additional links to sites of interest, and ACE self-tests.
- A management game called *Manager: A Simulation*, Third Edition, prepared by Jerald R. Smith and Peggy Golden, Florida Atlantic University, offers students the chance to act as managers themselves. The game simulates a business environment in which student management teams produce and market a product. Players make various management decisions and learn from the positive or negative outcomes.
- A free CD, *Real Deal Upgrade*, contains a variety of review materials as well as tips on improving study habits.

Instructor's Resource Manual

The *Instructor's Resource Manual*, prepared by Maria Muto-Porter, contains the chapter objectives, a lecture outline, case interpretation/solutions, answers to discussion questions along with PowerPoint slides for every chapter.

Acknowledgments

Countless people, including colleagues, students, and relatives, have contributed in many ways to the many editions of this book. For me, this project has been a dream come true; it is amazing where life's journey leads when you have a clear goal, the support of many good people, and a bone-deep belief in the concept of continuous improvement. Whether critical or reinforcing, everyone's suggestions and recommendations have been helpful and greatly appreciated.

While it is impossible to acknowledge every contributor here, some key people need to be identified and sincerely thanked. I particularly appreciate the help and thoughtful comments of my colleague, co-author, and good friend, Professor Angelo Kinicki. I am grateful for the cornerstone reviews of earlier editions by Professors Jack L. Mendleson and Angelo Kinicki. A hearty thank you to Professor Amit Shah, Frostburg State University, for a top-quality job on the *Test Bank*. Sincere thanks also to Maria Muto-Porter for her outstanding and creative work on the *Instructor's Resource Manual*.

Warmest thanks are also extended to the following colleagues who have provided valuable input for this and prior editions by serving as content advisers or manuscript reviewers:

Teshome Abebe
University of Southern Colorado

Benjamin Abramowitz
University of Central Florida

Raymond E. Alie
Western Michigan University

Stephen L. Allen
Northwest Missouri State University

Douglas R. Anderson
Ashland University

Mark Anderson
Point Loma Nazarene College

Eva Beer Aronson
Interboro Institute

Debra A. Arvanites
Villanova University

Robert Ash
Rancho Santiago College

Seymour Barcun
St. Frances College

R. B. Barton Jr.
Murray State University

Andrew J. Batchelor
Ohio University—Chillicothe

Walter H. Beck Sr.
Kennesaw State University and *Reinhardt College*

Roger Best
Louisiana College

Gerald D. Biby
Sioux Falls College

Glenn M. Blair
Baldwin-Wallace College

Bruce Bloom
DeVry University, Chicago

Bob Bowles
Cecils College

Barbara Boyington
Brookdale Community College

Steve Bradley
Austin Community College

Molly Burke
Rosary College

Marie Burkhead
University of Southwestern Louisiana

John Cantrell
Cleveland State Community College

Thomas Carey
Western Michigan University

Elaine Adams Casmus
Chowan College

David Chown
Minnesota State University, Mankato

Anthony A. Cioffi
Lorain County Community College

Richard Coe
Richard Stockton College of New Jersey

George M. Coggins
High Point College

Naomi Berger Davidson
California State University—Northridge

Pamela Davis
Eastern Kentucky University

Richard A. Davis
Rosary College

Thomas Daymont
Temple University—Philadelphia

Tim Donahue
Sioux Falls College

Thomas Duda
S.U.N.Y. Canton Tech College

Deborah J. Dwyer
University of Toledo

Gary Ernst
North Central College

Janice Feldbauer
Macomb Community College

Jacque Foust
University of Wisconsin—River Falls

Ellen Frank
Southern Connecticut State University

Edward Fritz
Nassau Community College

Phyllis Goodman
College of DuPage

Sue Granger
Jacksonville State University

Judith Grenkowicz
Kirtland Community College

John Hall
University of Florida

Susan C. Hanlon
University of Akron

Kimberly Harris
Durham Technical Community College

Nell Hartley
Robert Morris College

Lindle Hatton
University of Wisconsin—Oshkosh

Samuel Hazen
Tarleton State University

Rick Hebert
East Carolina University

Brian R. Hinrichs
Illinois Wesleyan University

Jerome Hufnagel
Horry Georgetown Tech

Cathy Jensen
University of Nebraska—Lincoln

Marvin Karlins
University of South Florida

Velta Kelly
University of Cincinnati

Sylvia Keyes
Bridgewater State College

Mary Khalili
Oklahoma City University

John Lea
Arizona State University

Charles Lee
Baldwin-Wallace College

Roger D. Lee
Salt Lake Community College

Bob Lower
Minot State University

James L. Mann
Ashland Community College

Randall Martin
Florida International University

Irvin Mason
Herkimer County Community College

Fredric L. Mayerson
CUNY—Kingsboro Community College

Daniel McAlister
University of Las Vegas

Ann McClure
Ft. Hays State University

Barbara McIntosh
University of Vermont

Debra Miller
Ashland Community College

Peggy M. Miller
Ohio University—Athens

Ray Moroye
University of Denver & Metropolitan State College

John Nagy
Cleary College

James Nead
Vincennes University

Joan Nichols
Emporia State University

Alice E. Nuttall
Kent State University

Darlene Orlov
New York University

Robert Ottemann
University of Nebraska—Omaha

Clyde A. Painter
Ohio Northern University

Herbert S. Parker
Kean College of New Jersey

Gus Petrides
Borough of Manhattan Community College

J. Stephen Phillips
Ohio University—Chillicothe

Allen H. Pike
Ferrum College

Khush Pittenger
Ashland University

Jyoti N. Prasad
Eastern Illinois University

Abe Qastin
Lakeland College

Lynn J. Richardson
Fort Lewis College

Robert W. Risteen
Ohio University—Chillicothe

Ralph Roberts
University of West Florida

Jake Robertson
Oklahoma State University

Robert Rowe
New Mexico State University–Alamogordo and *Park College, Holloman Air Force Base*

Daniel James Rowley
University of Northern Colorado, Monfort College of Business

Wendell J. Roye
Franklin Pierce College

Doug Rymph
Emporia State University

Nestor St. Charles
Dutchess County Community College

John T. Samaras
Central State University

Roger C. Schoenfeldt
Murray State University

C. L. Scott III
Indiana University NW—Gary

Kathryn Severance
Viterbo College

Jane Shuping
Western Piedmont Community College

Marc Siegall
California State University—Chico

G. David Sivak
Westmoreland County Community College

Mick Stahler
Stautzenberger College

Jacqueline Stowe
McMurray University

Sharon Tarnutzer
Utah State University

Margo Underwood
Brunswick College

John Valentine
Kean College of New Jersey

Joe F. Walenciak
John Brown University

Dorothy Wallace
Chowan College

Stanley Welaish
Kean College of New Jersey

Richard A. Wells
Aiken Technical College

Ty Westergaard
Lincoln University

Timothy Wiedman
Ohio University—Lancaster

Mary Williams
College of South Nevada

James Wittman
Rock Valley College

My partnership with Houghton Mifflin through the years has been productive and enjoyable. Many Houghton Mifflin Company people have contributed enormously to this project. I would like to offer a hearty thank you to everyone by acknowledging the following key contributors: George Hoffman, Lisé Johnson, Julia Perez, Rachel D'Angelo Wimberly, Steven Mikels, Lisa Boden, Marcy Kagan, Anthony D'Aries, Bonnie Melton, and Rich Brewer.

The discussion of mentoring in Chapter 15 is dedicated once again to Professor Fred Luthans, University of Nebraska-Lincoln, for getting me into the textbook business. His love for our field of study and incredible work ethic continue to inspire me. To Margaret—my wife, best friend, and hiking buddy—thanks for being my center of gravity and for keeping the spirit of the dancing bears alive. Our marriage is a cherished treasure.

Finally, I would like to thank the thousands of introductory management students I have had the pleasure of working with through the years for teaching me a great deal about tomorrow's managers. Best wishes for a rewarding career in management.

Bob Kreitner

PART ONE

The Management Challenge

CHAPTER 1
Managers and Entrepreneurs

CHAPTER 2
The Evolution of Management Thought

CHAPTER 3
The Changing Environment of Management: Diversity, Global Economy, and Technology

CHAPTER 4
International Management and Cross-Cultural Competence

CHAPTER 5
Management's Social and Ethical Responsibilities

1

Managers and Entrepreneurs

"Management is a practice that has to combine a good deal of craft, namely experience, with a certain amount of art, as vision and insight, and some science, particularly in the form of analysis and technique."[1]

HENRY MINTZBERG

OBJECTIVES

- **Define** the term *management,* and **explain** the managerial significance of the terms *effectiveness* and *efficiency*.
- **Identify** and **summarize** five major sources of change for today's managers.
- **Distinguish** between managerial functions and skills, and **identify** the eight basic managerial functions.
- **Demonstrate** your knowledge of Wilson's three managerial skill categories, and **explain** the practical significance of his research findings.
- **Explain** how managers learn to manage.
- **Challenge** two myths about small businesses, and **describe** entrepreneurs.

the changing workplace

Can the 10-Day Sofa Save American Jobs?

For Bruce Birnbach, the dining room may be the scariest part of the house.

It's not that he's insecure about his table manners. It's just that for Birnbach, the president and COO [chief operating officer] of Rowe Furniture Inc., the dining room represents a vision of a future he's struggling desperately to avoid. Since January 2001, at least 49 U.S. plants specializing in wood furniture—think dining tables and bedroom sets—have closed. Imports have seized 52% of the market.

Fortunately, Rowe makes upholstered furntiture—sofas, ottomans, and such. Because these can come in so many styles and fabrics, they've proven tougher for exporters like China to reproduce in bulk. Still, trouble is looming: Imports have snagged about 16% of this market, compared with 9% five years ago. Birnbach is determined not to cede the living room to foreign producers. He's determined not to close 58-year-old Rowe's factories, and he's determined to keep its 1,464 production jobs here in the United States. The only way to do that, Birnbach believes, is to offer more styles and fabrics, and better quality. But above all, Rowe desperately needs a 10-day sofa. . . .

Before 1983, Rowe could take up to six weeks to produce and deliver a sofa. By 1987, Rowe had trimmed that to 30 days, increasing revenue from $60 million to $90 million. Now, Rowe, which generates $176 million in annual sales, aims to slash turnaround by two-thirds over the next year, becoming as efficient at making furniture as Toyota is at making cars. "I want to show American manufacturers that there are other ways to compete than letting manufacturing go," Birnbach says.

For a manufacturing operation as antediluvian as Rowe's, the 10-day sofa is an audacious goal. The Virginia-based company supplies midlevel furniture in more than 600 fabrics to about 1,500 retailers across the country, including Storehouse, a chain owned by its parent, the Rowe Companies. It specializes in batch manufacturing:

Cutting, sewing, framing, and upholstering are dispersed throughout a plant with minimal interaction among departments. The goal is to have the maximum amount of work in progress, with batches of inventory for other departments. That keeps everyone busy and creates impressive-looking mountains of arm coverings and frames, but it also causes a host of problems. Overdue orders are held back to create a batch, then mixed with new orders, increasing the likelihood that they'll be even later. Materials are easily lost amid the messy stacks of inventory. Fred Stanley, who once oversaw six upholstery lines at Rowe's Elliston, Virginia, plant, would spend hours crisscrossing the enormous factory looking for missing supplies. "When you're searching," he says, "you're not making furniture." Mistakes would be put aside to be repaired later, littering the factory floor with incomplete furniture. It would take 27.5 hours for a cushion that required just 10 minutes to stitch to make it to stuffing, the next spot on the production line.

Despite all the inefficiency, management demands high productivity, and that means Rowe is a tough place to work. Notwithstanding its spacious new factory, gym, video store, and staff concierge, Rowe "was a sweatshop," says Stanley, 45, one of many second-generation employees.

Rowe's transformation began last year after Birnbach concluded that 10-day delivery would give the company a big edge. Mike Boggins, the vice president of engineering, and his staff researched lean manufacturing and came across a step-by-step guide called *Fast Track to Waste-Free Manufacturing: Straight Talk from a Plant Manager* (Productivity Press, 1999). The author, John W. Davis, has rescued a factory he managed by making the sort of radical changes that Rowe needed. Rowe began putting his ideas into practice with two new production lines, one in Elliston and another in its plant in Poplar Bluff, Missouri.

The new lines, dubbed "focus factories" because they're meant to be self-contained within the larger plant, eliminate wasted floor space and greatly reduce unnecessary walking and material handling. Cutters, sewers, framers, and upholsterers sit together, roughly in production sequence, close enough to hand some pieces to one another. Most are cross-trained so they can help each other out when needed.

The line is designed for continuous work flow within each department and between departments. Typically seated in a U-shaped station, surrounded by three types of machines, a sewer can reach for supplies and perform different operations in one place rather than walking to separate machines. That allows her to complete a single piece and pass it down the line. Piles, or work in progress, are kept to a minimum. Such measures dramatically reduce inventory, which Rowe expects will ultimately clear about 80,000 square feet of floor space in Elliston, making room for more lines.

The company sets the basic outlines of a focus factory, then the employees work with staff engineers to decide what goes where. Once the line is up and running, they're expected to continuously improve the operation. Stanley, who supervises the original focus factory in Elliston, gives a different team member a legal pad each week. The assignment: "Tell me five things we're doing right and five things we're doing wrong." . . .

Some workers were scared to try something new. Long-time employees in particular were skeptical, having seen previous attempts to change flop. And, of course, there were those who worried that becoming lean was a prelude to layoffs. Birnbach vowed that wasn't the case. True, the idea was to use fewer employees on the line, he said, but no one would be laid off. The staff would be trimmed over time through attrition.

Besides making a 10-day couch, Elliston's first focus factory produces 5% more furniture, 100 or more pieces a day, with 10% fewer workers. Because work gets inspected and repaired immediately, the error rate is 0.1%, compared with 3% plantwide. Quality is up in general, too: Because workers who sew arm pieces can now see firsthand how the upholsterers attach them to frames, for example, they recognize the need for a precise half-inch seam to make a snug fit.

Despite the increased productivity, the atmosphere in the focus factories is considerably less stressful. Absenteeism is nearly half what it is elsewhere in the plant. Employees feel a greater sense of job satisfaction. And there are other incentives. Each morning, the line is assigned a set number of pieces for that day. If it finishes the order early, everyone goes home early, but they still get paid for a full day. Eventually, each focus factory will operate like its own business; if it gets the job done with 50 employees instead of 56, some of the savings will get passed on to the team members.

Rowe expects to offer 10-day delivery to all of its retailers next year. . . .

Occasionally, as he describes how far Rowe has come, Birnbach's eyes well up. He blushes. He can't help it. He has known some of his employees for 25 years, since he started at Rowe the summers during college. "This is emotional for me," he says. "We have employees who have been here 20 and 30 years who are adapting to the changes. We have an obligation to them. I tell them we're not walking away from you or anybody else. Here's what we need to survive."

Source: *By Chuck Salter, © 2005 Gruner & Jahr USA Publishing. First published in* Fast Company Magazine. *Reprinted by permission.*

Bruce Birnbach is an inspiring example of a modern manager in action. His overriding goal is to do whatever it takes to achieve his organization's mission in a highly competitive world. Relative to our present challenge to learn more about management, Birnbach's story underscores four key realities of managing today:

1. The only certainty today is *change.* Challenging *goals* motivate people to strive for improvement and overcome obstacles and resistance to change.
2. *Speed, teamwork,* and *flexibility* are the orders of the day, from both strategic and operational standpoints.
3. Managers at all levels need to stay close to the *customer.* Product/service *quality* is the driving force in the battle to stay competitive.
4. Without *continuous improvement* and *lifelong learning,* there can be no true economic progress for individuals and organizations alike.

Keep these managerial realities in mind as you explore the world of management in this book.

Every one of us—whether as an employee, a customer, a stockholder, or a member of the surrounding community—has a direct stake in the quality of management. Joan Magretta, a management consultant who went on to become an editor at *Harvard Business Review,* offers this perspective:

> *Management's business is building organizations that work. Underneath all the theory and the tools, underneath all the specialized knowledge, lies a commitment to performance that has powerfully altered our economy and our lives. That, ultimately, is why management is everyone's business.*[2]

Accordingly, bad management is a serious threat to our quality of life. Terry Bragg, president of a management training company in Utah, recently put it this way: "For most employees, the immediate boss is the prime representative of the organization. . . . If they don't like their immediate boss, they don't like the company."[3]

Effective management is the key to a better world, but mismanagement squanders our resources and jeopardizes our well-being. Every manager, regardless of level or scope of responsibility, is either part of the solution or part of the problem. Management or mismanagement—the choice is yours. A basic knowledge of management theory, research, and practice will help prepare you for productive and gainful employment in a highly organized world in which virtually everything is managed.

Management Defined

management: *the process of working with and through others to achieve organizational objectives in a changing environment*

We now need to define management, in order to highlight the importance, relevance, and necessity of studying it. **Management** is the process of working with and through others to achieve organizational objectives in a changing environment. Central to this process is the effective and efficient use of limited resources.

Five components of this definition require closer examination: (1) working with and through others, (2) achieving organizational objectives, (3) balancing effectiveness and efficiency, (4) making the most of limited resources, and (5) coping with a changing environment (see Figure 1.1).

1. DEFINE the term *management,* and **EXPLAIN** the managerial significance of the terms *effectiveness* and *efficiency*.

Working with and Through Others

Management is, above all else, a social process. Many collective purposes bring individuals together—building cars, providing emergency health care, publishing books, and on and on. But in all cases, managers are responsible for getting things done by working with and through others.

Figure 1.1 Key Aspects of the Management Process

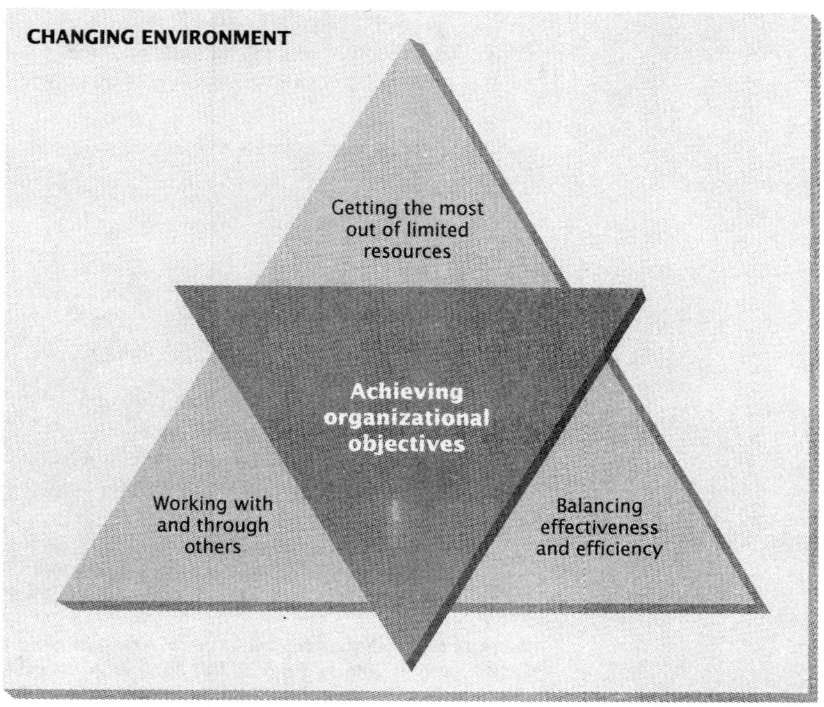

1a Do You Have What It Takes to Be a Great Boss?

Inc. magazine:

Integrity, poise, humility. Would your workers ascribe these qualities to you? However you see your role as boss—a parental figure, a coach, a general—your job ultimately boils down to directing people and, in some sense, serving them.

Source: Rod Kurtz, "How to . . . Be a Great Boss," Inc., *26 (October 2004): 90.*

QUESTIONS:

What is your personal experience with great (and/or not-so-great) managers? What enduring management lessons did you learn from what they did right or wrong?

For further information about the interactive annotations in this chapter, visit our Web site (**http://business.college.hmco.com/students/** and select Kreitner, *Management,* 10e).

Aspiring managers who do not interact well with others hamper their careers. This was the conclusion two experts reached following interviews with 62 executives from the United States, the United Kingdom, Belgium, Spain, France, Germany, and Italy. Each of the executives was asked to describe two managers whose careers had been *derailed.* Derailed managers were those who had not lived up to their peers' and superiors' high expectations. The derailed managers reportedly had these shortcomings:

- Problems with interpersonal relationships.
- Failure to meet business objectives.
- Failure to build and lead a team.
- Inability to change and adapt during a transition.[4]

Significantly, the first and third shortcomings involve failure to work effectively with and through others. Derailed managers experienced a number of interpersonal problems; among other things, they were perceived as manipulative, abusive, untrustworthy, demeaning, overly critical, not team players, and poor communicators. The former CEO of PeopleSoft tripped over this particular hurdle when he was fired by the board of directors in 2004 for a number of reasons, including "managing abrasively."[5]

Achieving Organizational Objectives

An objective is a target to be strived for and, one hopes, attained. Like individuals, organizations are usually more successful when their activities are guided by challenging, yet achievable, objectives. From an individual perspective, scheduling a course load becomes more systematic and efficient when a student sets an objective, such as graduating with a specific degree by a given date.

We create organizations to do what we cannot accomplish alone. This 555-seat Airbus A380 finally became reality in Toulouse, France, in 2005 thanks to the collective efforts of tens of thousands of contributors across four countries—France, Germany, Spain and Great Britain. Of course, the issue of profitability is still very much up in the air. (For more, visit* www.airbus.com.*)

Figure 1.2 Balancing Effectiveness and Efficiency.

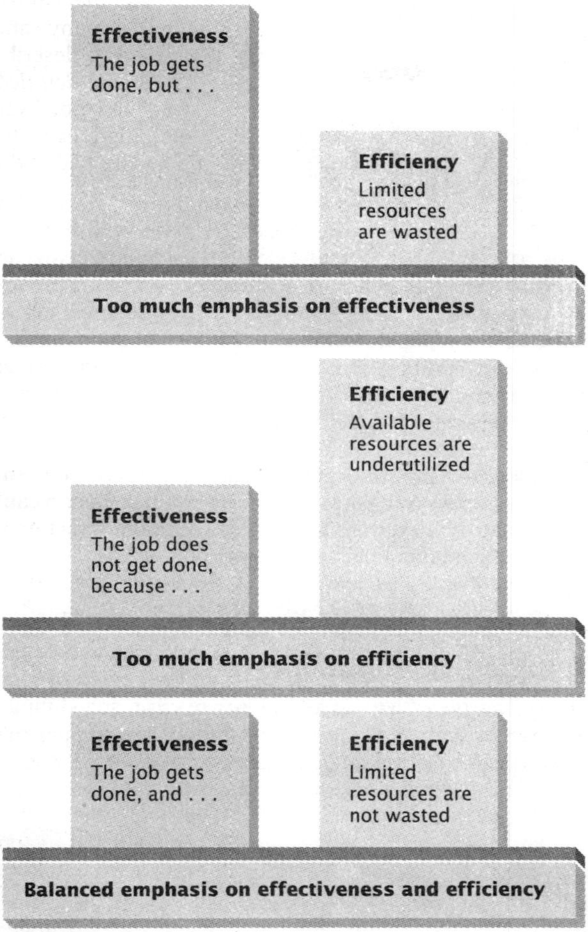

Although personal objectives are typically within the reach of individual effort, organizational objectives or goals always require collective action. For example, General Motors has announced an objective to increase its vehicle production in China to 1.3 million units by 2007.[6] That is an ambitious target, considering that GM produced only 65,000 vehicles in China in 2004. It will cost GM billions of dollars to become a major player in China. But its objective for 2007 will serve as a guiding star for building factories, hiring and motivating Chinese employees, and building vehicles that Chinese consumers will want to buy.

Organizational objectives also serve later as measuring sticks for performance. Without organizational objectives, the management process, like a trip without a specific destination, would be aimless and wasteful.

Balancing Effectiveness and Efficiency

Distinguishing between effectiveness and efficiency is much more than an exercise in semantics. The relationship between these two terms is important, and it presents managers with a never-ending dilemma. **Effectiveness** entails promptly achieving a stated objective. Swinging a sledgehammer against the wall, for example, would be an effective way to kill a bothersome fly. But given the reality of limited resources, effectiveness alone is not enough. **Efficiency** enters the picture when the resources required to achieve an objective are weighed against what was actually accomplished. The more favorable the ratio of benefits to costs, the greater the efficiency. Although a sledgehammer is an effective tool for killing flies, it is highly inefficient when the wasted effort and smashed walls are taken into consideration. A fly swatter is both an effective and an efficient tool for killing a single housefly.

effectiveness: *a central element in the process of management that entails achieving a stated organizational objective*

efficiency: *a central element in the process of management that balances the amount of resources used to achieve an objective against what was actually accomplished*

Managers are responsible for balancing effectiveness and efficiency (see Figure 1.2). Too much emphasis in either direction leads to mismanagement. On the one hand, managers must be effective by getting the job done. On the other hand, managers need to be efficient by reducing costs and not wasting resources. Of course, managers who are too stingy with resources may fail to get the job done.

At the heart of the quest for *productivity improvement* (a favorable ratio between inputs and output) is the constant struggle to balance effectiveness and efficiency.[7] Boeing, for example, hopes its productivity advantage will help it prevail against Europe's Airbus in the commercial airliner business.

> *[According to an airline analyst,] "Boeing's factories are more efficient than at any time in its history." Indeed, Boeing has cut the final assembly time of a 737 in half, to 11 days; Airbus has only been able to reduce its A320 final assembly from 40 days to 24.*[8]

■ Making the Most of Limited Resources

We live in a world of scarcity. Those who are concerned with such matters worry not only about running out of nonrenewable energy and material resources but also about the lopsided use of those resources. The United States, for example, with about 5 percent of the world's population, is currently consuming about 25 percent of the world's annual oil production and generating 23 percent of the greenhouse gases linked to global warming.[9]

Although experts and nonexperts alike may quibble over exactly how long it will take to exhaust our nonrenewable resources or come up with exotic new technological alternatives,[10] one bold fact remains: Our planet is becoming increasingly crowded.

Demographers who collect and study population statistics tell us the Earth's human population is growing by 2 1/3 people every *second*, 203,024 every *day*, and 6.2 million every *month*.[11] The present world population of over 6.4 billion people is projected to reach 9 billion within 70 years.[12] Meanwhile, our planet's carrying capacity is open to speculation. (For up-to-the-minute global and U.S. population statistics, go to: **www.census.gov/main/www/popclock.html**.)

Approximately 83 percent of the world's population in the year 2020 will live in relatively poor and less-developed countries. Developed and industrialized nations, consequently, will experience increasing pressure to divide the limited resource pie more equitably.[13]

Because of their common focus on resources, economics and management are closely related. Economics is the study of how limited resources are distributed among alternative uses. In productive organizations, managers are the trustees of limited resources, and it is their job to see that the basic factors of production—land, labor, and capital—are used efficiently as well as effectively. Management could be called "applied economics."

■ Coping with a Changing Environment

Successful managers are the ones who anticipate and adjust to changing circumstances rather than being passively swept along or caught unprepared. Employers today are hiring managers who can take unfamiliar situations in stride. *Business Week* served up this amusing but challenging profile of tomorrow's managers: "The next generation of corporate leaders will need the charm of a debutante, the flexibility of a gymnast, and the quickness of a panther. A few foreign languages and a keen understanding of technology won't hurt either."[14] Also in the mix are a sense of humor, passion, and the ability to make fast decisions.

2. IDENTIFY and **SUMMARIZE** five major sources of change for today's managers.

Chapter 3 provides detailed coverage of important changes and trends in management's social, political-legal, economic, and technological environments. At this point, it is instructive to preview major changes for managers doing business in the twenty-first century[15] (see Table 1.1). This particular collection of changes is the product of five overarching sources of change: globalization, the evolution of product quality, environmentalism, an ethical reawakening, and the Internet revolution. Together, these factors are significantly reshaping the practice of management.

■ **Globalization.** Figuratively speaking, the globe is shrinking in almost every conceivable way. Networks of transportation, communication, computers, music, and economics have tied the people of the world together as never before. Companies are having to become global players just to survive, let alone prosper. For example, McDonald's has "30,000 restaurants in 121 countries"[16] and Coca-Cola earns 76 percent of its operating profits from customers outside the United States.[17] Import and export figures are equally stunning. For instance, the United States currently imports about 60 percent of its oil, with 68 percent forecasted for the year 2025.[18] An even higher proportion (80 percent) of the seafood consumed in the United States is foreign-sourced.[19] On the export side, 3M, the maker of Scotch tape and Post-it notes, rings up more than half its sales outside the United States.[20]

Table 1.1 The Twenty-First-Century Manager: Ten Major Changes

	Moving away from	Moving toward
Administrative role	Boss/superior/leader	Team member/facilitator/teacher/sponsor/advocate/coach
Cultural orientation	Monocultural/monolingual	Multicultural/multilingual
Quality/ethics/environmental impacts	Afterthought (or no thought)	Forethought (unifying themes)
Power bases	Formal authority; rewards and punishments	Knowledge; relationships; rewards
Primary organizational unit	Individual	Team
Interpersonal dealings	Competition; win-lose	Cooperation; win-win
Learning	Periodic (preparatory; curriculum-driven)	Continuous (lifelong; learner-driven)
Problems	Threats to be avoided	Opportunities for learning and continuous improvement
Change and conflict	Resist/react/avoid	Anticipate/seek/channel
Information	Restrict access/hoard	Increase access/share

Business and job opportunities show little regard for international borders these days.

offshoring: *controversial practice of sending jobs to low-wage countries*

On the negative side is the controversial practice of **offshoring**, the outsourcing of jobs from developed countries to lower-wage countries.[21] This is a long-standing practice that has been going on for decades. Jobs in the textile, steel, and consumer electronics industries are long gone from the United States, and call-center jobs are going fast. Thanks to the broadband Internet, skilled jobs in areas such as hardware and software engineering, architecture, tax return preparation, and medical diagnosis are being outsourced to well-educated workers in India, China, the Philippines, and Russia.[22] A recent study puts the situation in perspective:

> *Meta Group Inc., a Stamford, Conn., consulting and research firm, says the outsourcing trend will grow by 20 percent per year through 2008 as more U.S. firms focus on cutting labor costs. Meta estimates that 60 percent of U.S. firms will send some technology work abroad by 2008. . . .*
>
> *"In the bigger picture, one job gain in India does not relate to one job in the United States," said Stan Lepeak of Meta Group.*
>
> *"The United States might employ fewer programmers here, but it will employ more managers and a variety of other new roles will be created to manage these new relationships."*[23]

Conclusion: A good education and marketable skills are the best insurance against having your job outsourced to a foreign country.

Also, some worry about giant global corporations eclipsing the economic and political power of individual nations and their citizens. Indeed, "half of the hundred largest budgets in the world now belong to corporations, not nations."[24]

Today's model manager is one who is comfortable transacting business in multiple languages and cultures.

There is a rapidly growing army of global managers from all corners of the world, and you can become a member of it through diligent effort and a clear sense of purpose. Chapter 4 is devoted to the topic of international management. The international cases, examples, and The Global Manager features throughout the text are intended to broaden your awareness of international management.

■ **The Evolution of Product Quality.** Managers have been interested in the quality of their products, at least as an afterthought, since the Industrial Revolution. But thanks to U.S. and Japanese quality gurus such as W. Edwards Deming and Kaoru Ishikawa[25] (more about them in Chapter 2), product/service quality has become both a forethought and a driving force in effective organizations of all kinds. Today's hospitals, hotels, universities, and government agencies are as interested in improving product/service quality as are factories, mines, airlines, and railroads.

In its most basic terms, the emphasis on quality has evolved through four distinct stages since World War II—from "fix it in" to "inspect it in" to "build it in" to "design it in." Progressive managers are moving away from the first two approaches and toward the build-it-in and design-it-in approaches.[26] Here are the key differences:

- ***The fix-it approach to quality.***
  Rework any defective products identified by quality inspectors at the end of the production process.
- ***The inspect-it-in approach to quality.***
  Have quality inspectors sample work in process and prescribe machine adjustments to avoid substandard output.
- ***The build-it-in approach to quality.***
  Make *everyone* who touches the product responsible for spotting and correcting defects. Emphasis is on identifying and eliminating *causes* of quality problems.
- ***The design-it-in approach to quality.***
  Intense customer and employee involvement drives the entire design-production cycle. Emphasis is on *continuous improvement* of personnel, processes, and product.

Notice how each stage of this evolution has broadened the responsibility for quality, turning quality improvement into a true team effort. Also, the focus has shift-

Greater awareness of the need to protect and nurture the natural environment translates to a growing desire to eat organic food. Sensing a business opportunity, Ronny Bell of Seattle started a business called Pioneer Organics. He is succeeding in home delivery, an area where mainstream grocers have generally failed.

MANAGEMENT ETHICS

PNC Financial Services Recycles Its Old Building

Pittsburgh—Nine tons of aluminum window frames, 350 tons of steel and 2,500 tons of concrete will be left after a seven-story downtown building is taken down.

Instead of ending in the scrap heap, the concrete will be ground up and used to fill the site, steel will be melted to create construction supports and the aluminum will be reused in cans and other products.

As companies become more environmentally aware, that attitude is reflected in the buildings in which they work and the ones they tear down.

Officials at PNC Financial Services, for example, plan to recycle 70 percent of the downtown building they began deconstructing, a trend being seen nationwide.

"Traditionally, if someone were to demolish a building, they would simply go in with a wrecking ball," said Gary Saulson, PNC's director of corporate real estate. The company is being more deliberate in how it takes down the building, a process taking two months.

PNC Financial bought the city's former Public Safety Building in 2004 for $4.2 million and announced plans to turn the space into a park. The company had previously built the world's largest certified green corporate building at a site near the building [being torn down].

Officials estimate the building will yield 11,000 tons of waste, 8,000 of which is recyclable. In addition to the steel and concrete, 24 tons of exterior steel will be used in other products and the foam-board ceiling tiles will be returned to the manufacturer. . . .

The demolition of buildings in the United States produces 124 million tons of debris every year, according to the Deconstruction Institute, a Florida-based group that encourages the recycling of buildings and the use of recycled materials. . . .

"We're going to save over $200,000 in dump fees alone," Saulson said.

Source: Jennifer C. Yates, "New Life for Piles of Old Scrap," Arizona Republic *(November 7, 2004): D4. Reprinted by permission of Reprint Management Services.*

ed from reactively fixing product defects to proactively working to prevent them and to satisfy the customer completely. Today's quality leaders strive to *exceed,* not just meet, the customer's expectations.

A popular label for the build-it-in and design-it-in approaches to quality is *total quality management* (TQM).[27] TQM is discussed in detail in Chapter 17.

■ **Environmentalism.** Environmental issues such as deforestation; global warming; depletion of the ozone layer; toxic waste; and pollution of land, air, and water are no longer strictly the domain of campus radicals.[28] Managers around the world are picking up the environmental banner and putting their creative ideas to work (see the Management Ethics feature). For example, Toyota's new 624,000–square-foot sales campus in Torrance, California, was designed and built with the environment in mind. Structural steel came primarily from recycled cars, solar panels generate enough electricity to power 500 homes, and recycled water is used to irrigate a drought-resistant landscape of native plants.[29] The so-called green movement is a cultural and political force in Europe and is gaining a foothold in North America and elsewhere. Managers are challenged to develop innovative ways to make a profit without unduly harming the environment in the process.[30] Terms such as *industrial ecology, sustainable business,* and *eco-efficiency* are heard today under the general umbrella of sustainable development.[31]

Also, cleaning up the environment promises to generate whole new classes of jobs and robust profits in the future. The debate over jobs versus the environment has been rendered obsolete by the need for both a healthy economy *and* a healthy environment. Authors William McDonough and Michael Braungart, while calling for a new Industrial Revolution, recently offered this fresh new perspective:

> *We see a world of abundance, not limits. In the midst of a great deal of talking about reducing the human ecological footprint, we offer a different vision.*

What if humans designed products and systems that celebrate an abundance of human creativity, culture, and productivity? That are so intelligent and safe, our species leaves an ecological footprint to delight in, not lament?

Consider this: All the ants on the planet, taken together, have a biomass greater than that of humans. Ants have been incredibly industrious for millions of years. Yet their productiveness nourishes plants, animals, and soil. Human industry has been in full swing for little over a century, yet it has brought about a decline in almost every ecosystem on the planet. Nature doesn't have a design problem. People do.[32]

Encouragingly, researchers recently found 80 percent higher stock market valuations for multinational corporations adhering to strict environmental standards, compared with those taking advantage of the lax environmental standards often found in less-developed countries.[33] In short, investors tend to reward "clean" companies and punish "dirty" ones.

■ **An Ethical Reawakening.** Managers are under strong pressure from the public, elected officials, and respected managers to behave better. This pressure has resulted from years of headlines about discrimination, illegal campaign contributions, accounting fraud, price fixing, insider trading, the selling of unsafe products, and other unethical practices. The results of a Gallup poll indicate how bad things have gotten: "just 17 % of Americans give execs high marks for honesty and ethics,"[34] a 32 percent drop from the prior year.

Traditional values such as honesty are being reemphasized in managerial decision making and conduct. A case in point: "When the *Economist* magazine published a Top 10 list of leadership qualities. . ., a sound ethical compass was No. 1."[35] Ethics and honesty are everyone's concern: *mine, yours,* and *ours.* Every day we have countless opportunities to be honest or dishonest. One survey of more than 4,000 employees uncovered the following ethical problems in the workplace (the percentage of employees observing the problem during the past year appears in parentheses):

- Lying to supervisors (56 percent)
- Lying on reports or falsifying records (41 percent)
- Stealing and theft (35 percent)
- Sexual harassment (35 percent)
- Abusing drugs or alcohol (31 percent)
- Conflict of interest (31 percent)[36]

Because of closer public scrutiny, ethical questions can no longer be shoved aside as irrelevant. The topic of managerial ethics is covered in depth in Chapter 5 and explored in the Management Ethics features throughout the text.

■ **The Internet and E-Business Revolution.** Like a growing child, the Internet first crawled, then walked, then ran too fast and fell, and now is running more wisely. In concept, the Internet began as a U.S. Department of Defense (DOD) research project during the Cold War era of the 1960s. The plan was to give university scientists a quick and inexpensive way to share their DOD research data. Huge technical problems, such as getting incompatible computers to communicate in a fail-safe network, were solved in 1969 at UCLA when researchers succeeded in getting two linked computers to exchange data. The Internet was born. Other universities were added to the Internet during the 1970s, and gradually applications such as e-mail emerged. By 1983, technology made it possible to share complex documents and graphics on the Internet, and the World Wide Web came into existence.[37] Time passed and improvements were made. During the early 1990s, individuals and businesses began to log on to the "Web" to communicate via e-mail and to buy, sell, and trade things.

Internet: *global network of servers and personal and organizational computers*

Growth of the **Internet** —the worldwide network of personal computers, routers and switches, powerful servers, and organizational computer systems—has been explosive. No one owns the Web, and anyone with a computer modem can be part of it.

1b It's a Wired, Wired World

The very ubiquity and addictiveness of the Internet is spreading the online world even deeper into every area of communication, commerce and human interaction. Don't try Googling the answer to where this will take us. We've long ago strayed off the map.

Source: Steven Levy, "No Net? We'd Rather Go Without Food." Newsweek (October 11, 2004): 14.

QUESTION:
In terms of your own work and leisure activities, what do you see ten years down the road for the Internet?

e-business: *a business using the Internet for greater efficiency in every aspect of its operations*

Within its digital recesses are both trash and treasure. According to Computer Industry Almanac Inc., the number of Internet users worldwide will exceed 1 billion by 2005, with 185 million of them in the United States.[38] The implications of this massive interconnectedness for all of us (especially managers) are profound and truly revolutionary. Indeed, eBay has 105 million registered users, and 430,000 of them reportedly make a full-time living trading on the site.[39] Legal, ethical, security, and privacy issues, however, remain largely unresolved.[40]

Within the business community, heads are still spinning from the dot-com crash of 2000–2001. Wild hype gave way to doubt as countless dot-com dreams simply vaporized. Internet portal Excite.com, purchased by At Home in 1999 for $6.7 *billion* and sold in 2001 for $10 *million*, is a sobering case in point.[41] Today, the e-business revolution is proceeding in a more measured way and with more realistic expectations.[42] Where their focus before the dot-com crash was primarily on business-to-consumer retailing, Internet strategists are now much more broadly focused. Thus, an **e-business** is one seeking efficiencies via the Internet in all basic business functions—production, marketing, and finance/accounting—and all support activities involving human, material, and financial resources. Craig Barrett, the chairman of Intel, the computer chip giant, explained how his firm evolved into what he calls an "Internet company":

> *. . . for Intel, being an Internet company meant turning ourselves into a 100% e-business from front to back—not just in terms of selling and buying, but also in terms of information transfer, education, and customer interaction. We wanted to improve our competitiveness and our productivity, to streamline our internal operations, and to save some money. We also wanted to show that we can use the technology that we sell to the rest of the world.*[43]

Aspects and implications of the Internet and e-business revolution are explored throughout this book, with detailed coverage of Internet strategy in Chapter 7.

Considering the variety of these sources of change in the general environment, managers are challenged to keep abreast of them and adjust and adapt as necessary.

What Do Managers Do?

managerial functions: *general administrative duties that need to be carried out in virtually all productive organizations to achieve desired outcomes*

managerial skills: *specific observable behaviors that effective managers exhibit*

3. DISTINGUISH between managerial functions and skills, and **IDENTIFY** the eight basic managerial functions.

Although nearly all aspects of modern life are touched at least indirectly by the work of managers, many people do not really understand what the management process involves. Management is much more, for example, than the familiar activity of telling employees what to do. Management is a complex and dynamic mixture of systematic techniques and common sense. As with any complex process, the key to learning about management lies in dividing it into readily understood pieces. There are two different ways we can analyze the management process for study and discussion. One approach, dating back to the early twentieth century, is to identify managerial functions. A second, more recent approach focuses more precisely on managerial skills.[44]

Managerial functions are general administrative duties that need to be carried out in virtually all productive organizations. **Managerial skills**, on the other hand, are specific observable behaviors that effective managers exhibit.[45] When we shift the focus from functions to skills, we are moving from general to specific. Stated another way, functions tell us *what* managers generally do while skills tell us more precisely *how* they carry out those functions. We shall examine both perspectives more closely and then have a frank discussion of some managerial facts of life.

Figure 1.3 Identifiable Functions in the Management Process

Managerial Functions

For nearly a century, the most popular approach to describing what managers do has been the functional view. It has been popular because it characterizes the management process as a sequence of rational and logical steps. Henri Fayol, a French industrialist turned writer, became the father of the functional approach in 1916 when he identified five managerial functions: planning, organizing, command, coordination, and control.[46] Fayol claimed that these five functions were the common denominators of all managerial jobs, whatever the purpose of the organization. Over the years Fayol's original list of managerial functions has been updated and expanded by management scholars. This book, even though it is based on more than just Fayol's approach, is organized around eight different managerial functions: planning, decision making, organizing, staffing, communicating, motivating, leading, and controlling (see Figure 1.3). A brief overview of these eight managerial functions will describe what managers do and will preview what lies ahead in this text.

■ **Planning.** Commonly referred to as the primary management function, planning is the formulation of future courses of action. Plans and the objectives on which they are based give purpose and direction to the organization, its subunits, and contributing individuals.

■ **Decision Making.** Managers choose among alternative courses of action when they make decisions. Making intelligent and ethical decisions in today's complex world is a major management challenge.

1c Back to the Opening Case

What evidence of the eight managerial functions can you detect in the Bruce Birnbach/Rowe Furniture case?

■ **Organizing.** Structural considerations such as the chain of command, division of labor, and assignment of responsibility are part of the organizing function. Careful organizing helps ensure the efficient use of human resources.

■ **Staffing.** Organizations are only as good as the people in them. Staffing consists of recruiting, training, and developing people who can contribute to the organized effort.

■ **Communicating.** Today's managers are responsible for communicating to their employees the technical knowledge, instructions, rules, and information required to get the job done. Recognizing that communication is a two-way process, managers should be responsive to feedback and upward communications.

■ **Motivating.** An important aspect of management today is motivating individuals to pursue collective objectives by satisfying needs and meeting expectations with meaningful work and valued rewards. Flexible work schedules can be motivational for today's busy employees.

4. ■ **DEMONSTRATE** your knowledge of Wilson's three managerial skill categories, and **EXPLAIN** the practical significance of his research findings.

■ **Leading.** Managers become inspiring leaders by serving as role models and adapting their management style to the demands of the situation. The idea of visionary leadership is popular today.

■ **Controlling.** When managers compare desired results with actual results and take the necessary corrective action, they are keeping things on track through the control function. Deviations from past plans should be considered when formulating new plans.

1d Back to the Opening Case

Which of Wilson's 12 managerial skills did Bruce Birnbach demonstrate in the Rowe Furniture case? Cite your evidence for each.

Managerial Skills

Thanks to Clark L. Wilson's 30 years of research involving tens of thousands of managers, we have a very clear picture of what it takes to be an effective manager. It takes three skill categories—technical, teambuilding, and drive—that branch into the 12 specific managerial skills listed in Figure 1.4. Unfortunately, according to Wilson's research, about one-third of managers at all levels do not achieve an appropriate *balance* of managerial skills and are thus ineffective. He explains:

> *Too many managers try to exercise control without providing the Technical and Teambuilding skills needed to achieve their goals. They must see that they cannot exercise effective control without first exercising their up-front responsibilities for communicating goals and coordinating teams.*[47]

This conjures up the image of effective managers as jugglers struggling to keep three balls in the air at once. Those balls are labeled technical skills, teambuilding skills, and drive skills. Not an easy chore, but today's and tomorrow's managers are challenged to get the job done amid constant change.

Figure 1.4 Wilson's Managerial Skills

SKILL CATEGORY	SKILLS	DESCRIPTION
TECHNICAL Applying your education, training, and experience to effectively organize a task, job, or project	**1. Technical expertise**	Skills you have acquired by education and experience; to understand and communicate key technical details
	2. Clarification of goals and objectives	Your ability to organize and schedule the work of your unit so it is achieved when expected, and meets established standards
	3. Problem solving	Your ability to resolve issues you confront in the day's work; to develop team collaboration in facing problems
	4. Imagination and creativity	You demonstrate an ability to originate ideas, to correct and develop ways to improve productivity
TEAMBUILDING Listening carefully and communicating clearly to develop and coordinate an effective group or team	**5. Listening for insights**	Keeping aware of activities of your team and units close to you; underpinning your ability to continue being a manager
	6. Directing and coaching	Meeting your goals and standards; keeping your team's skills up to target levels
	7. Solving problems as teams	An important role is helping your team contribute ideas to improve their performance
	8. Coordinating and cooperating	Demonstrating a willingness to work with others: your group, individuals, and units close to you
DRIVE Setting goals, maintaining standards, and evaluating performance to achieve effective outcomes involving costs, output, product quality, and customer service	**9. Standards of performance**	Your effort to keep your part of the organization moving, your willingness to be busy and keep aimed toward new accomplishments
	10. Control of details	Overseeing the performance of work at a close level, to meet performance goals and standards
	11. Energy	Demonstrating to your team and colleagues a readiness and willingness to work and that you expect their cooperation
	12. Exerting pressure	Urging others to perform, by shaping your activity to be perceived as teamwork, not domination

Source: *Quoted and adapted from Clark L. Wilson,* How and Why Effective Managers Balance Their Skills: Technical, Teambuilding, Drive, *2003, pp. 13, 18–20. Used by permission of the author.*

Source: *DILBERT © Scott Adams/Dist. by United Feature Syndicate, Inc.*

■ Some Managerial Facts of Life (with No Sugar Coating)

Managing is a tough and demanding job today. The hours are long and, at first anyway, the pay may not be generous. Worse yet, managers are visible authority figures who get more than their fair share of criticism and ridicule from politicians and Scott Adams's Dilbert cartoons.[48] Nevertheless, managing can be a very rewarding occupation for those who develop their skills and persist, as evidenced by American Management Association (AMA) research findings:

- Forty-six percent of U.S. managers say they feel more overwhelmed at work today than two years ago, and 22 percent more say they're "somewhat" more overwhelmed.
- Half of U.S. managers say they experience stress every day, but an even greater share—63 percent—say they feel enthusiasm for their jobs.[49]

■ A Hectic Pace. According to Henry Mintzberg's classic observational studies of actual managers, the average manager is not the reflective planner and precise "orchestra leader" that the functional approach suggests.[50] Mintzberg characterizes the typical manager as follows: "The manager is overburdened with obligations; yet he cannot easily delegate his tasks. As a result, he is driven to overwork and is forced to do many tasks superficially. Brevity, fragmentation, and verbal communication characterize his work."[51]

This retail clothing manager performs all the managerial functions and needs a complete set of managerial skills to succeed in today's hectic times.

1e "I Really Don't Like You, Now Let's Get The Job Done."

A survey of 173 managers found "Building relationships with people I dislike" to be the number one (73%) source of personal discomfort and stress.

Source: Adapted from "Do I Have To?" Business Week *(July 7, 2003): 14.*

QUESTION:
Putting yourself in the place of a manager "fresh out of school," how would you handle this challenge?

In addition, according to Mintzberg's research, constant interruptions are the order of the day. A more recent study supported Mintzberg's view and provided a somewhat surprising insight into the reality of nonstop interruptions. Stephanie Winston interviewed 48 top U.S. executives, including the late Katharine Graham, former chief executive of *The Washington Post,* and discovered that constant interruptions are not a threat to successful top executives. Indeed, interruptions are what the work of top managers is all about and actually constitute a valuable resource. Winston concluded, "They use a fluid time style to make abundant connections and draw in streams of information. . . . The torrent of questions, comments, updates, requests, and expectations is a rich resource to be mined."[52]

Thus, the typical manager's day involves a hectic schedule, with lots of brief interactions. Interruptions and fragmentation are the norm. Extended quiet periods for reflection and contemplation are rare. An even quicker pace is in store for future managers. However, in line with Wilson's advice to balance one's managerial skills, Mintzberg recently urged managers to balance reflective thought and action:

> *All effective managing has to be sandwiched between acting on the ground and reflecting in the abstract. Acting alone is thoughtless—we have seen enough of the consequences of that—just as reflecting alone is passive. Both are critical. But today, one—reflection—gets lost.*[53]

■ **Managers Lose Their Right to Do Many Things.** Mention the word *manager,* and the average person will probably respond with terms like *power, privilege, authority, good pay,* and so on. Although many managers eventually do enjoy some or all of these rewards, they pay a significant price for stepping to the front of the administrative parade.[54] According to one management expert, when you accept a supervisory or managerial position, you *lose* your right to do any of the following:

- Lose your temper
- Be one of the gang
- Bring your personal problems to work
- Vent your frustrations and express your opinion at work
- Resist change
- Pass the buck on tough assignments
- Get even with your adversaries
- Play favorites
- Put your self-interests first
- Ask others to do what you wouldn't do
- Expect to be immediately recognized and rewarded for doing a good job[55]

We tell you this not to scare you away from what could be a financially and emotionally rewarding career, but rather to present a realistic picture so you can choose intelligently. Management is not for everyone—it is not for the timid, the egomaniacal, or the lazy. Management requires clear-headed individuals who can envision something better and turn it into reality by working with and through others.

Learning to Manage

Students of management are left with one overriding question: "How do I acquire the ability to manage?" This question has stimulated a good deal of debate among those interested in management education. What is the key, theory or practice? Some contend that future managers need a solid background in management theory acquired through formal education. Others argue that managing, like learning to ride a bicycle, can be learned only by actually doing it.[56] We can leapfrog this debate

Figure 1.5 The Honeywell Study: How Managers Learn to Manage.

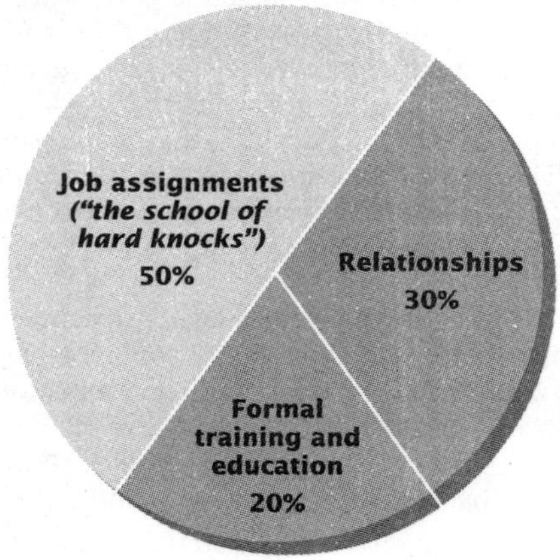

Source: *Data from Ron Zemke, "The Honeywell Studies: How Managers Learn to Manage,"* Training, *22 (August 1985): 46–51.*

by looking at how managers learn to manage, understanding how students learn about management, and considering how you can blend the two processes to your best advantage.

How Do Managers Learn to Manage?

We have an answer to this simple but intriguing question, thanks to the Honeywell study, which was conducted by a team of management development specialists employed by Honeywell.[57] In a survey, they asked 3,600 Honeywell managers, "How did you learn to manage?" Ten percent of the respondents were then interviewed for additional insights. Successful Honeywell managers reportedly acquired 50 percent of their management knowledge from job assignments (see Figure 1.5). The remaining 50 percent of what they knew about management reportedly came from relationships with bosses, mentors, and coworkers (30 percent) and from formal training and education (20 percent).

Fully half of what the Honeywell managers knew about managing came from the so-called school of hard knocks. To that extent, at least, learning to manage is indeed like learning to ride a bike. You get on, you fall off and skin your knee, you get back on a bit smarter, and so on, until you're able to wobble down the road. But in the minds of aspiring managers, this scenario raises the question of what classes are held in the school of hard knocks. A second study, this one of British managers, provided an answer. It turns out that the following are considered *hard knocks* by managers:

- Making a big mistake
- Being overstretched by a difficult assignment
- Feeling threatened
- Being stuck in an impasse or dilemma
- Suffering an injustice at work
- Losing out to someone else
- Being personally attacked[58]

As someone once said, "If you're not making mistakes, then you're not learning." Nike, for example, is a successful athletic apparel company because its managers learn from their mistakes and hard knocks:

> *In the mid-80s, Nike ordered a bowling shoe with nonslip soles—perfect for flinging your body, along with the ball, into the gutter. When the company entered the women's apparel market, its first commercial featured triathlete Joanne Ernst telling women, "It wouldn't hurt to stop eating like a pig." (The joke didn't go over well.) Forays into the golf and skateboarding worlds in the mid-90s similarly misfired. Its first golf product, basically leather shoes with spikes drilled in, was so uncomfortable that embarrassed Nike staffers dubbed it "air-blister." . . .*
>
> *Former Nike advertising VP Scott Bedbury . . . says the key to the company's success is its willingness to embrace "a culture of screw-ups. It does learn from its mistakes."*[59]

1f The Sink-or-Swim School of Management?

Michael Watkins, a Harvard Business School professor and author of the book *The First 90 Days: Critical Success Strategies for New Leaders at All Levels,* has the following concern:

> *Most new managers fail because they don't have a plan, they are not clear about the business situation and they assume that what made them successful in the past is going to work in the new job. . . . They lack the insight and support networks needed to succeed, and corporations lose millions of dollars due to the high failure rates.*

Source: As quoted in Gail Johnson, "Sink or Swim," Training, *41 (July 2004): 13.*

QUESTION:
What could cause a very successful college student to be a flop as a new manager? Explain.

Figure 1.6 Acquiring the Ability to Manage by Merging Theory and Practice

Theory → **Acquiring the ability to manage** ← **Practice**

Theory

- Definitions
- Relevant facts
- Concepts
- Techniques
- Guidelines

Source: *Textbooks, audiovisual presentations, and formal classroom instruction*

Acquiring the ability to manage

Systematic integration of theory and practice into personally meaningful and useful ways of managing
Source: *Self*

Imitating managerial role models
Source: *Practicing managers*

Practice

Simulated experience: Participating in instructor-aided experiential exercises, case studies, and role-playing
Source: *Semistructured classroom experience*

Real experience: Actually managing an organized endeavor
Source: *Part-time or full-time employment as a manager*

5. EXPLAIN how managers learn to manage.

How Can Future Managers Learn to Manage?

As indicated in Figure 1.6, students can learn to manage by integrating theory and practice and observing role models. Theory can help you systematically analyze, interpret, and internalize the managerial significance of practical experience and observations.[60] Although formal training and education contributed only 20 percent to the Honeywell managers' knowledge, they nonetheless can provide needed conceptual foundations. Returning to our bicycle example, a cross-country trip on a high-tech bike requires more than the mere ability to ride a bike. It requires a sound foundation of knowledge about bicycle maintenance and repair, weather and road conditions, and road safety. So, too, new managers who have a good idea of what lies ahead can go farther and faster with fewer foolish mistakes. The school of hard knocks is inevitable. But you can foresee and avoid at least some of the knocks.[61]

Ideally, an individual acquires theoretical knowledge and practical experience at the same time, perhaps through work-study programs or internships. Usually, though, full-time students get a lot of theory and little practice. This is when simulated experience and real experience become important. If you are a serious management student, you will put your newly acquired theories into practice wherever and whenever possible (for example, in organized sports; positions of leadership in fraternities, sororities, or clubs; and part-time and summer jobs). What really matters is your personal integration of theory and practice.

Small-Business Management

Small businesses have been called the "engine" of the U.S. economy. Consider, for example, the evolution of Wal-Mart. It began in 1945 as a single discount store in Arkansas run by Sam and Helen Walton.[62] Wal-Mart is now the largest company in the world, with revenues exceeding $263 *billion* and over 1.5 *million* employees.[63] Small businesses often are too small to attract much media attention, but collectively they (and their counterparts in other countries) are a *huge* and *vibrant* part of the global economy. As evidence, consider these facts about the 5.6 million small businesses in the United States:

- They represent 99 percent of the nation's employers.[64]
- Each year they account for more than one-quarter of the nation's $1.4 trillion in business capital investment.[65]

Interestingly, about 60 percent of them are "microbusinesses" with fewer than five employees, typically operating out of the owner's home[66] (1 out of every 13 workers in the United States is self-employed).[67] Free-enterprise capitalism is a rough-and-tumble arena where anyone can play, but only the very best survive. The only guaranteed result for those starting their own business is that they will be tested to their limit.

Few would dispute the facts and claims cited above, but agreement on the definition of a small business is not so easily reached. The many yardsticks used to distinguish small from large businesses include number of employees, level of annual sales, amount of owner's equity, and total assets. For our present purposes, a **small business** is defined as an independently owned and managed profit-seeking enterprise employing fewer than 100 people. (If the small business is incorporated, the owner/manager owns a significant proportion of the firm's stock.)

small business: *an independently owned and managed profit-seeking enterprise with fewer than 100 employees*

The health of every nation's economy depends on how well its small businesses are managed. To get a better grasp of the realm of small-business management, we will clear up two common misconceptions, explore small-business career options, and discuss entrepreneurship.

Exploding Myths About Small Business

Mistaken notions can become accepted facts if they are repeated often enough. Such is the case with failure rates and job creation for small businesses. Fortunately, recent research sets the record straight.

6. CHALLENGE two myths about small businesses and **DESCRIBE** entrepreneurs.

The 80-Percent-Failure-Rate Myth. An often-repeated statistic says that four out of five small businesses will fail within five years.[68] This 80 percent casualty rate is a frightening prospect for anyone thinking about starting a business. But a study by Bruce A. Kirchhoff of the New Jersey Institute of Technology found the failure rate for small businesses to be *only 18 percent during their first eight years.*[69] Why the huge disparity? It turns out that studies by the U.S. government and others defined business failures much too broadly. Any closing of a business, even if it occurred because someone died, sold the business, or retired, was recorded as a business failure. In fact, only 18 percent of the 814,000 small businesses tracked by Kirchhoff for eight years went out of business with unpaid bills. This should be a comfort to would-be entrepreneurs.

Entrepreneurs are driven by the mantra: "Find a need and fill it (profitably)." Malaysian-born Shoba Purushothaman detected a need among news outlets for fast, high-quality video footage. Now, as CEO of her own company, NewsMarket, she provides free Web-based video feeds to broadcasters. Corporations and government agencies pay her fees ranging up to $100,000 to get their news footage on the air.

The Low-Wage-Jobs Myth. When it came to creating jobs during the 1980s and 1990s, America's big businesses were put to shame by their small and mid-size counterparts. Eighty percent of the new job growth was generated by the smaller companies; massive layoffs were the norm at big companies.[70] Critics, meanwhile, claimed that most of the new jobs in the small-business sector went to low-paid clerks and hamburger flippers. Such was not the case, according to a Cambridge, Massachusetts, study by researcher David Birch.

After analyzing new jobs created in the United States between 1987 and 1992, Birch found that businesses with fewer than 100 employees had indeed created most new jobs. Surprisingly, however, only 4 percent of those small firms produced 70 percent of that job growth.[71] Birch calls these rapidly growing small companies "gazelles," as opposed to the "mice" businesses that tend to remain very small. For the period studied, the gazelles added more high-paying jobs than big companies eliminated. Gazelles are not mom-and-pop operations. They tend to be computer software, telecommunications, and specialized engineering or manufacturing firms.[72] Thus, although small businesses on average pay less than big companies do and are about half as likely to offer health insurance benefits, they are *not* low-wage havens.[73]

Again, as in the case of failure rates, the truth about the prospects of starting or working for a small company is different—and brighter—than traditional fallacies suggest.

■ Career Opportunities in Small Business

entrepreneurship: *process of pursuing opportunities without regard to resources currently under one's control*

Among the five small-business career options listed in Table 1.2, only franchises require definition. The other four are self-defining.[74] A franchise is a license to sell another company's products and/or to use another company's name in business. Familiar franchise operations include McDonald's, the National Basketball Association, and Holiday Inn.[75] Notice how each of the career options in Table 1.2 has positive and negative aspects. There is no one best option. Success in the small-business sector depends on the right combination of money, talent, hard work, luck, and opportunity.[76] Fortunately, career opportunities in small business are virtually unlimited.

1g Got a Good Business Idea? You've Got 45 Seconds

According to new-venture expert Elton B. Sherwin Jr., entrepreneurs who are trying to raise venture capital should be able to answer these "Seven Sacred Questions" in 45 seconds:

1. What is your product?
2. Who is the customer?
3. Who will sell it?
4. How many people will buy it?
5. How much will it cost to design and build?
6. What is the sales price?
7. When will you break even?

Source: Marc Ballon, "Hot Tips," Inc., *21 (April 1999): 104.*

QUESTION:

Can you pass this 45-second test with your idea for a new business? Give details.

■ Entrepreneurship

According to experts on the subject, "**entrepreneurship** is the process by which individuals—either on their own or inside organizations—pursue opportunities without regard to the resources they currently control."[77] In effect, entrepreneurs look beyond current resource constraints when they envision new possibilities. Entrepreneurs are preoccupied with "how to," rather than "why not." Entrepreneurs, as we discuss next, are risk takers—and all they want is a chance.

■ A Trait Profile for Entrepreneurs. Exactly how do entrepreneurs differ from general managers or administrators? According to the trait profiles in Table 1.3, entrepreneurs tend to be high achievers who focus more on future possibilities, external factors, and technical details. Also, compared with general

Table 1.2 Career Opportunities in Small Business

Small-business career options	Capital requirements	Likelihood of steady paycheck	Degree of personal control	Ultimate financial return
1. Become an independent contractor/consultant	Low to moderate	None to low	Very high	Negative to high
2. Take a job with a small business	None	Moderate to high	Low to moderate	Low to moderate
3. Join or buy a small business owned by your family	Low to high	Low to high	Low to high	Moderate to high
4. Purchase a franchise	Moderate to high	None to moderate	Moderate to high	Negative to high
5. Start your own small business	Moderate to high	None to moderate	High to very high	Negative to very high

Table 1.3 Contrasting Trait Profiles for Entrepreneurs and Administrators

Entrepreneurs tend to	Administrators tend to
Focus on envisioned futures	Focus on the established present
Emphasize external/market dimensions	Emphasize internal/cost dimensions
Display a medium to high tolerance for ambiguity	Display a low to medium tolerance for ambiguity
Exhibit moderate to high risk-taking behavior	Exhibit low to moderate risk-taking behavior
Obtain motivation from a need to achieve	Obtain motivation from a need to lead others (i.e., social power)
Possess technical knowledge and experience in the innovative area	Possess managerial knowledge and experience

Source: *Philip D. Olson, "Choices for Innovation-Minded Corporations,"* The Journal of Business Strategy, *11 (January–February 1990): Exhibit 1, p. 44. Reprinted from* Journal of Business Strategy *(New York: Warren, Gorham & Lamont). © 1990 Warren, Gorham & Lamont Inc. Used with permission.*

administrators, entrepreneurs are more comfortable with ambiguity and risk taking. It is important to note that entrepreneurs are not necessarily better or worse than other managers—they are just different. Jeff Bezos, the founder and CEO of Amazon.com, had this to say in a recent interview with *Inc.* magazine:

> *Entrepreneurship is really more about a state of mind than it is about working for yourself. It's about being resourceful, it's about problem solving. If you meet people who seem like really good problem solvers, step back, and you'll see that they are self-reliant. I spent summers on my grandfather's ranch, in a small town in Texas; from age four to 16 I probably missed only two summers. One of the things that you learn in a rural area like that is self-reliance. People do everything themselves. . . . If something is broken, let's fix it.*[78]

Bezos instructively calls himself a "realistic optimist." He explains:

> *I believe that optimism is an essential quality for doing anything hard—entrepreneurial endeavors or anything else. That doesn't mean that you're blind or unrealistic, it means that you keep focused on eliminating your risks, modifying your strategy, until it is a strategy about which you can be genuinely optimistic.*[79]

1h Look Out Below!

Fred Smith, founder and chairman of FedEx:

> *Being entrepreneurial doesn't mean you jump off a ledge and figure out how to make a parachute on the way down.*

Source: As quoted in Matthew Boyle, "Absolutely, Positively, Slow the Hell Down," Fortune *(November 15, 2004): 196.*

QUESTION:
What is the practical significance of Smith's comment for would-be entrepreneurs?

Guy Kawasaki, a California venture capitalist and author of the book *The Art of the Start*, offers a slightly different portrait of the entrepreneur: "It's confidence; it's also a little bit of denial. Part of being an entrepreneur is ignoring things too, because if you listen to all the naysayers, no one would ever start a company."[80]

■ **Entrepreneurship Has Its Limits.** Many successful entrepreneurs have tripped over a common stumbling block. Their organizations outgrow the entrepreneur's ability to manage them. In fact, according to "a poll by PriceWaterhouseCoopers, about 40% of CEOs at the fastest-growing companies said that their own ability to manage or reorganize their business could be an impediment to growth."[81] Some refer to this problem as "founder's disease." Moreover, entrepreneurs generally feel stifled by cumbersome and slow-paced bureaucracies.

One management consultant praised Microsoft's Bill Gates for knowing his limits in this regard:

> *In January [2000], Gates went from being CEO of the multibillion-dollar business he cofounded to naming himself "chief software architect" and handing over executive responsibility for his company to Steve Ballmer. . . . few people recognized it for what I think it was: a courageous leap into a self-esteem-threatening black hole.*[82]

The trick, according to a recent study of great entrepreneurs such as Southwest Airlines' Herb Kelleher, is for company founders to keep some psychological distance between themselves and their companies:

> *. . . it's all in their heads. It's their ability to avoid thinking of themselves as one with their companies. "The most successful entrepreneurs think of their companies as a separate entity from themselves," says Nancy Koehn, a historian of entrepreneurship who is a professor at Harvard Business School. "It's incongruous, but they have a sense that if they have done their work well, the proof will be in their companies outgrowing, outpacing—and even outliving—them."*[83]

Entrepreneurs who launch successful and growing companies face a tough dilemma: either grow with the company or have the courage to step aside and turn the reins over to professional managers who possess the administrative traits needed, such as those listed in Table 1.3.

SUMMARY

1. Formally defined, *management* is the process of working with and through others to achieve organizational objectives in a changing environment. Central to this process is the effective and efficient use of limited resources. An inability to work with people, not a lack of technical skills, is the main reason why some managers fail to reach their full potential. A manager is *effective* if he or she reaches a stated objective and *efficient* if limited resources are not wasted in the process.
2. Five overarching sources of change affecting the way management is practiced today are *globalization* (increased global commerce; controversy over offshoring of jobs to low-wage countries; greater need for global managers who can work effectively across cultures), *the evolution of product quality* (moving away from fix-it and inspect-it-in approaches; moving toward build-it-in and design-it-in approaches; emphasis on continuous improvement), *environmentalism* (greater emphasis on making money without destroying the natural environment; many profit opportunites in cleaning up the environment), *an ethical reawakening* (the public's low opinion of managers' ethical conduct is spurring renewed emphasis on honesty and ethical behavior), and *e-business on the Internet* (thanks to the Internet and the Web, e-commerce—buying and selling things over the Web—has evolved into e-business—using the Web to run the entire business).
3. Two ways to answer the question "What do managers do?" are the functional approach and the skills approach. *Managerial functions* generally describe *what* managers do, whereas *managerial skills* state in specific behavioral terms *how* they carry out those functions. This text is organized around eight managerial functions: planning, decision making, organizing, staffing, communicating, motivating, leading, and controlling.
4. Clark Wilson's three managerial skill categories are technical, teambuilding, and drive. His 30 years of research have uncovered an imbalance in managerial skills. About one-third of managers at all levels attempt to exercise control without first applying their technical and teambuilding skills. Thus, managers need to strive for an effective balance of skills.
5. Honeywell researchers found that managers learned 50 percent of what they know about managing from job assignments (" the school of hard knocks"). The remaining 50 percent of their management knowledge came from relationships (30 percent) and formal training and education (20 percent). A good foundation in management theory can give management students a running start and help them avoid foolish mistakes.

6. *Small businesses* (independently owned and managed profit-seeking companies with fewer than 100 employees) are central to a healthy economy. Contrary to conventional wisdom, 80 percent of new businesses do not fail within five years. In fact, one large study found only an 18 percent failure rate during the first eight years. The belief that small businesses create only low-wage jobs also has been shown to be a myth. Five career opportunities in the small-business sector are (1) becoming an independent contractor/consultant; (2) going to work for a small business; (3) joining or buying your family's business; (4) buying a franchise; and (5) starting your own business. Compared with general administrators, entrepreneurs tend to be high achievers who are more future-oriented, externally focused, ready to take risks, and comfortable with ambiguity.

TERMS TO UNDERSTAND

- Management, p. 5
- Effectiveness, p. 7
- Efficiency, p. 7
- Offshoring, p. 9
- Internet, p. 12
- e-Business, p. 13
- Managerial functions, p. 13
- Managerial skills, p. 13
- Small business, p. 20
- Entrepreneurship, p. 21

SKILLS & TOOLS

Career Tips for Today's and Tomorrow's Managers

How to Find the *Right* Job

1. **Assess yourself.**
"Job seekers need to emphasize the things they do best," says Diane Wexler of Career Transition Management in Palo Alto, California. Wexler takes clients through a process of examining goals, interests, skills, and resources. Questions include: What are the 20 things you love to do, both alone and with others? What are the roles you fill, and which aspects would you like to incorporate into a career?

2. **Draft a mission statement.**
Just as a company writes and adheres to a mission statement, create one for yourself. Thinking about your mission and putting it on paper will help define your job search.

3. **Brainstorm.**
Ask others about what your ideal job would be, and how you should go about landing that position. Nancy Nagel invited eight people with a variety of interests and careers to dinner. "I got these great ideas, ranging from being a talk show host to leading adventure travel," she says. "I ended up tossing most of them out, but the session reminded me that there was a great big world out there."

4. **Network.**
Conduct informational interviews. Yes, call those friends-of-friends and ask them for a few minutes of their time. Be prepared with some thoughtful questions.

5. **Research companies.**
Job seekers often accept positions without adequately researching their employers, says Valerie Frankel, co-author of the *I Hate My Job Handbook*. "Inevitably, after a year or two, the job becomes intolerable," she says. Before talking to anyone at a company, research its history, values, and priorities.

6. **Be aware of your abilities and the realities of work.**
"We have this entitlement problem, that we expect to be completely satisfied with our jobs," says Frankel. "I help people be humble when it comes to their job search," adds Elissa Sheridan of BSR. "You can't walk in with a BA or even an MBA and expect someone to be excited by your background without practical experience."

Source: *Excerpted from Mary Scott, "Finding the Perfect Job,"* Business Ethics, *10 (March–April 1996): 16. Reprinted with permission from* Business Ethics Magazine, *52 South 10th Street, #110, Minneapolis, Minn. 55403 (612-962-4700).*

Secrets to Success Once You've Found the Right Job

Investor's Business Daily has spent years analyzing leaders and successful people in all walks of life. Most have ten traits that, when combined, can turn dreams into reality.

1. How you think is everything. Always be positive. Think success, not failure. Beware of a negative environment.
2. Decide upon your true dreams and goals. Write down your specific goals and develop a plan to reach them.

3. Take action. Goals are nothing without action. Don't be afraid to get started now. Just do it.
4. Never stop learning. Go back to school or read books. Get training and acquire skills.
5. Be persistent and work hard. Success is a marathon, not a sprint. Never give up.
6. Learn to analyze details. Get all the facts, all the input. Learn from your mistakes.
7. Focus your time and money. Don't let other people or things distract you.
8. Don't be afraid to innovate; be different. Following the herd is a sure way to mediocrity.
9. Deal and communicate with people effectively. No person is an island. Learn to understand and motivate others.
10. Be honest and dependable; take responsibility. Otherwise, Numbers 1–9 won't matter.

Source: "IBD's 10 Secrets to Success," Investor's Business Daily *(June 8, 2000): A4.*

HANDS-ON EXERCISE

Do You Have the Right Stuff to Be an Entrepreneur?

Instructions: Entrepreneurship isn't just about a good business idea. It's a matter of temperament. Some have it, some don't. Do you? Test yourself. And be honest; there are no "right" answers.

1. Where do you think you'll be in 10 years' time?
   a. I don't think that far ahead; my short-term goals are clear, though.
   b. I have a career path in mind, and I'm going to stick to it.
   c. I live and work from day to day.
   d. I know where I want to be and have ideas on how to get there, but if a better idea comes along, I'll take it.

2. How would you describe your attitude toward competition?
   a. I relish it. Winning isn't everything, it's the only thing.
   b. I avoid it. Competition brings out the worst in people.
   c. I compete hard when I have to, but have been known to bluff my rivals.
   d. I compete hard, but my eye is always on the payoff.

3. Your boss says, "That's the way we do things here." How do you react?
   a. I respect established procedures, but I know when to ignore them.
   b. I begin to think I should be working somewhere else.
   c. I accept it and proceed accordingly. After all, I want to keep my job.
   d. I may try to change his mind, but if I don't succeed quickly, I'll go along.

4. Which statement comes closest to describing your personal finances?
   a. My checkbook is always balanced, and I pay my bills when they come in.
   b. I have an interest-bearing bank account, and I wait until the end of the statement period to pay my bills. That way the bank doesn't get the interest.
   c. I have multiple credit cards, and every one of them is about maxed out.
   d. I separate my business and personal expenses by using different credit cards.

5. What gives you the greatest personal satisfaction at work?
   a. Having an idea and being allowed to run with it.
   b. Receiving praise for a job well done.
   c. Coming out ahead of an office rival.
   d. Knowing my office status is secure.

6. How do you handle criticism at work?
   a. It throws me off track and makes my next task more difficult.
   b. Other perspectives are often helpful, so I listen carefully and adjust if the criticism makes sense to me.
   c. While maintaining my dignity, I try to shift at least some of the blame to others.
   d. I don't like it, but what can I do? I absorb the criticism and move on.

7. What's best about your current job?
   a. My salary and perks. I do OK compared with people like me.
   b. The fine reputation of my company.
   c. I enjoy a certain amount of freedom to start my own projects.
   d. I get regular promotions, and there's a clear career path to the top.

8. Which statement best describes your attitude toward your projects at work?
   a. I like to start projects, but I tend to lose interest and delegate things to other people.

b. I find myself moving on to new projects before I finish the current one.
c. I always finish what I start. Personally.
d. I've been known to put a project on hold if I run into difficulties.

9. How much time do you typically invest in your projects at work?
a. I take pride in being on schedule, so I put in however many hours it takes. Then I take a breather.
b. I work hard, but sometimes I'll take a day or two off in midproject.
c. I'm pretty much a 9-to-5er.
d. My work is my life.

10. If you had what you thought was a good idea for a start-up, how would you finance it?
a. A loan. That's why banks exist.
b. To hold down my exposure, I'd hit up friends and family.
c. I'd take out a second mortgage on my house.
d. I'd *sell* my house if it came to that.

Scoring: Add up your score, using the following key:

1. a-2	b-3	c-1	d-4
2. a-3	b-1	c-2	d-4
3. a-3	b-4	c-1	d-2
4. a-1	b-3	c-4	d-2
5. a-4	b-2	c-3	d-1
6. a-1	b-4	c-3	d-2
7. a-2	b-1	c-4	d-3
8. a-2	b-3	c-4	d-1
9. a-4	b-2	c-1	d-3
10. a-1	b-2	c-3	d-4

Results

10 TO 19 POINTS
You are probably a responsible employee, but not a self-starter. You wait to be assigned tasks. Security is important to you. Your tolerance of risk is relatively low. You may derive too much of your sense of self-worth from factors outside yourself, such as the prestige of the company you work for. Stay put.

20 TO 29 POINTS
You are capable of initiative, even if it doesn't seem that way. You try to advance your career, but are careful not to offend people along the way. You understand office politics, but are reluctant to make bold moves. If you aren't already in middle management, you may be a good candidate.

30 TO 35 POINTS
Lack of ambition is not one of your shortcomings. Neither is a willingness to work hard, and outside normal office hours. You may, however, be somewhat impatient, and reluctant to seek advice from others. These are not good qualities in an entrepreneur. Go for top management instead.

36 TO 40 POINTS
You have the makings of an excellent entrepreneur. You have a high tolerance for risk—an essential ingredient. You are passionate about your ideas. Equally important, you are able to balance your own ambition with interest in others' thoughts and regard for their feelings. Go for it.

Source: *From* Newsweek, *eLife Spring 2000*

For Consideration/Discussion

1. Well, do you have the right stuff to be an entrepreneur? Is this a valid assessment tool? Why or why not?
2. Do you know someone who is a successful entrepreneur? If so, how well does the interpretation for an individual scoring 36 to 40 points characterize that person?
3. What would happen if everyone in the business world scored high on this quiz?
4. Is it an insult to score low on this quiz? Explain.

INTERNET EXERCISES

1. Staying informed about management and managers: Business managers have their own culture—complete with heroes and villains, legends, myths, literature, and jargon. What better way to begin thinking like a manager than to read what they like to read? *Business Week* magazine offers an excellent collection of online resources at **www.businessweek.com**. Find a management-related article that interests you and read it. Clicking on the tab "Top News," "Small Biz," or "Careers" will produce lots of timely and useful information. You can access a full-text version of a particular article by selecting "Printer-Friendly Version" in the small box titled "Story tools." (*Note:* You may want to make a hard copy for later reference and/or discussion in class.)

Learning Points: 1. What linkages did you find between the article you selected and the material in Chapter 1? 2. What useful ideas did you learn about good management and/or mismanagement? 3. What interesting or useful things did you learn about specific managers, companies, industries, or current events? 4. Are you now more (or less) interested in being a manager?

2. Want to start and run your own business? When surveyed, nearly two-thirds of Americans say they either own their own business or have dreamed of being their own boss. If you are in that category, here is a must-visit on the Internet. Go to the home page of **www.morebusiness.com**. If your business is already up and running, explore the entire site for useful information and updates. If you are thinking of starting your own business, click on the main menu item "Start Up" and then select the link "Small Business Primer." Work your way through relevant parts of the primer.

If you are hungry for more information about starting your own business, get down to details with **www.inc.com**. This site is run by small-business–oriented *Inc.* magazine. You'll find lots of helpful advice and practical tips.

Learning Points: 1. Does starting your own business entail more than you expected? Explain. 2. Are you more or less inclined to start your own business after this Web exercise? Explain.

3. Check it out: The U.S. Small Business Administration provides a gold mine of free information for small-business owners and future entrepreneurs (**www.sba.gov**).

For updates to these exercises, visit our Web site (**http://business.college.hmco.com/students/** and select Kreitner, *Management,* 10e).

CLOSING CASE

Sudhaker Ghate: An Entrepreneur by Choice

Sudhaker Ghate, a successful entrepreneur and recipient of the 'Vijay Ratna' award, has been the Chairman of Miraj Pharmaceuticals since its inception. The award is given by the International Friendship Society every year to 20 people for the substantial contribution in their respective fields. Miraj Pharmaceuticals is a family managed organisation that was started by Sudhaker Ghate about 23 years back. Initially starting as a marketing organisation, he expanded his business by adding manufacturing units to it later on.

Ghate has three sons and a daughter; two sons are Chemical Engineers and the third is a Pharmacist and all of them have obtained postgraduate degree in management. His sons joined him as Vice-Presidents after 1982. His daughter has been looking after computer operations at the Corporate Office. All of the family members including his wife are board members and most of the decisions are restricted to the top management. The sales turnover of the company in the last financial year was Rs. 12 crores and had manpower of 600 people. The marketing network of the firm was covering almost the entire country having divisional offices at Mumbai, Kolkata, Delhi and Hyderabad. The sales force of 250 medical representatives was given 'detailing training' regularly as a part of staff development activity. Apart from inculcating professional skills and capabilities, it had contributed a lot in creating an environment where interaction and information sharing could take place easily amongst the executives and the staff. The marketing strategy was based on the review of the market through such meetings.

Ghate was born in a small village in Maharashtra in the year 1934. He was the youngest in a family of nine children. His father was a farmer and was educated upto the primary level. As his father was very particular about the education of his children, Ghate went to Nagpur after high school. He did his intermediate at Nagpur and then graduation from Mumbai. Being determined about progressing in life, he completed the Bachelor's degree in Pharmacy followed by a degree in law at Nagpur. During his college days he believed that he was of a different 'breed'. At that time he used to chalk out his future plan. He always wanted to do something of his own. Inspite of discouragement from his mother and an elder brother, he thought of starting and managing a pharmaceutical unit when he was a student. His father was all along a source of inspiration to him. He joined a pharmaceutical company as a medical representative in 1959 and rose to the position of Deputy Sales Manager in the span of seven years. He was transferred from Nagpur to Mumbai in 1966. By now he had seriously made up his mind to quit the job and start an enterprise of his own. Morally supported by his wife, he took the final decision and resigned in November 1967 from the company in which he had been working. The only financial resource available to Ghate at that time was gratuity and provident fund with which he made his initial investment of Rs. 55,000/-. His friends helped him in setting up the firm. Instead of venturing into manufacturing he thought of capturing the market share first and took a loan licence with another company. He used to get two types of tablets and a capsule manufactured by the company under the formula and supervision provided by him. He encountered many difficulties while marketing the products and realised that a common product that could be prescribed to every second patient would fetch a better market than the products he was offering. At this stage he was assisted by his wife in the secretarial work and two medical representatives in the field work.

He knew from his experience that a particular tonic called "Metatone" was doing well in the market. He went for an agreement with the concerned pharmaceutical company and then onwards used to get the tonic manufactured by them and marketed it under his own registered brand name 'ViTL tone'. Although he met with heavy losses during the first two financial years, he could reach the breakeven point in 1971. He applied for Government land in Mumbai to start a manufacturing unit and succeeded in getting a loan of Rs.1,98,000 from the Maharashtra State.

After acquiring the land and capital for investment, he went ahead with the manufacturing as well as marketing of ViTL tone. He achieved 100% annual growth for quite a few years. Encouraged by the performance, the firm came up with four more pharmaceutical manufacturing units at Nasik, by the year 1985. As suggested by his enthusiastic and change oriented sons, ten more products were added to the product line by now. Ghate was taken aback when the firm met with heavy losses during the financial year 1986-87. As it came to him as a shock, he went in for extensive market surveys only to find out why a few of his new products which were introduced in the recent past were not doing well in most of the regions. He restricted the market territories for such products and even stopped manufacturing some of them.

The strategy worked and he started to regain his position in the market. The main product of Miraj Pharmaceuticals, i.e., 'ViTL-tone' alone achieved 26 percent growth in the subsequent year. At the same time he continued to expand his product line by adding one product every year and came up with a new project every second year. The firm also diversified by acquiring a sick chemical unit in 1989, which started production in September 1990. Now, Ghate is planning to enter into a joint venture by starting and running a pharmaceutical unit at U.A.E.

For Discussion

1. How well does Sudhaker Ghate fit the entrepreneurial profile in Table 1.3? Explain.
2. What were the personal characteristics of Sudhaker Ghate which helped him to become an entrepreneur?
3. What led to heavy losses in the financial year 1986-87?
4. Does this case reveal anything about the vision of Sudhaker Ghate?

Source: Case Method in Management Education, Upinder Dhar & Santosh Dhar, Excel Books, New Delhi, 2002, pp. 132-134.

TEST PREPPER

True/False Questions

_____ **1.** If a company does not achieve its objective, it is effective but not efficient.

_____ **2.** Offshoring is the controversial practice of drilling for oil in the ocean.

_____ **3.** With the inspect-it-in approach to improving product quality, the emphasis is on continuous improvement of personnel and processes.

_____ **4.** By definition, e-business involves much more than business-to-consumer retailing on the Internet.

_____ **5.** Two managerial functions identified by French industrialist Henri Fayol in the early 1900s are planning and control.

_____ **6.** One of the three managerial skill categories identified by Clark L. Wilson is leadership.

_____ **7.** According to the Honeywell study, managers learned half of what they knew about managing from job assignments (the "school of hard knocks").

_____ **8.** Ninety-nine percent of the employers in the United States are small businesses.

_____ **9.** Eighty percent of small businesses fail within five years.

_____ **10.** Entrepreneurs tend to be high achievers who dislike ambiguity.

Multiple-Choice Questions

1. Management is the process of working with and through others to achieve _____ in a changing environment.
A. plans B. strategies
C. a mission D. success
E. organizational objectives

2. Which of these is(are) always required by organizational objectives or goals?
A. Management approval B. Job descriptions
C. Collective action D. Financial resources
E. Information gathering

3. What does "offshoring" involve?
A. Exporting goods to foreign countries
B. Outsourcing jobs to lower-wage countries
C. Hiring recent documented immigrants
D. Hiring undocumented immigrants
E. Sending employees on foreign assignments

4. The _____ stage in the evolution of product quality emphasizes _____
A. inspect-it-in; staffing and supervision
B. fix-it-in; quality training
C. design-it-in; continuous improvement
D. build-it-in; product redesign
E. work-it-in; engineering specifications

5. A business using the Internet for greater efficiency in every aspect is called a(n)
A. global business. B. integrated business.
C. small business. D. high-tech business.
E. e-business.

6. Which of these functions is commonly referred to as the primary management function?
A. Planning B. Leading
C. Controlling D. Staffing
E. Organizing

7. On the basis of his 30 years of research, Clark Wilson has identified the following three managerial skill categories:
A. motivating, communicating, and leading.
B. planning, checking, and regulating.
C. communicating, inspecting, and control.
D. teambuilding, motivating, and decision making.
E. technical, teambuilding, and drive.

8. In the Honeywell study, managers learned the *least* (20 percent of what they learned) about managing from
A. coworkers. B. internships.
C. job assignments. D. formal training and education.
E. role models.

9. Only _____ percent of small businesses tracked by Kirchhoff for _____ years went out of business with unpaid bills.
A. 50; 5 B. 80; 2
C. 25; 6 D. 75; 5
E. 18; 8

10. Entrepreneurship, by definition, is the process by which individuals pursue opportunities without regard to
A. risk.
B. plans.
C. the law.
D. resources under one's control.
E. the future.

ACE self-test

Want more questions? Visit the student website at **http://business.college.hmco.com/students/** (select Kreitner, *Management*, 10e) and take the ACE quizzes for more practice.,

2 The Evolution of Management Thought

"In the renewing society the historian consults the past in the service of the present and the future."[1]

JOHN W. GARDNER

OBJECTIVES

- **Identify** two key assumptions supporting the universal process approach, and briefly **describe** Henri Fayol's contribution.
- **Discuss** Frederick W. Taylor's approach to improving the practice of industrial management.
- **Identify** at least four key quality improvement ideas from W. Edwards Deming and the other quality advocates.
- **Describe** the general aim of the human relations movement, and **explain** the circumstances in which it arose.
- **Explain** the significance of applying open-system thinking to management.
- **Explain** the practical significance of adopting a contingency perspective.
- **Describe** what "management by best seller" involves, and **explain** what managers can do to avoid it.

the changing workplace

The Survivor

When Autodesk named Carol Bartz as its new chief executive in 1992, the then 43-year-old former Sun Microsystems sales manager was destined for corporate stardom. She was taking over one of the nation's fastest-growing software companies—maker of a groundbreaking program that allowed architects and engineers to abandon their T squares and pencils and design anything from a backyard arbor to a skyscraper on a personal computer. Her ascension instantly made her the most prominent female executive in technology—and one of the most buzzed-about up-and-comers in all of business.

But the storybook script ended there. Her second day on the job, Bartz learned she had breast cancer and began an arduous battle with the disease. Meanwhile, she had inherited a cabal of rebellious Autodesk programmers—led by a co-founder with a cult-like following—bent on humiliating the outsider. Worse, Bartz's first major product introduction was a dud, bringing Autodesk to the brink of collapse and raising questions about her competency.

A lot of people would have quit. Not Bartz. Between chemotherapy sessions, she worked doggedly to professionalize the company's amateurish business practices and to recruit desperately needed management depth. Ultimately, Bartz survived the cancer, and by the late 1990s it looked as though she had pumped new life into Autodesk too—only to see her world nearly collapse again. With Autodesk products slow to adapt to the Internet, Bartz endured a falling stock price, an exodus of talent, and a chorus of taunts about the company's future. At one meeting with stock analysts, she unloaded: "You'd be happier if we were selling plastic-wrapped fruit baskets over the Internet?"

Defying calls from analysts for her resignation, the tough-talking Bartz often lashed out at her executive team, opening some meetings with a taunt of her own: "Tell me why I shouldn't fire the whole lot of you." Her job, however, was never in serious jeopardy. During Autodesk's dog days, "we always asked what can be done differently," recalls board member Hal Dawson, an Autodesk director since 1988. "We always concluded we couldn't find anyone better than Carol."

Their faith has been rewarded. Every Fortune 100 company today uses Autodesk programs, which are as dominant among architects and engineers as Microsoft Word is with writers. The company ranks as the No. 1 performer in the S&P 500 for the past 12 months and has tripled in value since 2002. . . .

Bartz's tenacity wasn't forged solely by her struggles with disease and rebellious nerds. Her mother died when she was 8, and she was raised by her grandmother in a small Wisconsin town. She worked her way through high school as an assistant to the president of the local bank. Bartz earned a computer science degree at the University of Wisconsin—one of only two women to do so in 1971. That planted the seeds of a career that took her first to Digital Equipment Corp. and then to Sun. "Failure is not in her vocabulary," says Tony Peach, an Autodesk product manager.

Bartz excelled on the sales side at both DEC and Sun, and at Autodesk she has forged an effective leadership style out of her no-nonsense charm. Tech is full of swaggering CEOs; Bartz prefers poor-mouthing to pomposity. "She doesn't have an ego button to be pushed, thank God," Dawson says. Her periodic blue-streak outbursts are softened by an instinct for diplomacy and a folksy style that connects her with people of all sorts.

It's all on display one recent October morning at the company's headquarters in San Rafael, Calif., during an informal "coffee with Carol" gathering of about 250 employees. Autodesk's stock hit an all-time high this morning, and Bartz opens the meeting with trademark humor. Apologizing for arriving five minutes late, she quips, "My staff will tell you, never have a breakfast with Carol. That's when people tend to get fired."

The room erupts in laughter, and Bartz launches into an explanation of the company's recent success. Then she takes questions, the first of which is in her face: How much longer will she stay as CEO? Bartz, standing with a wireless mike, swings into her answer like a gameshow host. "There was a rumor I'd bail out when we got to a billion in annual sales," she says. "Comes from something I said 12 years ago. Well it's taken longer to reach a billion, but I don't see any change happening. As long as I'm learning, and I am, I want to stay." . . .

Everything that Bartz has been through has toughened her for the battles to come. And there's no questioning that toughness: She delayed the start of her seven-course chemotherapy treatment by a month, against her doctor's advice, so she could chart an initial course for Autodesk. Besides, no one believes more in the Autodesk mission than she does. At a recent employee meeting, she insists, "We are not a fluke." The company's current run, she says, is the start of a great new phase, not a final act. Then, raising her voice, she says, "We've got to believe in ourselves. Because if we believe, there's no stopping us." The room grows silent. Bartz's smile fades. She's getting serious. "So you'll hear this in the coming months: Do you believe? Over and over. Until you come up to me and say, 'I believe.'"

Source: *From G. Pascal Zachary, "The Survivor,"* Business 2.0, *5 (December 2004): 132–140.*

Carol Bartz did not start with a blank slate at Autodesk. The firm's founder, culture, and way of doing business all affected what she could and could not do to turn the company around. In short, history mattered. In a parallel sense, that is what this chapter is all about. Management historians believe that a better knowledge of the past will lead to a more productive future. They contend that students of management who fail to understand the evolution of management thought are destined to repeat past mistakes.[2] Moreover, historians and managers alike believe that one needs to know where management has been if one is to understand where it is going. For example, while participating in a Harvard Business School roundtable discussion on the value of management history, a top-level executive summarized:

> *It is always hard to communicate any sort of abstract idea to someone else, let alone get any acceptance of it. But when there is some agreement on the factual or historical background of that idea, the possibilities for general agreement expand enormously.*[3]

Historians draw a distinction between history and historical perspective. According to one management scholar,

> *Historical perspective is the study of a subject in light of its earliest phases and subsequent evolution. Historical perspective differs from history in that the object of historical perspective is to sharpen one's vision of the present, not the past.*[4]

This chapter qualifies as a historical perspective because it is part historical fact and part modern-day interpretation. Various approaches in the evolution of management thought are discussed relative to the lessons each can teach today's managers. The term *evolution* is appropriate here because management theory has developed in bits and pieces through the years. Moreover, pioneering contributors to management theory and practice have come from around the globe[5] (see Figure 2.1). A historical perspective puts these pieces together.

The Practice and Study of Management

The systemic study of management is relatively new. As an area of academic study, management is essentially a product of the twentieth century. Only three universities—Pennsylvania, Chicago, and California—offered business management courses before 1900.[6]

But the actual practice of management has been around for thousands of years. The pyramids of Egypt, for example, stand as tangible evidence of the ancient world's ability to manage. It reportedly took more than 100,000 individuals 20 years to construct the great pyramid honoring the Egyptian king Cheops nearly 5,000 years ago. This remarkable achievement was the result of systematically managed effort. Although the Egyptians' management techniques were crude by modern standards, many problems they faced are still around today. They, like today's managers, had to make plans, obtain and mobilize human and material resources, coordinate interdependent jobs, keep records, report their progress, and take corrective action as needed.

■ Information Overload

Since the building of the pyramids, entire civilizations have come and gone. In one form or another, management was practiced in each. Sadly, during those thousands of years of management experience, one modern element was missing: a systematically recorded body of management knowledge.[7] In early cultures, management was something one learned by word of mouth and trial and error—not something one studied in school, read about in textbooks and on the Internet, theorized about, experimented with, or wrote about.

Figure 2.1 Management Is a Global Affair: Selected Contributors to Management Theory

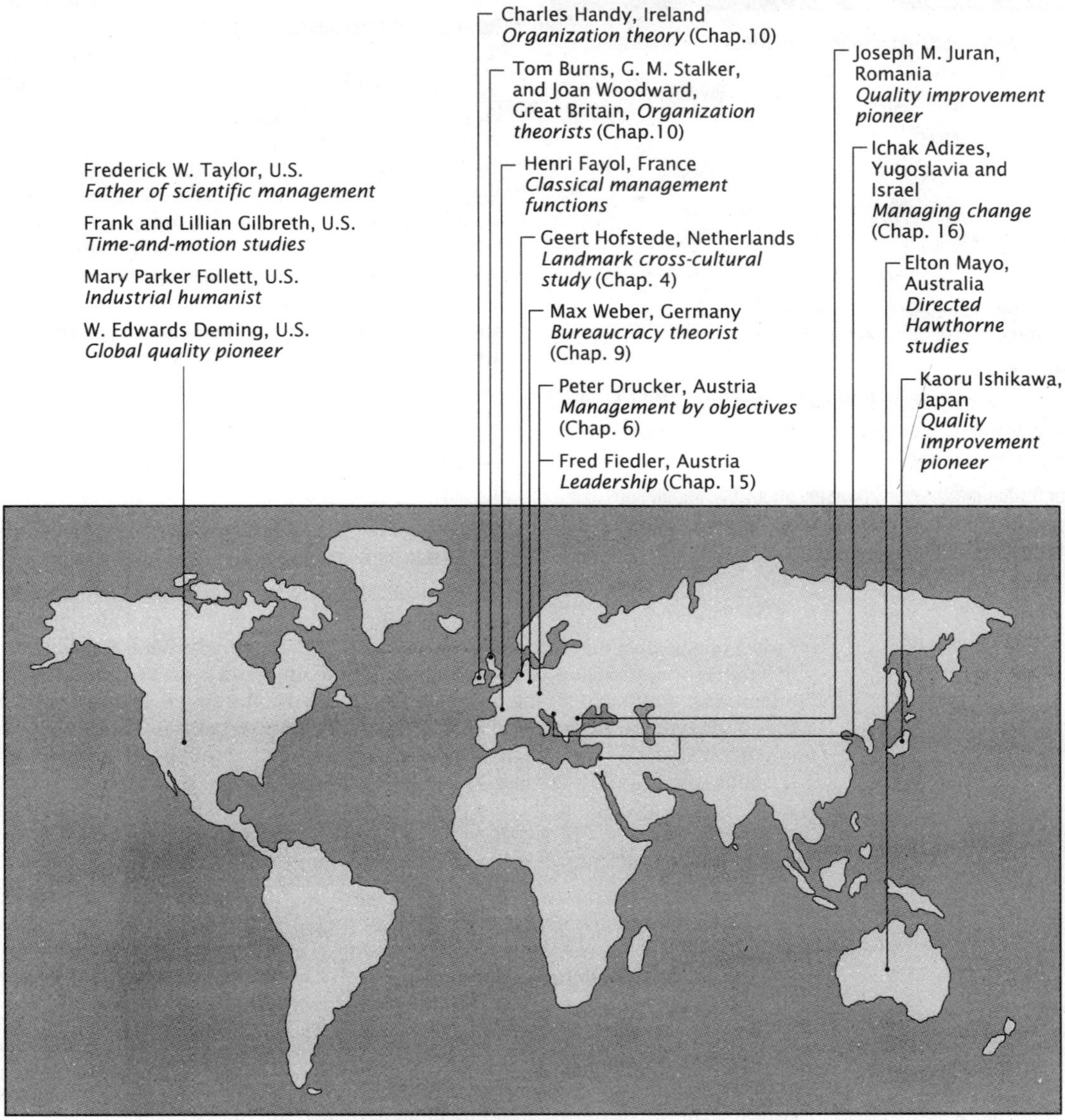

Thanks to modern print and electronic media, the collective genius of thousands of management theorists and practitioners has been compressed into a veritable mountain of textbooks, journals, research monographs, microfilms, movies, audio- and videotapes, and computer files. Never before have present and future managers had so much relevant information at their fingertips, as close as a Google search on the Web or the nearest library. As an indication of what is available, a 1990 study identified 54 journals dealing with just the behavioral side of management.[8] There are many, many others (see Skills & Tools at the end of this chapter). In fact, so much information on

2a How Do You Handle the Information Overload in *Your* Life?

In a survey, 2,096 employees categorized their workspace habits as follows:

Neat freaks	33%
Pilers	27%
Filers	23%
Pack rats	12%
Slobs	2%
Don't know	3%

Source: Data from Cheryl Comeau-Kirschner, "Neatness Counts for Many Employees," Management Review, *88 (April 1999): 7.*

QUESTIONS:

Are you experiencing information overload? Which category best describes your handling of the informational clutter in your life?

For further information about the interactive annotations in this chapter, visit our Web site (**http://business.college.hmco.com/students/** and select Kreitner, *Management*, 10e).

management theory and practice exists today that it is difficult, if not impossible, to keep abreast of all of it.[9]

An Interdisciplinary Field

A principal cause of the information explosion in management theory is its interdisciplinary nature. Scholars from many fields—including psychology, sociology, cultural anthropology, mathematics, philosophy, statistics, political science, economics, logistics, computer science, ergonomics, history, and various fields of engineering—have, at one time or another, been interested in management. In addition, administrators in business, government, religious organizations, health care, and education all have drawn from and contributed to the study of management. Each group of scholars and practitioners has interpreted and reformulated management according to its own perspective. With each new perspective have come new questions and assumptions, new research techniques, different technical jargon, and new conceptual frameworks.[10]

No Universally Accepted Theory of Management

We can safely state that no single theory of management is universally accepted today.[11] To provide a useful historical perspective that will guide our study of modern management, we shall discuss five different approaches to management: (1) the universal process approach, (2) the operational approach, (3) the behavioral approach, (4) the systems approach, and (5) the contingency approach. Understanding these general approaches to the theory and practice of management can help you appreciate how management has evolved, where it is today, and where it appears to be headed. Each of the five approaches to management represents a different conceptual framework for better understanding the practice of management. Cornell University professor Craig C. Lundberg explains the practical (and scientific) importance of conceptual frameworks:

> *When we have a known set of ideas, and the relationships among them are spelled out, we have a conceptual framework, or* model. . . . *In addition to helping us notice and comprehend something of interest as a frame of reference does, models also enable us to anticipate and discover relevant facts and to better understand how things really work. Over time, with continuing experiences and/or confirmation from research, models are modified by being fine-tuned to better and better represent the phenomena of interest, or they are discarded and replaced.*[12]

This chapter concludes with some cautionary words about slavishly following sure-fire success formulas in best-selling management books.

The Universal Process Approach

universal process approach: *assumes all organizations require the same rational management process*

The universal process approach is the oldest and one of the most popular approaches to management thought. It is also known as the universalist or functional approach. According to the **universal process approach,** the administration of all organizations, public or private and large or small, requires the same rational process. The universalist approach is based on two main assumptions. First, although the purpose of organizations may vary (for example, business, government, education, or religion), a core management process remains the same across all organizations. Successful managers, therefore, are assumed to be interchangeable among organizations of differing purpose. (This universality of management assumption drove the Pentagon's effort to recruit former corporate CEOs to help rebuild Iraq.)[13] Second, the universal management process can be reduced to a set of separate functions and related principles. Early universal process writers emphasized the specialization of labor (who does what), the chain of command (who reports to whom), and authority (who is ultimately responsible for getting things done).

■ Henri Fayol's Universal Management Process

1. IDENTIFY two key assumptions supporting the universal process approach, and briefly **DESCRIBE** Henri Fayol's contribution.

In 1916, at the age of 75, Henri Fayol published his now classic book *Administration Industrielle et Générale*, although it did not become widely known in Britain and the United States until an English translation became available in 1949.[14] Despite its belated appearance in the English-speaking world and despite its having to compete with enthusiastic scientific management and human relations movements in the United States, Fayol's work left a permanent mark on twentieth-century management thinking.

Fayol was first an engineer and later a successful administrator in a large French mining and metallurgical concern, which is perhaps why he did not resort to theory in his pioneering management book. Rather, Fayol was a manager who attempted to translate his broad administrative experience into practical guidelines for the successful management of all types of organizations.

As we mentioned in Chapter 1, Fayol believed that the manager's job could be divided into five functions, or areas, of managerial responsibility—planning, organizing, command, coordination, and control—that are essential to managerial success. (Some educators refer to them as the POC^3 functions.) His 14 universal principles of management, listed in Table 2.1, were intended to show managers how to

Table 2.1 Fayol's 14 Universal Principles of Management

1. **Division of work.** Specialization of labor is necessary for organizational success.
2. **Authority.** The right to give orders must accompany responsibility.
3. **Discipline.** Obedience and respect help an organization run smoothly.
4. **Unity of command.** Each employee should receive orders from only one superior.
5. **Unity of direction.** The efforts of everyone in the organization should be coordinated and focused in the same direction.
6. **Subordination of individual interests to the general interest.** Resolving the tug of war between personal and organizational interests in favor of the organization is one of management's greatest difficulties.
7. **Remuneration.** Employees should be paid fairly in accordance with their contribution.
8. **Centralization.** The relationship between centralization and decentralization is a matter of proportion; the optimum balance must be found for each organization.
9. **Scalar chain.** Subordinates should observe the formal chain of command unless expressly authorized by their respective superiors to communicate with each other.
10. **Order.** Both material things and people should be in their proper places.
11. **Equity.** Fairness that results from a combination of kindliness and justice will lead to devoted and loyal service.
12. **Stability and tenure of personnel.** People need time to learn their jobs.
13. **Initiative.** One of the greatest satisfactions is formulating and carrying out a plan.
14. **Esprit de corps.** Harmonious effort among individuals is the key to organizational success.

Source: *Adapted from Henri Fayol,* General and Industrial Management, *trans. Constance Storrs (London: Isaac Pitman & Sons, 1949). Copyright 1949 by Lake Publishing Company. Reprinted by permission.*

2b Back to the Opening Case

Which of Fayol's 14 universal principles of management in Table 2.1 are evident in the Carol Bartz case? Explain your reasoning for each principle selected.

carry out their functional duties. Fayol's functions and principles have withstood the test of time because of their widespread applicability. In spite of years of reformulation, rewording, expansion, and revision, Fayol's original management functions still can be found in nearly all management texts. In fact, after an extensive review of studies of managerial work, a pair of management scholars concluded:

> *The classical functions still represent the most useful way of conceptualizing the manager's job, especially for management education, and perhaps this is why it is still the most favored description of managerial work in current management textbooks. The classical functions provide clear and discrete methods of classifying the thousands of different activities that managers carry out and the techniques they use in terms of the functions they perform for the achievement of organizational goals.*[15]

Lessons from the Universal Process Approach

Fayol's main contribution to management thought was to show how the complex management process can be separated into interdependent areas of responsibility, or functions. Fayol's contention that management is a continuous process beginning with planning and ending with controlling also remains popular today. Contemporary adaptations of Fayol's functions offer students of management a useful framework for analyzing the management process. But as we noted in Chapter 1, this sort of rigid functional approach has been criticized for creating the impression that the management process is more rational and orderly than it really is. Fayol's functions, therefore, form a skeleton that needs to be fleshed out with concepts, techniques, and situational refinements from more modern approaches. The functional approach is useful because it specifies generally what managers *should* do, but the other approaches help explain *why* and *how*.

The Operational Approach

operational approach: *production-oriented field of management dedicated to improving efficiency and cutting waste*

The term **operational approach** is a convenient description of the production-oriented area of management dedicated to improving efficiency, cutting waste, and improving quality. Since the turn of the twentieth century, it has had a number of labels, including scientific management, management science, operations research, production management, and operations management. Underlying this somewhat confusing evolution of terms has been a consistent purpose: to make person-machine systems work as efficiently as possible. Throughout its historical development, the operational approach has been technically and quantitatively oriented.

Frederick W. Taylor's Scientific Management

Born in 1856 the son of a Philadelphia lawyer, Frederick Winslow Taylor was the epitome of the self-made man. Because a temporary problem with his eyes kept him from attending Harvard University, Taylor went to work as a common laborer in a small Philadelphia machine shop. In just four years he picked up the trades of pattern maker and machinist.[16]

2. DISCUSS Frederick W. Taylor's approach to improving the practice of industrial management.

Later, Taylor went to work at Midvale Steel Works in Philadelphia, where he quickly moved up through the ranks while studying at night for a mechanical engineering degree. As a manager at Midvale, Taylor was appalled at industry's unsystematic practices. He observed little, if any, cooperation between the managers and the laborers. Inefficiency and waste were rampant. Output restriction among groups of workers, which Taylor called "systematic soldiering," was widespread. Ill-equipped and inadequately trained workers were typically left on their own to determine how to do their jobs. Hence, the father of scientific management committed himself to the relentless pursuit of "finding a better way."[17] Taylor sought nothing less than what he termed a "mental revolution" in the practice of industrial management.[18]

scientific management: *developing performance standards on the basis of systematic observation and experimentation*

According to an early definition, **scientific management** is "that kind of management which *conducts* a business or affairs by *standards* established by facts or truths gained through *systematic* observation, experiment, or reasoning."[19] The word *experiment* deserves special emphasis because it was Taylor's trademark. While working at Midvale and later at Bethlehem Steel, Taylor started the scientific management movement in industry in four areas: standardization, time and task study, systematic selection and training, and pay incentives.[20]

Frederick W. Taylor, 1856–1915

■ **Standardization.** By closely studying metal-cutting operations, Taylor collected extensive data on the optimum cutting-tool speeds and the rates at which stock should be fed into the machines for each job. The resulting standards were then posted for quick reference by the machine operators. He also systematically catalogued and stored the expensive cutting tools that usually were carelessly thrown aside when a job was completed. Operators could go to the carefully arranged tool room, check out the right tool for the job at hand, and check it back in when finished. Taylor's approach caused productivity to jump and costs to fall.

■ **Time and Task Study.** According to the traditional rule-of-thumb approach, there was no "science of shoveling." But after thousands of observations and stopwatch recordings, Taylor detected a serious flaw in the way various materials were being shoveled—each laborer brought his own shovel to work. Taylor knew the company was losing, not saving, money when a laborer used the same shovel for both heavy and light materials. A shovel load of iron ore weighed about 30 pounds, according to Taylor's calculations, whereas a shovel load of rice coal weighed only 4 pounds. Systematic experimentation revealed that a shovel load of 21 pounds was optimum (permitted the greatest movement of material in a day). Taylor significantly increased productivity by having workers use specially sized and shaped shovels provided by the company—large shovels for the lighter materials and smaller ones for heavier work.

■ **Systematic Selection and Training.** Although primitive by modern standards, Taylor's experiments with pig iron handling clearly reveal the intent of this phase of scientific management. The task was to lift a 92-pound block of iron (in the steel trade, a "pig"), carry it up an incline (a distance of about 36 feet), and drop it into an open railroad car. Taylor observed that on the average, a pig iron handler moved about 12½ tons in a ten-hour day of constant effort. After careful study, Taylor found that if he selected the strongest men and instructed them in the proper techniques of lifting and carrying the pigs of iron, he could get each man to load 47 tons in a ten-hour day. Surprisingly, this nearly fourfold increase in output was achieved by having the pig iron handlers spend only 43 percent of their time actually hauling iron. The other 57 percent was spent either walking back empty-handed or sitting down. Taylor reported that the laborers liked the new arrangement because they were less fatigued and took home 60 percent more pay.

Management historians recently have disputed Taylor's pig iron findings, suggesting his conclusions were unfounded and/or exaggerated.[21] As mentioned earlier, our present historical perspective is an evolving blend of fact and interpretation.

2c Piece-Rate Puzzle

Suppose you are a college student about to take a part-time job in the school library. The job involves taking books and bound periodicals from the sorting room and returning them on a hand cart to their proper shelves throughout the library. Library officials have observed that an average of 30 items can be reshelved during one hour of steady effort. You have the option of being paid $9 an hour or 30 cents per item reshelved. The quality of your work will be randomly checked, and 30 cents will be deducted from your pay for each item found to be improperly shelved.

QUESTIONS:
How do you want to be paid? Why? Which pay plan is probably better for the library? Why?

■ **Pay Incentives.** According to Taylor, "What the workmen want from their employers beyond anything else is high wages."[22] This "economic man" assumption led Taylor to believe that piece rates were important to improved productivity. Under traditional piece-rate plans, an individual received a fixed amount of money for each unit of output. Thus, the greater the output, the greater the pay. In his

Figure 2.2 Taylor's Differential Piece-Rate Plan

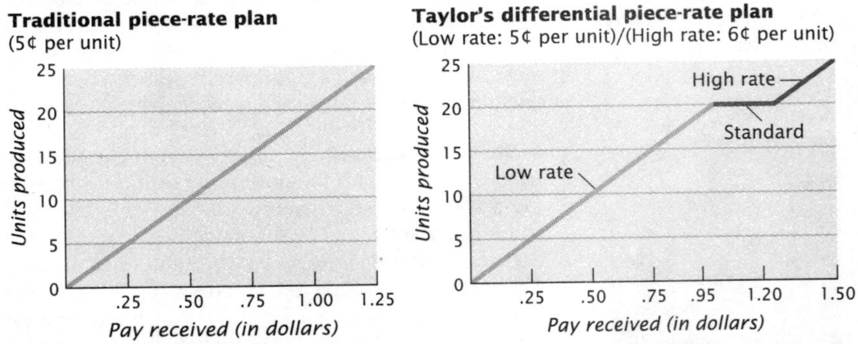

determination to find a better way, Taylor attempted to improve the traditional piece-rate scheme with his differential piece-rate plan.

Figure 2.2 illustrates the added incentive effect of Taylor's differential plan. (The amounts are typical rates of pay in Taylor's time.) Under the traditional plan, a worker would receive a fixed amount (for example, 5 cents) for each unit produced. Seventy-five cents would be received for producing 15 units and $1.00 for 20 units. In contrast, Taylor's plan required that a time study be carried out to determine the company's idea of a fair day's work. Two piece rates were then put into effect. A low rate would be paid if the worker finished the day below the company's standard, a high rate if the day's output met or exceeded the standard. As the lines in Figure 2.2 indicate, a hard worker who produced 25 units would earn $1.25 under the traditional plan and $1.50 under Taylor's plan.

■ Taylor's Followers

Among the many who followed in Taylor's footsteps, Frank and Lillian Gilbreth and Henry L. Gantt stand out.

■ Frank and Lillian Gilbreth. Inspired by Taylor's time studies and motivated by a desire to expand human potential, the Gilbreths turned motion study into an exact science. In so doing, they pioneered the use of motion pictures for studying and streamlining work motions. They paved the way for modern work simplification by cataloguing 17 different hand motions, such as "grasp" and "hold." These they called "therbligs" (actually the name *Gilbreth* spelled backwards with the *t* and *h* reversed). Their success stories include the following:

> *In laying brick, the motions used in laying a single brick were reduced from eighteen to five—with an increase in output, from one hundred and twenty bricks an hour to three hundred and fifty an hour, and with a reduction in the resulting fatigue. In folding cotton cloth, twenty to thirty motions were reduced to ten or twelve, with the result that instead of one hundred and fifty dozen pieces of cloth, four hundred dozen were folded, with no added fatigue.*[23]

Frank and Lillian Gilbreth were so dedicated to the idea of finding the one best way to do every job that 2 of their 12 children wrote *Cheaper by the Dozen*, a humorous recollection of scientific management and motion study applied to the Gilbreth household.[24]

Lillian M. Gilbreth, 1878–1972, at right, and Frank B. Gilbreth, 1868–1924, at left with 11 of their dozen children

Henry L. Gantt, 1861–1919

■ **Henry L. Gantt.** Gantt, a schoolteacher by training, contributed to scientific management by refining production control and cost control techniques. As illustrated in Chapter 6, variations of Gantt's work-scheduling charts are still in use today.[25] He also humanized Taylor's differential piece-rate system by combining a guaranteed day rate (minimum wage) with an above-standard bonus. Gantt was ahead of his time in emphasizing the importance of the human factor and in urging management to concentrate on service rather than profits.[26]

■ The Quality Advocates

Today's managers readily attach strategic importance to quality improvement. The road to this enlightened view, particularly for U.S. managers, was a long and winding one. It started in factories and eventually made its way through service businesses, not-for-profit organizations, and government agencies. An international cast of quality advocates took much of the twentieth century to pave the road to quality. Not until 1980, when NBC ran a television documentary titled *If Japan Can . . . Why Can't We?* did Americans begin to realize fully that *quality* was a key to Japan's growing dominance in world markets. Advice from the following quality advocates finally began to sink in during the 1980s.[27]

3. ■ **IDENTIFY** at least four key quality improvement ideas from W. Edwards Deming and the other quality advocates.

■ **Walter A. Shewhart.** A statistician for Bell Laboratories, Shewhart introduced the concept of statistical quality control in his 1931 landmark text *Economic Control of Quality of Manufactured Product.*

■ **Kaoru Ishikawa.** The University of Tokyo professor advocated quality before World War II and founded the Union of Japanese Scientists and Engineers (JUSE), which became the driving force behind Japan's quality revolution. Ishikawa proposed a preventive approach to quality. His expanded idea of the customer included both *internal and external customers.* Ishikawa's fishbone diagrams, discussed in Chapter 8, remain a popular problem-solving tool to this day.

W. Edwards Deming, 1900–1993

■ **W. Edwards Deming.** This Walter Shewhart understudy accepted an invitation from JUSE in 1950 to lecture on his principles of statistical quality control. His ideas, detailed later in Chapter 17, went far beyond what his Japanese hosts expected from a man with a mathematics Ph.D. from Yale. Japanese manufacturers warmly embraced Deming and his unconventional ideas about encouraging employee participation and striving for continuous improvement. His 1986 book *Out of the Crisis* is "a guide to the 'transformation of the style of American management,' which became a bible for Deming disciples."[28]

■ **Joseph M. Juran.** Juran's career bore a striking similarity to Deming's. Both were Americans (Juran was a naturalized U.S. citizen born in Romania) schooled in statistics, both strongly influenced Japanese managers via JUSE, and both continued to lecture on quality into their nineties. Thanks to extensive training by the Juran Institute, the concept of internal customers is well established today.[29] Teamwork, partnerships with suppliers, problem solving, and brainstorming are all Juran trademarks. "A specific term associated with Juran is *Pareto analysis*, a technique for separating major problems from minor ones. A Pareto analysis looks for the 20 percent of possible causes that lead to 80 percent of all problems."[30] (The 80/20 rule is discussed in Chapter 6 under the heading "Priorities.")

■ **Armand V. Feigenbaum.** While working on his doctorate at MIT, Feigenbaum developed the concept of *total quality control*. He expanded on his idea of an organizationwide program of quality improvement in his 1951 book *Total Quality Control*. He envisioned all functions of the business cycle—from purchasing and engineering, to manufacturing and finance, to marketing and service—as necessarily involved in the quest for quality. The *customer*, according to Feigenbaum, is the one who ultimately determines quality.[31]

■ **Philip B. Crosby.** The author of the 1979 best seller *Quality Is Free*, Crosby learned about quality improvement during his up-from-the-trenches career at ITT (a giant global corporation in many lines of business). His work struck a chord with top managers because he documented the huge cost of having to rework or scrap poor-quality products. He promoted the idea of *zero defects*, or doing it right the first time.[32]

2d The Deming Legacy

Author and management consultant Gary Hamel:

If you asked managers 40 years ago where quality comes from, they would have said it came from either the inspector at the end of the production line or from an artisan who could make beautiful products. Deming sought instead to make quality a systemic capability, everywhere and all the time. He told companies to give ordinary employees the authority to stop a million-dollar production line. They thought he was nuts.

Source: As quoted in David Kirkpatrick, "Innovation Do's & Don'ts," Fortune *(September 6, 2004): 239.*

QUESTIONS:
So who is ultimately responsible for product quality, according to Deming? Explain your rationale. Why were American managers so reluctant to accept this approach?

■ Lessons from the Operational Approach

Scientific management often appears rather unscientific to those who live in a world of genetic engineering, manned space flight, industrial robots, the Internet, and laser technology. *Systematic management* might be a more accurate label. Within the context of haphazard, turn-of-the-twentieth-century industrial practices, however, scientific management was indeed revolutionary. Heading the list of its lasting contributions is a much-needed emphasis on promoting production efficiency and combating waste. Today, dedication to finding a better way is more important than ever in view of uneven productivity growth and diminishing resources.

Nevertheless, Taylor and the early proponents of scientific management have been roundly criticized for viewing workers as unidimensional economic beings interested only in more money. These critics fear that scientific management techniques have dehumanized people by making them act like mindless machines. Not all would agree. According to one respected management scholar who feels that Taylor's work is widely misunderstood and unfairly criticized, Taylor actually improved working conditions by reducing fatigue and redesigning machines to fit people. A systematic analysis of Taylor's contributions led this same management scholar to conclude: "Taylor's track record is remarkable. The point is not, as is often claimed, that he was 'right in the context of his time' but is now outdated, but that *most of his insights are still valid today*."[33]

Contributions by the quality advocates are subject to less debate today. The only question is, Why didn't we listen to them earlier? (See Chapter 17.)

An important post–World War II outgrowth of the operational approach is operations management. Operations management, like scientific management, aims at promoting efficiency through systematic observation and experimentation. However, operations management (sometimes called production/operations management) tends to be broader in scope and application than scientific management was. Whereas scientific management was limited largely to hand labor and machine shops, operations management specialists apply their expertise to all types of production and service operations, such as the purchase and storage of materials, energy use, product and service design, work flow, safety, quality control, and data processing. Thus, **operations management** is defined as the process of transforming raw materials, technology, and human talent into useful goods and services.[34] Operations managers could be called the frontline troops in the battle for productivity growth.

operations management: *the process of transforming material and human resources into useful goods and services*

The Behavioral Approach

4. DESCRIBE the general aim of the human relations movement, and **EXPLAIN** the circumstances in which it arose.

Like the other approaches to management, the behavioral approach has evolved gradually over many years. Advocates of the behavioral approach to management point out that people deserve to be the central focus of organized activity. They believe that successful management depends largely on a manager's ability to understand and work with people who have a variety of backgrounds, needs, perceptions, and aspirations. The progress of this humanistic approach from the human relations movement to modern organizational behavior has greatly influenced management theory and practice.

The Human Relations Movement

human relations movement: *an effort to make managers more sensitive to their employees' needs*

The **human relations movement** was a concerted effort among theorists and practitioners to make managers more sensitive to employee needs. It came into being as a result of special circumstances that occurred during the first half of the twentieth century. As illustrated in Figure 2.3, the human relations movement may be compared to the top of a pyramid. Just as the top of a pyramid must be supported, so too the human relations movement was supported by three very different historical influences: (1) the threat of unionization, (2) the Hawthorne studies, and (3) the philosophy of industrial humanism.

Threat of Unionization. To understand why the human relations movement evolved, one needs first to appreciate its sociopolitical background. From the late 1800s to the 1920s, American industry grew by leaps and bounds as it attempted to satisfy the many demands of a rapidly growing population. Cheap immigrant labor was readily available, and there was a seller's market for finished goods. Then came the Great Depression in the 1930s, and millions stood in bread lines instead of pay lines. Many held business somehow responsible for the depression, and public sympathy swung from management to labor. Congress consequently began to pass prolabor legislation. When the Wagner Act of 1935 legalized union-management collective

Figure 2.3 The Human Relations Movement Pyramid

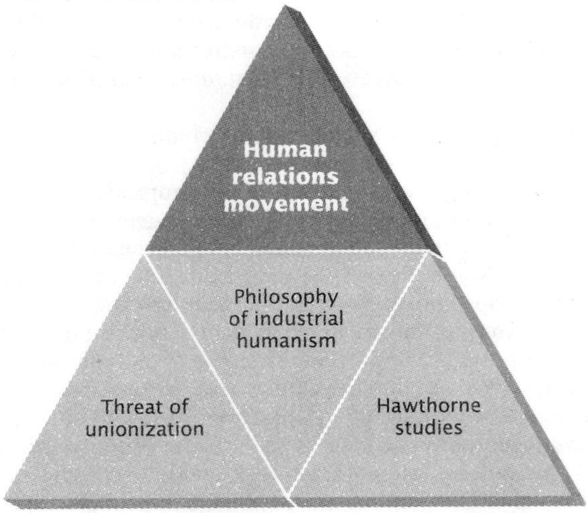

bargaining, management began searching for ways to stem the tide of all-out unionization. Early human relations theory proposed an enticing answer: satisfied employees would be less inclined to join unions. Business managers subsequently began adopting morale-boosting human relations techniques in an effort to discourage unionization.

■ **The Hawthorne Studies.** As the sociopolitical climate changed, a second development in industry took place. Behavioral scientists from prestigious universities began to conduct on-the-job behavior studies. Instead of studying tools and techniques in the scientific management tradition, they focused on people. Practical behavioral research such as the famous Hawthorne studies stirred management's interest in the psychological and sociological dynamics of the workplace.

The Hawthorne studies began in 1924 in a Western Electric plant near Chicago as a small-scale scientific management study of the relationship between light intensity and productivity. Curiously, the performance of a select group of employees tended to improve no matter how the physical surroundings were manipulated. Even when the lights were dimmed to mere moonlight intensity, productivity continued to climb! Scientific management doctrine could not account for what was taking place, and so a team of behavioral science researchers, headed by Elton Mayo, was brought in from Harvard to conduct a more rigorous study.

Elton Mayo, 1880–1949

By 1932, when the Hawthorne studies ended, more than 20,000 employees had participated in one way or another. After extensive interviewing of the subjects, it became clear to researchers that productivity was much less affected by changes in work conditions than by the attitudes of the workers themselves. Specifically, relationships between members of a work group and between workers and their supervisors were found to be more significant. Even though the experiments and the theories that evolved from them are criticized today for flawed methodology and statistical inaccuracies, the Hawthorne studies can be credited with turning management theorists away from the simplistic "economic man" model to a more humanistic and realistic view, the "social man" model.[35]

■ **The Philosophy of Industrial Humanism.** Although unionization prompted a search for new management techniques and the Hawthorne studies demonstrated that people were important to productivity, a philosophy of human relations was needed to provide a convincing rationale for treating employees better. Elton Mayo, Mary Parker Follett, and Douglas McGregor, although from very different backgrounds, offered just such a philosophy.

Mary Parker Follett, 1868–1933

Born in Australia, Elton Mayo was a Harvard professor specializing in psychology and sociology when he took over the Hawthorne studies. His 1933 book *The Human Problems of an Industrial Civilization,* inspired by what he had learned at Hawthorne, cautioned managers that emotional factors were a more important determinant of productive efficiency than physical and logical factors. Claiming that employees create their own unofficial yet powerful workplace culture complete with norms and sanctions, Mayo urged managers to provide work that fostered personal and subjective satisfaction. He called for a new social order designed to stimulate individual cooperation.[36]

Mary Parker Follett's experience as a management consultant and her background in law, political science, and philosophy shaped her strong conviction that

Douglas McGregor, 1906–1964

Theory Y: *McGregor's optimistic assumptions about working people*

managers should be aware that each employee is a complex collection of emotions, beliefs, attitudes, and habits. She believed that managers had to recognize the individual's motivating desires to get employees to work harder. Accordingly, Follett urged managers to motivate performance rather than simply demanding it. Cooperation, a spirit of unity, and self-control were seen as the keys to both productivity and a democratic way of life.[37] Historians credit Follett, who died in 1933, with being decades ahead of her time in terms of behavioral and systems management theory.[38] Her influence as a management consultant in a male-dominated industrial sector was remarkable as well.

A third philosophical rallying point for industrial humanism was provided by an American scholar named Douglas McGregor. In his 1960 classic, *The Human Side of Enterprise*, McGregor outlined a set of highly optimistic assumptions about human nature.[39] McGregor viewed the typical employee as an energetic and creative individual who could achieve great things if given the opportunity. He labeled the set of assumptions for this optimistic perspective **Theory Y**. McGregor's Theory Y assumptions are listed in Table 2.2, along with what he called the traditional Theory X assumptions. These two sets of assumptions about human nature enabled McGregor to contrast the modern or enlightened view he recommended (Theory Y) with the prevailing traditional view (Theory X), which he criticized for being pessimistic, stifling, and outdated. Because of its relative recency (compared with Mayo's and Follett's work), its catchy labels, and its intuitive appeal, McGregor's description of Theory X and Theory Y has left an indelible mark on modern management thinking.[40] Some historians have credited McGregor with launching the field of organizational behavior.

Organizational Behavior

organizational behavior: *a modern approach seeking to discover the causes of work behavior and develop better management techniques*

Organizational behavior is a modern approach to management that attempts to determine the causes of human work behavior and translate the results into effective management techniques. Accordingly, it has a strong research orientation and a robust collection of theories. In fact, a recent review uncovered "73 established organizational behavior theories."[41] Organizational behaviorists have borrowed an assortment of theories and research techniques from all the behavioral sciences and

2e Back to the Opening Case

Is Carol Bartz a Theory X or a Theory Y manager? Justify your conclusion.

Table 2.2 McGregor's Theories X and Y

Theory X: Some traditional assumptions about people	Theory Y: Some modern assumptions about people
1. Most people dislike work, and they will avoid it when they can.	1. Work is a natural activity, like play or rest.
2. Most people must be coerced and threatened with punishment before they will work. They require close direction.	2. People are capable of self-direction and self-control if they are committed to objectives.
3. Most people prefer to be directed. They avoid responsibility and have little ambition. They are interested only in security.	3. People will become committed to organizational objectives if they are rewarded for doing so.
	4. The average person can learn to both accept and seek responsibility.
	5. Many people in the general population have imagination, ingenuity, and creativity.

have applied them to people at work in modern organizations. The result is an interdisciplinary field in which psychology predominates.[42] In spite of its relatively new and developing state, organizational behavior has had a significant impact on modern management thought by helping to explain why employees behave as they do. Because human relations has evolved into a practical, how-to-do-it discipline for supervisors, organizational behavior amounts to a scientific extension of human relations. Many organizational behavior findings will be examined in Part Four of this text.

Lessons from the Behavioral Approach

Above all else, the behavioral approach makes it clear to present and future managers that *people* are the key to productivity.[43] According to advocates of the behavioral approach, technology, work rules, and standards do not guarantee good job performance. Instead, success depends on motivated and skilled individuals who are committed to organizational objectives.[44] Only a manager's sensitivity to individual concerns can foster the cooperation necessary for high productivity.

On the negative side, traditional human relations doctrine has been criticized as vague and simplistic. According to these critics, relatively primitive on-the-job behavioral research does not justify such broad conclusions. For instance, critics do not believe that supportive supervision and good human relations will lead automatically to higher morale and hence to better job performance. Also, recent analyses of the Hawthorne studies, using modern statistical techniques, have generated debate about the validity of the original conclusions.[45]

Fortunately, organizational behavior, as a scientific extension of human relations, promises to fill in some of the gaps left by human relationists, while at the same time retaining an emphasis on people. Today, organizational behaviorists are trying to piece together the multiple determinants of effective job performance in various work situations and across cultures.

The Systems Approach

system: *a collection of parts operating interdependently to achieve a common purpose*

A **system** is a collection of parts operating interdependently to achieve a common purpose. Working from this definition, the systems approach represents a marked departure from the past; in fact, it requires a completely different style of thinking.

Universal process, scientific management, and human relations theorists studied management by taking things apart. They assumed that the whole is equal to the sum of its parts and can be explained in terms of its parts. Systems theorists, in contrast, study management by putting things together and assume that the whole is greater than the sum of its parts. The difference is analytic versus synthetic thinking. According to one management systems expert, "Analytic thinking is, so to speak, outside-in thinking; synthetic thinking is inside-out. Neither negates the value of the other, but by synthetic thinking we can gain understanding that we cannot obtain through analysis, particularly of collective phenomena."[46]

Systems theorists recommend synthetic thinking because management is not practiced in a vacuum. Managers affect, and are in turn affected by, many organizational and environmental variables. Systems thinking has presented the field of management with an enormous challenge: to identify all relevant parts of organized activity and to discover how they interact. Two management writers predicted that systems thinking offers "a basis for understanding organizations and their problems which may one day produce a revolution in organizations comparable to the one brought about by Taylor with scientific management."[47]

Figure 2.4 Barnard's Cooperative System

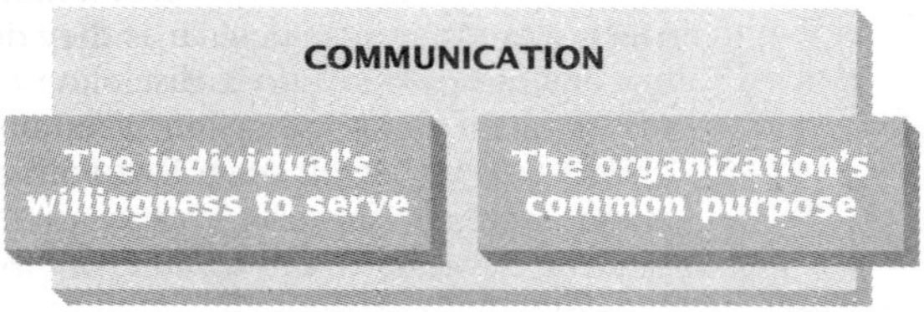

Chester I. Barnard's Early Systems Perspective

In one sense, Chester I. Barnard followed in the footsteps of Henri Fayol. Like Fayol, Barnard established a new approach to management on the basis of his experience as a top-level manager. But the approach of the former president of New Jersey Bell Telephone differed from Fayol's. Rather than isolating specific management functions and principles, Barnard devised a more abstract systems approach. In his landmark 1938 book *The Functions of the Executive*, Barnard characterized all organizations as cooperative systems: "A cooperative system is a complex of physical, biological, personal, and social components which are in a specific systematic relationship by reason of the cooperation of two or more persons for at least one definite end."[48]

According to Barnard, willingness to serve, common purpose, and communication are the principal elements in an organization (or cooperative system).[49] He felt that an organization did not exist if these three elements were not present and working interdependently. As illustrated in Figure 2.4, Barnard viewed communication as an energizing force that bridges the natural gap between the individual's willingness to serve and the organization's common purpose.

Barnard's systems perspective has encouraged management and organization theorists to study organizations as complex and dynamic wholes instead of piece by piece. Significantly, he was also a strong advocate of business ethics in his speeches and writings.[50] Barnard opened some important doors in the evolution of management thought.

General Systems Theory

general systems theory: *an area of study based on the assumption that everything is part of a larger, interdependent arrangement*

General systems theory is an interdisciplinary area of study based on the assumption that everything is part of a larger, interdependent arrangement. According to Ludwig von Bertalanffy, a biologist and the founder of general systems theory, "In order to understand an organized whole we must know the parts and the relations between them."[51] This interdisciplinary perspective was eagerly adopted by Barnard's followers because it categorized levels of systems and distinguished between closed and open systems.

5. EXPLAIN the significance of applying open-system thinking to management.

Levels of Systems. Envisioning the world as a collection of systems was only the first step for general systems theorists. One of the more important recent steps has been the identification of hierarchies of systems, ranging from very specific systems to general ones. Identifying systems at various levels has helped translate abstract general systems theory into more concrete terms.[52] A hierarchy of systems relevant to management is the seven-level scheme of living systems shown in Figure 2.5. Notice that each system is a subsystem of the one above it.

closed system: *a self-sufficient entity*

open system: *something that depends on its surrounding environment for survival*

Closed versus Open Systems. In addition to identifying hierarchies of systems, general systems theorists have distinguished between closed and open systems. A **closed system** is a self-sufficient entity, whereas an **open system** depends on the surrounding environment for survival. In reality, these two kinds of systems cannot be completely separated. The key to classifying a system as relatively closed or relatively open is to determine the amount of interaction between the system and its environment. A battery-powered digital watch, for example, is a relatively closed system; after the battery is in place, the watch operates without help from the outside environment. In contrast, a solar-powered clock is a relatively open system; it cannot operate without a continuous supply of outside energy. The human body is a highly

Figure 2.5 Levels of Living Systems

System level		Practical examples
Supranational	*General* ↑	United Nations
National		Canada
Organizational		Wal-Mart
Group		Family, work group
Organismic		Human being
Organic		Heart
Cellular	↓ *Specific*	Blood cell

open system because life depends on the body's ability to import oxygen and energy and to export waste. In other words, the human body is highly dependent on the environment for survival.

Along the same lines, general systems theorists say that all organizations are open systems because organizational survival depends on interaction with the surrounding environment. Just as no person is an island, no organization or organizational subsystem is an island, according to this approach (see The Global Manager).

■ New Directions in Systems Thinking

Two very different streams of thought are taking systems thinking in interesting new directions today. No one knows for sure where these streams will lead, but they promise to stimulate creative ideas about modern organizations.

2f Back to the Opening Case

Is Autodesk a closed or an open system? How can you tell?

■ Organizational Learning and Knowledge Management. An organizational learning perspective portrays the organization as a living and *thinking* open system. Like the human mind, organizations rely on feedback to adjust to changing environmental conditions. In short, organizations are said to learn from experience, just as humans and higher animals do. Organizations thus engage in complex mental processes such as anticipating, perceiving, envisioning, problem solving, and remembering. According to two organization theorists,

> *Some fo rms of organizational learning occur regularly in many organizations. Human resource development activities, strategic and other planning activities, and the introduction and mastering of new technologies for doing work are three common learning processes. They often do not fulfill their potential for true organizational learning, however.*
>
> *Organizational learning is more than the sum of the learning of its parts—more than cumulative individual learning. The training and development of individuals with new skills, knowledge bases, theories, and frameworks does not constitute organizational learning unless such individual learning is translated into altered organizational practices, policies, or design features. Individual learning is necessary but not sufficient for organizational learning.*[53]

When organizational learning becomes a strategic initiative to identify and fully exploit valuable ideas from both inside and outside the organization, a *knowledge management* program

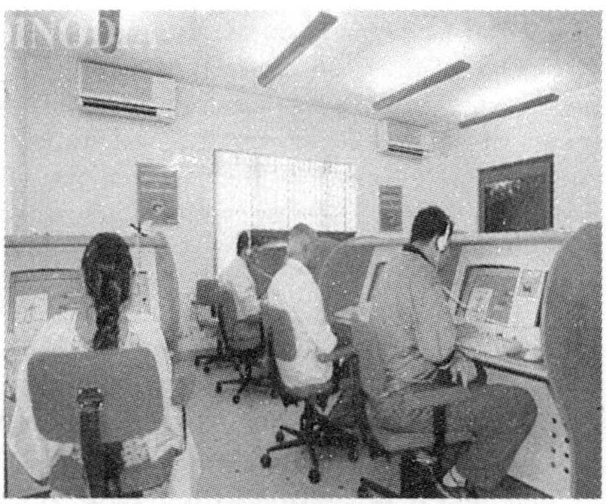

Dealing effectively with rapidly evolving telecommunications, computer, wireless and internet technologies requires lots of open-system technology.

THE GLOBAL MANAGER

Your Custom Car Is Ready

Nowadays . . . [Toyota] can build exactly to your specifications in just 14 days.

The secret is in the software. Toyota dealers can tap into the Dealer Pipeline Management System to quickly assemble and deliver special-order vehicles. The system gives a Toyota salesman a window into the future—what cars will be built for his dealership during the coming week at the company's four North American plants. If he wants a vehicle that's not earmarked for his showroom, he'll punch in his request and the software will immediately attempt a trade. Assuming, for example, that your dealer is willing to give up an Avalon in Desert Sand that's supposed to be coming his way, the system will match that with another dealer who doesn't want the Aspen Green he's been allotted. A simple swap makes everybody happy.

Should an exchange not be in the cards, there's still a 90 percent chance that you'll get what you want within two weeks. Toyota's software, which processes 700 special-order requests daily, triggers a chain of inquiries to see if one supplier can quickly provide an extra set of cowhide seats while another comes up with a sunroof. It took Toyota six years to convince reluctant suppliers that its new approach wouldn't gum up their manufacturing and cut into profits. Now special orders run as high as 11 percent, up from 2.5 percent in March 2003.

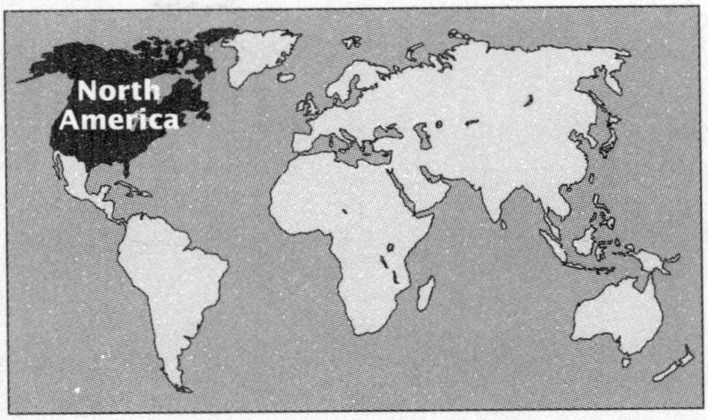

Toyota believes that the seven-month-old program will ultimately please everyone all the time. Buyers get their dream machines, suppliers receive more orders, dealers reduce inventory, and the carmaker gets a distinctive selling point for its brand. "Other companies are catching up to Toyota's quality," says Roy Vasher, general manager of production control at Toyota Motor Manufacturing for North America. "But if we give customers what they want when they want it, we'll have an edge."

Source: *Excerpted from Rachel Rosmarin, "Your Custom Car Is Ready,"* Business 2.0, *5 (October 2004): 150.*

exists.[54] You will find more about knowledge management in Chapter 8 and more about organizational learning in Chapter 9.

■ **Chaos Theory and Complex Adaptive Systems.** Chaos theory has one idea in common with organizational learning: systems are influenced by feedback. Work in the 1960s and 1970s by mathematicians Edward Lorenz and James Yorke formed the basis of modern chaos theory. So-called chaologists are trying to find order among the seemingly random behavior patterns of everything from weather systems to organizations to stock markets.[55] Behind all this is the intriguing notion that every complex system has a life of its own, with its own rule book. The challenge for those in the emerging field known as *complex adaptive systems theory* is to discover "the rules" in seemingly chaotic systems.

As indicated in Table 2.3, complex adaptive systems theory casts management in a very different light than do traditional models. Managers are challenged to be more flexible and adaptive than in the past.[56] They need to acknowledge the limits of traditional command-and-control management because complex systems have *self-organizing* tendencies. (For example, labor unions have historically thrived in eras when management was oppressive.) The twenty-first-century manager, profiled in the previous chapter (Table 1.1), is up to the challenge. Significantly, chaos theory and complex adaptive systems theory are launching pads for new and better management models, not final answers. Stay tuned.

Table 2.3 Complex Adaptive Systems Thinking Helps Managers Make Sense Out of Chaos

Complex adaptive systems theory	Classical management theory
Change and transformation are inherent qualities of dynamic systems. The goal of management is to increase learning and self-organizing in continuously changing contexts.	Organizations exist in equilibrium, therefore change is a nonnormal process. The goal of management is to increase stability through planning, organizing, and controlling behavior.
Organizational behavior is inherently nonlinear, and results may be nonproportional to corresponding actions. New models and methods are needed to understand change.	Organizational behavior is essentially linear and predictable, and results are proportional to causes. Thus linear regression models explain most of the variance of organizational change.
Inputs do not cause outputs. The elements of a system are interdependent and mutually causal.	System components are independent and can be analyzed by separating them from the rest of the system, as well as from their outcomes.
An organization is defined, first of all, according to its underlying order and principles. These give rise to surface-level organizing structures, including design, strategy, leadership, controls, and culture.	An organization can be completely defined in terms of its design, strategy, leadership, controls, and culture.
Change should be encouraged through embracing tension, increasing information flow, and pushing authority downwards.	Change should be controlled by minimizing uncertainty and tension, limiting information, and centralizing decision making
Long-term organizational success is based on optimizing resource flow and continuous learning. A manager's emphasis is on supporting structures that accomplish these goals.	Organizational success is based on maximizing resource utilization, to maximize profit and increase shareholder wealth. A manager's emphasis is on efficiency and effectiveness, and on avoiding both transformation and chaos.

Source: Academy of Management Executive: The Thinking Manager's Source *by Benjamin Bregmann Lichtenstein. Copyright 2000 by Academy of Management. Reproduced with permission of Academy of Management in the format Textbook via Copyright Clearance Center.*

■ Lessons from the Systems Approach

Because of the influence of the systems approach, managers now have a greater appreciation for the importance of seeing the whole picture. Open-system thinking does not permit the manager to become preoccupied with one aspect of organizational management while ignoring other internal and external realities. The manager of a business, for instance, must consider resource availability, technological developments, and market trends when producing and selling a product or service. Another positive aspect of the systems approach is how it tries to integrate various management theories. Although quite different in emphasis, both operations management and organizational behavior have been strongly influenced by systems thinking.

There are critics of the systems approach, of course. Some management scholars see systems thinking as long on intellectual appeal and catchy terminology and short on verifiable facts and practical advice.

The Contingency Approach

contingency approach: *research effort to determine which managerial practices and techniques are appropriate in specific situations*

A comparatively new line of thinking among management theorists has been labeled the contingency approach. Advocates of contingency management are attempting to take a step away from universally applicable principles of management and toward situational appropriateness. In the words of Fred Luthans, a noted contingency management writer, "The traditional approaches to management were not necessarily wrong, but today they are no longer adequate. The needed breakthrough for management theory and practice can be found in a contingency approach."[57] Formally defined, the **contingency approach** is an effort to determine through research which managerial practices and techniques are appropriate in specific situations. Imagine using Taylor's approach with a college-educated computer engineer! According to the contingency approach, different situations require different managerial responses.

Generally, the term *contingency* refers to the choice of an alternative course of action. For example, roommates may have a contingency plan to move their party indoors if it rains. Their subsequent actions are said to be contingent (or dependent) on the weather. In a management context, contingency management has become synonymous with situational management. As one contingency theorist put it, "The effectiveness of a given management pattern is contingent upon multitudinous factors and their interrelationship in a particular situation."[58] This means that the application of various management tools and techniques must be appropriate to the particular situation because each situation presents unique problems. A contingency approach is especially applicable in intercultural dealings, where customs and habits cannot be taken for granted.

6. EXPLAIN the practical significance of adopting a contingency perspective.

In real-life management, the success of any given technique is dictated by the situation. For example, researchers have found that rigidly structured organizations with many layers of management function best when environmental conditions are relatively stable. Unstable surroundings dictate a more flexible and streamlined organization that can adapt quickly to change. Consequently, traditional principles of management that call for rigidly structured organizations, regardless of the situation, have come into question.

Contingency Characteristics

Some management scholars are attracted to contingency thinking because it is a workable compromise between the systems approach and what can be called a purely situational perspective. Figure 2.6 illustrates this relationship. The systems

Figure 2.6 The Contingency View: A Compromise

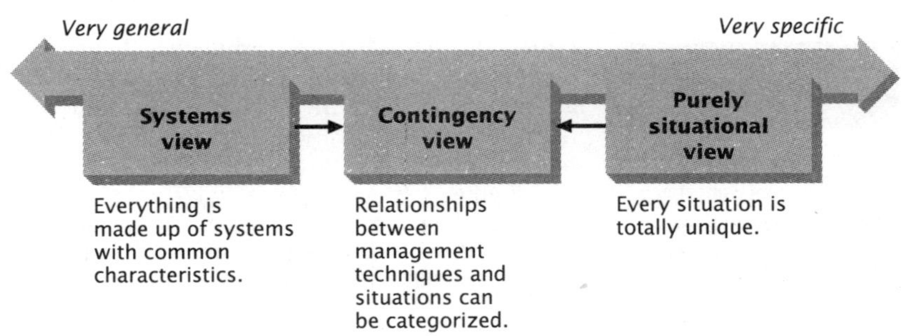

approach is often criticized for being too general and abstract, while the purely situational view, which assumes that every real-life situation requires a distinctly different approach, has been called hopelessly specific. Contingency advocates have tried to take advantage of common denominators without lapsing into simplistic generalization. Three characteristics of the contingency approach are (1) an open-system perspective, (2) a practical research orientation, and (3) a multivariate approach.

■ **An Open-System Perspective.** Open-system thinking is fundamental to the contingency view. Contingency theorists are not satisfied with focusing on just the internal workings of organizations. They see the need to understand how organizational subsystems combine to interact with outside social, cultural, political, and economic systems.

■ **A Practical Research Orientation.** Practical research is that which ultimately leads to more effective on-the-job management. Contingency researchers attempt to translate their findings into tools and situational refinements for more effective management.

■ **A Multivariate Approach.** Traditional closed-system thinking prompted a search for simple one-to-one causal relationships. This approach is called bivariate analysis. For example, the traditional human relations assumption that higher morale leads automatically to higher productivity was the result of bivariate analysis. One variable, morale, was seen as the sole direct cause of changes in a second variable, productivity. Subsequent multivariate analysis has shown that many variables, including the employee's personality, the nature of the task, rewards, and job and life satisfaction, collectively account for variations in productivity. **Multivariate analysis** is a research technique used to determine how a number of variables interact to cause a particular outcome. For example, if an employee has a conscientious personality, the task is highly challenging, and the individual is highly satisfied with his or her life and job, then analysis might show that productivity could be expected to be high. Contingency management theorists strive to carry out practical and relevant multivariate analyses.

Multivariate analysis: *research technique used to determine how a number of variables combine to cause a particular outcome*

■ Lessons from the Contingency Approach

Although still not fully developed, the contingency approach is a helpful addition to management thought because it emphasizes situational appropriateness. People, organizations, and problems are too complex to justify rigid adherence to universal principles of management. In addition, contingency thinking is a *practical* extension of the systems approach. Assuming that systems thinking is a unifying synthetic force in management thought, the contingency approach promises to add practical direction.

The contingency approach, like each of the other approaches, has its share of critics. One has criticized contingency theory for creating the impression that the organization is a captive of its environment.[59] If such were strictly the case, attempts to manage the organization would be in vain. In actual fact, organizations are subject to various combinations of environmental forces and management practices.

Whether the contingency management theorists have bitten off more than they can chew remains to be seen. At present they appear to be headed in a constructive direction. But it is good to keep in mind that the contingency approach is a promising step rather than the end of the evolution of conventional management thought.

2g Back to the Opening Case

What, if any, evidence of the contingency approach can you detect in Carol Bartz's management style? Explain.

The Era of Management by Best Seller: Proceed with Caution

An interesting thing happened to the field of management over the last 25 years or so. It went mainstream. A fledgling field that had been pretty much limited to college classrooms and management development seminars began having a broader appeal. Peter F. Drucker, an Austrian-born management consultant, writer, and teacher living in the United States, deserves to be considered the father of this trend.[60] His now-classic books, such as *The Concept of the Corporation* (1946), *The Practice of Management* (1954), and *The Effective Executive* (1967), along with his influential articles in *Harvard Business Review* and elsewhere, appealed to academics and practicing managers alike. Drucker became the first management guru whose sage advice was sought by executives trying to figure out how to manage in increasingly turbulent times. Others, such as quality advocates Juran and Deming, followed.

7. DESCRIBE what "management by best seller" involves, and **EXPLAIN** what managers can do to avoid it.

The popularization of management shifted into high gear in 1982 with the publication of Peters and Waterman's *In Search of Excellence*. This book topped the nonfiction best-seller lists for months, was translated into several foreign languages, and soon appeared in paperback. Just five years later, an astounding 5 million copies had been sold worldwide.[61] Others business management best sellers followed (see Table 2.4), and the popular appeal of management grew. The rest, as they say, is history. By 2004, best-selling authors such as Michael Hammer were collecting $82,000 per speaking engagement, worldwide sales of *The One Minute Manager* had reached 7 million copies,[62] and businessman Donald Trump was saying "You're fired!" on his reality TV hit *"The Apprentice."*[63] Certain academics, meanwhile, worried about the instant gurus and their best sellers encouraging shoddy research and simplistic thinking, to say nothing of pandering to busy managers' desire for quick fixes. Still, the era of management by best seller deserves serious discussion in any historical perspective of management thought, if for no other reason than the widespread acceptance of the books listed in Table 2.4.[64]

What's Wrong with Management by Best Seller?

Craig M. McAllaster, the Business School Dean at Florida's Rollins College, recently offered this instructive critique of managing by best seller:

> *An executive reads a management book written by a guru listed on the* New York Times *Bestseller List and decides that the concepts presented therein represent the magic bullet. This bestseller's concepts will solve the current problems of the organization and position her/him for greatness. Many times the manager sees the approach as working with minimal change and disruption, especially for her/him. Fired up and sure of the prognosis and treatment, the executive returns to the organization and orders a thousand copies of the book and calls a management meeting to announce the change. No diagnosis or assessment takes place to determine the real organizational problems. The executive buys off on a well-written book that captures the essence of problems in someone else's company and applies the one-size-fits-all solution to the organization.*[65]

The inevitable disappointment is not the fault of popular management books, which typically do contain some really good ideas; rather, the hurried and haphazard application of those ideas is at fault. Our challenge, then, is to avoid the quick-fix mentality that makes management by best seller so tempting.

How to Avoid the Quick-Fix Mentality

In a follow-up study of Peters and Waterman's *In Search of Excellence*, Michael Hitt and Duame Ireland conducted a *comparative* analysis of "excellent" companies and

Table 2.4 A Sampling of Business Management Best Sellers

Name of book, author(s), and year published	Main theme/lessons
Theory Z: How American Business Can Meet the Japanese Challenge, William Ouchi, 1981	UCLA professor finds successful "Theory Z." U.S. firms such as IBM exhibit a blend of American and Japanese traits (e.g., participative decision making; teamwork + individual responsibility).
In Search of Excellence: Lessons from America's Best-Run Companies, Thomas J. Peters and Robert H. Waterman Jr., 1982	Consultants' analysis of 36 companies, including Johnson & Johnson and McDonald's, finds eight "attributes of excellence." Excellent companies reportedly focus on action, customers, entrepreneurship, people, values, the core business, simplicity, and balanced control and decentralization.
The One Minute Manager, Kenneth Blanchard and Spencer Johnson, 1982	Short parable of a young man who learns from experienced managers about the power of on-the-spot goals, praise, and reprimands.
High Output Management, Andrew S. Grove, 1983	Respected CEO of Intel Corp. urges managers to be output-oriented, teambuilders, and motivators of individual peak performance.
Iacocca: An Autobiography, Lee Iacocca (with William Novak), 1984	Legendary president of Ford and CEO of Chrysler details how being a master salesman helped him save Chrysler Corp.
The 7 Habits of Highly Effective People: Powerful Lessons in Personal Change, Stephen R. Covey, 1989	Professor/consultant charts pathway to personal growth in terms of good habits formed by balancing one's knowledge, skills, and desires.
Reengineering the Corporation: A Manifesto for Business Revolution, Michael Hammer and James Champy, 1993	Consultants recommend using information technology to radically redesign basic business practices to achieve lower costs, higher quality, and speed.
Built to Last: Successful Habits of Visionary Companies, James C. Collins and Jerry I. Porras, 1994	After studying 18 "visionary"companies, including American Express and Marriott, these professors/consultants urge managers to "preserve the core" (with strong cultures and internal promotions) and "stimulate progress" (with difficult goals and a hunger for continuous change).
The Death of Competition: Leadership & Strategy in the Age of Business Ecosystems, James F. Moore, 1996	Consultant advises firms to be as good at cooperating as they are at competing, especially with others in their ecosystem (e.g., Microsoft and Intel).
Who Moved My Cheese? Spencer Johnson, 1998	Coauthor of *The One Minute Manager* spins a short fable about two mice who learn to adapt to change by facing their fears and enjoying the trip.
Fish! Stephen C. Lundin, Harry Paul, and John Christensen, 2000	Short story of a manager who turns her department around by applying four lessons learned at Seattle's Pike Place fish market.
Good to Great: Why Some Companies Make the Leap . . . and Others Don't, Jim Collins, 2001	Co-author of *Built to Last* returns with list of 11 companies, including Gillette and Walgreens, that jumped from good to great by hiring great people, confronting reality, and becoming the world's best.
Jack: Straight from the Gut, Jack Welch (with John A. Byrne), 2001	Legendary CEO of General Electric explains his concept of the "boundaryless" organization dedicated to sharing ideas, building people into winners, and fighting bureaucracy.
Execution: The Discipline of Getting Things Done, Larry Bossidy and Ram Charan (with Charles Burck), 2002	Retired CEO of Honeywell and professor/consultant tell how to get results by hiring good people who are taught to link strategy with operations.

Want to burn a couple of hours of extra time? Try browsing the business section at your local bookstore. You'll find a mountain of information with both trash and treasure. Be wary of quick fixes based on shoddy research while gathering those pearls of wisdom.

industry norms. Companies that satisfied all of Peters and Waterman's excellence criteria turned out to be no more effective than a random sample of *Fortune* 1000 companies.[66]This outcome prompted Hitt and Ireland to offer five tips for avoiding what they termed "the quick-fix mentality" (see Table 2.5).[67]

Putting What You Have Learned to Work

We need to put the foregoing historical overview into proper perspective. The topical tidiness of this chapter, while providing useful conceptual frameworks for students of management, generally does not carry over to the practice of management. Managers are, first and foremost, pragmatists. They use whatever works. Instead of faithfully adhering to a given school of management thought, successful managers tend to use a "mixed bag" approach. This chapter is a good starting point for you to begin building your own personally relevant and useful approach to management by blending theory, the experience and advice of others, and your own experience. A healthy dose of common sense would help as well.

2h Peter Drucker, Still Giving Wise Management Advice at Age 95

The greatest source of mistakes in top management is to ask the same questions most people ask. They all assume that there are the same "right answers" for everyone. But one does not begin with answers. One begins by asking, "What are our questions?"

Source: As quoted in Thomas Mucha, "How to Ask the Right Questions," Business 2.0, *5 (December 2004): 118.*

QUESTION:
What key questions should today's managers be asking?

Table 2.5 How to Avoid the Quick-Fix Mentality in Management

Our research suggests that practicing managers should embrace appealing ideas when appropriate but anticipate that solutions typically are far more complex than the type suggested by Peters and Waterman's search for excellence. To avoid the quick-fix mentality, managers should:

1. Remain current with literature in the field, particularly with journals that translate research into practice.
2. Ensure that concepts applied are based on science or, at least, on some form of rigorous documentation, rather than purely on advocacy.
3. Be willing to examine and implement new concepts, but first do so using pilot tests with small units.
4. Be skeptical when simple solutions are offered; analyze them thoroughly.
5. Constantly anticipate the effects of current actions and events on future results.

Source: *Michael A. Hitt and R. Duane Ireland, "Peters and Waterman Revisited: The Unended Quest for Excellence,"* Academy of Management Executive, *Vol. 2, no. 2 (May 1987): 96. Reprinted by permission.*

SUMMARY

1. Management is an interdisciplinary and international field that has evolved in bits and pieces over the years. Five approaches to management theory are (1) the universal process approach, (2) the operational approach, (3) the behavioral approach, (4) the systems approach, and (5) the contingency approach. Useful lessons have been learned from each.

   Henry Fayol's universal process approach assumes that all organizations, regardless of purpose or size, require the same management process. Furthermore, it assumes that this rational process can be reduced to separate functions and principles of management. The universal approach, the oldest of the various approaches, is still popular today.

2. Dedicated to promoting production efficiency and reducing waste, the operational approach has evolved from scientific management to operations management. Frederick W. Taylor, the father of scientific management, and his followers revolutionized industrial management through the use of standardization, time-and-motion study, selection and training, and pay incentives.

3. The quality advocates taught managers about the strategic importance of high-quality goods and services. Shewhart pioneered the use of *statistics* for quality control. Japan's Ishikawa emphasized *prevention* of defects in quality and drew management's attention to *internal* as well as external *customers.* Deming sparked the Japanese quality revolution with calls for *continuous improvement* of the entire production process. Juran trained many U.S. managers to improve quality through *teamwork, partnerships with suppliers,* and *Pareto analysis* (the 80/20 rule). Feigenbaum developed the concept of *total quality control,* thus involving all business functions in the quest for quality. He believed that the *customer* determined quality. Crosby, a champion of *zero defects,* emphasized how costly poor-quality products could be.

4. Management has turned to the human factor in the human relations movement and organizational behavior approach. Emerging from such influences as unionization, the Hawthorne studies, and the philosophy of industrial humanism, the human relations movement began as a concerted effort to make employees' needs a high management priority. Today, organizational behavior theory tries to identify the multiple determinants of job performance.

5. Advocates of the systems approach recommend that modern organizations be viewed as open systems. Open systems depend on the outside environment for survival, whereas closed systems do not. Chester I. Barnard stirred early interest in systems thinking in 1938 by suggesting that organizations are cooperative systems energized by communication. General systems theory, an interdisciplinary field based on the assumption that everything is systematically related, has identified a hierarchy of systems and has differentiated between closed and open systems. New directions in systems thinking are organizational learning and chaos theory.

6. A comparatively new approach to management thought is the contingency approach, which stresses situational appropriateness rather than universal principles. The contingency approach is characterized by an open-system perspective, a practical research orientation, and a multivariate approach to research. Contingency thinking is a practical extension of more abstract systems thinking.

7. Management by best seller occurs when managers read a popular book by a management guru and hastily try to implement its ideas and one-size-fits-all recommendations without proper regard for their organization's unique problems and needs. The quick-fix mentality that fosters this problem can be avoided by staying current with high-quality management literature, requiring rigorous support for claims, engaging in critical thinking, and running pilot studies.

TERMS TO UNDERSTAND

- Universal process approach, p. 34
- Operational approach, p. 36
- Scientific management, p. 37
- Operations management, p. 41
- Human relations movement, p. 41
- Theory Y, p. 43
- Organizational behavior, p. 43
- System, p. 44
- General systems theory, p. 45
- Closed system, p. 45
- Open system, p. 45
- Contingency approach, p. 49
- Multivariate analysis, p. 50

SKILLS & TOOLS

Recommended Periodicals for Staying Current in the Field of Management

Academic Journals (with a research orientation)
Academy of Management Journal
Academy of Management Review
Administrative Science Quarterly
Human Relations
Journal of Applied Psychology
Journal of Management
Journal of Organizational Behavior
Journal of Vocational Behavior
Journal of World Business
Nonprofit Management & Leadership

Scholarly Journals (with a practical orientation)
Academy of Management Executive
Business Horizons
Harvard Business Review
Journal of Organizational Excellence (formerly *National Productivity Review*)
Leadership Quarterly
MIT Sloan Management Review
Organizational Dynamics
Public Administration Review

General Periodicals
Business 2.0
Business Week
Canadian Business
The Economist
Fast Company
Forbes
Fortune
Industry Week
The Wall Street Journal

Practitioner Journals (special interest)
Black Enterprise
Business Ethics
CIO (information technology)
Entrepreneur
Healthcare Executive
Hispanic Business
HR Magazine (human resource management)
Inc. (small business)
Information Week (information technology)
Inside Supply Management (formerly *Purchasing Today*)
Macworld (Apple computer users)
Money (personal finance and investing)
NAFE Magazine (formerly *Executive Female*)
Nonprofit World (not-for-profit organizations)
PC World (personal computing and Internet)
Technology Review (new technology)
Training
T+D (training and development)
Web Bound (Web site directory)
Working Mother (work/family issues)

HANDS-ON EXERCISE

Managers Need Open-System Thinking to Deal with Global Terrorism

Instructions

To borrow a phrase from crisis management specialists, this is an exercise in "thinking about the unthinkable," with an eye toward being better prepared. After you have read the section on the systems approach to management (with special attention to Table 2.3), read the brief piece below about the threat of terrorism. The systems thinking you will need to get your mind around this huge issue will be enhanced by reading the description of organizations as open systems in Chapter 9 and the discussion of crisis management in Chapter 17. *Note:* An excellent background article on complex systems theory is "Simple, Yet Complex" by Megan Santosus in the April 15, 1998, issue of *CIO* magazine (available in full text on the Web at **www.cio.com/archive/**).

The Problem:

> *"The likelihood of cyberterrorism happening has gone from a possibility to almost a certainty."*
>
> *That assessment of the post–Sept. 11 world comes from Fred Rica, threat and vulnerability practice leader at PricewaterhouseCoopers. Rica is weighing the likelihood that the nation's economic arteries—banks, oil companies, communication companies, water systems, you name it—could be brought down by a terrorist hacker. And the reality, he says, is that "everybody is a potential target."...*
>
> *The very systems that have increased productivity and driven efficiencies have also made the United States more susceptible to attack. The electrical grid and telecommunications, for example, increasingly are connected to Internet protocol-based networks that have been opened by deregulation and, as a result, are shared by many competitors. On the corporate level, supply chains have expanded the reach of company networks—and multiplied the potential points of attack.*[68]

For Consideration/Discussion

1. From a personal standpoint, how could your life be disrupted by terrorism?
2. Focusing on a specific organization of your choice, determine its major vulnerabilities to terrorist acts.
3. What do today's managers need to do to protect their organizations, employees, and customers from acts of terrorism?
4. On a global scale, what needs to be done to make terrorism less likely in the first place?
5. Why is systems thinking useful for issues as complex as global terrorism?

INTERNET EXERCISES

1. Managerial shortcut to the information superhighway: Busy managers typically cannot afford the luxury of spending hours surfing the Internet for needed information. Fortunately, **www.ceoexpress.com** offers managers a handy one-stop information clearinghouse. Hundreds of "hot links" instantly tap into current information in relevant areas such as news, weather, technology, travel, health, investing, statistics, sports, and shopping. Breaktime can be made more interesting by spending time in the Dilbert Zone or reviewing comedian David Letterman's Top Ten Lists. Useful and interesting reference items include everything from a guide to writing and grammar, to a currency-exchange calculator, to an Internet public library, to a worldwide list of public holidays. Take some time to browse the links in this valuable Web site. Be sure to call up material of both managerial and personal interest.

Learning Points: 1. Which links would you recommend to a parent or a friend who is a manager? Why? 2. What useful or interesting things did you learn about management during this Internet session? 3. What personally relevant or useful things did you pick up during this exploratory session?

2. **Check it out:** There's only one thing better than useful information on the Internet, and that's *free* useful information! At the home page of **www.managementhelp.org**, you will find at least 75 topical areas relevant to modern management. Simply click through to a rich array of resources for topics such as business planning, supervision, crisis management, personal wellness, leadership development, career development, interpersonal skills, and systems thinking.

For updates to these exercises, visit our Web site (**http://business.college.hmco.com/students/** and select Kreitner, *Management,* 10e).

CLOSING CASE

Mr. Soni

Mr. Soni has recently joined as the Managing Director of a car manufacturing company which at present is incurring heavy losses. Mr. Soni has been entrusted with the formidable task of rejuvenating the company. He faces many challenges to achieve this task, such as controlling costs and expenses, increasing the productivity and boosting the morale of the employees so that they cooperate to achieve the set standards of output without any hesitation.

Mr. Soni, in his previous company that was also a car manufacturing company, as the Deputy Managing Director had proved to be a proficient manager and a talented leader who has successfully inspired his employees to increase the productivity. He was commended for his maximum concern for both people and production and also for bringing about an integration and harmony between the needs of employees and of the production.

In the new company also, Mr. Soni continued his policies of participative management and his high concern for production and people. With a view to reviving the company back to health, he introduced some major changes. First of all, he had decentralized the organization so that the subordinates could exercise their discretion and initiative in decision-making and their imagination and creativity in performing their other managerial functions. Furthermore, he empowered the junior managers to sanction expenditure upto an approved limit without seeking prior approval of the higher management. Communication system was also improved to facilitate free flow of the upward and downward communication.

Mr. Soni also adopted several measures to cut costs and wasteful expenditure. He banned donations to charitable institutions but increased the amount being spent on the welfare activities of the employees.

Will Mr. Soni's leadership style prove effective in ensuring bright future of the company? Some employees are of the view that a lot of things are being done but they might not be effective in the long-run. Others disagreed with them and said, 'Okay, we will give it a try'.

For Discussion

1. Is Mr. Soni a Theory X or a Theory Y manager? Give reasons for your answer. Will you advise Mr. Soni to change his assumptions about the nature of people at work? Give reasons.

2. In terms of the 'Managerial Grid' developed by Blake and Mouton, how would you describe Mr. Soni's leadership style? Is it the best style in the 'Managerial Grid'? Give reasons.

Source: Principles & Practice of Management by T.N. Chhabra, Dhanpat Rai & Co., Delhi, 2002, pp.851.

TEST PREPPER

True/False Questions

_____ **1.** The actual practice of management has been around for thousands of years.

_____ **2.** According to the universal process approach, a successful military commander should be able to run a business successfully.

_____ **3.** Henri Fayol was the father of scientific management.

_____ **4.** The idea of Pareto analysis, or doing it right the first time, was promoted by Elton Mayo.

_____ **5.** Taylor and the early proponents of scientific management have been praised for viewing workers as complex human beings who work for more than just money.

_____ **6.** McGregor's Theory Y assumes that people are capable of self-control.

_____ **7.** According to general systems theory, everything we know belongs to only one system—the earth's ecosystem.

_____ **8.** It is appropriate to characterize organizations as closed systems because they are managed internally.

_____ **9.** The most significant contribution of contingency theory has been its search for the one best way to manage.

_____ **10.** Peters and Waterman's book *In Search of Excellence* played a key role in the era of management by best seller.

Multiple-Choice Questions

1. Sharpening one's vision of ______ is the purpose of ______.
A. studying management theory; managerial practice
B. the present; historical perspective
C. management theory; what could be
D. history; the past
E. management; technology

2. ______ is *not* one of Fayol's 14 universal principles of management.
A. Esprit de corps B. Empowerment
C. Authority D. Equity
E. Centralization

3. When performance standards are developed on the basis of systematic observation and experimentation, what is involved?
A. Fayol's universal principle B. Therbligs
C. Gantt chart D. Total quality control
E. Scientific management

4. Which of these did Taylor's differential pay plan call for when the daily standard was met or exceeded?
A. Inclusion in a bonus pool
B. A higher per-unit rate
C. Permission to go home early
D. A ticket to a weekly prize drawing
E. A minimum wage

5. Which of these is also known as the 80/20 rule?
A. Linear programming B. Contingency planning
C. Pareto analysis D. Fishbone analysis
E. Strategic scanning

6. What did Mary Parker Follett urge managers to do?
A. Motivate rather than simply demand performance
B. Adopt a Theory X view of workers
C. Ignore the findings of the Hawthorne studies
D. Get rid of the traditional hierarchy of authority
E. Share profits equally with workers

7. Organizations can *best* be described as which of these?
A. Closed systems B. Specialized systems
C. Open systems D. Functional systems
E. Independent systems

8. Which of the following *best* describes the contingency approach?
A. Differential management B. Managerial uniformity
C. Continuous improvement D. Situational management
E. One best way to manage

9. Craig M. McAllaster criticizes "management by best seller" because
A. management books are not theory-driven.
B. only three authors have written all of the best sellers.
C. management books exhibit too much reliance on survey data.
D. Drucker's ideas keep being repeated over and over.
E. management books offer too many "one-size-fits-all" solutions.

10. Managers can avoid the quick-fix mentality by reading which sort of management journals?
A. Those that report nonquantitative studies
B. Those that report highly controlled laboratory studies
C. Those that report the results of public opinion polls
D. Those that specify how-to-do-it procedures
E. Those that translate research into practice

ACE self-test

Want more questions? Visit the student Web site at http://business.college.hmco.com/students/ (select Kreitner, *Management,* 10e) and take the ACE quizzes for more practice.

3

The Changing Environment of Management

Diversity, Global Economy, and Technology

"The best way to predict the future is to create it."[1]

ALAN KAYE

OBJECTIVES

- **Summarize** the demographics of the new American workforce.
- **Explain** how the social contract between employer and employee has changed in recent years.
- **Define** the term *managing diversity,* and **explain** why it is particularly important today.
- **Discuss** how the changing political-legal environment is affecting the practice of management.
- **Discuss** why business cycles and the global economy are vital economic considerations for modern managers.
- **Describe** the three-step innovation process, and **define** the term *intrapreneur*.

the changing workplace

Home Depot Goes Old School

As an engineer who spent 34 years at NASA's Johnson Space Center, Rob Roy has the kind of technical acumen that makes explaining the differences between competing washing machines a breeze. And he's spent half his adult life nurturing a passion for remodeling homes. "Name anything about a house and I've probably done it at least once," he says. "laying down carpets, installing gutters, roofing, plumbing . . . ." Roy is also 65 years old—and that, as much as anything else, makes him one of the most valuable new hires at $65 billion retailer Home Depot.

Roy, who makes $11 an hour selling kitchenware and appliances at a Home Depot store in Thornton, Colo., is part of an army of retirees being deployed to the company through a partnership with the 35-million-member AARP. The organization has begun recruiting more than 700 older workers like Roy—not for menial jobs, à la Wal-Mart's cadre of aged greeters and baggers, but as sales associates and managers who can help customers navigate Home Depot's towering, intimidating shelves. "We want them to have technical depth," says Cindy Milburn, Home Depot's senior hiring director. "That means plumbers, carpenters, electricians, people with millwork backgrounds, and people with design skills."

Believe it or not, workers like those are becoming difficult to find in the under-65 crowd. Like a growing number of companies today, Home Depot takes seriously recent projections of a future labor shortfall. The National Association of Manufacturers estimates that as baby boomers continue retiring and the economy grows, the country will have 7 million more jobs than workers by 2010. . . . That's why some firms are luring older workers back into their ranks. Already, about 17 percent of Home Depot's sales force is over 50, and Milburn expects that figure to keep rising.

But Home Depot isn't just thinking long-term. This year the company will open 175 new stores in North America. With rival Lowe's trumpeting its great customer service, the race is on to find reliable, knowledgeable workers. Seniors fit the bill: Home Deport says its older workers stay on the job longer and don't take as many sick days as their fresh-faced colleagues. Adds Jim Seith, director of AARP's Senior Community Service Employment Program, "They don't get pregnant, they come to work on time, they don't have rings all over their bodies, and they wear belts." More than two dozen major companies—including Anheuser-Busch, Barnes & Noble, and Sears—are now exploring similar partnerships with the AARP.

Roy, for his part, says this job is far more satisfying than the last two gigs he's taken since leaving NASA—a night job driving a bus, and as a baker at Safeway—and has no intention of retiring right now. "I get bored when I don't work," he says. "I put on weight and sit around the house. It's horrible." Home Depot might well be saving him from his misery—and, with experts like Roy on the floor, saving itself some misery as well.

Source: *From Melanie Warner, "Home Depot Goes Old School,"* Business 2.0, *5 (June 2004): 74.*

Like other successful companies today, Home Depot has learned to do more than merely cope with change; it has learned to thrive on it. Accordingly, present and future managers need to be aware of *how* things are changing in the world around them.

Ignoring the impact of general environmental factors on management makes about as much sense as ignoring the effects of weather and road conditions on high-speed driving. The general environment of management includes social, political-legal, economic, and technological dimensions. Changes in each area present managers with unique opportunities and obstacles that will shape not only the organization's strategic direction but also the course of daily operations.[2] This challenge requires forward-thinking managers who can handle change and accurately see the greater scheme of things.

The purpose of this chapter, then, is to prepare you for constant change and help you see the *big picture* by identifying key themes in the changing environment of management. It builds on our discussion in Chapter 1 of the five overarching sources of change for today's managers: globalization, the evolution of product quality, environmentalism, an ethical reawakening, and the e-business revolution.

The Social Environment

According to sociologists, society is the product of a constant struggle between the forces of stability and change. Cooperation promotes stability, whereas conflict and competition upset the status quo. The net result is an ever-changing society. Keeping this perspective in mind, we shall discuss four important dimensions of the social environment: demographics, the new social contract, inequalities, and managing diversity. Each presents managers with unique challenges.

Demographics of the New Workforce

demographics: *statistical profiles of human populations*

Demographics—statistical profiles of population characteristics—are a valuable planning tool for managers. Foresighted managers who study demographics can make appropriate adjustments in their strategic, human resource, and marketing plans. Selected demographic shifts reshaping the U.S. workforce are presented in Figure 3.1. (Other countries have their own demographic trends.)[3] The projections in Figure 3.1 are not "blue sky" numbers. They are based on people already born, most of whom are presently working. In short, the U.S. workforce demonstrates the following trends:

Figure 3.1 The Changing U.S. Workforce: 2002–2012

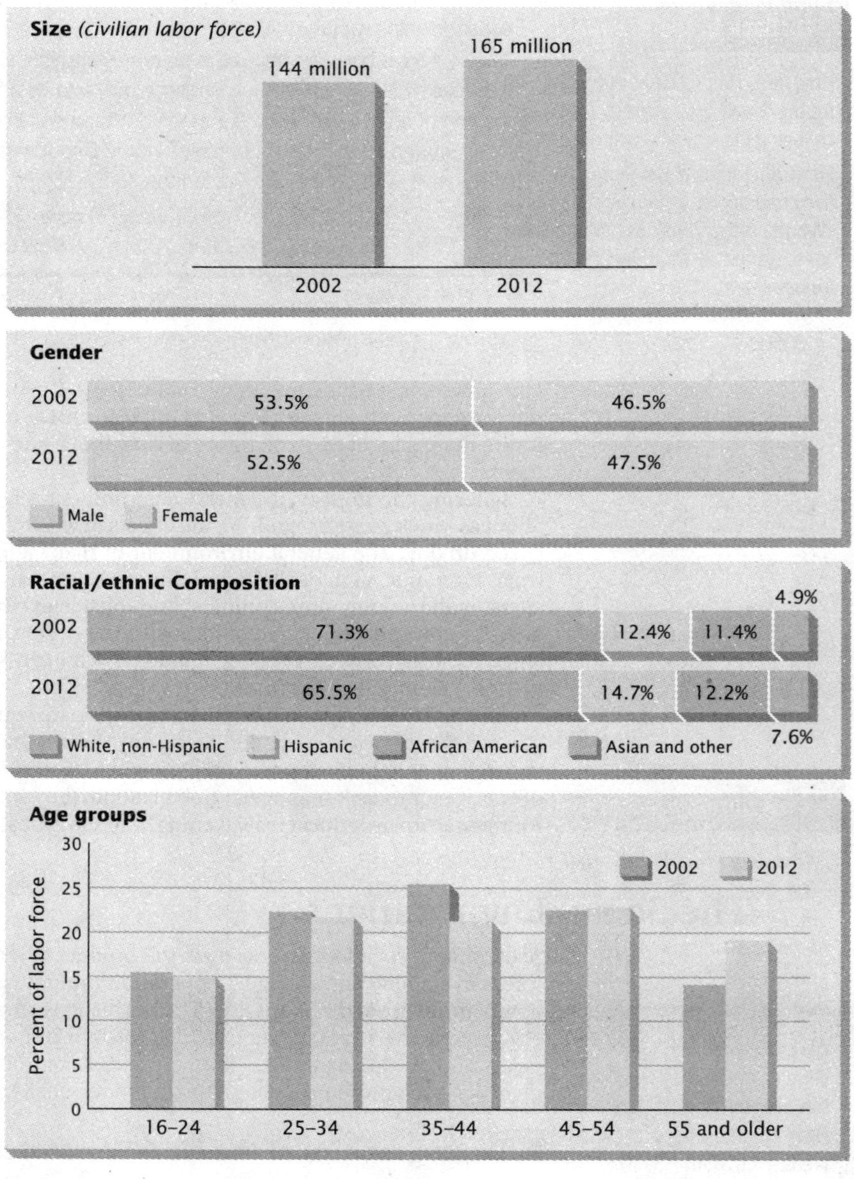

Source: *Data and bottom figure from U.S. Department of Labor, Bureau of Labor Statistics, "Tomorrow's Jobs,"* Occupational Outlook Handbook, *2004–2005 edition,* ***www.bls.gov****.*

1. SUMMARIZE the demographics of the new American workforce.

- *It is getting larger.* As in the previous two decades, the U.S. labor force will continue to grow at a faster rate than the national population. The resulting labor shortage will continue to be a magnet for legal and illegal immigration.
- *It is getting increasingly female.* Employment opportunities for both men and women will grow, but at a faster rate for women.
- *It is getting more racially and ethnically diverse.* The white, non-Hispanic majority of the U.S. workforce continues to shrink, and Hispanics have replaced African Americans as the second-largest segment. The "Asian and other" category is the most rapidly growing, but still the smallest, segment.
- *It is getting older.* The median age of U.S. employees will continue to increase, with most vigorous growth for the 55-and-older group. This mirrors an aging general population and, more specifically, the aging of the post–World War II baby-boom generation: "In 2011, the bubble of 77 million baby boomers will begin turning 65. By 2050, the 65-and-over population will grow from 12% to 21% of the population, the U.S. Census Bureau predicts."[4] (Japan and Italy will hit the 20% threshold for citizens 65 and older by 2008!)[5] This trend has major (some say troubling) implications for the viability of old-age assistance programs in developed countries, including the U.S. Social Security System.[6]

3a Back to the Opening Case

How does Home Depot's Rob Roy symbolize the "new" U.S. workforce? How is this changing the way America does business?

For further information about the interactive annotations in this chapter, visit our Web site (**http://business.college.hmco.com/students/** and select Kreitner, *Management,* 10e).

Parallel demographic shifts in the overall U.S. population have manufacturers redesigning products. Take refrigerators, for example:

> *Just 4% of refrigerators are sold with freezers on the bottom, but GE appliances is betting that the models are poised for a sales surge.*
>
> *The bottom freezers are gaining in popularity with two important demographic groups: retirees and Gen Xers, GE says.*
>
> *Older people like them because the food they reach for most often is up high, where they can see it and get at it. According to GE, consumers open their freezer once for every seven times they open their refrigerator. So having the freezer on the bottom actually means less bending over.*
>
> *Gen Xers like them because they're different.*
>
> *"They like the style and the look," says Robert Rogers, marketing manager for GE's refrigerator division."*[7]

Similarly, products, services, and advertising are being tailored to the rapidly growing Hispanic/Latino population. Many banks, including Bank of America and Wells Fargo, offer Spanish-language services at their teller windows, ATMs, and telephone and Internet service centers. Businesses cannot afford to ignore the estimated $1 trillion in buying power that the U.S. Hispanic/Latino community will have by 2007.[8]

3b A Curious Educational System

According to an international study completed in 1999, U.S. fourth-graders ranked among the world's best in math and science. By eighth grade, they fell below the international average. By 12th, they trailed students in nearly every other industrialized country.

Source: "Wanted: Next-Generation Scientists," USA Today (July 12, 2004): 5D.

QUESTIONS:

Why does this happen? What are the implications for the economy? What corrective steps need to be taken? How can the United States, a country with a supposedly weak educational system for kindergarten through grade 12, be a world leader in higher education?

■ **Needed: On-the-Job Remedial Education.** While demographics foretell possible labor shortages in the near term,[9] the picture for employers grows worse when the issue of labor force *quality* is considered. In the United States, the numbers are not encouraging. At present, the U.S. workforce is at a competitive disadvantage globally because of deficient reading, writing, science, and basic math skills.[10] In a 2004 survey of 119 manufacturers by the Federal Reserve Bank of Philadelphia, employers found 40 percent of their job applicants lacking in basic reading, math, and writing skills.[11]

Experts say about 20 percent of working adults in the United States are *functionally illiterate,* meaning that they have difficulty with basic life skills such as reading a newspaper, completing a job application, and interpreting a bus schedule.[12] In other words, 30 million U.S. workers could not comprehend the paragraph you are now reading. Another 15 million would struggle to do so. According to the National Jewish Coalition for Literacy, "illiteracy costs the USA about $225 billion a year in lost productivity."[13] Consequently, many businesses, often in partnership with local schools and colleges, have launched remedial education programs. A *Training* magazine survey of 1,652 companies with 100 or more employees found a broad corporate commitment to remedial education; the following skills were being taught at the indicated percentages of the companies surveyed:

- Basic life/work skills (71 percent)
- English as a second language (41 percent)
- Remedial math (42 percent)
- Remedial reading (37 percent)
- Remedial writing (41 percent)
- Welfare-to-work transition (35 percent)[14]

These remedial programs typically involve an intensive schedule of small-group sessions emphasizing practical, work-related instruction. Knowledge is the entry ticket to today's computerized service economy.

■ **Myths About Older Workers.** As we have noted, the U.S. workforce is getting older. Strengthening this tendency is the recent redefinition of the concept of retirement: "Sixty-eight percent of workers between the ages of 50 and 70 plan to work in retirement or never retire."[15] While we're on the subject, how old is old? According to a nationwide survey of 2,503 Americans between the ages of 18 and 75, the answer depends on how old *you* are! "Among those over 65, only 8 percent think of people under 65 as old, while 30 percent of those under 25 say 'old' is anywhere from 40 to 64."[16] Older workers, defined by the U.S. Department of Labor as those aged 55 and up, tend to be burdened by a negative image in America's youth-oriented culture.[17] Researchers have identified and disproved five stubborn myths about older workers:

Myth: Older workers are less productive than the average worker.

Fact: Research shows that productivity does not decline with a worker's age. Older employees perform as well as younger workers in most jobs. Moreover, older workers meet the productivity expectations.

Myth: The costs of employee benefits outweigh any possible gain from hiring older workers.

Fact: The costs of health insurance increase with age, but most other fringe benefits do not since they are tied to length of service and level of salary. A study at The Travelers Companies found that it was not safe to assume that older workers cost more or less than younger workers.

Myth: Older workers are prone to frequent absences because of age-related infirmities and above-average rates of sickness.

Fact: Data show that workers age 65 and over have attendance records that are equal to or better than most other age groups of workers. Older people who are *not* working may have dropped out of the workforce because of their health. Older workers who stay in the labor force may well represent a self-selected healthier group of older people.

Myth: Older workers have an unacceptably high rate of accidents at work.

Fact: Data show that older workers account for only 9.7 percent of all workplace injuries while they make up 13.6 percent of the labor force.

In our youth-obsessed culture, older people often are assumed to have obsolete skills and are pushed aside. That's not the case with 78-year-old Cecilia Bearchum from the Umatilla Indian Reservation in Oregon. A new Oregon law allows tribal elders who lack college degrees to teach Native American languages in public schools, using a special teaching permit. The idea is to revive interest in Native American languages. Ryan Branstetter, one-quarter Walla Walla Indian, appreciates Bearchum's teaching and wisdom.

Myth: Older workers are unwilling to learn new jobs and [are] inflexible about the hours they will work.

Fact: The truth depends on the individual. Studies of older employees' interest in alternative work arrangements found that many were interested in altering their work hours and their jobs. They were particularly interested in part-time work.[18]

Enlightened employers view older workers as an underutilized and valuable resource in an aging society facing a potential labor shortage.[19] Like all employees, older workers need to be managed according to their individual abilities, not as members of a demographic group.

> **3c Back to the Opening Case**
>
> Professor Gerard F. Anderson, Johns Hopkins University:
>
> *A strong feeling of "social solidarity," as Anderson sees it, makes Europeans inclined to be generous to older people, more willing to support them. "Their attitude is, we're in this together and sooner or later we're going to become older and we'll need some help," he says. "The U.S. attitude is, we're all rugged individualists and we're going to take care of ourselves, not others."*
>
> *Source: As quoted in Mike Edwards, "As Good As It Gets," AARP: The Magazine (November-December 2004): 48.*
>
> **QUESTIONS:**
>
> **Do you agree with this assessment? Explain. What is your own attitude toward older people? How should a younger manager handle an older employee such as Home Depot's Rob Roy?**

■ A New Social Contract Between Employer and Employee

Between World War II and the 1970s there was an implicit cultural agreement, a social contract, in the United States between employers and employees: "Be loyal to the company and the company will take care of you until retirement." But then the 1980s and 1990s brought restructuring, downsizing, and layoffs. With the dawn of the twenty-first century came a recession that only made matters worse. In 2001, 2.5 million

2. EXPLAIN how the social contract between employer and employee has changed in recent years.

employees in the United States were put out of work by "mass layoffs" involving 50 or more people.[20] As the economy bottomed out and began to grow again, the mass layoffs continued (involving more than 3 million people from 2002 to mid-2004).[21] The traditional social contract between employers and employees has been broken. In its place is a new social contract, framed in these terms:

> *In short, the rules of the game have changed, and they go something like this: Your career depends on you, and you had better work at increasing your own long-term value, because nobody is going to do it for you. Employers, in turn, have accepted this reality: In the new marketplace for talent, we must provide opportunities, resources, and rewards for the continual development of our workforce or risk losing our greatest competitive asset.*[22]

new social contract: *assumption that the employer-employee relationship will be a shorter-term one based on convenience and mutual benefit, rather than for life*

Thus, the **new social contract** is based not on the notion of lifetime employment with a single employer but rather on shorter-term relationships of convenience and mutual benefit.[23] The senior vice president of human resources at AT&T, Harold Burlingame, put it more bluntly:

> *There was a time when someone would come to the front door of AT&T and see an invisible sign that said,* AT&T: *a job for life. . . . That's over. Now it's a shared kind of thing. Come to us. We'll invest in you, and you invest in us. Together, we'll face the market, and the degree to which we succeed will determine how things work out.*[24]

■ Nagging Inequalities in the Workplace

Can the United States achieve full and lasting international competitiveness if a large proportion of its workforce suffers nagging inequalities? Probably not. Unfortunately, women, minorities, and part-timers often encounter barriers in the workplace. Let us open our discussion by focusing on women, because all minorities share their plight to some degree.[25]

■ Under the Glass Ceiling. As a large and influential minority, women are demanding—and getting—a greater share of workplace opportunities. Women occupy 50 percent of the managerial and professional positions in the U.S. workforce.[26] Still, a large inequity remains. *USA Today* summed up the situation:

> *For every dollar a man made in 2003, women made 75.5 cents, the Census Bureau said in its annual report on income. That was down from the record 76.6 cents that women earned vs. men's $1 in 2002. The median income for men working full time in 2003 was $40,668, not significantly different from the prior year, while the median income for women working full time was $30,724, down 0.6% from 2002.*
>
> *While the drop might appear minor, it was the first statistically significant decline in women's incomes since 1995, the Census Bureau said.*[27]

Also, according to a recent study, lifetime earnings for women in the United States equal, on average, 44 percent of the lifetime earnings for their male counterparts.[28] Across all job categories—from top business executives to lawyers, physicians, and office workers—the same sort of gender pay gap can be found.[29] This gap has expanded and contracted at various times since the 1950s in the United States, with the shortfall actually *growing* for women managers between 1995 and 2000.[30] In the United States, the gender pay gap can be summed up in two words: *large* and *persistent.* Comparatively well-paid men can grasp the significance of the gender wage gap by pondering the impact on their standard of living of a 25 percent pay cut. Moreover, men who share household expenses with a woman wage earner are also penalized by the gender wage gap.

glass ceiling: *the transparent but strong barrier keeping women and minorities from moving up the management ladder*

In addition to suffering a wage gap, women (and other minorities) bump up against the so-called glass ceiling when climbing the managerial ladder.[31] "The **glass ceiling** is a concept popularized in the 1980s to describe a barrier so subtle that it is transparent, yet so strong that it prevents women and minorities from moving up in the management hierarchy."[32] It is not unique to the United States.

Consider the situation going into 2004:

- The *Fortune* 500, America's largest corporations, were headed by 492 men (3 of them African Americans) and 8 women.[33]
- Women held 13.6 percent of the corporate board seats at *Fortune* 500 companies, up from 12.4 percent two years before. Women of color held 3 percent of those seats, up just 0.4 percent from 2001. (See Managing Diversity.)[34]

3d Is Race the Issue?

Kenneth Chenault, on being named CEO of American Express Corp.:

> *From a societal standpoint, it's a big deal; I won't minimize it. . . . But I want them to say, "He's a terrific CEO," not "He's a terrific black CEO."*

Source: As quoted in Nelson D. Schwartz, "What's in the Cards for AMEX?" Fortune (January 22, 2001): 60.

QUESTION:
What is the real message here?

Why is there a glass ceiling? According to *Working Woman* magazine, women are being held back by "the lingering perception of women as outsiders, exclusion from informal networks, male stereotyping and lack of experience."[35]

Another force is also at work here, siphoning off some of the best female executive talent part way up the corporate ladder. Many women are leaving the corporate ranks to start their own businesses. According to *Fortune* magazine, "Woman today control just under half of all the small businesses in America. In the past seven years the number of woman-owned firms with employees has grown by 28%—three times the growth rate among all employer firms."[36]

■ **Continuing Pressure for Equal Opportunity.** Persistent racial inequality is underscored by the fact that the unemployment rate for African Americans generally is about twice as high as that for whites during both good and bad economic times.[37] Women, African Americans, Hispanics/Latinos, Native Americans, the physically challenged, and other minorities who are overrepresented in either low-level, low-paying jobs or the unemployment line can be expected to press harder to become full partners in the world of work.[38] Equal employment opportunity (EEO) and affirmative action are discussed in Chapter 11.

contingent workers: *part-timers and other employees who do not have a long-term implicit contract with their ultimate employers*

■ **Part-Timer Promises and Problems.** An increasing percentage of the U.S. labor force is now made up of **contingent workers.** According to the U.S. Bureau of Labor Statistics, there are more than 2 million contingent workers in the U.S.[39] This "just-in-time" or "flexible" workforce includes a diverse array of part-timers, temporary workers, on-call employees, and independent contractors. "Their common denominator is that they do not have a long-term implicit contract with their ultimate employers, the purchasers of the labor and services they provide."[40] Employers are relying more on part-timers for two basic reasons. First, because they are paid at lower rates and often do not receive the full range of employer-paid benefits, part-timers are much less costly to employ than full-time employees. Second, as a flexible workforce, they can be let go when times are bad, without the usual repercussions of a general layoff. Starbucks is a refreshing exception to this state of affairs. As Howard Schultz, founder of the Seattle-based coffee company with 90,000 employees, recently noted in an interview,

> *Starbucks was the first company in America to give comprehensive health benefits and stock options to every single employee, including the over 65% that were part-time at the time. Starbucks has the lowest level of attrition of any national retailer. . . . The relationships that we have with our people are the driving force of innovation at Starbucks.*[41]

On the down side, a recent comprehensive analysis of 38 studies involving 51,231 employees found lower "job involvement" among part-timers, compared with their full-time coworkers. (There were no significant differences in job satisfaction and organizational commitment, however.)[42] Also, critics warn of the risk of creating a permanent underclass of employees burdened by low pay, inadequate health and retirement benefits, and low status. Although some highly skilled professionals do enjoy good pay and

MANAGING DIVERSITY

Finally in the Director's Chair

Standing before a small lecture hall in Chicago filled with nonstudents in September, Harvard Business School professor David Thomas drew laughter when he welcomed "one of the smallest groups in the world."

The group? Black board directors.

For the past few years, black executives who sit on corporate boards have started coming together in the hope of leveraging their collective clout and ultimately increasing their numbers. This year the directors allowed *Fortune* to sit in their hush-hush meeting.

The gathering was started informally two years ago by Charles Tribbett, managing director of Russell Reynolds, and John Rogers, CEO of Ariel Capital. At that first meeting there were just 30 directors; this year the summit drew 85 directors, including board members from Delta, Target, McDonald's, and Verizon. There are currently 185 black directors, and they hold a combined 321 of the 3,447 board seats available. . . .

Carl McCall, the former New York State comptroller who sits on the new Tyco board, also addressed the group. "This is a group of African Americans whom CEOs listen to," says Tribbett. "That's why developing this network is so important." . . .

The intense day and a half included hard-core networking (at one point Thomas forced directors who did not know one another into groups, giving them topics to discuss) and honest debate about general board issues such as CEO succession. The gathering stayed focused, though a few participants did have to sneak out for, well, board meetings.

Diversity was an underlying theme of the event, but talk went deeper than the typical "good business" rhetoric that is often bandied about in corporate settings. McCall told the group it was their obligation as black directors to always bring up issues of diversity in the boardroom. While some argued that they did not want to be typecast as the "black voice," others countered that such typecasting was inevitable. "It doesn't matter if we say anything or not—the conversation changes just by having us in the room," says Maceo Sloan, CEO of Sloan Financial Group and a member of the TIAA-CREF board. "That's why we have to get into those rooms."

Source: From Cora Daniels, "Finally in the Director's Chair," Fortune *(October 4, 2004): 42, 44.*

greater freedom by working part time,[43] most part-timers do not. The plight of part-timers could become a major social and political issue worldwide in the years to come.

Managing Diversity

The United States, a nation of immigrants, is becoming even more racially and ethnically diverse. The evidence is compelling:

- "Foreign-born workers make up about 11% of the U.S. population and 14% of the labor force. But their impact is outsized, accounting for more than half of total workforce growth from 1996 to 2002. In the western Midwest, New England, and Mid-Atlantic regions, foreign-born workers accounted for more than 90% of employment growth from 1996 to 2002."[44]
- "Thirteen states had more than a 100% rise in their foreign-born population in the 1990s. . . . An estimated 8 million to 10 million foreign-born people are in the USA illegally. . . ."[45]
- "The country will become a nation of minorities. Whites accounted for about 71% of the population . . . [in 2000,] but by 2050, the number will drop to 53%, blacks will increase one percentage point (to 13.2%), Asians will more than double to 8.9% (from 3.9%), and Hispanics will jump to 24.3% (from 11.8%)."[46]
- With a population growth rate seven times greater than that of any other group, Hispanics/Latinos passed African Americans in 2003 to become the country's largest minority.[47]

Accordingly, the U.S. workforce is becoming more culturally diverse. For example, the employees at some Marriott Hotels speak 30 different languages.[48] Some Americans decry what they consider to be an invasion of "their" national and organizational "terri-

managing diversity: *process of helping all employees, including women and minorities, reach their full potential*

tories." But many others realize that America's immigrants and minorities have always been a vitalizing, creative, hardworking force.[49] Progressive organizations are taking steps to better accommodate and more fully utilize America's more diverse workforce. **Managing diversity** is the process of creating an organizational culture that enables *all* employees, including women and minorities, to realize their full potential.[50]

3. DEFINE the term *managing diversity,* and **EXPLAIN** why it is particularly important today.

■ More than EEO. Managing diversity builds on equal employment opportunity (EEO) and affirmative action programs (discussed in Chapter 11). EEO and affirmative action are necessary to get more women and minorities into the workplace. But getting them in is not enough. Comprehensive diversity programs are needed to create more *flexible* organizations where *everyone* has a fair chance to thrive and succeed.[51] These programs need to include white males who have sometimes felt slighted or ignored by EEO and affirmative action; they, too, have individual differences (opinions, lifestyles, age, and schedules) that deserve fair accommodation. Managing diversity requires many of us to adjust our thinking. According to sociologist Jack McDevitt, "We don't want to have as a goal just tolerating people. We have to *value* them."[52] In addition to being the ethical course of action, managing diversity is a necessity; a nation cannot waste human potential and remain globally competitive.

3e Does Diversity Need a Push?

Anne Fisher, *Fortune* magazine:

> *Researchers surveyed more than 5,500 American workers, including managers and CEOs, and the results are thought-provoking. Just 32% of U.S. employees think their companies do a decent job of hiring and promoting people other than white males. Their bosses' view isn't much rosier: Fewer than half of executives (47%) think their own diversity efforts are working, and the majority (59%) say it's partly their fault for not being involved enough.*

Source: Anne Fisher, "How You Can Do Better on Diversity," Fortune (November 15, 2004): 60.

QUESTIONS:

Do you agree that diversity programs are coming up short? Explain. What needs to be done to strengthen diversity programs?

■ Promising Beginnings. Among the diversity programs in use today are the following:

- Teaching English as a second language.
- Creating mentor programs (an experienced employee coaches and sponsors a newcomer).
- Providing immigration assistance.
- Fostering the development of support groups for minorities.
- Training minorities for managerial positions.
- Training managers to value and skillfully manage diversity.
- Encouraging employees to contribute to and attend cultural celebrations and events in the community.
- Creating, publicizing, and enforcing discrimination and harassment policies.
- Actively recruiting minorities.[53]

The scope of managing diversity is limited only by management's depth of commitment and imagination. For example, a supervisor learns sign language to communicate with a hearing-impaired employee. Or a married male manager attends a diversity workshop and becomes aware of the difficulties of being a single working mother. Perhaps a younger manager's age bias is blunted after reading a research report documenting that older employees tend to be absent less often and have lower accident rates than younger ones.[54] Maybe other companies begin to follow Corning's diversity policy, whereby "new employees are no longer encouraged to adopt the dress, style, and social activities of the white male majority."[55]

The Political-Legal Environment

In its broadest terms, *politics* is the art (or science) of public influence and control. Laws are an outcome of the political process that differentiate good and bad conduct. An orderly political process is necessary because modern society is the product of an evolving consensus among diverse individuals and groups, often with conflicting interests and objectives. Although the list of special-interest groups is long and is

4. DISCUSS how the changing political-legal environment is affecting the practice of management.

still growing, not everyone can have his or her own way. The political system tries to balance competing interests in a generally acceptable manner.

Ideally, elected officials pass laws that, when enforced, control individual and collective conduct for the general good. Unfortunately, as we all know, variables such as hollow campaign promises, illegal campaign financing, and voter apathy throw sand into a democracy's political gears. Managers, as both citizens and caretakers of socially, politically, and economically powerful organizations, have a large stake in the political-legal environment. Two key pressure points for managers in this area are the politicization of management and increased personal legal accountability.

The Politicization of Management

Prepared or not and willing or not, today's managers often find themselves embroiled in issues with clearly political overtones. Just ask Slim-Fast. This was Slim-Fast's response when their spokesperson Whoopi Goldberg made off-color comments about President George W. Bush during the 2004 presidential race:

> *The West Palm Beach Fla.-based maker of diet aids said Wednesday that it is pulling the 8-month-old ad campaign that features Goldberg calling herself "a big loser." Terry Olson, Slim-Fast general manager and vice president of marketing, said the company regretted that Goldberg's remarks "offended some of our consumers."*[56]

This sort of political pressure has spurred the growth of a practice called *issues management.*

issues management: *ongoing process of identifying, evaluating, and responding to important social and political issues*

Issues Management.

Issues management (IM) is the ongoing organizational process of identifying, evaluating, and responding to relevant and important social and political issues. According to a pair of experts on the subject,

> *The purpose of IM is twofold. First, it attempts to minimize "surprises" which accompany social and political change by serving as an early warning system for potential environment threats and opportunities. IM analyzes the past development of an issue and assesses its importance for the firm. Second, IM attempts to prompt more systematic and effective responses to particular issues by serving as a coordinating and integrating force within the corporation. Once the issue has been analyzed, IM constructs alternative responses to deal with competing internal and external demands.*[57]

IM is not an exact science. It has been carried out in various ways in the name of strategic planning, public relations, community affairs, and corporate communications, among others. IM's main contribution to good management is its emphasis on systematic preparedness for social and political action. Take Wal-Mart, for example. In the face of a record class-action sex discrimination lawsuit on behalf of 1.6 million past and present female employees and a growing wave of local opposition to its "big box" stores,[58] Wal-Mart's CEO Lee Scott recently outlined a more proactive response:

> *"We have got to eliminate this constant barrage of negatives that cause people . . . to wonder if Wal-Mart will be allowed to grow," Scott said. "Our message has not gotten out to the extent that it should. I think that's management's failure. We thought we could sit in Bentonville, take care of customers, take care of associates, and the world would leave us alone."*
>
> *He said Wal-Mart must be "more sophisticated" than it was in the days of founder Sam Walton, who shunned politics and public speaking.*[59]

Indeed, Wal-Mart now has five lobbyists in Washington, D.C., and CEO Scott and other company executives give speeches and interviews. The company also has become a top campaign contributor (85 percent to Republicans in the 2004 election cycle).[60]

With this background in mind, let us turn our attention to three general political responses and four specific political strategies.

Source: *© 2004 Gary Markstein. Courtesy of the Milwaukee Journal Sentinel.*

■ **General Political Responses.** The three general political responses available to management can be plotted on a continuum, as illustrated in Figure 3.2. Managers who are politically inactive occupy the neutral zone in the middle and have a "wait and see" attitude. But few managers today can afford the luxury of a neutral political stance. Those on the extreme left of the continuum are politically active in defending the status quo and/or fighting government intervention. In contrast, politically active managers on the right end of the continuum try to identify and respond constructively to emerging political/legal issues.

In recent years, more and more business managers have swung away from being reactive and have become proactive. Why? In short, they view prompt action as a way to avoid additional governmental regulation. The wisdom of choosing a proactive stance is clearly illustrated by the recent experiences of Microsoft and Intel. Both are dominant players in their respective fields of software and computer chips. According to the *Harvard Business Review,*

Figure 3.2 Management's Political Response Continuum

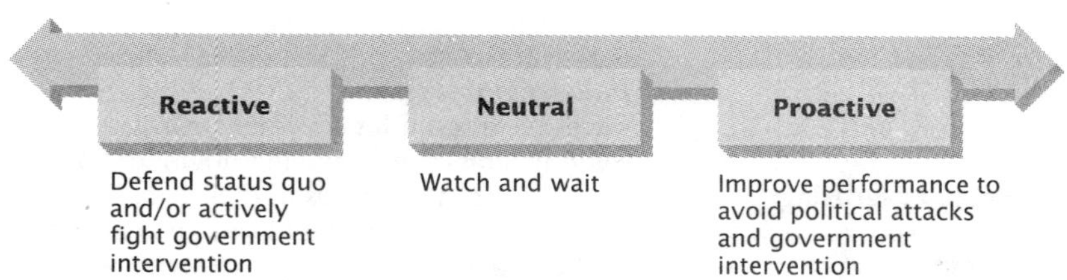

For years now, Microsoft has been mired in court, facing charges of predatory behavior by the U.S. Department of Justice and the attorneys general of more than a dozen states. It has seen its name and business practices dragged through the mud, its senior executives distracted and embarrassed, and its very future as a single company thrown into doubt. . . .

Intel, in stark contrast, has managed to avoid prolonged, high-profile antitrust cases. It's remained above the fray, its business focus largely undisturbed by trustbusters.

Intel's success is not a matter of luck. It's a matter of painstaking planning and intense effort. The company's antitrust compliance program, refined over many years, may not receive a lot of attention from the press and the public, but it's been an integral element in the chip maker's business strategy.[61]

■ **Specific Political Strategies.** Whether acting reactively or proactively, managers can employ four major strategies.[62]

1. ***Campaign financing.***
   Although federal law prohibits U.S. corporations from backing a specific candidate or party with the firm's name, funds, or free labor, a legal alternative is available. Corporations can form political action committees (PACs) to solicit volunteer contributions from employees biannually for the support of preferred candidates and parties. Significantly, PACs are registered with the Federal Election Commission and are required to keep detailed and accurate records of receipts and expenditures. Some criticize corporate PACs for having too great an influence over federal politics. But a recent MIT study found no positive correlation between corporate political giving and subsequent profitability. The researchers concluded that companies should spend their money in more productive ways.[63] Meanwhile, legislators are reluctant to tamper with a funding mechanism that tends to favor those already in office.
2. ***Lobbying.***
   Historically, lobbying has been management's most popular and successful political strategy. Secret and informal meetings between hired representatives and key legislators in smoke-filled rooms have largely been replaced by a more forthright approach. Today, formal presentations by well-prepared company representatives are the preferred approach to lobbying for political support. For example, consider eBay CEO Meg Whitman's 2004 trip to Washington:

   . . . Whitman and 51 eBay customers held 36 meetings with politicians in a single day. They had breakfast with Rep. Jesse Jackson Jr., D-Ill., lunch with Rep. David Dreier, R-Calif., and dinner with Sen. John McCain, R-Ariz. Their goal: keeping Internet sales tax-free.

   "We need to make sure the government understands and supports what we're doing," says eBay government relations head Tod Cohen.[64]

   Despite reform legislation from the U.S. Congress intended to correct abuses, loopholes, and weak penalties for inappropriate gifts, it is pretty much business as usual for corporate lobbyists.
3. ***Coalition building.***
   In a political environment of countless special-interest groups, managers are finding that coalitions built around common rallying points are required for political impact.
4. ***Indirect lobbying.***
   Having learned a lesson from unions, business managers now appreciate the value of grassroots lobbying. Members of legislative bodies tend to be more responsive to the desires of their constituents than to those of individuals who vote in other districts. Employee and consumer letter-writing, telephone, and e-mail campaigns have proved effective. **Advocacy advertising,** the controversial practice of promoting a point of view along with a product or service, is another

advocacy advertising: *promoting a point of view along with a product or service* form of indirect lobbying that has grown in popularity in recent years. The Internet is also becoming an effective indirect lobbying tool.

Auto makers launched saveleasing.com to defeat laws allowing companies to be held liable for damages caused by drivers in leased cars. By buying banner ads at local newspaper sites in Rhode Island, Connecticut, and New York, auto makers generated over 18,000 e-mails to legislators in those states. Connecticut and Rhode Island outlawed the suits.[65]

Increased Personal Legal Accountability

Recent changes in the political and legal climate have made it increasingly difficult for managers to take refuge in the bureaucratic shadows when a law has been broken. Managers in the United States who decide to take illegal courses of action stand a good chance of being held personally accountable in a court of law.

Things got even tougher in July 2002 when President George W. Bush signed the Sarbanes-Oxley Act into law. This sweeping corporate fraud bill garnered an unusually high degree of bipartisan support. The lawmakers were prodded into decisive action by public disgust over the fraud-tainted failures of corporate giants, including Enron, Andersen, WorldCom, and Adelphia.

The law, which passed the Senate by 99-0 and the House by 423-3, quadruples sentences for accounting fraud, creates a new felony for securities fraud that carries a 25-year prison term, places new restraints on corporate officers, and establishes a federal oversight board for the accounting industry.

"No more easy money for corporate criminals, just hard time," the president said. "The era of low standards and false profits is over, no boardroom in America is above or beyond the law."[66]

Guilty on all counts. Bernard Ebbers, the man who built a small Mississippi phone company into giant WorldCom, was convicted of massive accounting fraud in 2005. The jury didn't accept Ebbers' defense that he didn't know what was going on at his company when he was CEO. Ebbers could very well spend the rest of his life in prison.

This increases the likelihood of managers being held *personally responsible* for the illegal actions of their companies. Consider this stunning case in point:

. . . former Dynegy executive Jamie Olis was sentenced . . . [in 2004] to 24 years in prison for his role in a $300 million accounting scam at the Houston energy firm. . . .

Family and friends of the 38-year-old Olis wore yellow ribbons and cried when the sentence was ordered. His wife, Monica, and their baby daughter were in the packed Houston courtroom.[67]

The personal accountability trend is spreading to other countries as well.

Misguided folks who do not heed this warning can take some comfort in a Dallas, Texas, consulting service.

The company is the nation's only felon-run consulting service that preps newly convicted white-collar crooks on what to expect once they get to prison, coaching them about how to make their hard time easier—a sort of school for scoundrels. . . .

[According to the consultant, a three-time loser for investment scams,] a lot of white-collar crooks, represented by some of the nation's best lawyers, were utterly clueless about life behind bars. . . .[68]

3f Who, Me?

When companies break the law, the first thing chief executives typically do is plead ignorance and blame everything on rogue underlings. . . . But few have been quite as aggressive at it as ex-Enron CEO Kenneth L. Lay. A few days after his criminal indictment on July 7, [2004,] Lay offered up the perfect illustration of the deaf, dumb, and blind defense: "I cannot take responsibility for criminal conduct that I was not aware of," he told CNN's Larry King. "Enron was a company with about 30,000 employees in about 30 different countries."

Source: Mike France, "The New Accountability," Business Week (July 26, 2004): 30.

QUESTIONS:
How credible is Mr. Lay's defense? Explain.

Political-Legal Implications for Management

Managers will continue to be forced into becoming more politically astute, whether they like it or not. Support appears to be growing for the idea that managers can and should try to shape the political climate in which they operate. And the vigilant media and a wary public can be expected to keep a close eye on the form and substance of managerial politics to ensure that the public interest is served. Managers who abuse their political power and/or engage in criminal conduct while at work will increasingly be held accountable.

On the legal side, managers are attempting to curb the skyrocketing costs of litigation. Suing large companies with so-called deep pockets is common practice in the United States, a country with more than 1 million lawyers. In a recent survey of large-company CEOs, 24 percent said litigation costs were their primary economic concern.[69] Indicative of the current legal climate is the 2002 class-action suit against McDonald's. The fast-food giant was sued for advertising and selling to children food that tends to make them more likely to become overweight and plagued by diabetes and heart disease. Regardless of the outcome of the suit, *Fortune* issued this warning to the food industry:

> *Seasoned lawyers from both sides of past mass-tort disputes agree that the years ahead hold serious tobacco-like litigation challenges that extend beyond fast foods to snack foods, soft drinks, packaged goods, and dietary supplements.*[70]

Not surprisingly, U.S. business leaders are pushing hard for tort (noncriminal) reform in which some sort of legislated cap is put on jury awards and damage claims. Trial lawyers are pushing equally hard to squelch any such limitations, citing the need to protect the public. Meantime, managers can better prepare their companies and, it is hoped, avoid costly legal problems by performing legal audits. "A **legal audit** reviews all aspects of a firm's operations to pinpoint possible liabilities and other legal problems."[71] For example, a company's job application forms need to be carefully screened by the human resources department to eliminate any questions that could trigger a discriminatory-hiring lawsuit. Another approach, called **alternative dispute resolution** (ADR), strives to curb courtroom costs by settling disagreements out of court through techniques such as arbitration and mediation.

legal audit: *review of all operations to pinpoint possible legal liabilities or problems*

alternative dispute resolution: *avoiding courtroom battles by settling disputes with less costly methods, including arbitration and mediation*

> *The modern ADR phenomenon has led to much greater use of older methods such as arbitration and mediation, as well as the creation of many new methods such as mini-trial, summary jury trial, private judging, neutral evaluation, and regulatory negotiation. Variations and hybrids of these techniques are also commonly found today.*[72]

As a technical point, a third-party arbitrator makes a binding decision, whereas a mediator helps the parties reach their own agreement.

The Economic Environment

As we noted in Chapter 1, there is a close relationship between economics and management. Economics is the study of how scarce resources are used to create wealth and how that wealth is distributed. Managers, as trustees of our resource-consuming productive organizations, perform an essentially economic function. Unfortunately, economics is not a strong subject for the average American. In a recent nationwide survey by the University of Buffalo School of Management, "12th-graders answered only 52.3 percent of questions about personal finance and economics correctly."[73] A slight improvement over the 2002 results (50.2 percent of questions correctly answered) led the researcher to characterize U.S. high schoolers' knowledge of economics and finance as "dismal but improving."

Three aspects of the economic environment of management that deserve special consideration are jobs, business cycles, and the global economy.

The Job Outlook in Today's Service Economy, Where Education Counts

As in other important aspects of life, you have no guarantee of landing your dream job. However, as you move through college and into the labor force, one assumption is safe: you will probably end up with a service-producing job. Why? "According to the [U.S.] Bureau of Labor Statistics, the service economy is expected to account for 19.1 million of the 19.5 million total new wage and salary jobs generated over the 1998–2008 period."[74] Those concerned about having their future jobs outsourced to India, China, and elsewhere can take some comfort in knowing that the service-job category "general managers and operations managers" is one of the most rapidly growing job categories (*and* that it is resistant to being offshored).[75]

The traditional notion of the service sector as a low-wage haven of nothing but hamburger flippers and janitors is no longer valid. Well-paid doctors, lawyers, airline pilots, engineers, scientists, consultants, and other professionals are all service-sector employees enjoying the fruits of a good education. Economists at the U.S. Bureau of Labor Statistics see it this way: "Occupations that require a bachelor's degree are projected to grow the fastest, nearly twice as fast as the average for all occupations. All of the 20 occupations with the highest earnings require at least a bachelor's degree. . . . Education is essential in getting a high paying job."[76]

5. DISCUSS why business cycles and the global economy are vital economic considerations for modern managers.

Coping with Business Cycles

business cycle: *the up-and-down movement of an economy's ability to generate wealth*

The **business cycle** is the up-and-down movement of an economy's ability to generate wealth; it has a predictable structure but variable timing. Historical economic data from industrialized economies show a clear pattern of alternating expansions and recessions. In between have been peaks and troughs of varying magnitude and duration. According to Nobel economist Paul Samuelson, the four phases are like the changing seasons: "Each phase passes into the next. Each is characterized by different economic conditions: for example, during expansion we find that employment, production, prices, money, wages, interest rates, and profits are usually rising, with the reverse true in recession."[77]

Cycle-Sensitive Decisions. Important decisions depend on the ebb and flow of the business cycle (see Figure 3.3). These decisions include ordering inventory, borrowing funds, increasing staff, and spending capital for land, equipment, and energy.

Timing is everything when it comes to making good cycle-sensitive decisions. Just as a baseball batter needs to start swinging before the ball reaches home plate, managers need to make appropriate cutbacks prior to the onset of a recession. Failure to do so, in the face of decreasing sales, leads to bloated inventories and idle productive resources—both costly situations. On the other hand, managers cannot afford to get caught short during a period of rapid expansion. Prices and wages rise sharply when everyone is purchasing inventories and hiring at the same time.

The trick is to stay slightly ahead of the pack. This is particularly true during recessions, when corporate strategy is tested to the fullest. According to a leading management consultant, "Successful players in a downturn place counterintuitive bets in order to dramatically transform their market positions, but these bets are not lucky gambles that miraculously win big against the odds. Instead they are rigorous

Figure 3.3 Business Cycles Affect Managerial Decisions

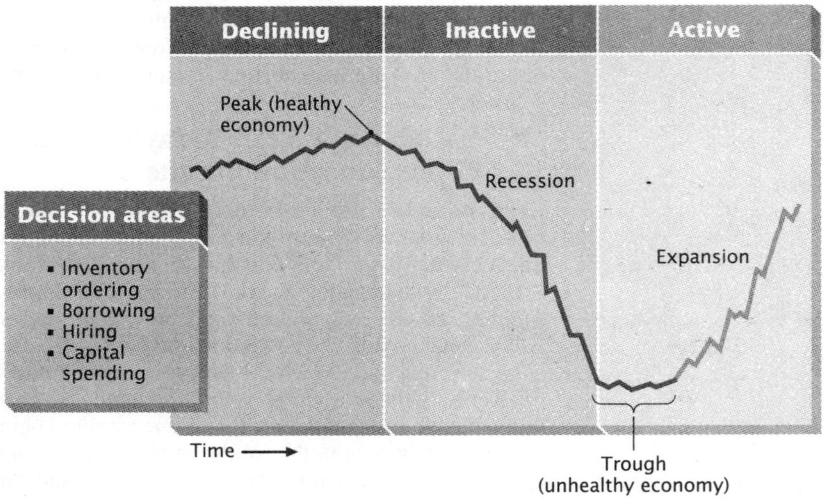

and systematic moves that shift the odds in management's favor."[78] Consider, for example, the strategy described by Wolfgang Hultner, CEO of Mandarin Oriental Hotel Group's North American properties:

> *The hotel business, like others, is cyclical, with the cycle lasting anywhere between four and seven years. You want to build hotels when the cycle is a little bit down. Of course, you can't always choose the timing, but to build in the downtime is good for a number of reasons. Number one, construction costs are normally 20% to 25% lower than at the height of the market. Two, it's easier to find a good staff, and today in the hotel business, it's all about finding the right staff. By the time the hotel opens—and most hotels take between three and five years from the time you sign a contract to the day the doors open—hopefully you are out of the cycle and ready for some good news.*[79]

Hultner's strategy is simple: take market share from more timid competitors. Time will tell whether it is a good cycle-sensitive strategy. As mentioned repeatedly in this text, successful managers are *foresighted* rather than hindsighted. Accurate economic forecasts can be very helpful in this regard.

■ **Benefiting from Economic Forecasts.** Thanks to some widely publicized bad calls, economic forecasting has come under fire in recent years.[80] A case in point:

> *In the fourth quarter of 2000 the 36 forecasters surveyed [by the Federal Reserve Bank of Philadelphia] predicted that the economy would grow at a 3.3% rate in the first quarter of 2001; it shrank by 0.6%. In late 2001 the gang that couldn't predict straight said the economy in the first quarter of 2002 would grow by just 0.1% ; it expanded at a whopping 5% pace.*[81]

3g The Economy: Surf's Up! Surf's Down!

James Morgan, former CEO of Applied Materials, maker of equipment for computer chip manufacturers:

> *. . . problems show up like the rocks in a bay when the tide is out. You can develop a navigation plan. When the water is up, you don't know where the rocks are. Use downturns to find areas that need to be improved. In an upturn you're responding to orders, meeting capacity, getting parts in. That's why when it starts to slow down, things unravel pretty quickly. I'm usually out of sync with the public. I'm focused on the next transition. I've developed the skill of anticipation.*

Source: Del Jones, "Use Recession to Plan for Next Level," USA Today (February 1, 2002): 6B.

QUESTION:
Why does it take *bad* economic times to make a truly *good* manager?

One wit chided economic forecasters by claiming they have predicted eight out of the last four recessions! How can managers get some value from the hundreds of economic forecasts they encounter each year?

A pair of respected forecasting experts recommends a *consensus approach.*[82] They urge managers to survey a wide variety of economic forecasts, taking the forecasters' track records into consideration, and to look for a consensus or average opinion. Cycle-sensitive decisions can then be made accordingly, and slavish adherence to a single forecast can be avoided. One sure formula for failure is naïvely to assume that the future will simply be a replication of the past. In spite of their imperfection, professional economic forecasts are better than no forecasts at all. One economist puts it this way: "Forecasters are very useful, in fact indispensable, because they give you plausible scenarios to help you think about the future in an organized way."[83]

■ The Challenge of a Global Economy

The global economy is expanding today as international trade increases. "International trade now accounts for almost 20% of global gross domestic product, up from just 10% a decade ago."[84] Greater economic interdependence and power shifts are the result. Here are some examples:

- 50 percent of tradable U.S. Treasury bonds are owned by foreigners, mostly Japanese and Chinese.[85]
- "About $450 billion of the roughly $700 billion in U.S. currency in circulation is used in foreign countries.[86]
- "In 2002, China surpassed the USA as the world's leading destination for foreign investment."[87]

Each of us is challenged to understand the workings and implications of the global economy better in light of its profound impact on our lives and work.

■ A Single Global Marketplace. Money spent on imported Japanese cars, French perfumes, Colombian coffee, New Zealand meat and produce, German beers, and Italian shoes may be evidence of an increasingly global economy. Deeper analysis, however, reveals more profound changes. First, according to observers, "The new global economy . . . must be viewed as the world moving from trade among countries to a single economy. One economy. One marketplace."[88] The North American Free Trade Agreement (NAFTA) among Mexico, Canada, and the United States, the 25-nation European Union, and the 147-nation World Trade Organization (WTO) represent steps toward that single global marketplace.[89] Second, the size of the global economy has expanded dramatically. *Fortune* explains why:

> *. . . the commercial world has been swelled by the former Soviet empire, China, India, Indonesia, and much of Latin America—billions of people stepping out from behind political and economic walls. This is the most dramatic change in the geography of capitalism in history.*[90]

Third, and an ominous sign to some, the business cycles of countries around the world show signs of converging in concert with the U.S. economy. International Monetary Fund economists recently documented this trend after studying 20 years of economic data from 170 countries: "They found that an increase of one percentage point in the growth of U.S. output per capita was associated with an increase of 0.8 to 1.0 percentage point in the average growth of other countries. Decreases in U.S. output likewise lowered growth elsewhere."[91] The prospect of global expansions and recessions gives new meaning to the old saying "We're all in the same boat."

■ Globalization Is Personal. Economic globalization is a huge concept, stretching the limits of the imagination. For instance, try to grasp what it means that more

Thanks to the Global Economy, while marketing across national and cultural boundaries care needs to be taken to 'think globally, but act locally' to avoid offending local tastes..

than $1 trillion moves through the global banking network in a single day![92] Ironically, globalization is also a very personal matter affecting where we work, how much we're paid, what we buy, and how much things cost. Let us explore two personal aspects of the global economy:

1. ***Working for a foreign-owned company.*** One of the most visible and controversial signs of a global economy is the worldwide trend toward foreign ownership. Consider the case of Toyota Motor, for example. By 2004, it was the eighth-biggest company in the world, employing 264,410 people around the globe. Toyota's eight U.S. factories (with two more under construction) manufactured more than one million vehicles annually. Those facilities employed more than 31,000 people and helped create at least 190,000 jobs at Toyota's dealerships and suppliers in the United States.[93] This sort of cross-border ownership raises fundamental questions. For instance, has the increase in foreign-owned companies in the United States been a positive or a negative? Economists have found evidence on the positive side:

   > *Americans who work in the USA for foreign companies typically make about 10% more than those who work for U.S. companies, just as foreigners who work for U.S. companies abroad make 10% more than domestic workers there, says Gary Hufbauer, senior economist with the Institute for International Economics.*
   >
   > *The reason, Hufbauer says, is that companies with the might to expand globally are the most productive, want the best workers and are willing to pay a premium.*[94]

2. ***Meeting world standards.*** One does not have to work for a foreign-owned company to be personally affected by the global economy. Many people today complain of having to work harder for the same (or perhaps less) money. Whether they realize it or not, they are being squeezed by two global economic trends: higher quality and lower wages. The "offshoring" of jobs discussed in Chapter 1 is a major by-product of these trends.[95] Only companies striking the right balance between quality and costs can be globally competitive.

The Technological Environment

Technology is a term that ignites passionate debates in many circles these days. Some blame technology for environmental destruction and cultural fragmentation. Others view technology as the key to economic and social progress. No doubt there are important messages in both extremes. See Table 3.1 for technologies likely to have significant effects on our lives in the future.

Table 3.1 Science Fiction Is Becoming Reality with These Seven New Technologies

- **Plastic solar cells:** "The new photovoltaics use tiny solar cells embedded in thin sheets of plastic to create an energy-producing material that is cheap, efficient, and versatile."
- **Printable mechatronics:** Researchers are "developing processes that adapt ink-jet printing technology to build ready-to-use products, complete with working circuitry, switches, and movable parts."
- **Memory drugs:** These drugs aim to help people with Alzheimer's and boost healthy peoples' memory by enhancing the brain's neural connections and functions.
- **Perpendicular magnetic storage:** "Today's hard drives store bits of data horizontally, like stalks of freshly cut corn. PMR stores them vertically, like cornstalks standing in a field. With perpendicular storage, each bit occupies less space on the surface of the disc, so more data can be stuffed into a smaller area." This technology also uses less power, thus prolonging battery life.
- **Microfluidic testing:** "Microfluidics is the science of moving fluids through tiny channels the thickness of a human hair. In microfluidic tests, blood, saliva, or urine samples are analyzed after coming into contact with tiny amounts of a chemical reagent."
- **Micro-opticals:** Combining the functions of several present-day chips on one integrated optical chip will make telecommunication faster and less expensive.
- **Software radio:** The goal of this new software is to create wireless communication devices that will work on all mobile networks—anywhere, anytime.

Source: *Adapted from G. Pascal Zachary, Om Malik, David Pescovitz, and Matthew Maier, "Seven New Technologies That Change Everything,"* Business 2.0, *5 (September 2004): 82–90.*

technology: *all the tools and ideas available for extending the natural physical and mental reach of humankind*

For our purposes, **technology** is defined as all the tools and ideas available for extending the natural physical and mental reach of humankind. A central theme in technology is the practical application of new ideas, a theme that is clarified by the following distinction between science and technology: "Science is the quest for more or less abstract knowledge, whereas technology is the application of organized knowledge to help solve problems in our society."[96] According to the following historical perspective, technology is facilitating the evolution of the industrial age into the information age, just as it once enabled the agricultural age to evolve into the industrial age.

> *Stephen R. Barley, a professor at Cornell's School of Industrial and Labor Relations, builds on the work of others to argue that until recently, "the economies of the advanced industrial nations revolved around electrical power, the electric motor, the internal combustion engine, and the telephone." The development of these "infrastructural technologies" made possible the shift from an agricultural to a manufacturing economy, in the process precipitating "urbanization, the growth of corporations, the rise of professional management. . . ."*
>
> *Now, Barley writes, the evidence suggests that another shift is taking place, with implications likely to be just as seismic: "Our growing knowledge of how to convert electronic and mechanical impulses into digitally encoded information (and vice versa) and how to transmit such information across vast distances is gradually enabling industry to replace its electromechanical infrastructure with a computational infrastructure."*[97]

Consequently, *information* has become a valuable strategic resource. Organizations that use appropriate information technologies to get the right information to the right people at the right time will enjoy a competitive advantage (Internet strategies are discussed in Chapter 7).

Two aspects of technology with important implications for managers are the innovation process and intrapreneurship.

■ The Innovation Process

innovation process: *the systematic development and practical application of a new idea*

Technology comes into being through the **innovation process**, the systematic development and practical application of a new idea.[98] According to a recent survey of 250 executives, this important area needs improvement: "... nearly seven out of ten cited innovation as a top priority and said they plan to hike R&D [research and development] spending. Yet 57% also said they aren't satisfied with the return on their innovation investments."[99]

A great deal of time-consuming work is necessary to develop a new idea into a marketable product or service. And many otherwise good ideas do not become technologically feasible, let alone marketable and profitable. According to one innovation expert, "only one of every 20 or 25 ideas ever becomes a successful product—and of every 10 or 15 new products, only one becomes a hit."[100] Nowhere is this uphill battle more apparent than in pharmaceutical research and development:

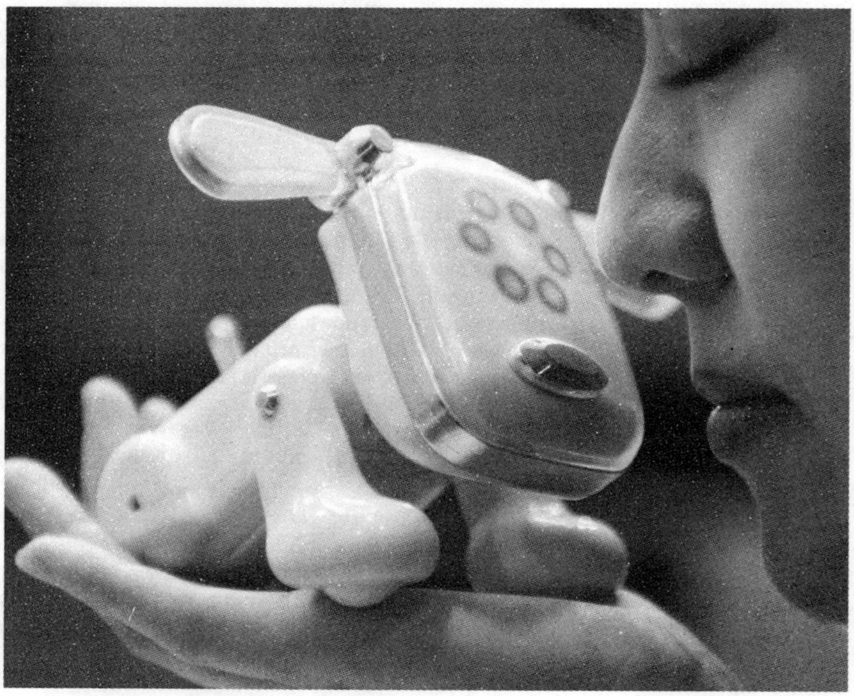

For better or for worse, technology keeps moving in new directions. Decades ago, people used now-primitive audio technology to listen to Elvis sing "You ain't nothin'; but a hound dog." Now with Sega Toys' new pet robot I-Dog, the hound dog can return the favor by singing an Elvis tune. Touch the Japanese firm's robot on the nose, tail, or top of the head and it will sing and, yes, even dance for you. Hmmm, they call it progress.

Drug discovery is a costly slog in which hundreds of scientists screen tens of thousands of chemicals against specific disease targets. After a remorseless round of testing, most of those compounds will prove to be unstable, unsafe, or otherwise unsuitable for human use. Pfizer spends $152 million a week *funding 479 early-stage, preclinical discovery projects; 96% of those efforts will ultimately bomb.*[101]

6. DESCRIBE the three-step innovation process, and **DEFINE** the term *intrapreneur*.

A better understanding of the innovation process can help improve management's chances of turning new ideas into profitable goods and services.

product technology: *second stage of innovation process, involving the creation of a working prototype*

production technology: *third stage of innovation process, involving the development of a profitable production process*

innovation lag: *time it takes for a new idea to be translated into satisfied demand*

■ A Three-Step Process. The innovation process has three steps (see Figure 3.4). First is the conceptualization step, when a new idea occurs to someone. Development of a working prototype is the second step, called **product technology.** This involves actually creating a product that will work as intended. The third and final step is developing a production process to create a profitable quantity-quality-price relationship. This third step is labeled **production technology.** Successful innovation depends on the right combination of new ideas, product technology, and production technology. A missing or deficient step can ruin the innovation process.

■ Innovation Lag. The time it takes for a new idea to be translated into satisfied demand is called **innovation lag.** The longer the innovation lag, the longer society must wait to benefit from a new idea. For example, fax machines came into wide use in the early 1990s. But the fax concept was patented by a Scottish clockmaker named Alexander Bain in 1843—an innovation lag of nearly a century and a half.[102] Over the years, the trend has been toward shorter innovation lags. For example, Britain's Imperial Chemical Industries has "slashed the time it takes to commercialize a technology from the industry norm of more than a decade to only five years."[103]

■ Shortening Innovation Lag. Reducing innovation lags should be a high priority for modern managers. Innovative companies generally rely on two sound management practices: *goal setting* and *empowerment.* These practices create the sense of urgency necessary for speedier innovation. Medtronic, the Minnesota-based leader in manufacturing heart pacemakers, uses goal setting skillfully. A powerful message is sent to its 25,000-plus employees worldwide about promptly getting new ideas to market when top management restates the "annual goal of gathering 70% of its sales from products introduced within the past two years."[104] That is a bold commitment!

Empowerment, discussed in Chapter 15, involves pushing decision-making authority down to levels where people with the appropriate skills can do the most good. Software giant Microsoft is strong in this regard, as illustrated by the following story told by the firm's recently retired chief operating officer:

Figure 3.4 The Three-Step Innovation Process

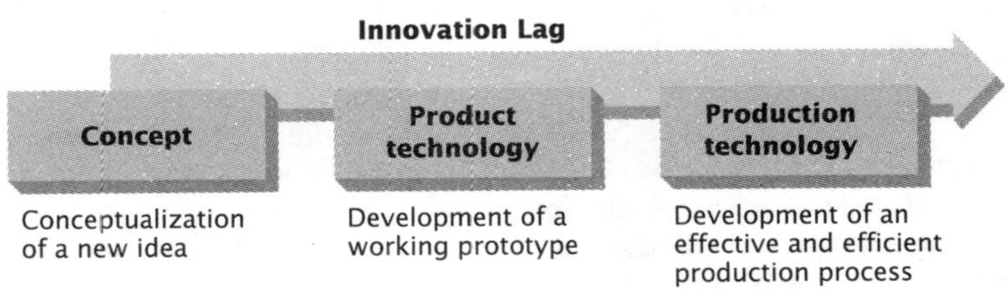

I was in a meeting where Bill Gates was quizzing a young manager—dressed in cutoffs, sandals, and a well-worn Microsoft T-shirt—about a new product proposal. After the meeting, I asked Bill, for whom this had been the first significant briefing on the product, what the next step would be. Would the manager prepare a memo summarizing the arguments, something top management could review before suggesting modifications to his proposal and granting final approval? Bill looked at me and smiled. "No, that's it. The key decisions got made," he said. "Now his group better hustle to implement things—or else."[105]

concurrent engineering: *team approach to product design involving specialists from all functional areas, including research, production, and marketing*

Another step in the right direction is a practice called *concurrent engineering.* Also referred to as parallel design, **concurrent engineering** is a team approach to product design. This approach lets research, design, production, finance, and marketing specialists have a direct say in the product design process from the very beginning.[106] This contrasts with the traditional, and much slower, practice of having a product move serially from research to design, from design to manufacturing, and so on down the line toward the marketplace. The time to hear about possible marketing problems is while a product is still in the conceptualization stage, not after it has become a warehouse full of unsold goods.

Promoting Innovation Through Intrapreneurship

When we hear someone called an entrepreneur, we generally think of a creative individual who has risked everything while starting his or her own business. Indeed, as we saw in Chapter 1, entrepreneurs are a vital innovative force in the economy. A lesser-known but no less important type of entrepreneur is the so-called intrapreneur.

intrapreneur: *an employee who takes personal responsibility for pushing an innovative idea through a large organization*

Gifford Pinchot, author of the book *Intrapreneuring,* defines an **intrapreneur** as an employee who takes personal "hands-on responsibility" for pushing any type of innovative idea, product, or process through the organization. Pinchot calls intrapreneurs "dreamers who do." But unlike traditional entrepreneurs, who tend to leave the organizational confines to pursue their dreams, intrapreneurs strive for innovation *within* existing organizations.[107] Intrapreneurs tend to have a higher need for security than entrepreneurs, who strike out on their own. They pay a price for being employees rather than owners. Pinchot explains:

Corporate entrepreneurs [or intrapreneurs], despite prior successes, have no capital of their own to start other ventures. Officially, they must begin from zero by persuading management that their new ideas are promising. Unlike successful independent entrepreneurs, they are not free to guide their next ventures by their own intuitive judgments; they still have to justify every move.[108]

Kathleen Synnott, a division marketing manager for Pitney Bowes Inc., is the classic intrapreneur. After seeing the potential of the versatile new Mail Center 2000, a computerized mail-handling and -stamping machine, Synnott became its enthusiastic champion. Just two things stood in her way: change-resistant managers and satisfied customers.

During the design process, for instance, Synnott helped protect the original blueprint from execs who wanted to break up the Mail Center 2000 and sell it as upgrading components to Pitney's existing mail-metering machines. She also guided it through a technical maze, insisting on 22 simulations to make sure potential customers liked what they saw. "There were naysayers who didn't think we were ready" for such a system, says Synnott. . . . "But they got religion."[109]

3h Advice for Future Intrapreneurs

Among Gifford Pinchot's ten commandments for intrapreneurs are the following:

- "Come to work each day willing to be fired."
- "Do any job needed to make your project work, regardless of your job description."
- "Remember it is easier to ask for forgiveness than for permission."

Source: Excerpted from Gifford Pinchot III, Intrapreneuring: Why You Don't Have to Leave the Corporation to Become an Entrepreneur (New York: Harper & Row, 1985), 22.

QUESTIONS:
How can these ideas enhance innovation in large organizations? Is this advice a formula for career success or sudden unemployment?

If today's large companies are to achieve a competitive edge through innovation, they need to foster a supportive climate for intrapreneurs like Synnott. According to experts on the subject, an organization can foster intrapreneurship if it does four things:

- Focuses on results and teamwork
- Rewards innovation and risk taking
- Tolerates and learns from mistakes
- Remains flexible and change-oriented[110]

Our discussions of creativity, participative management, and organizational cultures in later chapters contain ideas about how to encourage intrapreneurship of all types.

SUMMARY

1. Demographically, the U.S. workforce is becoming larger, older, more culturally diverse, and increasingly female. Remedial education programs are needed to improve the quality of the U.S. workforce. Researchers have disproved persistent myths that older workers are less productive and more accident-prone than younger coworkers.
2. A new social contract between employers and employees is taking shape because the tradition of lifetime employment with a single organization is giving way to shorter-term relationships of convenience and mutual benefit. The traditional paternalistic social contract between employer and employee, whereby lifetime job security was exchanged for loyalty, has been replaced by a shorter-term relationship of convenience. Today's employees are assumed to be responsible for their own employability.
3. The persistence of opportunity and income inequalities (and the so-called glass ceiling) among women and minorities is a strong stimulus for change. With part-timers playing a greater role in the U.S. workforce, there is genuine concern about creating a disadvantaged underclass of employees. Managing-diversity programs attempt to go a step beyond equal employment opportunity. The new goal is to tap *every* employee's *full* potential in today's diverse workforce.
4. Because of government regulations and sociopolitical demands from a growing list of special-interest groups, managers are becoming increasingly politicized. More and more believe that if they are going to be affected by political forces, they should be more active politically. Some organizations rely on issues management to systematically identify, evaluate, and respond to important social and political issues. Managers can respond politically in one of three ways: by being reactive, neutral, or proactive. Four political strategies that managers have found useful for pursuing active or reactive political goals are campaign financing, lobbying, coalition building, and indirect lobbying. There is a strong trend toward managers being held personally accountable for the misdeeds of their organizations. Alternative dispute resolution tactics such as arbitration and mediation can help trim management's huge litigation bill.
5. Managers can make timely decisions about inventory, borrowing, hiring, and capital spending during somewhat unpredictable business cycles by taking a consensus approach to economic forecasts. Business is urged to compete actively and creatively in the emerging global economy. By influencing jobs, prices, quality standards, and wages, the global economy affects virtually *everyone*.
6. Including conceptualization, product technology, and production technology, a healthy innovation process is vital to technological development. Innovation lags must be shortened. An organizational climate that fosters intrapreneurship can help. An intrapreneur is an employee who champions an idea or innovation by pushing it through the organization.

TERMS TO UNDERSTAND

- Demographics, p. 61
- New social contract, p. 66
- Glass ceiling, p. 66
- Contingent workers, p. 67
- Managing diversity, p. 69
- Issues management, p. 70
- Advocacy advertising, p. 72
- Legal audit, p. 74
- Alternative dispute resolution, p. 74
- Business cycle, p. 75
- Technology, p. 79
- Innovation process, p. 80
- Product technology, p. 81
- Production technology, p. 81
- Innovation lag, p. 81
- Concurrent engineering, p. 82
- Intrapreneur, p. 82

SKILLS & TOOLS

How Business Leaders Can Help Women Break the Glass Ceiling

Businesses need as much leadership, talent, quality, competence, productivity, innovation, and creativity as possible as they face more effective worldwide competition. Following are ten actions companies can take to ensure maximum use of women's business capability:

1. **Provide feedback on job performance.**
   Give frequent and specific appraisals. Women need and want candid reviews of their work. Clearly articulated suggestions for improvement, standards for work performance, and plans for career advancement will make women feel more involved in their jobs and help make them better employees.
2. **Accept women.**
   Welcome them as valued members of your management team. Include women in every kind of communication. Listen to their needs and concerns, and encourage their contributions.
3. **Ensure equal opportunities.**
   Give women the same chances you give talented men to grow, develop, and contribute to company profitability. Give them the responsibility to direct major projects, to plan and implement systems and programs. Expect them to travel and relocate and to make the same commitment to the company as do men who aspire to leadership positions.
4. **Provide career counseling.**
   Give women the same level of counseling on professional career advancement opportunities as you give to men.
5. **Identify potential.**
   Identify women as possible future managers early in their employment, and encourage their advancement through training and other developmental activities.
6. **Encourage assertiveness.**
   Assist women in strengthening their assertion skills. Reinforce strategic career planning to encourage women's commitment to their careers and long-term career plans.
7. **Accelerate development.**
   Provide "fast track" programs for qualified women. Either formally or informally, these programs will give women the exposure, knowledge and positioning they need for career advancement.
8. **Offer mentoring opportunities.**
   Give women the chance to develop mentoring relationships with other employees. The overall goal should be to provide advice, counsel, and support to promising female employees from knowledgeable, senior-level men and women.
9. **Encourage networking.**
   Promote management support systems and networks among employees of both genders. Sharing experiences and information with other men and women who are managers provides invaluable support to peers. These activities give women the opportunity to meet and learn from men and women in more advanced stages of their careers—a helpful way of identifying potential mentors or role models.

10. Increase women's participation.
Examine the feasibility of increasing participation of women in company-sponsored planning retreats, use of company facilities, social functions, and so forth. With notable exceptions, men are still generally more comfortable with other men, and as a result, women miss many of the career and business opportunities that arise during social functions. In addition, women may not have access to information about the company's informal political and social systems. Encourage male managers to include women when socializing with other business associates.

***Source:** Excerpted from Rose Mary Wentling, "Breaking Down Barriers to Women's Success,"* HR Magazine, *40 (May 1995). Reprinted with the permission of* HR Magazine, *published by the Society for Human Resource Management, Alexandria, Virginia.*

HANDS-ON EXERCISE

Crystal Ball Gazing

Instructions:

Read these predictions from *The Futurist* magazine and rate how probable each is, according to the scale below. (*Note:* Use the year 2020 if a specific time frame is not mentioned.)

No chance										Virtually guaranteed
0%	10%	20%	30%	40%	50%	60%	70%	80%	90%	100%

Prediction	Probability of occurrence
1. Globalization could make foods less safe to eat. As more food is imported from far-flung local producers, national food-safety standards will become harder to enforce. Growing demand for fresh foods year-round makes refrigeration and other safe-transport issues more of a concern.	__________
2. Falling language barriers could spur more travel. Automated translation systems could enable most of the world's people to communicate directly with one another—each speaking and hearing in his or her own language—by about 2020.	__________
3. No more textbooks? Printed and bound textbooks may disappear as more interactive coursework goes online.	__________
4. "Internet Universities" could lead to the demise of traditional institutions. Web-linked education services that offer franchised software and "college-in-a-box" courses from superstar teachers could lead to educational monopolies. Such "virtual" universities would have rigidly standardized curricula that undersell traditional courses in brick-and-mortar institutions.	__________
5. The era of cheap oil is NOT over. Not only is the world not running out of oil, but prices are likely to fall again and remain around $20 per barrel for the next decade. Reason: The current high prices make intensive exploration and development of new oil sources more attractive, thus ultimately increasing supply and lowering prices.	__________

6. **Water shortages will become more frequent and severe.** Most of the major cities in the developing world will face severe water shortages in the next two decades, as will one-third of the population of Africa. By 2040, at least 3.5 billion people will run short of water—almost 10 times as many as in 1995—and by 2050, two-thirds of the world's population could be living in regions with chronic, widespread shortages of water. ____________
7. **Tissue engineers may one day grow a "heart in a bottle."** Using a fibrous "scaffold" that is seeded with stem cells, researchers could coax the cells to grow into the needed organ. Skin and cartilage have already been grown this way. In the future, organ generation could help the tens of thousands of patients in need of organ transplants, predicts Vladimir Mironov, chief scientific officer with Cardiovascular Tissues Technology, Inc. ____________
8. **Nanomachines will enhance our brains.** Nanocomputers may soon be placed inside human brains to enhance memory, thinking ability, visualization, and other tasks, according to futurist consultant Michael Zey, author of *The Future Factor*. Technologies will also be developed that allow us to connect our brains to a computer and either download or upload data. ____________
9. **Touch-sensitive robots may make virtual reality more realistic.** The ability to collect and transmit tactile data—such as the way it feels to kick a soccer ball—could add to humans' ability to experience events ____________
10. **Hardware will soften up**. Instead of pounding on hard, plastic keyboards to do your computing, you'll soon be able to gently caress soft electronic fabrics. Among potential applications for smart textiles: tablecloths with piano keyboards and furniture slipcovers with TV remote controls. ____________

Source: *Originally published in the November-December 2001 issue of The Futurist. Used with permission from the World Future Society, 7910 Woodmont Avenue, Suite 450, Bethesda, Maryland 20814. Telephone: 301-656-8274; Fax: 301-951-0394;* ***http://www.wfs.org.***

For Consideration/Discussion

1. When you compare your ratings with those of others, do you envision things changing more rapidly or more slowly than they do? What does this imply about the way you, as a manager, would tend to deal with organizational and external changes?
2. What, if any, potentially profitable business ideas do you see in any of these predictions? Explain.
3. What are two or three of your own 10-year predictions for our sociocultural, political-legal, economic, or technological future?
4. What needs to be done to prepare for two or three selected predictions from *The Futurist*'s list (or from your own predictions)?

INTERNET EXERCISES

1. **Current events online:** Today's managers need to follow worldwide current events to track new markets, customer preferences, competitors, new technology, and investment opportunities. The Internet stands ready to fill this need 24 hours a day, 7 days a week. For example, select one of the following three general news Web sites and search it for a news story that updates one of the topical areas in this chapter (social-demographic, political-legal, economic, or technological). Read the news story and be prepared to take a copy of it to class if your instructor requests.

    - Go to the home page of the Cable News Network (**www.cnn.com**) and select one or more of the following main menu items: "World," "Politics," "Business," or "Science & Space."
    - At the home page of MSNBC (**www.msnbc.com**), start by clicking on "World News." After that, you may want to move on to the "Business" and "Tech/Science" pages.
    - The BBC, Britain's publicly funded and noncommercial radio, television, and Internet broadcaster (known in the U.K. as "The Beeb"), is a good source for news from around the world (**www.bbc.co.uk**). Browse "Business & Money," "News," "Science & Nature," and "Society & Culture."

2. **What does the job situation look like?** Getting (and keeping) the *right* job is a major quality-of-life issue for most of us. Thanks to the immense data-gathering capabilities of the U.S. Labor Department's Bureau of Labor Statistics (**stats.bls.gov**), you can put yourself on the right path toward a rewarding career. The idea is to prepare yourself with the right education and training for sectors of the economy with the greatest potential. A very useful and readable publication can be found online by going to the home page and selecting "Occupational Outlook Handbook" under the heading "Occupations." Then click on the tab titled "Tomorrow's Jobs."

    Learning Points: 1. Is your present program of study taking you in a fruitful direction for jobs? Explain. 2. Is the career you have in mind in a growing sector of the economy? Explain. 3. What are the most useful pieces of information you picked up from this handbook?

3. **Technology makes the world go 'round:** Technological developments are a window on tomorrow's world. For a general survey of what's new, go to **www.technologyreview.com**. Read one or two articles of personal interest. (Note: Be sure to print a hard copy if classroom discussion is planned.)

    Learning Points: 1. Will the technology you read about make the world a better or a worse place? Explain. 2. What, if any, are the implications of this technology for modern managers? For the world in general? 3. What was the most interesting bit of knowledge you picked up during this Web search?

4. **Check it out:** A treasure chest of free career information is available at the *Wall Street Journal's* Internet site (**www.careerjournal.com**). Be sure to review the helpful readings in the section tabs titled "Job-Hunting Advice" and "Manage Your Career."

    For updates to these exercises, visit our Web site (**http://business.college.hmco.com/students/** and select Kreitner, *Management,* 10e).

CLOSING CASE

Innovations at Wipro

"We are predominantly a service company, but we feel if we develop something of our own, it creates more value for our customer. We are not merely telling our customers we will do this or that, but are bringing something new to the table which is ready and available."

-Divakaran Mangalath (Divakaran), CTO, Wipro Technologies.[1]

Applying Thoughts'

In July 2001, Anurag Seth along with his team at Wipro Technologies (WT), the flagship company of Wipro, created workflow automation solutions for the publishing industry. This was a significant step as it resulted in a framework around which Wipro built a huge market for automation of business processes. In November 2001, the workflow automation solutions were named Content Commerce. Initially, Wipro focused on the publishing industry, but with the huge success of Content Commerce, the company decided to expand the solutions to other areas such as finance, insurance and manufacturing.

Wipro believed that innovation was essential to achieve growth and a competitive advantage. Innovation was one of the values in Wipro's promise statement (Refer Exhibit I). According to analysts, the deep-set culture of innovation in Wipro gave it an edge over others in the knowledge-based industry. The top management at Wipro believed that to achieve its goal of being among the top 10 IT services companies in the world by 2004, it had to focus on offering innovative solutions to the customers.

Commenting on the innovation process at Wipro, Divakaran said, "Have we done innovation in different parts of the organization? Yes, we have, but it was done in different parts of the organization. The individual business units looked at business opportunities from their own viewpoint. This time it is a corporation-wide initiative." [2]In 2003, Wipro was concentrating on innovative ideas in themes like Home Networking, Wireless telecommunications and Workplace Collaboration.

Background Note

Wipro was established in 1945 under the name Western India Vegetable Products Limited in Maharashtra and commenced operations in 1946. In 1947, the company set up an oil mill and hydrogenated cooking medium plant at Amalner in Maharashtra for manufacturing vegetable ghee, edible oil and laundry soap. In 1966, Azim Hasham Premji (Premji) became chairman of Wipro and charted an expansion plan for the company. This included diversification into manufacturing toiletries and baby care products.

In 1975, the company diversified into hydraulic cylinders and fluid power components and its factory at Amalner was used for production of soaps, toiletries, and baby care products. In later years, Wipro also entered the lighting products market through Wipro Bulbs. In 1980, Wipro entered the IT industry with its subsidiary WT being established in Bangalore (Refer Table I for Wipro's subsidiaries).

In the 1980s, in the Indian Institute of Science (IISc) lab, the company's team developed India's first mini-computer. It was first Indian company to design and develop multi-processor systems in India, to design and manufacture mini computers and write a compiler[3]

Table I Wipro Subsidiaries - Products & Services

Subsidiaries	Products & Services
Wipro Fluid Power	Hydraulic & pneumatic cylinders
Wipro Consumer Care & Lighting<None>	Soaps, Vanaspati, baby care products and toiletries. Incandescent and fluorescent lamps, industrial lighting
Wipro Infotech	Hardware Products
Wipro Technologies	Software Products
Wipro GE Medical Systems Ltd.	Health care Products
Wipro Health Science	Business solutions to hospitals and health insurance companies
Wipro e-peripherals	Manufacturing and Marketing of Computer peripherals

Source: *www.wiprocorporate.com*

[1] *How Wipro Incubates Business Ideas, Indian Management, April 2003.*

[2] *How Wipro Incubates Business Ideas, Indian Management, April 2003.*

[3] *A compiler, is a special program that processes statements written in a particular programming language and turns them into machine language or "code" that a computer'*

in India. In the later years, Wipro diversified into IT–related businesses such as IT peripherals.

By the mid-1990s, WT became the flagship company of the group. It was also one of the largest software exporters from India after Tata Consultancy Services[4] and Infosys Technologies[5]. Over the years, Wipro entered into various alliances with global IT majors (Refer Table II for Wipro's alliances). With increasing globalization, Wipro started focusing more on the IT - related products and services.

Table II: Wipro-Alliances & Areas of Business*

Alliances	Areas of Business
Vignette, Art Technology Group (ATG), Open Market, iPlanet	e-Business
Aether Systems	m-Commerce
IBM MQ Series, Mercator, SeeBeyond Vitria, WebMethods	Enterprise Application Integration
SAP, Oracle, PeopleSoft	ERP
Siebel, Clarify, Oracle, SAP	CRM
Computer Associates, Cisco; Nortet; Sun Microsystems	Technology Infrastructure Services
WebMethods	B2B Integration
Ariba	e-Procurement
BEA, Microsoft.Net	Web services

** This list is not exhaustive*

Over the years, Wipro implemented various quality processes in its organizations to ensure a high quality of products and services. The company paid special attention to attain high quality standards in WT and Wipro Infotech so as to gain a global market share. In 2001, the company successfully acquired the Six Sigma[6] certification and also became the first IT services company in the world to get the SEI –CMM[7] level 5[8] and People Capability Maturity Model (PCMM)[9] level 5 certifications. The same year, Wipro received the TL 9000 [10]certification for implementation of telecom projects and the Bluetooth[11] qualification from the Bluetooth Qualification Body (BQB). The qualification from BQB helped the company provide a complete set of Bluetooth solutions. In 2002, the company received the KM Reality award from KMWorld[12] for best practices in knowledge management.

By March 2003, Wipro had 30 offices in USA, Canada, Finland, Taiwan, France and UK for its global IT and IT enabled services and it was also listed in Forbes magazine's 'A' list of best big companies across the world. Even in the economic slowdown, Wipro posted healthy growth rates. For the FY 2002-03, Global IT services accounted for 66% of the total revenues, IT enabled services accounted for 4% and India & AsiaPac IT services & products accounted for 14% of the total revenues. The company's consumer care and lighting businesses accounted for 7% of the total revenues while Wipro Health Sciences accounted for 2% of total revenues (Refer Exhibit II for profit and loss statements).

Over the years, Wipro realized that along with its focus on implementation of quality standards it needed to come out with innovative products and services to gain acceptance in the global markets. It also realized that the innovation would provide the company with a platform to differentiate itself from the rest of the players in the industry. In order to come out with innovative products and services, the top management at Wipro

4 One of the Tata Group of companies involved in providing software solutions to the clients and it is the largest IT Company in India.

5 Bangalore based Infosys Technologies is one of the pioneers in the Indian IT industry and it is among the top 3 IT companies in India.

6 Six Sigma is a multi-faceted approach to process improvement, reduced costs, and increased profits. The fundamental principle is to improve customer satisfaction by reducing defects.

7 SEI was formed in 1984 to make acquisition, development, and sustainment of software intensive e-systems better, faster, and cheaper for the industry. It was sponsored by the US Department of Defense and operated by the CMU.

8 CMM standards developed by SEI access the processes implemented in the software companies. There are five levels to access the company's software processes and each level has some Key Process Areas associated with specific goals to be achieved by the organization.

9 PCMM standards are also developed by SEI with the aim to integrate workforce practices into a system and facilitate management involvement in people-related issues.

10 TL 9000 is a set of quality system requirements for suppliers of telecommunication systems: hardware, software and services. It includes a set of cost and performance-based metrics that measure reliability and quality of the products.

11 A specification for short-range radio links between mobile computers, mobile phones, digital cameras, and other portable devices.

12 KMWorld magazine presented the first KM Reality Awards at KMWorld 2001. The awards were designed to celebrate the success stories in knowledge management. KMWorld was the world's largest and most comprehensive conference and exposition dedicated to Content, Work, Collaboration, Knowledge and Intellectual Asset Management, and Business/Competitive Intelligence. KM Reality honor organizations that demonstrate leadership in the implementation of knowledge management practices and processes by realizing measurable benefits.

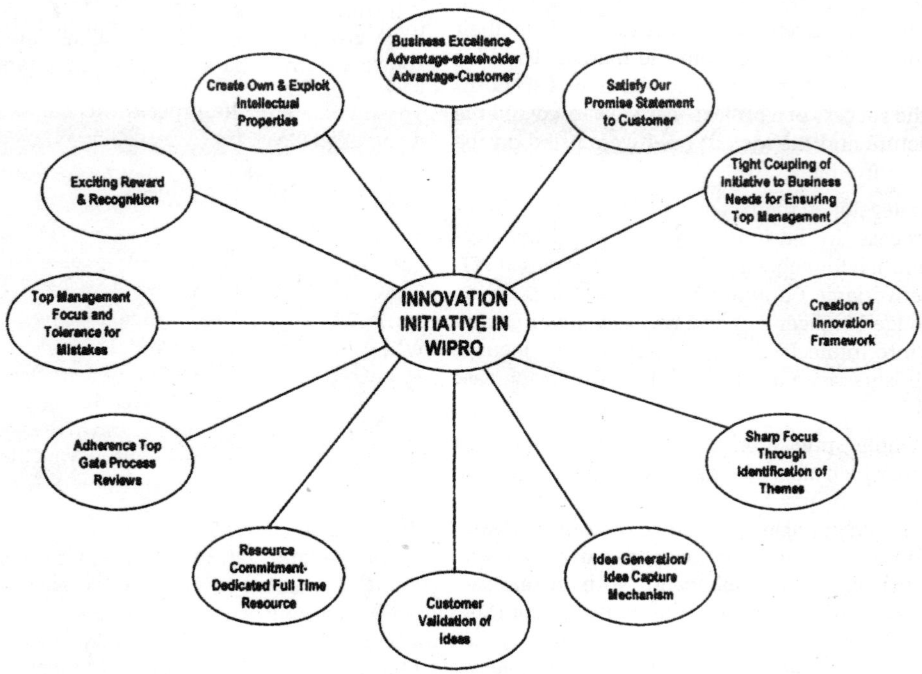

Figure I: Innovation Clock

Source: *www .wiprocorporate.com*

committed itself to fostering innovation in the organization and encouraging employees to come out with innovative ideas.

The Wipro management identified that innovation would be one of the major growth drivers, especially in the IT field. By 2000, a process to encourage innovation was implemented in all the group companies including WT and Wipro Infotech.

The Process of Innovation

Innovation was defined at Wipro as "the implementation of a new idea resulting into a marketable product or service." According to Wipro sources, an idea would be considered as a good innovation only when the company could get benefits out of it. So, in Wipro, commercial viability of an idea was also given importance along with innovation. Wipro's goal was to create components with Intellectual Properties that would generate revenues over a period of time rather than a one-time revenue from projects.

Innovation initiatives at Wipro were based on an in-depth study of methods for fostering innovation, in companies like Nike[13] , 3M[14] , and Home Depot[15] that were known for their innovative practices. The top management developed a framework for innovation and tried to foster innovation within it. The framework provided guidelines right from the idea at generation stage to commercialization of that idea. The innovation process at Wipro was represented through the ***Innovation Clock*** (Refer Figure I).

The Innovation Clock consisted of 12 steps. The initial step was the creation of an innovation framework followed by identifying the themes to be worked on. Another step involved generating ideas from the employees followed by a customer validation process for the ideas. Along with starting the innovation process, the top management at Wipro also realized the role played by rewards and recognition in motivating employees to come up with innovative ideas and

[13] *Nike is a leading US based international sports and casual wear brand.*

[14] *3M Technologies is a diversified technology company offering innovative and practical solutions. It has a presence in consumer and office products; display and graphics; electronics and telecommunications; health care; abrasives, adhesives, non-woven fibers, films, etc.*

[15] *Home Depot sells a wide range of building materials and home improvement, lawn and garden products. It is also the largest retailer of rainforest wood in the U.S.*

framed a detailed rewards policy. The rewards and recognition were given to employees based on their competence and response from the market. The idea generator and the team as a whole, which was accountable for the success of a project, were rewarded and the name, picture and the idea in brief were listed on the company's intranet.

Wipro developed themes on which it based its innovation process. In the initial phase, the top management identified four core areas called as Themes at WT-Home Networking, Content Commerce, Collaboration & Knowledge Management and Wireless (Refer Exhibit III). In Wipro Infotech, the innovation process focused on new businesses and products that would increase revenues.

The whole innovation process was enabled by Wipro web, which allowed employees to post new ideas on the intranet by just filling in simple questionnaires. In addition, Wipro also constituted innovative teams with the aim of generating innovative ideas in line with customer needs and market trends so as to increase customer satisfaction and bring in increased revenues for the company. The marketing team at Wipro helped the R&D team know about market demand by exploring the market. In order to encourage the innovative spirit among employees, Wipro even conducted workshops and brought in external consultants from specialized fields to help the employees refine their ideas. It also gave innovation process guidelines to all the middle level managers and department heads so that they would clearly understand the innovation process.

After an employee came up with an innovative idea, the idea had to go through five gates before it could be turned into a product or service. Wipro set up an Innovation Council (IC) in each business. It was headed by a Chief Technology Officer (CTO) and had five permanent members. The main responsibility of IC was to evaluate an idea and its commercial viability .An idea was approved after it passed through five levels of screening known as 'gateways' for evaluation. The first level was the ***Idea gate***, where the ideas were developed followed by the ***Evaluation gate*** where the new ideas were screened. The third level was the ***Commitment gate*** where the amount of resources for the project was allocated. The fourth level was the ***Development gate*** where the ideas were passed only if they had an order from a customer. At this gate, a detailed business plan and projected revenues had to be presented by an employee. The final gate of the process was called ***Volume gate,*** wherein an idea became ready for commercialization.

Wipro did not fix any time frame for the evaluation of ideas - it could even stretch over a few months. Divakaran said, "We don't want to kill any idea at an early state - usually in the first three to four months. That's when we want to be close to a go-no-go decision[16]. " The total time for an idea to be commercialized was estimated to be around 18 months. An idea was evaluated from all angles for the first six months. In the next 6-12 months, it was given funds and resources to be developed into a product, and in the six months after that, the idea was commercialized -the idea was expected to not only cover its costs but also bring in revenues for the company.

In addition, Wipro also organized TechForum, an annual technological event at which Wipro employees were allowed to showcase their new innovative products through paper presentations and demos to portray their competencies to the company's existing and prospective customers. The TechForum was conducted in all Wipro locations in India. Wipro also set up an innovation center in 2001 at Bangalore to encourage business ideas and entrepreneurial skills among employees. The corporate vice president, who reported to the chairman directly, headed the innovation center. By 2002, the innovation center employed around 200 people working on turning innovative ideas into products. The innovation center provided the funds, people and infrastructure needed to turn their ideas into products and services. Wipro also constituted an advisory board with top academicians, consultants and experts from the industry both in India and abroad to guide its innovation initiatives.

In addition, Wipro also established Research and Development Centers (Centers of Excellence) that worked towards meeting future technological challenges. The objective was to have expertise in the new technologies and come up with the products and productive services that could be patented by Wipro

[16] *How Wipro Incubates Business Ideas, Indian Management, April 2003.*

[17] *Symbian, a software licensing company owned by Ericsson, Nokia, Panasonic, Motorola, Psion, Samsung Electronics, Siemens and Sony Ericsson, was established in 1998. Symbian developed software technology for mobile computing devices and mobile phones.*

[18] *Siebel Systems, Inc., was a leading provider of eBusiness applications software. Siebel Systems provided organizations with industry-specific best practices, CRM applications, and business processes. Its sales and service facilities were located in more than 28 countries.*

Table III Centers of Excellence-Focus Areas

Embedded Solutions	Access Telecom	E-Commerce	Enterprise Application
Internet Protocols	IP Networks	Web Security	SAP
Access Technologies	IN Networks	Digital Marketplace	Siebel
Wireless Networks	Wireless Applications	e-infrastructure	12
Residential Gateways	OSS Service	Mobile Commerce	Oracle Applications
Bluetooth	--	--	PeopleSoft
System on Chip	--	--	--
VoIP	--	--	--

Source: www.wipro.com

(Refer Table III for focus areas of Centers of Excellence). These centers worked with research institutes and also with technology providers like Symbian[17], Siebel[18], etc. and provided a platform for the growth of Wipro employees.

By 2003, Wipro employees came up with various innovative products such as Flow-BriX, workflow solutions for publishing, i-Desk, the workplace collaboration tool enabling easier HR management by speeding up work processes, etc.

Future Prospects

According to Wipro sources, the innovation process enabled the company to come up with a strong product portfolio that assured the company of good revenue streams. Analysts felt that with its focus on innovation, Wipro would be able to achieve its goal of being one of the top 10 IT players in the world. They were also of the view that as the company was focusing on consultancy services, its innovative software solutions might enhance its image in the global software industry.

Table IV Innovative Products at Wipro

Theme based Innovation	Product
Home Networking	The Home Gateway Software was the first project under the innovation initiative to be commercialized. It enabled the customers to have a networked home. Its applications were Virtual Private Network Connectivity. Internet sharing, Video on Demand, IP Telephony and home security and surveillance. It comprised of CommEngine, VoceEngine and appEngine software addressing the Communication. Voice Over Broadband and Application Service Delivery Infrastructure needs of the Home Gateway devices
Content Commerce	Flow-brix was a workflow automation framework to provide prepress workflow solutions for the publishing industry. It also catered to the needs of cross-media publishing and Brand asset Management
Collaboration and Knowledge Management	i-desk was a web-based employee self-service framework that helped employees to access HR services and programmes.

Source: www.wipro.com

Wipro's innovative products not only enhanced the image of Wipro in the global IT market, but also had the potential of bringing in the revenues for the company (Refer Table IV for innovative products). For example, it was reported that the workflow solutions - Flow-BriX had commercial potential of $75,000-1 million.

With more and more high-end innovative solutions coming from the Wipro stable, analysts felt that it was just a matter of time before the company went up to the value chain by moving from its traditional software services business to consulting services.

For Discussion

1. Wipro promised to provide its customers with innovative solutions in its promise statement. In order to fulfill this promise, it focused on fostering innovation at its group companies. Discuss the process adopted by Wipro to launch its innovation strategy with particular reference to the innovation clock.

2. Discuss in detail the approach adopted by Wipro to foster innovation, to institutionalize innovation, and systems and procedures to ensure its success.
3. What was the role played by the top management in the initiative to launch innovation and how far was it responsible for its success?
4. What are the benefits that are likely to be derived from the innovation strategy and how will it contribute to corporate strategy, accelerating growth and achieving long term goals?

Exhibit I

Wipro Promise Statement

With utmost respect to human values, we promise to serve our customers with integrity through innovative, value for money solutions, by applying thought day after day.

Exhibit II Profit & Loss Statement of Wipro

	2003	2002	2001	2000	1999
Income					
Operating Income	29,920.19	34,253.88	30,569.88	22,858.96	17,817.31
Expenses					
Material Consumed	7,462.09	8,129.02	8,515.44	8,927.05	8,480.42
Manufacturing Expenses	3,105.80	1,657.13	757.91	252.43	251.66
Personnel Expenses	6,424.70	5,083.73	4,218.98	2,567.38	1,976.51
Selling Expenses	539.99	1,018.03	1,355.00	1,189.88	896.33
Administrative Expenses	12,634.70	8,780.51	7,903.26	5,873.96	3,806.10
Expenses Capitalized	-156.00	-76.27	-117.88	-130.61	-54.28
Cost of Sales	30,011.29	24,592.14	22,632.70	18,680.11	15,356.74
Operating Profit	9,908.90	9,661.73	7,937.18	4,178.85	2,460.58
Other Recurring Income	352.96	1,094.91	468.90	252.65	217.30
Adjusted PBDIT	10,261.86	10,756.64	8,406.08	4,431.50	2,677.88
Financial Expenses	29.30	28.94	68.89	286.68	355.88
Depreciation	1,379.45	1,418.90	979.42	698.54	645.30
Other Write Offs	0.00	0.00	0.00	0.00	0.00
Adjusted PBT	8,853.11	9,308.80	7,357.77	3,446.27	1,676.70
Tax Charges	893.02	732.60	914.00	501.00	62.00
Adjusted PAT	7,960.09	8,576.20	6,443.77	2,945.27	01,614.70
Non Recurring Items	334.97	76.64	154.79	-514.69	-576.27
Other Non Cash Adjustments	-162.74	8.24	-24.34	0.00	0.00
Reported Net Profit	8,395.02	8,661.09	6,663.49	2,482.59	1,702.34
Earnings Before Appropriation	8,132.32	8,661.09	6,574.23	2,430.59	1,038.44
Equity Dividend	232.56	232.47	116.22	68,75	68.75
Preference Dividend	0.00	0.00	18.04	25.63	7.58
Retained Earnings	7,869.96	8,428.63	6,426.13	2,325.82	954.47

Source: www.indiainfoline.com

Source: *Case Studies in Human Resource Management, Volume II, ICFAI Center for Management Research, Hyderabad, 2004, pp. 344 – 353.*

TEST PREPPER

True/False Questions

_____ **1.** The U.S. workforce is getting older, more diverse, and increasingly female.

_____ **2.** In 2004, only 24 *Fortune* 500 companies had female CEOs.

_____ **3.** Hispanics/Latinos are now the largest minority group in the United States.

_____ **4.** Managing diversity, by definition, is limited in scope to advancing women and minorities.

_____ **5.** A "defend status quo" attitude is adopted by managers on the neutral portion of the political response continuum.

_____ **6.** Settling legal disputes outside of court is referred to as legal auditing.

_____ **7.** Economic forecasts are a waste of time for managers because they have a poor track record.

_____ **8.** Researchers have found that in the United States employees of foreign-owned companies earn less than employees of domestic companies.

_____ **9.** The three steps in the innovation process are inspiration, development, and exploitation.

_____ **10.** Intrapreneurs typically do not quit their present job to pursue an innovative idea.

Multiple-Choice Questions

1. Demographics involves the study of
A. regional pay rates.
B. managerial influence.
C. male-female pay gaps.
D. work schedule variations.
E. population characteristics.

2. From a global perspective, the U.S. labor force is ________ relative to reading, writing, and basic math skills.
A. at a competitive disadvantage
B. far superior
C. about average
D. only slightly above average
E. average, but steadily improving

3. Which phrase *best* sums up the new social contract between employers and employees?
A. Mutual distrust
B. Lifetime employment
C. Cautious optimism
D. Shorter-term relationship of convenience
E. Loyalty and long-term obligations

4. The subtle yet strong barrier that has kept women and minorities from assuming top executive positions is called the
A. dual-track syndrome.
B. black hole.
C. glass ceiling.
D. wall.
E. career canyon.

5. ________ is the process of creating an organizational culture that enables all employees to realize their full potential.
A. Human asset accounting
B. Managing diversity
C. Constructive conflict
D. Issues management
E. Protectionism

6. When a chemical company replaced its underground storage tanks six years before the government's deadline, it demonstrated that it occupied which position on the political response continuum?
A. Neutral
B. Proactive
C. Anticipatory
D. Reactive
E. Entrenched

7. Which of the following is *not* one of the four political strategies available to management?
A. Indirect lobbying
B. Watchful waiting
C. Coalition building
D. Campaign financing
E. Lobbying

8. The global economy, generally speaking, has raised ________ and lowered ________.
A. financial standards; human tolerance
B. the cost of capital; prices
C. wages; tariff barriers
D. quality standards; wage standards
E. wages; protectionism

9. The three-step innovation process begins with
A. gathering necessary resources.
B. conducting a break-even analysis.
C. developing a working prototype.
D. doing a feasibility study.
E. conceptualization of a new idea.

10. Which of these phrases *best* describes concurrent engineering?
A. One-person product development cycle
B. Continuous improvement
C. Functional specialization
D. Garbage in, garbage out
E. Team approach to product design

ACE self-test

Want more questions? Visit the student Web site at http://business.college.hmco.com/students/ (select Kreitner *Management,* 10e) and take the ACE quizzes for more practice.

4 International Management and Cross-Cultural Competence

> *"I've always thought of travel as a university without walls."*[1]
>
> ANITA RODDICK, FOUNDER OF THE BODY SHOP

OBJECTIVES

- **Describe** the six-step internationalization process, and **distinguish** between a global company and a transnational company.
- **Define** the term *cultural intelligence*, and **contrast** ethnocentric, polycentric, and geocentric attitudes toward foreign operations.
- **Explain** from a cross-cultural perspective the difference between high-context and low-context cultures, and **identify** at least four of the GLOBE cultural dimensions.
- **Discuss** Hofstede's conclusion about the applicability of American management theories in foreign cultures, and **explain** the practical significance of the international study of work goals.
- **Summarize** the leadership lessons from the GLOBE Project.
- **Identify** the four leading reasons why U.S. expatriates fail to complete their assignments, and **discuss** the nature and importance of cross-cultural training in international management.
- **Summarize** the situation of North American women on foreign assignments.

the changing workplace

MTV's Passage to India

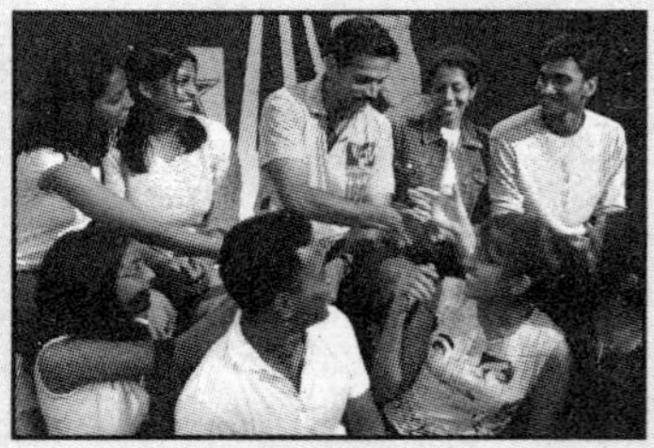

Seen from afar—say, from the executive suites atop Viacom's building in Times Square or NBC's Rockefeller Center headquarters or Disney's base camp in Burbank—India looks like a great place to be in the television business. More than one billion people live in India, and while most remain poor, the middle class is expanding rapidly. The economy grew by 8% last year; advertising grew faster. Consumers are getting their first credit cards and buying mobile phones, motor scooters, CD players, and of course TV sets. What's more, unlike China, where the central government tightly controls television and print, India enjoys a robust democracy, a boisterous press, and a vibrant film and music industry. So it's no surprise that every one of the global entertainment giants, whose businesses are maturing in the U.S. and in Western Europe, have journeyed to India—and to the rest of Asia—in search of growth.

What they have found upon arrival is a media landscape unlike any other—as noisy, chaotic, overcrowded, and impossible to navigate, at least for a stranger, as the streets of Mumbai, the nation's entertainment capital. Here the past, present, and future live side by side: Shiny new Mercedes swerve around the three-wheeled taxis powered by motorcycle engines and known as autorickshaws, whose drivers honk impatiently at men pulling ancient wooden carts piled high with mangoes and bananas. Roadside billboards advertise reality TV shows (*The Search for India's Smartest Kid*) and cable networks (cricket coverage on ESPN). You can almost see money being made. But each time my taxi stops at a traffic light, scrawny children cluster at the windows, tapping on the glass and pointing at their mouths, begging for money to buy something to eat.

I've come to Mumbai to see MTV India. Why MTV? Two reasons: first, because MTV has been doing business here since 1991, before most of its competitors arrived; second, because MTV has done better than any other global TV network—better than CNN or anything owned by Rupert Murdoch—at spreading its brand and programs into every nook and cranny of the globe. MTV Networks, a division of Viacom, operates 72 international channels, including versions of Nickelodeon and VH1, that reach 321 million homes in Europe, Asia, Latin America, Canada, and Australia, and generate nearly $1 billion in annual revenues from outside the U.S. If any global TV company could figure out how to build a business in India, MTV could.

And in fact, MTV India has built a business. It's just not a big business—not yet anyway—and therein lies a cautionary tale about operating in unfamiliar territory. Yes, the company figured out quickly that it couldn't simply blast its American programming at Indian teenagers, who don't like rock or rap music—and who were utterly mystified by *The Osbournes.* MTV knew it had to tailor operations to fit the market. But that has proven to be harder than it looks.

And it's not just a programming puzzle. India's freewheeling cable TV industry, it turns out, has too many channels chasing too few advertising dollars: The cable advertising market today amounts to about $600 million a year, which is divided among more than 100 channels. Prying revenue out of cable subscribers is hard, too—customers pay only about $3 a month for cable, leaving pennies, if that, for the networks. Finally, because most families own just one TV set, they tend to watch TV together, which means that MTV India has to compete with news, sports, and entertainment channels. India's top-rated TV show—a soap opera on Star Plus—generates ratings that dwarf anything on MTV. Who would have thought that one of the world's strongest brands would get crushed by *Kyonki Saas Bhi Kabhi Bahu Thi,* which means "The Mother-in-Law Was the Daughter-in-Law Once"?

Alex Kuruvilla, MTV's top man in Mumbai, is not deterred by any of that. Doing business in the developing world requires enormous patience, he tells me. There's an art to refashioning products made in the U.S. to suit local tastes. . . .

"The mistake a lot of multinationals have made here is looking at the size of the middle class, multiplying by *x* number of boxes per person or whatever, and seeing a business that looks enormous—until they discover, to their horror, that you have to do things differently. You need to reflect the local culture," [Kuruvilla says].

Indeed, one country's MTV looks very little like another's. Bill Roedy, the globetrotting president of MTV Networks International, says, "MTV India is very colorful, self-effacing, full of humor, a lot of street culture. China's is about family values, nurturing, a lot of love songs. In Indonesia, with our largest Islamic population, there's a call to prayer five times a day on the channel. Brazil is very sexy. Italy is stylish, elegant, with food shows because of the love of food there. Japan's very techie, a lot of wireless product." Of the 2,500 or so people who work for MTV International, fewer than 10% are Americans.

What MTV exports is a global brand, a culture driven by creativity and a handful of big events, like its annual Video Music Awards, that cross boundaries. (The conventional wisdom among antiglobalists—that America is shoving Britney Spears and Big Macs down people's throats everywhere—is neither supported by evidence nor respectful of the fact that people in the developing world decide for themselves what they want to consume.) The trouble is, once you decide, as MTV has, to build dozens of original channels, each with local programs and staffs, the economies of scale enjoyed by the global media giants dwindle. Still, every big media company—News Corp., Disney, Sony, Time Warner, Discovery Communications, and NBC—has jumped into the global game.

Source: *From Marc Gunther, "MTV's Passage to India,"* Fortune *(August 9, 2004): 116–125.*

Managers, such as those at Viacom's MTV Networks division, are moving from country to country as never before, meeting the challenges of international competition. The pull of new sources of low-cost but increasingly skilled labor and huge new markets is simply too strong to resist. India, for example, has a population now exceeding 1 billion and is projected to be more populous than China by 2025.[2] This global business tradition dates back farther than one might think:

> *In the antique shops of Shanghai's old French quarter, amid the German cameras, American radios, Russian crystal and other relics of a vanished past, lie tarnished reminders of just how long the world economy has been a global economy: rough-cast taels of South American silver and smooth-worn Mexican silver dollars.*
>
> *It was in 1571 that modern global commerce began, argues Dennis O. Flynn, head of the economics department of the University of the Pacific in Stockton, Calif. That year, the Spanish empire founded the city of Manila in the Philippines to receive its silver-laden galleons that made their way across the vast Pacific Ocean from the New World. The metal was bound not for Spain, but for imperial China. For the first time, all of the world's populated continents were trading directly—Asia with the Americas, Europe and Africa, and each with the others. They were highly interdependent: when silver depreciated in later decades, world-wide inflation ensued.*
>
> *"Some economists think the global economy is a World War II thing," says Prof. Flynn. "That just demonstrates an ignorance of history."*[3]

Both air travel and modern information technology have made the world a seemingly smaller place. A third globe-shrinking force steadily gaining momentum is *corporate globalism.* By creating globe-spanning organizations, this third force promises to be the main contributor to a smaller world with many similarities.

Striking evidence of the modern global marketplace is everywhere. Consider these recent examples:

- "More than 80% of the toys, bikes and Christmas tree ornaments sold in the USA come from China. About 90% of all sporting goods and 95% of shoes are foreign-made."[4]
- New York-based Citigroup, the world's largest banking and financial services company, "operates in 100 countries on six continents and has 275,000 employees."[5]
- Israel's publicly owned companies earn 90 percent of their revenues from outside the country, and Mexico sends 90 percent of its exports to the United States.[6]
- Ironically, U.S. Border Patrol agents responsible for curbing illegal immigration along the U.S.–Mexico border recently were issued new uniforms with "Made in Mexico" labels.[7]

This dizzying array of international commerce is simply business as usual in our global economy, which is projected to grow from $26 trillion in 1994 to $48 trillion in 2010. Over the same period, world trade is expected to quadruple, from $4 trillion to $16.6 trillion![8]

international management: *pursuing organizational objectives in international and cross-cultural settings*

Like any other productive venture, an international corporation must be effectively and efficiently managed. Consequently, **international management**, the pursuit of organizational objectives in international and intercultural settings, has become an important discipline. Indeed, Nancy Adler, a leading international management scholar at Canada's McGill University, sees it this way: "Managing the global enterprise and modern business management have become synonymous."[9] The purpose of this chapter is to define and discuss multinational and global corporations, stimulate global and cultural awareness, explore comparative management insights, and discuss the need for cross-cultural training.

Global Organizations for a Global Economy

Many labels have been attached to international business ventures over the years. They have been called international companies, multinational companies, global companies, and transnational companies. This section clarifies the confusion about terminology by reviewing the six-stage internationalization process as a foundation for contrasting global and transnational companies.

■ The Internationalization Process

There are many ways to do business across borders. At one extreme, a company may merely buy goods from a foreign source, or, at the other, it may actually buy the foreign company itself. In between is an internationalization process with identifiable stages. Companies may skip steps when pursuing foreign markets, so the following sequence should *not* be viewed as a lock step sequence.

■ **Stage 1: Licensing.** Companies in foreign countries are authorized to produce and/or market a given product within a specified territory in return for a fee.[10] For example, under the terms of a ten-year licensing agreement, South Korea's Samsung Electronics will get to use Texas Instruments' patented semiconductor technology for royalty payments exceeding $1billion.[11]

■ **Stage 2: Exporting.** Goods produced in one country are sold to customers in foreign countries. As documented in Chapter 3, exports amount to a large and growing slice of the U.S. economy.[12]

■ **Stage 3: Local Warehousing and Selling.** Goods produced in one country are shipped to the parent company's storage and marketing facilities located in one or more foreign countries.

Gordon Murray, director of advanced concepts at Caparo Vehicle Products with Angad Paul, Caparo's CEO. The £725m Caparo Group – a vehicle component supplier based largely in the UK, US and India – aims to realise its manufacturing ambitions of commoditizing lightweight composites for the car industry as quickly and efficiently as possible..

4a What Are the Three Scariest Words for American Manufacturers?

"The China price." They are the three scariest words in U.S. industry. In general, it means 30% to 50% less than what you can possibly make something for in the U.S. In the worst cases, it means below your cost of materials. Makers of apparel, footwear, electric appliances, and plastics products, which have been shutting U.S. factories for decades, know well the futility of trying to match the China price. It has been a big factor in the loss of 2.7 million manufacturing jobs since 2000. Meanwhile, America's deficit with China keeps soaring to new records [over $150 billion in 2004].

Source: Pete Engardio and Dexter Roberts, "The China Price," Business Week (December 6, 2004): 104.

QUESTION:

What are the implications of this situation for you, your nation's economy, and the global economy?

For further information about the interactive annotations in this chapter, visit our Web site (**http://business.college.hmco.com/students/** and select Kreitner, *Management*, 10e).

■ **Stage 4: Local Assembly and Packaging.** Components, rather than finished products, are shipped to company-owned assembly facilities in one or more foreign countries for final assembly and sales.

■ **Stage 5: Joint Ventures.** A company in one country pools resources with one or more companies in a foreign country to produce, store, transport, and market products, with resulting profits/losses shared appropriately. Joint ventures, also known as *strategic alliances* or *strategic partnerships*, have become very popular in recent years.[13] For example, consider this win-win alliance:

> *Industrial giants Honda Motor and General Electric are teaming up to produce an engine to power a new generation of smaller, lower-cost business jets. . . .*
>
> *GE, one of the largest makers of engines for big jets, would gain access to a market segment where it has been without a product: smaller business jets. Honda would fulfill a long-held plan to break into aviation.*[14]

International joint ventures/strategic alliances have tended to be fruitful for Japanese companies but disappointing for American and European partners.

> *Gary Hamel, a professor at the London Business School, regards partnerships as "a race to learn": The partner that learns fastest comes to dominate the relationship and can then rewrite its terms. Thus, an alliance becomes a new form of competition. The Japanese excel at learning from others, Hamel says, while Americans and Europeans are not so good at it.*[15]

Experts offer the following recommendations for successful international joint ventures/strategic alliances. First, exercise *patience* when selecting and building trust with a partner that has compatible (but not directly competitive) products and markets. Second, *learn* as fast and as much as possible without giving away core technologies and secrets. Third, establish firm *ground rules* about rights and responsibilities at the outset.[16]

1. **DESCRIBE** the six-step internationalization process, and **DISTINGUISH** between a global company and a transnational company.

■ **Stage 6: Direct Foreign Investments.** Typically, a company in one country produces and markets products through wholly owned subsidiaries in foreign countries. Global corporations are expressions of this last stage of internationalization.

Cross-border mergers are an increasingly popular form of direct foreign investment.[17] A cross-border merger occurs when a company in one country buys an entire company in another country. Unfortunately, cross-border mergers are not a quick and easy way to go global.

> *On top of the usual challenges of acquiring a company—paying a fair price, melding two management teams, and capturing the elusive "synergy" that's supposed to light up the bottom line—special risks and costs attach to cross-border mergers. They often involve wide differences in distance, language, and culture that can lead to serious misunderstandings and conflicts. . . .*
>
> *According to a study of cross-border mergers among large companies by consultants McKinsey & Co., nearly 40% end in total failure, with the acquiring company never earning back its cost of capital.*[18]

Source: www.CartoonStock.com

From Global Companies to Transnational Companies

global company: *a multinational venture centrally managed from a specific country*

transnational company: *a futuristic model of a global, decentralized network with no distinct national identity*

The difference between these two types of international ventures is the difference between actual and theoretical. That is to say, transnational companies are evolving and represent a futuristic concept. Meanwhile, global companies, such as the giants in Table 4.1, do business in many countries simultaneously. They have global strategies for product design, financing, purchasing, manufacturing, and marketing. By definition, a **global company** is a multinational venture centrally managed from a specific country.[19] For example, even though Coca-Cola earns most of its profit outside the United States, it is viewed as a U.S. company because it is run from a powerful headquarters in Atlanta, Georgia.[20] The same goes for McDonald's, Ford, IBM, and Wal-Mart, with their respective U.S. headquarters.

A **transnational company**, in contrast, is a global network of productive units with a decentralized authority structure and no distinct national identity.[21] Transnationals rely on a blend of global and local strategies, as circumstances dictate. Local values and practices are adopted whenever possible because, in the end, all *customer contacts* are local. Ideally, managers of transnational organizations "think globally, but act locally." Managers of foreign operations are encouraged to interact freely with their colleagues from around the world. Once again, this type of international business venture exists mostly in theory, although some global companies are moving toward transnationalism. For example, consider L. M. Ericsson, the

4b Back to the Opening Case

Is Viacom/MTV a global company or a transnational company? Explain.

Table 4.1 Corporate Giants Worldwide

Company	Home Country	Industry	2003 Sales (U.S. $, billions)
Petrobrás	Brazil	Petroleum products	31
BP	Britain	Petroleum products	233
Nokia	Finland	Electronics	33
AXAl	France	Insurance	112
DaimlerChrysler	Germany	Motor vehicles	157
Fiat	Italy	Motor vehicles	53
Toyota Motor	Japan	Motor vehicles	153
Pemex	Mexico	Petroleum products	49
ING	Netherlands	Insurance	96
Samsung Electronics	South Korea	Electronics	54
Nestlé	Switzerland	Food products	65
General Electric	United States	Electrical equipment/ Financial services	134

Source: *Adapted from data in "The Fortune Global 500,"* Fortune *(July 26, 2004): 159–180.*

Swedish telecommunications equipment manufacturer. As reported in *Business Week*, "Ericsson . . . moved its European headquarters to London to escape Sweden's high personal-income taxes, and to be closer to investors and customers."[22] Ericsson's decision to relocate its headquarters was not constrained by national identity, but rather guided by business and financial considerations.

Significantly, many experts are alarmed at the prospect of immense "stateless" transnational companies because of unresolved political, economic, and tax implications. If transnational companies become more powerful than the governments of even the largest countries in which they do business, who will hold them accountable in cases of fraud, human rights violations, and environmental mishaps?[23]

Toward Greater Global Awareness and Cross-Cultural Competence

Americans in general and American business students and managers in particular are often considered too narrowly focused for the global stage. Boris Yavitz, former dean of Columbia University's Graduate School of Business, observed that "unlike European and Asian managers, who grow up expecting to see international service, U.S. executives are required to prepare only for domestic experience, with English as their only language."[24] This state of affairs is slowly changing amid growth of international business and economic globalization. To compete successfully in a dynamic global economy, present and future managers need to develop their international and cross-cultural awareness. In this section we distinguish between travelers and settlers, examine attitudes toward international operations, and explore key sources of cultural diversity.

■ Travelers versus Settlers (Developing *Cultural Intelligence*)

One or more short visits to a foreign country do not make a person competent to transact business deals there. Accordingly, cross-cultural management experts distinguish between travelers and settlers. Travelers visit foreign countries, whether for work or pleasure, on a short-term basis (a few days to several weeks). They tend to have limited knowledge of the local history, culture, and customs. Their local language skills typically vary from none to weak. In contrast, settlers take foreign assignments lasting from two to five years or more.

> *The Settler has to deal with a variety of challenges, starting from pre-departure training to the hassles of relocating, transitional challenges to acclimatization, to culture shock to re-entry shock. . . . [Also,] the Settler must receive more in-depth insights into the host country's customs and culture. The language skills must be much more than conversational and a solid knowledge of the country's religion, politics, history, meaning of nature, morals, social structure, education, food and table manners, roles of man and woman, business ethics, negotiation techniques, humor and values is highly important. . . . The Settler should be extremely open-minded, flexible, friendly and honest . . . [and] adaptability is a valuable asset.*[25]

cultural intelligence (CQ): *ability to interpret and act in appropriate ways in unfamiliar cultural surroundings*

Settlers need to possess a characteristic called **cultural intelligence (CQ)**, the ability of an outsider to read individual behavior, group dynamics, and situations in a foreign culture as well as the locals do. (The initials CQ are a variation of the familiar label IQ, for intelligence quotient.) Just as a chameleon changes colors to blend in with its surroundings, a person with high CQ quickly analyzes an unfamiliar cultural situation and then acts appropriately and confidently. In short, CQ involves seeing the world as someone else sees it. CQ combines two topics we cover later—*impression management* (Chapter 14) and *emotional intelligence* (Chapter 15)—and puts them into a cross-cultural context. While noting that only 5 percent of managers studied possess high CQ, a pair of researchers shared this cautionary tale of a manager with low CQ:

> *Consider the example of the French manager transferred to the USA. After meeting his secretary (a woman) the first time, he greeted her with a European "hello" (an effusive and personal cheek-to-cheek kiss greeting). This greeting was, however, met with obvious discomfort. His secretary later filed a complaint for harassment.*[26]

The rest of this chapter will help boost your cultural intelligence.

2. DEFINE the term *cultural intelligence*, and **CONTRAST** ethnocentric, polycentric, and geocentric attitudes toward foreign operations.

Contrasting Attitudes Toward International Operations

Can a firm's degree of internationalization be measured? Some observers believe it can, and they claim a true global company must have subsidiaries in at least six nations. Others say that to qualify as a multinational or global company, a firm must have a certain percentage of its capital or operations in foreign countries. However, Howard Perlmutter insists that these measurable guidelines tell only part of the story and suggests that it is management's *attitude* toward its foreign operations that really counts.

> *The more one penetrates into the living reality of an international firm, the more one finds it is necessary to give serious weight to the way executives think about doing business around the world. The orientation toward "foreign people, ideas, resources," in headquarters and subsidiaries, and in host and home environments, becomes crucial in estimating the multinationality of a firm.*[27]

Perlmutter identified three managerial attitudes toward international operations, which he labeled ethnocentric, polycentric, and geocentric.[28] Each attitude is presented here in its pure form, but all three are likely to be found in a single multinational or global corporation (see Table 4.2). The key question is "Which attitude predominates?"

ethnocentric attitude: *view that assumes the home country's personnel and ways of doing things are best*

Ethnocentric Attitude. Managers with an **ethnocentric attitude** are home-country-oriented. Home-country personnel, ideas, and practices are viewed as inherently superior to those from abroad. Foreign nationals are not trusted with key decisions or technology. Home-country procedures and evaluation criteria are applied worldwide without variation. Proponents of ethnocentrism say that it makes

Table 4.2 Three Different Attitudes Toward International Operations

Organization design	Ethnocentric	Polycentric	Geocentric
Identification	Nationality of owner	Nationality of host country	Truly international company but identifying with national interests
Authority; decision making	High in headquarters	Relatively low in headquarters	Aim for a collaborative approach between headquarters and subsidiaries
Evaluation and control	Home standards applied for person and performance	Determined locally	Find standards that are universal and local
Communication; information flow	High volume to subsidiaries; orders, commands, advice	Little to and from headquarters; little between subsidiaries	Both ways and between subsidiaries; heads of subsidiaries part of management team
Perpetuation (recruiting, staffing, development)	Recruit and develop people of home country for key positions everywhere in the world	Develop people of local nationality for key positions in their own country	Develop best people everywhere in the world for key positions everywhere in the world

Source: *Excerpted from Howard V. Perlmutter, "The Tortuous Evolution of the Multinational Corporation,"* Columbia Journal of World Business, *4 (January-February 1969): 12. Used with permission.*

for a simpler and more tightly controlled organization. Critics believe this attitude makes for poor planning and ineffective operations because of inadequate feedback, high turnover of subsidiary managers, reduced innovation, inflexibility, and social and political backlash.

In U.S.–Japanese business relations, ethnocentrism cuts both ways. Procter & Gamble failed to do its cultural homework when it ran a series of advertisements for Pampers in Japan. Japanese customers were bewildered by the ads, in which a stork carried a baby, because storks have no cultural connection to birth in Japan.[29] Similarly, Japanese companies operating in the United States seem to be out of touch with the expectations of American managers. In a survey of American managers employed by 31 such companies, the common complaint was too few promotions and too little responsibility.[30]

Ethnocentric attitudes can also cause problems in ethnically diverse countries, such as the United States. (Hispanics/Latinos are projected to be nearly one-quarter of the U.S. population by 2050,[31] and more than 28 million U.S. residents currently speak Spanish.)[32]

> *When it comes to Hispanic marketing, a little knowledge is a dangerous thing. . . . Tropicana advertised* jugo de china *in Miami.* China *means orange to Puerto Ricans, but Miami's Cubans thought it was juice from the Orient. Jack in the Box goofed with a commercial featuring a band of Mexican mariachis accompanying a Spanish flamenco dancer. "That's like having Willie Nelson*

sing while Michael Jackson does the moonwalk," says Bert Valencia, a marketing professor at the American Graduate School of International Management in Glendale, Arizona.

Why do companies sometimes end up looking like idiotas? *Because learning this market takes more than a few lessons at Berlitz. An occasional blunder is forgivable. But many companies are designing advertising for the nation's . . . [more than 39] million Hispanics without understanding the differences among Mexicans, Puerto Ricans, Cubans, and the rich array of the other nationalities that make up the U.S. Hispanic population.*[33]

In fact, U.S. Hispanics and Latinos trace their roots to 22 different countries.

polycentric attitude: *view that local managers in host countries know best how to run their own operations*

■ **Polycentric Attitude.** This host-country orientation is based on the assumption that because cultures are so different, local managers know what is best for their operations. A **polycentric attitude** leads to a loose confederation of comparatively independent subsidiaries rather than to a highly integrated structure. Because foreign operations are measured in terms of ends (instead of means), methods, incentives, and training procedures vary widely from location to location.

On the negative side, wasteful duplication of effort occurs at the various units within the confederation precisely because they are independent. Such duplication can erode the efficiency of polycentric organizations. Moreover, global objectives can be undermined by excessive concern for local traditions and success. But there is a positive side: "The main advantages are an intensive exploitation of local markets, better sales since local management is often better informed, more local initiative for new products, more host-government support, and good local managers with high morale."[34]

geocentric attitude: *world-oriented view that draws on the best talent from around the globe*

■ **Geocentric Attitude.** Managers with a **geocentric attitude** are world-oriented. "As Sue Evens, senior manager of international human resources consulting at KPMG, New York, says, thinking globally means 'taking the best other cultures have to offer and blending that into a third culture.'"[35] Skill, not nationality, determines who gets promoted or transferred to key positions around the globe. In geocentric companies, local and worldwide objectives are balanced in all aspects of operation. Collaboration between headquarters and subsidiaries is high, but an effort is made to maintain a balance between global standards and local discretion. Thus, a geocentric attitude is essential in the transnational model discussed earlier. Bausch & Lomb, the Rochester, New York, maker of Ray-Ban sunglasses, fosters a geocentric attitude by telling its managers to "think globally, but act locally." Says international division senior vice president Ronald Zarella, "What we try to do today is set strategic goals and let local management take advantage of nuances in their market."[36] This has enabled Bausch & Lomb to satisfy European demand for more styles and costly sunglasses than is typical in the United States. "In Asia the company redesigned them to better suit the Asian face—with its flatter bridge and higher cheek bones—and sales took off."[37]

Of these three contrasting attitudes, only a geocentric attitude can help management take a long step toward success in today's vigorously competitive global marketplace.

■ The Cultural Imperative

4c Back to the Opening Case

Is MTV Networks an ethnocentric, polycentric, or geocentric company? Explain.

Culture has a powerful impact on people's behavior. For example, consider the everyday activity of negotiating a business contract.

To Americans, a contract signals the conclusion of negotiations; its terms establish the rights, responsibilities, and obligations of the parties involved. However, to the Japanese, a company is not forever bound to the terms of the contract. In fact, it can be renegotiated whenever there is a significant shift in the company's circumstances. For instance, an unexpected change in governmental tax policy,

Now here's a rockin' bunch. Bono with lead vocals, backed up by . . . . British Prime Minister Tony Blair? And Microsoft's Bill Gates? While this trio may not make great music together, they exercised their influence during a 2005 summit on the ethics of globalization in Davos, Switzerland. Geocentric Bono has worked tirelessly to break the global debt-poverty cycle.

> *or a change in the competitive environment, are considered legitimate reasons for contract renegotiation. To the Chinese, a signatory to an agreement is a partner with whom they can work, so to them the signing of a contract is just the beginning of negotiations.*[38]

Cross-cultural business negotiators who ignore or defy cultural traditions do so at their own risk. That means the risk of not making the sale or of losing a contract or failing to negotiate a favorable deal. Therefore, a sensitivity to cross-cultural differences is imperative for people who do business in other countries.

In this section, we define the term *culture* and address the fear of an "Americanized" world culture. Then, drawing primarily from the work of pioneering cultural anthropologist Edward T. Hall, we explore key sources of cross-cultural differences.

culture: *a population's taken-for-granted assumptions, values, beliefs, and symbols that foster patterned behavior*

■ **Culture Defined. Culture** is the pattern of taken-for-granted assumptions about how a given collection of people should think, act, and feel as they go about their daily affairs.[39] Regarding the central aspect of this definition, *taken-for-granted assumptions,* Hall noted that

> *Much of culture operates outside our awareness; frequently, we don't even know what we know. . . . This applies to all people. The Chinese or the Japanese or the Arabs are as unaware of their assumptions as we are of our own. We each assume that they're part of human nature. What we think of as "mind" is really internalized culture.*[40]

In Chapter 9, *organizational culture* is called the social glue binding members of an organization together. Similarly, at a broader level, *societal culture* acts as a social glue. That glue is made up of norms, values, attitudes, role expectations, taboos, symbols, heroes, beliefs, morals, customs, and rituals. Cultural lessons are imparted from birth to death via role models, formal education, religious teachings, and peer pressure.

Cultural undercurrents make international dealings immensely challenging. According to Fons Trompenaars and Charles Hampden-Turner, the Dutch and English authors of the landmark book *Riding the Waves of Culture,*

> *International managers have it tough. They must operate on a number of different premises at any one time. These premises arise from their culture of origin, the culture in which they are working, and the culture of the organization which employs them.*
>
> *In every culture in the world such phenomena as authority, bureaucracy, creativity, good fellowship, verification, and accountability are experienced in different ways. That we use the same words to describe them tends to make us unaware that our cultural biases and our accustomed conduct may not be appropriate, or shared.*[41]

■ **Are U.S. Global Corporations Turning the World into a Single "Americanized" Culture?** Protesters at World Trade Organization and global economic summit meetings in recent years have decried the growing global reach of McDonald's (in 120 countries) and other American corporate giants. They predict a homogenizing of the world's unique cultures into a so-called McWorld, where American culture prevails. Although they evoke much emotion, these concerns are *not* supported by University of Michigan researchers who have been tracking cultural values in 65 societies for more than 20 years. Citing evidence from their ongoing World Values Survey, the researchers recently reached the following conclusions:

> *The impression that we are moving toward a uniform "McWorld" is partly an illusion. The seemingly identical McDonald's restaurants that have spread throughout the world actually have different social meanings and fulfill different social functions in different cultural zones. Eating in a McDonald's restaurant in Japan is a different social experience from eating in one in the United States, Europe, or China.*
>
> *Likewise, the globalization of communication is unmistakable, but its effects may be overestimated. It is certainly apparent that young people around the world are wearing jeans and listening to U.S. pop music; what is less apparent is the persistence of underlying value differences.*
>
> *In short, economic development will cause shifts in the values of people in developing nations, but it will not produce a uniform global culture. The future may look like McWorld, but it won't feel like one.*[42]

Cultural roots run deep, have profound effects on behavior, and are not readily altered.

4d Big Wide World? What World?

More than 75% of the [U.S.] public supports requiring students to take courses addressing global issues. But college coursework of that nature is, at best, uneven. One study indicates that less than 7% of college students meet even basic standards of global preparedness.

Source: Mary Beth Marklein, "Colleges Lose Their Foreign Accent," USA Today (November 13, 2000): 7D.

QUESTIONS:

How do you rate your own awareness of global issues and preparedness to work in the global economy? How world-wise is your college coursework?

■ Understanding Cultural Diversity

Dealing effectively with both coworkers and customers in today's diverse workplaces requires a good deal of cultural intelligence. For instance, the standard all-too-revealing hospital gown caused a unique cross-cultural problem for the Maine Medical Center in Portland, Maine. When the hospital's staff realized that Muslim women were canceling appointments to avoid the shame of being inadequately clothed, they created gowns for modest patients who desire coverage of their legs and backside.[43] Making this sort of cultural accommodation is a little easier when you know about the following important sources of cultural diversity.

■ **High-Context and Low-Context Cultures.** People from European-based cultures typically assess people from Asian cultures

3. EXPLAIN from a cross-cultural perspective the difference between high-context and low-context cultures, and **IDENTIFY** at least four of the GLOBE cultural dimensions.

such as China and Japan as quiet and hard to figure out. Conversely, Asians tend to view Westerners as aggressive, insensitive, and even rude. True, language differences are a significant barrier to mutual understanding. But something more fundamental is involved, something cultural. Anthropologist Edward T. Hall prompted better understanding of cross-cultural communication by distinguishing between high-context and low-context cultures.[44] The difference centers on how much meaning one takes from what is actually said or written versus who the other person is.

high-context cultures: *cultures in which nonverbal and situational messages convey primary meaning*

In **high-context cultures**, people rely heavily on nonverbal and subtle situational messages when communicating with others. The other person's official status, place in society, and reputation say a great deal about the person's rights, obligations, and trustworthiness. In high-context cultures, people do not expect to talk about such "obvious" things. Conversation simply provides general background information about the other person. Thus, in high-context Japan, the ritual of exchanging business cards is a social necessity, and failing to read a card you have been given is a grave insult. The other person's company and position determine what is said and how. Arab, Chinese, and Korean cultures also are high-context.

low-context cultures: *cultures in which words convey primary meaning*

People from **low-context cultures** convey essential messages and meaning primarily with words. Low-context cultures in Germany, Switzerland, Scandinavia, North America, and Great Britain expect people to communicate their precise intended meaning. Low-context people do read so-called body language, but its messages are secondary to spoken and written words. Legal contracts with precisely worded expectations are important in low-context countries such as the United States. However, according to international communications experts, "in high-context cultures the process of forging a business relationship is as important as, if not more important than, the written details of the actual deal."[45] This helps explain why Americans tend to be frustrated with the apparently slow pace of business dealings in Japan. For the Japanese, the many rounds of meetings and social gatherings are necessary to collect valuable contextual information as a basis for judging the other party's character. For the schedule-driven American, anything short of actually signing the contract is considered a pointless waste of time. *Patience* is a prime virtue for low-context managers doing business in high-context cultures.

■ **Nine Dimensions of Culture from the GLOBE Project.** The GLOBE (Global Leadership and Organizational Behavior Effectiveness) project was conceived by Robert J. House, a University of Pennsylvania researcher. Beginning with a 1994 meeting in Calgary, Canada, the GLOBE project has grown to encompass an impressive network of over 150 researchers from 62 countries. It is a massive ongoing effort in which researchers assess organizations in their own cultures and languages with standardized instruments to collect data from around the world, building a comprehensive model. If things go as intended, the resulting data base will yield important new insights about both similarities and differences across the world's cultures.[46] More important, it promises to provide practical guidelines for international managers. Thanks to the first two phases of the GLOBE project, we have a research-based list of key cultural dimensions (see Table 4.3).

Interestingly, according to one GLOBE research report, mid-level managers in the United States scored high on assertiveness and performance orientation and moderately on uncertainty avoidance and institutional collectivism.[47]

■ **Other Sources of Cultural Diversity.** Managers headed for a foreign country need to do their homework on the following cultural variables to avoid awkwardness and problems.[48] There are no rights or wrongs here, only cross-cultural differences.

individualistic cultures: *cultures that emphasize individual rights, roles, and achievements*

- ***Individualism versus collectivism.***
  This distinction between "me" and "we" cultures deserves closer attention because it encompasses two of the nine GLOBE cultural dimensions in Table 4.3. People in **individualistic cultures** focus primarily on individual rights, roles, and achievements. The United States and Canada are highly individualistic cultures.

Table 4.3 Nine Cultural Dimensions from the GLOBE Project

Dimension	Description	Countries scoring highest	Countries scoring lowest
Power distance	Should leaders have high or low power over others?	Morocco, Argentina, Thailand	Denmark, Netherlands, South Africa (black sample)
Uncertainty avoidance	How much should social norms and rules be used to reduce future uncertainties?	Switzerland, Sweden, Germany (former West)	Russia, Hungary, Bolivia
Institutional collectivism	To what extent should society and institutions reward loyalty?	Sweden, South Korea, Japan	Greece, Hungary, Germany (former East)
In-group collectivism	To what extent do individuals value loyalty to their family or organization?	Iran, India, Morocco	Denmark, Sweden, New Zealand
Assertiveness	How aggressive and confrontational should one be with others?	Germany (former East), Austria, Greece	Sweden, New Zealand, Switzerland
Gender equality	How nearly equal are men and women?	Hungary, Poland, Slovenia	South Korea, Egypt, Morocco
Future orientation	How much should one work and save for the future, rather than just live for the present?	Singapore, Switzerland, Netherlands	Russia, Argentina, Poland
Performance orientation	How much should people be rewarded for excellence and improvement?	Singapore, Hong Kong, New Zealand	Russia, Argentina, Greece
Humane orientation	How much should people be encouraged to be generous, kind, and fair to others?	Philippines, Ireland, Malaysia	Germany (former West), Spain, France

Source: *Adapted from discussions in Mansour Javidan and Robert J. House, "Cultural Acumen for the Global Manager: Lessons from Project GLOBE,"* Organizational Dynamics, *29 (Spring 2001): 289–305; Robert House, Mansour Javidan, Paul Hanges, and Peter Dorfman, "Understanding Cultures and Implicit Leadership Theories Across the Globe: An Introduction to Project GLOBE,"* Journal of World Business, *37 (Spring 2002): 3–10; and Mansour Javidan, Robert J. House, and Peter W. Dorfman, "A Nontechnical Summary of GLOBE Findings," in Robert J. House, Paul J. Hanges, Mansour Javidan, Peter W. Dorfman, and Vipin Gupta, eds.,* Culture, Leadership, and Organizations: The GLOBE Study of 62 Societies *(Thousand Oaks, Calif.: Sage, 2004), pp. 29–48.*

collectivist cultures: *cultures that emphasize duty and loyalty to collective goals and achievements*

People in **collectivist cultures**—such as Egypt, Mexico, India, and Japan—rank duty and loyalty to family, friends, organization, and country above self-interests. Group goals and shared achievements are paramount to collectivists; personal goals and desires are suppressed. It is important to remember that individualism and collectivism are extreme ends of a continuum, along which people and cultures are variously distributed and mixed. For example, in the United States, one can find pockets of collectivism among Native Americans and recent immigrants from Latin America and Asia. This helps explain why a top-notch engineer born in China would be reluctant to attend an American-style recognition dinner where individual award recipients are asked to stand up for a round of applause.[49]

- ***Time.***

Hall referred to time as a silent language of culture. He distinguished between monochronic and polychronic time.[50] **Monochronic time** is based on the perception that time is a unidimensional straight line divided into standard units, such as seconds, minutes, hours, and days. In monochronic cultures, including North America and Northern Europe, everyone is assumed to be on the same clock, and

monochronic time: *a perception of time as a straight line broken into standard units*

polychronic time: *a perception of time as flexible, elastic, and multidimensional*

time is treated as money. The general rule is to use time efficiently, to be on time, and above all, not to waste time. In contrast, **polychronic time** involves the perception of time as flexible, elastic, and multidimensional. Latin American, Mediterranean, and Arab cultures are polychronic. Managers in polychronic cultures tend to view schedules and deadlines in relative rather than absolute terms. Different perceptions of time have caused many cultural collisions. For example, as the deadline for completion of the 2004 Olympic facilities in Athens approached, monochronic Americans fretted about the Greeks moving too slowly and missing the August deadline. But Brett Heyl, a U.S. kayaker who trained in Greece and became familiar with the local work habits, was not worried.

> *"You never see them working hard, but things seem to get done," Heyl says. "Don't ask me how."*
>
> *In April, Heyl took note of a seemingly idle crew of road workers, near the Athens airport.*
>
> *"You come back in a month, and you're driving on a new highway." Heyl says. "It's just astounding how quickly they can get things done. When I was here in April, I saw a city that could not possibly be ready for the Olympics. Now I see one that will be ready on Friday."*[51]

Sure enough, the Greeks pulled it off to rave reviews.

It is important to reset your mental clocks (and expectations) when living and working in a culture with a different time orientation or when working globally on a virtual team. (Virtual teams are discussed in Chapter 14.)[52]

- ***Interpersonal space.***
  People in a number of cultures prefer to stand close when conversing. Many Arabs and Asians fall into this group. An interpersonal distance of only six inches is very disturbing to a Northern European or an American who is accustomed to conversing at arm's length. Cross-cultural gatherings in the Middle East often involve an awkward dance as Arab hosts strive to get closer while their American and European guests shuffle backwards around the room to maintain what they consider a proper social distance.
- ***Language.***
  Foreign language skills are the gateway to true cross-cultural understanding. Translations are not an accurate substitute for conversational ability in the local language.[53] Consider, for example, the complexity of the Japanese language:

> *Japanese is a situational language and the way something is said differs with the relationship between speaker, listener, or the person about whom they are speaking; their respective families, ages, professional statuses, and companies all affect the way they express themselves.*
>
> *In this respect, Japanese isn't one language but a group of them, changing with a dizzying array of social conventions with which Americans have no experience. Japanese people are raised dealing with the shifting concepts of in group/out group, male and female speech patterns, appropriate politeness levels, and humble and honorific forms of speech. An unwary student, armed only with a few years of classroom Japanese, can pile up mistakes in this regard very quickly.*[54]

4e Pleased to Meet You. What Was Your Name Again?

U.S. managers—particularly driven, individualistic, technically minded personnel—seem to have trouble establishing effective relationships with colleagues abroad. Many quickly conclude that they understand the meaning and significance of relationships and check this subject off their list, but in fact they are neither fully aware of its implications nor committed to investing the time and personal sacrifices that will be required.

Source: Ernest Gundling, Working GlobeSmart: 12 People Skills for Doing Business Across Borders *(Palo Alto, Calif.: Davies-Black, 2003), pp. 11–12.*

QUESTIONS:

With your knowledge of individualism versus collectivism and monochronic versus polychronic time, how do you interpret this characterization? Is this a male-female divide, as well as a cross-cultural divide? Explain.

Language instructors who prepare Americans for foreign assignments say it takes from 150 to 350 hours of classroom work, depending on the difficulty of the language, to reach minimum proficiency (e.g., exchanging greetings, shopping and ordering meals, and asking for directions). The American Society for Testing and Materials has ranked the difficulty of learning foreign languages for native English speakers:

> *The easiest to learn are the Romance and Germanic languages, such as Spanish, German and Swedish. Next are African and Eastern European languages, such as Russian. Finally, the hardest languages are Middle Eastern and Asian languages, such as Arabic, Chinese and Japanese.*[55]

Indeed, of the 34 percent of U.S. public school students in grades 7 to 12 who were enrolled in a foreign language course in 2000, 69 percent were studying Spanish, 18 percent were studying French, and 5 percent were studying German. Less than 1 percent were learning Japanese.[56]

- ***Religion.***
  Awareness of a business colleague's religious traditions is essential for building a lasting relationship.[57] Those traditions may dictate dietary restrictions, religious holidays, and Sabbath schedules, which are important to the devout and represent cultural minefields for the uninformed. For instance, the official day of rest in Iran is Thursday; in Kuwait and Pakistan it is Friday.[58] In Israel, where the official day off is Saturday, "Burger King restaurants—unlike McDonald's—do not offer cheeseburgers in order to conform to Jewish dietary laws forbidding mixing milk products and meat."[59]

  Of course, it is important to be aware of and follow applicable laws regarding religion in the workplace (see the accompanying Managing Diversity feature, for example).

As always, these are turbulent and exciting times in the Middle East, where ethnic, religious, and cultural traditions collide with modern ways. Here Kuwaiti women demonstrate for broader rights in front of their nation's Parliament in Kuwait city. Expatriates working in countries such as Kuwait need to be fully aware of cross-cultural and religious differences if they are to get the job done.

MANAGING DIVERSITY

Dealing with Religion in the U.S. Workplace

For employers wanting to offer a more open environment for employees, it's important to know the laws and regulations. With some 97 percent of religious people practicing one of 20 religions and more than 2,200 individual religions and sects, according to Business for Social Responsibility, it's no wonder why religious discrimination complaints to the U.S. Equal Employment Opportunity Commission have risen by 50 percent since 1991.

Complaints are often about restrictions placed on workers who want to bring a small part of their religion into the workplace—whether it be a prayer time or particular garments. Simultaneously, employees complain about too much tolerance—those who get special treatment because of a particular religion or employees proselytizing.

Employers are prohibited from discriminating against individuals because of their religion, among other things, in hiring, firing and other parts of employment, according to Title VII of the Civil Rights Act of 1964. Employers are also expected to make reasonable accommodations for employees' religious practices.

In 1998, the Clinton administration, along with a religious coalition including the Christian Legal Society and the American Jewish Congress, sought to clarify Title VII in regard to religion. New guidelines stated that personal expression should be allowed as long as workplace productivity was not at risk. Employees, for example, can keep the Koran or Bible on their desks, talk to coworkers about religion and pray during breaks.

But like many laws, vagueness and uncertainty still exist. Business for Social Responsibility offers a few helpful hints to employers who want to stay accepting but legal of religion in the workplace.

Spread the Word. Either through employee orientation materials, bulletin boards or meetings, let employees know that your company is willing to make reasonable accommodations for their religious practices.

Be specific about what is reasonable and unreasonable.

Be fair. Don't exclude religions because they are new or widely unknown.

Review company policies for phrases that could be considered discriminating.

Educate yourself. Learn about other religions, along with their beliefs, holidays, and customs. Then share this information with employees.

Seek individualized solutions. Take time to work with employees on an individual basis to find the answers to specific problems.

Don't forget the nonreligious. Rather than offering time off for religious holidays, offer time off for personal needs.

Source: From Heather Johnson, "Spiritually Responsible," Training, *41 (April 2004): 26. © VNU Business Media, Inc. Reprinted with permission.*

Comparative Management Insights

comparative management: *study of how organizational behavior and management practices differ across cultures*

Comparative management is the study of how organizational behavior and management practices differ across cultures. In this relatively new field of inquiry, as in other fields, there is disagreement about theoretical frameworks and research methodologies.[60] Nevertheless, some useful lessons have been learned. This research-based foundation of understanding can come in handy for managers such as Nancy McKinstry, who lives and works across cultures. McKinstry, an American, is the CEO of Wolters Kluwer, a $4.3-billion-a-year Dutch publishing company based in Amsterdam. This is the sort of cultural mix she deals with daily as she oversees operations in 25 countries:

> *Cultures vary from country to country, so the most important thing is to have local management on the ground that understands the markets. There are actually more similarities between the U.S., Germany and Holland than there are between those countries and southern Europe. In southern Europe, decision-making is more collaborative, and developing long-term business relationships is essential to success.*[61]

4. **DISCUSS** Hofstede's conclusion about the applicability of American management theories in foreign cultures, and **EXPLAIN** the practical significance of the international study of work goals.

In this section, we focus on (1) the applicability of American management theories in other cultures, (2) work-goal diversity across cultures, and (3) a GLOBE matrix of leadership styles.

Made-in-America Management Theories Require Translation

In the 1970s, Geert Hofstede, a Dutch organizational behavior researcher, surveyed 116,000 IBM employees from 40 different countries.[62] He classified each of his 40 national samples according to four different cultural dimensions. Hofstede found a great deal of cultural diversity among the countries he studied. For example, as demonstrated in Table 4.4, employee needs were ranked differently from country to country.

The marked cultural differences among the 40 countries led Hofstede to recommend that American management theories be adapted to local cultures rather than imposed on them. As we saw in Chapter 2, many popular management theories were developed within the U.S. cultural context. Hofstede believes that it is naive to expect those theories to apply automatically in significantly different cultures. For example, American-made management theories that reflect Americans' preoccupation with individualism are out of place in countries such as Mexico, Brazil, and Japan, where individualism is discouraged.

Hofstede's research does not attempt to tell international managers *how* to apply various management techniques in different cultures. However, it does provide a useful cultural typology and presents a convincing case for the cultural adaptation of American management theory and practice.[63] In turn, Americans would do well to culturally adapt any management theories and practices acquired from other cultures.

Table 4.4 Top-Ranking Needs Vary from Country to Country

Security	Security and social	Social	Self-actualization
Switzerland	Iran	Singapore	Hong Kong**
Germany*	Thailand	Denmark	Great Britain
Austria	Taiwan	Sweden	India
Italy	Brazil	Norway	United States
Venezuela	Israel	Netherlands	Philippines
Mexico	France	Finland	Canada
Colombia	Spain		New Zealand
Argentina	Turkey		Australia
Belgium	Peru		South Africa
Japan	Chile		Ireland
Greece	Yugoslavia		
Pakistan	Portugal		

* At the time of this study, East and West Germany were separate countries. East Germany was not one of the 40 countries surveyed.
** Now reunited with China.

Source: *Paraphrased with permission from Geert Hofstede, "Motivation, Leadership, and Organization: Do American Theories Apply Abroad?" in* Organizational Dynamics, *9, no. 1 (Summer 1980): 54–56. This article summarizes Dr. Hofstede's research published in the book* Culture's Consequences: International Differences in Work-Related Values *(Beverly Hills, Calif.: Sage Publications, 1980).*

A Cross-Cultural Study of Work Goals

What do people want from their work? A survey of 8,192 employees from seven countries found general disagreement about the relative importance of 11 different work goals.[64] Respondents to the survey represented a broad range of professions and all levels of the organizational hierarchy. They were asked to rank 11 work goals. Those work goals are listed in Table 4.5, along with the average rankings for five countries. "Interesting work" got a consistently high ranking. "Opportunity for promotion" and "working conditions" consistently were at or very near the bottom of each country's rankings. Beyond those few consistencies, general disagreement prevailed.

The main practical implication of these findings is that managers need to adapt their motivational programs to local preferences.[65] Throughout this text, we consistently stress the importance of the contingency approach to management. In this case, an international contingency approach to motivation is called for. For instance, pay is less important in Japan than in the other four countries. And job security is much less important to Israelis than to American, British, German, and Japanese employees.

Table 4.5 Work Goals Vary from Country to Country.

	MEANS RANKINGS (BY COUNTRY)				
Work goals	**U.S.**	**Britain**	**Germany***	**Israel**	**Japan**
Interesting work	1	1	3	1	2
Pay	2	2	1	3	5
Job security	3	3	2	10	4
Match between person and job	4	6	5	6	1
Opportunity to learn	5	8	9	5	7
Variety	6	7	6**	11	9
Interpersonal relations	7	4	4	2	6
Autonomy	8	10	8	4	3
Convenient work hours	9	5	6**	7	8
Opportunity for promotion	10	11	10	8	11
Working conditions	11	9	11	9	10

* Formerly West Germany.
**Two goals tied for sixth rank.

Source: *Data from Itzhak Harpaz, "The Importance of Work Goals: An International Perspective,"* Journal of International Business Studies, *21 (First Quarter 1990): 81. Reprinted with permission.*

Lessons in Leadership from the GLOBE Project

The huge 62-society data base compiled by the GLOBE researchers provides valuable insights about the applicability of leadership styles around the world. As listed along the top of the matrix in Figure 4.1, the GLOBE researchers focused on the following five different leadership styles:

- *Charismatic/Value-based:* a visionary person who inspires high performance by exhibiting integrity and decisiveness.
- *Team-oriented:* an administratively competent person and team builder who diplomatically emphasizes common purposes and goals.
- *Participative:* a person who actively involves others in both making and carrying out decisions.
- *Humane-oriented:* a compassionate, generous, considerate, and supportive person.
- *Self-protective:* a self-centered and status-conscious person who tends to save face and stir conflict.[66]

The matrix in Figure 4.1 rates these five leadership styles as most acceptable, moderately acceptable, or least acceptable for ten cultural clusters.

5. SUMMARIZE the leadership lessons from the GLOBE Project.

According to the matrix, the charismatic/value-based and team-oriented leadership styles have the greatest cross-cultural applicability. The self-protective leadership style definitely is *not* acceptable, regardless of the cultural setting. Humane-oriented leadership is perceived around the world as being only moderately acceptable, except within the southern Asia cultural cluster. This is probably because humane-oriented leaders are perceived in most cultures as not pushing hard enough to achieve goals and solid results. The picture for participative leadership is mixed, despite its general popularity in North and South America and in Germanic, Latin, and Nordic Europe. A completely different study of employees in Russia's largest textile factory confirms the limited applicability of participative leadership in eastern Europe. That study documented how participative leadership triggered a *decrease* in output. Why? The researchers felt the Russians were influenced by their lack of faith in participative schemes that had proved untrustworthy during the communist era.[67] It takes time for people in new democracies to get used to participative management. For example, American entrepreneur Michael Smolens has taken it one step at a time at Danube Knitware Ltd., the textile mill he cofounded in Hungary. It has been a learning experience for all involved at the 950-employee company, which recently opened a sewing factory in neighboring Romania.

> *The first step was getting workers used to high Western production standards and motivating them to accept the company's priorities. Hungary's low wage base was seen as a big plus when the company was being formed, but absenteeism has been an ongoing problem. . . . Smolens realized he'd have to strengthen his wage structure to keep his workers from abandoning the company for the*

Figure 4.1 GLOBE Leadership Matrix

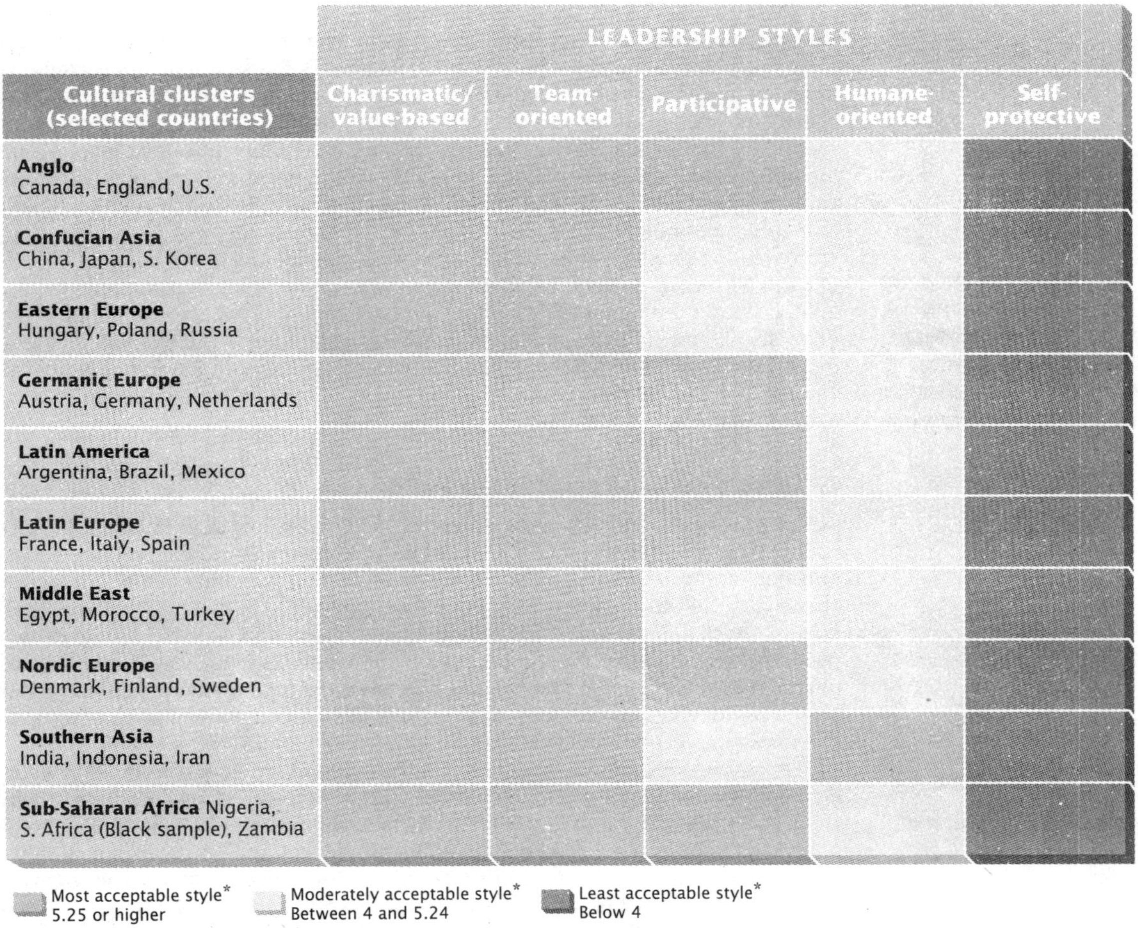

*Mean score on 1–7 scale of acceptability

Source: *Adapted from data in Peter W. Dorfman, Paul J. Hanges, and Felix C. Brodbeck, "Leadership and Cultural Variation: The Identification of Culturally Endorsed Leadership Profiles," in Robert J. House, Paul J. Hanges, Mansour Javidian, Peter W. Dorfman, and Vipin Gupta,* Culture, Leadership, and Organizations: The GLOBE Study of 62 Societies *(Thousand Oaks, Calif.: Sage, 2004), pp. 669–719; and Vipin Gupta and Paul J. Hanges, "Regional and Climate Clustering of Societal Cultures," in* Ibid., *pp. 178–218.*

family farms or the black market. He also moved from awarding attendance bonuses to providing other job incentives—in particular, cultivating a more comfortable, open work environment.

"We're actively soliciting comments from the workers day to day," says [cofounder Phil] Lightly. "They know what the problems are, but because of the way things used to be in this country, they're not always comfortable sharing them."

"It's a good approach," Smolens adds, "and we do see progress. They're starting to realize that what they say is being taken seriously."[68]

International managers need a full repertoire of leadership styles that they can use flexibly in a culturally diverse world.[69]

Staffing Foreign Positions

In our global economy, successful foreign experience is becoming a required stepping stone to top management. *Fortune* magazine's Marshall Loeb observed, "An assignment abroad, once thought to be a career dead end, has become a ticket to speedy advance. And an increasingly necessary one."[70] Unfortunately, Americans reportedly have a higher-than-average failure rate. Failure in this context means foreign-posted employees perform so poorly that they are sent home early or they voluntarily go home early. Estimates vary widely, from a modest 3.2 percent failure rate to an alarming 25 percent.[71] Whatever the failure rate, *any* turnover among employees on foreign assignments is expensive, considering that it costs an average of $1 to $2 million to send someone on a three–to-four-year foreign assignment.[72] Predeparture training for the employee and education allowances for children can drive the bill much higher. Managers are challenged not to waste this sort of investment. They need to do a better job of preparing employees for foreign assignments. Toward that end, let us examine why employees fail abroad and what can be done about it.

6. IDENTIFY the four leading reasons why U.S. expatriates fail to complete their assignments, and **DISCUSS** the nature and importance of cross-cultural training in international management.

Why Do U.S. Expatriates Fail?

Although it has historically been a term for banishment or exile from one's native country, *expatriate* today refers to those who live and work in a foreign country. Living outside the comfort zone of one's native culture and surroundings can be immensely challenging—even overwhelming. Expatriates typically experience some degree of **culture shock** defined as feelings of anxiety, self-doubt, and isolation brought about by a mismatch between one's expectations and reality. Psychologist Elisabeth Marx offered these insights: "On average, managers in my study experienced culture shock symptoms for about seven weeks: 70 percent of managers reported these lasting up to five weeks and 30 percent had symptoms for up to ten weeks."[73]

culture shock: *negative feelings triggered by an expectations-reality mismatch*

Those who view culture shock as a natural part of living and working in a foreign country are better equipped to deal with it. More precise knowledge of why U.S. expatriates fail also is helpful. Thanks to a recent survey of 74 large U.S. companies, encompassing a total of 3.6 million employees and 12,500 expatriates, we have a clearer picture[74] (see Table 4.6). Job performance—either so poor that it prompted recall (48.4 percent) or so good it attracted outside job offers (43.7 percent)—was the leading cause of expatriate failure. Also high on the list were factors related to culture shock (36.6 percent) and homesickness (31 percent). Other factors trailed in relative importance. As with culture shock, it behooves candidates for foreign assignments to prepare accordingly.

cross-cultural training: *guided experience that helps people live and work successfully in foreign cultures*

> **4f Looking for the Right Stuff**
>
> According to Robert Rosen, author and international management consultant, today's global businesses need leaders who
>
> - See the world's challenges and opportunities.
> - Think with an international mindset.
> - Act with fresh, global-centric leadership behaviors.
> - Mobilize a world-class team and company.
>
> *Source: Ruth E. Thaler-Carter, "Whither Global Leaders?"* HR Magazine, *45 (May 2000): 84.*
>
> **QUESTIONS:**
> **How do you measure up to this profile? Can you identify people you know personally who fit these requirements? Describe these people and assess their effectiveness.**

Cross-Cultural Training

As we have defined it, culture is the unique system of values, beliefs, and symbols that foster patterned behavior in a given population. It is difficult to distinguish the individual from his or her cultural context. Consequently, people tend to be very protective of their cultural identity. Careless defiance or ignorance of cultural norms or traditions by outsiders can result in grave personal insult and put important business dealings at risk. Fortunately, cultural sensitivity can be learned through appropriate cross-cultural training. **Cross-cultural training** is any

Table 4.6 Research Findings on Why U.S. Expatriates Go Home Early

Reason	Percentage in Agreement
Not performing job effectively	48.4
Received other, more rewarding offers from other companies	43.7
Expatriate or family not adjusting to culture	36.6
Expatriate or family missing contact with family and friends at home	31.0
Received other, more rewarding offers from our company	12.2
Unable to adjust to deprived living standards in country of assignment	10.3
Concerned with problems of safety and/or health care in foreign location	10.3
Believed children's education was suffering	7.1
Feared that assignment would slow career advancement	7.1
Spouse wanted career	6.1
Compensation package was inadequate	0.0

Source: *Reprinted from* Business Horizons, *45 (November-December 2002), Gary S. Insch and John D. Daniels, "Causes and Consequences of Declining Early Departures from Foreign Assignments," Table 2, p. 41, Copyright 2002, with permission from Elsevier.*

form of guided experience aimed at helping people live and work successfully in another culture. Experts say successful cross-cultural adaptation requires the following nine competencies:

1. Building relationships
2. Valuing people of different cultures
3. Listening and observation
4. Coping with ambiguity
5. Translating complex information
6. Taking action and initiative
7. Managing others
8. Adaptability and flexibility
9. Managing stress[75]

See the Skills & Tools section at the end of this chapter for additional details about these important cross-cultural competencies.

■ **Specific Techniques.** The nine competencies listed above involve the *what* of cross-cultural training. Let us now consider *how* those competencies can be taught. Following is a list of five basic cross-cultural training techniques, ranked in order of increasing complexity and cost.[76]

- ***Documentary programs.***
Trainees read about a foreign country's history, culture, institutions, geography, and economics. Videotaped and Web-based presentations are often used. For example, this is how Ambergris Solutions makes sure its 1,400 call center employees in the Philippines can comfortably converse with American clients of Texas-based companies:

> *. . . workers are given* USA Today *and the most recent Texas travel guide to read between calls. They watch the previous day's TV news from Texas during breaks in case conversation with a customer veers to current events.*
>
> *Operations manager Katherine Ann Fernando said it can help knowing the weather, the top stories—even how the Dallas Cowboys or Texas Rangers are doing.*
>
> *"We can't afford to sound like we don't know anything about Texas," she said.*[77]

- ***Culture assimilator.***
Cultural familiarity is achieved through exposure to a series of simulated intercultural incidents, or typical problem situations. This technique has been used to quickly train those who are given short notice of a foreign assignment.[78]
- ***Language instruction.***
Conversational language skills are taught through a variety of methods. Months, sometimes years, of study are required to master difficult languages. But as a cross-cultural communications professor noted, "To speak more than one language is no longer a luxury, it is a necessity."[79] A good role model is Tupperware's top management team, made up of nine executives (all with foreign experience) who speak from two to four languages each.[80]

In today's world, comprehensive cross cultural training is a vital step towards meeting the present day management challenges. When doing business in any part of the world, knowing the local language and culture are imperative.

- ***Sensitivity training.***
  Experiential exercises teach awareness of the impact of one's actions on others in cross-cultural situations.
- ***Field experience.***
  Extensive firsthand exposure to ethnic subcultures in one's own country or to foreign cultures can build cultural intelligence.[81] PricewaterhouseCoopers, the major accounting and consulting company, has developed an inspiring leadership development program involving cross-cultural field experience. The Ulysses Program sends mid-career employees to developing countries for eight-week community service projects. Here, for example, is the experience of Tahir Ayub:

  > *His job: helping village leaders in the Namibian outback grapple with their community's growing AIDS crisis. Faced with language barriers, cultural differences, and scant access to electricity, Ayub, 39, and two colleagues had to scrap their PowerPoint presentations in favor of a more low-tech approach: face-to-face discussion. The village chiefs learned that they needed to garner community support for programs to combat the disease, and Ayub learned important lessons as well: Technology isn't always the answer, "You better put your beliefs and biases to one side and figure out new ways to look at things," he said.*[82]

  PricewaterhouseCoopers considers the $15,000 per-person cost of the Ulysses Program to be a sound investment in human and social capital.

■ **Is One Technique Better Than Another?** A study of 80 (63 male, 17 female) managers from a U.S. electronics company attempted to assess the relative effectiveness of two different training techniques.[83] A documentary approach was compared with an interpersonal approach. The latter combined sensitivity training and local ethnic field experience. These techniques were judged equally effective at promoting cultural adjustment, as measured during the managers' three-month stay in South Korea. The researchers recommended a *combination* of documentary and interper-

4g Foreign Language Skills

Fact: Native English speakers are projected to be only 5 percent of the world's population by 2050, down from 9 percent in 1995.

Fact: Senior executives in the Netherlands speak an average of 3.9 languages. Their counterparts in both the United Kingdom and the United States speak an average of 1.5 languages.

Learning a foreign language is easier for some than for others. International business experts say it is worth the time and effort in order to

- Enhance the traveler's sense of mastery, self-confidence, and safety.
- Show respect for foreign business hosts or guests.
- Help build rapport and trust with foreign hosts or guests.
- Improve the odds of a successful foreign business venture.
- Build a base of confidence for learning other languages.
- Promote a deeper understanding of other cultures.
- Help travelers obtain the best possible medical care during emergencies.
- Minimize culture shock and the frustrations of being an outsider.

Source: Data from "English Declining as World Language," USA Today *(February 27, 2004): 7A; data from "Bilingual Business,"* USA Today *(April 11, 2000): 1B; adapted from Gary P. Ferraro, "The Need for Linguistic Proficiency in Global Business,"* Business Horizons, *39 (May-June 1996): 39–46.*

QUESTIONS:

Could you conduct a business meeting in one or more foreign languages? What has been your experience with trying to learn foreign languages? How strong is your desire to speak a foreign language? Which language(s)? Why? Would a strong second language help you get a better job? Explain.

sonal training. The importance of language training was diminished in this study because the managers dealt primarily with English-speaking Koreans.

Considering that far too many U.S. companies have no formal expatriate training programs, the key issue is not which type of training is better, but whether companies offer any systematic cross-cultural training at all.

■ An Integrated Expatriate Staffing System. Cross-cultural training, in whatever form, should not be an isolated experience. Rather, it should be part of an integrated, selection-orientation-repatriation process focused on a distinct career path.[84] The ultimate goal should be a positive and productive experience for the employee and his or her family and a smooth professional and cultural reentry back home.

During the selection phase, the usual interview should be supplemented with an orientation session for the candidate's family. This session gives everyone an opportunity to "select themselves out" before a great deal of time and money has been invested. Experience has shown that, upon the expatriate's arrival at the foreign assignment, family sponsors or assigned mentors are effective at reducing culture shock.[85] Sponsors and mentors ease the expatriate family through the critical first six months by answering naive but important questions and by serving as cultural translators.[86]

Finally, repatriation should be a forethought rather than an afterthought.[87] Candidates for foreign assignments deserve a firm commitment from their organization that a successful tour of duty will lead to a step up the career ladder upon their return. Expatriates who spend their time worrying about being leapfrogged while they are absent from headquarters are less likely to succeed.

■ What About North American Women on Foreign Assignments?

7. SUMMARIZE the situation of North American women on foreign assignments.

Historically, companies in Canada and the United States have sent very few women on foreign assignments. Between the early 1980s and the late 1990s, the representation of women among North American expatriates grew from 3 percent to a still small 14 percent.[88] Conventional wisdom—that women could not be effective because of foreign prejudice—has turned out to be a myth.[89] Recent research and practical experience have given us these insights:

- North American women have enjoyed above-average success on foreign assignments.
- The greatest barriers to foreign assignments for North American women have been self-disqualification and prejudice among *home-country* managers. A recent survey led to this conclusion: "We found that American women in management and executive roles in foreign countries can do just as well as American men. Their biggest problem was convincing their companies to give them the assignments."[90]

4h Ready to Pack Your Bags?

Survey of 516 senior executives: "Half of the executives would take a job in China, 34 percent said they would work in India, and the same number would accept a position in Russia."

Survey of 1,000 employees: When asked whether they would move if their mate were given a foreign assignment, 68 percent said "No," 30 percent said "Yes," and 2 percent weren't sure.

Sources: Ann Pomeroy, "Have Job, Will Travel," HR Magazine, *49 (June 2004): 20; and data from "Most Mates Not Willing to Move Abroad,"* USA Today *(July 21, 2004): 1B.*

QUESTIONS:
Questions: How would you respond to these two surveys? Explain.

- Culture is a bigger hurdle than gender. In other words, North American women on foreign assignments are seen as North Americans first and as women second.[91]

Testimonial evidence suggests that these last two factors are also true for African Americans, many of whom report smoother relations abroad than at home.[92] Thus, the best career advice for *anyone* seeking a foreign assignment is this: carefully prepare yourself, *go for it,* and don't take "no" for an answer![93]

Relying on Local Managerial Talent

In recent years, the expensive problem of expatriate failure and general trends toward geocentrism and globalism have resulted in a greater reliance on managers from host countries. Foreign nationals already know the language and culture and do not require huge relocation expenditures.[94] In addition, host-country governments tend to look favorably on a greater degree of local control. On the negative side, local managers may have an inadequate knowledge of home-office goals and procedures. The staffing of foreign positions is necessarily a case-by-case proposition.

SUMMARY

1. The study of international management is more important than ever as the huge global economy continues to grow. Doing business internationally typically involves much more than importing and/or exporting goods. The six stages of the internationalization process are licensing, exporting, local warehousing and selling, local assembly and packaging, joint ventures, and direct foreign investments. There are three main guidelines for success in international joint ventures: (a) Be patient while building trust with a carefully selected partner; (b) learn as much as fast as possible without giving away key secrets; and (c) establish clear ground rules for rights and responsibilities. Global companies are a present-day reality, whereas transnational companies are a futuristic vision. A global company does business simultaneously in many countries but pursues global strategies administered from a strong home-country headquarters. In contrast, a transnational company is envisioned as a decentralized global network of productive units with no distinct national identity. There is growing concern about the economic and political power that such stateless enterprises may acquire as they eclipse the power and scope of their host nations.
2. Cultural intelligence (CQ) is defined as the ability of an outsider to "read" individual behavior, group dynamics, and situations in a foreign culture as well as the locals do. Those with high CQ are cross-cultural chameleons who blend in with the local cultural situation. Experts, noting that American managers generally are prepared only for domestic service, recommend that present and future managers begin to think globally and cross-culturally. According to Howard Perlmutter, management tends to exhibit one of three general attitudes about international operations: an ethnocentric attitude (home-country-oriented), a poly centric attitude (host-country-oriented), or a geocentric attitude (world-oriented). Perlmutter claims that a geocentric attitude will lead to better product quality, improved use of resources, better local management, and more profit than the other attitudes.

3. In high-context cultures such as Japan, communication is based more on nonverbal and situational messages than it is in low-context cultures such as the United States. The nine cultural dimensions identified by the GLOBE project are power distance, uncertainty avoidance, institutional collectivism, in-group collectivism, assertiveness, gender equality, future orientation, performance orientation, and humane orientation.
4. Comparative management is a new field of study concerned with how organizational behavior and management practices differ across cultures. A unique study by Geert Hofstede of 116,000 IBM employees in 40 nations classified each country by its prevailing attitude toward four cultural variables. In view of significant international differences on these cultural dimensions, Hofstede suggests that American management theory and practice be adapted to local cultures rather than imposed on them. The cross-cultural study of work goals uncovered a great deal of diversity. Thus, motivational programs need to be tailored to the local culture.
5. Across 62 societies in the GLOBE study, the charismatic/value-based (goal-directed visionary) and team-oriented (competent team builder) leadership styles were found to be widely applicable. The self-protective (self-centered) leadership style was not acceptable in any culture. The participative leadership style (involving others in making and implementing decisions) had mixed applicability across cultures, as did the humane-oriented (supportive and nurturing) style. Global managers need to use a contingency approach to leadership, adapting their styles to the local culture.
6. Culture shock is a normal part of expatriate life. Job performance issues, family and/or individual culture shock, and homesickness are the leading reasons why U.S. expatriates go home early (a costly problem). Systematic cross-cultural training—ideally including development of interpersonal, observational, language, and stress management competencies—is needed. Expatriates also need to be flexible and able to handle ambiguity. Specific cross-cultural training techniques include documentary programs, culture assimilator, language instruction, sensitivity training, and field experience.
7. North American women fill a growing but still small share of foreign positions. The long-standing assumption that women will fail on foreign assignments because of foreigners' prejudice has turned out to be false. Women from the United States and Canada have been successful on foreign assignments but face two major hurdles at *home:* self-disqualification and prejudicial managers. Culture, not gender, is the primary challenge for women on foreign assignments. The situation for African Americans parallels that of women.

TERMS TO UNDERSTAND

- International management, p. 92
- Global company, p. 95
- Transnational company, p. 95
- Cultural intelligence (CQ) , p. 97
- Ethnocentric attitude, p. 97
- Polycentric attitude, p. 99
- Geocentric attitude, p. 99
- Culture, p. 100
- High-context cultures, p. 102
- Low-context cultures, p. 102
- Individualistic cultures, p. 102
- Collectivist cultures, p. 103
- Monochronic time, p. 103
- Polychronic time, p. 104
- Comparative management, p. 106
- Culture shock, p. 110
- Cross-cultural training, p. 110

SKILLS & TOOLS

Competencies You Need to Develop to Work Effectively in a Foreign Culture

Cross-Cultural Competency Cluster	Behavioral Indicator	Knowledge or Skill Required	Communication Ability
1. Building relationships	Interacts with others regularly, particularly members of the host culture	Ability to gain access to and maintain relationships with members of host culture	Recognizes and deals effectively with misunderstandings; a willingness to maintain contact with people even when communication is difficult
2. Valuing people of different cultures	Expresses interest in and respect for host culture, including its history, customs, beliefs, and politics	Empathy for difference; sensitivity to diversity	Initiates and engages in open conversation with friends and colleagues about host culture
3. Listening and observation	Spends time observing, reading about, and studying host culture, particularly with locals	Knows cultural history and reasons for certain cultural actions and customs	Asks questions; when possible, takes careful account of situations before taking action
4. Coping with ambiguity	Maintains work habits in the face of unexpected events, new experiences, or unfamiliar situations	Recognizes and interprets implicit behavior, especially nonverbal cues	Changes communication in response to nonverbal cues from others
5. Translating complex information	Translates personal thoughts into language of host culture	Knowledge of local language, symbols, or other forms of verbal language and written language	Demonstrates fluency in language of host country
6. Taking action and initiative	Takes action when appropriate, even when outcome is uncertain	Understands intended and potential unintended consequences of actions	Easily approaches and interacts with strangers
7. Managing others	Takes responsibility for accomplishing tasks related to the organizational goals	Ability to manage details of a job including maintaining cohesion in a group	Communicates implication of individual actions to others in the organizations
8. Adaptability and flexibility	Demonstrates acceptance of change, setbacks, and challenges	Views change from multiple perspectives	Can explain perspectives on a single issue
9. Managing stress	Maintains work habits during times of personal and environmental crisis or in the face of heavy emotional demands	Understands own and other's mood, emotions, and personality	Expresses personal feelings in an appropriate and nonthreatening way

Source: Academy of Management Learning & Education *by Yoshitaka Yamazaki and Christopher Kayes. Copyright 2004 by Academy of Management Learning & Education. Reproduced with permission of Academy of Management Learning & Education in the format Textbook via Copyright Clearance Center.*

HANDS-ON EXERCISE

Look into the Cultural Mirror

Instructions:

Culture, as defined in this chapter, involves *taken-for-granted* assumptions about how we should think, act, and feel (relative to both ourselves and the world in general). Here is an opportunity to bring those assumptions to the surface. Remember, there are no right or wrong answers. Moreover, because this exercise has no proven scientific validity, it is intended for instructional purposes only. The idea is to see where you stand in the world's rich mosaic of cultural diversity by rating yourself on the cultural variables discussed in this chapter.

Low-context ("Put it in writing.") — High-context ("The situation is more important than words.")

1................2................3................4................5

Individualistic ("Me first.") — Collectivist ("It's all about us.")

1................2................3................4................5

Monochronic ("Do one thing at a time and be on time.") — Polychronic ("There's a time to go fast and a time to go slow. Do more than one thing at a time.")

1................2................3................4................5

Power Distance

Low ("Leaders are no better than anyone else.") — High ("Authority and power of leaders should be respected.")

1................2................3................4................5

Uncertainty Avoidance

Low ("Take chances, bend the rules.") — High ("Take no chances, follow the rules.")

1................2................3................4................5

Future Orientation

Low ("Live for today; instant gratification.") — High ("Think long-term; save for the future.")

1................2................3................4................5

Performance Orientation

Low ("Loyalty and belonging are what really count.") — High ("Take the initiative; have a sense of urgency about getting results.")

1................2................3................4................5

Humane Orientation

Low ("Look out for yourself.") — High ("Help others, especially the weak and vulnerable.")

1................2................3................4................5

Masculinity ("Winning and material wealth are what count.") — Femininity ("Relationships and quality of life are what really matter.")

1................2................3................4................5

For Consideration/Discussion:

1. Did this exercise help you better understand any of the cultural variables discussed in this chapter? Explain.
2. Does your cultural profile help you better understand some of your family's traditions, values, rituals, or customs?
3. How does your cultural profile compare with that of others (spouse, friends, classmates)? Could the seeds of conflict and misunderstanding grow from any cultural differences with them?
4. Which of your positive cultural traits could become a negative if taken to extremes?

INTERNET EXERCISES

1. **Using the Internet to prepare for a foreign assignment (or travel adventure).** When your author was in graduate school, he was offered the chance to teach for six months in Micronesia. He accepted—and then ran to the university library to find out where Micronesia was (it turned out to be 2,200 islands in the Western Pacific, just north of the Equator). To make a long story short, he soon found himself standing at the airport in a pool of sweat on a tiny coral atoll in the Marshall Islands with his books, virtually no knowledge of the local culture, and a big lump in his throat. Six months, lots of mistakes and lessons, countless mosquito bites, and five islands later, he boarded a plane back to the United States, a grateful and wiser person. Thanks to the Internet, you can get to the grateful and wiser stage a lot more efficiently.

   Pick a foreign country you would like to know more about, perhaps visit, or even a place you would like to work. (For this exercise, it is preferable to select one where you would not be able to speak the local language.) An excellent source of national and cultural information about your selected country comes from the publishers of the somewhat offbeat *Lonely Planet* travel guides (**www.lonelyplanet.com**). From the home page menu, click on "Worldguide." At the "Destinations" page, follow the prompts to tap into useful information about the country you have in mind.

   If the local language for your selected country is not your native language, the Internet can get you headed in the right direction. At the home page of **www.travlang.com,** select "Foreign Languages for Travelers" in the "Travlang Sections" box, and then follow the two steps for your chosen language. Next, at your selected language page, click on the option "Basic Words." Practice your new vocabulary of essential greetings and questions. The quiz option is a good learning tool.

   Learning Points: 1. Does your selected country appear to be high-context or low-context? Individualistic or collectivist? Monochronic or polychronic? How can you tell? 2. How much culture shock are you likely to experience in your chosen country? Explain. 3. How well will your native language serve you? What language will you have to know to do business in your selected country? 4. If it is not your native language, how do you say "Yes," "No," "Hello," "Thank you," and "Goodbye" in the language of your selected country? 5. Based on your Internet studies, how strong is your desire to visit or work in the country you selected? Explain.

2. **Check it out:** Since the 2001 terrorist attacks on the United States, foreign business travelers have had a greater need than ever to know about potential trouble spots. At the home page of Air Security International (**www.airsecurity.com**), click on any of the news items under "Hotspots." You will find a daily briefing and useful information on travel alerts and trouble spots around the world. Featured countries are assigned a "country threat level" rating from 1 (reasonably safe) to 5 (high threat of physical harm). *Bon voyage!*

For updates to these exercises, visit our Web site (**http://business.college.hmco.com/students/** and select Kreitner, *Management,* 10e).

CLOSING CASE

A Clash of Cultures

Pradeep Singh sat in the parking lot watching the cars leave one by one. He needed to make up his mind before he left the premises of Balaji Global Group (BGG) for the day. At yesterday's particularly acrimonious meeting with the chief operating officer, K.R. Muthiah, Singh had burst his dam of patience and told him in no uncertain terms what he thought of BGG's policies.

It was not a sudden argument. Singh had been patient for the last 18 months. When he left Trilo Hygiene Products, a multinational corporation (MNC) where he was head of human resource development (HRD), to join BGG, it was to spearhead a change to professionalism and empowerment. Then Muthiah had said to him: "In five years, we have grown 100% and this year we are crossing the Rs 1,500-crore mark. With so many diverse businesses and a vast management team, we want to develop our managers to grow out of a task orientation to one of long-term business orientation. I want you to come in as the group's HRD director to institute the change process. We want you to work closely with the family in evolving a new culture and replicate the MNC model of effective and proactive business management here."

And while it meant relocating to an alien region with a totally alien culture, varied customs and habits, Singh felt it was worth the effort and emotional upheaval. With his 20 years' of exposure and experience in a multinational, he believed that if even a few like him entered the family-managed concerns (FMCs), Indian business houses could make a quantum leap in their contributions to the country's management development.

As if to reinforce his faith, one of the first things he was asked to work on was a performance bonus scheme for the business heads and CEOs, to grow their initiative and business drive. Two months later, when Singh discussed his scheme, Muthiah said: "You need to discuss this with the rest of the family and convince them. I suggest you meet them individually and discuss the matter."

Singh was confused; many of the family were not directly connected with the businesses - the various businesses were managed by professionals. But for the purpose of some internal structure, these professionals reported to some specified senior family member. Therefore, it made more sense to discuss with the CEOs first and get their commitment. After sometime, the responsibility for the division's success or failure was ultimately on them.

But later that year, when Singh presented his evaluation of the performance, G.K. Muthalingam, the president (corporate affairs), protested over excluding six business heads from the bonus. "These people have been with us for many years; we cannot be harsh on them. After all, it is the first year and if we do not encourage them with rewards, they are unlikely to perform well in the future," he said.

The family was indulgent as business heads enumerated reasons for non-delivery of goals, and Muthalingam insisted that as a gesture of encouragement, all business heads should be rewarded. Much to his chagrin, Singh found that while at the outset they were driven by goal-setting, when it came to looking at performances below norms, there was tremendous dilution. Thus, while they had the philosophy of a reward system, they lacked the political will to implement it.

In fact, felt Singh, it was this accent on the family that encouraged hereditary succession and diluted the much-needed focus on performance. This was also evident in the recruitment of people based on recommendation, rather than merit and experience. Family members were installed as heads for most businesses but the CEOs were professionals - chartered accountants and MBAs. In their recent drive to professionalize, BGG had hired four MBAs from MNCs to head the businesses. Apart from these, the general calibre of the managers left a lot to be desired. Many did not possess the competence and professional drive required for a senior manager. They were typically from within the region, with no broad based experience in larger companies or the other states in India.

And this did not augur well for BGG, felt Singh. Going by the recent acquisition spree, the diversification plans and investment commitments, mere financial clout was not enough and sustaining BGG's businesses would depend heavily on the calibre of the professionals, their ability to take independent decisions and develop a sound business orientation.

In fact, Singh often found the diversities in the businesses a strain. The calibre and variety of personnel needed to manage many of these were not available within the group but the family still insisted on using internal talent. Very often he was faced with a recruitment that was neither planned, nor necessary. However, the justifications offered never ceased to amaze him.

For instance, Vasu Muthalingam, who headed the textiles division, justified the hiring of a chartered accountant as: "He is a fine accountant and his father was our production supervisor in the cement division until he retired last year. We had promised his father that his son would be employed by BGG." It was this accent on personal promises and assurances that Singh found totally distanced from a business focus. No wonder then, he felt, that despite its turnover of Rs. 1,500 crore, BGG's profits were only a paltry 4%. A business ought not to be based on emotions and personal relationships. The employees should be employed on the basis of merit and qualification.

And it wasn't just recruitment. Other business decisions were similarly influenced by emotional considerations. Only recently, Deep Ahuja, the CEO of the electronics division was complaining to Singh about what he called "methodic madness". Ahuja, an engineer with an MBA from a leading business school in Delhi, was asked by the president R.V. Seshagiri, (grandson of the chairman), to allot 40% of the division's transport contracts to Velayudan & Sons. Ahuja was surprised. The new transporter came at a premium of 8% which translated to incremental costs of Rs. 25 lakh per annum. Ahuja felt this to be an unnecessary strain on the division's business. But Seshagiri reasoned that it was prudent business practice to develop an alternative source; besides which, the transporter was the grandson of the ex- financial controller and BGG needed to "take care" and show solidarity in strengthening his business.

Other similar practices surfaced from time to time and Singh was convinced it was time the group broke out of the traditional practice of nurturing unrelated causes. But Muthaiah refused to listen. And neither was he willing to consider Singh's proposal to streamline designations and rationalize the organizational structure. Each business unit was structured differently; some had a president, others a CEO and many also a business head, who was a family member. "If we are talking of a change, then it must be reflected in the way the organization is structured so that the lines of reporting and responsibility flow are homogeneous," said Singh. But the family said: "How can we take away a designation that has been given?" For the example clearly pointed to Muthalingam and Seshagiri, both of whom held the post of president.

But Singh was aware that if designations and reporting relationships were not streamlined, the current noise level in the multi-reporting relationships could create unnecessary dichotomies. For instance, Muthaiah, as chief operating officer (strategy) also headed the garments division, whose CEO was Dhiren Chinoy. Chinoy had to also report to Sambasivam, a nephew of the chairman, who had limited experience in knitwear. But Sambasivam was being groomed to take over as the business head and Chinoy was pulled in different directions between the two men.

Early in the year, Chinoy discussed with Sambasivam a proposal to dispose some Rs 60 lakh worth rejected knits lying idle in the warehouse. Sambasivam rejected the idea, and as luck would have it, a small fire at the warehouse destroyed the entire stock. The next evening in Muthaiah's office, in the presence of six others, Chinoy was pulled up for incompetence. "What kind of a business manager are you? If we had disposed them as scrap, we could have reduced our losses," shouted Muthaiah. When Chinoy pointed out that he had discussed the possibility with Sambasivam, Muthaiah blasted him some more. "I am the business head and if you value your job, you will talk to me!"

Chinoy obviously could not get over this humiliating incident. In a bitter note to Singh, he wrote: "I don't need to take this sort of humiliation. Managing a garments unit is not an easy task and this is the last thing I need. If I consulted Sambasivam, it was because they asked me to deal with him as the local business head at Tirupur. And, in any case, I refuse to be treated as a slave and be shouted at. I am a professional and I am sure I will find more dignified employment elsewhere. Kindly accept my resignation."

Singh realized that this style of management was fast percolating down the line. Younger family members, who witnessed their elders' style, nearly always found it successful in winning the obedience of the junior managers and emulated it. Singh could see there was a cultural dissonance and the newer crop of professional managers was not likely to accept it. But the question was how was he to communicate this to the management? He could see there was fear in the minds of many and most were even wary of speaking their mind. This also meant that the culture enabled retention of only mediocre senior executives and had not allowed development of any professional systems orientation at work.

And even if a CEO attempted to act independently, he was promptly hauled over the coals and publicly denounced for breaking the rules. Even day-to-day business decisions could not be taken without the family's permission, as Sudeep Krishnan who took over from Chinoy, discovered. When he changed suppliers for lack of quality, the original vendor complained, and Krishnan was derided for acting out of turn. The visible culture of the Balaji family was in total contrast to their style of management. While there was a show of wanting to empower, in fact, the family at every point sent subtle messages that they were the owners and demanded subservience.

Seemingly simple folks, most people lauded their simple eating, dressing and living habits. And the family believed austerity was a virtue. So they travelled in simple cars, but all of them had a choice of yes-men who followed them everywhere and waited on them at every meeting. Even the senior patriarch, G.D. Ramadurai, was almost never alone in his room. Two men always stood on either side to rush to his every bidding. The whole ambience and body language spoke of domination, control and of wanting complete subservience.

And Singh found this language and culture was not conducive to the growth of a democratic organization. "If the culture has to change," Singh told Muthaiah, "then it should start with shedding the aura of terror and promoting open discussions with the employees, without holding out threats. But the terrorization in the form of erratic, abrasive behaviour has only helped build clones and promoted passive acceptance. And unfortunately, senior executives have now come to believe that such behaviour begets results and is rewarded."

And that was enacted, when T.M. Kalyanasundaram, the financial controller of the electronics division, was promoted as the CEO of that division. As far as Singh could see, TMK, as he was known, was just a sharp financial man. No doubt he had delivered some results in his function, "but that is not enough to be a CEO," said Singh to Muthaiah, when he was told of the promotion. "What a CEO needs to have are clear leadership qualities, abilities to manage resources and motivate people. If anything, TMK has a track record of demoralizing and terrorizing his staff and most have not enjoyed working with him. All he brings to his new position is fine numbers acumen, but no business orientation."

Asked Singh: "What message are you sending down the line about your culture? That this is the style that will be rewarded and this is our role model?" But the refusal to debate and pro actively deliberate on alternatives to organizational problems was almost endemic. Led by the overall fear of the family and now the performance bonus scheme, business heads were risk-averse and quick to pass the buck.

Which is what happened at the domestic appliances division, which was headed by T. V. Murugan, a nephew of the chairman. When an export order for 50,000 mixers was received from a buyer in West Asia, Chetan Vyas, the chief accountant of the division, worked on a detailed pricing and projected a profit of 22%. When the order was completed, however, the actual profit delivered was a shockingly low 12%. Murugan quickly called in the auditors to investigate the accounts and found that rejects alone accounted for 7%. Further investigations revealed that the wastage was a function of sub-standard steel used in the order. It was found that the quality of steel supplied was not adequately tested for conformation to the norms, the required net weight and tensile strength of the alloy was communicated to the vendor but each supply was not tested, on the assumption that all batches would be as per specifications. More important, the clue lay in what the purchase manager said: "Palaniappan Steels has been our supplier for 20 years and we trusted them."

Trust, as Singh could see, was an emotion that underscored most business relationships at BGG. It transpired that the vendor was selected by Murugan despite knowing that he did not have the technology to continuously monitor the quality of his output. While it was clear that the erosion of the profits was due to raw material quality, Murugan blamed the purchase department for not ensuring good quality. He also blamed Vyas for exaggerating his projections by not building in wastages adequately in his pricing strategy. Vyas had, in fact, built in a nominal 2% for rejects but this was obviously not seen as adequate.

However, Singh was clear that the problem lay in quality control and vendor selection. He said: "We need to develop our vendors as partners in progress. This means educating them about our products and customer needs, the reasons for demanding certain specifications and testing this technology periodically to check if it fits with our needs. We take pride in saying that Palaniappan has been with us for 20 years. But in these 20 years, what value have you added to his business or processes? Have we invested in his business to ensure our interests?"

As Singh could see, as a culture there was no attempt to diagnose problem. Instead the terrorizing had led the focus to shift from problem analysis to penalty levying. There was tremendous suspicion, doubt and undermining of each other at work rather than a clear-cut discussion of the problems. For instance, in the case of the export order, the purchase manager had tried his level best to draw Murugan's attention to the sub-standard quality of the raw material. Instead of perceiving the problem, Murugan had felt his authority was being undermined and questioned by a subordinate. And both the purchase manager and Vyas were sacked for gross negligence.

Singh met Muthaiah to seek his intervention to stall the exit of the two sound managers. But Muthaiah was clear that it was the duty of the subordinates to strengthen the hands of the business heads and in this case, they were guilty of negligence. But Singh believed Muthaiah was not exercising his authority to question Murugan, on the other hand, he was exercising his power based on closeness to individual family members, He felt that by not judging the situation on its merits, Muthaiah had wasted a golden opportunity to set an example to inspire both Murugan and the other managers.

And this, Singh felt, was detrimental to the long-term interests of the group. Despite the fact that all earlier encounters had dampened his spirits, he decided to call a meeting of the senior family members. His note said: "Given the various diversifications and acquisitions we have entered into, it is necessary for us to look at BGG's culture towards empowering our managers and building the strengths necessary for future growth and success. A culture represents the values, beliefs and expectations shared by members of the group and exerts a normative pressure on the members to conform to the shared codes. Since it shapes the behaviour of people, the concept of culture will open up the possibility of bringing in changes in attitudes and behaviour. It is with this background that I request each of you to share your thoughts on how we can collectively articulate and craft a culture for BGG."

And Singh could see that the issue of culture needed to be addressed urgently. With newer family members being given stewardship of the new businesses, it seemed more critical to develop an inspirational role to emulate.

But more was in store for Singh. Muthaiah, the spokesperson of the family said: "Singh, while we appreciate your enthusiasm and concern, the family does not wish to discuss the subject. We want to retain total control, and empowerment is thus not suited to the needs of our group. We would always want the total involvement of all the family members in all matters. But yes, we were definitely going to increase the induction of professional managers from multinational companies, so that there is at least a subtle conversion in management styles."

And Muthaiah pulled out some papers pertaining to Rishi Dasgupta, the marketing controller of Dagwood Industries. Muthaiah had received his resume from a local head hunter and he now asked Singh to quickly hire Dasgupta.

The following week, Singh flew to Mumbai to meet Dasgupta. Dasgupta had close to 18 years in industrial marketing and strategic management. But he needed time to think about the offer of president (group marketing). As he said: "I have always worked for MNCs and I need to be sure before I move base to a FMC."

When, after four weeks of relentless chasing, Dasgupta declined the offer, Muthaiah was furious. He told Singh: "You have failed us miserably. After all the lengths we were willing to go on salary, other benefits and position, you, an MNC manager yourself, have been unable to market the group to Dasgupta adequately."

Singh was taken aback. This was the last thing he had expected to hear. He had done his best in marketing both BGG's image as well as the company's position to Dasgupta. "What has my being an MNC manager got to do with anything? I am not selling chocolates; I have to sell an image and Dasgupta will buy it only if that is what he wants. And as for the culture, I have not been able to make the desired dent. It is possible only over a period of time, through collective effort, cooperation and conviction. Building an image requires a sustained plan and commitment and certainly not coercion. But my request for a relook at the culture has been turned down."

And now, as he ran the last encounter over in his mind, Singh was convinced he could not spend any more time with BGG. He stepped out of the car, went to Muthaiah's cabin and handed his resignation to him.

For Discussion

1. Why do you think Pradeep Singh had to tender resignation from Balaji Global Group?
2. How can one prevent a clash of cultures with a view to foster consonance and cross-cultural understanding?

Source: *Businessworld, Special Collector's Issue, Selected Case Studies, April 2004, pp- 204-207*

TEST PREPPER

True/False Questions

_____ **1.** The first stage in the internationalization process is direct foreign investment.

_____ **2.** Geocentric companies staff all positions with the best available talent in the world.

_____ **3.** People from high-context countries such as Switzerland and the United States rely heavily on nonverbal cues when communicating.

_____ **4.** Individuals and countries scoring high on Project GLOBE's "future orientation" prefer to work and save for the future rather than just living for the present.

_____ **5.** Hofstede found American management theories to be universally applicable around the world.

_____ **6.** In a cross-cultural study of work goals, "interpersonal relations" got a consistently high ranking.

_____ **7.** GLOBE Project researchers found the team-oriented leadership style to have wide cross-cultural applicability.

_____ **8.** The number one reason why Americans fail in foreign assignments is "lack of motivation to work in another country."

_____ **9.** "Coping with ambiguity" and "managing stress" are among the nine competencies needed for successful cross-cultural adaptation.

_____ **10.** North American women have enjoyed above-average success on foreign assignments.

Multiple-Choice Questions

1. What is the final stage of the internationalization process?
A. Direct foreign investment
B. Exporting
C. Licensing
D. Local assembly and packaging
E. A joint venture

2. Because of unresolved political, economic, and tax implications, many experts are alarmed at the prospect of immense "stateless" ______ companies.
A. joint venture B. transnational
C. global D. multinational
E. cross-border

3. Which one of these creatures *best* characterizes someone with high cultural intelligence?
A. An elephant B. A tiger
C. A chameleon D. An eagle
E. A butterfly

4. Which type of organization relies heavily on home-country personnel, ideas, and practices?
A. Polycentric B. Polychronic
C. Ethnocentric D. Geocentric
E. Monochronic

5. ______ is(are) vital to communication in high-context cultures.
A. Being on time
B. Nonverbal and situational cues
C. Being polite
D. Having family ties
E. Written contracts

6. Which of these is *not* one of the nine GLOBE Project cultural dimensions?
A. Assertiveness B. Power distance
C. Gender equality D. Historical persective
E. Institutional collectivism

7. The perception of time as flexible, elastic, and multidimensional represents ______ time.
A. polychronic B. monochronic
C. natural D. low-context
E. traditional

8. The GLOBE Project researchers found the ______ leadership style to be widely applicable across cultures.
A. charismatic/value-based B. self-protective
C. competence-based D. humane-oriented
E. participative

9. According to a recent survey, what was the number one reason why U.S. employees go home early from foreign assignments?
A. Family not adjusting to culture
B. Not performing job effectively
C. Better offer from another company
D. Safety concerns
E. Inadequate compensation

10. Which of these phrases *best* sums up the status of North American women on foreign assignments?
A. Rapidly approaching gender parity
B. Better pay equality than at home
C. Underrepresented but successful
D. Greater administrative status than at home
E. Lower satisfaction with foreign experiences than male counterparts report

ACE self-test

Want more questions? Visit the student Web site at **http://business.college.hmco.com/students/** (select Kreitner, *Management,* 10e) and take the ACE quizzes for more practice.

5 Management's Social and Ethical Responsibilities

> *"I find a universal belief in fairness, kindness, dignity, charity, integrity, honesty, quality, and patience."*[1]
>
> STEPHEN R. COVEY

OBJECTIVES

- **Define** the term *corporate social responsibility* (CSR), and **specify** the four levels in Carroll's global CSR pyramid.
- **Contrast** the classical economic and socioeconomic models of business, and **summarize** the arguments for and against CSR.
- **Identify** and **describe** the four social responsibility strategies, and **explain** the concept of enlightened self-interest.
- **Summarize** the four practical lessons from business ethics research.
- **Distinguish** between instrumental and terminal values, and **explain** their relationship to business ethics.
- **Identify** and **describe** at least four of the ten general ethical principles.
- **Discuss** what management can do to improve business ethics.

the changing workplace

Money and Morals at GE

A few weeks ago, Jeffrey R. Immelt, the chairman and chief executive office of the world's most valuable and most admired company, stood before General Electric's 200 corporate officers and said it would take four things to keep the company on top. Three of those were predictable: execution, growth, and great people. The fourth was not: virtue. And it was at the top of his list.

Virtue is not the first thing that comes to mind when people think about GE. An industrial and financial services giant that is on track to generate $150 billion in [annual] revenues. . ., GE under Jack Welch was known for hard-driving management and for delivering market-beating shareholder returns. Immelt wants GE to stand for all that, and more. To be a great company today, he likes to say, you also have to be a good company. "The reason people come to work for GE," he tells *Fortune,* " is that they want to be about something that is bigger than themselves. People want to work hard, they want to get promoted, they want stock options. But they also want to work for a company that makes a difference, a company that's doing great things in the world."

Immelt's emphasis on values is one way he is putting his own stamp on the company, and it's having an impact throughout GE. It affects how the company runs itself and treats its employees; the kinds of companies and countries it chooses to do business with; and the technologies it invests in. Immelt takes it as a given that companies have an obligation not just to make money and obey the law but also to help solve the world's problems. "Good leaders give back," he says. "The era we live in belongs to people who believe in themselves but are focused on the needs of others."

Of course, GE isn't the first big company to wrestle with questions of corporate social responsibility. In fact, it has been slow to join the debate. But when GE talks, people listen. . . .

To be sure, no one's going to confuse GE with Ben & Jerry's as long as Immelt's in charge. A 6-foot-4 bear of a man who played football at Dartmouth and routinely works

14-hour days, he is every bit as tough as the legendary Welch. GE may well aspire to be virtuous, but only when it makes business sense. The company has been slow to clean up PCBs it discharged into the Hudson River, for example, and it fought off a shareholder group that wants GE to stop operating in the rogue state of Iran.

But there's no doubt a new attitude has taken hold at GE, one that reflects new realities. Immelt became CEO on Sept. 7, 2001—four days before the terrorist attacks in New York City and Washington, shortly after the stock market bubble burst, and just as Enron's collapse began what, even today, feels like an unending parade of corporate wrongdoing.

"The world's changed," Immelt says. "Businesses today aren't admired. Size is not respected. There's a bigger gulf today between haves and have-nots than ever before. It's up to us to use our platform to be a good citizen. Because not only is it a nice thing to do, it's a business imperative."

GE has changed too. In 2002, Immelt appointed GE's first vice president for corporate citizenship. Bob Corcoran, 48, a trusted ally who worked for Immelt when he ran . . . [G.E.'s] health-care business, now holds the job. Corcoran has spread the gospel to the company's far-flung business units. Today GE audits its suppliers in the developing world to make sure they comply with labor, environmental, health, and safety standards. It has performed 3,100 audits since the program began in 2002. The company has opened up discussions with so-called socially responsible investment funds. This fall GE was admitted to the Dow Jones sustainability index, a collection of 200 best-of-class firms that meet detailed criteria for environmental, social, and financial sustainability. Although Welch got GE going on diversity, Immelt moved the ball forward. The company this year won high-profile awards for promoting women and African Americans into its executive ranks. It granted domestic-partner benefits to its gay and lesbian employees. Meanwhile, GE has set out to globalize its philanthropy, notably by launching an ambitious health-care project in rural Ghana. And next spring GE will publish its first corporate citizenship report.

"It is not a radical approach," says Noel Tichy, a former GE executive who works with GE, Procter & Gamble, and 3M through his Global Corporate Citizenship Initiative at the University of Michigan. "But Jeff has moved the needle considerably."

As an old-line manufacturer, GE tended to view environmental rules as a cost or burden. Now Immelt sees growth opportunities in cleaning up the planet. He wants GE to be known as one of the few companies with the scale and know-how to tackle the world's toughest problems. Since 2001, GE has purchased a water-purification company, a maker of solar-energy equipment, and a wind-energy business. Last month GE Energy signed an agreement with the Shanghai Power Industrial & Commercial Co. to supply wind turbines to the first two utility-scale wind-energy projects in China.

"Wind, water, lowering emissions, having an environmental service business. . . . The economics of scarcity are going to drive lots of technological innovation over the next 20, 30 years," Immelt says. "This is an approach to growing the company faster."

Source: *From Marc Gunther, "Money and Morals at GE,"* Fortune *(November 15, 2004): 176, 178, 180.*

Major changes are never easy, particularly when entrenched practices and huge capital investments are involved. Just ask Jeff Immelt, who is attempting to guide General Electric to a higher moral ground while maintaining profitability. Meanwhile, important questions remain unanswered. Are Immelt's actions simply a public relations gimmick to keep government regulators and special-interest groups at bay? Or is he wisely crafting a strategy for the long-term survival of his company? Is this sort of corporate social responsibility an expedient luxury or a nonnegotiable necessity? What is the appropriate balance between profits and the public good? This chapter will help you tackle these tough questions.

As the social, political, economic, and technological environments of management have changed, the practice of management itself has changed. This is especially true for managers in the private business sector. Today, in the wake of the Enron, Tyco, and WorldCom debacles, it is far less acceptable for someone in business to stand before the public and declare that his or her only job is to make as much profit as possible. The public is wary of the abuse of power and the betrayal of trust, and business managers—indeed, managers of all types of organizations—are expected to make a wide variety of economic and social contributions. Demands on business that would have been considered patently unreasonable 30 or 40 years ago have become the norm today. The purpose of this chapter is to examine management's broader social and ethical responsibilities.

Social Responsibility: Definition and Perspectives

When John D. Rockefeller was at the zenith of his power as the founder of Standard Oil Company, he handed out dimes to rows of eager children who lined the street. Rockefeller did this on the advice of a public relations expert who believed the dime campaign would counteract his widespread reputation as a monopolist who had ruthlessly eliminated his competitors in the oil industry. The dime campaign was not a complete success, however, because Standard Oil was broken up under the Sherman Antitrust Act of 1890.[2] Conceivably, Rockefeller believed he was fulfilling some sort of social responsibility by passing out dimes to hungry children. Since Rockefeller's time, the concept of social responsibility has grown and matured to the point where many of today's companies are intimately involved in social programs that have no direct connection with the bottom line. These programs include everything from support of the arts and urban renewal to education reform and environmental protection. But like all aspects of management, social responsibility needs to be carried out in an effective and efficient manner.

What Does Corporate Social Responsibility (CSR) Involve?

corporate social responsibility (CSR): *idea that business has social obligations above and beyond making a profit*

Social responsibility, as defined in this section, is a relatively new concern of the business community. Like a child maturing through adolescence on the way to adulthood, the idea of corporate social responsibility is evolving. One expert defined **corporate social responsibility (CSR)** as "the notion that corporations have an obligation to constituent groups in society other than stockholders and beyond that prescribed by law or union contract."[3] As might be expected for any emerging area, disagreement remains over the exact nature and scope of management's *social* responsibilities.[4]

Nancy Lockwood, a researcher for the Society for Human Resource Management, recently framed CSR this way:

> *Simply put, the business case for CSR—establishing a positive company reputation and brand in the public eye through good work that yields a competitive edge while at the same time contributing to others—demands that organizations shift from solely focusing on making a profit to including financial, environmental and social responsibility in their core business strategies. Despite what the phrase* corporate social responsibility *suggests, the concept is not restricted to corporations but rather is intended for most types of organizations, such as associations, labor unions, organizations that serve the community for scientific, educational, artistic, public health or charitable purposes, and governmental agencies.*[5]

1. **DEFINE** the term *corporate social responsibility* (CSR), and **SPECIFY** the four levels in Carroll's global CSR pyramid.

Thus, Lockwood has expanded the domain of CSR. The global economy is expanding it even more.

■ CSR for Global and Transnational Corporations. Business ethics scholar Archie B. Carroll believes the burgeoning global economy requires a more encompassing perspective on CSR. According to his model in Figure 5.1, today's global and transnational companies have four main areas of responsibility: economic, legal, ethical, and philanthropic. Working from bottom to top, this means the global corporation should

- *Make a profit* consistent with expectations for international businesses;
- *Obey the law* of host countries as well as international law;
- *Be ethical in its practices,* taking host-country and global standards into consideration;
- *Be a good corporate citizen,* especially as defined by the host country's expectations.[6]

Carroll emphasizes that this is not a pick-and-choose approach to CSR. All four responsibilities are intertwined and need to be fulfilled if a global corporation—or *any* company in any situation, for that matter—is to be called socially responsible. However, over the long term, a company must consistently satisfy the bottom three levels before exercising philanthropic responsibility. Carroll describes *philanthropic responsibilities* as "social activities that are not mandated by law nor generally expected of business in an ethical sense."[7] Of course, expectations regarding philanthropic responsibilities vary from country to country.[8] This global perspective on CSR is summed up very nicely by Tachi Kiuchi, managing director of Japan's Mitsubishi Electric Corp.:

> *People talk about businesses needing to be responsible as if it's something new we need to do on top of everything else. But the whole essence of business should be responsibility. My philosophy is, we don't run companies to earn profits. We earn profits to run companies. Our companies need meaning and purpose if they're to fit into the world, or why should they live at all?*[9]

Figure 5.1 Carroll's Global Corporate Social Responsibility Pyramid

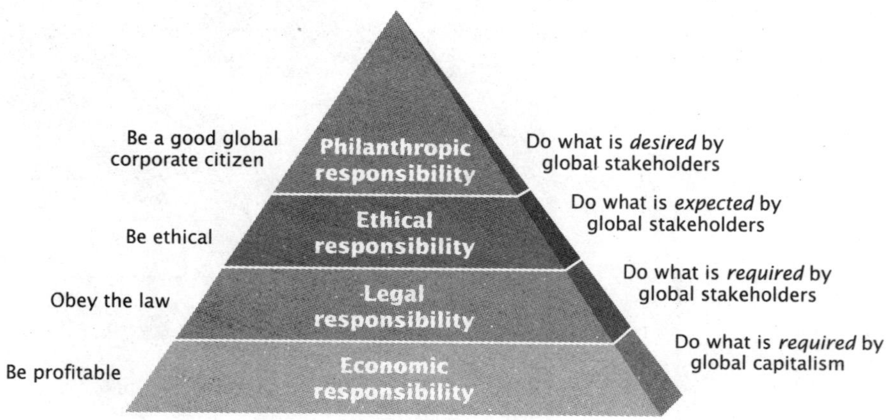

Source: Academy of Management Executive: The Thinking Manager's Source *by Archie B. Carroll. Copyright 2004 by Academy of Management. Reproduced with permission of Academy of Managment in the format Textbook via Copyright Clearance Center.*

■ **CSR Requires Voluntary Action.** An implicit feature of the above definition and perspective is that an action must be *voluntary* to qualify as socially responsible. For example, consider the actions of Paul Dolan at California's Fetzer Vineyards:

> *[He says,] "it's the way we farm. Everything is organic." Indeed, every single one of the 2,000 acres owned by Fetzer is certified organic. Dolan has sworn to convert all of his 200 outside grape growers to organic methods by the year 2010. And Fetzer is considered a "zero waste" business by the State of California. "It's just how business needs to be done," he says. . . .*
>
> *[In his new book on "sustainable business,"* True to Our Roots: Fermenting a Business Revolution*], Dolan urges all businesses to commit to the "triple bottom line," a measure of corporate success that takes into account not just profit and loss but also social and environmental impact, and he offers the story of Fetzer's own transformation as an example.*
>
> *To those who say that going organic, using alternative power sources, providing living wages for workers, and eliminating waste (all of which Fetzer does) are nice, fuzzy goals that don't make financial sense, Dolan simply points to his own success in a tough industry.*[10]

5a Back to the Opening Case

Based on what you have read so far, is General Electric a socially responsible company? Should we be asking for more from CEO Immelt and his company? Explain.

For further information about the interactive annotations in this chapter, visit our Web site (**http://business.college.hmco.com/students/** and select Kreitner, *Management*, 10e).

Fetzer Vineyards is socially responsible because Dolan has *voluntarily* taken a creative and inspiring leadership role in the winemaking business to strike a workable balance between profit and the greater good. His actions did not involve reluctant compliance with new laws or court orders, nor are his actions a cynical public relations ploy to keep regulators at bay.

Students from a local high school welcoming Senior Vice President, Chief Technology Officer and General Manager New Business and New Products Group, Mark Pinto as he arrived to open the new Digital Equalizer Center in Bangalore, India. Through collaboration with the American India Foundation (AIF), Applied Materials launched a center for local high school children in Bangalore, India, to increase student exposure to technology.

2. CONTRAST the classical economic and socioeconomic models of business, and **SUMMARIZE** the arguments for and against CSR.

What Is the Role of Business in Society?

Much of the disagreement over what social responsibility involves can be traced to a fundamental debate about the exact purpose of a business. Is a business an economic entity responsible only for making a profit for its stockholders? Or is it a socioeconomic entity obligated to make both economic and social contributions to society?[11] Depending on one's perspective, social responsibility can be interpreted either way.

The Classical Economic Model. The classical economic model can be traced to the eighteenth century, when businesses were owned largely by entrepreneurs or owner-managers. Competition was vigorous among small operations, and short-run profits were the sole concern of these early entrepreneurs. Of course, the key to attaining short-run profits was to provide society with needed goods and services. According to Adam Smith, father of the classical economic model, an "invisible hand" promoted the public welfare. Smith believed the efforts of competing entrepreneurs had a natural tendency to promote the public interest when each tried to maximize short-run profits. In other words, Smith believed the public interest was served by individuals pursuing their own economic self-interests.[12]

This model has survived into modern times. For example, *Business Week* quoted Robert J. Eaton, former chairman of Chrysler Corporation prior to the creation of DaimlerChrysler, as saying, "The idea of corporations taking on social responsibility is absolutely ridiculous. . . . You'll simply burden industry to a point where it's no longer competitive."[13] Thus, according to the classical economic model of business, short-run profitability and social responsibility are the same thing.

The Socioeconomic Model. Reflecting society's broader expectations for business (for example, safe and meaningful jobs, clean air and water, charitable donations, safe products), many think the time has come to revamp the classical economic model, which they believe to be obsolete. Enron, the company that took a spectacular tumble from number 7 on the 2001 *Fortune* 500[14] list to a scandalous bankruptcy in 2002, has been cited as a prime case in point. Economist Robert Kuttner bluntly explained:

> *The deeper scandal here is ideological. Enron epitomized an entire philosophy about the supposed self-cleansing nature of markets. . . .*
>
> *Enron, as a trading enterprise, claimed to be the quintessence of a pure free market. In practice, it was up to its ears in cronyism, influence-peddling, rigging the rules to favor insiders, and undermining the transparency on which efficient markets depend. . . .*
>
> *Enron is to the menace of market fundamentalism what September 11 was to the peril of global terror—a very costly wake-up call.*[15]

Enron's 21,000 former employees—most of whom lost their life's savings along with their jobs—would probably agree.[16] According to the socioeconomic model proposed as an alternative to the classical economic model, business is just one subsystem among many in a highly interdependent society.

Advocates of the socioeconomic model point out that many groups in society besides stockholders have a stake in corporate affairs. Creditors, current and retired employees, customers, suppliers, competitors, all levels of government, the community, and society in general have expectations, often conflicting, for management. Some companies go so far as to conduct a **stakeholder audit.**[17] This growing practice involves systematically identifying all parties that might possibly be affected by the company's performance (for an example, see Figure 5.2). According to the socioeconomic view, business has an obligation to respond to the needs of all stakeholders while pursuing a profit.[18] Debra Dunn, senior vice president of corporate affairs at Hewlett-Packard, speaks to the difficulty of this balancing act:

stakeholder audit: *identification of all parties that might be affected by the organization*

> *It begins with the way a company thinks about its role in the world. Does it simply exist to make as much money as possible? At Hewlett-Packard, the question*

we ask ourselves is this: How do we consistently address multiple stakeholders, including customers, employees, and the communities we're a part of?

Collaboration between sectors [e.g., government, business, and nonprofits] is critical, and it's also the biggest challenge we face.[19]

5b Jack Speaks

General Electric's legendary former CEO, Jack Welch, was asked how he defines 'social responsibility.' His response:

> *Win. By winning, being highly profitable. Only then can you be a socially responsible company. If you are worried about your job, you can't give anything back.*

Source: As quoted in Del Jones and David Kiley, "Welch Gives Book Launch Another Try," USA Today *(October 22, 2001): 7B.*

QUESTIONS:

How does Jack Welch's interpretation mesh with Carroll's global CSR pyramid? Explain. How does it align with the distinction between the classical economic and socioeconomic models of business? Do you agree or disagree with Welch? Explain.

■ Arguments for and Against Corporate Social Responsibility

As one might suspect, the debate about the role of business has spawned many specific arguments both for and against corporate social responsibility.[20] A sample of four major arguments on each side reveals the principal issues.

■ **Arguments For.** Convinced that a business should be more than simply a profit machine, proponents of social responsibility have offered these arguments:

1. *Business is unavoidably involved in social issues.* As social activists like to say, business is either part of the solution or part of the problem. There is no denying that private business shares responsibility for such societal problems as unemployment, inflation, and pollution. Like everyone else, corporate citizens must balance their rights and responsibilities.

Figure 5.2 A Sample Stakeholder Audit for Wal-Mart, the World's Largest Retailer

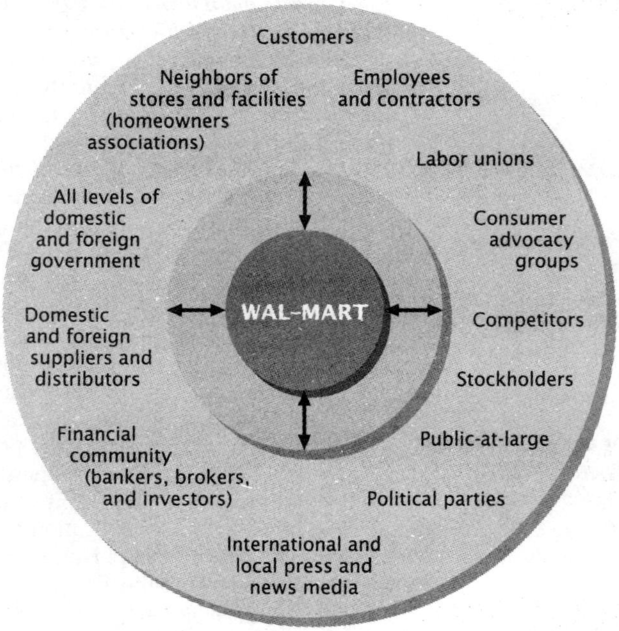

2. *Business has the resources to tackle today's complex societal problems.* With its rich stock of technical, financial, and managerial resources, the private business sector can play a decisive role in solving society's more troublesome problems. After all, without society's support, business could not have built its resource base in the first place.
3. *A better society means a better environment for doing business.* Business can enhance its long-run profitability by making an investment in society today. Today's problems can turn into tomorrow's profits.
4. *Corporate social action will prevent government intervention.* As evidenced by waves of antitrust, equal employment opportunity, and pollution-control legislation, government will force business to do what it fails to do voluntarily.

Arguments like these four give business a broad socioeconomic agenda.

■ **Arguments Against.** Remaining faithful to the classical economic model, opponents of corporate social responsibility rely on the first two arguments below. The third and fourth arguments have been voiced by those who think business is already too big and powerful.

1. *Profit maximization ensures the efficient use of society's resources.* By buying goods and services, consumers collectively dictate where assets should be deployed. Social expenditures amount to theft of stockholders' equity.
2. *As an economic institution, business lacks the ability to pursue social goals.* Gross inefficiencies can be expected if managers are forced to divert their attention from their pursuit of economic goals.
3. *Business already has enough power.* Considering that business exercises powerful influence over where and how we work and live, what we buy, and what we value, more concentration of social power in the hands of business is undesirable.
4. *Because managers are not elected, they are not directly accountable to the people.* Corporate social programs can easily become misguided. The market system effectively controls business's economic performance but is a poor mechanism for controlling business's social performance.

These arguments are based on the assumption that business should stick to what it does best—pursuing profit by producing marketable goods and services. Social goals should be handled by other institutions, such as the family, school, religious organizations, or government.

Toward Greater Social Responsibility

iron law of responsibility: *those who do not use power in a socially responsible way will eventually lose it*

Is it inevitable that management will assume greater social responsibility? Some scholars believe so. It has been said that business is bound by an **iron law of responsibility,** which states that "in the long run, those who do not use power in a way that society considers responsible will tend to lose it."[21] This is an important concept, considering that cynicism about business runs deep today, despite a more probusiness political climate worldwide. As *Training* magazine recently observed, "We are living in a time of low trust and high suspicion. 'Trusted leader' is an oxymoron."[22] The demand for business to act more responsibly is clear. If this challenge is not met voluntarily, government reform legislation is likely to force business to meet it. In this section, we look at four alternative social responsibility strategies and some contrasting expressions of corporate social responsibility.

■ Social Responsibility Strategies

Similar to management's political response continuum, discussed in Chapter 3, is its social responsibility continuum (see Figure 5.3), marked by four strategies: reaction, defense, accommodation, and proaction.[23] Each involves a distinctly different approach to demands for greater social responsibility.

Figure 5.3 A Continuum of Social Responsibility Strategies

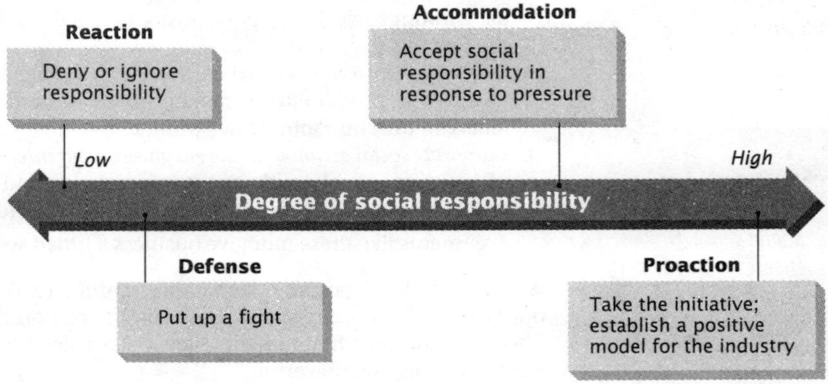

reactive social responsibility strategy: *denying responsibility and resisting change*

■ **Reaction.** A business that follows a **reactive social responsibility strategy** will deny responsibility while striving to maintain the status quo. This strategy has been a favorite one for the tobacco industry, intent on preventing any legal liability linkage between smoking and cancer. When European countries showed signs of adopting U.S.-style bans on secondhand smoke, Philip Morris launched a rather odd reactive strategy:

3. **IDENTIFY** and **DESCRIBE** the four social responsibility strategies, and **EXPLAIN** the concept of enlightened self-interest.

> *In a Western European ad campaign that backfired, Philip Morris suggested that inhaling secondhand smoke is less dangerous than eating a cookie or drinking milk. The campaign was banned from France after the National Union of Biscuit Makers and the National Committee Against Tobacco Use filed separate suits against Philip Morris.*[24]

defensive social responsibility strategy: *resisting additional responsibilities with legal and public relations tactics*

■ **Defense.** A **defensive social responsibility strategy** uses legal maneuvering and/or a public relations campaign to avoid assuming additional responsibilities. A case in point is this recent news item in *Business Week*:

> *The auto industry has decided to fight California's efforts to regulate greenhouse gas emissions. The industry's lobby group, the Alliance of Automobile Manufacturers, along with General Motors, Ford, Chrysler, and Toyota and a few others, have filed a lawsuit in federal court in Fresno, Calif. They're challenging a rule enacted by the California Air Resources Board in September [2004] that would force the industry to cut carbon dioxide emissions by about 30%, starting in 2009.*[25]

accommodative social responsibility strategy: *assuming additional responsibilities in response to pressure*

■ **Accommodation.** The organization must be pressured into assuming additional responsibilities when it follows an **accommodative social responsibility strategy.** Some outside stimulus, such as pressure from a special-interest group or threatened government action, is usually required to trigger an accommodative strategy. For example, consider this turn of events:

> *[Office supply] superstore Staples agreed to stop purchasing paper that originated in endangered forests and to increase the fraction of recycled paper in its products to 30 percent. Activists had picketed Staples stores, heckled executives at shareholder meetings, and issued critical reports and press releases in a campaign led by ForestEthics and the Dogwood Alliance.*[26]

proactive social responsibility strategy: *taking the initiative with new programs that serve as models for the industry*

■ **Proaction.** A **proactive social responsibility strategy** involves taking the initiative with a progressive program that serves as an inspiring role model for the industry. Sportswear maker Patagonia is a prime example. Founder Yvon Chouinard describes one recent initiative.

> *We did an analysis of all the different fibers that we use in making clothes and found that the most damaging was just plain old industrial cotton—dripping with pesticides. I gave the company 18 months to get out of making any product out of industrial-grown cotton—25% of our business. We had to reinvent the way we made clothing to accomplish it, but what the switchover to organically grown cotton did was mobilize the company in a direction, and it's been more profitable because it puts us in a unique position. The Gap is coming here this week to learn how they can get more into organic cotton; we've influenced Nike, Levi's, and a bunch of companies to begin switching because we worked to make the stuff available. Now we're in the forefront of a new way of making clothes.*[27]

Proponents of corporate social responsibility[28] would like to see proactive strategies become management's preferred response in both good times and bad.[29]

5c The *Perfect* Hamburger?

Two hormone-free, grass-fed beef patties. Special low-cal, nonfat sauce. Organic red-leaf lettuce. Reduced-fat cheese. Low-sodium pickles. Vidalia onions. On a low-carb, multigrain bun.

Source: Matthew Boyle, "Can You Really Make Fast Food Healthy?" Fortune *(August 9, 2004): 134.*

QUESTIONS:
Would you even try this hamburger? What does this tongue-in-cheek product specification say about the risk of a company taking proactive social responsibility too far?

■ Who Benefits from Corporate Social Responsibility?

altruism: *unselfish devotion to the interests of others*

Is it accurate to say of social responsibility what used to be said about home medicine, "It has to taste bad to be good"? In other words, does social responsibility have to be a hardship for the organization? Those who answer *yes* believe that social responsibility should be motivated by **altruism,** an unselfish devotion to the interests of others.[30] This implies that businesses that are not socially responsible are motivated strictly by self-interest. In short-run economic terms, the tobacco industry's foot dragging has saved it billions of dollars. In contrast, 3M's decision to pull its popular Scotchgard fabric protector spray cans from the marketplace as soon as the company became aware of a possible health hazard cost the company an estimated $500 million in annual sales.[31] On the basis of this evidence alone, one would be hard pressed to say that social responsibility pays. But research paints a brighter picture.

- A study of 243 companies for two years found a positive correlation between industry leadership in environmental protection/pollution control and profitability. The researchers concluded, "It pays to be green."[32]
- A second study found a good reputation for corporate social responsibility to be a competitive advantage in recruiting talented people.[33]

enlightened self-interest: *a business ultimately helping itself by helping to solve societal problems*

corporate philanthropy: *charitable donation of company resources*

■ **Enlightened Self-Interest. Enlightened self-interest,** the realization that busi-ness ultimately helps itself by helping to solve societal problems, involves balancing short-run costs and long-run benefits. Advocates of enlightened self-interest contend that social responsibility expenditures are motivated by profit. Research into **corporate philanthropy,** the charitable donation of company resources ($12 billion in the United States in 2002),[34] supports this contention.

After analyzing Internal Revenue Service statistics for firms in 36 industries, researchers concluded that corporate giving is a form of *profit-motivated advertising.* They went on to observe that "it would seem ill-advised to use philanthropy data to

Is this an act of enlightened self-interest on behalf of BMW and its co-sponsors, or simply a tricky form of advertising? Whatever your opinion, the effort is certainly appreciated by those striving to cure breast cancer.

measure altruistic responses of corporations."[35] This profit-motivated advertising thesis was further supported by a study of 130 large manufacturing firms in the United States. Companies that had committed significant crimes but donated a good deal of money had better responsibility ratings than companies that had committed no crimes but donated very little money.[36]

As U.S. companies earn increasingly more from foreign operations (22 percent in 2004), their philanthropy has gone global. Here are some recent examples of global enlightened self-interest in action:

> *Intel Corp. now has computer clubhouses providing Internet access and technology training to children in 32 countries, including South Africa, India, and, in the West Bank, the Ramallah Clubhouse. Avon Products Inc. provides breast cancer programs in 50 countries, sponsoring research, donating medical gear, and subsidizing mammograms. This year, General Electric Co. pledged $20 million to construct 11 hospitals in Ghana. Total corporate giving abroad rose 13.82% from 2002 to 2003, according to the Conference Board's annual report on corporate contributions. International programs now account for 16% of U.S. corporate giving.*[37]

What benefits are these companies likely to reap from their global philanthropy?

■ **An Array of Benefits for the Organization.** In addition to the advertising effect, other possible long-run benefits for socially responsible organizations include the following:

5d Back to the Opening Case

What role, if any, does enlightened self-interest play in the GE case? Explain.

- Tax-free incentives to employees (such as buying orchestra tickets and giving them to deserving employees).
- Retention of talented employees by satisfying their altruistic motives.
- Help in recruiting talented and socially conscious personnel.
- Swaying public opinion against government intervention.
- Improved community living standards for employees.
- Attracting socially conscious investors.
- A nontaxable benefit for employees in which company funds are donated to their favorite causes. Many companies match employees' contributions to their college alma maters, for example.

Social responsibility can be a win-win proposition; both society and the socially responsible organization can benefit in the long run. Meanwhile, in today's age of increased corporate accountability, efforts are underway to weigh the benefits of philanthropy. According to one consultant, "Giving is an investment and it should be every bit as strategic as, say, marketing or a new business development."[38]

The Ethical Dimension of Management

Highly publicized accounts of corporate misconduct in recent years have led to widespread cynicism about business ethics. Here is just a small sampling of corporate misdeeds from the period 2003–2004:

- Twelve investment banks agreed to pay $1.4 billion to settle conflict-of-interest charges brought by New York State Attorney General Eliot Spitzer.
- The U.S. Securities and Exchange Commission (SEC) fined WorldCom a record $750 million for accounting fraud.
- A federal jury convicted Tyson Foods of market manipulation and ordered it to pay cattle producers $1.3 billion.
- Pharmaceutical giant Bristol-Myers Squibb was fined $150 million by the SEC for accounting fraud.
- Three mutual fund companies (Putnam, Janus, and Strong) were collectively fined $295 million by the SEC for illegal trading; Strong's CEO, Richard Strong, was barred from the industry for life.
- Chipmaker Infineon Technologies was fined $160 million for price fixing.[39]

Subsequent public disgust has surfaced in opinion pools: "In Harris Interactive's 2004 Annual Corporation Reputation Survey, 74% say corporate America's reputation is 'not good' or 'terrible.'"[40] Managers seem to be getting the message. A recent survey of 1,600 executives found 57 percent paying more attention to manager and supervisor ethics.[41] Indeed, the subject of ethics certainly deserves serious attention in management circles these days.[42]

ethics: *study of moral obligation involving right versus wrong*

Ethics is the study of moral obligation involving the distinction between right and wrong.[43] *Business ethics*, sometimes referred to as management ethics or organizational ethics, narrows the frame of reference to productive organizations.[44] However, as a pair of ethics experts noted, business ethics is not a simple matter:

> *Just being a good person and, in your own way, having sound personal ethics may not be sufficient to handle the ethical issues that arise in a business organization. Many people who have limited business experience suddenly find themselves making decisions about product quality, advertising, pricing, hiring practices, and pollution control. The values they learned from family, church, and school may not provide specific guidelines for these complex business decisions. For example, is a particular advertisement deceptive? Should a gift to a customer be considered a bribe, or is it a special promotional incentive?... Many business ethics decisions are close calls. Years of experience in a particular industry may be required to know what is acceptable.*[45]

With this realistic context in mind, we turn to a discussion of business ethics research, personal values, ethical principles, and steps that management can take to foster ethical business behavior.

5e We're Not Impressed!

[A] survey of 933 graduate students and 807 MBA graduates of top business schools found that 66.9 percent of the female students and 56.9 percent of the males feel U.S. companies are not run honestly or ethically.

Source: Excerpted from Diane E. Lewis, "Business School Graduates Find Ethics Lacking," Arizona Republic *(October 24, 2004): D7.*

QUESTIONS:
What is your general opinion about the present state of business ethics? Explain. What needs to be done to improve business ethics? What can *you* do to improve the situation?

Practical Lessons from Business Ethics Research

Empirical research is always welcome in a socially relevant and important area such as business ethics.[46] It permits us to go beyond mere intuition and speculation to determine more precisely who, what, and why. On-the-job research of business ethics among managers has yielded practical insights in four areas: (1) ethical hot spots, (2) pressure from above, (3) discomfort with ambiguity, and (4) the rationalization of unethical conduct.

4. SUMMARIZE the four practical lessons from business ethics research.

■ Ethical Hot Spots. In a survey of 1,324 U.S. employees from all levels across several industries, 48 percent admitted to having performed (during the prior year) at least one illegal or unethical act from a list of 25 questionable practices. The list included everything from calling in sick when feeling well to cheating on expense accounts, forging signatures, and giving or accepting kickbacks, to ignoring violations of environmental laws. Also uncovered in the study were the top ten workplace hot spots responsible for triggering unethical and illegal conduct:

- Balancing work and family
- Poor internal communications
- Poor leadership
- Work hours, workload
- Lack of management support
- Need to meet sales, budget, or profit goals
- Little or no recognition of achievements
- Company politics
- Personal financial worries
- Insufficient resources[47]

■ Pressure from Above. A number of studies have uncovered the problem of perceived pressure to achieve results. As discussed later in Chapter 14, pressure from superiors can lead to unhealthful conformity. How widespread is the problem? Very widespread, according to the ethical hot spots survey just discussed:

- Most workers feel some pressure to act unethically or illegally on the job (56 percent), but far fewer (17 percent) feel a high level of pressure to do so. . . .
- Mid-level managers most often reported a high level of pressure to act unethically or illegally (20 percent). Employees of large companies cited such pressure more than those at small businesses (21 percent versus 14 percent).
- High levels of pressure were reported more often by those with a high school diploma or less (21 percent) versus college graduates (13 percent).[48]

By being aware of this problem of pressure from above, managers can (1) consciously avoid putting undue pressure on others and (2) prepare to deal with excessive organizational pressure.

An instructive case in point is Walt Pavlo, a former MCI employee who spent 18 months in prison for his part in a fraudulent scheme:

> *Working as a collection manager for high-risk accounts, Pavlo discovered that MCI executives, who were loading up on stock options, didn't want anything to happen that would cause the stock price to drop. So, Pavlo says, when he brought them bad news, they didn't want to hear it; Pavlo says he felt he was being told to fudge the numbers, which he did. . . .*
>
> *"I was under a lot of pressure," Pavlo recalls. "Thinking about doing something wrong, but wanting to be accepted by my bosses, a team member, part of the inner circle."*[49]

Excessive pressure to achieve results is a serious problem because it can cause otherwise good and decent people to take ethical shortcuts just to keep their jobs. The challenge for managers is to know where to draw the line between creating motivation to excel and exerting undue pressure.[50]

■ Ambiguous Situations. In a recent survey of 111 executives (27 percent female) from a diverse array of large companies, 78 percent said the existence of "ambiguous rules" was a common rationale for "bending the rules."[51] Surveys of purchasing managers and field sales personnel showed that respondents were uncomfortable with ambiguous situations in which there were no clear-cut ethical guidelines. As one research team noted, "A striking aspect of the responses to the questionnaire is the degree to which the purchasing managers desire a stated pol-

"THE DOG ATE OUR QUARTERLY STATEMENT? I LIKE IT."

Source: *John Caldwell*/Harvard Business Review.

icy."[52] In other words, those who often face ethically ambiguous situations want formal guidelines to help sort things out. Ethical codes, discussed later, can satisfy this need for guidelines.

■ **Rationalization: How Good People End Up Doing Bad Things** Rationalization is a fundamental part of everyday life. "They say chocolate is good for you. I think I'll have another big piece of that delicious chocolate cake." "Of course I cheat a little on my expense report, doesn't everybody? Besides, the company owes me." Such rationalizations involve perceiving an objectively questionable action as normal and acceptable. Rationalization may occur before and/or after the fact. A team of management researchers recently reviewed the behavioral science literature and came up with a list of six rationalization strategies that employees commonly use to justify misdeeds in the workplace (see Table 5.1). Those misdeeds can range from slightly wrong (e.g., exaggerating your knowledge of a software program to your coworkers) to absolutely criminal (e.g., accepting a bribe from a vendor). Both managers and nonmanagers need to be aware of these common rationalizations and not overuse them. New employees are particularly vulnerable to socialization tactics and influences infected with unhealthful rationalizations. The researchers' conclusion:

> *The pressure and temptations to cut ethical corners and to continue questionable practices instigated by others are strong indeed. And given the ambiguity, complexity, and dynamism that pervade contemporary environments, there is often*

Table 5.1 How Employees Tend to Rationalize Unethical Conduct

Strategy	Description	Examples
Denial of responsibility	The actors engaged in corrupt behaviors perceive that they have no other choice than to participate in such activities.	"What can I do? My arm is being twisted." "It is none of my business what the corporation does in overseas bribery."
Denial of injury	The actors are convinced that no one is harmed by their actions; hence the actions are not really corrupt.	"No one was really harmed." "It could have been worse."
Denial of victim	The actors counter any blame for their actions by arguing that the violated party deserved whatever happened.	"They deserved it." "They chose to participate."
Social weighting	The actors assume two practices that moderate the salience of corrupt behaviors: 1. Condemn the condemner, 2. Selective social comparison.	"You have no right to criticize us." "Others are worse than we are."
Appeal to higher loyalties	The actors argue that their violation of norms is due to their attempt to realize a higher-order value.	"We answered to a more important cause." "I would not report it because of my loyalty to my boss."
Metaphor of the ledger	The actors rationalize that they are entitled to indulge in deviant behaviors because of their accrued credits (time and effort) in their jobs.	"We've earned the right." "It's all right for me to use the Internet for personal reasons at work. After all, I do work overtime."

Source: Academy of Management Executive: The Thinking Manager's Source *by Vikas Anand, Blake Ashforth, Mahendra Jo. Copyright 2004 by Academy of Management. Reproduced with permission of Academy of Management in the format Textbook via Copyright Clearance Center.*

ample room to rationalize such transgressions as unavoidable, commonplace, and even laudable. In this context, organizations need to be especially conscious in guarding against the onset of such tactics within the organization. Employee education and the establishment of independent ethics ombudspersons could go a long way toward protecting against the onset of rationalization/socialization tactics.[53]

■ **A Call to Action.** Corporate misconduct and the foregoing research findings underscore the importance of the following call to action. It comes from Bill George, the highly respected former CEO of Medtronic, manufacturer of heart pacemakers and other medical devices: "Each of us needs to determine . . . where our ethical boundaries are and, if asked to violate (them), refuse. . . . If it means refusing a direct order, we must be prepared to resign."[54] George's call is *personal.* It requires *courage.*[55] His words suggest that each of us can begin the process of improving business ethics by looking in a mirror.[56]

5f Where Do You Draw the Line?

Kevin Gibson, philosophy professor, Marquette University:

Morality is not a question of counting heads, and opinion polls do not reflect moral correctness. The fact that most people in a company feel that mocking obese coworkers is morally acceptable will not make it morally correct.

Source: Kevin Gibson, "Excuses, Excuses: Moral Slippage in the Workplace," Business Horizons, *43 (November-December 2000): 67.*

QUESTIONS:

What instances of the majority being morally wrong have you observed lately? Do you have the courage to act on your convictions, or do you pretty much just go along with the crowd to avoid being seen as a troublemaker? Explain.

■ Personal Values as Ethical Anchors

Values are too often ignored in discussions of management.[57] This oversight is serious because personal values can play a pivotal role in managerial decision making and ethics. Take J.M. Smucker Co., for example:

> *Timothy P. and Richard K. Smucker, the brothers who serve as co–chief executives of J.M. Smucker Co., are unabashedly old-fashioned. The deeply religious pair refuse to advertise their jams, jellies, peanut butter, and cooking oil on some of television's biggest hits because they deem the content offensive.*[58]

Contemporary social observers complain that many managers lack character and have turned their backs on ethical values such as honesty. MIT management scholar Michael Schrage has observed:

> *If there's a single issue that frightens me about the workplace future, it's the rising willingness of people to blame institutional imperatives for betraying their own values. . . . There's no shortage of talent and intelligence; character may be the scarcer and more valuable commodity. That's the one to watch.*[59]

values: *abstract ideals that shape one's thinking and behavior*

Defined broadly, **values** are abstract ideals that shape an individual's thinking and behavior.[60] Let us explore two different types of values that act as anchors for our ethical beliefs and conduct.

instrumental value: *enduring belief in a certain way of behaving*

terminal value: *enduring belief in the attainment of a certain end-state*

5. DISTINGUISH between instrumental and terminal values, and **EXPLAIN** their relationship to business ethics.

■ Instrumental and Terminal Values. Each manager, indeed each person, values various means and ends in life. Recognizing this means-ends distinction, behavioral scientists have identified two basic types of values. An **instrumental value** is an enduring belief that a certain way of behaving is appropriate in all situations. For example, the time-honored saying "Honesty is the best policy" represents an instrumental value. A person who truly values honesty will probably behave in an honest manner under all circumstances. A **terminal value,** in contrast, is an enduring belief that a certain end-state of existence is worth striving for and attaining.[61] Whereas one person may strive for eternal salvation, another may strive for social recognition and admiration. Instrumental values (modes of behavior) help people achieve terminal values (desired end-states).

Because a person can hold a number of different instrumental and terminal values in various combinations, individual value systems are somewhat like fingerprints: each of us has a unique set. No wonder managers who face the same ethical dilemma often differ in their interpretations and responses.

■ Identifying Your Own Values. To help you discover your own set of values, refer to the Rokeach value survey in the Hands-On Exercise at the end of this chapter. Take a few moments now to complete this survey. (As a reality check on the "fit" between your intentions and your actual behavior, have a close friend, relative, or spouse evaluate you later with the Rokeach survey.)

If your results surprise you, it is probably because we tend to take our basic values for granted. We seldom stop to arrange them consciously according to priority. For the sake of comparison, compare your top five instrumental and terminal values with the value profiles uncovered in a survey of 220 eastern U.S. managers. On average, those managers ranked their instrumental values as follows: (1) honest, (2) responsible, (3) capable, (4) ambitious, and (5) independent. The most common terminal value rankings were (1) self-respect, (2) family security, (3) freedom,

(4) a sense of accomplishment, and (5) happiness.[62] These managerial value profiles are offered for purposes of comparison only; they are not necessarily an index of desirable or undesirable priorities. When addressing specific ethical issues, managers need to consider each individual's personal values.

■ General Ethical Principles

6. IDENTIFY and DESCRIBE at least four of the ten general ethical principles.

Like your highly personalized value system, your ethical beliefs have been shaped by many factors, including family and friends, the media, culture, schooling, religious instruction, and general life experiences.[63] This section brings taken-for-granted ethical beliefs, generally unstated, out into the open for discussion and greater understanding. It does so by exploring ten general ethical principles. Even though we may not necessarily know how ethics scholars label them, we use ethical principles both consciously and unconsciously when dealing with ethical dilemmas.[64] Each of the ten ethical principles is followed by a brief behavioral guideline.

1. *Self-interests.* "Never take any action that is not in the *long-term* self-interests of yourself and/or of the organization to which you belong."
2. *Personal virtues.* "Never take any action that is not honest, open, and truthful and that you would not be proud to see reported widely in national newspapers and on television."
3. *Religious injunctions.* "Never take any action that is not kind and that does not build a sense of community, a sense of all of us working together for a commonly accepted goal."
4. *Government requirements.* "Never take any action that violates the law, for the law represents the minimal moral standards of our society."
5. *Utilitarian benefits.* "Never take any action that does not result in greater good than harm for the society of which you are a part."

Representatives of an NGO raising awareness of HIV/AIDS amongst Indian women construction workers. Their projects range from implementing vital HIV/AIDS eradication programmes and pro-poor initiatives to studies for institutional strengthening, sector reform and impact evaluation.

5g Does God Belong in the Workplace?

Gregory F. A. Pearce, author of the book *Spirituality@Work*:

Why would we want to look for God in our work... ? The simple answer is most of us spend so much time working, it would be a shame if we couldn't find God there. A more complex answer is that there is a creative energy in work that is somehow tied to God's creative energy. If we can understand that connection, perhaps we can use it to transform the workplace into something remarkable.

Source: As quoted in Marc Gunther, "God & Business," Fortune *(July 9, 2001), 61.*

QUESTIONS:

Is it time to change the traditional practice of keeping spirituality out of the workplace? Explain. What implications does your answer have for business ethics?

6. *Universal rules.* "Never take any action that you would not be willing to see others, faced with the same or a closely similar situation, also be free to take."
7. *Individual rights.* "Never take any action that abridges the agreed-upon and accepted rights of others."
8. *Economic efficiency.* "Always act to maximize profits subject to legal and market constraints, for maximum profits are the sign of the most efficient production."
9. *Distributive justice.* "Never take any action in which the least [fortunate people] among us are harmed in some way."
10. *Contributive liberty.* "Never take any action that will interfere with the right of all of us for self-development and self-fulfillment."[65]

Source: *Excerpted from Hosmer, Moral Leadership in Business, pp. 39–41, © 1994, McGraw-Hill. Reproduced with permission of The McGraw-Hill Companies.*

Which of these ethical principles appeals most to you in terms of serving as a guide for making important decisions? Why? The best way to test your ethical standards and principles is to consider a *specific* ethical question and see which of these ten principles is most likely to guide your *behavior*. Sometimes, in complex situations, a combination of principles would be applicable.

Encouraging Ethical Conduct

7. DISCUSS what management can do to improve business ethics.

Simply telling managers and other employees to be good will not work. Both research evidence and practical experience tell us that words must be supported by action. Four specific ways to encourage ethical conduct within the organization are ethics training, ethical advocates, ethics codes, and whistle-blowing. Each can make an important contribution to an integrated ethics program.

Ethics Training

amoral managers: *managers who are neither moral nor immoral, but ethically lazy*

Managers lacking ethical awareness have been labeled *amoral* by CSR and ethics researcher Archie B. Carroll. **Amoral managers** are neither moral nor immoral, but indifferent to the ethical implications of their actions. Carroll contends that managers in this category far outnumber moral or immoral managers.[66] If his contention is correct, there is a great need for ethics training and education, a need that too often is not adequately met. Consider these recent research findings:

- According to a survey of human resource executives, only 27 percent of large U.S. companies provide ethics training for corporate directors.[67]
- Only 28 percent of a sample of 1,001 employees in the U.S. had received any ethics training during the prior year.[68]
- An analysis of the core curricula at 50 leading U.S. business schools "found only 40% require an ethics or social responsibility course."[69]

These are surprising and disappointing statistics, in view of the tidal wave of corporate misconduct in recent years (see the accompanying Management Ethics feature for an inspiring exception).

Some say ethics training is a waste of time because ethical lessons are easily shoved aside in the heat of competition.[70] For example, Dow Corning's model ethics program included ethics training but did not keep the company from getting

MANAGEMENT ETHICS

MBAs Majoring in Morality

As the stereotype goes, business students are single-minded in their career goals: Make money, more money, and still more money.

Don't tell that to Daron Horwitz. He spent spring break in Iraq, where he visited schools that will be helped by a non-profit group he and other students formed at Northwestern University's Kellogg School of Management.

Experts say they're part of a new breed of MBA students, influenced by everything from corporate scandal to the dot-com bust to concerns about the effects of globalization on everyday people.

They also note that the curriculum at business schools across the country has been changing in recent years, placing more emphasis on ethics, non-profit work and "corporate social responsibility."

"Our data suggests that the students are more interested in thinking about the role of business in society . . . and, as a generation, are saying, 'We want to do a better job,'" said Nancy McGraw, deputy director of the New York-based Aspen Institute Business and Society Program.

Every two years since the late 1990s, her organization, which has been tracking the trend, and another organization, the Word Resources Institute, have surveyed business schools and students worldwide for a report titled "Beyond Grey Pinstripes."

She said the most marked growth in MBA programs emphasizing "social and environmental stewardship" came between the 2001 survey and the most recent, completed last year.

For Horwitz, the Northwestern student, the inspiration to start a non-profit organization came a year ago, after the fall of Baghdad.

"I was watching this historic moment on TV and wanting to make some sort of contribution," said the 29-year-old, who also earned a law degree at Northwestern.

Soon after, he was approaching his peers to help him form an organization, which they christened Americans Supporting Iraqi Students.

They've done all the work to organize the non-profit in their free time, including securing a large corporate sponsor, not yet identified publicly.

"Whichever side of the war you're on—whether for or against—it's an easy rallying cry," said Yaser Moustafa, a 28-year-old MBA student whose duties have included raising funds for the organization in Arab-American communities.

The money they raise goes directly to a relief organization called Mercy Corps, which is helping students and schools amid the turmoil in Iraq.

Source: Martha Irvine, "MBAs Majoring in Morality," Arizona Republic *(April 18, 2004): D7. Reprinted by permission of Reprint Management Services.*

embroiled in costly charges of selling leaky breast implants.[71] Ethics training is often halfhearted and intended only as window dressing.[72] Hard evidence that ethics training actually improves behavior is lacking. Nonetheless, carefully designed and administered ethics training courses can make a positive contribution. Key features of effective ethics training programs include the following:

- Top-management support
- Open discussion of realistic ethics cases or scenarios
- A clear focus on ethical issues specific to the organization
- Integration of ethics themes into all training
- A mechanism for anonymously reporting ethical violations (Companies have had good luck with e-mail and telephone hot lines.)
- An organizational climate that rewards ethical conduct[73]

■ Ethical Advocates

ethical advocate: *ethics specialist who plays a role in top-management decision making*

An **ethical advocate** is a business ethics specialist who is a full-fledged member of the board of directors and acts as the board's social conscience.[74] This person may also be asked to sit in on top-management decision deliberations. The idea is to assign someone the specific role of critical questioner (see Table 5.2 for

Table 5.2 Twelve Questions for Examining the Ethics of a Business Decision

1. Have you defined the problem accurately?
2. How would you define the problem if you stood on the other side of the fence?
3. How did this situation occur in the first place?
4. To whom and to what do you give your loyalty as a person and as a member of the corporation?
5. What is your intention in making this decision?
6. How does this intention compare with the probable results?
7. Whom could your decision or action injure?
8. Can you discuss the problem with the affected parties before you make your decision?
9. Are you confident that your position will be as valid over a long period of time as it seems now?
10. Could you disclose without qualm your decision or action to your boss, your CEO, the board of directors, your family, society as a whole?
11. What is the symbolic potential of your action if understood? If misunderstood?
12. Under what conditions would you allow exceptions to your stand?

Source: *Reprinted by permission of the* Harvard Business Review. *Exhibit from "Ethics Without the Sermon," by Laura L. Nash (November-December 1981). Copyright © 1981 by the President and Fellows of Harvard College; all rights reserved.*

recommended questions). Problems with groupthink and blind conformity, discussed in Chapter 14, are less likely to arise when an ethical advocate tests management's thinking about ethical implications during the decision-making process.

■ Codes of Ethics

An organizational code of ethics is a published statement of moral expectations for employee conduct. Some codes specify penalties for offenders. As in the case of ethics training, growth in the adoption of company codes of ethics has stalled in recent years.

Recent experience has shown codes of ethics to be a step in the right direction, but not a cure-all.[75] To encourage ethical conduct, formal codes of ethics for organization members must satisfy two requirements. First, they should refer to specific practices, such as kickbacks, payoffs, receiving gifts, record falsification, and misleading claims about products. For example, Xerox Corporation's 15-page ethics code says, "We're honest with our customers. No deals, no bribes, no secrets, no fooling around with prices. A kickback in any form kicks anybody out. Anybody."[76] General platitudes about good business practice or professional conduct are ineffective—they do not provide specific guidance, and they offer too many tempting loopholes.

The second requirement for an organizational code of ethics is that it be firmly supported by top management and equitably enforced through the reward-and-punishment system. Selective or uneven enforcement is the quickest way to undermine the effectiveness of an ethics code. The effective development of ethics codes and monitoring of compliance are more important than ever in today's complex legal environment.[77]

Whistle-Blowing

Detailed ethics codes help managers deal swiftly and effectively with employee misconduct. But what should a manager do when a superior or an entire organization is engaged in misconduct? Yielding to the realities of organizational politics, many managers simply turn their backs or claim they were "just following orders." (Nazi war criminals who based their defense at the Nuremberg trials on the argument that they were following orders ended up with ropes around their necks.) Managers with leadership and/or political skills may attempt to work within the organizational system for positive change.[78] Still others will take the boldest step of all, whistle-blowing. **Whistle-blowing** is the practice of reporting perceived unethical practices to outsiders such as the news media, government agencies, or public-interest groups. Several whistle-blowers made headlines in recent years. Sherron Watkins foresaw Enron's financial collapse, and FBI agent Coleen Rowley went public with allegations of a mishandled terrorist lead. Noreen Harrington blew the whistle on illegal trading at Canary Capital Partners, resulting in a scandal that rocked the entire mutual fund industry. Military policeman Joseph Darby blew the whistle on the abuse of Iraqi prisoners by his fellow U.S. soldiers.[79]

whistle-blowing: *reporting perceived unethical organizational practices to outside authorities*

Not surprisingly, whistle-blowing is a highly controversial topic among managers, many of whom believe that whistle-blowing erodes their authority and decision-making prerogatives. Because loyalty to the organization is still a cherished value in some quarters, whistle-blowing is criticized as the epitome of disloyalty. Consumer advocate Ralph Nader disagrees: "The willingness and ability of insiders to blow the whistle is the last line of defense ordinary citizens have against the denial

No doubt, it took ethical courage for CPA Sherron Smith Watkins to confront Enron's leadership with her concerns about accounting irregularities and questionable financial deals. She even passed her concerns along to the firm's auditor, Arthur Andersen, to little avail. Unfortunately, Enron soon unraveled and took Andersen with it. Although rightly praised in the popular media for being an honest "whistle-blower," Watkins technically wasn't a whistle-blower, as the term is defined in this chapter. Whistle-blowers report corporate misdeeds to outsiders such as the media and government watchdog agencies.

5h An Uphill Battle?

Stephen Covey, former professor and best-selling author:

I'm convinced that 90% of failures in life are character failures, not ability failures.

After studying the ethical principles and ethical behavior of 674 business students at a U.S. university, a pair of researchers drew this rather somber conclusion:

While ethical behavior can be taught to our business students in the classroom, their resolve will be challenged on the job. Faced with pressure from above, platitudinous ethical codes, spotty enforcement, and no discernible link to the reward system, many will revert to expedience.

News item:

When San Diego State University instructor Brian Cornforth received an anonymous tip in March that students were cheating in his undergraduate business-ethics course, he decided to make a case study of his own class. The tipster said students in one class had obtained answer keys for the multiple-choice quizzes from earlier test-takers, so Cornforth scrambled the questions for the later class. "I was horrified," Cornforth says: 25 of 75 students simply cribbed the pirated test key, even though many answers were clearly nonsense. Punishment came swiftly. He flunked all 25, and several management majors won't graduate until they retake the required course. "Students really want that piece of paper and apparently they are willing to do anything to get it," says Julie Logan, the school's judicial officer.

Source: As quoted in "This Week's Question," USA Today *(February 6, 2004): 4B; Larry R. Watts and Joseph G. Ormsby, "Ethical Frameworks and Ethical Behavior: A Survey of Business Students,"* International Journal of Value-Based Management, *73, no. 3 (1994): 233; and Jamie Reno, "Need Someone in Creative Accounting?"* Newsweek *(May 17, 1999): 51.*

QUESTIONS:

Is it a waste of time to teach business ethics to college students? Explain. How can colleges and universities do a better job of improving business ethics? What does the business community need to do to improve ethics in the workplace?

of their rights and the destruction of their interests by secretive and powerful institutions."[80] Still, critics worry that whistle-blowers may be motivated by revenge.

Whistle-blowing generally means putting one's job and/or career on the line, even though the federal government and many states have passed whistle-blower protection acts.[81] A few whistle-blowers strike gold, such as the former Warner-Lambert employee who was awarded $26.6 million,[82] but most do not. After reviewing a wide variety of whistle-blower cases, *USA Today* reached the following conclusion:

> *Whistle-blowers might be heroes to people tired of the scandals that have swept Corporate America, but they often find themselves near-penniless, their home lives and emotional well-being in shambles, and followed by private investigators.*
>
> *Whistle-blowers persist because that's the way they are—a breed apart, driven by a desire to expose dirty executives, protect consumers or avenge wrongs they feel have been done to them.*[83]

The challenge for today's management is to create an organizational climate in which the need to blow the whistle is reduced or, ideally, eliminated. Constructive steps include the following:

- Encourage the free expression of controversial and dissenting viewpoints.
- Streamline the organization's grievance procedure so that those who point out problems receive a prompt and fair hearing.
- Find out what employees think about the organization's social responsibility policies and make appropriate changes.
- Let employees know that management respects and is sensitive to their individual consciences.
- Recognize that the harsh treatment of a whistle-blower will probably lead to adverse public opinion.[84]

In the final analysis, individual behavior makes organizations ethical or unethical. Organizational forces can help bring out the best in people by clearly identifying and rewarding ethical conduct.

SUMMARY

1. Corporate social responsibility is the idea that management has broader responsibilities than just making a profit. A strict interpretation holds that an action must be voluntary to qualify as socially responsible. Accordingly, reluctant submission to court orders or government coercion is not an example of social responsibility. Carroll's global corporate social responsibility pyramid encompasses, from bottom to top, four responsibilities: economic, legal, ethical, and philanthropic.
2. The debate over the basic purpose of the corporation is long-standing. Those who embrace the classical economic model contend that business's social responsibility is to maximize profits for stockholders. Proponents of the socioeconomic model disagree, saying that business has a responsibility, above and beyond making a profit, to improve the general quality of life. The arguments *for* corporate responsibility say businesses are members of society with the resources and motivation to improve society and avoid government regulation. Those arguing *against* call for profit maximization because businesses are primarily economic institutions run by unelected officials who have enough power already.
3. Management scholars who advocate greater corporate social responsibility cite the iron law of responsibility. This law states that if business does not use its socioeconomic power responsibly, society will take away that power. A continuum of social responsibility includes four strategies: reaction, defense, accommodation, and proaction. The reaction strategy involves *denying* social responsibility, whereas the defense strategy involves actively *fighting* additional responsibility with political and public relations tactics. Accommodation occurs when a company must be *pressured into* assuming additional social responsibilities. Proaction occurs when a business *takes the initiative* and becomes a positive model for its industry. In the short run, proactive social responsibility usually costs the firm money. But according to the notion of enlightened self-interest, both society and the company will gain in the long run. Research indicates that corporate philanthropy actually is a profit-motivated form of advertising.
4. Business ethics research has taught these four practical lessons: (1) 48 percent of surveyed workers reported engaging in illegal or unethical practices; (2) perceived pressure from above can erode ethics; (3) employees desire clear ethical standards in ambiguous situations, and (4) rationalization sometimes enables good people to do bad things. The call for better business ethics is clearly a *personal* challenge.
5. Managers cannot afford to overlook each employee's personal value system; values serve as anchors for one's beliefs and conduct. Instrumental values are related to desired behavior, whereas terminal values involve desired end-states. Values provide an anchor for one's ethical beliefs and conduct.
6. The ten general ethical principles that consciously and unconsciously guide behavior when ethical questions arise are self-interests, personal virtues, religious injunctions, government requirements, utilitarian benefits, universal rules, individual rights, economic efficiency, distributive justice, and contributive liberty.
7. The typical manager is said to be *amoral*—neither moral nor immoral—just ethically lazy or indifferent. Management can encourage ethical behavior in the following four ways: conduct ethics training; use ethical advocates in high-level decision making; formulate, disseminate, and consistently enforce specific codes of ethics; and create an open climate for dissent in which whistle-blowing becomes unnecessary.

TERMS TO UNDERSTAND

- Corporate Social Responsibility (CSR), p. 124
- Stakeholder audit, p. 127
- Iron law of responsibility, p. 129
- Reactive social responsibility strategy, p. 130
- Defensive social responsibility strategy, p. 130
- Accommodative social responsibility strategy, p. 130
- Proactive social responsibility strategy, p. 131
- Altruism, p. 131
- Enlightened self-interest, p. 131
- Corporate philanthropy, p. 131
- Ethics, p. 133
- Values, p. 137
- Instrumental value, p. 137
- Terminal value, p. 137
- Amoral managers, p. 139
- Ethical advocate, p. 140
- Whistle-blowing, p. 142

SKILLS & TOOLS

An International Code of Ethics

Developed in 1994 by the Caux Round Table in Switzerland, these Principles for Business are believed to be the first international ethics code. This code was created through the collaboration of business leaders in Europe, Japan, and the United States.

Principle 1.
The Responsibility of Businesses: Beyond Shareholders Toward Stakeholders. The value of a business to society is the wealth and employment it creates and the marketable products and services it provides to consumers at a reasonable price commensurate with quality. To create such value, a business must maintain its own economic health and viability, but survival is not a sufficient goal.

Businesses have a role to play in improving the lives of all their customers, employees, and shareholders by sharing with them the wealth they have created. Suppliers and competitors as well should expect businesses to honor their obligations in a spirit of honesty and fairness. As responsible citizens of the local, national, regional, and global communities in which they operate, businesses share a part in shaping the future of those communities.

Principle 2.
The Economic and Social Impact of Business: Toward Innovation, Justice, and World Community. Businesses established in foreign countries to develop, produce, or sell should also contribute to the social advancement of those countries by creating productive employment and helping to raise the purchasing power of their citizens. Businesses also should contribute to human rights, education, welfare, and vitalization of the countries in which they operate.

Businesses should contribute to economic and social development not only in the countries in which they operate, but also in the world community at large, through effective and prudent use of resources, free and fair competition, and emphasis upon innovation in technology, production methods, marketing, and communications.

Principle 3.
Business Behavior: Beyond the Letter of Law Toward a Spirit of Trust. While accepting the legitimacy of trade secrets, businesses should recognize that sincerity, candor, truthfulness, the keeping of promises, and transparency contribute not only to their own credibility and stability but also to the smoothness and efficiency of business transactions, particularly on the international level.

Principle 4.
Respect for Rules. To avoid trade frictions and to promote freer trade, equal conditions for competition, and fair and equitable treatment for all participants, businesses should respect international and domestic rules. In addition, they should recognize that some behavior, although legal, may still have adverse consequences.

Principle 5.
Support for Multilateral Trade. Businesses should support the multilateral trade systems of the World Trade Organization and similar international agreements. They should cooperate in efforts to promote the progressive and judicious liberalization of trade, and to relax those domestic measures that unreasonably hinder global commerce, while giving due respect to national policy objectives.

Principle 6.
Respect for the Environment. A business should protect and, where possible, improve the environment, promote sustainable development, and prevent the wasteful use of natural resources.

Principle 7.
Avoidance of Illicit Operations. A business should not participate in or condone bribery, money laundering, or other corrupt practices; indeed, it should seek cooperation with others to eliminate them. It should not trade in arms or other materials used for terrorist activities, drug traffic, or other organized crime.

Source: *Excerpted from "Principles for Business,"* Business Ethics, *10 (May-June 1996): 16–17. Reprinted with permission from* Business Ethics Magazine, *52 South 10th Street, #110, Minneapolis, MN 55403. 612/962–4700.*

HANDS-ON EXERCISE

The Rokeach Value Survey

Instructions

Study the two lists of values presented below. Then rank the instrumental values in order of importance to you (1 = most important, 18 = least important). Do the same with the list of terminal values.

Instrumental values	Terminal values
Rank	**Rank**
___ Ambitious (hardworking, aspiring)	___ A comfortable life (a prosperous life)
___ Broadminded (open-minded)	___ An exciting life (a stimulating, active life)
___ Capable (competent, effective)	___ A sense of accomplishment (lasting contribution)
___ Cheerful (lighthearted, joyful)	___ A world at peace (free of war and conflict)
___ Clean (neat, tidy)	___ A world of beauty (beauty of nature and the arts)
___ Courageous (standing up for your beliefs)	___ Equality (brotherhood, equal opportunity for all)
___ Forgiving (willing to pardon others)	___ Family security (taking care of loved ones)
___ Helpful (working for the welfare of others)	___ Freedom (independence, free choice)
___ Honest (sincere, truthful)	___ Happiness (contentedness)
___ Imaginative (daring, creative)	___ Inner harmony (freedom from inner conflict)
___ Independent (self-sufficient)	___ Mature love (sexual and spiritual intimacy)
___ Intellectual (intelligent, reflective)	___ National security (protection from attack)
___ Logical (consistent, rational)	___ Pleasure (an enjoyable, leisurely life)
___ Loving (affectionate, tender)	___ Salvation (saved, eternal life)
___ Obedient (dutiful, respectful)	___ Self-respect (self-esteem)
___ Polite (courteous, well-mannered)	___ Social recognition (respect, admiration)
___ Responsible (dependable, reliable)	___ True friendship (close companionship)
___ Self-controlled (restrained, self-disciplined)	___ Wisdom (a mature understanding of life)

Source: *Copyright 1967, by Milton Rokeach, and reproduced by permission of Halgren Tests, 873 Persimmon Avenue, Sunnyvale, Calif. 94087.*

For Consideration/Discussion

1. How does this value survey help you better understand yourself? Or others?
2. Do you believe that values drive behavior (including ethical and unethical behavior)? Explain.
3. Value *conflict* can make life troublesome in three ways. First, there can be incompatibility among one's highly ranked instrumental values (e.g., honest vs. polite; courageous vs. obedient). Second, it may be difficult to achieve one's top terminal values via one's highly ranked instrumental values (e.g., ambitious and responsible vs. happiness and an exciting life). Third, your important instrumental and terminal values may clash with those of significant others—such as friends, spouse, coworkers, or an organization. What sorts of potential or actual value conflict do you detect in your survey responses? Explain. What can you do to minimize these conflicts?

INTERNET EXERCISES

1. Learning more about the world of corporate social responsibility (CSR). *Business Ethics* magazine (**www.business-ethics.com**) calls the Business for Social Responsibility Web site (**www.bsr.org**) the best CSR site of all. This site has a wealth of information to inspire and challenge all of us to take CSR to new heights. First go to the home page and browse the news items under "Global News." Next, click on the home page "CSR Resources" tab and read the available material.

Learning Points: 1. What new and/or useful ideas did you acquire about CSR? 2. Do you like or dislike how encompassing the field of CSR has become? Explain. 3. What, if any, social responsibility spark (for making the world a better place) has been ignited in you? Explain.

2. Check it out: Many people believe that today's large and powerful corporations need to be monitored carefully (and held accountable) to make sure they are behaving effectively, responsibly, and ethically. An excellent one-stop Web site for checking up on corporate saints and sinners alike is **www.corpwatch.org**. This is a must-see site for politically and socially conscious people who are out to "save the world"—or at least are intrigued by the idea.

For updates to these exercises, visit our Web site (**http://business.college.hmco.com/students/** and select Kreitner, *Management,* 10e).

CLOSING CASE

The Loyal Employee

Raman is the Sales Manager of a reputed Corporation. He has 25 employees in his Department, and all are paid commission for their sales in their territories. For the past three years, the market for the company's goods has been steadily growing and the majority of Raman's staff have met this growth with increased sales. However, one employee in particular, Krishnan has not kept up with the pace.

Krishnan has been with this Corporation for over 20 years and is now 56 years old. Krishnan is a friendly man and is liked by his peers and those to whom he sells the company's products on a regular basis. The company has always considered Krishnan dependable and loyal. Through the years Krishnan has been counted as an asset to the company, but at the age of 56 he has gone into a state of semi-retirement. Krishnan's sales have not increased as the others have and he does not have the determination to acquire a significant increase in sales.

Raman wishes to change this situation. He wants to motivate Krishnan into increasing his sales to match that of his younger peers. To accomplish this, Krishnan must begin to do more than put in his time, but Raman is not sure how to go about trying to motivate him. Unlike the majority of the new employees Krishnan is an old man, who within a few years will reach the age of retirement. If you were Raman what would you do?

For Discussion

1. Would you threaten to fire him?
2. Would you increase his commission?
3. Would you increase the retirement benefits for Krishnan rather than offer him the increased commission rate?
4. Would you offer him more status by way of a new title or a new company car or place his table in a better position in the office?
5. Is there some way in terms of appraisal and rewards with which you can motivate Krishnan?

Source: *Management Text and Cases, V S P Rao & V Hari Krishna, Excel Books, 2002, pp-952*

TEST PREPPER

True/False Questions

_____ **1.** The top level of Carroll's global corporate social responsibility pyramid is ethical responsibility.

_____ **2.** An argument in favor of corporate social responsibility is that business is unavoidably involved in social issues.

_____ **3.** By definition, a stakeholder audit identifies all parties with financial ties to the organization.

_____ **4.** When an organization follows an accommodative social responsibility strategy, it must be pressured into assuming additional responsibilities.

_____ **5.** Helping others is what altruistic people and organizations strive to do.

_____ **6.** Managers who believe in enlightened self-interest think that, ultimately, the best way to help themselves is to help create a better society.

_____ **7.** According to research, the number one workplace "hot spot" responsible for triggering unethical and illegal conduct is trying to meet unrealistic deadlines.

_____ **8.** According to researchers, one way in which people rationalize their unethical conduct is to say that their victims deserved what they got.

_____ **9.** Economic efficiency is one of the ten general ethical principles.

_____ **10.** An effective code of ethics does not get bogged down in the details of specific behavior but, rather, needs to be stated in general terms.

Multiple-Choice Questions

1. Socially responsible acts, by definition, generally
A. are not voluntary.
B. are performed in response to legal pressure.
C. take the form of a public relations campaign.
D. are a reaction to public pressure.
E. are voluntary and above and beyond the stockholders' needs.

2. _____ responsibility is *not* one of the four levels in Carroll's global corporate social responsibility pyramid.
A. Economic B. Ethical
C. Legal D. Philanthropic
E. Cultural

3. Systematically identifying all parties that might be affected by a company's actions is the goal of performing a(n)
A. social responsibility profile. B. stakeholder audit.
C. corporate audit. D. internal audit.
E. SWOT analysis.

4. Which of these is an argument in favor of corporate social responsibility?
A. Ensuring the most efficient use of society's resources
B. Profitability improvement
C. Preventing government intervention
D. Giving business more power
E. Management accountability

5. Say a Swiss drug company denies responsibility for the dangerous side effects of a profitable new drug for anxiety, despite convincing scientific evidence of problems with the drug. Which social responsibility strategy is this company following?
A. Proactive B. Accommodating
C. Traditional D. Political/legal
E. Reactive

6. What type of self-interest do businesses acknowledge when they realize that they ultimately help themselves by helping to solve society's problems?
A. Progressive B. Proactive
C. Enlightened D. Sociocentric
E. Neo-economic

7. Which one of these is *not* among the top ten workplace "hot spots" for triggering unethical or illegal conduct?
A. Work hours, workload
B. Employees with undisclosed criminal records
C. Lack of management support
D. Personal financial worries
E. Poor leadership

8. According to research, which one of these is a strategy that people tend to use to rationalize unethical conduct?
A. Reverse logic
B. Inductive reasoning
C. Denial of injury
D. Metaphor of the clock
E. Groupthink

9. "Honesty is the best policy" reflects which type of personal value?
A. Instrumental B. Procedural
C. Behavioral D. Terminal
E. Cultural

10. _____ is what an employee does if he reports his employer's falsified safety records to government regulators.
A. Social auditing
B. Whistle-blowing
C. Amoralizing
D. Exhibiting civil disobedience
E. Indulging in moral deconstruction

ACE self-test

Want more questions? Visit the student Web site at **http://business.college.hmco.com/students/** (select Kreitner *Management,* 10e) and take the ACE quizzes for more practice.

Managers-in-Action Videos

1A Milton Rodriguez, the Passionate Entrepreneur

Born in Puerto Rico, Milton Rodriguez moved to the United States with his parents and grew up to embody "the American Dream." He invented an antitheft labeling system for motor vehicles and built a thriving business that he operated for 15 years. Today, as co-owner of a Chevrolet dealership in Southington, Connecticut, he is a positive and inspiring role model for his employees and customers. You will enjoy meeting Milton Rodriguez.

Learning Objectives: To see how a start-from-nothing entrepreneur with a positive attitude energizes a business and its employees.

Links to Textual Material: **Chapter 1:** Management defined; The twenty-first century manager; Managerial functions and roles; Small-business management and entrepreneurship; **Chapter 14:** Teamwork; **Chapter 15:** Influence tactics; Leadership

Discussion Questions:

1. How does Milton Rodriguez exemplify the definition of management?
2. Which characteristics of the twenty-first-century manager (see Table 1.1) are evident in this video profile?
3. Which of the eight managerial functions (Figure 1.3) and which of Wilson's twelve managerial skills (Figure 1.4)are evident in this video profile? Explain.
4. How well does Milton Rodriguez fit the entrepreneurial trait profile in Table 1.3? Explain, trait by trait.

1B Hewlett-Packard Leverages Global Diversity

Three global managers at HP—Christian Foerg, Daisy Ng, and Gerard Brossard—discuss the unique challenges of communicating, evaluating performance, and leading across cultures. HP seeks to make its rich diversity a strategic advantage by focusing on character, capability, and collaboration within various cultural contexts.

Learning Objectives: To show how a large global corporation strives to make the diversity of its employees a competitive advantage.

Links to Textual Material: **Chapter 1:** Managerial roles and skills; **Chapter 3:** Managing diversity; **Chapter 4:** Cross-cultural competence; **Chapter 11:** Performance appraisal; **Chapter 15:** Leadership

Discussion Questions:

1. Which of the eight managerial functions (Figure 1.3) and which of Wilson's twelve managerial skills (Figure 1.4) are evident in this video profile? Explain.
2. Why is it important for HP's management to focus on character, capability, and collaboration?
3. If you were one of the three HP managers in this video, how would you explain to a group of visitors why managing diversity is important?
4. Which of the GLOBE leadership styles (Figure 4.1) appear to be most apparent in this video? Explain.

PART TWO

Planning and Decision Making

6 The Basics of Planning and Project Management

> *"Management is a balancing act between the short term and the long term, between different objectives at different times."*[1]
>
> PETER F. DRUCKER

OBJECTIVES

- **Distinguish** among state, effect, and response uncertainty.
- **Identify** and **define** the three types of planning.
- **Write** good objectives, and **discuss** the role of objectives in planning.
- **Describe** the four-step management by objectives (MBO) process, and **explain** how it can foster individual commitment and motivation.
- **Discuss** project planning within the context of the project life cycle, and **list** six roles played by project managers.
- **Compare** and **contrast** flow charts and Gantt charts, and **discuss** the value of PERT networks.
- **Explain** how break-even points can be calculated.

the changing workplace

Plan B (and C and D and. . .)

Management experts advise entrepreneurs to revisit their business plans regularly. After all, circumstances change, and if tactics and goals don't change along with them, a business strategy can grow stale awfully fast.

Still, it's hard not to wonder whether Craig Knouf has taken such advice a tad too far. The CEO of Associated Business Systems, an office-equipment supplier based in Portland, Oreg., simply cannot keep his hands off his business plan. Since founding his company in 1997, Knouf figures he's revised his original business plan more than 120 times, revisiting the 30-page document on a monthly, quarterly, and annual basis. Running his company any other way, Knouf says, "would be like driving a car with no steering wheel."

Knouf is in the minority. In fact, most business owners reexamine their business plans only once a year, unless they are applying for a loan or seeking investment capital, says Ed Rogoff, author of *Bankable Business Plans.* After that, the plans go back in a drawer until the next annual checkup. Yet many experts warn that once or twice a year is not enough. "The world turns; things change," says Eric Siegel, a lecturer at the Wharton School and president of Siegel Management Co., a consulting firm in Bryn Mawr, Pa. "What you commit to a document on Dec. 19 is not necessarily appropriate on Jan. 19."

Knouf couldn't agree more. So every 30 days, he distributes Associated's business plan to his seven vice presidents. The VPs review the plan, comparing their divisions' current results with goals established the previous month. If the two don't match, they consider why and rewrite the business plan accordingly. Quarterly reviews take the same approach to three-month goals. Plus, there's an annual two-day meeting to discuss and refine long-term objectives. Such relentless planning, Knouf says, helped the 110-employee company reach $21.5 million in sales in 2003. "If you only looked at the plan every quarter, by the time you realize the mistake, you're five months off," says the 45-year-old entrepreneur. "You're done. You're not going to get back on track."

The strategy has a tendency to send Knouf's business in unanticipated directions. He never guessed that sales of scanning software would be a big part of his business, for example. But several years ago, with each monthly checkup, Knouf noticed a slight uptick in demand for scanning capability. Because he updates his business plan every month, he was able to react quickly, adding such software—which had not even been part of his original strategy—to Associated's array of products. The result: In 2004, Knouf expects such sales to reach $3.1 million, double that of 2003.

What's more, the plans provide a highly detailed, written record of his company's evolution—something that banks love, says Knouf, who claims never to have had a problem getting a loan. That doesn't surprise Dana Drago, president of small-business banking at Bank of America. "If he gets into trouble, he's got a plan," which is exactly what lenders like to see, she says.

Associated's management team recently emerged from its 2004 planning meetings with ambitious goals for the year—these include 20% internal growth, as well as an acquisition to boost market share. For now, such milestones seem reachable. But if things change, Knouf is ready to change right along with them.

Source: *By Nicole Gull, © 2004 Gruner & Jahr USA Publishing. First published in* Inc. *Magazine. Reprinted with permission.*

In the age of Internet speed, more and more managers are finding they have a lot in common with Craig Knouf. Small and large, public and private organizations are struggling to stay relevant and responsive. A standing joke among managers is that they are responsible for "doing the impossible by yesterday!" Indeed, virtually all of today's managers are asked to do a lot with limited budgets, resources, and time. All this takes thoughtful planning and a healthy dose of courage in the face of nerve-wracking uncertainty.

planning: *coping with uncertainty by formulating courses of action to achieve specified results*

Planning is the process of coping with uncertainty by formulating future courses of action to achieve specified results. Planning enables humans to achieve great things by envisioning a pathway from concept to reality. The greater the mission, the longer and more challenging the pathway. For example, imagine the challenges awaiting Walgreens, the drugstore chain, as it pursues its ambitious growth plan. As *Fortune* magazine reported: "The company's aim is to nearly double its stores, to around 6,000, within five years."[2] Planning is a never-ending process because of constant change, uncertainty, new competition, unexpected problems, and emerging opportunities.[3]

Because planning affects all downstream management functions (see Figure 6.1), it has been called the primary management function. With this model in mind, we shall discuss uncertainty, highlight five essential aspects of the planning function, and take a close look at management by objectives and project planning. We shall also introduce four practical tools (flow charts, Gantt charts, PERT networks, and break-even analysis).

Coping with Uncertainty

Ben Franklin said the only sure things in life are death and taxes. Although this is a gloomy prospect, it does capture a key theme of modern life: We are faced with a great deal of uncertainty. Organizations, like individuals, are continually challenged to accomplish something in spite of general uncertainty.[4] Organizations meet this

Figure 6.1 Planning: The Primary Management Function

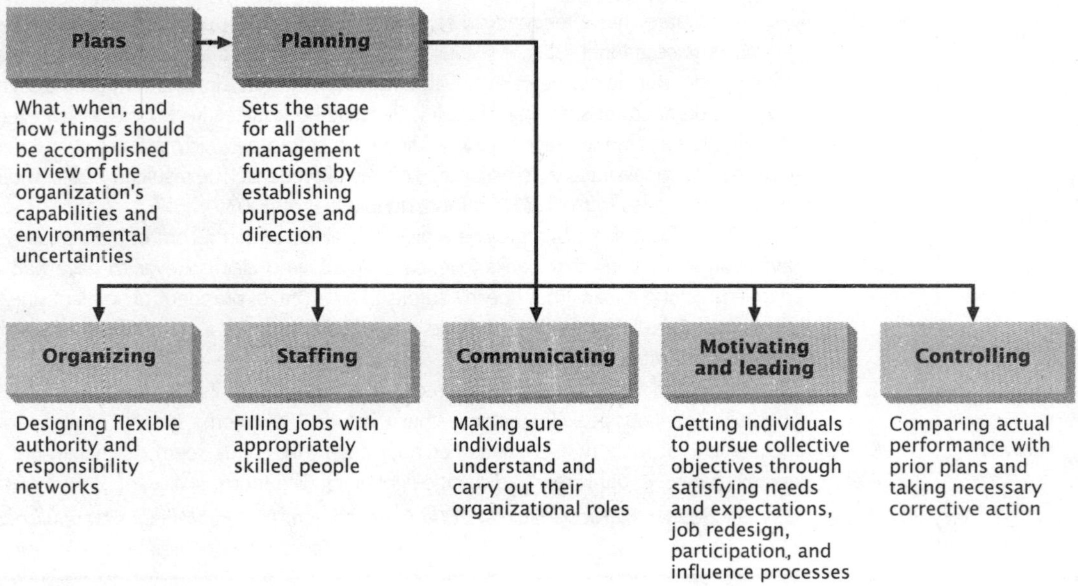

challenge largely through planning. As a context for our discussion of planning in this and the following chapter, let us explore environmental uncertainty from two perspectives: (1) types of uncertainty and (2) organizational responses to environmental uncertainty.

■ Three Types of Uncertainty

Through the years, *environmental uncertainty* has been a catch-all term among managers and researchers. However, research indicates that people actually perceive three types of environmental uncertainty: state uncertainty, effect uncertainty, and response uncertainty. **State uncertainty** occurs when the environment, or a portion of the environment, is considered unpredictable. A manager's attempt to predict the *effects* of specific environmental changes or events on his or her organization involves **effect uncertainty. Response uncertainty** is inability to predict the *consequences* of a particular decision or organizational response.[5]

state uncertainty: *environment is unpredictable*

effect uncertainty: *impacts of environmental changes are unpredictable*

response uncertainty: *consequences of decisions are unpredictable*

A simple analogy can help us conceptually sort out these three types of uncertainty. Suppose you are a golfer, and on your way to the course you wonder whether it is going to rain; this is *state uncertainty.* Next, you experience *effect uncertainty* because you are not sure whether it will rain hard enough, if it does rain, to make you quit before finishing nine holes. Soon you begin weighing your chances of making par if you have to adjust your choice of golf clubs to poor playing conditions; now you are experiencing *response uncertainty.* Each of the three types of perceived uncertainty could affect your golfing attitude and performance. Similarly, managers are affected by their different perceptions of environmental factors. Their degree of uncertainty may vary from one type of uncertainty to another. A manager may, for example, be unsure about whether a key employee is about to quit (considerable state uncertainty) but very sure that productivity would suffer without that individual (little effect uncertainty).[6]

1. DISTINGUISH among state, effect, and response uncertainty.

San Francisco, Christmas Eve: Thanks to stormy weather in the Midwest, UPS driver Doug Lamb ended up working through the night. Weather is a major source of uncertainty for the package delivery giant because it is a highly-integrated, tightly-scheduled global system. Weather-related delays for planes and trucks in one region inevitably impact delivery schedules in other regions.

6a Back to the Opening Case

Will Knouf's detailed approach to planning help his company deal more effectively with each of the three types of uncertainty–state, effect, and response uncertainty? Explain.

For further information about the interactive annotations in this chapter, visit our Web site (**http://business.college.hmco.com/students/** and select Kreitner, *Management,* 10e).

■ Organizational Responses to Uncertainty

Some organizations do a better job than others of planning amid various combinations of uncertainty. This is due in part to differing patterns of response to environmental factors beyond the organization's immediate control. As outlined in Table 6.1, organizations cope with environmental uncertainty by adopting one of four positions vis-à-vis the environment in which they operate. These are the positions taken by defenders, prospectors, analyzers, and reactors,[7] and each position has its own characteristic impact on planning.

■ **Defenders.** A defender can be successful as long as its primary technology and narrow product line remain competitive. But Defenders can become stranded on a dead-end road if their primary market seriously weakens. A prime example of a defender is Harley-Davidson, which sold its recreational vehicle division and other nonmotorcycle businesses to get back to basics. Harley-Davidson enjoys such fierce brand loyalty among Hog riders that many sport a tattoo of the company's logo. Can you imagine a Coca-Cola or a Wal-Mart tattoo? But Harley-Davidson runs the risk of having its narrow focus miss the mark in an aging America. Specifically, the median age of Harley buyers rose from 35 in 1987 to 46 in 2002. Harley-Davidson is therefore seeking to lure younger riders who prefer sleek bikes away from Honda and other Japanese rivals.[8]

■ **Prospectors.** Prospector organizations are easy to spot because they have a reputation for aggressively making things happen rather than waiting for them to happen. But life is challenging for prospectors such as Genentech, the fast-growing San Francisco biotech company.

Table 6.1 Different Organizational Responses to an Uncertain Environment

Type of organizational response	Characteristics of response
1. Defenders	Highly expert at producing and marketing a few products in a narrowly defined market
	Opportunities beyond present market not sought
	Few adjustments in technology, organization structure, and methods of operation because of narrow focus
	Primary attention devoted to efficiency of current operations
2. Prospectors	Primary attention devoted to searching for new market opportunities
	Frequent development and testing of new products and services
	Source of change and uncertainty for competitors
	Loss of efficiency because of continual product and market innovation
3. Analyzers	Simultaneous operations in stable and changing product/market domains
	In relatively stable product/market domain, emphasis on formalized structures and processes to achieve routine and efficient operation
	In changing product/market domain, emphasis on detecting and copying competitors' most promising ideas
4. Reactors	Frequently unable to respond quickly to perceived changes in environment
	Make adjustments only when finally forced to do so by environmental pressures

Source: *Adapted from* Organizational Strategy, Structure, and Process, *by Raymond E. Miles and Charles C. Snow. Copyright © 1978, McGraw-Hill Book Company, p. 29. Used with permission of McGraw-Hill Book Company.*

> *In an industry that sets its sights on the bet-the-farm blockbuster approach to drug development, it sometimes pays to step back and take aim before firing. "That can mean not going after the huge markets that everybody's going after, where all the science has been picked over," says consultant Michael Treachy, author of* Double-Digit Growth. *"Sometimes that involves going after market segments where perhaps there's been a lot less effort." . . . Genentech is doing just that: moving away from the mob-chasing, big-market, one-size-fits-all opportunities, and instead innovating through "targeted therapies"—that is, treatments for specific sets of patients, mostly in the areas of oncology and immunology.*[9]

Prospectors (or pioneers) traditionally have been admired for their ability to gain what strategists call a *first-mover advantage.* In other words, the first one to market wins. Following the Internet crash, when many dot-com pioneers were the first to go bankrupt, the first-mover advantage was given a second look. Two researchers, one from the United States and the other from France, recently offered this insight about both industrial and consumer goods companies: ". . . we found that over the long haul, early movers are considerably *less* profitable than later entrants. Although pioneers do enjoy sustained revenue advantages, they also suffer from persistently *high* costs, which eventually overwhelm the sales gains."[10] Prospectors need to pick their opportunities very carefully, selecting those with the best combination of feasibility and profit potential. This is especially true for entrepreneurs starting small businesses.[11]

■ **Analyzers.** An essentially conservative strategy of following the leader marks an organization as an analyzer. It is a "me too" response to environmental uncertainty. Analyzers let market leaders take expensive R&D risks and then imitate or build upon what works. This slower, more studied approach can pay off when the economy turns down and prospectors stumble. A classic example is Israel's Teva Pharmaceuticals, a maker of generic drugs that sell for much less than brand-name drugs:

You may never have heard of the Israeli company. But you could very well be taking one of its drugs. One in every 15 prescriptions in the U.S. is a Teva product, making the company this country's largest drug supplier. With $3.3 billion in revenues, it sells more than 450 drugs in North America, Europe, and Israel—everything from antibiotics to heart medicines. . . .

Chief executive Israel Makov doesn't have any illusions about turning Teva into a brand-name producer. . . . His goal is to double sales every four years by remaining largely a maker of me-too medications.[12]

Although analyzers such as generic drug companies may not get a lot of respect, they perform the important economic function of breaking up overly concentrated industries. Customers appreciate the resulting lower prices, too.

■ **Reactors.** The reactor is the exact opposite of the prospector. Reactors wait for adversity, such as declining sales, before taking corrective steps. They are slow to develop new products to supplement their tried-and-true ones. Their strategic responses to changes in the environment are often late. An instructive example in this area is Kodak:

Kodak continues to grapple with one of the harshest corporate transitions of the past decade. Its 100–year-old film business is waning in the face of digital photography, which exploded [in 2003]. . . .

The company cautiously moved into digital photography in the mid-1990s but never made the transition away from film. Now, it might be too late.

"Kodak saw this coming," says Michael Raynor, co-author of management best-seller The Innovator's Solution. *But instead of driving a transition earlier and building up a digital business, it's now "leaping on a train when it's going 70 miles per hour," Raynor says.*[13]

Not surprisingly, Kodak's global workforce has been cut by one-third (about 31,000 employees) over the last decade.[14] According to one field study, reactors tended to be less profitable than defenders, prospectors, and analyzers.[15]

6b A Quick Quiz

Jeff Bezos, CEO, Amazon.com:

. . . one type of competitive-focused strategy that can be very effective is called "close following," and it has a lot of advantages. You don't have to go down as many blind alleys. You watch and let a competitor go down a bunch of blind alleys, and when it finds something successful, you try to copy it very quickly and out-execute them. It's a perfectly valid strategy—it just happens not to be who we are. Pioneering is in our corporate DNA, so we'd rather go down those blind alleys ourselves. In my opinion, there are strong rewards for being a pioneer that more than compensate us for all the blind alleys. Plus, me-too strategies don't work very well on the Internet.

Source: As quoted in Melanie Warner, "How to Think Competitively," Business 2.0, *5 (December 2004): 111.*

QUESTION:
Which labels should be attached to the two strategies Bezos mentions: defender, prospector, analyzer, or reactor?

■ Balancing Planned Action and Spontaneity in the Twenty-First Century

In the obsolete command-and-control management model, plans were considered destiny. Top management formulated exacting plans for every aspect of operations and then kept everything under tight control to "meet the plan." All too often, however, plans were derailed by unanticipated events, and success was dampened by organizational inflexibility. Today's progressive managers see plans as general guidelines for action, based on imperfect and incomplete information. Planning is no longer the exclusive domain of top management; it now typically involves those who carry out the plans because they are closer to the customer. Planning experts say managers need to balance planned action with the flexibility to take advantage of surprise events and unexpected opportunities. A good analogy is to an improvisational comedy act.[16] The stand-up comic has a plan for the introduction, structure of the act, some tried-and-true jokes, and closing remarks. Within this planned framework, the comic will play off the audience's input and improvise as necessary. Accordingly, 3M Corporation had a plan for encouraging innovation that allowed it to capitalize on the spontaneous success of the Post-it Note.[17] Planning should be a springboard to success, not a barrier to creativity.

The Essentials of Planning

Planning is an ever-present feature of modern life, although there is no universal approach. Virtually everyone is a planner, at least in the informal sense. We plan leisure activities after school or work; we make career plans. Personal or informal plans give purpose to our lives. In a similar fashion, more formalized plans enable managers to mobilize their intentions to accomplish organizational purposes. A **plan** is a specific, documented intention consisting of an objective and an action statement. The objective portion is the end, and the action statement represents the means to that end. Stated another way, objectives give management targets to shoot at, whereas action statements provide the arrows for hitting the targets. Properly conceived plans tell *what, when,* and *how* something is to be done.

plan: *an objective plus an action statement*

In spite of the wide variety of formal planning systems that managers encounter on the job, we can identify some essentials of sound planning. Among these common denominators are organizational mission, types of planning, objectives, priorities, and the planning/control cycle.

If you want a Big Mac, fries, a chocolate shake, and a prayer of forgiveness, this is the man to see. He's the Reverend Joe Ratliff, senior pastor of the Brentwood Baptist Church in Houston, Texas. Reverend Ratliff saw McDonald's outlets popping up in unusual places such as gas stations, schools, and hospitals. So why not have one for the church's 10,000-member congregation? After all, on-site dining fit the church's mission of helping people and a restaurant fit nicely into the plans for a huge new multi-purpose building. "Good idea," said McDonald's, and the rest is history. Did you say, "Hold the onions?"

■ Organizational Mission

To some, defining an organization's mission might seem to be an exercise in the obvious. But exactly the opposite is true. Some organizations drift along without a clear mission. Others lose sight of their original mission. Sometimes an organization, such as the U.S. Army Corps of Engineers, finds its original mission no longer acceptable to key stakeholders. In fact, the Corps is stepping back from its tradition of building dams and levees, in favor of more environmentally sensitive projects. It has tackled "a 30-year, $7.8 billion restoration of the Florida Everglades"[18] that will involve tearing down levees to restore the natural flow of the Kissimmee River. Periodically redefining an organization's mission is both common and necessary in an era of rapid change.

A clear, formally written, and publicized statement of an organization's mission is the cornerstone of any planning system that will effectively guide the organization through uncertain times. The satirical definition by Scott Adams, the Dilbert cartoonist, tells us how *not* to write an organizational mission statement: "A Mission Statement is defined as a long, awkward sentence that demonstrates management's inability to think clearly."[19] This sad state of affairs, too often true, can be avoided by a well-written mission statement that does the following things:

6c A Model Mission Statement?

Alan Brunacini, the long-time chief of the Phoenix, Arizona, Fire Department, has a reputation as a great manager. He boiled his department's mission down to five words: "Prevent harm, survive, be nice."

Source: As quoted in Jon Talton, "What in Blazes Has the Chief Done? Create a Model for Managers," The Arizona Republic *(January 27, 2002): D1.*

QUESTIONS:

Based on what you have just read, is this an effective organizational mission statement? Why or why not?

1. *Defines* your organization for key stakeholders
2. Creates an *inspiring vision* of what the organization can be and can do
3. Outlines *how* the vision is to be accomplished
4. Establishes key *priorities*
5. States a *common goal* and fosters a sense of togetherness
6. Creates a *philosophical anchor* for all organizational activities
7. Generates *enthusiasm* and a "can do" attitude
8. *Empowers* present and future organization members to believe that *every* individual is the key to success[20]

A good mission statement provides a focal point for the entire planning process. When Vincent A. Sarni took the top job at PPG, the large glass and paint company, he created a document he called "Blueprint for the Decade." In it he specified the company's mission and corporate objectives for such things as service, quality, and financial performance.

> *Sarni . . . trudged from plant to plant preaching the virtues in his Little Blue Book. "My first two or three years I always started with a discussion of the Blueprint," he says. "I don't have to do that anymore. The Blueprint's on the shop floor, and it has meaning."*[21]

2. IDENTIFY and **DEFINE** the three types of planning.

■ Types of Planning

Ideally, planning begins at the top of the organizational pyramid and filters down. The rationale for beginning at the top is the need for coordination. It is top management's job to state the organization's mission, establish strategic priorities, and draw up major policies. After these statements are in place, successive rounds of strategic, intermediate, and operational planning can occur. Figure 6.2 presents an idealized picture of the three types of planning, as carried out by different levels of management.

strategic planning: *determining how to pursue long-term goals with available resources*

intermediate planning: *determining what contributions subunits can make with allocated resources*

operational planning: *determining how to accomplish specific tasks with available resources*

planning horizon: *time that elapses between planning and execution*

■ Strategic, Intermediate, and Operational Planning. **Strategic planning** is the process of determining how to pursue the organization's long-term goals with the resources expected to be available. A well-conceived strategic plan communicates much more than general intentions about profit and growth. It specifies *how* the organization will achieve a competitive advantage, with profit and growth as necessary by-products. **Intermediate planning** is the process of determining the contributions that subunits can make with allocated resources. Finally, **operational planning** is the process of determining how specific tasks can best be accomplished on time with available resources. Each level of planning is vital to an organization's success and cannot effectively stand alone without the support of the other two levels.

■ Planning Horizons. As Figure 6.2 illustrates, planning horizons vary for the three types of planning. The term **planning horizon** refers to the time that elapses between the formulation and the execution of a planned activity. As the planning process evolves from strategic to operational, planning horizons shorten and plans become increasingly specific. Naturally, management can be more confident—and hence more specific—about the near future than about the distant future.

Notice, however, that the three planning horizons overlap, their boundaries being elastic rather than rigid. The trend today is toward involving employees from all levels in the strategic planning process. Also, it is not uncommon for top and lower managers to have a hand in formulating intermediate plans. Middle managers often help lower managers draw up operational plans as well. Hence Figure 6.2 is an ideal instructional model with countless variations in the workplace.

Figure 6.2 Types of Planning

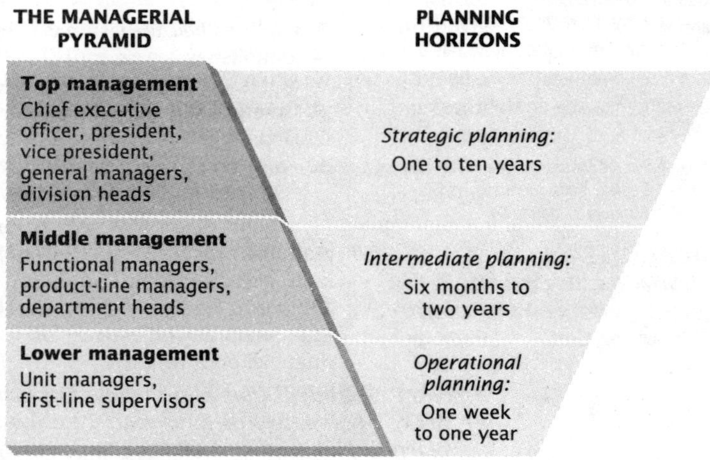

■ Objectives

Just as a distant port is the target or goal for a ship's crew, objectives are targets that organizational members steer toward. Although some theorists distinguish between goals and objectives, managers typically use the terms interchangeably. A goal or an **objective** is defined as a specific commitment to achieve a measurable result within a given time frame. Many experts view objectives as the single most important feature of the planning process. They help managers and entrepreneurs build a bridge between their dreams, aspirations, and visions and an achievable *reality.* Dan Sullivan, a consultant for entrepreneurs, explains:

objective: *commitment to achieve a measurable result within a specified period*

> *[Objectives and goals] should be achievable by definition. If you are setting functional goals, at useful increments, they should be both real and realizable. The distance between where you actually are now and your goal can be measured objectively, and when you achieve your goal, you know it. Think of the distinction this way: no matter how fast you run toward the horizon, you'll never get there, but if you run more quickly toward a goalpost, you will get there faster. Sounds simplistic, but I'm constantly amazed at how many people—and entrepreneurs in particular—confuse their goals with their ideals.*[22]

It is important for present and future managers to be able to write good objectives, to be aware of their importance, and to understand how objectives combine to form a means-ends chain.

Source: *DILBERT © Scott Adams/Dist. by United Feature Syndicaate, Inc.*

3. WRITE good objectives, and **DISCUSS** the role of objectives in planning.

■ Writing Good Objectives. An authority on objectives recommends that "as far as possible, objectives [should be] expressed in quantitative, measurable, concrete terms, in the form of a written statement of desired results to be achieved within a given time period."[23] In other words, objectives represent a firm commitment to accomplish something specific. A well-written objective should state what is to be accomplished and when it is to be accomplished. In the following sample objectives, note that the desired results are expressed *quantitatively*, in units of output, dollars, or percentage of change.

- To increase subcompact car production by 240,000 units during the next production year
- To reduce bad-debt loss by $50,000 during the next six months
- To achieve an 18 percent increase in Brand X sales by December 31 of the current year

For actual practice in writing good objectives and plans, see the Hands-On Exercise at the end of this chapter.

■ The Importance of Objectives. From the standpoint of planning, carefully prepared objectives benefit managers by serving as targets and measuring sticks, fostering commitment, and enhancing motivation.[24]

- *Targets.* As mentioned earlier, objectives provide managers with specific targets. Without objectives, managers at all levels would find it difficult to make coordinated decisions. People quite naturally tend to pursue their own ends in the absence of formal organizational objectives.
- *Measuring sticks.* An easily overlooked, after-the-fact feature of objectives is that they are useful for measuring how well an organizational subunit or individual has performed. When appraising performance, managers need an established standard against which they can measure performance. Concrete objectives enable managers to weigh performance objectively on the basis of accomplishment rather than subjectively on the basis of personality or prejudice.
- *Commitment.* The very process of getting an employee to agree to pursue a given objective gives that individual a personal stake in the success of the enterprise. Thus objectives can be helpful in encouraging personal commitment to collective ends. Without individual commitment, even well-intentioned and carefully conceived strategies are doomed to failure.
- *Motivation.* Good objectives represent a challenge—something to reach for. Accordingly, they have a motivational aspect. People usually feel good about themselves and what they do when they successfully achieve a challenging objective. Moreover, objectives give managers a rational basis for rewarding performance. Employees who believe they will be equitably rewarded for achieving a given objective will be motivated to perform well.

6d Okay Now, Everybody S-t-r-e-t-c-h!

Jack Welch, retired General Electric CEO:

In a stretch environment the . . . field team is asked to come in with "operating plans" that reflect their dreams—the highest numbers they think they have a shot at: their "stretch." The discussion revolves around new directions and growth, energizing stuff.

Source: Jack Welch, Jack: Straight from the Gut *(New York: Warner Books, 2001), p. 386.*

QUESTION:
What are the positives and negatives of this approach to planning?

■ The Means-Ends Chain of Objectives. Like the overall planning process, objective setting is a top-to-bottom proposition. Top managers set broader objectives with longer time horizons than do successively lower levels of managers. In effect, this downward flow of objectives creates a means-ends chain. Working from bottom to top in Figure 6.3, supervisory-level objectives provide the means for achieving middle-level objectives (ends) that, in turn, provide the means for achieving top-level objectives (ends).

The organizational hierarchy in Figure 6.3 has, of course, been telescoped and narrowed at the middle and lower levels for illustrative purposes. Usually, two or three layers of management would separate the president and the product-line managers.

Figure 6.3 A Typical Means-Ends Chain of Objectives

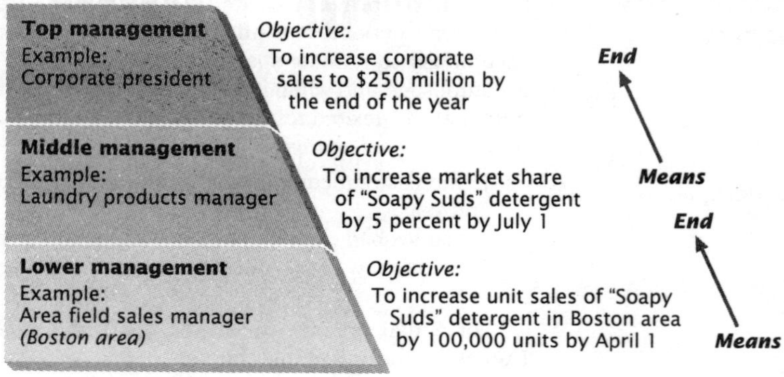

Another layer or two would separate product-line managers from area sales managers. But the telescoping helps show that lower-level objectives provide the means for accomplishing higher-level ends or objectives.

■ Priorities

priorities: *goals, objectives, or activities ranked in order of importance*

Defined as a ranking of goals, objectives, or activities in order of importance, **priorities** play a special role in planning. By listing long-range organizational objectives in order of their priority, top management prepares to make later decisions regarding the allocation of resources. Limited time, talent, and financial and material resources need to be channeled into more important endeavors and away from other areas in proportion to the relative priority of the areas. Establishment of priorities is a key factor in managerial and organizational effectiveness. Strategic priorities give both insiders and outsiders answers to the questions "Why does the organization exist?" and "How should it act and react during a crisis?" An inspiring illustration of the latter occurred for American Express after the September 11, 2001, terrorist attacks:

> *The hundreds of ad hoc decisions made by [new CEO Kenneth I.] Chenault and his team were guided by two overriding concerns: employee safety and customer service. AmEx helped 560,000 stranded cardholders get home, in some cases chartering airplanes and buses to ferry them across the country. It waived millions of dollars in delinquent fees on late-paying cardholders and increased credit limits to cash-starved clients. . . .*
>
> *Most telling, Chenault gathered 5,000 American Express employees at the Paramount Theater in New York on Sept. 20 for a highly emotional "town hall meeting." During the session, Chenault demonstrated . . . poise, compassion, and decisiveness.*[25]

■ The A-B-C Priority System. Despite time-management seminars, day planners, and computerized "personal digital assistants," establishing priorities remains a subjective process affected by organizational politics and value conflicts.[26] Although there is no universally acceptable formula for carrying out this important function, the following A-B-C priority system is helpful.

A: "Must do" objectives *critical* to successful performance. They may be the result of special demands from higher levels of management or other external sources.

B: "Should do" objectives *necessary* for improved performance. They are generally vital, but their achievement can be postponed if necessary.

C: "Nice to do" objectives *desirable* for improved performance, but not critical to survival or improved performance. They can be eliminated or postponed to achieve objectives of higher priority.[27]

Home Depot uses an interesting and effective color-coded variation of this approach. According to *Business Week*: ". . . when a to-do list for managers arrives electronically, it is marked in green. If it isn't done by the set date, it changes to red—and district managers can pounce."[28]

80/20 principle: *a minority of causes, inputs, or effort tend to produce a majority of results, outputs, or rewards*

■ **The 80/20 Principle.** Another proven priority-setting tool is the 80/20 principle (or Pareto analysis, as mentioned in Chapter 2). "The **80/20 principle** asserts that a minority of causes, inputs, or effort usually leads to a majority of the results, outputs, or rewards."[29] Care needs to be taken not to interpret the 80/20 formula too literally—it is approximate. Consider this situation, for example:

> *Market Line Associates, an Atlanta financial consultancy, estimates that the top 20% of customers at a typical commercial bank generate up to six times as much revenue as they cost, while the bottom fifth cost three to four times more than they make for the company.*[30]

For profit-minded banks and other businesses, all customers are not alike. Indeed, ING Bank, the U.S. subsidiary of the Dutch insurance giant ING, "'fires' about 3,600 of its 2 million customers every year. Ditching clients who are too time-consuming saves the company at least $1 million annually."[31] How would business purists who say "The customer is always right" feel about this practice?

■ **Avoiding the Busyness Trap.** These two simple yet effective tools for establishing priorities can help managers avoid the so-called *busyness trap*.[32] In these fast-paced times, managers should not confuse being busy with being effective and efficient. *Results* are what really count. Activities and speed, without results, are an energy-sapping waste of time. By slowing down a bit, having clear priorities, and taking a strategic view of daily problems, busy managers can be successful *and* "get a life."[33]

Finally, managers striving to establish priorities amid lots of competing demands would do well to heed management expert Peter Drucker's advice—that the most important skill for setting priorities and managing time is simply learning to say "no."

6e Urgent versus Important?

Urgent issues are easy to address. They are the ones that get everyone in the room for the final go-ahead. They are the ones we need to decide on right now, before it's too late. . . .

Smart organizations ignore the urgent. Smart organizations understand that important issues are the ones to deal with. If you focus on the important stuff, the urgent will take care of itself.

Source: Seth Godin, "If It's Urgent, Ignore It," Fast Company, no. 81 (April 2004): 101.

QUESTIONS:

Is this distinction between "urgent" and "important" a useful one? Either on the job or in your personal affairs, what "important" decisions do you need to make now to keep them from growing into "urgent" problems?

■ The Planning/Control Cycle

To put the planning process in perspective, it is important to show how it is connected with the control function. Figure 6.4 illustrates the cyclical relationship between planning and control. Planning gets things headed in the right direction, and control keeps them headed in the right direction. (Because of the importance of the control function, it is covered in detail in Chapter 17.) Basically, each of the three levels of planning is a two-step sequence followed by a two-step control sequence.

The initial planning/control cycle begins when top management establishes strategic plans. When those strategic plans are carried out, intermediate and operational plans are formulated, thus setting in motion two more planning/control cycles. As strategic, intermediate, and operational plans are carried out, the control function begins. Corrective action is necessary when either the preliminary or the final results deviate from plans. For planned activities still in progress, the

Figure 6.4 The Basic Planning/Control Cycle

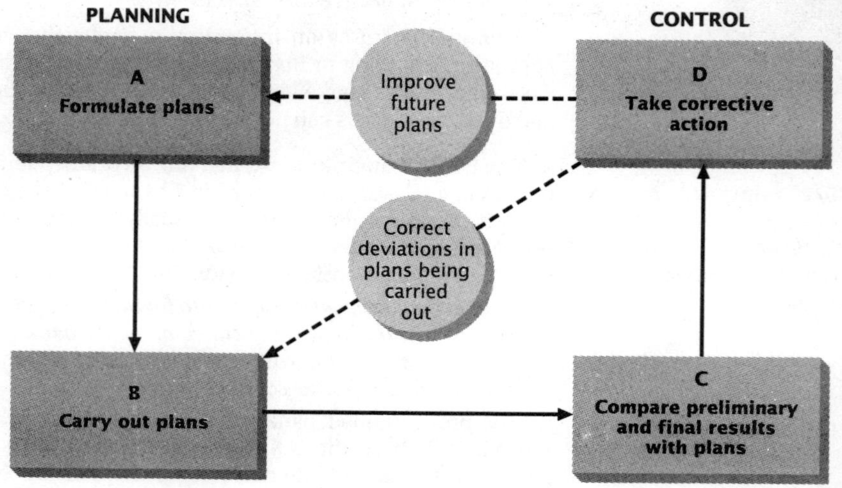

corrective action can get things back on track before it is too late. Deviations between final results and plans, on the other hand, are instructive feedback for the improvement of future plans. The broken lines in Figure 6.4 represent the important sort of feedback that makes the planning/control cycle a dynamic and evolving process. (See The Global Manager.) Our attention now turns to some practical planning tools.

Management by Objectives and Project Planning

In this section we examine a traditional planning technique and a modern planning challenge. Valuable lessons about planning can be learned from each.

Management by Objectives

management by objectives (MBO): *comprehensive management system based on measurable and participatively set objectives*

Management by objectives (MBO) is a comprehensive management system based on measurable and participatively set objectives. MBO has come a long way since it was first suggested by Peter Drucker in 1954 as a means of promoting managerial self-control.[34] MBO theory[35] and practice subsequently mushroomed and spread around the world. In one form or another, and under various labels, MBO has been adopted by most public and private organizations of any significant size. For example, at Cypress Semiconductor Corporation, the San Jose, California, electronics firm, computerization paved the way for high-tech MBO. T. J. Rodgers, the company's founder and chief executive officer, explains:

> *All of Cypress's 1,400 employees have goals, which, in theory, makes them no different from employees at most other companies. What makes our people different is that every week they set their own goals, commit to achieving them by a specific date, enter them into a database, and report whether or not they completed prior goals. Cypress's computerized goal system is an important part of our managerial infrastructure. It is a detailed guide to the future and an objective record of the past. In any given week, some 6,000 goals in the database come due. Our ability to meet those goals ultimately determines our success or failure....*
>
> *I developed the goal system long before personal computers existed. It has its roots in management-by-objectives techniques I learned in the mid-1970s at American Microsystems.*[36]

THE GLOBAL MANAGER

Culture Affects How Planning and Control Are Perceived: Russian versus Western Views

VIEWS OF PLANNING IN ORGANIZATIONS

Russians	Westerners
The plan is an ultimate end-task.	The plan is only a starting point and articulates alternative courses of action.
The plan must be executed by all means in the way that it was initially defined.	The plan needs to be adjusted continuously.
Only short-term planning is meaningful.	Planning is a long-term activity.
Success is measured according to whether the plan has been executed.	In order to be successful, one needs to reassess and readjust the plan.

VIEWS OF CONTROL IN ORGANIZATIONS

Russians	Westerners
Prefer the notion of control instead of feedback.	Prefer the notion of feedback instead of control.
Control is top-down.	Control is intrinsic to all organizational members' actions.
Control is focused on formalized bureaucracy.	Control is oriented toward involvement.
Control is exercised by using rewards and punishments.	Control is related to monitoring processes.
Control is a discrete activity.	Control is continuous.

The common denominator that has made MBO programs so popular in management theory and practice is the emphasis on objectives that are both *measurable* and *participatively set.*

■ **The MBO Cycle.** Because MBO combines planning and control, the four-stage MBO cycle corresponds to the planning/control cycle outlined in Figure 6.4. Steps 1 and 2 make up the planning phase of MBO, and steps 3 and 4 are the control phase.

4. DESCRIBE the four-step management by objectives (MBO) process, and **EXPLAIN** how it can foster individual commitment and motivation.

1. *Step 1: Setting objectives.* A hierarchy of challenging, fair, and internally consistent objectives is the necessary starting point for the MBO cycle and serves as the foundation for all that follows. All objectives, according to MBO theory, should be reduced to writing and put away for later reference during steps 3 and 4. Consistent with what was said earlier about objectives, objective setting in MBO begins at the top of the managerial pyramid and filters down, one layer at a time.

MBO's main contribution to the objective-setting process is its emphasis on the participation and involvement of people at lower levels. There is no place in MBO for the domineering manager ("Here are the objectives I've written for you") or for the passive manager ("I'll go along with whatever objectives you set"). MBO calls for a give-and-take negotiation of objectives between the manager and those who report directly to him or her.[37]

2. *Step 2: Developing action plans.* With the addition of action statements to the participatively set objectives, the planning phase of MBO is complete. Managers at each level develop plans that incorporate objectives established in step 1. Higher managers are responsible for ensuring that their direct assistants' plans complement one another and do not work at cross-purposes.
3. *Step 3: Periodic review.* As plans turn into action, attention turns to step 3, monitoring performance. Advocates of MBO usually recommend face-to-face meetings between a manager and his or her people at three-, six-, and nine-month intervals. (Some organizations, such as Cypress, rely on shorter cycles.) These periodic checkups permit those who are responsible for a particular set of objectives to reconsider them, checking their validity in view of unexpected events—added duties or the loss of a key assistant—that could make them obsolete. If an objective is no longer valid, it is amended accordingly. Otherwise, progress toward valid objectives is assessed. Periodic checkups also afford managers an excellent opportunity to give their people needed and appreciated feedback.
4. *Step 4: Performance appraisal.* At the end of one complete cycle of MBO, typically one year after the original goals were set, final performance is compared with the previously agreed-upon objectives. The pairs of superior and subordinate managers who mutually set the objectives one year earlier meet face to face once again to discuss how things have turned out. MBO emphasizes results, not personalities or excuses. The control phase of the MBO cycle is completed when success is rewarded with promotion, merit pay, or other suitable benefits and when failure is noted for future corrective action.

After one round of MBO, the cycle repeats itself, with each cycle contributing to the learning process. A common practice in introducing MBO is to start at the top and to pull a new layer of management into the MBO process each year. Experience has shown that plunging several layers of management into MBO all at once often causes confusion, dissatisfaction, and failure. In fact, even a moderate-sized organization usually takes five or more years to evolve a full-blown MBO system that ties together such areas as planning, control, performance appraisal, and the reward system. MBO programs can be facilitated by using off-the-shelf software programs. Such programs offer helpful spreadsheet formats for goal setting, timelines, at-a-glance status boards, and performance reports. MBO proponents believe that effective leadership and greater motivation—through the use of realistic objectives, more effective control, and self-control—are the natural by-products of a proper MBO system.[38]

■ **Strengths and Limitations of MBO.** Any widely used management technique is bound to generate debate about its relative strengths and weaknesses, and MBO is no exception.[39] Present and future managers will have more realistic expectations for MBO if they are familiar with both sides of this debate. The four primary strengths of MBO and four common complaints about it are compared in Figure 6.5.

This debate will probably not be resolved in the near future. Critics of MBO, such as the late quality expert W. Edwards Deming, point to both theoretical and methodological flaws.[40] Meanwhile, MBO advocates insist that it is the misapplication of MBO, not the MBO concept itself, that leads to problems. In the final analysis, MBO will probably work when organizational conditions are favorable and will probably fail when those conditions are unfavorable. A favorable climate for MBO includes top-management commitment, openness to change, Theory Y management, and employees who are willing and able to shoulder greater responsibility.[41] Research justifies

Figure 6.5 MBO's Strengths and Limitations

Strengths	Limitations
• MBO blends planning and control into a rational system of management. • MBO forces an organization to develop a top-to-bottom hierarchy of objectives. • MBO emphasizes end results rather than good intentions or personalities. • MBO encourages self-management and personal commitment through employee participation in setting objectives.	• MBO is too often sold as a cure-all. • MBO is easily stalled by authoritarian (Theory X) managers and inflexible bureaucratic policies and rules. • MBO takes too much time and effort and generates too much paperwork. • MBO's emphasis on measurable objectives can be used as a threat by overzealous managers.

putting *top-management commitment* at the top of the list. In a review of 70 MBO studies, researchers found that "when top-management commitment was high, the average gain in productivity was 56 percent. When such commitment was low, the average gain in productivity was only 6 percent."[42] A strong positive relationship was also found between top-management commitment to MBO program success and employee job satisfaction.[43] The greater management's commitment, the greater the satisfaction.

Project Planning and Management

Project-based organizations are becoming the norm today. Why? Drawing-board-to-market times are being honed to the minimum in today's technology-driven world.[44] Typically, cross-functional teams of people with different technical skills are brought together on a temporary basis to complete a specific project as swiftly as possible. According to the Project Management Institute, "A **project** is a temporary endeavor undertaken to achieve a particular aim."[45] Projects, like all other activities within the management domain, need to be systematically planned and managed. What sets project planning/management apart is the *temporary* nature of projects, as opposed to the typical ongoing or continuous activities in organizations. Projects may be pursued within the organization or performed for outside clients. When the job is done, project members disband and move on to other projects or return to their usual work routines. Time is usually of the essence for project managers because of tight schedules and deadlines. For example, put yourself in the shoes of Larry Crain, who has been the floral director for the Academy Awards ceremony for the past twelve years:

project: *a temporary endeavor undertaken to achieve a particular aim*

6f Back to the Opening Case

Is Knouf's approach to planning an effective application of MBO? Why or why not?

> *It takes 70,000 flowers, 1,500 potted plants, 500 buckets, 65 people and 20 floral designers to give the biggest event in entertainment a simple, elegant look.*
>
> *More that 90% of the blooms are California-grown, and they arrive within 24 hours of being cut. But Crain has gone as far as Ecuador for roses, Thailand for orchids, and Holland and Israel for tulips.*[46]

Project management is the usual thing on Hollywood movie sets and at construction companies building homes, roads, and skyscrapers. But it is new to manufacturers, banks, insurance companies, hospitals, and government agencies. Unfortunately, much of this Internet-age project management leaves a lot to be desired. For example, consider the dismal track record for information technology (IT) projects, typically involving conversion of an old computer system to new hardware, software, and work methods.

> *Most large IT projects are delivered late and over budget because they are inefficiently managed. A study by the Hackett Group, a Hudson, Ohio–based benchmarking firm, found that the average company completes only 37 percent of large IT projects on time and only 42 percent on budget.*[47]

A broader and deeper understanding of project management is in order.

Project managers face many difficult challenges. First and foremost, they work outside the normal organizational hierarchy or chain of command because projects are ad hoc and temporary. Consequently, they must rely on excellent "people management skills" instead of on giving orders. Those skills include, but are not limited to, communication, motivation, leadership, conflict resolution, and negotiation (see Chapters 12–16).

A UFO? No, it's the first of three 85-foot domes where peanuts will be stored in nitrogen-enriched air. Farmer-owned Tifton Quality Peanuts in Tifton, Georgia, hopes construction of this peanut shelling facility will be complete in time for the new crop. Many loose ends need to be neatly tied together in a schedule-driven project of this size.

Project *planning* deserves special attention in this chapter because project managers have the difficult job of being both intermediate/tactical and operational planners. They are responsible for both the big picture and the little details of their project. A project that is not well planned is a project doomed to failure. So let us take a look at the project life cycle, project management software, the six roles project managers play, and guidelines for project managers.

5. DISCUSS project planning within the context of the project life cycle, and **LIST** six roles played by project managers.

■ **The Project Life Cycle.** Every project, from developing a new breakfast cereal to staging a benefit rock concert, has a predictable four-stage life cycle. As shown in Figure 6.6, the four stages are conceptualization, planning, execution, and termination. Although they are shown equally spaced in Figure 6.6, the four stages typically involve varying periods of time. Sometimes the borders between stages blur. For example, project goal setting actually begins in the conceptualization stage and often carries over to the planning stage. During this stage, project managers turn their attention to facilities and equipment, personnel and task assignments, and scheduling. Work on the project begins in the execution stage, and additional resources are acquired as needed. Budget demands are highest during the execution stage because everything is in motion. To some, the label "termination" in stage 4 might suggest a sudden end to the project. But more typically, the completed project is turned over to an end user (e.g., a new breakfast cereal is turned over to manufacturing) and project resources are phased out.[48]

6g A Work of Art

At a conference this week I ran into a high-school classmate I hadn't seen in 26 years. I remember her winning all the art awards. Now she's in satellite communications. "Still painting?" I asked. "No," she said, "but managing a complex project uses the same creativity."

Source: Thomas Petzinger Jr., *"Some Thoughts on All I've Learned from You as New Fronts Beckon,"* Wall Street Journal *(May 21, 1999): B1.*

QUESTION:
What do you think she meant?

■ **Project Management Software.** Recall from our earlier discussion of the basic planning/control cycle (Figure 6.4) how planning and control are intertwined. One cannot occur without the other. The same is true for project planning. Making sure planned activities occur when and where appropriate and taking corrective action when necessary can be an overwhelming job for the manager of a complex project. Fortunately, a host of computer software programs

Figure 6.6 The Project Life Cycle and Project Planning Activities

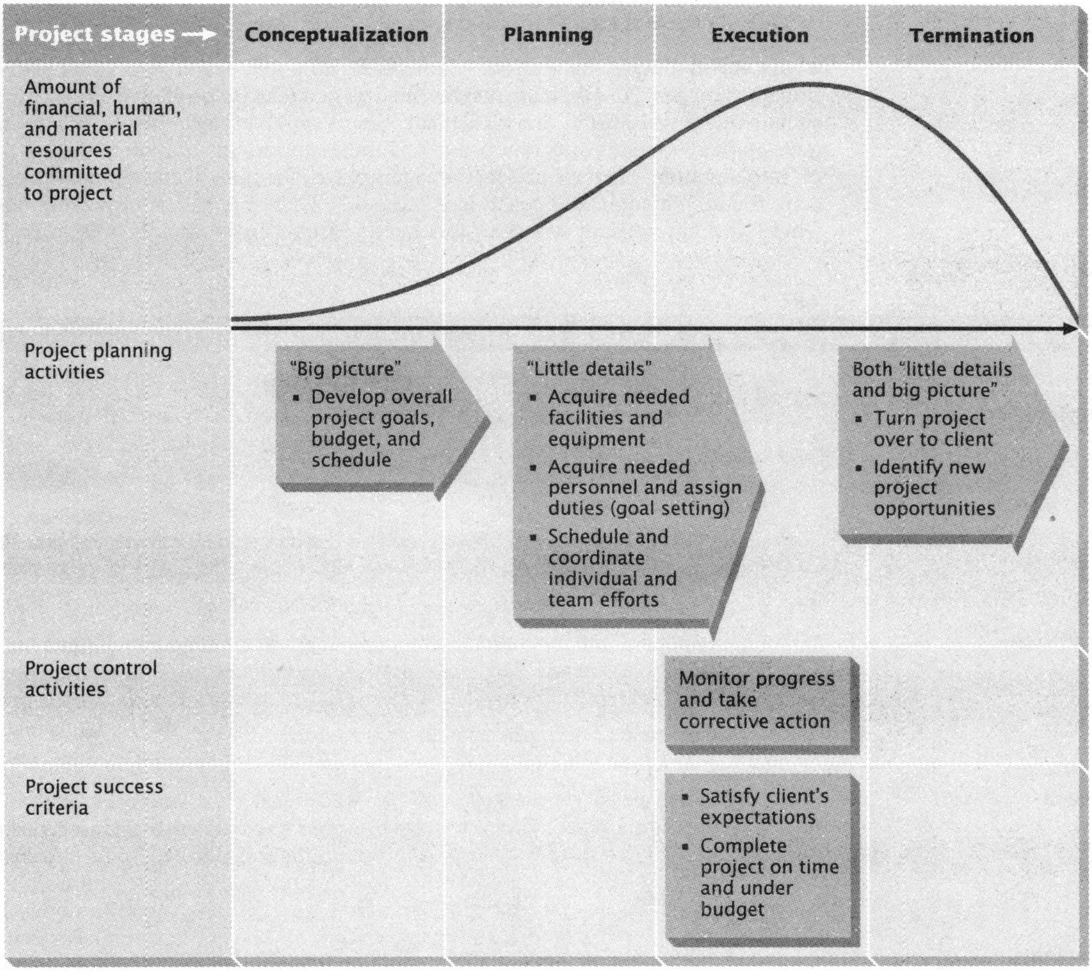

Source: *Adapted in part from Figure 1.2 and discussion in Jeffrey K. Pinto and O. P. Kharbanda,* Successful Project Managers: Leading Your Team to Success *(New York: Van Nostrand Reinhold, 1995), pp. 17–21.*

can make the task manageable. But which one of the many available programs—such as Microsoft Project for Windows—should a project manager use? Thanks to project management experts, we have a handy list of screening criteria for selecting the right tool. Judging from the list that follows, the overriding attributes of good project management software packages are *flexibility* and *transparency* (meaning quick and up-to-date status reports on all important aspects of the project).[49]

- Identify and ultimately schedule need-to-do activities
- Ability to dynamically shift priorities and schedules, and view resulting impact
- Provide critical path analysis
- Provide flexibility for plan modifications
- Ability to set priority levels
- Flexibility to manage all resources: people, hardware, environments, cash

- Ability to merge plans
- Management alerts for project slippage
- Automatic time recording to map against project
- Identification of time spent on activities[50]

■ **Six Roles Played by Project Managers.** In a new study, interviews with 40 project managers (and their clients) revealed what it takes to be effective.[51] The managers studied were working with outside clients on IT projects involving software development, systems integration, and technical support. In addition to the key role of "implementer," effective project managers played the roles of entrepreneur, politician, friend, marketer, and coach (see Table 6.2). Each role has its own set of challenges and appropriate strategies for meeting those challenges. It takes a highly

Table 6.2 Roles, Challenges, and Strategies for Effective Project Managers

Project manager role	Challenges	Strategies
Implementer	– Effectively plan, organize, and accomplish the project goals.	– Extend this role to include the newly identified roles described.
Entrepreneur	– Navigate unfamiliar surroundings. – Survive in a "sink or swim" environment. – Manage the unexpected.	– Build relationships with a number of different stakeholders. – Use persuasion to influence others. – Be charismatic in the presentation of new approaches.
Politician	– Understand two diverse corporate cultures (parent and client organizations). – Operate within the political system of the client organization.	– Align with the powerful individuals. – Obtain a senior/politically savvy client sponsor to promote and support the project.
Friend	– Determine the important relationships to build and sustain outside the team itself. – Be a friend to the client.	– Build friendships with key project managers and functional managers. – Identify common interests and experiences to bridge a friendship with the client.
Marketer	– Access client corporate strategic information. – Understand the strategic objectives of the client organization. – Determine future business opportunities.	– Develop a strong relationship with the primary client contact and with top management in the client organization. – Align new ideas/proposals with the strategic objectives of the client organization.
Coach	– Blend team members from multiple organizations. – Motivate team members without formal authority. – Reward and recognize team accomplishments with limited resources.	– Identify mutually rewarding common objectives. – Provide challenging tasks to build the skills of the team members. – Promote the team and its members to key decision makers.

Source: Academy of Management Executive: The Thinking Manager's Source *by Sheila Simsarian Webber and Maria Torti. Copyright 2004 by Academy of Management. Reproduced with permission of Academy of Management in the format Textbook via Copyright Clearance Center.*

6h Oh, My Aching Deadline!

QUESTIONS:
How do you respond to deadlines? Which types of deadlines motivate you and which types do not? Why are deadlines such a powerful motivational tool?

skilled and motivated person to play all these roles successfully in today's business environment. As one project management educator put it,

> *In today's harsh business economy, executives want to know one thing about any project management initiative: "What's the value?" More than ever, every dollar invested must be justified, and every initiative must deliver tangible results.*[52]

■ **Project Management Guidelines.** Project managers need a working knowledge of basic planning concepts and tools, as presented in this chapter. Beyond that, they need to be aware of the following special planning demands of projects.[53]

- *Projects are schedule-driven and results-oriented.* By definition, projects are created to accomplish something specific by a certain time. Project managers require a positive attitude about making lots of quick decisions and doing things in a hurry. They tend to value results more than process.
- *The big picture and the little details are of equal importance.* Project managers need to keep the overall project goal and deadline in mind when attending to day-to-day problems and personnel issues. This is difficult because distractions are constant.
- *Project planning is a necessity, not a luxury.* Novice project managers tend to get swept away by the pressure for results and fail to devote adequate time and resources to project planning.
- *Project managers know the motivational power of a deadline.* A challenging (but not impossible) project deadline is the project manager's most powerful motivational tool. The final deadline serves as a focal point for all team and individual goal setting.[54]

Graphical Planning/Scheduling/Control Tools

6. **COMPARE** and **CONTRAST** flow charts and Gantt charts, and **DISCUSS** the value of PERT networks.

Management science specialists have introduced needed precision into the planning/control cycle through graphical analysis. Three graphical tools for planning, scheduling, and controlling operations are flow charts, Gantt charts, and PERT networks. They can be found in project management software programs.

■ Sequencing with Flow Charts

Flow charts have been used extensively by computer programmers for identifying task components and by TQM (total quality management) teams for *work simplification* (eliminating wasted steps and activities). Beyond that, flow charts are a useful sequencing tool with broad application.[55] Sequencing is simply arranging events in the order of their actual or desired occurrence. For instance, this book had to be purchased before it could be read. Thus the event "purchase book" would come before the event "read book" in flow-chart sequence.

A sample flow chart is given in Figure 6.7. Notice that the chart consists of boxes and diamonds in addition to the start and stop ovals. Each box contains a major event, and each diamond contains a yes-or-no decision.

Managers at all levels and in all specialized areas can identify and properly sequence important events and decisions with flow charts of this kind. User-friendly computer programs make flow-charting fun and easy today. Flow charts force people to consider all relevant links in a particular endeavor as well as their proper sequence. This is an advantage because it encourages analytical thinking. But flow charts have two disadvantages. First, they do not indicate the time dimension— that is, the varying amounts of time required to complete each step and make each

Figure 6.7 A Sample Flow Chart

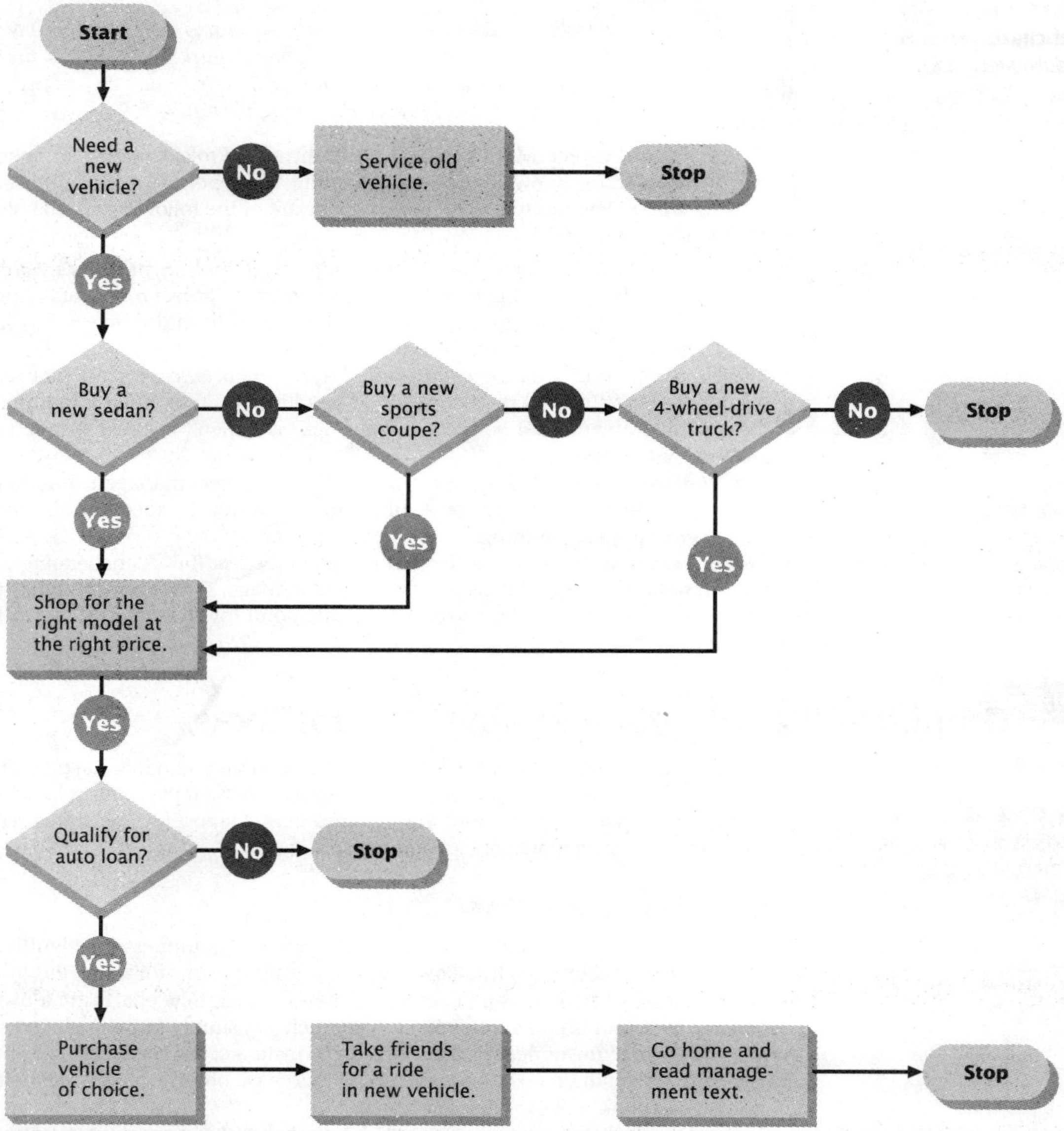

decision. Second, the use of flow charts is not practical for complex endeavors in which several activities take place at once.

■ Scheduling with Gantt Charts

Scheduling is an important part of effective planning. When later steps depend on the successful completion of earlier steps, schedules help managers determine when and where resources are needed. Without schedules, inefficiency creeps in as equipment and people stand idle. Also, like any type of plan or budget, schedules provide management with a measuring stick for corrective action. Gantt charts, named for Henry L. Gantt, who developed the technique, are a convenient scheduling tool for managers.[56] Gantt worked with Frederick W. Taylor at Midvale Steel beginning in 1887 and, as discussed in Chapter 2, helped refine the practice of scientific management. A **Gantt chart** is a graphical scheduling technique historically used in production operations. Things have changed since Gantt's time, and so have Gantt chart applications. Updated versions like the one in Figure 6.8 are widely used today for planning and scheduling all sorts of organizational activities. They are especially useful for large projects such as moving into a new building or installing a new computer network.[57]

Gantt chart: *graphical scheduling technique*

Figure 6.8 also shows how a Gantt chart can be used for more than just scheduling the important steps of a job. Filling in the timelines of completed activities makes it possible to assess *actual* progress at a glance. Like flow charts, Gantt charts force managers to be analytical as they reduce jobs or projects to separate steps. Moreover, Gantt charts improve on flow charts by allowing the planner to specify the time to be spent on each activity. A disadvantage Gantt charts share with flow charts is that overly complex endeavors are cumbersome to chart.

PERT Networks

The more complex the project, the greater the need for reliable sequencing and scheduling of key activities. Simultaneous sequencing and scheduling amounts to programming. One of the most widely recognized programming tools used by managers is a technique referred to simply as PERT. An acronym for **Program Evaluation and Review Technique, PERT** is a graphical sequencing and scheduling tool for large, complex, and nonroutine projects.

Program Evaluation and Review Technique, PERT: *graphical sequencing and scheduling tool for complex projects*

Figure 6.8 A Sample Gantt Chart

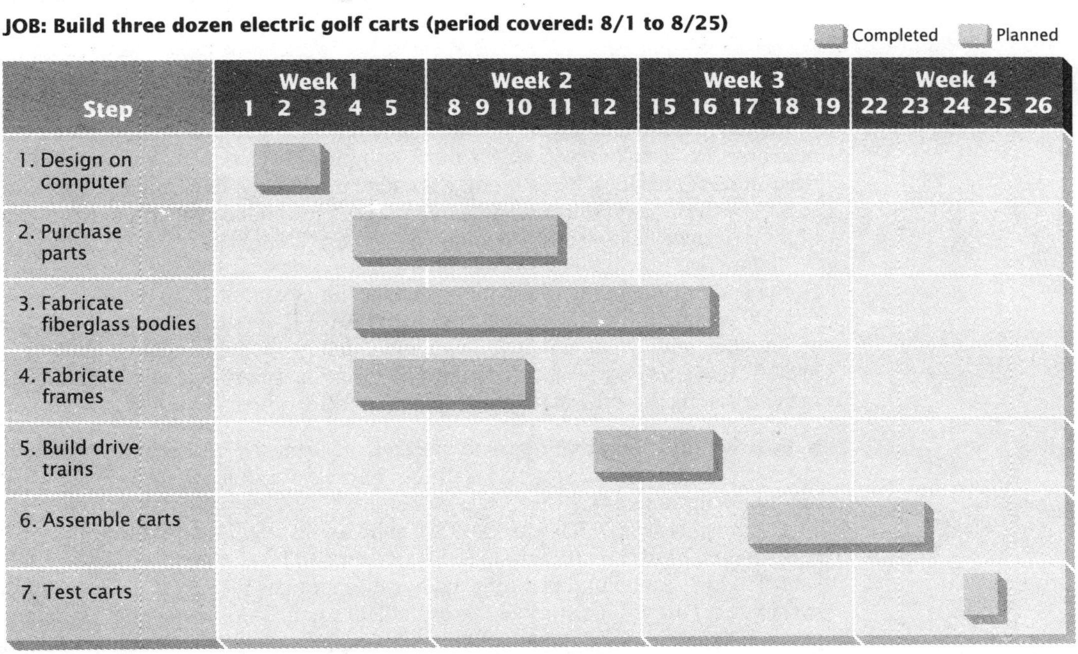

History of PERT. PERT was developed in 1958 by a team of management consultants for the U.S. Navy Special Projects Office. At the time, the navy was faced with the seemingly insurmountable task of building a weapon system that could fire a missile from the deck of a submerged submarine. PERT not only contributed to the development of the Polaris submarine project but also was credited with helping to bring the system to combat readiness nearly two years ahead of schedule. News of this dramatic administrative feat caught the attention of managers around the world. But, as one user of PERT reflected, "No management technique has ever caused so much enthusiasm, controversy, and disappointment as PERT."[58] Realizing that PERT is not a panacea, but rather a specialized planning and control tool that can be appropriately or inappropriately applied, helps managers accept it at face value.[59]

PERT Terminology. Because PERT has its own special language, four key terms must be understood.

PERT event: *performance milestone; start or finish of an activity*

PERT activity: *work in process*

PERT times: *weighted time estimates for completion of PERT activities*

- *Event.* A **PERT event** is a performance milestone representing the start or finish of some activity. Handing in a difficult management exam is an event.
- *Activity.* A **PERT activity** represents work in process. Activities are time-consuming jobs that begin and end with an event. Studying for a management exam and taking the exam are activities.
- *Time.* **PERT times** are estimated times for the completion of PERT activities. PERT times are weighted averages of three separate time estimates: (1) *optimistic time* (T_o)—the time an activity should take under the best of conditions; (2) *most likely time* (T_m)—the time an activity should take under normal conditions; and (3) *pessimistic time* (T_p)—the time an activity should take under the worst possible conditions. The formula for calculating estimated PERT time (T_e) is

$$T_e = \frac{T_o + 4T_m + T_p}{6}$$

critical path: *most time-consuming route through a PERT network*

- *Critical path.* The **critical path** is the most time-consuming chain of activities and events in a PERT network. In other words, the longest path through a PERT network is critical because if any of the activities along it are delayed, the entire project will be delayed accordingly.[60]

PERT in Action. A PERT network is shown in Figure 6.9. The task in this example, the design and construction of three dozen customized golf carts for use by physically challenged adults, is relatively simple for instructional purposes. PERT networks are usually reserved for more complex projects with hundreds or even thousands of activities. PERT events are coded by circled letters, and PERT activities, shown by the arrows connecting the PERT events, are coded by number. A PERT time (T_e) has been calculated and recorded for each PERT activity.

Before reading on, see if you can pick out the critical path in the PERT network in Figure 6.9. By calculating which path will take the most time from beginning to end, you will see that the critical path turns out to be A-B-C-F-G-H-I. This particular chain of activities and events will require an estimated 21.75 workdays to complete. The overall duration of the project is dictated by the critical path, and a delay in any of the activities along this critical path will delay the entire project.

Positive and Negative Aspects of PERT. During the nearly 50 years that PERT has been used in a wide variety of settings, both its positive and its negative aspects have become apparent.

On the plus side, PERT is an excellent scheduling tool for large, nonroutine projects, ranging from constructing an electricity generation station to launching a space vehicle. PERT is a helpful planning aid because it forces managers to envision projects in their entirety. It also gives them a tool for predicting resource needs, potential problem areas, and the impact of delays on project completion. If an activity runs over or under its estimated time, the ripple effect of lost or gained time on down-

Figure 6.9 A Sample PERT Network

TASK: Build three dozen customized golf carts for use by physically challenged adults

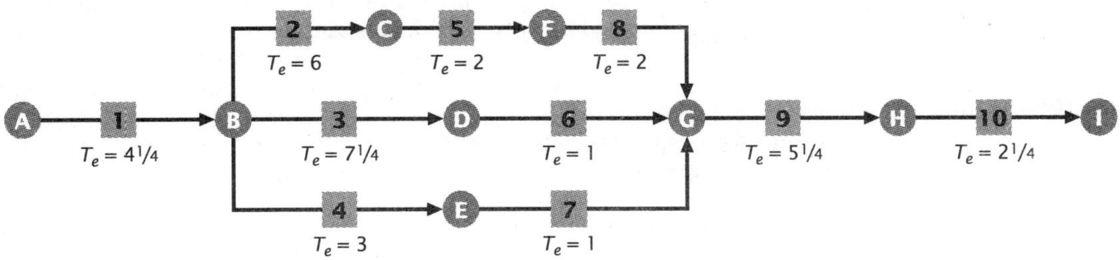

PERT events
A. Receive contract
B. Begin construction
C. Receive parts
D. Bodies ready for testing
E. Frames ready for testing
F. Drive trains ready for testing
G. Components ready for assembly
H. Carts assembled
I. Carts ready for shipment

PERT activities and times

Activities	T_o	T_m	T_p	T_e*
1. Prepare final design	3	4	6	4 1/4
2. Purchase parts	4	5	12	6
3. Fabricate bodies	5	7 1/2	9	7 1/4
4. Fabricate frames	2 1/2	3	4	3
5. Build drive trains	1 1/2	2	3	2
6. Test bodies	1/2	1	1 1/2	1
7. Test frames	1/2	1	1 1/2	1
8. Test drive trains	1	1 1/2	5	2
9. Assemble carts	3	5	9	5 1/4
10. Test carts	1	2	5	2 1/4

Rounded to nearest 1/4 workday

stream activities can be calculated. PERT also gives managers an opportunity, through the calculation of optimistic and pessimistic times, to factor in realistic uncertainties about planning horizons.

On the minus side, PERT is an inappropriate tool for repetitive assembly-line operations in which scheduling is dictated by the pace of machines. PERT also shares with other planning and decision-making aids the disadvantage of being only as good as its underlying assumptions. False assumptions about activities and events and miscalculations of PERT times can render PERT ineffective. Despite the objective impression of numerical calculations, PERT times are derived rather subjectively. Moreover, PERT's critics say it is too time-consuming: A complex PERT network prepared by hand may be obsolete by the time it is completed, and frequent updates can tie PERT in knots. Project management software with computerized PERT routines is essential for complex projects because it can greatly speed the graphical plotting process and updating of time estimates.

Break-Even Analysis

In well-managed businesses, profit is a forethought rather than an afterthought. A widely used tool for projecting profits relative to costs and sales volume is break-even analysis. In fact, break-even analysis is often referred to as cost-volume-profit analysis. By using either the algebraic method or the graphical method, planners can calculate the **break-even point,** the level of sales at which the firm neither suffers a loss nor realizes a profit. In effect, the break-even point is the profit-making threshold. If sales are below that point, the organization loses money. If sales go beyond the break-even point, it makes a profit. Break-even points, as discussed later, are often expressed in units. For example, Airbus Industrie, based in France, is moving forward on its plan to have a huge 555-passenger commercial airliner in service by 2006. The break-even point for the \$290 million double-deck A380 reportedly is about 250 units.

break-even point: *level of sales at which there is no loss or profit*

7. EXPLAIN how break-even points can be calculated.

From a procedural standpoint, a critical part of break-even analysis is separating fixed costs from variable costs.

Fixed versus Variable Costs

Some expenses, called fixed costs, must be paid even if a firm fails to sell a single unit. Other expenses, termed variable costs, are incurred only as units are produced and sold. **Fixed costs** are contractual costs that must be paid regardless of the level of output or sales. Typical examples include rent, utilities, insurance premiums, managerial and professional staff salaries, property taxes, and licenses. **Variable costs** are costs that vary directly with the firm's production and sales. Common variable costs include costs of production (such as labor, materials, and supplies), sales commissions, and product delivery expenses. As output and sales increase, fixed costs remain the same but variable costs accumulate. Looking at it another way, fixed costs are a function of *time* and variable costs are a function of *volume.* You can now calculate the break-even point.

fixed costs: *contractual costs that must be paid regardless of output or sales*

variable costs: *costs that vary directly with production and sales*

The Algebraic Method

Where the following abbreviations are used,

$$FC = \text{total fixed costs}$$
$$P = \text{price (per unit)}$$
$$VC = \text{variable costs (per unit)}$$
$$BEP = \text{break-even point}$$

the formula for calculating break-even point (in units) is

$$BEP \text{ (in units)} = \frac{FC}{P - VC}$$

The difference between the selling price P and per-unit variable costs VC is referred to as the **contribution margin.** In other words, the contribution margin is the portion of the unit selling price that falls above and beyond the variable costs and that can be applied to fixed costs. Above the break-even point, the contribution margin contributes to profits.

contribution margin: *selling price per unit minus variable costs per unit*

Variable costs are normally expressed as a percentage of the unit selling price. As a working example of how the break-even point (in units) can be calculated, assume that a firm has total fixed costs of \$30,000, a unit selling price of \$7, and variable costs of 57 percent (or \$4 in round numbers):

$$BEP \text{ (in units)} = \frac{30{,}000}{7 - 4} = 10{,}000$$

This calculation shows that 10,000 units must be produced and sold at \$7 each if the firm is to break even on this particular product.

Price Planning. Break-even analysis is an excellent "what-if" tool for planners who want to know what impact price changes will have on profit. For instance, what

Jacky Cheung, Hong Kong Disneyland's spokesperson, gets some help from his friends during the castle-topping ceremony in 2004. From groundbreaking in January 2003 through its targeted opening in 2005–2006, this has been no Mickey Mouse operation. Hong Kong officials project $19 billion in benefits over the next 40 years. A break-even analysis to determine how many paid visits it will take to turn a profit will facilitate planning and operations.

would the break-even point be if the unit selling price were lowered to match a competitor's price of $6?

$$BEP \text{ (in units)} = \frac{30{,}000}{6 - 4} = 15{,}000$$

In this case, the $1 drop in price to $6 means that 15,000 units must be sold before a profit can be realized.

■ **Profit Planning.** Planners often set profit objectives and then work backward to determine the required level of output. Break-even analysis greatly assists such planners. The modified break-even formula for profit planning is

$$BEP \text{ (in units)} = \frac{FC + \text{desired profit}}{P - VC}$$

Assuming that top management has set a profit objective for the year at $30,000 and that the original figures above apply, the following calculation results:

$$BEP \text{ (in units)} = \frac{30{,}000 + 30{,}000}{7 - 4} = 20{,}000$$

To meet the profit objective of $30,000, the company would need to sell 20,000 units at $7 each.

■ The Graphical Method

If you place the dollar value of costs and revenues on a vertical axis and unit sales on a horizontal axis, you can calculate the break-even point by plotting fixed costs, total costs (fixed + variable costs), and total revenue. As illustrated in Figure 6.10, the break-even point is where the total costs line and the total sales revenue line intersect.

Figure 6.10 Graphical Break-Even Analysis

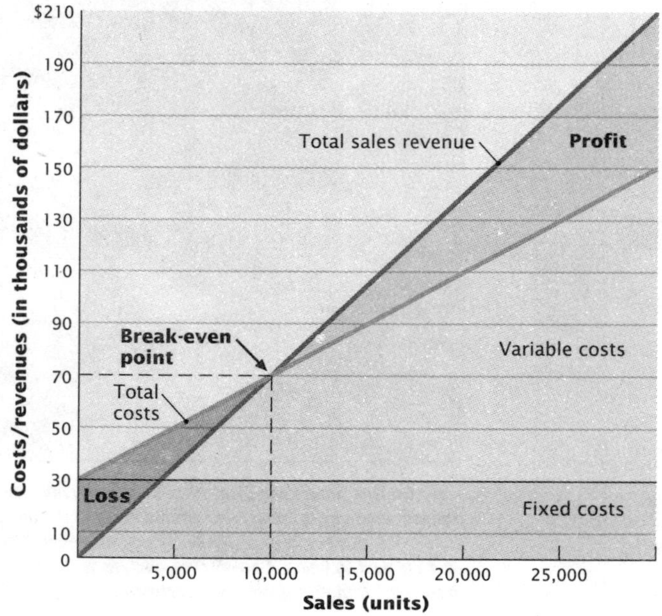

> **6i Meet Me at the Margin**
>
> Jeffrey Dachis, cofounder and former CEO of Razorfish, a Web-based marketing company, on lessons learned during the dot-com crash:
>
> *... the rules of business never changed. You have fixed costs, you have variable costs, and you have profit margin. And that's it. If you don't have a handle on that stuff, then there's nothing else to talk about. If there is no profit margin, you're in trouble.*
>
> *Source: As quoted in* Fast Company, *no. 80 (March 2004): 51.*
>
> **QUESTION:**
> **What is the connection between this statement and break-even analysis?**

Although the algebraic method does the same job, some planners prefer the graphical method because it presents the various cost-volume-profit relationships at a glance, in a convenient visual format.

Break-Even Analysis: Strengths and Limitations

Like the other planning tools discussed in this chapter, break-even analysis is not a cure-all. It has both strengths and limitations.

On the positive side, break-even analysis forces planners to acknowledge and deal realistically with the interrelatedness of cost, volume, and profit. All three variables are connected such that a change in one sends ripples of change through the other two. As mentioned earlier, break-even analysis allows planners to ask what-if questions concerning the impact of price changes and varying profit objectives.

The primary problem with break-even analysis is that neatly separating fixed and variable costs can be very difficult. General managers should enlist the help of accountants to isolate relevant fixed and variable costs. Moreover, because of complex factors in supply and demand, break-even analysis is not a good tool for setting prices. It serves better as a general planning and decision-making aid.

SUMMARY

1. Planning has been labeled the primary management function because it sets the stage for all other aspects of management. Along with many other practical reasons for planning, managers need to plan in order to cope with an uncertain environment. Three types of uncertainty are state uncertainty ("What will happen?"), effect uncertainty ("What will happen to our organization?"), and response uncertainty ("What will be the outcome of our decisions?"). To cope with environmental uncertainty, organizations can respond as defenders, prospectors, analyzers, or reactors.

2. A properly written plan tells what, when, and how something is to be accomplished. A clearly written organizational mission statement tends to serve as a useful focus for the planning process. Strategic, intermediate, and operational plans are formulated by top-, middle-, and lower-level management, respectively.

3. Objectives have been called the single most important feature of the planning process. Well-written objectives spell out, in measurable terms, what should be accomplished and when it is to be accomplished. Good objectives help managers by serving as targets, acting as measuring sticks, encouraging commitment, and strengthening motivation. Objective setting begins at the top of the organization and filters down, thus forming a means-ends chain. Priorities affect resource allocation by assigning relative importance to objectives. Plans are formulated and executed as part of a more encompassing planning/control cycle.

4. Management by objectives (MBO), an approach to planning and controlling, is based on measurable and participatively set objectives. MBO basically consists of four steps: (1) setting objectives participatively, (2) developing action plans, (3) periodically reevaluating objectives and plans and monitoring performance, and (4) conducting annual performance appraisals. Objective setting in MBO flows from top to bottom. MBO has both strengths and limitations and requires a supportive climate favorable to change, participation, and the sharing of authority.

5. Project planning occurs throughout the project life cycle's four stages: conceptualization, planning, execution, and termination. "Big-picture" tactical planning—project goal, budget, and schedule—occurs during stage 1 and into stage 2. During stage 2 and into the execution phase in stage 3, project planning deals with the "little details" of facilities and equipment, personnel and job assignments, and scheduling. Starting near the end of stage 3 and carrying into the termination stage, both little-details and big-picture planning are required to pass the project along and identify new project opportunities. Planning is central to project success because projects are schedule-driven and results-oriented. Project planners need to keep constantly abreast of both the big picture and the little details. Novice project managers too often shortchange planning. Challenging but realistic project deadlines are project managers' most powerful motivational tool. Six roles performed by effective project managers are implementer, entrepreneur, politician, friend, marketer, and coach.

6. Flow charts, Gantt charts, and PERT networks, found in project management software packages, are three graphical tools for more effectively planning, scheduling, and controlling operations. Flow charts visually sequence important events and yes-or-no decisions. Gantt charts, named for Frederick W. Taylor's disciple Henry L. Gantt, are a graphical scheduling technique used in a wide variety of situations. Both flow charts and Gantt charts have the advantage of forcing managers to be analytical. But Gantt charts realistically portray the time dimension, whereas flow charts do not. PERT, which stands for Program Evaluation and Review Technique, is a sequencing and scheduling tool appropriate for large, complex, and nonroutine projects. Weighted PERT times enable managers to factor in their uncertainties about time estimates.

7. Break-even analysis, or cost-volume-profit analysis, can be carried out algebraically or graphically. Either way, it helps planners gauge the potential impact of price changes and profit objectives on sales volume. A major limitation of break-even analysis is that specialized accounting knowledge is required to identify relevant fixed and variable costs.

TERMS TO UNDERSTAND

- Planning, p. 153
- State uncertainty, p. 154
- Effect uncertainty, p. 154
- Response uncertainty, p. 154
- Plan, p. 158
- Strategic planning, p. 159
- Intermediate planning, p. 159
- Operational planning, p. 159
- Planning horizon, p. 159
- Objective, p. 160
- Priorities, p. 162
- 80/20 principle, p. 163
- Management By Objectives (MBO), p. 164
- Project, p. 167
- Gantt chart, p. 173
- Program Evaluation and Review Technique, PERT, p. 173
- PERT event, p. 174
- PERT activity, p. 174
- PERT times, p. 174
- Critical path, p. 174
- Break-even point, p. 176
- Fixed costs, p. 176
- Variable costs, p. 176
- Contribution margin, p. 176

SKILLS & TOOLS

Ten Common Errors to Avoid When Writing a Plan for a New Business

Here are errors in business plan preparation that almost certainly will result in denial of a loan application by a bank.

- Submitting a "rough copy," perhaps with coffee stains on the pages and crossed-out words in the text, tells the banker that the owner doesn't take his idea seriously.
- Outdated historical financial information or industry comparisons will leave doubts about the entrepreneur's planning abilities.
- Unsubstantiated assumptions can hurt a business plan; the business owner must be prepared to explain the "whys" of every point in the plan.
- Too much "blue sky"—a failure to consider prospective pitfalls—will lead the banker to conclude that the idea is not realistic.
- A lack of understanding of the financial information is a drawback. Even if an outside source is used to prepare the projections, the owner must fully comprehend the information.
- Absence of any consideration of outside influences is a gap in a business plan. The owner needs to discuss the potential impact of competitive factors as well as the economic environment prevalent at the time of the request.
- No indication that the owner has anything at stake in the venture is a particular problem. The lender will expect the entrepreneur to have some equity capital invested in the business.
- Unwillingness to personally guarantee any loans raises a question: If the business owner isn't willing to stand behind his or her company, then why should the bank?
- Introducing the plan with a demand for unrealistic loan terms is a mistake. The lender wants to find out about the viability of the business before discussing loan terms.
- Too much focus on collateral is a problem in a business plan. Even for a cash-secured loan, the banker is looking toward projected profits for repayment of the loan. The emphasis should be on cash flow.

Source: *J. Tol Broome Jr., "Mistakes to Avoid in Drafting a Plan,"* Nation's Business, *81 (February 1993): 30. Reprinted by permission,* Nation's Business, *February 1993. Copyright 1993, U.S. Chamber of Commerce.*

HANDS-ON EXERCISE

How to Write Good Objectives and Plans (Plan = What + When + How)

Instructions:

Well-written objectives are the heart of effective planning. An objective should state *what* is to be accomplished (in measurable terms) and *when* it will be accomplished. An objective becomes a plan when the *how* is added. Here is an everyday example of a well-written plan: "I will ("what?") lose 5 pounds ("when?") in 30 days ("how?") by not eating desserts and walking a mile four days a week."

Remember the following handy three-way test to assess how well your plans are written.

- Test 1: Does this plan specify *what* the intended result is and is it stated in *measurable* terms?
- Test 2: Does this plan specify *when* the intended result is to be accomplished?
- Test 3: Does this plan specify *how* the intended result is to be accomplished?

Write a plan that passes all three tests for each of the following areas of your life.

Self-improvement plan:	What? ______
	When? ______
	How? ______
Work-related plan:	What? ______
	When? ______
	How? ______
Community-service plan:	What? ______
	When? ______
	How? ______

For Consideration/Discussion

1. In terms of the above three-way test, which of your plans is the best? Why? Which is the worst? Why?
2. What is the hardest part of writing good plans? Explain.
3. From a managerial standpoint, why is it important to have plans written in measurable terms?
4. What is the managerial value of formally written plans, as opposed to verbal commitments?
5. Why would some employees resist writing plans according to the specifications in this exercise? Explain.

INTERNET EXERCISES

1. **All about project management.** Project management software, as covered in this chapter, belongs in virtually every modern manager's tool kit. The purpose of this exercise is to explore the different features of the most widely used project management software package: Microsoft Project. The journey begins at Microsoft Project's Web page (**www.microsoft.com/office/project**), where you first need to click on "Frequently asked questions" under the heading "Discover Project 2003." Browse the rest of the site to get a feel for how this software can help managers plan and control a project. (*Note:* By the time you read this, a new version of Microsoft Project may have been released. In that case, simply

follow the prompts to view the material mentioned above.)

Learning Points: 1. Have you ever used project management software? Was it Microsoft Project? If you used something else, does Microsoft Project appear to be superior or inferior? Explain. 2. If you have never used project management software, which of the features of Microsoft Project do you like best? Why? 3. Why is project management software essential for today's complex projects?

2. **How to write a business plan.** Got a great new product or service idea? Thinking of starting your own business? You need a plan, not only to sharpen your focus but to obtain financing as well. *Inc.* magazine's Web site (**www.inc.com**) offers an excellent selection of resources for both future and present small-business owners. At the home page, scroll down to the bottom section titled "Inc.com How-To" and click on "Writing a Business Plan." A good place to begin your self-education program is at the heading "Build a Strong Business Plan, Section by Section." How much time you have and your level of interest will determine how many of the other useful topics you access.

   Learning Points: 1. Is there a lot more to a basic business plan than you first thought? Explain. 2. Which part of the business plan would be the most difficult for you to prepare? Why? Which would be the easiest? Why? 3. Does this exercise make you more or less interested in starting your own business? Explain.

3. **Check it out.** Are you overloaded? Do you have too much to do and too little time in which to do it? Then perhaps you could use the 10 practical tips for setting priorities at **www.score.org/om_2.html**.

For updates to these exercises, visit our Web site (**http://business.college.hmco.com/students/** and select Kreitner, *Management*, 10e).

CLOSING CASE

Ford's Hybrid SUV Team Races to the Finish

In the Spring of 2003, Phil Martens saw trouble down the road. As head of product development for Ford, he was supervising the creation of what could be one of the most important vehicles in company history. While the car wasn't due to come out until the fall of 2004, the team needed to be in launch mode right then to stay on schedule.

It wasn't. It was still pulling marathon hours just trying to get the thing running properly.

The vehicle was the much-anticipated gas-electric hybrid that CEO Bill Ford Jr. had been touting for a couple of years as emblematic of the new, environmentally friendly Ford. The Ford Escape Hybrid would be the first hybrid SUV; it would handle like a muscular V-6, yet sip gas—36 miles per gallon, about 50% better than a standard Escape; its emissions would be minuscule. It was the most technically advanced product the automaker had ever attempted to put into mass production.

The hybrid team was packed with PhDs, but for all of their technical prowess, the brainiacs had one weakness: little launch experience. Martens needed someone to crack the whip without destroying morale, someone to persuade the scientists to stop perfecting and start finishing the vehicle. That someone was Mary Ann Wright—part spark plug, part disciplinarian, and all Ford.

A self-described "car nut," Wright, 42, has launched Sables, Tauruses, and Lincolns. Her discipline is legendary. Twelve-plus-hour days. Five hours of sleep. Four A.M. workouts. She has blond bangs, blue eyes, a firm handshake, and the confidence of someone who doesn't miss deadlines. "My launches are really, really good," she says. Somehow this doesn't come across as a boast.

Even with Wright on board, staying on schedule wasn't a sure thing. Introducing one major technology is a challenge. The Escape Hybrid contains nine such technologies. By the time Ford sends it to dealers in September, this SUV will have been in the works for a little more than five years. In addition to overcoming herculean technical hurdles, Ford collaborated with suppliers around the globe. "This is an unusually complex team with little or no experience with hybrid technology," says Martens, "and they're introducing this unusually complex technology into a mainstream manufacturing system without any flaws."...

Creating a dramatically different product is a staggering challenge for any organization, but for the oldest and second-largest American automaker, it's a higher, steeper mountain to scale. Ford Motor Co. has been making cars for 101 years—cars with one motor. Open the hood of a hybrid, and you'll find two: one gas, the other electric.

As a "full" hybrid, the Escape can run on either motor. Its network monitors an array of computers to determine which motor can drive the wheels most efficiently. In an instant, the vehicle balances the dueling demands for power and acceleration and for high mileage and low emissions. For team member Tom Gee, Ford's announcement of a mass-produced hybrid was "the equivalent of Kennedy saying, 'We're going to the moon by the end of the decade.'" At Ford, vehicle programs are typically ranked 1 to 10, according to the complexity of the power train. "This was a 20," says longtime researcher Mike Tamor.

The stakes are particularly high because Honda and Toyota introduced their hybrids in the United States first—in 1999 and 2000, respectively. Although they lacked the power and roominess of conventional cars, the first gas-electric models found a niche audience. Last year, Toyota released a zippier Prius, but Ford insists that its Escape is going where no hybrid has gone before: into the mainstream. The pitch? No compromises on acceleration, towing capacity, cargo space, fuel economy, or emissions. Not only is it the first hybrid manufactured by an American automaker, but it's also the first hybrid SUV. Ford has plenty of competition in the rearview mirror, though; over the next three years, the major automakers plan to release 20 new hybrids, many of them SUVs and trucks. . . .

Ford's Escape Hybrid program got its start in a Toyota Prius, of all places. After being tapped to head the team in late 1998, Prabhaker Patil went for a test drive with then-chairman Alex Trotman. As the two had suspected, the soon-to-be-released Prius sacrificed too much performance. Trotman insisted that Ford's hybrid do better.

To develop its unconventional vehicle, Ford created an unconventional team. Typically, researchers and product engineers don't work closely together. At Ford, in fact, they work in different buildings. Researchers act as consultants; they share their expertise while commuting from the Ford Scientific Research Laboratory. But Ford's team would itself be a hybrid: scientists and product engineers inventing and building software and hardware together, then shepherding their creation through production. "The people story is as interesting as the technology story," says Wright.

Patil, 54, was a hybrid himself, a PhD scientist who worked in Ford's lab for more than 15 years and then in product development for the past four. He sought team members he knew would be open to collaboration. They included Anand Sankaran, 39, who holds a doctorate in electrical engineering and is a nine-year veteran of the research lab. "It has always been my wish to take something into product production," he says. Still, Sankaran was curious about the fit. "There was a little bit of concern, because I come from a background where I deal more with solving problems technically but it's not fine-tuned to be put easily into production."

The creative tension often centered on deadlines. "On one side, you have people with program discipline who said, 'This has to happen at this point and at this point,'" Patil says, "and the other side would say, 'Oh you want to time an invention?'" . . .

Internally, the hybrid team is simply Team U293. It occupies a long stretch of gray cubicles a one-minute walk from the tinted glass door of one of Bill Ford's offices. The bulletin board celebrates new babies and new patents ("Method for controlling an internal combustion engine during engine shutdown to reduce evaporative emissions"). Schedules wallpaper the conference room, along with a banner that says, "By When?"

The office feels ordinary, but for Ford it is revolutionary. Engineers and scientists work in adjacent cubicles. "Before, it might have been a half a mile apart, but even one building away is a barrier compared with what we have now," says Gee. "It makes a huge difference." Group lunches in the nearby cafeteria evolve into meetings. Hallway chats lead to impromptu problem solving. Once, a couple of engineers at the soda machine discovered a discrepancy in a power-train specification and corrected the issue before the code was written. With thousands of tasks on the to-do list, preventing a problem is as sweet as solving one.

The hybrid group has become the envy of other Ford engineers. "I have engineers who say, 'I wish I could be on that team,'" says Craig Rigby, a technical support supervisor. "Then I tell them the hours." As a way of motivating his weary team, Patil would remind them how fortunate they were. "This was a product that if you did it right, it was going to do a great deal for customers and the company and the country and the environment," he says. "You rarely get a chance to go after something like this in your career. It's what I call the nobility of the cause." . . .

After putting his foot down in the spring of 2003 about the Escape Hybrid's launch, Martens gave the team a rare gift: no outside interruptions. From May through December, it wouldn't have to do management reviews and other presentations. Martens would check in periodically and test-drive the latest prototype so he could keep his bosses informed. "I was getting questions from above," he says. "Weekly." A grin. "Daily."

During this "dark period," Martens says, "I allowed them to be entrepreneurial, and they doubled their productivity." Issues that had been stalled for months got resolved: reaching the fuel economy goal and building the first preproduction model. "The same people who had been coming into my office saying, 'I don't know how we're going to get there,' were saying within weeks and months, 'My God, we can get there,'" Wright recalls. . . .

Wright put the pedal to the metal. "Every day is a lost day," she would tell the team. She quickly established a launch plan and a "meeting cadence": daily get-togethers at 8 A.M. for two hours, with suppliers in Germany and Japan participating by video. There were also weekly meetings with chief engineers and technical forums to tackle specific issues. Wright devoured the details. "Most chiefs won't do that. I find it helps motivate people and helps educate me."

Launch mode meant acting as an even more integrated team. During the design phase, small groups had focused on each system to master its separate technology. Now the challenge was orchestrating the interaction between systems. "I told them, 'If one person is struggling, we're all struggling,'" says Wright. She could be tough, but Martens believed she was what the team needed, just as Patil and his more collegial style had been effective in development. She was the hybrid team's second motor; if Patil's job was to inspire invention, hers was to wrap it up.

Letting go didn't come naturally to scientists like Sankaran. One of his goals was eliminating extraneous engine noise. Like a conductor with extraordinary hearing, he could detect an occasional, almost imperceptible high-pitched tone even though the transmission met the noise requirements. Technically—officially—it was good to go. But, Sankaran says, "as an engineer I wanted to say, 'What are the physics behind this sound? I can do better.'" Ultimately, though, he was persuaded to let it go by taking consolation in another of Wright's reminders: "This isn't the only one we'll do." There will be more hybrids down the road.

Source: *Excerpted from Chuck Salter, "Ford's Escape Route,"* Fast Company, *no. 87 (October 2004): 106–110. Reprinted by permission.*

For Discussion

1. Which stages of the project life cycle in Figure 6.6 are evident in this case? Explain.
2. Was it a good idea for Phil Martens, head of product development, to have two project managers—first Prabhaker Patil and then Mary Ann Wright—to head the Escape Hybrid project? Explain.
3. From a project manager's standpoint, what are the toughest challenges with this sort of high-visibility, high-risk project? Explain.
4. Which of the project manager roles in Table 6.2 did Mary Ann Wright play in this case? Explain.
5. Would you have liked to have been a member of this team? Why or why not?

TEST PREPPER

Tru e/ False Questions

_____ **1.** State, effect, and response uncertainty are three types of environmental uncertainty that people perceive, according to research.

_____ **2.** Analyzer organizations have a reputation for aggressively making things happen rather than waiting for them to happen.

_____ **3.** Mission statements have little practical value today because everything is changing so fast.

_____ **4.** By definition, an objective deals with achieving a measurable result without regard to time.

_____ **5.** "C" objectives are in the 'nice to do' category in the A-B-C priority system.

_____ **6.** Monitoring performance, step 2 in the MBO cycle, is the most important step.

_____ **7.** Among the six roles that project managers play are friend and marketer.

_____ **8.** Planned as well as actual progress can be plotted on a Gantt chart.

_____ **9.** Work in process is represented by a PERT event.

_____ **10.** Both fixed costs and variable costs need to be calculated when doing a break-even analysis.

Multiple-Choice Questions

1. Which sort of uncertainty is related to being unable to predict the consequences of a particular decision?
A. Effect
B. State
C. Response
D. Economic
E. Macro

2. A good example of a(n) _____ is motorcycle maker Harley-Davidson because it successfully produces and markets a few products in a narrowly defined market.
A. reactor
B. prospector
C. defender
D. opportunist
E. analyzer

3. Two key components of a plan are
A. an objective and an action statement.
B. a budget and an alternative plan.
C. a strategy and an estimated budget.
D. a sales forecast and an operations analysis.
E. a time line and an action statement.

4. Which type of planning involves determining how specific tasks can best be accomplished on time with available resources?
A. Budgetary
B. Operational
C. Strategic
D. Intermediate
E. Contingency

5. Objectives are both targets and
A. barriers.
B. measuring sticks.
C. threats.
D. priorities.
E. flow charts.

6. The _____ asserts that a minority of causes, inputs, or effort usually is responsible for a majority of the results, outputs, or rewards.
A. MBO cycle
B. principle of diminishing returns
C. project life cycle
D. PERT network
E. 80/20 principle

7. _____ is the second step in the MBO process.
A. Reviewing plans
B. Performance appraisal
C. Task analysis
D. Developing action plans
E. Setting objectives

8. _____ is *not* one of the roles played by project managers.
A. Entrepreneur
B. Friend
C. Politician
D. Scheduler
E. Marketer

9. The boxes on a flow chart contain
A. cost estimates.
B. time estimates.
C. major events.
D. potential barriers.
E. key decisions.

10. If a candle factory has fixed costs of $40,000, a unit selling price of $10, and a variable cost per unit of $6, its break-even point in units is
A. 13,000.
B. 3,000.
C. 10,000.
D. impossible to determine without more data.
E. 2,500.

ACE self-test

Want more questions? Visit the student Web site at http://business.college.hmco.com/students/ (select Kreitner, *Management*, 10e) and take the ACE quizzes for more practice.

7

Strategic Management

Planning for Long-Term Success

> *"The only sustainable competitive advantage any business has is its reputation."*[1]
>
> LAUREL CUTLER

OBJECTIVES

- **Define** the term *strategic management,* and **explain** its relationship to strategic planning, implementation, and control.
- **Explain** the concept of synergy, and **identify** four kinds of synergy.
- **Describe** Porter's model of generic competitive strategies.
- **Identify** and **explain** the major contribution the business ecosystems model makes to strategic thinking.
- **Identify** seven basic Internet business models and four Internet strategy lessons.
- **Identify** and **describe** the four steps in the strategic management process.
- **Explain** the nature and purpose of a SWOT analysis.
- **Describe** the three types of forecasts.

the changing workplace

Starbucks Tries to Hum a New Strategic Tune

So this girl walks into a bar. She holds a tall iced coffee in one hand, and her blond hair is piled high in a ponytail, neon bikini strings peeking out from her tank top. At this bar, however, headphones hang above the stools, and computer screens are embedded in the countertop. The girl looks at the "bartender" quizzically. "So you can burn music here and it's, like, legal and everything?" she asks. The bartender smiles and nods. "Omigod, so you have, like, every song, ever?" Well, not every song, but quite a few: approaching 150,000—about 20,000 albums' worth. The girl settles onto a stool and grabs a headset, taking a long drag on the straw in her drink as she starts tapping away on a screen. "That's awwwesome."

It's awesome indeed, this new-concept music store on the trendy Third Street Promenade in Santa Monica, California. It's a beautiful space with warm lighting and wood paneling—a place where you can buy regular old CDs, or linger with a drink while you listen to music and sift through thousands of songs stored in a computer database to create your very own personalized, mixed-CD masterpiece. In about five minutes, a freshly burned CD, complete with your chosen title and funky artwork on both the disc and the jacket (plus liner notes!) will be ready to take home. It all happens very smoothly, and yet it's a novel and startling experience. But what's most startling about this remarkable new place to buy music is this: It's a Starbucks.

The Hear Music Coffeehouse, as it's known, opened . . . [in 2003] as the first of several fully integrated café-music stores that Starbucks is launching with its wholly owned subsidiary, retailer Hear Music. . . . [In 2004,] Starbucks will install individual music-listening stations, with CD-burning capabilities, in 10 existing Starbucks locations in Seattle. From there, the concept rolls out to Texas in the fall, including Starbucks stores in the music mecca of Austin. With the help of technology partner Hewlett-Packard, Starbucks plans to have 100 coffee shops across the country enabled with Hear Music CD-burning stations by next Christmas, and more than 1,000 locations up and running by the end of 2005. Think iTunes meets Tower Records. With lattes.

Chairman and chief global strategist Howard Schultz's ambitions for this new business operation are vast: it's not just about selling a few CDs from a coffee shop (Starbucks has been doing that, successfully, for about five years already). Schultz wants Starbucks customers to make their own CDs, yes, but he also thinks they will someday use Starbucks' enormous Wi-Fi footprint to buy and store music from the network on any device imaginable—from laptops and iPods to phones and PDAs. He hopes record labels will develop proprietary material just for the Starbucks network. And that Starbucks itself may help break new artists and develop original material. Indeed, Howard Schultz plans nothing less than to turn the entire music industry upside down. "We are the most frequented retailer in the world," he says. "With hundreds of thousands of songs digitally filed and stored, these Hear Music coffeehouses combined with our existing locations can become the largest music store in any city that we have a Starbucks in. And because of the traffic, the frequency, and the trust that our customers have in the experience and the brand, we believe strongly that we can transform the retail record industry."

There's something even more intriguing going on here, though. This push into music is the start of a daring effort to reinvent one of the world's best-known brands. It is an experiment that asks whether that brand is powerful enough, and Starbucks' relationships with the 30 million customers who pass through its 8,000 stores every week durable enough, that they can be used to completely transform the business.

"Great companies are defined by their discipline and their understanding of who they are and who they are not," Schultz says. "But also, great companies must have the courage to examine strategic opportunities that are transformational—as long as they are not inconsistent with the guiding principles and values of the core business." And so Schultz finds himself on a precipice, at the edge of just such an opportunity, where he celebrates coffee as both the origins and the core of his business, and yet has dreams of transcending those origins to become something much more.

In effect, Schultz is asking the question famously posed by Theodore Levitt, the Harvard Business School professor and father of modern marketing: What business are you really in? Levitt explained that the once-powerful railroads, for example, were blindsided first by automobiles and then by the airlines. It happened because they had defined themselves too narrowly as being in the railroad business rather than the transportation business. As railroads, they were entrenched and invulnerable; as transportation, they were wide open to attack. Theirs was a failure of imagination—the inability to reconceive themselves based on the business they were really in. . . .

[Schultz] aims to achieve what so few are able to do—to reimagine his company as something bigger, better, and more significant than it has ever been. In fact, forget joining them. Schultz plans to surpass them all. "We have the potential to become the most recognizable and respected brand in the world," he says flatly.

Source: *By Alison Overholt, © 2005 Gruner & Jahr USA Publishing. First published in* Fast Company Magazine. *Reprinted by permission. Also see Stanley Holmes, "Starbucks Waltzes into Music,"* Business Week *(March 22, 2004): 13.*

Strategic management drives the effort to succeed amid constant change, uncertainty, and obstacles. If Starbucks stands still or rests on its remarkable accomplishments, it will fail. Thus, Howard Schultz and his coworkers are constantly on the lookout both for threats to their core business and for potentially profitable new markets. Without the discipline of a strategic management orientation, Starbucks's 74,000 employees[2] would tend to work at cross-purposes, with no unified direction.[3] In fact, a statistical analysis of 26 published studies documented the positive impact of strategic planning on business performance.[4]

Executives responding to a recent Gallup Poll said they spend the largest proportion of their time (39 percent) on "strategic thinking/planning."[5] For instance, this is Michael Dell's assessment of his role at the computer company he founded in his college dorm room 20 years ago:

> *I spend more time thinking about the future and the challenges and how to avoid making mistakes, how to keep growing and how to conquer new markets and succeed in places where we haven't.*[6]

Accordingly, many people assume that strategy is the exclusive domain of top-level management. But that simply is not true.[7] Its relevance for those lower in the organization may not be as apparent, but it is relevant for *everyone* in the organization. A management student who is 10 to 20 years away from a top-level executive position might reasonably ask, "If top managers formulate strategies and I'm headed for a supervisory or staff position, why should I care about strategic management?" There are three good reasons why staff specialists and managers at all levels need a general understanding of strategic management.

First, in view of widespread criticism that American managers tend to be shortsighted, a strategic orientation encourages farsightedness (see Table 7.1). Second, employees

Table 7.1 Key Dimensions of Strategic Farsightedness

	Shortsighted	Farsighted
1. Organizational strategy	No formally documented strategies.	A formally written and communicated statement of long-term organizational mission.
2. Competitive advantage	"Follow the leader." No attention devoted to long-term competitive edge.	"Be the leader." Emphasis on gaining and holding a strategic competitive edge.
3. Organizational structure	Rigid structure emphasizing status quo, downward communication, and predictability.	Flexible structure encouraging change, upward and lateral communication, adaptability, and speed.
4. Research and development	Emphasis on applying competitors' good ideas.	Heavy emphasis on developing new products and services and on innovations in production, marketing, and human resource management.
5. Return	Emphasis on short-term profits.	Emphasis on increased market share, growth, and future profit potential.
6. Human resources	Emphasis on stopgap hiring and training. Labor viewed as a commodity. Layoffs common.	Emphasis on long-term development of employees. Labor viewed as a valuable human resource. Layoffs seen as a last resort.
7. Problem solving	Emphasis on chasing symptoms and blaming scapegoats.	Emphasis on finding solutions to emerging problems.
8. Management style	Emphasis on day-to-day firefighting, owing to short-term orientation.	Multilevel strategic thinking that encourages managers to consider long-term implications of their actions and decisions.

who think in strategic terms tend to understand better how top managers think and why they make the decisions they do. In other words, the rationale behind executive policies and decisions is more apparent when things are put into a strategic perspective. Unfortunately, as a 2002 study revealed, things seem to be headed in the wrong direction: "Only 49 percent of U.S. workers surveyed this year say they understand the steps that their firms are taking to reach their business goals, down from 69 percent of workers surveyed two years ago."[8]

A third reason for promoting a broader understanding of strategic management is related to a recent planning trend. Specifically, greater teamwork and cooperation throughout the planning/control cycle are eroding the traditional distinction between those who plan and those who implement plans. In terms of the five strategy-making modes shown in Table 7.2, there is a clear trend *away from* the command, symbolic, and rational modes and *toward* the transactive and generative modes.[9] In other words, the traditional idea of top-management strategists as commanders, coaches, or bosses is giving way to a view of them more as participative facilitators and sponsors. In each of the traditional modes, people below the top level must be obedient, passive, and reactive. In the *transactive* strategy-making mode, continuous improvement is the order of the day, as middle- and lower-level managers and staff specialists actively participate in the process. They go a step further, becoming risk-taking entrepreneurs, in the *generative* mode. Here is a case in point:

> *J. M. Smucker Co., the Ohio-based maker of jams and jellies, . . . enlisted a team of 140 employees—7 percent of its workforce—who devoted nearly 50 percent of their time to a major strategy exercise for more than six months. "Instead of having just 12 minds working it, we really used the team of 140 as ambassadors to solicit input from all 2,000 employees," says President [now co-CEO] Richard K. Smucker. "It gave us a broader perspective, and it brought to the surface a lot of people with special talents." The company, which has struggled to grow in a mature market, now has a dozen viable initiatives that could double its $635 million revenues over the next five years.*[10]

7a Are You Future-Focused?

Annette Verschuren, president of Home Depot Canada:

> *I don't look in the rear-view mirror. I don't care what happened yesterday. I care about what is going to happen tomorrow.*

Source: As quoted in Zena Olijnyk, "The Home Depot Boss on Small Wins," Canadian Business *(November 8, 2004):* **www.canadianbusiness.com**.

QUESTIONS:
On a scale of 1 = low to 10 = high, how future-focused are you? Is it possible for a manager to be too future-focused? Explain.

For further information about the interactive annotations in this chapter, visit our Web site (**http://business.college.hmco.com/students/** and select Kreitner, *Management,* 10e).

Table 7.2 Five Different Strategy-Making Modes

	TRADITIONAL MODES			MODERN MODES	
	Command	**Symbolic**	**Rational**	**Transactive**	**Generative**
Style	*Imperial* Strategy driven by leader or small top team	*Cultural* Strategy driven by mission and a vision of the future	*Analytical* Strategy driven by formal structure and planning systems	*Procedural* Strategy driven by internal process and mutual adjustment	*Organic* Strategy driven by organizational actors' initiative
Role of Top Management	*Commander* Provide direction	*Coach* Motivate and inspire	*Boss* Evaluate and control	*Facilitator* Empower and enable	*Sponsor* Endorse and support
Role of Organizational Members	*Soldier* Obey orders	*Player* Respond to challenge	*Subordinate* Follow the system	*Particpant* Learn and improve	*Entreprenuer* Experiment and take risks

Source: *Adapted from Stuart L. Hart, "An Integrative Framework for Strategy-Making Processes,"* Academy of Management Review, *17 (April 1992): 334. Reprinted by permission.*

This strategic exercise certainly paid off because some key purchases, including Crisco oil and Jif peanut butter from Procter & Gamble, helped boost Smucker's annual sales to over $2 billion eight years later.[11]

Thus you, today's management student, are not as far away from the strategic domain as you may think. The time to start thinking strategically is *now*. This chapter defines strategic management, looks at ways to think strategically (including e-business strategy), explores the strategic management process, and discusses forecasting.

Strategic Management = Strategic Planning + Implementation + Control

strategic management: *seeking a competitively superior organization-environment fit*

strategy: *integrated, externally oriented perception of how to achieve the organization's mission*

1. DEFINE the term *strategic management,* and **EXPLAIN** its relationship to strategic planning, implementation, and control.

Strategic management is the ongoing process of ensuring a competitively superior fit between an organization and its changing environment.[12] In a manner of speaking, strategic management is management on a grand scale, management of the "big picture." Accordingly, **strategy** has been defined as an integrated and externally oriented perception of how the organization will achieve its mission.[13] The strategic management perspective is the product of a historical evolution and is now understood to include budget control, long-range planning, and strategic planning.[14]

Significantly, strategic management does not do away with earlier, more restricted approaches. Instead, it synthesizes and coordinates them all in a more systematic fashion. For example, consider the relationship between strategic planning, as defined in Chapter 6, and strategic management. Recall that *strategic planning* is the process of determining how to pursue the organization's long-term goals with the resources expected to be available. Notice that nothing is said in this definition about adjustment or control. But just as astronauts and space scientists need to make midflight corrections to ensure that space shuttles reach their distant destinations, strategic adjustment and control are necessary. The more encompassing strategic management concept is useful today because it effectively merges strategic planning, implementation, and control.

Today's competitive pressures necessitate a dynamic strategic management process. According to *Fortune*,

> *The old methods won't do. At too many companies strategic planning has become overly bureaucratic, absurdly quantitative, and largely irrelevant. In executive suites across America, countless five-year plans, updated annually and solemnly clad in three-ring binders, are gathering dust—their impossibly specific prognostications about costs, prices, and market share long forgotten.*[15]

Managers who adopt a strategic management perspective appreciate that strategic plans are living documents. They require updating and fine-tuning as conditions change. They also need to draw upon all available talent in the organization.

The strategic management process is discussed in greater detail later in this chapter. But first we need to consider alternative ways to encourage strategic thinking.

Thinking Strategically (Including E-Business Strategies)

Effective strategic management involves more than just following a few easy steps. It requires *every* employee, on a daily basis, to consider the "big picture" and think strategically about gaining and keeping a competitive edge. ABB Power Technologies, based in Alamo, Tennessee, uses a teambulding business simulation to get its employees to think strategically:

> *ABB, along with its management consultancy, The Hayes Group, created "Learn or Burn: Making The Right Business Decisions," a one-day workshop required of all employees. Working in teams of four, employees participate in a simula-*

tion in which they must run a manufacturing business for three years. They purchase materials, move products through production, pay for overhead, complete profit and loss statements and analyze financial ratios. The idea is that employees will be able to more clearly see the direct impact that their decisions have on an organization.

"It's everyone's responsibility to make decisions, not just management," says Eduardo Miller, ABB manager and workshop co-instructor. "If all of us are not learning to make the right decisions, we can burn the business."[16]

This section presents four alternative perspectives for thinking innovatively about strategy in today's fast-paced global economy: synergies, Porter's generic strategies, business ecosystems, and e-business strategies.

■ Synergy

synergy: *the concept that the whole is greater than the sum of its parts*

Although not necessarily a familiar term, *synergy* is a well-established and valuable concept. **Synergy** occurs when two or more variables (for example, chemicals, drugs, people, and organizations) interact to produce an effect greater than the sum of the effects of any of the variables acting independently. Some call this the 1 + 1 = 3 effect; others prefer to say that with synergy, the whole is greater than the sum of its parts. Either definition is acceptable as long as one appreciates the bonus effect in synergistic relationships. In strategic management, managers are urged to achieve as much *market, cost, technology,* and *management synergy*[17] as possible when making strategic decisions. Those decisions may involve mergers, acquisitions, new products, new technology or production processes, or executive replacement. When Procter & Gamble bought pet-food maker Iams, executives trumpeted the potential synergies. Five years later, unique synergies have materialized and the acquisition has proved to be a wise one.

P&G, being P&G, flexed its marketplace muscle immediately: Using 3,000 trucks to move Iams into 25,000 mass retail outlets, it increased distribution nearly 50% overnight. Then, armed with research indicating that pet owners fear that their four-footed family members will die before they do, Iams's R&D folks began collaborating with Procter's scientists who study human hearts, bones, muscles, teeth, and gums. Iams unleashed a stream of new foods aimed at lengthening pets' lives—weight-control formulas, antioxidant blends, tartar-fighting "dental defense" ingredients.

It paid off: Iams has moved from the nation's No. 5 pet-food brand to No. 1. Worldwide sales have doubled to $1.6 billion; profits have tripled.[18]

2. EXPLAIN the concept of synergy, and **IDENTIFY** four kinds of synergy.

■ Market Synergy. When one product or service fortifies the sales of one or more other products or services, market synergy has been achieved. Examples of market synergy are common in the business press. For example, consider how FedEx's acquisition of Kinko's in 2003 provides busy customers with the convenience of one-stop shopping:

Kinko's business centers are popularly known as offices on the road for many frequent business travelers. FedEx CEO Fred Smith says services that Kinko's provides—storing, printing and electronically delivering corporate documents—complement FedEx's package-delivery services.[19]

7b Tasty Synergy

Some people think Reese's Peanut Butter Cups are a great example of synergy.

QUESTIONS:
Why would they say that? Are they right? Explain.

■ Cost Synergy. This second type of synergy can occur in almost every dimension of organized activity. When two or more products can be designed by the same engineers, produced in the same facilities, distributed through the same channels, or sold by the same salespeople, overall costs will be lower than they would be if each product received separate treatment. In an interesting example of cost synergy, major hotels are trying to squeeze more value from their costly real estate. "At Miami Airport, Marriott has three hotels on the same plot of land. There's the Marriott Hotel, a full-service hotel. Behind the hotel are a Courtyard by Marriott, a midprice hotel, and a Fairfield Inn, an economy brand."[20]

Cost synergy also can be achieved by recycling by-products and hazardous wastes that would normally be thrown away. Human imagination is the only limit to creating cost synergies through recycling. For example, Stampp Corbin's fast-growing company, RetroBox, recycles electronic waste including PCs and laptops, printers, servers, cables, and Palm Pilots tossed out by *Fortune* 500 companies.

> *Launched in 1997, Corbin's company picks up the gear, trucks it to a warehouse in Columbus, [Ohio,] strips it of all information and programming, then refurbishes and resells over the Internet those products that still have a useful life. It disassembles and recycles those that do not. Companies pay about $35 for each product they no longer want; RetroBox rebates a portion of the proceeds from those that are sold. "Our goal is to have every client break even or make money," Corbin says. (See what's for sale at* ***www.RetroBox.com****.)*[21]

Cost synergy through waste recycling is good business ethics, too.

■ Technological Synergy. The third variety of synergy involves transferring technology from one application to another, thus opening up new markets. For example, consider an emerging technology called broadband over powerline (BPL) that has electric power companies excited:

> *One day soon, getting a broadband connection at home could be as easy as plugging a cord into an electrical outlet in the wall. The same power lines that deliver electricity to light rooms and run refrigerators will transport messages, music, and video across cyberspace. To link up computers, music players, and TV set top boxes in a home network, people will no longer have to mess with a tangle of wires or Wi-Fi settings. Over the powerlines, they'll have the convenience of plug-and-play—something that still isn't readily available from telephone or cable companies.*[22]

On top of all this, the resulting "smart" electric lines will enable the power companies to monitor demand more accurately and charge higher rates during peak hours to encourage conservation. Thanks to this sort of technological synergy, profitable new markets can be tapped with existing equipment and technical know-how.

7c Back to the Opening Case

What kind of synergy is Starbucks attempting to achieve? Explain.

■ Management Synergy. This fourth type of synergy occurs when a management team is more productive because its members have complementary rather than identical skills. Management synergy also is achieved when an individual with multiple skills or talents is hired for an administrative position. For example, Intel's top salesperson in its vitally important China operations is Jason Chen, someone who works comfortably across Chinese and North American cultures.[23]

You may find it difficult, if not impossible, to take advantage of all four types of synergy when developing new strategies. Nonetheless, your strategies are more likely to be realistic and effective if you give due consideration to all four types of synergy as early as possible.[24]

3. DESCRIBE Porter's model of generic competitive strategies.

■ Porter's Generic Competitive Strategies

In 1980, Michael Porter, a Harvard University economist, developed a model of competitive strategies. During a decade of research, Porter's model evolved to encompass these four generic strategies: (1) cost leadership, (2) differentiation, (3) cost focus, and (4) focused differentiation.[25] As shown in Figure 7.1, Porter's model combined two variables, *competitive advantage* and *competitive scope*.

differentiation: *buyer perceives unique and superior value in a product*

On the horizontal axis is competitive advantage, which can be achieved via low costs or differentiation. A competitive advantage based on low costs, which means lower prices, is self-explanatory. **Differentiation**, according to Porter, "is the ability to provide unique and superior value to the buyer in terms of product quality, special

Figure 7.1 Porter's Generic Competitive Strategies

		COMPETITIVE ADVANTAGE	
		Lower cost	**Differentiation**
COMPETITIVE SCOPE	**Broad target**	Cost leadership	Differentiation
	Narrow target	Cost focus	Focused differentiation

Source: *Adapted with permission of The Free Press, a Division of Simon & Schuster Adult Publishing Group, from* The Competitive Advantage of Nations *by Michael E. Porter. Copyright © 1990, 1998 by Michael E. Porter. All rights reserved.*

features, or after-sale service."[26] Differentiation helps explain why consumers willingly pay more for branded products such as Sunkist oranges or Crest toothpaste.[27] On the vertical axis is competitive scope. Is the firm's target market broad or narrow? Dell, which sells many types of computers all around the world, serves a very broad market. A neighborhood pizza parlor offering one type of food in a small geographical area has a narrow target market.

" DESPITE IT ALL, I'M STILL FEELING THE SYNERGY. HOW ABOUT YOU GUYS?"

*Source: John Caldwell/*Harvard Business Review

Like the concept of synergy, Porter's model helps managers think strategically: it enables them to see the big picture as it affects the organization and its changing environment. Each of Porter's four generic strategies deserves a closer look.

■ **Cost Leadership Strategy.** Managers pursuing this strategy have an overriding concern for keeping costs, and therefore prices, lower than those of competitors. Normally, this means extensive production or service facilities with efficient economies of scale (low unit costs of making products or delivering services). Productivity improvement is a high priority for managers following the cost leadership strategy. Wal-Mart Stores, Inc., is a prime example of the cost leadership strategy.

> *The Wal-Mart formula is deceptively simple: Sell good-quality, name-brand, modestly priced merchandise in a clean, no-frills setting that offers one-stop family shopping. Rather than entice shoppers with an ever-changing array of discounts and sales, Wal-Mart operates from an "everyday low price" philosophy.*[28]

Wal-Mart's computerized warehousing network gives it an additional cost advantage over its less efficient competitors. When rival Kmart declared bankruptcy in 2002, a retail industry consultant bluntly observed, "Kmart is simply another piece of retail roadkill in Wal-Mart's march to dominance."[29]

In manufacturing firms, the preoccupation with minimizing costs flows beyond production into virtually all areas: purchasing, wages, overhead, R&D, advertising, and selling. A relatively large market share is required to accommodate this high-volume, low-profit-margin strategy.

Some people think air travel has gone to the dogs. But that's just fine with Julie, the English Setter who's all dressed up and ready to fly on Midwest Airlines. Meanwhile, Midwest's CEO Tim Hoeksema announces a frequent flier program for pets. This is part of a differentiation strategy to get people talking and set Midwest Airlines apart from the pack. Everyone in favor, raise your right paw.

■ **Differentiation Strategy.** For this strategy to succeed, a company's product or service must be considered unique by most of the customers in its industry. Advertising and promotion help the product to stand out from the crowd. Specialized design (BMW automobiles), a widely recognized brand (Crest toothpaste), leading-edge technology (Intel), or reliable service (Caterpillar) also may serve to differentiate a product in the industry. Because customers with brand loyalty will usually spend more for what they perceive to be a superior product, the differentiation strategy can yield larger profit margins than the low-cost strategy.[30] But if a brand's image is not carefully nurtured and protected, brand loyalty and customers' willingness to pay a premium price can erode (see The Global Manager). For businesses sticking to a differentiation strategy, it is important to note that cost reduction is not ignored; it simply is not the highest priority.

■ **Cost Focus Strategy.** Organizations with a cost focus strategy attempt to gain a competitive edge in a narrow (or regional) market by exerting strict control. For instance, Foot Locker has become a powerhouse in athletic footwear and apparel by selling off unrelated businesses, such as San Francisco Music Box, and focusing on what it does best.

THE GLOBAL MANAGER

The Ultimate Fairly Inexpensive Driving Machine

Helmut Panke, chairman of BMW, hates to say the word. He's in his stark, white office at the company's headquarters near Munich [Germany], describing a future vehicle his team is developing. A precise man who has a doctorate in nuclear science as well as a deep appreciation for exquisite engineering, Panke is fond of talking about the "DNA" of BMW. When he talks about the company's tradition and values, his entire body contorts with emotion. "A BMW will always be true BMW," he says. "We will never build a boring BMW." And yet the more he describes his new dream machine, the more the word he's avoiding hangs in the air. This means of conveyance will be large and roomy. *(Min . . .)* It will have the utility of an SUV yet the handling of a BMW. *(Miniv . . .)* As Panke talks, it's hard not to think "juice boxes" and "soccer practice." It can't be. *A minivan?*

Actually, Panke would prefer you use the term "space-functional concept." But in essence, yes, BMW is planning a minivan. It won't be out until the end of the decade, which will come as some relief to Beemer purists, but still. A BMW minivan?

Panke's loathing of the m-word has less to do with snobbery than with the fact that he's forcing the company through a major change. The minivan is just one part of a strategy to transform BMW from a specialized producer of sporty rides for high-income aesthetes into a full-line automaker, with a complete range of sedans, wagons, SUVs, roadsters, all of it. (Except pickup trucks. There's no danger that there will ever be a BMW pickup truck.) He has pledged to boost sales of the BMW group, which includes MINI and Rolls-Royce, from 1.1 million cars . . . [in 2003] to 1.4 million by 2008. And his latest step in that direction is to head into unfamiliar territory: downmarket. In . . . [2004], BMW added a new, entry-level model called the 1 Series. The 1 Series won't be a small-volume promotional leader either—BMW expects to sell some 120,000 . . . [in 2005]. After that will come the space-functional concept.

Panke is walking a dangerous line. On the one hand, he knows growth means expanding into new markets with new kinds of products. BMW ranks only 14th among the world's automakers, ahead of Mazda and behind Mitsubishi in global unit sales, which severely limits its economies of scale. . . .

On the other hand, there's the high-end BMW cachet to protect. The company is revered by millions of owners and fans for engineering cars that put the driver first. For many customers, buying a BMW is like joining a semi-exclusive club. . . .

Panke's mass-with-class strategy puts that cachet in peril. BMWs command premium prices partly because of their scarcity. Once BMWs turn up at every mall and hockey rink, the snob appeal will disappear.

Source: From Alex Taylor III, "The Ultimate Fairly Inexpensive Driving Machine," Fortune *(November 1, 2004): 131–132.*

> *With an 18% (and growing) share of the athletic retail market—nearly twice that of its nearest competitor—Foot Locker uses its weight to negotiate advantageous deals with manufacturers like Nike and Reebok. It gets the hottest products earlier and cheaper than its peers.*[31]

Foot Locker plans to increase its 3,600-store chain by 1,000 in the years ahead.

■ **Focused Differentiation Strategy.** This generic strategy involves achieving a competitive edge by delivering a superior product and/or service to a limited audience. The Mayo Clinic's world-class health care facilities—in Rochester, Minnesota; Jacksonville, Florida; and Scottsdale, Arizona—are an expression of this strategy.[32]

A contingency management approach is necessary for determining which of Porter's generic strategies is appropriate. Research on Porter's model indicates a positive relationship between long-term earnings growth and a good fit between strategy and environment.[33]

7d Back to the Opening Case

Overall, which of Porter's four generic competitive strategies is Starbucks pursuing? Explain your rationale.

■ Business Ecosystems

Researchers recently have given new meaning to the saying "It's a jungle out there." They have extended the concept of ecosystems from nature to business. In his best-seller *The Death of Competition: Leadership and Strategy in the Age of Business Ecosystems,* James F. Moore writes, "It is my view that executives need to think of

business ecosystem: *economic community of organizations and all their stakeholders*

themselves as part of organisms participating in an ecosystem in much the same way that biological organisms participate in a biological ecosystem."[34] A **business ecosystem** is an economic community of organizations and all their stakeholders, including suppliers and customers.[35] This evolving model makes one very important contribution to modern strategic thinking: *organizations need to be as good at cooperating as they are at competing if they are to succeed.*

4. IDENTIFY and EXPLAIN the major contribution the business ecosystems model makes to strategic thinking.

■ **A Business Ecosystem in Action.** Within a dominant business ecosystem, key organizations selectively cooperate and compete to achieve both their individual and their collective goals. A prime example is the relationship between Microsoft and Intel. In fact, the so-called Wintel technology (the combination of Microsoft Windows software and Intel microprocessors) dominates the personal computer market. Yet make no mistake about it—Microsoft and Intel are competitors in all other respects.[36] In the language of business ecosystems, Microsoft and Intel have *coevolved* to a dominant position in the personal computer ecosystem (along with Dell Computer). Meanwhile, Marc Benioff, CEO of Salesforce.com in San Francisco, tells companies not to buy expensive software. His rationale is simple: "Why buy cumbersome hardware and software to do routine back-office chores when you can purchase comparable technology as an online service?"[37] The Wintel ecosystem has responded by slashing the cost of personal computers and insisting that PCs are not obsolete in the Internet age. In ten years, will the Wintel ecosystem, with its reliance on personal computers packed with expensive software, still be dominant? Or will Benioff be able to pull together a successful community of organizations and individuals to create a new dominant ecosystem in which inexpensive information appliances are used to pull low-cost software applications off the Internet on an as-needed basis? Only time will tell; an epic battle is on in the business jungle.

■ **Needed: More Strategic Cooperation.** Through the years, the terms *strategy* and *competition* have become synonymous.[38] Business ecologists now call for greater cooperation, even among the toughest of competitors. Moore puts it this way: "The major factor today limiting the spread of realized innovation is not a lack of good ideas, technology, or capital. It is the inability to command cooperation across broad, diverse communities of players who must become intimate parts of a far-reaching process of coevolution."[39] In ecosystem terms, companies need to "coevolve" with key strategic partners (and sometimes even with their competitors) if they are to thrive today. A prime example is OnStar, the 24-hour emergency satellite communication system developed by General Motors. Chet Huber, president of OnStar, originally startled his bosses at GM when he suggested offering the service to other auto companies, rather than keeping it a GM exclusive. "Huber's mold-breaking strategy worked. Today, OnStar provides its service to Lexus, Audi, Isuzu, Acura, Volkswagen, and Subaru cars, in addition to GM's own lines. OnStar now controls 70% of the market."[40]

■ E-Business Strategies for the Internet

The recent boom-bust-recovery cycle for dot-coms, although painful for many, has been an excellent learning laboratory. We now see the Internet not as some sort of miracle but rather as a powerful business tool requiring thoughtful application.[41] Janey Place, e-business manager for Mellon Financial Corp. in Pittsburgh, put the situation into proper perspective:

- ***The Internet changes everything—but it doesn't change everything overnight....*** The Internet changes everything: how we get information, how we learn, how we conduct business. But I was alarmed by the hype of the late 1990s, when the mind-set was "Fire, then aim"—you didn't ever have to be ready....
- ***Some of the old rules still rule....*** Technology, in and of itself, isn't enough of a reason to invest in the Internet. There has to be a reasonable, logical business model. Either you're saving money or you're making money....

eBay goes bricks-and-clicks. iSold It, a rapidly-growing chain of stores affiliated with online auction giant eBay, is successfully blending the old and new economies. Rather than doing an entire transaction alone online, a customer can get personalized help and a convenient place to drop off goods for sale at iSold It stores like this one in Huntington, New York.

- ***First, we overestimated the Internet; don't underestimate it now. . . .*** Looking ahead, I am convinced that the Internet will exceed our expectations.[42]

A broad, strategic perspective of the Internet is needed. Recall from our definition in Chapter 1 that e-business involves using the Internet to make *all* business functions—from sales to human resource management—more efficient, more responsive, and speedier. The purpose of this section is to build a framework of understanding for squeezing maximum value from the Internet.

■ Evolving Internet Technologies and Applications. The Internet is not a fixed thing. It is a complex bundle of emerging technologies at various stages of development.[43] Corporate strategists and entrepreneurs are challenged to build business models based on *where they expect these technologies to be* X years down the road. This exercise is akin to hitting a moving target from a moving platform—very difficult, at best. But Amazon.com's founder and CEO Jeff Bezos proved it can be done:

> *. . . he was one of the few dot-com leaders to understand that sweating the details of Internet technologies would make all the difference. Amazon wasn't the first store on the Web. But Bezos beat rivals in inventing or rolling out new Internet technologies that made shopping online faster, easier, and more personal than traditional retail. He offered customized recommendations based on other buyers' purchases, let people buy an item with just one mouse click, and created personalized storefronts for each customer.*[44]

E-business experts predict major changes ahead for several industries, including software development and distribution, real estate, telecommunications, bill payment, jewelry, and advertising.[45]

■ Basic Internet Business Models. Relative to buying, selling, and trading things on the Internet, it is possible to fashion a strategy around one or a combination of seven basic business models (see Table 7.3).[46] eBay, for example, has been

Table 7.3 Seven Basic Internet Business Models

Type	Features and Content	Sources of Competitive Advantage
Commission-based	Commissions charged for brokerage or intermediary services. Adds value by providing expertise and/or access to a wide network of alternatives.	Search Evaluation Problem solving Transaction
Advertising-based	Web content paid for by advertisers. Adds value by providing free or low-cost content—including customer feedback, expertise, and entertainment programming—to audiences that range from very broad (general content) to highly targeted (specialized content).	Search Evaluation
Markup-based	Reselling marked-up merchandise. Adds value through selection, distribution efficiencies, and by leveraging brand image and reputation. May use entertainment programming to enhance sales.	Search Transaction
Production-based	Selling manufactured goods and custom services. Adds value by increasing production efficiencies, capturing customer preferences, and improving customer service.	Search Problem solving
Referral-based	Fees charged for referring customers. Adds value by enhancing a company's product or service offering, tracking referrals electronically, and generating demographic data. Expertise and customer feedback are often included with referral information.	Search Problem solving Transaction
Subscription-based	Fees charged for unlimited use of service or content. Adds value by leveraging strong brand name, providing high-quality information to specialized markets or access to essential services. May consist entirely of entertainment programming.	Evaluation Problem solving
Fee-for-service-based	Fees charged for metered services. Adds value by providing service efficiencies, expertise, and practical outsourcing solutions.	Problem solving Transaction

Source: *Reprinted from* Organizational Dynamics, *33, no. 2, G. T. Lumpkin and Gregory G. Dess, "E-Business Strategies and the Internet Business Models: How the Internet Adds Value," p.169, Copyright 2004, with permission from Elsevier.*

hugely successful with the commission-based model.[47] Google, on the other hand, makes its money via an advertising-based model.[48] As indicated in Table 7.3, each of the Internet business models has its own unique set of opportunities for strategic competitive advantage. Our challenge is to take what we have learned about synergy, Porter's competitive strategies, and business ecosystems and develop a winning strategy. Guiding us in the right direction are the following four Internet strategy lessons learned in recent years.

5. IDENTIFY seven basic Internet business models and four Internet strategy lessons.

■ There Is No One-Size-Fits-All Internet Strategy. Harvard's Michael Porter, whose generic competitive strategies we just covered, cautions us to avoid putting Internet strategies into one basket. Instead, he sees two major categories:

> *At this critical juncture in the evolution of Internet technology, dot-coms and established companies face different strategic imperatives. Dot-coms must develop real strategies that create economic value. They must recognize that current ways of competing are destructive and futile and benefit neither themselves nor, in the end, customers. Established companies, in turn, must stop deploying the Internet on a stand-alone basis and instead use it to enhance the distinctiveness of their strategies.*[49]

Mellon's Janey Place calls these two types of businesses dot-coms and dot-corps. Porter urges established "bricks-and-mortar" businesses to weave the Internet into the very fabric of their operations—in short, to become true e-businesses.

■ Customer Loyalty Is Built with Reliable Brand Names and "Sticky" Web Sites. Web surfers have proved to have very short attention spans. Seemingly attractive Web sites can have many visitors ("hits"), but few or no sales. When doing business at Internet speed, Web sites need to satisfy three criteria: (1) high-quality layout and graphics; (2) fast, responsive service; and (3) complete and up-to-date information.[50] A trusted brand name can further enhance what e-business people call the *stickiness* of a Web site—that is, the ability to draw the same customer back again and again. A great deal of work is needed in this area, considering the results of one study: two-thirds of the visitors to online stores did not return within a year.[51] Even though e-retailing might appear to be a quick-and-easy and impersonal process, loyal customers still expect a personal touch and some "hand holding" when they have questions, problems, or suggestions.

■ Bricks and Clicks: Blending the Best of Two Worlds. Popular accounts of e-business conjure up visions of "virtual organizations" where an entrepreneur and a handful of employees run a huge business with little more than an Internet hookup and a coffee maker. Everything—including product design, production, marketing, shipping, billing, and accounting—is contracted out. As discussed in Chapter 10, these network or virtual organizations *do* exist, but they are more the exception than the rule. More typically, companies with bricks-and-mortar facilities such as factories, warehouses, retail stores, and showrooms are blending the Internet into their traditional business models. In fact, some retailers are using a so-called "three-tailing"[52] concept whereby a retailer such as Lands' End (acquired by Sears in 2002) serves the customer in three ways—mail-order catalog, Web site, and stores. With the *clicks-and-bricks* strategy used by Lands' End, customers have a lot of freedom in how and when they shop. Conceivably, after seeing something they liked in the Lands' End mail catalog, customers could place an order over the phone, by mail, or over the Internet. Later, if dissatisfied with the purchase, they could mail it back or take it back to the nearest Sears store for a refund or exchange. Lands' End now does over one-third of its business via the Internet.[53]

7e Back to the Opening Case

Acting as a management consultant, explain what role, if any, the Internet should ultimately play in Starbucks's Hear Music Coffeehouse concept? Explain.

■ **E-Business Partnering Should Not Dilute Strategic Control or Ethical Standards.** Whenever uncompetitive assets are sold and tasks contracted out, care needs to be taken to maintain ethical and quality standards. Do both domestic and foreign subcontractors follow applicable labor laws and ethical labor practices, or do sweatshop conditions prevail? Are subcontractors ruining the natural environment to reduce costs? Is a product designed properly before it is manufactured by an outside contractor? Are product quality standards faithfully met? These ethical and technical questions can be answered only through systematic monitoring and strategic oversight. Tough sanctions are also needed. Informed consumers are holding the sellers of goods and services to higher standards these days. And in doing so, they include a company's *entire* supply chain, foreign and domestic. Sweatshop-produced goods sold via sophisticated e-business networks are still dirty business.[54]

The Strategic Management Process

6. IDENTIFY and DESCRIBE the four steps in the strategic management process.

Strategic plans are formulated during an evolutionary process with identifiable steps. In line with the three-level planning pyramid covered in Chapter 6, the strategic management process is broader and more general at the top and filters down to narrower and more specific terms. Figure 7.2 outlines the four major steps of the strategic management process: (1) formulation of a grand strategy, (2) formulation of strategic plans, (3) implementation of strategic plans, and (4) strategic control. Corrective action based on evaluation and feedback takes place throughout the entire strategic management process to keep things headed in the right direction.[55]

It is important to note that this model represents an ideal approach for instructional purposes. Because of organizational politics, as discussed in Chapter 14, and different planning orientations among managers, a somewhat less systematic process typically results. Nevertheless, it is helpful to study the strategic management process

Since he started in the music business as a teenager, British businessman Richard Branson has had a flair for envisioning grand strategies and making them happen. Now the knighted billionaire wants to extend his Virgin empire beyond music and commercial air travel to include commercial space travel. If everything goes according to plan, Virgin spacecraft carrying five passengers per trip will be headed for space by 2007. Ticket price: $198,000 (round trip, of course).

Figure 7.2 The Strategic Management Process

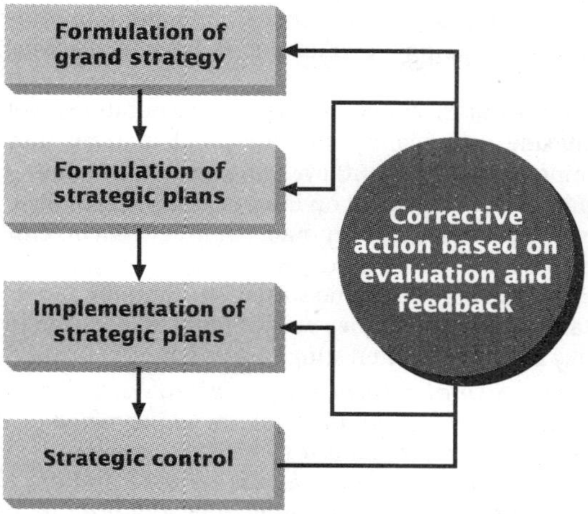

as a systematic and rational sequence in order to better understand what it involves. Although he noted that rational strategic planning models should not be taken literally, Henry Mintzberg acknowledged their profound instructional value. They teach necessary vocabulary and implant the notion "that strategy represents a fundamental congruence between external opportunity and internal capability."[56]

Formulation of a Grand Strategy

As pointed out in Chapter 6, a clear statement of organizational mission serves as a focal point for the entire planning process. Key stakeholders inside and outside the organization are given a general idea of why the organization exists and where it is headed.[57] Working from the mission statement, top management formulates the organization's **grand strategy**, a general explanation of *how* the organization's mission is to be accomplished. Grand strategies are not drawn out of thin air. They are derived from a careful *situational analysis* of the organization and its environment. A clear vision of where the organization *is* headed and of where it *should be* headed is the gateway to competitive advantage.

grand strategy: *how the organization's mission will be accomplished*

situational analysis: *finding the organization's niche by performing a SWOT analysis*

Situational Analysis. A **situational analysis** is a technique for matching organizational strengths and weaknesses with environmental opportunities and threats to determine the right niche for the organization (see Figure 7.3). Many strategists refer to this process as a SWOT analysis. SWOT stands for **S**trengths, **W**eaknesses, **O**pportunities, and **T**hreats. (You can perform an actual SWOT analysis in the Hands-On Exercise at the end of this chapter.) Every organization should be able to identify the purpose for which it is best suited. But this matching process is more difficult than it may at first appear. Strategists are faced not with snapshots of the environment and the organization but with a movie of rapidly changing events. As one researcher said, "The task is to find a match between opportunities that are still unfolding and resources that are still being acquired."[58] For example, Google CEO Eric Schmidt explains how his company tackles this task:

> *There's tremendous opportunity before us, so we're organized around taking advantage of . . . technology discontinuities as they occur. And therefore we spend a lot of time trying to make sure that we're busy seeing them. And that's our competitive advantage. You have to be set up to shift your focus quickly so that you spend most of your energies inventing the new business instead of blindly optimizing the old one.*[59]

Figure 7.3 Determining Strategic Direction Through Situational (SWOT) Analysis

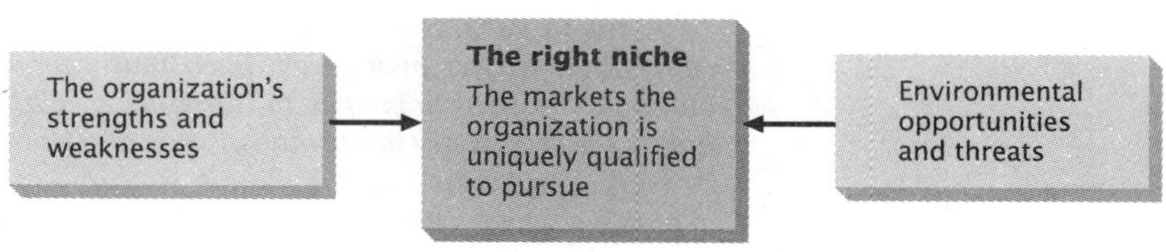

Forecasting techniques, such as those reviewed later in this chapter, help managers cope with uncertainty about the future while conducting situational analyses.

7. EXPLAIN the nature and purpose of a SWOT analysis.

Strategic planners, whether top managers, key operating managers, or staff planning specialists, have many ways to scan the environment for opportunities and threats. They can study telltale shifts in the economy, recent technological innovations, growth and movement among competitors, market trends, labor availability, and demographic patterns.[60]

Unfortunately, according to a survey of executives at 100 U.S. corporations, not enough time is spent looking outside the organization: "Respondents said they spend less than half of their planning time (44 percent) evaluating external factors—competition and markets—compared with 48 percent on internal analysis—budget, organizational factors, human resources. 'That's the corporate equivalent of contemplating one's navel,'"[61] says the researcher.

Environmental opportunities and threats need to be sorted out carefully. A perceived threat may turn out to be an opportunity, or vice versa. Steps can be taken to turn negatives into positives. Pitney Bowes is an interesting case in point:

> *In February [2004], after eBay went looking for a company to create a system for online postage, it didn't turn to Stamps.com or any other dotcom whippersnapper. Rather, the nine-year-old Internet upstart tapped 84-year-old graybeard Pitney Bowes, a firm based in Stamford, Conn., that dominates the world of postal meters. Now millions of sellers on eBay download postage and print it out—with Pitney Bowes earning a click fee each time.*
>
> *It's the latest ratification of Pitney's business model, which many believed would be rendered obsolete by e-mail and the Internet. Instead, the $4.6 billion company has bolstered its 80 percent share of the domestic postal-meter market with new revenue streams from the digital world. Profits are growing at a clip of 13 percent a year.*[62]

7f Back to the Opening Case

Based on the facts of this case and any reasonable assumptions you might make about Starbucks, what would a situational (SWOT) analysis suggest that the future strategic direction of Starbucks should be? *Hint:* First arrange your evidence under these four headings: organizational strengths, organizational weaknesses, environmental opportunities, and environmental threats.

Capability Profile. After scanning the external environment for opportunities and threats, management's attention turns inward to identifying the organization's strengths and weaknesses.[63] This subprocess is called a creating a **capability profile**. The following are key capabilities for today's companies:

- Quick response to market trends
- Rapid product development
- Rapid production and delivery
- Continuous cost reduction
- Continuous improvement of processes, human resources, and products
- Greater flexibility of operations[64]

Diversity initiatives are an important way to achieve continuous improvement of human resources.[65] Also, notice the clear emphasis on *speed* in this list of key organizational capabilities.

capability profile: *identifying the organization's strengths and weaknesses*

The Strategic Need for Speed. Speed has become an important competitive advantage. Warren Holtsberg, a Motorola corporate vice president, recently offered this perspective:

> *I find the impatience of the new economy refreshing. The concept that fast is better than perfect bodes well, particularly for the technology industry. At Motorola, we used to be able to introduce a cellular telephone, and it would have a life expectancy in the marketplace of about two years. Now we face cycle times of four to six months. People continue to demand new things. They demand change. They're impatient. Bringing that into a big corporation is invigorating.*[66]

reengineering: *radically redesigning the entire business cycle for greater strategic speed*

Accordingly, the new strategic emphasis on speed involves more than just doing the same old things faster. It calls for rethinking and radically redesigning the entire business cycle, a process called **reengineering**[67] (see Skills & Tools). The idea is to have cross-functional teams develop a whole new—and better—production process, one that does not let time-wasting mistakes occur in the first place. (The related topic of horizontal organizations is covered in Chapter 10.)

■ Formulation of Strategic Plans

In the second major step in the strategic management process, general intentions are translated into more concrete and measurable strategic plans, policies, and budget allocations.[68] This translation is the responsibility of top management, although staff planning specialists and middle managers often provide input. From our discussion in the last chapter, we recall that a well-written plan consists of both an objective and an action statement. Plans at all levels need to specify who, what, when, and how things are to be accomplished and for how much. Many managers prefer to call these specific plans "action plans" to emphasize the need to turn good intentions into action. Even though strategic plans may have a time horizon of one or more years, they must meet the same criteria that shorter-run intermediate and operational plans meet. They should do the following:

1. Develop clear, results-oriented objectives in measurable terms.
2. Identify the particular activities required to accomplish the objectives.
3. Assign specific responsibility and authority to the appropriate personnel.
4. Estimate times to accomplish activities and their appropriate sequencing.
5. Determine resources required to accomplish the activities.
6. Communicate and coordinate the above elements and complete the action plan.[69]

All of this does not happen in a single quick-and-easy session. Specific strategic plans usually evolve over a period of months as top management consults with key managers in all areas of the organization to gather their ideas and recommendations and, one hopes, to win their commitment.

Strategic Implementation and Control

As illustrated earlier in Figure 7.2, the third and fourth stages of the strategic management cycle involve implementation and control. The entire process is only as strong as these two traditionally underemphasized areas.

■ Implementation of Strategic Plans

Because strategic plans are too often shelved without adequate attention to implementation, top managers need to do a better job of facilitating the implementation process and building middle-manager commitment.[70]

■ A Systematic Filtering-Down Process. Strategic plans require further translation into successively lower-level plans. Top-management strategists can do some groundwork to ensure that the filtering-down process occurs smoothly and efficiently. Planners need answers to four questions, each tied to a different critical organizational factor:

1. *Organizational structure.* Is the organizational structure compatible with the planning process, with new managerial approaches, and with the strategy itself?
2. *People.* Are people with the right skills and abilities available for key assignments, or must attention be given to recruiting, training, management development, and similar programs?
3. *Culture.* Is the collective viewpoint on "the right way to do things" compatible with strategy, must it be modified to reflect a new perspective, or must top management learn to manage around it?

4. *Control systems.* Is the necessary apparatus in place to support the implementation of strategy and to permit top management to assess performance in meeting strategic objectives?[71]

Strategic plans that successfully address these four questions have a much greater chance of helping the organization achieve its intended purpose than those that do not. In addition, field research indicates the need to *sell* strategies to all affected parties. New strategies represent change, and people tend to resist change for a variety of reasons. "The strategist thus faces a major selling job; that is, trying to build and maintain support among key constituencies for a plan that is freshly emerging."[72] FedEx founder and CEO Fred Smith explains how strategy is "sold" throughout his company:

> *We have meetings each year to review our strategy, to make sure we're not drifting out of our core competencies, and to make sure we're correctly seeing where the markets are going. Once we've bought into that as a senior management team, we then communicate that in every way we can think of. We put it in the mission statement. We put it in the employee handbooks. We tie our business plans to it. We tie our incentive plans to it. We have one of the biggest industrial TV networks in the world and we use it to make sure our employees understand what we're trying to do and why we're trying to do it.*[73]

This brings us to the challenge of obtaining commitment among middle managers.

■ **Building Middle-Manager Commitment.** Resistance among middle managers can kill an otherwise excellent strategic management program. A study of 90 middle managers who wrote 330 reports about instances in which they had resisted strategic decisions documented the scope of this problem. It turned out that to protect their own self-interests, the managers in the study frequently derailed strategies. This finding prompted the researchers to conclude as follows:

> *If general management decides to go ahead and impose its decisions in spite of lack of commitment, resistance by middle management can drastically lower the efficiency with which the decisions are implemented, if it does not completely stop them from being implemented. Particularly in dynamic, competitive environments, securing commitment to the strategy is crucial because rapid implementation is so important.*[74]

Participative management (see Chapter 13) and influence tactics (see Chapter 15) can foster middle-management commitment.[75]

■ Strategic Control

Strategic plans, like our more informal daily plans, can go astray. But a formal control system helps keep strategic plans on track. Software programs (such as Performance eWorkbench by PerformaWorks)[76] that synchronize and track all contributors' goals in real time are indispensable today. And strategic control systems need to be carefully designed ahead of time, not merely tacked on as an afterthought.[77] Before strategies are translated downward, planners should set up and test channels for information on progress, problems, and strategic assumptions about the environment or organization that have proved to be invalid. If a new strategy varies significantly from past

7g When Does a Good Strategy Become the Wrong Strategy?

Bob Nardelli, CEO of Home Depot:

> *Lay a strategy, lay a course, and stay with it. Not blindly stay with it, but believe in it and mobilize. . . .*

Source: As quoted in Patricia Sellers and Julie Schlosser, "It's His Home Depot Now," Fortune *(September 20, 2004): 116.*

QUESTIONS:

How can managers tell when it is time to significantly revise or abandon a successful strategy? What factors weigh against this type of corrective action?

Winter in Yellowstone National Park, where the buffalo (more precisely, American bison) roam. Actually, that's the problem—the buffalo do indeed roam, into neighboring private and public grazing lands. Sometimes they carry diseases harmful to cattle. A comprehensive strategic control program attempts to maintain a healthy herd within the Park and minimize damage elsewhere. Predictably, no stakeholders—including ranchers, hunters, and environmentalists—are totally happy with the program.

ones, then new production, financial, or marketing reports will probably have to be drafted and introduced.

The ultimate goal of a strategic control system is to detect and correct downstream problems in order to keep strategies updated and on target, without stifling creativity and innovation in the process. A survey of 207 planning executives found that in high-performing companies there was no tradeoff between strategic control and creativity. Both were delicately balanced.[78]

Corrective Action Based on Evaluation and Feedback

As illustrated in Figure 7.2, corrective action makes the strategic management process a dynamic cycle. A rule of thumb is that negative feedback should prompt corrective action at the step immediately before.[79] Should the problem turn out to be more deeply rooted, then the next earlier step also may require corrective action. The key is to detect problems and initiate corrective action, such as updating strategic assumptions, reformulating plans, rewriting policies, making personnel changes, or modifying budget allocations, as soon as possible. In the absence of prompt corrective action, problems can rapidly worsen.

Let us now turn to forecasting. Without the ability to obtain or develop reliable environmental forecasts, managerial strategists have a minimal chance of successfully negotiating their way through the strategic management process.

Forecasting

forecasts: *predictions, projections, or estimates of future situations*

An important aspect of strategic management is anticipating what will happen. **Forecasts** may be defined as predictions, projections, or estimates of future events or conditions in the environment in which the organization operates.[80] Forecasts may be little more than educated guesses, or they may be the result of highly sophisticated statistical analyses. They vary in reliability. (Consider the track record of television weather forecasters!)[81] They may be relatively short run—a few hours to a year—or long run—five or more years. A combination of factors determines a forecast's relative sophistication, time horizon, and reliability. These factors include the type of forecast required, management's knowledge of forecasting techniques, and how much money management is willing to invest.[82]

Types of Forecasts

There are three types of forecasts: (1) event outcome forecasts, (2) event timing forecasts, and (3) time series forecasts.[83] Each type answers a different general question

event outcome forecasts: *predictions of the outcome of highly probable future events*

event timing forecasts: *predictions of when a given event will occur*

time series forecasts: *estimates of future values in a statistical sequence*

(see Table 7.4). **Event outcome forecasts** are used when strategists want to predict the outcome of highly probable future events. For example: "How will an impending strike affect output?"

Event timing forecasts predict when, if ever, given events will occur. Strategic questions in this area might include "When will the prime interest rate begin to fall?" or "When will our primary competitor introduce a certain product?" Timing questions such as these typically can be answered by identifying leading indicators that historically have preceded the events in question. For instance, a declining inflation rate often prompts major banks to lower their prime interest rate, or a competitor may flag the introduction of a new product by conducting market tests or ordering large quantities of a new raw material.

Time series forecasts seek to estimate future values in a sequence of periodically recorded statistics. A common example is the sales forecast for a business. Sales forecasts need to be as accurate as possible because they impact decisions all along the organization's supply chain. As Cisco Systems learned the hard way, sales forecasts based on poor input can be very costly.

> *In May 2001, Cisco Systems announced the largest inventory write-down in history: $2.2 billion erased from its balance sheet for components it ordered but couldn't use. . . .*
>
> *To lock in supplies of scarce components during the [Internet] boom, Cisco ordered large quantities well in advance, based on demand projections from the company's sales force. What the forecasters didn't notice, however, was that many of their projections were inflated artificially. With network gear hard to come by, many Cisco customers also ordered similar equipment from Cisco's competitors, knowing that they'd ultimately make just one purchase—from whoever could deliver the goods first.*[84]

8. DESCRIBE the three types of forecasts.

Forecasting Techniques

Modern managers may use one or a combination of four techniques to forecast future outcomes, timing, and values. These techniques are informed judgment, scenario analysis, surveys, and trend analysis.

Informed Judgment.

Limited time and money often force strategists to rely on their own intuitive judgment when forecasting. Judgmental forecasts are both fast and inexpensive, but their accuracy depends on how well informed the strategist is. Frequent visits with employees—in sales, purchasing, and public relations, for example—who regularly tap outside sources of information are a good way of staying informed. A broad reading program to stay in touch with current events and industry trends and refresher training through management development programs are also helpful. Additionally, customized news clipping services (delivered by e-mail), spreadsheet forecasting software, and a competitive intelligence-gathering opera-

Table 7.4 Types of Forecasts

Type of forecast	General question	Example
1. Event outcome forecast	"What will happen when a given event occurs?"	"Who will win the next World Series?"
2. Event timing forecast	"When will a given event occur?"	"When will a human set foot on Mars?"
3. Time series forecast	"What value will a series of periodic data have at a given point in time?"	"What will the closing Dow Jones Industrial Average be on January 5, 2010?"

tion[85] can help keep strategic decision makers up to date. The trick is to separate key bits of information from extraneous background noise. For example, "Apple watchers used Hitachi's announcement of its 1-inch hard drive to accurately predict the arrival of the iPod mini."[86]

Of course, informed judgment is no panacea. It generally needs to be balanced with data from other forecasting techniques and formal market research.[87]

scenario analysis: *preparing written descriptions of equally likely future situations*

longitudinal scenarios: *describing how the future will evolve from the present*

cross-sectional scenarios: *describing future situations at a given point in time*

■ **Scenario Analysis.** This technique also relies on informed judgment, but it is more systematic and disciplined than the approach just discussed. **Scenario analysis** (also called scenario planning) is the preparation and study of written descriptions of *alternative* but *equally likely* future conditions.[88] Scenarios are visions of what "could be." The late futurist Herman Kahn is said to have first used the term *scenario* in conjunction with forecasting during the 1950s. The two types of scenarios are longitudinal and cross-sectional. **Longitudinal scenarios** describe how the present is expected to evolve into the future. **Cross-sectional scenarios**, the most common type, simply describe possible future situations at a given time.

While noting that *multiple forecasts* are the cornerstone of scenario analysis, one researcher offered the following perspective:

> *Scenario writing is a highly qualitative procedure. It proceeds more from the gut than from the computer, although it may incorporate the results of quantitative models. Scenario writing is based on the assumption that the future is not merely some mathematical manipulation of the past, but the confluence of many forces, past, present and future, that can best be understood by simply thinking about the problem.*[89]

The same researcher recommends developing two to four scenarios (three being optimal) for narrowly defined topics.[90] Likely candidates for scenario analysis are specific products, industries, or markets. For example, a grain-exporting company's strategists might look five years into the future by writing scenarios for three different likely situations: (1) above-average grain harvests, (2) average harvests, and (3) below-average harvests. These scenarios could serve as focal points for strategic plans concerning construction of facilities, staffing and training, and so on. As the future unfolds, the strategies written to accompany the more realistic scenario would be followed.

This approach has been called "no surprise" strategic planning. The results of a recent poll uncovered a crying need for such an approach: "fully two-thirds of 140 corporate strategists . . . admitted that their organizations had been surprised by as many as three high-impact events in the past five years."[91] Amazingly, 97 percent of the respondents "stated that their companies have no early warning system in place."[92] *Business Week* framed the case for scenario planning this way:

> *If you envision multiple versions of the future and think through their implications, you will be better prepared for whatever ends up happening. In effect, you won't be seeing the future for the first time. You'll be remembering it. The alternative won't cut it: Those who cannot remember the future are condemned to be taken by surprise.*[93]

The key to good scenario writing is to focus on the few readily identifiable but unpredictable factors that will have the greatest impact on the topic in question. Because scenarios look far into the future, typically five or more years, they need to be written in general and rather imprecise terms.[94]

7h Give Me the Bad News.

Jeffrey Pfeffer, Stanford University business professor:

> *At one company where I'm a board member, people constantly ask the CEO what might go wrong, what the problems are, and what keeps him up at night. It's not done to be negative or critical but to ensure that there's planning in place for every scenario—good, bad, and downright ugly.*

Source: Jeffrey Pfeffer, "The Whole Truth and Nothing But," Business 2.0, *5 (October 2004): 78.*

QUESTIONS:
In your view, how typical is this situation? What needs to be done to make it more common in today's organizations?

■ **Surveys.** Surveys are a forecasting technique involving face-to-face or telephone interviews and mailed, fax, or e-mail questionnaires.

They can be used to pool expert opinion or to fathom consumer tastes, attitudes, and opinions. When carefully constructed and properly administered to representative samples, surveys can give management comprehensive and fresh information. They suffer the disadvantages, however, of being somewhat difficult to construct, time-consuming to administer and interpret, and expensive. Although costs can be trimmed by purchasing an off-the-shelf or "canned" survey, standardized instruments too often either fail to ask precisely the right questions or ask unnecessary questions.

trend analysis: *hypothetical extension of a past series of events into the future*

■ **Trend Analysis.** Essentially, a **trend analysis** is the hypothetical extension of a past pattern of events or time series into the future. An underlying assumption of trend analysis is that past and present tendencies will continue into the future.[95] Of course, surprise events such as the September 11, 2001, terrorist attacks can destroy that assumption. Trend analysis can be fickle and cruel to reactive companies. As a case in point, Chrysler's commitment to fuel-efficient, four-cylinder cars in the early 1980s was based on the assumption that the 1970s trend toward higher gas prices would continue. However, when the price of gasoline stabilized during the 1980s, Chrysler came up short as U.S. car buyers demanded more horsepower.[96] By the time Chrysler had geared up its production of more powerful V-6 engines, Iraq's 1990 invasion of Kuwait sent the price of gasoline skyward and car buyers scrambling for four-cylinder cars. Again Chrysler tripped over a faulty trend analysis. If sufficient valid historical data are readily available, trend analysis can, barring disruptive surprise events, be a reasonably accurate, fast, and inexpensive strategic forecasting tool. An unreliable or atypical database, however, can produce misleading trend projections.

Each of these forecasting techniques has inherent limitations. Consequently, strategists are advised to cross-check one source of forecast information with one or more additional sources.

SUMMARY

1. Strategic management sets the stage for virtually all managerial activity. Managers at all levels need to think strategically and to be familiar with the strategic management process for three reasons: farsightedness is encouraged, the rationale behind top-level decisions becomes more apparent, and strategy formulation and implementation are more decentralized today. Strategic management is defined as the ongoing process of ensuring a competitively superior fit between the organization and its ever-changing environment. Strategic management effectively merges strategic planning, implementation, and control.
2. Strategic thinking, the ability to look ahead and spot key organization-environment interdependencies, is necessary for successful strategic management and planning. Four perspectives that can help managers think strategically are synergy, Porter's model of competitive strategies, the concept of business ecosystems, and e-business strategic signposts. Synergy has been called the 1 + 1 = 3 effect because it focuses on situations where the whole is greater than the sum of its parts. Managers are challenged to achieve four types of synergy: market synergy, cost synergy, technological synergy, and management synergy.
3. According to Porter's generic competitive strategies model, four strategies are (1) cost leadership, (2) differentiation, (3) cost focus, and (4) focused differentiation. Porter's model helps managers create a profitable "fit" between the organization and its environment.
4. Contrary to the traditional assumption that strategy automatically equates to competition, the business ecosystems model emphasizes that organizations need to be as good at *cooperating* as they are at competing. By balancing competition and cooperation, competitors can *coevolve* into a dominant economic community (or business ecosystem).
5. Seven basic Internet business models are the commission-based, advertising based, markup-based, production-based, referral-based, subscription-based, and fee-for-service-based models. Each model affords its own opportunities for competitive advantage. Four Internet strategy lessons have been learned in recent years: (1) there is no one-size-fits-all strategy; (2) reliable brand names and "sticky" Web sites are needed to build customer loyalty, (3) a bricks-and-clicks strategy effectively blends the old (bricks-and-mortar facilities such as stores and warehouses) with the new (a presence on the Web),

and (4) strategic control and high ethical standards are more important than ever with today's virtual global partnerships on the Web.

6. The strategic management process consists of four major steps: (1) formulation of a grand strategy, (2) formulation of strategic plans, (3) implementation of strategic plans, and (4) strategic control. Corrective action based on evaluation of progress and feedback helps keep the strategic management process on track. Results-oriented strategic plans that specify what, when, and how are then formulated and translated downward into more specific and shorter-term intermediate and operational plans. Participative management can build needed middle-manager commitment during implementation. Problems encountered along the way should be detected by the strategic control mechanism or by ongoing evaluation and subjected to corrective action.

7. Strategists formulate the organization's grand strategy after conducting a SWOT analysis. The organization's key capabilities and appropriate niche in the marketplace become apparent when the organization's strengths (S) and weaknesses (W) are cross-referenced with environmental opportunities (O) and threats (T). Strategic speed has become an important capability today, sometimes necessitating radical reengineering of the entire business cycle.

8. Event outcome, event timing, and time series forecasts help strategic planners anticipate and prepare for future environmental circumstances. Popular forecasting techniques among today's managers are informed judgment, scenario analysis, surveys, and trend analysis. Each technique has its own limitations, so forecasts need to be crosschecked against one another.

TERMS TO UNDERSTAND

- Strategic management, p. 190
- Strategy, p. 190
- Synergy, p. 191
- Differentiation, p. 192
- Business ecosystem, p. 196
- Grand strategy, p. 201
- Situational analysis, p. 201
- Capability profile, p. 202
- Reengineering, p. 203
- Forecasts, p. 205
- Event outcome forecasts, p. 206
- Event timing forecasts, p. 206
- Time series forecasts, p. 206
- Scenario analysis, p. 207
- Longitudinal scenarios, p. 207
- Cross-sectional scenarios, p. 207
- Trend analysis, p. 208

SKILLS & TOOLS

Reengineering

Reengineering, a.k.a. process innovation and core process redesign, is the search for, and implementation of, radical change in business processes to achieve breakthrough results. Its chief tool is a clean sheet of paper. Most change efforts start with what exists and fix it up. Reengineering, adherents emphasize, is not tweaking old procedures and certainly not plain-vanilla downsizing. Nor is it a program for bottom-up continuous improvement. Reengineers start from the future and work backward, as if unconstrained by existing methods, people, or departments. In effect they ask, "If we were a new company, how would we run this place?" Then, with a meat ax and sandpaper, they conform the company to their vision.

That's how GTE looks at its telephone operations, which account for four-fifths of the company's $20 billion in annual revenues. Facing new competitive threats, GTE figured it had to offer dramatically better customer service. Rather than eke out steady gains in its repair, billing, and marketing departments, the company examined its operations from the outside in. Customers, it concluded, wanted one-stop shopping—one number to fix an erratic dial tone, question a bill, sign up for call waiting, or all three, at any time of day.

GTE set up its first pilot "customer care center" in Garland, Texas, late last year and began to turn vision into fact. The company started with repair clerks, whose job had been to take down information from a customer, fill out a trouble ticket, and send it on to others who tested lines and switches until they found and fixed the problem. GTE wanted that done while the customer was still on the phone—something that happened just once in 200 calls. The first step was to move testing and switching equipment to the desks of the repair clerks—now called "front-end technicians"—and train them to use it. GTE stopped measuring how fast they handled calls and instead tracked how often they cleared up a problem without passing it on. Three out of ten now, and GTE is shooting for upward of seven.

The next step was to link sales and billing with repair, which GTE is doing with a push-button phone menu that allows callers to connect directly to any service. It has given operators new software so their computers can get into databases that let the operators handle virtually any customer request. In the process, says GTE vice president Mark Feighner, "we eliminated a tremendous amount of work—in the pilots, we've seen a 20 percent or 30 percent increase in productivity so far."

GTE's rewired customer-contact process—one of eight similar efforts at the company—displays most of the salient traits of reengineering: It is occurring in a dramatically altered competitive landscape; it is a major change, with big results; it cuts across departmental lines; it requires hefty investment in training and information technology; and layoffs result. . . .

It ain't cheap, and it ain't easy. At Blue Cross of Washington and Alaska, where redesigning claims processing raised labor productivity 20 percent in 15 months, CEO Betty Woods says the resource she drew on most was courage: "It was more difficult than we ever imagined, but it was worth it."

Therein lies the most important lesson from business's experience with reengineering: Don't do it if you don't have to. Says Thomas H. Davenport, head of research for Ernst & Young: "This hammer is incredibly powerful, but you can't use it on everything." Don't reengineer your buggy whip business; shut it. If you're in decent shape but struggling with cost or quality problems or weak brand recognition, by all means juice up your quality program and fire your ad agency, but don't waste money and energy on reengineering. Save reengineering for big processes that really matter, like new-product development or customer service, rather than test the technique someplace safe and insignificant.

Source: *From Thomas A. Stewart, "Reengineering: The Hot New Managing Tool,"* Fortune *(August 23, 1993): 41–42.*

HANDS-ON EXERCISE

Thinking Strategically: A SWOT Analysis

Instructions

This exercise is suitable for either an individual or a team. First, pick an organization as the focal point of the exercise. It can be a large company, a unit of a large company, a small business, or a nonprofit organization such as a college, government agency, or religious organization. Next, look inward and list the organization's strengths and weaknesses. Turning the analysis outward, list opportunities and threats in the organization's environment. Finally, envision workable strategies for the organization by cross-referencing the two sets of factors. Be sure to emphasize organizational strengths that can exploit environmental opportunities and neutralize or overcome outside threats. Also think about what needs to be done to correct organizational weaknesses. The general idea is to create the best possible fit between the organization and its environment (the "right niche").

Note: A SWOT analysis also can be a powerful career guidance tool. Simply make *yourself* the focus of the exercise and go from there.

Organization or Unit: ______________________

Organization (Unit)

Strengths	Weaknesses

Environment (Unit's Situation)

Opportunities	**Threats**

For Consideration/Discussion

1. Which of the four elements—strengths, weaknesses, opportunities, threats—turned out to be the most difficult to develop? Why? Which was the easiest? Why?
2. What valuable insights about your focal organization did you gain during your SWOT analysis?
3. Why should every manager know how to do a SWOT analysis?
4. What "right niche" did your SWOT analysis yield?
5. How can a personal SWOT analysis improve your career prospects?

INTERNET EXERCISES

1. **Get the BIG Picture with BIG Ideas:** Strategic management is all about looking forward and thinking big. Busy students and managers can stretch their minds and jump-start their imaginations by going online. A good place to begin is at *Fast Company* magazine's excellent Web site. Any article published in paper form by the magazine can be found in its Internet archive. Go to **www.fastcompany.com/backissues** and click on "Browse archives by topic." At the "Articles by Topic" page, select a category such as "Internet in Business" or "Strategy." (*Note:* If these listings have changed, simply select one or more related to the topics in this chapter on strategic management.) Read two or three of the articles you have selected to identify a BIG idea about strategic management and/or making sense of an uncertain future. Your instructor may want you to print a hard copy of your key article if it is part of a formal assignment or class presentation.
   Learning Points: 1. What is the BIG idea you selected and how is it relevant to strategic management? 2. How should managers respond appropriately to your BIG idea (understand, exploit, avoid, etc.)? 3. Is your BIG idea a threat or an opportunity? Explain. 4. Does your BIG idea represent an opportunity to start a new business? Explain.
2. **Check it out:** Go to the home page of the World Future Society (**www.wfs.org**) and search for forecasts and predictions. Make sure you click on the society's publication, *The Futurist,* to scan article titles past and present. Select "Top 10 Forecasts" for interesting reading.

For updates to these exercises, visit our Web site (**http://business.college.hmco.com/students/** and select Kreitner, *Management,* 10e).

CLOSING CASE

Reviving Khadi in India

"Khadi has fallen to disrepair. It had to be repackaged, upgraded, cleaned up."

-Vasundhara Raje, Minister for Small Scale Industries, 2001.

"Khadi is a natural fabric and unique. The rustic, no machine look of the fabric is both sophisticated and bohemian."

-Ritu Kumar, Fashion Designer

"If the supply chain and production can be streamlined, the potential for Khadi is high."

- B.S.Nagesh, CEO, Shoppers' Stop.

Khadi Loses Its Sheen

Khadi[1] , which symbolized self reliance and emancipation during the freedom struggle in India[2] has lost its sheen over the years. And there are several reasons for the same. Post 1947, India opted for state led large scale industrialization. With many Indian industrialists setting up huge textile mills, the mass production of fine cloth led to the availability of cloth at lower prices. People began to buy machine made textiles and thus Khadi began losing out to the mill fabric.

In January 1953, the All India Khadi and Village Industries Board was set up to provide employment to thousands of spinners all over India. In 1957, the Khadi and Village Industries Commission (KVIC) was established to take over the work of the board. KVIC was formed as a nodal agency to promote Khadi all over India through its exclusive outlets known as Khadi Bhandars[3]. The Government of India (GoI) has ever since continued its support to Khadi.

However, there were a few problems. According to designers, the production of Khadi was inconsistent and the cloth was prone to shrinkage and fabric stretch. Besides, fabric colours in Khadi were also limited. Red tapism and bureaucracy prevalent in the Indian system, further hampered the growth of the Khadi sector.

Inspite of having a wide distribution network, there were problems, especially middlemen. Corruption was rampant. There were many bogus Khadi units operating in the country, which made it extremely difficult to claim rebates from the Government of India (GoI). KVIC received huge financial assistance from the GoI in the form of subsidies and rebates.

In May 2000, the Ministry of Small Scale Industries, announced a special package of Rs.12.16 billion to the industry. In order to face the challenges of globalization and strengthen its position in the market, KVIC launched two separate brands, Sarvodaya and Khadi in August 2001.

Sarvodaya comprised consumer goods like incense sticks, spices, honey, and pickles. The Khadi brand included products like essential oils, herbal oil & soaps, face scrubs, dry fruit, honey, designer garments etc. The Khadi brand was introduced exclusively for exports and upmarket. The fabric was being promoted as a fashion fabric.

Many high profile fashion designers were roped in to create garments using the fabric. KVIC allotted huge funds into research and development to improve the quality of Khadi. It allotted around Rs. 0.4 billion for promoting the fabric emphasizing its Unique Selling Proposition (USP), eco-friendliness.

Background Note

Khadi has its roots in the freedom struggle of India. Khadi, the home spun cloth was central to Gandhi's vision of self-reliance and self-rule. Gandhi wanted Indians to spin their own cotton thread and to weave Khadi, thereby, providing employment to many Indians and contributing to the country's self-sufficiency. Post independence, Khadi fabrics were woven on handlooms from cotton, silk, and woollen yarn, which were hand-spun.

The production of Khadi is labour intensive as the weaving has to be done manually. The pure cotton collected from cotton farms is first ginned and bales are made. These bales are then converted into rowings and distributed to different spinning units. In the spinning units, the cotton fibre is manually converted into yarn using charkas[4]. The yarn is then woven into fabric using handlooms.

[1] *Khadi is a cloth produced by interlacement of handspun yarn. The soft twist imparted by the hand gives the yarn 'hairiness' which gives maximum comfort to the wearer. The loom used in weaving of Khadi interlaces the threads in a manner that allows maximum air to permeate to body and soothes the body. Khadi is acknowledged to be one of the coolest and the most comfortable fabric.*

[2] *Instead of exporting raw cotton and importing fine Manchester-made cloth, freedom fighters in India led by Mahatma Gandhi wanted all Indians to spin their own cloth and boycott imports to weaken the British rule in India and make India self-reliant.*

[3] *Khadi Bhandars are exclusive outlets opened by the KVIC to retail all its products.*

[4] *Charka is the Indian version of the spinning wheel.*

During the post-independence era, Indian industrialists set up capital intensive textile mills. Due to mass production, these mills could offer fine cloth at lower prices. Synthetic material like polyester was available at a very low price compared to Khadi. Thus despite all policy incentives to popularize Khadi, people bought machine made textiles.

In order to popularize Khadi among the masses, in 1957, the government set up the KVIC. It had the following broad objectives:

- The social objective of providing employment
- The economic objective of producing saleable articles, and
- The wider objective of creating self-reliance amongst the poor and developing a strong rural community spirit

Besides Khadi, KVIC also dealt with other products such as toilet soaps, detergents, honey, pickles, spices, incense sticks, handmade paper, leather, ceramics, and many other agro-based products. To keep the spirit of Khadi alive and promote it as a national fabric, KVIC has set up many outlets across India.

As a result thousands of spinners, who wove the fabric could sell their output through the vast network of KVIC retail outlets. However, the situation did not improve much. The poor quality of garments sold through the KVIC outlets, resulted in customers' dissatisfaction. People even complained that the quality of Khadi had deteriorated and hence it faded easily.

In the 1990s, very few people bought Khadi. Khadi was bought only during the annual discount sale. Synthetic material was quickly replacing the hand made fabric. People who had got used to the high quality of imported materials, felt that Khadi was rough and coarse and associated it with shapeless kurtas[5] , mostly worn by politicians. And therefore, in spite of the GoI's financial assistance to thousands of traditional spinners in India, they had tough time selling their product.

Reviving Khadi: From Freedom Fabric to Fashion Fabric

In 1985, designer Devika Bhojwani pioneered the Swadeshi label of Khadi ensembles. Those were distributed through nearly 5000 Khadi Emporia. To display Khadi's potential, KVIC organized a fashion show in Mumbai in 1989. Nearly 85 dazzling garments created by Devika Bhojwani were presented at the show.

This was the first step towards changing Khadi's earlier image of being unfashionable. Commenting on the poor state of Khadi, Devika Bhojwani said that failures in the Khadi sector were a result of red tapism and bureaucracy prevalent in the Indian system.

Even though the country had a wide distribution network, the middlemen, commissions and cuts had gradually weakened the system. She further said that though the government was taking the initiative to revive Khadi, nothing much would improve until the implementation, and the cost per garment etc. were controlled.

In 1990, the Delhi based designer, Ritu Kumar presented her first Khadi collection, Tree of Life, which helped put Khadi in the fashion circuit. With increasing interest of the western world in use of handloom and Khadi, many Indian designers began to use Khadi for their designs.

The government also made efforts to promote Khadi. In September 2000, Vasundhara Raje, Minister for Small Scale Industries, initiated a movement to revive all the 7,000 KVIC shops in India and make Khadi more fashionable and affordable. The KVIC Board hired the services of leading fashion designers to help create a new range and brand of Khadi wear.

In May 2001, KVIC set up the first air-conditioned shop in New Delhi. The decor was modern and the clothes were neat and fashionable. The outlet sold Khadi garments designed by high profile designers. On the opening of this outlet, well-known fashion designer, Rohit Bal commented, Khadi is the Indian alternative for linen. It is as comfortable and now, we've proved that it is as fashionable[6].

In January 2002, a high-profile textile exhibition, featuring Khadi ensembles designed by prominent Indian designers, was launched in New Delhi to popularise the traditional hand-spun cotton. The idea of the exhibition was to promote wholly hand spun, hand woven and hand patterned fabric, as a unique luxury product.

The exhibition displayed western as well as traditional Indian attire made from the finest Khadi available in the country. Besides, nearly 110 varieties of the fabric (from the sheerest to the coarsest) were showcased. Designer Rakesh Thakore, whose collection was showcased in the exhibition commented, if packaged well, Khadi can be sold internationally[7] .

[5] *Kurta is a loose fitting shirt.*

[6] *Sengupta, Hindol, Khadi-Much More than a Fabric, Indo-Asian -News -Service.*

[7] *'Glamour platform for Gandhian cotton,' news.bbc.co.uk, Wednesday, January 30, 2002.*

[8] *Volkart Foundation, a Swiss charitable trust, is devoted to funding sustainable development. Marking its 150th anniversary, in February 2001, the Volkart Foundation pledged US $ 1 million as a cultural and social grant. The Khadi exhibition which formed a part of this, was meant for the revival of the old cotton business, Khadi as well as to highlight the non-violence movement.*

The exhibition was sponsored by a Swiss charitable trust, Volkart Foundation[8] in association with the Indian National Trust for Art and Cultural Heritage (INTACH)[9]. With many designers experimenting with Khadi, the designs are no longer as simple as they used to be.

A great deal of emphasis was given to the details of the designs and many new colours were introduced. Eco-friendly vat dyes were used. In March 2002, Preyasi[10], the official designer for KVIC, launched the Khadi Range Collection-2002. In the collection, Khadi was used to create apparel such as, casual shirts, waist coats, skirts, wrap-arounds, trousers, parallels, and tops for women.

Government Support to Khadi

The GoI had been providing huge subsidies and grants to the Khadi sector. Khadi was given a rebate[11] of Rs. 1.49 billion and Rs. 1.4 billion in 1998-99 and 1999-2000 respectively. In 2000-2001, funds to the tune of Rs. 1.29 billion were released for the same. During the same time, concerted efforts were made to root out corruption in the payment of rebate.

Regular vigilance raids were conducted in various parts of the country to detect malpractices in claiming of Khadi rebates and to distinguish between genuine and bogus Khadi and Village Industries. In May 2000, the Ministry of Small Scale Industries announced a special package of Rs.12.15 billion for KVIC. Of this, Rs.0.3 billion had been allocated for renovation of the existing outlets, while Rs 0.4 billion was sanctioned for promotional activities.

Though the GoI provided huge financial assistance to KVIC, the funds did not produce the desired result. It was also being felt that the structure of KVIC needed to be changed to enable it to face the challenges of globalization. Therefore, in 2000, the global consulting firm, Arthur Anderson was hired to suggest restructuring strategies for KVIC.

According to the report, submitted to the Ministry of Small Scale Industries, KVIC should be a policy-making body and play a strategic role rather than being involved in the operations. It also suggested that KVIC should be made a market-oriented organization, and given the freedom to decide on the issues of rebate. In order to improve the marketing and retailing aspects of the sector, it was proposed that an independent marketing company should be formed, which would be disintegrated from the existing Khadi and Village Industries structure.

This company would also deal with improvements in the quality of products, packaging and marketing. It also recommended that the special rebate on Khadi products be made available in the first week of every month, instead of the usual 90-day period after the month of October. The declining production, sales, rural employment opportunities and share of Khadi in the total business of KVIC had become a matter of serious concern for the government (Refer table I)

This had assumed greater significance as the population and per capita consumption of clothes in India had considerably increased over the years. Keeping this in view, the GoI took many initiatives to promote the sector and exploit the full potential of Khadi as a product category in all its forms. As a part of these initiatives, KVIC registered Khadi as a brand name, thereby, protecting it legally.

Table I Khadi Production

Year	Quantity (in million square meters)	Value (in Rs billion)
1998 - 1999	98.2	6.35
1999 - 2000	84.32	5.51
2000 - 2001	69.39	4.31
2001 - 2002	58.89	4.11

Source: www.kvic.org.in

Table II Share of Khadi in The Total Proudction at KVIC (In Rs Billion)

Year	Total production at KVIC*	Share of Khadi
1997 – 1998	45.19	6.24
1998 – 1999	51.12	6.35
1999 – 2000	61.65	5.51
2000 – 2001	69.23	4.31

Source: www.kvic.org.in

** The total production and sales at KVIC includes all the products.*

[9] *INTACH is an NGO that seeks to make strategic and timely intervention in order to conserve and promote India's natural and cultural heritage. INTACH has a nation-wide network of volunteers, who spread awareness about heritage, prevent acts likely to degrade their region's cultural and natural wealth and act positively to preserve and enhance local heritage. INTACH is the nation's largest NGO working in the field of culture.*

[10] *Preyasi is a certified designer by the Ministry of Handicrafts and Textiles - Govt. of India. It claims to be the world's best Wardrobe Management Company. Since fifteen years, Preyasi has been involved in delivering designer-wear and consultancy services to clients in over 48 countries. In 2001, it signed up with KVIC as their official designer to design and promote Khadi garments in the national and international market.*

[11] *These rebates are the discounts given by the Khadi outlets to the consumers, which can be later claimed back from the KVIC.*

Table III Share of Khadi to The Total Sales at KVIC (In Rs Billion)

Year	Total Sales at KVIC*	Share of Khadi
1997 – 1998	50.65	7.45
1998 – 1999	56.01	6.47
1999 – 2000	61.69	6.31
2000 – 2001	79.55	5.7

Source: www.kvic.org.in

In order to compete with other varieties of textile and make it more acceptable in the market, improvisation was needed and new products and designs had to be developed. Keeping this objective in mind, in October 2001, KVIC signed a memorandum of understanding with the Ahmedabad-based National Institute of Design (NID) to provide it design support in order to improve the diminishing market-share of Khadi.

Under the agreement, a special cell would be set up at NID (financed by the KVIC) to provide design support services in Khadi, Village Industries, packaging, marketing, communication, publicity, disseminating materials and other design-related activities.

Khadi goes for a Facelift

Over the years, the Khadi Boards of different states have been experimenting on blending of Khadi with other materials and improving its quality. In July 2002, a collection of ensembles in 'Tencel Khadi' (a blend of Tencel and Khadi in the ratio 30:70) was created by Bangalore-based designer, Deepika Govind, in association with the Karnataka Khadi Board. Tencel is a lyocell fiber natural in origin and hence, environment friendly.

It offers the comfort and luxury of a natural fiber as well as the performance and practicality of a man-made fabric. Tencel Khadi showed lesser shrinkage (4-5%) as compared to the high shrinkage seen in Khadi garments (about 7 %). Due to Tencel's softness, it would become easier to work with Khadi and lend better drape quality to finished garments. Tencel Khadi would provide excellent scope for exports.

In 2002, the Austria-based company, Lenzing AG, proposed to make Khadi more eco-friendly by blending the bio-degradable 'modal fibre' with Khadi. This blend would absorb 50 per cent more humidity than cotton. The blend, besides strengthening the Khadi yarn, would make it easy to wash and maintain.

Future of Khadi

The saleability of any textile depends on its USP and performance. For many years, the promotion for Khadi had been on emotional and political grounds while its quality and variety had been ignored completely. Khadi has very little to offer in terms of fabric performance.

It looks attractive when starched and kept in showrooms but, it does not remain the same after washing. Even finer counts and blends of Khadi cannot withstand many washes and thus, cannot be used for day-to-day purposes. It was becoming extremely difficult for Khadi to compete with the high-tech, colour-fast, wrinkle-free, mill-made cottons and blends available today.

According to analysts, Khadi requires government sanction in every single activity and has therefore been stuck in a bureaucratic swamp, unable to increase its output or raise the quality of the fabric. In 2002, Khadi formed less than half per cent of India's textiles. In order to grow, the production of Khadi needs to be decentralized.

A research and development wing should also be established by KVIC to experiment with new patterns and colours. Besides, weavers can also be given grants to enable creating new designs. KVIC must allot a special advertising budget to promote the fabric.

KVIC plans to launch an advertising campaign in India and abroad to create awareness among people about Khadi and its uses. For this, it allocated an advertising and promotional budget of about Rs. 0.4 billion. It also plans to set up Khadi shops at all the international airports in India.

KVIC is also exploring the possibilities of using e-commerce to market its products. However, Khadi, like any other craft of India, would need to face the challenge of quality and produce contemporary designs, which suit the tastes of the present generation.

For Discussion

1. Khadi is handspun from natural fibers thus, making it eco-friendly, pure and fully bio-degradable. This has made it popular in the overseas market. However, Khadi is not very popular in India. Why is Khadi unable to create a substantial market for itself in India? What are the factors that are responsible for the declining sales of Khadi?
2. According to analysts, the Khadi sector was unable to grow because of the loopholes present in the Indian system. What are the initiatives taken by KVIC and the GoI to address these issues and thereby, boost the sales of Khadi?
3. In order to revive Khadi, KVIC followed the strategy of repositioning it as a fashion fabric and aiming it towards customers at the premium end. Do you think following this strategy alone would suffice? What are the other areas where KVIC can improve?

Source: *http://www.icmr.icfai.org/casestudies*

**Source: Website www.icmrindia.org*

TEST PREPPER

True/False Questions

_____ **1.** Finding solutions to emerging problems reveals a farsighted management style.

_____ **2.** In the two modern modes of strategy making, top managers act as commander and coach rather than as sponsor or facilitator.

_____ **3.** Synergy has been called the 2 + 1 = 3 effect.

_____ **4.** Competitive advantage and competitive scope are the two major variables in Porter's generic competitive strategies model.

_____ **5.** Two of the seven basic Internet business models are advertising-based models and entertainment-based models.

_____ **6.** Writing a formal code of ethics is the first step in the strategic management process.

_____ **7.** The "O" in a SWOT analysis stands for "outlook."

_____ **8.** Strategic planning is a bottom-up process, as opposed to a top-down process.

_____ **9.** Time series forecasts seek to estimate future values in a sequence of periodically recorded statistics.

_____ **10.** The key to good scenario writing is to focus on the few readily identifiable but unpredictable factors that will have the greatest impact on the topic in question.

Multiple-Choice Questions

1. _____ is *not* a key dimension of strategic farsightedness.
A. Emphasizing the development of new products
B. Emphasizing increased market share
C. Writing a formal mission statement
D. Viewing labor as a commodity
E. Relying on upward communication

2. There is a trend away from the _____ mode and toward the _____ mode in strategy making.
A. command; rational B. symbolic; rational
C. transactive; symbolic D. symbolic; generative
E. generative; command

3. Strategic management =
A. operational planning + intermediate planning + strategic planning.
B. resources + opportunities + results.
C. top-management commitment + results.
D. strategic planning + implementation + control.
E. strategic planning.

4. What does the term *synergy* refer to?
A. The 1 + 1 = 2 effect
B. Situational analysis
C. The additive effect
D. The 1 + 1 = 3 effect
E. Forecasting

5. Which of these, according to Porter, is the ability to provide unique and superior value to the buyer in terms of product quality, special features, or after-sales service?
A. Competitive scope B. Cost leadership
C. Market segmentation D. Economies of scale
E. Differentiation

6. The seven basic Internet business models include all *except* which one of these?
A. Transaction-based models
B. Commission-based models
C. Referral-based models
D. Subscription-based models
E. Mark-up-based models

7. One of four key lessons that managers have learned about Internet strategy is that when doing business on the Internet, it is especially important to ensure that e-business partnering does not dilute
A. profitability.
B. strategic control and ethical standards.
C. executive leadership.
D. employee morale.
E. communication and teamwork.

8. _____ serves as the focal point for the entire planning process.
A. Product/service quality
B. A performance appraisal system
C. The customer
D. A code of ethics
E. A mission statement

9. The "W" in a SWOT analysis stands for
A. weaknesses. B. workers.
C. window of opportunity. D. workability.
E. willingness.

10. _____ analysis has been called "no surprise" strategic planning.
A. Rational B. Trend
C. Market D. Scenario
E. Economic

ACE self-test

Want more questions? Visit the student Web site at **http://business.college.hmco.com/students/** (select Kreitner, *Management*, 10e) and take the ACE quizzes for more practice.

8

Decision Making and Creative Problem Solving

"Every now and then, I'm reminded that the difference between success and failure in business is often one decision. You make the right one, and you survive. You make the wrong one, and you don't."[1]

NORM BRODSKY, ENTREPRENEUR

OBJECTIVES

- **Specify** at least five sources of decision complexity for modern managers.
- **Explain** what a *condition of risk* is and what managers can do to cope with it.
- **Define** and **discuss** the three decision traps: framing, escalation of commitment, and overconfidence.
- **Discuss** why programmed and nonprogrammed decisions require different decision-making procedures, and **distinguish** between the two types of knowledge in knowledge management.
- **Explain** the need for a contingency approach to group-aided decision making.
- **Identify** and briefly **describe** five of the ten "mental locks" that can inhibit creativity.
- **List** and **explain** the four basic steps in the creative problem-solving process.
- **Describe** how causes of problems can be tracked down with fishbone diagrams.

the changing workplace

The Stats Wonk Who Runs a Pro Sports Team

When Paul DePodesta watches his Los Angeles Dodgers play baseball, it's through a lens that has nothing to do with cutting down the glare of the Southern California sun. He sees numbers and calculations everywhere on the field, and it's that distinct vision that [in 2004] made him, at the tender age of 31, the general manager of one of baseball's most storied franchises.

Unlike many front-office vets, DePodesta never played in the big leagues. But he loves the sport and happens to be fluent in statistical analysis. "My dad taught me a board game called Big League Manager when I was 7," DePodesta says. "From then on I started thinking about baseball more and more in percentage terms."

How does a mathlete find his way into one of professional sports' most prestigious posts? Odd as it sounds, he stuck with his strengths. In 1996, after leaving Harvard with an economics degree, DePodesta landed an internship with the Cleveland Indians. He instantly stood out: Here was a geek who had analyzed the numbers from every baseball team in the 20th century—and had concluded that a player's value was tied to the arcane stat of on-base percentage (how often someone reaches base safely). He also found that players with high OBPs, rather than marquee numbers like home runs or runs batted in, often could be picked up on the cheap.

The Indians embraced some of DePodesta's theories and pushed him to scour his spreadsheets for more. He rose quickly. "They challenged me to do things differently," DePodesta says. "That's become the foundation for my career."

His iconoclastic views drew attention around the league, and he was hired away by the Oakland As in 1998. He says it wasn't just for his number crunching. He'd learned that everything about the business of baseball—from the age at which schoolboys get contracts to the reliability of a scout's gut calls—should be questioned. "Analysis in any business can change," he says. "Don't be wed to conventional thought. Always think critically."

Update DePodesta was fired after the Dodgers had 71 wins and 91 losses in 2005. His approach was critized for ignoring team chemistry.

As an assistant GM [general manager] in Oakland, DePodesta was instrumental in consistently building low-cost, championship-caliber teams. He found prospects by mining the Internet for stats of obscure college players. But landing the Tinsel Town dream job (reportedly a five-year deal worth $800,000 annually) required one more insight: Hear out your elders, of which there are many with the Dodgers. "Those who've achieved before you? Soak up as much of their knowledge as possible," he says.

Being young, unconventional, and in charge of his own team hasn't been easy. Sportswriters have dubbed him General Manager.com and savaged him for his trades. But the Dodgers made the playoffs . . . [in 2004] for the first time since 1996. However they fare in the . . . [future], DePodesta won't pause to gloat—or to doubt. "I'm going to stick to my guns," he says. "That's to never be satisfied with the status quo."

Source: *From Paul DePodesta, "The Stats Wonk Who Runs a Pro Sports Team,"* Business 2.0, *5 (November 2004): 103.*

decision making: *identifying and choosing among alternative courses of action*

Decision making is the process of identifying and choosing among alternative courses of action in a manner appropriate to the demands of the situation.[2] The act of choosing implies that alternative courses of action must be weighed and weeded out. That is precisely what the Dodgers' Paul DePodesta does as he studies the records of many baseball players before extending offers and cutting players. He needs to make important decisions amid lots of change and uncertainty, despite incomplete information. No matter how sophisticated DePodesta's statistical analysis is, reason and judgment are still necessary. Thus judgment and discretion are fundamental to decision making. This chapter highlights major challenges for decision makers, introduces a general decision-making model, discusses group-aided decision making, and examines creativity and problem solving.

Challenges for Decision Makers

Though decision making has never been easy, it is especially challenging for today's managers. In an era of accelerating change, the pace of decision making also has accelerated. According to a survey of 479 managers, 77 percent reported making *more decisions* during the previous three years, and 43 percent said they had *less time* to make each of those decisions.[3] A stunning example of this second trend occurred in 2004 when AT&T was in the middle of a bidding war for its wireless unit:

> *With time running out in the high-stakes poker match for AT&T wireless, the CEOs for BellSouth and SBC Communications agreed . . . to throw one last chip on the table. At just past 2 a.m. . . ., the telecom giants authorized their investment bankers to increase their all-cash offer for AT&T to $41 billion with just one condition: AT&T's board had one minute to decide. . . . Finally, after a flurry of e-mail messages, AT&T said yes to the gambit, then yes to the offer.*[4]

In addition to having to cope with this acceleration, today's decision makers face a host of tough challenges. Those that we will discuss here are (1) complex streams of decisions, (2) uncertainty, (3) information-processing styles, and (4) perceptual and behavioral decision traps.

8a What Do You Stand For?

Michael Useem, director, Center for Leadership and Change Management, University of Pennsylvania:

> *When you have to make a fast decision with significant stakes, you better know what you stand for, because the temptation to violate your basic commitments in life can be large because of the stress of the moment.*

Source: Michael Useem, "How Do Values Relate to Courage?" Fast Company, *no. 86 (September 2004): 102.*

QUESTIONS:

Is this a major ethics problem for today's managers? Explain. How about in your own personal life? Explain.

For further information about the interactive annotations in this chapter, visit our Web site (**http://business.college.hmco.com/students/** and select Kreitner, *Management,* 10e).

1. SPECIFY at least five sources of decision complexity for modern managers.

Dealing with Complex Streams of Decisions

Above all else, today's decision-making contexts are not neat and tidy. A pair of experts lent realism to the subject by using the analogy of a stream:

> *If decisions can be viewed as streams—streams containing countless bits of information, events, and choices—then how should decision makers be viewed? . . . The streams flowing through the organization do not wait for them; they flow around them. The streams do not serve up problems neatly wrapped and ready for choice. Rather, they deliver the bits and pieces, the problems and choices, in no particular order. . . .*
>
> *In short, decision makers in an organization are floating in the stream, jostled capriciously by problems popping up, and finding anchors through action at a given time in a given place.*[5]

It is important to note that the foregoing is a recognition of complexity, *not* an admission of hopelessness. A working knowledge of eight intertwined factors contributing to decision complexity can help decision makers successfully navigate the stream (see Figure 8.1).

1. ***Multiple criteria.*** Typically, a decision today must satisfy a number of often-conflicting criteria representing the interests of different groups. For example, the new Denver International Airport was designed and built with much more than airplanes in mind:

   > *Denver's is the first airport to be built for maximum accessibility for the disabled. During construction, the city took blind people, deaf people and those who use wheelchairs and canes through the terminal and concourses to road-test the layout.*
   >
   > *"They wanted to make sure a sign wasn't too low or a drinking fountain sticking out too far," says Thom Walsh, project manager at Fentress Bradburn. "It's a completely accessible building and uses Braille and voice paging."*[6]

Figure 8.1 Sources of Complexity for Today's Managerial Decision Makers

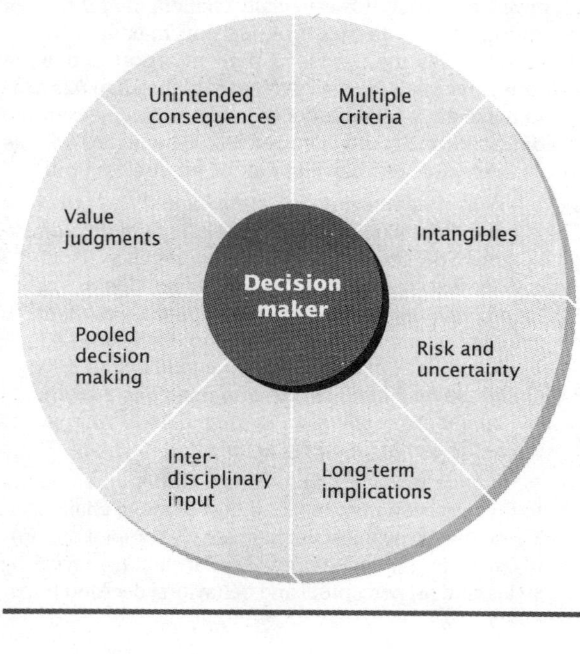

Identifying stakeholders and balancing their conflicting interests is a major challenge for today's decision makers.

2. ***Intangibles.*** Factors such as customer goodwill, employee morale, increased bureaucracy, and aesthetic appeal (for example, negative reaction to a billboard on a scenic highway), although difficult to measure, often determine decision alternatives.
3. ***Risk and uncertainty.*** Along with every decision alternative goes the chance that it will fail in some way. Poor choices can prove costly. Yet the right decision, as illustrated in this legendary example, can open up whole new worlds of opportunity:

   > *In 1967, seven dry holes on Alaska's harsh North Slope had left Atlantic Richfield Chairman Robert O. Anderson facing a costly choice. Should he try one more? The consummate wildcatter, Anderson pushed ahead, making one of the [greatest] strategic decisions in U.S. oil history.*
   >
   > *The day after Christmas, oil historian Daniel Yergin recounts, a sound like four jumbo jets flying just overhead*

announced a plume of spewing natural gas. Prudhoe Bay turned out to be the largest petroleum discovery ever in North America.[7]

Because of the importance of this particular aspect of decision complexity, we shall devote special attention to it in the next section.

4. ***Long-term implications.*** Major decisions generally have a ripple effect, with today's decisions creating the need for later rounds of decisions. For example, remember Airbus's 555-seat A380 jetliner, mentioned in our Chapter 6 discussion of break-even analysis? Consider these long-term implications for the world's largest commercial airplane now moving from concept to production in Europe:

   The Airbus A380 is so large that it cannot park at a terminal designed for a row of Boeing 747s. It is so long that it will handle some taxiways like a tractor-trailer truck turning into a suburban driveway. It is so heavy that it cannot taxi across some culverts and bridges.

   Its engines are spaced so far apart that their exhaust could fry a runway's guide lights. Its body is so wide and tall that tower controllers may have to ban aircraft from nearby runways and taxiways before the plane lands or takes off.[8]

   Airports will have to be significantly redesigned to accommodate the A380.

5. ***Interdisciplinary input.*** Decision complexity is greatly increased when technical specialists such as lawyers, consumer advocates, tax advisers, accountants, engineers, and production and marketing experts are consulted before making a decision. This process can become even more complex and time-consuming in traditional societies such as China, for example, where it is common practice to consult *feng shui* experts about superstitious beliefs. "*Feng shui* (pronounced 'fung schway') literally means wind (*feng*) and water (*shui*) and refers to the ancient Chinese art of creating harmony between inhabitants and their environment."[9] Perhaps a tree needs to be removed, the roof painted a different color, or the alignment of doorways changed. Foreigners who ignore what they deem to be superstitious nonsense do so at the peril of their business dealings with their Chinese partners.

This oddball Kentucky billboard conveys a very serious message from the owners of local small businesses. They fear being driven out of business by look-alike, big-box stores. The giant mass-retail chains, in turn, consider the failure of some local businesses to be an unintended consequence of their low-price strategy. Where do you stand on this issue?

MANAGING DIVERSITY

Are You a Biased Decision Maker?

Are you willing to bet that you feel the same way toward European-Americans as you do toward African-Americans? How about women versus men? Or older people versus younger ones? Think twice before you take that bet. Visit **implicit.harvard.edu** or **www.tolerance.org/hidden_bias** to examine your unconscious attitudes.

The Implicit Association Tests available on these sites reveal unconscious beliefs by asking takers to make split-second associations between words with positive or negative connotations and images representing different types of people. The various tests on these sites expose the differences—or the alignment—between test takers' conscious and unconscious attitudes toward people of different races, sexual orientation, or physical characteristics. Data gathered from over 2.5 million online tests and further research tell us that unconscious biases are

- **widely prevalent.** At least 75% of test takers show an implicit bias favoring the young, the rich, and whites.
- **robust.** The mere conscious desire not to be biased does not eliminate implicit bias.
- **contrary to conscious intention.** Although people tend to report little or no *conscious* bias against African-Americans, Arabs, Arab-Americans, Jews, gay men, lesbians, or the poor, they show substantial biases on implicit measures.
- **different in degree depending on group status.** Minority group members tend to show less implicit preference for their own group than majority group members show for theirs. For example, African-Americans report strong preference for their group on explicit measures but show relatively less implicit preference in the tests. Conversely, white Americans report a low explicit bias for their group but a higher implicit bias.
- **consequential.** Those who show higher levels of bias on the IAT are also likely to behave in ways that are more biased in face-to-face interactions with members of the group they are biased against and in the choices they make, such as hiring decisions.
- **costly.** Research currently under way in our lab suggests that implicit bias generates a "stereotype tax"—negotiators leave money on the table because biases cause them to miss opportunities to learn about their opponent and thus create additional value through mutually beneficial tradeoffs.

Source: Reprinted by permission of the Harvard Business Review. *An exhibit from "How (Un)Ethical Are You?" vol. 81, p. 59.*

6. ***Pooled decision making.*** Rarely is a single manager totally responsible for the entire decision process. For example, consider the approach of Brian Ruder, the successful president of Heinz's U.S. unit:

   > *[He] has collected a number of mentors and advisers over the course of his career. Ruder, in fact, has elected a group of people, including his father, to a personal board of directors. He canvasses them whenever he's faced with a major decision, such as introducing plastic ketchup bottles. . . . "I rely on them," he says, "for total frankness and objectivity." Obviously, it's helped.*[10]

   After pooled input, complex decisions wind their way through the organization, with individuals and groups interpreting, modifying, and sometimes resisting. Minor decisions set the stage for major decisions, which in turn are translated back into local decisions. Typically, many people's fingerprints are on final decisions in the organizational world.
7. ***Value judgments.*** As long as decisions are made by people with differing backgrounds, perceptions, aspirations, and values, the decision-making process will be marked by disagreement over what is right or wrong, good or bad, and ethical or unethical (see Managing Diversity).

law of unintended consequences: *results of purposeful actions are often difficult to predict*

8. ***Unintended consequences.*** The **law of unintended consequences**, according to an expert on the subject, "states that you cannot always predict the results of purposeful action."[11] In other words, there can be a disconnect between intentions and actual results. Although unintended consequences can be positive, negative ones are most troublesome and have been called the Frankenstein monster effect.[12] For example, did the designers of motor vehicle airbags, in their quest to save lives, adequately

anticipate how lethal the devices would be for small children and frail adults? Evidently not. And therein lies the crux of the problem of unintended consequences. Namely, *hurried decision makers typically give little or no consideration to the broader consequences of their decisions.* Unintended consequences cannot be altogether eliminated in today's complex world.[13] Still, they can be moderated to some extent by giving them creative and honest consideration when making important decisions.

8b Back to the Opening Case

Based on the facts of this case and any reasonable assumptions, how many of the eight sources of decision complexity are evident in the Dodger baseball case? Explain.

Coping with Uncertainty

Among the valuable contributions of decision theorists are classification schemes for types and degrees of uncertainty. (Recall our discussion in Chapter 6 about state, effect, and response uncertainty.) Unfortunately, life is filled with varying degrees of these types of uncertainties. Managers are continually asked to make the best decisions they can, despite uncertainties about both present and future circumstances. For example, this is how Richard Branson, the flamboyant British founder and CEO of Virgin, recently described a key strategic decision:

> *When we did Virgin Mobile four years ago, it was a big investment for us—$300 million. I looked at the percentage of people in America with prepaid phones, and it was 8%. Yet in England it was 83%, in France 78%, and so on. And yet we had long debates before making the decision. I decided to push on with it—and it's been one of the best investment decisions we've ever made. So sometimes you just have to go on gut feeling. To start Virgin Mobile, I sold assets that I loved, that I'd had since I was 20 years old, in order to take one opportunity.*[14]

Managers who are able to assess the degrees of certainty in a situation—whether conditions are certain, risky, or uncertain—are able to make more effective decisions. As illustrated in Figure 8.2, there is a negative correlation between uncertainty and the decision maker's confidence in a decision. In other words, the more uncertain a manager is about the principal factors in a decision, the less confident he or

While transportation officials in Malibu, California, were deciding what to do about this huge boulder in the road in early 2005, utility crews worked to restore electricity and telephone service. Mud and rock slides are common during heavy rains in southern California, but local utility companies still face great uncertainty about exactly where and when various types of problems will occur.

Figure 8.2 The Relationship Between Uncertainty and Confidence

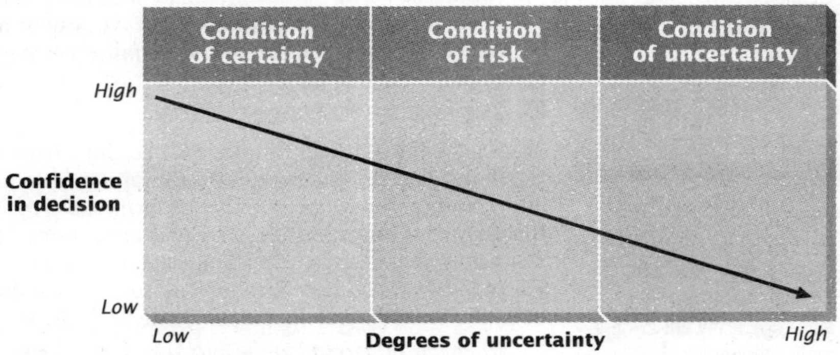

she will be about the successful outcome of that decision. The key, of course, lies not in eliminating uncertainty, which is impossible, but rather in learning to work within an acceptable range of uncertainty.[15]

condition of certainty: *solid factual basis allows accurate prediction of decision's outcome*

■ **Certainty.** A **condition of certainty** exists when there is no doubt about the factual basis of a particular decision and its outcome can be predicted accurately. Much like the economic concept of pure competition, the concept of certainty is useful mainly as a theoretical anchor point for a continuum. In a world filled with uncertainties, certainty is relative rather than absolute. For example, the decision to order more rivets for a manufacturing firm's fabrication department is based on the relative certainty that the current rate of use will exhaust the rivet inventory on a specific date. But even in this case, uncertainties about the possible misuse or theft of rivets creep in to reduce confidence. Because nothing is truly certain, conditions of risk and uncertainty are the general rule for managers, not the exception.

condition of risk: *decision made on basis of incomplete but reliable information*

■ **Risk.** A **condition of risk** is said to exist when a decision must be made on the basis of incomplete but reliable factual information.[16] Reliable information, though incomplete, is still useful to managers coping with risk because they can use it to calculate the probability that a given event will occur and then to select a decision alternative with favorable odds.

objective probabilities: *odds derived mathematically from reliable data*

subjective probabilities: *odds based on judgment*

The two basic types of probabilities are objective and subjective probabilities. **Objective probabilities** are derived mathematically from reliable historical data, whereas **subjective probabilities** are estimated on the basis of one's past experience or judgment. Decision making based on probabilities is common in all areas of management today. For instance, laundry product manufacturers would not think of launching a new detergent without determining the probability of its acceptance via consumer panels and test marketing. A number of inferential statistical techniques can help managers objectively assess risks.[17]

condition of uncertainty: *no reliable factual information available*

■ **Uncertainty.** A **condition of uncertainty** exists when little or no reliable factual information is available. Still, judgmental or subjective probabilities can be estimated. Decision making under conditions of uncertainty can be both rewarding and nerve-racking for managers. Just ask executives in the biotechnology industry: "It costs tens of millions of dollars and can take five to 15 years to get a drug from the test tube to the clinic—and many drugs simply don't make it."[18] Decision confidence is lowest when a condition of uncertainty prevails because decisions are then based on educated guesses rather than on hard factual data.

2. ■ **EXPLAIN** what a *condition of risk* is and what managers can do to cope with it.

8c Great Mistake!

Geraldine Laybourne, creator of Oxygen, a cable TV channel for women:

You learn a hell of a lot more from a mistake than from an early success.

Source: As quoted in Nadine Heintz, "Thinking Inside the Box," Inc.*, 26 (July 2004): 93.*

QUESTIONS:

How does this perspective help managers deal with the risk-taking aspect of decision making?

Information-Processing Styles

Thinking is one of those activities we engage in constantly yet seldom pause to examine systematically.[19] But within the context of managerial decision making and problem solving, it is important that one's thinking not get into an unproductive rut. The quality of our decisions is a direct reflection of how we process information.

Researchers have identified two general information-processing styles: the thinking style and the intuitive style.[20] One is not superior to the other. Both are needed during organizational problem solving. Managers who rely predominantly on the *thinking* style tend to be logical, precise, and objective. They prefer routine assignments requiring attention to detail and systematic implementation. Conversely, managers who are predominantly *intuitive* find comfort in rapidly changing situations in which they can be creative and follow their hunches and visions. Intuitive managers see things in complex patterns rather than as logically ordered bits and pieces. They typically rely on their own mental shortcuts and detours.[21] An interesting example of intuitive thinking involves brothers Harvey and Bob Weinstein, who founded and head Disney's Miramax film unit.

> Bob: *I used to wonder how Harvey viewed a movie; what was the quality he was looking for in making a decision to buy? He gave me an answer I've never forgotten. He said, "I actually watch a movie for the movie's sake, just as if I'd paid my seven bucks to see it. Whether it was costing me $2 million or $7 million to acquire it, that wasn't in my mind. It was just, literally, did I enjoy the movie for its own sake?" You follow your instincts and enjoyment rather than a formula in your head; you buy it on your gut.*[22]

8d How Intuitive Are You?

Rate yourself on each item with the following "1 to 5" scale. The higher your total score, the more intuitive you are.

Not at all like me 1—2—3—4—5 ***Very much like me***

1. You can identify something you haven't seen clearly.
2. You look at a cloud and many images come to mind.
3. You always know when it's the ideal time to strike.
4. You're good at hunches.
5. You're good at detective work; you know what elements fit together.

Total score: _____

Source: Questionnaire items excerpted from Daniel Cappon, "The Anatomy of Intuition," Psychology Today*, 26 (May-June 1993): 42–43.*

QUESTIONS:

How intuitive are you? Would your close friends and relatives agree with your score? How do others tend to react to your level of intuition? How can your intuition (or lack of it) help or hinder you as a manager?

Of course, not every manager falls neatly into one of these two categories; many people process information through a combination of the two styles. For example, Bonnie Reitz, a senior vice president for sales at Continental Airlines, told *Fast Company* magazine, "I believe in unshakable facts. Get as many facts as you can. Don't spend forever on it, but if you have enough facts and the gut intuition, you're going to get it right most of the time."[23] (See Table 8.1.)

The important thing to recognize here is that managers can approach decision making and problem solving in very different ways, depending on their information-processing styles.[24] It is a matter of diversity. Their approaches, perceptions, and recommendations vary because their minds work differently. In traditional pyramid work organizations, where the thinking style tends to prevail, intuitive employees may be criticized for being imprecise and rocking the boat. A concerted effort needs to be made to tap the creative skills of "intuitives" and the implementation abilities of "thinkers." An appreciation for alternative information-processing styles needs to be cultivated because they complement one another.

Avoiding Perceptual and Behavioral Decision Traps

Behavioral scientists have identified some common human tendencies capable of eroding the quality of decision making. Three well-documented ones are framing, escalation, and overconfidence. Awareness and conscious avoidance of these traps can give decision makers a competitive edge.

Table 8.1 How to Sharpen Your Intuition

Recommendation	Description
1. Open up the closet	To what extent do you: experience intuition; trust your feelings; count on intuitive judgments; suppress hunches; covertly rely upon gut feel?
2. Don't mix up your I's	Instinct, insight, and intuition are not synonymous; practice distinguishing between your instincts, your insights, and your intuitions.
3. Elicit good feedback	Seek feedback on your intuitive judgments; build confidence in your gut feel; create a learning environment in which you can develop better intuitive awareness.
4. Get a feel for your batting average	Benchmark your intuitions; get a sense for how reliable your hunches are; ask yourself how your intuitive judgment might be improved.
5. Use imagery	Use imagery rather than words; literally visualize potential future scenarios that take your gut feelings into account.
6. Play devil's advocate	Test out intuitive judgments; raise objections to them; generate counter-arguments; probe how robust gut feel is when challenged.
7. Capture and validate your intuitions	Create the inner state to give your intuitive mind the freedom to roam; capture your creative intuitions; log them before they are censored by rational analysis.

Source: Academy of Management Executive: The Thinking Manager's Source *by Eugene Sadler-Smith and Erella Sheffy, Copyright 2004 by Academy of Management. Reproduced with permission of Academy of Management in the format Textbook via Copyright Clearance Center.*

framing error: *how information is presented influences one's interpretation of it*

■ **Framing Error.** One's judgment can be altered and shaped by how information is presented or labeled. In other words, labels create frames of reference with the power to bias our interpretations. **Framing error** is the tendency to evaluate positively presented information favorably and negatively presented information unfavorably.[25] Those evaluations, in turn, influence one's behavior. A study with 80 male and 80 female University of Iowa students documented the framing-interpretation-behavior linkage. Half of each gender group was told about a cancer treatment with a 50 percent success rate. The other two groups heard about the same cancer treatment but were told it had a 50 percent failure rate. The researchers summed up the results of the study as follows:

> *Describing a medical treatment as having a 50 percent success rate led to higher ratings of perceived effectiveness and higher likelihood of recommending the treatment to others, including family members, than describing the treatment as having a 50 percent failure rate.*[26]

Framing thus influenced both interpretations and intended behavior. Given the importance of the information in this study (cancer treatment), ethical questions arise about the potential abuse of framing error.

3. ■ **DEFINE** and **DISCUSS** the three decision traps: framing, escalation of commitment, and overconfidence.

In organizations, framing error can be used constructively or destructively. Advertisers, for instance, take full advantage of this perceptional tendency when attempting to sway consumers' purchasing decisions. A leading brand of cat litter boasts of being 99 percent dust-free. Meanwhile, a shampoo claims to be fortified with 1 percent natural protein. Thanks to framing error, we tend to perceive very little dust in the cat litter and a lot of protein in the shampoo. Managers who couch their proposals in favorable terms hope to benefit from framing error. And who can blame them? On the negative side, prejudice and bigotry thrive on framing error. A male manager who believes women can't manage might frame interview results so that John looks good and Mary looks bad.

escalation of commitment: *people get locked into losing courses of action to avoid the embarrassment of quitting or admitting error*

■ **Escalation of Commitment.** Why are people slow to write off bad investments? Why do companies stick to unprofitable strategies? And why has the U.S. government typically continued to fund over-budget and behind-schedule programs? Escalation of commitment is a possible explanation for these diverse situations.[27] **Escalation of commitment** is the tendency of individuals and organizations to get locked into losing courses of action because *quitting is personally and socially difficult.* This decision-making trap has been called the "throwing good money after bad" dilemma. Those victimized by escalation of commitment are often heard talking about "sunk costs" and "too much time and money invested to quit now." Within the context of management, psychological, social, and organizational factors conspire to encourage escalation of commitment[28] (see Figure 8.3).

The model in Figure 8.3 can be brought to life by using it to analyze a highly unusual decision by the Pentagon in 1991. Two giant defense contractors, McDonnell Douglas and General Dynamics, were under contract to design and build the A-12 attack plane. All told, 620 of the aircraft carrier–based bombers were to be built for the U.S. Navy at a cost of $60 billion. With the A-12 program 18 months behind schedule and $2.7 billion over budget, then–Secretary of Defense Dick Cheney terminated the contract. It was the Pentagon's biggest cancellation ever. An appreciation of the contributing factors shown in Figure 8.3 underscores how truly unusual Cheney's decision was. Psychologically, his termination decision flew in the face of three possible motives for throwing good money after bad. Cheney went against the social grain as well by publicly admitting the Defense Department's mistake and doing something culturally distasteful to Americans: giving up. (American folk heroes tend to be persistent to the bitter end.) Finally, Cheney had to overcome bureaucratic resistance in the defense establishment. He also had to withstand political opposition from the

Figure 8.3 Why Escalation of Commitment Is So Common

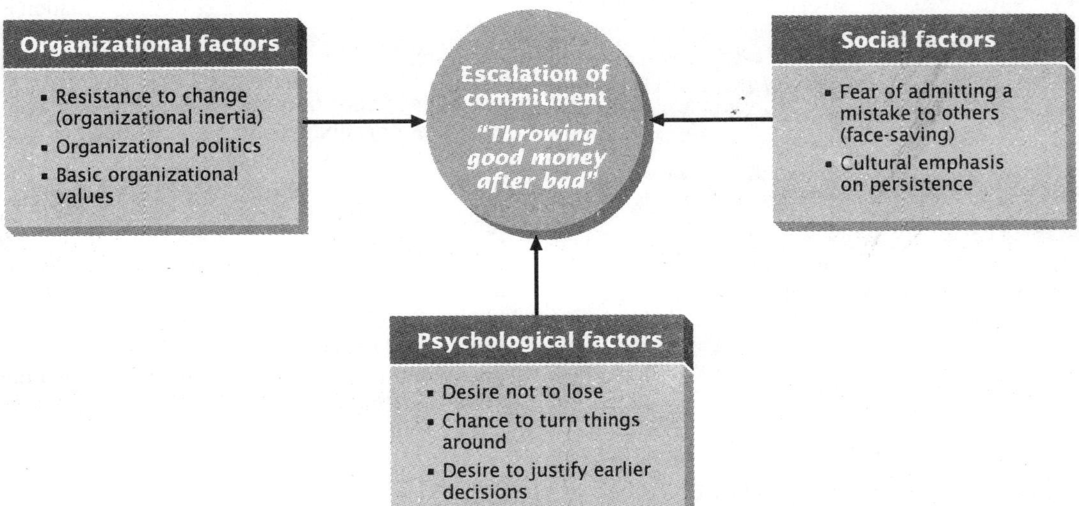

Source: *Adapted from discussion in Barry M. Staw and Jerry Ross, "Understanding Behavior in Escalation Situations,"* Science, *246 (October 13, 1989): 216–220.*

contractors about their having to lay off 8,000 A-12 project employees. Nevertheless, despite many pressures to continue the program, Cheney refused to let the forces of escalation carry the day.

Reality checks, in the form of comparing actual progress with effectiveness and efficiency standards, are the best way to keep escalation in check.[29] In Cheney's case, he concluded, "No one can tell me exactly how much more it will cost to keep this [A-12] program going. And I do not believe that a bailout is in the national interest. If we cannot spend the taxpayers' money wisely, we will not spend it."[30] This is an instructive lesson for all potential victims of escalation.

■ **Overconfidence.** The term *overconfidence* is commonplace and requires no formal definition. We need to comprehend the psychology of overconfidence because it can expose managers to unreasonable risks. For example, in his book *Why Smart Executives Fail—and What You Can Learn from Their Mistakes,* Sydney Finkelstein offers this helpful caution:

> *Movies, television shows, and journalists all offer us instantly recognizable vignettes of the dynamic executive making a dozen decisions a minute, snapping out orders that will redirect huge enterprises, dealing with numerous crises at once, and taking only seconds to size up situations that have obviously stumped everyone else for days. . . .*
>
> *The problem with this picture of executive competence is that it is really a fraud. In a world where business conditions are constantly changing and innovations often seem to be the only constant, no one can "have all the answers" for long. Leaders who are invariably crisp and decisive tend to settle issues so quickly that they have no opportunity to grasp the ramifications. Worse, because these leaders need to feel that they already have all the answers, they have no way to learn* new *answers. Their instinct, whenever something truly important is at stake, is to push for rapid closure, allowing no periods of uncertainty, even when uncertainty is appropriate.*[31]

Ironically, researchers have found a positive relationship between overconfidence and task difficulty. In other words, the more difficult the task, the greater the tendency for people to be overconfident.[32] Easier and more predictable situations foster confidence, but generally not unrealistic overconfidence. People may be overconfident about one or more of the following: accuracy of input data; individual, team, or organizational ability; and the probability of success. There are various theoretical explanations for overconfidence. For example, overconfidence may often be necessary to generate the courage needed to tackle difficult situations.[33]

As with the other decision traps, managerial awareness of this problem is the important first step toward avoiding it. Careful analysis of situational factors, critical thinking about decision alternatives, and honest input from stakeholders can help managers avoid overconfidence.[34]

8e I Think I'll Sleep on It

It's good to be cautious, but mulling over a decision usually boosts confidence without actually improving accuracy. Unless you expect to get fresh information, it rarely helps to "sleep on it," particularly given the human tendencies to focus on confirming information and to discount contrary facts.

Source: J. Wesley Hutchinson and Joseph W. Alba, "When Business Is a Confidence Game," Harvard Business Review, *79 (June 2001): 21.*

QUESTION:

People in the United States have a reputation for hasty decision making. How can they strike the right balance between speed and the overconfidence trap described here?

Making Decisions

It stands to reason that if the degree of uncertainty varies from situation to situation, there can be no single way to make decisions.[35] Managers do indeed make decisions in every conceivable way. One of the oddest examples is how the stacked potato

4. DISCUSS why programmed and nonprogrammed decisions require different decision-making procedures, and **DISTINGUISH** between the two types of knowledge in knowledge management.

chips we know as Pringles got their name. It seems that employees at Procter & Gamble pulled it out of a phone book.[36] Even doing nothing can qualify as decision making. Behavioral economists explain: "Postponement, delay, procrastination. They may seem like the path of least resistance, but they are in their own way as consequential as any other choice."[37] How often a particular decision is made is another important consideration. Some decisions are made frequently, perhaps several times a day. Others are made infrequently or just once. Consequently, decision theorists have distinguished between programmed and nonprogrammed decisions.[38] Each of these types of decisions requires a different procedure.

Making Programmed Decisions

programmed decisions: *repetitive and routine decisions*

Programmed decisions are those that are repetitive and routine. Examples include hiring decisions, billing decisions in a hospital, supply reorder decisions in a purchasing department, consumer loan decisions in a bank, and pricing decisions in a university bookstore. Managers tend to devise fixed procedures for handling these everyday decisions. Most decisions made by the typical manager on a daily basis are of the programmed variety.

decision rule: *tells when and how programmed decisions should be made*

At the heart of the programmed decision procedure are decision rules. A **decision rule** is a statement that identifies the situation in which a decision is required and specifies how the decision will be made. Behind decision rules is the idea that standard, recurring problems need to be solved only once. Decision rules permit busy managers to make routine decisions quickly without having to go through comprehensive problem solving over and over again. Generally, decision rules should be stated in "if-then" terms. A decision rule for a consumer loan officer in a bank, for example, might be: *If* the applicant is employed, has no record of loan default, and can put up 20 percent collateral, *then* a loan not to exceed $15,000 can be authorized." Carefully conceived decision rules can streamline the decision-making process by allowing lower-level managers to shoulder the responsibility for programmed decisions and freeing higher-level managers for relatively more important, nonprogrammed decisions.

Making Nonprogrammed Decisions

nonprogrammed decisions: *decisions made in complex and nonroutine situations*

Nonprogrammed decisions are those made in complex, important, and nonroutine situations, often under new and largely unfamiliar circumstances. This kind of decision is made much less frequently than programmed decisions. Examples of nonprogrammed decisions include deciding whether to merge with another company, how to replace an executive who died unexpectedly, whether a foreign branch should be opened, and how to market an entirely new kind of product or service. The following six questions need to be asked prior to making a nonprogrammed decision:

1. What decision needs to be made?
2. When does it have to be made?
3. Who will decide?
4. Who will need to be consulted prior to the making of the decision?
5. Who will ratify or veto the decision?
6. Who will need to be informed of the decision?[39]

The decision-making process becomes more sharply focused when managers take the time to answer these questions.

One respected decision theorist has described nonprogrammed decisions as follows: "There is no cut-and-dried method for handling the problem because it hasn't arisen before, or because its precise nature and structure are elusive or complex, or because it is so important that it deserves a custom-tailored treatment."[40]

Nonprogrammed decision making calls for creative problem solving. The four-step problem-solving process introduced later in this chapter helps managers make effective and efficient nonprogrammed decisions.

Location: ***Puno, Peru.*** **Situation:** ***Alpacas, prized for their luxurious wool, are being stolen and smuggled.*** **Nonprogrammed decision:** ***Identification microchips are implanted in the animals—a common practice among North American pet owners—to help keep track of them and foil criminals. Nice high-tech solution to a low-tech problem.***

8f Back to the Opening Case

Does Paul DePodesta lean more toward programmed or nonprogrammed decision making when selecting players for the Dodgers? Explain. What are the relative advantages and disadvantages of his decision-making style?

A General Decision-Making Model

Although different decision procedures are required for different situations, it is possible to construct a general decision-making model. Figure 8.4 shows an idealized, logical, and rational model of organizational decision making. Significantly, it describes how decisions can be made, but it does not portray how managers actually make decisions.[41] In fact, on-the-job research found that managers did not follow a rational and logical series of steps when making decisions.[42] Why, then, should we even consider a rational, logical model? Once again, as in the case of the strategic management process in Chapter 7, a rational descriptive model has instructional value because it identifies key components of a complex process.[43] It also suggests a better way of doing things.

The first step, a scan of the situation, is important, although it is often underemphasized or ignored altogether in discussions of managerial decision making. Scanning answers the question "How do I know a decision should be made?" More than 65 years ago, Chester I. Barnard gave one of the best answers to this question, stating that "the occasions for decision originate in three distinct fields: (a) from authoritative communications from superiors; (b) from cases referred for decision by subordinates; (c) from cases originating in the initiative of the [manager] concerned."[44] In addition to signaling when a decision is required, scanning reveals the degree of uncertainty and provides necessary information for pending decisions.[45]

When the need for a decision has been established, the manager must determine whether the situation is routine. If it is routine and there is an appropriate decision rule, the rule is applied. But if it turns out to be a new situation demanding a nonprogrammed decision, comprehensive problem solving begins. In either case, the results of the final decision need to be monitored to see whether any follow-up action is necessary.

Figure 8.4 A General Decision-Making Model

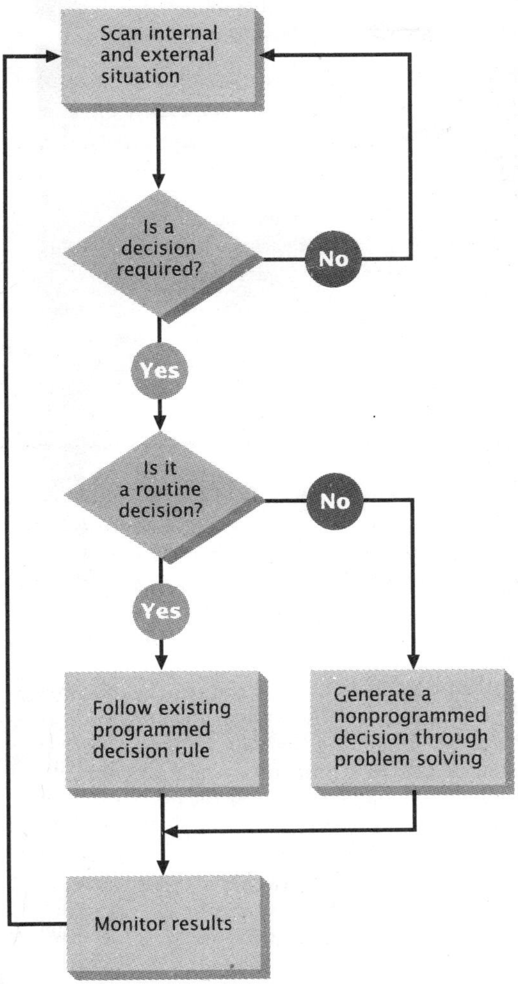

■ Knowledge Management: A Tool for Improving the Quality of Decisions

An army of academics, consultants, and managers have rallied around the concept of knowledge management during the last decade. Although some may dismiss it as a passing fad, knowledge management is a powerful and robust concept that deserves a permanent place in management theory and practice.[46] Authorities on the subject define **knowledge management** (KM) as "the development of tools, processes, systems, structures, and cultures explicitly to improve the creation, sharing, and use of knowledge critical for decision-making."[47] KM is at the heart of *learning organizations,* a topic we cover in the next chapter. Our purpose here is to explore the basics of KM, with an eye toward better organizational decisions. After all, decisions are only as good as the information on which they are based.

■ Two Types of Knowledge KM specialists draw a fundamental distinction between two types of knowledge: tacit knowledge and explicit knowledge (see Figure 8.5). **Tacit knowledge** is personal, intuitive, and undocumented information about how to skillfully perform tasks, solve problems, and make decisions. People who are masters of their craft have tacit knowledge (or "deep smarts") accumulated through years of experience.

> *Experts who encounter a wide variety of situations over many years accumulate a storehouse of knowledge and, with it, the ability to reason swiftly and without a lot of conscious effort. Those with keen managerial or technical intuition can rapidly determine whether current cases fit any patterns that have emerged in the past; they're also adept at coherently (though not always consciously) assembling disparate elements into a whole that makes sense. . . . In fact, when asked to explain a decision, experts often cannot re-create all the pathways their brains checked out and so cannot give a carefully reasoned answer. They chalk up to gut* feel *what is really a form of gut* knowledge.[48]

Experts with deep smarts simply "do" the task; they have a "feel" for the job; they know when they are "in the zone." For example, ask really good golfers how they swing their clubs.[49]

knowledge management: *developing a system to improve the creation and sharing of knowledge critical for decision making*

tacit knowledge: *personal, intuitive, and undocumented information*

explicit knowledge: *documented and sharable information*

Meanwhile, **explicit knowledge** is readily sharable information because it is in verbal, textual, visual, or numerical form. It can be found in presentations and lectures, books and magazines (both hard copy and online), policy manuals, technical specifications, training programs, databases, and software programs. In short, explicit knowledge is public (to varying degrees), whereas tacit knowledge is private.

■ Improving the Flow of Knowledge As indicated in Figure 8.5, knowledge resides in different places and needs to be shared. Each type of knowledge is important in its own way. Each needs to be carefully cultivated. The sharing of constructive tacit knowledge between coworkers is a top priority, as indicated in Figure 8.5. Organizational support is needed to help individuals feel comfortable about giving and receiving useful task-related knowledge on demand.[50]

Sophisticated new KM software is proving very useful and cost-effective in large organizations for sharing both tacit and explicit knowledge.[51] For example, consider

Figure 8.5 Key Dimensions of Knowledge Management

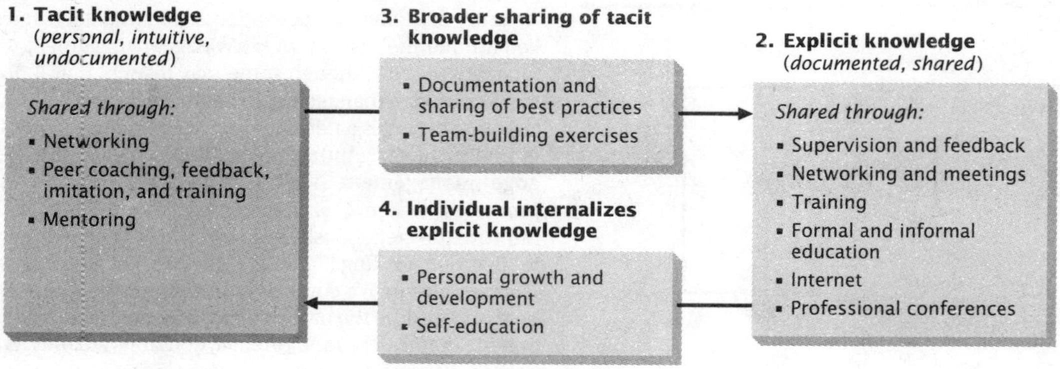

Source: *Adapted from discussion in Kiujiro Nonaka, "The Knowledge-Creating Company,"* Harvard Business Review on Knowledge Management, *(Boston: Harvard Business School Publishing, 1998), pp. 21–45; and Roy Lubit, "Tacit Knowledge and Knowledge Management: The Key to Sustainable Competitive Advantage,"* Organizational Dynamics, *29 (Winter 2001): 164–178.*

8g Let's Hear It for Ignorance

The concept is Ignorance Management, or IM. Like its knowledge management counterpart, IM is the process by which ignorance, in all of its various and sundry forms, is captured, tagged, stored, mapped, manipulated, and last but certainly not least, corrected.

Source: Tammy Galvin, "Ignorance Management," Training, *41 (June 2004): 4.*

QUESTIONS:

Is a formal organizational IM program a waste of time? Why or why not? What knowledge or skills should you possess that you presently do *not* have?

the recent experience of Werner Hinz, a lead engineer at defense contractor Northrop Grumman:

> *[He] had to prepare a design bid for a next-generation unmanned airplane for the Pentagon—one that travels at several times the speed of sound. To do this, Hinz needed some high-level expertise on hypersonics. But no one he knew, or knew of, had what he needed.*
>
> *So Hinz turned to [ActiveNet, a KM software application Northrup had purchased]. . . . The program combs through thousands of employee profiles and millions of internal documents—from e-mails to PowerPoint slides—and suggests synergistic matchups between workers, based on what the software's algorithms perceive as someone's interests and expertise. After Hinz typed in a few phrases and keywords, the program fired back a message listing two colleagues in his building—people Hinz had met, but whose backgrounds he didn't know—who might be good sources. Hinz called the first one; two minutes later he knew he'd found the right person.*[52]

KM software is sort of like an Internet dating service—but for informational rather than romantic purposes. According to KM advocates, it is important to know what you know, to know what you don't know, and to know how to find what you need to know. The result: better and more timely decisions.

You will encounter many topics in this book to improve the various knowledge flows in Figure 8.5.[53] Among them are organizational learning, organizational cultures, training, communication, empowerment, participative management, virtual teams, transformational leadership, and mentoring.

Group-Aided Decision Making: A Contingency Perspective

Decision making, like any other organizational activity, does not take place in a vacuum. Typically, decision making is a highly social activity with committees, study groups, review panels, or project teams contributing in a variety of ways.

Nina Niu-Ok, employed by health-care provider Kaiser Permanente, appreciates the power of group-aided decision making. During this session in Palo Alto, California, she successfully tapped the creative energy of a mix of coworkers ranging from doctors to administrators. The idea was to map out scenarios to guide future strategy and decision making at Kaiser Permanente. Typically a six-month ordeal, this intense cooperative effort got the job done in three days. Cooperation and participation—just what the doctor ordered for these turbulent times in health care.

■ Collaborative Computing

collaborative computing: *teaming up to make decisions via a computer network programmed with groupware*

Computer networks, the Internet, and the advent of **collaborative computing** guarantee even broader participation in the decision-making process.

> *Collaborative computing is a catchphrase for a new body of software and hardware that helps people work better together. A collaborative system creates an environment in which people can share information without the constraints of time and space.*
>
> *Network groupware applications link workgroups across a room or across the globe. The software gives the group a common, online venue for meetings, and it lets all members labor on the same data simultaneously.*
>
> *Collaborative applications include calendar management, video teleconferencing, computer teleconferencing, integrated team support, and support for business meetings and group authoring. Messaging and e-mail systems represent the most basic type of groupware.*[54]

Unfortunately, according to research, groupware is typically plagued by low-quality implementation. Sixty-five percent of the survey respondents used it simply as a communication tool, to send and receive e-mail, which is analogous to using a personal computer for word processing only. Groupware users need to be taught how to *collaborate* via computer (for instance, jointly identifying and solving problems). "When implemented correctly, the benefits are astounding. Groupware had twice the impact on individual job performance and nearly three times the impact on customer satisfaction at the organizations with the highest-quality implementation compared with the organization with the lowest."[55]

Group Involvement in Decisions

Whether the situation is a traditional face-to-face committee meeting or a global e-meeting, at least five aspects of the decision-making process can be assigned to groups:

1. Analyzing the problem
2. Identifying components of the decision situation
3. Estimating components of the decision situation (for example, determining probabilities, feasibilities, time estimates, and payoffs)
4. Designing alternatives
5. Choosing an alternative[56]

Assuming that two (or more) heads may be better than one and that managers can make better use of their time by delegating various decision-making chores, there is a strong case for turning to groups when making decisions. But before bringing others into the decision process, managers need to be aware of the problem of dispersed accountability and consider the tradeoff between the advantages and disadvantages of group-aided decision making. In view of these problems and of research evidence comparing individual and group performance, a contingency approach is recommended.

The Problem of Dispersed Accountability

There is a critical difference between group-aided decision making and group decision making. In the first instance, the group does everything except make the final decision. In the second instance, the group actually makes the final decision. Managers who choose the second route face a dilemma. Although a decision made by a group will probably reflect the collective experience and wisdom of all those involved, personal accountability is lost. Blame for a joint decision that fails is too easily passed on to others. For example, Robert Palmer, hired to turn Digital Equipment around, inherited the following situation: "This was a company run by committee, by consensus. No one actually made a decision. When things went well, there would be a number of people willing to take credit. But when things went wrong, it was impossible to fix responsibility on anyone."[57] This legacy of dispersed accountability proved too much for Palmer, and Digital was sold to Compaq Computer.

The traditional formula for resolving this problem is to make sure that a given manager is personally accountable for a decision when the responsibility for it has to be traced. According to this line of reasoning, even when a group is asked to recommend a decision, the responsibility for the final outcome remains with the manager in charge. For managers who want to maintain the integrity of personal accountability, there is no such thing as group decision making; there is only group-*aided* decision making. There are three situations in which individual accountability for a decision is necessary:

- The decision will have significant impact on the success or failure of the unit or organization.
- The decision has legal ramifications (such as possible prosecution for price-fixing, antitrust, or product safety violations).
- A competitive reward is tied to a successful decision. (For example, only one person can get a promotion.)

In less critical areas, the group itself may be responsible for making decisions.[58]

5. EXPLAIN the need for a contingency approach to group-aided decision making.

Advantages and Disadvantages of Group-Aided Decision Making

Various combinations of positive and negative factors are encountered when a manager brings others into the decision-making process. The advantages and disadvantages are listed in Table 8.2. If there is a conscious effort to avoid or at least minimize the disadvantages, managers can gain a great deal by sharing the decision-making process with peers, outside consultants, and team members.[59] However, some important contingency factors need to be taken into consideration.

8h Collective Wisdom

James Surowiecki, author of the book *The Wisdom of Crowds*:

> *... under the right circumstances, groups are remarkably intelligent, and are often smarter than the smartest people in them. ... The best collective decisions are the product of disagreement and contest, not consensus or compromise.*

Source: As quoted in Brad Wieners, "Why It Pays to Heed the Herd," Business 2.0, *5 (May 2004): 32.*

QUESTIONS:
Do you agree or disagree? Explain.

A Contingency Approach Is Necessary

Are two or more heads actually better than one? The answer depends on the nature of the task, the ability of the contributors, and the form of interaction (see Figure 8.6). An analysis of dozens of individual-versus-group performance studies conducted over a 61-year period led one researcher to the following conclusions: (1) groups tend to do quantitatively and qualitatively better than the *average* individual; and (2) *exceptional* individuals tend to outperform the group, particularly when the task is complex and the group is made up of relatively low-ability people.[60]

Consequently, busy managers need to delegate aspects of the decision-making process (specified earlier) according to the contingencies in Figure 8.6. More is said about delegation in Chapter 10.

Table 8.2 Advantages and Disadvantages of Group-Aided Decision Making and Problem Solving

Advantages	Disadvantages
1. **Greater pool of knowledge.** A group can bring much more information and experience to bear on a decision or problem than can an individual acting alone.	1. **Social pressure.** Unwillingness to "rock the boat" and pressure to conform may combine to stifle the creativity of individual contributors.
2. **Different perspectives.** Individuals with varied experience and interests help the group see decision situations and problems from different angles.	2. **Domination by a vocal few.** Sometimes the quality of group action is reduced when the group gives in to those who talk the loudest and longest.
3. **Greater comprehension.** Those who personally experience the give-and-take of group discussion about alternative courses of action tend to understand the rationale behind the final decision.	3. **Logrolling.** Political wheeling and dealing can displace sound thinking when an individual's pet project or vested interest is at stake.
4. **Increased acceptance.** Those who play an active role in group decision making and problem solving tend to view the outcome as "ours" rather than "theirs."	4. **Goal displacement.** Sometimes secondary considerations such as winning an argument, making a point, or getting back at a rival displace the primary task of making a sound decision or solving a problem.
5. **Training ground.** Less experienced participants in group action learn how to cope with group dynamics by actually being involved.	5. **"Groupthink."** Sometimes cohesive "in groups" let the desire for unanimity override sound judgment when generating and evaluating alternative courses of action. (Groupthink is discussed in Chapter 14.)

Figure 8.6 Individual versus Group Performance: Contingency Management Insights from 61 Years of Research

Nature of task	Insights from research
Problem-solving task	Individuals are faster, but groups tend to produce better results
Complex task	Best results achieved by polling the contributions of individuals working alone
Brainstorming task	Same as for complex task
Learning task	Groups consistently outperform individuals
Concept mastery/ creative task	Contributions from average-ability group members tend to improve when they are teamed with high-ability group members

Source: *Based in part on research conclusions found in Gayle W. Hill, "Group versus Individual Performance: Are N + 1 Heads Better than One?"* Psychological Bulletin, *91 (May 1982): 517–539.*

Managerial Creativity

Demands for creativity and innovation make the practice of management endlessly exciting (and often extremely difficult).[61] Nearly all managerial problem solving requires a healthy measure of creativity as managers mentally take things apart, rearrange the pieces in new and potentially productive configurations, and look beyond normal frameworks for new solutions. This process is like turning the kaleidoscope of one's mind. Thomas Edison used to retire to an old couch in his laboratory to do his creative thinking. Henry Ford reportedly sought creative insights by staring at a blank wall in his shop. Although the average manager's attempts at creativity may not be as dramatically fruitful as Edison's or Ford's, workplace creativity needs to be understood and nurtured.[62] As a steppingstone for the next section on creative problem solving, this section defines creativity, discusses the management of creative people, and identifies barriers to creativity.

What Is Creativity?

creativity: *the reorganization of experience into new configurations*

Creativity is a rather mysterious process known chiefly by its results and is therefore difficult to define. About as close as we can come is to say that **creativity** is the reorganization of experience into new configurations.[63] According to a management consultant specializing in creativity, "Creativity is a function of *knowledge, imagination,* and *evaluation.* The greater our knowledge, the more ideas, patterns, or combinations we can achieve. But merely having the knowledge does not guarantee the formation of new patterns; the bits and pieces must be shaken up and interrelated in new ways. Then, the embryonic ideas must be evaluated and developed into usable ideas."[64] Donna Kacmar, an architect in Houston, Texas, exemplifies our definition of creativity:

My creativity lies in trying to explore new possibilities for what might be considered a dumb or mundane problem. We all think we know how to make an office building or a townhouse or some run-of-the-mill thing like that. Well, do we? Let's question the assumptions that we have and see if there are some new things we can try. . . .

What I'm able to do is help people see things a different way. I think I'm able to see things a little bit more openly—to find relationships between things that aren't as readily apparent and then make something of those relationships. My version of creativity is more like a quest for understanding.[65]

Creativity is often subtle and may not be readily apparent to the untrained eye. But the combination and extension of seemingly insignificant day-to-day breakthroughs lead to organizational progress.

Identifying general types of creativity is easier than explaining the basic process. One pioneering writer on the subject isolated three overlapping domains of creativity: art, discovery, and humor.[66] These have been called the "ah!" reaction, the "aha!" reaction, and the "haha!" reaction, respectively.[67]

The discovery ("aha!") variation is the most relevant to management. Entirely new businesses can spring from creative discovery. A prime example is Donald L. Beaver Jr.'s low-tech discovery that grew into a thriving multimillion-dollar business.[68] He found that nylon stockings stuffed with ground-up corncobs could soak up oil and grease spills faster than any known technique and at much less cost. Machine shops and gas stations, where slippery oil spills are a costly occupational hazard, clamored for Beaver's new product. Beaver's creativity did not stop there. It extended to the company's name: New PIG Corp. According to Beaver, PIG stands for "Partners in Grime." Creative ideas can spring from unexpected places and unlikely people.

Workplace Creativity: Myth and Modern Reality

Recent research has shattered a long-standing myth about creative employees. According to the myth, creative people are typically nonconformists. But Alan Robinson's field research paints a very different picture:

"HE TRIED THINKING ON HIS FEET AND OUTSIDE OF THE BOX AT THE SAME TIME."

Source: *Scott Arthur Masear/*Harvard Business Review.

"We went to 450 companies in 13 countries and spoke to 600 people who'd done highly creative things, from big new innovations to tiny improvements," he explains. Only three out of the 600 were true nonconformists. The rest were more like your average corporate Joe, much more "plodding and cautious" than most managers would expect. Other creativity studies have had similar results, he says.

One reason for the mismatch between popular perception and reality, he believes, is that so many steps are needed to bring most new ideas to fruition. Those who succeed must be able to build support for the idea among other team members, and they sometimes need a lot of patience as well. Corporate nonconformists may not have a great deal of either.[69]

Thus, creative self-expression through unconventional dress and strange behavior does not necessarily translate into creative work.

Today's managers are challenged to create an organizational culture and climate capable of evoking the often hidden creative talents of *every* employee.[70] Consider, for instance, the birth of Frappuccino at Starbucks, as related by founder and CEO Howard Schultz:

Frappuccino was created by a store manager in West L.A. This person was fooling around one day in our store, blending beverages with a blender she bought on her own. We started sampling that, and the people in our Southern California region were very intrigued. We tested it, named it, and Frappuccino today is a multi-hundred-million-dollar business in our stores. A ready-to-drink joint venture with Pepsi-Cola is a $500 million business unto itself. The employee who came up with it? She is now god. *She still works with Starbucks.*[71]

■ Learning to Be More Creative

6. IDENTIFY and briefly **DESCRIBE** five of the ten "mental locks" that can inhibit creativity.

Some people naturally seem to be more creative than others. But that does not mean that those who feel the need cannot develop their creative capacity. It does seem clear that creative ability can be learned, in the sense that our creative energies can be released from the bonds of convention, lack of self-confidence, and narrow thinking. We all have the potential to be more creative.

The best place to begin is by trying consciously to overcome what creativity specialist Roger von Oech calls *mental locks*. The following mental locks are attitudes that get us through our daily activities but tend to stifle our creativity*:

1. ***Looking for the "right" answer.*** A given problem may have several right answers, depending on one's perspective.
2. ***Always trying to be logical.*** Logic does not always prevail, given human emotions and organizational inconsistencies, ambiguity, and contradictions.
3. ***Strictly following the rules.*** If things are to be improved, arbitrary limits on thinking and behavior need to be questioned.
4. ***Insisting on being practical.*** Impractical answers to "what-if" questions can become steppingstones to creative insights.
5. ***Avoiding ambiguity.*** Creativity can be stunted by too much objectivity and specificity.
6. ***Fearing and avoiding failure.*** Fear of failure can paralyze us into not acting on our good ideas. This is unfortunate because we learn many valuable and lasting lessons from our mistakes.[72]
7. ***Forgetting how to play.*** The playful experimentation of childhood too often disappears by adulthood.
8. ***Becoming too specialized.*** Cross-fertilization of specialized areas helps in defining problems and generating solutions.

8i A Bad Idea Turned Inside Out

Linda Kaplan Thaler, CEO of the ad agency responsible for the popular AFLAC duck:

Believe it or not, the best ideas usually come from the really bad ones turned inside out. So we encourage people to be fearless in offering up ideas, no matter how weird, wild, or wacky. The important thing is to reward people for having a voice, because it's that constant input of vocal energy that helps big bangs to explode.

Source: As quoted in Charles Decker, "Find Your 'Inner Bang,'" Fast Company, *no. 79 (February 2004): 39.*

QUESTIONS:

What is your personal experience with bad ideas turned inside out? How can a manager keep a "wild and wacky" group of employees on a productive track?

9. ***Not wanting to look foolish.*** Humor can release tensions and unlock creative energies. Seemingly foolish questions can enhance understanding.
10. ***Saying "I'm not creative."*** By nurturing small and apparently insignificant ideas, we can convince ourselves that we are indeed creative.[73]

* Source: *List adapted from* A Whack on the Side of the Head *by Roger von Oech, Warner Books, 1983. Reprinted by permission.*

(Try the creativity exercise in the Hands-On Exercise at the end of this chapter.) If these mental locks are conquered, the creative problem-solving process discussed in the next section can be used to its full potential.

Creative Problem Solving

7. LIST and EXPLAIN the four basic steps in the creative problem-solving process.

We are all problem solvers. But this does not mean that all of us are good problem solvers or even, for that matter, that we know how to solve problems systematically. Most daily problem solving is done on a haphazard, intuitive basis. A difficulty arises, we look around for an answer, jump at the first workable solution to come along, and move on to other things. In a primitive sense, this sequence of events qualifies as a problem-solving process, and it works quite well for informal daily activities. But in the world of management, a more systematic problem-solving process is required for tackling difficult and unfamiliar nonprogrammed decisions. In the context of management, **problem solving** is the conscious process of bringing the actual situation closer to the desired situation.[74] Managerial problem solving consists of a four-step sequence: (1) identifying the problem, (2) generating alternative solutions, (3) selecting a solution, and (4) implementing and evaluating the solution (see Figure 8.7).

problem solving: *conscious process of closing the gap between actual and desired situations*

Identifying the Problem

As strange as it may seem, the most common problem-solving difficulty lies in the identification of problems. Busy managers have a tendency to rush into generating and selecting alternative solutions before they have actually isolated and understood the real problem. According to Peter Drucker, the respected management scholar, "The greatest source of mistakes in top management is to ask the same questions most people ask. They all assume that there are the same 'right answers' for everyone. But one does not begin with answers. One begins by asking, 'What are our questions?'"[75] When problem finding, managers should probe for the right questions.[76] Only then can the right answers be found.

Problem finding can be a great career booster, too, as Michael Iem discovered. It all started with his love of tough challenges.

> *This bricklayer's son has no formal job title and no office, but his career at Tandem Computers [now part of Hewlett-Packard] is on a tear. He personifies the advice that executive recruiter Robert Horton offers all who want to advance: "Find the biggest business problem your employer faces for which you and your skills are the solution."... [Iem's problem-solving ability] made him known throughout Tandem, bringing promotions and a doubling of his $32,000 starting salary.... The company lets him decide what projects to take on, making him the youngest of perhaps a dozen employees with the broad mandate.*[77]

What Is a Problem? Ask half a dozen people how they identify problems, and you are likely to get as many answers. Consistent with the definition given earlier for problem solving, a **problem** is defined as the difference between an actual state of affairs and a desired state of affairs. In other words, a problem is the gap between where one is and where one wants to be. Problem solving is meant to close this gap. For example, a person in New York who has to make a presentation in San Francisco

problem: *the difference between an actual and a desired state of affairs*

Figure 8.7 The Problem-Solving Process

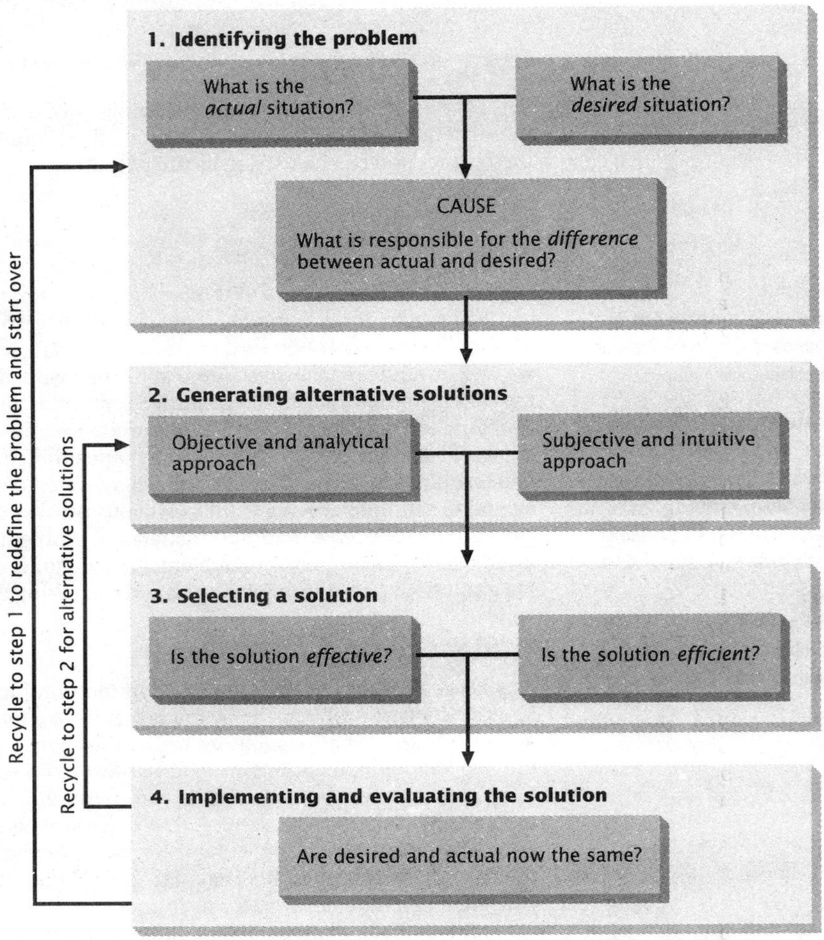

in 24 hours has a problem. The problem is not being in New York (the actual state of affairs), nor is it presenting in San Francisco in 24 hours (the desired state of affairs). Instead, the problem is the distance between New York and San Francisco. Flying would be an obvious solution. But thanks to modern communications technology such as videoconferencing, there are ways to overcome the 2,934-mile gap without having to travel.

Managers need to define problems according to the gaps between the actual and the desired situations. A production manager, for example, would be wise to concentrate on the gap between the present level of weekly production and the desired level. This focus is much more fruitful than complaining about the current low production or wishfully thinking about high production. The challenge is discovering a workable alternative for closing the gap between actual and desired production.[78]

■ **Stumbling Blocks for Problem Finders.** There are three common stumbling blocks for those attempting to identify problems:

1. ***Defining the problem according to a possible solution.*** One should be careful not to rule out alternative solutions in the way one states a problem. For example, a manager in a unit plagued by high absenteeism who says, "We have a problem with low pay," may prevent management from discovering that tedious and boring work is the real cause. By focusing on how to close the gap between actual and desired attendance, instead of simply on low pay, management stands a better chance of finding a workable solution.
2. ***Focusing on narrow, low-priority areas.*** Successful managers are those who can weed out relatively minor problems and reserve their attention for problems that really make a difference. Formal organizational goals and objectives provide a useful framework for determining the priority of various problems. Don't be concerned with cleaning the floor when the roof is caving in.
3. ***Diagnosing problems in terms of their symptoms.*** As a short-run expedient, treating symptoms rather than underlying causes may be appropriate. Buying a bottle of aspirin is cheaper than trying to find a less stressful job, for example. In the longer run, however, symptoms tend to reappear and problems tend to get worse. There is a two-way test for discovering whether one has found the cause of a problem: "If I *introduce* this variable, will the problem (the gap) disappear?" or "If I *remove* this variable, will the problem (the gap) disappear?" **Causes** are variables that, because of their presence in or absence from the situation, are primarily responsible for the difference between the actual and the desired conditions. For example, the *absence* of a key can cause a problem with a locked door, and the *presence* of a nail can cause a problem with an inflated tire.[79]

causes: *variables responsible for the difference between actual and desired conditions*

8. DESCRIBE how causes of problems can be tracked down with fishbone diagrams.

■ **Pinpointing Causes with Fishbone Diagrams.** Fishbone diagrams, discussed in Chapter 17 as a TQM process improvement tool, are a handy way to track down causes of problems. They work especially well in group problem-solving situations. Construction of a fishbone diagram begins with a statement of the problem (the head of the fish skeleton). "On the bones growing out of the spine one lists possible causes of . . . problems, in order of possible occurrence. The chart can help one see how various separate problem causes might interact. It also shows how possible causes occur with respect to one another, over time, helping start the problem-solving process."[80] (A sample fishbone diagram appears in Skills & Tools at the end of this chapter.)

■ Generating Alternative Solutions

After the problem and its most probable cause have been identified, attention turns to generating alternative solutions. This is the creative step in problem solving. Unfortunately, as the following statement points out, creativity is often shortchanged.

> *The natural response to a problem seems to be to try to get rid of it by finding an answer—often taking the first answer that occurs and pursuing it because of one's reluctance to spend the time and mental effort needed to conjure up a rich storehouse of alternatives from which to choose.*[81]

It takes time, patience, and practice to become a good generator of alternative solutions: a flexible combination of analysis and intuition is helpful. A good sense of humor can aid the process as well. Several popular and useful techniques can stimulate individual and group creativity. Among them are the following approaches:

- ***Brainstorming.*** This is a group technique in which any and all ideas are recorded, in a *nonjudgmental* setting, for later critique and selection.[82] Computerized brainstorming on computer network systems is proving worthwhile now that sophisticated groupware is available.[83]
- ***Free association.*** Analogies and symbols are used to foster unconventional thinking. For example, think of your studies as a mountain requiring special climbing gear and skills.

- ***Edisonian method.*** Named for Thomas Edison's tedious and persistent search for a durable light bulb filament, this technique involves trial-and-error experimentation.

  > *On a Sunday evening in 1897, Thomas Edison and his assistants powered up an electric bulb and took turns watching it. Over the past 18 months their quest for a workable filament had generated nothing but 1,200 failures and $40,000 in expenses. But this time the carbonized sewing thread inside was still glowing more than 13 hours later.*[84]

  The rest, as they say, is history.
- ***Attribute listing.*** Ideal characteristics of a given object are collected and then screened for useful insights.
- ***Scientific method.*** Systematic hypothesis testing, manipulation of variables, situational controls, and careful measurement are the essence of this rigorous approach.
- ***Creative leap.*** This technique involves thinking up idealistic solutions to a problem and then working back to a feasible solution.

Selecting a Solution

Simply stating that the best solution should be selected in step 3 (refer to Figure 8.7) can be misleading. Because of time and financial constraints and political considerations, *best* is a relative term. Generally, alternative solutions should be screened for the most appealing balance of effectiveness and efficiency in view of relevant constraints and intangibles. Russell Ackoff, a specialist in managerial problem solving, contends that three things can be done about problems: they can be resolved, solved, or dissolved.[85]

satisfice: *to settle for a solution that is good enough*

Resolving the Problem.

When a problem is resolved, a course of action that is good enough to meet the minimum constraints is selected. The term **satisfice** has been applied to the practice of settling for solutions that are good enough rather than the best possible.[86] A badly worn spare tire may satisfice as a replacement for a flat tire for the balance of the trip, although getting the flat repaired is the best possible solution. According to Ackoff, most managers rely on problem resolving. This non-quantitative, subjective approach is popular because managers claim they do not have the information or time necessary for the other approaches. Satisficing, however, has been criticized as a shortsighted and passive technique emphasizing expedient survival instead of improvement and growth.

optimize: *to systematically identify the solution with the best combination of benefits*

Solving the Problem.

A problem is solved when the best possible solution is selected. Managers are said to **optimize** when, through scientific observation and quantitative measurement, they systematically research alternative solutions and select the one with the best combination of benefits.

idealize: *to change the nature of the situation in which a problem has arisen*

Dissolving the Problem.

A problem is dissolved when the situation in which it occurs is changed so that the problem no longer exists. Problem dissolvers are said to **idealize** because they actually change the nature of the system in which a problem resides. Managers who dissolve problems rely on whatever combination of non-quantitative and quantitative tools is needed to get the job done. The replacement of automobile assembly-line welders with robots, for instance, has dissolved the problem of costly absenteeism among people in that job category.

Whatever approach a manager chooses, the following advice from Ackoff should be kept in mind: "Few if any problems. . . are ever permanently resolved, solved, or dissolved; every treatment of a problem generates new problems."[87] A Japanese manager at the General Motors-Toyota joint venture auto plant in California put it this way: "No problem is a problem."[88] And, as pointed out by the cofounder of a successful import business, an administrative life made up of endless problems is cause for optimism, not pessimism: "Spare yourself some grief. Understand that, in business, you will always have problems. They are where the opportunities lie."[89] Hence the need for continuous improvement.

8j Quick Quiz

After 40 years of making people stand in lines (lots of lines) at its parks, Disney woke up and instituted Fastpass, which allows visitors to reserve a spot in line and eliminate the wait. An astonishing 95% of its visitors like the change. [Says Dale Stafford, a Disney VP,] "We have been teaching people how to stand in line since 1955, and now we are telling them they don't have to."

Source: Seth Godin, "If It's Broke, Fix It," Fast Company, *no. 75 (October 2003): 131.*

QUESTIONS:

Did Disney resolve, solve, or dissolve a problem at its theme parks? Explain your choice.

Implementing and Evaluating the Solution

Time is the true test of any solution. Until a particular solution has had time to prove its worth, the manager can rely only on his or her judgment concerning its effectiveness and efficiency. Ideally, the solution selected will completely eliminate the difference between the actual and the desired in an efficient and timely manner. Should the gap fail to disappear, two options are open. If the manager remains convinced that the problem has been correctly identified, he or she can recycle to step 2 to try another solution that was identified earlier. This recycling can continue until all feasible solutions have been given a fair chance or until the nature of the problem changes to the extent that the existing solutions are obsolete. If the gap between actual and desired persists in spite of repeated attempts to find a solution, then it is advisable to recycle to step 1 to redefine the problem and engage in a new round of problem solving.

SUMMARY

1. Decision making is a fundamental part of management because it requires choosing among alternative courses of action. In addition to having to cope with an era of accelerating change, today's decision makers face the challenges of dealing with complexity, uncertainty, the need for flexible thinking, and decision traps. Eight factors that contribute to decision complexity are multiple criteria, intangibles, risk and uncertainty, long-term implications, interdisciplinary input, pooled decision making, value judgments, and unintended consequences.
2. Managers must learn to assess the degree of certainty in a situation—whether conditions are certain, risky, or uncertain. Confidence in one's decisions decreases as uncertainty increases. Managers can respond to a condition of risk—incomplete but reliable factual information—by calculating objective or subjective probabilities. Today's managers need to tap the creative potential of intuitive employees and the implementation skills of those who process information as thinkers.
3. Researchers have identified three perceptual and behavioral decision traps that can undermine the quality of decisions. Framing error occurs when people let labels and frames of reference sway their interpretations. People fall victim to escalation of commitment when they get locked into losing propositions for fear of quitting and looking bad. Oddly, researchers find that overconfidence tends to grow with the difficulty of the task.
4. Decisions, generally, are either programmed or nonprogrammed. Because programmed decisions are relatively clear-cut and routinely encountered, fixed decision rules can be formulated for them. In contrast, nonprogrammed decisions require creative problem solving because they are novel and unfamiliar. Decision making can be improved with a knowledge management (KM) program. KM is a systematic approach to creating and sharing critical information throughout the organization. Two types of knowledge are *tacit* (personal, intuitive, and undocumented) and *explicit* (documented and sharable) knowledge.
5. Managers may choose to bring other people into virtually every aspect of the decision-making process. However, when a group rather than an individual is responsible for making the decision, personal accountability is lost. Dispersed accountability is undesirable in some key decision situations. Group-aided decision making has both advantages and disadvantages. Because group performance does not always exceed individual performance, a contingency approach to group-aided decision making is advisable.
6. Creativity requires the proper combination of knowledge, imagination, and evaluation to reorganize experience into new configurations. The domains of

creativity may be divided into art, discovery (the most relevant to management), and humor. Contrary to myth, researchers have found only a weak link between creativity and nonconformity. A fun and energizing workplace climate can tap *every* employee's creativity. By consciously overcoming ten mental locks, we can become more creative.

7. The creative problem-solving process consists of four steps: (1) identifying the problem, (2) generating alternative solutions, (3) selecting a solution, and (4) implementing and evaluating the solution. Inadequate problem finding is common among busy managers. By seeing problems as gaps between an actual situation and a desired situation, managers are in a better position to create more effective and efficient solutions. Depending on the situation, problems can be resolved, solved, or dissolved. It is important to remember that today's solutions often become tomorrow's problems.

8. A clear and concise statement of the problem forms the "head" of the fishbone skeleton. Each of the "bones" extending out from the backbone of the fishbone diagram represents a possible cause of the problem. More likely causes are located closer to the head of the diagram. Possible explanations for each cause are attached to each particular "bone."

TERMS TO UNDERSTAND

- Decision making, p. 215
- Law of unintended consequences, p. 218
- Condition of certainty, p. 220
- Condition of risk, p. 220
- Objective probabilities, p. 220
- Subjective probabilities, p. 220
- Condition of uncertainty, p. 220
- Framing error, p. 222
- Escalation of commitment, p. 223
- Programmed decisions, p. 225
- Decision rule, p. 225
- Nonprogrammed decisions, p. 225
- Knowledge management, p. 227
- Tacit knowledge, p. 227
- Explicit knowledge, p. 227
- Collaborative computing, p. 229
- Creativity, p. 232
- Problem solving, p. 235
- Problem, p. 235
- Causes, p. 237
- Satisfice, p. 238
- Optimize, p. 238
- Idealize, p. 238

SKILLS & TOOLS

How to Construct a Fishbone Diagram

Tips

- Reduce a complex web of problems to a distinct, high-priority problem.
- Create fishbones for the main categories of causes.
- Chart the most recent causes nearest the head (problem).
- Fill in specific causes.

POSSIBLE CAUSES

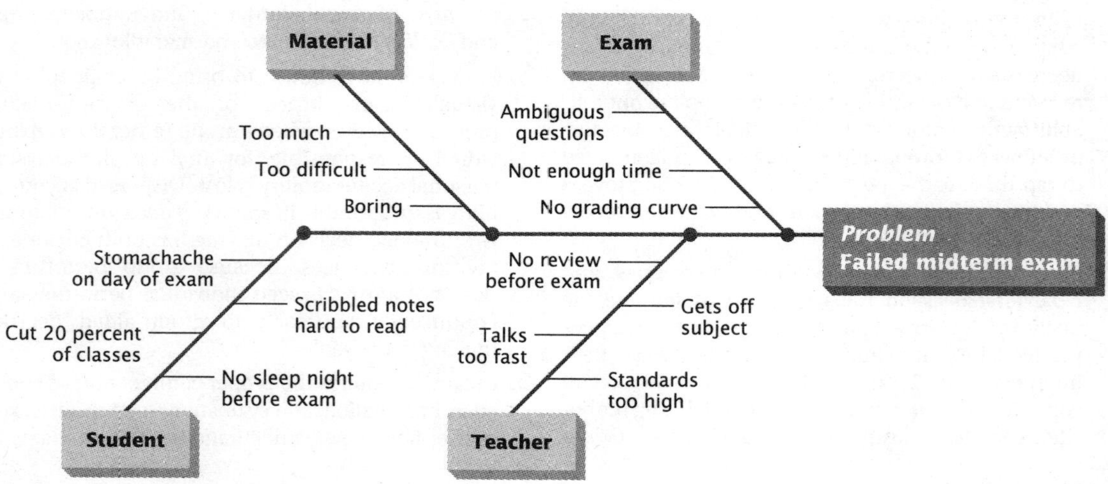

HANDS-ON EXERCISE

How Creative Are You?

Instructions

This exercise is for both individuals and teams. Assume that a steel pipe is embedded in the concrete floor of a bare room as shown below. The inside diameter is .06″ larger than the diameter of a ping-pong ball (1.50″) which is resting gently at the bottom of the pipe. You are one of a group of six people in the room, along with the following objects:

- 100′ of clothesline
- Carpenter's hammer
- Chisel
- Box of Wheaties
- File
- Wire coat hanger
- Monkey wrench
- Light bulb

List as many ways you can think of (in five minutes) to get the ball out of the pipe without damaging the ball, tube, or floor.

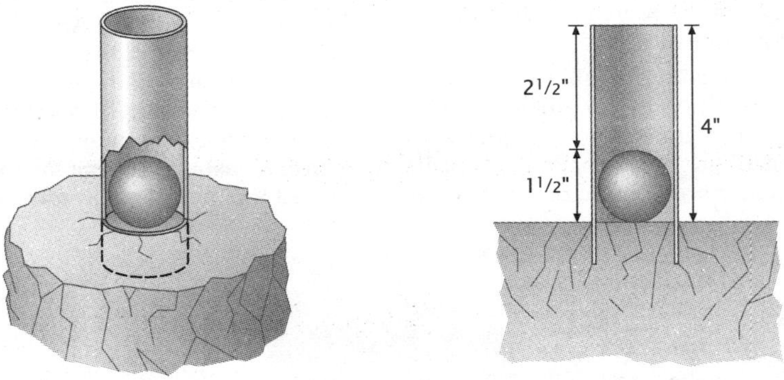

Source: *From* Conceptual Blockbusting *by James L. Adams. © 1986 by James L. Adams. Reprinted by permission of Perseus Books PLC, a member of Perseus Books, L.L.C.*

For Consideration/Discussion

1. In terms of the definition in this chapter, what is the "problem" here?
2. What assumptions did you make about any of the objects?
3. How would you rate your creativity on this exercise on a scale of 1 = low to 10 = high?
4. How many of the eight resource objects did you manage to employ? Which was the most useful? Why?
5. How many solutions did you develop? Which one is the "best"? Why?

INTERNET EXERCISES

1. **More about decision making, creativity, and problem solving:** Want to learn more about how managers make decisions, strive to be creative, and solve tough problems? Go to *Fast Company* magazine's Online Archives at **www.fastcompany.com/backissues** and type the key word *decision* into the Search box. Browse the list of articles for one or two worth reading. (Be sure to print a hard copy if you will need to refer to your selection(s) later, perhaps for class discussion.) Follow the same procedure for the key word *creativity*. *Note*: "The Creativity Issue" (no. 89, December 2004) is an excellent resource for anyone interested in better understanding and managing creativity. For instructive and interesting reading on the topic of problem solving, type the key word *problem* into the Search box and select a *Fast Company* article or two to read.

   - *Learning Points:* 1. What useful information about decision making, creativity, and/or problem solving did you pick up? Did it reinforce or contradict what you learned in this chapter? Explain. 2. What major barriers or obstacles for effective managerial decision making, creativity, and/or problem solving cropped up in your reading? What can be done to overcome them? 3. Why is creativity of central importance in both managerial decision making and problem solving? 4. When it comes to on-the-job creativity, how important is plain old persistence? Explain.

2. **Check it out:** Sometimes our creativity needs a boost and our inspiration needs a jump start. A good departure point is **www.queendom.com**, a richly stocked Web site created by and for women but equally valuable to men. Get your creativity cranked up by selecting the section "Brain Tools" from the main menu. Among the fun and challenging mind-stretching exercises are lots of trivia quizzes, jigsaw puzzles, and puzzles. *Note:* This Internet resource also has a great selection of automatically scored self-assessment and personality tests under the main menu heading "Tests and Profiles."

For updates to these exercises, visit our Web site (**http://business.college.hmco.com/students/** and select Kreitner, *Management*, 10e).

CLOSING CASE

Hindustan Motors' Struggle for Survival

Troubled Waters?

In October 1998, Hindustan Motors (HM), makers of one of India's best known cars, the Ambassador launched a new car, the Mitsubishi Lancer (Lancer). The launch of Lancer, a new car from the HM stable after nearly two decades, was reported to be very important for the company, whose market share was on the decline. HM was reportedly banking heavily on the Lancer's success to fight competition from other car companies.

Lancer was positioned in the mid-size luxury car segment, which was dominated by Maruti Udyog's (MUL) Maruti Esteem and Honda's Honda City. Lancer was received very well by automobile experts throughout the country, largely due to its technical finesse. The cars sales reached 2,866 units by the end of the fiscal 1998-99.

Much to HM's delight, Lancer was even ranked as the top vehicle in India for the three consecutive years (1999, 2000 and 2001) by J. D. Powers[1] for the least number of defects and high customer satisfaction in a countrywide survey of car owners. However, the company's euphoria was short-lived as Lancer's sales failed to pick up as expected.

While 7,621 cars were sold in 1999, HM managed to sell only 7,635 cars in 2000-01 against a forecast of 8,000[2]. On the other hand, sales of Honda City increased to 10,011 in 2001 from 9631 in 1999 (Refer Exhibit I for the sales comparison). Meanwhile, HM's other offerings Ambassador and Contessa were also faring badly.

In 1999, Ambassador's sales were down to 15,374 from 18,312 in 1998 and Contessa's to 285 from 575 in 1998. This poor performance took a heavy toll on the company's bottom-line and HM reported a net loss of

[1] *J. D. Power and Associates is a global marketing information services firm established in 1968. The firm provides clients with relevant and actionable market research, forecasting, consulting and training services.*

[2] *A portion of the lost sales was accounted for by supply related problems in April and May 2001.*

Rs 615.8 million for the fiscal 1999-00. (Refer Table I). The company had reportedly accumulated losses worth Rs 1.1 billion during 1999-2001.[3]

In late 2001, HM announced its plans to launch another car, the Mitsubishi Pajero. The company planned to import fully assembled cars and sell them by early 2002. Analysts remarked that the Pajero could do little to revive the company's fortunes as despite many efforts to turn itself around, HM had failed to regain its 4-decade long leadership in the Indian passenger car market. Its 3.3% market share in the half-year ending September 2001, proved beyond doubt that the company was struggling to stay afloat.

Background Note

HM was incorporated in 1942 by the GP-CK Birla Group of companies in collaboration with General Motors (GM),[4] USA. The CK Birla group was one of the well known family-owned business houses in India, with 17 companies in businesses such as automobiles, engineering, paper, and auto-components.

Some of them were Hyderabad Industries Ltd., Oriented Papers & Industries Ltd., National Engineering Industries Ltd., Gujarat Instruments Ltd., Hindustan Power Plus Ltd., India Gypsum Ltd., Malabar Building Products Ltd., Birla Horizons International Ltd., and Birla Techneftegas Ltd.

Table I Hindustan Motors—Financial Performance (In Rs million)

	Mar-98	Mar-99	Mar-00	1-Mar
Total income	10,124.90	12,297.30	15,085.50	14.977.4
Cost of material	5,864.40	8,126.20	10,707.30	10,272.90
Employee cost	1,393.30	1,463.40	1,545.60	1,558.60
Power & Fuel	236.1	224.2	279.2	2.669
Advertising/promotion/public	12.1	21.8	11.6	5.8
Other expenses	1,305.20	1,588.40	1,652.00	1,608.10
Cost of sales	8,809.10	11,423.96	14,195.80	13,712.40
PBIDT	1,315.80	873.3	889.7	1,265.00
Interest &finance changes	583.2	834.6	1,082.10	1,001.30
PBDT	732.6	38.8	-192.4	263.7
Depreciation	249.6	320.5	429.4	452.5
PBT	483.1	-281.7	-621.8	-188.8
Provision for taxation	89.5	0.8	1	0.9
Extraordinary items/Prior year adj.	85.9	407	7	210.5
Adjusted PAT	479.5	-277.8	-615.8	20.8

Source: www.indiainfoline.com

HM's manufacturing facilities were located at Uttarpara in West Bengal, Pithampur in Madhya Pradesh, Thiruvallur and Hosur in Tamil Nadu, and Pondicherry. Over the years, HM built up a vast dealer network comprising 115 dealers, 50 service and parts dealers and 60 additional exclusive parts dealers.

Initially, the company concentrated on its auto components business, producing its first car only in 1949. In 1954, HM started production of the Landmaster in technical collaboration with UK-based Morris Motors Ltd. (Morris). The company upgraded the Oxford model of Morris and launched it as the Ambassador in 1957 – the car went on to become the flagship brand of the company in the years to come. In 1963, HM commenced the production of Ambassador Mark 2, made available in two variants – diesel and Ambassador ISZ. HM entered the earth moving equipment business in 1971 and the power products business in 1983 .

Until the 1980s, HM's Ambassador and Premier Automobiles Ltd's[5] (PAL) Padmini were the only two cars available in the Indian market. Ambassador was the vehicle of choice of Government of India, and the official car for almost every Indian Prime Minister after independence. Though there was no executive order that said that the government departments have to buy only Ambassador cars HM derived a major part of its sales from senior politicians, top civil servants, bank managers and defence personnel. Ambassador was very popular in the taxi segment as well. Even in 2001, the segment accounted for almost 65% of Ambassador's

[3] *In September 2002, Rs 48 equaled 1 US $.*

[4] *GM was the world's largest car manufacturer with a host of successful popular brands and facilities in over 100 countries across the world.*

[5] *PAL was established in 1944 by the Walchand Hirachand family in technical collaboration with the Italian automobile major Fiat.*

sales. This was because of the perception that the Ambassador was better suited for the rough Indian roads and its strong structure was believed to be able to withstand the impact of accidents much better than any other car.

However in 1981, with the entry of MUL, the scenario changed drastically. MUL's small, fuel-efficient and well-designed car, Maruti 800, became a huge success. By the late 1980s, MUL became the market leader, leaving Hindustan Motors way behind in the war for market share.

During the 1980s, HM was in the news only because of its tie-ups with GM and its subsidiary Vauxhall Motors (VM). In 1984, HM launched the Contessa, which was labeled one of the first 'upmarket' cars in India, in technical collaboration with VM. In 1987, the company launched the Contessa Classic that was considered as the most powerful car available then. The Contessa was a reasonably successful car, though it never managed to match Ambassador's success.

In 1995, HM entered into collaboration with the Japanese automobile major Mitsubishi Motor Corporation (Mitsubishi), wherein Mitsubishi agreed to provide technical assistance to HM to manufacture its products in India. HM produced a mid-size luxury car, Opel Astra in collaboration with GM in 1996. In 1997, the Contessa GXL version with power steering was launched. HM terminated the GM joint venture in 1999, by selling off its stake to GM.

The Turnaround Efforts - Phase I

In the early 1990s, when the Indian economy was opened up for foreign players, many multinational automobile companies entered the country. In the 1990s, companies including Daewoo, General Motors, Daimler Benz, Hyundai and Honda entered India through joint ventures and partnerships with Indian firms.

HM was one of the worst affected companies due to this inflow of competitors. Forced to react due to the poor performance of its vehicles, HM launched the Ambassador Nova in 1990 (with better interiors) and an improved Ambassador 1800 ISZ (with better engine performance) in 1993. The company also appointed consultants McKinsey & Co for a restructuring plan to turn around its business.

McKinsey asked HM to focus on the marketing of components, refurnish the Ambassador model and upgrade other vehicles, speed up the delivery process and improve productivity through reengineering on the floor shop and reduce the workforce in its production plant at Uttarpara. The company began to implement the recommendations.

HM decided to tap new segments to ease the competitive pressures it was facing in the passenger car market. In 1995, the company collaborated with Oka Motor Co[6] to develop a vehicle specifically targeted at rural markets. This led to the launch of the Trekker (also referred to as the Rural Transport Vehicle RTV) in 1995. Launched in three northern states, the Trekker was received well in the rural markets. However, the vehicle soon came under criticism owing to a host of technical problems.

By late 1998, Trekkers sales dropped by two-thirds of its initial volumes to around 800 a year. In 1999, HM launched the redesigned Trekker and an upgraded version of the Ambassador. Despite all the product upgradations and restructuring efforts, HM could not stem the decline in sales. (Refer Table II).

Analysts opined that HM's dismal condition was a result of its lax management policies and shortsightedness. Before MUL entered the market, HM was the market leader. It was able to sell whatever it produced and therefore it did not care to upgrade the technology or production facilities. However, pressure from competition was just one aspect of HM's problems. The company had a host of internal problems particularly human resource troubles at the Uttarpara plant.

Table II Hindustan Motors Passenger Car Sales

Year	1994	1995	1996	1997	1998
Sales	25,150	27,517	25,942	24,711	20,109

Source: *www.indiainfoline.com*

The Uttarpara plant had workforce of 14,000 employees and the wage bill alone constituted 22% of plant's expenditure. Against the standard output of 8-10 cars per employee per annum, the plants output was as low as 3 cars. Analysts claimed that with the 1999 production level of 2500 cars, the plant should have been staffed with no more than 3,000 personnel. Annual production at the plant declined from 30,822 cars in 1995-96 to 26,684 cars in 1996-97. In November 1997, 2835 Ambassadors and 146 Contessas were produced. The numbers came down to 1385 and 33 respectively by October 1998.

In its bid to turn around the plant, HM invested around Rs 750 million to modernize the assembly line, build new body and paint shops and purchase new equipment. The company also embarked on a cost-cutting exercise and announced a Voluntary Retirement Scheme (VRS) for workers in April 1998 and again in November 1998, offering a Rs. 0.1 million package.

[6] *A West Australian automotive company specializing in designing and building four-wheel drive vehicles.*

However, the VRS was not received well by the strong Center of Indian Trade Union (CITU) and the Indian National Trade Union Congress (INTUC)[7] led employee unions. Commenting on a similar VRS offered by the Fiat management at its Kurla, (Maharashtra) plant, employees said workers at the Fiat factory at Mumbai have got an average of Rs.0.35 million per worker while we are fobbed off with such measly sums. The strong political patronage to the employee unions made it tough for the management to convince workers about the VRS.

Both the CITU and INTUC union leaders refused to accept the VRS offered by the company. The unions were confident that the West Bengal State Government would back them on the issue. As employee protests intensified, HM approached the state government with a proposal to run the plant for only three days in a week, in an attempt to save Rs. 0.32 million every week. The company also promised that it would continue to pay the workforce full wages for an entire week.

However, the government rejected HM's proposal, following which the company decided to seek legal recourse. In January 1999, HM filed a writ petition in the Calcutta High Court, claiming that its decision was not prompted by industrial relations, but by the company's poor financial position. It also stated that the layoff in the Uttarpara plant was temporary in nature and the company would resume normal production as soon as demand picked up. The High Court then ordered the state government to reconsider the issue.

In May 1999, instead of reconsidering the issue, the state government filed an appeal before the division bench of the Calcutta High Court, claiming that HM had suppressed facts and figures during its meeting with them to settle the issue. The division bench directed that the matter should be referred to the Industrial Tribunal. In July 1999, the Industrial Tribunal dismissed the company's proposal. HM again filed a writ petition against the Tribunal's order in the division bench of Calcutta High Court and the division bench upheld the Tribunal's order. In response to the division bench's order, HM moved to the Supreme Court in July 1999.[8] During all this time, productivity at the plant suffered considerably, this added to company's woes.

The Turnaround Efforts - Phase II

When its attempts to reorganize its operations did not pay off, HM decided to look beyond its existing product portfolio to come out of its problems. As per McKinsey's recommendations, the company explored the global auto components business in 2000 and established a unit at Indore to assemble engines and gearboxes.

Analysts said that this was a wise move because HM with its expertise, could easily become a component supplier for both domestic and global car majors. HM's executive director Sarkar Narayanan said, "We are open to such opportunities. It brings in extra cash and it is an inexpensive way to upgrade our skills by working with different customers".

In order to use its design and engineering skills to enter new businesses, HM entered into an agreement with Mahindra & Mahindra (M&M) for developing petrol engine for M&M vehicles. The company also tied up with GM to market the entire range of transmission equipment manufactured by Allison Automatics (a company owned by GM).

HM then overhauled its distribution system in order to become more market-friendly and dealer-friendly (HM was accused of offering very few dealer incentives and poor after-sales services). In 1999, the company unveiled a new distribution strategy, wherein dealers were divided into three tiers - red, blue, and green depending on their location and performance records. While the red-tier catered to the metros for selling and servicing Lancers, the blue-tier catered to the semi-urban areas for Contessas and Ambassadors and the green-tier catered to the rural markets for Trekkers.

HM also decided to explore the overseas markets for its products and began by exporting around 150 RTVs to Bangladesh in 2001. The company also managed to secure an export order for 300 petrol engines from a UK-based company, in addition to the 1,800 engines already supplied.

In February 2001, HM sold its earthmoving equipment manufacturing division to a wholly-owned Indian subsidiary of Caterpillar Inc. for Rs 3.3 billion. After the deal, HM was able to bring down its high interest debts from Rs 255.5 million in the first quarter of the 1999-00 to Rs 156.9 million in the corresponding quarter of the 2000-01 fiscal. The company used this money to repay debts worth Rs 2.25 billion from its long-term borrowings of Rs 6.2 billion.

This helped reduce the gross loss in 2000-01 to Rs 152.2 million from Rs 255.5 million in the corresponding quarter of 1999-00. The remaining sum of Rs1.05 billion after the repayment of debt from the sale was used for working capital requirements and automotive business. HM continued its customer relations enhancement initiatives with the launch of the click and customize service for Lancer customers in September 2001.

[7] Two of the biggest trade unions in the country, the CITU was affiliated to the CPI-M party, while the INTUC was an affiliate of the Congress party.

[8] After another VRS, which closed in July 2001, the Uttarpara plan workforce had come down to 9,200. The plant, suffering a loss of Rs. 70 million per month had stopped functioning on two weekdays. In August 2001, HM was asked by the State Government to submit a comprehensive plan for reviving the plant. The situation at the plant continued to be grim even in late 2001.

The company set up kiosks in six cities (New Delhi, Bangalore, Chennai, Hyderabad, Chandigarh and Pune) that had computer terminals displaying the features of the petrol and diesel versions of the Lancer. HM had invested Rs 2.5 million in the software and Rs 0.1 million on each kiosk. Customers could pick and choose the car color, the interior, accessories and the wheels, and take delivery within three weeks.

HM made this facility available on the Internet also, becoming the first carmaker to offer such a service to its customers in India. The company planned to install 16 such computer kiosks at its dealers premises across the country by the end of fiscal 2001-02. According to company sources, after the launch of the service, Lancer's market share had gone up by 4%.

In November 2001, HM announced its plans to emerge as a major player in the engine manufacturing business for other companies. The company was awaiting the outcome of its bid to make the engines for Ford's Ikon. With the second phase of the restructuring efforts in place, HM hoped to improve its growth in the automotive division and offset the losses from the passenger car segment.

The Road Ahead

The company's moves seemed to be finally bearing fruits as it was able to narrow down the losses in the first quarter of 2001-02 by around 30%.

HM was banking on the Ambassador's niche markets (government and taxi) and hoped to retain the segment by launching new variants. The Trekker was also poised to do well after the relaunch and HM hoped to sell 3,200 vehicles in 2001-02. Analysts however remained skeptical about HM's future prospects and its ability to make a turnaround as a passenger carmaker.

They felt that the only way out for HM was to turn itself into auto-component supplier to multi-nationals producing passenger cars in the country. HM on the other hand, seemed confident that with Pajero's launch in early 2002, it would regain its position in the Indian car market.

For Discussion

1. The responsibility of Hindustan Motors having failed to sustain its leadership position in the post-liberalization era was primarily the company's own. Critically comment on the above statement while analyzing the factors that led to the company's downfall.
2. Study HM's restructuring initiatives. Do you agree that despite all the turnaround efforts and new launches, HM has no chance in the Indian passenger car market? Give reasons to support your stand.

Exhibit I Comparing Car Sales Figures

Period	Sales		
	Lancer(HM)	Esteem (MUL)	Honda City (Honda)
1998-99	2,866	16,744	9,631
1999-00	8,300	16,031	9,772
2000-01	7,635	12,000	10,011

Source: *www.cybersteering.com*

Source: *http://www/icmr.icfai.org/casestudies*

✔ TEST PREPPER

True/False Questions

_____ **1.** One of the eight intertwined factors that contribute to decision complexity is governmental regulation.

_____ **2.** By definition, a condition of risk exists when there is little or no reliable factual information available.

_____ **3.** One way to sharpen your intuition is to get good feedback on your intuitive judgments.

_____ **4.** Throwing good money after bad is involved in escalation of commitment.

_____ **5.** "If-then" decision rules are used when one is making programmed decisions.

_____ **6.** There are two types of knowledge: implicit knowledge and tactical knowledge.

_____ **7.** "Logrolling" is a disadvantage of group-aided decision making.

_____ **8.** According to recent field research, creative people tend to be extreme nonconformists.

_____ **9.** A problem is defined as any sort of deficiency.

_____ **10.** "Satisficing" involves finding a solution to a problem that is "good enough," rather than finding the best possible solution.

Multiple-Choice Questions

1. As defined, decision making involves
A. eliminating uncertainty. B. leadership.
C. information technology. D. choosing.
E. overcoming fears.

2. Which of these, according to the author, is a contributor to decision complexity?
A. Culture B. Personality conflicts
C. Poor leadership D. Interdisciplinary input
E. Government regulation

3. Which one of these is *not* among the seven recommendations for sharpening your intuition?
A. Play devil's advocate.
B. Use imagery.
C. Open up the closet.
D. Get a feel for your batting average.
E. Engage in circular reasoning.

4. _____ is the tendency to evaluate positively presented information favorably and negatively presented information unfavorably.
A. Short-term thinking B. Overconfidence
C. Framing error D. Escalation of commitment
E. Satisficing

5. _____ are those that are repetitive and routine.
A. Reality checks
B. Nonprogrammed decisions
C. Programmed decisions
D. Semiprogrammed decisions
E. Contingent decisions

6. _____ knowledge is personal, intuitive, and undocumented information about how to skillfully perform tasks, solve problems, and make decisions.
A. Explicit B. Tacit
C. Job D. Conditional
E. Implicit

7. Which of the following is *not* cited as an advantage of group-aided decision making?
A. More ethical decisions
B. Training ground
C. Greater pool of knowledge
D. Increased acceptance
E. Greater comprehension

8. _____ is defined as the reorganization of experience into new configurations.
A. Forecasting B. Groupthink
C. Conceptualization D. Decision making
E. Creativity

9. Which of the following is *not* among the ten mental locks on creativity?
A. Strictly following the rules
B. Not being logical or rational
C. Insisting on being practical
D. Avoiding ambiguity
E. Not wanting to look foolish

10. When the situation in which a problem occurs is changed so that the problem no longer exists, the problem is
A. dissolved. B. created.
C. optimized. D. resolved.
E. satisfied.

ACE self-test

Want more questions? Visit the student Web site at http://business.college.hmco.com/students/ (select Kreitner, *Management,* 10e) and take the ACE quizzes for more practice.

Managers-in-Action Videos

2A Mary Guerrero-Pelzel, Contractor

Since 1982, when Mary Guerrero-Pelzel became a general contractor in Austin, Texas, Pelzel Construction has faced lots of tough challenges. Although heavy construction historically has been a male-dominated field, Guerrero-Pelzel has thrived because her suppliers, subcontractors, and customers trust her to get the job done properly and on time. She earned that trust by carefully watching costs, keeping her employee teams motivated, and maintaining tight control.

Learning Objectives: To learn more about the marriage of planning and control. To appreciate how a project manager needs to balance the little details and the big picture.

Links to Textual Material: **Chapter 6:** Planning/control cycle; Project planning; **Chapter 7:** Porter's generic competitive strategies; **Chapter 8:** Decision complexity

Discussion Questions:

1. Using Figure 6.4 as a guide, explain how the planning/control cycle is illustrated in this video case.
2. Referring to Figure 6.6, explain why Guerrero-Pelzel is an effective project manager.
3. Which of Porter's generic competitive strategies (see Figure 7.1) is Pelzel Construction using?
4. Which sources of decision complexity (see Figure 8.1) are evident in this video case? Explain your choices.

2B Planning and Decision Making at Percy Inn

Not everyone in Portland, Maine, is on vacation. This video takes us to that charming seaside city to see how an entrepreneur turned a crumbling historical landmark into a popular bed and breakfast. Dale Northrup, founder and innkeeper, and his assistant, Phyliss Rogers, give us the history and operational details of the Percy Inn. For more background, visit **www.percyinn.com**.

Learning Objectives: To learn more about international strategic management. To understand how a small business owner's life involves nonstop planning and decision making.

Links to Textual Material: **Chapter 1:** Entrepreneurs; **Chapter 6:** Planning and project management; **Chapter 7:** Strategic management; **Chapter 8:** Decision making; Creativity; Problem solving

Discussion Questions:

1. Which entrepreneurial traits (Table 1.3) does Northrup exemplify? Explain.
2. How is the planning/control cycle (Figure 6.4) apparent in this video? Explain.
3. Thinking strategically, what kinds of synergies can be achieved at the Percy Inn?
4. Which of the eight sources of decision complexity (Figure 8.1) did Northrup have to deal with when constructing and operating the Percy Inn? Explain.
5. How creative was Northrup when his bed and breakfast was being built? Explain

PART THREE

Organizing, Managing Human Resources, and Communicating

9

Organizations

Structure, Effectiveness, and Cultures

Equip people to make decisions by clearly defining the culture.[1]

KEVIN AND JACKIE FREIBERG

OBJECTIVES

- **Identify** and **describe** four characteristics common to all organizations.
- **Identify** and **explain** the two basic dimensions of organization charts.
- **Contrast** the traditional and modern views of organizations.
- **Describe** a business organization in terms of the open-system model.
- **Explain** the term *learning organization*.
- **Explain** the time dimension of organizational effectiveness.
- **Explain** the role of complacency in organizational decline, and **discuss** the ethics of downsizing.
- **Describe** at least three characteristics of organizational cultures, and **explain** the cultural significance of stories.

the changing workplace

Southwest Finds Trouble in the Air

Back in the days when Herb Kelleher was doing killer Elvis impersonations and wisecracking flight attendants had passengers rolling in the aisles, a scrappy Texas airline was built on a culture of fun. That worked so well that Southwest is now the nation's biggest carrier, in terms of passengers, and has the largest market cap [the total value of all outstanding shares of stock]. But where has the fun gone? After a grim tenure, Kelleher's successor, Jim Parker, recently quit as CEO. Now it's former CFO Gary Parker who must come up with some answers to a very unfunny question: Is success spoiling Southwest?

The problem with being the one profitable major airline, post-9/11, is that airline workers get avaricious. At the six bedraggled "legacy" carriers, unions have been making big wage concessions. At Southwest they've been making big demands. Its 7,200 flight attendants, whose starting pay was just $14,000, spent two bitter years seeking big raises and work-rule changes. They bridled against cleaning cabins between flights, for instance, which is one of those things that's given Southwest the industry's most productive workforce.

As long as Kelleher was around, employees would go the extra mile in the name of Herb. Prior to his retirement in 2001, "he was able to implement Southwest's unique cost structure and work rules," says an executive at another airline. "If you were a union leader, you couldn't badmouth Kelleher; he was an icon. But anybody new was going to be just another corporate executive."

The 73-year-old Kelleher was pressed back into service . . . [in 2004] in the stalemated, embittered flight-attendant negotiations. He got the deal done finally, but expensively: a 31% raise over the contract's six years. It's settlements like that—and a 2002 pilots' contract raising their pay a minimum of 20% over the past two years—that have sent

Southwest's costs soaring. Its cost per average seat-mile of 8 cents is creeping closer to that of the legacy carriers—which is no way to continue being a successful discounter.

"It's worth asking whether Southwest is finally facing the same issues and challenges that legacy carriers have experienced for some time," wrote Morgan Stanley analyst William Greene on the day Parker quit and Southwest missed its second-quarter earnings number. "We believe there is a risk that as a generational change occurs and the oldest Southwest employees retire (who remember the early years of struggle), the company's low-cost culture will change."

To Michael Roach, airline consultant and former America West president, that has already happened. Southwest workers once saw themselves as industry outsiders and were motivated partly by feeling embattled. Now they mainly feel entitled. The result isn't exactly a midlife crisis, because Southwest is still the healthiest, richest U.S. airline. But it does represent the passing of a corporate culture and era. "The miracle at Southwest," says Roach, "is that it's gone on so long."

Source: *From John Helyar, "Southwest Finds Trouble in the Air,"* Fortune *(August 9, 2004): 38.*

Organizations are an ever-present feature of modern society. We look to organizations for food, clothing, education, employment, entertainment, health care, transportation, and protection of our basic rights. Southwest Airlines, for its part, serves 65 million passengers a year with 2,800 daily flights to 60 airports.[2] For better or for worse, virtually every aspect of modern life is influenced in one way or another by organizations. Douglas Smith, a management consultant/author who is concerned about ethics and values in our era of giant global corporations, offers this perspective on organizations:

> *Organizations are not just places where people have jobs. They are our neighborhoods, our communities. They are where we join with other people to make a difference for ourselves and others. If we think of them only as the places where we have jobs, we not only lose the opportunity for meaning, but we endanger the planet.*[3]

Smith calls for increased corporate transparency and accountability to make sure the greater good is served.

In Chapter 1 we said the purpose of the management process is to achieve *organizational* objectives in an effective and efficient manner. Organizations are social entities that enable people to work together to achieve objectives they normally could not achieve alone. This chapter explores the organizational context in which managers operate. It serves as an introduction, laying the foundation for the discussion of organization design alternatives in Chapter 10. Specifically, this chapter defines the term *organization* and discusses different types of organizations and organization charts. It contrasts traditional and modern (open-system) views in the evolution of organization theory and explores the concept of learning organizations. The chapter also examines organizational effectiveness as a backdrop for a discussion of organizational decline. Finally, it looks at organizational cultures.

What Is an Organization?

organization: *cooperative and coordinated social system of two or more people with a common purpose*

An **organization** is defined as a cooperative social system involving the coordinated efforts of two or more people pursuing a shared purpose.[4] In other words, when people gather and formally agree to combine their efforts for a common purpose, an organization is the result.

There are exceptions, of course, such as when two individuals agree to push a car out of a ditch. This task is a one-time effort based on temporary expediency. But if the same two people decide to pool their resources to create a towing service, an organization would be created. The "coordinated efforts" portion of our definition, which implies a degree of formal planning and division of labor, is present in the second instance but not in the first.

Characteristics Common to All Organizations

According to Edgar Schein, an organizational psychologist, all organizations share four characteristics: (1) coordination of effort, (2) common goal or purpose, (3) division of labor, and (4) hierarchy of authority.[5]

1. IDENTIFY and DESCRIBE four characteristics common to all organizations.

Coordination of Effort. As we noted in the last chapter, two heads are sometimes better than one. Individuals who join together and coordinate their mental and/or physical efforts can accomplish great and exciting things. Building the great pyramids, conquering polio, sending astronauts to the moon—all these achievements far exceeded the talents and abilities of any single individual. Coordination of effort multiplies individual contributions.

Common Goal or Purpose. Coordination of effort cannot take place unless those who have joined together agree to strive for something of mutual interest. A common goal or purpose gives the organization focus and its members a rallying point.

Division of Labor. By systematically dividing complex tasks into specialized jobs, an organization can use its human resources efficiently. Division of labor permits each organization member to become more proficient by repeatedly doing the same specialized task. (But, as is discussed in Chapter 13, overspecialized jobs can breed boredom and alienation.)

The advantages of dividing labor have been known for a long time. One of its early proponents was the pioneering economist Adam Smith. While touring an eighteenth-century pin-manufacturing plant, Smith observed that a group of specialized laborers could produce 48,000 pins a day. This was an astounding figure, considering that each laborer could produce only 20 pins a day when working alone.[6]

Hierarchy of Authority. According to traditional organization theory, if anything is to be accomplished through formal collective effort, someone should be given the authority to see that the intended goals are carried out effectively and efficiently. Organization theorists have defined **authority** as the right to direct the actions of others. Without a clear hierarchy of authority, coordination of effort is difficult, if not impossible, to achieve. Accountability is also enhanced by having people serve in what is often called, in military language, the *chain of command.* For instance, a grocery store manager has authority over the assistant manager, who has authority over the produce department head, who in turn has authority over the employees in the produce department. Without such a chain of command, the store manager would have the impossible task of directly overseeing the work of every employee in the store.

authority: *right to direct the actions of others*

The idea of hierarchy has many critics, particularly among those who advocate flatter organizations with fewer levels of management.[7] An organization theorist answered those critics as follows:

> *At first glance, hierarchy may seem difficult to praise. Bureaucracy is a dirty word even among bureaucrats, and in business there is a widespread view that managerial hierarchy kills initiative, crushes creativity, and has therefore seen its day. Yet 35 years of research have convinced me that managerial hierarchy is the most efficient, the hardiest, and in fact the most natural structure ever devised for large organizations. Properly structured, hierarchy can release energy and creativity, rationalize productivity, and actually improve morale.*[8]

"YOU KNOW, EVER SINCE I STARTED WORKING HERE, I'VE HAD THIS CRAVING FOR CHEESE."

Source: *Published* Harvard Business *April 2004. Permission by Dave Carpenter*

9a Lighten Up!

A legal secretary at the Atlanta-based law firm Alston & Bird (number 4 on *Fortune* magazine's 2005 list of "The 100 Best Companies to Work For"):

> *There is no pecking-order mentality here. Folks have a sense of humor without regard to status.*

Source: As quoted in Robert Levering and Milton Moskowitz, "The 100 Best Companies to Work For," Fortune *(January 24, 2005): 86.*

QUESTIONS:

Is this type of organizational climate important today? Why or why not?

For further information about the interactive annotations in this chapter, visit our Web site (**http://business.college.hmco.com/students/** and select Kreitner, *Management,* 10e).

■ **Putting All the Pieces Together.** All four of the foregoing characteristics are necessary before an organization can be said to exist. Many well-intentioned attempts to create organizations have failed because something was missing. In 1896, for example, Frederick Strauss, a boyhood friend of Henry Ford, helped Ford set up a machine shop, supposedly to produce gasoline-powered engines. But while Strauss was busy carrying out his end of the bargain by machining needed parts, Ford was secretly building a horseless carriage in a workshop behind his house.[9] Although Henry Ford eventually went on to become an automobile-industry giant, his first attempt at organization failed because not all of the pieces of an organization were in place. Ford's and his partner's efforts were not coordinated, they worked at cross-purposes, their labor was vaguely divided, and they had no hierarchy of authority. In short, they had organizational intentions, but no organization.

■ Classifying Organizations

Because organizations are created to pursue particular purposes, they can be classified accordingly. The classification by organizational purpose discussed here has four categories: business, nonprofit service, mutual-benefit, and commonweal organizations.[10] Some of today's large and complex organizations overlap categories. For example, religious organizations are both nonprofit service organizations and mutual-benefit organizations. Nevertheless, classifying organizations by their purpose helps clarify the variety of roles they play in society and the similar problems shared by organizations with similar purposes (see Table 9.1).

■ **Business Organizations.** Business organizations such as General Mills, Southwest Airlines, and the Washington Post all have one underlying purpose: to make a profit in a socially acceptable manner. Businesses cannot survive, let alone grow, without earning a profit, and profits are earned by efficiently satisfying demand for products and services. This economic production function is so important to society that many think immediately of business when the word *management* is mentioned.

■ **Nonprofit Service Organizations.** Unlike businesses, many organizations survive, and even grow, without making any profits at all. They need to be solvent, of course, but they measure their success not in dollars and cents but by how well they provide a specific service for some segment of society.[11] The American Heart Association, Notre Dame University, and Massachusetts General Hospital are examples of nonprofit service organizations. The 12 million people who work for 1.8 million nonprofit service organizations in the United States constitute a $700 billion slice of the economy.[12] Because the services of such organizations are usually in great demand, one of their biggest problems lies in screening large numbers of applicants to determine who qualifies for service. Another problem for most nonprofit service organizations is securing a reliable stream of funds through fees, donations, grants, or

Table 9.1 Classifying Organizations by Their Intended Purpose

Purpose	Primary beneficiary	Common examples	Overriding management problem
Business	Owners	Computer manufacturers Newspapers Railroads Fast-food restaurant chains	Must make a profit
Nonprofit service	Clients	Universities Welfare agencies Hospitals (nonprofit)	Must selectively screen large numbers of potential clients
Mutual-benefit	Members	Unions Clubs Political parties Trade associations Cooperatives	Must satisfy members' needs
Commonweal	Public at large	U.S. Postal Service Police departments Fire departments Public schools	Must provide standardized services to large groups of people with diverse needs

Malaysian superstar Michelle Yeoh and Razali Ismail, Malaysia's special envoy for tsunami aid (back row, far right), posed with some famous musicians in Kuala Lumpur, Malaysia, in 2005 to build support for the Force of Nature Aid Foundation. Can you pick out any of your favorites from The Backstreet Boys, the Black Eyed Peas, and Boyz II Men? Their concert for Tsunami Relief, and the nonprofit organization behind it, raised millions of dollars for victims of the Indian Ocean disaster.

appropriations. Given today's limited resources, both private-sector and public-sector nonprofit service organizations are under pressure to operate more efficiently.[13]

■ **Mutual-Benefit Organizations.** Often, as in the case of labor unions or political parties, individuals join together strictly to pursue their own self-interests. In other cases—the National Association of Manufacturers, for example—organizations may feel compelled to join together in an umbrella organization. Mutual-benefit organizations, like all other types of organizations, need to be effectively and efficiently managed if they are to survive. In this instance, survival depends on satisfying members' needs.

■ **Commonweal Organizations.** Like nonprofit service organizations, commonweal organizations offer public services without attempting to earn a profit. But unlike nonprofit service organizations, which serve some *segment* of society, a **commonweal organization** offers standardized service to *all* members of a given population. The Canadian Army, for example, protects everyone within Canada's borders, not just a select few. The same can be said for local police and fire departments. Commonweal organizations are generally large, and their great size makes them unwieldy and difficult to manage. The U.S. federal government, for example, has 2.7 million civilian employees.[14] Competing demands from a diverse array of clients also complicate matters. Members of the New York City Fire Department, for example, stand ready to do everything from fighting fires to administering emergency medical treatment to providing disaster assistance to rescuing pets.[15]

commonweal organization: *nonprofit organization serving all members of a given population*

organization chart: *visual display of an organization's positions and lines of authority*

Organization Charts

An **organization chart** is a diagram of an organization's official positions and formal lines of authority. In effect, an organization chart is a visual display of an organization's structural skeleton. With their familiar pattern of boxes and connecting lines, these charts (some call them tables) are a useful management tool because they are an organizational blueprint for deploying human resources.[16] Organization charts are common in both profit and nonprofit organizations.

■ Vertical and Horizontal Dimensions

2. IDENTIFY and **EXPLAIN** the two basic dimensions of organization charts.

Every organization chart has two dimensions, one representing *vertical hierarchy* and one representing *horizontal specialization*. Vertical hierarchy establishes the chain of command, or who reports to whom. Horizontal specialization establishes the division of labor. A short case tracing the growth of a new organization will help demonstrate the relationship between vertical hierarchy and horizontal specialization.

■ A Case Study: The Growth of an Organization

For years, George Thomas was an avid trout fisherman.[17] The sight of George loading up his old camper with expensive fly-casting gear and heading out to the nearest trout stream was familiar to his family and neighbors. About six years ago, George tried his hand at the difficult task of tying his own trout flies. Being a creative individual and a bit of a handyman, George soon created a fly that trout seemingly fought over to bite. Word spread rapidly among local and regional fishing enthusiasts. Eventually, George was swamped with orders for his newly patented Super Flies at $3.50 each. What had started out as a casual hobby turned into a potentially lucrative

Figure 9.1 The Evolution of an Organization Chart

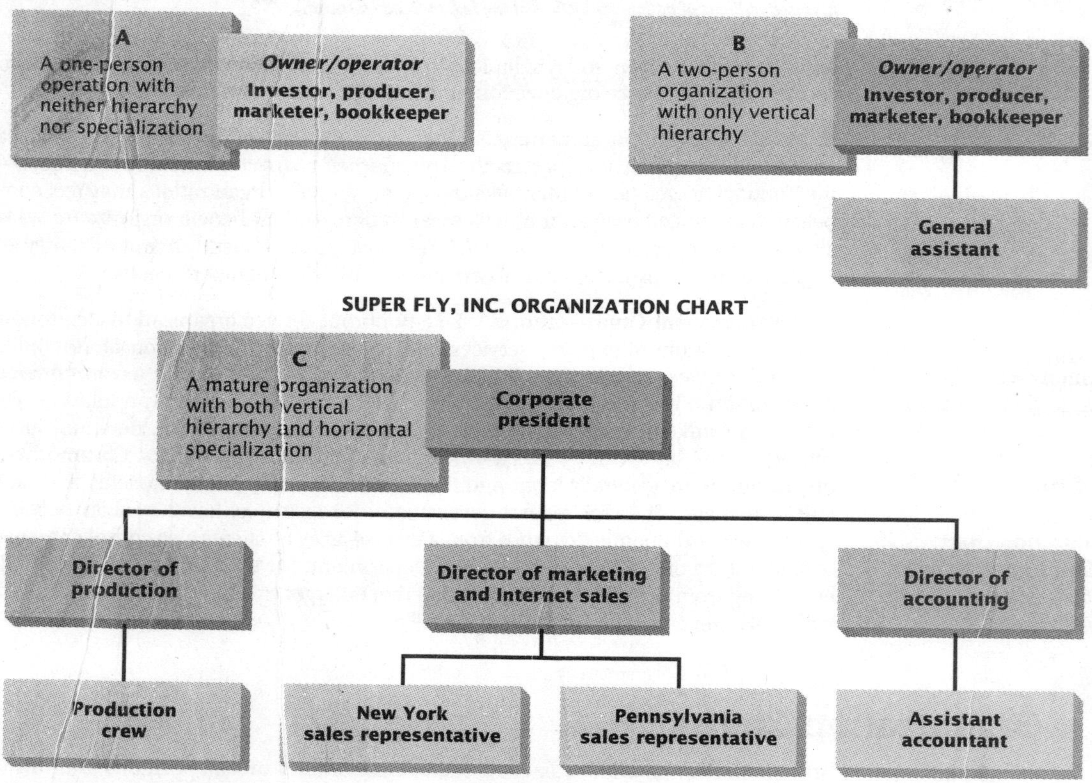

business bringing in roughly $500 per week. George no longer found any time to fish; all his time was taken up tying and selling Super Flies. An organization chart at that point would have looked like the one in Figure 9.1A. George was the entire operation and, technically, an organization did not yet exist. There was no vertical hierarchy or horizontal specialization at that early stage.

George soon found it impossible to tie more than a couple hundred flies a week and still visit fishing-tackle retailers who might carry his Super Flies. To free up some time, George hired and trained a family friend named Amy to help him run the operation in a small building he had leased. An organization chart could have been drawn up at that time because an organization came into existence when Amy was hired. (Remember that it takes at least two people to make an organization.) The chart would have resembled the one in Figure 9.1B. Vertical hierarchy had been introduced because Amy was George's subordinate. However, there still was no horizontal specialization because Amy did many different things.

As business picked up, George had to hire and train four full-time employees to work under Amy tying flies. He also hired Fred, a computer salesman and an old fishing buddy, to head the marketing operation, recruit and train two regional sales representatives, and create a Web site. Shortly afterward, an accountant was brought into the organization to set up and keep the books. Today, Super Fly, Inc., is recording annual sales in excess of $2.5 million. George has finally gotten around to formally organizing the company he built in patchwork fashion through the years. His current organization chart is displayed in Figure 9.1C.

Notice that the company now has three layers in the vertical hierarchy and three distinct forms of horizontal specialization. The three specialized directors now do separately what George used to do all by himself. George's job of general management will become progressively more difficult as additional vertical layers and horizontal specialists are added. Coordination is essential; the "right hand" must operate in concert with the "left hand." *Generally, specialization is achieved at the expense of coordination when designing organizations.* A workable balance between specialization and coordination can be achieved through contingency design, as discussed in the next chapter.

Contrasting Theories of Organization

3. CONTRAST the traditional and modern views of organizations.

The study of organization theory is largely a twentieth-century development. As one organization theorist philosophically observed, "The study of organizations has a history but not a pedigree."[18] This history is marked by disagreement rather than uniformity of thinking. A useful way of approaching the study of organization theory is to contrast the traditional view with a modern view, two very different ways of thinking about organizations.

In the traditional view, the organization is characterized by closed-system thinking. This view assumes that the surrounding environment is fairly predictable and that uncertainty within the organization can be eliminated through detailed planning and strict control. An organization's primary goal is seen to be economic efficiency. In contrast, a prevailing modern view characterizes the organization as an open system interacting continuously with an uncertain environment. Both the organization and its surrounding environment are assumed to be filled with variables that are difficult to predict or control. As the open-system theorists see it, the organization's principal goal is survival in an environment of uncertainty and surprise. These contrasting approaches are summarized in Table 9.2.

■ The Traditional View

Let us explore the evolution of traditional organization theory by first reviewing the contributions of the early management writers and Max Weber's concept of

Table 9.2 Contrasting Theories of Organization

	Traditional view	Modern view
General perspective	Closed-system thinking	Open-system thinking
Primary goal of organization	Economic efficiency	Survival in an environment of uncertainty and surprise
Assumption about surrounding environment	Predictable	Generally uncertain
Assumptions about organizations	All causal, goal-directed variables are known and controllable. Uncertainty can be eliminated through planning and controlling.	The organizational system has more variables than can be comprehended at one time. Variables often are subject to influences that cannot be controlled or predicted.

Source: *Adapted, by permission, from James D. Thompson,* Organizations in Action *(New York: McGraw-Hill, 1967), pp. 4–7.*

bureaucracy. Then a look at challenges to these traditional models will prepare the way for our examination of the modern open-system model of organizations.

■ **The Early Management Writers.** Early contributors to management literature, such as Henri Fayol and Frederick W. Taylor, treated organizing as a subfield of management. You will recall from Chapter 1 that organizing was among Fayol's five universal functions of management. Taylor's narrow task definitions and strict work rules implied a tightly structured approach to organization design.

In general, Fayol and the other pioneering management writers who followed in his footsteps endorsed closely controlled authoritarian organizations. For instance, managers were advised to have no more than six immediate subordinates. Close supervision and obedience were the order of the day. Emphasis in these organizations was on the unrestricted downward flow of authority in the form of orders and rules. Four traditional principles of organization that emerged were (1) a well-defined hierarchy of authority, (2) unity of command,[19] (3) authority equal to responsibility, and (4) downward delegation of authority but not of responsibility (see Table 9.3).

bureaucracy: *Weber's model of a rationally efficient organization*

■ **Max Weber's Bureaucracy.** Writing more than a hundred years ago, a German sociologist named Max Weber described what he considered to be the most rationally efficient form of organization, to which he affixed the label **bureaucracy**. According to Weber's model, bureaucracies are efficient because of the following characteristics: (1) division of labor, (2) hierarchy of authority, (3) a framework of rules, and (4) impersonality.[20] By *impersonality,* Weber meant hiring and promoting people on the basis of *what* they know, not *whom* they know. It is important to realize that Weber's ideas about organizations were shaped by prevailing circumstances. In the late 1800s, Germany was a semifeudal state struggling to adjust to the pressures of the Industrial Revolution. Weber was appalled at the way public administrators relied on subjective judgment, emotion, fear tactics, and nepotism (the hiring and promotion of one's relatives) rather than on sound management practices.[21] He used the widely respected and highly efficient Prussian army as the model for his bureaucratic form of organization.

In theory, Weber's bureaucracy was supposedly the epitome of efficiency. But experience with bureaucracies has shown that they can be slow, insensitive to indi-

Table 9.3 Traditional Principles of Organization

1. **A well-defined hierarchy of authority.** This principle was intended to ensure the coordinated pursuit of organizational goals by contributing individuals.
2. **Unity of command.** It was believed that the possibility of conflicting orders, a serious threat to the smooth flow of authority, could be avoided by making sure that each individual answered to only one superior.
3. **Authority equal to responsibility.** *Authority* was defined as the right to get subordinates to accomplish something. *Responsibility* was defined as the obligation to accomplish something. The traditionalists cautioned against holding individuals ultimately accountable for getting something done unless they were given formal authority to get it done.
4. **Downward delegation of authority but not of responsibility.** Although a superior with the requisite authority and responsibility can pass along the *right* to get something accomplished to subordinates, the *obligation* for getting it done remains with the superior. This arrangement was intended to eliminate the practice of "passing the buck."

vidual needs, and grossly inefficient.[22] Today, the term *bureaucracy* has a strongly negative connotation. According to Jack Welch, the former head of General Electric: "Bureaucracy frustrates people, distorts their priorities, limits their dreams and turns the face of the enterprise inward."[23] This bureaucratic paradox can be reconciled somewhat by viewing bureaucracy as a matter of degree.

Every systematically managed organization, regardless of its size or purpose, is to some extent a bureaucracy. Bureaucratic characteristics are simply more pronounced or advanced in some organizations than in others.[24] Trying to eliminate bureaucracy is impractical. The real challenge is keeping bureaucratic characteristics within functional limits. As Table 9.4 indicates, a moderate degree of bureaucratization can enhance organizational efficiency, but taken too far, each dimension of bureaucracy can hinder efficiency. Managers who learn to read and retreat from the symptoms of dysfunction can reap the benefits of functional bureaucracy.[25]

9b Unruly Rules

Fire Chief Alan Brunacini, Phoenix, Arizona:

"When I got here, all our rules were the size of a bushel," he says. "Now they're on one sheet of paper. How many rules do you need? It only takes 10 to get into heaven."

Source: As quoted in Jon Talton, "What in Blazes Has the Chief Done? Create a Model for Managers," Arizona Republic *(January 27, 2002): D1.*

QUESTIONS:
Do today's organizations have too many rules? Explain. Which rules should stay and which should go?

■ Challenges to the Traditional View of Organizations

Because the traditionalists' rigid recommendations for organizing and managing did not work in all situations, their recommendations were eventually challenged. Prescriptions for machinelike efficiency that worked in military units and simple shop operations often failed to work in complex organizations. Fayol's universal functions and principles turned out to be no guarantee of success. Similarly, experience proved that organizing was more than just the strict obedience to authority that Taylor had emphasized. In spite of Weber's rationally efficient organizational formula, bureaucracy in practice often became the epitome of inefficiency. In addition, challenges to traditional thinking about organizations arose from two other sources.

■ **Bottom-Up Authority.** Traditionalists left no doubt about the origin of authority in their organizational models. Authority was inextricably tied to property ownership and therefore naturally flowed from the top of the organization to the bottom. In businesses, those farthest removed from the ownership of stock were entitled to the least amount of authority. Naturally, this notion appealed strongly to those interested

Table 9.4 Functional versus Dysfunctional Bureaucracy: A Matter of Degree

	Indications of functional bureaucracy	Symptoms of dysfunctional bureaucracy
Degree of bureaucratization	Moderate	High
Division of labor	More work, of higher quality, can be completed faster because complex tasks are separated into more readily mastered jobs.	Grievances, absenteeism, and turnover increase as a result of overly fragmented jobs that people find boring and dehumanizing. Poor performance leads to customer complaints.
Hierarchy of authority	A generally accepted chain of command serves to direct individuals' efforts toward accomplishment of organizational goals.	Due to a fear of termination, a climate of blind obedience to authority, whether right or wrong, exists.
Framework of rules	Individual contributions to the collective effort are directed and coordinated by rules that answer important procedural questions.	Pursuit of the organization's mission is displaced by the practice of formulating and enforcing self-serving rules that protect status, create unnecessary work, hide incompetence and inefficiencies, or disperse accountability.
Impersonality	Hiring, promotion, and other personnel decisions are made on the basis of objective merit rather than favoritism or prejudice.	Employees and clients complain about being treated like numbers by bureaucrats who fail to respond to the full range of human needs.

in maintaining the power base of society's more fortunate members. But when Chester I. Barnard described organizations as cooperative systems, he questioned the traditional assumption about the automatic downward flow of authority. Instead, he proposed a more democratic **acceptance theory of authority**. According to Barnard's acceptance theory, a leader's authority is determined by his or her subordinates' willingness to comply with it. Barnard believed that a subordinate recognizes a communication from above as being authoritative and decides to comply with it only when all of the following conditions apply:

acceptance theory of authority: *Barnard's theory that authority is determined by subordinates' willingness to comply*

1. The message is understood.
2. The subordinate believes it is consistent with the organization's purpose.
3. It serves the subordinate's interest.
4. The subordinate is able to comply.[26]

Barnard's acceptance theory opened the door for a whole host of ideas, such as upward communication and the informal organization that is based on friendship rather than work rules. Prior to Barnard's contribution, such concepts had been discussed only by human relationists. In effect, Barnard humanized organization theory by characterizing workers as active controllers of authority, not mere passive recipients. Interestingly, Barnard's empowerment theme has resulted in a distaste for the term *subordinate*, which many today regard as a demeaning label.

■ **Environmental Complexity and Uncertainty.** Although traditionalists liked to believe that rigid structure and rational management were important to organizational effectiveness and efficiency, environmental complexity and uncertainty often undermined companies' efforts to achieve these goals. As Charles Perrow observed in writing about the history of organization theory, "The increasing complexity of markets, variability of products, increasing number of branch plants, and changes in technology all required more adaptive organizations."[27] Plans usually have to be made on the basis of incomplete or imperfect information, and consequently, things do not always work out according to plan. Similarly, many of the traditional principles of organization, such as the number of people a manager can effectively manage, have proved to be naive.

The net result of these and other challenges to traditional thinking was a desire to look at organizations in some new ways. When open-system thinking appeared on the management horizon, as discussed in Chapter 2, many embraced it eagerly because it emphasized the need for flexibility and adaptability in organization structure.

■ Organizations as Open Systems: A Modern View

Open-system thinking fosters a more realistic view of the interaction between an organization and its environment.[28] Traditional closed-system perspectives—such as Fayol's universal process approach, scientific management, and bureaucracy—largely ignored environmental influences. Today's managers cannot afford that luxury. Intense competition in a fast-changing world prompted Intel's Andy Grove to offer this view: "A corporation is a living organism, and it has to continue to shed its skin."[29]

Organizations are systems made up of interacting subsystems. Organizations are themselves subsystems that interact with larger social, political-legal, and economic systems. Those who take an open-system perspective realize that system-to-system

According to the open-system concept of equifinality, there is more than one way to get the job done. Dramatic evidence of equifinality was spotted by race fans in 1989 at the Golden Gate Fields track in Albany, California. As Nate Hubbard, a 19-year-old apprentice jockey, guided Sweetwater Oak into the final stretch, the filly stumbled on the muddy track and Hubbard lurched out of the saddle, holding on to the horse's mane. Hubbard finished second. Officials declared it a legal ride because the jockey remained aboard the horse.

interactions are often as important as the systems themselves. Among these interactions are movements of people into and out of the labor force (for example, unemployment), movements of capital (for example, stock exchanges and corporate borrowing), and movements of goods and services (for example, international trade). A highly organized and vigorously interactive world needs realistically dynamic models. In this area, particularly, open-system thinking can make a contribution to organization theory.

■ **Some Open-System Characteristics.** According to general systems theory, all open systems—whether the human body, an organization, a society, or the solar system—share certain characteristics. At the same time, the theory recognizes significant differences among the various kinds of open systems. Four characteristics that emphasize the adaptive and dynamic nature of all open systems are (1) interaction with the environment, (2) synergy, (3) dynamic equilibrium, and (4) equifinality.

- ***Interaction with the environment.*** Open systems have permeable boundaries, whereas closed systems do not. Open systems, such as the human body, are not self-sufficient. Life-sustaining oxygen, nutrients, and water must be imported from the surrounding environment, and waste must be exported. Similarly, organizations depend on the environment for survival.
- ***Synergy.*** As discussed in Chapter 7, synergy is the 1 + 1 = 3 effect. In other words, an open system adds up to more than the sum of its parts. A winning athletic team is more than its players, coaches, plays, and equipment. Only when all parts are in place and working in concert can the winning edge be achieved. Likewise, a successful business is more than the traditional factors of production—land, labor, and capital. Synergistic thinking emphasizes that a firm's competitive edge is dictated as much by how the factors of production are mobilized as by what those factors are.

dynamic equilibrium: *process whereby an open system maintains its own internal balance with help from its environment*

- ***Dynamic equilibrium.*** In open systems, **dynamic equilibrium** is the process of maintaining the internal balance necessary for survival by importing needed resources from the environment.[30] Proper blood chemistry in the human body is maintained through dynamic equilibrium. When a person's blood sugar drops below normal, a craving for sugar prompts the ingestion of something sweet, thus increasing the blood-sugar level. Similarly, management can take out a loan when operations have drained the organization's cash reserves.

equifinality: *open systems can achieve similar ends through different means*

- ***Equifinality.*** Open systems are made up of more than fixed cause-and-effect linkages. **Equifinality** means reaching the same result by different means. In their landmark book *Organization and Management*, Fremont Kast and James Rosenzweig summarize: "The concept of equifinality suggests that the manager can utilize a varying bundle of inputs into the organization, can transform them in a variety of ways, and can achieve satisfactory output."[31] For example, Nucor, a rapidly growing and highly profitable steel producer, is almost totally unlike traditional steel companies. Nucor builds its own mills, avoids debt, makes steel from scrap rather than ore, uses the latest energy-saving technology, and ties its nonunion employees' weekly bonuses to productivity.[32] Whereas America's steel giants have had to retrench in the face of stiff foreign competition, Nucor has thrived because of equifinality. In short, Nucor found a different (and better) way of getting the job done.

4. DESCRIBE a business organization in terms of the open-system model.

■ **Developing an Open-System Model.** An open-system model encourages managers to think about organization-environment interaction (see Figure 9.2). A business must acquire various *inputs:* capital, either through selling stock or borrowing; labor, through hiring people; raw materials, through purchases; and market information, through research. On the *output* side of the model, goods and services are marketed, profits (or losses) are realized, and waste materials are discarded (if not recycled).[33]

Figure 9.2 Open-System Model of a Business

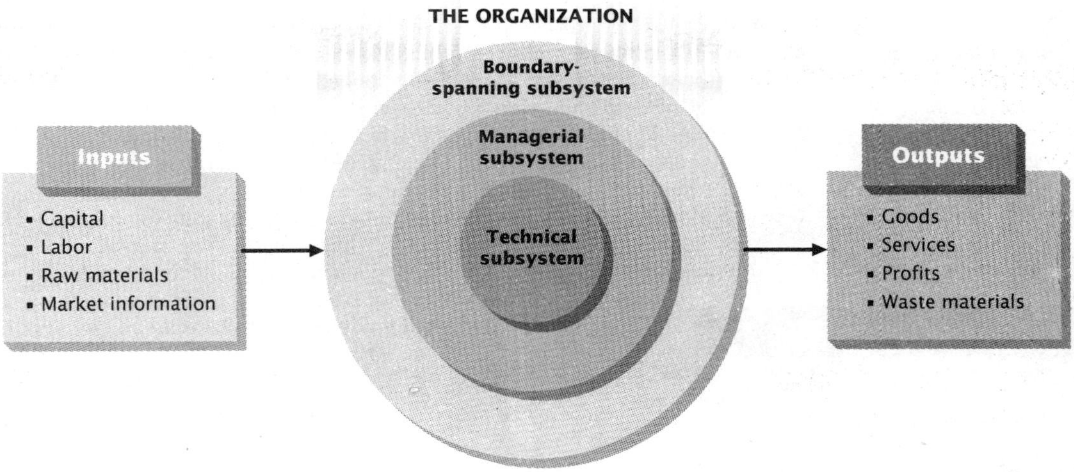

9c Back to the Opening Case

Using Figure 9.2 as a guide (and drawing on your general knowledge), how would you describe Southwest Airlines in open-system terms?

There are other inputs and outputs as well. This open-system model, although descriptive of a business organization, readily generalizes to all types of organizations.

By using the open-system premise that systems are made up of interacting subsystems, we can identify three prominent organizational subsystems: technical, boundary-spanning, and managerial. Sometimes called the production function, the technical subsystem physically transforms raw materials into finished goods and services. But the ability to turn out a product does not in itself guarantee organizational survival. Other supporting subsystems working in concert are also needed.

Whereas technical subsystems may be viewed as being at an organization's very core, boundary-spanning subsystems are directed outward toward the general environment. Most boundary-spanning jobs, or interface functions, as they are sometimes called, are easily identified by their titles. Purchasing and supply-chain specialists are responsible for making sure the organization has a steady and reliable flow of raw materials and subcomponents. Public relations staff are in charge of developing and maintaining a favorable public image of the organization. Strategic planners have the responsibility of surveying the general environment for actual or potential opportunities and threats. Sales personnel probe the environment for buyers for the organization's goods or services. Purchasing agents, public relations staff, strategic planners, and sales personnel have one common characteristic: they all facilitate the organization's interaction with its environment. Each, so to speak, has one foot inside the organization and one foot outside.

Although the technical and boundary-spanning subsystems are important and necessary, one additional subsystem is needed to tie the organization together. As Figure 9.2 indicates, the managerial subsystem serves as a bridge between the other two subsystems. The managerial subsystem controls and directs the other subsystems in the organization. It is within this subsystem that the subject matter of this book is practiced as a blend of science and art.

■ **Extending the Open-System Model: The Learning Organization.** The idea of organizational learning, and its companion topic of knowledge management discussed in Chapter 8, dates back to the 1970s.[34] It took Peter Senge's 1990 best-seller, *The Fifth*

5. EXPLAIN the term *learning organization.*

learning organization: *one that turns new ideas into improved performance*

Discipline, to popularize this extension of open-system thinking.[35] Many management writers and consultants then jumped on the bandwagon and confusion prevailed.

Fortunately, Harvard's David A. Garvin did a good job of sorting things out. According to Garvin, "A **learning organization** is an organization skilled at creating, acquiring, and transferring knowledge, and at modifying its behavior to reflect new knowledge and insights."[36] One could view Garvin and the others as having extended the open-system model of organizations by putting a human head on the biological (open-system) model. Garvin believes that organizational learning, just like human learning, involves three stages (see Figure 9.3): (1) cognition (learning new concepts), (2) behavior (developing new skills and abilities), and (3) performance (actually getting something done). All three stages are necessary to erase the infamous gap between theory and practice.

Also illustrated in Figure 9.3 are five organizational skills that Garvin claims are needed to turn new ideas into improved organizational performance. Each skill is important if today's organizations are to *thrive*, not just survive.

- ***Solving problems.*** Problems, as discussed in Chapter 8, are the gap between actual and desired situations. Everyone in the organization needs to be skilled at identifying problems and creatively solving them.
- ***Experimenting.*** W. Edwards Deming's plan-do-check-act (PDCA) cycle, covered in Chapter 17, is an excellent tool for learning through systematic experimentation.
- ***Learning from organizational experience/history.*** Role models and oft-told stories of success and failure embedded in the organization's culture teach vital lessons. Also, as recently pointed out, creating an organization "that can concurrently harness innovation, initiative, and competence-building is a difficult task that often requires significant 'unlearning' of previous organizational practices."[37]
- ***Learning from others.*** Two prime sources of valuable knowledge in this regard are benchmarking, also discussed in Chapter 17, and customer input and feedback.
- ***Transferring and implementing.*** All the other skills are for naught if actions are not taken to make the organization perform better. Training (Chapter 11) and effective communication (Chapter 12) are key bridges spanning the gap between ideas and skills and superior organizational performance.

9d Never Too Early to Learn

For more than a decade, the Pfizer Education Initiative (PEI) . . . [has] sought to bridge the gap between the classroom and the pharmaceutical industry by promoting the idea that science and chemistry are fun. Through tutoring, internships, lectures and resources for teachers, PEI reaches more than 21,000 kindergarten through twelfth-grade students and 500 teachers throughout 40 schools in the United States and Europe.

Source: Heather Johnson, "Training Top 100: Pfizer," Training, *41 (March 2004): 45.*

QUESTION:

How does this corporate social responsibility initiative help Pfizer become a more effective learning organization?

Figure 9.3 Garvin's Model of the Learning Organization

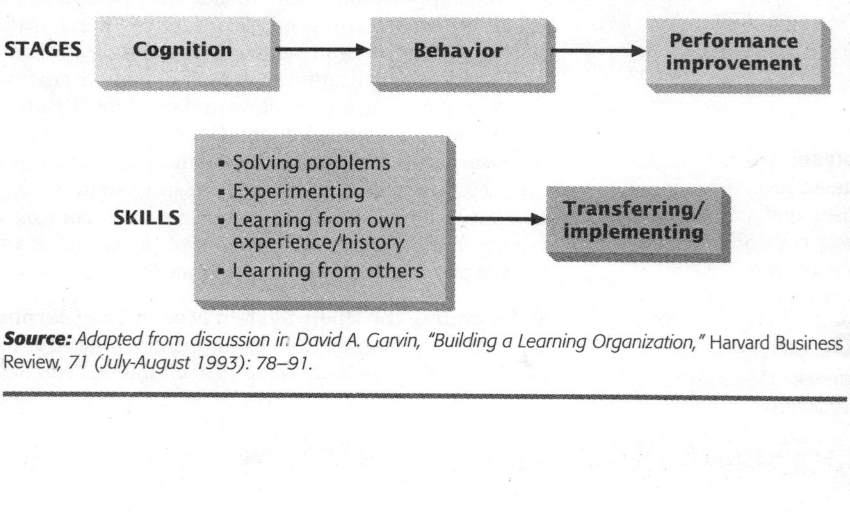

Source: *Adapted from discussion in David A. Garvin, "Building a Learning Organization,"* Harvard Business Review, *71 (July-August 1993): 78–91.*

The concept of learning organizations is a valuable addition to organization theory because it explains how managers can deal with today's only certainty—*change.*[38] (For more, see the Skills & Tools feature at the end of this chapter.)

Organizational Effectiveness

The practice of management, as defined in Chapter 1, challenges managers to use organizational resources effectively and efficiently. Effectiveness is a measure of whether organizational objectives are accomplished. In contrast, efficiency is the relationship between outputs and inputs. Only monopolies can get away with being effective but not efficient. Moreover, in an era of diminishing resources and increasing concern about civil rights, society is reluctant to label "effective" any organization that wastes scarce resources or tramples on civil rights. Management's definition of organizational effectiveness therefore needs to be refined. The related issue of organizational decline also needs to be understood and skillfully managed.

■ No Silver Bullet

According to one management scholar, "no single approach to the evaluation of effectiveness is appropriate in all circumstances or for all organizational types."[39] More and more, the effectiveness criteria for modern organizations are being prescribed by society in the form of explicit expectations, regulations, and laws. In the private sector, profitability is no longer the sole criterion of effectiveness.[40] Winslow Buxton, CEO of Pentair, Inc., a Minnesota manufacturing company with $2 billion in annual revenue and 10,000 employees, offered this perspective:

> *One of the most challenging aspects of my job is balancing the differing expectations of employees, management, customers, financial analysts, and investors. The common denominator for all these groups is growth. But this seemingly simple term has different connotations for each constituency, and a successful company must satisfy all of those meanings.*[41]

Moreover, today's managers are caught up in an enormous web of laws and regulations covering employment practices, working conditions, job safety, pensions, product safety, pollution, and competitive practices. To be truly effective, today's productive organizations need to strike a generally acceptable balance between organizational and societal goals. Direct conflicts, such as higher wages for employees versus lower prices for customers, are inevitable (see Management Ethics). Therefore, the process of determining the proper weighting of organizational effectiveness criteria is an endless one requiring frequent review and updating.[42]

■ A Time Dimension

organizational effectiveness: *being effective, efficient, and satisfying today, adapting and developing in the intermediate future, and surviving in the long term*

6. EXPLAIN the time dimension of organizational effectiveness.

To build a workable definition of organizational effectiveness, we shall introduce a time dimension. As indicated in Figure 9.4, the organization needs to be effective in the near, intermediate, and distant future. Consequently, **organizational effectiveness** can be defined as meeting organizational objectives and prevailing societal expectations in the near future, adapting and developing in the intermediate future, and surviving into the distant future.[43]

Most people think only of the near future. It is in the near future that the organization has to produce goods or render services, use resources efficiently, and satisfy both insiders and outsiders with its activity. But this is just the beginning, not the end. To grow and be effective, an organization must adapt to new environmental demands and mature and learn in the intermediate future (two to four years).[44]

MANAGEMENT ETHICS

Should We Admire Wal-Mart?

There is an evil company in Arkansas, some say. It's a discount store—a very, very big discount store—and it will do just about anything to get bigger. You've seen the headlines. Illegal immigrants mopping its floors. Workers locked inside overnight. A big gender discrimination suit. Wages low enough to make other companies' workers go on strike. And we know what it does to weaker suppliers and competitors. Crushing the dream of the independent proprietor—an ideal as American as Thomas Jefferson—it is the enemy of all that's good and right in our nation.

There is another big discount store in Arkansas, yet this one couldn't be more different from the first. Founded by a folksy entrepreneur whose notions of thrift, industry, and the square deal were pure Ben Franklin, this company is not a tyrant but a servant. Passing along the gains of its brilliant distribution system to consumers, its farsighted managers have done nothing less than democratize the American dream. Its low prices are spurring productivity and helping win the fight against inflation. It is America's most admired company.

Weirdest part is, both these companies are named Wal-Mart Stores Inc.

The more America talks about Wal-Mart, it seems, the more polarized its image grows. Its executives are credited with the most expansive of visions and the meanest of intentions; its CEO is presumed to be in league with Lex Luthor *and* St. Francis of Assisi. It's confusing. Which should we believe in: good Wal-Mart or evil Wal-Mart? . . .

Where you stand on Wal-Mart, then, seems to depend on where you sit. If you're a consumer, Wal-Mart is good for you. If you're a wage earner, there's a good chance it's bad. If you're a Wal-Mart shareholder, you want the company to grow. If you're a citizen, you probably don't want it growing in your backyard. So, which one are you?

And that's the point: Chances are, you're more than one. And you may think each role is important. Yet America has elevated one above the rest. . . .

Wal-Mart swore fealty to the consumer and rode its coattails straight to the top. Now we have more than just a big retailer on our hands, though. We have a servant-king—one powerful enough to place everyone else in servitude to the consumer too. Gazing up at this new order, we wonder if our original choices made so much sense after all. . . .

Now Wal-Mart has been brought face to face with its own contradiction: Its promises of the good life threaten to ring increasingly hollow if it doesn't pay its workers enough to have that good life.

It's important that this debate continue. But in holding the mirror up to Wal-Mart, we would do well to turn it back on ourselves. Sam Walton created Wal-Mart. But we created it, too.

Source: From Jerry Useem, "Should We Admire Wal-Mart?" Fortune *(March 8, 2004): 118, 120. © 2004 Time Inc. All rights reserved.*

■ Organizational Decline

Prior to the mid-1970s, North American managers sped along a one-way street to growth. Fueled by strong demand, corporations mushroomed in size and diversity of operations as they achieved ever-greater market shares. In recent years, however, unsteady economic growth, resource shortages, mismanagement, global competition, and the end of the Cold War have taken their toll among industrial giants. Layoffs, retrenchments, cutbacks, and plant closings have become commonplace in the United States. During the last decade, the figures have been stunning, in both good times and bad. Consider these illustrative examples: Between 2000 and 2003, AT&T cut its employee payroll from 148,000 to 61,600. On its way to bankruptcy, United Airlines shed 44,000 employees. Canada's Nortel Networks went from 95,500 employees in 2000 to less than 33,000 in 2004.[45]

Turnaround specialists, hired to restore companies to health, have come to use terms such as *downsizing, demassing,* and *reengineering* when shrinking and breaking up companies. This organizational revolution points up a fundamental shortcoming of modern management theory and practice: We know a lot about striving for growth when times are good, but precious little about retreating when times are bad. Logic says what goes up must come down. According to a pair of experts on the subject, "Corporate performance almost always declines following a period of success."[46]

Figure 9.4 The Time Dimension of Organizational Effectiveness

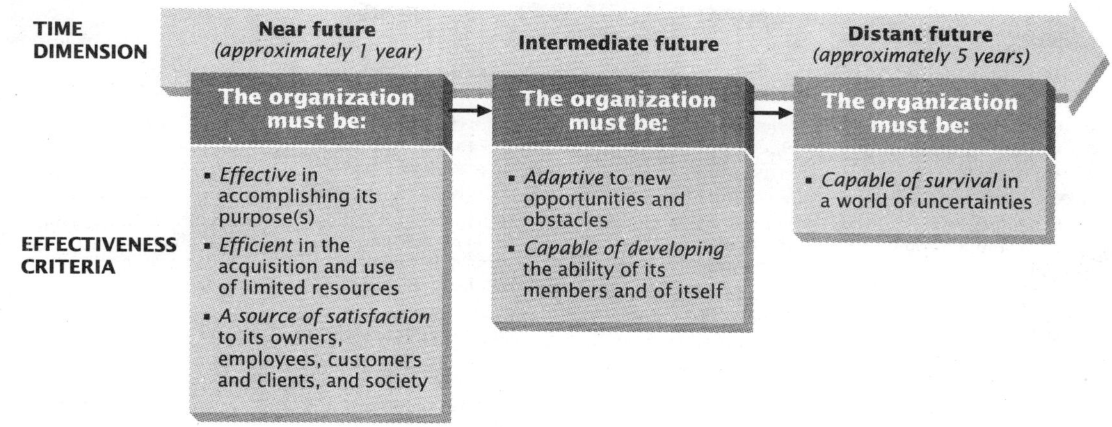

Source: *Adapted from James L. Gibson, John M. Ivancevich, and James H. Donnelly Jr.,* Organizations: Behavior, Structure, Processes, *5th ed. (Homewood, Ill.: Richard D. Irwin, Inc.), p. 37. © 1991.*

9e Back to the Opening Case

How does Southwest Airlines measure up to the six organizational effectiveness criteria in Figure 9.4? Is Southwest headed for decline? Explain.

These experts believe that *management complacency* is largely responsible for turning success into decline (see Figure 9.5). Once allowed to take root, complacency is hard to eliminate. According to Everett Stoub of Germany's Siemens, "Complacency often rules until the death rattle."[47] The remedy? Jay Desai, a management consultant who worked for Jack Welch at General Electric, urges companies to engage in "continuous reinvention."[48]

If allowed to persist, organizational decline can mean failure and bankruptcy. As the Enron debacle demonstrated, organizational decline can be remarkably swift and brutal. In January 2001, Enron was number 7 on the *Fortune* 500 list, it was number 22 on *Fortune*'s "One Hundred Best Companies" list, and its stock was selling for $83 a share. Just one year later, the company was bankrupt and its stock fetched a mere 67 cents a share before being delisted.[49] Worse yet, tens of thousands of people were left to deal with unemployment and worthless retirement accounts. Today's managers must be adept at expanding, remaking, and sometimes shrinking their organizations, as conditions warrant.

organizational decline: *organization is weakened by resource or demand restrictions and/or mismanagement*

Organizational decline is a weakened condition resulting from resource or demand restrictions and/or mismanagement. It typically involves a reduction in the size or scope of the organization.[50] For example, Lee Iacocca's turnaround team had to reduce Chrysler's size by 50 percent during its 1979–1981 brush with bankruptcy. Because that management era was preoccupied with growth, Iacocca had no textbook models, research base, or collection of proven techniques from which to learn. Thanks to recent interest in the management of organizational decline, an instructive body of theory, research, and practice is taking shape. Let us review that body of knowledge to better understand how managers can steer their organizations through the bad times that typically follow the good times.

7. EXPLAIN the role of complacency in organizational decline, and **DISCUSS** the ethics of downsizing.

Characteristics of Organizational Decline

What are the characteristics or indicators of an organization in decline? A partial answer to this question came from a survey of 3,406 administrators at 334 four-year colleges in the United States.[51] Kim Cameron and his colleagues used six years of revenue data to divide the schools into three categories: growing, stable, and declining.

Figure 9.5 Complacency Can Lead to Organizational Decline

They found that nine attributes (listed in Table 9.5) were statistically significant characteristics of organizational decline. The researchers were surprised to find that the same characteristics were associated with stable organizations, suggesting that all organizations are actually in one of two phases—either growth or decline. In short, an organization that has entered a period of stability has taken the first step toward decline.

Table 9.5 Nine Characteristics of Organizational Decline

Characteristic	Description
Centralization	Decision making is passed upward, participation decreases, control is emphasized.
No long-term planning	Crisis and short-term needs drive out strategic planning.
Innovation curtailed	No experimentation, risk aversion, and skepticism about noncore activities.
Scapegoating	Leaders are blamed for the pain and uncertainty.
Resistance to change	Conservatism and turf protection lead to rejection of new alternatives.
Turnover	The most competent leaders tend to leave first, causing leadership anemia.
Low morale	Few needs are met, and infighting is predominant.
Nonprioritized cuts	Attempts to ameliorate conflict lead to attempts to equalize cutbacks.
Conflict	Competition and infighting for control predominate when resources are scarce.

Source: *Characteristics and Descriptions excerpted from Kim S. Cameron, David A. Whetten, and Myung U. Kim, "Organizational Dysfunction of Decline,"* Academy of Management Journal, *30 (March 1987): 128. Reprinted by permission.*

■ **Decline Dilemmas.** Among the nine characteristics of organizational decline presented in Table 9.5, five particularly troublesome dilemmas emerge. First, the leaders most needed by the organization tend to be the first to leave. For example, Lucent Technologies lost many key players during its 2001–2002 slump.[52]

> *Management experts say multiple executive departures are often a sign a company is in trouble. When too many talented leaders leave at once, it can indicate dissension or a loss of faith, they say. "It could be the rats leaving the sinking ship," says Daniel Lyons, president of leadership development firm Team Concepts.*[53]

Second, control is achieved at the expense of employee participation and morale. Third, when management needs to take long-term risks, short-term thinking and risk avoidance prevail. Fourth, conflict intensifies when teamwork is most needed. Finally, at precisely the time when changes are required, resistance to change is the greatest. A prime example of this last organizational decline dilemma is Scott McNealy, CEO of Sun Microsystems, where sales slumped 48 percent in recent years:

> *It's a classic management tragedy, and to a striking degree the responsibility lies with the 49-year-old McNealy. His greatest strengths—the uncompromising determination, sharp-tongued irreverence, and unblushing idealism—turned out to be critical flaws. . . . As Sun's situation deteriorated, McNealy was bucking not just the counsel of outsiders but also that of his own lieutenants. After the tech industry went into its long slide in late 2000, virtually his entire management team . . . pleaded with McNealy to scale back his vision [of a quick economic recovery] and adjust to meaner times.*
>
> *Time and again, McNealy refused. . . . Preparing for the next upturn, he felt, was much more important than whittling expenses for a brief lull.*[54]

No surprise, then, that nearly a dozen of McNealy's top executives have left the firm. Organizational decline is a cycle that feeds on itself and only gets worse if left unmanaged.[55]

■ **Decline Is a Never-Ending Challenge.** More research is required in this important area.[56] Meanwhile, to avoid being caught by surprise, managers need to anticipate and counteract the characteristics of decline (again see Figure 9.5). Seeds of decline are sown during periods of success, when management is most likely to become overconfident, arrogant, and complacent. At these times, Peter Drucker recommends stirring things up.

> *One strategy is practically infallible: Refocus and change the organization when you are successful. When everything is going beautifully. When everybody says, "Don't rock the boat. If it ain't broke, don't fix it." At that point, let's hope, you have some character in the organization who is willing to be unpopular by saying, "Let's* improve *it." If you don't improve it, you will go downhill pretty fast.*[57]

Kaizen, the Japanese philosophy of continuous improvement, is the best weapon against organizational decline.[58] Just ask the people at Boeing, a leading manufacturer of commercial jet aircraft fighting to keep pace with Europe's Airbus. The president of Boeing's Commercial Airplane Group is clear about the challenge: "We are dedicated to not doing what IBM, Sears Roebuck, and General Motors have done—which is to get to the top, be the best, and then get fat and lazy."[59] Boeing is reinventing itself by shortening product development cycles, shrinking inventories, and training *every* employee to be a world-class competitor.

■ Downsizing: An Ethical Perspective

downsizing: *planned elimination of positions or jobs*

Downsizing has been defined simply as "the planned elimination of positions or jobs."[60] Mergers and acquisitions can prompt downsizing, especially when jobs and/or facilities become redundant. For example, when Bank of America merged with neighboring Security Pacific Bank, unnecessary branches had to be closed.[61]

A layoff by any other name (such as downsizing, rightsizing, etc.) is still a layoff. Here, city of Detroit employees who belong to the American Federation of State, County, and Municipal Employees union protest the Mayor's service cuts and layoffs. Managers in both public- and private-sector organizations need to hire carefully and manage skillfully in order to avoid treating employees like throw-away objects.

Whether due to decline or merger, the net result is the same—people lose their jobs. Ethical implications abound.

■ **Does Downsizing Work?** According to researchers, the short answer is *not nearly as well as expected.* An analysis of annual nationwide surveys by the American Management Association revealed the following:

> *. . . only 30 percent of companies implementing job cuts since 1990 reported an increase in worker productivity over the next year, and only 40 percent report an increase in subsequent years.*
>
> *Similarly, just 45 percent of job-cutters experienced a rise in operating profits . . . in either the year following a workforce reduction or over the longer term.*[62]

Another survey of 1,000 companies found that downsizings yielded the expected savings only 34 percent of the time. This was because the companies tended to go through cycles of overstaffing, laying off, overstaffing, laying off, and so on.[63] If this scenario reminds you of the unhealthful weight control strategy of overeating and then crash dieting, you understand the problem.

Critics remind us that layoffs are traumatic for *everyone*—those who lose their jobs, the managers who must decide who stays and who goes, the community, and the survivors.[64] Managers who see their employees as a commodity to be hired when times are good and fired when times are bad are rightfully criticized for being shortsighted and unethical. The pre-

9f You're Killin' Me!

A study of layoff survivors among municipal workers in Finland during a severe recession:

> *Those who survived the downsizing had to assume greater work loads. . . . The only difference in mortality was in cardiovascular deaths. Those in work units with the most downsizing suffered twice the death rate from heart attack and stroke.*

Source: Anne Underwood, "For a Happy Heart," Newsweek *(September 27, 2004): 54.*

QUESTIONS:

Based on this information and on what you have just read about the ethics of downsizing, what would you say to a top executive who is thinking about resorting to a big layoff?

ferred model today views employees as valuable human resources whose skills should be nurtured and who deserve career assistance in the event of a last-resort layoff.[65]

■ Making Layoffs a Last Resort. Managers who view employees as valuable human resources have several progressive alternatives to sudden, involuntary layoffs.

- ***Redeployment.*** Displaced employees are retrained and/or transferred. This approach amounts to a recycling program for human resources.
- ***Downgrading.*** To prevent a layoff, the organization moves displaced employees to unstaffed, lower-level jobs, avoiding pay cuts if possible.[66]
- ***Work sharing.*** Instead of laying off a portion of its workforce, management divides the available work among all employees, who take proportional cuts in hours and pay. This approach has been called "share the gain, share the pain."[67]
- ***Job banks.*** Work that would normally be outsourced is kept in-house for employees caught in a downturn. For example, Harman International Industries, the Washington, D.C., maker of JBL and Infinity audio systems, calls its job bank program Off-Line Enterprises (OLÉ). At any time, a total of 15 to 20 jobs are available through OLÉ in four general categories:
  1. Manufacturing products usually purchased from external suppliers
  2. Providing services such as security, which usually is contracted out
  3. Converting waste by-products into marketable products, such as making clocks from scrap wood
  4. Training and employing plant employees in Harman's nearby retail outlet[68]
- ***Employee sharing.*** This unique approach to redeployment involves finding laid-off employees temporary jobs with another company. For example, consider this situation reported in 2001: "About 12 employees at MLT Vacations' call center in Minot, N. D., are working on loan to Sykes, a computer support firm in the area. The MLT employees work several months for Sykes, which pays MLT for the use of its workers."[69]
- ***Voluntary early retirement and voluntary layoffs ("Buyouts").*** Employees are induced to leave the organization with offers of accelerated retirement benefits, severance pay, bonuses, and/or prepaid health insurance. For example, in 2004, amid hard times in the airline industry, Southwest Airlines "offered voluntary buyout packages, including cash, health care and travel, to [33,000] employees who . . . [had] worked for the low-cost carrier at least a year."[70] But this tactic can backfire if valued employees leave and poor performers stay. For example, "Eastman Kodak had to scurry to refill the jobs of 2,000 of the 8,300 workers who unexpectedly took its 1991 buyout offer."[71]
- ***Early warning of facility closings.*** Imagine the pain of an unsuspecting employee who goes to work only to find a permanently locked gate. Several state legislatures in the United States have passed laws requiring companies to provide employees with some sort of advance warning of factory or office closings.[72] The Worker Adjustment and Retraining Notification Act, a federal law that went into effect in 1989, requires U.S. companies with 100 or more employees to give 60 days' notice of a closing or layoff.[73] Early warnings give displaced employees time to prepare financially and emotionally for a job change.
- ***Outplacement.*** The practice of **outplacement** involves helping laid-off workers polish their job-seeking skills to increase their chances of finding suitable employment promptly.[74] Although this ethical practice can be costly, a recent survey of 1,200 human resource (HR) managers in North America highlighted a number of positive outcomes:

  > *[It] found that 78 percent believe that outplacement consulting and career transition services improve the organization's internal and external image. Seventy-two percent said these services help reduce litigation.*

outplacement: *the ethical practice of helping displaced employees find new jobs*

> ### 9g Loyalty Is a Two-Way Street
>
> Dan DiMicco, CEO of Nucor, a steel company with a no-layoff policy:
>
> *"How can you build loyalty when you pat people on the back when times are good and when times are tough, you show them the door?"*
>
> Northwestern Mutual:
>
> *The life insurer hasn't laid off a single person in 145 years.*
>
> *Sources: Stephanie Armour, "Some Companies Choose No-Layoff Policy,"* USA Today *(December 17, 2001): 1B; and Robert Levering and Milton Moskowitz, "The 100 Best Companies to Work For,"* Fortune *(January 12, 2004): 76.*
>
> **QUESTION:**
>
> **Why aren't corporate no-layoff policies more common?**

Two-thirds of HR leaders said outplacement assistance reduces stress on managers responsible for implementing organizational changes; nearly as many HR professionals said these services provide a good return on investment; and 59 percent said outplacement efforts improve the morale of remaining employees.[75]

- ***Helping layoff survivors.*** The needs of these people have traditionally been ignored because, after all, they are the "lucky ones who still have their jobs." But research indicates that layoff survivors are stressed by overwork, uncertainty about future layoffs, and guilt over not suffering the same fate as their friends. Psychological and career counseling and retraining are appropriate and ethical options.[76]

Our discussions of organizational structure, effectiveness, and decline teach valuable lessons about the functioning of modern organizations. But the picture is not complete. A more subtle yet influential dimension of organizations remains to be explored. Managers who ignore this key dimension of organizations have little chance of success. So let's turn our attention to the interesting topic of organizational cultures to see what makes otherwise static structures come alive.

Organizational Cultures

organizational culture: *shared values, beliefs, and language that create a common identity and sense of community*

The notion of organizational culture is rooted in cultural anthropology.[77] **Organizational culture** is the collection of shared (stated or implied) beliefs, values, rituals, stories, myths, and specialized language that foster a feeling of community among organization members.[78] Culture, although based largely on taken-for-granted or "invisible" factors, exerts a potent influence on behavior. For example, a six-year study of more than 900 newly hired college graduates found significantly lower turnover among those who joined public accounting firms with cultures emphasizing respect for people and teamwork. New hires working for accounting firms whose cultures emphasized detail, stability, and innovation tended to quit 14 months sooner than their counterparts in the more people-friendly organizations. According to the researcher's estimate, the companies with people-friendly cultures saved $6 million in human resources expenses because of lower turnover rates.[79]

Unfortunately, there is a dark side to organizational cultures as well. Dysfunctional cultures anchored to irresponsible values and supportive of (or blind to) unethical conduct have been blamed for the collapse of Enron, Arthur Andersen, and WorldCom and for the crash of NASA's space shuttle *Columbia* that took the lives of its seven crew members.[80] The problem of "groupthink," discussed in Chapter 14, is associated with cultural misdirection. Today's managers need to understand the subtle yet powerful influence of organizational culture and appropriately manage it.

Some call organizational (or corporate) culture the "social glue" that binds an organization's members together. Accordingly, this final section binds together all we have said about organizations in this chapter. Without an appreciation for the cultural aspect, an organization is just a meaningless collection of charts, tasks, and people. An anthropologist-turned-manager offered these cautionary words:

> *Corporate culture is not an ideological gimmick to be imposed from above by management or management consulting firms but a stubborn fact of human social organization that can scuttle the best of corporate plans if not taken into account.*[81]

Characteristics of Organizational Cultures

Given the number of variables involved, organizational cultures can vary widely from one organization to the next. Even so, authorities on the subject have identified six characteristics that most organizational cultures exhibit.[82] Let us briefly examine these common characteristics to gain a fuller understanding of organizational cultures.

8. DESCRIBE at least three characteristics of organizational cultures, and **EXPLAIN** the cultural significance of stories.

1. ***Collective.*** Organizational cultures are *social* entities. An individual may exert a cultural influence, but it takes collective agreement and action for an organization's culture to assume a life of its own. Organizational cultures are truly synergistic (1 + 1 = 3). Jeffrey R. Immelt offered this companywide perspective soon after becoming the new head of General Electric: "We run a multibusiness company with common cultures, with common management . . . where the whole is always greater than the sum of its parts. Culture counts."[83]
2. ***Emotionally charged.*** People tend to find their organization's culture a comforting security blanket that enables them to deal with (or sometimes mask) their insecurities and uncertainties. Not surprisingly, people can develop a strong emotional attachment to their cultural security blanket. They will fight to protect it, often refusing to question its basic values. Corporate mergers often get bogged down in culture conflicts.[84]
3. ***Historically based.*** Shared experiences, over extended periods of time, bind groups of people together. We tend to identify with those who have had similar life experiences. Trust and loyalty, two key components of culture, are earned by consistently demonstrating predictable patterns of words and actions.
4. ***Inherently symbolic.*** Actions often speak louder than words. Memorable symbolic actions are the lifeblood of organizational culture. For instance, consider what has been going on at Procter & Gamble:

Imagine you're applying for a job at Internet search company Ask Jeeves. You show up for your interview at the firm's Oakland, California, headquarters and you encounter this lively scene in the lunchroom. What does it tell you about the company's culture, the "feel" of the place?

> *From the outside, Procter & Gamble Co's Cincinnati headquarters looks unchanged. But on the top floor—the haunt of P&G's top brass for 50 years—there's a major overhaul under way. Wood paneling and an executive cafeteria are making way for a training center that will bring employees from around the world within earshot of CEO Alan G. Lafley. "I have made a lot of symbolic, very physical changes so people understand we are in the business of leading change," says Lafley.*[85]

The changes at P&G symbolically tell top executives to focus less on power and privilege and more on employee development and open communication.

5. ***Dynamic.*** In the long term, organizational cultures promote predictability, conformity, and stability. Just beneath this apparently stable surface, however, change boils as people struggle to communicate and comprehend subtle cultural clues. A management trainee who calls the president by her first name after being invited to do so may be embarrassed to learn later that "no one actually calls the president by her first name, even if she asks you to."
6. ***Inherently fuzzy.*** Ambiguity, contradictions, and multiple meanings are fundamental to organizational cultures. Just as a photographer cannot capture your typical busy day in a single snapshot, it takes intense and prolonged observation to capture the essence of an organization's culture.

Forms and Consequences of Organizational Cultures

Figure 9.6 lists major forms and consequences of organizational cultures. To the extent that people in an organization share symbols, a common language, stories, and practices, they will tend to experience the four consequences. The degree of sharing and the intensity of the consequences determine whether the organization's culture is strong or weak.

organizational values: *shared beliefs about what the organization stands for*

Shared values are a pivotal factor. Unlike instrumental and terminal values, discussed in Chapter 5 as *personal* beliefs, **organizational values** are *shared* beliefs about what the organization stands for.[86] Shared values, when deeply embedded in the organization's culture, become the equivalent of its DNA. Just as DNA in the cells of our bodies determines who we are, shared values define an organization. For example, Houston-based Bridgeway Funds stood out as a positive role model in the recent mutual fund trading scandal. Founder and president John Montgomery explained why:

Figure 9.6 Forms and Consequences of Organizational Cultures

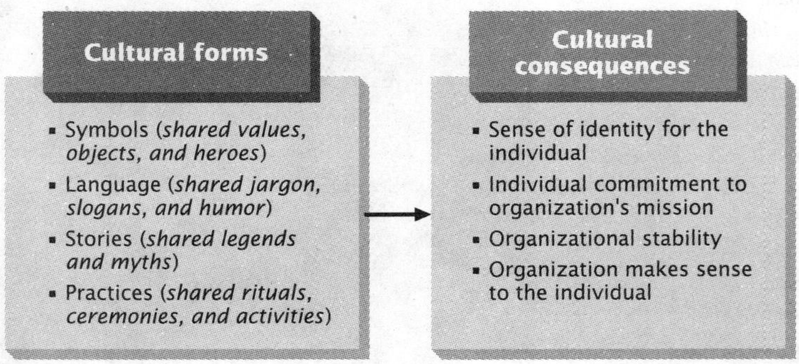

Source: *Forms adapted from Harrison M. Trice and Janice M. Beyer,* The Cultures of Work Organizations *(Englewood Cliffs, N.J.: Prentice-Hall, 1993), pp. 77–128. Consequences adapted from Linda Smircich, "Concepts of Culture and Organizational Analysis,"* Administrative Science Quarterly, *28 (September 1983): 339–358.*

The biggest safeguard is a very strong culture . . . of integrity. We have four business values we've had from day one, in order: integrity, investment performance, low cost and service. Another guideline we have is answering the question, "What's in the long-term interest of current shareholders?"[87]

Not surprisingly, Bridgeway does not own any tobacco stocks, and half the firm's profits are donated to charity.

The Organizational Socialization Process

organizational socialization: *process of transforming outsiders into accepted insiders*

Organizational socialization is the process through which outsiders are transformed into accepted insiders.[88] In effect, the socialization process helps newcomers make sense of their new situation and integrate into the organization's culture.

The culture asserts itself when the taken-for-granted cultural assumptions are in some way violated by the uninitiated and provoke a response. As the uninitiated bump into one after another taken-for-granted assumption, more acculturated employees respond in a variety of ways (tell stories, offer advice, ridicule, lecture, shun, and so forth) that serve to mold the way in which the newcomer thinks about his or her role and about "how things are done around here."[89]

Orientations. *Orientation programs*—in which newly hired employees learn about their organization's history, culture, competitive realities, and compensation and benefits—are an important first step in the socialization process. Too often today, however, orientations are hurried or nonexistent, and new employees are left to "sink or swim." This is a big mistake, according to workplace research:

One study at Corning Glass Works (in Corning, New York) found that new employees who went through a structured orientation program were 69 percent more likely to be with the company after three years than those who were left on their own to sort out the job. A similar two-year study at Texas Instruments concluded that employees who had been carefully oriented to both the company and their jobs reached full productivity two months sooner than those who weren't.[90]

Storytelling. *Stories* deserve special attention here because, as indicated in Figure 9.6, they are a central feature of organizational socialization and culture. Company stories about heroic or inspiring deeds let newcomers know what "really counts."[91] For example, 3M's eleventh commandment—"Thou shalt not kill a new product idea"—has been ingrained in new employees through one inspiring story about the employee who invented transparent cellophane tape.

According to the story, an employee accidentally discovered the tape but was unable to get his superiors to buy the idea. Marketing studies predicted a relatively small demand for the new material. Undaunted, the employee found a way to sneak into the board room and tape down the minutes of board members with his transparent tape. The board was impressed enough with the novelty to give it a try and experienced incredible success.[92]

Upon hearing this story, a 3M newcomer has believable, concrete evidence that innovation and

9h An American Indian Art Form Goes Corporate Mainstream

As a child, retired Citgo CEO David Tippeconnic sat on the porch of his Oklahoma farmhouse and listened to the stories of his Comanche elders.

Tippeconnic, 64, recalls a lesson handed down to his grandfather, to his father and then to himself that he says can be summarized: "Don't trust a red-faced white man."

In business, Tippeconnic has interacted primarily with white men. But he's interpreted the boyhood lesson to mean that he should avoid dealing with anyone, of any race, who angers easily, and that he should maintain his cool. It has served him well. . . .

Companies in their never-rest quest for the hot strategy have inadvertently backed into the art of Indian storytelling.

Source: Del Jones, "Indian Art of Storytelling Seeps into Boardroom," USA Today *(September 20, 2004): 1B.*

QUESTIONS:

What family stories that were passed on to you during your childhood have served you well (or not so well) in life? Why are stories such a powerful form of communication?

persistence pay off at 3M. It has been said that stories are "social roadmaps" for employees, telling them where to go and where not to go and what will happen when they get there. Moreover, stories are remembered longer than abstract facts or rules and regulations. How many times have you recalled a professor's colorful story but forgotten the rest of the lecture?

Strengthening Organizational Cultures

Given the inherent fuzziness of organizational cultures, how can managers identify cultural weak spots that need improvement? Symptoms of a weak organizational culture include the following:

- ***Inward focus.*** Has internal politics become more important than real-world problems and the marketplace?
- ***Morale problems.*** Are there chronic unhappiness and high turnover?
- ***Fragmentation/inconsistency.*** Is there a lack of "fit" in the way people behave, communicate, and perceive problems and opportunities?
- ***Ingrown subcultures.*** Is there a lack of communication among subunits?
- ***Warfare among subcultures.*** Has constructive competition given way to destructive conflict?
- ***Subculture elitism.*** Have organizational units become exclusive "clubs" with restricted entry? Have subcultural values become more important than the organization's values?[93]

9i Back to the Opening Case

What are the practical business implications of a weakened organizational culture at Southwest Airlines?

Evidence of these symptoms may encourage a potential recruit to look elsewhere. Each of these symptoms of a weak organizational culture can be a formidable barrier to organizational effectiveness. Organizations with strong cultures do a good job of avoiding these symptoms.[94]

SUMMARY

1. Organizations need to be understood and intelligently managed because they are an ever-present feature of modern life. Whatever their purpose, all organizations exhibit four characteristics: (1) coordination of effort, (2) common goal or purpose, (3) division of labor, and (4) hierarchy of authority. If even one of these characteristics is absent, an organization does not exist. One useful way of classifying organizations is by their intended purpose. Organizations can be classified as business, nonprofit service, mutual-benefit, or commonweal organizations.
2. Organization charts are helpful visual aids for managers. Representing the organization's structural skeleton, organization charts delineate vertical hierarchy and horizontal specialization. Vertical hierarchy is the so-called chain of command. Horizontal specialization involves the division of labor.
3. There are both traditional and modern views of organizations. Traditionalists such as Fayol, Taylor, and Weber subscribed to closed-system thinking and ignored the impact of environmental forces. Modern organization theorists tend to prefer open-system thinking because it realistically incorporates organizations' interdependence with their environment. Early management writers proposed tightly controlled, authoritarian organizations. Max Weber, a German sociologist, applied the label *bureaucracy* to his formula for the most rationally efficient type of organization. When bureaucratic characteristics, which are present in all organizations, are carried to an extreme, however, efficiency gives way to inefficiency. Chester I. Barnard's acceptance theory of authority and growing environmental complexity and uncertainty questioned traditional organization theory.
4. Open-system thinking became a promising alternative because it was useful in explaining the necessity of creating flexible and adaptable, rather than rigid, organizations. Although the analogy between natural systems and human social systems (organizations) is imperfect, there are important parallels. Organizations, like all open systems, are unique because of their (1) interaction with the environment, (2) synergy, (3) dynamic equilibrium, and (4) equifinality. In open-system terms, business organizations are made up of interdependent technical, boundary-spanning, and managerial subsystems.
5. Harvard's David A. Garvin characterizes learning organizations as those capable of turning new ideas

into improved performance. Five skills required to do this are (1) solving problems, (2) experimenting, (3) learning from organizational experience and history, (4) learning from others, and (5) transferring and implementing knowledge for improved performance.

6. Because there is no one criterion for organizational effectiveness, for-profit as well as nonprofit organizations need to satisfy different effectiveness criteria in the near, intermediate, and distant future. In the near term, effective organizations accomplish their purposes, are efficient, and are a source of satisfaction to all stakehholders. They are adaptive and developing in the intermediate term. Ultimately, in the long term, effective organizations survive.

7. The management of organizational decline has only recently received the attention it deserves. Decline is often attributable to managerial complacency. Decline is characterized by interlocking dilemmas that foster organizational self-destruction. To avoid decline as much as possible, or at least lessen its frequency, organizations should adopt preventive safeguards that counteract complacency. Continuous improvement is the primary tool for fighting decline. Downsizing tends to yield disappointing results. Among the ethical alternatives to layoffs are redeployment and work sharing.

8. Organizational culture is the "social glue" binding people together through shared symbols, language, stories, and practices. Organizational cultures can commonly be characterized as collective, emotionally charged, historically based, inherently symbolic, dynamic, and inherently fuzzy (or ambiguous). Diverse outsiders are transformed into accepted insiders through the process of organizational socialization. Orientations and stories are powerful and lasting socialization techniques. Systematic observation can reveal symptoms of a weak organizational culture.

TERMS TO UNDERSTAND

- Organization, p. 249
- Authority, p. 250
- Commonweal organization, p. 253
- Organization chart, p. 253
- Bureaucracy, p. 256
- Acceptance theory of authority, p. 258
- Dynamic equilibrium, p. 260
- Equifinality, p. 260
- Learning organization, p. 262
- Organizational effectiveness, p. 263
- Organizational decline, p. 265
- Downsizing, p. 267
- Outplacement, p. 269
- Organizational culture, p. 270
- Organizational values, p. 272
- Organizational socialization, p. 273

SKILLS & TOOLS

How to Build Your Organization's Learning Capability

"**Learning capability** represents the capacity of managers within an organization to generate and generalize ideas with *impact*."

Managerial Actions to Ensure Learning Capability

Step 1: Build a commitment to learning capability.

- Make learning a visible and central element of the strategic intent.
- Invest in learning.
- Publicly talk about learning.
- Measure, benchmark, and track learning.
- Create symbols of learning.

Step 2: Work to generate ideas with impact.

- Continuous improvement (improve it).
- Competence acquisition (buy or hire it).
- Experimentation (try it).
- Boundary spanning (adapt it).

Step 3: Work to generalize ideas with impact.

- Teach leaders to coach.
- Teach leaders to facilitate.
- Select leaders who teach.
- Select leaders with vision.
- Walk the talk.

Source: *Reprinted from* Organizational Dynamics, *Autumn 1993, Dave Ulrich, Todd Jick, and Mary Ann Von Glinow, "High-Impact Learning: Building and Diffusing Learning Capability," Copyright 1993, with permission from Elsevier.*

HANDS-ON EXERCISE

An Organizational X Ray: Capturing the "Feel" of an Organization's Culture

Instructions:

Working either alone or as part of a team, select an organization you are personally familiar with (such as your college or university or a place of present or past employment). Alternatively, you may choose to interview someone about an organization of their choice. The key is to capture a knowledgeable "insider's" perspective. Complete Parts A and B of this exercise with your target organization in mind. (*Notes:* This instrument is for instructional purposes only because it has not been scientifically validated. Also, you may want to disguise the organization in any class discussion if your cultural profile could offend someone or is strongly negative.)

Part A

For each of the following adjective pairs, circle the number that best describes the "feel" of the organization, and then calculate a sum total.

Rejecting	1······2······3······4······5······6······7······8······9······10	Accepting
Destructive	1······2······3······4······5······6······7······8······9······10	Constructive
Uncomfortable	1······2······3······4······5······6······7······8······9······10	Comfortable
Unfair	1······2······3······4······5······6······7······8······9······10	Fair
Unsupportive	1······2······3······4······5······6······7······8······9······10	Supportive
Demeaning	1······2······3······4······5······6······7······8······9······10	Empowering
Dishonest	1······2······3······4······5······6······7······8······9······10	Honest
Dull, boring	1······2······3······4······5······6······7······8······9······10	Challenging
Declining	1······2······3······4······5······6······7······8······9······10	Improving
Untrustworthy	1······2······3······4······5······6······7······8······9······10	Trustworthy
		Total score = _____

Interpretive scale

1. 10–39 = Run for your life!
2. 40–69 = Needs a culture transplant.
3. 70–100 = Warm and fuzzy!

Part B

Write a brief statement for each of the following:

1. What are the organization's key values (as enacted, not simply as written or stated)?
2. What story (or stories) best conveys what the organization is "really" like?
3. Does the organization have legends or heroes that strongly influence how things are done? Describe.
4. What traditions, practices, or symbols make the organization's culture stronger?
5. Does the organization have a larger-than-life reputation or mythology? Explain.

For Consideration/Discussion

1. Is the organization's culture strong or weak? How can you tell?
2. Is the organization's culture people-friendly? Explain.
3. Does the strength (or weakness) of the culture help explain why the organization is thriving (or suffering)? Explain.
4. Will the organization's culture attract or repel high-quality job applicants? Explain.
5. What can or should be done to improve the organization's culture?

INTERNET EXERCISES

1. **Earthlink's down-to-earth corporate values:** Internet service provider Earthlink has published a list of its corporate values. You can view them at **www.earthlink.com** by scrolling to the bottom of the home page and clicking on "About Us." Select "Our Values" and then read the single-page proclamation of the company's mission, purpose, and core values and beliefs.

Learning Points: 1. What do you like or dislike about these values? 2. Is this type of statement of corporate values a good way to improve individual and company performance, or just a useful public relations ploy? Explain. 3. Does reading this list make you more or less likely to be an Earthlink customer and/or to apply for a job there? Explain. 4. What do Earthlink's managers need to do to make the corporate values become business-as-usual?

2. **Patagonia knows the power of a good story:** As discussed in this chapter, stories can be a powerful way to socialize newcomers and reinforce the organization's core cultural values. For a really interesting story about the founding and growth of a unique company, go to **www.patagonia.com** and select "Company History" under the heading "Our Culture." Read "Patagonia Company History." Remember to print a copy if this exercise will be discussed in class.

   Learning Points: 1. What specific organizational values are communicated by this story? 2. How would reading this story help socialize a new Patagonia employee? 3. Does this story make you want to work for Patagonia and/or buy its products? Explain. 4. Why is a well-told story such a powerful cultural tool?

3. **Check it out:** Want to learn more about organizational cultures? Go to **www.fastcompany.com/backissues**. In the blank search box, type "corporate culture" and hit the "Search" button. You will find several informative and interesting *Fast Company* magazine articles involving organizational cultures. Who knows, you might even find a great place to work!

For updates to these exercises, visit our Web site (**http://business.college.hmco.com/students/** and select Kreitner, *Management,* 10e).

CLOSING CASE

Change Management @ICICI

"What role am I supposed to play in this ever-changing entity? Has anyone worked out the basis on which roles are being allocated today?"

- A middle level ICICI manager, in 1998.

"We do put people under stress by raising the bar constantly. That is the only way to ensure that performers lead the change process."

- K.V. Kamath, MD & CEO, ICICI, in 1998.

The Change Leader

In May 1996, K.V. Kamath (Kamath) replaced Narayan Vaghul (Vaghul), CEO of India's leading financial services company Industrial Credit and Investment Corporation of India (ICICI). Immediately after taking charge, Kamath introduced massive changes in the organizational structure and the emphasis of the organization changed - from a development bank[1] mode to that of a market-driven financial conglomerate.

Kamath's moves were prompted by his decision to create new divisions to tap new markets and to introduce flexibility in the organization to increase its ability to respond to market changes. Necessitated because of the organization's new-found aim of becoming a financial powerhouse, the large-scale changes caused enormous tension within the organization. The systems within the company soon were in a state of stress. Employees were finding the changes unacceptable as learning new skills and adapting to the process orientation was proving difficult.

The changes also brought in a lot of confusion among the employees, with media reports frequently carrying quotes from disgruntled ICICI employees. According to analysts, a large section of employees began feeling alienated.

The discontentment among employees further increased, when Kamath formed specialist groups within ICICI like the 'structured projects' and 'infrastructure' group.

Doubts were soon raised regarding whether Kamath had gone 'too fast too soon,' and more importantly, whether he would be able to steer the employees and the organization through the changes he had initiated.

Background Note

ICICI was established by the Government of India in 1955 as a public limited company to promote industrial development in India. The major institutional shareholders were the Unit Trust of India (UTI), the Life Insurance Corporation of India (LIC) and the General Insurance Corporation of India (GIC) and its subsidiaries. The equity of the corporation was supplemented by

[1] *Developmental Financial Institutions were set up with principal objective of providing term finance for fixed asset formation in Industry.*

borrowings from the Government of India, the World Bank, the Development Loan Fund (now merged with the Agency for International Development), Kreditanstalt fur Wiederaufbau (an agency of the Government of Germany), the UK government and the Industrial Development Bank of India (IDBI).

The basic objectives of the ICICI were to

- assist in creation, expansion and modernization of enterprises
- encourage and promote the participation of private capital, both internal and external
- take up the ownership of industrial investment; and
- expand the investment markets.

Since the mid 1980s, ICICI diversified rapidly into areas like merchant banking and retailing. In 1987, ICICI co-promoted India's first credit rating agency, Credit Rating and Information Services of India Limited (CRISIL), to rate debt obligations of Indian companies. In 1988, ICICI promoted India's first venture capital company - Technology Development and Information Company of India Limited (TDICI) - to provide venture capital for indigenous technology-oriented ventures.

In the 1990s, ICICI diversified into different forms of asset financing such as leasing, asset credit and deferred credit, as well as financing for non-project activities. In 1991, ICICI and the Unit Trust of India set up India's first screen-based securities market, the Over-The-Counter Exchange of India (OTCEI). In 1992 ICICI tied up with J P Morgan of the US to form an investment banking company, ICICI Securities Limited.

In line with its vision of becoming a universal bank, ICICI restructured its business based on the recommendations of consultants McKinsey & Co in 1998. In the late 1990s, ICICI concentrated on building up its retail business through acquisitions and mergers. It took over ITC Classic, Anagram Finance and merged the Shipping Credit Investment Corporation of India (SCICI) with itself. ICICI also entered the insurance business with Prudential plc of UK.

ICICI was reported to be one of the few Indian companies known for its quick responsiveness to the changing circumstances. While its development bank counterpart IDBI was reportedly not doing very well in late 2001, ICICI had major plans of expanding on the anvil. This was expected to bring with it further challenges as well as potential change management issues. However, the organization did not seem to be much perturbed by this, considering that it had successfully managed to handle the employee unrest following Kamath's appointment.

Change Challenges - Part I

ICICI was a part of the club of developmental finance institutions (DFIs - ICICI, IDBI and IFCI) who were the sole providers of long-term funds to the Indian industry. If the requirement was large, all three pooled in the money. However, the deregulation beginning in the early 1990s, allowed Indian corporates' to raise long-term funds abroad, putting an end to the DFI monopoly. The government also stopped giving DFIs subsidized funds. Eventually in 1997, the practice of consortium lending by DFIs was phased out.

It was amidst this newfound independent status that Kamath, who had been away from ICICI for eight years working abroad[2], returned to the helm. At this point of time, ICICI had limited expertise, with its key activity being the disbursement of eight-year loans to big clients like Reliance Industries and Telco through its nine zonal offices. In effect, the company had one basic product, and a customer orientation, which was largely regional in nature.

Kamath, having seen the changes occurring in the financial sector abroad, wanted ICICI to become a one-stop shop for financial services. He realized that in the deregulated environment ICICI was neither a low-cost player nor was it a differentiator in terms of customer service. The Indian commercial banks' cost of funds was much lower, and the foreign banks were much more savvy when it came to understanding customer needs and developing solutions. Kamath identified the main problem as the company's ignorance regarding the nuances of lending practices in newly opened sectors like infrastructure.

The change program was initiated within the organization, the first move being the creation of the 'infrastructure group (IIG),' 'oil & gas group (O&G),' 'planning and treasury department (PTD)' and the 'structured products group (SPG)', as the lending practices were quite different for all of these. Kamath picked up people from various departments, who he was told were good, for these groups.

The approach towards creating these new skill sets, however, led to one unintended consequence. As these new groups took on the key tasks, a majority of the work, along with a lot of good talent, shifted to the corporate center. While the zonal offices continued to do the same work - disbursing loans to corporates in the same region - their importance within the organization seemed to have diminished. An ex-employee remarked, "The way to get noticed inside ICICI after 1996 has been to attach yourself to people who were heading these (IIG, PTD, SPG, O&G) departments. These groups were seen as the thrust areas and if you worked in the zones it was difficult to be noticed."

[2] *Non performing Assets (NPAs) are loans on which interest payments have been due for more than one quarter (3 months) and in the case of monthly installments have been due for more than 3 installments.*

Refuting this, Kamath remarked, "This may be said by people who did not make it. And there will always be such people." Some of the people who did not fit in this set-up were quick to leave the organization. However, this was just the beginning of change-resistance at ICICI.

Another change management problem surfaced as a result of ICICI's decision to focus its operations much more sharply around its customers. In the system prevailing, if a client had three different requirements from ICICI[3], he had to approach the relevant departments separately. The process was time consuming, and there was a danger that the client would take a portion of that business elsewhere. To tackle this problem, ICICI set up three new departments: major client group (MCG), growth client group (GCG) and personal finance group. Now, the customer talked only to his representative in MCG or GCG. And these representatives in turn found out which ICICI department could do the job.

Though the customers seemed to be happy about this new arrangement, people within the organization found it unacceptable. In the major client group, a staff of about 30-40 people handled the needs of the top 100 customers of ICICI. On the other hand, about 60 people manned the growth client group, which looked after the needs of mid-size companies. Obviously, the bigger clients required more diverse kinds of services. So working in MCG offered better exposure and bigger orders. The net effect was that the MCG executive ended up doing more business than the GCG executive. A middle-level manager at ICICI commented, "The bosses may call it handling growth clients but the GCG manager is actually chasing non-performing assets (NPA)[4] and Board of Industrial and Financial Restructuring (BIFR)[5] cases."

Kamath was quick to deny this allegation as well, "Just because somebody is within the MCG does not guarantee him success. And these assignments are not permanent. Today's MCG man could easily be tomorrow's GCG person and vice-versa."

Complaints against these changes were put in continuously and ICICI was blamed for not putting in adequate systems in place to develop the right people. The manner, which ICICI recognized an individual's efforts - the feedback process - was also questioned. A manager remarked, "Last year the bonuses varied from Rs 30,000 to Rs 250,000 depending on the performance. In many cases the appraisal scores were same but the bonus amount was not. And we were not told why."

With Kamath's stated objective to make ICICI provide almost every financial service, separating the customer service people from the product development groups was another problem area. In the current scheme of things, an MCG or GCG person acted as a clients' representative inside ICICI.

The MCG or GCG person understood the client's need and got the relevant internal skill department to develop a solution. Unlike foreign banks, there were no demarcations between these internal skill groups and client service person. (Demarcation helped in preventing an internal skills person from cannibalizing business being developed by the client service group.) With no such systems in place at ICICI, this distorted the compensation packages between the competing divisions.

While Kamath's comments in the media seemed to dismiss many of the employee complaints, ICICI was in fact, putting in place a host of measures to check this unrest. One of the first initiatives was regarding imparting new skills to existing employees. Training programmes and seminars were conducted for around 257 officers by external agencies, covering different areas.

In addition, in-house training programmes were conducted in Pune and Mumbai. During 1995-96, around 35 officers were nominated for overseas training programmes organized by universities in the US and Europe. ICICI also introduced a two-year Graduates' Management Training Programme (GMTP) for officers in the Junior Management grades.

Along with the training to the employees, management also took steps to set right the reward system. To avoid the negative impact of profit center approach, wherein pressure to show profits might affect standards of integrity within an organization, management ensured that rewards were related to group performance and not individual performances. To reward individual star performers, the method of selecting a star performer was made transparent. This made it clear that there would be closer relationship between performance and reward.

However, it was reported that pressure on accountability triggered off some levels of anxiety within ICICI which resulted in a lot of stress in human relationships. Dismissing reports of upsetting people, Kamath said, 'much of the restructuring plan has come from the bottom.'

ICICI also reviewed the compensation structure in place. Two types of remuneration were considered - a contract basis which would attract risk-takers and a tenure-based compensation which would be appealing

3. *The Board for Industrial and Financial Reconstruction (BIFR) is responsible for the revival of companies declared sick. A company is declared sick if it has incurred losses continuously for 3 years and its networth turns negative.*

4. *Though Kamath had started his career with ICICI, he had left the bank to join Asian Development Bank (ADB) in Manila in 1988.*

5. *For instance, an eight-year loan, merger and acquisition advice and working capital requirements.*

to employees who wanted security. Kamath accepted that ICICI had been a bit slow on completing the employee feedback process. Soon, a 360-degree appraisal system was put in place, whereby an individual was assessed by his peers, seniors and subordinates. As a result of the above measures, the employee unrest gradually gave way to a much more relaxed atmosphere within the company.

By 2000, ICICI had emerged as the second largest financial institution in India with assets worth Rs 582 billion. The company had eight subsidiaries providing various financial services and was present in almost all the areas of financial services: medium and long term lending, investment and commercial banking, venture capital financing, consultancy and advisory services, debenture trusteeship and custodial services.

Change Challenges - Part II

ICICI had to face change resistance once again in December 2000, when ICICI Bank was merged with Bank of Madura (BoM). Though ICICI Bank was nearly three times the size of BoM, its staff strength was only 1,400 as against BoM's 2,500. Half of BoM's personnel were clerks and around 350 were subordinate staff.

There were large differences in profiles, grades, designations and salaries of personnel in the two entities. It was also reported that there was uneasiness among the staff of BoM as they felt that ICICI would push up the productivity per employee, to match the levels of ICICI. BoM employees feared that their positions would come in for a closer scrutiny. They were not sure whether the rural branches would continue or not as ICICI's business was largely urban-oriented.

The apprehensions of the BoM employees seemed to be justified as the working culture at ICICI and BoM were quite different and the emphasis of the respective management was also different. While BoM management concentrated on the overall profitability of the Bank, ICICI management turned all its departments into individual profit centers and bonus for employees was given on the performance of individual profit center rather than profits of whole organization.

ICICI not only put in place a host of measures to technologically upgrade the BoM branches to ICICI's standards, but also paid special attention to facilitate a smooth cultural integration. The company appointed consultants Hewitt Associates to help in working out a uniform compensation and work culture and to take care of any change in management problems.

ICICI conducted an employee behavioral pattern study to assess the various fears and apprehensions that employees typically went through during a merger. (Refer Table I).

Table I 'Post-Merger' Employee Behavioral Pattern

Period	Employee Behavior
Day 1	Denial, fear, no improvement
After a month	Sadness, slight improvement
After a Year	Acceptance, significant improvement
After 2 Years	Relief, liking, enjoyment, business development activities

Source:*www.sibm.edu*

Based on the above findings, ICICI established systems to take care of the employee resistance with action rather than words. The 'fear of the unknown' was tackled with adept communication and the 'fear of inability to function' was addressed by adequate training. The company also formulated an 'HR blue print' to ensure smooth integration of the human resources. (Refer Table II).

Table II Managing HR During the ICICI-BoM Merger

The HR Blueprint	Areas of HR integration Focussed on
• A data base of the entire HR structure	• Employee communication
• Road map of career	• Cultural integration
• Determining the blue print of HR moves	• Organization structuring
• Communication of milestones	• Recruitment & Compensation
• IT Integration - People Integration - Business Integration.	• Training
• Performance management	• Employee relations

Source: *www.sibm.edu*

To ensure employee participation and to decrease the resistance to the change, management established clear communication channels throughout to avoid any kind of wrong messages being sent across. Training programmes were conducted which emphasized on knowledge, skill, attitude and technology to upgrade skills of the employees. Management also worked on contingency plans and initiated direct dialogue with the employee unions of the BoM to maintain good employee relations.

By June 2001, the process of integration between ICICI and BoM was started. ICICI transferred around 450 BoM employees to ICICI Bank, while 300 ICICI employees were shifted to BoM branches. Promotion schemes for BoM employees were initiated and around 800 BoM officers were found to be eligible for the promotions. By the end of the year, ICICI seemed to have successfully handled the HR aspects of the BoM merger. According to a news report, "The win-win situation created by....HR initiatives have resulted in high level of morale among all sections of the employees from the erstwhile BoM."

Even as the changes following the ICICI-BoM merger were stabilizing, ICICI announced its merger with ICICI Bank in October 2001. The merger, to be effective from March 2002, was expected to unleash yet another series of changes at the organization. With Kamath still heading ICICI, analysts were hopeful that the bank would come out successfully in the task of integrating the operations of both the entities this time as well.

For Discussion

1. 'The changed focus of ICICI to become a one-stop shop for financial services necessitated the changes in the organization culture and goals.' Analyze the changes implemented by Kamath in mid-1990s and comment briefly on the necessity and efficacy of these changes.
2. Compare and contrast the changed management process at ICICI initiated after Kamath became the CEO with the one following the ICICI-BoM merger. Also explain the rationale behind the employee resistance in both the cases.

Source: *Case Studies in Human Resource Management, Volume II, ICFAI Center for Management Research, Hyderabad, 2004, pp. 209 -217.*

TEST PREPPER

True/False Questions

_____ **1.** By definition, it takes at least seven people to make an organization.

_____ **2.** The primary beneficiaries of a commonweal organization are its owners and members.

_____ **3.** Closed-system thinking dominated the traditional view of organizations.

_____ **4.** Responsibility and authority are identical concepts.

_____ **5.** It is appropriate to say bureaucracy is really a matter of degree.

_____ **6.** *Dynamic equilibrium,* the open-system term, means maintaining internal balance with environmental assistance.

_____ **7.** Cognition, behavior, and performance are the three stages in Garvin's model of organizational learning.

_____ **8.** It is possible for an organization to be effective in the near future but not in the distant future.

_____ **9.** According to research, downsizing has worked far better than expected.

_____ **10.** Symbolism plays a large part in organizational culture.

Multiple-Choice Questions

1. _____ is *not* a characteristic common to all organizations.
A. Coordination of effort
B. Division of labor
C. Hierarchy of authority
D. Equal authority and responsibility
E. Common goal or purpose

2. Who are the primary beneficiaries of mutual-benefit organizations such as unions and political parties?
A. The public at large B. Members
C. Customers D. Stockholders
E. Owners

3. What are the two dimensions of an organization chart?
A. People and tasks
B. Economic and social power
C. Vertical hierarchy and horizontal specialization
D. Division of labor and coordination
E. Boxes and lines

4. _____ is the primary goal of an organization, according to the modern view.
A. Economic efficiency
B. Survival in the face of uncertainty
C. Continuous growth
D. Adaptation to change
E. Human satisfaction

5. Chester I. Barnard's theory of authority is unique because it
A. is drawn from the legal authority of the corporation.
B. merges authority and responsibility into one concept.
C. is derived from closed-system theory.
D. is drawn from the legal authority of the state.
E. is based on subordinates' willingness to comply.

6. In open-system terminology, which of these means reaching the same result by different means?
A. Boundary-spanning system B. Equifinality
C. Synergy D. Self-efficacy
E. Dynamic equilibrium

7. In Garvin's model of organizational learning, _____ is *not* one of the needed organizational skills.
A. learning from experience/history
B. learning from others
C. hiring expert talent
D. experimenting
E. solving problems

8. Which of the following must the organization be if it is to be effective specifically in the intermediate term?
A. Adaptive and developing
B. Efficient
C. A source of satisfaction for employees and customers
D. Large and growing
E. Capable of survival

9. _____ can be used to help layoff victims polish their job-seeking skills.
A. Outplacement
B. An employee assistance program
C. An EEO program
D. Redeployment
E. Work sharing

10. Which of these is *not* a characteristic of organizational cultures?
A. Dynamic B. Inherently symbolic
C. Collective D. Focused on the future
E. Emotionally charged

ACE self-test

Want more questions? Visit the student Web site at http://business.college.hmco.com/students/ (select Kreitner *Management,* 10e) and take the ACE quizzes for more practice.

10 Organizing in the Twenty-First Century

> "... You have to think small to grow big."[1]
>
> **SAM WALTON**

OBJECTIVES

- **Explain** the concept of contingency organization design.
- **Distinguish** between mechanistic and organic organizations.
- **Discuss** the roles that differentiation and integration play in organization structure.
- **Identify** and briefly **describe** the five basic departmentalization formats.
- **Describe** how a highly centralized organization differs from a highly decentralized one.
- **Define** the term *delegation*, and **list** at least five common barriers to delegation.
- **Explain** how the traditional pyramid organization is being reshaped.

the changing workplace

Business NOT as Usual at W. L. Gore: Part 1 (see the Closing Case in Chapter 15 for Part 2)

Pound for pound, the most innovative company in America is W. L. Gore & Associates.

You've no doubt heard of its most famous product: Gore-Tex fabrics, which have a transparent plastic coating that makes them waterproof and windproof but keeps them breathable. Gore is big—with $1.58 billion in annual revenues and 6,300 employees—but not gargantuan like 3M or IBM. Still, Gore makes so many products that the total is hard to pin down—with all the variations, the count rises above 1,000. Gore's medical products, such as heart patches and synthetic blood vessels, have been implanted in more than 7.5 million patients. Its cutting-edge fabrics are worn by astronauts and soldiers, as well as trekkers at the North and South Poles and on the world's highest mountains. It makes the number-one products in industrial and electronics niches ranging from filters for reducing air pollution at large factories to the assemblies for fuel cells that convert hydrogen to electricity. Gore, a privately owned company, doesn't release its annual financial data, but a spokesperson says that the company has had "double digit" revenue growth for the past couple of years. In many businesses, Gore has come out of nowhere and seized the market lead, as it did with its smooth Glide dental floss, the first floss that resisted shredding, and its Elixir guitar strings, which last three to five times longer than normal strings. When Gore's people think they can create a much better product, they're fearless about attacking new markets.

Gore is a strikingly contradictory company: a place where nerds can be mavericks; a place that's impatient with the standard way of working, but more than patient with nurturing ideas and giving them time to flourish; a place that's humble in its origins, yet ravenous for breakthrough ideas and, ultimately, growth. Gore's uniqueness comes from being as innovative in its operating principles as it is in its diverse product lines. This is a company that has kicked over the rules that most other organizations live by. It is tucked away in the mid-Atlantic countryside, 3,000 miles from Silicon Valley and even further (in its mind-set) from Wall Street. And in its quietly revolutionary way, it is doing something almost magical: fostering ongoing, consistent, breakthrough creativity. . . .

What really distinguishes Gore is its culture, which goes back to 1958, when Wilbert ("Bill") L. Gore left DuPont, where he had worked as an engineer for 17 years, and launched his start-up. Bill liked to say that "communication really happens in the car pool." At a hierarchical company, the car pool is the only place where people talk to one another freely without regard for the chain of command. He also observed that when there's a crisis, a company creates a task force and throws out the rules. That's when organizations take risks and make big breakthroughs. Why, he wondered, should you have to wait for a crisis?

So Bill Gore threw out the rules. He created a place with hardly any hierarchy and few ranks and titles. He insisted on direct, one-on-one communication; anyone in the company could speak to anyone else. In essence, he organized the company as though it were a bunch of small task forces. To promote this idea, he limited the size of teams—keeping even the manufacturing facilities to 150 to 200 people at most. That's small enough so that people can get to know one another and what everyone is working on, and who has the skills and knowledge they might tap to get something accomplished—whether it's creating an innovative product or handling the everyday challenges of running a business.

Gore doesn't have an impressive campus that proclaims the company's success. It consists of several dozen bland, low-rise buildings scattered near the Delaware-Maryland border. They're separated far enough from one another so that each can house a small, autonomous team. Often, the buildings are set back from country roads. You can drive by and think you're passing farmland rather than corporate sites.

What goes on inside those nondescript buildings is hard to understand unless you've actually worked there for at least a year or two. Consider the case of Diane Davidson, whom the company hired to work on Citywear, an effort that has persuaded designers such as Prada, Hugo Boss, and Polo to use Gore-Tex fabrics in clothing that people can wear to the office or out to a party. Nothing in Davidson's 15 years of experience as a sales executive in the apparel industry, including a stint at Bostonian, prepared her for life in a place where there are no bosses and no clear-cut roles.

"I came from a very traditional male-dominated business—the men's shoe business," she recalls. "When I arrived at Gore, I didn't know who did what. I wondered how anything got done here. It was driving me crazy." Like all new hires, Davidson was given a "starting sponsor" at Gore—a mentor, not a boss. But she didn't know how to work without someone telling her what to do.

"Who's my boss?" she kept asking.

"Stop using the B-word," her sponsor replied.

As an experienced executive, Davidson assumed that Gore's talk was typical corporate euphemism rather than real practice.

"Secretly, there are bosses, right?" she asked.

There weren't. She eventually figured out that "your team is your boss, because you don't want to let them down. Everyone's your boss, and no one's your boss."

What's more, Davidson saw that people didn't fit into standard job descriptions. They had all made different sets of "commitments" to their team, often combining roles that remained segregated in different fiefdoms at conventional companies, such as sales, marketing, and product design. It took a long time to get to know people and what they did—and for them to get to know her and trust her with responsibilities. Eventually, Davidson went on to oversee the sales force and product development for Citywear. She describes herself as a "category champion." She's involved in marketing, sales, and sponsorship—a good example of how Gore's associates create roles that aren't easily defined by traditional corporate departments.

Her experience is commonplace. "You join a team and you're an idiot," says John Mongan, who has switched into new teams five times over a 20-year tenure. "It takes 18 months to build credibility. Early on, it's really frustrating. In hindsight, it makes sense. As a sponsor, I tell new hires, 'Your job for the first six months is to get to know the team,' but they have trouble believing it—and not contributing when other people are." . . .

The Gore organization isn't as fanatically flat as some idealized accounts have made it out to be. There is indeed a president and CEO, Chuck Carroll. . . . And the company necessarily has some structure. The four divisions (fabrics, medical, industrial, and electronic products) each have a recognized "leader," as do certain companywide support functions (human resources, information technology) and specific businesses and cells. But there is no codified set of ranks and positions as there is in the typical corporation. As a Gore "associate," you're supposed to morph your role over time to match your skills. You're not expected to fit into some preconceived box or standardized organizational niche. Your compensation is tied to your "contribution" and decided by a committee, much the way it's done in law firms. The company looks at your past and present performance as well as your future prospects, which takes away the potential disincentive for investing time and effort in speculative projects. Gore encourages risk taking. When Gore people pull the plug on a failing initiative, they'll still have a "celebration" with beer or champagne, just as they would if it had been a success.

"We were a lot more radical compared to the norm in 1958," says Brad Jones, who leads the industrial-products division. "The gap between Gore and other companies has narrowed. But we're still different. Companies may have fewer layers today, but they still have pyramids and reporting structures. You can still feel the difference in an organization when the only person speaking in a meeting is the top person. It's easier to compare us to a start-up company." . . .

But a $1.6 billion company can't run on hope. Gore's next big challenge is to keep up its double-digit growth rate even as its gets bigger. That means venturing into the hazards of the greater world, where Gore might find it difficult to safeguard its unusual culture. It means teaming up with giants like GM, the quintessential hierarchical organization. It means expanding overseas to tap new markets and new sources of talent. While the Gore culture is progressive for U.S. business, it's radical almost everywhere else. "Europeans generally like hierarchies, job specs, and knowing who the boss is," says Doak. He had a career in the British government before joining Gore. Recently, he met with a member of Parliament who asked, "How are you getting along at Gore? Is it still the Moonies?"

Gore isn't a cult. But its culture is much like Gore-Tex, its most famous product. As Gore grows from nearly 7,000 employees to 14,000 and then 21,000, it must continue to invent ways to protect its people from the harsh outside elements, even as it lets their big and creative ideas breathe—and prosper.

Source: *Excerpted from Alan Deutschman, "The Fabric of Creativity,"* Fast Company, *no. 89 (December 2004): 54–62. Reprinted by permission.*

Many of us have been to picnics where everyone brings a bottle of ketchup but no one brings the mustard. Although too much of one thing and too little of another may be laughable at a picnic, such disorganized situations can spell disaster for an organization that needs to manage human and material resources effectively and efficiently in order to survive. W. L. Gore may appear to be disorganized at first glance, but the company actually has evolved a strong, team-oriented organization that is highly innovative. Some traditional "rules" of organization had to be broken along the way.[2] As a testimony to Gore's unique organizational style, it is one of only 22 companies appearing on every one of *Fortune* magazine's "100 Best Companies to Work For" lists (1998–2005).[3]

organizing: *creating a coordinated authority and task structure*

Organizing is the structuring of a coordinated system of authority relationships and task responsibilities. By spelling out who does what and who reports to whom, organization structure can translate strategy into an ongoing productive operation. Structure always follows strategy in well-managed organizations. Tasks and interrelationships cannot be realistically and systematically defined without regard for the enterprise's overall direction. Furthermore, strategy determines the required technologies and the resources likely to be available.[4]

Unfortunately, as pointed out in *Harvard Business Review*, the current state of organization structure and design leaves a lot to be desired:

> *Organizational structures rarely result from systematic, methodical planning. Rather, they evolve over time, in fits and starts, shaped more by politics than by policies. The haphazard nature of the resulting structures is a source of constant frustration to senior executives. Strategic initiatives stall or go astray because responsibilities are fragmented or unclear. Turf wars torpedo collaboration and knowledge sharing. Promising opportunities die for lack of managerial attention. Overly complex structures, such as matrix organizations, collapse because of lack of clarity about responsibilities.*[5]

The modern open-system view, with its emphasis on organization-environment interaction and learning organizations, has helped underscore the need for more flexible organization structures. A term used today by organizational scholars is *ambidextrous organizations*. Just as an ambidextrous person can perform a task with either hand, ambidextrous organizations are organized both to satisfy today's situational demands and to prepare for meeting tomorrow's new demands.[6] These more flexible organizations are adaptable to sudden changes and are also interesting and challenging for employees. Traditional principles of organization are severely bent or broken during the design of flexible and adaptive organizations, and managers need new formulas for drawing up these designs. This is where the contingency approach enters the picture. The contingency approach permits the custom tailoring of organizations to meet unique external and internal situational demands.[7]

In this chapter we introduce and discuss organization design alternatives that enhance situation appropriateness and, hence, organizational effectiveness. We also discuss the related topic of delegation and explore the dramatic reshaping of today's organizations.

Contingency Design

Recall from our discussion in Chapter 2 that contingency thinking amounts to situational thinking. Specifically, the contingency approach to organizing involves taking special steps to make sure the organization fits the demands of the situation. In direct contrast to traditional bureaucratic thinking, contingency design is based on the assumption that there is no single best way to structure an organization.

contingency design: *fitting the organization to its environment*

Contingency design is the process of determining the degree of environmental uncertainty and adapting the organization and its subunits to the situation. This does not mean that all contingency organizations necessarily differ from each other.

1. EXPLAIN the concept of contingency organization design.

Instead, it means that managers who take a contingency approach select from a number of standard design alternatives to create the most situationally effective organization possible. Contingency managers typically start with the same basic collection of design alternatives but end up with unique combinations of them as dictated by the demands of their situations.

The contingency approach to designing organizations boils down to two questions: (1) How much environmental or state uncertainty is there? (See Table 10.1 for a handy way to answer this question.) (2) What combination of structural characteristics is most appropriate? We will examine two somewhat different contingency models to establish the validity of the contingency approach. Each model presents a scheme for systematically matching structural characteristics with environmental demands.

■ The Burns and Stalker Model

mechanistic organizations: *rigid bureaucracies*

organic organizations: *flexible, adaptive organization structures*

Tom Burns and G. M. Stalker, both British behavioral scientists, proposed a useful typology for categorizing organizations by structural design.[8] They distinguished between mechanistic and organic organizations. **Mechanistic organizations** tend to be rigid in design and have strong bureaucratic qualities. In contrast, **organic organizations** tend to be quite flexible in structure and adaptive to change. Actually, these two organizational types are the extreme ends of a single continuum. Pure types are difficult to find, but it is fairly easy to check off the characteristics listed in Table 10.2 to determine whether a particular organization (or subunit) is relatively mechanistic or relatively organic. It is notable that a field study found distinctly different communication patterns in mechanistic and organic organizations. Communication tended to be the formal command-and-control type in the mechanistic factory and to be participative in the organic factory.[9]

2. DISTINGUISH between mechanistic and organic organizations.

■ Telling the Difference. Here is a quick test of how well you understand the distinction between mechanistic and organic organizations. Read the following description of how an Emeryville, California, company maximizes the security of its clients' Web site data, and then attach a mechanistic or organic label.

SiteROCK employees . . . are required to read through several three-inch-thick binders of standard operating procedures before they can work in the com-

Table 10.1 Determining Degree of Environmental Uncertainty

	Low	Moderate	High
1. How strong are social, political, and economic pressures on the organization?	Minimal	Moderate	Intense
2. How frequent are technological breakthroughs in the industry?	Infrequent	Occasional	Frequent
3. How reliable are resources and supplies?	Reliable	Occasional, predictable shortages	Unreliable
4. How stable is the demand for the organization's product or service?	Highly stable	Moderately stable	Unstable

Table 10.2 Mechanistic versus Organic Organizations

Characteristic	Mechanistic organizations	Organic organizations
1. Task definition for individual contributors	Narrow and precise	Broad and general
2. Relationship between individual contribution and organization purpose	Vague	Clear
3. Task flexibility	Low	High
4. Definition of rights, obligations, and techniques	Clear	Vague
5. Reliance on hierarchical control	High	Low (reliance on self-control)
6. Primary direction of communication	Vertical (top to bottom)	Lateral (between peers)
7. Reliance on instructions and decisions from superior	High	Low (superior offers information and advice)
8. Emphasis on loyalty and obedience	High	Low
9. Type of knowledge required	Narrow, technical, and task-specific	Broad and professional

Source: *Adapted from Tom Burns and G. M. Stalker,* The Management of Innovation *(London: Tavistock, 1961), pp. 119–125. Reprinted by permission.*

mand center. As each shift turns over, the staff must shuffle through 90 minutes of paperwork before handing over the keys. "Not everyone would be able to do this job. You have to be able to follow directions and follow the processes," says Lori Perrine, a customer-support specialist at siteROCK.[10]

If you said mechanistic, you're right. Using Table 10.2 as a guide, we see evidence of precise task definition, low task flexibility, clear definition of techniques, and high emphasis on obedience. Indeed, siteROCK is staffed mostly by former military personnel and is run with military precision. An organic organization would have basically the opposite characteristics. One example is Sterling Bank in Houston, Texas. "This commercial and retail bank has an unusual inverted pyramid hierarchy. Workers essentially manage themselves. Promotions, for example, are determined by a panel of peers, rather than by managers."[11]

Situational Appropriateness. Burns and Stalker's research uncovered distinct organization-environment patterns indicating the relative appropriateness of both mechanistic and organic organizations. They discovered that *successful organizations in relatively stable and certain environments tended to be mechanistic.* Conversely, they also discovered that *relatively organic organizations tended to be the successful ones when the environment was unstable and uncertain.*

For practical application, this means that mechanistic design is appropriate for environmental stability, and organic design is appropriate for high environmental uncertainty. Today, the trend necessarily is toward more organic organizations because uncertainty is the rule. *Management Review* summed up the situation this way:

> *Products, companies, and industries all have shorter life cycles, which means that product launches, corporate realignments, and other*

10a Back to the Opening Case

Employees, dubbed "associates," have "sponsors," who serve as mentors, not bosses. Associates decide for themselves what new commitments to take on. Committees evaluate an associate's contribution and decide on compensation. There are no standardized job descriptions or categories: Everyone is supposed to be like an amoeba, taking on a unique shape.

Source: Alan Deutschman, "The Fabric of Creativity," Fast Company, *no. 89 (December 2004): 59.*

QUESTIONS:

Is W. L. Gore a mechanistic or an organic organization? How can you tell? What problems might this type of organization likely have? What could be done to avoid those problems? Would you like to work for this sort of organization? Why or why not?

For further information about the interactive annotations in this chapter, visit our Web site (**http://business.college.hmco.com/students/** and select Kreitner, *Management,* 10e).

initiatives may take place in months rather than years. The global span of today's companies, which have employees, customers, and suppliers throughout the world, also multiplies the complexities of change. And let us not forget another complicator—technology. Companies must constantly upgrade systems, evaluate new technology, and adopt new ways of doing business.[12]

This is not to say that organic is good and mechanistic is bad. Mechanistic organizations do have their appropriate places. SiteROCK's mechanistic structure, for example, makes it highly resistant to human error, technical failures, and attacks by hackers and terrorists.

■ **Woodward's Study.** Since Burns and Stalker's pioneering study, several different contingency models have been proposed. Some, such as Joan Woodward's study of the relationship among technology, structure, and organizational effectiveness, focused on a single environmental variable rather than on general environmental certainty-uncertainty. Applying her own scale of technological complexity to 100 British firms, Woodward found distinctly different patterns of structure in effective and ineffective organizations. When technological complexity was either low or high, Woodward found that effective organizations tended to have organic structure. Mechanistic structure was associated with effectiveness when technological complexity was moderate.[13] In spite of criticism of weak methodology, Woodward's study added to the case against the traditional notion of a universally applicable organization design.

■ The Lawrence and Lorsch Model

differentiation: *tendency of specialists to think and act in restricted ways*

Paul R. Lawrence and Jay W. Lorsch, researchers from Harvard University, made a valuable contribution to contingency design theory by documenting the relationship between two opposing structural forces and environmental complexity. The opposing forces they isolated were labeled *differentiation* and *integration*. **Differentiation** is the tendency among specialists to think and act in restricted ways. This structural

These computer assembly employees in Manus, Brazil, work in what Burns and Stalker call a mechanistic organization. Otherwise, poor-quality products would result from people deviating from precise product design and assembly specifications.

integration: *collaboration needed to achieve a common purpose*

force results from division of labor and technical specialization. Differentiation tends to fragment and disperse the organization (see Figure 10.1). **Integration,** in opposition to differentiation, is the collaboration among specialists that is needed to achieve a common purpose.[14] Integration can be partially achieved through a number of mechanisms, including hierarchical control, standard policies and procedures, departmentalization, computer networks, cross-functional teams and committees, better human relations, and liaison individuals and groups. As illustrated in Figure 10.1, integration is a unifying and *coordinating* force.

3. DISCUSS the roles that differentiation and integration play in organization structure.

According to Lawrence and Lorsch, every organization needs to achieve an appropriate *dynamic equilibrium* (an open-system term) between differentiation and integration. Moreover, their comparison of successful and unsuccessful firms in three different industries demonstrated that in the successful firms, *both differentiation and integration increased as environmental complexity increased.* These findings applied not only to the overall organization but also to organizational subunits such as departments or divisions. Lawrence and Lorsch also found that "the more differentiated an organization, the more difficult it is to achieve integration."[15]

These findings suggest that organizational failure in the face of environmental complexity probably results from a combination of high differentiation and inadequate integration.[16] Under these conditions, specialists in different areas within the organization work at cross-purposes and get embroiled in counterproductive jurisdictional conflicts. Greater integration (coordination) certainly was on the minds of 360 senior executives in the United States when responding to one survey. Among the four key ways to boost profits, according to the executives, was to: "Implement cross-functional coordination throughout the organization to increase customer retention."[17] Such action could prove fruitful because, in another study of 39 companies, productivity increased when organizational integration was improved. One source of improvement involved increased contact and coordination between product design and manufacturing specialists.[18] Yahoo's CEO Terry Semel knows the value of increased organizational integration:

10b Back to the Opening Case

Using Figure 10.1 as a guide, what evidence of organizational integration can you find at W. L. Gore? Explain.

Figure 10.1 Differentiation and Integration: Opposing Organizational Forces

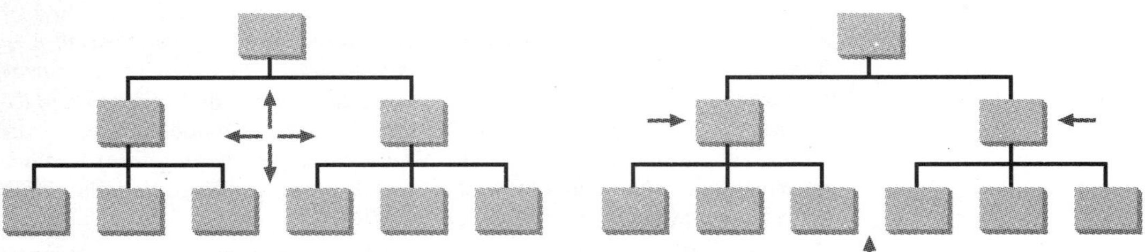

Differentiation (fragmentation)

Differentiating mechanisms:
Forces pushing the organization apart

- Division of labor
- Technical specialization

Integration (coordination)

Integrating mechanisms:
Forces pulling the organization together

- Formal hierarchy (chain of command)
- Standard policies, rules, and procedures
- Departmentalization
- Computer networks
- Cross-functional teams and committees
- Human relations training for managers (to help avoid interpersonal conflict)
- Liaison individuals and groups (to bridge gaps between specialists)

THE GLOBAL MANAGER

A Globe-Trotting Organizational Thinker Looks at the Future of Work Organizations

About Charles Handy: A native of Dublin, Ireland, he is the author of well-regarded books such as *The Age of Unreason* and, more recently, *The Hungry Spirit*. His diverse background includes being the executive of an oil company and a London Business School professor. He and his wife, a professional photographer, shuttle between residences in England and Italy.

Here are excerpts from an interview by Barbara Ettorre, senior editor of *Management Review:*

Q. The corporation as we know it is approximately 100 years old. Will it survive the twenty-first century?

Handy: Not in its present form. The twentieth century will be known as the century of the organization. The next one will not be known as that. We are seeing the withering of the employment organization. It won't totally disappear, but it will be reduced to an organizing core. Organizations will live up to the name—they will organize. [They won't] have to employ everybody being organized, only the organizers. So my formula is half-by-two-by-three: Half the workers paid twice as well, producing three times as much.

The other half will be outside the organization. And because those on the inside are working very hard to be paid twice as well, they will have short lives in the organization, 20 or 30 years, instead of 50 years. It could be 15. It's a hell of a reduction. I try not to frighten people too much. But I would say 15 to 20.

This upper half of society, those with competent skills, will become independent workers, selling back into the organization for the most part, but also into several organizations at the same time. At the bottom level you will still need people because most of the jobs for the less skilled will be in the service world, giving people food and drink, keeping places clean, [taking care of old] folks. They will probably be organized by what I call intermediary employers.

Q. If the future consists of virtual corporations, portfolio workers, and knowledge as the competitive edge, what of the vast majority that cannot be a part of this? Are we creating an even larger underclass, large groups without salable portfolios?

Handy: To some extent, there's no way out of that. Wealth doesn't trickle down as it used to. If you don't make the poor rich, the rich are not going to have any customers before long.

Source: Management Review *by Barbara Ettorre. Copyright 1996 by American Management Association (J). Reproduced with permission of American Management Association (J) in the format Textbook via Copyright Clearance Center.*

[He] puts all new ideas through a rigorous sounding board, composed of managers from various corners of the company, which requires that all new businesses mesh with existing ones. This has paid dividends in the ultra-competitive Internet search industry. When Yahoo relaunched its search service in early 2003, managers explored how they could inject Yahoo-generated content directly into the search results. Now, users get everything from weather reports to stock charts directly on their search-results pages—at least one click faster than on Google or Microsoft Corp.'s MSN.[19]

Although contingency design models may differ in perspective and language, two conclusions stand out. First, research has proved time and time again that *there is no single best organization design*. Second, research generally supports the idea that the more uncertain the environment, the more flexible and adaptable the organization structure must be.[20] (See The Global Manager.) With this contingency perspective in mind, we now consider five basic structural formats.

Basic Structural Formats

As we noted earlier, differentiation occurs in part through division of labor. When labor is divided, complex processes are reduced to distinct and less complex jobs. But because differentiation tends to fragment the organization, some sort of integration must be introduced to achieve the necessary coordination. Aside from the hier-

departmentalization: *grouping related jobs or processes into major organizational subunits*

archical chain of command, one of the most common forms of integration is departmentalization. It is through **departmentalization** that related jobs, activities, or processes are grouped into major organizational subunits. For example, all jobs involving staffing activities such as recruitment, hiring, and training are often grouped into a human resources department. Grouping jobs through the formation of departments, according to management author James D. Thompson, "permits coordination to be handled in the least costly manner."[21] A degree of coordination is achieved through departmentalization because members of the department work on interrelated tasks, are guided by the same departmental rules, and report to the same department head. It is important to note that although the term *departmentalization* is used here, it does not always literally apply; managers commonly use labels such as *division, group,* or *unit* in large organizations.

4. IDENTIFY and briefly **DESCRIBE** the five basic departmentalization formats.

Five basic types of departmentalization are functional departments, product-service departments, geographic location departments, customer classification departments, and work flow process departments.[22]

Functional Departments

Functional departments categorize jobs according to the activity performed. Among profit-making businesses, variations of the functional production-finance-marketing arrangement in Figure 10.2A are the most common forms of departmentalization. Functional departmentalization is popular because it permits those with similar technical expertise to work in a coordinated subunit. Of course, functional departmentalization is not restricted to profit-making businesses. Functional departments in a nonprofit hospital might be administration, nursing, housekeeping, food service, laboratory and x ray, admission and records, and accounting and billing.

A negative aspect of functional departmentalization is that it creates "technical ghettos," in which local departmental concerns and loyalties tend to override strategic organizational concerns. For example, look what Bruce L. Claflin, head of IBM's newly formed mobile computing division, ran into when he called a planning meeting for the Think-Pad 700C.

> *Everybody cared more about how their own area—say, marketing—would fare than for what was best for IBM. The marketing people knew [the 700C] would be competitive, but they had made commitments to sell only 6,000 worldwide. They didn't believe the development group would build it anyway. The development people knew they could design it, but they said, "Well, marketing won't sell it, and anyway, manufacturing can't build it." And manufacturing figured it would never be developed. It was complete gridlock.*[23]

Situations like this prompted a major reorganization at IBM and the eventual sale of its PC unit to a Chinese company in 2004.[24]

Product-Service Departments

Because functional departmentalization has been criticized for encouraging differentiation at the expense of integration, a somewhat more organic alternative has evolved. It is called product-service departmentalization because a product (or service), rather than a functional category of work, is the unifying theme. As diagrammed in Figure 10.2B, the product-service approach permits each of, say, two products to be managed as semiautonomous businesses. Organizations rendering a service instead of turning out a tangible product might find it advantageous to organize around service categories. In reality, however, many of today's companies turn out *bundles* of products and services for customers. General Electric, for example, was recently reorganized around these major product/service categories: energy (power generation equipment), transportation (aircraft engines and rail locomotives),

Figure 10.2 Alternative Departmentalization Formats

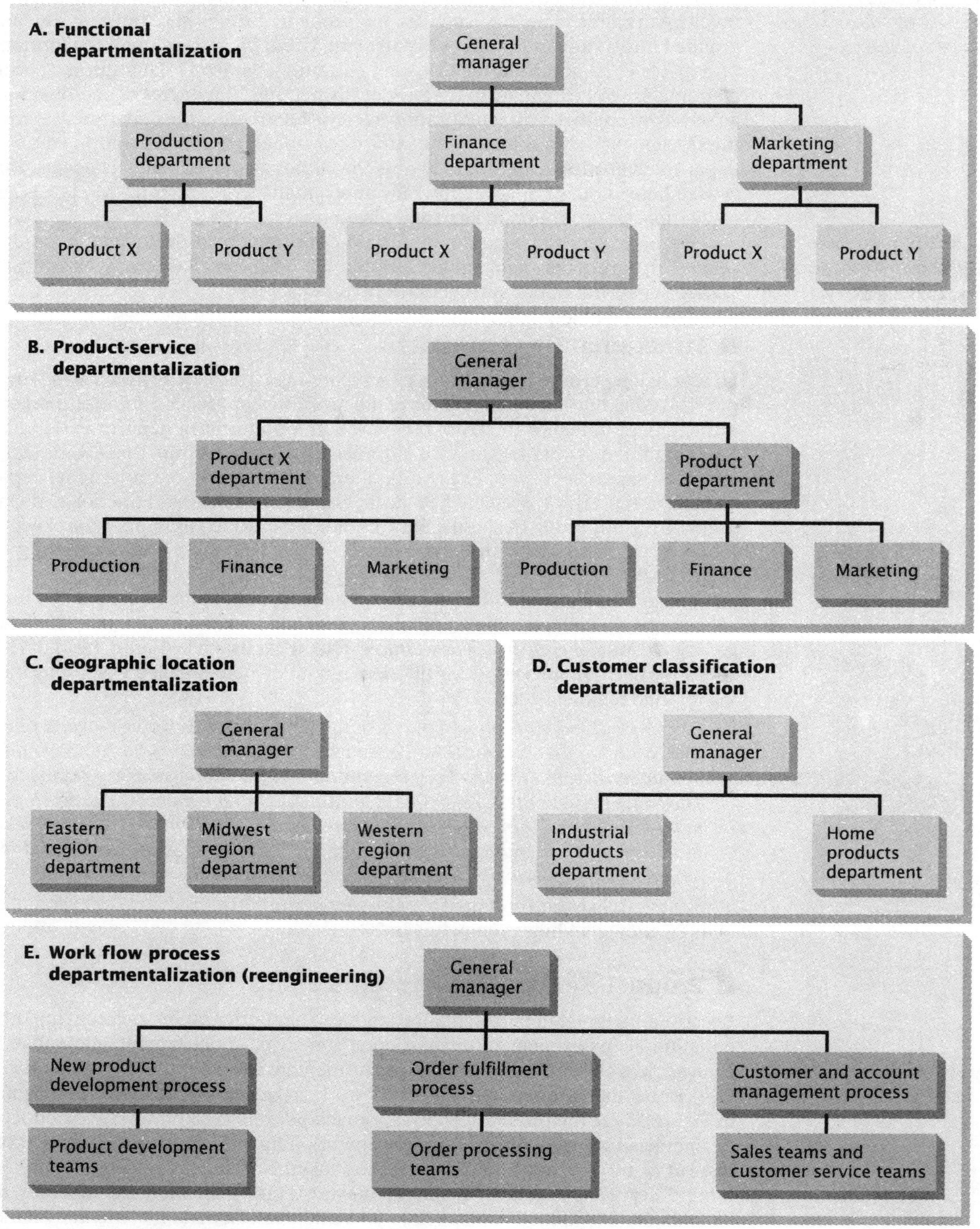

NBC-Universal (television and films), health care (diagnostic equipment), and consumer and industrial products and services.[25] Ideally, those working in this sort of product-service structure have a broad "business" orientation rather than a narrow functional perspective. As Figure 10.2B shows, it is the general manager's job to ensure that these minibusinesses work in a complementary fashion, rather than competing with one another.[26]

■ Geographic Location Departments

Sometimes, as in the case of organizations with nationwide or worldwide markets, geography dictates structural format (see Figure 10.2C). Geographic dispersion of resources (for example, mining companies), facilities (for example, railroads), or customers (for example, chain supermarkets) may encourage the use of a geographic format to put administrators "closer to the action." One can imagine that drilling engineers in a Houston-based petroleum firm would be better able to get a job done in Alaska if they actually went there. Similarly, a department-store marketing manager would be in a better position to judge consumer tastes in Florida if working out of a regional office in Orlando rather than out of a home office in Salt Lake City or Toronto.

Long lines of communication among organizational units have traditionally been a limiting factor with geographically dispersed operations. But space-age telecommunications technology has created some interesting regional advantages. A case in point is Omaha, Nebraska. Its central location, along with the absence of a distinct regional accent among Nebraskans, has made Omaha the 1-800 capital of the country. Every major hotel chain and most of the big telemarketers have telephone service centers in Omaha.[27]

Global competition is pressuring managers to organize along geographic lines. This structure allows multinational companies to serve local markets better.

How big was that fish you caught? Whole Foods' Jacob Perea lets everyone know at the grand opening of the firm's new 80,000 square-foot headquarters store in Austin, Texas. Whole Foods has become the world's largest retailer of organic and natural foods with 167 supermarkets around the U.S. Its geographic location organization structure allows Whole Foods to be close to the customer. Nothing fishy about that arrangement.

Customer Classification Departments

A fourth structural format centers on various customer categories (see Figure 10.2D). Intel is a good case in point. As Paul Otellini was getting ready to assume the CEO post at Intel in 2005, he reorganized the computer-chip maker to sharpen its focus on the customer:

> *He believes that to keep Intel growing, every idea and technical solution should be focused on meeting customers' needs from the outset. So rather than relying on its engineering prowess, Intel's reorganization will bring together engineers, software writers, and marketers into five market-focused units: corporate computing, the digital home, mobile computing, health care, and channel products—PCs for small manufacturers.*[28]

Customer classification departmentalization shares a weakness with the product-service and geographic location approaches: all three can create costly duplication of personnel and facilities. Functional design is the answer when duplication is a problem.

Work Flow Process Departments in Reengineered Organizations

In Chapter 7, we introduced the concept of reengineering, which involves starting with a clean sheet of paper and radically redesigning the organization into cross-functional teams that speed up the entire business process. The driving factors behind reengineering are lower costs, better quality, greater speed, better use of modern information technology, and improved customer satisfaction.[29] Organizations with work flow process departments are called *horizontal organizations* because emphasis is on the smooth and speedy horizontal flow of work between two key points: (1) identifying customer needs and (2) satisfying the customer.[30] This is a distinct *outward* focus, as opposed to the inward focus of functional departments. Here is what happens inside the type of organization depicted in Figure 10.2E:

> *Rather than focusing single-mindedly on financial objectives or functional goals, the horizontal organization emphasizes customer satisfaction. Work is simplified and hierarchy flattened by combining related tasks—for example, an account-management process that subsumes the sales, billing, and service functions—and eliminating work that does not add value. Information zips along an internal superhighway. The knowledge worker analyzes it, and technology moves it quickly across the corporation instead of up and down, speeding up and improving decision making.*[31]

Each of the preceding design formats is presented in its pure form, but in actual practice, hybrid versions occur frequently. For example, Coca-Cola created a mix of three geographic location units and a functional unit in 2001 to make the global company more responsive to both customers and product trends. The four units: "Americas, Asia, Europe/Africa, and New Business Ventures."[32] From a contingency perspective, the five design formats are useful starting points rather than final blueprints for organizers. A number of structural variations show how the basic formats can be adapted to meet situational demands.

10c How Reengineering Got a Bad Name

A manager reportedly told James Champy, coauthor of the landmark book on reengineering,

> *We don't really know how to do reengineering in our company; so what we do is, we regularly downsize and leave it to the three people who are left to figure out how to do their work differently.*

Source: As quoted in "Anything Worth Doing Is Worth Doing from Scratch," Inc. *(20th Anniversary Issue), 21 (May 18, 1999): 51–52.*

QUESTIONS:

Does the term *reengineering* have a positive or a negative connotation for you? Explain. How often do you think misapplication or misinterpretation gives otherwise sound management practices a bad name? Explain.

Contingency Design Alternatives

Contingency design requires managers to select from a number of situationally appropriate alternatives instead of blindly following fixed principles of organization.[33] Managers who face a relatively certain environment can enhance their effectiveness by drawing on comparatively mechanistic alternatives. Those who must cope with high uncertainty will do better to select organic alternatives. Design alternatives include span of control, decentralization, line and staff, and matrix design.

Span of Control

span of control: *number of people who report directly to a given manager*

The number of people who report directly to a manager represents that manager's **span of control**. (Some scholars and managers prefer the term *span of management.*) Managers with a narrow span of control oversee the work of a few people, whereas those with a wide span of control have many people reporting to them (see Figure 10.3). Generally, narrow spans of control foster tall organizations (many levels in the hierarchy). In contrast, flat organizations (few hierarchical levels) have wide spans of control. Everything else being equal, it stands to reason that an organization with narrow spans of control needs more managers than one with wide spans. Management theorists and practitioners have devoted a good deal of time and energy through the years in an effort to answer the question "What is the ideal span of control?"[34] Ideally, the right span of control strikes an efficient balance between too little and too much supervision, important considerations in the era of lean organizations.

Is There an Ideal Span of Control? Early management theorists confidently specified exactly how many individuals should be in a manager's span of control. In the words of one early management scholar, "No superior can supervise directly the work of more than five or, at the most, six subordinates whose work interlocks."[35]

As time went by, research results began to supersede strictly intuitive judgments, and evidence supported wider spans of control. James C. Worthy, a vice president of Sears, Roebuck and Co., reported that his company had gotten good results with spans of control far in excess of six. Specifically, Worthy found morale and effectiveness were higher in one department store in which 36 department managers reported to a single manager than in a second store in which the span of control averaged only five.[36]

Figure 10.3 Narrow and Wide Spans of Control

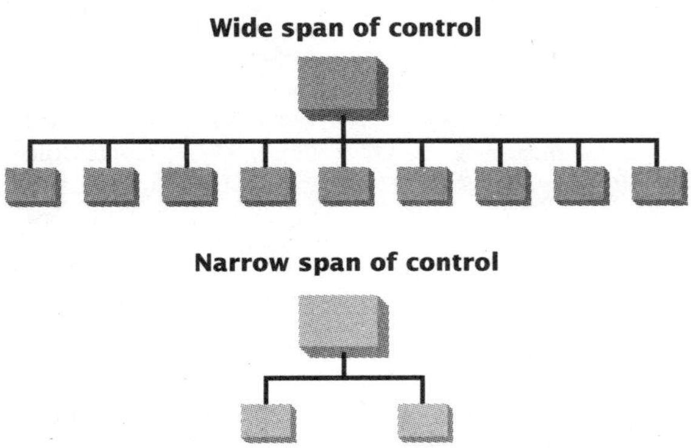

Today's emphasis on contingency organization design, combined with evidence that wide spans of control can be effective, has made the question of an ideal span obsolete. The relevant question is no longer how wide spans of control *should* be but instead "How wide *can* one's span of control be?" Wider spans of control mean less administrative expense and more self-management, both popular notions today.

The Contingency Approach to Spans of Control. Both overly narrow and overly wide spans of control are counterproductive. Overly narrow spans create unnecessarily tall organizations plagued by such problems as oversupervision; long lines of communication; slow, multilevel decision making; limited initiative due to minimal delegation of authority; restricted development among managers who devote most of their time to direct supervision; and increased administrative cost.[37] In contrast, overly wide spans can erode

10d Wider Is Better, for the Head of Cisco Systems

Says John Chambers, CEO of Cisco Systems Inc.: "I learned a long time ago that a team will always defeat an individual. And if you have a team of superstars, then you have a chance to create a dynasty." That's one reason why Chambers has two to three times as many people reporting to him as does the average executive in his company: It forces him to empower those directly under him with greater autonomy, because he can't possibly keep up with every detail of their work.

Source: John Byrne, "The Global Corporation Becomes the Leaderless Corporation," Business Week *(August 30, 1999): 90.*

QUESTION:
What is the key to making Chambers's wide span of control work?

efficiency and inflate costs due to workers' lack of training, behavioral problems among inadequately supervised workers, and lack of coordination. Clearly, a rationale is needed for striking a workable balance.

Situational factors such as those listed in Figure 10.4 are a useful starting point. The narrow, moderate, and wide span-of-control ranges in Figure 10.4 are intended to be illustrative benchmarks rather than rigid limits. Each organization must do its own on-the-job experimentation. At Federal Express, for example, the span of control varies with different areas of the company. Departments that employ many people doing the same job or very similar jobs—such as customer service agents, handlers/sorters, and couriers—usually have a span of control of 15 to 20 employees per manager. Groups performing multiple tasks, or tasks that require only a few people, are more likely to have spans of control of five or fewer.[38] No ideal span of control exists for all kinds of work.

■ Centralization and Decentralization

centralization: *the retention of decision-making authority by top management*

decentralization: *management's sharing of decision-making authority with lower-level employees*

Where are the important decisions made in an organization? Are they made strictly by top management or by middle- and lower-level managers? These questions are at the heart of the decentralization design alternative. Centralization is at one end of a continuum, and at the other end is decentralization. **Centralization** is defined as the relative retention of decision-making authority by top management. Almost all decision-making authority is retained by top management in highly centralized organizations. In contrast, **decentralization** is the granting of decision-making authority by management to lower-level employees. Decentralization increases as

Figure 10.4 Situational Determinants of Span of Control

	Wide span of control appropriate (10 or more) →	Moderate span of control appropriate (5 to 9) →	Narrow span of control appropriate (2 to 4)
1. Similarity of work performed by subordinates	Identical		Distinctly different
2. Dispersion of subordinates	Same work area		Geographically dispersed
3. Complexity of work performed by subordinates	Simple and repetitive		Highly complex and varied
4. Direction and control required by subordinates	Little and/or infrequent		Intensive and/or constant
5. Time spent coordinating with other managers	Little		A great deal
6. Time required for planning	Little		A great deal

the degree, importance, and range of lower-level decision making *increase* and the amount of checking up by top management *decreases* (see Figure 10.5).

5. DESCRIBE how a highly centralized organization differs from a highly decentralized one.

The Need for Balance. When we speak of centralization or decentralization, we are describing a comparative degree, not an absolute. The challenge for managers, as one management consultant observed, is to strike a workable balance between two extremes.

> *The modern organization in transition will recognize the pull of two polarities: a need for greater centralization to create low-cost shared resources; and, a need to improve market responsiveness with greater decentralization. Today's winning organizations are the ones that can handle the paradox and tensions of both pulls. These are the firms that analyze the optimum organizational solution in each particular circumstance, without prejudice for one type of organization over another. The result is, almost invariably, a messy mixture of decentralized units sharing cost-effective centralized resources.*[39]

Support for greater decentralization in the corporate world has come and gone over the years in faddish waves. Today, the call is for the type of balance just discussed. The case against extreme decentralization can be summed up in three words: *lack of control.* Balance helps neutralize this concern. Again, the contingency approach dictates which end of the continuum needs to be emphasized.[40] Centralization, because of its mechanistic nature, generally works best for organizations in relatively stable situations.[41] A more organic, decentralized approach is appropriate for firms in complex and changing conditions.[42]

Decentralization Through Strategic Business Units. Because of their growing popularity, particularly among very large businesses attempting to become more entrepreneurial, strategic business units deserve special mention. A **strategic business unit** (SBU) is an organizational subunit that acts like an independent business in all major respects, including the formulation of its own strategic plans. To qualify as a full-fledged SBU, an organizational unit must meet four criteria:

strategic business unit: *organizational subunit that acts like an independent business*

Figure 10.5 Factors in Relative Centralization/Decentralization

	Highly centralized organization	Highly decentralized organization
How many decisions are made at lower levels in the hierarchy?	Very few, if any	Many or most
How important are the decisions that are made at lower levels *(i.e., do they impact organizational success or dollar values)?*	Not very important	Very important
How many different functions *(e.g., production, marketing, finance, human resources)* rely on lower-level decision making?	Very few, if any	All or most
How much does top management monitor or check up on lower-level decision making?	A great deal	Very little or not at all

10e Quick Quiz

. . . no, it won't do you much good to show up at the Wal-Mart Super Center in your town and try to pitch your product to the manager there. "You'll still have to go through the new-supplier development division," says [executive vice president Don] Harris. . . . The company receives 2,000 inquiries a week, says Harris, and it manages to review "every single one."

Source: John Anderson, "How Wal-Mart Says You Should Sell to Wal-Mart," Inc., *25 (November 2003): 99.*

QUESTION:
Is this an example of centralization or decentralization? Explain.

1. It must serve a specific market outside the parent organization, rather than being simply an internal supplier.
2. It must face outside competitors.
3. It should be in a position of controlling its own destiny, especially through strategic planning and new product development. However, SBUs may choose to share the parent organization's resources, such as manufacturing facilities or sales personnel. The important point here is that the SBU, not the parent organization, makes the key choices.
4. It should be a profit center, with its effectiveness measured in terms of profit and loss.[43]

Like the underlying concept of decentralization, SBUs vary in degree. Units that fail to meet the above criteria are still called SBUs by some managers. A true SBU is highly decentralized from the parent organization.

In addition to encouraging organizational units to take greater entrepreneurial risk, SBUs can foster customer-centeredness. That was the idea at Nordstrom, the Seattle-based department-store chain with a reputation for excellent customer service. The CEO "reorganized the company into five separate operating units: department stores, outlet stores, consumer finance, online, and private-label, each with its own profit-and-loss statement."[44]

Interference by the parent organization is the surest way to render SBUs ineffective. Research shows that the more decentralized SBUs are from the parent organization, the more effective they are.[45] Ironically, to succeed, SBUs need the freedom to fail.

Line and Staff Organizations

Through the years, managers of large mechanistic organizations have struggled to strike a balance between technical specialization and unity of command. Remember that unity of command was emphasized by traditional management theorists. According to the unity-of-command principle, people should have only one immediate superior to avoid receiving conflicting orders. Unfortunately, in highly differentiated organizations there is often a mismatch between technical expertise and authority. For example, a production manager with the appropriate authority to take constructive action may not perceive sloppy inventory control as the source of runaway production costs. But an assistant accounting manager who has the technical expertise to identify and solve the inventory problem does not have the authority to take direct action in the production area. This is a common and frustrating situation. Line and staff organization design helps management apply technical expertise where it is most needed while maintaining relative unity of command.

line and staff organization: *organization in which line managers make decisions and staff personnel provide advice and support*

Line versus Staff. In a **line and staff organization**, a distinction is made between line positions, those in the formal chain of command, and staff positions, those serving in an advisory capacity outside the formal chain of command. Line managers have the authority to make decisions and give orders to those lower in the chain of command. In contrast, those who occupy staff positions merely advise and support line managers. Staff authority is normally restricted to immediate assistants. The line-staff distinction is relatively clear in mechanistic organizations but tends to blur in organic organizations.

As one might suspect, line and staff distinctions are a natural setting for conflict. Disagreement and conflict, as discussed in Chapter 16, are inevitable when two groups have different backgrounds, goals, and perspectives on the organization. For instance, line managers tend to emphasize decisiveness and deadlines, whereas staff members prefer to analyze problems systematically and thoroughly. Thus, line managers often criticize staff for taking too much time, and staff in turn complain of line managers' impatience and hasty decisions. A study of 207 Israeli police officers found yet another potential source of line-versus-staff conflict. Line employees were found to have greater job commitment than their staff coworkers.[46] The differing levels of commitment could cause line managers to question staff members' loyalty to the organization's mission. Teamwork and trust could become casualties in the conflict over loyalties. Fortunately, the recent emphasis on *internal service,* often in conjunction with total quality management, promises to reduce line-staff conflict. According to a pair of respected organization theorists, "... it is reasonable to expect that as the line operations of organizations develop and perfect their own concepts of how to deliver high quality, they will in turn demand high-quality service from their staff organizations. Line managers are likely to expect staff organizations to treat them as customers."[47]

■ **Personal versus Specialized Staff.** There are two general types of staff, personal and specialized.[48] Personal staff are individuals assigned to a specific manager to provide research support, specialized technical expertise, and counsel. For example, in Figure 10.6, the strategic planning specialist and legal counsel are on the president's personal staff. But unlike the president's line authority, which extends to all functions, the authority of personal staff is normally limited to those working in their technical areas.

In contrast, specialized staff are "a reservoir of special knowledge, skills, and experience which the entire organization can use."[49] Consider the organization in Figure 10.6. Because it is primarily a manufacturing firm, manufacturing is a line function, whereas research and development, marketing, finance/accounting, and human resources are specialized staff functions. Notice that each of the four specialized staff functions supports but does not directly control the manufacturing function.

■ **Functional Authority.** Strict distinctions between line and staff tend to disappear in relatively organic organizations. A device called functional authority helps prevent the collapse of unity of command. **Functional authority** is an organic design alternative that gives staff personnel temporary, limited line authority for specified tasks. In Figure 10.6, for example, the president's personal legal counsel may be given functional authority for negotiating a new union contract with factory personnel.

functional authority: *gives staff temporary and limited authority for specified tasks*

Figure 10.6 A Line and Staff Organization

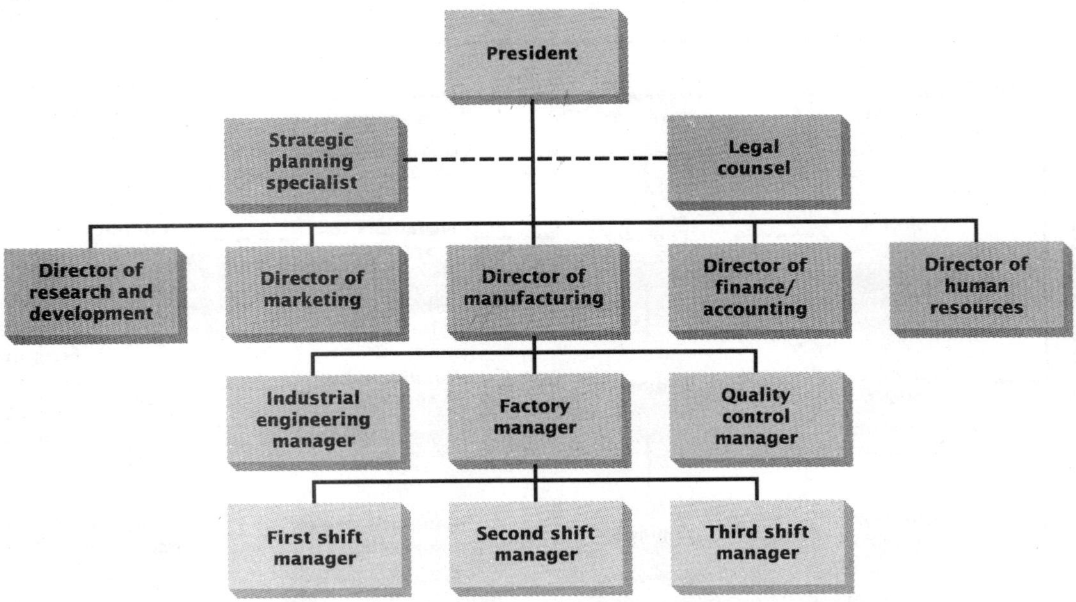

When acting in that capacity, the legal counsel's authority would override that of cooperating line managers such as the manufacturing and human resources directors. By giving knowledgeable staff the direct authority to get something done, functional authority can reduce bureaucratic delays and enhance organizational flexibility.

■ Matrix Organization

matrix organization: *a structure with both vertical and horizontal lines of authority*

This last design alternative was originally called *project management.*[50] In a **matrix organization**, vertical and horizontal lines of authority are combined in checkerboard fashion. Authority flows both down and across the organization structure.

Matrix design originally became popular in the construction and aerospace industries. Imagine how difficult it would be for a construction firm to complete, simultaneously and in a cost-effective manner, several huge projects such as hydroelectric dams. (Recall our discussion of project managment in Chapter 6.)[51] Because each major project has its own situational and technical demands, mechanistic bureaucracies have not worked out well as principal contractors of airports and other large projects. A more organic alternative had to be found. Likewise, aerospace giants such as Lockheed, Grumman, and General Dynamics had to turn to a more organic structure to build complex weapons systems and space vehicles for the federal government. Consequently, the matrix format evolved.[52]

Take a moment to study the matrix organization chart in Figure 10.7. Notice the checkerboard configuration. In effect, the project managers borrow specialists

Figure 10.7 A Simplified Matrix Organization Chart

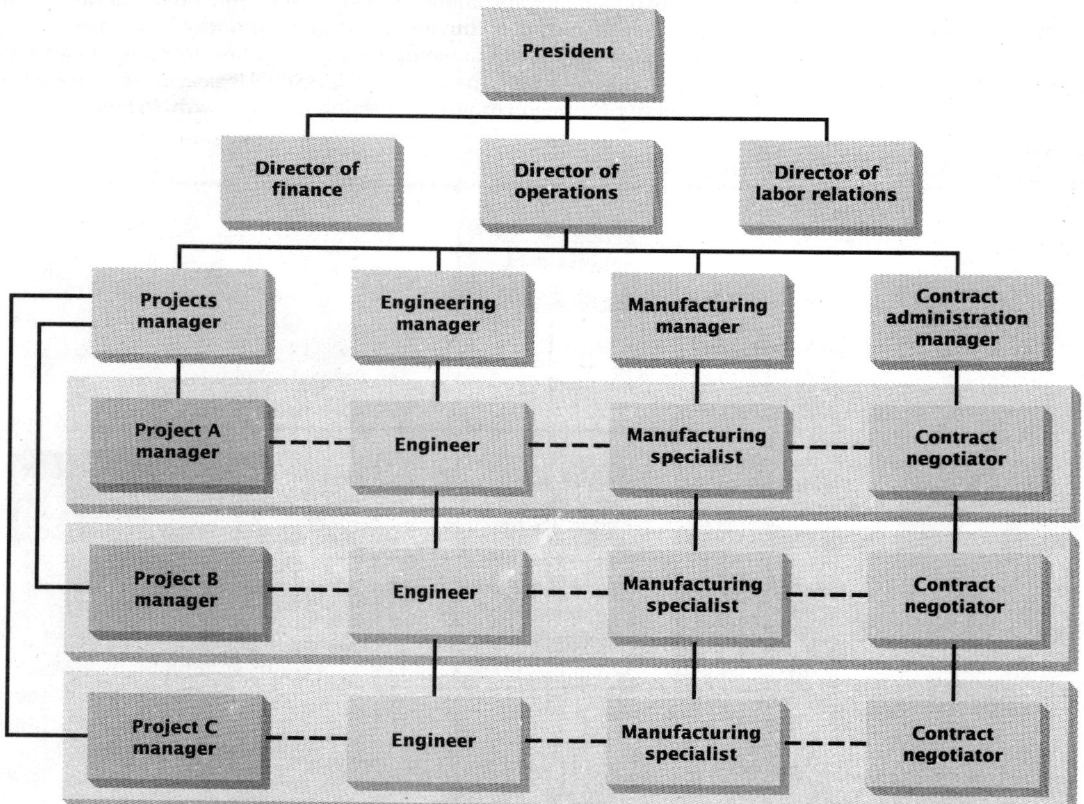

Table 10.3 Advantages and Disadvantages of Matrix Organizations

Advantages	Disadvantages
Efficient use of resources: Individual specialists as well as equipment can be shared across projects.	**Power struggles:** Conflict occurs because boundaries of authority and responsibility overlap.
Project integration: There is a clear and workable mechanism for coordinating work across functional lines.	**Heightened conflict:** Competition over scarce resources occurs, especially when personnel are being shared across projects.
Improved information flow: Communication is enhanced both laterally and vertically.	**Slow reaction time:** Heavy emphasis on consultation and shared decision making retards timely decision making.
Flexibility: Frequent contact between members from different departments expedites decision making and adaptive responses.	**Difficulty in monitoring and controlling:** Multidiscipline involvement heightens information demands and makes it difficult to evaluate responsibility.
Discipline retention: Functional experts and specialists are kept together even though projects come and go.	**Excessive overhead:** Double management by creating project managers.
Improved motivation and commitment: Involvement of members in decision making enhances commitment and motivation.	**Experienced stress:** Dual reporting relations contribute to ambiguity and role conflict.

Source: *From Erik W. Larson and David H. Gobeli, "Matrix Management: Contradictions and Insights." Copyright © 1987, by the Regents of the University of California. Reprinted from the* California Management Review, *vol. 29, no. 4. By permission of the Regents.*

from the line managers in charge of engineering, manufacturing, and contract administration. Technical needs dictate how many specialists will be borrowed from a given functional area at a given time. It is important to note that project managers have only limited (project-related) authority over the specialists, who otherwise report to their line managers. Matrix design has both advantages and disadvantages (see Table 10.3).

■ **Advantages.** Increased *coordination* is the overriding advantage of matrix design. The matrix format places a project manager in a good position to coordinate the many interrelated aspects of a particular project, both inside and outside the organization.[53] In mechanistic organizations, the various aspects of a project normally would be handled in a fragmented fashion by functional units, such as production and marketing, with no single person being in charge of the project.

Improved information flow, the third advantage listed in Table 10.3, needs to be interpreted carefully. Research has found that matrix design increases the *quantity* of communication but decreases its *quality*.[54]

■ **Disadvantages.** First and foremost, matrix design flagrantly violates the traditional unity-of-command principle. A glance at Figure 10.7 reveals that an engineer, for instance, actually has two supervisors at the same time. This special arrangement can and sometimes does cause power struggles and conflicts of interest. Only frequent and comprehensive communication between functional and project managers (integration) can minimize unity-of-command problems. A corollary of the unity-of-command problem is the "authority gap" facing project managers who must complete projects in spite of a lack of formal line authority. Research has shown that project managers tend to use negotiation, persuasive ability, technical competence, and the exchange of favors to compensate for their lack of authority.[55] All of these challenges might explain why project managers, in a recent study of a matrix organization, reported significantly higher job satisfaction than did their line-manager colleagues.[56]

Finally, matrix organizations have turned out to be too complex and cumbersome for some organizations. After years of serving as a model for matrix design, Texas Instruments scrapped its complex matrix structure in favor of a more decentralized arrangement approximating strategic business units.[57] However, to conclude that matrix design was a passing fad of the 1970s and early 1980s, as some have done, would be a mistake. According to a study reported in the late 1980s, 89 percent of 387 U.S. and Canadian companies with matrix management experience said they would continue using it.[58]

10f Philips Flips the Switch on Matrix

In the 1990s, Dutch electronics giant Philips experimented with matrix management, which organizes the company along product lines and country sector. But the scheme sparked too much conflict. "We killed the matrix. It was too slow—it put the management board in a referee role," says Jan Oosterveld, board member in charge of strategy at Philips. Now Philips is trying something more flexible: Managers of individual businesses have primary global responsibility, while regional bosses or global account managers for key clients play a role as well.

Source: Gail Edmondson, "See the World, Erase Its Borders," Business Week *(August 28, 2000): 114.*

QUESTIONS:

Why would matrix design be especially difficult for a huge global corporation? What arguments could you present in favor of a *well-run* matrix design for Philips? Does Philips's new arrangement sound good to you? Explain.

Effective Delegation

delegation: *assigning various degrees of decision-making authority to lower-level employees*

6. DEFINE the term *delegation,* and **LIST** at least five common barriers to delegation.

Delegation is an important common denominator that runs through virtually all relatively organic design alternatives. It is vital to successful decentralization. Formally defined, **delegation** is the process of assigning various degrees of decision-making authority to lower-level employees.[59] As this definition implies, delegation is not an all-or-nothing proposition. There are at least five different degrees of delegation[60] (see Figure 10.8).

A word of caution about delegation is necessary, because there is one thing it does *not* include. Former President Harry Truman is said to have had a little sign on his White House desk that read, "The Buck Stops Here!"[61] Managers who delegate should keep this idea in mind because, although authority may be passed along to people at lower levels, ultimate responsibility cannot be passed along. Thus delegation is the sharing of authority, not the abdication of responsibility. Chrysler's former CEO Lee Iacocca admittedly fell victim to this particular lapse:

> *When the company started to make money, it spent its cash on stock buybacks and acquisitions. For his part, Iacocca was distracted by nonautomotive concerns.*

Figure 10.8 The Delegation Continuum

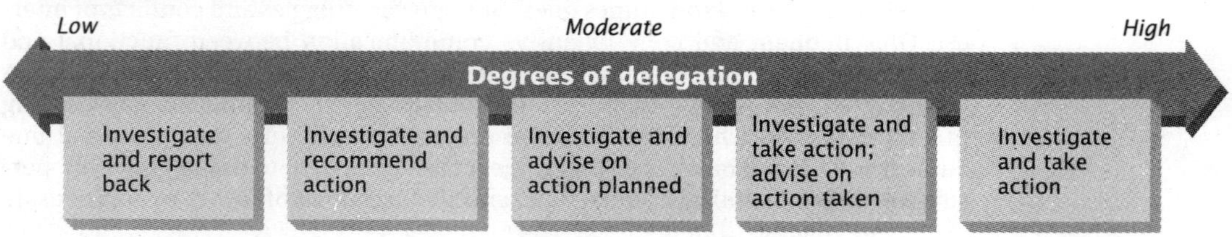

President George W. Bush knows how to delegate. His job is simply too big to do alone. But when it came to selecting special envoys to spearhead the U.S. relief efforts for tsunami and hurricane victims in 2005, he outdid himself. He tapped the unlikely team of former Presidents George H.W. Bush and Bill Clinton. So add this item to the list of advantages of delegation: these former political adversaries not only got the job done, they became good friends and golfing buddies in the process.

> *[Iacocca] concedes that while he kept his finger on finance and marketing, he should have paid closer attention to new model planning. "If I made one mistake," he says now, "it was delegating all the product development and not going to one single meeting."*[62]

Iacocca corrected this mistake prior to his retirement, and customers liked Chrysler's bold new designs.

■ The Advantages of Delegation

Managers stand to gain a great deal by adopting the habit of delegating. By passing along well-defined tasks to lower-level people, managers can free more of their time for important chores such as planning and motivating. Regarding the question of exactly *what* should be delegated, Intel's former chairman, Andy Grove, made the following recommendation: "Because it is easier to monitor something with which you are familiar, if you have a choice you should delegate those activities you know best."[63] Grove cautions that delegators who follow his advice will experience some psychological discomfort because they will quite naturally want to continue doing what they know best.

In addition to freeing valuable managerial time,[64] delegation is also a helpful management training and development tool. Moreover, lower-level managers who desire more challenge generally become more committed and satisfied when they are given the opportunity to tackle significant problems. Conversely, a lack of delegation can stifle initiative. Consider the situation of a California builder:

> *[The founder and chairman] personally negotiates every land deal. Visiting every construction site repeatedly, he is critical even of details of cabinet*

> *construction. "The building business is an entrepreneurial business," he says. "Yes, you can send out people. But you better follow them. You have to manage your managers."*
>
> *Says one former . . . executive: "The turnover there's tremendous. He hires bright and talented people, but then he makes them eunuchs. He never lets them make any decisions."*[65]

Perfectionist managers who avoid delegation have problems in the long run when they become overwhelmed by minute details.

10g Two Types of Delegation?

There are two types of delegating that managers need to consider before passing the workload to their employees: delegating for results and delegating for employee development.

Source: Sharon Gazda, "The Art of Delegating," HR Magazine, *47 (January 2002): 75*

QUESTIONS:
How do you feel about this distinction? Do you think it is valid? Explain. How can a manager effectively blend the two types of delegation?

■ Barriers to Delegation

There are several reasons why managers generally do not delegate as much as they should:

- Belief in the fallacy expressed in the advice "If you want it done right, do it yourself"
- Lack of confidence and trust in lower-level employees
- Low self-confidence
- Fear of being called lazy
- Vague job definition
- Fear of competition from those below
- Reluctance to take the risks involved in depending on others
- Lack of controls that provide early warning of problems with delegated duties
- Poor example set by bosses who do not delegate[66]

Managers can go a long way toward effective delegation by recognizing and correcting these tendencies both in themselves and in their fellow managers.[67] Since successful delegation is habit forming, the first step usually is the hardest. Properly trained and motivated people who know how to take initiative in challenging situa-

Source: *Published* Harvard Business Review, *June 2004. Permission by Dave Carpenter.*

tions (see Skills & Tools at the end of this chapter) often reward a delegator's trust with a job well done.[68]

Once managers have developed the habit of delegating, they need to remember this wise advice from Peter Drucker: "Delegation . . . requires that delegators follow up. They rarely do—they think they have delegated, and that's it. But they are still accountable for performance. And so they have to follow up, have to make sure that the task gets done—and done right."[69]

The Changing Shape of Organizations

Management scholars have been predicting the death of traditional pyramid-shaped bureaucracies for nearly 40 years.[70] Initial changes were slow in coming and barely noticeable. Observers tended to dismiss the predictions as naïve and exaggerated. However, the pace and degree of change have picked up dramatically since the 1980s. All of the social, political-legal, economic, and technological changes discussed in Chapter 3 threaten to make traditional organizations obsolete. Why? Because they are too slow, unresponsive, uncreative, costly, and hard to manage. It is clear today that no less than a reorganization revolution is under way. Traditional pyramid organizations, though still very much in evidence, are being questioned as never before. General Electric's legendary CEO Jack Welch put it this way:

> *The old organization was built on control, but the world has changed. The world is moving at such a pace that control has become a limitation. It slows you down. You've got to balance freedom with some control, but you've got to have more freedom than you ever dreamed of.*[71]

7. EXPLAIN how the traditional pyramid organization is being reshaped.

Consequently, to be prepared for tomorrow's workplace, we need to take a look at how organizations are being reshaped.

Characteristics of the New Organizations

Three structural trends, already well established, are paving the way for new and different organizations. Layers are being eliminated, teamwork is becoming the norm, and size is being compartmentalized. Let us explore each of these exciting and sometimes troublesome trends.

Fewer Layers. As documented in the last chapter, the dramatic downsizing of large U.S. businesses continues. Well-paid middle managers have been particularly hard hit. The plain truth is that companies can no longer afford layer upon layer of costly managerial talent in today's global economy. *Fortune* magazine offered this instructive historical perspective:

> *Middle managers have always handled two main jobs: supervising people, and gathering, processing, and transmitting information. But in growing numbers of companies, self-managed teams are taking over such standard supervisory duties as scheduling work, maintaining quality, even administering pay and vacations. Meanwhile, the ever-expanding power and dwindling cost of computers have transformed information handling from a difficult, time-consuming job to a far easier and quicker one. Zap! In an instant, historically speaking, the middle manager's traditional functions have vaporized.*
>
> *That's bad enough. At the same time, competition is forcing many companies to squeeze costs without mercy. Guess who looks like a big, fat target?*[72]

The so-called delayering of corporate America during the past decade has been remarkable. General Electric stripped away six layers of management, from ten to four.[73] America's second biggest copper company, Asarco, compressed 13 layers of management down to only five, thus helping to save the company $100 million.[74] Does delayering mean that hierarchies are unnecessary? According to motivation expert Edward Lawler, hierarchies are necessary, but less hierarchy is better:

Hierarchies perform some very important organizational functions that must be done in some way if coordinated, organized behavior is to take place. On the other hand, if an organization design is adopted that includes work teams, new reward systems, extensive training, and . . . various other practices . . ., organizations can operate effectively with substantially less hierarchy.[75]

Some organizations have already proved Lawler's point. Federal Express, for example, created a whole new overnight delivery industry with only five layers of management.[76]

■ **More Teams.** Envisioning tomorrow's organizations, Peter Drucker mentioned three characteristics: they will have fewer layers, be information-based, and be structured around teams.[77] Common team formats include project teams, quality circles, cross-functional teams, self-managed teams, and virtual teams.[78] We pay close attention to each of these in later chapters. Greater emphasis on teamwork demands more effective communication, greater interpersonal trust, negotiating skills, and efficient conflict management. These topics also are discussed in later chapters.

■ **Smallness Within Bigness.** When it comes to organizations, how big is too big? Is small beautiful? Is bigger better? These questions continue to stir lively debate in management circles. Research has not produced clear-cut answers.[79] Today, however, many have come to realize that the issue is not the size of the organization. Rather, *complexity* seems to be the key issue. As organizations grow, they tend to become more complex and unmanageable. The trick for managers is to strike a balance to jointly reap the benefits of large size and small scale. A prime example is Cleveland's Parker Hannifin Corporation, the successful maker of hydraulics and other heavy equipment.

"When a division gets to a point where its general manager can't know and understand the business and be close to the customer, we split it off," says [now retired] Chief Executive Paul G. Schloemer. Typically, that means plants of 300 to 400 workers, but there is no hard-and-fast rule on size. It has more to do with how well managers can deal with the organization's complexity. Parker Hannifin now has more than 200 plants in some 80 divisions.[80]

We can expect to see many attempts to create entrepreneurial units within the financial security blanket of big companies in the years ahead. General Electric's Jack Welch observed, "Well, in the end, that's what it's all about, trying to create a small-company soul in a big-company body. If you can do that and use the leverage and power, the global reach and human resources of a big company, you can create massive amounts of opportunity."[81]

10h A World Turned Upside Down

Harvard Business School Professor Rosabeth Moss Kanter:

The companies that are role models talk about themselves as inverted pyramids, with the executives being there to support the people on the ground.

Source: As quoted in Sheila M. Puffer, "Changing Organizational Structures: An Interview with Rosabeth Moss Kanter," Academy of Management Executive, *18 (May 2004): 104.*

QUESTIONS:

Have you seen any evidence of this in your own work experience or in what you have read or heard about today's business leaders? Explain the practical implications of your answer. Is this one of those "easy-to-say-but-hard-to-do" managerial tasks? Explain.

■ New Organizational Configurations

Figure 10.9 illustrates three different ways in which the traditional pyramid organization is being reshaped.[82] They are the hourglass organization, the cluster organization, and the virtual organization. In various combinations, these three configurations embody the characteristics just discussed. They also may overlap, as when an hourglass organization relies extensively on teams. The new structures have important implications for both the practice of management and the quality of work life. Let us examine them and take an imaginary peek into the not-too-distant future of work organizations.

Figure 10.9 Reshaping the Traditional Pyramid Organization

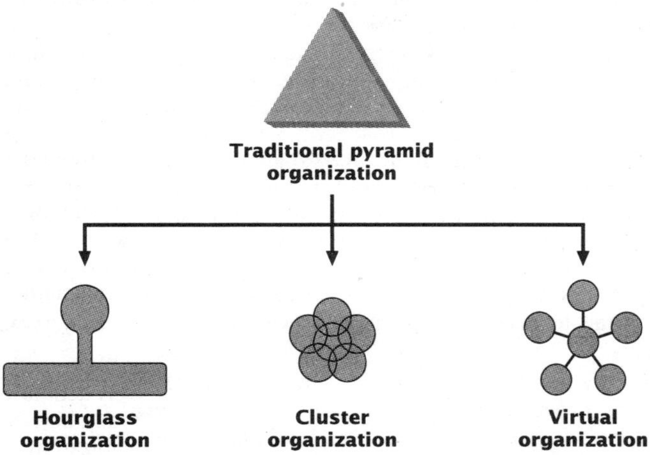

■ **Hourglass Organizations.** The **hourglass organization** consists of three layers, with the middle layer distinctly pinched. A strategic elite is responsible for formulating a vision for the organization and making sure it becomes reality. A significantly shrunken middle-management layer carries out a coordinating function for diverse lower-level activities. Thanks to computer networks that flash information directly from the factory floor or retail outlet to the executive suite and back again, middle managers are no longer simply conduits for warmed-over information. Also unlike traditional middle managers, hourglass middle managers are generalists rather than narrow specialists. They are comfortable dealing with complex interfunctional problems. A given middle manager might deal with an accounting problem one day, a product design issue the next, and a marketing dilemma the next—all within cross-functional team settings.

hourglass organization: *three-layer structure with a constricted middle layer*

At the bottom of the hourglass is a broad layer of technical specialists who act as their own supervisors much of the time. Consequently, the distinction between supervisors and rank-and-file personnel is blurred. Employees at this operating level complain about a very real lack of promotion opportunities. Management tries to keep them motivated with challenging work assignments, lateral transfers, skill-training opportunities, and pay-for-performance schemes. Union organizers attempt to exploit complaints about employees "having to act like managers, but not being paid like managers."

cluster organization: *collaborative structure in which teams are the primary unit*

■ **Cluster Organizations.** Another new configuration shown in Figure 10.9 is the **cluster organization**. This label is appropriate because teams are the primary structural unit.[83]

For instance, Oticon Inc., a Danish hearing-aid manufacturer that also has operations in Somerset, NJ, abolished its formal organizational structure several years ago as part of a strategic turnaround. The old way of doing things has been replaced with a flexible work environment and project-based work processes. Self-directed teams have become the defining unit of work, disbanding and forming again as the work requires. Oticon typically has 100 projects running at any time, and most of its 1,500 employees work on several projects at once.[84]

Imagining ourselves working in a cluster organization, we see multiskilled people moving from team to team as projects dictate. Pay for knowledge is a common practice. Motivation seems to be high, but some complain about a lack of job security because things are constantly changing. Stress levels rise when the pace of change quickens. Special training efforts, involving team-building exercises, are aimed at enhancing everyone's communication and group involvement skills.[85]

10i A Radical Approach to Virtual Organizations

Advice from management guru Michael Hammer:

> *See your business not as a self-contained company but as part of an extended enterprise of companies that work together to create customer value.*

Source: Michael Hammer, The Agenda: What Every Business Must Do to Dominate the Decade *(New York: Crown Business, 2001), p. 221.*

QUESTIONS:

But what about quaint notions such as loyalty and company pride? How prepared are you to work in this sort of fluid and uncertain environment? Explain.

virtual organizations: *Internet-linked networks of value-adding subcontractors*

■ **Virtual Organizations.** From the time of the Industrial Revolution until the Internet age, the norm was to build an organization capable of designing, producing, and marketing products. Bigger was assumed to be better. And this approach worked as long as large batches of look-alike products were acceptable to consumers. But then along came the Internet, e-business, and mass customization, discussed in Chapters 1 and 7. *Speed*—in the form of faster market research, faster product development, faster production, and faster delivery—became more important than organizational size. Meanwhile, global competition kept a lid on prices. Suddenly, consumers realized they could get exactly what they wanted, at a good price, and fast. Many lumbering organizational giants of the past were not up to the task. Enter **virtual organizations**, flexible networks of value-adding subcontractors, linked by the Internet, e-mail, fax machines, and telephones.[86] Probably the most extreme example of a virtual organization that we can find today is Linux. What started in 1991 as Linus Torvalds's student project at Finland's University of Helsinki has evolved into a huge global enterprise with a product competing head-to-head with Microsoft's Windows operating system. *Business Week* explains:

> *There's no headquarters, no CEO, and no annual report. And it's not a single company. Rather, it's a cooperative venture in which employees at about two dozen companies [including industry giants IBM, Intel, and Hewlett-Packard],*

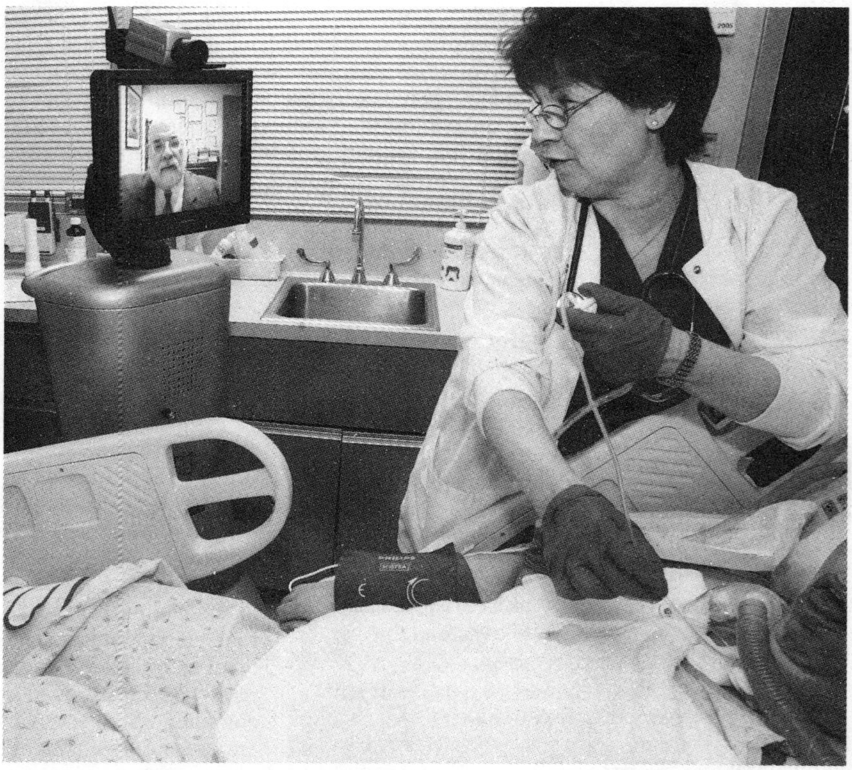

Sometimes it's very instructive and comforting to have an expert peering over your shoulder while you work. Thanks to modern technology, experts in "virtual organizations" can be in more than one place at a time. Here, R.N. Kathy Trimble attends to an intensive care patient at the Detroit Medical Center with the guidance of Harper University Hospital's Dr. Joseph Bander, via a RP-6 robot.

along with thousands of individuals [including volunteers], work together to improve Linux software. The tech companies contribute sweat equity to the project, largely by paying programmers' salaries, and then make money by selling products and services around the Linux operating system. They don't charge for Linux itself, since under the cooperative's rules the software is available to all comers for free. . . .

Distributors, including Red Hat Inc. and Novell Inc., package Linux with helpful user manuals, regular updates, and customer service, and then charge customers annual subscription fees for all the extras. . . .

IBM, HP, and others capitalize on the ability to sell machines without any up-front charge for an operating-system license, which can range up to several thousand dollars for some versions of Windows. . . .[87]

Torvalds studiously monitors the quality of changes to his open-source software from his home in Oregon via the Internet. Aside from the Torvalds legacy, what holds this far-ranging virtual organization together is a common passion for creating world-class software.[88]

Other virtual organizations are taking shape as large companies strive to cut costs by outsourcing functions ranging from manufacturing and shipping to payroll and accounting.[89] (See the Closing Case for a look at how United Parcel Service has made a thriving business out of taking over a wide range of supply chain functions for many companies.)

From a personal perspective, life in virtual organizations is *hectic*. Everything moves at Internet speed. Change and learning are constant. Cross-functional teams are the norm, and job reassignments are frequent. Project specialists rarely see a single project to completion because they are whisked off to other projects. Unavoidable by-products of constant change are stress and burnout. Unexpectedly, the need for face-to-face contact increases as geographically dispersed team members communicate via e-mail, instant messaging, groupware, and voice mail.[90] Only face-to-face interaction, both on and off the job, can build the rapport and trust necessary to get something done quickly with people you rarely see. The growing gap between information haves and have-nots produces resentment and alienation among low-paid workers employed by factory, data-processing, and shipping subcontractors.

SUMMARY

1. Contingency organization design has grown in popularity as environmental complexity has increased. The idea behind contingency design is structuring the organization to fit situational demands. Consequently, contingency advocates contend that there is no one best organizational setup for all situations. Diagnosing the degree of environmental uncertainty is an important first step in contingency design. Field studies have confirmed the validity of the assumption that organization structure should vary according to the situation.
2. Burns and Stalker discovered that mechanistic (rigid) organizations are effective when the environment is relatively stable and that organic (flexible) organizations are best when unstable conditions prevail.
3. Lawrence and Lorsch found that differentiation (division of labor) and integration (cooperation among specialists) increased in successful organizations as environmental complexity increased. Today's organizations tend to suffer from excessive differentiation and inadequate integration.
4. There are five basic departmentalization formats, each with its own combination of advantages and disadvantages. Functional departmentalization is the most common approach. The others are product-service, geographic location, customer classification, and work flow process departmentalization.

In actual practice, these pure types of departmentalization are usually combined in various ways.

5. Design variables available to organizers are span of control, decentralization, line and staff, and matrix. As organizers have come to realize that situational factors dictate how many people a manager can directly supervise, the notion of an ideal span of control has become obsolete. Decentralization, the delegation of decision authority to lower-level managers, has been praised as being democratic and criticized for reducing top management's control. Strategic business units foster a high degree of decentralization. Line and staff organization helps balance specialization and unity of command. Functional authority serves to make line and staff organi-zations more organic by giving staff specialists temporary and limited line authority. Matrix organizations are highly organic because they combine vertical and horizontal lines of authority to achieve coordinated control over complex projects.

6. Delegation of authority, although generally resisted for a variety of reasons, is crucial to decentralization. Effective delegation permits managers to tackle higher-priority duties while helping train and develop lower-level managers. Although delegation varies in degree, it never means abdicating primary responsibility. Successful delegation requires that lower-level managers display plenty of initiative.

7. Many factors, with global competition leading the way, are forcing management to reshape the traditional pyramid bureaucracy. These new organizations are characterized by fewer layers, extensive use of teams, and manageably small subunits. Three emerging organizational configurations are the hourglass organization, the cluster organization, and the virtual organization. Each has its own advantages and pitfalls.

TERMS TO UNDERSTAND

- Organizing, p. 283
- Contingency design, p. 283
- Mechanistic organizations, p. 284
- Organic organizations, p. 284
- Differentiation, p. 286
- Integration, p. 287
- Departmentalization, p. 289
- Span of control, p. 293
- Centralization, p. 294
- Decentralization, p. 294
- Strategic business unit, p. 295
- Line and staff organization, p. 296
- Functional authority, p. 297
- Matrix organization, p. 298
- Delegation, p. 300
- Hourglass organization, p. 305
- Cluster organization, p. 305
- Virtual organizations, p. 306

SKILLS & TOOLS

If You Want to Be Delegated Important Duties, Then Demonstrate a Lot of Initiative

Instructions: Assess yourself with this checklist for taking initiative. What areas need improvement?

Going Beyond the Job

- I make the most of my present assignment.
- I do more than I am asked to do.
- I look for places where I might spot problems and fix them.
- I fix bugs that I notice in programs or at least tell someone about them.
- I look for opportunities to do extra work to help the project move along more quickly.

New Ideas and Follow-Through

- I try to do some original work.
- I look for places where something that's already done might be done better.
- I have ideas about new features and other technical projects that might be developed.
- When I have an idea, I try to make it work and let people know about it.
- I try to document what my idea is and why it's a good idea.
- I think about and try to document how my idea would save the company money or bring in new business.
- I seek advice from people who have been successful in promoting ideas.
- I construct a plan for selling my idea to people in the company.

Dealing Constructively with Criticism

- I tell colleagues about my ideas to get their reactions and criticisms.
- I use their comments and criticisms to make my ideas better.
- I consult the sources of criticisms to help find solutions.
- I continue to revise my ideas to incorporate my colleagues' concerns.

Planning for the Future

- I spend time planning what I'd like to work on next.
- I look for other interesting projects to work on when my present work gets close to the finish line.
- I talk to people to find out what projects are coming up and will need people.

Source: *Reprinted by permission of* Harvard Business Review. *An exhibit from "How Bell Labs Creates Star Performers," by Robert Kelly and Janet Caplan, 71 (July-August 1993).*

HANDS-ON EXERCISE

A Field Study: Sizing Up an Organization's Structure and Design

Instructions:

This exercise is designed to help you better understand organization design by getting you out into the real world to interview a manager. (*Note:* If you *are* a manager—meaning you are responsible for directly overseeing the work of others in a formal organization—simply complete the exercise yourself.) Higher-level managers are best for this exercise because their perspective will tend to be broader and more strategic. If you interview a first-line supervisor, on the other hand, be sure to remind him or her to respond from an organizationwide perspective. The only materials you will need are photocopies of Table 10.1, Table 10.2, Figure 10.4, Figure 10.5, and Figure 10.8 to share with your interviewee to explain the questions.

If the manager you interview works for a large organization, the unit of analysis can be a division, group, department, or stand-alone facility such as a factory, bank, restaurant, or store. Otherwise, the focus should be on the whole organization. (*Tip:* This exercise can give you a better feel for an organization where you might want to apply for a job.)

A. *What is the degree of environmental uncertainty?* (Table 10.1)
Low 1—2—3—4—5—6—7—8—9—10 High

B. *Is the organization relatively mechanistic or organic?* (Table 10.2)
Mechanistic 1—2—3—4—5—6—7—8—9—10 Organic

C. *How wide is the typical span of control?* (Figure 10.4)
_____ Narrow (2 to 4) _____ Moderate (5 to 9) _____ Wide (10 or more)

D. *How centralized or decentralized is the organization?* (Figure 10.5)
Highly Centralized 1—2—3—4—5—6—7—8—9—10 Highly Decentralized

E. *What is the typical degree of delegation?* (Figure 10.8)
Low 1—2—3—4—5—6—7—8—9—10 High

F. *How effective is the organization* (profitability and/or customer satisfaction)?
Not effective 1—2—3—4—5—6—7—8—9—10 Effective

G. *How strong are employee morale and job satisfaction?*
Weak 1—2—3—4—5—6—7—8—9—10 Strong

For Consideration/Discussion

1. According to Burns and Stalker's research findings about mechanistic and organic organizations, is this organization appropriately structured for its environment? Explain.
2. What sort of connection do you see between this organization's design and its overall effectiveness?
3. What sort of connection do you see between this organization's design and employee morale and job satisfaction?
4. How were the degree of centralization/decentralization and the degree of delegation related in this study?
5. In your opinion, is the design of this organization a strategic strength or weakness?
6. Would you like to work for this organization (if you don't already)? Why?
7. What was the most interesting, useful, or important thing you learned from this exercise?

INTERNET EXERCISES

1. **Let's get really organic:** Safe to say, there's probably no other company quite like W. L. Gore & Associates (**www.gore.com**). As profiled in the chapter-opening case, the maker of Gore-Tex fabrics, popular among sportspeople, consistently makes *Fortune*'s "100 Best Companies to Work For" list. This exercise gives you an additional peek inside an extraordinarily organic organization. Select the main menu heading "About Us" and then explore the material under the headings "About Gore," "Corporate Culture," "Diversity," and "Fast Facts."

Learning Points: 1. Using Table 10.2 as a guide, try to figure out what features characteristic of the organic organization are evident at Gore. 2. What

INTERNET EXERCISES

types of people would, and what types would not, be comfortable working at W. L. Gore? Would you like to work at Gore? 3. What are the main risks of being too organic?

2. Check it out: *Fast Company* magazine (**www.fastcompany.com/backissues**) always has interesting and provocative ideas for modern managers. Starting with the most recent issue of *Fast Company,* scan the contents of three or four issues for a topic relevant to this chapter. Read the full text of an article or two. Chances are very good you'll find something instructive and interesting about the design and management of today's organizations.

For updates to these exercises, visit our Web site (**http://business.college.hmco.com/students/** and select Kreitner, *Management,* 10e).

CLOSING CASE

A Virtually Great New Business for UPS

They call it the "end of the runway," although technically speaking, it's on the wrong side of the fence surrounding Louisville International Airport. And it's across the street. But close enough. This is prime real estate for companies, as advantageous as rail position at Churchill Downs. The closer they are to the airport, the closer they are to customers. Got a last-minute order? Not a problem. Throw it on a plane. Naturally, UPS has a sprawling campus here. No surprise there. But what is surprising is what the world's largest delivery company is doing for customers inside the six unmarked, off-white monolithic buildings.

April Bell, who used to load packages for UPS, works in an emergency room for electronics in Building One. Her specialty is repairing printers. A few desks over, Jason Bennett is diagnosing digital projectors. Other technicians are rescuing faulty laptops and cell phones. In another building, Shana Phillips, who used to drive a UPS truck, is supervising distribution of sports apparel. Her team puts shirts and jackets on hangers, attaches labels, rearranges cartons of basketball shoes by size or style. And in yet another building, UPS is packaging Nikon digital cameras with a CD-ROM, camera strap, and operating instructions.

Where are the brown trucks? The snappy brown uniforms? Not here. This is a little-known subsidiary of the giant delivery company. It goes by the unwieldy name of UPS Supply Chain Solutions, and it performs what are, for UPS, some very peculiar functions—everything from fixing busted electronics to answering customer phone calls to issuing corporate credit cards. Although SCS, as it is sometimes referred to in company shorthand, is largely invisible—which suits many of its customers just fine—it represents the company's aggressive play for new business and deeper, more lucrative relationships with companies. For those companies, it offers ways to become faster, more efficient, more competitive.

UPS is tapping into a powerful trend. For years, Peter Drucker and other management gurus have argued that companies are better off focusing on the front office and leaving the back office and similar functions to someone else who specializes in those areas. In other words, find a company whose front office is your back office. By offering to take on many of the various tasks known as the "supply chain"—which can encompass every step in producing a product or service and getting it to customers—UPS is trying to be that company.

Unlike the outsourcing of manufacturing, which has caused a massive migration of American jobs overseas, much outsourced supply-chain work stays in the United States, or wherever the customers are. The idea is to make the chain shorter and simpler, not longer, so that companies can operate quickly and efficiently. The best way to do that is to have raw materials, finished products, and repair technicians close to the people who need them. Or, if that's not feasible because the customers are spread out, then close to the next best thing: the end of the runway. . . .

One of the attractions of SCS is that it allows small companies to have a big-league supply chain. Take AND 1, a sports-apparel company based outside Philadelphia.

Despite its modest size ($175 million in revenue in 2002), it has logistics experts around the globe, the latest inventory tracking technology, and two state-of-the-art warehouses in California and Kentucky. That's because SCS's resources are AND 1's resources, which is what persuaded AND 1's chief operating officer, Christina Houlahan, to give SCS her entire supply chain. "I compete on how rapidly I get our product out the door of the manufacturer and in the store," she says. . . .

United Parcel Service Inc. still gets the vast majority of its annual revenue—$31 billion in 2002—the old-fashioned way, by picking up and dropping off boxes of stuff. With $2.5 billion in annual revenue in 2002, SCS represents just 8% of the company's total business. But UPS CEO Mike Eskew is gambling that these sophisticated behind-the-scenes services will be the company's next big moneymaker. SCS is now UPS's fastest-growing division. It has more than 750 locations worldwide, and UPS has acquired 19 companies, including a bank, in an effort to beef up its offerings. There's no question that the demand for outsourcing supply-chain services is growing. In his annual surveys of large American manufacturers, Northeastern University professor Bob Lieb reports that 82% used third-party logistics providers . . . [in 2003], up from 38% in 1991, the first year of the survey.

Source: *Excerpted from Chuck Salter, "Surprise Package,"* Fast Company, *no. 79 (February 2004): 62, 66. Reprinted by permission.*

For Discussion

1. Would it make sense to break SCS into strategic business units? Explain.
2. Why is open-system thinking, as covered in Chapters 2 and 9, especially important for the executives at SCS?
3. Based on what you have learned in this case, what are the growth prospects for virtual organizations? Explain.
4. What are the greatest challenges for managers in today's virtual organizations? What specific skills do they need to succeed?
5. Relative to your own career plans, what do you like or dislike about the trend toward virtual organizations? Explain.

TEST PREPPER

True/False Questions

_____ **1.** Strategy always follows structure in well-managed organizations.

_____ **2.** Contingency design researchers have found the traditional bureaucracy to be the best overall approach.

_____ **3.** Organic organizations put little emphasis on loyalty and obedience.

_____ **4.** Lawrence and Lorsch's research suggests that inadequate integration can be a problem when environmental complexity is high.

_____ **5.** Functional departments categorize jobs according to the activity performed.

_____ **6.** Organizations with work flow process departments have a distinct outward focus.

_____ **7.** The trend today is toward narrow spans of control.

_____ **8.** Strategic business units reflect a high degree of organizational centralization.

_____ **9.** Project managers in matrix organizations need good negotiation skills.

_____ **10.** New organizations are eliminating layers, becoming compartmentalized, and using more teams.

Multiple-Choice Questions

1. The _____ approach permits the custom tailoring of organizations to meet unique situational demands.
A. organic B. traditional
C. differentiation D. contingency
E. integration

2. Communication tends to be _____ in the organic organization and _____ in the mechanistic organization.
A. lateral; top-to-bottom
B. vertical; lateral
C. lateral; participative
D. command-and-control; vertical
E. top-down; bottom-up

3. Lawrence and Lorsch concluded that as environmental complexity increased for successful companies,
A. differentiation replaced integration.
B. both differentiation and integration increased.
C. both differentiation and integration decreased.
D. there was more differentiation and less integration.
E. differentiation and integration were unrelated.

4. Which of the following is *not* a basic type of departmentalization?
A. Functional B. Operational
C. Geographic location D. Work flow process
E. Customer classification

5. Horizontal organizations have _____ departments.
A. geographic location B. customer classification
C. work flow process D. product-service
E. line and staff

6. _____ is *not* a situational determinant of spans of control.
A. Dispersion of subordinates
B. Dominant technology
C. Time required for planning
D. Complexity of work performed by subordinates
E. Time spent coordinating with other managers

7. In a highly decentralized candy factory, who makes many of the important decisions?
A. Middle and lower managers
B. Top management
C. Outside consultants
D. Customers
E. The corporate board of directors

8. In a matrix organization, which way does authority flow?
A. Only horizontally
B. Nowhere, because there is no authority dimension in matrix organizations
C. Only vertically
D. Both vertically and horizontally
E. Diagonally

9. An instruction to _____ represents the highest degree of delegation.
A. "investigate and report back"
B. "investigate and recommend action"
C. "investigate and advise on action planned"
D. "investigate, take action, and advise on action taken"
E. "investigate and take action"

10. _____ are Internet-linked networks of value-adding subcontractors.
A. Hourglass structures
B. Matrix systems
C. Virtual organizations
D. Cluster organizations
E. Functional structures

ACE self-test

Want more questions? Visit the student Web site at **http://business.college.hmco.com/students/** (select Kreitner, *Management*, 10e) and take the ACE quizzes for more practice.

11 Human Resource Management

> *"From the outside, my guess is most people think about the incredible technology we have. But what really matters is our people."* [1]
>
> DAN ROSENSWEIG, CHIEF OPERATING OFFICER, YAHOO.

OBJECTIVES

- **Explain** what human resource management involves.
- **Define** the term *human capital,* and **identify** at least four of Pfeffer's people-centered practices.
- **Identify** and briefly **explain** the seven steps in the PROCEED model of employee selection.
- **Distinguish** among equal employment opportunity, affirmative action, and managing diversity.
- **Explain** how managers can be more effective interviewers.
- **Discuss** how performance appraisals can be made legally defensible.
- **Compare** and **contrast** the ingredients of good training programs for both skill and factual learning.
- **Specify** the essential components of an organization's policies for dealing with sexual harassment and alcohol and drug abuse.

the changing workplace

Finding Workers Who Fit

Since founders Kip Tindell and Garrett Boone opened the first Container Store in Dallas in 1978, containing growth has turned out to be their most daunting challenge. The privately held company has quietly expanded into a 33-store nationwide chain with projected 2004 revenue of $370 million and annual sales growth that has topped 20 percent in all of its 26 years. Behind much of that success, analysts say, aren't just the popular knicknacks the Container Store sells for Type A neat freaks. Just as important is the company's organizing principle for human resources: turning its best customers into loyal, top-performing employees.

In an industry with an average employee turnover rate of more than 70 percent, worker churn at the Container Store is less than 10 percent for full-time employees and 30 to 35 percent for part-timers. And nearly a third of the company's 2,500 workers come from referrals. "To be a great place to shop, you need to be a great place to work," says Doug Fleener, president of Massachusetts-based retail consultancy Dynamic Experiences Group. "This company is in total harmony, from the sales floor to the distribution center." Forget the closet—here's how the Container Store organizes its talent.

1. **In-Store Head-Hunting** Tindell and Boone make recruiting part of everybody's job by offering all staff members handsome bonuses. Workers get $500 for every full-time hire and $200 for every part-timer. All employees, from stockers to managers, carry recruiting cards to pull out when chatting up customers in the aisles. The program is so successful, says Kevin Fuller, director of training and recruiting, that the company often goes six to eight months without placing a single classified ad.
2. **All-Hands Interviews** Applicants who get a call back submit to a group interview with as many as 10 fellow job candidates. There, potential hires often make a pitch for a product that solves an organizational challenge—a key indicator of enthusiasm and sales skills. The group setting offers managers a glimpse of how candidates function as part of a team. "We want to see how people encourage one another, because that's our environment," Fuller says.

3. **Continuous Training** New hires begin a 241-hour training program that stretches out over a year. (The retail-industry average for training new workers is eight hours.) Newbies are paired up with training "buddies" who give them crash courses in everything from sales techniques to the ins and outs of Elfa, the company's best-selling modular storage system. The company won't disclose how much it spends on training, but "we know it's expensive," Fuller says. Still, the training helps ensure better service—which results in fewer lost customers and a lot more sales: The Container Store rings up an average of $400 per square foot, compared with $125 for the rest of the housewares industry.

Source: *From Vicki Powers, "Finding Workers Who Fit,"* Business 2.0, *5 (November 2004): 74.*

human resource management: *acquisition, retention, and development of human resources*

1. EXPLAIN what human resource management involves.

Staffing has long been an integral part of the management process. Like other traditional management functions, such as planning and organizing, the domain of staffing has grown throughout the years. This growth reflects increasing environmental complexity and greater organizational sophistication, as the Container Store case illustrates. Early definitions of staffing focused narrowly on hiring people for vacant positions. Today, the traditional staffing function is just one part of the more encompassing human resource management process. **Human resource management** involves the acquisition, retention, and development of human resources necessary for organizational success. This broader definition underscores the point that people are valuable *resources* requiring careful nurturing. In fact, what were once called personnel departments are now called human resource departments. In a more folksy manner, the top human resources executive at Wal-Mart is called the "senior vice president of people."[2] This people-centered human resource approach emphasizes the serious moral and legal issues involved in viewing labor simply as a commodity to be bought, exploited to exhaustion, and discarded when convenient. Moreover, global opportunities and competitive pressures have made the skillful management of human resources more important than ever.[3]

Progressive and successful organizations treat all employees as valuable human resources. They go out of their way to accommodate their employees' full range of needs. A prime example is Analytical Graphics Inc. in Exton, Pennsylvania:

> *Its aerospace, electrical and software engineers develop mission-critical software that helps analyze and visualize data from missiles, jets, rockets and satellites for commercial and military aerospace uses, including NASA's space shuttle. . . .*
>
> *The company serves [free] daily breakfasts, lunches and dinners, to which family members are invited. Its kitchen and pantries offer free snack foods and drinks. The entire headquarters staff meets Friday for hot lunches and "story time"—during which the CEO and other employees update everyone on company performance figures, activities and news.*
>
> *The free-flowing food encourages teamwork and camaraderie, employees say, while making their work lives easier and more productive.*
>
> *Other free family-style perks include a laundry room with free washers, dryers and supplies; a well-equipped fitness room; and free holiday gift wrapping. For nominal fees, employees can take advantage of other services, such as dry cleaning, oil changes, car washes, flower delivery and shoeshines.*[4]

Field research indicates that employees tend to return the favor when they are treated with dignity and respect. For instance, one study compared steel mills with either "control" or "commitment" human resource systems. Emphasis at the control-oriented steel mills was on cost cutting, rule compliance, and efficiency. Meanwhile, the other steel mills encouraged psychological commitment to the company with a climate of trust and participation. "The mills with commitment systems had higher productivity, lower scrap rates, and lower employee turnover than those with control systems."[5]

Figure 11.1 presents a model for the balance of this chapter; it reflects this strategic orientation. Notice how a logical sequence of human resource management activities—human resource strategy, recruiting, selection, performance appraisal, and training—all derive from organizational strategy and structure. Without a strategic orientation, the management of people becomes haphazardly inefficient and ineffective. Also, as indicated in Figure 11.1, an ongoing process following the hiring decision involves identifying and solving human resource problems. Two contemporary human resource problems, explored in the last section of this chapter, are discouraging sexual harassment and controlling alcohol and drug abuse.

Human Resource Strategy: A People-Centered Approach

Conventional wisdom about how employees should be perceived and managed has evolved greatly over the last 60 years. The pendulum has swung from reactive to proactive. Following World War II, personnel departments filled hiring requisitions and handled disciplinary problems submitted by managers. During the 1970s and 1980s, human resource (HR) departments became the norm, and a more encompassing approach evolved. HR departments attempted to forecast labor supply and demand, recruit and hire, manage payrolls, and conduct training and development programs. Too often, however, HR was treated as a support-staff function with only an indirect link to corporate strategy. Today, in well-managed companies, HR is being embedded in organizational strategy.[6] Other major HR trends: traditional HR functions are being decentralized throughout the enterprise and, in a more controversial move, being outsourced;[7] and HR is adapting to globalization.[8] But these transitions are far from complete, as indicated by this observation: "Some business pundits have likened the current status of HR to an awkward adolescent. The profession is just beginning to come of age but isn't quite sure where it's heading."[9] This section outlines a strategic agenda for human resource management.

Figure 11.1 A General Model for Human Resource Management

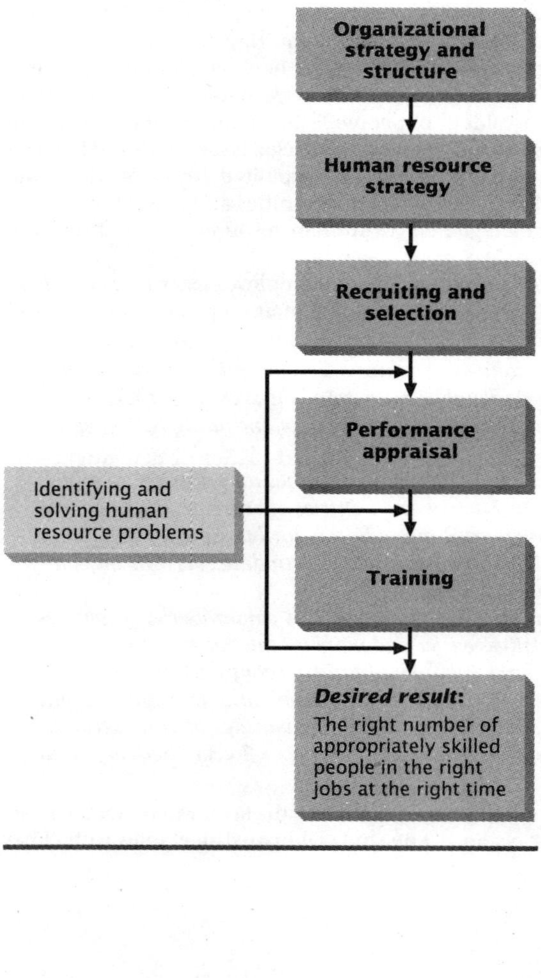

■ The Age of Human Capital

This perspective requires open-system thinking, as discussed in Chapters 2 and 9. It is a "big picture" approach to managing people and staying competitive. According to the authors of *The HR Scorecard: Linking People, Strategy, and Performance,*

> *We're living in a time when a new economic paradigm—characterized by speed, innovation, short cycle times, quality, and customer satisfaction—is highlighting the importance of intangible assets, such as brand recognition, knowledge, innovation, and particularly human capital.*[10]

human capital: *the need to develop to their fullest potential all present and future employees*

2. **DEFINE** the term *human capital,* and **IDENTIFY** at least four of Pfeffer's people-centered practices.

11a Back to the Opening Case

What role does the concept of "human capital" play in the Container Store case?

The term **human capital** encompasses all present and future workforce participants and emphasizes the need to develop their fullest potential for the benefit of everyone. Central to this perspective is the assumption that every employee is a valuable asset, not merely an expense item.[11] This broad concern for possible *future* employees is a marked departure from traditional "employees-only" perspectives.

Intel, the Santa Clara, California–based maker of computer microprocessors, is committed to developing human capital. The company "adopts" primary and secondary schools—providing computers, teaching talent, and money—and encourages its employees to help. "For every 20 hours workers volunteer at local schools, Intel donates $200."[12] As might be expected from a high-tech company, the emphasis is on math and science. Additionally, Intel matches employees' donations to their college alma maters up to $10,000 a year and awards $1,250,000 in school grants and scholarships each year to winners in a national science competition for high school seniors. Most of those who benefit from these initiatives will *not* end up working for Intel. That's what developing the *world's* human capital is all about—thinking big! (For more, see the Internet Exercises at the end of this chapter.)

People-Centered Organizations Enjoy a Competitive Advantage

In an era of nonstop layoffs, the often-heard slogan "Employees are our most valuable asset" rings hollow. In fact, Dilbert cartoonist Scott Adams calls that statement "The First Great Lie of Management."[13] But such cynicism can be countered by looking at how leading companies build a bridge from progressive human resource practices to market success. Take, for instance, Southwest Airlines. Cofounder and former CEO Herb Kelleher told *Fortune* magazine, "My mother taught me that your employees come first. If you treat them well, then they treat the customers well, and that means your customers come back and your shareholders are happy."[14] Well, Herb's mom was right! Solid research support for this approach comes from Stanford's Jeffrey Pfeffer, who reported a strong connection between *people-centered practices* and higher profits and lower employee turnover. Pfeffer identified these seven people-centered practices:

- Protection of job security (including a no-layoff policy)
- Rigorous hiring process
- Employee empowerment through decentralization and self-managed teams
- Compensation linked to performance
- Comprehensive training
- Reduction of status differences
- Sharing of key information

11b Back to the Opening Case

How well does the Container Store measure up against Pfeffer's list of people-centered practices? Explain your evidence.

Pfeffer sees these practices as an integrated package and cautions against implementing them piecemeal. Unfortunately, according to Pfeffer's calculations, only about 12 percent of today's organizations qualify as being systematically people-centered.[15] Thus, we have a clear developmental agenda for human resource management. Ideas about how to enact people-centered practices can be found throughout the balance of this book.

Recruitment and Selection

Jim Collins, in his best-seller *Good to Great: Why Some Companies Make the Leap . . . and Others Don't,* uses the metaphor of a bus when referring to the organization and its employees.[16] He believes a busload of great people can go just about anywhere it wants.[17] But a bus filled with confused and unruly passengers is destined for the ditch. A survey of CEOs reinforces the importance of getting the right people on the bus and keeping them there. When the CEOs were asked what they probably will look

Stock broker Merrill Lynch uses its famous Wall Street bull to give diversity a boost in this advertisement. (And there's only one race—the human race.)

back on five years from now as the key to their success, the number one response was "Getting and retaining talent."[18] This section deals with that important challenge.

■ Recruiting for Diversity

The ultimate goal of recruiting is to generate a pool of qualified applicants for new and existing jobs. Everyday recruiting tactics include internal job postings, referrals by present and past employees, campus recruiters, newspaper ads, Web sites, public and private employment agencies, so-called headhunters, job fairs, temporary-help agencies, and union halls. Meanwhile, an underlying reality makes today's recruiting extremely challenging. Specifically, applicant pools need to be demographically representative of the population at large if diversity is to be achieved. One *Fortune* 500 company CEO recently stated the business case for diversity this way:

> *What's most important is understanding that having a long-term commitment to diversity isn't an option. It's a requirement. It isn't something that you can turn on and off. It has to be built into the fabric of the business. Diversity is a business objective with real payoff, not a "nice-to-do." As soon as people get it into their heads that diversity is a "nice-to-do," I think it's the kiss of death.*
>
> *Diversity is the right thing to do, but it also is an imperative for businesses that intend to be successful over the long term. So you do it because it's a have-to-do.*[19]

A casual review of today's recruiting ads reveals abundant evidence of corporate diversity initiatives.[20] Companies strive hard to make *Fortune*'s annual "50 Best Companies for Minorities" list so that they can cite the honor in their recruiting ads. Among the major names high on the most recent list are McDonald's (no. 1), U.S. Postal Service (no. 6), and PepsiCo (no. 7).[21]

Recent research holds a major surprise about recruiting for diversity (see Table 11.1). Significantly, the study turned the tables and took a *job hunter's* perspective. Within the top five categories of search methods, corporate Web sites[22] had the distinction of being the most frequently used but *least successful* job-hunting method. Referrals turned out to be the best way to land a job. So we have one word of advice for job hunters in all walks of life: *network.*

> *Especially in a tough economy, networking is the key. Resume-deluged employers are posting job openings only as a last resort, says Kirsten*

11c Do You Have a Bulletproof Résumé?

News Item: *[The] chairman of gunmaker Smith & Wesson is forced to resign when newspaper reporters discover that, before becoming a corporate exec, he'd spent 15 years behind bars for a string of armed robberies and an attempted prison escape.*

Source: Adam Horowitz, Mark Athitakis, Mark Lasswell, and Owen Thomas, "101 Dumbest Moments in Business," Business 2.0, *6 (January-February 2005): 104.*

QUESTION:

Could *your* résumé successfully withstand close scrutiny for lies, misrepresentations, and critical omissions that could come back to haunt you?

Table 11.1 How Diverse Candidates Search for and Find Jobs

Top 5 Search Methods	
1. Corporate Web sites	70%
2. General job-listing sites	67
3. Classified ads	53
4. Referrals	52
5. Headhunters/agencies	35
Top 5 Ways Candidates Found Jobs	
1. Referrals	25%
2. General job-listing sites	17
3. Headhunters/agencies	17
4. Classified ads	15
5. Corporate Web sites	6

Source: HR Magazine *by Ruth Thaler-Carter. Copyright 2001 by* Society for Human Resource Management. *Reproduced with permission of* Society for Human Resource Management *in the format Textbook via Copyright Clearance Center.*

Watson, president of HireTopTalent. Rather, job leads come from "a friend who had a friend who had an uncle."...

To network effectively, start with friends, family, and others who know you well and can help present your case, says Bob Critchley, executive VP for global relationships at outplacement firm Drake Beam Morin.[23]

For more job-hunting tips, see Internet Exercise 3 at the end of the chapter.

■ The Selection Process: An Overview

HR experts commonly compare the screening and selection process to a hurdle race. Equal employment opportunity (EEO) legislation in the United States and elsewhere attempts to ensure a fair and unprejudiced race for all job applicants.[24] The first two hurdles are résumé screening and reference checking. Both are very important because of discouraging evidence such as this:

ADP Screening and Selection Services, a unit of the Roseland, N.J.-based ADP payroll and benefits managing company, says that in performing 2.6 million background checks in 2001, it found that 44 percent of applicants lied about their work histories, 41 percent lied about their education, and 23 percent falsified credentials or licenses.[25]

Background checks for criminal records and citizenship/immigration status are more crucial than ever amid concerns about workplace violence and international terrorism. Consider this: "Between January 1998 and October 2000, American Background Information Services Inc. (ABI), based in Winchester, Va., found undisclosed criminal backgrounds on 12.6 percent of the people it screened."[26] In 2004, Wal-Mart began to perform criminal background checks on all of its job applicants.[27] Other hurdles may include psychological tests, physical examinations, interviews, work-sampling tests, and drug tests. The whole selection process can become quite complex and drawn out at companies such as Google, where 25 people are hired each week:

A team of nearly 50 recruiters divided by specialty combs through résumés, which applicants must submit online, then dumps them into a program that routes those selected for interviews to the proper hiring committee and throws

the rest in the electronic trash. Interviewing for a job is a grueling process that can take months. Every opening has a hiring committee of seven to nine Googlers who must meet you. Engineers may be asked to write software or debug a program on the spot. Marketers are often required to take a writing test. No matter how long you have been out of school, Google requires that you submit your transcripts to be considered. The rigorous process is important partly for the obvious reason that in high tech, as on Wall Street, being the smartest and the cleverest at what you do is a critical business advantage.[28]

3. IDENTIFY and briefly **EXPLAIN** the seven steps in the PROCEED model of employee selection.

Del J. Still, a respected author and trainer, summarizes the overall employee selection process with the acronym PROCEED, where each letter represents one of the seven steps involved (see Table 11.2). This model encourages managers to take a systems perspective, all the way from preparation to the final hiring decision. Before examining key elements of the PROCEED model in depth, we need to clarify what is involved in the first three action items for step 1. This is where job analysis and job descriptions come into play. **Job analysis** is the process of identifying basic task and skill requirements for specific jobs by studying superior performers. A **job description** is a concise document outlining the role expectations and skill requirements for a specific job. Although some say they have become obsolete in today's fast-paced world, up-to-date job descriptions foster discipline in selection and performance appraisal by offering a formal measuring stick.[29]

job analysis: *identifying task and skill requirements for specific jobs by studying superior performers*

job description: *document outlining role expectations and skill requirements for a specific job*

■ Equal Employment Opportunity

Although earlier legislation selectively applies, the landmark EEO law in the United States is Title VII of the Civil Rights Act of 1964. Subsequent amendments, presidential executive orders, and related laws have expanded EEO's coverage. EEO law now

Table 11.2 The Employee Selection Process: Still's PROCEED Model

Step 1: PREPARE

- Identify existing superior performers
- Create a job description for the position
- Identify the competencies or skills needed to do the job
- Draft interview questions

Step 2: REVIEW

- Review questions for legality and fairness

Step 3: ORGANIZE

- Select your interview team and your method of interviewing
- Assign roles to your team and divide the questions

Step 4: CONDUCT

- Gather data from the job candidate

Step 5: EVALUATE

- Determine the match between the candidate and the job

Step 6: EXCHANGE

- Share data in a discussion meeting

Step 7: DECIDE

- Make the final decision

Source: *Del J. Still,* High Impact Hiring: How to Interview and Select Outstanding Employees, *2nd edition, revised (Dana Point, CA.: Management Development Systems, 2001), pp. 43–44. Reprinted by permission.*

provides a broad umbrella of employment protection for certain categories of disadvantaged individuals:

> *The result of this legislation has been that in virtually all aspects of employment, it is unlawful to discriminate on the basis of race, color, sex, religion, age, national origin,... [disabilities], being a disabled veteran, or being a veteran of the Vietnam Era.*[30]

What all this means is that managers cannot refuse to hire, promote, train, or transfer employees simply on the basis of the characteristics listed above. Nor can they lay off or discharge employees on these grounds. Sexual preference has been added to the list in some local jurisdictions.[31] Selection and all other personnel decisions must be made solely on the basis of objective criteria such as ability to perform or seniority. Lawsuits and fines by agencies such as the U.S. Equal Employment Opportunity Commission (EEOC) are a powerful incentive to comply with EEO laws. In fact, racial discrimination settlements cost Texaco $176 million in 1996 and Coca-Cola $192.5 million in 2000.[32] In 2004, Boeing agreed to pay $72.5 million to settle a class-action lawsuit covering 29,000 women who claimed the aircraft maker discriminated against them when making pay and promotion decisions.[33]

4. DISTINGUISH among equal employment opportunity, affirmative action, and managing diversity.

affirmative action program (AAP): *making up for past discrimination by actively seeking and employing minorities*

■ **Affirmative Action.** A more rigorous refinement of EEO legislation is affirmative action. An **affirmative action program (AAP)** is a plan for actively seeking out, employing, and developing the talents of those groups historically discriminated against in employment.[34] Affirmative action amounts to a concerted effort to make up for *past* discrimination. EEO, in contrast, is aimed at preventing *future* discrimination. Typical AAPs attack employment discrimination with the following four methods: (1) *active* recruitment of women and minorities, (2) elimination of prejudicial questions on employment application forms, (3) establishment of specific goals and timetables for minority hiring, and (4) statistical validation of employment testing procedures.

Like any public policy with legal ramifications, the EEO/AAP area is fraught with complexity.[35] Varying political and legal interpretations and inconsistent court decisions have sometimes frustrated and confused managers.[36] Researchers have uncovered both negative and positive findings about affirmative action. On the negative side, "people believed to be hired through affirmative action programs carry a stigma of incompetence no matter how qualified they are for the job."[37] On the positive side, a study based on nationwide U.S. Census Bureau data found that affirmative action had enhanced the promotion opportunities of black workers in both government and business organizations. In fact, according to the researcher, "with the exception of women in the public sector, women and blacks enjoyed better promotion opportunities than equally qualified and situated white male workers."[38] These findings disturb some white males, who claim to be the victims of "reverse discrimination."[39] At the same time, some minority employees complain of swapping one injustice for another when they take advantage of affirmative action. Legislated social change, however necessary or laudable, is not without pain. Much remains to be accomplished to eliminate the legacy of unfair discrimination in the workplace.

■ **From Affirmative Action to Managing Diversity.** As discussed in Chapter 3, the "managing-diversity" movement promises to raise the discussion of equal employment opportunity and affirmative action to a higher plane. One authority on the subject, R. Roosevelt Thomas Jr., put it this way:

> *Managers usually see affirmative action and equal employment opportunity as centering on minorities and women, with very little to offer white males. The diversity I'm talking about includes not only race, gender, creed, and ethnicity but also age, background, education, function, and personality differences. The objective is not to assimilate minorities and women into a dominant white male culture but to create a dominant heterogeneous culture.*[40]

MANAGING DIVERSITY

Diversity Goes Global

Two out of three U.S. companies have broadened their diversity programs because of increasing globalization, according to a survey of 1,780 human resource and training executives by Boston-based consulting firm Novations/J. Howard & Associates. Of those that have not done so, most expect to update diversity efforts in the near future.

Sixty-three percent of training and human resource executives surveyed report a need to broaden the scope of their company's diversity programs, and 22 percent plan to in the near future. Fifteen percent of respondents have no plans to expand their diversity programs.

"American-style diversity training, which has typically focused on race issues, isn't suitable for Latin America or Europe," says Mike Hyter, president and CEO of Novations/J. Howard. "Instead, multinational employers want and need an integrated solution that works organizationwide."

U.S. diversity programs were originally based on redressing past grievances, explains Hyter. "Early on, diversity meant meeting the needs of African-American employees or women, and then it moved to include Hispanics too. But these specific needs aren't so relevant in other regions of the world. In Latin America, the issues are more social or economic and have to do with cultural conflict. In Northern Europe, on the other hand, the main challenge stems from immigration and increasing ethnic minorities. The specifics are different everywhere and it's hard to generalize."

Hyter observes that the gender issue is still a stumbling block in some countries. "Management will say diversity training is for inclusion, but they will be in denial that women need to be part of the outreach effort," he says. "Wherever a program is delivered, it's necessary for the diversity trainer to ask questions, and not presume too much about the local situation. In fact, the very term 'diversity' communicates a U.S.-centric issue."

Pressure for a more comprehensive approach to diversity, says Hyter, is increasing because so many executives are constantly being shifted from location to location. "This has brought about a more worldly perspective by senior management and [led] to a change in U.S.-based training. This has meant that diversity programs have steadily become more about inclusion for everyone, and less about traditional diversity."

Hyter says the key to success is to have an approach to diversity and inclusion that is broad and not only meets the varied requirements of organizations in the United States, but also may be expanded to organizations overseas.

Source: From Gail Johnson, "Time to Broaden Diversity," Training, *41 (September 2004): 16. © VNU Business Media, Inc. Reprinted with permission.*

In short, diversity advocates want to replace all forms of bigotry, prejudice, and intolerance with tolerance and, ideally, *appreciation* of interpersonal differences.[41] They also want to broaden the message of *inclusion* to make it globally applicable (see Managing Diversity).

■ **Accommodating the Needs of People with Disabilities.** From the perspective of someone in a wheelchair, the world can be a very unfriendly place. Curbs, stairways, and inward-swinging doors in small public toilet stalls all symbolically say, "You're not welcome here; you don't fit in." Prejudice and discrimination worsen the situation. Cheri Blauwet, a world-class wheelchair racer from Larchwood, Iowa, who was paralyzed below the waist in a farm accident at 15 months of age, recently offered this perspective:

> *The thing that bothers me most is the low expectations strangers have of me. The first thing people see is not a 24-year-old woman who's strong and capable. They don't see a Stanford medical school student. What they see is the wheelchair.*[42]

Human disabilities vary widely, but historically, disabled people have had one thing in common—unemployment. Consider these telling statistics:

> *Today, more than 54 million Americans are disabled, nearly 20 percent of the U.S. population. One in five disabled adults has not graduated from high*

The world changed for Carmen Jones when a car accident during her junior year at Virginia's Hampton University left her in a wheelchair for life. After months of painful rehabilitation, an inspiring boost from the University's president helped her eliminate deep self-doubts and earn a marketing degree with honors. It's been onward and upward ever since. Now she's the founding president of Solutions Marketing Group in Arlington, Virginia. The company helps businesses reach and better serve disabled people—a group Jones believes is seriously underserved.

school, and more than 70 percent of disabled people between ages 18 and 55 are unemployed.[43]

Reducing the unemployment rate for people with disabilities is not just about jobs and money. It is about self-sufficiency, hopes, and dreams.[44] With enactment of the Americans with Disabilities Act of 1990 (ADA), disabled Americans hoped to get a real chance to take their rightful place in the workforce.[45] But according to research, this hope remains unfulfilled. In fact, added government regulation reportedly has discouraged some employers from hiring disabled people. The disappointing findings: "analysis of Census Bureau survey data from 1987 to 1996 indicates that the act's impact on employment of the disabled was negative."[46] Also, in a 2004 survey of 2,000 disabled Americans, "64% said the Americans with Disabilities Act has made no difference in their lives, up from 58% in 2000."[47]

The ADA, enforced by the EEOC, requires employers to make *reasonable* accommodations to the needs of present and future employees with physical and mental disabilities. As the ADA was being phased in to cover nearly all employers, many feared their businesses would be saddled with burdensome expenses and many lawsuits. But a 1998 White House–sponsored survey "determined that the mean cost of helping disabled workers to overcome their impairments was a mere $935 per person."[48]

New technology is also making accommodation easier.[49] Large-print computer screens for the partially blind, braille keyboards and talking computers for the blind, and telephones with visual readouts for the deaf

11d The Word "Ability" Is the Most Important Part of Disability

Don't call people without disabilities 'normal.' They're 'nondisabled.' Indeed, some would add that those without disabilities are 'temporarily nondisabled.'

Source: Marc Hequet, "ADA Etiquette," Training, *30 (April 1993): 33.*

QUESTIONS:

What are the implications of these statements for people with disabilities? What sorts of accommodations to disabled people have you observed recently? How do any of these accommodations affect your life?

are among today's helpful technologies. Here are some general policy guidelines for employers:

- Audit all facilities, policies, work rules, hiring procedures, and labor union contracts to eliminate barriers and bias.
- Train all managers in ADA compliance and all employees in how to be sensitive to coworkers and customers with disabilities.[50]
- Do not hire anyone who cannot safely perform the basic duties of a particular job with reasonable accommodation.

With lots of low-tech ingenuity, a touch of high tech, and support from coworkers, millions of disabled people can help their employers win the battle of global competition.

Employment Selection Tests

employment selection test: *any procedure used in the employment decision process*

EEO guidelines in the United States have broadened the definition of an **employment selection test** to include any procedure used as a basis for an employment decision. This means that in addition to traditional pencil-and-paper tests, numerous other procedures qualify as tests, such as unscored application forms; informal and formal interviews; performance tests; and physical, educational, or experience requirements.[51] This definition of an employment test takes on added significance when you realize that in the United States, the federal government requires all employment tests to be statistically valid and reliable predictors of job success.[52] Historically, women and minorities have been victimized by invalid, unreliable, and prejudicial employment selection procedures. Similar complaints have been voiced about the use of personality tests, polygraphs, drug tests, and AIDS and DNA screening during the hiring process[53] (see Table 11.3). Despite questions about the practice, and despite its potential drawbacks, the Association of Test Publishers recently noted that "overall employment testing, including personality tests, has been growing at a rate of 10% to 15% in each of the past three years."[54]

Effective Interviewing

Interviewing warrants special attention here because it is the most common employee selection tool.[55] Line managers at all levels are often asked to interview candidates for job openings and promotions and should be aware of the weaknesses of the traditional unstructured interview. The traditional unstructured or informal interview, which has no fixed question format or systematic scoring procedure, has been criticized on grounds such as the following:

5. EXPLAIN how managers can be more effective interviewers.

- It is highly susceptible to distortion and bias.
- It is highly susceptible to legal attack.
- It is usually indefensible if legally contested.
- It may have apparent validity, but no real validity.
- It is rarely totally job-related and may incorporate personal items that infringe on privacy.
- It is the most flexible selection technique, thereby being highly inconsistent.
- There is a tendency for the interviewer to look for qualities he or she prefers, and then to justify the hiring decision based on these qualities.
- Often the interviewer does not hear about the selection mistakes.
- There is an unsubstantiated confidence in the traditional interview.[56]

The Problem of Cultural Bias. Traditional unstructured interviews are notorious for being culturally insensitive. Evidence of this problem surfaced in a study of the interviewing practices of 38 general managers employed by nine different fast-food chains. According to the researcher:

Table 11.3 Employment Testing Techniques: An Overview

Type of test	Purpose	Comments
Pencil-and-paper psychological and personality tests	Measure attitudes and personality characteristics such as emotional stability, intelligence, and ability to deal with stress.	Renewed interest based on claims of improved validity. Can be expensive when scoring and interpretations are done by professionals. Validity varies widely from test to test.
Pencil-and-paper honesty tests (integrity testing)	Assess the degree of risk of a candidate's engaging in dishonest behavior.	Inexpensive to administer. Promising evidence of validity. Growing in popularity since recent curtailment of polygraph testing. Women tend to do better than men.
Job skills tests (clerical and manual dexterity tests, math and language tests, assessment centers, and simulations)	Assess competence in actual "hands-on" situations.	Generally good validity if carefully designed and administered. Assessment centers and simulations can be very expensive.
Polygraph (lie detector) tests	Measure physical signs of stress, such as rapid pulse and perspiration.	Growing use in recent years severely restricted by federal (Employee Polygraph Protection Act of 1988), state, and local laws. Questionable validity.
Drug tests	Check for controlled substances through urine, blood, or hair samples submitted to chemical analysis.	Rapidly growing in use despite strong employee resistance and potentially inaccurate procedures.
Handwriting analysis (graphoanalysis)	Infer personality characteristics and styles from samples of handwriting.	Popular in Europe and growing in popularity in the United States. Sweeping claims by proponents leave validity in doubt.
AIDS/HIV antibody tests	Find evidence of AIDS virus through blood samples.	An emerging area with undetermined legal and ethical boundaries. Major confidentiality issue.
Genetic/DNA screening	Use tissue or blood samples and family history data to identify those at risk of costly diseases.	Limited but growing use strongly opposed on legal and moral grounds. Major confidentiality issue.

> *Considering the well-known demographics of today's workforce, it's amazing that 9 percent of those receiving a negative hiring decision are turned down for inappropriate eye contact. To give a firm handshake and look someone straight in the eyes is a very important lesson taught by Dad to every middle-class male at a tender age. Not only do nonmainstream groups miss the lesson from Dad, some are taught that direct eye contact is rude or worse. Girls are frequently taught that direct eye contact is unbecoming in a female. In reality, having averted or shifty eyes may indicate mostly that the job applicant is not a middle-class male.*[57]

Managers can be taught, however, to be aware of and to overcome cultural biases when interviewing. This is particularly important in today's era of managing diversity and greater sensitivity to disabled people.

structured interview: *set of job-related questions with standardized answers*

behavior-based interview: *detailed questions about specific behavior in past job-related situations*

■ **Structured Interviews.** Structured interviews are the recommended alternative to traditional unstructured or informal interviews.[58] A **structured interview** is a set of job-related questions with standardized answers applied consistently across all interviews for a specific job.[59] Structured interviews are constructed, conducted, and scored by a committee of three to six members to try to eliminate individual bias. The systematic format and scoring of structured interviews eliminate the weaknesses inherent in unstructured interviews. Four types of questions typically characterize structured interviews: (1) situational, (2) job knowledge, (3) job sample simulation, and (4) worker requirements (see Table 11.4).

11e Caution! Tough Interview Questions Ahead

1. What was the last product or service you saw that took your breath away?
2. Is the customer always right?
3. Have you learned more from your mistakes or your successes?
4. On what occasions are you tempted to lie?
5. Tell me about yourself in words of one syllable.

Source: Excerpted from John Kador, How to Ace the Brainteaser Interview *(New York : McGraw-Hill, 2005), pp. 213–214.*

QUESTIONS:

How would you handle these "think-on-your-feet" questions in a job interview? Playing the interviewer's role, what kinds of answers would you like to hear?

■ **Behavioral Interviewing.** Behavioral scientists tell us that past behavior is the best predictor of future behavior. We are, after all, creatures of habit. Situational-type interview questions can be greatly strengthened by anchoring them to actual past behavior (as opposed to hypothetical situations).[60] Structured, job-related, behaviorally specific interview questions keep managers from running afoul of the problems associated with unstructured interviews, as listed above.

> *In a* ***behavior-based interview,*** *candidates are asked to recall specific actions they have taken in past job-related situations and describe them in detail. . . .*
>
> *Behavior-based interviews are rich with verifiable data. Candidates are required to include details such as names, dates, times, locations, and numbers.*
>
> *Candidates are reminded to use the word "I" rather than using "we" or "they" as they describe past experiences. This helps the candidate remain focused on their role in each situation and helps the interviewer evaluate the presence or absence of specific competencies.*[61]

If the questions are worded appropriately, the net result should be a good grasp of the individual's relevant skills, initiative, problem-solving ability, and ability to recover from setbacks and learn from mistakes. (For practice, see the Hands-On Exercise at the end of this chapter.)

Table 11.4 Types of Structured Interview Questions

Type of question	Method	Information sought	Sample question
Situational	Oral	Can the applicant handle difficult situations likely to be encountered on the job?	"What would you do if you saw two of your people arguing loudly in the work area?"
Job knowledge	Oral or written	Does the applicant possess the knowledge required for successful job performance?	"Do you know how to do an Internet search?"
Job sample simulation	Observation of actual or simulated performance	Can the applicant actually do essential aspects of the job?	"Can you show us how to compose and send an e-mail message?"
Worker requirements	Oral	Is the applicant willing to cope with job demands such as travel, relocation, or hard physical labor?	"Are you willing to spend 25 percent of your time on the road?"

Source: *Updated from "Structured Interviewing: Avoiding Selection Problems," by Elliott D. Pursell, Michael A. Campion, and Sarah R. Gaylord, copyright November 1980. Reprinted with permission of* Personnel Journal, *Costa Mesa, California; all rights reserved.*

Performance Appraisal

Annual performance appraisals are such a common part of modern organizational life that they qualify as a ritual. As with many rituals, the participants repeat the historical pattern without really asking the important questions: "Why?" and "Is there a better way?" Both appraisers and appraisees tend to express general dissatisfaction with performance appraisals. According to HR specialist Susan Jespersen, "Giving performance feedback is the No. 1 dreaded task of managers."[62] In fact, nearly 75 percent of the companies responding to a survey expressed major dissatisfaction with their performance appraisal system.[63] This is not surprising, in view of the following observation:

> *The annual performance review process, touted by some as the gateway to future prosperity, is, in reality for many companies, nothing more than a fill-in-the-blank, form-completing task that plots an individual's performance against a sanitized list of often generic corporate expectations and required competencies.*[64]

Considering that experts estimate the average cost of a *single* performance appraisal to be $1,500, the waste associated with poorly administered appraisals is mind boggling.[65]

Performance appraisal can be effective and satisfying if systematically developed and implemented techniques replace haphazard methods. For our purposes, **performance appraisal** is the process of evaluating individual job performance as a basis for making objective personnel decisions.[66] This definition intentionally excludes occasional coaching, in which a supervisor simply checks an employee's work and gives immediate feedback. Although personal coaching is fundamental to good management, formally documented appraisals are needed both to ensure equitable distribution of opportunities and rewards and to avoid prejudicial treatment of protected minorities.[67]

performance appraisal: *evaluating job performance as a basis for personnel decisions*

In this section, we will examine two important aspects of performance appraisal: (1) legal defensibility and (2) alternative techniques.

Making Performance Appraisals Legally Defensible

6. DISCUSS how performance appraisals can be made legally defensible.

Lawsuits challenging the legality of specific performance appraisal systems and resulting personnel actions have left scores of human resource managers asking themselves, "Will my organization's performance appraisal system stand up in court?" From the standpoint of limiting legal exposure, it is better to ask this question when developing a formal appraisal system than after it has been implemented. Managers need specific criteria for legally defensible performance appraisal systems. Fortunately, researchers have discerned some instructive patterns in court decisions.

After studying the verdicts in 66 employment discrimination cases in the United States, one pair of researchers found that employers could successfully defend their appraisal systems if these systems satisfied four criteria:

1. A *job analysis* was used to develop the performance appraisal system.
2. The appraisal system was *behavior-oriented*, not trait-oriented.
3. Performance evaluators followed *specific written instructions* when conducting appraisals.
4. Evaluators *reviewed the results* of the appraisals with the ratees.[68]

Each of these conditions has a clear legal rationale. Job analysis, discussed earlier relative to employee selection, anchors the appraisal process to specific job duties, not to personalities. Behavior-oriented appraisals properly focus management's attention on *how* the individual actually performed his or her job.[69] Performance appraisers who follow specific written instructions are less likely to be plagued by vague performance standards and/or personal bias. Finally, by reviewing performance appraisal results with those who have been evaluated, managers provide the feedback necessary for learning and improvement. Managers who keep these criteria for legal defensibility and the elements in Table 11.5 in mind are better equipped to select a sound appraisal system from alternative approaches and techniques.

Alternative Performance Appraisal Techniques

The list of alternative performance appraisal techniques is long and growing. Appraisal software programs also are proliferating. Unfortunately, many are simplistic, invalid, and unreliable. In general terms, an *invalid* appraisal instrument does not accurately measure what it is supposed to measure. *Unreliable* instruments do not measure criteria in a consistent manner. Many other performance appraisal techniques are so complex that they are impractical and burdensome to use. But armed with a working knowledge of the most popular appraisal techniques, a good manager can distinguish the strong from the weak. Once again, the strength of an appraisal technique is gauged by its conformity to the criteria for legal defensibility discussed previously. Following are some of the techniques used through the years:

- ***Goal setting.*** Within an MBO framework, performance is typically evaluated in terms of formal objectives set at an earlier date. This is a comparatively strong technique if desired outcomes are clearly linked to specific behavior. For example, a product design engineer's "output" could be measured in terms of the number of product specifications submitted per month.
- ***Written essays.*** Managers describe the performance of employees in narrative form, sometimes in response to predetermined questions. Evaluators often criticize this technique for consuming too much time. This method is also limited by the fact that some managers have difficulty expressing themselves in writing.[70]

11f Strong Words About Performance Reviews

Stephen Covey, former professor and best-selling author:

It's a repugnant process. It's insulting to people and unnecessary. I'm more in favor of open accountability against previously decided criteria that everyone agrees upon. . . . If you have real-time information, against the goals you've established together, then people can evaluate their own performance, and you can become a source of help to them.

Source: As quoted in Elizabeth Fenner, "The Secrets of His Success," Fortune *(November 29, 2004): 158.*

QUESTIONS:
Do you agree? Why or why not?

Table 11.5 Elements of a Good Performance Appraisal

Appraisals can be used to justify merit increases, document performance problems or simply "touch base" with employees. Experts say HR first must decide what it wants the appraisal to accomplish, then customize the form and the process to meet that goal.

Elements to consider include:

1. Objectives set by the employee and manager at the last appraisal.
2. List of specific competencies or skills being measured, with examples of successful behaviors.
3. Ratings scale appropriate to the organization.
4. Space for employee's self-appraisal.
5. Space for supervisor's appraisal.
6. Space for specific comments from the supervisor about the employee's performance.
7. Suggestions for employee development.
8. Objectives to meet by the next appraisal date.

Source: HR Magazine *by* Carla Johnson. *Copyright 2001 by* Society for Human Resource Management. *Reproduced with permission of* Society for Human Resource Management *in the format Textbook via Copyright Clearance Center.*

- ***Critical incidents.*** Specific instances of inferior and superior performance are documented by the supervisor when they occur. Accumulated incidents then provide an objective basis for evaluations at appraisal time. The strength of critical incidents is enhanced when evaluators document specific behavior in specific situations and ignore personality traits.[71]
- ***Graphic rating scales.*** Various traits or behavior are rated on incremental scales. For example, "initiative" could be rated on a 1(= low)—2—3—4—5(= high) scale. This technique is among the weakest when personality traits are employed. However, **behaviorally anchored rating scales (BARS)**, defined as performance rating scales divided into increments of observable job behavior determined through job analysis, are considered to be one of the strongest performance appraisal techniques. For example, managers at credit card issuer Capital One use performance rating scales with behavioral anchors such as "Do you get things done well through other people? Do you play well as a team member?"[72]

behaviorally anchored rating scales (BARS): *performance appraisal scales with notations about observable behavior*

- ***Weighted checklists.*** Evaluators check appropriate adjectives or behavioral descriptions that have predetermined weights. The weights, which gauge the relative importance of the randomly mixed items on the checklist, are usually unknown to the evaluator. Following the evaluation, the weights of the checked items are added or averaged to permit interpersonal comparisons. As with the other techniques, the degree of behavioral specificity largely determines the strength of weighted checklists.
- ***Rankings/comparisons.*** Coworkers in a subunit are ranked or compared in head-to-head fashion according to specified accomplishments or job behavior. A major shortcoming of this technique is that the absolute distance between ratees is unknown. For example, the employee ranked number one may be five times as effective as number two, who in turn is only slightly more effective than number three. Rankings/comparisons are also criticized for causing resentment among lower-ranked, but adequately performing, coworkers. *Fortune* offered this overview:

  > *In companies across the country, from General Electric to Hewlett-Packard, such grading systems—in which all employees are ranked against one another and grades are distributed along some sort of bell curve—are creating a firestorm of controversy. In the past 15 months employees have filed class-action suits against Microsoft and Conoco as well as Ford, claiming that the companies discriminate in assigning grades. In each case, a different group of disaffected employees is bringing the charges: older workers at Ford, blacks and women at Microsoft, U.S. citizens at Conoco.*[73]

  Ford has since dropped its forced ranking system.[74] This technique can be strengthened by combining it with a more behavioral technique, such as critical incidents or BARS.
- ***Multirater appraisals.*** This is a general label for a diverse array of nontraditional appraisal techniques involving more than one rater for the focal person's performance. The rationale for multirater appraisals is that "two or more heads are less biased than one." One approach that enjoyed faddish popularity in recent years involves 360-degree feedback. In a **360-degree review**, a manager is evaluated by his or her boss, peers, and subordinates. The results may or may not be statistically pooled and are generally fed back anonymously.[75] The use of 360–degree reviews as a performance appraisal tool has produced mixed results.[76] But research reveals that 360–degree *feedback* is an effective management development technique, especially when paired with coaching.[77] Consider, for example, how 360–degree feedback is used at Wachovia, the Charlotte, North Carolina–based bank:

360-degree review: *pooled, anonymous evaluation by one's boss, peers, and subordinates*

  > *For the past year, [extensively trained internal and external] coaches have been supporting participants in the company's 360 Assessment Process, which*

Source: *DILBERT © Scott Adams/Distributed by United Feature Syndicate, Inc.*

is based on Wachovia's executive leadership competency model. The coaches deliver the 360 feedback, assist participants in understanding the results, support them in developing individual development plans, and provide ongoing coaching and support for a four-month period after the 360 in conjunction with the participant's manager and human resource business partner.[78]

Training

No matter how carefully job applicants are screened and selected, typically a gap remains between what employees *do* know and what they *should* know. Training is needed to fill in this knowledge gap. In 2004, U.S. companies with 100 or more employees spent $51.4 billion on training, according to *Training* magazine's annual industry survey.[79] Huge as this number sounds, it still is not nearly enough, as we will see in a moment.

Training and life-long learning are constant facts of life today in both business and government organizations. These law enforcement officials are learning how to solve crimes with digital evidence at the FBI's new Silicon Valley Regional Computer Forensics Lab in Menlo Park, California. Do you suppose they have to watch CSI television reruns for homework?

training: *using guided experience to change employee behavior and/or attitudes*

Formally defined, **training** is the process of changing employee behavior and/or attitudes through some type of guided experience. We now focus on a looming skills gap in the United States and on current training methods, the ingredients of a good training program, and the important distinction between skill and factual learning.

■ A Shortage of Skilled Workers?

Could a shortage of skilled workers in the United States be around the corner? *Yes*, because experts say the U.S. labor force will come up short in terms of both numbers and quality in the years ahead. Driving this situation is a "perfect storm" of demographic and technological trends. Demographically, the huge post–World War II baby-boom generation is hitting retirement age. Jeff Taylor, founder of Monster.com, the Internet job-search leader, frames the demographic dilemma this way: "About 70 million baby boomers, some highly skilled, will exit the workforce over the next 18 years with only 40 million workers coming in."[80] Meanwhile, technological change will continue to increase the need for so-called "knowledge workers," people who are comfortable with math, science, and technology. Consequently, education and training are more important than ever.[81] Edward E. Gordon, author of the book *The 2010 Crossroad: The New World of People and Jobs*, explains the unfolding situation:

> *In the short term (2005–2010), U.S. business will likely move more jobs offshore, keep some older workers for a few extra years, and continue replacing people with technology. But none of these strategies are long-term solutions.*
>
> *U.S. employers must begin to ramp up their training investment in the current workforce—and they must do it now. By 2015 the situation may become so critical that the United States will have little choice but to support massive career preparation efforts that will still lag far behind new employment opportunities.*[82]

Some farsighted companies, such as David Weekley Homes, in Houston, Texas, have made training a top strategic priority. The 1,234-employee "homebuilder spends at least $4,500 a year per employee on training; that's more than $5 million each year."[83]

■ Today's Training Methods

Training magazine's 2004 survey of companies with at least 100 employees gives us a revealing snapshot of current training practices (see Table 11.6). Surprisingly, despite all we read and hear about e-learning via the Internet, the majority of today's training is remarkably low-tech. "Instructor-led classroom training continues to be the dominant method of delivery; 70 percent of training was delivered this way."[84] We anticipate growth in e-learning and other nontraditional methods as trainers become

Table 11.6 Content and Delivery of Today's Training

Method	E-learning	Traditional	Both	Do not provide
Communication skills	4%	62%	25%	10%
Computer systems/applications	8%	33%	57%	2%
Computer systems/programming	7%	20%	45%	28%
Customer service	2%	54%	25%	18%
Executive development	1%	51%	25%	23%
Management skills/development	3%	58%	32%	8%
Personal growth	5%	39%	31%	25%
Sales	1%	32%	23%	44%
Supervisory skills	3%	59%	30%	9%
Technological skills/knowledge	4%	42%	45%	9%

Source: *From Holly Dolezalek, "Industry Report 2004,"* Training, *41 (October 2004): 36. © VNU Business Media, Inc. Reprinted with permission.*

more tech-savvy and new training products such as realistic computer simulations come to market.[85] Meanwhile, the old standbys—classroom PowerPoint presentations, workbooks/manuals, videotapes/CDs, and seminars—are still the norm. For better or for worse, the typical college classroom is still a realistic preview of what awaits you in the world of workplace training.

Which instructional method is best? There are probably as many answers to this question as there are trainers. Given variables such as interpersonal differences, budget limitations, and instructor capabilities, it is safe to say that there is no one best training technique. Whatever method is used, trainers need to do their absolute best because they are key facilitators for people's hopes and dreams.

■ The Ingredients of a Good Training Program

Although training needs and approaches vary, managers can get the most out of their training budgets by following a few guidelines. According to two training specialists, every training program should be designed along the following lines to maximize retention and transfer learning to the job:

1. Maximize the similarity between the training situation and the job situation.
2. Provide as much experience as possible with the task being taught.
3. Provide for a variety of examples when teaching concepts or skills.
4. Label or identify important features of a task.
5. Make sure that general principles are understood before expecting much transfer.
6. Make sure that the trained behaviors and ideas are rewarded in the job situation.
7. Design the training content so that the trainees can see its applicability.
8. Use adjunct questions to guide the trainee's attention.[86]

7. COMPARE and CONTRAST the ingredients of good training programs for both skill and factual learning.

11g Subject: Sleeping in Class

Professor Roger Schank, Carnegie Mellon University, Pittsburgh, identifies three major training flaws that dampen motivation:

> *One, it's boring. . . .Second, it's not obvious why you need what you're being trained to do. And third, you're being trained in what you need, but not when you need it.*

Source: As quoted in Dianne Molvig, "Yearning for Learning," HR Magazine, 47 (March 2002): 68.

QUESTION:

Drawing on your many years of being a "consumer" of classroom instruction, what would you do as a trainer to avoid these three flaws?

■ Skill versus Factual Learning

The ingredients of a good training program vary according to whether skill learning or factual learning is involved.

> *Effective skill learning should incorporate four essential ingredients: (1) goal setting, (2) modeling, (3) practice, and (4) feedback. Let's take as an example the task of training someone to ride horseback. How would you do it? It basically must entail telling someone specifically what you want them to do (goal setting), showing them how you want them to do it (modeling), giving them the opportunity to try out what you have told them and shown them (practice), and then telling them what they are doing correctly (feedback).*[87]

When factual learning is involved, the same sequence is used, except that in step 2, "meaningful presentation of the materials" is substituted for modeling. Keep in mind that the object of training is *learning*. Learning requires thoughtful preparation, carefully guided exposure to new ideas or behavior, and motivational support.[88] Let us turn our attention to modern human resource management problems that have serious implications for the well-being of today's organizations and employees.

Contemporary Human Resource Challenges and Problems

Modern organizations are a direct reflection of society in general. People take societal influences to work (such as attitudes toward the opposite sex). Along with these predispositions, they take their social, emotional, behavioral, and health-related problems to work. Like it or not and prepared or not, managers face potential problems such as sexual harassment and alcohol and drug abuse. Today's challenge to deal effectively with human resource problems of this nature cannot be ignored because organizational competitiveness is at stake.

Discouraging Sexual Harassment

sexual harassment: *unwanted sexual attention that creates an offensive or intimidating work environment*

A great deal of misunderstanding surrounds the topic of sexual harassment because of sexist attitudes, vague definitions, differing perceptions,[89] and inconsistent court findings. **Sexual harassment**, defined generally as unwanted sexual attention or conduct, has both behavioral and legal dimensions (see Table 11.7). Important among these are the following:

- Although typically it is female employees who are the victims of sexual harassment, both women and men (in the United States) are protected under Title VII of the Civil Rights Act of 1964.
- Sexual harassment includes, but is not limited to, unwanted physical contact. Gestures, displays, joking, and language also may create a sexually offensive or hostile work environment. "Courts generally regard a work environment as hostile if there is behavior that is physically threatening or humiliating, interferes unreasonably with an employee's work performance and affects an employee's psychological well-being."[90]
- It is the manager's job to be aware of and correct cases of sexual harassment. Ignorance of such activity is not a valid legal defense.[91]

8. SPECIFY the essential components of an organization's policies for dealing with sexual harassment and alcohol and drug abuse.

Research evidence indicates that sexual harassment is commonplace. In one recent survey, 35 percent of women and 17 percent of men reported having been sexually harassed at work.[92] Employees who use e-mail systems must also contend with problems of sexual harassment in the form of rape threats and obscene words and graphics. In 2000, "Dow Chemical fired 50 employees and disciplined 200 others after an e-mail investigation turned up hard-core pornography and violent subject matter. . . .'This sort of activity creates a harassment environment that we can't tolerate,' [said a company official]."[93] Sexual harassment begins early, with 83 percent of high school girls and 60 percent of high school boys reportedly experiencing it.[94] According to research, people generally agree that unwanted sexual propositions, promises, or threats tied to sexual favors, lewd comments/gestures/jokes, and touching/grabbing/brushing qualify as sexual harassment. Beyond that, opinions differ.[95] Personal tastes and sensibilities vary widely from individual to individual. In view of the foregoing evidence, corrective action needs to be taken by both the victims of sexual harassment and management.

Table 11.7 Behavioral and Legal Dimensions of Sexual Harassment

What exactly is sexual harassment? The Equal Employment Opportunity Commission (EEOC) says that unwelcome sexual advances, requests for sexual favors, and other verbal or physical conduct of a sexual nature constitute sexual harassment when submission to such conduct is made a condition of employment; when submission to or rejection of sexual advances is used as a basis for employment decisions; or when such conduct creates an intimidating, hostile, or offensive work environment. These EEOC guidelines interpreting Title VII of the Civil Rights Act of 1964 further state that employers are responsible for the actions of their supervisors and agents and that employers are responsible for the actions of other employees if the employer knows or should have known about the sexual harassment.

Source: *"Sexual Harassment, 1: Discouraging It in the Work Place," by B. Terry Thornton. Reprinted by permission of the publisher, from* Personnel, *April 1986, © 1986. American Management Association, New York, N.Y. All rights reserved.*

Sexual harassment is not only a threat to human dignity, but a drain on human capital and productivity as well. These Indian women from the All India Progressive Women's association observed International Women's Day 2005 in New Delhi by urging the government to give women the constitutional right to work and legal protection from sexual harassment in the workplace.

■ **What Can the Victim Do?** Employees who believe they are victims of sexual harassment can try to live with it, fight back, complain to higher-ups, find another job, or sue their employer. Those who choose to file a lawsuit need to know how to arrange the odds in their favor. An analysis of sexual harassment cases revealed that the following five factors are likely to lead to success. Victims of sexual harassment tended to win their lawsuits when

- The harassment was severe.
- There were witnesses.
- Management had been notified.
- There was supporting documentation.
- Management had failed to take action.[96]

The more of these factors that apply, the greater the chances that a sexual harassment lawsuit will be successful. Courtrooms are the last line of defense for victims of sexual harassment. Preventive and remedial actions are also needed. Harassers need to be told by their victims, coworkers, and supervisors that their actions are illegal, unethical, and against company policy. As more organizations develop and enforce sexual harassment policies, the problem can be greatly reduced without costly court battles and the loss of valued employees.

■ **What Can the Organization Do?** Starting with top management, an organizationwide commitment to eliminating sexual harassment should be established. A clear policy statement, with behavioral definitions of sexual harassment and associated penalties, is essential. As with all policies, sexual harassment policies need to be disseminated and uniformly enforced if they are to have the desired impact. Appropriate training, particularly for new employees, can alert people to the problem and consequences of sexual harassment.[97] Finally, in accordance with EEOC guidelines, management can remain adequately informed of any sexual harassment in the organization by establishing a grievance procedure. Harassed employees should be able to get a fair hearing of their case without fear of retaliation.

Controlling Alcohol and Drug Abuse

Statistics tell a grim story about the number one drug problem—alcohol. In the United States, 70 percent of adults consume alcohol and 43 percent of the population claim to have an alcoholic spouse or blood relative.[98] "An estimated 8 million Americans are alcoholics; another 6 million abuse alcohol but aren't physically dependent on it. Half of all alcoholics who get treatment relapse at least once."[99] Once believed to be a character disorder, **alcoholism** is now considered a disease in which an individual's normal social and economic roles are disrupted by the consumption of alcohol. Very few alcoholics are actually the skid row–bum type; the vast majority are average citizens with jobs and families. Alcoholism cuts across all age, gender, racial, and ethnic categories. Experts say a glance in the mirror shows what the average alcoholic looks like.

alcoholism: *a disease in which alcohol abuse disrupts one's normal life*

Close on the heels of employee alcoholism is workplace drug abuse. As a general point of reference, a 2002 survey of people 12 and older by the U.S. Department of Health and Human Services found that 46 percent had used illicit drugs during their lifetime. "Illicit drugs include marijuana, hashish, cocaine, crack, heroin, hallucinogens, inhalants, or any prescription-type psychotherapeutic (non-medical usage)."[100]

Because drug fads come and go, the drug problem is a moving target. For example, when one workplace drug-testing company began an ecstasy screening program, "the number of positives in the methamphetamine category (where ecstasy resides) almost doubled."[101] Experts say 8 to 12 percent of the general population is at risk of drug addiction. Seventy percent of illegal drug users in the United States are employed.[102] Compared with nonabusers, alcoholic employees and drug abusers are significantly less productive, ten times more likely to be absent, and three times more likely either to have or to cause an accident.[103] In terms of lost productivity due to absenteeism, accidents, shoddy work, sick leave, and theft of organizational resources, employee drug abuse costs the U.S. economy an estimated $100 billion a year.[104] Employers can play a key role in curbing this tragic and costly erosion of our human resources.

The Legal Side of Workplace Substance Abuse. Businesses doing contract work for the U.S. government are squeezed on two sides by the law. On the one side, alcoholics and drug addicts are protected from employment discrimination by the Vocational Rehabilitation Act of 1973. They are presumed to have the same employment rights as any disabled person.[105] On the other side, employers with federal contracts exceeding $25,000 are subject to the Federal Drug-Free Workplace Act of 1988. These employers "must certify that they will maintain a drug-free workplace."[106] The idea is to rid federal contractors' workplaces of the production, distribution, and possession of controlled substances. Alcohol is not considered a controlled substance by the 1988 act. Companies found to be in violation of the act may lose their right to do business with the U.S. government.

Do these two legal thrusts work in opposite directions? Actually, the two laws work in combination because they make *rehabilitation* the best option.

11h Time to Get MADD About Drunk Drivers

Fact: More than 40 percent of all college students qualify as binge drinkers.

Fact: "In a recent survey, . . . 30.2 percent of students have ridden with a driver who had been drinking alcohol."

Fact: "[In the U.S.] in 2003, 17,013 people were killed in alcohol-related crashes–an average of one almost every half hour. These deaths constituted approximately 40 percent of the 42,642 total traffic fatalities."

Source: Mothers Against Drunk Driving, **www.madd.org/stats**, *February 1, 2005.*

QUESTION:
What can *you* do about this terrible problem?

Referral and Rehabilitation. Alcoholism and drug abuse typically reveal themselves to the manager in the form of increased absenteeism, tardiness, sloppy work, and complaints from coworkers. As soon as a steady decline in performance is observed, the manager should confront the individual with his or her poor performance record. Experts advise supervisors *not* to make accusations about alcohol or drug abuse. It is the employee's challenge to admit having such a problem. Management's job is to refer troubled employees to appropriate sources of help.[107] Managers are cautioned against "playing doctor" when trying to help the alcohol- or drug-abusing employee. If the organization has an *employee assistance program (EAP)*, counselors, or a company doctor, an in-house referral can be made.[108] One study, "which tracked 25,000 employees over a four-year period, showed that the company's EAP saved $4 in health claims and absentee rates for every dollar it spent."[109]

Managers in small organizations without sophisticated employee services can refer the alcoholic employee to community resources such as Alcoholics Anonymous. Similar referral agencies for drug abusers exist in most communities. The overriding objective for the manager is to put troubled employees in touch with trained rehabilitation specialists as soon as possible.

SUMMARY

1. Human resource management involves human resource acquisition, retention, and development. Four key human resource management activities necessarily linked to organizational strategy and structure are (1) human resource strategy, (2) recruitment and selection, (3) performance appraisal, and (4) training. After an employee has joined the organization, part of the human resource management process involves dealing with human resource problems such as sexual harassment and alcohol and drug abuse.
2. A systems approach to human resource strategy views both present and future employees as human capital that needs to be developed to its fullest potential. Pfeffer's seven people-centered practices can serve as a strategic agenda for human resource management. The seven practices are provision of job security, rigorous hiring practices, employee empowerment, performance-based compensation, comprehensive training, reduction of status differences, and sharing of key information.
3. Managers need to recruit for diversity to increase their appeal to job applicants and customers alike. The hurdle-like selection process can be summed up in the seven-step PROCEED model. The seven steps are (1) prepare (job analysis, job descriptions, and interview questions), (2) review (ensure the legality and fairness of the questions), (3) organize (assign the questions to an interview team), (4) conduct (collect information from the candidate), (5) evaluate (judge the candidate's qualifications), (6) exchange (meet and discuss information about the candidate), and (7) decide (extend a job offer or not).
4. Federal equal employment opportunity laws require managers to make hiring and other personnel decisions on the basis of ability to perform rather than personal prejudice. Affirmative action (making up for past discrimination) is evolving into managing diversity. Appreciation of interpersonal differences within a heterogeneous organizational culture is the goal of managing-diversity programs. The Americans with Disabilities Act of 1990 (ADA) requires employers to make reasonable accommodations so that disabled people can enter the workforce.
5. All employment tests must be valid predictors of job performance. Because interviews are the most popular employee screening device, experts recommend structured rather than traditional, informal interviews.
6. Legally defensible performance appraisals enable managers to make objective personnel decisions. Four key legal criteria are job analysis, behavior-oriented appraisals, specific written instructions, and discussion of results with ratees. Seven common performance appraisal techniques are goal setting, written essays, critical incidents, graphic rating scales, weighted checklists, rankings/comparisons, and 360-degree reviews.
7. Today, training is a huge business in itself. Unfortunately, most training dollars are being spent where they are least needed: to train well-educated managers and professionals. Managers can ensure that their training investment pays off by using techniques appropriate to the situation. Training programs should be designed with an eye toward maximizing the retention of learning and its transfer to the job. Successful skill learning and factual learning both depend on goal setting, practice, and feedback. But skills should be modeled, whereas factual information should be presented in a logical and meaningful manner.
8. Sexual harassment and alcohol and drug abuse are contemporary human resource problems that require top-management attention and strong policies. A sexual harassment policy needs to define the problem behaviorally, specify penalties, and be disseminated and enforced. Referral to professional help and rehabilitation is the key to fighting substance abuse in the workplace.

TERMS TO UNDERSTAND

- Human resource management, p. 315
- Human capital, p. 317
- Job analysis, p. 320
- Job description, p. 320
- Affirmative Action Program (AAP), p. 321
- Employment selection test, p. 324
- Structured interview, p. 326
- Behavior-based interview, p. 326
- Performance appraisal, p. 327
- Behaviorally Anchored Rating Scales (BARS), p. 329
- 360-degree review, p. 329
- Training, p. 331
- Sexual harassment, p. 333
- Alcoholism, p. 335

SKILLS & TOOLS

How to Handle the Job Interview Successfully

1. **Thoroughly pre-scout the employer.** Spy discreetly on the company to learn about its activities, characteristics, strengths, trends, and market position. Review newsletters, product literature, financial and annual reports, brochures, news articles, and anything else you can find about the company in the library or on the Internet. For personal accounts, visit the company on a pre-interview day or arrive early for your appointment and casually converse with departing or arriving employees. . . .
2. **Ask permission to take notes.** Your interviewer won't refuse this request, so have paper and a pen handy for jotting down important facts during the meeting. Not only will this help you make a good impression, but it also will provide ammunition for your interview summary and follow-up letter.

   Examples of what you should write down include the final hiring deadline, details about the job description, information about the company and its policies, the name of your prospective manager, product information, and advice on next steps you can take.
3. **Ask pertinent questions.** This underutilized strategy may, in fact, be the most valuable of all to candidates. By asking questions, you'll show what you've learned about the company and find out more about the job requirements and where you stand. Questions you might want to ask include the following:

   "Would you take a few moments to give me a more comprehensive description of the job requirements?"

   "What do you think are the most important qualities that candidates for this job should have?"

   "What opportunities exist in the future for someone who performs successfully in this position?". . .
4. **Ask the interviewer to rate your qualifications for the job.** From this reply, you'll learn which way the wind is blowing and possibly uncover a potentially fatal problem or weakness the interviewer didn't plan to discuss with you. . . .

   You've made an impression, gained information, and set the stage to politely and briefly summarize the strengths and assets you'd bring to the job. This is where the notes you've taken during the interview come in handy.

   Quoting the interviewer's job description and specifications whenever possible, repeat each requirement for the position as you understand them. Then cite the strengths, experience, and values you'd bring to each area. Candidly admit to any weaknesses, but promise to embark on a vigorous training program to overcome them. State that the company's training strengths and your attitude are a winning combination.

   As you finish your summary, be sure to ask for the job confidently and pleasantly. If you're enthusiastic and polite, you won't be labeled as overly aggressive. Employers prefer you to be results-oriented because they think you'll act the same way on the job. . . .
5. **Always follow up.** Write and mail a follow-up letter to the interviewer within 12 to 24 hours of your meeting, with a copy to any other executives who are involved in the decision. [An e-mail can get lost in the clutter, unless the interviewer expressly prefers to communicate via e-mail.]

   Your letter should state:
   - What you liked most about the company.
   - The assets you'd bring to the position.
   - Your availability and enthusiasm.
   - Your hope of meeting other decision-makers as soon as possible.

Source: National Business Employment Weekly *[Only Staff-Produced Materials May Be Used] by Milton Gralla. Copyright 1997 by Dow Jones & Co Inc in the format Textbook via Copyright Clearance Center.*

HANDS-ON EXERCISE

Writing Behavioral Interview Questions

Instructions

Working either alone or as a member of a team, select a specific job and write *two* behavioral interview questions for at least *five* of these categories.

Being a self-starter and demonstrating initiative

Being a leader

Being an effective communicator

Being ethical

Being able to make a hard decision

Being a team player

Being able to handle conflict

Being able to handle a setback, disappointment, or failure

Tips: If you pick a higher-level job, this exercise will be easier because people at higher levels have more responsibility and engage in a broader range of behavior. Be sure to prepare by rereading the Behavioral Interviewing section in this chapter.

For Consideration/Discussion

1. How well will each of your questions uncover *actual past job-related behavior*?
2. Would any of your questions put the candidate at a disadvantage because of his or her gender, race, ethnicity, religion, disability, marital status, or sexual preference?
3. When others hear your questions, are they judged to be *fair* questions?
4. Which question is your absolute best? Why? Which is your weakest? Why?
5. What (if anything) do you like about behavioral interviews? What (if anything) do you dislike about them?

INTERNET EXERCISES

1. **A case study in diversity:** Computer maker Dell takes diversity very seriously. It is of major strategic importance to the company's success. At Dell's home page (**www.dell.com**), click on "About Dell." Next, select "Diversity" and read "Our Mission." Then browse the link "The Soul of Dell" while keeping the following questions in mind.

   Learning Points: 1. How embedded is diversity in Dell's overall corporate strategy? How can you tell? 2. Which particular diversity initiative or program appeals most to you? Why? 3. If you were on Dell's diversity program staff, how would you justify the firm's diversity efforts to Dell stockholders? 4. Would you like to work for Dell? Why or why not?

2. **Intel is very serious about human capital:** The investment Intel is making in students and educational programs around the world is amazing. At Intel's home page (**www.intel.com**), select "Education Resources" under "Featured Intel Links." Explore Intel's various human capital programs, while keeping the following questions in mind.

   Learning Points: 1. Putting yourself in the place of the company's CEO, how would you justify this huge expenditure of time and money on people who probably will end up working somewhere else? 2. In your view, which of Intel's investments in human capital is the best? Why? Which is the most questionable? Why? 3. Thinking back to what you read in Chapter 5, explain the role of "enlightened self-interest" in Intel's investment in education. 4. Would you like to work at Intel? Why or why not?

3. **Check it out:** The popular Internet job site **www.monster.com** has lots of great material to help you prepare for the job-hunting experience. Click on "Career Advice" at the home page and explore from there. You also can use this site to check out employment opportunities in foreign countries (and take the instructive and fun "Culture Quizzes" for various countries in the "Self-Assessment Center").

For updates to these exercises, visit our Web site (**http://business.college.hmco.com/students/** and select Kreitner, *Management,* 10e).

CLOSING CASE

Indian Airlines - HR Problems

"There could scarcely be a more undisciplined bunch of workers than IA's 22,000 employees."

- ***Business India,* January 25, 1999.**

Flying Low

Indian Airlines (IA) – the name of India's national carrier conjured up an image of a monopoly gone berserk with the absolute power it had over the market. Continual losses over the years, frequent human resource problems and gross mismanagement were just some of the few problems that plagued the company.

Widespread media coverage regarding the frequent strikes by IA pilots not only reflected the adamant attitude of the pilots, but also resulted in increased public resentment towards the airline. IA's recurring human resource problems were attributed to its lack of proper manpower planning and underutilization of existing manpower.

The recruitment and creation of posts in IA was done without proper scientific analysis of the manpower requirements of the organization. IA's employee unions were rather infamous for resorting to industrial action on the slightest pretext and their arm-twisting tactics to get their demands accepted by the management.

During the 1990s, the Government took various steps to turn around IA and initiated talks for its disinvestment. Amidst strong opposition by the employees, the disinvestment plans dragged on endlessly well into mid 2001.

The IA story shows how poor management, especially in the human resources area, could spell doom even for a Rs 40 bn monopoly.

Background Note

IA was formed in May 1953 with the nationalization of the airlines industry through the Air Corporations Act. Indian Airlines Corporation and Air India International were established and the assets of the then existing nine airline companies were transferred to these two entities. While Air India provided international air services, IA and its subsidiary, Alliance Air, provided domestic air services. In 1990, Vayudoot, a low-capacity and short-haul domestic airline with huge long-term liabilities, was merged with IA.

IA's network ranged from Kuwait in the west to Singapore in the east, covering 75 destinations (59 within India, 16 abroad). Its international network covered Kuwait, Oman, UAE, Qatar and Bahrain in West Asia; Thailand, Singapore and Malaysia in South East Asia; and Pakistan, Nepal, Bangladesh, Myanmar, Sri Lanka and Maldives in the South Asian subcontinent. Between themselves, IA and Alliance Air carried over 7.5 million passengers annually. In 1999, the company had a fleet strength of 55 aircraft - 11 Airbus A300s, 30 Airbus A320s, 11 Boeing B737s and 3 Dorniers D0228.

In 1994, the Air Corporation Act was repealed and air transport was thrown open to private players. Many big corporate houses entered the fray and IA saw a mass exodus of its pilots to private airlines. To counter increasing competition IA launched a new image building advertisement campaign. It also improved its services by strictly adhering to flight schedules and providing better in-flight and ground services. It also launched several other new aircraft, with a new, younger, and more dynamic in-flight crew. These initiatives were soon rewarded in form of 17% increase in passenger revenues during the year 1994.

However, IA could not sustain these improvements. Competitors like Sahara and Jet Airways (Jet) provided better services and network. Unable to match the performance of these airlines IA faced severe criticism for its inefficiency and excessive expenditure by human resources. Staff cost increased by an alarming Rs 5.9 bn during 1994-98. These costs were responsible to a great extent for the company's frequent losses. By 1999 the losses touched Rs 7.5 bn.

In the next few years, private players such as East West, NEPC, and Damania had to close shop due to huge losses. Jet was the only player that was able to sustain itself. IA's market share, however continued to drop. In 1999, while IA's market share was 47%, the share of private airlines reached 53%.

Unnecessary interference by the Ministry of Civil Aviation was a major cause of concern for IA. This interference ranged from deciding on the crew's quality to major technical decisions in which the Ministry did not even have the necessary expertise. IA had to operate flights in the North-East at highly subsidized fares to fulfill its social objectives of connecting these regions with the rest of the country. These flights contributed to the IA's losses over the years. As the carrier's balance sheet was heavily skewed towards debt with an equity base of Rs 1.05 bn in 1999 as against long term loans of Rs 28 bn, heavy interest outflows of Rs 1.99 bn further increased the losses.

IA could blame many of its problems on competitive pressures or political interference; but it could not deny responsibility for its human resource problems. A report by the Comptroller and Auditor General of India stated, "Manpower planning in any organization should depend on the periodic and realistic assessment of the manpower needs, need-based recruitment, optimum utilization of the recruited personnel and abolition of surplus and redundant posts. Identification of the qualifications appropriate to all the posts is a basic requirement of efficient human resource management. IA was found grossly deficient in all these aspects."

'Fighter' Pilots?

IA's eight unions were notorious for their defiant attitude and their use of unscrupulous methods to force the management to agree to all their demands. Strikes, go-slow agitations and wage negotiations were common.

For each strike there was a different reason, but every strike was about pressurizing IA for more money. From November 1989 to June 1992, there were 13 agitations by different unions. During December 1992-January 1993, there was a 46-day strike by the pilots and yet another one in November 1994. The cavalier attitude of the IA pilots was particularly evident in the agitation in April 1995.

The pilots began the agitation demanding higher allowances for flying in international sectors. This demand was turned down. They then refused to fly with people re-employed on a contract basis. Thereafter they went on a strike, saying that the cabin crew earned higher wages than them and that they would not fly until this issue was addressed.

Due to adamant behaviour of pilots many of the cabin crew and the airhostesses had to be off-loaded at the last moment from aircrafts. In 1996, there was another agitation, with many pilots reporting sick at the same time. Medical examiners, who were sent to check these pilots, found that most of these were false claims.

Some of the pilots were completely fit; others somehow managed to produce medical certificates to corroborate their claims. In January 1997, there was another strike by the pilots, this time asking for increased foreign allowances, fixed flying hours, free meals and wage parity with Alliance Air.

Though the strike was called off within a week, it again raised questions regarding IA's vulnerability. April 2000 saw another go-slow agitation by IA's aircraft engineers who were demanding pay revision and a change in the career progression pattern[1]. The strategies adopted by IA to overcome these problems were severely criticized by analysts over the years. Analysts noted that the people heading the airline were more interested in making peace with the unions than looking at the company's long-term benefits.

Russy Mody (Mody), who joined IA as chairman in November 1994, made efforts to appease the unions by proposing to bring their salaries on par with those of Air India employees. This was strongly opposed by the board of directors, in view of the mounting losses. Mody also proposed to increase the age of retirement from 58 to 60 to control the exodus of pilots.

However, government rejected Mody's plans[2]. When Probir Sen (Sen) took over as chairman and managing director, he bought the pilot emoluments on par with emoluments of other airlines, thereby successfully controlling the exodus. In 1994, the IA unions opposed the re-employment of pilots who had left IA to join private carriers and the employment of superannuated fliers on contract.

Sen averted a crisis by creating Alliance Air, a subsidiary airline company where the re-employed people were utilized. He was also instrumental in effecting substantial wage hikes for the employees. The extra financial burden on the airline caused by these measures was met by resorting to a 10% annual hike in fares. (Refer Table I)

Table I Impact of Staff Cost Hike in Fare Increase (%)

Date of fare increase	Impact (%)
25/07/1994	16.22
1/10/1995	25
22/09/1996	36
15/10/1997	13.44
1/10/1998	8.8

Source: *IATA-World Air Transport Statistics*

Initially, Sen's efforts seemed to have positive effects with an improvement in aircraft utilization figures. IA also managed to cut losses during 1996-97 and reported a Rs 140 mn profit in 1997-98. But recessionary trends in the economy and its mounting wage bill pushed IA back into losses by 1999. Sen and the entire board of directors were sacked by the government.

[1] *These engineers were already earning Rs 60,000 per month, excluding perks.*

[2] *The government claimed that Mody had failed to turn IA around. It appointed a seven-member committee under the chairmanship of Vijay Kelkar, the then petroleum secretary to make suggestions regarding turnaround. In its report submitted in November 1996, the committee declared that IA's losses were caused by factors that were beyond the control of IA. It recommended that the government provide substantial financial aid to the carrier and revamp its fleet. This report was later evaluated by P.S.Brar, the joint Comptroller General of Accounts in the Department of Expenditure of the Finance Ministry. Brar severely criticized the Kelkar recommendations, saying that any money given to IA would 'go down the drain' and said that IA had to go for massive cost-cutting and human resource management initiatives if it wanted to get back on the tracks. The hard-hitting Brar report received criticism from IA and Kelkar's supporters.*

In the late 1990s, in yet another effort to appease its employees, IA introduced the productivity-linked scheme. The idea of the productivity linked incentive (PLI) scheme was to persuade pilots to fly more in order to increase aircraft utilization. But the PLI scheme was grossly misused by large sections of the employees to earn more cash. For instance, the agreement stated that if the engineering department made 28 Airbus A320s available for service every day, PLI would be paid.

This number was later reduced to 25 and finally to 23. There were also reports that flights leaving 30 - 45 minutes late were shown as being on time for PLI purposes. Pilots were flying 75 hours a month, while they have to fly only 63 hours. Eventually, the PLI schemes raised an additional annual wage bill of Rs 1.8 bn for IA. It was alleged that IA employees did no work during normal office hours; this way they could not work overtime and earn more money.

Though experts agreed that IA had to cut its operation costs. To survive the airline continued to add to its costs, by paying more money to its employees. (Refer Table II). The payment of overtime allowance (OTA) which included holiday pay to staff, increased by 109% during 1993-99. It was also found that the payment of OTA always exceeded the budget provisions.

Between 1991-92 and 1995-96, the increase in pay and allowances of the executive pilots was 842% and that of non-executive pilots was 134%. Even the lowest paid employee in the airline, either a sweeper or a peon, was paid Rs 8,000 – 10,000 per month with overtime included.

Table II Increase in Staff Costs

Year	Staff cost (in Rs bn)	No. of employees	Per employee cost (in mn) (in Rs bn)	Total expenditure	Staff cost as percentage of total operational expenditure	Effective fleet size
1993-94	2.85	22182	0.13	20.75	15%	54
1994-95	3.74 (31.18%)*	22683	0.16	22.59	19%	58
1995-96	5.71 (52.59%)	22582	0.25	26	25%	55
1996-97	7.10 (24.35%)	22153	0.32	29.29	26%	40
1997-98	8.17 (15.03%)	21990	0.37	32.21	27%	40
1998-99	8.75 (7.12%)	21922	0.39	34.31	28%	41

Source: *IATA-World Air Transport Statistics*
** Figures in brackets indicate increase over the previous year.*
 # Excludes 4 aircraft grounded from 1993-94 to 1995-96 as well as 12 aircraft leased to Airline Allied Services Ltd. from 1996-97 to 1998-99.

In 1998, IA tried to persuade employees to cut down on PLI and overtime to help the airline weather a difficult period; however there efforts failed.

Though IA incurred losses during 1995-96 and 1996-97 and made only marginal profits during 1997-98 and 1998-99, heavy payments were made on account of PLI. A net loss of Rs 641.8 mn was registered during the period 1995-99. PLI payments alone amounted to Rs 6.66 bn, during the same period. According to unofficial reports, arrears to be paid to employees on account of PLI touched nearly Rs 7 bn by 1999.

Over the years, the number of employees at IA increased steadily. IA had the maximum number of employees per aircraft. (Refer Table III). It was reported that the airline's monthly wage bill was as high as of Rs 680 mn, which doubled in the next three years. There were 150 employees earning above Rs 0.3 mn per annum in 1994-95 and the number increased to 2,109 by 1997-98. The Brar committee attributed this abnormal increase in staff costs to inefficient manpower planning, unproductive deployment of manpower and unwarranted increase in salaries and wages of the employees.

Table III A Comparison of Various Airlines

Name of Airlines	Number of aircraft in fleet	No. of employees	ATKm[3] (in Million)	ATKm per Employee	Employees per aircraft
Singapore Airlines	84	13,549	14418.324	1064161	161
Thai Airways International	76	24,186	6546.627	270678	318
Indian Airlines	51	21,990	2113.671	398204	431
Gulf Air	30	5,308	1416.235	245831	177
Kuwait Airways	22	5,761	345.599	92853	261
Jet Airways	19	3,722	1094.132	49756	196

Source: *IATA-World Air Transport Statistics*

Analysts criticized the way posts were created in IA. In 1999, six new posts of directors were created of which three were created by dividing functions of existing directors. Thus, in place of 6 directors in departments prior April 1998, there were 9 directors by 1999 overseeing the same functions. There were 30 full time directors, who in turn had their retinue of private secretaries, drivers and orderlies. The posts in non-executive cadres were to be created after the assessment by the Manpower Assessment Committee. But analysts pointed that in the case of cabin crew, 40 posts were introduced in the Southern Region on an ad-hoc basis, pending the assessment of their requirement by the Staff Assessment Committee.

Another problem was that no basic educational qualifications were prescribed for senior executive posts. Even a matriculate could become a manager, by acquiring the necessary job-related qualifications and experience. Illiterate IA employees drew salaries that were on par with senior civil servants. After superannuation, several employees were re-employed by the airline in an advisory capacity. According to reports, IA employed 132 retired employees as consultants during 1995-96 on contract basis. With each strike/go-slow and subsequent wage negotiations, IA's financial woes kept increasing. Though at times the airline did put its foot down, by and large, it always acceded to the demands for wage hikes and other perquisites.

Troubled Skies

Frequent agitations was not the only problem that IA faced in the area of human resources. There were issues that had been either neglected or mismanaged.

For instance, the rates of highly subsidized canteen items were not revised even once in three decades and there was no policy on fixing rates. Various allowances such as out-of-pocket expenses, experience allowance, simulator allowance etc. were paid to those who were not strictly eligible for these. Excessive expenditure was incurred on benefits given to senior executives such as retention of company car, and room air-conditioners even after retirement. All these problems had a negative impact on divestment procedure.

This did not augur well for any of the parties involved, as privatization was expected to give the IA management an opportunity to make the venture a commercially viable one. Freed from its political and social obligations, the carrier would be in a much better position to handle its labor problems. The biggest beneficiaries would be perhaps the passengers, who would get better services from the airline.

For Discussion

1. Analyze the developments in the Indian civil aviation industry after the sector was opened up for the private players. Evaluate IA's performance. Why do you think IA failed to retain its market share against competitors like Jet Airways?
2. IA's human resource problems can largely be attributed to its poor human resource management policies. Do you agree? Give reasons to support your stand.

Source: *http://www.icmr.icfai.org/casestudies*

[3] *ATKm, i.e. Available Tonne Kilometers (ATKm) is used to measure the productivity of an airline. It denotes the total number of tonne kilometers produced by an airline during a particular period.*

TEST PREPPER

True/False Questions

_____ **1.** The human capital perspective is a "big picture" approach to managing people and staying competitive.

_____ **2.** According to Jeffrey Pfeffer, only about 12 percent of today's organizations qualify as being systematically people-centered.

_____ **3.** The process of identifying basic task and skill requirements for specific jobs by studying superior performers is called job analysis.

_____ **4.** Title VII of the Civil Rights Act of 1964 is the landmark equal employment opportunity law in the United States.

_____ **5.** Disabled Americans and able-bodied citizens have the same unemployment rate.

_____ **6.** Today, polygraphs (lie detectors) are in wide use in the United States because of strong government support.

_____ **7.** Trait-oriented performance appraisals, from a legal viewpoint, are more defensible than behavior-oriented appraisals.

_____ **8.** Despite what is published about computer-based training and e-learning via the Internet, the vast bulk of today's training is remarkably low-tech.

_____ **9.** Verbal misconduct cannot be considered sexual harassment.

_____ **10.** Employee assistance programs for substance abusers can end up saving companies money.

Multiple-Choice Questions

1. What did researchers find when comparing "control" human resource systems and "commitment" human resource systems?
A. Employees preferred control systems over commitment systems.
B. Productivity was high and employee turnover was low with commitment systems.
C. Employee turnover was much higher with commitment systems.
D. Productivity was identical under both systems.
E. Productivity and turnover were significantly lower with control systems.

2. Which of the following is *not* one of the seven people-centered practices identified by Pfeffer?
A. Sharing of key information
B. Compensation linked to performance
C. Protection of job security
D. Rigorous hiring process
E. Emphasis on status differences

3. _____, according to research, is(are) the most frequently used but least successful job-hunting method.
A. Corporate Web sites B. Internal job posting
C. Referrals D. Job fairs
E. Temporary-help agencies

4. What does the R stand for in the PROCEED model of employee selection?
A. Repeat interview B. Request references
C. Review interview questions D. Register with EEOC
E. Reject unqualified applicants

5. Research suggests that affirmative action programs in the United States
A. actually helped white males the most.
B. doubled female employment between 1965 and 1985.
C. helped black workers get promoted in government and business.
D. had the greatest positive impact on Native Americans.
E. tripled the percentage of Asian Americans in the workforce.

6. A(n) _____ interview is subject to distortion and bias and open to legal attack.
A. traditional unstructured B. structured
C. virtual D. lengthy
E. objective

7. Which of the following is *not* a criterion for legally defensible performance appraisals in the United States?
A. Specific written instructions for evaluators
B. Results reviewed with ratees
C. Based on job analysis
D. Results linked with compensation decisions
E. Behavior-oriented

8. A convergence of demographic and technological trends is predicted to have which impact on the U.S. labor force?
A. Too many job seekers
B. Unemployment
C. Shortage of skilled workers
D. Racism
E. Proportionately fewer women

9. Individuals who believe they are being sexually harassed at work and would like to file a lawsuit should follow which bit of advice?
A. Find witnesses.
B. Threaten the harasser with dire consequences.
C. Wait until you're physically assaulted.
D. Just ignore it.
E. Make sure a manager is the aggressor.

10. What is the preferred strategy for dealing with employee substance abusers?
A. Ignoring the problem B. Referral and rehabilitation
C. Imprisonment D. Stiff fines
E. Drug testing and punishment

ACE self-test

Want more questions? Visit the student Web site at http://business.college.hmco.com/students/ (select Kreitner, *Management,* 10e) and take the ACE quizzes for more practice.

12 Communicating in the Internet Age

> *"It is a luxury to be understood."*[1]
>
> RALPH WALDO EMERSON

OBJECTIVES

- **Identify** each major link in the communication process.
- **Explain** the concept of media richness and the Lengel-Daft contingency model of media selection.
- **Identify** the five communication strategies, and **specify** guidelines for using them.
- **Discuss** why it is important for managers to know about grapevine and nonverbal communication.
- **Explain** ways in which management can encourage upward communication.
- **Identify** and **describe** four barriers to communication.
- **List** two practical tips for each of the three modern communication technologies (e-mail, cell phones, and videoconferences), and **summarize** the pros and cons of telecommuting.
- **List** at least three practical tips for improving each of the following communication skills: listening, writing, and running a meeting.

the changing workplace

How to Start Turning Around a Behemoth CEO Ed Zander

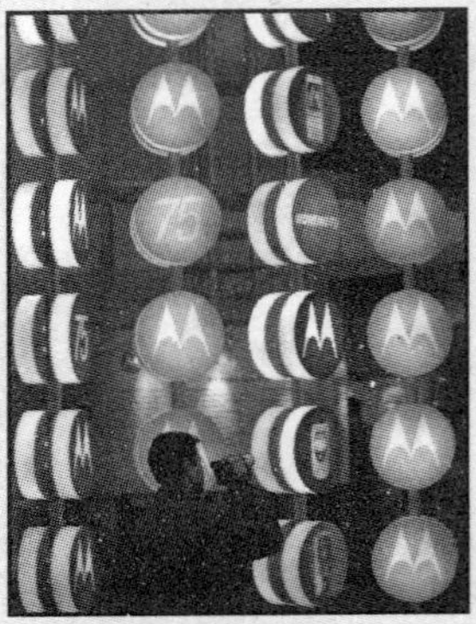

You replaced Chris Galvin as CEO of Motorola in January [2004]. What's the first thing an outsider does to run a legendary high-tech company that has seen better days? I knew I was coming in at the top of an 85,000-employee company without any support structure. I showed up the first day and wondered, Whom do you trust? I didn't even have my own administrator. Over Christmas, I read three books: Jim Collins's *Good to Great*; the first 100 pages of Lou Gerstner's memoir on turning around IBM; and *Execution*, by Lawrence Bossidy, because I'd heard Motorola was only so-so in execution. I also called CEO friends of mine for advice. I had lunch with John Chambers of Cisco. I flew to D.C. and talked with Michael Capellas at MCI. And Pat Russo at Lucent.

I came in with a plan of action, but I also knew I'd better live in the house for a little while before I jump to conclusions and start firing people. In the first week, I had one-on-ones with everyone, letting them talk. As much as I like to talk, for the first month I tried to listen. I held one or two "town hall" meetings a week, all across the country.

How did you think about the message that you wanted to deliver? I wanted the employees to understand my hot buttons, so I kept my messages very simple. Basically it was the five reasons I joined Motorola: the market opportunity; the technical prowess, with one of the strongest labs on the planet and a great patent portfolio; the brand, which, while tarnished, is an awesome franchise; the company's great customers; and finally, the employees themselves. We've got great people who want to win. I didn't want to provoke them. I didn't attack the culture.

The decisions I made that first month were another way of communicating the message. I quickly validated the decision to spin off the company's semiconductor operations—that showed I wouldn't second-guess everything that happened before I got here. I also made a big decision to change the compensation plan for management to include criteria for quality and customer satisfaction. And to back it up, I hired a chief quality officer and a vice president for customer advocacy.

What was your biggest surprise when you arrived on the job? That customers weren't a high priority at Motorola. I sat around my first three weeks, and no one asked me to make a sales call. So I picked up the phone and called two of Motorola's largest customers, Brian Roberts at Comcast and Tim Donahue at Nextel. I introduced myself and asked to go see them. That helped make my game plan very specific. Any advice I had for Motorola in the first months had better be right, or I'd spend the next six months undoing my mistakes. I knew the worst thing you can do as a CEO is to guess wrong. Your credibility goes to zero.

Source: *From G. Pascal Zachary, "How to Start Turning Around a Behemoth,"* Business 2.0, *5 (December 2004): 100.*

One of the most difficult challenges for management is getting individuals to understand and voluntarily pursue organizational objectives. Effective communication, as used by Ed Zander to get everyone at Motorola on the same page, is vital to meeting this challenge. Organizational communication takes in a great deal of territory—virtually every management function and activity can be considered communication in one way or another. Planning and controlling require a good deal of communicating, as do organization design and development, decision making and problem solving, leadership, and staffing. Organizational cultures would not exist without communication. Studies have shown that both organizational and individual performance improve when managerial communication is effective.[2] Given today's team-oriented organizations where things need to be accomplished with and through people over whom a manager has no direct authority, communication skills are more important than ever. In fact, a recent survey of 133 executives yielded this evidence:

> *The most-desired management skill is good communication, followed by a sense of vision, honesty, decisiveness, and ability to build good relationships with employees.*[3]

Thanks to modern technology, we can communicate more quickly and less expensively. But the ensuing torrent of messages has proved to be a mixed blessing for managers and nonmanagers alike. Complaints of information overload are common today. As an extreme example, how about Microsoft's cofounder and chairman Bill Gates? He reportedly receives 4 million e-mails a day![4] Worse yet, managers have a growing suspicion that more communication is not necessarily better. Research validates this suspicion: "Executives say 14 percent of each 40-hour workweek is wasted because of poor communication between staff and managers. . . . That amounts to a staggering seven workweeks of squandered productivity a year."[5] The challenge to improve this situation is both immense and immediate. But before managers, or anyone else for that matter, can become more effective communicators, they need to appreciate that

12a Attention, Please!

[Microsoft vice president Linda] Stone is a creative thinker who has coined the term *continuous partial attention* to describe the way we cope with the barrage of communication coming at us. It's not the same as multitasking, Stone says; that's about trying to accomplish several things at once. With continuous partial attention, we're scanning incoming alerts for the best thing to seize upon: "How can I tune in in a way that helps me sync up with the most interesting, or important, opportunity?"

Source: Jill Hecht Maxwell, "Stop the Net, I Want to Get Off," Inc., *24 (January 2002): 93.*

QUESTION:

What are the pros and cons of this technique relative to communicating in the workplace?

For further information about the interactive annotations in this chapter, visit our Web site (**http://business.college.hmco.com/students and select Kreitner, *Management,* 10e**).

communication is a complex process subject to a great deal of perceptual distortion and many problems. This is especially true for the apparently simple activity of communicating face to face.

The Communication Process

communication: *interpersonal transfer of information and understanding*

Management scholar Keith Davis defined **communication** as "the transfer of information and understanding from one person to another person."[6] Communication is inherently a social process. Whether one communicates face to face with a single person or with a group of people via television, it is still a social activity involving two or more people. By analyzing the communication process, one discovers that it is a chain made up of identifiable links (see Figure 12.1). Links in this process include sender, encoding, medium, decoding, receiver, and feedback.[7] The essential purpose of this chainlike process is to send an idea from one person to another in a way that will be understood by the receiver. Like any other chain, the communication chain is only as strong as its weakest link.[8]

1. IDENTIFY each major link in the communication process.

Encoding

Thinking takes place within the privacy of your brain and is greatly affected by how you perceive your environment. But when you want to pass along a thought to someone else, an entirely different process begins. This second process, communication, requires that you, the sender, package the idea for understandable transmission. Encoding starts at this point. The purpose of encoding is to translate internal thought patterns into a language or code that the intended receiver of the message will probably understand.

Managers usually rely on words, gestures, or other symbols for encoding. Their choice of symbols depends on several factors, one of which is the nature of the message itself. Is it technical or nontechnical, emotional or factual? Perhaps it could be expressed better with colorful PowerPoint slides than with words, as in the case of a budget report. To express skepticism, merely a shrug might be enough. More fundamentally, will the encoding help get the attention of busy and distracted people?[9]

Greater cultural diversity in the workplace also necessitates careful message encoding. Trudy Milburn, an American Management Association program coordinator, offers this perspective:

> *Communication becomes problematic when organizations adopt a narrow perspective of communication that focuses on a single normative standard. Some African-American employees, for example, may be discouraged from speaking in a dialect defined as "black English" and may be mandated to adopt proper business grammar. When companies deem their standard to be the only acceptable one, they will not be able to appreciate different ways of interacting.*[10]

Has modern telecommunications technology made communicating easier or harder? Both, really. This young Indian woman could be talking to anyone anywhere on the planet. But language barriers, inappropriate media, and incompatible equipment remain problematic.

Figure 12.1 The Basic Communication Process

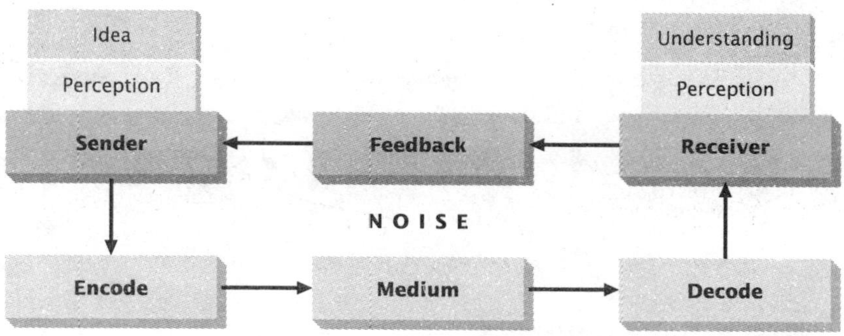

In the global marketplace, where language barriers hamper communication, e-mail translation programs promise to make the encoding process a bit easier.

Selecting a Medium

Managers can choose among a number of media: face-to-face conversations, telephone calls, e-mails, memos, letters, computer reports and networks, photographs, bulletin boards, meetings, organizational publications, and others. Communicating with those outside the organization opens up further possibilities, such as news releases, press conferences, and advertising on television and radio or in magazines, in newspapers, and on the Internet.

Media Selection in Cross-Cultural Settings. The importance of selecting an appropriate medium is magnified when one moves from internal to cross-cultural dealings. Recall the distinction between low-context and high-context cultures that we made in Chapter 4; managers moving from low-context cultures to high-context cultures need to select communication media with care.

> *The United States, Canada, and northern European nations are defined as low-context cultures, meaning that the verbal content of a message is more important than the medium—the setting through which the message is delivered. In such cultures, a videoconference or an e-mail is usually accepted as an efficient substitute for an in-person meeting.*
>
> *But in other countries—including many in Asia and the Middle East—context, or setting, with its myriad nonverbal cues, can convey far more meaning than the literal words of a given message. In such high-context cultures, business transactions are ritualized, and the style in which the rituals are carried out matters more than the words. A high value is placed on face-to-face interaction, and after-hours socialization with customers and colleagues is almost a daily occurrence.*[11]

media richness: *a medium's capacity to convey information and promote learning*

A Contingency Approach. A contingency model for media selection has been proposed by Robert Lengel and Richard Daft.[12] It pivots on the concept of media richness. **Media richness** describes the capacity of a given medium to convey information and promote learning. As illustrated in the top portion of Figure 12.2, media vary in richness from high (or rich) to low (or lean). Face-to-face conversation is a rich medium because it (1) simultaneously provides *multiple information cues,* such as message content, tone of voice, facial expressions, and so on; (2) facilitates immediate *feedback;* and (3) is *personal* in focus. In contrast, bulletins and general computer reports are lean media; that is, they convey limited information and foster

Figure 12.2 The Lengel-Daft Contingency Model of Media Selection

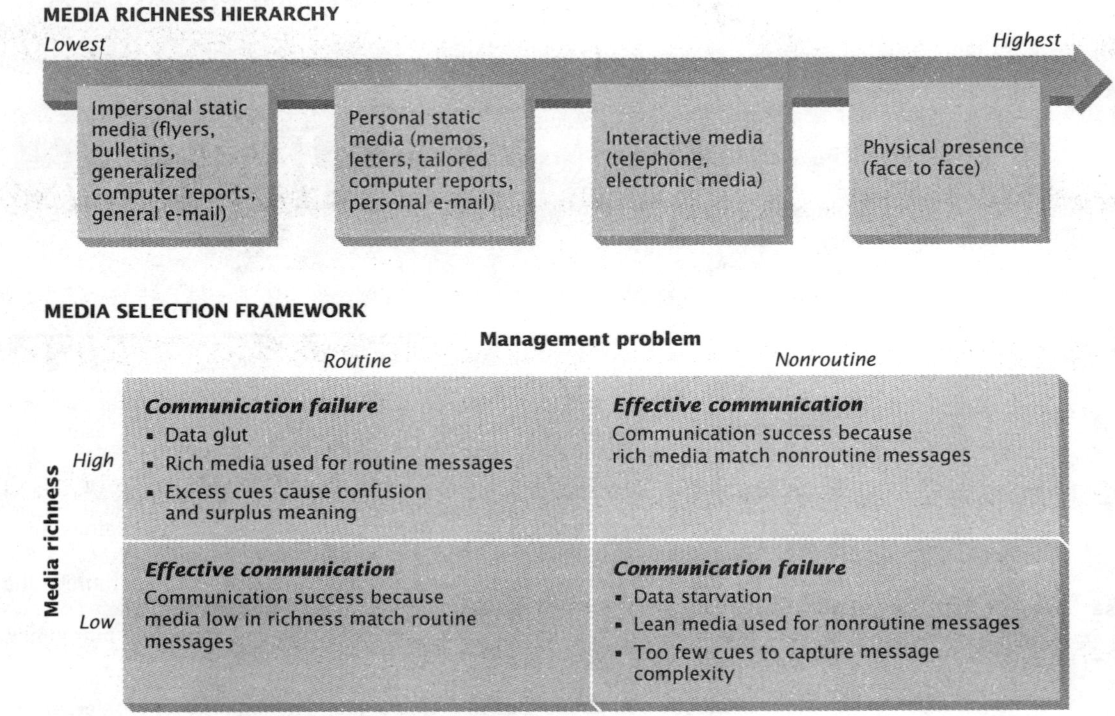

Source: *Based on Robert H. Lengel and Richard L. Daft, "The Selection of Communication Media as an Executive Skill,"* Academy of Management Executive, *2 (August 1988): 226, 227, exhibits 1 and 2. Reprinted by permission.*

2. EXPLAIN the concept of media richness and the Lengel-Daft contingency model of media selection.

limited learning. Lean media, such as general e-mail bulletins, provide a single cue, do not facilitate immediate feedback, and are impersonal.

Management's challenge, indicated in the bottom portion of Figure 12.2, is to match media richness with the situation. Nonroutine problems are best handled with rich media such as face-to-face, telephone, or video interactions.[13] Lean media are appropriate for routine problems. Examples of mismatched media include reading a corporate annual report at a stockholders' meeting (data glut) or announcing a massive layoff with an impersonal e-mail (data starvation).

■ Decoding

Even the most expertly fashioned message will not accomplish its purpose unless it is understood. After physically receiving the message, the receiver needs to comprehend it. If the message has been properly encoded, decoding is supposed to take place rather routinely. But perfect encoding is nearly impossible in our world of many languages and cultures.[14] (In fact, India alone has 17 official languages.)[15] Also in the mix are countless individual differences that affect perception:

> *Speakers and writers think they are delivering clear, cogent messages. Listeners and readers think—whatever they want to think. And what they want to think is influenced by the astonishing assortment of preexisting ideas, associations, and assumptions bumping around inside their skulls.*[16]

12b Back to the Opening Case

How would you rate Motorola's Ed Zander in terms of media selection? Explain.

At the core, the receiver's willingness to receive the message is a principal prerequisite for successful decoding. Successful decoding is more likely if the receiver knows the language and terminology used in the message. It helps, too, if the receiver understands the sender's purpose and background situation. Effective listening is given special attention later in this chapter.

■ Feedback

Some sort of verbal or nonverbal feedback from the receiver to the sender is required to complete the communication process. Appropriate forms of feedback are determined by the same factors that govern the sender's encoding decision. Without feedback, senders have no way of knowing whether their ideas have been accurately understood. Knowing whether others understand us significantly affects both the form and the content of our follow-up communication.

Employee surveys consistently underscore the importance of timely and personal feedback from management. For example, one survey of 500,000 employees from more than 300 firms contrasted satisfaction with "coaching and feedback from boss" for two groups of employees: (1) committed employees who planned to stay with their employer for at least five years and (2) those who intended to quit within a year. Satisfaction with coaching and feedback averaged 64 percent among the committed employees, whereas it dropped to 34 percent among those ready to quit.[17]

■ Noise

noise: *any interference with the normal flow of communication*

Noise is not an integral part of the chainlike communication process, but it may influence the process at any or all points. As the term is used here, **noise** is any interference with the normal flow of understanding from one person to another. This is a very broad definition. Thus, a speech impairment, garbled technical transmission, negative attitudes, lies,[18] misperception, illegible print or pictures, telephone static, partial loss of hearing, and poor eyesight all qualify as noise. Understanding tends to diminish as noise increases. In general, the effectiveness of organizational communication can be improved in two ways. Steps can be taken to make verbal and written messages more understandable. And at the same time, noise can be minimized by foreseeing and neutralizing sources of interference.

Dynamics of Organizational Communication

As a writer on the subject pointed out, "civilization is based on human cooperation and without communication, no effective cooperation can develop."[19] Accordingly, effective communication is essential for cooperation within productive organizations. At least four dynamics of organizational communication—communication strategies, the grapevine, nonverbal communication, and upward communication—largely determine the difference between effectiveness and ineffectiveness in this important area.

■ Communication Strategies

3. ■ **IDENTIFY** the five communication strategies, and **SPECIFY** guidelines for using them.

A good deal of effort goes into plotting product development, information technology, financial, and marketing strategies these days. Much less, if any, attention is devoted to organizational communication strategies.[20] Hence, organizational communication tends to be haphazard and often ineffective. A more systematic approach is needed. This section introduces five basic communication strategies, with an eye toward improving the overall quality of communication.

■ **A Communication Continuum with Five Strategies.** A team of authors led by communication expert Phillip G. Clampitt created the useful communication

Figure 12.3 Clampitt's Communication Strategy Continuum

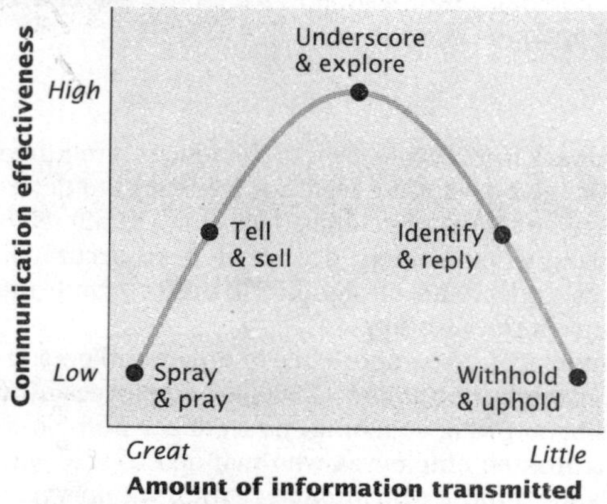

Source: Academy of Management Executive: The Thinking Manager's Source *by Phillip Clampitt. Copyright 2000 by Academy of Management. Reproduced with permission of Academy of Management in the format Textbook via Copyright Clearance Center.*

strategy continuum shown in Figure 12.3. Communication effectiveness is the vertical dimension of the model, ranging from low to high. A message communicated via any of the media discussed earlier is effective if one's intended meaning is conveyed fully and accurately to the receiver. The horizontal dimension of Clampitt's model is the amount of information transmitted, ranging from great to little. Plotted on this quadrant are five common communication strategies. Let us examine each one more closely.

- ***Spray & Pray.*** This is the organizational equivalent of a large lecture section where passive receivers are showered with information in the hope that some of it will stick. Managers employing the Spray & Pray strategy assume "more is better." Unfortunately, as employees who are swamped by corporate e-mail directives and announcements will attest, more is *not* necessarily better. This strategy suffers from being one-way, impersonal, and unhelpful because it leaves receivers to sort out what is actually important or relevant.
- ***Tell & Sell.*** This strategy involves communicating a more restricted set of messages and taking time to explain their importance and relevance. Top executives often rely on Tell & Sell when introducing new strategies, merger plans, and reorganizations. A potentially fatal flaw arises when more time is spent polishing the presentation than assessing the receivers' actual needs.
- ***Underscore & Explore.*** Key information and issues closely tied to organizational success are communicated with this give-and-take strategy. Priorities are included and justifications are offered. Unlike the first two strategies, this one is two-way. Receivers are treated as active rather than passive participants in the process. Feedback is generated by "allowing employees the creative freedom to explore the implications of those ideas in a disciplined way."[21] Listening, resolving misunderstandings, building consensus and commitment, and addressing actual or potential obstacles are fundamental to success with the Underscore & Explore strategy.
- ***Identify & Reply.*** This is a reactive and sometimes defensive strategy. Employee concerns about prior communications are the central focus here. Employees are not only viewed as active participants; they essentially drive the process because they are assumed to know the key issues. According to Clampitt and his colleagues, "Employees set the agenda, while executives respond to rumors, innuendoes, and leaks."[22] Those using the Identify & Reply strategy need to be good listeners.
- ***Withhold & Uphold.*** With this communication strategy, you tell people what you think they need to know only when you believe they need to know it. Secrecy and control are paramount. Because information is viewed as power, it is rationed and restricted. Those in charge uphold their rigid and narrow view of things when challenged or questioned. If you think this sounds like the old Theory X command-and-control style of management, you're right. The Withhold & Uphold communication strategy virtually guarantees rumors and resentment.

In organizational life, one can find hybrid combinations of these five strategies. But usually there is a dominant underlying strategy that may or may not be effective.

■ **Seeking a Middle Ground.** Both ends of the continuum in Figure 12.3 are problematic.

> *On one extreme, employees receive all the information they could possibly desire, while at the other, they are provided with little or no communication. Strategies at the extremes have a similar quality: employees have difficulty*

12c Back to the Opening Case

Which communication strategy did Ed Zander rely on most heavily during his early days at Motorola? Was it an appropriate strategy? Explain.

framing and making sense out of organizational events. Discovering salient information, focusing on core issues, and creating the proper memories are left to employees' personal whims.[23]

Accordingly, managers need to follow this set of guidelines when selecting a communication strategy appropriate to the situation: (1) avoid Spray & Pray and Withhold & Uphold; (2) use Tell & Sell and Identify & Reply sparingly; and (3) use Underscore & Explore as much as possible.

■ Merging Communication Strategies and Media Richness. Present and future managers who effectively blend lessons from Figure 12.2 (media selection) and Figure 12.3 (communication strategies) are on the path toward improved organizational communication. The trick is to select the richest medium possible (given resource constraints) when employing the Tell & Sell, Identify & Reply, and Underscore & Explore strategies.

■ The Grapevine

In every organization, large or small, there are actually two communication systems, one formal and the other informal. Sometimes these systems complement and reinforce each other; at other times they come into direct conflict. Although theorists have found it convenient to separate the two, distinguishing one from the other in real life can be difficult. Information required to accomplish official objectives is channeled throughout the organization via the formal system. By definition, official or formal communication flows in accordance with established lines of authority and structural boundaries. Media for official communication include all of those discussed earlier. But intertwined with this formal network is the **grapevine**, the unofficial and informal communication system. The term *grapevine* can be traced back to Civil War days, when vinelike telegraph wires were strung from tree to tree across battlefields. *Inc.* magazine recently offered this comment about the grapevine: "Good news travels fast, bad news travels faster, and embarrassing news travels at warp speed. So long as people have mouths to speak and fingers to type they will gossip."[24] All the more reason to learn more about the grapevine and how to deal with it.

grapevine: *unofficial and informal communication system*

4. DISCUSS why it is important for managers to know about grapevine and nonverbal communication.

■ Words of Caution About The E-Grapevine and "Blogs" Modern Internet and communication technologies—including e-mail, cell phones, and instant messaging—have been a boon for the grapevine, vastly and instantly extending its reach. But this new communication landscape holds some nasty surprises for the unwary. As a pair of business writers recently pointed out,

> *E-mail allows workplace tales to spread faster than ever. But without the opportunity for nonverbal cues and interactivity, e-mail makes it even harder for employees to accurately interpret the message. Because in many if not most work environments e-mail messages are stored and subject to inspection (by people for whom the message was not intended), the savviest employees will not engage in e-gossip. Indeed, companies have pursued legal action to deal with some of the more harmful aspects of their e-grapevines.*[25]

So a bit of gossip shared by the water cooler is not the same as a bit of gossip shared online, because the latter leaves an electronic trail that could be read by anyone. The same goes for *blogs* (short for Web logs) that amount to online diaries.[26] For example, Jonathan Schwartz, the president of Sun Microsystems, considers blogging a crucial tool for getting out his company's story. "About 35,000 people read his blog (**http://blogs.sun.com**) in a typical month, including customers, employees, and competitors. Schwartz encourages all Sun's 32,000 employees to blog, though only about 100 are doing it so far."[27] About 1,000 Microsoft employees reportedly do so (see Management Ethics). The e-grapevine is one more area where lawmakers, ethics specialists, and company policy makers are racing to catch up with new technology.

MANAGEMENT ETHICS

Keeping Blogs in Check

The popularity of web logs, or "blogs," got a tremendous boost . . . [in 2003] when reporters covering the war in Iraq began posting their personal experiences. Blogs have been around for a few years, but their value as a communication tool is just starting to grab the attention of employers.

"Employer interest currently is the highest that I've ever seen it, and it seems to be growing every day," said Jason Shellen, associate program manager of Blogger, the web log division of Google Inc., which operates one of the Internet's most popular search engines. "The interest is mainly in developing blogs as external communication tools with customers and clients, though some employers are beginning to consider ways they can use blogs internally."

Blogs can be a very flexible way to communicate daily with clients and customers about product releases and new services. "Many employers have found blogs are extremely useful in getting up-to-date feedback and input from their customers," said Shellen, referring to interactive blogs.

Blogs also may help to forge better working relationships among staff.

"We began running blogs about six or seven months ago to discuss product development and work out technical problems in software development," said Ben Saitz, senior director of operations, global technical service for DoubleClick Inc. in New York. "We're spread out all over the world, but the blogs have helped us to develop a cohesion among the staff. We have software engineers and programmers in our office in Denver now interacting with our staff in Dublin. Six months ago, they didn't even know [the others] existed, but they now are working together. It's been a very interesting process to watch."

There is, however, as much potential for misuse of blogs as there is for any other form of electronic communication. "The topics should really be business-related for a blog to be really effective," said Kathryn Yates, communication global practice leader for Watson Wyatt Worldwide in Chicago.

"We have both a code of conduct and a well-written computer usage policy," Saitz said. "Our employees understand and follow those policies, and I think we all know these policies should cover the use of blogs both internally and externally."

Still, Watson Wyatt's Yates cautions employers not to take a laissez faire attitude when it comes to usage policies for blogs. "Most employers already have e-mail and computer use policies and should probably just review them before developing blogs for internal or external communications," she said. "Adding the words 'web logs' or 'text messaging' or a term like 'all computer-based electronic communications' to your written policy is probably a good idea."

Even with a good computer usage policy in place, employers should screen their blogs to ensure employees aren't posting inappropriate comments and material. And they should make it perfectly clear that they will review and remove any offensive material.

Lack of oversight ruined one employer's attempt at creating an internal blog, which allowed employees to post questions to senior-level managers who would then respond on the blog. The employees were allowed to post anonymously, which immediately led to problems.

Source: From Bill Leonard, "Blogs Begin to Make Mark on Corporate Communication," HR Magazine, *48 (September 2003): 30. Reprinted with the permission of* HR Magazine, *published by the Society for Human Resource Management, Alexandria, VA.*

■ **Managerial Attitudes Toward the Grapevine.** One survey of 341 participants in a management development seminar uncovered predominantly negative feelings among managers toward the grapevine. Moreover, first-line supervisors perceived the grapevine to be more influential than did middle managers. This second finding led the researchers to conclude that "apparently the grapevine is more prevalent, or at least more visible, at lower levels of the managerial hierarchy where supervisors can readily feel its impact."[28] Finally, the survey found that employees of relatively small organizations (fewer than 50 people) viewed the grapevine as less influential than did those from larger organizations (more than 100 people). A logical explanation for this last finding is that smaller organizations are usually more informal.

In spite of the negative attitude that many managers have toward it, the grapevine does have a positive side. In fact, experts estimate that grapevine communication is about 75 percent accurate.[29] Even though the grapevine has a reputation among managers as a bothersome source of inaccurate information and gossip, it helps satisfy a natural desire to know what is really going on and gives employees a sense of belonging. The grapevine also serves as an emotional outlet for employee fears and apprehensions.[30] Consider, for example, what happened when investor Laurence A. Tisch became chairman of CBS:

> *Tisch's reputation as a ferocious cost cutter, which he despises, forces him to watch every word and gesture. Simple questions—such as why a department needs so many people—are sometimes interpreted as orders to slash. One day Tisch and [the CBS News department head] were talking outside CBS's broadcast center on Manhattan's West 57th Street when Tisch pointed to a tower atop the building, asking what it was. Apparently staffers at a window saw him pointing in their general direction, and the next day newspaper reporters called CBS checking out a rumor that Tisch planned to sell the building.*[31]

Nevertheless, grapevine communication can carry useful information through the organization with amazing speed. Moreover, grapevine communication can help management learn how employees truly feel about policies and programs.[32]

■ **Coping with the Grapevine.** Considering how the grapevine can be an influential and sometimes negative force, what can management do about it? First and foremost, the grapevine *cannot be extinguished.* In fact, attempts to stifle grapevine communication may serve instead to stimulate it. Subtly monitoring the grapevine and officially correcting or countering any potentially damaging misinformation is about all any management team can do.[33] "Management by walking around" is an excellent way to monitor the grapevine in a nonthreatening manner. Some managers selectively feed information into the grapevine. For example, a health care administrator has admitted, "Sure, I use the grapevine. Why not? The employees sure use it. It's fast, reaches everyone, and employees believe it—no matter how preposterous. I limit its use, though."[34] Rumor-control hotlines and Web sites with answers to frequently asked questions (FAQs) have proved useful for neutralizing disruptive and inaccurate rumors and grapevine communication.[35]

For their part, individuals would do well to follow this time-honored advice recently passed along by *Training* magazine's editor-in-chief, Tammy Galvin:

> *Whether it's something you're hearing or something you're telling, ask yourself: Is it the truth? Is it fair to all concerned? Will it build goodwill and better friendships? And finally, will it be beneficial to all concerned? If you answer "no" to even one of those questions, don't open your mouth. If you're on the receiving end, you are equally responsible. You should decline to participate in the conversation, and the onus is also on you to try to cut it off at the source.*[36]

body language: *nonverbal communication based on facial expressions, posture, and appearance*

■ Nonverbal Communication

In today's hurried world, our words are often taken to have meanings that were not intended. Facial expressions and body movements that accompany our words can either enhance communication or worsen matters. This nonverbal communication, sometimes referred to as **body language**, is an important part of the communication process.[37] In fact, one expert contends that only 7 percent of the impact of our face-to-face communication comes from the words we utter; the other 93 percent comes from our vocal intonations, facial expressions, posture, and appearance.[38] Even periods of silence can carry meaning. Consider this advice:

> *Your job as a manager is to learn to hear not only what people are saying, but also what they*

12d Hmmmm. Should I or Shouldn't I?

Letter to *Business 2.0* magazine's advice column:

> *I spotted a memo from the CEO on my boss's desk–and proceeded to find out who will be the targets of downsizing. I don't need a lecture about wandering eyes, but I wonder if I should tell my co-worker that he's on the list.*

Source: As quoted in Evelyn Nussenbaum, "I Know Something I Shouldn't Know," Business 2.0, *5 (January-February 2004): 115.*

QUESTIONS:
What is the *ethical* thing to do here? What would *you* do? Explain your rationale.

How important is nonverbal communication? Try giving directions to someone just verbally, no gesturing. This manager points a customer in the right direction during the grand opening of Wal-Mart's 3,000th U.S. store in San Antonio, Texas.

may not be saying in a conversation. So the next time you encounter someone's silence during an interview or a meeting, don't interrupt unless the person is clearly anxious or having a hard time responding.[39]

Silence may indicate doubt, lack of understanding, or polite disagreement. Even the whole idea of "dressing for success" is an attempt to send a desired nonverbal message about oneself.[40] Image consultants have developed a thriving business helping aspiring executives look the part:

Vanda Sachs had a problem. The 35-year-old senior marketing executive for a well-known fashion magazine had her sights set on the publisher's office. Her trouble? Projecting enough authority to be considered for the job. "I'm petite and blonde and I'm baby-faced," she says, "none of which goes over very well in a world of 45-year-old men who are 6-foot-2." Being short, in particular, is a "major liability," she adds, "more so than being a woman."

Beyond wearing high heels, Sachs (a pseudonym) couldn't do much about her height, but she decided she could improve on her appearance. The first step was to hire a personal image consultant. Her choice: Emily Cho, founder of New Image, a respected New York City personal-image shopping service that for 19 years has been helping women choose clothes compatible with their private and professional aspirations. Four days and $3,000 later, Sachs had a knockout wardrobe and a newly acquired savvy that would help her look the part of a publisher. "Like it or not," she explains, "we're a society that's built on first impressions."[41]

■ **Types of Body Language.** There are three kinds of body language: facial, gestural, and postural.[42] Without the speaker or listener consciously thinking about it, seemingly insignificant changes in facial expressions, gestures, and posture send various messages. A speaker can tell whether a listener is interested by monitoring a combination of nonverbal cues, including an attentive gaze, an upright posture, and confirming or agreeing gestures. Unfortunately, many people in positions of authority—parents, teachers, and managers—ignore or misread nonverbal feedback. When this happens, they become ineffective communicators.

■ **Receiving Nonverbal Communication.** Like any other interpersonal skill, sensitivity to nonverbal cues can be learned (see Table 12.1).

Listeners need to be especially aware of subtleties, such as the fine distinctions between an attentive gaze and a glaring stare and between an upright posture and a stiff one. Knowing how to interpret a nod, a grimace, or a grin can be invaluable to managers.[43] If at any time the response seems inappropriate to what one is saying, it is time to back off and reassess one's approach. It may be necessary to explain things more clearly, adopt a more patient manner, or make other adjustments.

Nonverbal behavior can also give managers a window on deep-seated emotions. For example, consider the situation Michael C. Ruettgers encountered shortly after joining EMC Corp., a leading manufacturer of computer data storage equipment:

> *Four months into Ruettgers' new job as head of operations and customer service, EMC's product quality program erupted into a full-blown crisis. Every piece of equipment the company sold was crashing because EMC engineers [had] failed to detect faulty disk drives supplied by NEC Corp. Ruettgers made a series of marathon swings across the country to meet personally with customers. In Denver and Salt Lake City, he came face to face with the scope of the catastrophe when managers broke down in tears because their computer operations were in shambles. "Nothing can really prepare you for that," Ruettgers says.*[44]

Table 12.1 Reading Body Language

Unspoken message	Behavior
"I want to be helpful."	Uncrossing legs Unbuttoning coat or jacket Unclasping hands Moving closer to other person Smiling face Removing hands from pockets Unfolding arms from across chest
"I'm confident."	Avoiding hand-to-face gestures and head scratching Maintaining an erect stance Keeping steady eye contact Steepling fingertips below chin
"I'm nervous."	Clearing throat Expelling air (such as "Whew!") Placing hand over mouth while speaking Hurried cigarette smoking
"I'm superior to you."	Peering over tops of eyeglasses Pointing a finger Standing behind a desk and leaning palms down on it Holding jacket lapels while speaking

Source: *Adapted from William Friend, "Reading Between the Lines,"* Association Management, *36 (June 1984): 94–100. Reprinted by permission of the publisher.*

After his promotion to CEO, Ruettgers helped make EMC a leader in product quality. No doubt his face-to-face interaction with frustrated customers, who conveyed powerful nonverbal emotional messages, drove home the need for improvement.

■ **Giving Nonverbal Feedback.** What about the nonverbal feedback that managers give rather than receive? A research study carried out in Great Britain suggests that nonverbal feedback from authority figures significantly affects employee behavior. Among the people who were interviewed, those who received nonverbal approval from the interviewers in the form of smiles, positive head nods, and eye contact behaved quite differently from those who received nonverbal disapproval through frowns, head shaking, and avoidance of eye contact. Those receiving positive nonverbal feedback were judged by neutral observers to be significantly more relaxed, more friendly, more talkative, and more successful in creating a good impression.[45]

Positive nonverbal feedback to and from managers is a basic building block of good interpersonal relations. A smile or nod of the head in the appropriate situation tells the individual that he or she is on the right track and to keep up the good work. Such feedback is especially important for managers, who must avoid participating in the subtle but powerful nonverbal discrimination experienced by women in leadership positions.[46] When samples of men and women leaders in one study offered the same arguments and suggestions in a controlled setting, the women leaders received more negative and less positive nonverbal feedback than the men.[47] Managing-diversity workshops target this sort of "invisible barrier" to women and minorities. Similarly, cross-cultural training alerts employees bound for foreign assignments to monitor their nonverbal gestures carefully. For example, the familiar thumbs-up sign tells American employees to keep up the good work. Much to the embarrassment of poorly informed expatriates, that particular nonverbal message does not travel well. The same gesture would be a vulgar sign in Australia, would say "I'm winning" in Saudi Arabia, and would signify the number one in Germany and the number five in Japan. Malaysians use the thumb, instead of their forefinger, for pointing.[48]

Two other trends in nonverbal communication are offering etiquette classes for students and management trainees[49] and teaching sign language to coworkers of deaf employees.

upward communication: *encouraging employees to share their feelings and ideas with management*

■ Upward Communication

As used here, the term **upward communication** refers to a process of systematically encouraging employees to share their feelings and ideas with management. Although upward communication is more important than ever, a recent survey of 25,000 employees at 17 companies in the United States found it lacking: "Less than half of workers, 45 percent, said their senior managers both talk and listen. And almost half said there was no procedure to raise questions and answers with upper management."[50] A refreshing exception is IBM's CEO, Sam Palmisano:

> *[His lofty position as the head of a company with 320,000 employees] doesn't stop him from reading every single e-mail message sent to him by IBM employees, aides say, or from calling midlevel managers just to ask them what they think.*[51]

At least seven different options are open to managers who want to improve upward communication.

12e Hey, Poker Face!

Improv, that domain of theater students, has become the latest discipline taught at the nation's top business schools. The goal: to improve listening skills, speech delivery, and responsiveness. At New York University's Stern School of Business, for example, students . . . don featureless face masks to hone their body language.

Source: Stephanie Clifford, "It's Official: MBAs Are a Bunch of Clowns," Inc., 27 (February 2005): 23.

QUESTIONS:
How much of your nonverbal communication is facial? How good are you at reading the facial expressions of other people? Explain.

■ **Formal Grievance Procedures.** When unions represent rank-and-file employees, provisions for upward communication are usually spelled out in the collective bargaining agreement. Typically, unionized employees utilize a formal grievance procedure for con-

5. EXPLAIN ways in which management can encourage upward communication.

testing managerial actions and oversights. Grievance procedures usually consist of a series of progressively more rigorous steps.[52] For example, union members who have been fired may talk with their supervisor in the presence of the union steward. If the issue is not resolved at that level, the next step may be a meeting with the department head. Sometimes the formal grievance process includes as many as five or six steps, with a third-party arbitrator as the last resort. Formal grievance procedures are also found in nonunion situations.

A promising alternative to the traditional grievance process is the *peer review* program. Originally developed in the early 1980s by General Electric at its Appliance Park factory in Columbia, Maryland, peer reviews have been adopted by a growing number of organizations. At GE, the three specially trained coworkers and two managers on the panel listen to the grievance, conduct a majority-rule secret ballot, and render a final decision. Certain issues, including those involving work rules, performance appraisal results, and pay rates, are not handled by GE's peer review panels. GE created this process as a union-avoidance tactic.[53]

■ **Employee Attitude and Opinion Surveys.** Both in-house and commercially prepared surveys can bring employee attitudes and feelings to the surface. Thanks to commercial software packages, time-saving and paperless electronic surveys are popular in today's workplaces.[54] Employees will usually complete surveys if they are convinced meaningful changes will result. Consider this chain of events, for example:

> *Taking time to implement action plans based on survey results "translates into big bucks, says Gregg Campa, director of client relations at the Business Research Lab in Houston, which conducts about 70 employee surveys a year. He cites a financial services client that had a turnover rate of 55 percent. After the company acted on results from a survey that pinpointed the source of its retention problems, the turnover rate the next year dropped to 22 percent and then down to 14 percent following a second survey. The firm documented savings of $2 million annually by reducing turnover, Campa says.*[55]

Surveys with no feedback or follow-up action tend to alienate employees, who feel the surveys are just wasting their time.[56] On the other hand, a researcher found that unionized companies conducting regular attitude surveys were less likely to experience a labor strike than companies failing to survey their employees.[57]

■ **Suggestion Systems.** Who knows more about a job than someone who performs that job day in and day out? This rhetorical question is the primary argument for suggestion systems, which can be a wellspring of good ideas. At Ernst & Young, the New York-based accounting firm, "a new confidential ethics hotline came from an employee suggestion."[58] Fairness and prompt feedback are keys to successful suggestion systems. Monetary incentives can help, too. Take, for example, this success story at Winnebago Industries, the recreational vehicle maker in Forest City, Iowa:

> *The program works because employees take it seriously. All reasonable suggestions submitted—an impressive 10,355 since the program began in 1991—are investigated by two full-time employees. The company has ended up implementing fully a third of these ideas, and employees have won more than $500,000 (they receive 10 percent of what the company saves in the first year). Winnebago says the program's first-year savings have added up to $5.8 million.*[59]

Nice return on investment! (The 10 percent rule is also used at Chicago's famous chewing gum and candy company, Wm. Wrigley Jr.)[60] A study of U.S. government employees found a positive correlation between suggestions and productivity.[61]

■ **Open-Door Policy.** The open-door approach to upward communication has been both praised and criticized. Proponents say problems can be nipped in the bud when managers keep their doors open and employees feel free to walk in at any time and talk with them. But critics contend that an open-door policy encourages

Source: *Miller. Dist. by UNIVERSAL PRESS SYNDICATE. Reprinted with permission.*

employees to leapfrog the formal chain of command (something that happens a lot these days because of e-mail and blogs). They argue further that it is an open invitation to annoying interruptions when managers can least afford them. A limited open-door policy—afternoons only, for example—can effectively remedy this particular problem. Another problem that needs to be overcome is the tendency for hard-charging managers and entrepreneurs to be too defensive. *Inc.* magazine explains:

> *. . . research shows that entrepreneurs are adept at "internalizing" success, taking full personal credit when things go right, and "externalizing" failure, blaming setbacks on outside factors. This psychological dynamic leads to certain less than helpful responses: Some managers become defensive and lash out; others find themselves wracked with self-doubt.*
>
> *There's only one way to approach the problem and it's pretty simple: Remind yourself that even if the feedback feels personal, your reaction to it has to be anything but. Tell yourself . . . that a business mistake is not the same thing as a moral failing. [California Internet entrepreneur Christine] White, for example, has now created an "open door" policy to invite negative feedback. When she feels herself getting defensive, she remembers that it's all just part of doing business.*[62]

■ **Informal Meetings.** Employees may feel free to air their opinions and suggestions if they are confident management will not criticize or penalize them for being frank. But they need to be given the right opportunity.[63] Here is an excellent case in point:

> *Employees at the Lodge at Vail are instructed to treat guests like treasured friends, anticipating and meeting their needs with the hope that they return season after season. HR director Mandy Wulfe's job is to ensure that the Vail, Colo., hotel's 280 workers feel the same way about their employer.*
>
> *To bolster employee relations, Wulfe and her boss, hotel manager Wolfgang Triebnig, last spring started a "lunch with the boss" program to give each employee the opportunity to interact with Triebnig in a casual setting.*
>
> *. . . Wulfe developed "Wolfgang's Lunch Gang," a series of monthly employee lunches in which eight staff members are invited to dine with Triebnig in the hotel's five-star restaurant. Over time, each employee will have a turn at the table.*[64]

■ **Internet Chat Rooms.** In the Internet age, a convenient way for management to get candid feedback is to host a meeting place on the Web. These so-called "virtual water coolers" give employees unprecedented freedom of speech. Dave Barram, head of the huge General Services Administration (GSA) in Washington, D.C., offered this assessment:

> *. . . GSA has set up a Web-based "chat line," in which employees exchange uncensored thoughts and ideas. "If we have honest conversations about what's working and what isn't, we can become really good," Barram says. "If we don't, we'll never help each other."*[65]

This approach takes lots of managerial courage, if the rough-and tumble "cyberventing" on unauthorized Web sites aimed at specific companies is any indication.[66]

exit interview: *brief, structured interview with a departing employee*

■ **Exit Interviews.** An employee leaving the organization, for whatever reason, no longer fears possible recrimination from superiors and so can offer unusually frank and honest feedback, obtained in a brief, structured **exit interview**.[67] On the other hand, exit interviews have been criticized for eliciting artificially negative feedback because the employee may have a sour-grapes attitude toward the organization. Research finds the use of exit interviews to be spotty and haphazard, although many employers claim to use them. "If done well, managers and consultants said, exit interviews can show trends and point to potential problems that need to be addressed."[68]

12f Straight Talk at CarMax

Employees at this chain of used-car superstores know their opinions count: CEO Austin Ligon opens frequent Q&A sessions with them by asking, "What are we doing that is stupid, unnecessary, or doesn't make sense?"

Source: Robert Levering and Milton Moskowitz, "The 100 Best Companies to Work For," Fortune (January 24, 2005): 78.

QUESTIONS:

If your present (or a former) boss asked you these questions, what would you say? How many of today's executives would be comfortable with this upward communication technique? Explain.

Systematic use of exit interviews is recommended, not only for feedback purposes, but also for "harvesting" valuable knowledge from retiring experts. This needs to be done within the context of a comprehensive *knowledge management* (KM) program, as discussed in Chapter 8. In the following recommendation from *Business 2.0* magazine, we discover how Halliburton, the oil-services and military contractor, collects and shares vital knowledge from exit interviews:

> *Target the gurus in a particular field, prolific inventors, or people in charge of a set of relationships either inside or outside the company. In particular, seize those who haven't groomed obvious successors. Halliburton's knowledge harvesters focused on a chemical division manager who had juggled suppliers and bundled contracts. He'd never shown anyone else his tricks of the trade....*
>
> *Halliburton picks key lessons and designs online flowcharts that are so rich in graphics that viewing them is like playing a game of Chutes and Ladders.*[69]

This use of exit interviews for KM is especially important in view of the coming wave of post–World War II baby boom retirees, discussed in Chapter 11.

In general, attempts to promote upward communication will be successful only if employees truly believe that their contributions will have a favorable impact on their employment. Halfhearted or insincere attempts to get employees to open up and become involved will do more harm than good.

Communication Problems and Promises in the Internet Age

Because communication is a complex, give-and-take process, problems will occur. Managers who are aware of common barriers to communication and who are sensitive to the problems of sexist and racist communication are more likely to be effective communicators. In addition, managers who want to be effective communicators need to be aware of opportunities and obstacles in Internet-age communication systems.

■ Barriers to Communication

Do intended messages actually have the desired impact on employee behavior? This is the true test of organizational communication. Emerson Electric, the successful maker of electric motors, has a simple but effective way of testing how well its organizational communication is working. According to the head of the company,

In addition to the barriers to communication covered here are two others: time and money. For example, at failing inner city schools in New York City parent-teacher communication is a big problem. Enter Brady Keys Jr., a former NFL star with the Pittsburgh Steelers, who helped create a telephone/Internet communications network linking parents and teachers. Positive results at 29 schools include greater parental involvement and higher test scores.

> *As a measure of communication at Emerson, we claim that every employee can answer four essential questions about his or her job:*
>
> 1. *What cost reduction are you currently working on?*
> 2. *Who is the "enemy" (who is the competition)?*
> 3. *Have you met with your management in the past six months?*
> 4. *Do you understand the economics of your job?*
>
> *When I repeated to a business journalist the claim that every employee can answer these questions, he put it to the test by randomly asking those questions of different employees at one of our plants. Each employee provided clear and direct answers, passing both the journalist's test and ours.*[70]

6. IDENTIFY and DESCRIBE four barriers to communication.

Emerson Electric evidently has done a good job of overcoming the four main types of communication barriers: (1) process barriers, (2) physical barriers, (3) semantic barriers, and (4) psychosocial barriers.

■ Process Barriers. Every step in the communication process is necessary for effective communication. Blocked steps become barriers. Consider the following situations:

- ***Sender barrier.*** A management trainee with an unusual new idea fails to speak up at a meeting for fear of criticism.

- ***Encoding barrier.*** This is a growing problem in today's culturally diverse workplace:

  William D. Fleet, human-resources director at the Seattle Marriott, where employees speak 17 languages, once fired a Vietnamese kitchen worker for wrongly accusing a chef of assault. Only after another employee was attacked by a kitchen worker did Fleet figure out that the Vietnamese employee had used the word "chef" to refer to all kitchen workers with white uniforms. The misunderstanding had led to the firing of a good staffer and delayed the arrest of a dangerous one....

  That's why ... [Fleet] instituted a comprehensive ESL [English as a second language] program for staffers to take on company time. After all, workers who know English interact better with guests.[71]
- ***Medium barrier.*** After getting no answer three times and a busy signal twice, a customer concludes that a store's consumer hot line is a waste of time.
- ***Decoding barrier.*** A restaurant manager does not understand unfamiliar computer jargon during a sales presentation for laptop computers.
- ***Receiver barrier.*** A manager who is preoccupied with the preparation of a budget asks a team member to repeat an earlier statement.
- ***Feedback barrier.*** During on-the-job training, the failure of the trainee to ask any questions causes a manager to wonder whether any real understanding has taken place.

The complexity of the communication process itself is a potentially formidable barrier to communication. Malfunctions anywhere along the line can singly or collectively block the transfer of understanding.

■ **Physical Barriers.** Sometimes a physical object blocks effective communication. For example, a riveter who wears ear protectors probably could not hear someone yelling "Fire!" Distance is another physical barrier. Thousands of miles and differing time zones traditionally made international business communication difficult. So today's global managers appreciate how the Internet and modern telecommunications technology have made the planet a seemingly smaller place. Although people often take physical barriers for granted, they can sometimes be removed. Perhaps an inconveniently positioned wall in an office can be torn out. Architects and office layout specialists called "organizational ecologists" are trying to redesign buildings and offices with more effective communication in mind. An interesting example is Timex's eye-catching new headquarters building in Middlebury, Connecticut:

> *All of the 275 employees—including the CEO—work in a single, open room roughly the size of a football field: No walls, no partitions, no cubes divide them....*
>
> *By opening up space, Timex hopes to promote all of the usual behavior expected from workspace design these days: collaboration, interaction, spontaneous meetings.*[72]

semantics: *study of the meaning of words*

■ **Semantic Barriers.** Formally defined, **semantics** is the study of the meaning of words. Words are indispensable, although they can cause a great deal of trouble. In a well-worn army story, a growling drill sergeant once ordered a frightened recruit to go out and paint his entire jeep. Later, the sergeant was shocked to find that the private had painted his *entire* jeep, including the headlights, windshield, seats, and dashboard gauges. Obviously, the word *entire* meant something different to the recruit than it did to the sergeant.

In today's highly specialized world, managers and professionals in such fields as accounting, computer science, advertising, medicine, and law may become so accustomed to their own technical jargon that they forget that people outside their field may not understand them. (For instance, viewers of Donald Trump's television show,

12g Watch Your #@~*&$% Language!

While the latitude of acceptable language varies across companies, managers should know that there are legal implications to cursing in the workplace. Anna Segobia Masters, chair of the labor and employment practice at McKenna and Cuneo LLP, Los Angeles, says that profane words uttered in the context of sex, race, age, or religion could be considered a form of harassment. If left unchecked, such language could be the basis of an employee complaint about a hostile work environment. . . .

To minimize the risks of lawsuits, Masters suggests creating a written policy stating that harassment can be verbal and establishing procedures for employees who want to seek corrective action.

Source: Excerpted from Louisa Wah, "Profanity in the Workplace," Management Review, *88 (June 1999): 8.*

QUESTIONS:
Do you hear more profanity in the workplace today? Is it a problem? Does it create a hostile work environment? Explain.

The Apprentice, are bombarded with business jargon such as "bottom line," "synergy," "face time," "scenario," "proactive," and "on the same page.")[73] Unexpected reactions or behavior by others may signal a semantic barrier when jargon is used. It may become necessary to reencode the message using more familiar terms. Sometimes, if the relationship among specialists in different technical fields is an ongoing one, remedial steps can be taken. For example, hospital administrators often take a special course in medical terminology to better understand the medical staff.

■ **Psychosocial Barriers.** Psychological and social barriers are probably responsible for more blocked communication than any other type of barrier.[74] People's backgrounds, perceptions, values, biases, needs, and expectations differ. Childhood experiences may result in negative feelings toward authority figures (such as supervisors), racial prejudice, distrust of the opposite sex, or lack of self-confidence. Family and personal problems, including poor health, alcoholism, lack of sleep, and emotional strain, may be so upsetting that an employee is unable to concentrate on work. Experience on present or past jobs may have created anger, distrust, and resentment that speak more loudly in the employee's mind than any work-related communication. Sincere sensitivity to the receiver's needs and personal circumstances goes a long way toward overcoming psychosocial barriers to communication.

■ Sexist and Racist Communication

In recent years the English language has been increasingly criticized for being sexist and racist. Words such as *he, chairman, brotherhood, mankind,* and the like have traditionally been used in reference to both men and women. The usual justification is that everyone understands that these words refer to both sexes, and it is simpler to use the masculine form. Critics maintain that wholly masculine wording subtly denies women a place and image worthy of their equal status and importance in society.[75] This criticism is largely based on psychological and sociological considerations. Calling the human race *mankind,* for instance, is seldom a real barrier to understanding. But a Stanford University researcher found that "males appear to use 'he' in response to male-related imagery, rather than in response to abstract or generic notions of humanity."[76] In other words, *he* is commonly interpreted to mean literally *he* (a man), not *they* (men and women).

These same cautions carry over to the problem of racist communication for both ethical and legal reasons.

> *Words spoken at work that aren't literally racist—such as "you people," "poor people," and "that one in there"—now can be grounds for employment discrimination lawsuits [in the United States].*
>
> *They're called "code words."...*
>
> *It's not just the words, says Herman Cain, the black CEO of Godfather's Pizza and author of* Leadership Is Common Sense. *"It's body language. Tone of voice. How people talk to you. Over the years you can develop a sixth sense."*[77]

Progressive and ethical managers are weeding sexist and racist language out of their vocabularies and correspondence to eliminate both intentional and inadvertent demeaning of women and racial minorities.[78]

7. LIST two practical tips for each of the three modern communication technologies (e-mail, cell phones, and videoconferences), and **SUMMARIZE** the pros and cons of telecommuting.

■ Communicating in the Online Workplace

Computers speak a simple digital language of 1s and 0s. Today, every imaginable sort of information— including text, numbers, still and moving pictures, and sound—is being converted into a digital format. This process has meant nothing short of a revolution for the computer, telecommunications, consumer electronics, publishing, and entertainment industries. Organizational communication, already significantly reshaped by computer technology, is undergoing its own revolutionary change. This section does *not* attempt the impossible task of describing all the emerging communication technologies, ranging from speech recognition computers to Wi-Fi networks to virtual reality.[79] Rather, it explores the impact of some established Internet-age technologies on workplace communications. Our goal is to use more effectively the technologies we have and to prepare for those to come.

■ Getting a Handle on E-Mail and Instant Messaging. E-mail via the Internet has precipitated a communication revolution akin to those brought about by the printing press, telephone, radio, and television. If you are on the Internet, you are ultimately linked to each of hundreds of millions of people on Earth capable of sending and receiving e-mail. Both on and off the job, e-mail is more than a way of communication—it is a lifestyle! Jim Keyes, CEO of the 7-Eleven convenience store chain, "burns three to four hours of his day on 200 e-mails and is such a heavy user that if a top field executive or licensee were to phone him, he might not recognize the voice."[80] Shifting the focus from individual to organization, we run into astonishing numbers. After discovering that many of its 88,000 employees worldwide were spending about 2½ hours each day exchanging 3 million e-mails, Intel decided to act:

> *The chipmaker recently started classes on how to manage e-mail. Some tips: Put short messages in the subject line so recipients don't have to open it to read the note. Intel also is asking workers to sparingly use graphics and attachments and get off unnecessary distribution lists.*
>
> *"We're not discouraging e-mail, just better use," spokesman Chuck Mulloy says.*[81]

E-mail is a two-headed beast: easy and efficient, while at the same time grossly abused[82] and mismanaged.[83] By properly managing e-mail, the organization can take a big step toward properly using the Internet. An organizational e-mail policy, embracing these recommendations from experts, can help:

- The e-mail system belongs to the company, which has the legal right to monitor its use. (*Never* assume privacy with company e-mail.)[84]
- Workplace e-mail is for business purposes only.
- Harassing and offensive e-mail will not be tolerated.
- E-mail messages should be concise (see Table 12.2). As in all correspondence, grammar and spelling count because they reflect on your diligence and credibility. Typing in all capital letters makes the message hard to read and amounts to SHOUTING in cyberspace. (All capital letters can be appropriate, for contrast purposes, when adding comments to an existing document.)
- Lists of bullet items (similar to the format you are reading now) are acceptable because they tend to be more concise than paragraphs.
- Long attachments defeat the quick-and-easy nature of e-mail.
- Recipients should be told when a reply is *unnecessary.*

12h Does *E*-Mail Stand For *Evidence*-Mail?

[When building criminal cases in the investment banking and insurance industries, New York attorney general Eliot] Spitzer uses whistle-blowers and even newspaper articles for leads. Yet the crucial proof comes later, when he subpoenas that modern-day treasure trove of evidence: e-mails stored on computer hard drives. They provide unscripted insights into what people really think, showing their intent, a necessary ingredient for proving fraud.

Source: Charles Gasparino, "Top of His Game," Newsweek *(November 1, 2004): 36.*

QUESTIONS:

Are your workplace e-mails "clean"? Or are you unwittingly building a case against you and/or your employer? When you delete an e-mail, where does it go?

Table 12.2 How to Compose a CLEAR E-Mail Message

Concise. A brief message in simple conversational language is faster for you to write and more pleasant for your readers to read.

Logical. A message in logical steps, remembering to include any context your readers need, will be more easily understood.

Empathetic. When you identify with your readers, your message will be written in the right tone and in words they will readily understand.

Action-oriented. When you remember to explain to your readers what you want them to do next, they are more likely to do it.

Right. A complete message, with no important facts missing, with all the facts right, and with correct spelling, will save your readers having to return to you to clarify details.

Source: *Joan Tunstall,* Better, Faster Email: Getting the Most Out of Email *(St. Leonards, Australia: Allen & Unwin, 1999), p. 37. Reprinted by permission.*

- An organization-specific priority system should be used for sending and receiving all e-mail. *Example:* "At Libit, a company in Palo Alto, Calif., that makes silicon products for the cable industry, e-mail is labeled as either informational or action items to avoid time wasting."[85]
- "Spam" (unsolicited and unwanted e-mail) that gets past filters should be deleted without being read. Despite passage of a federal anti-spam law in the United States, spam still constitutes about 60 to 70 percent of all e-mail.[86] So-called spyware and adware should be blocked and should be uninstalled when a system has been infected.[87]
- To avoid file clutter, messages unlikely to be referred to again should not be saved.[88]

IBM has responded to e-mail overload by encouraging the use of *instant messaging* (IM), because it is faster and supposedly less of a burden on the network.[89] But instant messaging, especially when it is not managed by the organization, has its own drawbacks. A survey of 840 companies, conducted by the American Management Association, uncovered some disturbing information about the uses and abuses of IM:

> *. . . only 11 percent of organizations have IM gateway/management software to control the 31 percent of employees who IM in the office. That's a dangerous prospect, given that 70 percent of these IMers have downloaded free IM software from the Internet, increasing legal, compliance, productivity and security issues.*
>
> *The survey, "2004 Workplace E-Mail and Instant Messaging Survey," also reveals that of those who IM at work, 58 percent engage in personal chats. Within these chats, 19 percent send attachments; 16 percent send jokes, gossip, rumors or disparaging remarks; 9 percent share confidential information about the company, coworkers or clients; and 6 percent exchange sexual, romantic or pornographic content.*[90]

Like e-mail, IM requires standards, policy guidelines, and management oversight.

■ Hello! Can We Talk About Cell Phone Etiquette? According to industry data, there were over 175 million wireless subscribers in the United States in early 2005.[91] The market penetration rate for cell phones in the United States is around 60 percent, with much higher figures for other countries, such as Italy.[92] As a sign of things to come, an entire 8,000-person engineering group at Ford Motor Company recently traded in their desktop phones for cell phones.[93] Like e-mail, cell phones have proved to be both a blessing and a curse. Offsetting the mobility and convenience are concerns about distracted drivers and loud and obnoxious phone conversations in public places.[94] Managers need to be particularly sensitive to the risk of inadvertently broadcasting proprietary company information, names, and numbers. Competitors could be standing in the same airport line or sitting in the next restaurant booth. Table 12.3 offers some practical tips to help make the use of cell phones more effective, secure, and courteous.[95]

Camera phones, expected to make up more than 25 percent of worldwide cell phone sales by 2006, also require restrictions in the workplace because of concerns about privacy and information security. At DaimlerChrysler, for example, neither visitors nor employees are allowed to have camera phones on company property.[96]

videoconference: *live television or broadband Internet video exchange between people in different locations*

■ **Videoconferences.** A **videoconference** is a live television or broadband Internet video exchange between people in different locations. The decreasing cost of steadily improving videoconferencing technologies and the desire to reduce costly travel time have fostered wider use of this approach to organizational communication.[97] Consider this case in point:

> *As part of its knowledge-management initiative, British Petroleum rolled out some videoconferencing technology for rapidly sharing ideas. Soon after, one of their gas drills broke down in the North Slope of Alaska. BP's leading expert in gas turbines was working in the North Sea; it would have taken him 20 hours to fly to Alaska. Instead of putting him on a plane, BP patched him into the North Slope via videoconference, and he worked with on-site technicians to pinpoint the problem and get the drill back onstream. They finished the job in just 30 minutes.*[98]

As a sample of what is available, it now is possible to go to one of 150 Kinko's stores and rent a videoconferencing room for either a meeting or a "virtual interview."[99] Moreover, "companies turned off by the $30,000 bulky systems of a decade ago can outfit a broadband-connected conference room for $5,000."[100]

Communication pointers for videoconference participants include the following:

- Test the system before the meeting convenes.
- Dress for the occasion. The video image is distorted by movement of wild patterns and flashy jewelry. Solid white clothing tends to "glow" on camera.
- Make sure everyone is introduced.
- Check to make sure everyone can see and hear the content of the meeting.
- Do not feel compelled to direct your entire presentation to the camera or monitor. Directly address those in the same room.
- Speak loudly and clearly. Avoid slang and jargon in cross-cultural meetings where translations are occurring.

Table 12.3 Five Commandments of Cell Phone Etiquette

1. ***Thou shalt not subject defenseless others to cell phone conversations.*** [Cell phone etiquette, like all forms of etiquette, centers on having respect for others.]
2. ***Thou shalt not set thy ringer to play La Cucaracha every time thy phone rings.*** [It's a phone, not a public address system.]
3. ***Thou shalt turn thy cell phone off during public performances.*** [Set your phone on vibrate when in meetings or in the company of others and, if necessary, take or return the call at a polite distance.]
4. ***Thou shalt not dial while driving.*** [If you must engage in cell phone conversations while driving, use a hands-off device.]
5. ***Thou shalt not speak louder on thy cell phone than thou would on any other phone.*** [It's called "cell yell" and it's very annoying to others.]

Source: *Five basic commandments excerpted from Dan Briody, "The Ten Commandments of Cell Phone Etiquette,"* InfoWorld, *February 5, 2005,* ***www.infoworld.com***.

Table 12.4 Telecommuting: Promises and Problems

Promises	Potential problems
1. Significantly boosts individual productivity.	1. Can cause fear of stagnating at home.
2. Saves commuting time and travel expenses (lessens traffic congestion).	2. Can foster sense of isolation due to lack of social contact with coworkers.
3. Taps broader labor pool (such as mothers with young children, disabled and retired persons, and prison inmates).	3. Can result in competition or interference with family duties, thus causing family conflict.
4. Eliminates office distractions and politics.	4. Can disrupt traditional manager-employee relationship.
5. Reduces employer's cost of office space.	5. Can cause fear of being "out of sight, out of mind" at promotion time.

- Avoid exaggerated physical movements that tend to blur on camera.
- Adjust your delivery to any transmission delay, pausing longer than usual when waiting for replies.
- Avoid side conversations, which are disruptive.
- Do not nervously tap the table or microphone or shuffle papers.[101]

telecommuting: *sending work to and from one's office via computer modem while working at home*

■ **Telecommuting.** Years ago, futurist Alvin Toffler used the term *electronic cottage* to refer to the practice of working at home on a personal computer connected—typically by telephone in those days—to an employer's place of business. More recently, this practice has been labeled **telecommuting** because work, rather than the employee, travels between a central office and the employee's home, reaching the computer via telephone or cable modem. The advent of overnight delivery services, low-cost facsimile (fax) machines, e-mail, and high-speed modems, combined with wireless and traditional telephone communication, has broadened the scope of telecommuting. According to a recent study, about 15 percent of the U.S. workforce telecommutes one or more days a week.[102] At computer services giant IBM, 40 percent of its employees telecommute from home or remote locations on a typical workday.[103] Despite some compelling advantages, telecommuting has enough drawbacks to make it unsuitable for many employees as well as employers (see Table 12.4). Telecommuting can disrupt the normal social and communication patterns in the workplace, as this manager has discovered:

> *Jack Kramer, sales vice president at Pathlore Software, a provider of online learning systems, works from home in Chester Springs, Pa., rather than corporate headquarters in Columbus, Ohio. Family was a key reason for his reticence to move: After relocating previously for work, he'd promised his children . . . they wouldn't have to move again.*
>
> *Technology also enables the setup. Through virtual technology, his employees can view a desktop at the same time he does, despite the distance: Before a recent national kickoff event, he was able to show them all a PowerPoint presentation even though he was nearly 400 miles away. "The biggest challenge is 'face time.' We have to schedule in cups of coffee remotely," [he says].*[104]

Telecommuting will not become the prevailing work mode anytime soon, but it certainly is more than a passing fad.[105]

Becoming a Better Communicator

Three communication skills as important as ever in today's rapidly changing world are listening, writing, and running meetings. Managers who master these skills generally have fewer interpersonal relations problems. Moreover, effective communica-

8. LIST at least three practical tips for improving each of the following communication skills: listening, writing, and running a meeting.

tors tend to move up the hierarchy faster than poor ones do. *Training* magazine recently summed up the importance of communication this way:

> *One of the biggest challenges managers face is communication . . . [and] communication is also one of the most critical aspects of leadership. Without good communication, managers can fail to gain commitment from employees, fail to achieve business goals and fail to develop rapport with the people on their team. In short, they can fail as leaders no matter how good their intentions may be.*[106]

■ Effective Listening

Almost all training in oral communication in high school, college, and management development programs is in effective speaking. But what about listening, the other half of the communication equation? Listening is the forgotten factor in communication skills training. This is unfortunate because the most glowing oration is a waste of time if it is not heard. Interestingly, a Cornell University researcher asked 827 employees in the hospitality industry to rate their managers' listening ability. Managers considered to be good listeners by employees tended to be female, under 45 years of age, and relatively new to their position.[107]

Listening takes place at two steps in the verbal communication process. First, the receiver must listen in order to decode and understand the original message. Then the sender becomes a listener when attempting to decode and understand subsequent feedback. Identical listening skills come into play at both ends.

We can hear and process information much more quickly than the normal speaker can talk. According to researchers, our average rate of speaking is about 125 words per minute, whereas we are able to listen to about 400 to 600 words a minute.[108] Thus, listeners have up to 75 percent slack time during which they can daydream or, alternatively, analyze the information and plan a response. Effective listeners know how to put that slack time to good use. Here are some practical tips for more effective listening:

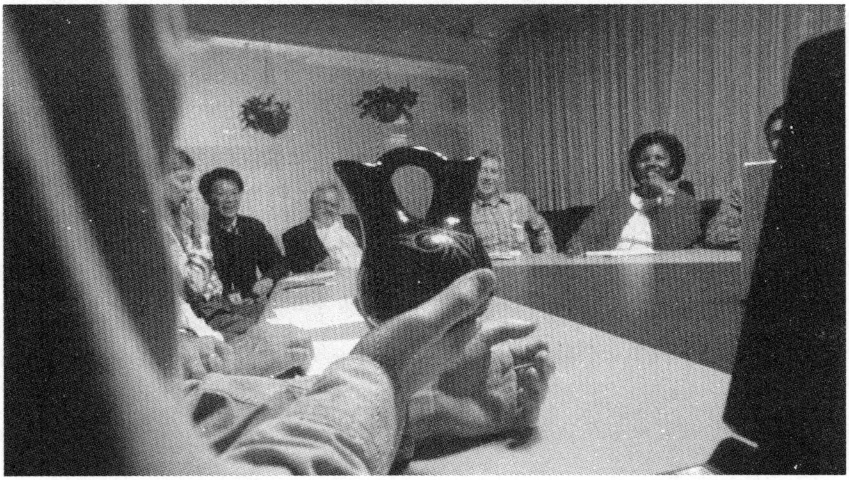

Listen to this! Native American tradition calls for giving each person in a "talking circle" an uninterrupted opportunity to speak. It is referred to as "passing the rock." The person holding the object speaks without interference, then passes the rock and shifts into a listening mode. Here a group of Xerox employees in Rochester, New York, pass the rock in their talking circle. Of course, you don't have to work for Xerox to copy this tradition.

- Tolerate silence. Listeners who rush to fill momentary silences cease being listeners.
- Ask stimulating, open-ended questions, ones that require more than merely a yes-or-no answer.
- Encourage the speaker with attentive eye contact, alert posture, and verbal encouragers such as "umhum," "yes," and "I see." Occasionally repeating the speaker's last few words also helps.
- Paraphrase. Periodically restate in your own words what you have just heard.
- Show emotion to demonstrate that you are a sympathetic listener.
- Know your biases and prejudices and attempt to correct for them.
- Avoid premature judgments about what is being said.
- Summarize. Briefly highlight what the speaker has just finished saying to bring out possible misunderstandings.[109]

For their part, speakers need to randomly insert comprehension checks. John Baldoni, a Michigan communication consultant, offers this tip: "Implement the 'brief-back.' Make sure people understand what you say. Ask your listeners to tell you what you have just told them."[110] Are you listening? Wal-Mart has developed an admired "culture of listening." All of Wal-Mart's senior managers, including the CEO, try to devote two days each week to visiting stores across the United States and listening to employees' concerns.[111] The valuable information gathered more than makes up for the Wal-Mart managers' hectic travel schedules.

■ Effective Writing

Managers often complain about poor writing skills. A recent example:

> *Larry Kensington, president of Kentwood, Mich.-based Bananza Air Management Systems, sifted through scores of résumés to hire three workers this year. One of his biggest gripes: Job applications riddled with spelling errors. "They can't even express themselves in a simple sentence," he says, noting employees need to be able to write so they can fill out quality-control data and other reports.*[112]

Writing difficulties stem from an educational system that requires students to do less and less writing. Essay tests have given way in many classes to the multiple-choice variety, and term papers are being pushed aside by team activities and projects. Quick-and-dirty e-mails, instant messages, and cell phone text messaging at home, school, and the workplace also have contributed to the erosion of writing quality in recent years. Moreover, spelling and grammar checkers used by those who compose at the computer keyboard are not cure-alls. (There really is no adequate substitute for careful proofreading.) As a learned skill, effective writing is the product of regular practice.[113] Students who do not get the necessary writing practice in school are at a disadvantage when they enter the job market.

Good writing is a key form of encoding in the basic communication process. If it is done skillfully, potentially troublesome semantic and psychosocial barriers can be surmounted. Caterpillar's publications editor offered four helpful reminders:

1. ***Keep words simple.*** Simplifying the words you use will help reduce your thoughts to essentials; keep your readers from being "turned off" by the complexity of your letter, memo, or report; and make it more understandable.
2. ***Don't sacrifice communication to rules of composition.*** Most of us who were sensitized to the rules of grammar and composition in school never quite recovered from the process. As proof, we keep trying to make our writing conform to rigid rules and customs without regard to style or the ultimate purpose of the communication. (Of course, managers need to be sensitive to the stylistic preferences of their bosses.)
3. ***Write concisely.*** This means expressing your thoughts, opinions, and ideas in the least number of words consistent with composition and smoothness. But don't

confuse conciseness with mere brevity; otherwise, you may write briefly without being clear or complete.

4. ***Be specific.*** Vagueness is one of the most serious flaws in written communication because it destroys accuracy and clarity, leaving the reader to wonder about your meaning or intent.[114]

Also, avoid irritating your readers with useless phrases such as "to be perfectly honest," "needless to say," "as you know," and "please be advised that."[115]

Running a Meeting

Meetings are an ever-present feature of modern organizational life. Whether they are convened to find facts, solve problems, or pass along information, meetings typically occupy a good deal of a manager's time. This is particularly true in the United States, where employees in general have an average of 7.2 face-to-face meetings and 2.1 telephone conferences a week. Those figures were the highest among five countries in a recent study that also included Canada, the United Kingdom, Germany, and France (listed in diminishing order of meeting frequency).[116] Meetings are the principal format for committee action. Too often, as illustrated by this research insight, meetings are a waste of valuable time. "The typical professional attends more than 60 meetings per month—and more than one-third are rated unproductive."[117] A good first step toward better meetings, according to author Patrick M. Lencioni, is to categorize meetings for a sharper focus. Four general categories that he recommends using are:

> ***Daily check-in****. A five-minute morning huddle to report on activities that day.*
>
> ***Weekly tactical****. A 45– to 90–minute meeting to review the firm's critical metrics (revenue, expenses, etc.) and solve problems.*
>
> ***Monthly strategic****. Executives wrestle with, debate, analyze and decide the big critical issues that will affect the bottom line.*
>
> ***Quarterly off-site review****. These reviews focus on four areas—strategy, team, personnel, and competitors—to help avoid turning into the 'touchy-feely boondoggle' that such meetings can become.*[118]

Whatever the reason for a meeting, managers who convene meetings owe it to themselves and their organization to use everyone's time and talent efficiently. Here are ten pointers for conducting successful meetings:

- Meet for a specific purpose, not simply as a ritual.
- Create an agenda and distribute it at least one day in advance.
- Communicate expectations for attendees to help them come prepared with proper data and documentation.
- Limit attendance to essential personnel.
- Open the meeting with a brief overview of what has been accomplished and what lies ahead.
- Deal with the most difficult/challenging agenda items fairly early in the meeting while the energy level is still high.
- Encourage broad participation while sticking to the agenda.
- Selectively use stimulating visual aids to make key points and, according to one expert, do not use more than three PowerPoint slides for every 10 minutes of presentation.[119]

12i That's All Folks!

John Clemens, management professor and author:

> *. . . managers have to develop a sixth sense as to when a major moment is at hand so that employees walk out [of a meeting] jazzed up–and never discount the natural high of exiting a meeting early.*

Source: Patrick J. Sauer, "What Time Is the Next Meeting?" Inc.*, 26 (May 2004): 75.*

QUESTIONS:

How does a manager develop such a sixth sense? Taking the role of a management consultant, discuss how often (and when) the early-finish tactic should be used.

- Make sure everyone understands what action items they are responsible for after the meeting.
- Begin and end the meeting on time and follow up as necessary.[120]

With practice, these guidelines will become second nature. Running a meeting brings into focus all the components of the communication process, including coping with noise and barriers. Effective meetings are important to organizational communication and, ultimately, to organizational success in today's team-oriented workplaces.

SUMMARY

1. Modern technology has made communicating easier and less costly, with the unintended side effect of information overload. Managers are challenged to improve the *quality* of their communication because it is a core process for everything they do. Communication is a social process involving the transfer of information and understanding. Links in the communication process include sender, encoding, medium, decoding, receiver, and feedback. Noise is any source of interference.
2. According to the Lengel-Daft contingency model, media richness is determined by the amount of information conveyed and the amount of learning promoted. Rich media such as face-to-face communication are best for nonroutine problems. Lean media such as impersonal bulletins are suitable for routine problems.
3. Organizational communication is typically too haphazard. Clampitt's communication continuum indicates that the five basic strategies are not equally effective. The Spray & Pray and Withhold & Uphold strategies are generally ineffective and should be avoided. The Tell & Sell and Identify & Reply strategies should be used sparingly. Managers need to use the Underscore & Explore strategy as much as possible. Media richness needs to be as high as possible if the preferred communication strategies are to be effective.
4. The unofficial and informal communication system that sometimes complements and sometimes disrupts the formal communication system has been labeled the grapevine. A sample of managers surveyed had predominantly negative feelings toward it. Recognizing that the grapevine cannot be suppressed, managers are advised to monitor it constructively. Nonverbal communication, including facial, gestural, and postural body language, accounts for most of the impact of face-to-face communication. Managers can become more effective communicators by doing a better job of receiving and giving nonverbal communications.
5. Upward communication can be stimulated by using formal grievance procedures, employee attitude and opinion surveys, suggestion systems, an open-door policy, informal meetings, Internet chat rooms, and exit interviews.
6. Managers need to identify and overcome four barriers to communication. Process barriers can occur at any one of the basic links in the communication process. Physical barriers, such as walls and distance between two points, can block effective communication. Semantic barriers are encountered when there is confusion about the meaning of words. Psychosocial barriers to communication involve the full range of human perceptions, prejudices, and attitudes that can interfere with understanding. Care needs to be taken to eliminate subtle forms of sexist and racist communication.
7. E-mail, supposedly a real time saver, has quickly become a major time waster. Organizations need to create and enforce a clear e-mail policy to improve message quality and curb abuses. Cell phone users need to be discreet and courteous to avoid broadcasting privileged information and/or

offending others. Videoconferencing restricts how people communicate because televised contacts are more mechanical than face-to-face meetings. Although telecommuting can reduce travel time and expense and can offer employment to nontraditional employees, it restricts normal social contact and face-to-face communication in the workplace.

8. Listening does not get sufficient attention in communications training. Active, cooperative listening is to be encouraged. Writing skills are no less important in the computer age. Written messages need to be specific, simply worded, and concise. Meetings, an ever-present feature of organizational life, need to be focused and agenda-driven if time is to be used wisely.

TERMS TO UNDERSTAND

- Communication, p. 344
- Media richness, p. 345
- Noise, p. 347
- Grapevine, p. 349
- Body language, p. 351
- Upward communication, p. 354
- Exit interview, p. 357
- Semantics, p. 359
- Videoconference, p. 363
- Telecommuting, p. 364

SKILLS & TOOLS

How You Speak Shows Where You Rank

Popular discussion of communication style in recent years has centered on differences between the sexes. The subject has been fodder for TV talk shows, corporate seminars, and best-sellers, notably Deborah Tannen's *You Just Don't Understand* and John Gray's *Men Are from Mars, Women Are from Venus.* But Sarah McGinty, a teaching supervisor at Harvard University's School of Education, believes language style is based more on power than on gender—and that marked differences distinguish the powerful from the powerless loud and clear. As a consultant, she is often called on to help clients develop more effective communication styles. *Fortune*'s Justin Martin spoke with McGinty about her ideas:

What style of speaking indicates that someone possesses power?
A person who feels confident and in control will speak at length, set the agenda for conversation, stave off interruptions, argue openly, make jokes, and laugh. Such a person is more inclined to make statements, less inclined to ask questions. They are more likely to offer solutions or a program or a plan. All this creates a sense of confidence in listeners.

What about people who lack power? How do they speak?
The power deficient drop into conversations, encourage other speakers, ask numerous questions, avoid argument, and rely on gestures such as nodding and smiling that suggest agreement. They tend to offer empathy rather than solutions. They often use unfinished sentences. Unfinished sentences are a language staple for those who lack power.

How do you figure out what style of communication you lean toward?
It's quite hard to do. We're often quite ignorant about our own way of communicating. Everyone comes home at night occasionally and says, "I had that idea, but no one heard me, and everyone thinks it's Harry's idea." People like to pin that on gender and a lot of other things as well. But it's important to find out what really did happen. Maybe it was the volume of your voice, and you

weren't heard. Maybe you overexplained, and the person who followed up pulled out the nugget of your thought.

But it's important to try to get some insight into what your own language habits are so that you can be analytical about whether you're shooting yourself in the foot. You can tape your side of phone calls, make a tape of a meeting, or sign up for a communications workshop. That's a great way to examine how you conduct yourself in conversations and in meetings.

Does power language differ from company to company?
Certainly. The key is figuring out who gets listened to within your corporate culture. That can make you a more savvy user of language. Try to sit in on a meeting as a kind of researcher, observing conversational patterns. Watch who talks, who changes the course of the discussion, who sort of drops in and out of the conversation. Then try to determine who gets noticed and why.

One very effective technique is to approach the person who ran the meeting a couple of days after the fact and ask for an overall impression. What ideas were useful? What ideas might have a shot at being implemented?

How can you get more language savvy?
You can start by avoiding bad habits, such as always seeking collaboration in the statements you make. Try to avoid "as Bob said" and "I pretty much agree with Sheila." Steer clear of disclaimers such as "I may be way off base here, but. . . ." All these serve to undermine the impact of your statements.

The amount of space you take up can play a big part in how powerful and knowledgeable you appear. People speaking before a group, for instance, should stand with their feet a little bit apart and try to occupy as much space as possible. Another public-speaking tip: Glancing around constantly creates a situation in which nobody really feels connected to what you're saying.

Strive to be bolder. Everyone tends to worry that they will offend someone by stating a strong opinion. Be bold about ideas, tentative about people. Saying "I think you're completely wrong" is not a wise strategy. Saying "I have a plan that I think will solve these problems" is perfectly reasonable. You're not attacking people. You're being bold about an idea.

Source: *Justin Martin, "How You Speak Shows Where You Rank,"* Fortune *(February 2, 1998): 156.*

HANDS-ON EXERCISE

Oh, No! What Have I Done?

Situation:
It's almost 6 P.M. and you're back at your office putting the finishing touches on next week's annual presentation to top management. Your stomach is churning, partly from hunger and partly from the stress of having missed another one of your twins' soccer matches. As the corporate director of product design at a large multinational company, you don't need to be reminded about the importance of next week's presentation. Between 3 P.M. and a few minutes ago, you had hidden out in a remote conference room fine-tuning it. Your cell phone was with you but had a dead battery, as you just noticed.

Right now, you are staring in disbelief at an e-mail message on your computer screen. The three-word message "WHERE WERE YOU!" burns into your mind. This particular e-mail is from your firm's director of marketing. She e-mailed an hour ago from her home after a late-afternoon meeting with two executives from a company that has been a customer for over ten years. During a quick chat in the hallway yesterday, you had promised the marketing director you'd attend today's meeting to provide technical support. This customer is one of your smaller accounts, but there is potential for a big jump in business this year. The marketing director's idea was to have a brief "let's explore possibilities" meeting.

The plain truth is you simply forgot about the meeting. You've been on major overload. You never bothered to put it on your electronic calendar because the commitment was made just yesterday and you thought you'd surely remember it. Well, you didn't!

Your mind races, weighing the situation and what to do about it. Losing this customer would be very bad for your career because your CEO is a table-pounder about customer service. Whom should you contact first—the marketing director, your boss, the customer, your family? And how should you communicate with them? It's dinnertime now. What about calling later tonight? Can everything but your family wait until tomorrow? What about e-mails? You know both your boss and the marketing director check their e-mails later each evening at home. Should you stop by anybody's home tonight to deliver a personal apology and explanation? What should you do? What should you say? How should you say it? Your stomach tightens a couple more notches.

Instructions:

Working either alone or as a member of a team, quickly develop a communication plan for this awkward situation. Your plan should involve (1) specifying your assumptions and objectives, (2) choosing an appropriate medium for each message (face-to-face, cell phone, telephone/voice mail, or e-mail), and (3) composing messages to the relevant parties.

For Consideration/Discussion

1. What assumptions did you make in this case? How did they influence your response?
2. What were your priorities in this situation? How did they influence your actions?
3. Whom did you contact first? How and why?
4. How did you communicate with each party? Why did you choose that way?
5. What practical lessons about communication did you learn from this exercise? Explain.

INTERNET EXERCISES

1. **Assessing your communication style and skills:** Communication is such an everyday activity that we seldom pause to review how we're actually doing. Here's an opportunity to systematically evaluate your communication style and skills, with the goal of becoming a more effective communicator. Once again, as we did in Chapter 8, let's visit QueenDom's unique Web site (**www.queendom.com**) and take advantage of the excellent collection of free self-assessment questionnaires. At the home page, select the main menu category "Tests & Profiles." At the "tests, tests, tests" page, select "Communication Skills" under the Heading "top tests." Next, click on the "GO!" button under the heading "non-members take the test." (*Note:* You do not have to register or purchase anything to take the communication skills test. Also, if the site has been revised by the time you read this, simply search the site for the free communication skills test. It is well worth the effort.) This 34-item assessment instrument is designed to take about 15 to 20 minutes to complete. It is self-paced, so you might complete it in less time. Score the test and read the brief free interpretation.

   Learning Points: 1. Are you surprised by the result of this assessment test? Explain. 2. What are your communication strengths? 3. What are your communication weaknesses or limitations? 4. What do you need to do to improve? 5. How motivated are you to improve your communication skills? Explain.

2. **Some timeless advice on good writing:** Most literary scholars say the best primer on English composition ever written is William Strunk Jr.'s *The Elements of Style.* This masterful little book was originally published in 1918. Nearly 90 years later, after revision by E. B. White and countless reprintings, it is still essential reading for college students. The current 105-page hardcover version is William Strunk Jr., E. B. White, and Roger Angell, *The Elements of Style,* 4th ed. (Upper Saddle River, N.J.: Pearson Higher Education, 1999.) Thanks to the Internet, the original version is available free on-line. Go to (**www.bartleby.com**), click on the tab "Reference," scroll down the list of authors and titles and, under the heading "English Usage: Language, Style, & Composition," select "The Elements of Style" next to the name "Strunk, William, Jr." Browse through the topics in Part III, Elementary Principles of Composition, with the objective of answering the following questions.

   Learning Points: 1. Is this nearly 90-year-old book instructive for e-mail users? How? 2. By Strunk's standards, which principles of composition are your strengths? 3. What elements of composition do you need to improve? 4. How important are writing skills in the Internet age? Explain.

3. **Check it out:** Public speaking can be a dreadful experience for those who are unprepared. On the other hand, a well-delivered oral presentation is a very gratifying accomplishment. Next time you are preparing an oral presentation, be sure to tap the extensive collection of resources at the Advanced Public Speaking Institute's Web site (**www.public-speaking.org**). You will find lots of practical tips on everything from handouts and humor to room setup and stage fright.

4. **Check it out:** Want to create your own blog (Web log)? Get details from these sources: **www.typepad.com**; **www.blogger.com**; and **www.modblog.com**.

   For updates to these exercises, visit our Web site (**http://business.college.hmco.com/students/** and select Kreitner, *Management,* 10e).

CLOSING CASE

Communication Gap

It was 9.30 a.m. when two trucks brought some large crates to the assembly shop. Everyone saw the truck crew unloading the boxes quickly; leave them piled near the gate of the stores department and drive away. Mohan, a worker, watched and approached the foreman and pointed to the boxes. The foreman stopped, shrugged his shoulders and walked away.

Mohan came across another worker who asked: "What's in the boxes?" "I don't know", was the reply, "and the foreman doesn't know either or at least, he doesn't want to tell me." Mohan went over his work but continued to wonder: "What could be in those boxes? And why does not the foreman want to tell us? May be it is new machines say, that's probably what is, those new automated machines. All you have to do is push the button and the machine does the rest. There won't be many jobs in the assembly shop if these machines are installed."

Mohan became more nervous. He got up and went over to the water cooler where two other workers were gossiping: "The foreman doesn't want to tell us what's in those crates because it is new automatic machinery. That will mean fewer jobs for us." Mohan saw fear and anger creep across the workers' faces.

Words spread like wildfire. Soon no one was working, all were talking and their voices grew angrier and angrier. Finally, a worker stood on his bench and shouted, "If this is the way the management treats us, then let's teach them a lesson. If they fire us, we'll fire the boxes."

Just then the Superintendent came running and stood in the middle of the men.

"'What's the matter? What happened?"

"You are trying to replace us with new machines."

"What new machinery ?"

"The new machinery in those boxes."

"Oh, my God ! That's equipment for our new plant. We're only keeping these here for a few days."

Everyone looked very foolish and tempers quickly cooled. "You should have told us", one man said dejectedly. Mohan quietly slipped away.

For Discussion

1. What is the problem in this case?
2. Who is responsible for this episode?
3. Do you feel that the workers would have not agitated if there were two-way communication between the management and the workers?

***Source:** Principles & Practice of Management by T.N. Chhabra, Dhanpat Rai & Co., Delhi, 2002, pp.852*

TEST PREPPER

True/False Questions

_____ **1.** Feedback is one of the links in the basic communication process.

_____ **2.** According to the Lengel-Daft model, e-mail communication ranks highest on the media richness scale.

_____ **3.** In the "Withhold & Uphold" communication strategy, managers tell what they think people need to know only when they believe people need to know it.

_____ **4.** The organizational grapevine is an even bigger problem today thanks to e-mail, cell phones, and Web logs (blogs).

_____ **5.** Most of the impact of our communication comes from the implied meaning of our words.

_____ **6.** With an open-door policy, an employee is free to leave the workplace at any time.

_____ **7.** Psychological and social barriers are responsible for most blocked communication.

_____ **8.** Videoconference participants should look directly at the camera when speaking.

_____ **9.** Effective listeners ask simple yes-or-no questions.

_____ **10.** One key to conducting a successful meeting is to create an agenda and distribute it at least one day in advance.

Multiple-Choice Questions

1. Which of these *best* describes the basic communication process?
A. A chain with identifiable links B. Noninstructive
C. Inherently flawed D. A computer network
E. A bush

2. Media richness involves the capacity to
A. achieve organizational results.
B. justify decisions.
C. convince and persuade.
D. convey information and promote learning.
E. build personal relationships.

3. Which of the following is *not* one of the basic communication strategies?
A. Spray & Pray B. Underscore & Restate
C. Identify & Reply D. Withhold & Uphold
E. Tell & Sell

4. Judging on the basis of what you read in this chapter, what advice would you give a bookstore manager about the grapevine?
A. Extinguish it as soon as possible.
B. Pretend it doesn't exist.
C. Don't try to kill it.
D. Make it the official communication network.
E. Weed out the troublemakers.

5. In a recent survey of 25,000 employees in the United States, _____ said that their senior managers both talk *and* listen.
A. 45 percent B. slightly more than half
C. only 7 percent D. 75 percent
E. about 25 percent

6. Which of these is *most* effective in making employees more willing to complete attitude and opinion surveys?
A. Promise of specific results
B. Early time off with pay
C. Money
D. Likelihood of meaningful changes
E. None of these; employees are very resistant to surveys today.

7. All of these are suggestions by Joan Tunstall for composing a clear e-mail message *except*
A. making the message action-oriented.
B. sending copies to all relevant parties.
C. ensuring that the message unfolds in logical steps.
D. expressing empathy with readers through appropriate tone and choice of words.
E. keeping the message concise.

8. The text sums up the future of telecommuting as
A. a serious threat to productivity.
B. just a passing fad.
C. already obsolete.
D. more than a passing fad.
E. certain to be the standard work routine in 20 years.

9. Asking _____ questions is among the practical tips for effective listening.
A. easy-to-answer B. yes-or-no
C. many D. open-ended
E. no more than two

10. _____ is *not* among the four types of meetings discussed in this chapter.
A. Quarterly off-site review B. Monthly strategic
C. Weekly tactical D. Daily check-in
E. Annual employee recognition

ACE self-test

Want more questions? Visit the student Web site at http://business.college.hmco.com/students/ (select Kreitner, *Management,* 10e) and take the ACE quizzes for more practice.

Managers-in-Action Videos

3A Organization Structures at Green Mountain Coffee Roasters

CEO and chairman Bob Stiller and his executive team provide a strategic overview of this 670-employee business based in Waterbury, Vermont. Functional departments are effectively blended with cross-functional teams. A culture of collaboration and cooperation, driven by principles and values, is a point of pride at this leading specialty coffee company. Decentralization is encouraged despite the company's growth. The organization is kept as flat as possible by relying on virtual teamwork via e-mail. For more background, see **www.greenmountaincoffee.com**.

Learning Objective: To show the importance of organization structure and design to overall organizational success.

Links to Textual Material: **Chapter 9:** Organizational characteristics; Organizational culture **Chapter 10:** Mechanistic and organic organizations; Differentiation and integration; Decentralization; Characteristics of the "new organizations" **Chapter 12:** E-mail communication

Discussion Questions:

1. Which of the four common characteristics of organizations, presented in Chapter 9, are evident in this video? Explain.
2. Explain how the culture at Green Mountain Coffee acts as a "social glue," as the term is used in Chapter 9.
3. Where does Green Mountain Coffee fit on the mechanistic-organic continuum? Explain.
4. How are Lawrence and Lorsch's concepts of differentiation and integration balanced in this video?
5. What are the arguments for and against decentralization, as practiced at Green Mountain Coffee?
6. Which characteristics of the "new organizations," discussed in Chapter 10, can you detect in this video? Explain.

3B Managing Human Capital at Accenture

Gill Rider, chief leadership officer at the 100,000-employee consulting and computer outsourcing firm, explains her role as head of all corporate human resource functions. The strategic goal is to deploy the right people with the right skills at the right time. We learn about the company's fluid and virtual organization structure. An overriding goal is to create "authentic leaders" who are value creators, good at developing people, and good business operators.

Learning Objective: To appreciate the central importance of effective human resource management.

Links to Textual Material: **Chapter 9:** Learning organizations **Chapter 10:** Organic organizations; New organizations **Chapter 11:** Human capital; Human resource management **Chapter 15:** Leadership

Discussion Questions:

1. Why is it important to make Accenture a "learning organization" (Figure 9.3)?
2. Which organic characteristics (Table 10.2) are evident in this video? What difficulties might they cause?
3. What evidence of a "virtual organization" can you detect at Accenture? What associated problems might be encountered?
4. How are the concepts of human capital and authentic leaders interrelated at Accenture?

PART FOUR

Motivating and Leading

13

Motivating Job Performance

"There are no simple, cookbook formulas for working with people."[1]

KEITH DAVIS

OBJECTIVES

- **Explain** the motivational lessons taught by Maslow's theory, Herzberg's theory, and expectancy theory.
- **Describe** how goal setting motivates performance.
- **Discuss** how managers can improve the motivation of personnel who perform routine tasks.
- **Explain** how job enrichment can be used to enhance the motivating potential of jobs.
- **Distinguish** extrinsic rewards from intrinsic rewards, and **list** four rules for administering extrinsic rewards effectively.
- **Explain** how quality control circles, open-book management, and self-managed teams promote employee participation.
- **Explain** how companies are striving to motivate today's diverse workforce with quality-of-work-life programs.

the changing workplace

Pat McGovern Motivates Through Respect

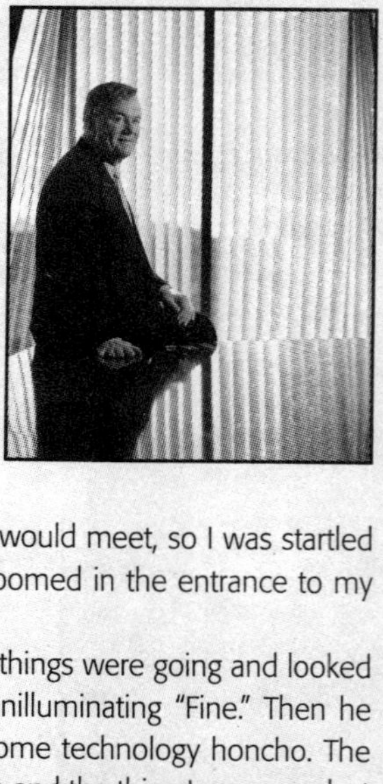

Leigh Buchanan, senior editor, *Harvard Business Review*:

The genius of Pat McGovern is the way he makes things all about you. That impressed me hugely, because when I first met Pat back in 1989 I wasn't the sort of person anything was all about. I was a new copy editor at *CIO* magazine; Pat was (still is) the founder and chairman of *CIO*'s parent, International Data Group, a then $400 million technology publishing and research empire. It hadn't occurred to me that the twain would meet, so I was startled (confused, marginally freaked) when a tall, ruddy man loomed in the entrance to my cubicle a few weeks before Christmas.

Pat thanked me for my contributions. He asked how things were going and looked vaguely disappointed when all I could muster was an unilluminating "Fine." Then he complimented me on a column I had ghostwritten for some technology honcho. The column was my most substantive accomplishment to date and the thing I was proudest of. But my name didn't appear on it anywhere, so how did he know? After three or four minutes, he handed me my bonus and proceeded to the next cubicle.

The formula for Pat's Christmas calls—expression of gratitude/request for feedback/congratulations on specific achievement/delivery of loot—never varied, even as IDG grew into the $2.4 billion global behemoth it is today. To personally thank most every person in every business unit in the U.S., more than 1,500 employees, takes almost four weeks, he told me years later: Managers provide him with a list of accomplishments for all their reports, and Pat memorizes them the night before his visits. He does this because he wants employees to know that he sees them—really sees them—as individuals, and that he considers what they do all day to be meaningful.

Not only does Pat care about his people; he also believes in them. His commitment to decentralization has created a constellation of motivated business units that make their own decisions about everything from how to reward staff to what new businesses to launch. He also treats his end customers—the readers of such publications as *Computerworld, PC World,* and *Macworld*—with consummate respect. At IDG the quality of content is sacrosanct, a tough ideal to sustain when advertising pays so many of the bills.

Did I mention that he's giving $350 million to MIT to create an institute for brain research? Maybe I shouldn't: I don't want to lay it on too thick.

Another small-company tradition Pat has kept up over the years is taking each employee out for a meal at the Ritz on his or her 10th anniversary with IDG. I left *CIO* after only seven years (to work for *Inc.,* where I could write about people like Pat and not just work for them), so I never got my anniversary dinner. Too bad—it would have been a class act. And I'm not talking about the restaurant.

Source: *From Leigh Buchanan, "For Knowing the Power of Respect,"* Inc Magazine, *26, April 2004, p. 143. Reprinted by permission of the author.*

motivation: *psychological process giving behavior purpose and direction*

The complex webs of factors that motivate our work efforts are as varied as our occupations. Still, as Pat McGovern's deft personal touches and respect for his coworkers illustrate, some motivational techniques are widely applicable. As used here, the term **motivation** refers to a psychological process that gives behavior purpose and direction. By appealing to this process, managers attempt to get individuals to pursue organizational objectives willingly. Motivation theories are generalizations about the "why" and "how" of purposeful behavior.[2]

Figure 13.1 is an overview model for this chapter. The final element in this model, job performance, is the product of a combination of an individual's motivation and ability. Both are necessary. All the motivation in the world, for example, will not enable a computer-illiterate person to sit down and create a computer spreadsheet. Ability and skills, acquired through training and/or on-the-job experience, are also required. The individual's motivational factors—needs, satisfaction, expectations, and goals—are affected by challenging work, rewards, and participation.[3] We need to take a closer look at each key element in this model. A review of four basic motivation theories is a good starting point.

Figure 13.1 Individual Motivation and Job Performance

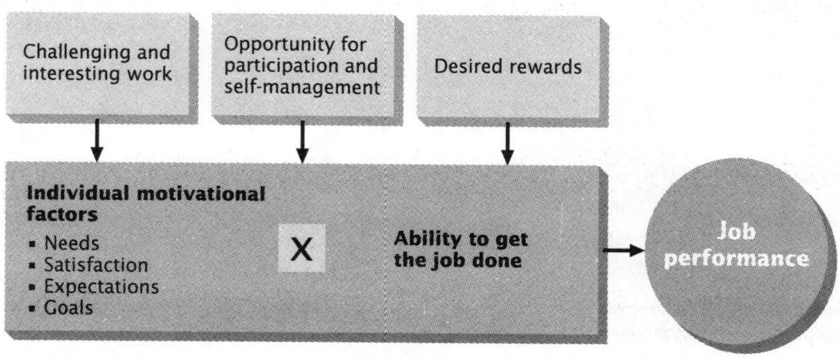

Motivation Theories

1. EXPLAIN the motivational lessons taught by Maslow's theory, Herzberg's theory, and expectancy theory.

Although there are dozens of different theories of motivation, four have emerged as the most influential: Maslow's needs hierarchy theory, Herzberg's two-factor theory, expectancy theory, and goal-setting theory. Each approaches the motivation process from a different angle, each has supporters and detractors, and each teaches important lessons about motivation to work.

■ Maslow's Hierarchy of Needs Theory

In 1943 psychologist Abraham Maslow proposed that people are motivated by a predictable five-step hierarchy of needs.[4] Little did he realize at the time that his tentative proposal, based on an extremely limited clinical study of neurotic patients, would become one of the most influential concepts in the field of management. Perhaps because it is so straightforward and intuitively appealing, Maslow's theory has strongly influenced those interested in work behavior. Maslow's message was simply this: people always have needs, and when one need is relatively fulfilled, others emerge in a predictable sequence to take its place. From bottom to top, Maslow's needs hierarchy includes physiological, safety, love, esteem, and self-actualization needs (see Figure 13.2). According to Maslow, most individuals are not consciously aware of these needs; yet we all supposedly proceed up the hierarchy of needs, one level at a time.

■ Physiological Needs. At the bottom of the hierarchy are needs based on physical drives, including the need for food, water, sleep, and sex. Fulfillment of these lowest-level needs enables the individual to survive, and nothing else is important when these bodily needs have not been satisfied. As Maslow observed, "It is quite true that man lives by bread alone—when there is no bread."[5] But today the average employee experiences little difficulty in satisfying physiological needs. Figuratively speaking, the prospect of eating more bread is not motivating when one has plenty of bread to eat.

■ Safety Needs. After our basic physiological needs have been relatively well satisfied, we next become concerned about our safety from the elements, enemies, and other threats. For reasons that are not entirely clear (terrorism? workplace violence?), researchers have documented a recent jump in the need for "feeling safe at work." "Overall, feeling safe at work was ranked as a 'very important factor' in job satisfaction by 62 percent of all employees surveyed . . . [in 2004], up from around 36 percent in 2002."[6] Yet most of us, by virtue of earning a living, achieve a reasonable degree of fulfillment in this area. Unemployment assistance is a safety net for those between jobs. Insurance also helps fulfill safety needs, a point not lost on Coca-Cola Femsa, Mexico's primary bottler of Coke:

> *Many of the store owners in Mexico, Coke's second-biggest market, turned out to be single mothers and retirees who couldn't afford health insurance. Armed with that intelligence, Femsa was able to create an incentive program that rewards shopkeepers who sell enough Cokes with access to group insurance—a move that helped boost Coke's sales volume in Mexico 13 percent last year.*[7]

Figure 13.2 Maslow's Hierarchy of Needs Theory

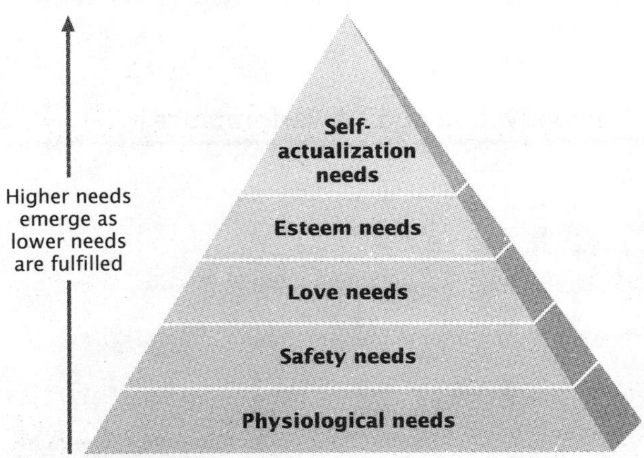

Source: *Data for diagram drawn from A. H. Maslow, "A Theory of Human Motivation,"* Psychological Review, *50 (July 1943): 370–396.*

13a Quick Quiz

Howard Schultz, chairman of Starbucks, explains his company's formula for "exceeding employee expectations" so that they, in turn, will do the same for customers:

> *We provided comprehensive health care as well as equity in the form of stock options to all employees. For the first time in America's history, not only did part-time workers have a stake in the financial outcome of the company, but they had the kind of health-care programs that gave them the sense of security and a psychological contract with the company that the company was not going to leave people behind.*

Source: As quoted in Jeremy B. Dann, "How to Find a Hit as Big as Starbucks," Business 2.0, *5 (May 2004): 66.*

QUESTIONS:

Starbucks is trying to satisfy which particular needs in Maslow's hierarchy? Explain. Is this an effective approach to motivating today's employees?

For further information about the interactive annotations in this chapter, visit our Web site (**http://business.college.hmco.com/students**) and select Kreitner, *Management,* 10e.

■ **Love Needs.** A physiologically satisfied and secure person focuses next on satisfying needs for love and affection. This category is a powerful motivator of human behavior. People typically strive hard to achieve a sense of belonging with others. As with the first two levels of needs, relative satisfaction of love needs paves the way for the emergence of needs at the next higher level.

■ **Esteem Needs.** People who perceive themselves as worthwhile are said to possess high self-esteem.[8] Self-respect is the key to esteem needs. Much of our self-respect, and therefore our esteem, comes from being accepted and respected by others. It is important for those who are expected to help achieve organizational objectives to have their esteem needs relatively well fulfilled. But esteem needs cannot emerge if lower-level needs go unattended.

■ **Self-Actualization Needs.** At the very top of Maslow's hierarchy is the open-ended category *self-actualization needs.* It is open-ended because, as Maslow pointed out, it reflects the need "to become more and more what one is, to become everything that one is capable of becoming."[9] One may satisfy this need by striving to become a better homemaker, plumber, rock singer, or manager. For example, this is what Grammy Award-winning singer and song writer Alicia Keys told an interviewer who asked how she would follow up her hit *Fallin'* that got a lot of radio play:

> *"'I have to find the truth in everything I do, and I have to make sure it means something for me," she says. "That's how I write, and that's who I am. I can't say, Oh, let's get this radio song.' All I know how to do is what I feel and what I love."*[10]

Now here's someone who can tell school children a thing or two about self-actualization needs. Grammy Award-winning singer and song writer Alicia Keys fires up a classroom of 8th graders at the Betty Shabazz International Charter School in Chicago. If Ms. Keys ever tires of entertaining, she obviously would make a great teacher!

According to one management writer, the self-actualizing manager has the following characteristics:

1. Has warmth, closeness, and sympathy.
2. Recognizes and shares negative information and feelings.
3. Exhibits trust, openness, and candor.
4. Does not achieve goals by power, deception, or manipulation.
5. Does not project own feelings, motivations, or blame onto others.
6. Does not limit horizons; uses and develops body, mind, and senses.
7. Is not rationalistic; can think in unconventional ways.
8. Is not conforming; regulates behavior from within.[11]

Granted, this is a rather tall order to fill. It has been pointed out that "a truly

THE GLOBAL MANAGER

Paying Employees to Go on a Global Search for Self-Actualization

Most employees don't have time to spend one hour on community service, let alone a whole week. But that is what employees at Creative Consumer Concepts (C3), an Overland Park, Kan.–based marketing company, are doing—in other countries. Better yet, the company pays for their overseas trip and continues to pay their salary.

Bob Cutler, CEO of C3, developed the Global Community Service Program to allow employees to travel overseas to do community work in foreign countries for a week at a time. Cutler started this program after visiting Russia and Jerusalem. "After coming back from this trip I realized I wouldn't have had that opportunity if it hadn't been for all the support and hard work from all the people I work with," he says. "I wanted to make the same opportunity available to our employees."

C3 already had a program in place where staff could work up to 40 hours in the local community, but the participation rate wasn't what Cutler expected. "I decided to raise the bar a little and made the community service program international."

During the first two months of the program, 10 out of 40 employees went overseas, and more are planning to go, including Derek Rippe. "I'm going to work in an elephant refuge in Thailand, where I hope to learn a lot about the culture," says Rippe, an illustrator and designer at C3. "I'm going where I don't speak the language, so I think my communication skills and my patience will be better after this experience."

Joy Merrit, associate art director for C3, is going to a small town called Tutova in northeast Romania. She will work in a hospital with infants who are failing to thrive. "I think it will be a labor of love as well as a fulfilling experience," she says. "Volunteerism is very important, and if you can't do it on a global level, it's important to do it locally or any way you can."

Cutler says community service brings balance and new skills to his workforce. By encouraging his employees to volunteer overseas, Cutler hopes to foster pride, self-actualization and self-purpose. "Those things are pretty powerful but they're difficult to teach," he says. "We train our associates to live full lives of purpose and meaning."

Cutler hopes to refine his idea and see the impact of the program on his organization more clearly. He also hopes that small- to medium-sized companies will follow his lead. "Maybe we'll create a new model for some larger organizations to eventually engage within their own communities," he says.

Source: From "Culture of Community," Training, *41 (December 2004): 14 © VNU Business Media, Inc., Reprinted with permission.*

self-actualized individual is more of an exception than the rule in the organizational context."[12] Whether productive organizations need more self-actualized individuals is subject to debate. On the positive side, self-actualized employees might help break down barriers to creativity and steer the organization in new directions (see The Global Manager). On the negative side, too many unconventional nonconformists could wreak havoc with the typical administrative setup dedicated to predictability.

■ **Relevance of Maslow's Theory for Managers.** Behavioral scientists who have attempted to test Maslow's theory in real life claim it has some deficiencies.[13] Even Maslow's hierarchical arrangement has been questioned. Practical evidence points toward a two-level rather than a five-level hierarchy. In this competing view, physiological and safety needs are arranged in hierarchical fashion, as Maslow contends. But beyond that point, any one of a number of needs may emerge as the single most important need, depending on the individual. Edward Lawler, a leading motivation researcher, observed, "Which higher-order needs come into play after the lower ones are satisfied and in which order they come into play cannot be predicted. If anything, it seems that most people are simultaneously motivated by several of the same-level needs."[14]

Although Maslow's theory has not stood up well under actual testing, it teaches managers one important lesson: a *fulfilled* need does not motivate an individual. For example, the promise of unemployment benefits may partially fulfill an employee's need for economic security (the safety need). But the added security of additional unemployment benefits will probably not motivate fully employed individuals to work any harder. Effective managers anticipate each employee's personal need profile and provide opportunities to fulfill *emerging* needs. Because challenging and worthwhile jobs and meaningful recognition tend to enhance self-esteem, the esteem level presents managers with the greatest opportunity to motivate better performance.

■ Herzberg's Two-Factor Theory

During the 1950s, Frederick Herzberg proposed a theory of employee motivation based on satisfaction.[15] His theory implied that a satisfied employee is motivated from within to work harder and that a dissatisfied employee is not self-motivated. Herzberg's research uncovered two classes of factors associated with employee satisfaction and dissatisfaction (see Table 13.1). As a result, his concept has come to be called Herzberg's two-factor theory.

■ Dissatisfiers and Satisfiers. Herzberg compiled his list of dissatisfiers by asking a sample of about 200 accountants and engineers to describe job situations in which they felt exceptionally bad about their jobs. An analysis of their responses revealed a consistent pattern. Dissatisfaction tended to be associated with complaints about the job context or factors in the immediate work environment.

Herzberg then drew up his list of satisfiers, factors responsible for self-motivation, by asking the same accountants and engineers to describe job situations in which they had felt exceptionally good about their jobs. Again, a patterned response emerged, but this time different factors were described: the opportunity to experience achievement, receive recognition, work on an interesting job, take responsibility, and experience advancement and growth. Herzberg observed that these satisfiers centered on the nature of the task itself. Employees appeared to be motivated by *job content*—that is, by what they actually did all day long. Consequently, Herzberg concluded that enriched jobs were the key to self-motivation. The work itself—not pay, supervision, or some other environmental factor—was the key to satisfaction and motivation.

Table 13.1 Herzberg's Two-Factor Theory of Motivation

Dissatisfiers: Factors mentioned most often by dissatisfied employees	**Satisfiers: Factors mentioned most often by satisfied employees**
1. Company policy and administration	1. Achievement
2. Supervision	2. Recognition
3. Relationship with supervisor	3. Work itself
4. Work conditions	4. Responsibility
5. Salary	5. Advancement
6. Relationship with peers	6. Growth
7. Personal life	
8. Relationship with subordinates	
9. Status	
10. Security	

Source: *Adapted and reprinted by permission of the* Harvard Business Review. *An exhibit from "One More Time: How Do You Motivate Employees?" by Frederick Herzberg (January-February 1968). Copyright © 1968 by the President and Fellows of Harvard College; all rights reserved.*

Implications of Herzberg's Theory. By insisting that satisfaction is not the opposite of dissatisfaction, Herzberg encouraged managers to think carefully about what actually motivates employees. According to Herzberg, "the opposite of job satisfaction is not job dissatisfaction, but rather *no* job satisfaction; and similarly, the opposite of job dissatisfaction is not job satisfaction, but *no* dissatisfaction,"[16] Rather, the dissatisfaction-satisfaction continuum contains a zero midpoint at which both dissatisfaction and satisfaction are absent. An employee stuck on this midpoint, though not dissatisfied with pay and working conditions, is not particularly motivated to work hard because the job itself lacks challenge. Herzberg believes that the most managers can hope for when attempting to motivate employees with pay, status, working conditions, and other contextual factors is to reach the zero midpoint. But the elimination of dissatisfaction is not the same as truly motivating an employee. To satisfy and motivate employees, an additional element is required: meaningful, interesting, and challenging work. Herzberg believed that money is a weak motivational tool because, at best, it can only eliminate dissatisfaction.

Like Maslow, Herzberg triggered lively debate among motivation theorists. His assumption that job performance improves as satisfaction increases has been criticized for having a weak empirical basis. But a recent analysis of studies encompassing a total of 7,939 business units at 36 companies lends weight to Herzberg's model. The researchers' conclusion: "One implication is that changes in management practices that increase employee satisfaction may increase business-unit outcomes, including [greater productivity, fewer accidents, less turnover, and more] profit."[17] On the negative side, other researchers found that one person's dissatisfier may be another's satisfier (for example, money).[18] Nonetheless, Herzberg made a major contribution to motivation theory by emphasizing the motivating potential of enriched work. (Job enrichment is discussed in detail in the next section.)

13b I Quit!

"People quit managers, not companies."

Source: Ed Boswell, CEO of The Forum Corp., a Boston management development firm, as quoted in Gail Johnson, "Retention Reality Check," Training, *41 (September 2004): 17.*

QUESTIONS:
Do you agree with this statement? Why or why not? How is the statement related to Herzberg's "dissatisfiers" and "satisfiers"? Explain.

Expectancy Theory

Both Maslow's and Herzberg's theories have been criticized for making unsubstantiated generalizations about what motivates people. Practical experience shows that people are motivated by lots of different things. Fortunately, expectancy theory, based largely on Victor H. Vroom's 1964 classic *Work and Motivation*, effectively deals with the highly personalized rational choices individuals make when faced with the prospect of having to work to achieve rewards. Individual perception, though secondary in the Maslow and Herzberg models, is central to expectancy theory. Accordingly, **expectancy theory** is a motivation model based on the assumption that motivational strength is determined by perceived probabilities of success. The term **expectancy** refers to the subjective probability (or expectation) that one thing will lead to another. Work-related expectations, like all other expectations, are shaped by ongoing personal experience. For instance, an employee's expectation of a raise, diminished after being turned down, later rebounds when the supervisor indicates a willingness to reconsider the matter.

expectancy theory: *model that assumes that motivational strength is determined by perceived probabilities of success*

expectancy: *one's belief or expectation that one thing will lead to another*

A Basic Expectancy Model. Although Vroom and other expectancy theorists developed their models in somewhat complex mathematical terms, the descriptive model in Figure 13.3 is helpful for basic understanding. In this model, one's motivational strength increases as one's perceived effort-performance and performance-reward probabilities increase. All this is not as complicated as it sounds. For example, estimate your motivation to study if you expect to do poorly on a quiz no matter how hard you study (low effort-performance probability) and you know the quiz will not be graded (low performance-reward probability). Now contrast that estimate with your motivation to study if you believe that you can do well on the quiz with minimal

Figure 13.3 A Basic Expectancy Model

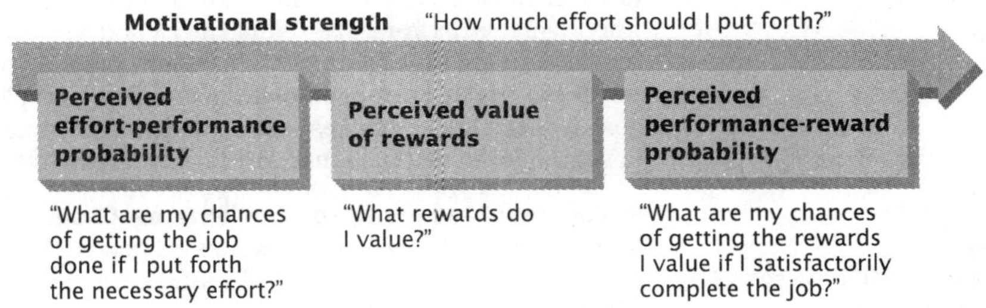

study (high effort-performance probability) and that doing well on the quiz will significantly improve your grade in the course (high performance-reward probability). Like students, employees are motivated to expend effort when they believe it will ultimately lead to rewards they themselves value. This expectancy approach not only appeals strongly to common sense; it also has received encouraging empirical support from researchers.[19]

■ Relevance of Expectancy Theory for Managers. According to expectancy theory, effort → performance → reward expectations determine whether motivation will be high or low. Although these expectations are in the mind of the employee, they can be influenced by managerial action and organizational experience. Training, combined with challenging but realistic objectives, gives people reason to believe that they can get the job done if they put forth the necessary effort. But perceived effort-performance probabilities are only half the battle. Listening skills enable managers to discover each individual's perceived performance-reward probabilities. Employees tend to work harder when they believe they have *a good chance* of getting *personally meaningful* rewards. Both sets of expectations require managerial attention. Each is a potential barrier to work motivation.

■ Goal-Setting Theory

Think of the three or four most successful people you know personally. Their success may have come via business or professional achievement, politics, athletics, or community service. Chances are they got where they are today by being goal-oriented. In other words, they committed themselves to (and achieved) progressively more challenging goals in their professional and personal affairs.[20] A prime example is Noël Forgeard, who helped put France-based Airbus on an equal footing with Boeing in the commercial airliner business. According to one of his former colleagues,

> *He appears low-key, but can be very tough, and when he has set a goal, nothing can distract him from it. He has an impressive ability to set priorities, to focus on his goals, and then set up a very strong team to achieve those goals.*[21]

Biographies and autobiographies of successful people in all walks of life generally attest to the virtues of goal setting. Accordingly, goal setting is acknowledged today as a respected and useful motivation theory.

goal setting: *process of improving performance with objectives, deadlines, or quality standards*

Within an organizational context, **goal setting** is the process of improving individual or group job performance with formally stated objectives, deadlines, or quality standards.[22] Management by objectives (MBO), discussed in Chapter 6, is a specific application of goal setting that advocates participative and measurable objectives. Also, recall from Chapter 6 how managers tend to use the terms *goal* and *objective* interchangeably.

■ **A General Goal-Setting Model.** Thanks to motivation researchers such as Edwin A. Locke, there is a comprehensive body of knowledge about goal setting.[23] Goal setting has been researched more rigorously than the three motivation theories just discussed.[24] Important lessons from goal-setting theory and research are incorporated in the general model in Figure 13.4. This model shows how properly conceived goals trigger a motivational process that improves performance. Let us explore the key components of this goal-setting model, while keeping in mind that a recent Franklin Covey survey of workers in the United States found that only 19 percent had "clearly defined work goals."[25]

2. DESCRIBE how goal setting motivates performance.

■ **Personal Ownership of Challenging Goals.** In Chapter 6, the discussion of MBO and writing good objectives stressed how goal effectiveness is enhanced by *specificity, difficulty*, and *participation*. Measurable and challenging goals encourage an individual or group to stretch while trying to attain progressively more difficult levels of achievement. For instance, parents who are paying a college student's tuition and expenses are advised to specify a challenging grade point goal rather than simply to tell their son or daughter, "Just do your best." Otherwise, the student could show up at the end of the semester with two Cs and three Ds, saying, "Well, I did my best!" It is important to note that goals need to be difficult enough to be challenging, but not impossible. Impossible goals hamper performance; they are a handy excuse for not even trying.[26]

Participation in the goal-setting process gives the individual *personal ownership*. From the employee's viewpoint, it is "something I helped develop, not just my boss's wild idea." Feedback on performance operates in concert with well-conceived goals. Feedback lets the person or group know if things are on track or if corrective action is required to reach the goal. An otherwise excellent goal-setting program can be compromised by lack of timely and relevant feedback from managers. Researchers have documented the motivational value of matching *specific goals* with *equally specific feedback*.[27] Sam Walton, the founder of Wal-Mart, was a master of blending goals and feedback. For example, consider this exchange between Sam Walton and an employee during one of his regular store visits:

A manager rushes up with an associate in tow.

"Mr. Walton, I want you to meet Renee. She runs one of the top ten pet departments in the country."

"Well, Renee, bless your heart. What percentage of the store [sales] are you doing?"

"Last year it was 3.1 percent," Renee says, "but this year I'm trying for 3.3 percent."

"Well, Renee, that's amazing," says Sam. "You know our average pet department only does about 2.4 percent. Keep up the great work."[28]

Figure 13.4 A Model of How Goals Can Improve Performance

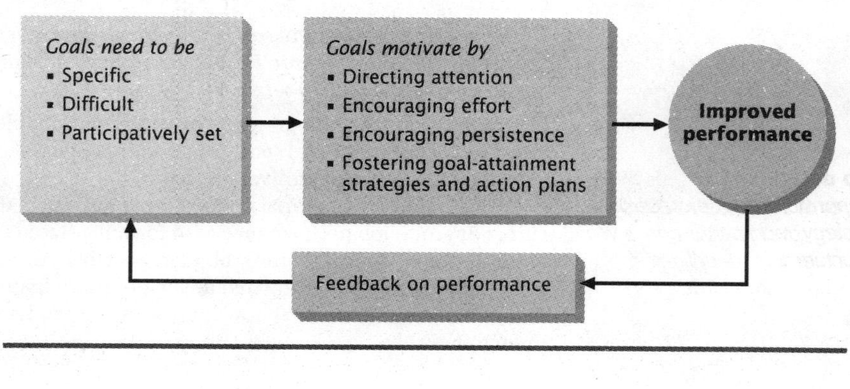

How Do Goals Actually Motivate? Goal-setting researchers say goals perform a motivational function by doing the four things listed in the center of Figure 13.4. First, a goal is an exercise in selective perception because it directs one's *attention* to a specific target. Second, a goal encourages one to exert *effort* toward achieving something specific. Third, because a challenging goal requires sustained or repeated effort, it encourages *persistence*. Fourth, because a goal creates the problem of bridging the gap between actual and desired, it fosters the creation of *strategies and action plans*. Consider, for example, how all these motivational components were activated by the following program at Marriott's hotel chain.

> *For years, Marriott's room-service business didn't live up to its potential. But after initiating a 15-minute-delivery guarantee for breakfast in 1985, Marriott's breakfast business—the biggest portion of its room-service revenue—jumped 25 percent. [Hotel guests got their breakfast free if it was delivered late.] Marriott got employees to devise ways to deliver the meals on time, including having deliverers carry walkie-talkies so they [could] receive instructions more quickly.*[29]

13c Aiming Too Low? It's Time to Stretch

Robert Nardelli, CEO of Home Depot:

I think what has served us well is setting not unrealistic but challenging goals. If you set aggressive stretch goals and develop a plan and put the right leadership in place, you start to see realization. Now, will we get there as fast as we want? Maybe not. But we will get there faster than we would have.

Source: As quoted in Patricia Sellers and Julie Schlosser, "It's His Home Depot Now," Fortune *(September 20, 2004): 116.*

QUESTIONS:
How often in your school work and/or on the job have you penalized yourself by aiming too low? Which of your goals need to be adjusted upward? Is it possible to aim too high? Explain.

Marriott's goal, increased room-service revenue, was the focal point for this program. In effect, the service-guarantee program told Marriott employees that prompt room service was important, and they rose to the challenge with persistent and creative effort. Clear, reasonable, and challenging goals, reinforced by specific feedback and meaningful rewards, are indeed a powerful motivational tool.[30]

Practical Implications of Goal-Setting Theory. Because the model in Figure 13.4 is a generic one, the performance environment may range from athletics to academics to the workplace. The motivational mechanics of goal setting are the same, regardless of the targeted performance. If you learn to be an effective goal setter in school, that ability will serve you faithfully throughout life.

Anyone tempted to go through life without goals should remember the smiling Cheshire Cat's good advice to Alice when she asked him to help her find her way through Wonderland:

> *"Would you tell me, please, which way I ought to walk from here?"*
> *"That depends a good deal on where you want to get to," replied the Cat.*
> *"I don't much care where—" said Alice.*
> *"Then it doesn't matter which way you walk," said the Cat.*
> *"—so long as I get somewhere," Alice added as an explanation.*
> *"Oh, you're sure to do that," said the Cat, "if you only walk long enough."*[31]

Motivation Through Job Design

job design: *creating task responsibilities based upon strategy, technology, and structure*

A job serves two separate but related functions. It is a productive unit for the organization and a career unit for the individual. Thus **job design**, the delineation of task responsibilities as dictated by organizational strategy, technology, and structure, is a key determinant of individual motivation and ultimately of organizational success. Considering that the average adult spends about half of his or her waking life at work, jobs are a central feature of modern existence. A challenging and interesting job can add zest and meaning to one's life. Boring and tedious jobs, on the other hand, can become a serious threat to one's motivation to work hard, not to mention the effect

"Really, I'm fine. It was just a fleeting sense of purpose—I'm sure it will pass."

Source: *© The New Yorker Collection 2000 Tom Cheney from cartoonbank.com. All Rights Reserved.*

on one's physical and mental health.[32] Concern about uneven productivity growth, product quality, and declining employee satisfaction has persuaded managers to consider two job design strategies.[33]

■ Strategy One: Fitting People to Jobs

For technological or economic reasons, work sometimes must be divided into routine and repetitive tasks. Imagine, for example, doing Paula Villalta's job at Chung's Gourmet Foods in Houston, Texas:

> *Quickly wrapping one egg roll after another, Paula Villalta becomes rapt herself.*
>
> *Her fingers move with astonishing speed, placing a glutinous vegetable mixture on a small sheet of pastry before rolling it closed in one smooth stroke. But the secret to her swiftness lies not just in her nimble hands.*
>
> *The real key, says Ms. Villalta, pointing to her head, is staying completely focused throughout an eight-hour shift. . . .*
>
> *The results are stunning. The average wrapper at Chung's Gourmet churns out about 4,000 shrimp, pork, vegetable, or chicken egg rolls per shift. Ms. Villalta typically tops 6,000.*[34]

In routine-task situations, steps can be taken to avoid chronic dissatisfaction and bolster motivation.[35] Three proven alternatives are realistic job previews, job rotation, and limited exposure. Each involves adjusting the person rather than the job in the person-job equation. Hence, each entails creating a more compatible fit between an individual and a routine or fragmented job. (In line with this approach is the employment of mentally disadvantaged workers, often in sheltered workshops.)

■ Realistic Job Previews. Unrealized expectations are a major cause of job dissatisfaction, low motivation, and turnover. Managers commonly create unrealistically

3. DISCUSS how managers can improve the motivation of personnel who perform routine tasks.

high expectations in job applicants to entice them to accept a position. This has proved particularly troublesome with regard to routine tasks. Dissatisfaction too often sets in when lofty expectations are brought down to earth by dull or tedious work. **Realistic job previews** (RJPs), honest explanations of what a job actually entails, have been successful in helping to avoid employee dissatisfaction resulting from unrealized expectations. On-the-job and laboratory research have demonstrated the practical value of giving a realistic preview of both positive and negative aspects to applicants for highly specialized and/or difficult jobs.

realistic job previews: *honest explanations of what a job actually entails*

A recent statistical analysis of 40 different RJP studies revealed these patterns: fewer dropouts during the recruiting process, lower initial expectations, and lower turnover and higher performance once on the job. The researcher recommended a contingency approach regarding the form and timing of RJPs. *Written* RJPs are better for reducing the dropout rate during the recruiting process, whereas *verbal* RJPs more effectively reduce post-hiring turnover (quitting). "RJPs given just *before* hiring are advisable to reduce attrition [dropouts] from the recruitment process and to reduce . . . turnover, but organizations wishing to improve employee performance should provide RJPs *after* job acceptance, as part of a realistic socialization effort."[36]

job rotation: *moving people from one specialized job to another*

■ **Job Rotation.** As the term is used here, **job rotation** involves periodically moving people from one specialized job to another. Such movement prevents stagnation. Other reasons for rotating personnel include compensating for a labor shortage, enhancing safety, training, and preventing fatigue.[37] *Carpal tunnel syndrome* and other painful and disabling injuries stemming from repetitive-motion tasks can be reduced significantly through job rotation. For example, Nissan, at its U.S. vehicle assembly plants, "has workers do four different jobs during a typical eight-hour shift, to try to cut down on repetitive-motion injuries. Nissan claims that injury rates have fallen 60% in the past two years."[38] Meanwhile, the FBI rotates its agents off the drug squad periodically to discourage corruption.[39] If highly repetitious and routine jobs are unavoidable, job rotation, by introducing a modest degree of novelty, can help prevent boredom and resulting alienation. Of course, a balance needs to be achieved—people should be rotated often enough to fight boredom and injury but not so often that they feel unfairly manipulated or disoriented.

■ **Limited Exposure.** Another way of coping with the need to staff a highly fragmented and tedious job is to limit the individual's exposure to it. A number of organizations have achieved high productivity among personnel doing routine tasks by allowing them to earn an early quitting time.[40] This technique, called **contingent time off** (CTO) or earned time off, involves establishing a challenging yet fair daily performance standard, or quota, and letting employees go home when it is reached. The following CTO plan was implemented at a large manufacturing plant where the employees were producing about 160 units a day with 10 percent rejects:

contingent time off: *rewarding people with early time off when they get the job done*

> *If the group produced at 200 units with three additional good units for each defective unit, then they could leave the work site for the rest of the day. Within a week of implementing this CTO intervention, the group was producing 200+ units with an average of 1.5 percent rejects. These employees, who had formerly put in an 8-hour day, were now working an average of 6.5 hours per day and, importantly, they increased their performance by 25 percent.*[41]

Some employees find the opportunity to earn eight hours of pay for six hours of steady effort extremely motivating.

Companies using contingent time off report successful results. Impressive evidence comes from a large-scale survey of 1,598 U.S. companies employing about 10 percent of the civilian workforce. Among nine nontraditional reward systems, "earned time off" ranked only eighth in terms of use (5 percent of the companies). But among those using it, earned time off ranked *second* in terms of posi-tive impact on job performance—an 85 percent approval rating.[42] Thus, the use of contingent time off has not yet reached its excellent potential as a motivational tool.

> **13d They're Rockin' in Utah!**
>
> Autoliv's airbag assembly factory in Ogden, Utah:
>
> *Each [of 88 production cells] consists of a group of workstations staffed by a handful of employees. A screw is tightened, the finished piece scanned and registered in inventory, and then it's handed off to the next associate, who tags it and drops it into a box to be picked up and shipped. There are cells for driver airbags, passenger airbags, and side-curtain airbags. . . .*
>
> *Every 24 minutes, loud rock music from the 1970s group Steam blares through the public address system: "Na, na, na, na, hey, hey, hey, goodbye." It signals job change: Each person rotates down the line to a different task.*
>
> *Source: Abrahm Lustgarten, "Elite Factories,"* Fortune *(September 6, 2004): 240[F].*
>
> **QUESTIONS:**
>
> **From a production manager's standpoint, what do you like or dislike about the motivational potential of this arrangement? From a production employee's standpoint, what do you like or dislike about this situation?**

■ Strategy Two: Fitting Jobs to People

The second job-design strategy calls for managers to consider changing the job instead of the person. Two job-design experts have proposed that managers address the question "How can we achieve a fit between persons and their jobs that fosters *both* high work productivity and a high-quality organizational experience for the people who do the work?"[43] Two techniques for moving in this direction are job enlargement and job enrichment.

■ Job Enlargement. As used here, **job enlargement** is the process of combining two or more specialized tasks in a work flow sequence into a single job. Aetna used this technique to give some of its office employees a measure of relief from staring at a video display terminal (VDT) all day:

> *Aetna Life & Casualty in Hartford . . . reorganized its payroll department to combine ten full-time data-entry jobs with ten jobs that involve paperwork and telephoning. Now nobody in the department spends more than 70 percent of [the] day on a VDT. Morale and productivity have gone up dramatically since the change, says Richard Assunto, Aetna's payroll services manager.*[44]

job enlargement: *combining two or more specialized tasks to increase motivation*

A moderate degree of complexity and novelty can be introduced in this manner. But critics claim that two or more potentially boring tasks do not necessarily make one challenging job. Furthermore, organized labor has criticized job enlargement as a devious ploy for getting more work for the same amount of money. But if pay and performance are kept in balance, boredom and alienation can be kept somewhat at bay by job enlargement.

job enrichment: *redesigning jobs to increase their motivational potential*

■ Job Enrichment. In general terms, **job enrichment** is redesigning a job to increase its motivating potential.[45] Job enrichment increases the challenge of one's work by reversing the trend toward greater specialization. Unlike job enlargement, which merely combines equally simple tasks, job enrichment builds more complexity and depth into jobs by introducing planning and decision-making responsibility normally carried out at higher levels. Thus, enriched jobs are said to be *vertically loaded*, whereas enlarged jobs are *horizontally loaded*. Managing an entire project can be immensely challenging and motivating thanks to vertical job loading. Scott Nichols, a home construction foreman, had this to say about his job:

> *I find it very rewarding. Just building something, creating something, and actually seeing your work. . . . You start with a bare, empty lot with grass growing up and then you build a house. A lot of times you'll build a house for a family, and you see them move in, that's pretty gratifying. . . . I'm proud of that.*[46]

4. EXPLAIN how job enrichment can be used to enhance the motivating potential of jobs.

Jobs can be enriched by upgrading five core dimensions of work: (1) skill variety, (2) task identity, (3) task significance, (4) autonomy, and (5) job feedback. Each of these core dimensions deserves a closer look.

- ***Skill variety.*** The degree to which the job requires a variety of different activities in carrying out the work, involving the use of a number of different skills and talents of the person
- ***Task identity.*** The degree to which the job requires completion of a "whole" and identifiable piece of work; that is, doing a job from beginning to end with a visible outcome

Why would someone want to work on their hands and knees doing menial labor in the sizzling hot, dusty desert near Cairo, Egypt? If you're this antiquities expert, you do it for the work itself, for the challenge, for the love of discovery. Job enlargement and job enrichment can give a similar motivational boost to less exotic jobs.

- ***Task significance.*** The degree to which the job has a substantial impact on the lives of other people, whether those people are in the immediate organization or in the world at large
- ***Autonomy.*** The degree to which the job provides substantial freedom, independence, and discretion to the individual in scheduling the work and in determining the procedures to be used in carrying it out
- ***Job feedback.*** The degree to which carrying out the work activities required by the job provides the individual with direct and clear information about the effectiveness of his or her performance[47]

Figure 13.5 shows the theoretical connection between enriched core job characteristics and high motivation and satisfaction. At the heart of this job-enrichment model are three psychological states that highly specialized jobs usually do not satisfy: meaningfulness, responsibility, and knowledge of results.

It is important to note that not all employees will respond favorably to enriched jobs. Personal traits and motives influence the connection between core job characteristics and desired outcomes. Only those with the necessary knowledge and skills plus a desire for personal growth will be motivated by enriched work.

Figure 13.5 How Job Enrichment Works

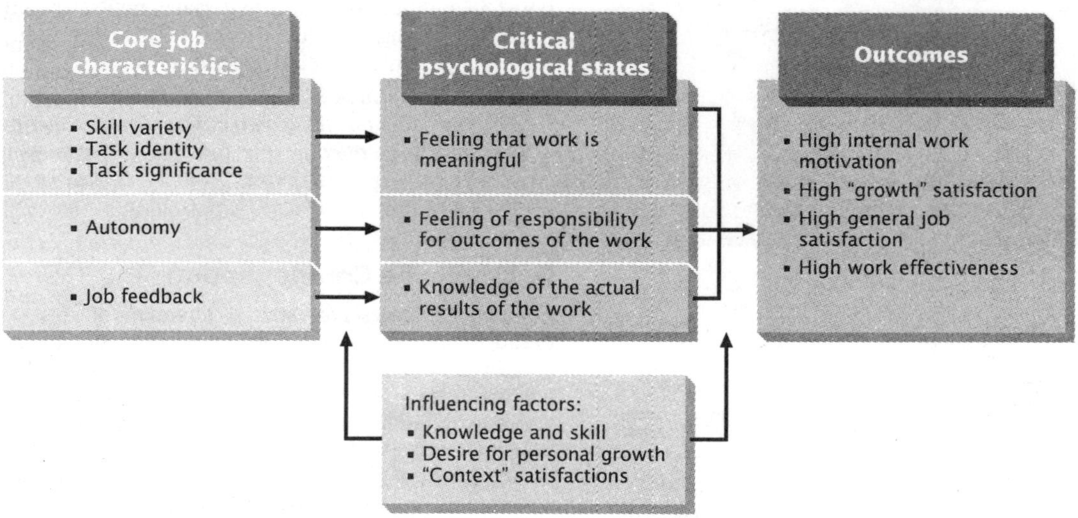

Source: *J. Hackman /G. Oldham,* Work Redesign *(Figure 4.6). © 1980. Reprinted by permission of Pearson Education, Inc., Upper Saddle River, New Jersey.*

Furthermore, in keeping with Herzberg's two-factor theory, dissatisfaction with factors such as pay, physical working conditions, or supervision can neutralize enrichment efforts. Researchers have reported that fear of failure, lack of confidence, and lack of trust in management's intentions can stand in the way of effective job enrichment. But job enrichment can and does work when it is carefully thought out, when management is committed to its long-term success, and when employees desire additional challenge.[48]

rewards: *material and psychological payoffs for working*

Motivation Through Rewards

extrinsic rewards: *payoffs, such as money, that are granted by others*

intrinsic rewards: *self-granted and internally experienced payoffs, such as a feeling of accomplishment*

All workers, including volunteers who donate their time to worthy causes, expect to be rewarded in some way for their contributions. **Rewards** can be defined broadly as the material and psychological payoffs for performing tasks in the workplace. Managers have found that job performance and satisfaction may be improved by properly administered rewards. Today, rewards vary greatly in both type and scope, depending on one's employer and geographical location. One indicator of the vastness of this topic is the book titled *The 1001 Rewards & Recognition Fieldbook.*[49]

In this section, we distinguish between extrinsic and intrinsic rewards, review alternative employee compensation plans, and discuss the effective management of extrinsic rewards.

To help personalize and boost the motivating potential of employee rewards, companies such as Marriott now offer gift-certificate reward programs to employers. What is more motivating, a useless dust-collecting trinket, or the opportunity for a relaxing vacation?

Extrinsic versus Intrinsic Rewards

There are two different categories of rewards. **Extrinsic rewards** are payoffs granted to the individual by other people. Examples include money, employee benefits, promotions, recognition, status symbols, and praise. The second category consists of **intrinsic rewards**, which are self-granted and internally experienced payoffs. Among intrinsic rewards are a sense of accomplishment, self-esteem, and self-actualization.[50] Usually, on-the-job extrinsic and intrinsic rewards are intermingled. For instance, employees often experience a psychological boost, in addition to reaping material benefits, when they complete a big project. Harvard Business School's Abraham Zaleznik offered this perspective:

> *I think a paycheck buys you a baseline level of performance. But one thing that makes a good leader is the ability to offer people intrinsic rewards, the tremendous lift that comes from being aware of one's own talents and wanting to maximize them.*[51]

Employee Compensation

Compensation deserves special attention at this point because money is the universal extrinsic reward.[52] Moreover, since "labor costs are about two-thirds of total business expenses,"[53] compensation practices need to be effective and efficient. Employee compensation is a complex area fraught with legal and tax implications.[54] Although an exhaustive treatment of employee compensation plans is beyond our present purpose, we can identify major types. Table 13.2 lists and briefly describes ten different pay plans. Two are nonincentive plans, seven qualify as incentive plans, and one plan is in a category of its own. Each type of

Table 13.2 Guide to Employee Compensation Plans

Pay plan	Description/calculation	Main advantage	Main disadvantage
		Nonincentive	
Hourly wage	Fixed amount per hour worked	Time is easier to measure than performance	Little or no incentive to work hard
Annual salary	Contractual amount per year	Easy to administer	Little or no incentive to work hard
		Incentive	
Piece rate	Fixed amount per unit of output	Pay tied directly to personal output	Negative association with sweatshops and rate-cutting abuses
Sales commission	Fixed percentage of sales revenue	Pay tied directly to personal volume of business	Morale problem when sales personnel earn more than other employees
Merit pay	Bonus granted for outstanding performance	Gives salaried employees incentive to work harder	Fairness issue raised when tied to subjective appraisals
Profit sharing	Distribution of specified percentage of bottom-line profits	Individual has a personal stake in firm's profitability	Profits affected by more than just performance (for example, by prices and competition)
Gain sharing	Distribution of specified percentage of productivity gains and/or cost savings	Encourages employees to work harder *and* smarter	Calculations can get cumbersome
Pay-for-knowledge	Salary or wage rates tied to degrees earned or skills mastered	Encourages lifelong learning	Tends to inflate training and labor costs
Stock options	Selected employees earn right to acquire firm's stock free or at a discount	Gives individual a personal stake in firm's financial performance	Can be resented by ineligible personnel; morale tied to stock price
		Other	
Cafeteria compensation (life-cycle benefits)	Employee selects personal mix of benefits from an array of options	Tailored benefits package fits individual needs	Can be costly to administer

5. DISTINGUISH extrinsic rewards from intrinsic rewards, and **LIST** four rules for administering extrinsic rewards effectively.

pay plan has advantages and disadvantages. Therefore, there is no single best plan suitable for all employees. Indeed, two experts at the U.S. Bureau of Labor Statistics say the key words in compensation for the next 25 years will be "flexible" and "varied." A diverse workforce will demand an equally diverse array of compensation plans.[55]

Improving Performance with Extrinsic Rewards

Extrinsic rewards, if they are to motivate job performance effectively, need to be administered in ways that (1) satisfy operative needs, (2) foster positive expectations, (3) ensure equitable distribution, and (4) reward results. Let us see how these four criteria can be met relative to the ten different pay plans in Table 13.2.

13e Back to the Opening Case

How many different extrinsic rewards can you identify in the IDG case? Explain. Why is Pat McGovern a good motivator?

cafeteria compensation: *plan that allows employees to select their own mix of benefits*

Rewards Must Satisfy Individual Needs. Whether it is a pay raise or a pat on the back, a reward has no motivational impact unless it satisfies an operative need.[56] Not all people need the same things, and one person may need different things at different times. Money is a powerful motivator for those who seek security through material wealth. But the promise of more money may mean little to a financially secure person who seeks ego gratification from challenging work. People's needs concerning when and how they want to be paid also vary.

Because cafeteria compensation is unique and particularly promising, we shall examine it more closely. **Cafeteria compensation** (also called life-cycle benefits) is a plan that allows each employee to determine the makeup of his or her benefit package.[57] Because today's nonwage benefits are a significant portion of total compensation, the motivating potential of such a privilege can be sizable.

> *Under these plans, employers provide minimal "core" coverage in life and health insurance, vacations, and pensions. The employee buys additional benefits to suit [his or her] own needs, using credit based on salary, service, and age.*
>
> *The elderly bachelor, for instance, may pass up the maternity coverage he would receive, willy-nilly, under conventional plans and "buy" additional pension contributions instead. The mother whose children are covered by her husband's employee health insurance policy may choose legal and dental care insurance instead.*[58]

Although some organizations have balked at installing cafeteria compensation because of added administrative expense, the number of programs in effect in the United States has grown steadily. Cafeteria compensation enhances employee satisfaction, according to at least one study,[59] and represents a revolutionary step toward fitting rewards to people, rather than vice versa.

Employees Must Believe Effort Will Lead to Reward. According to expectancy theory, an employee will not strive for an attractive reward unless it is perceived as being attainable. For example, the promise of an expenses-paid trip to Hawaii for the leading salesperson will prompt additional efforts at sales only among those who feel they have a decent chance of winning. Those who believe they have little chance of winning will not be motivated to try any harder than usual. Incentive pay plans, especially merit pay, profit sharing, gain sharing, and stock options, need to be designed and communicated in a way that will foster believable effort-reward linkages.[60]

13f Does Money Buy Happiness?

Gallup poll: Even if they won a $10 million lottery jackpot, 55 percent of working Americans would continue to work.

George Lucas, director of Star Wars: "Money can buy *pleasure*, but pleasure isn't happiness. Happiness is a feeling that goes beyond pleasure."

Source: Data from "The Stat," Business Week *(October 4, 2004): 16; and Lucas as quoted in Craig Wilson, "How Much Would Make You Smile?"* USA Today *(December 27, 2004): 2B.*

QUESTIONS:

Some management theorists say money isn't a motivator. Do you agree or disagree? Why? When it comes to motivating you to do your best, what role does money play?

Rewards Must Be Equitable. Something is equitable if people perceive it to be fair and just. Each of us carries in our head a pair of scales upon which we weigh equity.[61] Figure 13.6 shows one scale for *personal equity* and another for *social equity*. The personal equity scale tests the relationship between effort expended and rewards received. The social equity scale, in contrast, compares our own effort-reward ratio with that of someone else in the same situation. We are motivated to seek personal and social equity and to avoid inequity.[62] An interesting aspect of research on this topic is its demonstration that inequity is perceived by those who are *overpaid* as well as by those who are underpaid.[63] Since perceived inequity is associated with feelings of dissatisfaction and anger, jealousy, or guilt, inequitable reward schemes tend to be counterproductive and are ethically questionable. Record-setting executive pay in recent years of painful downsizings and massive layoffs has been roundly criticized as inequitable and unfair.[64] In fact, when 400 college-educated people were recently asked, "What has undermined your trust in companies?" 60 percent said "Excessive compensation for executives."[65] One notable exception to this trend occurred at Xilinx, the San Jose, California, semiconductor maker: "Xilinx survived the recent tech downturn by cutting salaries across the board—the CEO took a 27% hit—instead of resorting to mass layoffs."[66]

Figure 13.6 Personal and Social Equity

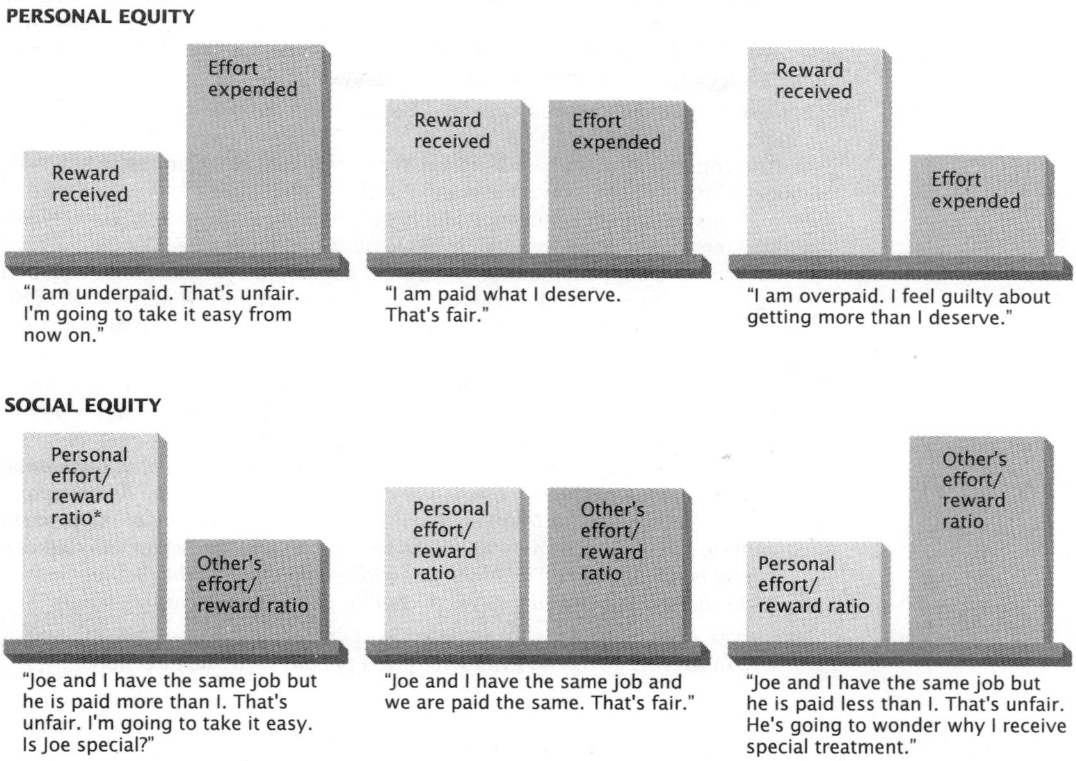

* The lower the effort/reward ratio, the greater the motivation.

■ **Rewards Must Be Linked to Performance.** Ideally, there should be an if-then relationship between task performance and extrinsic rewards. Traditional hourly wage and annual salary pay plans are weak in this regard. They do little more than reward the person for showing up at work. Managers can strengthen motivation to work by making sure that those who give a little extra get a little extra. In addition to piece-rate and sales-commission plans, merit pay, profit sharing, gain sharing, and stock option plans are popular ways of linking pay and performance.[67] Cash bonuses, when paid promptly to maximize the *positive reinforcement* effect, can boost motivation:

> *If an employee's performance has been exceptional—such as filling in for a sick colleague, perhaps, or working nights or weekends or cutting costs for the company—the employer may reward the worker with a one-time bonus of $50, $100 or $500 shortly after the noteworthy actions.*
>
> *"Your boss walking by and saying, 'That's a great job,' and showing up the next day with a check or gift certificate really underscores the*

13g What's Fair?

Fact: The average CEO in the United States had to work 1.5 *days* "in 2003 to earn the equivalent of a typical employee's yearly salary."

Survey finding: ". . . 64% of workers who call in sick to the office aren't actually ill."

Source: "The Stat," Business Week *(December 6, 2004): 16; and Elise Soukup, "Surveys,"* Newsweek *(January 17, 2005): 11.*

QUESTIONS:

Is publicity about excessive CEO pay likely to have any effect on employee motivation these days? Explain. Does the concept of equity have anything to do with employees calling in sick when they aren't? Explain.

> *specific thing you just did," says Salary.com's [senior vice president of compensation Bill] Coleman. That differentiates spot bonuses from more structured programs such as annual bonuses: While those larger yearly awards can be a crucial part of an overall compensation package, annual bonuses are often distributed so long after the fact that employees have forgotten the impressive behavior for which they're being paid, he says.*[68]

Positive reinforcement is discussed in Chapter 15, in the context of behavior modification.

The concept of team-based incentive pay as a way of rewarding teamwork and cooperation has been slow to take hold in the United States for two reasons: (1) it goes against the grain of an individualistic culture, and (2) poorly conceived and administered plans have given team-based pay a bad reputation.[69]

All incentive pay plans should be carefully conceived because undesirable behavior may inadvertently be encouraged. Consider, for example, what the head of Nucor Corporation, a successful minimill steel company, had to say about his firm's bonus system:

> *[Nucor's] bonus system . . . is very tough. If you're late even five minutes, you lose your bonus for the day. If you're late more than 30 minutes, or you're absent because of sickness or anything else, you lose your bonus for the week. Now, we do have what we call four "forgiveness" days during the year when you can be sick or you have to close on a house or your wife is having a baby. But only four. We have a melter, Phil Johnson, down in Darlington, and one of the workers came in one day and said that Phil had been in an automobile accident and was sitting beside his car off of Route 52, holding his head. So the foreman asked, "Why didn't you stop and help him?" And the guy said, "And lose my bonus?"*[70]

Like goals, incentive plans foster selective perception.[71] Consequently, managers need to make sure goals and incentives point people in ethical directions.

Motivation Through Employee Participation

participative management: *empowering employees to assume greater control of the workplace*

While noting that the term *participation* has become a "stewpot" into which every conceivable kind of management fad has been tossed, one management scholar helpfully identified four key areas of participative management. Employees may participate in (1) setting goals, (2) making decisions, (3) solving problems, and (4) designing and implementing organizational changes.[72] Thus, **participative management** is defined as the process of empowering employees to assume greater control of the workplace.[73] When personally and meaningfully involved, above and beyond just doing assigned tasks, employees are said to be more motivated and productive. In fact, a study of 164 New Zealand companies with at least 100 employees found lower employee turnover and higher organizational productivity among firms using participative management practices.[74]

This section focuses on three approaches to participation. They are quality control circles, open-book management, and self-managed teams. After taking a closer look at each, we consider four keys to successful employee participation programs.

Quality Control Circles

quality control circles: *voluntary problem-solving groups committed to improving quality and reducing costs*

Developed in Japan during the early 1960s, this innovation took the U.S. industrial scene by storm during the late 1970s and early 1980s. Today, thousands of quality control circles (carrying all sorts of names) can be found in hundreds of North American and European companies. **Quality control circles**, commonly referred to as QC circles or simply quality circles, are voluntary problem-solving groups of five to ten employees from the same work area who meet regularly to discuss quality improvement and ways to reduce costs.[75] A weekly one-hour meeting, during company time, is common practice. By relying on *voluntary* participation, QC circles attempt to tap the creative potential every employee possesses. Although QC circles do not work in every situation, benefits such as direct cost savings, improved worker-management relations, and greater individual commitment have been reported.[76]

QC circles should be introduced in evolutionary fashion rather than by management edict. Training, supportive supervision, and team building are all part of this evolutionary development. The idea is to give those who work day in and day out at a specific job the tools, group support, and opportunity to have a say in nipping quality problems in the bud. Each QC circle is responsible not only for recommending solutions but also for actually implementing and evaluating those solutions. According to one observer, "The invisible force behind the success of QC's [quality circles] is its ability to bring the psychological principles of Maslow, McGregor, and Herzberg into the workplace through a structured process."[77]

6. EXPLAIN how quality control circles, open-book management, and self-managed teams promote employee participation.

Open-Book Management

open-book management: *sharing key financial data and profits with employees who are trained and empowered*

Open-book management (OBM) involves "opening a company's financial statements to all employees and providing the education that will enable them to understand how the company makes money and how their actions affect its success and bottom line."[78] Clearly, this is a bold break from traditional management practice. Many companies claim to practice OBM, but few actually do.[79] Why? OBM asks managers to correct three typical shortcomings by (1) displaying a high degree of trust in employees, (2) having a deep and unwavering commitment to employee training, and (3) being patient when waiting for results.[80] Once again, as we saw earlier with his masterful blending of goals and feedback, Wal-Mart's founder Sam Walton was a pioneer in open-book management and employee participation. Here is how former Wal-Mart CEO David Glass remembers it:

> *Sam felt we were all partners, and he wanted to share everything. And he was absolutely right. He believed that everyone should be an entrepreneur. If you ran the toy department in Harrison, Ark., you'd have all your financial information. So you're just like the toy entrepreneur of Harrison: You know what your sales are, what your margins are, what your inventory is. And then we had another philosophy where we had grass-roots meetings in every store. And there was an absolute belief that the best ideas ever at Wal-Mart came from the bottom up. Ideas would come up from those meetings and be implemented companywide. The door greeter, for example, was the idea of a hourly associate in Louisiana.*[81]

A four-step approach to OBM is displayed in Figure 13.7. The STEP acronym stands for *share, teach, empower,* and *pay.* Skipping or inadequately performing a step virtually guarantees failure. A systematic process is needed. Experts tell us it takes at least two complete budget cycles (typically two years) to see positive results. In step 1, employees are exposed to eye-catching public displays of key financial data. Sales, expense, and profit data for both the organization and relevant business units are shared in hallways, in cafeterias, and on internal Web sites. Of course, without step 2, step 1 would be meaningless. Comprehensive, ongoing training gives *all* employees a working knowledge of the firm's business model. Here is what Jelly Belly Candy Co. does:

> *Through Jelly Belly University, employees from the upper-most management level to administrative support personnel learn the art of candymaking, evaluate the results and conduct product evaluations, production scheduling and inventory control.*[82]

Thus, Jelly Belly's employees not only learn how to make great jelly beans; they also learn what it takes to make a profit in the process. In OBM companies, finance specialists teach other employees how to read and interpret basic financial documents such as profit-loss statements. Entertaining and instructive business board games and computer simulations have proved effective. Remedial education is provided when needed. Armed with knowledge about the company's workings and financial health,

Figure 13.7 The Four S.T.E.P. Approach to Open-Book Management

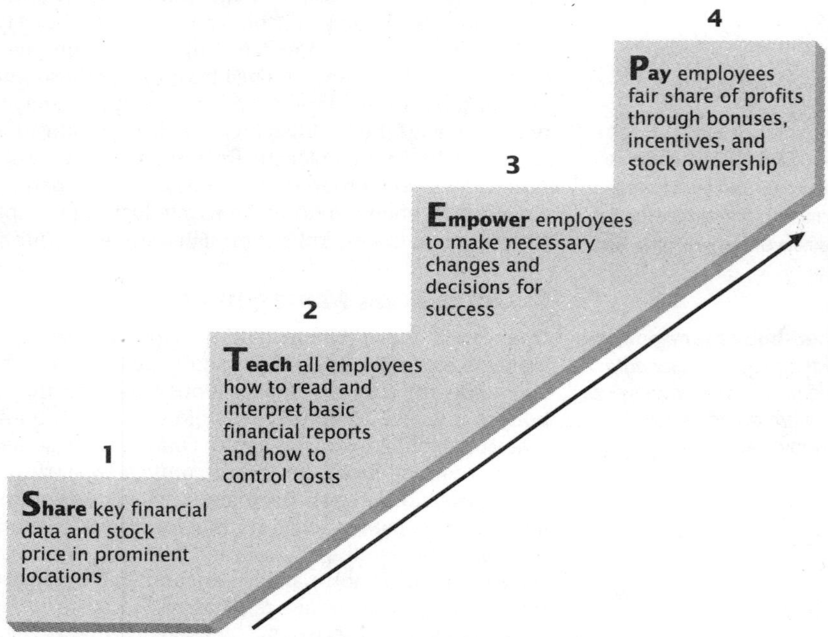

Source: *Based on Raj Aggarwal and Betty J. Simkins, "Open Book Management—Optimizing Human Capital,"* Business Horizons, *44 (September-October 2001): 5–13.*

employees are ready for step 3. Managers find it easier to trust empowered employees to make important decisions when the employees are adequately prepared (more on empowerment in Chapter 15). In step 4, employees enjoy the fruits of their efforts by sharing profits and/or receiving bonuses and incentive compensation. There is no magic to OBM. It simply involves doing *important* things in the *right* way.[83]

■ Self-Managed Teams

self-managed teams: *high-performance teams that assume traditional managerial duties such as staffing and planning*

According to the logic of this comprehensive approach to participation, self-management is the best management because it taps people's full potential. Advocates say self-management fosters creativity, motivation, and productivity. **Self-managed teams**, also known as autonomous work groups or high-performance work teams, take on traditional managerial tasks as part of their normal work routine.[84] They can have anywhere from 5 to more than 30 members, depending on the job. Unlike QC circles, which are staffed with volunteers, employees are assigned to self-managed teams. Cross-trained team members typically rotate jobs as they turn out a complete product or service. Any supervision tends to be minimal, with managers acting more as *facilitators* than as order givers.

■ Vertically Loaded Jobs. In the language of job enrichment, team members' jobs are vertically loaded. This means nonmanagerial team members assume duties traditionally performed by managers. But specifically which duties? A survey of industry practices at 1,456 U.S. companies by *Training* magazine gave us some answers. Over 60 percent of the companies using self-managed teams let team members determine work schedules, deal directly with customers, and conduct training. Between 30 and 40 percent of the teams were allowed to manage budgets, conduct performance appraisals, and hire people. Only 15 percent of the teams were permitted to fire coworkers. The researchers concluded that *true* self-managed teams are still in the early growth stage.[85] Still, Google Inc., creator of the popular Internet search engine, shows how far the concept can go:

> *When [chief engineer Wayne] Rosing started at Google in 2001, "we had management in engineering. And the structure was tending to tell people, No you can't do that." So Google got rid of the managers. Now most engineers work in teams of three, with project leadership rotating among team members. If something isn't right, even if it's in a product that has already gone public, teams fix it without asking anyone.*
>
> *"For a while," Rosing says, "I had 160 direct reports. No managers. It worked because the teams knew what they had to do. That set a cultural bit in people's heads: You are the boss. Don't wait to take the hill. Don't wait to be managed."*
>
> *And if you fail, fine. On to the next idea. "There's faith here in the ability of smart, well-motivated people to do the right thing," Rosing says. "Anything that gets in the way of that is evil."*[86]

Consequently, Google hires very carefully, putting applicants through a rigorous screening process. *Fortune* quoted the head of Texas Instruments as saying, "No matter what your business, these teams are the wave of the future."[87]

■ **Managerial Resistance.** Not surprisingly, managerial resistance is the number one barrier to self-managed teams. More than anything else, self-managed teams represent *change*, and lots of it.

> *Adopting the team approach is no small matter; it means wiping out tiers of managers and tearing down bureaucratic barriers between departments. Yet companies are willing to undertake such radical changes to gain workers' knowledge and commitment—along with productivity gains that exceed 30 percent in some cases.*[88]

Traditional authoritarian supervisors view autonomous teams as a threat to their authority and job security. For this reason, *new* facilities built around the concept of self-managed teams, so-called greenfield sites, tend to fare better than reworked existing operations.

Managers who take the long view and switch to self-managed teams are finding it well worth the investment of time and money. Self-managed teams even show early promise of boosting productivity in the huge service sector.[89] (Teamwork is discussed in the next chapter.)

13h Author Stephen Covey's "Declaration of Independence" for Employees

The industrial age was about control, and the information age, or knowledge-worker age, is about release. And release means helping people find their voice, so they can do what they love doing and what they do well.

Have you ever had that kind of a job or role? What kind of supervision did it require? Right. You supervised yourself. You didn't need anyone to motivate you.

Source: As quoted in Susanna Hamner, "How to Find a New Answer," Business 2.0, *5 (December 2004): 118.*

QUESTIONS:
Some believe the best form of management is self-management. Do you agree or disagree? Why? What practical boundaries would you put on Covey's position?

■ Keys to Successful Employee Participation Programs

According to researchers, four factors build the *employee* support necessary for any sort of participation program to work:

1. A profit-sharing or gain-sharing plan
2. A long-term employment relationship with good job security
3. A concerted effort to build and maintain group cohesiveness
4. Protection of the individual employee's rights[90]

Working in combination, these factors help explain motivational success stories such as that of Genencor in the Closing Case for this chapter.

It should be clear by now that participative management involves more than simply announcing a new program, such as open-book management. To make sure a supportive climate exists, a good deal of background work often needs to be done.[91] This is particularly important in view of the conclusion drawn by researchers who analyzed 41 participative management studies:

> *Participation has . . . [a positive] effect on both satisfaction and productivity, and its effect on satisfaction is somewhat stronger than its effect on productivity. . . . Our analysis indicates specific organizational factors that may enhance or constrain the effect of participation. For example, there is evidence that a participative climate has a more substantial effect on workers' satisfaction than participation in specific decisions.*[92]

In the end, effective participative management is as much a managerial attitude about sharing power as it is a specific set of practices. In some European countries, such as Germany, the supportive climate is reinforced by government-mandated participative management.[93]

Motivation Through Quality-of-Work-Life Programs

Workforce diversity has made *flexibility* and *accommodation* top priorities for managers today. This chapter concludes with a look at ways of accommodating emerging employee needs. For example, a big concern these days involves striking a proper balance between work and life beyond the workplace. The dilemmas facing Dan Rosensweig, Yahoo's chief operating officer, and teacher Carmen Alvarez are typical today:

> ***Rosensweig**: The biggest challenge is, when you're given an opportunity like this, how do you give it everything you have because it deserves it, and also recognize and appreciate that the most important things in your life are your wife and daughters. I'm envious of people who have been able to find better balance.*[94]
>
> ***Alvarez**: Each day after teaching fourth graders, Carmen Alvarez, 35, cooks for her three daughters, helps them with their homework and finds time to attend at least one of their games. "I feel responsible for everything." Alvarez, who is separated from the girls' father, finished Ph.D. coursework at Boston College. Now she's trying to complete her dissertation. "How do you find time to put yourself first?"*[95]

7. EXPLAIN how companies are striving to motivate today's diverse workforce with quality-of-work-life programs.

Harvard's Rosabeth Moss Kanter believes employers need to be part of the solution: "If we don't make it possible for people to have highly flexible lives, I think we won't get the mutual benefits to our society of all the talent there is. At least now there are role-model companies that offer more flexibility, sabbaticals, family leaves, and the like. But a lot more needs to be done."[96] By meeting these needs in creative ways, such as flexible work schedules, family support services, wellness programs, and sabbaticals, managers hope to enhance motivation and job performance.[97]

■ Flexible Work Schedules

flextime: *allows employees to choose their own arrival and departure times within specified limits*

The standard 8 A.M. to 5 P.M., 40-hour workweek has come under fire as dual-income families, single parents, and others attempt to juggle hectic schedules. Taking its place is **flextime**, a work-scheduling plan that allows employees to determine their own arrival and departure times within specific limits.[98] All employees must be present during a fixed core time (see the center portion of Figure 13.8). If an eight-hour day is required, as in Figure 13.8, an early bird can put in the required eight hours by arriving at 7:00 A.M., taking half an hour for lunch, and departing at 3:30 P.M. Alternatively, a late starter can come in at 9:00 A.M. and leave at 5:30 P.M. Some progressive organizations, such as Mitre, in McLean, Virginia, take flextime to an extreme: "The nonprofit technology consultant for the Pentagon allows the most flexible of schedules: Create your own as long as you hit 40 hours in a seven-day peri-

Figure 13.8 Flextime in Action

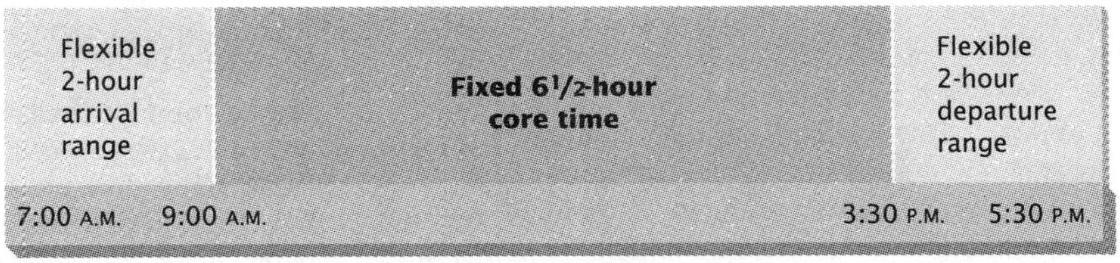

od."[99] When given the choice of "flexible work hours" versus an "opportunity to advance" in a survey, 58 percent of the women opted for flexible hours. Forty-three percent of the men chose that option.[100] The growing use of flextime and other alternative work arrangements, such as telecommuting, is partly due to employer self-interest. Employers want to cut the cost of unscheduled absenteeism. A 2001 survey found the average annual cost for each employee's unscheduled absenteeism (68 percent of which was *not* for illness) to be $775.[101] Flextime can also be used to accommodate the special needs of disabled employees.[102]

■ **Benefits.** In addition to many anecdotal reports citing the benefits of flextime, research studies have uncovered promising evidence. Flextime has several documented benefits:

- Better employee-supervisor relations
- Reduced absenteeism
- Selective positive impact on job performance (for example, a 24 percent improvement for computer programmers over a two-year period but no effect on the performance of data-entry workers).[103]

Flextime, though very popular among employees because of the degree of freedom it brings, is not appropriate for all situations. Problems reported by adopters include greater administrative expense, supervisor resistance, and inadequate coverage of jobs.

■ **Alternatives.** According to organizations promoting a better quality of work-life—such as Alliance for Work-Life Progress and Families and Work Institute—the concept of flextime is taking on a much broader meaning:

> *Traditionally, flexibility means being allowed to start and end work at employee-determined times, usually within a preset band of times. Nowadays, it's a bigger concept involving reduced time, options for moving between part- and full-time, paid leave for family or personal reasons, telecommuting and more. One new idea is career flexibility, or the ability to move in and out of active work, entering and re-entering the workforce over the course of a working life.*[104]

A good case in point is Brenda Barnes. In 1997, she quit as CEO of PepsiCo's North America division to spend more time with her three children, a career-ending move according to some observers at the time. Such was not the case, however, and Barnes was named the new CEO of Sara Lee, the $20 billion-a-year food and apparel company, in 2005.[105] Other work-scheduling variations include *compressed workweeks* (40 or more hours in fewer than five days)[106] and *permanent part-time* (workweeks with fewer than 40 hours). *Job sharing* (complementary scheduling that allows two or more part-timers to share a single full-time job), yet another work-scheduling innovation, is growing in popularity among employers of working parents.[107]

Under the heading of unintended consequences, a European study suggests that employees may be paying a price for the freedom of flexible work scheduling. Compared with a control group of employees on fixed schedules, employees with compressed workweeks, rotating shifts, irregular schedules, and part-time jobs

13i In Search of a Balanced Life

There's a better way to think about all this, one that requires us to embrace imbalance. Instead of trying to balance all of our commitments and passions at any one time, let's acknowledge that anything important, and anything done well, demands our full investment. At some times, it may be a demanding child or an unhappy spouse, and the office will suffer. At others, it may be winning the McWhorter account, and child and spouse will have to fend for themselves. Only over time can we really balance a portfolio of diverse experiences.

Source: Keith H. Hammonds, "Balance Is Bunk!" Fast Company, *no. 87 (October 2004): 70.*

QUESTIONS:

Why is this an acceptable or unacceptable logic? What relative weights do you apply to work, family, and leisure in your life? What sort of rebalancing do you need for a less stressful life? How?

experienced significantly more health, psychological, and sleeping problems.[108]

Family Support Services

family-friendly companies: *companies that recognize and accommodate employees' nonwork lives and priorities*

Family-friendly companies recognize that employees have lives and priorities outside the workplace and make appropriate accommodations. They strive to help their employees achieve a productive and satisfying work/life balance with supportive policies, programs, and culture. This last factor—culture—is particularly important because it is driven by the organization's core values. A company that claims to be family-friendly, yet promotes only those who log 60-hour weeks, values total dedication more than work/life balance. A recent study by the Society for Human Resource Management identified "the top five family-friendly benefits": 1. "Dependent care flexible spending accounts" (71 percent); 2. "Flextime" (55 percent); 3. "Family leave above required leave of the federal Family and Medical Leave Act" (39 percent); 4. "Telecommuting on a part-time basis" (34 percent); and 5. "Compressed workweeks" (31 percent).[109] It is important to note that the U.S. Family and Medical Leave Act (FMLA), which took effect in 1993, has significant holes and limitations. First, only companies with 50 or more employees are required to comply with the law mandating up to 12 weeks of unpaid leave per year for family

One big happy family! At least that's what Frank Guerra has tried to create by making his San Antonio advertising, marketing, and public relations company a family-friendly employer. On-site day care has proven to be a big hit with the firm's working parents and their children, pictured here with Mr. Guerra.

events such as births, adoptions, or sickness. Because the vast majority of U.S. businesses (95 percent) employ fewer than 50 people, millions of working Americans (43 percent) are left unprotected by FMLA. Second, employees can be required by their employer to exhaust their sick leave and vacation allotments before taking FMLA leave. Fortunately, states and businesses have plugged some of the holes in FMLA.[110]

True family-friendly companies go way beyond the legal minimum, as these inspiring examples show:

- **Station Casinos, Las Vegas**: "... this gaming company was the first in Las Vegas to offer full-service on-site dentistry and 24–hour child care."
- **First Horizon National, Memphis, Tennessee**: "[This bank is] parent-friendly. Each school year, parents get unlimited time off to visit their kids' classrooms."
- **MBNA, Wilmington, Delaware**: "Benefits keep flowing at this credit-card issuer: eight child-care centers, generous reimbursement for tuition, up to $20,000 per child for adoption, and even a paid week off for new grandparents."
- **Pfizer, New York City**: "[The 44,000–employee drug company offers] an elder-care program that includes counseling."
- **CDW, Vernon Hills, Illinois**: "Adoptive parents have special benefits at this computer and electronics seller. Agency and placement fees, legal fees, foreign adoption charges, and related travel expenses are reimbursed up to $3,000 per child."
- **Container Store, Coppell, Texas**: "Everyone who works at least 18 hours a week gets some health coverage, and special schedules are available for those with children: 9A.M. to 2P.M., Monday through Friday."[111]

As more and more companies offer family-friendly benefits,[112] cost-conscious managers properly ask, "What is the return on our investment?" Recent studies of companies with family-friendly practices have documented financial payoffs from easier recruitment, lower absenteeism and turnover, and greater productivity.[113] In fact, accounting and consulting giant Deloitte & Touche claims that its flexible work schedule programs "helped the company avoid $41.5 million in turnover-related costs in 2003."[114]

Wellness Programs

Stress and burnout are all too common consequences of modern work life.[115] (See the Skills & Tools feature at the end of this chapter.) Family-versus-work conflict, long hours, overload, hectic schedules, deadlines, frequent business travel, and accumulated workplace irritations are taking their toll. Progressive companies are coming to the rescue with *wellness programs* featuring a wide range of offerings. Among them are stress reduction, healthy eating and living clinics, quit-smoking and weight-loss programs, exercise facilities, massage breaks, behavioral health counseling, and health screenings. The ultimate objective is to help employees achieve a sustainable balance between their personal lives and work lives, with win-win benefits all around.[116] A good example is Fieldale Farms, a chicken processor in Baldwin, Georgia, where the $50,000 tab each time an employee had a heart attack was making health insurance unaffordable:

> *... the company went on a campaign to make its 4,600 employees healthier. It paid for gym memberships and offered free health screenings, one-on-one nutritional counseling and educational sessions at work about heart disease, diabetes and other preventable health problems....*
>
> *Since Fieldale Farms started its wellness program in 1992, its cost for health insurance has grown at an average annual rate of just 2.5 percent, below the national average of 12 percent. The company health insurance plan spends less than $3,000 a year per employee, compared to the national average of $5,800. The program costs $200,000 a year, but the company insists it is worth it.*[117]

13j High-Octane Wellness

Mel Zuckerman, owner of the Canyon Ranch Resort and Spa in Tucson, Arizona:

Your body is like a car.... Both require regular servicing, premium fuel, and care and maintenance. The main difference is you have no trade-in value, so you'd better take care of what you've got.

Source: As quoted in Jen Laing, "Mel Zuckerman, Canyon Ranch: For Showing the Way," Inc., *26 (April 2004): 130.*

QUESTIONS:

Do you treat your body like a race car or an old junker? How can you improve your overall wellness?

Sabbaticals

Some progressive companies in the United States (about 2 percent) give selected employees paid sabbaticals after a certain number of years of service. Here is a sampling to illustrate the many variations:

- **Adobe Systems and Men's Wearhouse**: Three weeks every five years.
- **Silicon Graphics**: Six weeks every four years.
- **Genentech**: Six weeks every six years.
- **American Century**: Four weeks every seven years.
- **Intel**: Eight weeks every seven years.[118]
- **Timberland**: "It offers a six-month, fully paid sabbatical for those who want 'to pursue a personal dream that benefits the community in a meaningful way.'"[119]

An extended period of paid time off gives the employee time for family, recreation, service, or travel. The idea is to refresh dedicated employees and, it is hoped, bolster their motivation and loyalty in the process.[120]

SUMMARY

1. Maslow's five-level hierarchy of needs, although empirically criticized, makes it clear to managers that people are motivated by emerging rather than fulfilled needs. Assuming that job satisfaction and performance are positively related, Herzberg believes that the most that wages and working conditions can do is eliminate sources of dissatisfaction. According to Herzberg, the key to true satisfaction, and hence motivation, is an enriched job that provides an opportunity for achievement, responsibility, and personal growth. Expectancy theory is based on the idea that the strength of one's motivation to work is the product of perceived probabilities of acquiring personally valued rewards. Both effort-performance and performance-reward probabilities are important in expectancy theory.
2. Goals can be an effective motivational tool when they are specific, difficult, participatively set, and accompanied by feedback on performance. Goals motivate performance by directing attention, encouraging effort and persistence, and prompting goal-attainment strategies and action plans.
3. Managers can counteract the boredom associated with routine-task jobs through realistic job previews, job rotation, and limited exposure. This third alternative involves letting employees earn an early departure time.
4. Job enrichment vertically loads jobs to meet individual needs for meaningfulness, responsibility, and knowledge of results. Personal desire for growth and a supportive climate must exist for job enrichment to be successful.
5. Both extrinsic (externally granted) and intrinsic (self-granted) rewards, when properly administered, can have a positive impact on performance and satisfaction. There is no single best employee compensation plan. A flexible and varied approach to compensation will be necessary in the coming years because of workforce diversity. The following rules can help managers maximize the motivational impact of extrinsic rewards: (1) rewards must satisfy individual needs, (2) one must believe that one's effort will lead to reward, (3) rewards must be equitable, and (4) rewards must be linked to performance. Gain-sharing plans have great motivational potential because they emphasize participation and link pay to actual productivity.
6. Participative management programs foster direct employee involvement in one or more of the following areas: goal setting, decision making, problem solving, and change implementation. Quality control circles are teams of volunteers who meet regularly on company time to discuss ways to improve product/service quality. The S.T.E.P. model of open-book management encourages employee participation when managers (1) *share* key financial data with all employees, (2) *teach* employees how to interpret financial statements and control costs, (3) *empower* employees to make improvements and decisions, and (4) *pay* a fair share of profits to employees. Employees assigned to self-managed teams participate by taking on tasks that have traditionally been performed by management. Profit sharing or gain sharing, job security, cohesiveness, and protection of employee rights are keys to building crucial employee support for participation programs.
7. Quality-of-work-life programs are being used to accommodate and motivate today's diverse workforce. Flextime, a flexible work-scheduling scheme that allows employees to choose their own arrival and departure times, has been effective in improving employee-supervisor relations while reducing absen-

teeism. Employers are increasingly providing family-friendly services such as child care, elder care, parental leaves, and adoption benefits. Employee wellness programs and sabbaticals are offered by some companies to reduce health insurance costs, build loyalty, and boost motivation.

TERMS TO UNDERSTAND

- Motivation, p. 377
- Expectancy theory, p. 382
- Expectancy, p. 382
- Goal setting, p. 383
- Job design, p. 385
- Realistic job previews, p. 387
- Job rotation, p. 387
- Contingent time off, p. 387
- Job enlargement, p. 388
- Job enrichment, p. 388
- Rewards, p. 390
- Extrinsic rewards, p. 390
- Intrinsic rewards, p. 390
- Cafeteria compensation, p. 392
- Participative management, p. 394
- Quality control circles, p. 394
- Open-book management, p. 395
- Self-managed teams, p. 396
- Flextime, p. 398
- Family-friendly companies, p. 400

SKILLS & TOOLS

Stress Management 101

Feeling burned out? You're not alone. According to a survey of 7,000 senior executives in the United States and 12 other countries, burnout is on the rise in the executive ranks, and many companies fail to handle the problem properly.

"All leaders are at risk for burnout, but too often companies are embarrassed by the phenomenon and have no idea how to address it," says Andrew Kakabadse, director of the survey and professor of management at the Cranfield University School of Management, Bedford, UK.

Even if companies aren't addressing the issue of burnout, there are some steps individuals can take on their own. Lois Tamir, vice president of Personnel Decisions International in Minneapolis, Minnesota, offers a number of suggestions for the busy executive who needs to stay focused during a tough time (see list). In a nutshell, managers can reduce stress by thinking big and treating themselves better.

How to Avoid Burnout

- ***Pace yourself.*** Don't put in extra hours because you probably won't get much done anyway.
- ***Laugh more.*** Humor relieves a great deal of physiological and psychological stress.
- ***Be good to yourself.*** Do something that you enjoy, such as going to the movies.
- ***Keep it simple.*** Separate your work into small tasks that can be accomplished easily. It's important to feel a sense of achievement.
- ***Stay true to your values.*** Think about the larger values in your work and personal life. Integrity, family priorities, and kindness to others will keep you grounded and put things in perspective.
- ***Keep expectations in check.*** Forget about changing the world or achieving your greatest goal at work. Some things will have to be postponed until you are better equipped to handle your own situation.
- ***Don't try to be perfect.*** Everyone experiences difficult times in his or her professional and personal life.

Source: Management Review *by Cheryl Comeau-Kirschner. Copyright 1999 by* American Management Association *(J). Reproduced with permission of* American Management Association *(J) in the format Textbook via Copyright Clearance Center.*

HANDS-ON EXERCISE

Quality-of-Work-Life Survey

Instructions:
Think of your present job, or one you had in the past, and circle one number for each of the following items. Add the circled numbers to get a total quality-of-work-life score. Alternatively, you can use this survey to interview another jobholder to determine his or her quality of work life. (*Note:* This survey is for instructional purposes only because it has not been scientifically validated.)

General Job Satisfaction
Most of the time, my job satisfaction is

Very low						Very high
1	2	3	4	5	6	7

Quality of Supervision
The person I report to respects me, listens to me, and supports me.

Never						Always
1	2	3	4	5	6	7

Quality of Communication
The organization keeps me well informed about its mission and pending changes.

Never						Always
1	2	3	4	5	6	7

Organizational Climate
My workplace generally feels like

A cold, rainy day						A warm, sunny day
1	2	3	4	5	6	7

Job Design
The work I do is

Routine and boring						Varied and challenging
1	2	3	4	5	6	7

Unimportant						Important
1	2	3	4	5	6	7

Feedback and Compensation
I am given timely and constructive feedback.

False						True
1	2	3	4	5	6	7

I am paid fairly for what I do.

False						True
1	2	3	4	5	6	7

Coworkers
My coworkers are

Negative and unfriendly						Positive and friendly
1	2	3	4	5	6	7

Work Hours and Schedules
My work hours and schedules are flexible and accommodate my lifestyle.

Never						Always
1	2	3	4	5	6	7

Organizational Identification
I have a strong sense of commitment and loyalty to my work organization.

False						True
1	2	3	4	5	6	7

Stress
The degree of unhealthy stress in my workplace is

Very high						Very low
1	2	3	4	5	6	7

Total quality-of-work-life score = _______

Scale
12–35 = Warning—this job could be hazardous to your health
36–60 = Why spend half your waking life settling for average?
61–84 = T.G.I.M. (Thank goodness it's *Monday*!)

For Consideration/Discussion

1. Which of these various quality-of-work-life factors is of overriding importance to you? Why? Which are least important? Why?
2. How strongly does your quality-of-work-life score correlate with the amount of effort you put into your job? Explain the connection.
3. How helpful would this survey be in your search for a better job? Explain.
4. How much does your total score reflect your attitude about life in general?
5. What should your managers do to improve the quality-of-work-life scores for you and your coworkers?
6. How important is quality of worklife to your overall lifestyle and happiness? Explain.

INTERNET EXERCISES

1. **More on open-book management (OBM):** As discussed in this chapter, OBM is an underused way to reap the benefits of participative management. It requires managers to rethink some of their assumptions about managing people. A good place to begin is with a free tutorial at **www.bizcenter.com**. At the home page, click on "Open-Book Management" in the Alphabetical Index. Next, scroll down and select "To Book Excerpt" and read the brief tutorial on OBM.

   Learning Points: 1. Name two or three useful insights about OBM that you gained from this tutorial. 2. Does OBM appeal to you? Explain. 3. Do you believe OBM has great promise in the business world? Why or why not? 4. What are the major stumbling blocks for OBM in today's typical organizations? How can they be overcome?

2. **More on wellness: Getting the upper hand on heart disease:** According to the American Heart Association, "nearly 62 million Americans have some form of cardiovascular disease, and nearly 1 million die from it each year. . . . Heart disease ranks as the No. 1 killer in the USA, although one-third of those deaths could be prevented if people ate better diets and exercised more."[121] A good place to start your personal battle against heart disease is with a risk assessment. You can do that free online at **www.yourdiseaserisk.harvard.edu**. At the home page, click on "What's your heart disease risk?" and complete the questionnaire. Simply follow the prompts to interpret your score and to discover what you're doing right and what things you need to do to lower your risk of heart disease. If you have the time to take them, you will find the other disease-risk quizzes very instructive as well.

   Learning Points: 1. Are you surprised at the results of your quiz? Why? 2. What do you need to do to lower your risk of heart disease? What is your action plan?

3. **Check it out:** Are you underpaid? Need supporting evidence to ask for a raise? Want to know how much you could make if you switched jobs or careers? Like to know how much someone else makes? Go online to **www.salary.com** and put the Salary Wizard to work.

For updates to these exercises, visit our Web site (**http://business.college.hmco.com/students/** and select Kreitner, *Management*, 10e).

CLOSING CASE

The Taj's People Philosophy and STAR System

"The employee at Taj is viewed as an asset and is the real profit center. He or she is the very reason for our survival. The creation of the Taj People Philosophy displays our commitment to and belief in our people. We want an organization with a very clear philosophy, where we can treasure people and build from within."

- Bernard Martyris, Senior Vice-President, HR, Indian Hotels Company Limited (IHCL).

Introduction

In March 2001, the Taj Group[1] launched an employee loyalty program called the 'Special Thanks and Recognition System' (STARS). STARS was an initiative aimed at motivating employees to transcend their usual duties and responsibilities and have fun during work. This program also acknowledged and rewarded hard working employees who had done excellent work.

The Taj Group had always believed that their employees were their greatest assets and the very reason for the survival of their business. In 2000, to show its commitment to and belief in employees, the Taj Group developed the 'Taj People Philosophy' (TPP), which covered all the people practices of the group. TPP considered every aspect of employees' organizational career planning, right from their induction into the company till their superannuation.

TPP offered many benefits to the Taj Group. It helped the company boost the morale of its employees and improve service standards, which in turn resulted in repeat customers for many hotels in the group. The STAR system also led to global recognition of the Taj Group of hotels in 2002 when the group bagged the 'Hermes Award'[2] for 'Best Innovation in Human Resources' in the global hospitality industry.

The Taj People Philosophy

Since its establishment, the Taj Group had a people-oriented culture. The group always hired fresh graduates from leading hotel management institutes all over India so that it could shape their attitudes and develop their skills in a way that fitted its needs and culture. The management wanted the new recruits to pursue a long-term career with the group. All new employees were placed in an intensive two-year training program, which familiarized them with the business ethos of the group, the management practices of the organization, and the working of cross-functional departments.

The employees of the Taj Group were trained in varied fields like sales and marketing, finance, hospitality and service, front office management, food and beverages, projects, HR and more. They also had to take part in various leadership programs, so that they could develop in them a strong, warm and professional work culture. Through these programs, the group was able to assess the future potential of the employees and the training required to further develop their skills. The group offered excellent opportunities to employees both on personal as well as organizational front[3] . In order to achieve 'Taj standards,' employees were made to undergo a rigorous training program. The group strove hard to standardize all its processes and evolve a work culture, which appealed to all its employees universally.

The group believed that talent management[4] was of utmost importance to develop a sustainable competitive advantage. The group aimed at making the HR function a critical business partner, rather than just a support function. To further show its commitment to and belief in employees, the group created the 'Taj People Philosophy' (TPP) covering all people practices of the group. The concept of TPP, developed in 1999, was the brainchild of Bernard Martyris (Martyris), Senior Vice-President, HR, IHCL, and his core team. The concept, originally planned to be called as 'The Womb to Tomb Approach,' covered all the aspects of an employee's career, from joining the group until his/her retirement. TPP was based on the key points of the Taj employee charter (Refer Table I). It was developed in line with the Tata Business Excellence Model (TBEM).[5] Explaining the rationale for implementing the philosophy, Martyris said, "It is to achieve that international benchmarking in hospitality, and HR must fit into it." According to him, the three major areas of TPP included work systems and processes; learning and development; and employee welfare.

As part of the TPP, the Taj Group introduced a strong performance management[6] system, called the Balanced Scorecard System (BSS) that linked individual performance with the group's overall strategy. BSS was based on a model developed by Kaplan and Nortan[7], and focused on enhancing both individual as well as enterprise performance. BSS measured the performance of employees across all hierarchical levels against a set of predefined targets and identified their variances. Martyris explained, "We are looking at a matrix form of organization which cuts across hierarchy. It is important to understand the potential of people." Therefore, BSS was implemented even at the lowest levels of the hierarchy.

[1] *The Taj Group of Hotels is run by IHCL, a part of the Tata Group. IHCL was founded by Jamsetji Nusserwanji Tata on April 1, 1902. The hotels in the Taj Group fall into three categories - hotels owned by IHCL and its subsidiaries; hotels owned by associate companies; and hotels with third party management contracts in which IHCL has no stake.*

[2] *The 'Hermes Award' is decided by a 22-member jury, which includes representatives from top hospitality chains from all over the world. This is the only award given for human resources in the hospitality industry and is also one of the most prestigious awards in the hospitality industry. 120 applications were received for the award for the year 2002, among which five were short-listed for the final round. The Taj Group won the award for its innovative 'STAR' program.*

[3] *On personal front, the Taj Group offered its employees personal counseling and empathized with their problems. On organizational front, it offered its employees ample scope for career advancement, training programs, excellent opportunities for learning and sharing, and self-development programs.*

[4] *The strategic and tactical management of talent in the organization. Talent Management is a strategic business function that involves an organization's ability to attract, recruit, hire and retain the right talent at the right time and align it with its business goals.*

[5] *TBEM provides guidelines for the introduction of business systems into the organization and correlates business performance and rewards to individuals. The TBEM includes systems for reviewing talent and offering opportunities across various functions within the group companies.*

[6] *Performance management is the process of creating a work environment or setting in which people are enabled to perform to the best of their abilities. Performance management is a total work system that begins when a job is defined as needed. It ends when an employee leaves the organization.*

[7] *Professors at the Harvard Business School (HBS).*

Table I Key Points of the Taj Charter

Some of the key points of the Taj Charter are given below:
- Every employee of the Taj Group would be an important member in the Taj family.
- The Taj family would always strive to attract, retain and reward the best talent in the industry.
- The Taj family would commit itself to formal communication channels, which would foster transparency.

The BSS included an Employee Satisfaction Tracking System (ESTS), which solved employees' problems on a quarterly basis. As a part of ESTS, Taj carried out an organization wide employee satisfaction survey in mid 2000 of about 9000 employees. According to this survey, the reported satisfaction level was about 75 percent. The group aimed to increase this level to 90-95 percent, and eventually to 100 percent.

The group also took strong measures to weed out under-performers. The group adopted the 360-degree feedback system to evaluate the performance of all top officials, from the Managing Director to departmental managers, in which they were evaluated by their immediate subordinates. The 360-degree feedback was followed by personal interviews of individuals to counsel them to overcome their deficiencies.

The Taj Group also established Centers of Excellence for its 14,000 employees at five locations in India including Jaipur, Bangalore, Ernakulam, Chennai and Hyderabad. At these centers, departmental heads in each functional area were trained. These departmental heads later trained their own staff. The training included foundation modules and accreditation programs that familiarized the employees with Taj standards.

Apart from adopting stringent measures to improve performance, Taj also recognized and rewarded its best employees across all levels of the organization. For this purpose, Taj created a unique employee loyalty and reward program known as STARS. Describing the program, Martyris said, "It's an HR initiative aimed at creating an association between our star performers and our brand, the Taj."

The STAR System

The STAR system (STARS) was the brainchild of Martyris. The system was developed in accordance with Taj's core philosophy that 'happy employees lead to happy customers.' STARS, operative throughout the year (from April to March), was open to all employees across the organization, at all hierarchical levels. It aimed to identify, recognize and reward those employees who excelled in their work. STARS was actively promoted across the group's 62 chain of hotels and among its 18,000 employees globally, out of which 15,000 were from India.

STARS had five different levels. Though employees did not receive any cash awards, they gained recognition by the levels they attained through the points they accumulated for their acts of kindness or hospitality. 'Level 1' was known as the 'Silver Grade'. To reach this level, employees had to accumulate 120 points in three months. To attain 'Level 2', known as the 'Gold Grade,' employees had to accumulate 130 points within three months of attaining the silver grade. To reach 'Level 3', called the 'Platinum Grade', employees had to accumulate 250 points within six months of attaining the gold grade. To attain 'Level 4', employees had to accumulate 510 or more points, but below 760 points, to be a part of the Chief Operating Officer's club. 'Level 5' which was the highest level in STARS, enabled employees to be a part of the MD's club, if they accumulated 760 or more points.

Points were granted to employees on the basis of parameters like integrity, honesty, kindness, respect for customers, environmental awareness, teamwork, coordination, cooperation, excellence in work, new initiatives, trustworthiness, courage and conviction, among others. Suggestions by employees that benefited the organization fetched them significant points. Such suggestions in each hotel of the Taj Group were examined by the General Manager, HR Manager and training manager of the hotel the employee worked in. The suggestions could also be posted on the web, which were constantly monitored.

Employees could also earn points through appreciation by customers, 'compliment-a-colleague' forums[8] and various suggestion schemes. Employees could also get 'default points' if the review committee did not give feedback to the employee within two days of his/her offering a suggestion for the betterment of the organization. In such cases, the employee concerned was awarded '20 default points.' Hence, in an indirect manner, the system compelled judges of the review committee to give feedback to employees as early as possible.

STARS helped employees work together as a team and appreciate fellow employees for their acts of kindness and excellence. It enhanced their motivation levels and led to increased customer satisfaction. In one case, a bellboy in one of the group's hotel who received an American customer went out of his way to care for the customer. Noticing that the customer, who had arrived late at night, was suffering from cold, he offered to bring him a doctor. However, the customer refused the boy's offer. The bellboy then, on his own, offered a glass of

[8] *The program encourages the employees to work together and compliment each other.*

warm water mixed with ginger and honey, a traditional Indian home remedy for cough and cold. The customer felt surprised and also happy at the bellboy's gesture. He left a note of appreciation for him, which added to his existing points.

According to the number of points accumulated, employees would receive a star, which could be pinned on to their coat. When a certain number of points were collected, employees received gift hampers, cash vouchers or a vacation in a Taj Hotel of their choice in India. The winners of STARS were felicitated at a function held in Taj, Mumbai. The winners' photographs were displayed on a big screen at the function and they received awards given by the MD of the Taj Group. This awards ceremony significantly boosted their morale.

The Future Plans

The STARS program had generated lot of attention among the employees at the Taj Group. During the initial phase, not every hotel seemed to be serious about adopting STARS, but after the first awards ceremony was conducted, every hotel in the group reportedly became very serious about the implementation of STARS. Reportedly, customer satisfaction levels increased significantly after the implementation of STARS. Commenting on the success of STARS, Martyris said, "After the campaign was launched, a large number of employees have started working together in the true spirit of teams and this helps us value our human capital. There are stars all around us but very often we look only at stars outside the system. Many employees do that extra bit and go that extra mile, out of the way to dazzle the customer satisfaction with employee recognition. Employee recognition is, hence, directly linked to customer satisfaction. It is recognition for the people, of the people and by the people." STARS was also used by the group as an appraisal system, in addition to its regular appraisal system.

The STARS was not only successful as an HR initiative, but it brought many strategic benefits to the group as well. The service standards at all hotels of the group improved significantly because the employees felt that their good work was being acknowledged and appreciated. This resulted in repeat customers for Taj hotels. Because of STARS, the Group won the 'Hermes Award 2002' for 'best innovation in HR' in the hospitality industry. Analysts felt that the fame and recognition associated with the winning of the Hermes Award would place the Taj Group of Hotels at the top of the list of the best hotels in the world. The group also received requests for setting up hotels in Paris (France), where the 'Hermes award' function took place.

The HR practices at the Taj Group attracted several Human Resources and Organizational Behavior experts' world over. In late 2001, Thomas J. Delong, a professor of Organizational Behavior from Harvard Business School (HBS), visited India and interviewed various employees in the Taj Group. After his visit, the Taj Group was "envisioned as an example of organizational transformation wherein key dimensions of cultural change went into the making of global managers." Analysts also felt that social responsibility and people-centric programs were the core values at Taj Group, which were well demonstrated through the 'Taj People Philosophy.' Martyris said, "The challenges here lay in retaining the warmth and relationship focus of the Taj and inculcating a systems-driven approach to service."

Analysts felt that the Taj Group had been highly successful because of its ability to provide better opportunities and give greater recognition to its employees, which motivated them to work to the best of their abilities. The Employee Retention Rate (ERR) of the Taj Group was the highest in the hospitality industry because of its employee-oriented initiatives. In spite of the highest ERR; Martyris felt that the retention of talent was Taj's major challenge. He said, "Our staff is routinely poached by not just industry competitors but also banks, call centers and others. In 2002, in the placements process at the hotel management institute run by the Taj, more than half of those passing out were hired by non-hospitality companies. While we are happy to see the growth and opportunity for this sector, we also feel there is a need for introspection. Are we offering swift and smooth career paths to our employees? How am I to retain staffers from moving across industries?"

In late 2002, the Taj Group, to demonstrate its strong belief in employees, announced plans to make further investments in training, development, career planning and employee welfare. The group also tried to standardize its various processes and develop a common work culture. After winning the Hermes Award in 2002, the group also planned to nominate the BSS for the Hermes Awards 2003.

For Discussion

1. "The Taj People Philosophy was developed to show the Taj Group's commitment to and belief in employees." What did the philosophy entail and what were its key components? Explain.
2. The STARS program was created to reward employees to deliver their best at the workplace. In what way did this program acknowledge the work of its employees, and what were the various levels of recognition it offered to its best employees? How did the program achieve its goal? Explain.
3. STARS was not only successful as an HR initiative, but it brought several strategic benefits to the Taj Group. What were the various benefits brought about by the STARS program to the employees and the group? How? Discuss.

Source: *Case Studies in Human Resource Management, Volume II, ICFAI Center for Management Research, Hyderabad, 2004, pp. 402-409.*

TEST PREPPER

True/False Questions

_____ **1.** On Maslow's hierarchy of needs, social needs rank above self-actualization needs.

_____ **2.** According to Herzberg's theory of motivation, salary and supervision are dissatisfiers.

_____ **3.** Rewards play a role in the expectancy model of motivation.

_____ **4.** Participative goals are less effective than imposed goals.

_____ **5.** Contingent time off involves letting employees go home when they do not feel like working.

_____ **6.** A critical psychological state in the job enrichment model is "Feeling that the work is meaningful."

_____ **7.** Perceived inequity can be experienced by employees who are either underpaid or overpaid.

_____ **8.** The S.T.E.P. acronym, in open-book management, stands for share, teach, empower, and perform.

_____ **9.** In a flextime program, workers can arrive at work whenever they choose.

_____ **10.** By definition, family-friendly companies help employees achieve a productive and satisfying balance between work and life outside the workplace.

Multiple-Choice Questions

1. What needs rank at the very top of Maslow's hierarchy of needs?
A. Esteem
B. Love
C. Physiological needs
D. Safety
E. Self-actualization

2. Which of the following motivate(s) employees *most* effectively, according to Herzberg?
A. Good working conditions
B. The work itself
C. Money
D. Supportive supervision
E. Supportive coworkers

3. How do rewards influence motivational strength in the expectancy model?
A. Rewards do not play a role in expectancy theory.
B. They erode intrinsic motivation.
C. They have little impact on motivation.
D. They motivate effort but not results.
E. Through the perception that effort will lead to valued rewards.

4. Goals motivate performance by doing all of the following *except*
A. directing attention.
B. fostering action plans.
C. fostering teamwork.
D. encouraging effort.
E. encouraging persistence.

5. _____ involve(s) telling recruits about both the good and the bad aspects of a particular job.
A. Realistic job previews
B. Job enlargement
C. Job enrichment
D. Job rotation
E. Cafeteria compensation

6. Doing a "whole" piece of work from beginning to end is the defining characteristic of which of the following?
A. Job feedback
B. Task significance
C. Autonomy
D. Skill variety
E. Task identity

7. According to the experts at the U.S. Bureau of Labor Statistics, the term(s) _____ will apply to future compensation plans.
A. time-based
B. lean and uniform
C. flexible and varied
D. uniform and standardized
E. skill-based

8. The equity of rewards is said to be weighed by people on which two scales?
A. Intrinsic and extrinsic
B. Short-term and long-term
C. Personal and organizational
D. Technical and social
E. Personal and social

9. The "S" in the S.T.E.P. approach to open-book management stands for
A. share.
B. separate.
C. sales.
D. strength.
E. success.

10. How does the text characterize the U.S. Family and Medical Leave Act that took effect in 1993?
A. Long overdue universal coverage
B. More generous than state laws
C. The first law to require paid leave for everyone
D. Probably unconstitutional
E. Has significant holes and limitations

ACE self-test

Want more questions? Visit the student Web site at **http://business.college.hmco.com/students/** (select Kreitner, *Management,* 10e) and take the ACE quizzes for more practice.

14 Group Dynamics and Teamwork

> *"Business is a team sport."*[1]
>
> **GREGORY D. BRENNEMAN, CEO, BURGER KING**

OBJECTIVES

- **Define** the term *group.*
- **Explain** the significance of cohesiveness, roles, norms, and ostracism in regard to the behavior of group members.
- **Identify** and briefly **describe** the six stages of group development.
- **Define** *organizational politics,* and **summarize** relevant research insights.
- **Explain** how groupthink can lead to blind conformity.
- **Define** and **discuss** the management of virtual teams.
- **Discuss** the criteria and determinants of team effectiveness.
- **Explain** why trust is a key ingredient of teamwork, and **discuss** what management can do to build trust.

the changing workplace

Do Business and Friendship Mix in the Workplace?

Penny Baker always considered himself the "huggy, touchy" type. Indeed, the 38-year-old Austin [Texas] entrepreneur—a former car salesman whose first business consisted of selling "Bad Cop, No Donut" T shirts in the back of *Rolling Stone* magazine—is the opposite of stuffy. So in 1997, when he founded National Bankcard Systems, he wanted the provider of credit card terminals and Internet payment systems to be as friendly as possible. He hired close friends for key positions and socialized with his staff on a regular basis, going out for happy hour or dinner as often as four nights a week. The company thrived, growing to 75 employees and $5.3 million in sales in just three years.

But Baker began to sense that his huggy, touchy managing style was no longer working. A number of employees, all of them perfectly pleasant as drinking buddies or dinner companions, had grown complacent, behaving as though they had earned some kind of tenure. Even some longtime friends were slacking off. "I figured if I hired my buddies, they'd work their butts off for me," Baker says. Instead, he had to fire two of them. The last straw came one night at happy hour when one of his salespeople—the brother of a college pal—got drunk and proclaimed that he could do a better job than Baker and was starting a rival business. It was then that Baker realized he had a lot to learn about the difference between being a friend and being a boss.

The fact is, there are no clear-cut rules when it comes to mixing business and buddies. At big corporations, with their often elaborate and rigid hierarchies, this isn't much of a problem. But small companies tend to be far less formal, often behaving more like families. That puts entrepreneurs in a tough spot. Act too chummy and you risk losing employees' respect. But behave too formally and you sacrifice the team spirit and bonhomie on which small companies thrive. "When you show employees that you care about them as people, they may feel an emotional attachment to you and work harder," says Glenn Okun, a professor at New York University's Leonard N. Stern School of Business who advises CEOs. "But there's also a significant risk involved."

In Baker's case, "hugginess" felt perfectly appropriate when his company was small. But once National Bankcard reached new levels of size and sophistication, he knew it was time to separate the ranks. "It's not that I think I'm better than my employees," he says. "But I don't want people to feel like I owe them anything because we're friends." The happy-hour incident only served to drive that point home. So Baker changed his approach. He still prides himself on being a nice boss who encourages employees to have fun—say, throwing officewide pizza parties to celebrate strong sales. But he says he keeps employees at "arm's length" now, behaving in a more businesslike manner, and avoiding any involvement in their personal affairs. . . .

Of course, forming close, personal bonds in the workplace sometimes can be a smart management strategy. Employees with a strong connection to their bosses are more likely to be loyal, work harder, and stick around longer, says Denise Rousseau, a professor of organizational behavior at Carnegie Mellon University, who recently asked top executives at 80 start-ups about their human resources strategies. Most of the CEOs surveyed, she says, found a friendly and congenial office atmosphere to be a competitive advantage. Such an environment "can beat off alternative job offers and itchy feet," Rousseau says, and is as effective a motivator as bonuses, raises, and other typical perks. That's especially true at small companies, where entrepreneurs often expect employees to work long hours and be willing to wear many different hats.

That said, Rousseau is not suggesting bosses open up about the nitty-gritty details of their personal lives. "But if you're having a bad week because your son's been sick," she says, "better to let them know than have them wonder if the company's in trouble." Meanwhile, explaining your personal motivations for founding the business encourages employees to buy in to the company's mission. And taking an interest in employees' home lives or kids' soccer teams conveys that you're interested not only in their professional success, but in their personal struggles, as well—another great motivator, Rousseau says. . . .

[A]fter two years, . . . [Baker] recently broke his own rule against hiring friends and reluctantly brought on a longtime pal who wouldn't take no for an answer. He made it clear that working together could mean the end of the friendship if, say, the business starts to falter. "We're rolling the dice," he warned him. "If it doesn't work out, you, your parents, and your wife may blame it on me." So far, Baker is happy to report, it's going pretty well. "I think there are exceptions," he says. "But is it worth losing a friend to find that out?"

Source: *By Nadine Heintz, © 2004 Gruner & Jahr, USA Publishing. First published in* Inc. Magazine. *Reprinted with permission.*

As in daily life itself, relationships rule in modern organizations. The more managers know about building and sustaining good working relationships, the better. A management consultant put it this way:

> *At the end of the day, a company's only sustainable competitive advantage is its relationships with customers, business partners, and employees. After all, we provide products and services to people, not to companies. A commitment to developing effective relationships strengthens the fabric of the organization in the long run.*[2]

social capital: *productive potential of strong relationships, goodwill, trust, and cooperation*

What is involved here is the concept of **social capital**, "productive potential resulting from strong relationships, goodwill, trust, and cooperative effort."[3] In line with our discussion of human capital in Chapter 11, managers need to build social capital by working on strong, constructive, and mutually beneficial relationships. This often involves delicate balancing acts, as entrepreneur Penny Baker learned the hard way. The purpose of this chapter is to build a foundation of understanding about how groups and teams function in today's organizations.

Fundamental Group Dynamics

According to one organization theorist, "All groups may be collections of individuals, but all collections of individuals are not groups."[4] This observation is more than a play on words; mere togetherness does not automatically create a group. Consider, for example, this situation. Half a dozen people who worked for different companies in the same building often shared the same elevator in the morning. As time passed, they introduced themselves and exchanged pleasantries. Eventually, four of the elevator riders discovered that they all lived in the same suburb. Arrangements for a car pool were made, and they began to take turns picking up and delivering one another. A group technically came into existence only when the car pool was formed. To understand why this is so, we need to examine the definition of the term *group*.

What Is a Group?

group: *two or more freely interacting individuals with a common identity and purpose*

1. DEFINE the term *group*.

From a sociological perspective, a **group** can be defined as two or more freely interacting individuals who share a common identity and purpose.[5] Careful analysis of this definition reveals four important dimensions (see Figure 14.1). First, a group must be made up of two or more people if it is to be considered a social unit. Second, the individuals must freely interact in some manner. An organization may qualify as a sociological group if it is small and personal enough to permit all its members to interact regularly with each other. Generally, however, larger organizations with bureaucratic tendencies are made up of many overlapping groups. Third, the interacting individuals must share a common identity. Each must recognize himself or herself as a member of the group. Fourth, these interacting individuals who have a common identity must also have a common purpose. That is, there must be at least a rough consensus on why the group exists.

Types of Groups

Human beings belong to groups for many different reasons. Some people join a group as an end in itself. For example, an accountant may enjoy the socializing that is part of belonging to a group at a local health club. That same accountant's membership in a work group is a means to a professional end. Both the exercise group and the work group satisfy the sociological definition of a group, but they fulfill very different needs. The former is an informal group, and the latter is a formal group.

Figure 14.1 What Does It Take to Make a Group?

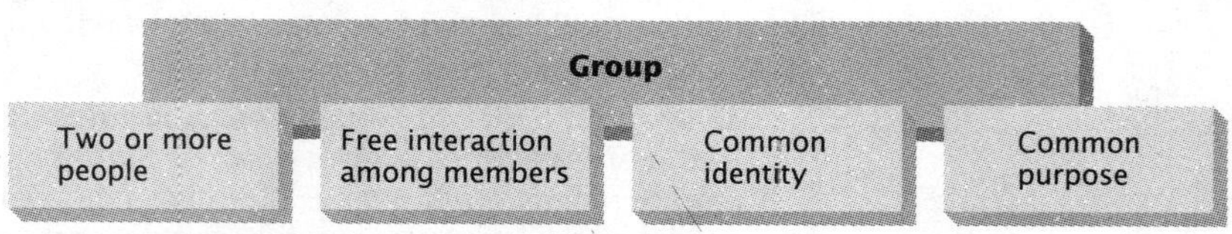

14a An Uphill Battle?

Max De Pree, former CEO of Herman Miller, the Michigan office furniture maker:

In our group activities, intimacy is betrayed by such things as politics, short-term measurements, arrogance, superficiality, and an orientation toward self rather than toward the good of the group.

Source: Max De Pree, Leadership Is an Art *(New York: Dell, 1989), p. 56.*

QUESTIONS:

Which of the various barriers to effective group action mentioned by De Pree is the most difficult for managers to overcome? Why? Is De Pree being too negative, or is he just being realistic? Explain.

For further information about the interactive annotations in this chapter, visit our Web site (**http://business.college.hmco.com/students**) and select Kreitner, *Management,* 10e.

■ **Informal Groups.** As Abraham Maslow pointed out, a feeling of belonging is a powerful motivator. People generally have a great need to fit in, to be liked, to be one of the gang. Whether a group meets at work or during leisure time, it is still an **informal group** if the principal reason for belonging is friendship.[6] Informal groups usually evolve spontaneously. They serve to satisfy esteem needs because one develops a better self-image when accepted, recognized, and liked by others. Sometimes, as in the case of a group of friends forming an investment club, an informal group may evolve into a formal one.

informal group: *collection of people seeking friendship*

Managers cannot afford to ignore informal groups because grassroots social networks can either advance or threaten the organization's mission.[7] As experts on the subject explained,

> *These informal networks can cut through formal reporting procedures to jump-start stalled initiatives and meet extraordinary deadlines. But informal networks can just as easily sabotage companies' best-laid plans by blocking communication and fomenting opposition to change unless managers know how to identify and direct them. . . .*
>
> *If the formal organization is the skeleton of a company, the informal is the central nervous system driving the collective thought processes, actions, and reactions of its business units. Designed to facilitate standard modes of production, the formal organization is set up to handle easily anticipated problems. But when unexpected problems arise, the informal organization kicks in. Its complex web of social ties forms every time colleagues communicate and solidif[ies] over time into surprisingly stable networks. Highly adaptive, informal networks move diagonally and elliptically, skipping entire functions to get work done.*[8]

By definition, these people qualify as a formal group because they are assembled to do a job. Sharing some laughs while working makes them a more cohesive group. If they socialize together after work, they could also qualify as an informal group. For better or for worse, formal and informal groups often overlap.

formal group: *collection of people created to do something productive*

■ **Formal Groups.** A **formal group** is a group created for the purpose of doing productive work. It may be called a team, a committee, or simply a work group. Whatever its name, a formal group is usually formed for the purpose of contributing to the success of a larger organization. Formal groups tend to be more rationally structured and less fluid than informal groups. Rather than joining formal task groups, people are assigned to them according to their talents and the organization's needs. One person normally is granted formal leadership responsibility to ensure that the members carry out their assigned duties. Informal friendship groups, in contrast, generally do not have officially appointed leaders, although informal leaders often emerge by popular demand. For the individual, the formal group and an informal group at the place of employment may or may not overlap. In other words, one may or may not be friends with one's coworkers.

14b Back to the Opening Case

Where should a manager draw the line between business and friendship in the workplace? Are the "rules" different for an entrepreneur such as Penny Baker and a manager at a large company?

■ Attraction to Groups

What attracts a person to one group but not to another? And why do some groups' members stay whereas others leave? Managers who can answer these questions can take steps to motivate others to join and remain members of a formal work group. Individual commitment to either an informal or a formal group hinges on two factors. The first is *attractiveness*, the outside-looking-in view.[9] A nonmember will want to join a group that is attractive and will shy away from a group that is unattractive. The second factor is **cohesiveness**, the tendency of group members to follow the group and resist outside influences. This is the inside-looking-out view. In a highly cohesive group, individual members tend to see themselves as "we" rather than "I." Cohesive group members stick together.[10]

cohesiveness: *tendency of a group to stick together*

2. EXPLAIN the significance of cohesiveness, roles, norms, and ostracism in regard to the behavior of group members.

Factors that either enhance or destroy group attractiveness and cohesiveness are listed in Table 14.1. It is important to note that each factor is a matter of degree. For example, a group may offer the individual little, moderate, or great opportunity for prestige and status. Similarly, group demands on the individual may range from somewhat disagreeable to highly disagreeable. What all this means is that both the decision to join a group and the decision to continue being a member depend on a net balance of the factors in Table 14.1. Naturally, the resulting balance is colored by one's perception and frame of reference, as it was in the case of Richard Dale, a former manager of distribution at Commodore International, during his first meeting with the company's founder, Jack Tramiel.

Table 14.1 Factors That Enhance or Detract from Group Attractiveness and Cohesiveness

Factors that enhance	Factors that detract
1. Prestige and status	1. Unreasonable or disagreeable demands on the individual
2. Cooperative relationship	2. Disagreement over procedures, activities, rules, and the like
3. High degree of interaction	3. Unpleasant experience with the group
4. Relatively small size	4. Competition between the group's demands and preferred outside activities
5. Similarity of members	5. Unfavorable public image of the group
6. Superior public image of the group	6. Competition for membership by other groups
7. A common threat in the environment	

Source: *Table adapted from* Group Dynamics: Research and Theory, *2nd ed., by Dorwin Cartwright and Alvin Zander. New York: HarperCollins Publishers, Inc.*

14c Toward a Sense of *Community* in the Workplace

Carolyn Schaffer and Kristin Anundsen, authors of the book *Creating Community Anywhere: Finding Support and Connection in a Fragmented World*:

> *Community is a dynamic whole that emerges when a group of people:*
> - *Participate in common practices;*
> - *Depend upon one another;*
> - *Make decisions together;*
> - *Identify themselves as part of something larger than the sum of their individual relationships; and*
> - *Commit themselves for the long term to their own, one another's, and the group's well-being.*

Source: Quoted in Ron Zemke, "The Call of Community," Training, *33 (March 1996): 27.*

QUESTIONS:
How important is it to build this sense of community in today's work groups and organizations? Explain. What is your personal experience with a genuine feeling of community? Are we naïve to expect a sense of community in today's hurried and rapidly changing workplace? Explain.

> *Dale's first meeting with Tramiel began with a summons to appear at Tramiel's office. Dale flew from his office in Los Angeles to Santa Clara . . ., only to find that Tramiel had decided to visit him instead.*
>
> *Terrified, Dale caught a plane back to find his secretary shaking in her shoes and the burly Tramiel sitting at his desk. For an hour Tramiel grilled Dale on his philosophy of business, pronounced it all wrong, and suggested a tour of the warehouse. When they passed boxes of . . . [computers] waiting for shipment, recalls Dale, Tramiel seemed to "go crazy," pounding the boxes with his fists and yelling, "Do you think this is bourbon? Do you think it gets better with age?"*[11]

Dale's departure within a few months of this episode is not surprising in view of the fact that Tramiel's conduct destroyed work group attractiveness and cohesiveness.

■ Roles

According to Shakespeare, "All the world's a stage, and all the men and women merely players." In fact, Shakespeare's analogy between life and play-acting can be carried a step further—to organizations and their component formal work groups. Although employees do not have scripts, they do have formal positions in the organizational hierarchy, and they are expected to adhere to company policies and rules. Furthermore, job descriptions and procedure manuals spell out how jobs are to be done. In short, every employee has one or more organizational roles to play. An organization that is appropriately structured, in which everyone plays his or her role(s) effectively and efficiently, will have a greater chance for organizational success.

A social psychologist has described the concept of *role* as follows:

> *The term role is used to refer to (1) a set of expectations concerning what a person in a given position must, must not, or may do, and (2) the actual behavior of the person who occupies the position. A central idea is that any person occupying a position and filling a role behaves similarly to anyone else who could be in that position.*[12]

role: *socially determined way of behaving in a specific position*

A **role**, then, is a socially determined prescription for behavior in a *specific* position. Roles evolve out of the tendency for social units to perpetuate themselves, and roles are socially enforced. Role models are a powerful influence. They are indispensable to those trying to resolve the inherent conflicts between work and family roles, for example.[13]

■ Norms

norms: *general standards of conduct for various social settings*

Norms define "degrees of acceptability and unacceptability."[14] More precisely, **norms** are general standards of conduct that help individuals judge what is right or wrong or good or bad in a given social setting (such as work, home, play, or religious organization). Because norms are culturally derived, they vary from one culture to another. For example, public disagreement and debate, which are normal in Western societies, are often considered rude in Eastern countries such as Japan.

Figure 14.2 Norms Are Enforced for Different Reasons

Sample norms	Why these norms would be enforced
"Don't criticize the work of our Celebrating Diversity Task Force in front of the director of finance, a person who thinks we're wasting time and money."	Helps the group survive
"Make sure you've done your homework before meeting with the division head."	Clarifies role expectations
"Don't discuss religion in the company cafeteria."	Avoids embarrassment and protects self-images
"Listen carefully to complaints from minority employees because, unlike the other shifts, the second-shift supervisors have never had a discrimination complaint filed against them."	Emphasizes key values and enhances group's identity

Norms have a broader influence than roles, which focus on a specific position. Although usually unwritten, norms influence behavior enormously.[15]

Every mature group, whether informal or formal, generates its own pattern of norms that constrains and directs the behavior of its members. Norms are enforced for at least four different reasons:

1. To facilitate survival of the group
2. To simplify or clarify role expectations
3. To help group members avoid embarrassing situations (protect self-images)
4. To express key group values and enhance the group's unique identity[16]

As illustrated in Figure 14.2, norms tend to go above and beyond formal rules and written policies. Compliance is shaped with social reinforcement in the form of attention, recognition, and acceptance.[17] Those who fail to comply with the norm may be criticized or ridiculed. For example, consider the pressure Gwendolyn Kelly experienced in medical school:

> *The word among students is that if you've got any brains, "tertiary" medicine—which involves complex diagnostic procedures and comprehensive care—is where it's at. Instructors often refer to the best students as "future surgeons" and belittle the family-practice specialty. These attitudes trickle down. I've heard my peers say the reason so many women choose pediatrics is that "they want to be mommies." And students who take a family-practice residency may be maligned by colleagues who say the choice is a sign of subpar academic credentials.*[18]

Reformers of the U.S. health care system, who want to increase the number of primary care (family practice) doctors from one-third to one-half, need to begin by altering medical school norms.

ostracism: *rejection from a group*

Worse than ridicule is the threat of being ostracized. **Ostracism**, or rejection from the group, is figuratively the capital punishment of group dynamics. Informal groups derive much of their power over individuals through the ever-present threat of ostracism. Thus, informal norms play a pivotal role in on-the-job ethics.[19] Police officers, for example, who honor the traditional "code of silence" norm that demands *total* loyalty to one's fellow officers, face a tough moral dilemma.

Group Development

Like inept youngsters who mature into talented adults, groups undergo a maturation process before becoming effective. We have all experienced the uneasiness associated with the first meeting of a new group, be it a class, club, or committee. Initially, there is little mutual understanding, trust, or commitment among the new group members, and their uncertainty about objectives, roles, and leadership doesn't help. The prospect of cooperative action seems unlikely in view of defensive behavior and differences of opinion about who should do what. Someone steps forward to assume a leadership role, and the group is off and running toward eventual maturity (or perhaps premature demise). A working knowledge of the characteristics of a mature group can help managers envision a goal for the group development process.

Characteristics of a Mature Group

If and when a group takes on the following characteristics, it can be called a mature group.

1. Members are aware of their own and each other's assets and liabilities vis-à-vis the group's task.
2. These individual differences are accepted without being labeled as good or bad.
3. The group has developed authority and interpersonal relationships that are recognized and accepted by the members.
4. Group decisions are made through rational discussion. Minority opinions and dissension are recognized and encouraged. Attempts are not made to force decisions or a false unanimity.
5. Conflict is over substantive group issues such as group goals and the effectiveness and efficiency of various means for achieving those goals. Conflict over emotional issues regarding group structure, processes, or interpersonal relationships is at a minimum.
6. Members are aware of the group's processes and their own roles in them.[20]

Group development is both important and a bit more challenging in today's diverse workplaces. People from different backgrounds bring different perspectives, values, and issues to the table. Here, Nike's Ethnic Diversity Council meets to gather ideas and plot strategy.

Effectiveness and productivity should increase as the group matures. Recent research with groups of school teachers found positive evidence in this regard. The researchers concluded, "Faculty groups functioning at higher levels of development have students who perform better on standard achievement measures."[21] This finding could be fruitful for those seeking to reform and improve the American education system.

A hidden but nonetheless significant benefit of group maturity is that individuality is strengthened, not extinguished.[22] Protecting the individual's right to dissent is particularly important in regard to the problem of blind obedience, which we shall consider later in this chapter. Also, as indicated in the fifth item on the list above, members of mature groups tend to be emotionally mature.[23] This paves the way for building much-needed social capital.

14d The Business of Golf

Ask people why they golf with business associates, and the answer is always the same: It's a great way to build relationships. They say this far more about golf than about going to dinner or attending a baseball game, and for good reason. Indeed, this may be the central fact about corporate golf, though it's rarely said: When people golf together, they see one another humiliated. At least 95% of all golfers are terrible, which means that in 18 holes everyone in the foursome will hit a tree, take three strokes in one bunker, or four-putt, with everyone else watching. Bonding is simply a matter of people jointly going through adversity, and a round of golf will furnish plenty of it.

Source: Geoffrey Colvin, "Why Execs Love Golf," Fortune (April 30, 2001): 46.

QUESTIONS:

Why does shared adversity foster strong relationships and bonding? How can managers get task group members to bond like this without playing golf?

■ Six Stages of Group Development

Experts have identified six distinct stages in the group development process[24] (see Figure 14.3). During stages 1 through 3, attempts are made to overcome the obstacle of uncertainty over power and authority. Once this first obstacle has been surmounted, addressing uncertainty over interpersonal relations becomes the challenge. This second obstacle must be cleared during stages 4 through 6 if the group is to achieve maturity. Each stage confronts the group's leader and contributing members with a unique combination of problems and opportunities.

■ **Stage 1: Orientation.** Attempts are made to "break the ice." Uncertainty about goals, power, and interpersonal relationships is high. Members generally want and accept any leadership at this point. Emergent leaders often misinterpret this "honeymoon period" as a mandate for permanent control.

■ **Stage 2: Conflict and Challenge.** As the emergent leader's philosophy, objectives, and policies become apparent, individuals or subgroups advocating alternative courses of action struggle for control. This second stage may be prolonged while members strive to clarify and reconcile their roles as part of a complete redistribution of power and authority. Many groups never continue past stage 2 because they get bogged down as a consequence of emotionalism and political infighting. Organizational committees often bear the brunt of jokes (we've all heard that a camel is a horse designed by a committee) because their frequent failure to mature beyond stage 2 prevents them from accomplishing their goals.[25]

3. **IDENTIFY** and briefly **DESCRIBE** the six stages of group development.

■ **Stage 3: Cohesion.** The shifts in power started in stage 2 are completed, under a new leader or the original leader, with a new consensus on authority, structure, and procedures. A "we" feeling emerges as everyone becomes truly involved. Any lingering differences over power and authority are resolved quickly. Stage 3 is usually of relatively short duration. If not, the group is likely to stall.

■ **Stage 4: Delusion.** A feeling of "having been through the worst of it" prevails after the rather rapid transition through stage 3. Issues and problems that threaten to break this spell of relief are dismissed or treated lightly. Members seem committed to fostering harmony at all costs. Participation and camaraderie run high because members believe that all the difficult emotional problems have been solved.

■ **Stage 5: Disillusion.** Subgroups tend to form as the illusion of unlimited goodwill wears off, and there is a growing disenchantment with how things are turning out. Those with unrealized expectations challenge the group to perform better and are prepared to reveal their personal strengths and weaknesses if necessary. Others hold back. Tardiness and absenteeism are symptomatic of diminishing cohesiveness and commitment.

■ **Stage 6: Acceptance.** It usually takes a trusted and influential group member who is concerned about the group to step forward and help the group move from conflict to cohesion. This individual, acting as the group catalyst, is usually someone other than the leader. Members are encouraged to test their self-perceptions against the reality of how others perceive them. Greater personal and mutual understanding helps members adapt to situations without causing problems. Members' expectations are more realistic than ever before. Since the authority structure is generally accepted, subgroups can pursue different matters without threatening group cohesiveness. Consequently, stage 6 groups tend to be highly effective and efficient.

Figure 14.3 Group Development from Formation to Maturity

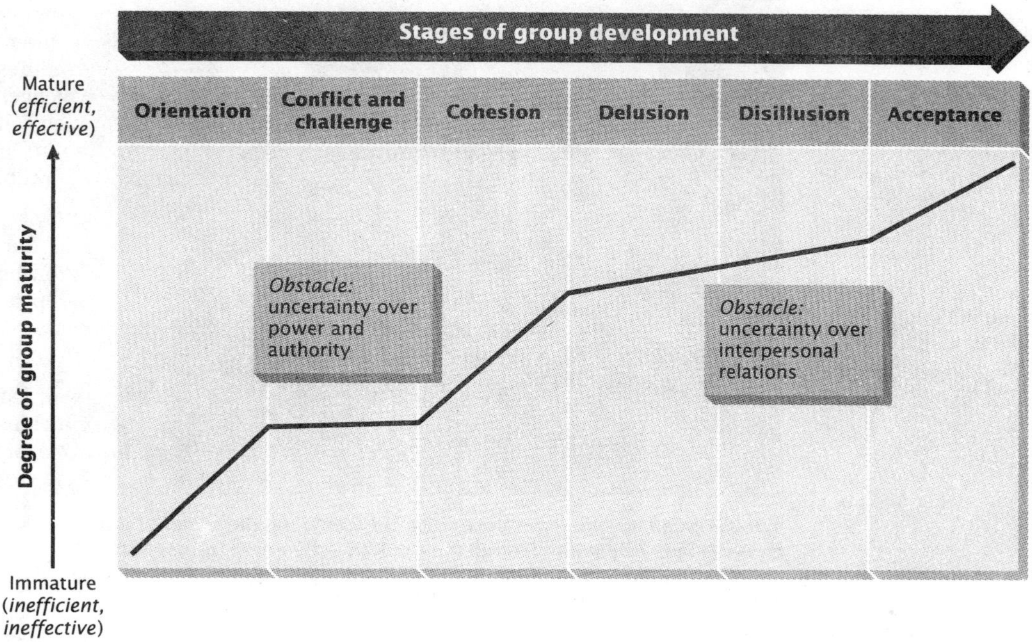

Source: Group Effectiveness in Organizations, *by Linda N. Jewell and H. Joseph Reitz, p. 20. Used with permission of the authors.*

Time-wasting problems and inefficiencies can be minimized if group members are consciously aware of this developmental process. Just as it is impossible for a child to skip being a teenager on the way to adulthood, committees and other work groups will find there are no shortcuts to group maturity. Some emotional stresses and strains are inevitable along the way.[26]

Organizational Politics

Only in recent years has the topic of organizational politics (also known as impression management) begun to receive serious attention from management theorists and researchers.[27] But as we all know from practical experience (and the back-stabbing on Donald Trump's television show *The Apprentice*),[28] organizational life is often highly charged with political wheeling-and-dealing. For example, consider this complaint:

> *I've been working at my current job as a marketing manager for about a year now, and one thing is bugging me. Every time I propose a strategy or a solution in a meeting, someone else at the table repeats it, in somewhat altered form—and ends up getting the credit for having thought of it. This is no trivial problem, since in my department, year-end bonuses are based on how many of each person's ideas have been put into (profitable) practice.*[29]

4. DEFINE *organizational politics,* and **SUMMARIZE** relevant research insights.

Workplace surveys reveal that organizational politics can hinder effectiveness and be an irritant to employees. A three-year study of 46 companies attempting to establish themselves on the Internet "found that poor communication and political infighting were the No. 1 and No. 2 causes, respectively, for slowing down change."[30] Meanwhile, 44 percent of full-time employees and 60 percent of independent contractors listed "freedom from office politics" as extremely important to their job satisfaction.[31]

It created quite a stir when former nurse Cecilia Fire Thunder was elected the first woman president of the Oglala Sioux Tribe in 2004. Meanwhile, she redirected attention to the need for the tribal council members of the Pine Ridge Reservation in South Dakota to stop playing political games and instead get busy enacting positive changes for the betterment of their people.

Whether they themselves are politically motivated or not, managers need to be knowledgeable about organizational politics because their careers will be affected by it.[32] New managers, particularly, should be aware of the political situation in their organization. As "new kids on the job," they might be more easily taken advantage of than other, more experienced managers. Certain political maneuvers also have significant ethical implications[33] (see Management Ethics).

■ What Does Organizational Politics Involve?

organizational politics: *the pursuit of self-interest in response to real or imagined opposition*

As the term implies, self-interest is central to organizational politics. In fact, **organizational politics** has been defined as "the pursuit of self-interest at work in the face of real or imagined opposition."[34] Political maneuvering is said to encompass all self-serving behavior above and beyond competence, hard work, and luck.[35] For example, consider this clip from the *Wall Street Journal*:

> *A former Wall Street analyst, a veteran of several investment banks who knows the value of that most ludicrous of achievements—performing "better than expected"—advises us to list easy goals and just make them sound hard. That way next year you can say you "achieved 100% of goals" last year.*
>
> *All year long, she would collect kudos as ammo, dumping them into folders she named "Success" and "Yay." The latter was for praise from colleagues. "Getting messages from my boss's boss—or anyone else he respected and was also slightly intimidated by—was even better," she confides.*
>
> *Brownie points, we all know, come from personally saving a few pennies. "Point out in the [annual performance] review—not in writing!—that the rest of the team stayed at the Four Seasons and flew American," the analyst says. Then wipe your fingerprints from the knives you stuck in everyone's backs.*[36]

Although self-serving people such as this have given the term *organizational politics* a negative connotation, researchers have identified both positive and negative aspects:

MANAGEMENT ETHICS

How Do You Feel About "Hard Ball" Organizational Politics?

Circle one number for each item, total your responses, and compare your score with the scale below:

	Unacceptable attitude/conduct				*Acceptable attitude/conduct*
1. The boss is always right.	1	2	3	4	5
2. If I were aware that an executive in my company was stealing money, I would use that information against him or her in asking for favors.	1	2	3	4	5
3. I would invite my boss to a party in my home even if I didn't like that person.	1	2	3	4	5
4. Given a choice, take on only those assignments that will make you look good.	1	2	3	4	5
5. I like the idea of keeping a "blunder (error) file" about a company rival for future use.	1	2	3	4	5
6. If you don't know the correct answer to a question asked by your boss, bluff your way out of it.	1	2	3	4	5
7. Why go out of your way to be nice to any employee in the company who can't help you now or in the future?	1	2	3	4	5
8. It is necessary to lie once in a while in business in order to look good.	1	2	3	4	5
9. Past promises should be broken if they stand in the way of one's personal gain.	1	2	3	4	5
10. If someone compliments you for a task that is another's accomplishment, smile and say thank you.	1	2	3	4	5

Scale

10–20 = Straight arrow with solid ethics.

21–39 = Closet politician with elastic ethics.

40–50 = Hard ball politician with no ethics.

Total score = _____

Source: "Measuring Your Political Tendencies," adapted from Winning Office Politics *by Andrew J. Dubrin, copyright © 1990 by Prentice-Hall, Inc. Used by permission of Portfolio, an imprint of Penguin Group (USA) Inc.*

> *Political behaviors widely accepted as legitimate would certainly include exchanging favors, "touching bases," forming coalitions, and seeking sponsors at upper levels. Less legitimate behaviors would include whistle-blowing, revolutionary coalitions, threats, and sabotage.*[37]

Recall our discussion of whistle-blowing in Chapter 5.[38]

Employees resort to political behavior when they are unwilling to trust their career solely to competence, hard work, and luck. One might say that organizational politicians help luck along by relying on political tactics. Whether employees will fall back on political tactics has a lot to do with an organization's climate or culture. A culture that presents employees with unreasonable barriers to individual and group success tends to foster political maneuvering. Consider this situation, for example: "A cadre of Corvette lovers inside General Motors lied, cheated, and stole to keep the legendary sports car from being eliminated during GM's management turmoil and near-bankruptcy in the late 1980s and early 1990s."[39] The redesigned Corvette finally made it to market in 1997, thanks in part to the Corvette team giving high-level GM executives thrilling unauthorized test rides in the hot new model.

Research on Organizational Politics

Researchers in one widely cited study of organizational politics conducted structured interviews with 87 managers employed by 30 electronics firms in southern California. Included in the sample were 30 chief executive officers, 28 middle managers, and 29 supervisors. Significant results included the following:

- The higher the level of management, the greater the perceived amount of political activity.
- The larger the organization, the greater the perceived amount of political activity.
- Personnel in staff positions were viewed as more political than those in line positions.
- People in marketing were the most political; those in production were the least political.
- "Reorganization changes" reportedly prompted more political activity than any other type of change.
- A majority (61 percent) of those interviewed believed that organizational politics helps advance one's career.
- Forty-five percent believed that organizational politics distracts from organizational goals.[40]

Regarding the last two findings, it was clear that political activities were seen as helpful to the individual. On the other hand, the interviewed managers were split on the question of the value of politics to the organization. Managers who believed political behavior had a positive impact on the organization cited the following reasons: "gaining visibility for ideas, improving coordination and communication, developing teams and groups, and increasing *esprit de corps*. . . ."[41] As listed above, the most-often-cited negative effect of politics was its distraction of managers from organizational goals. Misuse of resources and conflict were also mentioned as typical problems.

14e Ouch, That Hurts!

Paul Argenti, Dartmouth business professor:

"You can't get ahead back-stabbing."

Source: As quoted in Del Jones and Bill Keveney, "10 Lessons of 'The Apprentice,'" USA Today *(April 15, 2004): 5A.*

QUESTIONS:
Do you agree or disagree? Explain.

Political Tactics

As defined earlier, organizational politics takes in a lot of behavioral territory. The following six political tactics are common expressions of politics in the workplace:

- ***Posturing.*** Those who use this tactic look for situations in which they can make a good impression. "One-upmanship" and taking credit for other people's work are included in this category.
- ***Empire building.*** Gaining and keeping control over human and material resources is the principal motivation behind this tactic. Those with large budgets usually feel more safely entrenched in their positions and believe they have more influence over peers and superiors.
- ***Making the supervisor look good.*** Traditionally referred to as "apple polishing," this political strategy is prompted by a desire to favorably influence those who control one's career ascent. Anyone with an oversized ego is an easy target for this tactic.
- ***Collecting and using social IOUs.*** Reciprocal exchange of political favors can be done in two ways: (1) helping someone look good or (2) preventing someone

Table 14.2 One Manager's Rules for Winning at Office Politics

1. Find out what the boss expects.
2. Build an information network. Knowledge is power. Identify the people who have power and the extent and direction of it. Title doesn't necessarily reflect actual influence. Find out how the grapevine works. Develop good internal public relations for yourself.
3. Find a mentor. This is a trusted counselor who can be honest with you and help train and guide you to improve your ability and effectiveness as a manager.
4. Don't make enemies without a very good reason.
5. Avoid cliques. Keep circulating in the office.
6. If you must fight, fight over something that is really worth it. Don't lose ground over minor matters or petty differences.
7. Gain power through allies. Build ties that bind. Create IOUs, obligations, and loyalties. Do not be afraid to enlist help from above.
8. Maintain control. Don't misuse your cohorts. Maintain the status and integrity of your allies.
9. Mobilize your forces when necessary. Don't commit your friends without their approval. Be a gracious winner when you do win.
10. Never hire a family member or a close friend.

Source: *Adapted from David E. Hall, "Winning at Office Politics,"* Credit & Financial Management*, 86 (April 1984): 23. Reprinted with permission from* Credit & Financial Management*, Copyright April 1984, published by the National Association of Credit Management, 475 Park Avenue South, New York, NY 10016.*

from looking bad by ignoring or covering up a mistake. Those who rely on this tactic feel that all favors are coins of exchange rather than expressions of altruism or unselfishness.

- ***Creating power and loyalty cliques.*** Because there is power in numbers, the idea here is to face superiors and competitors as a cohesive group rather than alone.
- ***Engaging in destructive competition.*** As a last-ditch effort, some people will resort to character assassination through suggestive remarks, vindictive gossip, or outright lies. This tactic also includes sabotaging the work of a competitor.[42]

Obvious illegalities notwithstanding, one's own values and ethics as well as organizational sanctions are the final arbiters of whether these tactics are acceptable. (See Table 14.2 for a practicing manager's advice on how to win at office politics.)

14f Bring It On, Boss!

Letter to *Fortune* magazine:

I am a 31-year-old executive at a company headed by a friendly but fiercely competitive CEO. We get along fine, but here's the thing: We both play racquetball, and he's mentioned repeatedly that we should play sometime. I keep putting off setting a date for a game because I'm an excellent player and I'm pretty sure I would crush him, which I'm afraid would be career suicide. Should I agree to play? If so, should I play to win?—Killer Backhand

Source: Anne Fisher, "Will I Lose If I Beat the Boss at Racquetball?" Fortune *(January 24, 2005): 36.*

QUESTIONS:
If you were in this person's position, what would you do? How "political" is your answer?

Antidotes to Political Behavior

Each of the foregoing political tactics varies in degree. The average person will probably acknowledge using at least one of these strategies. But excessive political maneuvering can become a serious threat to productivity when self-interests clearly override the interests of the group or organization. Organizational politics can be kept within reasonable bounds by applying the following five tips:

- Strive for a climate of openness and trust.
- Measure performance results rather than personalities.
- Encourage top management to refrain from exhibiting political behavior that will be imitated by employees.
- Strive to integrate individual and organizational goals through meaningful work and career planning.

- Practice job rotation to encourage broader perspectives and understanding of the problems of others.[43]

This is how Nokia, Finland's cell phone giant, does a good job of curbing organizational politics:

> *[CEO Jorma] Ollila has a reputation for being animated and funny—not traditional Finnish traits, say Nokia's Finnish employees. But like many Finns, he is blunt and direct. He gives executives tough assignments, then gives them leeway to get them done or risk his ire. He particularly hates corporate politics.*
>
> *"It is a plague that has to be weeded out at the first signs," he says. Ollila and his top managers "will tell you what's on their minds—it's very black and white," says Susan Macke, an American who joined Nokia as a vice president earlier this year. "Everybody has an opinion, and they're not afraid to voice it. But at the end of the day, the leader makes a decision and everybody buys in. There's no posturing."*
>
> *There's not much bureaucracy or hierarchy. Ollila wants Nokia to seem like a small, intimate organization even though it has 57,000 employees spread from Japan to India to Silicon Valley.*[44]

Conformity and Groupthink

conformity: *complying with prevailing role expectations and norms*

Conformity means complying with the role expectations and norms perceived by the majority to be appropriate in a particular situation. Conformity enhances predictability, which is generally thought to be good for rational planning and productive enterprise. How can anything be accomplished if people cannot be counted on to perform their assigned duties? On the other hand, why do so many employees actively participate in or passively condone illegal and unethical organizational practices involving discrimination, environmental degradation, accounting fraud, and unfair competition?[45] The answers to these questions lie along a continuum with anarchy at one end and blind conformity at the other. Socially responsible management is anchored to a point somewhere between them.

Research on Conformity

Social psychologists have discovered much about human behavior by studying individuals and groups in controlled laboratory settings. One classic laboratory study conducted by Solomon Asch was designed to answer the following question: How often will an individual take a stand against a unanimous majority that is obviously wrong?[46] Asch's results were both intriguing and unsettling.

Figure 14.4 The Asch Line Experiment

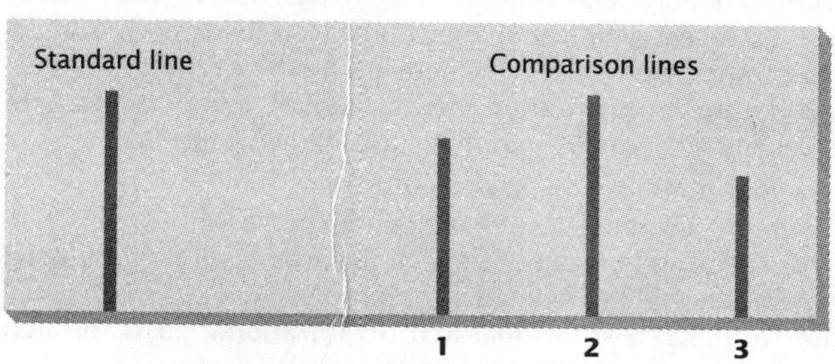

The Hot Seat. Asch began his study by assembling groups of seven to nine college students, supposedly to work on a perceptual problem. Actually, though, Asch was studying conformity. All but one member of each group were Asch's confederates, and Asch told them exactly how to behave and what to say. The experiment was really concerned with the reactions of the remaining student—called the naïve subject—who didn't know what was going on.

All the students in each group were shown cards with lines similar to those in Figure 14.4. They were instructed to match the line on the left with the one on the right that was closest to it in length. The differences in length among the lines on the right were obvious. Each group went through 12 rounds of the matching process, with a different set of lines for every round. The researcher asked one group member at a time to announce his or her choice to the group. Things proceeded normally for the first two rounds as each group member voiced an opinion. Agreement was unanimous. Suddenly, on the third round only one individual, the naïve subject, chose the correct pair of lines. All the other group members chose a different (and obviously wrong) pair. During the rounds in which there was disagreement, all of Asch's confederates conspired to select an incorrect pair of lines. It was the individual versus the rest of the group.

■ **Following the Immoral Majority.** Each of the naïve subjects was faced with a personal dilemma. Should he or she fight the group or give in to the obviously incorrect choice of the overwhelming majority? Among 31 naïve subjects who made a total of 217 judgments, two-thirds of the judgments were correct. The other one-third were incorrect; that is, they were consistent with the majority opinion. Individual differences were great, with some subjects yielding to the incorrect majority opinion more readily than others. *Only 20 percent of the naïve subjects remained entirely independent in their judgments.* All the rest turned their backs on their own perceptions and went along with the group at least once. In other words, 80 percent of Asch's subjects knuckled under to the pressure of group opinion at least once, even though they knew the majority was dead wrong.

Replications of Asch's study in the Middle East (Kuwait) and in Japan have demonstrated that this tendency toward conformity is not unique to American culture.[47] Indeed, a recent statistical analysis of 133 Asch conformity studies across 17 countries concluded that blind conformity is a greater problem in collectivist ("we") cultures than in individualist ("me") cultures. Japan is strongly collectivist, whereas the United States and Canada are highly individualistic cultures.[48] (You may find it instructive to ponder how you would act in such a situation.)

Because Asch's study was a contrived laboratory experiment, it failed to probe the relationship between cohesiveness and conformity. Asch's naïve subjects were outsiders. But more recent research on "groupthink" has shown that a cohesive group of insiders can fall victim to blind conformity.

■ Groupthink

groupthink: *Janis's term for blind conformity in cohesive in-groups*

5. ■ **EXPLAIN** how groupthink can lead to blind conformity.

After studying the records of several successful and several unsuccessful American foreign policy decisions, psychologist Irving Janis uncovered an undesirable by-product of group cohesiveness. He labeled this problem **groupthink** and defined it as a "mode of thinking that people engage in when they are deeply involved in a cohesive in-group, when the members' strivings for unanimity override their motivation to realistically appraise alternative courses of action."[49] Groupthink helps explain how intelligent policymakers, in both government and business, can sometimes make incredibly unwise decisions.

One dramatic result of groupthink in action was the Vietnam War. Strategic advisers in three successive administrations unwittingly rubber-stamped battle plans laced with false assumptions. Critical thinking, reality testing, and moral judgment were temporarily shelved as decisions to escalate the war were enthusiastically railroaded through. Although Janis acknowledges that cohesive groups are not inevitably victimized by groupthink, he warns group decision makers to be alert for the signs of groupthink—the risk is always there.

■ **Symptoms of Groupthink.** According to Janis, the onset of groupthink is foreshadowed by a definite pattern of symptoms. Among these are excessive optimism, an assumption of inherent morality, suppression of dissent, and an almost desperate quest for unanimity.[50] Given such a decision-making climate, the probability of a poor decision is high. Managers face a curious dilemma here. While a group is still in

"Damn it, Hopkins, didn't you get yesterday's memo?"

stage 1 or stage 2 of development, its cohesiveness is too low to get much accomplished because of emotional and time-consuming power struggles. But by the time, in stage 3, that the group achieves enough cohesiveness to make decisions promptly, the risk of groupthink is high. The trick is to achieve needed cohesiveness without going to the extreme of groupthink.

■ **Preventing Groupthink.** According to Janis, one of the group members should periodically ask, "Are we allowing ourselves to become victims of groupthink?"[51] More fundamental preventive measures include the following:

- Avoiding the use of groups to rubber-stamp decisions that have already been made by higher management.
- Urging each group member to be a critical evaluator.
- Bringing in outside experts for fresh perspectives.
- Assigning someone the role of devil's advocate to challenge assumptions and alternatives.[52]
- Taking time to consider possible side effects and consequences of alternative courses of action.[53]

Ideally, decision quality improves when these steps become second nature in cohesive groups. But groupthink remains a constant threat in management circles.

One major area ripe for abuse is corporate governance. Corporate boards of directors are supposed to represent the interests of stockholders and hold top executives accountable for results. Too often, however, domineering CEOs and pliable boards create the perfect environment for groupthink.[54] For example, consider Al Dunlap, as profiled in the book *Bad Leadership*, by Harvard's Barbara Kellerman. Dunlap, nicknamed "chainsaw Al" and "Rambo in pinstripes" by the business press, was hired as CEO of Sunbeam Corporation in 1996 to turn the company around. Less than two years later, after Dunlap had slashed 40 percent of Sunbeam's payroll while richly rewarding himself, the company was deeply in debt and on the verge of bankruptcy. Dunlap was fired amid claims of financial trickery. Kellerman explains how Dunlap fostered a climate conducive to groupthink:

14g It's My Way or the Highway

Letter to *Fast Company* magazine:

I'm a lawyer, and I have just joined my first corporate board. The chairman, a client of mine, runs meetings as if only his ideas matter; he seems more interested in impressing us than in using our counsel.

Source: *Kerry J. Sulkowicz, "The Corporate Shrink,"* Fast Company, *no. 82 (May 2004): 54.*

QUESTIONS:

What is the risk of groupthink in this type of situation? Explain. How would you handle the situation if you were the lawyer? What are the ethical implications of your answer?

Dunlap's original contract gave him the right to immediately select three new board members and eventually to replace nearly every director with one of his own choosing. Consequently, until nearly the end of his reign, the majority of board members supported him; they were not overly curious, nor did they seek to interfere with the way he ran the business. Sunbeam's board unanimously approved his plans for restructuring, no matter its draconian measures. And whatever their personal reservations, board members continued nearly for the duration to acquiesce in what Dunlap wanted and when he wanted it. . . .

On paper, Sunbeam's board of directors, like all boards of directors, was officially in charge, but in fact, it was not. By empowering Dunlap to do what he wanted when he wanted, board members became followers, even groupies.[55]

Disturbing? Yes. Unusual? Not really, especially when groupthink prevails.

Managers who cannot imagine themselves being victimized by blind conformity are prime candidates for groupthink.[56] Dean Tjosvold of Canada's Simon Fraser University recommends "cooperative conflict" (see Skills & Tools at the end of this chapter). The constructive use of conflict is discussed further in Chapter 16.

Teams, Teamwork, and Trust

Virtually all executives sing the praises of teamwork today. But for Jerry Perenchio, the head of Univision Communications Inc., the leading Hispanic/Latino broadcaster in the United States, being a team player is a passion that he has driven deep into his company.

> *At Univision, Perenchio rules with a 20-point manifesto that demands that employees think big, avoid mistakes, practice teamwork, and "hire people smarter than you." The No. 1 rule: "Stay clear of the press. Stay out of the spotlight. It fades your suit. Only promote the brands." . . .*
>
> *When a top lieutenant gave an unauthorized interview to the press in 1995, Perenchio fined him $25,000.*[57]

Perenchio clearly wants the emphasis at Univision on "we," not "me," because he knows teamwork is a key factor in success today.[58] Unfortunately, team skills in today's typical organization tend to lag far behind technical skills.[59] It is one thing to be a creative software engineer, for example. It is quite another for that software specialist to be able to team up with other specialists in accounting, finance, and marketing to beat the competition to market with a profitable new product. In this final section, we explore teams and teamwork by discussing cross-functional teams, virtual teams, a model of team effectiveness, and the importance of trust.

Cross-Functional Teams

cross-functional team: *task group staffed with a mix of specialists pursuing a common objective*

A **cross-functional team** is a task group staffed with a mix of specialists focused on a common objective. This structural innovation deserves special attention here because cross-functional teams are becoming commonplace.[60] They may or may not be self-managed, although self-managed teams (as discussed in Chapter 13) generally are cross-functional. Cross-functional teams are based on assigned rather than voluntary membership. Quality control (QC) circles made up of volunteers, also discussed in Chapter 13, technically are in a different category. Cross-functional teams stand in sharp contrast to the tradition of lumping specialists into functional departments, thereby creating the problem of integrating and coordinating those

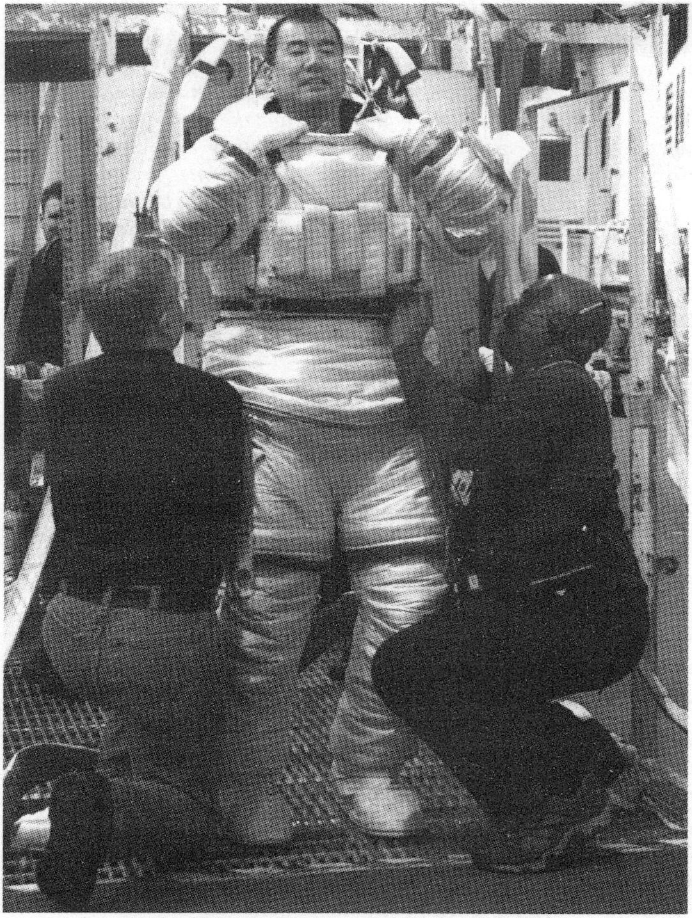

Talk about the need for teamwork and trust! Japanese astronaut Soichi Noguchi prepares for a space shuttle trip by doing some underwater training at NASA's Neutral Buoyancy Lab in Houston. It takes a sophisticated support team just to get him dressed for the occasion.

departments. Boeing, for example, relies on cross-functional teams to integrate its various departments to achieve important strategic goals. The giant aircraft manufacturer thus accelerated its product development process for the Boeing 777 jetliner. Also, Boeing engineer Grace Robertson turned to cross-functional teams for faster delivery of a big order of customized jetliners to United Parcel Service:

> *When UPS ordered 30 aircraft, Boeing guaranteed that it could design and build a new, all-cargo version of the 767 jet in a mere 33 months—far faster than the usual cycle time of 42 months. The price it quoted meant slashing development costs dramatically.*
>
> *Robertson's strategy has been to gather all 400 employees working on the new freighter into one location and organize them into "cross-functional" teams. By combining people from the design, planning, manufacturing, and tooling sectors, the teams speed up development and cut costs by enhancing communication and avoiding rework.*[61]

This teamwork approach helped Robertson's group stay on schedule and within its budget, both vitally important achievements in Boeing's quest to be the world's leading aircraft maker.

Cross-functional teams have exciting potential. But they present management with the immense challenge of getting technical specialists to be effective boundary spanners.

■ Virtual Teams

virtual team: *task group members from dispersed locations who are electronically linked*

6. DEFINE and **DISCUSS** the management of virtual teams.

Along with the move toward virtual organizations, discussed in Chapter 10, have come virtual teams. A **virtual team** is a physically dispersed task group linked electronically.[62] Face-to-face contact is usually minimal or nonexistent. E-mail, voice mail, videoconferencing, Web-based project software, and other forms of electronic interchange allow members of virtual teams from anywhere on the planet to accomplish a common goal.[63] It is commonplace today for virtual teams to have members from different organizations, different time zones, and different cultures.[64] Because virtual organizations and teams are so new, paced as they are by emerging technologies, managers are having to learn from the school of hard knocks rather than from established practice.

Just as we saw (in Chapter 10) of virtual organizations, one reality of managing virtual teams is clear. *Periodic face-to-face interaction, trust building, and team building are more important than ever when team members are widely dispersed in time and space.* Although faceless interaction may work in Internet chat rooms, it can doom a

14h No Team Is an Island

Martha Rogers, partner, Peppers and Rogers Group, Bowling Green, Ohio:

You can't say, "teams work because of this" or "teams don't work because of that"–because it depends. But if you're looking for one quality that most good teams share, I'd have to say that it's the culture of the company in which the team exists. Is the culture one that rewards groups? Is it one that rewards individuals? Or is it a culture where no one gets rewarded? Look around. Watch how people act and interact, regardless of whether they're on a team. Do people do things for one another? Do they pick up coffee for others when they're going out? If the culture is full of give and take–if it's supportive and trusting–there's a good chance that you'll see successful teams at work.

Source: As quoted in Regina Fazio Maruca, "What Makes Teams Work?" Fast Company, *no. 40 (November 2000): 109.*

QUESTIONS:

Do you agree? Explain. How can management build a supportive and trusting organizational culture?

virtual team with a crucial task and a pressing deadline. Additionally, special steps need to be taken to clearly communicate role expectations, performance norms, goals, and deadlines (see Table 14.3). Virtual teamwork may be faster than the traditional face-to-face kind, but it is by no means easier[65] (see this chapter's Closing Case).

What Makes Workplace Teams Effective?

Widespread use of team formats—including QC circles, self-managed teams, cross-functional teams, and virtual teams—necessitates greater knowledge of team effectiveness.[66] A model of team effectiveness criteria and determinants is presented in Figure 14.5 on p. 429. This model is the product of two field studies involving 360 new product-development managers employed by 52 high-tech companies.[67] It is a generic model that applies equally well to all workplace teams.[68]

The five criteria for effective team performance in Figure 14.5 parallel the criteria for organizational effectiveness discussed in Chapter 9. Thus, team effectiveness feeds organizational effectiveness. For example, if the Boeing 777 product development teams had not been effective, the entire corporation could have stumbled.

7. DISCUSS the criteria and determinants of team effectiveness.

Determinants of team effectiveness, shown in Figure 14.5, are grouped into people-, organization-, and task-related factors. Considered separately, these factors involve rather routine aspects of good management. But the collective picture reveals each factor to be part of a complex and interdependent whole. Managers cannot maximize just a few of them, ignore the rest, and hope to have an effective team. In the spirit of the Japanese concept of *kaizen,* managers and team leaders need to strive for "continuous improvement" on all fronts. Because gains on one front will inevitably be offset by losses in another, the pursuit of team effectiveness and teamwork is an endless battle with no guarantees of success.[69]

Let's focus on trust, one of the people-related factors in Figure 14.5 that can make or break work teams.

Trust: A Key to Team Effectiveness

trust: *belief in the integrity, character, or ability of others*

Trust, a belief in the integrity, character, or ability of others, is essential if people are to achieve anything together in the long run.[70] Participative management programs are very dependent on trust.[71] According to Stanford's Jeffrey Pfeffer, "one of the most important factors in employee retention and motivation is trust in management."[72] Sadly, trust is not one of the hallmarks of the current U.S. business scene. Harris Interactive polls in the United States in 2000 and 2004 found that the public's "confidence in executives" had plunged from an already low 28 percent to 12 percent.[73] To a greater extent than they may initially suspect, managers determine the level of trust in the organization and its component work groups and teams. Experts in the area of social capital tell us that

> *No one can manufacture trust or mandate it into existence. When someone says, "You can trust me," we usually don't, and rightly so. But leaders can make deliberate investments in trust. They can give people reasons to trust one another instead of reasons to watch their backs. They can refuse to reward successes that are built on untrusting behavior. And they can display trust and trustworthiness in their own actions, both personally and on behalf of the company.*[74]

14i Back to the Opening Case

What are the dynamics of trust in this case?

Table 14.3 It Takes More Than E-Mail to Build a Virtual Team

Teams need a structure to work successfully across time and distance. In *Mastering Virtual Teams: Strategies, Tools, and Techniques That Succeed*, authors Deborah Duarte and Nancy Tennant Snyder list six steps for creating a virtual team, of which each acts as a support beam that helps uphold the structure.

1. **Identify the team's sponsors, stakeholders, and champions.** These are the people who connect the team to the power brokers within the organizations involved.
2. **Develop a team charter that includes its purpose, mission, and goals.** The authors say it's best to do this in a face-to-face meeting that includes the team's leader, management, and other stakeholders.
3. **Select team members.** Most virtual teams have at least three types of members: *core* members who regularly work on the project; *extended* members who provide support and advice; and *ancillary* members who review and approve work.
4. **Contact team members and introduce them to each other.** During this initial meeting, team leaders should make sure members understand why they've been selected, use computers that are compatible, and have a forum in which to ask and get answers to questions. Duarte says leaders should use this time to find out what other projects members are working on. "It's easy to put people on a team when you can't see them," she says. "People don't say 'no,' but then they find themselves on five or six teams and don't have time for any of them."
5. **Conduct a team-orientation session.** This is one of the most important steps. Duarte says an eyeball-to-eyeball meeting is essential, unless team members are working on a very short task or have worked together in another capacity and know each other. "This forms the basis for more natural dialogue later if problems arise," she says. At this getting-to-know-you session, which often includes some type of team-building activity, the leader should provide an overview of the team's charter so members understand the task they are charged with and their roles in achieving it.

   Leaders also should provide guidance in developing team norms. This includes discussing telephone, audio- and videoconference etiquette; establishing guidelines for sending and replying to e-mail and returning phone calls; determining which meetings members must attend in person and which can be done by audio- or videoconference; outlining how work will be reviewed; and discussing how meetings will be scheduled.

   Team leaders also can use this session to decide which technologies the team will use and discuss how members will communicate with each other, with the leader, and with management.
6. **Develop a team process.** Leaders should explain how the team's work will be managed, how information will be stored and shared, and who will review documents and how often.

Duarte says teams that follow these steps often have a better sense of clarity about their goals, the roles of each member, how the work will get done, and how the team will communicate. "They don't feel as though they've been left floating."

Source: *Kim Kiser, "Building a Virtual Team,"* Training *36 (March 1999): 34. Reprinted with permission from the March 1999 issue of* Training *magazine. Copyright 1999. Bill Communications, Minneapolis, MN. All rights reserved. Not for resale.*

8. EXPLAIN why trust is a key ingredient of teamwork, and **DISCUSS** what management can do to build trust.

■ **Zand's Model of Trust.** Trust is not a free-floating variable. It affects, and in turn is affected by, other group processes. Dale E. Zand's model of work group interaction puts trust into proper perspective (see Figure 14.6). Zand believes that trust is the key to establishing productive interpersonal relationships.[75]

Primary responsibility for creating a climate of trust falls on the manager. Team members usually look to the manager, who enjoys hierarchical advantage and greater access to key information, to set the tone for interpersonal dealings. Threatening or intimidating actions by the manager will probably encourage the group to bind together in cohesive resistance. Therefore, trust needs to be developed right from the beginning, when team members are still receptive to positive managerial influence.

Trust is initially encouraged by a manager's openness and honesty. Trusting managers talk *with* their people rather than *at* them. A trusting manager, according to Zand's model, demonstrates a willingness to be influenced by others and to change if the facts indicate a change is appropriate. Mutual trust between a manager and team members encourages *self-control*, as opposed to control through direct supervision.

Figure 14.5 A Model of Team Effectiveness

Source: *Reprinted from* Journal of Product Innovation Management*, 7, Hans J. Thamhain, "Managing Technologically Innovative Team Efforts Toward New Product Success," pp. 5–18. Copyright 1990, with permission from Elsevier Science.*

Paradoxically, managerial control actually expands when committed group or team members enjoy greater freedom in pursuing consensual goals. Those who trust each other generally avoid taking advantage of others' weaknesses or shortcomings.[76]

■ **Six Ways to Build Trust.** Trust is a fragile thing. As most of us know from personal experience, trust grows at a painfully slow pace yet can be destroyed in an instant with a thoughtless remark. Mistrust can erode the long-term effectiveness of work teams and organizations. According to management professor and consultant Fernando Bartolomé, managers need to concentrate on six areas: communication, support, respect, fairness, predictability, and competence.

- ***Communication.*** Keep your people informed by providing accurate and timely feedback and explaining policies and decisions. Be open and honest about your own problems. Do not hoard information or use it as a political device or reward.
- ***Support.*** Be an approachable person who is available to help, encourage, and coach your people. Show an active interest in their lives and be willing to come to their defense.
- ***Respect.*** Delegating important duties is the sincerest form of respect, followed closely by being a good listener.
- ***Fairness.*** Evaluate your people fairly and objectively and be liberal in giving credit and praise.

Figure 14.6 Trust and Effective Group Interaction

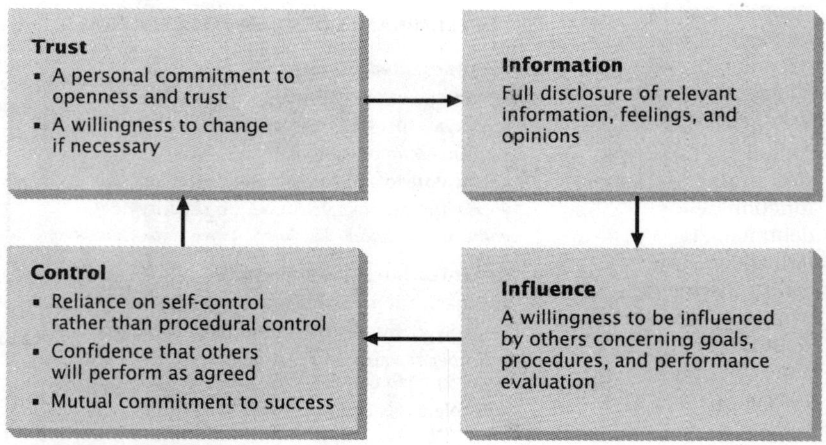

Source: *Reprinted from "Trust and Managerial Problem Solving," by Dale E. Zand and published in* Administrative Science Quarterly, *17, no. 2 (June 1972), by permission of* Administrative Science Quarterly. *© 1972 by Cornell University.*

- ***Predictability.*** Be dependable and consistent in your behavior and keep all your promises.
- ***Competence.*** Be a good role model by exercising good business judgment and being technically and professionally competent.[77]

Managers find that trust begets trust. In other words, those who feel they are trusted tend to trust others in return.[78]

SUMMARY

1. Managers need a working understanding of group dynamics because groups are the basic building blocks of organizations. Generating social capital through strong, constructive, and win-win relationships is essential to success today. Both informal (friendship) and formal (work) groups are made up of two or more freely interacting individuals who have a common identity and purpose.

2. After someone has been attracted to a group, cohesiveness—a "we" feeling—encourages continued membership. Roles are social expectations for behavior in a specific position, whereas norms are more general standards for conduct in a given social setting. Norms are enforced because they help the group survive, clarify role expectations, protect self-images, and enhance the group's identity by emphasizing key values. Compliance with role expectations and norms is rewarded with social reinforcement; noncompliance is punished by criticism, ridicule, and ostracism.

3. Mature groups are characterized by mutual acceptance, encouragement of minority opinion, and minimal emotional conflict. They are the product of a developmental process with identifiable stages. During the first three stages—orientation, conflict and challenge, and cohesion—power and authority problems are resolved. Groups are faced with the obstacle of uncertainty over interpersonal relations during the last three stages—delusion, disillusion, and acceptance. Committees have a widespread reputation for inefficiency and ineffectiveness because they tend to get stalled in an early stage of group development.

4. Organizational politics centers on the pursuit of self-interest. Research shows greater political activity to be associated with higher levels of management, larger organizations, staff and marketing personnel, and reorganizations. Political tactics such as posturing, empire building, making the boss look good, collecting and using social IOUs, creating power and loyalty cliques, and engaging in destructive competition need to be kept in check if the organization is to be effective.

5. Although a fairly high degree of conformity is necessary if organizations and society in general are to function properly, blind conformity is ultimately dehumanizing and destructive. Research shows that individuals have a strong tendency to bend to the will of the majority, even if the majority is clearly wrong. Cohesive decision-making groups can be victimized by groupthink when unanimity becomes more important than critical evaluation of alternative courses of action.

6. Teams are becoming the structural format of choice. Today's employees generally have better technical skills than team skills. Cross-functional teams are particularly promising because they facilitate greater strategic speed. Although members of virtual teams by definition collaborate via electronic media, there is still a need for periodic face-to-face interaction and team building. Three sets of factors—relating to people, organization, and task—combine to determine the effectiveness of a work team.

7. Trust, a key ingredient of effective teamwork, is disturbingly low in the American workplace today. When work group members trust one another, there will be a more active exchange of information, more interpersonal influence, and hence greater self-control. Managers can build trust through communication, support, respect (primarily in the form of delegation), fairness, predictability, and competence.

TERMS TO UNDERSTAND

- Social capital, p. 410
- Group, p. 410
- Informal group, p. 411
- Formal group, p. 412
- Cohesiveness, p. 412
- Role, p. 413
- Norms, p. 413
- Ostracism, p. 414
- Organizational politics, p. 418
- Conformity, p. 422
- Groupthink, p. 423
- Cross-functional team, p. 425
- Virtual team, p. 426
- Trust, p. 427

SKILLS & TOOLS

How to Use *Cooperative Conflict* to Avoid Groupthink

Guides for Action

- Elaborate positions and ideas.
- List facts, information, and theories.
- Ask for clarification.
- Clarify opposing ideas.
- Search for new information.
- Challenge opposing ideas and positions.
- Reaffirm your confidence in those who differ.
- Listen to all ideas.
- Restate opposing arguments that are unclear.
- Identify strengths in opposing arguments.
- Change your mind only when confronted with good evidence.
- Integrate various information and reasoning.
- Create alternative solutions.
- Agree to a solution responsive to several points of view.
- Use a new round of cooperative conflict to develop and refine the solution.

Pitfalls to Avoid

- Assume your position is superior.
- Prove your ideas are right and must be accepted.
- Interpret opposition to your ideas as a personal attack.
- Refuse to admit weaknesses in your position.
- Pretend to listen.
- Ridicule to weaken the others' resolve to disagree.
- Try to win over people to your position through charm and exaggeration.
- See accepting another's ideas as a sign of weakness.

Source: *Reprinted from* Learning to Manage Conflict: Getting People to Work Together Productively *by Dean Tjosvold. Copyright © 1993 Dean Tjosvold. First published by Lexington Books. All rights reserved. All correspondence should be sent to Lexington Books, 4720 Boston Way, Lanham, Md., 20706.*

HANDS-ON EXERCISE

Management Teamwork Survey

Instructions:

Think of your present job (or a past one) and check one box for each of the following 10 questions. Alternatively, you can ask a manager to complete this survey. The idea is to assess the organization's commitment to building cooperation and teamwork among managers. This instrument also pinpoints weak spots needing attention.

TO WHAT EXTENT DO...	Never	To a Limited Extent	To a Great Extent	Always
1. Our managers pursue common goals that focus on our customers and profitability?	☐	☐	☐	☐
2. We have team-based performance measurements and feedback devices?	☐	☐	☐	☐
3. Our top managers demonstrate and foster cooperation in their approach to leadership?	☐	☐	☐	☐
4. We provide incentives and rewards that encourage management cooperation?	☐	☐	☐	☐
5. We engage in ongoing team-building activities and skill development among our managers?	☐	☐	☐	☐
6. We identify and resolve problems/conflicts among managers in a timely fashion?	☐	☐	☐	☐
7. We create management team ownership of decision processes and outcomes?	☐	☐	☐	☐
8. We clarify each manager's roles and goals to each other?	☐	☐	☐	☐
9. We integrate planning, problem-solving, and communication activities among managers?	☐	☐	☐	☐
10. We build consensus and understanding around work processes and systems?	☐	☐	☐	☐

Interpretation:

Scores in Columns 1 and 2 represent areas that damage management cooperation and teamwork; these areas should be systematically addressed to enhance organizational performance. Scores in Columns 3 and 4 represent practices that can and should be continued and improved to increase management cooperation and teamwork.

Source: *Clinton O. Longenecker and Mitchell Neubert, "Barriers and Gateways to Management Cooperation and Teamwork." Reprinted with permission from* Business Horizons, 43 (September-October 2000).

For Consideration/Discussion

1. Why are cooperation and teamwork among managers so important today?
2. Overall, how does this organization measure up in terms of fostering managerial cooperation and teamwork?
3. Which areas are strongest? How can they be made even stronger?
4. Which areas are weakest and what needs to be done?
5. Which factors in this survey are most critical to organizational success today? Explain.

INTERNET EXERCISES

1. ***What's new with teams and teamwork?*** Things are changing rapidly in this area because teams have become such an important part of organizational life. Lots of new ideas can be found on the Internet by those willing to search a bit. Here is a way to jump-start your Web search for updates on teams and teamwork. Go to *Fast Company* magazine's online archives (**www.fastcompany.com/backissues**) and type "Teamwork" into the "Search" box. Read at least two of the full-text articles, with the goal of picking up at least three good ideas about managing workplace teams. You may have to select and read additional articles if you don't find enough good ideas right away. *Note:* You may want to make hard copies of the articles you selected and notes on your good ideas for possible class discussion.

   Learning Points: 1. Why did you select those particular articles? 2. Among your "good ideas" about managing teams, which idea stands out as the best? Why? 3. Did other class members tend to focus on the same articles and ideas as you, or did they select different ones? 4. After comparing notes with your classmates, indicate which of their "good ideas" are superior to the ones on your list.

2. ***Getting "street smart" about organizational politics:***

   Step 1: How savvy are you about organizational politics? For a general indication, take the 5-item multiple-choice quiz at **www.fortune.com/fortune/careers**. Scroll down to the "Quizzes" heading and click on "Could You Make It to CEO?" Be sure to read the interpretation for each of your responses.

   Step 2: Ethical managers today "play clean" in the game of business but are street smart enough to avoid getting hurt by those who fight dirty. For good background reading, go to *Fast Company* magazine's online archives (**www.fastcompany.com/backissues**). Scroll down to the April-May 1998 issue (no. 14). From the table of contents for that issue, select and read the articles titled "The Bad Guy's (and Gal's) Guide to Office Politics" and "The Good Guy's (and Gal's) Guide to Office Politics." Also look up Polly LaBarre's article "The New Face of Office Politics" in the October 1999 issue (no. 28). While you're in *Fast Company*'s online archives, you may want to search recent issues for articles related to organizational and office politics.

   Learning Points: 1. How political are you, according to the quiz? 2. Why is it fair to say that organizational politics can be both good and bad? 3. What new ideas or useful tips did you learn about workplace politics? 4. Is political maneuvering an inescapable part of life on the job? Explain. 5. Is organizational politics a fun aspect of organizational life for you, or do you find it distasteful? Explain. 6. Why is it important to know about political tactics in the workplace even if you don't enjoy engaging in them?

3. ***Check it out:*** Are you a team player or a solo act? Find out by taking the free 10-item quiz at **http://tools.monster.com/archives/selfassessment**. You will receive a score, a general analysis, and an item-by-item analysis.

For updates to these exercises, visit our Web site (**http://business.college.hmco.com/students**) and select Kreitner, *Management,* 10e.

CLOSING CASE

The Sales Girls

The Roopchand Departmental Stores, New Delhi, has a separate section to sell winter garments. This section consists of two groups: permanent clerks and temporary clerks appointed during winter season. Unfortunately, this section has always witnessed a tug-of-war situation between permanent and temporary clerks. The story begins thus.

The permanent clerks, by virtue of their long and fruitful association in the Departmental Store, had developed intimate social relations among themselves.

Usually, they take their lunch and tea together. They worked, like a well-knit group, in close proximity and not surprisingly, developed close relations even after the work is over. The slack period starting from April to September every year had given them wonderful opportunity to sit together, discuss about matters of common interest, peep into each other's minds and if possible, solve their problems to mutual advantage. Presently, all of them are unmarried with the exception of two.

The temporary clerks were school girls, who are normally appointed before the commencement of winter. Often, they have complained about their work in the Winter Garments Section and two of the clerks even desired transfer to some other section after a short stay. The reasons are quite obvious. The permanent clerks bothered little about helping the newcomers. If the newcomer is not able to strike a deal with a customer, often, the permanent clerks joined hands in throwing arrows of uncharitable criticism before the Section-in-charge. Being small in number, the temporary clerks could not resist the frequent onslaughts which were at times irritating and insinuating. The temporary clerks had very little scope to blow off their 'steam'.

In this heated atmosphere, the determination of commission on sales remained a contentious issue. The permanent clerks had, through an informal understanding, agreed not to boost up sales. They feared, inherently, that fluctuations in sales would lead to fluctuations in employment. At the same time, they could not tolerate the sight of a temporary sales person pocketing a fair share of commission. They always felt that the temporary ones do not deserve any commission, because they have not contributed anything on a continual basis for the development of the Department. Suffering from an inflated ego, they also believed that they had the right temperament and skill to boost up sales. Thus, in every way, the temporary sales clerk are inferior to them. Recently, an unhappy situation has developed when one of the temporary clerks was able to make a substantial sale to one of her acquaintances. Now the permanent clerks began to make a hue and cry regarding the commission payment. The poor sales clerk came to the Assistant Sales Manager with tears after having been scolded bitterly by the permanent clerks for having sold a few sweaters in their absence.

The temporary clerks were always anxious to show good performance so as to earn a position in the Department. To prevent this, the permanent clerks used to furnish false information about garments' quality; negotiable price etc. Whenever the temporary clerk sought the help of a senior in selling the garments to the customer, the latter would take over and claim the commission on sales herself. The temporary clerks were often assigned to insignificant tasks like arranging displays, rearranging garments, bringing garments from stores etc., and were prevented from striking it rich with customers. At every stage, the temporary ones are taken for a ride by the senior clerks.

For Discussion

1. How do you explain the behaviour of permanent clerks in the Winter Garments Section?
2. Does the management derive any benefits from the increased cohesiveness of permanent clerks?
3. Is it realistic to find employees doing average or below average work and still consider themselves as top notch sales persons as in the above case?
4. What could you do if you were the Assistant Sales Manager in this case?

Source: *Management Text and Cases, V S P Rao & V Hari Krishna, Excel Books, 2002, pp-839-840*

TEST PREPPER

True/False Questions

_____ **1.** Jean is a member of both a formal group and an informal group if she socializes with her coworkers.

_____ **2.** Members of a cohesive group tend to see themselves as "we" rather than "I."

_____ **3.** Roles have a broader influence than norms, which focus on behavior in a specific position.

_____ **4.** The first stage in the six-stage group development process is acceptance.

_____ **5.** According to research, people in marketing were the least political, whereas people in production were the most political.

_____ **6.** According to research, the more conformity in organizations, the better.

_____ **7.** Too often, domineering CEOs and pliable corporate boards create the perfect environment for groupthink.

_____ **8.** Quality control circles and cross-functional teams are the same thing.

_____ **9.** Much more than goal accomplishment is involved in the model of team effectiveness.

_____ **10.** According to a management professor and consultant who has suggested six ways in which managers can build trust, one of the best ways to show respect for subordinates is to delegate important duties.

Multiple-Choice Questions

1. Which of the following is *not* one of the four definitional dimensions of a group?
A. Trust B. Common identity
C. Free interaction D. Two or more people
E. Common purpose

2. How do people become members of formal groups in the workplace?
A. Volunteering B. Demotion
C. Lottery drawing D. Luck
E. Assignment

3. The tendency of group members to follow the group and resist outside influences is called
A. attractiveness. B. cohesiveness.
C. ostracism. D. conformity.
E. groupthink.

4. Which of the following is the *best* description of norms?
A. General standards of conduct
B. Prescriptions for behavior in specific positions
C. Individually determined principles
D. Laws
E. Culturally neutral principles

5. A "we" feeling becomes apparent during the _____ stage of the group development process.
A. delusion B. acceptance
C. orientation D. agreement
E. cohesion

6. How do experts describe political behavior at work?
A. Universally positive
B. Inevitably destructive
C. Usually negative
D. Both positive and negative
E. At first neutral but eventually positive

7. Which one of these was *not* found by researchers to be associated with increased political activity?
A. Smaller organizations
B. People in marketing
C. Higher levels of management
D. Reorganizations
E. Staff personnel

8. What was the major finding in Asch's line experiments?
A. Employees engage in organizational politics when they fear for their jobs.
B. Americans hold stronger opinions than Japanese.
C. People tend to yield to the majority opinion, even if it is wrong.
D. Groupthink is not a problem in smaller companies.
E. Women tend to make more ethical decisions than men.

9. A cross-functional team can *best* be described as
A. a mix of employees and outside consultants.
B. people assigned to play the role of devil's advocate.
C. containing no more than three members.
D. both managers and nonmanagers from the same department.
E. a mix of specialists.

10. Which of the following is *not* among the areas that managers should concentrate on as they attempt to build trust?
A. Predictability B. Competence
C. Fairness D. Communication
E. Friendship

ACE self-test

Want more questions? Visit the student Web site at http://business.college.hmco.com/students/ (select Kreitner, *Management,* 10e) and take the ACE quizzes for more practice.

15 Influence, Power, and Leadership

> *"As for leadership, some of the most important attributes are inspiration and motivation and coaching. That's 80% to 90% of my job."*[1]
>
> **ANNETTE VERSCHUREN, PRESIDENT, HOME DEPOT CANADA**

OBJECTIVES

- **Identify** and **describe** eight generic influence tactics used in modern organizations.
- **Identify** the five bases of power, and **explain** what it takes to make empowerment work.
- **Explain** the concept of emotional intelligence in terms of Goleman's four leadership traits.
- **Summarize** what the Ohio State model and the Leadership Grid® have taught managers about leadership.
- **Describe** the path-goal theory of leadership, and **explain** how the assumption on which it is based differs from the assumption on which Fiedler's contingency theory is based.
- **Describe** a transformational leader, and **explain** Greenleaf's philosophy of the servant leader.
- **Identify** the two key functions that mentors perform, and **explain** how a mentor can develop a junior manager's leadership skills.
- **Explain** the management of antecedents and consequences in behavior modification.

the changing workplace

eBay's Secret Weapon

Meg Whitman is on the last lap of a two-day, if-it's-noon-it-must-be-Rotterdam investor road show. She's pitched eBay's global growth to six rapt audiences in three Dutch cities in eight hours. As we fly into Frankfurt, [Germany,] Whitman is beat, but she gamely engages in a discussion about a topic she professes to dislike: power. "I don't actually think of myself as powerful," she says. When Rajiv Dutta, a native Indian who is eBay's chief financial officer, tosses out a profundity—"To have power, you must be willing to not have any of it"—she agrees. You'd expect Whitman to be glad the talk is over when we touch ground, but as she climbs into the back seat of a black Mercedes, she doesn't let it go: "Ask anyone about me, and they would never think of power. You know, you say, 'sky,' and they say 'blue.' Say 'power,' and no one would say 'Meg Whitman.'"

Well, we would, so here goes: Meg Whitman, 48, is the most powerful woman in American business. . . . Since she arrived as CEO and president almost seven years ago, eBay has grown from $5.7 million to $3.2 billion in estimated 2004 revenues. To put that into perspective, hers is the fastest-growing company in history—faster than Microsoft, Dell, or any other company during the first eight years of its existence. That $3.2 billion in revenues will probably produce more than $1 billion in operating income this year. eBay has such high margins partly because it has no factories or inventory, but also because its customers do the work. Some 48 million active users will select, price, buy, sell, and ship $32 billion worth of merchandise [in 2004]. . . . If eBay were a retailer, rather than the world's largest online marketplace, it would be bigger than Best Buy and almost the size of Lowe's. If eBay employed the 430,000 people who earn all or most of their income selling on its site, it would be the second-largest employer on the FORTUNE 500, after Wal-Mart.

Despite all that, it's easy to underestimate Whitman's power. As she likes to say, "It's our customers who have built eBay." eBay's business model looks so simple—take an online trading platform, let sellers attract buyers, buyers attract more sellers, and so on—that people say things like, "A monkey could run this thing." Which is exactly what a hotshot MBA, new to eBay, told Whitman to her face. (She laughed; the MBA still has his job.) One of her board members, Scott Cook, the founder of Intuit, jokes that Whitman found "a parade and ran in front of it."

But the idea that anyone with a pulse could run eBay is naïve. It's a lot harder than it looks. The fact is, Whitman and her team are building and tuning what many consider to be the company of tomorrow—a model 21st-century organization of minimal staff and maximal profitability. Whitman has steered the company in surprising directions and made counterintuitive strategic choices. Running eBay is an act of imagination; it is the opposite of some straightforward exercise in the caretaker arts.

Her power is unconventional too. Whitman doesn't have the kind of raw, command-and-control power of, say, Exxon Mobil's Lee Raymond. . . . Whitman had to amass a more complex, subtle kind of power. As one of her admirers, A. G. Lafley, CEO of Procter & Gamble, says of power, "It's not about control, and I don't think it's about size. The measure of a powerful person is that their circle of influence is greater than their circle of control."

Of course, there are some basic steps you need to take before you widen your circle of influence. Like, for instance, establishing credibility by doing what you say you're going to do. That sounds like a no-brainer, but it's amazing how few CEOs actually follow the rule. . . .

Running eBay has proved a lot more complicated than Whitman ever figured. She runs a company *and* an enormous, rowdy swarm of sellers who live off it. She has to do right by her shareholders, of course, but she also has to keep the swarm happy. Doing all that means Whitman has as many managerial roles as Pez has dispensers.

At eBay Live! you see Meg as celebrity—working the throngs (10,000 eBay users attended in June [2004]) and autographing T-shirts and trading cards that picture a cartoon version of her while fly-fishing—her hobby. Here, Whitman is not only eBay's living icon but, at the same time, the users' best friend. "Where are you from? . . . What do you sell?" she asks each customer who walks up to her, from a long line that snakes through the New Orleans convention center. Everybody calls her "Meg," and when anyone boasts about his growing business on eBay, she reflexively replies, "There you go!"—like a mom who tells her kid that she knew he could do it, and gosh darn it, he did. Taking the stage before several thousand customers, she tells them, "eBay's success will always be based on your success. . . . eBay reaffirms my faith in humanity. eBay is proof that people are basically good." Somehow she manages to say it without sounding fake or sappy. She means it.

All this up-with-people stuff (wedding of two eBay users, soaring gospel choir) makes Whitman come across like another powerful woman who talks about enabling her followers: Oprah. "I do use the word 'enable' a lot," Whitman says, liking the comparison. "Enable, not direct. Use carrots, not sticks." Whitman lacks Oprah's glam, of course. When I impolitely ask whether she has been wearing the same clothes for three days straight, she replies, "Two shirts, two pairs of pants." She wears the same outfit, navy polo shirt and khaki pants, as other eBay employees—it's "egalitarian." She happily invents a self-effacing tagline for herself: "She's frumpy, but she delivers." . . .

Whitman has one more important role inside eBay: Meg as den mother, nurturing her ambitious scouts with proper values. Yes, it sounds warm, fuzzy, and most un–Captain of Industry-esque, but it works to her advantage. Benchmark's [Bob] Kagle likes her soft touch. "People aren't threatened by her," he says. (Her one dictatorial habit, say colleagues: instructing people where to sit at meetings. "My mother has always said that the right seating is the secret of a good dinner party," she says.) Whitman is so unrelentingly pleasant that a cynic can't help but wonder: Is she for real? Could it all be just a shtick? When asked this question, [Yahoo's CEO] Terry Semel laughs. "Meg is Meg. She is who you meet. She's smart, straight, and to the point. She's just really nice to do business with."

Source: *Excerpted from Patricia Sellers, "eBay's Secret Weapon,"* Fortune *(October 18, 2004): 161–178.* *For more on eBay, see Erick Schonfeld, "The World According to eBay,"* Business 2.0, *6 (January-February 2005): 76–84.*

What do the following situations have in common?

- A magazine editor praises her supervisor's new outfit shortly before asking for the afternoon off.
- A milling-machine operator tells a friend that he will return the favor if his friend will watch out for the supervisor while he takes an unauthorized cigarette break.
- An office manager attempts to head off opposition to a new Internet-use policy by carefully explaining how it will be fair and will increase productivity.

Aside from the fact that all of these situations take place on the job, the common denominator is "influence." In each case, someone is trying to get his or her own way by influencing someone else's behavior. eBay's Meg Whitman is an inspiring role model for the skillful and responsible use of influence, power, and leadership.

influence: *any attempt to change another's behavior*

Influence is any attempt by a person to change the behavior of superiors, peers, or lower-level employees. Influence is not inherently good or bad. As the foregoing situations illustrate, influence can be used for purely selfish reasons, to subvert organizational objectives, or to enhance organizational effectiveness. Managerial success is firmly linked to the ability to exercise the right sort of influence at the right time. A good example is Andrea Jung, CEO of Avon, as she was working her way up the executive ladder:

> *Jung had little business experience in foreign markets, but as the daughter of immigrants from Hong Kong and China (she was born in Toronto), she had a feel for different cultures. . . . She once flew to Mexico to unveil a new line of products. [Former CEO Jim] Preston recalls that Avon's executive team in Latin America expected her to bomb, that her Manhattan-glam look would make it hard for her to connect with the local sales staff. But Jung sprinkled a little Spanish into her talk and connected, says Preston, who heard glowing reports back from the team.*[2]

Jung's influence skills eventually paid off when she was named the first woman CEO of Avon in its 118-year history.

The purpose of this chapter is to examine different approaches to influencing others. We focus specifically on influence tactics, power, leadership, mentoring, and behavior modification.

Influence Tactics in the Workplace

1. IDENTIFY and DESCRIBE eight generic influence tactics used in modern organizations.

A replication and refinement of an earlier groundbreaking study provides useful insights about on-the-job influence.[3] Both studies asked employees basically the same question: "How do you get your boss, coworker, or subordinate to do something you want?" The following eight generic influence tactics emerged:

You might say Jamaican-born Michael Lee-Chin is a world-class expert on influence. After all, he turned a $150,000 investment in AIC Ltd., a Canadian mutual fund company, into a financial services giant with $9.5 billion under management. His personal net worth has grown to $1.1 billion. He is a master at earning people's trust; enough trust to have them turn over their life savings to be managed by AIC. If Lee-Chin can't win over new clients, then perhaps the two parrots in his corporate lobby can do the trick. They've been trained to say "Buy" and "Hold."

1. ***Consultation.*** Seeking someone's participation in a decision or change
2. ***Rational persuasion.*** Trying to convince someone by relying on a detailed plan, supporting information, reasoning, or logic
3. ***Inspirational appeals.*** Appealing to someone's emotions, values, or ideals to generate enthusiasm and confidence
4. ***Ingratiating tactics.*** Making someone feel important or good before making a request; acting humble or friendly before making a request
5. ***Coalition tactics.*** Seeking the aid of others to persuade someone to agree
6. ***Pressure tactics.*** Relying on intimidation, demands, or threats to gain compliance or support
7. ***Upward appeals.*** Obtaining formal or informal support of higher management
8. ***Exchange tactics.*** Offering an exchange of favors; reminding someone of a past favor; offering to make a personal sacrifice[4]

These influence tactics are *generic* because they are used by various organizational members to influence lower-level employees (downward influence), peers (lateral influence), or superiors (upward influence). Table 15.1 indicates what the researchers found out about patterns of use for the three different directions of influence. Notice that consultation, rational persuasion, and inspirational appeals were the three most popular tactics, regardless of the direction of influence.[5]

15a How Do You Get Your Way?

Profound change has taken place both inside modern organizations and in the environments in which those organizations reside. Many of these changes have greatly increased the importance of the topic of organizational influence processes. This is because so many of the changes have led us toward organizational situations that are much more complex, more ambiguous, more fluid or temporary, and more uncertain—all preconditions for an increase in the role of influence processes, including political behavior.

Source: Lyman W. Porter, Harold L. Angle, and Robert W. Allen, eds. Organizational Influence Processes, *2nd ed. (Armonk, N.Y.: M. E. Sharpe, 2003), pp. xvi–xvii.*

QUESTIONS:

In your daily affairs both inside and outside the workplace, which influence tactics do you rely on the most? Are you an effective influencer? In these changing times, how can you become more effective at influencing others?

For further information about the interactive annotations in this chapter, visit our Web site (**http://business.college.hmco.com/students**) and select Kreitner, *Management,* 10e.

Meanwhile, pressure tactics, upward appeals, and exchange tactics consistently were the least used influence tactics. Ingratiating and coalition tactics fell in the midrange of use.[6] This is an encouraging pattern from the standpoint of getting things done through collaborative problem solving rather than through intimidation and conflict in today's team-oriented workplaces.

For example, Frank Squillante, an IBM vice president, has only four direct reports. To do his job—devising the strategy for the company's intranet, and then developing and deploying applications for 325,000 people and 100,000 business partners—he must be a master at cajoling people over whom he has no real power. "I use 'collaborative influence' every minute of every day," he says. "If I tried to pull one of these 'I'm in charge so you have to do this' maneuvers, the whole thing would break down."[7]

Do women and men tend to rely on different influence tactics? Available research evidence reveals no systematic gender-based differences relative to influencing others.[8] In contrast, the tactics used by employees to influence their bosses were found to vary with different leadership styles. Employees influencing authoritarian managers tended to rely on ingratiating tactics and upward appeals. Rational persuasion was used most often to influence participative managers.[9]

Power

Power is inevitable in modern organizations. According to one advocate of the positive and constructive use of power,

Table 15.1 Use of Generic Organizational Influence Tactics

	Rank order (by direction of influence)		
Tactic	**Downward**	**Lateral**	**Upward**
Consultation	1	1	2
Rational persuasion	2	2	1
Inspirational appeals	3	3	3
Ingratiating tactics	4	4	5
Coalition tactics	5	5	4
Pressure tactics	6	7	7
Upward appeals	7	6	6
Exchange tactics	8	8	8

Source: *Adapted from discussion in Gary Yukl and Cecilia M. Falbe, "Influence Tactics and Objectives in Upward, Downward, and Lateral Influence Attempts,"* Journal of Applied Psychology, *75 (April 1990): 132–140.*

> *Power must be used because managers must influence those they depend on. Power also is crucial in the development of managers' self-confidence and willingness to support subordinates. From this perspective, power should be accepted as a natural part of any organization. Managers should recognize and develop their own power to coordinate and support the work of subordinates; it is powerlessness, not power, that undermines organizational effectiveness.*[10]

As a manager, if you understand power, its bases, and empowerment, you will have an advantage when it comes to getting things accomplished with and through others.[11]

■ What Is Power?

power: *ability to marshal resources to get something done*

Power is "the ability to marshal the human, informational, and material resources to get something done."[12] Power affects organizational members in the following three areas:

1. ***Decisions.*** A packaging engineer decides to take on a difficult new assignment after hearing her boss's recommendations.
2. ***Behavior.*** A hospital lab technician achieves a month of perfect attendance after receiving a written warning about absenteeism from his supervisor.
3. ***Situations.*** The productivity of a product design group increases dramatically following the purchase of project management software.[13]

Another instructive way of looking at power is to distinguish between "power over" (ability to dominate), "power to" (ability to act freely), and "power from" (ability to resist the demands of others).[14]

By emphasizing the word *ability* in our definition and discussion of power, we can contrast power with authority. As defined in Chapter 9, authority is the "right" to direct the activities of others.[15] Authority is an officially sanctioned privilege that may or may not get results. In contrast, power is the demonstrated *ability* to get results. As illustrated in Figure 15.1, one may possess authority but have no power, possess no authority yet have power, or possess both authority and power. The first situation, authority but no power, was experienced by Albanian police in 1997, when Europe's poorest nation fell into anarchy over dissatisfaction with a corrupt government. According to *Newsweek*, "An angry mob surrounded one group of police, stripped them to their underpants, and burned their gear."[16] At the other end of the model in Figure 15.1, it is possible for an individual to have power but no authority. For example, employees may respond to the wishes of the supervisor's spouse.[17] Finally, a manager who gets employees to work hard on an important project has both authority and power.[18]

reward power: *gaining compliance through rewards*

coercive power: *gaining compliance through threats or punishment*

2. IDENTIFY the five bases of power, and **EXPLAIN** what it takes to make empowerment work.

■ The Five Bases of Power

Essential to the successful use of power in organizations is an understanding of the various bases of power. One widely cited classification of power bases identifies five types of power: reward, coercive, legitimate, referent, and expert.[19]

Figure 15.1 The Relationship Between Authority and Power

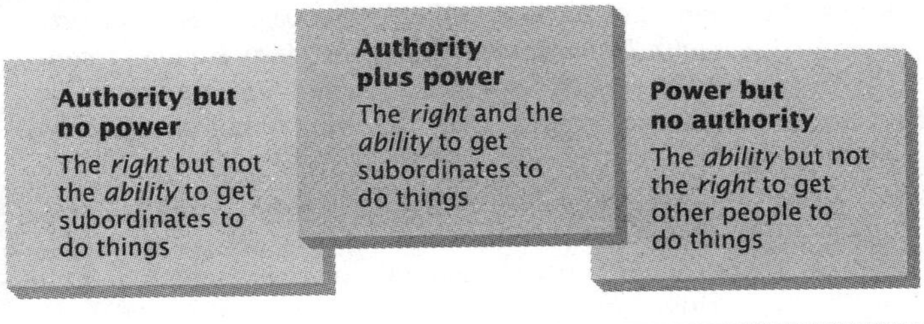

■ Reward Power. One's ability to grant rewards to those who comply with a command or request is the key to **reward power**. Management's reward power can be strengthened by linking pay raises, merit pay, and promotions to job performance. Sought-after expressions of friendship or trust also enhance reward power.

■ Coercive Power. Rooted in fear, **coercive power** is based on threatened or actual punishment. For example, a

It may be her husband, Hosni Mubarak, who is the President of Egypt and wields immense legitimate power; but make no mistake, Suzanne Mubarak is a very powerful person in her own right. When she addressed the Arab women's forum for science and technology in Cairo recently, she exercised a good deal of referent and expert power.

manager might threaten a habitually tardy employee with a demotion if he or she is late one more time.

■ **Legitimate Power.** **Legitimate power** is achieved when a person's superior position alone prompts another person to act in a desired manner. This type of power closely parallels formal authority, as discussed above. Parents, teachers, religious leaders, and managers who expect or demand obedience by virtue of their superior social position are attempting to exercise legitimate power. Note, however, the following warning about legitimate power:

> *Trying to control others solely by directing them and on the basis of the power associated with one's position simply will not work—first, because managers are always dependent on some people over whom they have no formal authority, and second, because virtually no one in modern organizations will passively accept and completely obey a constant stream of orders from someone just because he or she is the "boss."*[20]

One might reasonably conclude that legitimate power has been eroded by its frequent abuse (or overuse) through the years.[21] Moreover, legitimate power may exact a price that fewer are willing to pay these days. According to a recent survey, "60 percent of executives don't want to be CEO. That's double the number (27 percent) who had no interest in the top job in 2001."[22]

legitimate power: *compliance based on one's formal position*

referent power: *compliance based on charisma or personal identification*

■ **Referent Power.** An individual has **referent power** over those who identify with him or her if they comply on that basis alone. Personal attraction is an elusive thing to define, let alone consciously cultivate. *Charisma* is a term often used in conjunction with referent power. Although leaders with the personal magnetism of Abraham Lincoln, John Kennedy, or Martin Luther King Jr., are always in short supply, charisma in the workplace can be problematic. *Fortune* magazine offered this perspective:

> *Used wisely, it's a blessing. Indulged, it can be a curse. Charismatic visionaries lead people ahead—and sometimes astray. They can be impetuous, unpredictable, and exasperating to work for, like [media mogul Ted] Turner. [Donald] Trump. Steve Jobs. Ross Perot. Lee Iacocca. "Often what begins as a mission becomes an obsession," says John Thompson, president of Human Factors, a leadership consulting service in San Rafael, California. "Leaders can cut corners on values and become driven by self-interest. Then they may abuse anyone who makes a mistake."*
>
> *Like pornography, charisma is hard to define. But you know it when you see it. And you don't see much of it in the Fortune 500.*[23]

Still, as we will see in our discussion of transformational leadership later in this chapter, charisma does have its positive side.

"Whoa! Sorry Ed. Is there a power control on these laser pointers?"

Source: *Chris Wildt.*

expert power: *compliance based on ability to dispense valued information*

■ **Expert Power.** Those who possess and can dispense valued information generally exercise **expert power** over those in need of such information. Information technology experts, for instance, are in a position today to wield a great deal of expert power. Anyone who has ever been taken advantage of by an unscrupulous automobile mechanic knows what expert power in the wrong hands can mean.

15b Quick Quiz

A snapshot of Jeffrey Greenberg, who stepped down as CEO of insurance broker Marsh & McLennan in 2004 amid charges his company had paid illegal kickbacks:

> *Marsh executives entered Jeffrey's office on the 44th floor of a midtown Manhattan skyscraper with trepidation. . . . Jeffrey didn't hesitate to raise his voice when he was displeased. "If you got summoned up there, he was either going to anoint you with the key to the kingdom," says a former senior vice president, "or he was going to rip the floor out from under you."*

Source: Devin Leonard, "Greenberg & Sons," Fortune *(February 21, 2005): 114.*

QUESTIONS:
Which power base is evident here? Is it a good idea to rely heavily on this particular power base today?

■ Empowerment

Empowerment (see p. 444 for definition) occurs when employees are adequately trained, provided with all relevant information and the best possible tools, fully involved in key decisions, and fairly rewarded for results.[24] Those who endorse this key building block of progressive management view power as an unlimited resource. Frances Hesselbein, the widely respected former head of the Girl Scouts of the USA, offered this perspective: "The more power you give away, the more you have."[25] This can be a difficult concept to grasp for traditional authoritarian managers who see empowerment as a threat to their authority and feeling of being in control. Today, the issue is not empowerment versus no empowerment. Rather, the issue is how empowerment should take place. As indicated in Skills & Tools at the end of this chapter, employee empowerment is like a seed requiring favorable growing conditions. Much of the burden for successful empowerment falls on the *individual.* No amount of empowerment and

empowerment: *making employees full partners in the decision-making process and giving them the necessary tools and rewards*

supportive management can overcome dishonesty, untrustworthiness, selfishness, and inadequate skills.[26] Moreover, as we learned in the Enron case, empowerment without proper oversight can lead to very bad consequences.

> *Young people, many just out of undergraduate or MBA programs, were handed extraordinary authority, able to make $5 million decisions without higher approval. . . .*
>
> *At Enron, however, the pressure to make the numbers often overwhelmed the pretext of "tight" controls. "The environment was ripe for abuse," says a former manager in Enron's energy services unit. "Nobody at corporate was asking the right questions. It was completely hands-off management. A situation like that requires tight controls. Instead, it was a runaway train."*[27]

Once again, rigorous employee selection and training and ethics training, as discussed in Chapters 5 and 11, come to the forefront.

Leadership

Leadership has fascinated people since the dawn of recorded history. The search for good leaders has been a common thread running through human civilization.[28] In view of research evidence that effective leadership is associated with both better performance and more ethical performance, the search for ways to identify (or develop) good leaders needs to continue.[29] As Peter Drucker recently pointed out, leadership is a difficult topic because great leaders come in all sizes, shapes, and temperaments. The legendary management scholar helpfully offered the following leader *effectiveness* criteria:

> *. . . some of the best business and nonprofit CEOs I've worked with over a 65-year consulting career were not stereotypical leaders. They were all over the map in terms of their personalities, attitudes, values, strengths, and weaknesses. They ranged from extroverted to nearly reclusive, from easygoing to controlling, from generous to parsimonious.*
>
> *What made them all effective is that they followed the same eight practices:*
>
> - *They asked, "What needs to be done?"*
> - *They asked, "What is right for the enterprise?"*
> - *They developed action plans.*
> - *They took responsibility for decisions.*
> - *They took responsibility for communicating.*
> - *They were focused on opportunities rather than problems.*
> - *They ran productive meetings.*
> - *They thought and said "we" rather than "I."*[30]

leadership: *social influence process of inspiring and guiding others in a common effort*

Let us keep these effectiveness criteria in mind as we explore the topic of leadership, while resisting the temptation to embrace a one-size-fits-all leadership model.[31]

15c Repeal the Golden Rule?

Marshall Goldsmith, executive coach and author:

> *The golden rule ["Treat others as you want to be treated."] doesn't always work in leadership. If you manage your people the way you'd want to be managed, you're forgetting: You're not managing you!*

Source: Marshall Goldsmith, "When the Golden Rule Doesn't Work," Fast Company, *no. 90 (January 2005): 90.*

QUESTIONS:
Do you agree or disagree with this proposition? Why?

Leadership Defined

Research on leadership has produced many definitions of the term. Much of the variation is semantic; the definition offered here is a workable compromise. **Leadership** is the process of inspiring, influencing, and guiding others to participate in a common effort.[32] In today's highly interconnected world, leadership extends beyond the office door or factory gate.

> *Leaders bear the responsibility of guiding a host of constituents toward the accomplishment of an overarching goal, whether this be leading employees toward greater productivity, guiding suppliers toward a better understanding of ways to cooperate in order to*

> *better serve the firm's customers, or helping investors appreciate the firm's strategy and how achievement of that strategy will result in enhanced shareholder value. All require a solid grounding in a vision that guides the leader and, ultimately, the organization toward better performance.*[33]

To encourage such broad participation, leaders supplement any authority and power they possess with their personal attributes, imagination, and social skills. Colin Powell, a leader admired in both military and civilian circles, offers his own definition: "Leadership is the art of accomplishing more than the science of management says is possible."[34]

Formal and Informal Leaders

formal leadership: *the process of influencing others to pursue official objectives*

informal leadership: *the process of influencing others to pursue unofficial objectives*

Experts on leadership distinguish between formal and informal leadership. **Formal leadership** is the process of influencing relevant others to pursue official organizational objectives. **Informal leadership**, in contrast, is the process of influencing others to pursue unofficial objectives that may or may not serve the organization's interests. Formal leaders generally have a measure of legitimate power because of their formal authority, whereas informal leaders typically lack formal authority. Beyond that, both types rely on expedient combinations of reward, coercive, referent, and expert power. Informal leaders who identify with the job to be done are a valuable asset to an organization. Conversely, an organization can be brought to its knees by informal leaders who turn cohesive work groups against the organization.

The Issue of Leaders versus Managers: A Middle Ground

A long-standing debate about the differences between leaders and managers sprang from Abraham Zaleznik's 1977 article in *Harvard Business Review* titled "Managers and Leaders: Are They Different?" Over the years, stereotypes developed characterizing leaders and managers in very different ways. Leaders are typically viewed as farsighted and even heroic visionaries who boldly blaze new trails. They can't be bothered with details. In contrast, a less-flattering portrayal of the manager is that of a facilitator who tends to the details of turning the leader's vision into reality. Accordingly, it has been said that leaders make chaos out of order and managers make order out of chaos. This dueling-sterotypes debate may be a fun academic exercise, but it misses one important *practical* point: Today's leaner and continuously evolving organizations require people who can both lead *and* manage—in other words, the total package.[35] The future belongs to those who can effectively blend the characteristics in Table 15.2. JetBlue's CEO David Neeleman, explains how his airline strives to strike the right balance:

> *JetBlue's officers don't act aloof and sit at their desks all day. We roll up our sleeves to understand what's going on, because our leaders shouldn't treat others as inferiors. A couple of years ago, we promoted our middle managers without giving them leadership training. They became little dictators, and favoritism started to creep in.*
>
> *So we had to create a leadership program to reset the expectations of what leaders should do. But we didn't hire a bunch of slick facilitators to talk about principles. Instead, the people who were actually living [those principles] at JetBlue were the ones teaching the courses. Now 40 of our top managers spend two days a year leading the group.*[36]

No one ever said leadership was easy.

The study of leadership has evolved as theories have been developed and refined by successive generations of researchers.[37] Something useful has been learned at each stage of development. We now turn to significant milestones in the evolution of leadership theory by examining the trait, behavioral styles, situational, and transformational approaches (see Figure 15.2).

Table 15.2 Lead or Manage? Good Leaders Must Do Both

Being a leader means	Being a manager means
Motivating, influencing and changing behavior.	Practicing stewardship, directing and being held accountable for resources.
Inspiring, setting the tone, and articulating a vision.	Executing plans, implementing and delivering the goods and services.
Managing people.	Managing resources.
Being charismatic.	Being conscientious.
Being visionary.	Planning, organizing, directing and controlling.
Understanding and using power and influence.	Understanding and using authority and responsibility.
Acting decisively.	Acting responsibly.
Putting people first. The leader knows, responds to, and acts for his or her followers.	Putting customers first. The manager knows, responds to, and acts for his or her customers.
Leaders can make mistakes when: 1. they choose the wrong goal, direction or inspiration, due to incompetence or bad intentions; or 2. they over-lead; or 3. they are unable to deliver on [or] implement the vision due to incompetence or a lack of follow through commitment.	Managers can make mistakes when: 1. they fail to grasp the importance of people as the key resource; or 2. they under-lead; they treat people like other resources [or like] numbers; or 3. they are eager to direct and to control but are unwilling to accept accountability.

Source: *Reprinted from* Organizational Dynamics, *Vol. 33, Peter Lorenzi, "Managing for the Common Good: Prosocial Leadership," p. 286, Copyright 2004, with permission from Elsevier.*

Trait Theory

During most of recorded history, the prevailing assumption was that leaders are born and not made. Leaders such as Alexander the Great, Napoleon Bonaparte, and George Washington were said to have been blessed with an inborn ability to lead. This so-called great-man approach to leadership[38] eventually gave way to trait theory. According to one observer, "under the influence of the behavioristic school of psychological thought, the fact was accepted that leadership traits are not completely inborn but can also be acquired through learning and experience. Attention turned to the search for universal traits possessed by leaders."[39]

As the popularity of the trait approach mushroomed during the second quarter of the twentieth century, literally hundreds of physical, mental, and personality traits were said to be the key determinants of successful leadership. Unfortunately, few

Figure 15.2 The Evolution of Leadership Theory

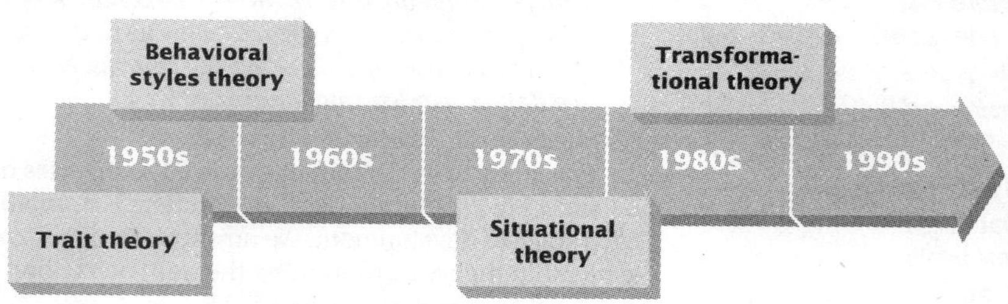

theorists agreed on the most important traits of a good leader. The predictive value of trait theory was severely limited because traits tend to be a chicken-and-egg proposition: Was George Washington a good leader because he had self-confidence, or did he have self-confidence because he was thrust into a leadership role at a young age? In spite of inherent problems, trait profiles provide a useful framework for examining what it takes to be a good leader.

■ **An Early Trait Profile.** Not until 1948 was a comprehensive review of competing trait theories conducted. After comparing more than 100 studies of leader traits and characteristics, the reviewer uncovered moderate agreement on only five traits. In the reviewer's words, "the average person who occupies a position of leadership exceeds the average member of his group in the following respects: (1) intelligence, (2) scholarship, (3) dependability in exercising responsibilities, (4) activity and social participation, and (5) socioeconomic status."[40]

■ **A Modern Trait Profile: Leaders with Emotional Intelligence.** Daniel Goleman's 1995 book *Emotional Intelligence* popularized a concept that psychologists had talked about for years.[41] Whereas standard intelligence (IQ) deals with thinking and reasoning, emotional intelligence (EQ) deals more broadly with building social relationships and controlling one's emotions. **Emotional intelligence** has been defined as

emotional intelligence: *the ability to monitor and control one's emotions and behavior in complex social settings*

> *. . . good old street smarts—knowing when to share sensitive information with colleagues, laugh at the boss's jokes or speak up in a meeting. In more scientific terms, . . . [emotional intelligence] can be defined as an array of noncognitive skills, capabilities and competencies that influence a person's ability to cope with environmental demands and pressures.*[42]

Higher EQ scores indicate more polished social skills and greater emotional maturity (try the Hands-On Exercise at the end of this chapter). Interestingly, Goleman says that emotional intelligence should be evaluated by others because it is difficult to be objective about oneself in such an important domain.

3. EXPLAIN the concept of emotional intelligence in terms of Goleman's four leadership traits.

Goleman and his colleagues recently cast emotional intelligence in terms of four leadership traits:

- ***Self-awareness.*** This essential component of emotional intelligence involves the ability to read one's own emotions and hence be better equipped to assess one's strengths and limitations.
- ***Self-management.*** Those who possess this trait do not let their moods and emotions disrupt honest and straightforward relationships.
- ***Social awareness.*** Those who possess this trait are able to read others' emotions and reactions and subsequently adapt in a constructive and caring fashion.
- ***Relationship management.*** Leaders who possess this trait are clear, enthusiastic, and convincing communicators who can defuse conflicts. They rely on kindness and humor to build strong relationships.[43]

Each of these traits can be learned, according to Goleman. A big step in the right direction is for managers to fully appreciate how their emotional outbursts and foul moods can poison the work environment. Leaders and followers alike need to exhibit greater emotional intelligence in order to build social capital in today's hectic and often stressful workplaces.[44]

15d Take a Good Look Inside Yourself

Jeff Immelt, CEO, General Electric:

Leadership is an intense journey into yourself. You can use your own style to get anything done. It's about being self-aware. Every morning, I look in the mirror and say, "I could have done three things better yesterday."

Source: As quoted in "Top 10 Leadership Tips from Jeff Immelt," Fast Company, *no. 81 (April 2004): 96.*

QUESTIONS:

What does this say about Immelt's emotional intelligence? Explain. How would you rate your own self-awareness?

■ **The Controversy over Female and Male Leadership Traits.** A second source of renewed interest in leadership traits is the ongoing debate about female versus male leadership traits. In an often-cited survey by Judy B. Rosener, female leaders were found to be better than their male counterparts at sharing power and information.[45] Critics have chided Rosener for reinforcing this traditional feminine stereotype.[46] Actually, a comprehensive review of 162 different studies found *no significant difference* in leadership styles exhibited by women and men. In real-life organizational settings, women did *not* fit the feminine stereotype of being more relationship- oriented, and men did *not* fit the masculine stereotype of being more task-oriented.[47] As always, it is bad practice to make prejudicial assumptions about individuals on the basis of their membership in some demographic category.

■ Behavioral Styles Theory

During World War II, the study of leadership took on a significant new twist. Rather than concentrating on the personal traits of successful leaders, researchers working with the military began turning their attention to patterns of leader behavior (called leadership styles). In other words, attention turned from who the leader was to how the leader actually behaved. One early laboratory study of leader behavior demonstrated that followers overwhelmingly preferred managers who had a democratic style to those with an authoritarian style or a laissez-faire (hands-off) style.[48] An updated review of these three classic leadership styles can be found in Table 15.3.

For a number of years, theorists and managers hailed democratic leadership as the key to productive and happy employees. Eventually, however, their enthusiasm was dampened when critics noted how the original study relied on children as subjects and virtually ignored productivity. Although there is general agreement that these basic styles exist, debate has been vigorous over their relative value and appropriateness. Practical experience has shown, for example, that the democratic style does not always stimulate better performance. Some employees prefer to be told what to do rather than participating in decision making. This can be the result of cultural differences, as was the case recently when the world's largest television maker was created by the merger of China's TCL Corp. and France's Thomson.

Table 15.3 The Three Classic Styles of Leadership

	Authoritarian	Democratic	Laissez-faire
Nature	Leader retains all authority and responsibility	Leader delegates a great deal of authority while retaining ultimate responsibility	Leader grants responsibility and authority to group
	Leader assigns people to clearly defined tasks	Work is divided and assigned on the basis of participatory decision making	Group members are told to work things out themselves and do the best they can
	Primarily a downward flow of communication	Active two-way flow of upward and downward communication	Primarily horizontal communication among peers
Primary strength	Stresses prompt, orderly, and predictable performance	Enhances personal commitment through participation	Permits self-starters to do things as they see fit without leader interference
Primary weakness	Approach tends to stifle individual initiative	Democratic process is time-consuming	Group may drift aimlessly in the absence of direction from leader

Figure 15.3 Basic Leadership Styles from the Ohio State Study

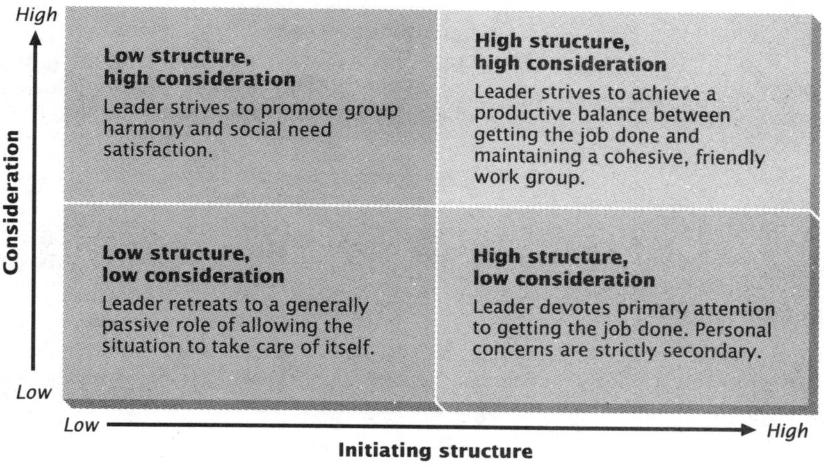

In China, says one TCL official, "if the leader says something is right, even if he is wrong, employees will agree with him. But in foreign companies, they will not agree with him. We have two different cultures.[49]

4. SUMMARIZE what the Ohio State model and the Leadership Grid® have taught managers about leadership.

The Ohio State Model. While the democratic style of leadership was receiving attention, a slightly different behavioral approach to leadership emerged. This second approach began in the late 1940s when a team of Ohio State University researchers defined two independent dimensions of leader behavior.[50] One dimension, called "initiating structure," was the leader's efforts to get things organized and get the job done. The second dimension, labeled "consideration," was the degree of trust, friendship, respect, and warmth that the leader extended to subordinates. By making a matrix out of these two independent dimensions of leader behavior, the Ohio State researchers identified four styles of leadership (see Figure 15.3).

This particular scheme proved to be fertile ground for leadership theorists, and variations of the original Ohio State approach soon appeared.[51] Leadership theorists began a search for the "one best style" of leadership. The high-structure, high-consideration style was generally hailed as the best all-around style. This "high-high" style has intuitive appeal because it embraces the best of both categories of leader behavior. But one researcher cautioned in 1966 that although there seemed to be a positive relationship between consideration and employee satisfaction, a positive link between the high-high style and work group performance had not been proved conclusively.[52]

15e A Leadership Tightrope Act

James McNerney, CEO, Boeing:

"Some people feel you either have a demanding command-and-control style or you have a nurturing, encouraging style. I believe you have to have both."

Source: As quoted in Michael Arndt, "3M's Rising Star," Business Week *(April 12, 2004): 74.*

QUESTION:
What is the take-away lesson here for present and future leaders?

The Leadership Grid®. Developed by Robert R. Blake and Jane S. Mouton, and originally called the Managerial Grid®, the Leadership Grid® is a trademarked and widely recognized typology of leadership styles.[53] Today, amid the growing popularity of situational and transformational leadership theories, Blake's followers remain convinced that there is one best style of leadership.[54] As we will see, they support this claim with research evidence.

As illustrated in Figure 15.4, the Leadership Grid® has "concern for production" on the horizontal axis and "concern for people" on the vertical axis. Concern for production involves a desire to achieve greater output, cost-effectiveness, and profits in

Figure 15.4 Blake and McCanse's Leadership Grid®

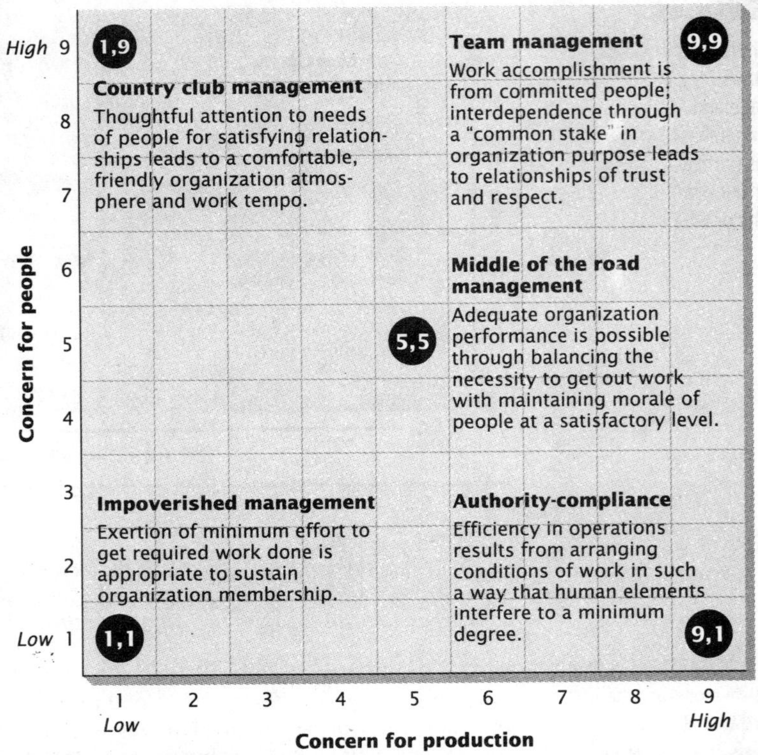

Source: *From Blake, R. R. & A. A. McCanse.* Leadership Dilemmas—Grid Solutions *Houston: Gulf Publishing, 1991.*

profit-seeking organizations. Concern for people involves promoting friendship, helping coworkers get the job done, and attending to things that matter to people, such as pay and working conditions. When a scale from 1 to 9 is marked on each axis, five major styles emerge on the grid:

9,1 style: primary concern for production; people secondary

1,9 style: primary concern for people; production secondary

1,1 style: minimal concern for either production or people

5,5 style: moderate concern for both production and people to maintain the status quo

9,9 style: high concern for both production and people as evidenced by personal commitment, mutual trust, and teamwork

Although they stress that managers and leaders need to be versatile enough to select the courses of action appropriate to the situation, Blake and his colleagues contend that a 9,9 style correlates positively with better results, better mental and physical health, and effective conflict resolution. They believe there *is* one best leadership style. As they see it, the true 9,9 style has never been adequately tested by the situationalists. In a more recent study by Blake and Mouton, 100 experienced managers overwhelmingly preferred the 9,9 style, regardless of how the situation varied.[55]

15f Back to the Opening Case

Where would you plot eBay's Meg Whitman on Blake and McCanse's Leadership Grid®? Why? Is this particular style the best for her present situation? Why or why not?

Consequently, Blake's management training and organization development programs were designed to help individuals and entire organizations move into the 9,9 portion of the Leadership Grid®.

A 9,9 leadership style certainly worked well for Lawrence R. Johnston, CEO of grocery giant Albertsons Inc., when he worked for Jack Welch at General Electric:

> *Welch dispatched him to Paris in 1997 to fix the [medical services] business, which was losing $100 million a year, or dump it.*
>
> *In less than three years, the division was making a $100 million operating profit. According to Welch, Johnston succeeded because he quickly realized his chief task was reenergizing the employees. "This was a cynical group of French and German engineers," Welch recalls. "But he engaged them incredibly." Every month Johnston traveled to a different European city, conducting sales meetings in the mornings and taking his team to visit hospitals in the afternoons. And at nights he studied French. "Larry can lead people over the hill," Welch says. "He put us on the map in Europe."*[56]

Situational Theory

Convinced that no one best style of leadership exists, some management scholars have advocated situational or contingency thinking. Although a number of different situational-leadership theories have been developed, they all share one fundamental assumption: successful leadership occurs when the leader's style matches the situation. Situational-leadership theorists stress the need for flexibility. They reject the notion of a universally applicable style. Research is under way to determine precisely when and where various styles of leadership are appropriate. Fiedler's contingency theory and the path-goal theory are introduced and discussed here because they represent distinctly different approaches to situational leadership.

Fiedler's Contingency Theory. Among the various leadership theories proposed so far, Fiedler's is the most thoroughly tested. It is the product of more than 30 years of research by Fred E. Fiedler and his associates. Fiedler's contingency theory gets its name from the following assumption:

> *The performance of a leader depends on two interrelated factors: (1) the degree to which the situation gives the leader control and influence—that is, the likelihood that [the leader] can successfully accomplish the job; and (2) the leader's basic motivation—that is, whether [the leader's] self-esteem depends primarily on accomplishing the task or on having close supportive relations with others.*[57]

Regarding the second factor, the leader's basic motivation, Fiedler believes leaders are either task-motivated or relationship-motivated. These two motivational profiles are roughly equivalent to initiating structure (or concern for production) and consideration (or concern for people).

A consistent pattern has emerged from the many studies of effective leaders carried out by Fiedler and others.[58] As illustrated in Figure 15.5, task-motivated leaders seem to be effective in extreme situations when they have either very little control or a great deal of control over situational variables. In moderately favorable situations, however, relationship-motivated leaders tend to be more effective. Consequently, Fiedler and one of his colleagues summed up their findings by noting that "everything points to the conclusion that there is no such thing as an ideal leader."[59] Instead, there are leaders, and there are situations. The challenge, according to Fiedler, is to analyze a leader's basic motivation and then match that leader with a suitable situation to form a productive combination. He believes it is more efficient to move leaders to a suitable situation than to tamper with their personalities by trying to get task-motivated leaders to become relationship-motivated, or vice versa.

Figure 15.5 Fiedler's Contingency Theory of Leadership

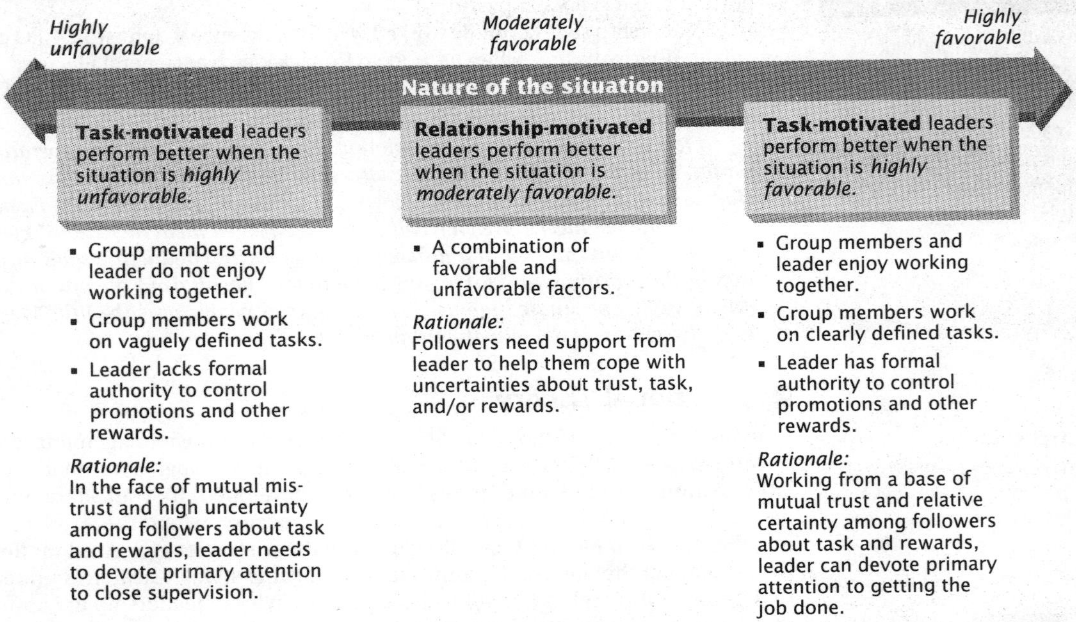

5. DESCRIBE the path-goal theory of leadership, and **EXPLAIN** how the assumption on which it is based differs from the assumption on which Fiedler's contingency theory is based.

■ **House's Updated Path-Goal Theory.** Another situational-leadership theory is the path-goal theory, a derivative of expectancy motivation theory (see Chapter 13). Path-goal theory gets its name from the assumption that effective leaders can enhance employee motivation by (1) clarifying the individual's perception of work goals, (2) linking meaningful rewards to goal attainment, and (3) explaining how goals and desired rewards can be achieved. In short, leaders should motivate their followers by providing clear goals and meaningful incentives for reaching them. Path-goal theorists believe that motivation is essential to effective leadership.

According to path-goal theorists Robert J. House and Terence R. Mitchell, leaders can enhance motivation by "increasing the number and kinds of personal payoffs to subordinates for work-goal attainment and making paths to these payoffs easier to travel by clarifying the paths, reducing road blocks and pitfalls, and increasing the opportunities for personal satisfaction en route."[60] The path-goal perspective is clearly evident in the following profile, offered by best-selling author Marcus Buckingham, who has studied leaders for 20 years:

> *As a leader, your job is to make people more confident about the future you're dragging them into. To that end, you need to tell them why they're going to win. There are many competitors out there. Why will we beat them? There are many obstacles in our path. Why will we overcome them? The more clearly you can answer these questions, the more confident we will be, and therefore the more resilient, the more persistent, and the more creative.*[61]

Personal characteristics of employees, environmental pressures, and demands on employees will all vary from situation to situation. Thus, House's updated path-goal model advises managers to rely contingently on eight categories of leader behavior:

- **Path-goal clarifying behaviors** (Make it clear how goal attainment is linked with meaningful rewards.)

15g Back to the Opening Case

Which of the eight path-goal leader behaviors did Meg Whitman exhibit in the eBay case? Explain. Which one did she use most effectively? Explain.

- **Achievement-oriented behaviors** (Set challenging goals, emphasize excellence, and seek continuous improvement while maintaining a high degree of confidence that employees will meet difficult challenges in a responsible manner.)
- **Work facilitation behaviors** (Plan and coordinate work, make decisions, provide feedback and coaching, provide resources, remove roadblocks, and empower employees.)
- **Supportive behaviors** (Be friendly and approachable, and show concern for employees' well-being.)
- **Interaction facilitation behaviors** (Resolve disputes and encourage collaboration, diverse opinions, and teamwork.)
- **Group decision behaviors** (Encourage group input, problem solving, and participation.)
- **Networking behaviors** (Build bridges to influential people and represent the group's best interests to others.)
- **Value-based behaviors** (Self-confidently formulate and passionately support a vision.)[62]

The assumption that managers can and do shift situationally from one behavior pattern to another clearly sets path-goal theory apart from Fiedler's model. Recall that Fiedler claims managers cannot and do not change their basic leadership styles.

transformational leaders: *visionaries who challenge people to do exceptional things*

Limited research on the path-goal model has yielded mixed results.[63] One valuable contribution of path-goal theory is its identification of achievement-oriented leadership behavior. As managers deal with an increasing number of highly educated and self-motivated employees in advanced-technology industries, they will need to become skilled facilitators rather than just order givers or hand holders.

Steve Jobs is a true transformational leader and he has the resume to prove it. His vision, charisma, and communication skills are part of Silicon Valley legend. In the 1970s, he cofounded Apple Computer with his buddy Steve Wozniak. In the 1980s, he bought Pixar, the animated movie studio responsible for such hits as Finding Nemo. In the 1990s, he rejoined Apple as CEO and launched the iPod revolution. What's next?

Transformational Leadership Theory

In his 1978 book *Leadership*, James McGregor Burns drew a distinction between transactional and transformational leadership. Burns characterized **transformational leaders** as visionaries who challenge people to achieve exceptionally high levels of morality, motivation, and performance.[64] Only transformational leaders, Burns argued, are capable of charting necessary new courses for modern organizations. Why? Because they are masters of change (see Managing Diversity).[65] They can envision a better future, effectively communicate that vision, and get others to willingly make it a reality.

Transactional versus Transformational Leaders. Extending the work of Burns, Bernard Bass emphasized the importance of charisma in transformational leadership. Transformational leaders rely heavily on referent power. Wendy's Dave Thomas, Wal-Mart's Sam Walton, and Southwest Airlines' Herb Kelleher exemplify charismatic leaders who engineered great success at their respective companies.[66] While acknowledging that transformational leaders exhibit widely different styles and tend to stir their fair share of controversy, Bass rounded out Burns's distinction between transactional and transformational leaders (see Table 15.4 on p. 455). Transactional leaders monitor people so that they do the expected, according to plan. In contrast, transformational leaders inspire people to do the unexpected, above and beyond the plan. This distinction can mean the difference between maintaining the status quo and fostering creative and productive growth.

Positive Evidence. It is important to note that the distinction in Table 15.4 is not between bad and good leaders—both types are needed today.

MANAGING DIVERSITY

A Native American's Vision for a Better Future

It started as a simple business matter: The people needed jobs and nobody was providing them. Nothing is simple though, when your community is wilting under endemic poverty, when your ancestors left their footprints on forced removals from Wisconsin to Iowa to Minnesota to South Dakota to Nebraska, when your people have few options outside the federal government, when tribal politicians pull the strings on the local economy, and when the only available start-up funds come one pull of a handle, one rake of the chips, at a time. Or is it? Can a driven visionary entrepreneur change the fate of his people? In the case of Lance Morgan, the answer is yes.

"We've done it," says Morgan, "and other tribes have just as much talent as the Winnebagos, but they don't have the model . . . yet." The model is Ho-Chunk Inc., the $100 million tribe-owned corporation that employs 355 people in a variety of businesses including housing construction, hotels, convenience stores, e-commerce hot spot Allnative.com, Web design, tobacco distribution, community development, and Indianz.com, a news site for all things Native American. After graduating from Harvard Law School and spending two unhappy years at a corporate firm in Minneapolis, Morgan returned to the Winnebago reservation in 1995 to start Ho-Chunk with $8 million in seed money from a casino (although the company hasn't taken a nickel of gaming money since). "I don't think much of gaming," says Morgan, "but it was a means to an end."

The idea is no less than to create an economy, and it wouldn't have taken off if Morgan hadn't convinced the tribal council to break with the norm and allow Ho-Chunk to operate somewhat autonomously. (Ho-Chunk and the Winnebago tribal council meet quarterly and are partners in a business whose model is being studied and adopted by tribes across the country.) Morgan is currently embedded in an ambitious project to literally build a better community from the ground up. Houses and businesses are being erected in Ho-Chunk Village, a new urbanism/small town combination created to replace dilapidated, random government housing and where, Morgan says, "we can have a warm, safe place to raise a family, like any other neighborhood, except nicer and everyone will be brown."

Like most go-getters, Morgan, 35, has time for work and family and not much else—[University of Nebraska] Cornhuskers football is one of his few diversions from building a 21st-century economic model for Indian peoples nationwide who have been shut out of the entrepreneurial arena. "We've taken control of our destiny, gotten a taste of independence, and don't plan on giving it up," says Morgan. "Government-led economies have been a total failure. I refuse to believe the Winnebagos are Karl Marx's last hope."

Ho-Chunk (which loosely translates to "the people") has spoken.

This is where transformational leadership theory effectively combines the behavioral styles and situational approaches just discussed. To the traditional behavioral patterns of initiating structure and consideration have been added charismatic and other behaviors.[67] Transformational leadership also needs to be situationally appropriate. Specifically, transformational leadership is needed in rapidly changing situations; transactional leaders can best handle stable situations.[68]

Available laboratory and field research evidence generally supports the transformational-leadership pattern. Followers of transformational leaders tend to perform better and to report greater satisfaction than those of transactional leaders.[69]

Putting to Work What You've Learned by Using "Practical Intelligence" and Becoming a "Servant Leader"

6. DESCRIBE a transformational leader, and **EXPLAIN** Greenleaf's philosophy of the servant leader.

Finding ways to practice leadership both on and off the job can help present and future managers develop their abilities. Serving in campus, community, or religious organizations, for example, will give you an opportunity to experiment with different leadership styles in a variety of situations. Leading effectively, like riding a bike, is learned only by doing. This section offers some inspiration for polishing your leadership abilities.

Table 15.4 Transactional versus Transformational Leaders

Transactional leader		Transformational leader	
Contingent reward	Contracts exchange of rewards for effort, promises rewards for good performance, recognizes accomplishments.	**Charisma**	Provides vision and sense of mission, instills pride, gains respect and trust.
Management by exception (active)	Watches and searches for deviations from rules and standards, takes corrective action.	**Inspiration**	Communicates high expectations, uses symbols to focus efforts, expresses important purposes in simple ways.
Management by exception (passive)	Intervenes only if standards are not met.	**Intellectual stimulation**	Promotes intelligence, rationality, and careful problem solving.
Laissez-faire	Abdicates responsibilities, avoids making decisions.	**Individualized consideration**	Gives personal attention, treats each employee individually, coaches, advises.

Source: *Reprinted from* Organizational Dynamics *(Winter 1990). Bernard M. Bass et al., "From Transactional to Transformational Leadership: Learning to Share the Vision." Copyright 1990, with permission from Elsevier Science.*

■ **Practical Intelligence.** Yale University's Robert J. Sternberg believes that good leaders effectively blend three things: wisdom, intelligence, and creativity. What sort of intelligence? He explains:

> *Practical intelligence is the ability to solve everyday problems by utilizing knowledge gained from experience in order to purposefully adapt to, shape, and select environments. It thus involves changing oneself to suit the environment (adaptation), changing the environment to suit oneself (shaping), or finding a new environment within which to work (selection). One uses these skills to (a) manage oneself, (b) manage others, and (c) manage tasks.*[70]

Because practical intelligence is a broad concept—involving both relationships and tasks—it includes and goes beyond emotional intelligence, discussed earlier. Significantly, Sternberg rejects the notion of "born leaders." Leadership, he contends, is learned because wisdom, practical intelligence, and creativity all can be learned.

■ **Servant Leaders.** In addition to a working knowledge of the various leadership theories we have discussed in this chapter, aspiring leaders need a philosophical anchor point.[71] This is where Robert K. Greenleaf's philosophy of the *servant leader* enters the picture as an instructive and inspiring springboard. The servant leader is an ethical person who puts *others*—not herself or himself—in the foreground. As a devout Quaker with years of real-world experience at AT&T, Greenleaf wove humility and a genuine concern for the whole person into his philosophy of leadership.[72] He portrayed the servant leader as one who, in addition to putting others first, has a clear sense of purpose in life, is a good listener,

15h What About Courage?

Bill George, the respected former CEO of Medtronic and author of the book *Authentic Leadership*:

> *What's missing, George says, is authentic leadership—that is, business leaders who demonstrate integrity, values, and conviction. Leaders who put customers and employees before Wall Street, speak out to right a wrong, and admit their mistakes. In other words, leaders with courage. "Authenticity and courage go hand in hand," he says. "You need one to have the other."*

Source: Chuck Salter, "Mr. Inside Speaks Out," Fast Company, *no. 86 (September 2004): 93.*

QUESTIONS:
How are George's comments related to transformational and servant leadership? Explain. How would you rate your own courage, in this regard?

is trustworthy, and accepts others at face value. The servant leader tries to improve the world, first and foremost, through *self*-improvement. One person who embodies the servant leader philosophy is John Wooden, who coached the UCLA men's basketball team to an astounding ten national championships: "The great thing about Coach Wooden is that he is what he is," former player Bill Walton says. "This is a man with no pretensions. He is a humble, giving person who wants nothing in return but to see other people succeed."[73]

Mentoring

In spite of mountains of leadership research, much remains to be learned about why some people are good leaders whereas many others are not.[74] One thing is clear, though: mentors can make an important difference. Take Michael Dell, for example. How was he able to take a personal computer business he started in his dorm room at the University of Texas and build it into a giant company with $50 billion in annual sales? And all before his 40th birthday! *Business Week* offered this insight: ". . . most amazing of all to his peers is Dell's near egoless management. From the start, he has sought out gray-haired mentors to help show him the way."[75] Let us explore this interesting process whereby leadership skills are acquired by exposure to role models.

Mentoring is one of those gifts that keeps on giving. For Connie Lindsey (left), a senior vice president at The Northern Trust Co. in Chicago, the giving began back in the early '90s when a mentor who took note of her leadership skills advised her to leave marketing and move into sales management. She thrived and now passes along the gift of mentoring to others such as Linda Nolan, pictured here.

Learning from a Mentor

mentor: *someone who develops another person through tutoring, coaching, and guidance*

The many obstacles and barriers blocking the way to successful leadership make it easy to understand why there is no simple formula for developing leaders. Abraham Zaleznik, the respected sociologist mentioned earlier, insists that leaders must be nurtured under the wise tutelage of a mentor. A **mentor** is an individual who systematically develops another person's abilities through intensive tutoring, coaching, and guidance.[76] Zaleznik explains the nature of this special relationship:

> *Mentors take risks with people. They bet initially on talent they perceive in [junior] people. Mentors also risk emotional involvement in working closely with their juniors. The risks do not always pay off, but the willingness to take them appears crucial in developing leaders.*[77]

A survey of 246 health care industry managers found higher satisfaction, greater recognition, and more promotion opportunities among managers with mentors than among those without.[78] Other research suggests that *informal* relationships that arise naturally work better than formally structured pairings.[79] Wal-Mart prefers the structured approach. In the following example, notice how the world's number one retailer has integrated formal mentors into a comprehensive human resources program:

> *[T]he company has modified its human resources philosophy from "getting, keeping, and growing" employees to "keeping, growing, and getting" them. The shift isn't just semantics, says Coleman Peterson, senior vice president of Wal-Mart's people division. It indicates an increased emphasis on retaining and developing the talent Wal-Mart already has, rather than the "hire, hire, hire" strategy Peterson says characterized the company in the past.*
>
> *To that end, Wal-Mart focuses intensively on how employees adapt during their first 90 days with the company. To make sure new hires don't feel lost at the mammoth company, they are assigned veteran employees as mentors. They are also assessed on their progress at the 30-, 60-, and 90-day marks. These efforts have helped reduce attrition rates by 25 percent. Wal-Mart employees who exhibit leadership potential are sent for training to the Sam Walton Development Center, at company headquarters in Bentonville, Arkansas.*[80]

Whatever approach is taken to mentoring, a recent survey of senior executives revealed a major shortfall. "Just one in nine had a mentor or buddy to help them get acclimated to the position and the company."[81] Not surprisingly, 61 percent expressed dissatisfaction with their integration into their new positions.

Dynamics of Mentoring

According to Kathy Kram, who conducted intensive biographical interviews with both members in 18 different senior manager-junior manager mentor relationships, mentoring fulfills two important functions: (1) a career enhancement function and (2) a psychological and social support function (see Table 15.5). Mentor relationships were found to average about five years in length.[82] Thus, a manager might have a series of mentors during the course of an organizational career. Also, as explained recently by a team of researchers, there is a growing need for having more than one mentor at a time.

> *Forces such as rapidly changing technology, shifting organizational structures, and global marketplace dynamics have transformed mentoring into a process that by necessity extends beyond the services of a single mentor. As knowledge continuously changes and evolves, it becomes difficult if not impossible for individuals—or individual*

15i Mentoring Turned Upside Down

Procter & Gamble, Cincinnati, Ohio:

The consumer-products giant pairs junior female employees with a senior manager for reverse mentoring to help the mostly male higher-ups understand the issues women face.

Source: Robert Levering and Milton Moskowitz, "The 100 Best Companies to Work For," Fortune *(January 24, 2005): 74.*

QUESTIONS:
What are the pros and cons of this approach to mentoring? On balance, do you endorse this practice? Explain.

Table 15.5 Mentors Serve Two Important Functions

Career functions*	Psychosocial functions**
Sponsorship	Role modeling
Exposure and visibility	Acceptance and confirmation
Coaching	Counseling
Protection	Friendship
Challenging assignments	

* Career functions are those aspects of the relationship that primarily enhance career advancement.
** Psychosocial functions are those aspects of the relationship that primarily enhance a sense of competence, clarity of identity, and effectiveness in the managerial role.

Source: *Kathy E. Kram, "Phases of the Mentor Relationship,"* Academy of Management Journal, *26 (December 1983): 614 (Exhibit 1). Reprinted by permission.*

7. IDENTIFY the two key functions that mentors perform, and **EXPLAIN** how a mentor can develop a junior manager's leadership skills.

mentors—to possess all the requisite knowledge within themselves. Having multiple mentors facilitates the building of knowledge in the people who then become the primary assets and sources of competitive advantage to the firm.[83]

Interestingly, the junior member of a mentor relationship is not the only one to benefit. Mentors often derive great intrinsic pleasure from seeing their protégés move up through the ranks and conquer difficult challenges. Moreover, by passing along their values and their technical and leadership skills to promising junior managers, mentors can wield considerable power. Mentor relationships do sometimes turn sour, however. A mentor can become threatened by a protégé who surpasses him or her. Also, cross-gender[84] and cross-race mentor relationships can fall victim to bias and social pressures.[85]

Behavior Modification

behaviorism: *belief that observable behavior is more important than inner states*

This last approach to influencing behavior can be traced to two psychologists, John B. Watson and Edward L. Thorndike, who did their work in the early twentieth century. From Watson came the advice to concentrate on observable behavior. Accordingly, the philosophy of **behaviorism** maintains that observable behavior is more important than hypothetical inner states such as needs, motives, and expectations.[86] From Thorndike came an appreciation of the way in which consequences control behavior. According to Thorndike's classic law of effect, favorable consequences encourage behavior, whereas unfavorable consequences discourage behavior.[87] However, it remained for B. F. Skinner, the late Harvard psychologist, to integrate Watson's and Thorndike's contributions into a precise technology of behavior change.

What Is Behavior Modification?

Skinner was the father of *operant conditioning*, the study of how behavior is controlled by the surrounding environment.[88] Although some find Skinner's substitution of environmental control for self-control repulsive and dehumanizing,[89] few deny that operant conditioning actually occurs. Indeed, much of our behavior is the product of environmental shaping. Rather, the debate centers on whether or not natural shaping processes should be systematically managed to alter the course of everyday behavior.[90] Advocates of behavior modification in the workplace believe they should be.[91]

behavior modification: *systematic management of the antecedents and consequences of behavior*

Behavior modification is the practical application of Skinnerian operant-conditioning techniques to everyday behavior problems. **Behavior modification** (B. Mod.) involves systematically managing environmental factors to get people to do the right things more often and the wrong things less often. This is accomplished by managing the antecedents and/or consequences of observable behavior.

■ Managing Antecedents

antecedent: *an environmental cue for a specific behavior*

An **antecedent** is an environmental cue that prompts an individual to behave in a given manner. Antecedents do not automatically *cause* the person to behave in a predictable manner, as a hot stove causes you to withdraw your hand reflexively when you touch it. Rather, we learn through experience to interpret antecedents as signals telling us it is time to behave in a certain way if we are to get what we want or to avoid what we do not want. This process is sometimes referred to as *cue control.* Domino's Pizza Inc. makes effective use of cue control for maintaining product quality.

> *[Every Domino's] features a myriad of strategically placed, visually appealing posters displaying helpful, job-related tips and reminders. . . .*
>
> *Centrally located, particularly for the benefit of the oven tender who slices and boxes the just-baked pizza, are two photos, one of "The Perfect Pepperoni" pizza, the other showing a pizza with ten common flaws, one per slice.*[92]

8. EXPLAIN the management of antecedents and consequences in behavior modification.

Although it is often overlooked, the management of antecedents is a practical and simple way of encouraging good performance. As Table 15.6 indicates, there are two ways to manage antecedents. Barriers can be removed, and helpful aids can be offered. These steps ensure that the path to good performance is clearly marked and free of obstacles (which meshes with the path-goal theory of leadership).

■ Managing Consequences

Managing the consequences of job performance is more complex than dealing strictly with antecedents, because there are four different classes of consequences. Each type of consequence involves a different process. Positive reinforcement and negative reinforcement both encourage behavior, but they do so in different ways. Extinction and punishment discourage behavior but, again, in different ways. These four terms have precise meanings that are often confused by casual observers.

positive reinforcement: *encouraging a behavior with a pleasing consequence*

■ Positive Reinforcement. **Positive reinforcement** encourages a specific behavior by immediately following it with a consequence the individual finds pleasing. For example, a machine operator who maintains a clean work area because he or she is praised for doing so has responded to positive reinforcement. As the term implies, positive reinforcement reinforces or builds behavior in a positive way.

Table 15.6 Managing Antecedents

Barriers: remove barriers that prevent or hinder the completion of a good job. For example:	**Aids: provide helpful aids that enhance the opportunity to do a good job. For example:**
Unrealistic objectives, plans, schedules, or deadlines	Challenging yet attainable objectives
Uncooperative or distracting coworkers	Clear and realistic plans
Training deficiencies	Understandable instructions
Contradictory or confusing rules	Constructive suggestions, hints, or tips
Inadequate or inappropriate tools	Clear and generally acceptable work rules
Conflicting orders from two or more managers	Realistic schedules and deadlines
	Friendly reminders
	Posters or signs with helpful tips
	Easy-to-use forms
	Nonthreatening questions about progress
	User-friendly computer software and hardware

■ **Negative Reinforcement.** *Negative reinforcement* encourages a specific behavior by immediately withdrawing or terminating something a particular person finds displeasing. Children learn the power of negative reinforcement early in life when they discover that the quickest way to get something is to cry and scream until their parents give them what they want. In effect, the parents are negatively reinforced for complying with the child's demand by the termination of the crying and screaming. In other words, the termination or withdrawal of an undesirable state of affairs (for example, the threat of being fired) has an incentive effect. In a social context, negative reinforcement amounts to blackmail. "Do what I want, or I will continue to make your life miserable" are the bywords of the person who relies on negative reinforcement to influence behavior.

■ **Extinction.** Through *extinction*, a specific behavior is discouraged by ignoring it. For example, managers sometimes find that the best way to keep employees from asking redundant questions is simply not to answer them. Just as a plant will wither and die without water, behavior will fade away without occasional reinforcement.

■ **Punishment.** *Punishment* discourages a specific behavior by the immediate presentation of an undesirable consequence or the immediate removal of something desirable. For example, a manager may punish a tardy employee by either assigning the individual to a dirty job or docking the individual's pay.

It is important to remember that positive and negative reinforcement, extinction, and punishment all entail the manipulation of the *immediate* or *direct* consequences of a desired or undesired behavior. If action is taken before the behavior, behavior control is unlikely. For instance, if a manager gives an employee a cash bonus *before* a difficult task is completed, the probability of the task being completed declines because the incentive effect has been removed. In regard to managing consequences, behavior modification works only when there is a contingent ("if . . . then") relationship between a specific behavior and a given consequence.

15j Quick Quiz

Catherine Muther, who in the mid-1990s retired early from Cisco Systems with millions of dollars in company stock:

In that male-dominated company, Muther pushed for a change. She gave other executives electronic "zappers" with flashing red lights. They were used to make a buzzing sound whenever someone made a sexist remark during management meetings, says Cisco Chairman John Morgridge. "She certainly was a major factor in bringing the gender issue to Cisco," he says.

Source: Jim Hopkins, "Philanthropist Nurtures Tech Start-Ups by Women," USA Today *(January 22, 2002): 12B.*

QUESTIONS:
Which behavior modification tactic did Muther use? Explain. Why was it apparently effective?

■ Positively Reinforce What Is Right About Job Performance (the Art of "Bucket Filling")

Proponents of behavior modification prefer to build up desirable behaviors rather than tearing down undesirable ones. Every undesirable behavior has a desirable counterpart that can be reinforced. For example, someone who comes in late once a week actually comes in on time four days a week. To encourage productive behaviors, managers are advised to focus on the positive aspects of job performance when managing consequences. Thus, positive reinforcement is the preferred consequence strategy.[93] This positive approach was effectively taken to heart by Preston Trucking, a Maryland shipping company:

> *Preston, years ago, had terrible relations between management and labor. Then, one day, top management resolved to bury the hatchet. All sorts of reforms were announced, including the Four-to-One Rule: For every criticism a manager made about a driver's performance, he had to give him four compliments. You can imagine how this went over. "It was like a . . . like a marriage encounter," says Teamster Nick Costa, rolling his eyes. Eventually, though, drivers discovered that the rule really did reflect a change of heart.*[94]

This positive approach to modifying behavior is the central theme in the long-standing best-seller *The One Minute Manager,* which extols the virtues of "catching people doing something *right!*"[95] Positive reinforcement also is the core message in Tom Rath and Donald O. Clifton's recent best-selling book *How Full Is Your Bucket? Positive Strategies for Work and Life.* Rath and his now-deceased grandfather use the metaphor of a *bucket* to represent how a person feels and acts. One's bucket is filled by praise and other forms of positive reinforcement. Criticism and negativity empty one's bucket. On the basis of their Gallup surveys of a worldwide sampling of over 4 million employees, Rath and Clifton claim that "regular recognition and praise" boost productivity and satisfaction while reducing accidents and turnover. But they caution managers to use "positive interactions" to an appropriate extent—not too little, not too much. Citing recent research evidence, they recommend a ratio of positive to negative interactions (both at work and at home) of between 3 to 1 and 13 to 1. Less than a 3-to–1 ratio is flirting with corrosive negativity. A ratio greater than 13 to 1 communicates false optimism and lacks realism. Their conclusion: ". . . most of us don't have to worry about breaking the upper limit. The positive-to-negative ratios in most organizations are woefully inadequate and leave substantial room for improvement." (See Internet Exercise 5 at the end of this chapter.)[96]

Schedule Positive Reinforcement Appropriately

continuous reinforcement: *every instance of a behavior is rewarded*

intermittent reinforcement: *rewarding some, but not all, instances of a behavior*

Both the type and the timing of consequences are important in successful B. Mod. When a productive behavior is first tried out by an employee, a continuous schedule of reinforcement is appropriate. Under **continuous reinforcement** every instance of the desired behavior is reinforced. For example, a bank manager who is training a new loan officer to handle a difficult type of account should praise the loan officer after every successful transaction until the behavior is firmly established. After the loan officer is able to handle the transaction, the bank manager can switch to a schedule of intermittent reinforcement. As the term implies, **intermittent reinforcement** calls for reinforcing some, rather than all, of the desired responses.

The more unpredictable the payoff schedule is, the better the results will be. One way to appreciate the power of intermittent reinforcement is to think of the enthusiasm with which people play slot machines; these gambling devices pay off on an unpredictable intermittent schedule. In the same way, occasional reinforcement of established productive behaviors with meaningful positive consequences is an extremely effective management technique.[97] To spark your imagination, consider these examples from *Fortune* magazine's 2005 list of "The 100 Best Companies to Work For:"

- **San Juan, Puerto Rico-based Popular Bank**: "Employees at [subsidiary] Banco Popular North America . . . have the power to recognize coworkers' extraordinary efforts with On the Spot awards of up to $100."[98]
- **Perkins Coie, a Seattle law firm**: "Employees who are singled out for outstanding performance enter a raffle for free airline tickets."[99]
- **Baptist Health Care, Pensacola, Florida**: "Employees at this hospital must attend a periodic open-forum meeting in which everyone is urged to address the crowd. Those brave enough to do so are entered in a raffle for free rides on the company helicopter."[100]
- **Arbitron, New York City**: "At this radio market research firm, workers recognize one another for a job well done with $100 American Express gift cards (there's no restriction on how many you can bestow). Last year nearly 300 employees received $50,000 worth."[101]

(Now go do something nice for yourself as positive reinforcement for reading this chapter.)

SUMMARY

1. Influence is fundamental to management because individuals must be influenced to pursue collective objectives. Researchers have identified eight generic influence tactics used on the job: consultation (seeking participation of others), rational persuasion (reasoning with logic), inspirational appeals (appealing to someone's values or ideals), ingratiating tactics (using flattery or humility prior to a request), coalition tactics (seeking help in persuading others), pressure tactics (using intimidation, demands, or threats), upward appeals (seeking the support of higher management), and exchange tactics (trading favors).
2. The five basic types of power are reward, coercive, legitimate, referent, and expert power. Empowerment cannot work without a supporting situation such as a skilled individual, an organizational culture of empowerment, an emotionally mature individual with a well-developed character, and empowerment opportunities such as delegation, participation, and self-managed teams.
3. Formal leadership consists of influencing relevant others to voluntarily pursue organizational objectives. Informal leadership can work for or against the organization. Leadership theory has evolved through four major stages: trait theory, behavioral styles theory, situational theory, and transformational theory. A promising trait approach is based on Goleman's four dimensions of emotional intelligence: self-awareness, self-management, social awareness, and relationship management.
4. Researchers who differentiated among authoritarian, democratic, and laissez-faire leadership styles concentrated on leader behavior rather than personality traits. Leadership studies at Ohio State University isolated four styles of leadership based on two categories of leader behavior: initiating structure and consideration. A balanced high-structure, high-consideration style was recommended. According to Blake and his colleagues, a 9,9 style (high concern for both production and people) is the best overall style because it emphasizes teamwork.
5. Situational-leadership theorists believe there is no single best leadership style; rather, different situations require different styles. Many years of study led Fiedler to conclude that task-motivated leaders are more effective in either very favorable or very unfavorable situations, whereas relationship-motivated leaders are better suited to moderately favorable situations. The favorableness of a situation is dictated by the degree of the leader's control and influence in getting the job done. Path-goal leadership theory, an expectancy perspective, assumes that leaders are effective to the extent that they can motivate followers by clarifying goals and clearing the paths to achieving those goals and valued rewards. Unlike Fiedler, path-goal theorists believe that managers can and should adapt their leadership behavior to the situation.
6. In contrast to transactional leaders who maintain the status quo, transformational leaders are visionary, charismatic leaders dedicated to change. Greenleaf's philosophy of the servant leader helps aspiring leaders integrate what they have learned about leadership. The servant leader is motivated to serve rather than lead. Clear goals, trust, good listening skills, positive feedback, foresight, and self-development are the characteristics of a servant leader.
7. Mentors help develop less experienced people by fulfilling career and psychosocial functions. Mentors engage in intensive tutoring, coaching, and guiding. Mentors are role models for aspiring leaders.
8. Behavior modification (B. Mod.) is the practical application of Skinner's operant conditioning principles. B. Mod. involves managing antecedents (removing barriers and providing helpful aids) and consequences to strengthen desirable behavior and weaken undesirable behavior. Proponents of B. Mod. prefer to shape behavior through positive reinforcement rather than negative reinforcement, extinction, and punishment. Continuous reinforcement is recommended for new behavior and intermittent reinforcement for established behavior.

TERMS TO UNDERSTAND

- Influence, p. 438
- Power, p. 441
- Reward power, p. 441
- Coercive power, p. 441
- Legitimate power, p. 442
- Referent power, p. 442
- Expert power, p. 443
- Empowerment, p. 444
- Leadership, p. 444
- Formal leadership, p. 445
- Informal leadership, p. 445
- Emotional intelligence, p. 447
- Transformational leaders, p. 453
- Mentor, p. 457
- Behaviorism, p. 458
- Behavior modification, p. 458
- Antecedent, p. 459
- Positive reinforcement, p. 459
- Continuous reinforcement, p. 461
- Intermittent reinforcement, p. 461

SKILLS & TOOLS

Putting the Empowerment Puzzle Together

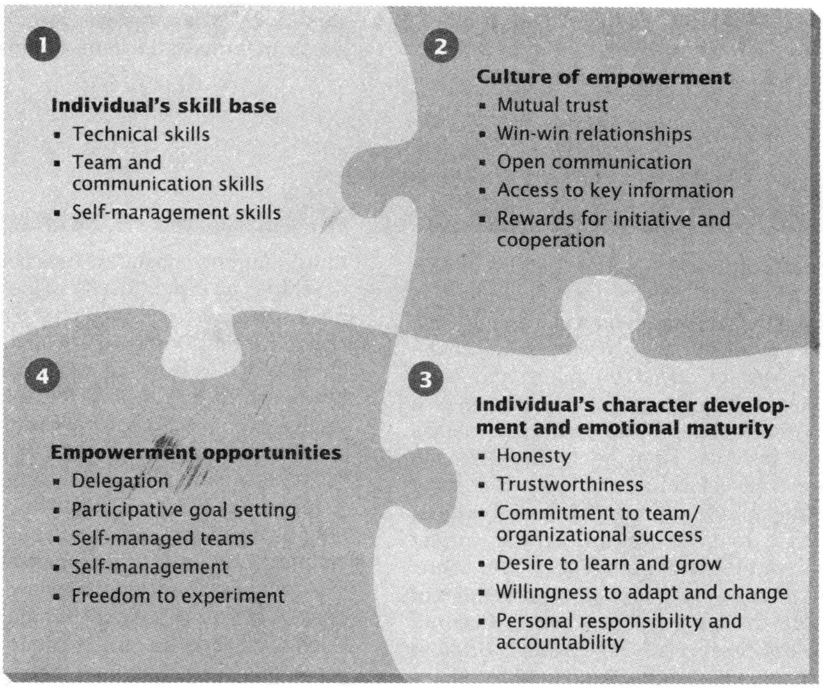

Source: *Adapted in part from discussion in Stephen R. Covey,* Principle-Centered Leadership *(New York: Simon & Schuster, 1991), pp. 212–216.*

HANDS-ON EXERCISE

What Is Your Emotional Intelligence (EQ)?[102]

Instructions:

Evaluate each statement about your emotional intelligence on a scale of 1 = "not at all like me" to 10 = "very much like me." Try to be objective by viewing yourself through the eyes of key people in your life such as family members, close friends, coworkers, and classmates. (*Note*: This instrument is for instructional purposes only because it was derived from a 25-item survey of unknown validity.)

_____ **1.** I usually stay composed, positive, and unflappable in trying situations.

_____ **2.** I am able to admit my own mistakes.

_____ **3.** I usually or always meet commitments and keep promises.

_____ **4.** I hold myself accountable for meeting my goals.

_____ **5.** I can smoothly handle multiple demands and changing priorities.

_____ **6.** Obstacles and setbacks may delay me a little, but they don't stop me.

_____ **7.** I seek fresh perspectives, even if that means trying something totally new.

_____ **8.** My impulses or distressing emotions don't often get the best of me at work.

_____ **9.** I usually don't attribute setbacks to a personal flaw (mine or somebody else's).

_____ **10.** I operate from an expectation of success rather than from a fear of failure.

Total = _____

Interpretation:

A score below 70 indicates a need for improvement. With sincere effort, one's emotional intelligence can be improved. It is part of a natural process of "growing up" and becoming mature in challenging social situations. People with low EQ scores are like porcupines—they're hard to hug.

For Consideration/Discussion

1. What do you like or dislike about the concept of emotional intelligence?
2. Have you ever worked with or for someone who had high emotional intelligence? If so, describe them and rate their effectiveness. Do the same for someone with low emotional intelligence.
3. What, if any, connection do you see between the concepts of emotional intelligence and servant leader? Explain.
4. How could you improve your emotional intelligence, in terms of the items on this test?

INTERNET EXERCISES

1. More on social influence: Robert B. Cialdini, author of the book *Influence: The Science of Persuasion,* says we are exposed to countless good and evil influence tactics every day of our lives. As a researcher, he knows the power of social influence and fears that this power is often abused. A combination Web and library search will provide instructive details and practical insights. First, go to his Web site (**www.influenceatwork.com**) and take the short quiz by clicking on "What's Your Influence Quotient (NQ)?" Be sure to click forward to the correct answers and read the interpretation of your score. Next, read Cialdini's ideas about the six principles of influence in the following article: Robert B. Cialdini, "Harnessing the Science of Persuasion," *Harvard Business Review,* 79 (October 2001): 72–79.

Learning Points: 1. Are you surprised at how pervasive social influence is in modern life? 2. Generally speaking, do you view social influence as a positive or a negative aspect of modern life? Explain. 3. What useful lessons did you learn from this exercise? 4. Are you better equipped to handle unwanted influence attempts now that you have completed this exercise? Explain. 5. How can and should managers use influence ethically?

2. More on power: The topic of power is an intriguing one for most of us. It is complex. It isn't an either/or thing. Author/consultant/teacher Janet Hagberg developed an insightful way of looking at power. Her book (*Real Power: Stages of Personal Power in Organizations*)[103] is a must-read for anyone seriously interested in learning about personal power and how to use it responsibly. To discover her six-stage model of power, go to **www.janethagberg.com**, scroll down and select "Site Map," and click on "6 Stages of power."

Learning Points: 1. What has Hagberg's model taught you about power that you didn't learn in this chapter? Explain. 2. Which stage of Hagberg's power cycle are you at during this phase of your life? How do you know? 3. What stage would you like to reach? Why? 4. What do you need to do to get to the stage of power you seek? 5. From a managerial perspective, what do you like or dislike about Hagberg's approach to power? Explain.

3. More on emotional intelligence: Did you find the coverage of Goleman's four dimensions of emotional intelligence (EQ) and the Hands-On Exercise interesting? If so, and you want to know more, go to **www.fortune.com/careers**, scroll down to "Quizzes," and select "What's Your EQ at Work?" You will find the complete 25-item survey from which the Hands-On Exercise was excerpted. This longer version is more job-oriented. Complete the survey and submit your responses for scoring. Alternatively, you may find it instructive to have a relative or close acquaintance evaluate your emotional intelligence with this survey.

Learning Points: 1. Is it really possible to take an objective outsider's view of yourself and your behavior with this type of instrument? Explain. 2. How useful is Goleman's concept of emotional intelligence within a management context? 3. If you would like to improve your EQ, what is your plan for doing so? 4. What is your personal experience with leaders who were high or low on emotional intelligence? What impact did their EQ have on their effectiveness?

4. **Check it out:** The Women's Organization for Mentoring Education and Networking, sponsored by WOMEN Unlimited Inc., is dedicated to enhancing diversity and achieving gender parity in the workplace. For instructive resources and readings on mentoring and related topics, go to the organization's home page at **www.women-unlimited.com** and click on "Resources." Both women and men can pick up useful career tips from this Web site.

5. **Check it out:** If our discussion (in the behavior modification section of this chapter) of Rath and Clifton's best-selling book *How Full Is Your Bucket? Positive Strategies for Work and Life* whetted your appetite for more, go to **www.bucketbook.com**, take the "Positive Impact Test," and then explore the rest of this fun and instructive Web site.

For updates to these exercises, visit our Web site (**http://business.college.hmco. com/students/** and select Kreitner, *Management*, 10e).

CLOSING CASE

Leadership Style

Rasayan Ltd., established in 1970, is a chemical company, having Head Office at Mumbai, and manufacturing plant at Pune. Its human resources include 450 workers and 45 officers/managers. Ms. Shalini, daughter of the Chairman of the company was appointed as Managing Director three years ago. Ms. Shalini who received management education from a prestigious business management school in U.K. and took over this command in her thirties was perceived by employees as a 'harsh and rash' Managing Director as compared with her father's style of managing. She operates from the Head Office but is regular in visiting plant atleast twice a month.

Ms. Shalini's approach towards 'managing people' was 'rough and tough'. She never used to spare anyone in the organization for the mistake committed. In one of the business meetings with senior managers and departmental heads of the plant, she commented, "I see no manager in this company takes decision". Taking a clue from this comment, a young administrative manager, Mr. Patel, who joined the company recently, took a couple of minor administrative decisions, after proper consultation with the Regional Manager and informed M.D. about the same by written communication. In the next visit of the M.D. to the plant, the admn. manager had to listen this from her: "Since when you have started taking decisions? You should have taken my permission before taking such decisions."

Once she had urged the workers' union leaders that they should clean the shopfloors instead of whiling away the time, and quoted example of Japanese workers. President of the workers' union Mr. Chandrakant refused to accept such a 'novel' idea and informed her that the comparison should be made on equal terms and suggested that the workers should also get comparable remuneration and perks as that of Japanese workers and then the union would accept her proposal of cleaning the shopfloors. She ignored the suggestion.

While addressing union leaders, Ms. Shalini used to refer that "Ours is a family and you all should work as a team". But the perception amongst union leaders was totally different. One of the union leaders had commented that "She (M.D.) considers us as a family, but gives 'step-motherly treatment'.

Her visit to Pune plant used to be a 'Firing day' for many managers including OM and Director. In fact, no officer had observed her talking and discussing about company's future plans and objectives in such meetings. On the contrary the meetings were conducted for 'post-mortem' of certain events.

Because of such internal atmosphere, the environment in the manufacturing plant was not at all conducive and dynamic. This was hampering the growth and progress of the Company. In fact, most of the employees developed a concept of "Two punch and

One lunch" i.e. in and out punch for attendance and a subsidized lunch during working hours, but no significant contribution in the achievement of company goals.

For Discussion

1. Analyze the behavioural pattern and leadership style of Ms. Shalini.
2. Were the workers satisfied with the internal climate of the company?
3. What steps should Ms. Shalini take to improve the present situation and motivate the workforce?

Source: *Principles & Practice of Management by T.N. Chhabra, Dhanpat Rai & Co., Delhi, 2002, pp.848.*

TEST PREPPER

True/False Questions

_____ **1.** According to research, consultation and rational persuasion are the most widely used influence tactics on the job.

_____ **2.** Negative power, based on threatened or actual punishment, is one of the five bases of power.

_____ **3.** Despite differing characteristics between leaders and managers, we need people who can lead *and* manage today.

_____ **4.** Higher EQ scores indicate more polished social skills and greater emotional maturity.

_____ **5.** Blake and Mouton, through their research with the Leadership Grid, believe that no one best style of leadership exists.

_____ **6.** The ideal leader is relationship-motivated, according to Fiedler's contingency theory.

_____ **7.** Transactional leaders characteristically offer a lot of personal attention and advice to employees.

_____ **8.** Within the context of practical intelligence, Yale's Robert J. Sternberg rejects the notion of "born leaders."

_____ **9.** One of the psychosocial functions of mentoring is role modeling.

_____ **10.** Both positive and negative reinforcement can be used to encourage specific target behaviors.

Multiple-Choice Questions

1. Which of the following is *not* among the generic influence tactics described in the text?
A. Upward appeals B. Exchange tactics
C. Coalition tactics D. Participative tactics
E. Consultation

2. _____ power closely parallels formal authority.
A. Rational B. Referent
C. Legitimate D. Traditional
E. Functional

3. All *except* which one of these are among Peter Drucker's criteria for assessing the effectiveness of leaders?
A. They knew when to say "no."
B. They asked, "What needs to be done?"
C. They developed action plans.
D. They ran productive meetings.
E. They took responsibility for communicating.

4. _____ leadership involves influencing others to pursue objectives that may or may not serve the organization's interests.
A. Corollary B. Formal
C. Informal D. Ad hoc
E. Decentralized

5. _____ can be defined as an array of noncognitive skills, capabilities, and competencies that influence a person's ability to cope with environmental demands and pressures.
A. Self-management B. Emotional intelligence
C. Behavior modification D. Empowerment
E. IQ

6. In the Ohio State leadership model, the term _____ *best* characterizes "consideration."
A. trust B. goals
C. results D. techniques
E. authority

7. According to Fiedler's contingency theory, _____ leaders tend to perform better when the situation is _____ favorable.
A. achievement-oriented; moderately
B. authoritarian; highly
C. relationship-motivated; moderately
D. social; highly
E. task-motivated; moderately

8. Which of thefollowing is *not* one of the eight categories of leader behavior in House's updated path-goal theory?
A. Work facilitation behaviors
B. Group decision behaviors
C. Achievement-oriented behaviors
D. Value-based behaviors
E. Mentoring behaviors

9. _____ is(are) the center of attention in Greenleaf's servant-leadership theory.
A. Others B. God
C. The leader D. Top management
E. The mission

10. In their best-selling book *How Full Is Your Bucket?* Rath and Clifton point to research evidence that the right ratio of positive to negative interactions with others is somewhere between _____ to 1 and _____ to 1.
A. 2; 4 B. 3; 13
C. 5; 10 D. 6; 12
E. 2; 8

ACE self-test

Want more questions? Visit the student Web site at http://business.college.hmco.com/students/ (select Kreitner, *Management,* 10e) and take the ACE quizzes for more practice.

16 Change, Conflict, and Negotiation

> "Change begets conflict, conflict begets change."[1]
>
> DEAN TJOSVOLD

OBJECTIVES

- **Identify** and **describe** four types of organizational change according to the Nadler-Tushman model.
- **Explain** how people tend to respond differently to changes they like and those they dislike.
- **List** at least six reasons why employees resist change, and **discuss** what management can do about resistance to change.
- **Describe** how the unfreezing-change-refreezing metaphor applies to organization development (OD).
- **Describe** tempered radicals, and **identify** the 5Ps in the checklist for grassroots change agents.
- **Contrast** the competitive and cooperative conflict styles.
- **Identify** and **describe** five conflict resolution techniques.
- **Identify** and **describe** the elements of effective negotiation, and **explain** the advantage of added value negotiating (AVN).

the changing workplace

What CEO Anne M. Mulcahy Learned from Turning Around Xerox

Background: Mulcahy, 51, was named president of Xerox in May 2000, and CEO a year later. The company was a shambles, its core copier business decimated. Today [2005], Xerox is still no one's idea of a hot growth company—but profits are up sharply and its stock price has more than doubled in two years. Mulcahy told *Fast Company* what she has learned in four years under the gun.

Change is the most difficult thing. You know how tough it is to basically wipe out your office manufacturing and outsource it? To invest in global services and R&D while we were being ruthless about taking cost out of other parts of the business? It's easy to talk about, tough to do.

In a crisis, you have the opportunity to move quickly and change a lot—and you have to take advantage of that.

Change doesn't happen if you don't work at it. You've got to get out there, give people the straight scoop, and get buy in. It's not just good-looking presentations; it's doing town meetings and letting people ask the tough questions. It's almost got to be done one person at a time.

Storytelling is hugely important. At our town meetings, the most frequently asked question wasn't whether we'd survive, but what we would look like when we did. I got great advice: Write a story. We wrote a *Wall Street Journal* article, because they had been particularly nasty about us, dated five years out. It was about where we could be if we really stood up to the plate. And people loved it. No matter where I go, people pull that article out. They personalized it.

Stories exist at all levels of the corporation. You talk to tech reps, and they'll tell you what they did to help turn this company around. Whether it was saving a buck here, or doing something different for customers, everyone has a story. That creates powerful momentum—people's sense that they're able to do good things. It's much more powerful than the precision or elegance of the strategy.

Risk taking gets a little easier when you've been where we've been. The downside is lower, and you can't stand still. So you have to make choices, and you can take risks.

I communicate good news in the same way I do the bad news. I thank people and make sure they feel a sense of recognition for their contribution. But the trick is to always use the opportunity to talk about what's next, to pose the next challenges. Where do we want to go? How do we want to build on it?

My strengths and weaknesses haven't changed a whole hell of a lot. At 51 years of age, you're pretty well formed. The important thing is to recognize the things you don't do well and build a team that reflects what you know the company needs that you yourself don't bring to the table.

There's not a lot of room anymore for senior people to be managers. They have to be leaders. I want people who create organizations that get aligned, get passionate, get really inspired about delivering.

I don't hold back in meetings. I always had great respect for Paul Allaire, my predecessor. He would sit back, and hours of debate would go by, and you'd never be able to tell what he thought. Then he'd finally play his card. I play my card much quicker than that.

One of the most extraordinary things was the support I got from employees. If I had to make a tough decision, I would get emails saying, "Keep your chin up, you're doing the right things," It was like, "Whoa, isn't that my job?" I'll always be grateful for that.

Source: *Keith H. Hammonds, "What I Know Now,"* Fast Company, *no. 92 (March 2005): 96. Reprinted by permission of* Fast Company.

Being competitive in today's fast-paced global economy means managers must be able to understand and manage constant change. High among the top ten challenges for CEOs, according to a 2004 worldwide survey, was "Speed, flexibility and adaptability to change."[2] As a case in point:

> *Every year, PepsiCo adds more than 200 product variations to its global portfolio of brands that includes Frito-Lay snacks, Pepsi-Cola sodas, Gatorade sports drinks, and Tropicana juice. Many are aimed at wooing ethnic tastes as well as satisfying health-conscious consumers.*[3]

Quick revolutionary changes and more deliberate evolutionary changes[4] need to be balanced so that people both inside and outside the organization can handle them. Also, as Xerox's Anne Mulcahy learned from the school of hard knocks, it helps to be proactive rather than reactive. She told an interviewer, "It's hard to know exactly when change is needed, but better early than late."[5] The purpose of this chapter, then, is to explore the dynamics of organizational change and its natural by-product, conflict. We discuss change from organizational and individual perspectives, address resistance to change, and examine how to make change happen. We then consider the nature and management of conflict and conclude with a discussion of negotiation.

Change: Organizational and Individual Perspectives

Researchers report a constant tension between opposing forces for stability and change in today's work organizations.[6] A productive balance is required. Too much stability and organizational decline begins. Too much change and the mission blurs and employees burn out. Today's managers need a robust set of concepts and skills to juggle stability and change. Let us tackle this major challenge for managers by looking at four types of organizational change and also at how individuals tend to respond to significant changes. These twin perspectives are important because organizational changes unavoidably have personal impacts.

anticipatory changes: *planned changes based on expected situations*

reactive changes: *changes made in response to unexpected situations*

incremental changes: *subsystem adjustments required to keep the organization on course*

strategic changes: *altering the overall shape or direction of the organization*

1. IDENTIFY and DESCRIBE four types of organizational change according to the Nadler-Tushman model.

■ Types of Organizational Change

Consultant David A. Nadler and management professor Michael L. Tushman together developed an instructive typology of organizational change (see Figure 16.1). On the vertical axis of their model, change is characterized as either anticipatory or reactive. **Anticipatory changes** are any systematically planned changes intended to take advantage of expected situations. By contrast, **reactive changes** are those necessitated by unexpected environmental events or pressures. The horizontal axis deals with the scope of a particular change, either incremental or strategic. **Incremental changes** involve subsystem adjustments needed to keep the organization on its chosen path. **Strategic changes** alter the overall shape or direction of the organization. For instance, adding a night shift to meet unexpectedly high demand for the company's product is an incremental change. Switching from building houses to building high-rise apartment complexes would be a strategic change. Four resulting types of organizational change in the Nadler-Tushman model are tuning, adaptation, re-orientation, and re-creation.[7] These types of organizational changes—listed in order of increasing complexity, intensity, and risk—require a closer look.

■ Tuning. Tuning is the most common, least intense, and least risky type of change. Other names for it include preventive maintenance and the Japanese concept of *kaizen* (continuous improvement).[8] The key to effective tuning is to actively anticipate and avoid problems rather than passively waiting for things to go wrong before taking action. For example, Du Pont tuned its marketing efforts by developing an Adopt-a-Customer program. The program "encourages blue-collar workers to visit a customer once a month, learn his needs, and be his representative on the factory floor."[9] This is a refreshing alternative to the traditional practice of waiting for customer complaints and only then trying to figure out how to fix them.

Figure 16.1 Four Types of Organizational Change

	Incremental	Strategic
Anticipatory	Tuning	Re-orientation
Reactive	Adaptation	Re-creation

Source: *David A. Nadler and Michael L. Tushman, "Beyond the Charismatic Leader: Leadership and Organizational Change." Copyright ©1990 by the Regents of the University of California. Reprinted from the* California Management Review, *vol. 32, no. 2. By permission of the Regents. All rights reserved.*

■ Adaptation. Like tuning, adaptation involves incremental changes.[10] But this time, the changes are in reaction to external problems, events, or pressures. For example, after Ford had great success with its aerodynamic styling, General Motors and Chrysler followed suit. In turn, Ford and GM broadened their product lines to compete with Chrysler's trend-setting minivans.

■ Re-orientation. This type of change is anticipatory and strategic in scope. Nadler and Tushman call re-orientation "frame bending" because the organization is significantly redirected. Importantly, there

As a sign of the times, this Washington, D.C.-area radio station recently did some "frame bending" by switching from a rock format to Spanish language music. Anyone wondering why simply needs to consider the demographics involved: the U.S. Hispanic/Latino population is the country's largest minority group and is projected to make up 25 percent of the population by the year 2050. Look for lots more changes with a Latin twist.

is not a complete break with the organization's past. Consider these examples of frame bending in New York City:

> *Big retailers known more for giant stores in suburbs are resizing stores, reformatting layouts and remixing merchandise to make it big in the Big Apple.*
>
> *Home Depot recently joined Toys R Us, Kmart, Best Buy and The Container Store here in exploring ways to adapt their formulas to an urban environment.*[11]

The Wall Street Journal also did some frame bending when it decided to add a Saturday edition in 2005.[12]

■ **Re-Creation.** Competitive pressures normally trigger this most intense and risky type of organizational change. Nadler and Tushman say it amounts to "frame breaking." A stunning example of frame breaking is the software giant Microsoft. Cofounder and CEO Bill Gates tied his company's future to the Internet in the mid-1990s after initially dismissing it as a passing fad. According to observers at the time,

16a Quick Quiz

Business news item:

> *IBM said . . . that it would sell its PC [personal computer] business to Lenovo, China's No. 1 PC maker, in a $1.75 billion deal that marks the end of an era.*
>
> *Lenovo will pay IBM up to $1.25 billion in cash and equity for IBM's PC division, which produced the first IBM PC in 1981.*

Source: Michelle Kessler, "It's Official: IBM Sells PC Unit to Chinese Company," USA Today *(December 8, 2004): 1B.*

QUESTION:
In terms of the Nadler-Tushman model in Figure 16.1, what type of change is this? Explain.

For further information about the interactive annotations in this chapter, visit our Web site (**http://business.college.hmco.com/students/**) and select Kreitner, *Management,* 10e.

Indeed, in just six months, Gates has done what few executives have dared. He has taken a thriving, $8 billion, 20,000-employee company and done a massive about-face. "I can't think of one corporation that has had this kind of success and after 20 years, just stopped and decided to reinvent itself from the ground up," says Jeffrey Katzenberg, a principal of DreamWorks SKG, which has a joint venture with Microsoft. "What they're doing is decisive, quick, breathtaking."[13]

Frame breaking helped Bill Gates to re-create Microsoft's strategy and products around the Internet.

■ Individual Reactions to Change

Ultimately, workplace changes of all types become a *personal* matter for employees. A merger, for example, means a new job assignment for one person and a new boss for another. The first person may look forward to the challenge of a new assignment, whereas the second may dread the prospect of adjusting to a new boss. Researchers tell us these two people will tend to exhibit distinctly different response patterns.[14] Specifically, people tend to respond to changes they *like* differently than they do to changes they *dislike*. Let us explore these two response patterns with the goal of developing a contingency model for managers. Importantly, both models are generic; that is, they apply equally to on-the-job and off-the-job changes.

■ How People Respond to Changes They Like. According to Figure 16.2, a three-stage adjustment is typical when people encounter a change they like. New college graduates, for instance, often see their unrealistic optimism (stage A) give way to the reality shock (stage B) of earning a living before getting their life and career on track (stage C). Key personal factors —including attitude, morale, and desire to make the change work—dip during stage B. Sometimes the dip is so severe or prolonged that the person gives up, as, say, when newlyweds head for the divorce court. Stage B is thus a critical juncture where leadership can make a difference.[15]

■ How People Respond to Changes They Fear and Dislike. Although exact statistics are not available, the situation in Figure 16.3 is probably more common in the workplace than the one in Figure 16.2. In other words, on-the-job change generally is more feared than welcomed. Changes, particularly sudden ones, represent the unknown. Most of us fear the unknown. We can bring the model in Figure 16.3 to life by walking through it with Maria, a production supervisor at a dairy products cooperative. She and her coworkers face a major reorganization involving a switch to team-based production.

2. EXPLAIN how people tend to respond differently to changes they like and those they dislike.

Figure 16.2 How People Tend to Respond to Changes They *Like*

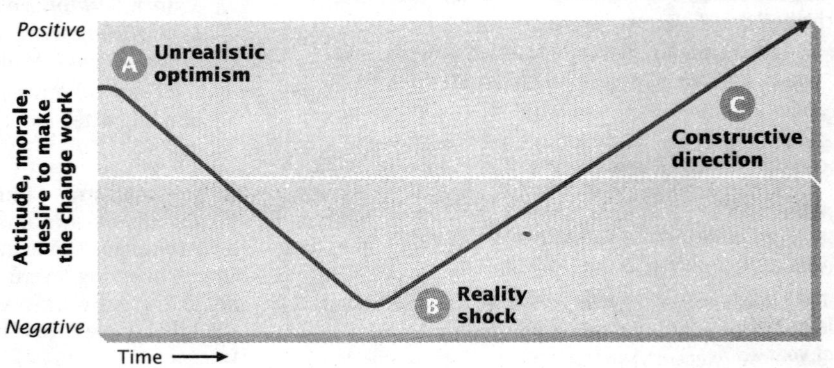

Figure 16.3 How People Tend to Respond to Changes They *Fear* and *Dislike*

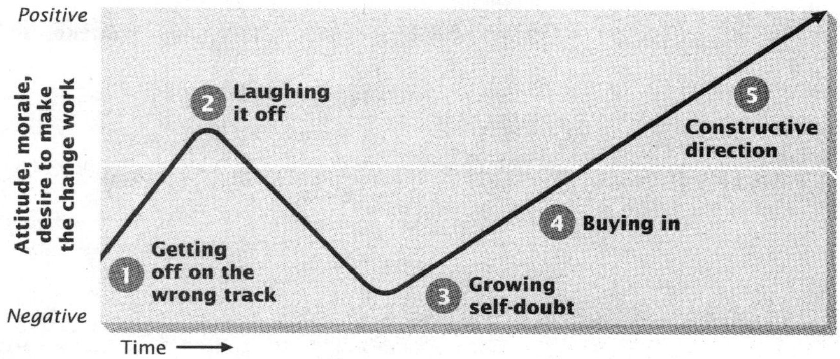

In stage 1, Maria feels a bit unsure and somewhat overwhelmed by the sudden switch to teams. She needs a lot more information to decide whether she really likes the idea. She feels twinges of fear. Stage 2 finds Maria joking with the other supervisors about how upper management's enthusiasm for teams will blow over in a few days, so there's no need to worry. Her attitude, mood, and desire for change improve a bit. After an initial training session on team-based management and participation, Maria begins to worry about her job security. Even if she keeps her job, she wonders if she is up to the new way of doing things. Her morale drops sharply in stage 3. In stage 4, after a stern but supportive lecture from her boss about being a team player, Maria comes to grips with her resistance to the team approach. She resolves to stop criticizing management's "fad of the week" and help make the switch to teams a success. Her attitude turns positive, and her morale takes an upswing in stage 5, as she tries participative management techniques and gets positive results. Additional training and some personal research and reading on team-based management convince Maria that this approach is the wave of the future.

Ten months after the switch to teams was announced, Maria has become an outspoken advocate for teams and participative management. Her job security is strengthened by a pending promotion to the training department, where she will coordinate all team training for supervisors. Unbeknownst to upper management, Maria has even toyed with the idea of starting her own consulting business, specializing in team management. Maria's transition from fear to full adaptation has taken months and has not been easy. But the experience has been normal and positive, including a timely boost from her manager between stages 3 and 4.

16b First Things First

Seth Godin, expert on organizational change:

> *You will succeed in the face of change when you make the difficult decisions first.*

Source: Seth Godin, "If It's Urgent, Ignore It," Fast Company, *no. 81 (April 2004): 101.*

QUESTIONS:

How does this advice tie in with one's values and priorities? Do you tend to make tough decisions sooner rather than later? What are the practical implications of your actions?

■ A Contingency Model for Getting Employees Through Changes. Contingency managers, once again, adapt their techniques to the situation. The response patterns in Figures 16.2 and 16.3 call for different managerial actions. Managerial action steps for both situations are listed in Table 16.1. When employees understand that stages B and 3 are normal and expected responses, they will be less apt to panic and more likely to respond favorably to managerial guidance through action steps C and 4 and 5.[16]

Table 16.1 How to Help Individuals Deal with Change: A Contingency Approach

Situation: The person *likes* the change.

Stage	Managerial Action Steps
A. Unrealistic optimism "What a great idea! It will solve all our problems."	Encourage enthusiasm while directing attention to potential problems and the cooperation and work necessary to get the job done.
B. Reality shock "This is going to be a lot harder than it seemed."	Listen supportively to negative feelings and neutralize unreasonable fears. Set realistic short-term goals. Build self-confidence. Recognize and reward positive comments and progress.
C. Constructive direction "This won't be easy, but we can do it."	Set broader and longer-term goals. Encourage involvement. Emphasize group problem solving and learning. Celebrate individual and group achievements. Prepare for bigger and better things.

Situation: The person *fears* and *dislikes* the change.

Stage	Managerial Action Steps
1. Getting off on the wrong track "What a dumb idea!"	Be a positive role model for the vision of a better way. Be a supportive listener and correct any misunderstanding.
2. Laughing it off "Just another wild idea that won't go anywhere. Don't worry about it."	Same as action step A above.
3. Growing self-doubt "I don't think I have what it takes."	Same as action step B above.
4. Buying in "Okay, I'll give this thing a try."	Encourage the person to let go of the past and look forward to a better future. Build personal commitment. Recognize and reward positive words and actions.
5. Constructive direction "This won't be easy, but we can do it."	Same as action step C above.

Overcoming Resistance to Change

Dealing with change is an integral part of modern management.[17] Change expert Ichak Adizes puts it this way:

> *Living means solving problems, and growing up means being able to solve bigger problems.*
>
> *The purpose of management, leadership, parenting, or governing is exactly that: to solve today's problems and get ready to deal with tomorrow's problems. This is necessary because there is change. No management is needed when there are no problems, and there are no problems only when we are dead. To manage is to be alive, and to be alive means to experience change with the accompanying problems it brings.*[18]

Within the change typology just discussed, organizational change comes in all sizes and shapes. Often it's new and unfamiliar technology, such as the evolving wireless Internet.[19] It could be a reorganization, a merger, a new pay plan, or perhaps a new performance appraisal program. Whatever its form, change is like a stone tossed into a still pond. The initial impact causes ripples to radiate in all directions, often with unpredictable consequences. A common consequence of change in organizations is resistance from those whose jobs are directly affected. Both rational and irrational resistance can bring the wheels of progress to a halt. Management faces the challenge of foreseeing and neutralizing resistance to change. The question is, how? To answer that question, we need to examine why employees resist change.

3. **LIST** at least six reasons why employees resist change, and **DISCUSS** what management can do about resistance to change.

■ Why Do Employees Resist Change?

Employees resist change for many reasons.[20] The following are the most common:

■ **Surprise.** Significant changes that are introduced on the spur of the moment or with no warning can create a threatening sense of imbalance in the workplace. Regarding this problem, an executive task force at J. C. Penney Co., the well-known retailer, had this recommendation: "Schedule changes in measurable, comfortable stages. Too much, too soon can be counterproductive."[21]

■ **Inertia.** Many members of the typical organization desire to maintain a safe, secure, and predictable status quo. The bywords of this group are "But we don't do things that way here." Technological inertia also is a common problem. Consider, for example, the history of the standard typewriter keyboard (referred to as the Qwerty keyboard because *Q, W, E, R, T,* and *Y* are the first six letters in the upper-left-hand corner).

> *The ungainly layout of the Qwerty keyboard was introduced in 1873 to slow down typists so they wouldn't jam keys. That design imperative quickly disappeared, yet Qwerty has turned back all attempts—including one by its own inventor—to replace it with something faster. The productive cost? Undoubtedly billions of dollars.*[22]

Thanks to resistance to change, the latest high-tech marvels in personal computing come out of the box today complete with an 1873-style keyboard! Supervisors and middle managers who fall victim to unthinking inertia can effectively kill change programs.

■ **Misunderstanding/Ignorance/Lack of Skills.** Without adequate introductory or remedial training, an otherwise positive change may be perceived in a negative light. This is precisely the situation Ann Fudge encountered in 2003 when she was hired as chair and CEO of Young & Rubicam, a troubled ad agency known for its turf battles. Fudge envisioned a more collaborative, efficient, and client-focused organization. But, as reported by *Business Week*, the transition has not been smooth:

> *Fudge's message of discipline is . . . bruising [senior managers'] egos. Many openly snicker at her attempts to introduce Six Sigma, the rigid and almost religious quality-control program long associated with General Electric Co. (where Fudge sits on the board). They call it Sick Sigma. She calls the initiative FIT—for focus, innovation, and teamwork—and says it's tailored to simplifying processes in the ad industry. She now has staffers trained as Six Sigma "green belts," who tackle everything from sourcing supplies to honing the process for developing creative strategies. Despite resistance, several converts are already excited about the results, with Y&R account manager Kathryn Burke arguing: "This really needed to be done."*[23]

■ **Emotional Side Effects.** Those who are forced to accept on-the-job changes can experience a sense of powerlessness and even anger. The subsequent backlash can be passive (stalling, pretending not to understand) or active (vocal opposition, sabotage, or aggression).

"THE 'SUBSEQUENT BACKLASH' IS HERE TO SEE YOU."

Source: *P. C. Vey*

- **Lack of Trust.** Promises of improvement are likely to fall on deaf ears when employees do not trust management. Conversely, managers are unlikely to permit necessary participation if they do not trust their people.

- **Fear of Failure.** Just as many college freshmen have doubts about their chances of ever graduating, challenges presented by significant on-the-job changes can also be intimidating.

- **Personality Conflicts.** Managers who are disliked by their people are poor conduits for change.

- **Poor Timing.** In every work setting, internal and/or external events can conspire to create resentment about a particular change. For example, an otherwise desirable out-of-state transfer would only make things worse for an employee with an ailing elderly parent.

- **Lack of Tact.** As we all know, it is not necessarily what is said that shapes our attitude toward people and events. *How* it is said is often more important. Tactful and sensitive handling of change is essential.

- **Threat to Job Status/Security.** Because employment fulfills basic needs, employees can be expected to resist changes with real or imaginary impacts on job status or job security.

- **Breakup of Work Group.** Significant changes can tear the fabric of on-the-job social relationships. Accordingly, members of cohesive work groups often exert peer pressure on one another to resist changes that threaten to break up the group.[24]

- **Passive-Aggressive Organizational Culture.** This subtle but potent form of resistance hides behind smiling faces. Passive-aggressive behavior becomes a major barrier to change when it becomes embedded in the organization's culture.

16c Resistance? Don't Be Silly

Jeffrey Pfeffer, Stanford business professor:

The notion that workers resist change is just . . . silly. Employees will always change when the change makes them and their companies more successful and is consistent with a more enjoyable work experience.

Source: Jeffrey Pfeffer, "Tech Answers No Prayers," *Business 2.0*, 5 (January-February 2004): 58.

QUESTIONS:

Do you agree or disagree with this statement? Explain. What is the take-away lesson for managers?

Meetings are a good way for employees to determine if they work for a passive-aggressive company. They go like this: Everyone is pleasant and agreeable. There's little debate. Heads nod when someone with power says it's time to introduce something new.

The meeting ends with everyone seemingly on the same page, but then the quips begin about the flavor of the month. Most go back and do their jobs as they always have, or procrastinate, hoping the proposed change will blow over.[25]

■ **Competing Commitments.** Employees may not have a problem with the change itself, but rather with how it disrupts their pursuit of other goals. Such competing commitments are often unconscious and need to be skillfully brought to the surface to make progress. Consider this situation: "[Y]ou find that the person who won't collaborate despite a passionate and sincere commitment to teamwork is equally dedicated to avoiding the conflict that naturally attends any ambitious team activity."[26]

These reasons for resisting change help demonstrate that participation is not a panacea. For example, imagine the futility of trying to gain the enthusiastic support of a team of assembly-line welders for a robot that will eventually take over their jobs. In extreme form, each reason for resisting change can become an insurmountable barrier to genuine participation. Therefore, managers need a broad array of methods for dealing with resistance to change.

■ Strategies for Overcoming Resistance to Change

Only in recent years have management theorists begun to give serious attention to alternative ways of overcoming resistance to change.[27] At least six options, including participation, are available in this area:

1. ***Education and communication.*** This strategy is appealing because it advocates prevention rather than cure. The idea here is to help employees understand the true need for a change as well as the logic behind it. Various media may be used, including face-to-face discussions, formal group presentations, or special reports or publications.
2. ***Participation and involvement.*** Once again, personal involvement through participation tends to defuse both rational and irrational fears about a workplace change. By participating in both the design of a change and its implementation, one acquires a personal stake in its success.
3. ***Facilitation and support.*** When fear and anxiety are responsible for resistance to doing things in a new and different way, support from management in the form of special training, job stress counseling, and compensatory time off can be helpful. According to the CEO of Medtronic, this is how the heart pacemaker company facilitates employees' acceptance of a constant stream of product innovations:

   We set up venture teams of people who aren't emotionally invested in the old product. Once the new one has enough strength to stand on its

Doctors and medical students in New Delhi, India on strike in protest against the government affirmative action plan. The nation faces a polarizing totem of public policy: a government plan to extend college admission quotas to certain "backward" castes. It will take some carefully crafted strategies to overcome this resistance to change.

own, we reintegrate the doubters. That's key. If you just tell them that "here's the new product," it demoralizes people. You have to go from the venture team to integrating it into the mainstream business.[28]

4. ***Negotiation and agreement.*** Sometimes management can neutralize potential or actual resistance by exchanging something of value for cooperation. An hourly clerical employee may, for instance, be put on a salary in return for learning how to operate a new Internet workstation.
5. ***Manipulation and co-optation.*** Manipulation occurs when managers selectively withhold or dispense information and consciously arrange events to increase the chance that a change will be successful. Co-optation normally involves token participation. Those who are co-opted with token participation cannot claim they have not been consulted, yet the ultimate impact of their input is negligible.
6. ***Explicit and implicit coercion.*** Managers who cannot or will not invest the time required for the other strategies can try to force employees to go along with a change by threatening them with termination, loss of pay raises or promotions, transfer, and the like.

16d Back to the Opening Case

How would you rate Anne Mulcahy's ability to overcome resistance to change at Xerox? Explain.

As shown in Table 16.2, each of these strategies for overcoming resistance to change has advantages and drawbacks. Appropriateness to the situation is the key to success.
Now we turn our attention to implementing changes in organizations.

Table 16.2 Dealing with Resistance to Change

Approach	Commonly used in situations	Advantages	Drawbacks
1. Education + communication	Where there is a lack of information or inaccurate information and analysis	Once persuaded, people will often help with the implementation of the change	Can be very time-consuming if lots of people are involved
2. Participation + involvement	Where the initiators do not have all the information they need to design the change, and where others have considerable power to resist	People who participate will be committed to implementing change, and any relevant information they have will be integrated into the change plan	Can be very time-consuming if participators design an inappropriate change
3. Facilitation + support	Where people are resisting because of adjustment problems	No other approach works as well with adjustment problems	Can be time-consuming, expensive, and still fail
4. Negotiation + agreement	Where someone or some group will clearly lose out in a change, and where that group has considerable power to resist	Sometimes it is a relatively easy way to avoid major resistance	Can be too expensive in many cases if it alerts others to negotiate for compliance
5. Manipulation + co-optation	Where other tactics will not work or are too expensive	It can be a relatively quick and inexpensive solution to resistance problems	Can lead to future problems if people feel manipulated
6. Explicit + implicit coercion	Where speed is essential, and the change initiators possess considerable power	It is speedy and can overcome any kind of resistance	Can be risky if it leaves people mad at the initiators

Source: *Reprinted by permission of the* Harvard Business Review. *From "Choosing Strategies for Change," by John P. Kotter and Leonard A. Schlesinger (March-April 1979, p. 111). Copyright © 1979 by the President and Fellows of Harvard College; all rights reserved.*

Making Change Happen

In these fast-paced times, managers need to be active agents of change rather than passive observers or, worse, victims of circumstances beyond their control. This active role requires foresight, responsiveness, flexibility, and adaptability.[29] In this section, we focus on two approaches to making change happen: (1) organization development, a formal top-down approach, and (2) grassroots change, an unofficial and informal bottom-up approach.

Planned Change Through Organization Development (OD)

Organization development has become a convenient label for a host of techniques and processes aimed at making sick organizations healthy and healthy organizations healthier.[30] According to experts in the field:

organization development (OD): *planned change programs intended to help people and organizations function more effectively*

> ***Organization development (OD)*** *consists of planned efforts to help persons work and live together more effectively, over time, in their organizations. These goals are achieved by applying behavioral science principles, methods, and theories adapted from the fields of psychology, sociology, education, and management.*[31]

Others simply call OD *planned change.* Regarding the degree of change involved, OD consultant and writer Warner Burke contends that

> *Organization development is a process of fundamental change in an organization's culture. By fundamental change, as opposed to fixing a problem or improving a procedure, I mean that some significant aspect of the organization's culture will never be the same.*[32]

OD programs generally are facilitated by hired consultants,[33] although inside OD specialists can also be found.[34]

The Objectives of OD. OD programs vary because they are tailored to unique situations. What is appropriate for one organization may be totally out of place in another. In spite of this variation, certain objectives are common to most OD programs. In general, OD programs develop social processes such as trust, problem solving, communication, and cooperation to facilitate organizational change and enhance personal and organizational effectiveness. More specifically, the typical OD program tries to achieve the following seven objectives:

1. Deepen the sense of organizational purpose (or vision) and align individuals with that purpose.
2. Strengthen interpersonal trust, communication, cooperation, and support.
3. Encourage a problem-solving rather than a problem-avoiding approach to organizational problems.
4. Develop a satisfying work experience capable of building enthusiasm.
5. Supplement formal authority with authority based on personal knowledge and skill.
6. Increase personal responsibility for planning and implementing.
7. Encourage personal willingness to change.[35]

Critics of OD point out that there is nothing really new in this list of objectives. Directly or indirectly, each of these objectives is addressed by one or another general management technique. OD advocates respond by saying general management lacks a systematic approach. They claim that the usual practice of teaching managers how to plan, solve problems, make decisions, organize, motivate, lead, and control contributes to a haphazard, bits-and-pieces management style. According to OD thinking, organization development gives managers a vehicle for systematically introducing change by applying a broad selection of management techniques as a unified and consistent package. This, they claim, leads to greater personal, group, and organizational effectiveness.

The OD Process. A simple metaphor helps introduce the three major components of OD.[36] Suppose someone hands you a coffee cup filled with clear, solid ice. You look down through the ice and see a penny lying tails up on the bottom of the cup. Now suppose that for some reason you want the penny to be frozen in place in a heads-up position. What can you do? There is really only one practical solution. You let the ice in the cup melt, reach in and flip the penny over, and then refreeze the cup of water. This is precisely how social psychologist Kurt Lewin recommended that change be handled in social systems. Specifically, Lewin told change agents to unfreeze, change, and then refreeze social systems.[37]

unfreezing: *neutralizing resistance by preparing people for change*

4. DESCRIBE how the unfreezing-change-refreezing metaphor applies to organization development (OD).

Unfreezing prepares the members of a social system for change and then helps neutralize initial resistance. Sudden, unexpected change, according to Lewin, is socially disruptive.[38] For example, Brooklyn Union Gas held a mock funeral when it became KeySpan. Deregulation had forced the former monopoly to reinvent itself to compete in the marketplace, a wrenching change. Corporate ombudsman Kenny Moore, a former priest who came up with the funeral idea, explains what took place with about 70 key managers in the room:

> *In one corner, I put two tombstones from our Halloween display and a funeral urn. I wore my priestly stole and played a tape of Gregorian chants. "Dearly beloved," I said, "we are gathered here today to bid farewell to the Brooklyn Union Gas of old." Then I asked people to write what was over for the company on index cards and put them in the urn. People wrote things like "lifetime employment" and "monopoly."...*
>
> *In the next corner was a steamer trunk for the things we needed to keep on our journey. We wrote things like "great people," and "dedication to the community" on cards and threw them in. Finally, I had a stork from our Valentine's display to symbolize our birth as KeySpan. I made everyone draw what the future of the company might look like with crayons on poster paper. By then, everyone was participating.*[39]

refreezing: *systematically following up a change program for lasting results*

16e Back to the Opening Case

What sort of "unfreezing" did Anne Mulcahy do while trying to turn around Xerox? How would you rate her effectiveness? Explain. Now what does she need to do in the way of "refreezing?"

Once the change has been introduced, **refreezing** is necessary to follow up on problems, complaints, unanticipated side effects, and any lingering resistance. This seemingly simple approach to change spells the difference between systematic and haphazard change.

The OD model introduced here is based on Lewin's approach to handling change (see Figure 16.4). Diagnosis is carried out during the unfreezing phase. Change is then carefully introduced through tailor-made intervention. Finally, a systematic follow-up refreezes the situation. Each phase is critical to successful organizational change and development. Still, it takes continual recycling through this three-phase sequence to make OD an ongoing system of planned change.

Figure 16.4 A General Model of OD

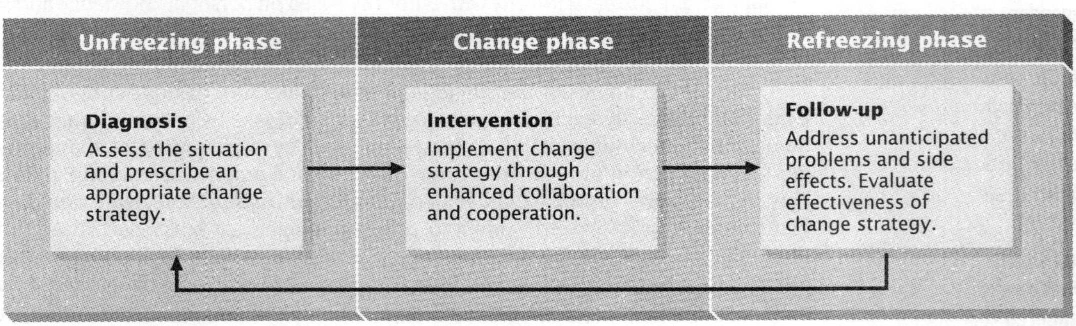

Unofficial and Informal Grassroots Change

OD is rationally planned, formal, systematic, and initiated by top management. As a sign of the times, many of today's organizations cannot be described in those terms. They tend to be spontaneous, informal, experimental, and driven from within. (Interestingly, employees in some of these modern organizations were empowered by earlier OD programs.)[40] Unusual things can happen when empowered employees start to take the initiative. Consider the unconventional language in this recent description of change:

> *Change starts with finding a backer—someone who can sell your plan to the senior team. Change dies without a fighter—someone smart enough and skilled enough to win over the opposition. Change kicks in when people start to trust—in the plan and in one another. Trust is the glue that invariably holds a change effort together. Change just might work when people are focused—on the goal, and on each step that's necessary to achieve it.*
>
> *Getting the buy-in. Overcoming resistance. Building trust. Zeroing in on the objective. These are the critical skills that every change team must leverage if it is to have any hope of succeeding.*[41]

This is not top-down change in the tradition of OD. Rather, it involves change from inside the organization. Let us explore two perspectives on unofficial and informal grassroots change: tempered radicals and the 5P model.

tempered radicals: *people who quietly try to change the dominant organizational culture in line with their convictions*

Tempered Radicals. This intriguing term and the concept it embraces come from Stanford professor Debra E. Meyerson. She defines **tempered radicals** as

> *people who want to succeed in their organizations yet want to live by their values or identities, even if they are somehow at odds with the dominant culture of their organizations. Tempered radicals want to fit in and they want to retain what makes them different. They want to rock the boat, and they want to stay in it.*[42]

Meyerson's research has found many "square pegs in round holes" who identify powerfully with her concept of the tempered radical. They tend to work quietly yet relentlessly to advance their vision of a better organization. If progressive managers are to do a good job of managing diversity, then they need to handle their tempered radicals in win-win fashion (see Managing Diversity). Too often those with different ideas are marginalized and/or trivialized. When this happens, the organization's intellectual and social capital suffer greatly.

Four practical guidelines for tempered radicals stem from Meyerson's research:

1. ***Think small for big results.*** Don't try to change the organization's culture all at once. Start small and build a string of steadily larger victories. Learn as you go. Encourage small, nonthreatening experiments. Trust and confidence in you and your ideas will grow with the victories.
2. ***Be authentic.*** Base your actions on your convictions and thoughtful preparation, not on rash emotionalism. Anger, aggression, and arrogance give people an easy excuse to dismiss you and your ideas.
3. ***Translate.*** Build managerial support by explaining the business case for your ideas.
4. ***Don't go it alone.*** Build a strong support network of family, friends, and co-workers to provide moral support and help advance your cause.[43]

16f Celebrating the Unexpected

Legendary management writer and consultant Peter F. Drucker:

> *If you start out by looking at change as threats, you will never innovate. Don't dismiss something simply because this is not what you had planned. The unexpected is often the best source of innovation.*

Source: As quoted in James Daly, "Sage Advice," Business 2.0, *1 (August 22, 2000): 142.*

QUESTION:
What does this perspective teach us about dealing with tempered radicals?

MANAGING DIVERSITY

Tempered Radicals as Everyday Leaders

In the course of their daily actions and interactions, tempered radicals teach important lessons and inspire change. In so doing, they exercise a form of leadership within organizations that is less visible than traditional forms—but just as important.

The trick for organizations is to locate and nurture this subtle form of leadership. Consider how Barry Coswell, a conservative, yet open-minded lawyer who headed up the securities division of a large, distinguished financial services firm, identified, protected, and promoted a tempered radical within his organization. Dana, a left-of-center, first-year attorney, came to his office on her first day of work after having been fingerprinted—a standard practice in the securities industry. The procedure had made Dana nervous: What would happen when her new employer discovered that she had done jail time for participating in a 1960s-era civil rights protest? Dana quickly understood that her only hope of survival was to be honest about her background and principles. Despite the difference in their political proclivities, she decided to give Barry the benefit of the doubt. She marched into his office and confessed to having gone to jail for sitting in front of a bus.

"I appreciate your honesty," Barry laughed, "but unless you've broken a securities law, you're probably okay." In return for her small confidence, Barry shared stories of his own about growing up in a poor county and about his life in the military. The story swapping allowed them to put aside ideological disagreements and to develop a deep respect for each other. Barry sensed a budding leader in Dana. Here was a woman who operated on the strength of her convictions and was honest about it but was capable of discussing her beliefs without self-righteousness. She didn't pound tables. She was a good conversationalist. She listened attentively. And she was able to elicit surprising confessions from him.

Barry began to accord Dana a level of protection, and he encouraged her to speak her mind, take risks, and, most important, challenge his assumptions. In one instance, Dana spoke up to defend a female junior lawyer who was being evaluated harshly and, Dana believed, inequitably. Dana observed that different standards were being applied to male and female lawyers, but her colleagues dismissed her "liberal" concerns. Barry cast a glance at Dana, then said to the staff, "Let's look at this and see if we are being too quick to judge." After the meeting, Barry and Dana held a conversation about double standards and the pervasiveness of bias. In time, Barry initiated a policy to seek out minority legal counsel, both in-house and at outside legal firms. And Dana became a senior vice president.

In Barry's ability to recognize, mentor, and promote Dana there is a key lesson for executives who are anxious to foster leadership in their organizations. It suggests that leadership development may not rest with expensive external programs or even with the best intentions of the human resources department. Rather, it may rest with the open-minded recognition that those who appear to rock the boat may turn out to be the most effective of captains.

Source: Reprinted by permission of Harvard Business Review. *From Debra E. Meyerson, "Radical Change the Quiet Way," October 2001. Copyright © 2001 by the President and Fellows of Harvard College; all rights reserved.*

5. DESCRIBE tempered radicals, and **IDENTIFY** the 5Ps in the checklist for grassroots change agents.

■ **The 5P Checklist for Grassroots Change Agents (Turning Ideas into Action).** The 5P model consists of an easy-to-remember list for anyone interested in organizational change: *preparation, purpose, participation, progress,* and *persistence* (see Figure 16.5). The model is generic, which means that it applies to all levels in profit and nonprofit organizations of all sizes. Let us examine each item more closely.

- ***Preparation:*** Is the concept or problem clearly defined? Has adequate problem *finding* taken place? Are underlying assumptions sound? Will the end result be worth the collective time, effort, and expense? Can the change initiative be harnessed to another change effort with a high probability of success, or should it stand alone? Does the proposed change have a *champion* or a *driver* who has the passion and persistence to see the process through to completion?
- ***Purpose:*** Can the objective or goal of the change initiative be expressed in clear, measurable terms? Can it be described quickly to busy people? What are the specific progress milestones and critical deadlines?

Figure 16.5 The 5P Checklist for Change Agents

	Key action steps
✓ Preparation	Develop concept; test assumptions; weigh costs and benefits; identify champion or driver.
✓ Purpose	Specify measurable objectives, milestones, deadlines.
✓ Participation	Refine concept while building broad and powerful support.
✓ Progress	Keep things moving forward despite roadblocks.
✓ Persistence	Foster realistic expectations and a sense of urgency while avoiding impatience.

- ***Participation:*** Have key people been involved in refining the change initiative to the extent of having personal "ownership" and willingness to fight for it? Have potential or actual opponents been offered a chance to participate? Have powerful people in the organization been recruited as advocates and defenders?
- ***Progress:*** Are performance milestones and intermediate deadlines being met? If not, why? Is support for the initiative weakening? Why? Have unexpected roadblocks been encountered? How can they be removed or avoided?
- ***Persistence:*** Has a reasonable sense of urgency been communicated to all involved? (*Note:* Extreme impatience can fray relationships and be stressful.) Has the change team drifted away from the original objective as time passed? Does everyone on the team have realistic expectations about how long the change process will take?

With situational adjustments for unique personalities and circumstances, the 5P approach can help ordinary employees create extraordinary change.[44] So sharpen your concept and take your best shot!

Managing Conflict

Conflict is intimately related to change and interpersonal dealings. Harvard's Abraham Zaleznik offered this perspective:

> *Because people come together to satisfy a wide array of psychological needs, social relations in general are awash with conflict. In the course of their interactions, people must deal with differences as well as similarities, with aversions as well as affinities. Indeed, in social relations, Sigmund Freud's parallel of humans and porcupines is apt: like porcupines, people prick and injure one another if they get too close; they will feel cold if they get too far apart.*[45]

The term *conflict* has a strong negative connotation, evoking words such as *opposition, anger, aggression,* and *violence.*[46] But conflict does not have to be a negative experience. Based on research evidence that most organizational conflict occurs within a cooperative context, Dean Tjosvold offered this more positive definition: "**Conflict** involves incompatible behaviors; one person interfering, disrupting, or in some other way making another's actions less effective."[47] This definition sets the scene for an

conflict: *incompatible behaviors that make another person less effective*

Students who want to argue for a higher grade may not want to tackle this particular professor. He's Bruce Patton, who teaches conflict management seminars in Harvard Law School's Program on Negotiation. For better or for worse, he calls conflict "a growth industry." He advises managers to not waste their time minimizing conflict, but rather to harness it in creative and constructive ways. Now, about that grade. . . .

important distinction between *competitive* (or destructive) conflict and *cooperative* (or constructive) conflict. Cooperative conflict is based on the win-win negotiating attitude discussed later in this chapter. Also, recall our discussion, in Chapter 14, of cooperative conflict as a tool for avoiding groupthink.

16g Let's Start a Good Clean Fight!

Jeff Weiss and Jonathan Hughes, management consultants:

> *Clashes between parties are the crucibles in which creative solutions are developed and wise trade-offs among competing objectives are made.*

Larry Whitney, vice president, Federal Reserve Bank of New York:

> *You have to get people upset. When things get disruptive, people really get work done, and learning takes place.*

Sources: Jeff Weiss and Jonathan Hughes, "Want Collaboration? Accept—and Actively Manage—Conflict," Harvard Business Review, *83 (March 2005): 93; and as quoted in Fiona Haley, "Tough-Love Leadership,"* Fast Company, *no. 86 (September 2004): 110.*

QUESTIONS:

Should managers try to stimulate conflict? How should they do it and how will they know if they've gone too far?

■ Dealing with the Two Faces of Conflict

Tjosvold contrasts competitive and cooperative conflict as follows:

> *The assumption that conflict is based on opposing interests leads to viewing conflict as a struggle to see whose strength and interests will dominate and whose will be subordinated. We must fight to win, or at least not lose. The assumption that you have largely cooperative goals leads to viewing the conflict as a common problem to be solved for mutual benefit, which in turn makes it more likely that the conflict will be constructive and that people will improve their abilities to deal with conflict.*[48]

Figure 16.6 Competitive versus Cooperative Conflict

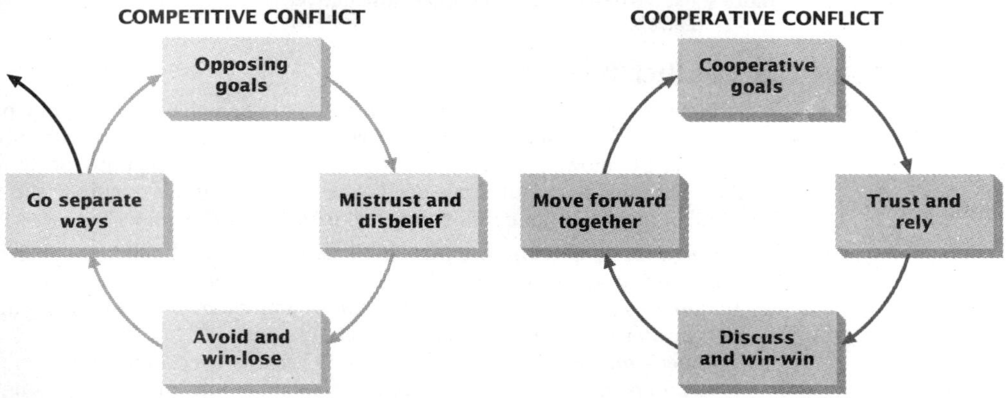

Source: (right figure): *Reprinted from* Learning to Manage Conflict: Getting People to Work Together Productively *by Dean Tjosvold. Copyright © 1993 by Dean Tjosvold. First published by Lexington Books. All rights reserved. All correspondence should be sent to Lexington Books, 4720 Boston Way, Lanham, Md. 20706.*

6. CONTRAST the competitive and cooperative conflict styles.

Figure 16.6 graphically illustrates the difference between competitive and cooperative conflict. In the competitive mode, the parties pursue directly opposite goals. Each mistrusts the other's intentions and disbelieves what the other party says. Both parties actively avoid constructive dialogue and have a win-lose attitude. Unavoidably, the disagreement persists and they go their separate ways.[49] Does this self-defeating cycle sound familiar? Probably, because most of us at one time or another have suffered through a broken relationship or destructive conflict with someone else.

In sharp contrast, the *cooperative* conflict cycle in Figure 16.6 is a mutually reinforcing experience serving the best interests of both parties. Cooperative conflict is standard practice at Anheuser-Busch, brewer of Budweiser beer:

> *When the policy committee of that company considers a major move—getting into or out of a business, or making a big capital expenditure—it sometimes assigns teams to make the case for each side of the question. There may be two teams or even three. Each is knowledgeable about the subject; each has access to the same information. Occasionally someone in favor of the project is chosen to lead the dissent, and an opponent to argue for it. Pat Stokes, who heads the company's beer empire, describes the result: "We end up with decisions and alternatives we hadn't thought of previously," sometimes representing a synthesis of the opposing views. "You become a lot more anticipatory, better able to see what might happen, because you have thought through the process."*[50]

When *Business Week* recently recognized Intel as a Silicon valley legend, it pointed out the semiconductor maker's use of cooperative conflict: "The process, dubbed 'disagree and commit,' encouraged engineers to constantly think of new ways of doing things faster, cheaper, and more reliably."[51] Cooperative conflict thus can give creativity and innovation a boost.

As a skill-building exercise, you might want to use the cooperative conflict model in Figure 16.6 to salvage a personal relationship mired in competitive conflict. Show the cooperative model to the other party and suggest starting over with a new set of ground rules. Cooperative goals are the necessary starting point. This process can be difficult, yet very rewarding (see the Hands-On Exercise at the end of this chapter). Win-win conflict is not just a good idea; it is one of the keys to a better world. (See Skills & Tools at the end of this chapter for tips on how to express anger.)

There are two sets of tools available for managing conflict.[52] The first we call conflict triggers, for stimulating conflict; the second involves conflict resolution techniques, used when conflict becomes destructive.

■ Conflict Triggers

conflict trigger: *any factor that increases the chances of conflict*

A **conflict trigger** is a circumstance that increases the chances of intergroup or interpersonal conflict. As long as a conflict trigger appears to stimulate constructive conflict, it can be allowed to continue. But as soon as the symptoms of destructive conflict[53] become apparent, steps need to be taken to remove or correct the offending conflict trigger. Major conflict triggers include the following:

- ***Ambiguous or overlapping jurisdictions.*** Unclear job boundaries often create competition for resources and control. Reorganization can help to clarify job boundaries if destructive conflict becomes a problem (refer to the organization design alternatives discussed in Chapter 10).
- ***Competition for scarce resources.*** As the term is used here, *resources* include funds, personnel, authority, power, and valuable information. In other words, anything of value in an organizational setting can become a competitively sought-after scarce resource. Sometimes, as in the case of money and people, destructive competition for scarce resources can be avoided by enlarging the resource base (such as increasing competing managers' budgets or hiring additional personnel).[54]
- ***Communication breakdowns.*** Because communication is a complex process beset by many barriers, these barriers often provoke conflict. It is easy to misunderstand another person or group of people if two-way communication is hampered in some way. The battle for clear communication never ends.
- ***Time pressure.*** Deadlines and other forms of time pressure can stimulate prompt performance or trigger destructive emotional reactions. When imposing deadlines, managers should consider individuals' ability to cope.
- ***Unreasonable standards, rules, policies, or procedures.*** These triggers generally lead to dysfunctional conflict between managers and the people they manage. The best remedy is for the manager to tune into employees' perceptions of fair play and correct extremely unpopular situations before they mushroom.
- ***Personality clashes.*** It is very difficult to change one's personality on the job. Therefore, the practical remedy for serious personality clashes is to separate the antagonistic parties by reassigning one or both to a new job.[55]
- ***Status differentials.*** As long as productive organizations continue to be arranged hierarchically, this trigger is unavoidable. But managers can minimize dysfunctional conflict by showing a genuine concern for the ideas, feelings, and values of lower-level employees.[56]
- ***Unrealized expectations.*** Dissatisfaction grows when expectations are not met. Conflict is another by-product of unrealized expectations. Destructive conflict can be avoided in this area by taking time to discover, through frank discussion, what people expect from their employment. Unrealistic expec-tations can be countered before they become a trigger for dysfunctional conflict.

Managers who understand these conflict triggers will be in a much better position to manage conflict in a systematic and rational fashion. Those who passively wait for things to explode before reacting will find conflict managing them.

■ Resolving Conflict

7. IDENTIFY and DESCRIBE five conflict resolution techniques.

Even the best managers sometimes find themselves in the middle of destructive conflict, whether it is due to inattention or to circumstances beyond their control. In such situations, they may choose to do nothing (some call this an *avoidance* strategy) or try one or more of the following conflict resolution techniques.[57]

16h Please, Let's Be More Respectful. Thank You.

We are not, sad to say, born kind and tolerant. Survival instincts still push us to fight or flee, dominate or submit. Just watch children at play. The good news is we're trainable. We learn our behaviors. We can develop different ways of interacting. We can be taught to play nice. . . .

Learning to develop respectful relationships at work is perhaps the most important work-related skill we can develop. Our successes will be a measure of how far we've come as a society. Our failures will end up as headlines in the morning newspaper.

Source: Robert Rosell, "The Respectful Workplace," Training, *38 (November 2001): 80.*

QUESTIONS:

Do you think standards of social conduct have declined in recent years? If so, can you give examples? Are disrespect and incivility conflict triggers in the workplace? Explain. What can managers (and you) do to improve the situation?

■ **Problem Solving.** When conflicting parties take the time to identify and correct the source of their conflict, they are engaging in problem solving. This approach is based on the assumption that causes must be rooted out and attacked if anything is really to change. Problem solving (refer to our discussion of creative problem solving in Chapter 8) encourages managers to focus their attention on causes, factual information, and promising alternatives rather than on personalities or scapegoats. The major shortcoming of the problem-solving approach is that it takes time, but the investment of extra time can pay off handsomely when the problem is corrected instead of ignored and allowed to worsen.

■ **Superordinate Goals.** "Superordinate goals are highly valued, unattainable by any one group [or individual] alone, and commonly sought."[58] When a manager relies on superordinate goals to resolve destructive conflict, he or she brings the conflicting parties together and, in effect, says, "Look, we're all in this together. Let's forget our differences so we can get the job done." For example, a company president might remind the production and marketing department heads who have been arguing about product design that the competition is breathing down their necks. Although this technique often works in the short run, the underlying problem tends to crop up later to cause friction once again.

■ **Compromise.** This technique generally appeals to those living in a democracy. Advocates of compromise say everyone wins because compromise is based on negotiation, on give-and-take.[59] However, as discussed in the next section, most people do not have good negotiating skills. They approach compromise situations with a win-lose attitude. Thus compromises tend to be disappointing, leaving one or both parties feeling cheated. Conflict is only temporarily suppressed when people feel cheated. Successful compromise requires skillful negotiation.

■ **Forcing.** Sometimes, especially when time is important or a safety issue is involved, management must simply step into a conflict and order the conflicting parties to handle the situation in a particular manner. Reliance on formal authority and the power of a superior position is at the heart of forcing. Consider this recent example involving Burger King's new CEO Gregory D. Brenneman: ". . . after hearing of nasty e-mails flying between feuding execs, he told perpetrators to cut it out or they would be fired."[60] As one might suspect, forcing does not resolve the conflict and, in fact, may serve to compound it by hurting feelings and/or fostering resentment and mistrust.

■ **Smoothing.** A manager who relies on smoothing says to the conflicting parties something like "Settle down. Don't rock the boat. Things will work out by themselves." This approach may tone down conflict in the short run, but it does not solve the underlying problem. Just like each of the other conflict resolution techniques, smoothing has its place. It can be useful when management is attempting to hold things together until a critical project is completed or when there is no time for problem solving or compromise and forcing is deemed inappropriate.

Problem solving and skillfully negotiated compromises are the only approaches that remove the actual sources of conflict. They are the only resolution techniques capable of improving things in the long run. The other approaches amount to short-run, stopgap measures. And managers who fall back on an avoidance strategy are simply running away from the problem. Nonetheless, as we have noted, problem solving and full negotiation sessions can take up valuable time— time that managers may not be willing or able to spend at the moment. When this is the case, management may choose to fall back on superordinate goals, forcing, or smoothing, whichever seems most suitable.[61]

Negotiating

Negotiating is a fact of everyday life. Our negotiating skills are tested when we begin a new job, rent an apartment, live with a roommate, buy a house, buy or lease a car, ask for a raise or promotion, live with a spouse, divorce a spouse, or fight for custody of a child. Managers have even more opportunities to negotiate. Salespeople, employees, labor unions, other managers, and customers all have wishes that the organization may not be able to grant without some give-and-take. Sadly, most of us are rather poor negotiators. Negotiating skills, like any other crucial communication skill, need to be developed through diligent study and regular practice.[62] In fact, subjects in a study who had been trained in negotiating tactics negotiated more favorable outcomes than did those with no such training.[63]

negotiation: *decision-making process among interdependent parties with different preferences*

Experts from Northwestern University define **negotiation** as "a decision-making process among interdependent parties who do not share identical preferences." They go on to say, "It is through negotiation that the parties decide what each will give and take in their relationship."[64] The scope of negotiations spans all levels of human interaction, from individuals to organizations to nations. Two common types of negotiation are *two-party* and *third-party negotiation.* This distinction is evident in common real estate transactions. If you sell your home directly to a buyer after set-

Thanks to some negotiated compromises with Safeway, Kroger, and Albertsons, 30,000 unionized employees got back to work in 2005. Grocery workers Laurie Piazza (left) and Elise Blazek are seen here in San Jose, California, explaining the position of their labor organization, the United Food and Commercial Workers Local 428 Bay Area Coalition.

8. IDENTIFY and **DESCRIBE** the elements of effective negotiation, and **EXPLAIN** the advantage of added value negotiating (AVN).

tling on a mutually agreeable price, that is a two-party negotiation. It becomes a third-party negotiation when a real estate broker acts as a go-between for seller and buyer. Regardless of the type of negotiation, the same basic negotiating concepts apply. This final section examines three elements of effective negotiation and introduces a useful technique called *added value negotiating.*

Elements of Effective Negotiation

A good way to learn about proper negotiation is to start from zero. This means confronting and neutralizing one's biases and faulty assumptions. Sports and military metaphors, for example, are usually inappropriate. Why? Because effective negotiators are not bent on beating the opposition or wiping out the enemy.[65] They have a much broader agenda. For instance, effective negotiators not only satisfy their own needs, they also enhance the other party's readiness to negotiate again. Trust is important in this regard.[66] Using this "clean slate" approach to learning, let us explore three common elements of effective negotiation.

Adopting a Win-Win Attitude. Culture, as discussed in Chapter 4, has a powerful influence on individual behavior. In America, for example, the prevailing culture places a high value on winning and shames losing. You can be number one or be a loser, with little or nothing in between. America's cultural preoccupation with winning, while sometimes an admirable trait, can be a major barrier to effective negotiation.[67] A win-win attitude is preferable.

> **16i Negotiating a Pay Raise**
>
> *. . . suggests [ExecuNet CEO] Dave Opton, "Pull together the data you need to position yourself, including what your peers elsewhere are making and what you've contributed to the company. Think of yourself as a brand you have to sell. Explain the features." Many managers, he says, make the mistake of waiting to bring up money during a formal evaluation. "It's never a good idea, because those discussions tend to focus on how you can improve. Start a discussion about pay a few months beforehand."*
>
> *Source: Anne Fisher, "How to Ask For—and Get—a Raise Now,"* Fortune *(December 27, 2004): 47.*
>
> **QUESTIONS:**
> **Do you dislike asking for a pay raise? Why? How well would this advice work for you? Explain.**

Stephen R. Covey, author of the best-selling books *The Seven Habits of Highly Effective People* and *The 8th Habit,* offered this instructive perspective:

> *Win/Win is a frame of mind and heart that constantly seeks mutual benefit in all human interactions. Win/Win means that agreements or solutions are mutually beneficial, mutually satisfying. With a Win/Win solution, all parties feel good about the decision and feel committed to the action plan. Win/Win sees life as a cooperative, not a competitive, arena. Most people tend to think in terms of dichotomies: strong or weak, hardball or softball, win or lose. But that kind of thinking is basically flawed. It's based on power and position rather than on principle. Win/Win is based on the paradigm that there is plenty for everybody, that one person's success is not achieved at the expense or exclusion of the success of others.*
>
> *Win/Win is a belief in the Third Alternative. It's not your way or my way; it's a better way, a higher way.*[68]

Replacing a culturally based win-lose attitude with a win-win attitude is quite difficult; deeply ingrained habits are hard to change. But change they must if American managers are to be more effective negotiators in today's global marketplace.[69] Tom's of Maine, famous for its toothpaste and other all-natural products, is a good role model. Founder and CEO Tom Chappell has built a values-driven company that pays its manufacturing employees in Maine 15 percent above the going rate and donates 10 percent of pretax profits to charity. He relies on a win-win attitude to grow his business:

> *. . . rather than compromising as it grows, Tom's has figured out how to convince mass-market retailers [such as Wal-Mart and Rite-Aid] that its values-centered business practices are good for the bottom line—a clever tactic that has helped the company expand its reach steadily over the course of three decades . . .*
>
> *To create new opportunities, Chappell and COO [chief operating officer] Tom O'Brien approach potential distributors by going right to the top, meeting with the retailer's CEO or COO. To prepare for these sessions, they dig through*

annual reports and press releases to find statements that describe the retailer's values—goals that can be cited during the meetings to establish a foundation of shared beliefs. Tom's execs then describe their customers, making the pitch that these shoppers—who O'Brien says spend more and shop more frequently than the average consumer—are looking for retailers who share their values.[70]

■ **Knowing Your BATNA.** This odd-sounding label represents the anchor point of effective negotiations. It is an abbreviation for *best alternative to a negotiated agreement.* In other words, what will you settle for if negotiations do not produce your desired outcome(s)? Members of the Harvard Negotiation Project, responsible for the concept, call BATNA "the standard against which any proposed agreement should be measured. That is the only standard which can protect you both from accepting terms that are too unfavorable and from rejecting terms it would be in your interest to accept."[71] In today's popular language, it adds up to "What is your bottom line?" For example, a business seller's BATNA becomes the measuring stick for accepting or rejecting offers.

A realistic BATNA is good insurance against the three decision-making traps discussed in Chapter 8—framing error, escalation of commitment, and overconfidence. To negotiate without a BATNA is to stumble along aimlessly in the dark.

bargaining zone: *the gap between two parties' BATNAs*

■ **Identifying the Bargaining Zone.** Negotiation is useless if the parties involved have no common ground (see the top portion of Figure 16.7). At the other extreme, negotiation is unnecessary if both parties are satisfied with the same outcome. Midway, negotiation is necessary when there is a degree of overlap in the ranges of acceptable outcomes. Hence, the **bargaining zone** can be defined as the gap between the two BATNAs— the area of overlapping interests where agreement is possible[72] (see the middle portion of Figure 16.7). Because negotiators keep their BATNAs secret, each party needs to *estimate* the other's BATNA when identifying the likely bargaining zone.

■ Added Value Negotiating

Win-win negotiation[73] is a great idea that can be difficult to implement on a daily basis. Managers and others tend to stumble when they discover that a win-win attitude is necessary but not enough to get through a tough round of negotiations. A

Figure 16.7 The Bargaining Zone for Negotiators

Transaction: The sale of a used mountain bike with an appraised value of $475.

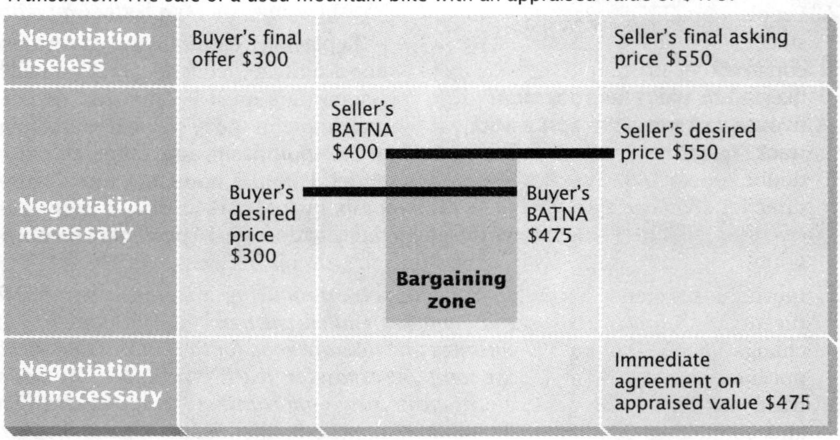

added value negotiating: *five-step process involving development of multiple deals*

step-by-step process is needed. Karl and Steve Albrecht's added value negotiating process bridges the gap between win-win theory and practice. **Added value negotiating** (AVN) is a five-step process involving the development of *multiple deals* that add value to the negotiating process.[74] This approach is quite different from traditional "single-outcome" negotiating that involves "taking something" from the other party. AVN comprises the following five steps:

1. ***Clarify interests.*** Both subjective (judgmental) and objective (observable and measurable) interests are jointly identified and clarified by the two parties. The goal is to find some *common ground* as a basis for negotiation.
2. ***Identify options.*** What sorts of value—in terms of money, property, actions, rights, and risk reduction—can each party offer the other? This step creates a *marketplace of value* for the negotiators.
3. ***Design alternative deal packages.*** Rather than tying the success of the negotiation to a single win-win offer, create a number of alternatives from various combinations of value items. This vital step, which distinguishes AVN from other negotiation strategies, fosters *creative agreement.*
4. ***Select a deal.*** Each party tests the various deal packages for value, balance, and fit. Feasible deals are then discussed jointly, and a *mutually acceptable deal* is selected.
5. ***Perfect the deal.*** Unresolved details are hammered out by the negotiators. Agreements are put in writing. *Relationships* are strengthened for future negotiations. Added value negotiating, according to the Albrechts, "is based on openness, flexibility, and a mutual search for the successful exchange of value. It allows you to build strong relationships with people over time."[75]

SUMMARY

1. Managers need to do a much better job of managing the process of change. Nadler and Tushman's model identifies four types of organizational change by cross-referencing anticipatory and reactive change with incremental and strategic change. Four resulting types of change are tuning, adaptation, re-orientation (frame bending), and re-creation (frame breaking).

2. People who like a change tend to go through three stages: unrealistic optimism, reality shock, and constructive direction. When someone fears or dislikes a change, a more complex process involving five stages tends to occur: getting off on the wrong track, laughing it off, experiencing growing self-doubt, buying in, and moving in a constructive direction. Managers are challenged to help employees deal effectively with reality shock and self-doubt.

3. Inevitable resistance to change must be overcome if the organization is to succeed. Employees resist change for many different reasons, including (but not limited to) surprise, inertia, ignorance, lack of trust, fear of failure, passive-aggressive behavior, and competing commitments. Modern managers facing resistance to change can select from several strategies, including education and communication, participation and involvement, facilitation and support, negotiation and agreement, manipulation and co-optation, and explicit and implicit coercion.

4. Organization development (OD) is a systematic approach to planned organizational change. The principal objectives of OD are increased trust, better problem solving, more effective communication, improved cooperation, and greater willingness to change. The typical OD program is a three-phase process of unfreezing, change, and refreezing.

5. Unofficial and informal grassroots change can be initiated by tempered radicals, who quietly follow their convictions when trying to change the dominant organizational culture. Four guidelines for tempered radicals are (1) think small for big results, (2) be authentic, (3) translate, and (4) don't go it alone. The 5P checklist for grassroots change agents—*preparation, purpose, participation, progress,* and *persistence*—is a generic model for people at all levels in all organizations. Ordinary employees can achieve extraordinary changes by having a clear purpose, a champion or driver for the change initiative, a measurable objective, broad and powerful support achieved through participation, an ability to overcome roadblocks, and a persistent sense of urgency.

6. Competitive conflict is characterized by a destructive cycle of opposing goals, mistrust and disbelief, and avoidance of discussion coupled with a win-lose attitude. In contrast, cooperative conflict involves a constructive cycle of cooperative goals, trust and reliance, and discussion coupled with a win-win attitude.

7. Conflict triggers can cause either constructive or destructive conflict. Destructive conflict can be resolved through problem solving, superordinate goals, compromise, forcing, or smoothing.

8. Three basic elements of effective negotiations are a win-win attitude, a BATNA (best alternative to a negotiated agreement) to serve as a negotiating standard, and the calculation of a bargaining zone to identify overlapping interests. Added value negotiating (AVN) improves on standard negotiation strategies by fostering a creative range of possible solutions.

TERMS TO UNDERSTAND

- Anticipatory changes, p. 470
- Reactive changes, p. 470
- Incremental changes, p. 470
- Strategic changes, p. 470
- Organization Development (OD), p. 479
- Unfreezing, p. 480
- Refreezing, p. 480
- Tempered radicals, p. 481
- Conflict, p. 483
- Conflict trigger, p. 486
- Negotiation, p. 488
- Bargaining zone, p. 490
- Added value negotiating, p. 491

SKILLS & TOOLS

How to Express Anger

Although not every angry feeling should be expressed to the person held accountable, this approach is direct and has the most potential to initiate a productive conflict. There are several rules to keep in mind when expressing anger.

- **Check assumptions.** No matter how convinced employees are that someone has deliberately interfered and tried to harm them, they may be mistaken. People can ask questions and probe. It may be that the other person had no intention and was unaware that others were frustrated. The incident may just dissolve into a misunderstanding.
- **Be specific.** People find being the target of anger stressful and anxiety provoking. They fear insults and rejection. The more specific the angry person can be, the less threatening and less of an attack on self-esteem the anger is. Knowing what angered the other can give the target of the anger concrete ways to make amends.
- **Be consistent.** Verbal and nonverbal messages should both express anger. Smiling and verbally expressing anger confuses the issue.
- **Take responsibility for anger.** Persons expressing anger should let the target know that they are angry and . . . [why they] feel unjustly frustrated.
- **Avoid provoking anger.** Expressing anger through unfair, insinuating remarks ("I can't believe someone can be as stupid as you!") can make the target of the anger angry too. Such situations can quickly deteriorate.
- **Watch for impulsivity.** Anger agitates and people say things they later regret.
- **Be wary of self-righteousness.** People can feel powerful, superior, and right; angry people can play "Now I got 'ya and you will pay." But anger should be used to get to the heart of the matter and solve problems, not for flouting moral superiority.
- **Be sensitive.** People typically underestimate the impact their anger has on others. Targets of anger often feel defensive, anxious, and worried. It is not usually necessary to repeat one's anger to get people's attention.
- **Make the expression cathartic.** Anger generates energy. Telling people releases that energy rather than submerges it. Anger is a feeling to get over, not to hang on to.
- **Express positive feelings.** Angry people depend upon and usually like people they are angry with. People expect help from people who have proved trustworthy, and are angry when it is not forthcoming.
- **Move to constructive conflict management.** Feeling affronted, personally attacked, and self-righteous should not side-track you from solving the underlying problems. Use the anger to create positive conflict.

- **Celebrate joint success.** Anger tests people's skills and their relationship. Be sure to celebrate the mutual achievement of expressing and responding to anger successfully.

Source: *Dean Tjosvold,* The Conflict-Positive Organization *(pp. 133–134).*

HANDS-ON EXERCISE

Putting Conflict on Ice[76]

Instructions:
Working alone or as a member of a team, read the following material on the iceberg of conflict. As instructed in the reading, focus on a specific conflict and then answer the seven sets of questions. Alternatively, both parties in a conflict can complete this exercise and then compare notes to establish interconnections and move toward resolution.

The Iceberg of Conflict

One way of picturing the hidden layers and complexities of conflict is through the metaphor of the iceberg, as depicted in the following chart. You may want to identify additional layers besides the ones we cite, to reveal what is below the surface for you.

ICEBERG OF CONFLICT

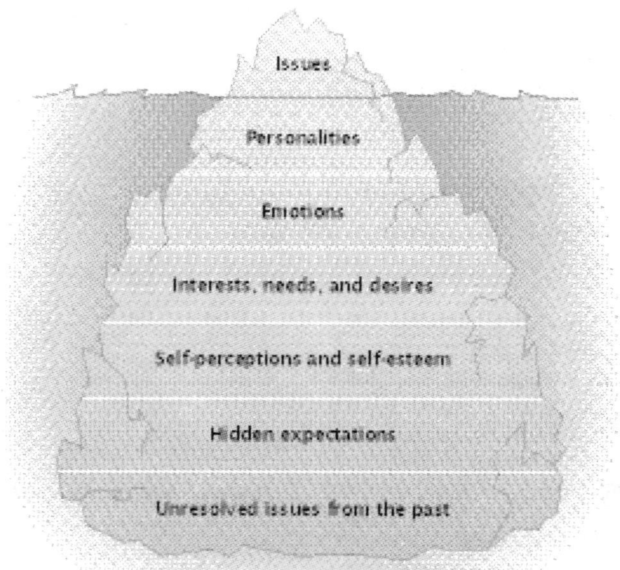

Exploring Your Iceberg

Each level of the iceberg represents something that does not appear on the surface, yet adds weight and immobility to our arguments when we are in conflict. Beneath the iceberg, the chart identifies an "awareness of interconnection," meaning that we all have the capacity, when we go deep enough and are not stuck on the surface of our conflicts, to experience genuine empathy and awareness of our interconnection with each other—including the person who is upsetting us.

To understand the deeper layers of your iceberg and get to an awareness of interconnection, consider a conflict in which you are now engaged. Try to identify the specific issues, problems, and feelings that exist for you at each level of the iceberg. As you probe deeper, notice whether your definition of the conflict changes, and how it evolves. Become aware of any emotions that emerge as you look deeper. Fear or resistance to these feelings can keep the conflict locked in place and block you from reaching deeper levels. Allow yourself to experience these feelings, whatever they are, and identify them to yourself or to someone you trust, so you can let them go. Try to answer the following questions for yourself and your opponent:

- *Issues:* What issues appear on the surface of your conflict?
- *Personalities:* Are differences between your personalities contributing to misunderstanding and tension? If so, what are they and how do they operate?
- *Emotions:* What emotions are having an impact on your reactions? How are they doing so? Are you communicating your emotions responsibly, or suppressing them?
- *Interests, needs, desires:* How are you proposing to solve the conflict? Why is that your proposal? What deeper concerns are driving the conflict? What do you really want? Why? What needs or desires, if satisfied, would enable you to feel good about the outcome? Why is that important? What does getting what you want have to do with the conflict?
- *Self-perceptions and self-esteem:* How do you feel about yourself and your behavior when you are engaged in the conflict? What do you see as your strengths and weaknesses?
- *Hidden expectations:* What are your primary expectations of your opponent? Of yourself? Have you clearly, openly, and honestly communicated your expectations to the other person? What would happen if you did? How might you release yourself from false expectations?
- *Unresolved issues from the past:* Does this conflict remind you of anything from your past relationships? Are there any unfinished issues remaining from the past that keep you locked in this conflict? Why?

For Consideration/Discussion

1. Did the issues and your perception of the conflict change as you worked through the iceberg? Explain.
2. Was there more (or less) to this conflict than you initially thought? Explain.
3. Which level of the iceberg was the most difficult to address? Why? Which was the easiest? Why?
4. What interconnections surfaced? How can they be used as a foundation for resolving the conflict?
5. How will this exercise affect the way you try to understand and resolve (or avoid) conflicts in the future?

Source: *From Kenneth Cloke and Joan Goldsmith,* Resolving Conflicts at Work: A Complete Guide for Everyone on the Job, *pp. 114–116. Copyright © 2000. Reprinted with permission of John Wiley & Sons, Inc.*

INTERNET EXERCISES

1. Ready, set, change: This practical application exercise has three parts: (a) think of an organizational change you would like to champion at your present or past place of work; (b) draw up an action plan based on the 5P checklist in Figure 16.5; and (c) search the Internet for good ideas about being an effective change agent. (*Note:* An alternative approach in the first step is to "borrow" a change proposal from a manager you know.) To jump-start your Internet search, go to **www.fastcompany.com/backissues**, scroll down to issue number 5 (October-November 1996), and read Nicholas Morgan's short article "9 Tips for Change Agents." Next, scroll up to recent issues of *Fast Company* magazine, and find and read two or three more articles dealing with change.

Learning Points: 1. Is your proposed change realistic? What do others think about it? 2. What sort of "unfreezing" will need to be done? 3. What sort of resistance is likely to be encountered? From whom? 4. How can the resistance to your change be avoided or neutralized? 5. Which powerful people do you need to recruit for your change team? How will you recruit them? 6. What helpful tips and guidelines about being a change agent did you acquire from your Internet search?

2. Building your tool kit for handling conflict: Society suffers and our general quality of life is eroded because of poor conflict management skills. Daily reports in the news media about domestic and workplace violence, road rage, school violence, and international warfare attest to the need for peaceful ways of resolving conflicts. The National Crime Prevention Council has a very useful Web site (**www.ncpc.org**) that offers advice and resources for dealing with conflict. Click on the tab "Topics in Crime Prevention" and then, within the "Browse by Subject" category, select "Violence Prevention." Read "Calling All Hotheads: Tips on Keeping Cool in an Angry World" and other topics of personal interest.

Learning Points: 1. What was the best piece of advice you acquired? 2. What was the most unusual bit of advice you read? 3. What proportion of the material that you read dealt with cooperative, as opposed to competitive, conflict (refer to Figure 16.6)? 4. How would you rate your ability to handle interpersonal conflict between yourself and someone else? Between two other people? 5. What do you need to do to improve your conflict-handling skills?

3. Check it out: In discussing the political implications for managers back in Chapter 3, we introduced the practice of *alternative dispute resolution* (ADR). Two common forms of ADR are arbitration and mediation. In arbitration, a third party gathers information from disputing parties and renders a binding decision, much like an informal court. Mediation, on the other hand, occurs when a third party facilitates a constructive dialogue between conflicting parties, who then create their own settlement. Both approaches can save time and money and avoid further clogging the court system. Being an effective mediator is a key conflict-handling skill for managers. To learn more about mediation, visit the Web site sponsored by Stephen R. Marsh (**www.adrr.com**), a lawyer and mediator from Dallas, Texas. Find "Mediation Essays," click on "Beginning," and read the material under the headings "What Is Mediation?" and "Negotiation in Mediation." Also worth reading, in the "Intermediate" category, are "Ethics and the Role of the Mediator" and "Ten Commandments."

For updates to these exercises, visit our Web site (**http://business.college.hmco.com/students/**) and select Kreitner, *Management,* 10e.

CLOSING CASE

Exit of Reddy

Sunder Motors Private Limited was established in the year 1959 at Ghaziabad by Babulal Sunder with a small investment of Rs 19 lakhs to manufacture tractors. In view of the success of this company, the promotor in the year 1978, diversified the business to the manufacturing and marketing of light commercial vehicles (LCVs), automotive gears, motorcycles aggregates and components. In 1986, the company set up with another plant for manufacturing LCVs at Pune in collaboration with the Yokumi of Japan.

For the first five years, the plant was dependent on the mother plant for designing and development of the product and the training of employees. But now the plant had become self sufficient in every respect. It had also broken up its ties with Yokumi. The company was now expanding in a big way, manufacturing the heavy commercial vehicles (HCVs). This led to an increase in number of workers upto 600.

In 1994, as a step to meet the challenges of liberalization, the family owned business of Babulal Sunder, headed by his son Rajan Sunder at that time appointed Sanjeev Mishra as the Chairman of the company. This was a rare phenomenon that a family owned company was headed by a professional who was not from the family indicating the preference for professionalism over sentiments. Mishra had an extensive experience in different industries and was a person of high repute in the corporate world. He being a professional initiated change in the culture of the organization. Among the many changes, emphasis was given to employee development through HRD mechanisms, such as the performance appraisal system, training and sensitivity to the organizational issues and the consequent corrective measures.

The appraisal system (Individual Development Process - IDP) was conducted in three stages namely, pre IDP dialogue between the coach and the coachee where the superior facilitated the subordinate in identifying his specific interests, his view about his own performance and how and what he wished to do in the future. The second stage was the discussion between IDP group which comprised of the immediate superior, superior's superior and the internal customers of the employee. Here the employee's strengths and weaknesses were assessed, development plans were formed in the form of training, job rotation and job enrichment and the tasks and targets of the individual employee were freezed, keeping in view, the overall organizational objectives. The IDP concluded with the post IDP dialogue wherein the superior let the employee know about the targets and tasks set for him. The organization had also created forums like the monthly departmental meetings to discuss issues, elicit feedback and look for possible solutions through consultative processes. Informal get-togethers and departmental picnics with families were organized besides a face to face dialogue with Ravi Kumar, Managing Director, wherein a group of randomly selected employees met him irrespective of their hierarchical level. Satisfaction surveys were occasionally conducted. The company also introduced the concept of movement boards on which the employees of every department mentioned their movement plans for a particular week, specifically the destination, the time of leaving, the person to be contacted with, his phone number and his purpose of the visit.

In one of the forums, keeping in view the tough competition, the need of launching HCV was felt. The idea emerged from a two day real time visioning exercise of 350 people drawn from different cross sections of the organization, to discuss the future of Sunder Motors. To put this plan into action, Rs 125 crores was spent on the upgradation of the plant. For HCV, the launch of an engine was crucial and to do so, tooling had to be done. The plant had a unique engine design development and testing centre but for the manufacturing of jigs and fixtures of this specific kind, it had to depend on different ancillary units within the plant.

Ramesh Reddy, the senior engineer who was incharge of the engines was given the responsibility of developing the jigs and fixtures. Reddy had been with the organization for seven years now and had the reputation of knowing his job well. He was reporting to the senior manager and had been promoted to this position a year before from the junior engineer's post inspite of the resistance from his colleagues on the pretext that he lacked interpersonal skills.

Keeping in view, the urgent need to launch HCV, Reddy and his team were communicated the deadlines for completion of the jigs and fixtures. Suddenly everybody in the department started feeling the brunt of excessive work as they were required to stretch out time on working days as well as Sundays. Reddy's team members at times felt handicapped in the absence of appropriate data handling devices like the computers and were unable to provide the necessary designing information required by Reddy. As a result, he started feeling that things were not happening as planned. In the quest to meet deadlines, Reddy started doing everything by himself. Inspite of his best efforts, he could not deliver the results on time. After three months, the top management realized that Reddy's inability had led to a huge wastage and loss, and the opportunity to launch HCV was delayed by three months.

Thinking that he was being blamed for none of his fault, Reddy decided to quit. Realizing that the company would lose a dedicated and competent employee, he was counselled to stay back but it was all in vain. In his exit interview, he highlighted the following points

(a) Inadequate infrastructure
(b) Unplanned expansion
(c) Unrealistic targets
(d) Non-cooperation from the immediate superiors and subordinates of his department and the colleagues from other departments

While Reddy's issue was being discussed with Ravi Kumar, the results of satisfaction survey were put before him which showed that the company lacked the technological and the functional focus and focused on the behavioural issues only.

For Discussion

1. Who do you think should be blamed for the heavy loss, Reddy, his superior or the top management?
2. Do you think Reddy's self criticism was reasonable? Discuss.
3. Do you think that the periodic review would have prevented this loss. What should be the stand of the top management?
4. How far does the unplanned change lead to the employee stress?

**Source: Case Method in Management Education, Upinder Dhar & Santosh Dhar, Excel Books, New Delhi, 2002, pp.287-289*

TEST PREPPER

True/False Questions

_____ **1.** Because the organization is significantly redirected, Nadler and Tushman call adaptation "frame bending."

_____ **2.** Poor timing and lack of trust are among the reasons why employees resist change.

_____ **3.** Managers can tell when resistance to change is caused by a passive-aggressive culture because everyone is unpleasant and disagreeable.

_____ **4.** Organization development (OD) involves planned change.

_____ **5.** Top-level managers are the only ones who should use the 5P checklist for change agents.

_____ **6.** A practical guideline for tempered radicals is "think big for small results."

_____ **7.** Mistrust and disbelief are involved in the cycle of competitive conflict.

_____ **8.** The superordinate goals technique involves identifying the causes of problems.

_____ **9.** Negotiation, by definition, is a decision-making process.

_____ **10.** Added value negotiating (AVN) is useful because it forces the parties into single-outcome negotiating.

Multiple-Choice Questions

1. What type of changes are planned and based on expected situations?
A. Exponential B. Incremental
C. Anticipatory D. Strategic
E. Reactive

2. _____ is the low point of the response to change when employees are responding to changes they like.
A. Self-doubt B. Laughing it off
C. Dissatisfaction D. Reality shock
E. Attitude adjustment

3. _____ is typically an employee's first response when coping with a change that he or she dislikes or fears.
A. Low self-esteem
B. Unrealistic optimism
C. Laughing it off
D. Getting off on the wrong track
E. Self-doubt

4. _____ is *not* a strategy for overcoming resistance to change, as described in the text.
A. Facilitation and support
B. Manipulation and co-optation
C. Participation and involvement
D. Education and communication
E. Divide and conquer

5. Which of the following is a good description of organization development (OD)?
A. Frame bending B. Employee renewal
C. Expectation shaping D. Planned change
E. Organizational modification

6. During what phase of OD does diagnosis occur?
A. Preparation B. Planning
C. Research D. Search
E. Unfreezing

7. Relative to the 5P checklist for change agents, measurable objectives, milestones, and deadlines are specified in which P?
A. Purpose B. Persistence
C. Participation D. Programming
E. Preparation

8. Personality clashes, communication breakdowns, and time pressure are
A. superordinate goals.
B. OD trouble spots.
C. OD failure factors.
D. examples of constructive conflict.
E. conflict triggers.

9. The attitude that effective negotiators need is *best* described as
A. compromising. B. win-win.
C. self-confident. D. single-minded.
E. carefree.

10. According to the added value negotiating (AVN) model, what should the last step in the process do?
A. Strengthen relationships for future negotiations.
B. Pinpoint the single best outcome.
C. Involve an exchange of BATNAs.
D. Involve selecting at least three possible alternatives.
E. Comfort the losing party.

ACE self-test

Want more questions? Visit the student Web site at http://business.college.hmco.com/students/ (select Kreitner, *Management,* 10e) and take the ACE quizzes for more practice.

Managers-in-Action Videos

4A Alternative Work Arrangement at Hewlett-Packard

Three managers introduce us to the nature and benefits of flexible work scheduling and nontraditional work arrangements at HP. Sid Reel is vice president of diversity and work life. Kristy Ward is a marketing manager who formerly was in a job-sharing arrangement. Karen Lee is a real estate and workspace services delivery manager. By accommodating its employees' diverse and complex lives, HP hopes to reap motivational benefits. Among the alternative work arrangements illustrated are flextime, job sharing, telecommuting, and "free-address" offices.

Learning Objective: To demonstrate the rich array (and motivational impacts) of alternatives to the traditional 9-to-5 workday in a single location.

Links to Textual Material: **Chapter 3 and 11:** Managing diversity **Chapter 10:** Virtual organizations
Chapter 13: Motivation; Quality-of-work-life programs

Discussion Questions:

1. What is the practical business linkage between the concepts of managing diversity and alternative work arrangements?
2. Briefly, what are the pros and cons of flextime, job sharing, and free-address offices?
3. What is the connection between virtual organizations and alternative work arrangements?
4. What is the motivational case for alternative work arrangements?
5. Which alternative work arrangement appeals most to you? Why?

4B Entrepreneurial Leadership

This inspiring 11-minute video introduces Jayson Goltz, president of Artist's Frame Service, based in Chicago, Illinois, and documents how an entrepreneur's leadership style must grow with the business. For more background, see **www.artistsframeservice.com.**

Learning Objective: To demonstrate how modern leaders must constantly learn and adapt to meet new challenges. To illustrate why successful inspirational leaders are not cookie-cutter imitations, but unique individuals who dare to be different.

Links to Textual Material: **Chapter 1:** Entrepreneurship **Chapter 12:** Communication **Chapter 13:** Motivating
Chapter 15: Influence tactics; Power; Leadership **Chapter 16:** Managing change
Chapter 17: Product/service quality

Discussion Questions:

1. How well does Jayson Goltz fit the entrepreneur trait profile in Table 1.3? Explain.
2. What influence tactics, as discussed in Chapter 15, are evident in this case?
3. In terms of House's updated path-goal leadership model in Chapter 15, which categories of leader behavior does Goltz seem to rely on the most?
4. Would you label Goltz a transactional or a transformational leader (see Table 15.4)? Explain.
5. Is Goltz a good leader? Explain. Would you like to work for him? Why or why not?

PART FIVE

Organizational Control Processes

17 Organizational Control and Quality Improvement

> *"Our business is so dynamic, you have to get everyone to think, to be strategic, to create, to innovate, and to always think about what our customers and suppliers are looking for from us."*[1]
>
> CHERYL ROSNER, PRESIDENT, HOTELS.COM

OBJECTIVES

- **Identify** three types of control and the components common to all control systems.
- **Discuss** organizational control from a strategic perspective.
- **Identify** the four key elements of a crisis management program.
- **Identify** five types of product quality.
- **Explain** how providing a service differs from manufacturing a product, and **identify** the five service-quality dimensions.
- **Define** *total quality management (TQM)*, and **specify** the four basic TQM principles.
- **Describe** at least three of the seven TQM process improvement tools.
- **Explain** how Deming's PDCA cycle can improve the overall management process.
- **Specify** and **discuss** at least four of Deming's famous 14 points.

the changing workplace

Ronald Gets Back in Shape

McDonald's built its business selling burgers and fries and more burgers and fries. While there were occasional nods to changing tastes—the Filet-O-Fish and Chicken McNuggets among them—for most of its five decades, McDonald's stuck to its "one-menu-fits-all" business model and feasted on the profits.

By 2001, though, McDonald's had gone flabby. Bad service and boring food were driving customers to Burger King, Subway, and Wendy's. Making matters worse, the best-selling book *Fast Food Nation* cast Ronald McDonald as the leading culprit behind America's obesity epidemic. Comparable-store sales dipped 1.3 percent in 2001 and 2.1 percent in 2002. In January 2003, the company's CEO announced its first quarterly loss since 1955. "The world has changed," Jim Cantalupo declared. "Our customers have changed, and we have to change too."

Cantalupo laid out what became known as the Plan to Win—an effort to woo back the chain's core customers: moms, 20-somethings, and kids. Analysts were skeptical; the plan required close cooperation from thousands of franchisees, as well as a nimbleness rarely found at $38 billion firms. . . . [In 2004], however, despite Cantalupo's unexpected death and the illness that forced his chosen successor, Charlie Bell, to hand the reins to current CEO Jim Skinner, it became clear that the Plan to Win is a winner. By any measure—same-store sales, customer satisfaction, profits, share price—McDonald's has successfully reinvented its fast-food recipe.

As at many corporations raised on a diet of rapid expansion, top managers at McDonald's had been reluctant to acknowledge that it was no longer a growth company. "We became too focused on building the next restaurant and missed some important customer trends," CFO [chief financial officer] Matt Paull says. "The brand was losing relevance because we were way too internally focused." So McDonald's slammed on the brakes, opening just 450 outlets worldwide last year, 80 percent fewer than in 2000. And it turned to a new obsession: boosting sales at existing restaurants.

At the core of the Plan to Win are menu changes designed to lure health-conscious customers. New items include salads, all-white-meat chicken strips, and apple slices for dessert. The salads haven't been huge sellers, but they've effectively broadened McDonald's appeal. One independent analyst found that some moms who in pre-salad days wouldn't have set foot inside a Mickey D's now order half the greens McDonald's sells while their kids scarf cheeseburgers.

Even better, the new menu additions are pricey—about $4 for a salad or the five-strip Chicken Selects. McDonald's continues to promote its Dollar Menu fare, but the new items have helped boost the average customer check in the United States by as much as 6 percent in the last 20 months. "Driving traffic with the Dollar Menu and profits with premium items has paid off handsomely," says Mark Kalinowski of Citigroup Smith Barney.

Service is improving too. Some 8,000 stores now take credit cards, and most outlets have added employees, so drive-through and counter wait times have declined by 8.5 and 12.4 percent, respectively, since 2001. Many restaurants have added lounges and replaced the nursery-school decor with blond wood. Finally, the hugely successful "I'm Lovin' It" advertising campaign, featuring Destiny's Child, Justin Timberlake, and Yao Ming, has helped reposition McDonald's as an energetic lifestyle brand.

The results have been impressive. Same-store sales for 2004 are up 10 percent in the United States and 7 percent worldwide. In the first half of 2004, the complaint rate on McDonald's toll-free customer-contact line dropped 11 percent, while compliments rose 18 percent. Wall Street is also happier, as earnings per share have doubled, and McDonald's stock is up a mind-blowing 167 percent since early 2003.

It'll be a challenge to keep up the pace. But for now, McDonald's has put the magic back in its secret sauce.

Source: *From Michael V. Copeland, "Ronald Gets Back in Shape,"* Business 2.0, *6 (January-February 2005): 46–47. © 2005 Time Inc. All rights reserved. Also see Jerry Shriver, "Twinkies at 75, McDonald's at 50,"* USA Today *(April 15, 2005): 1D.*

Recent events at McDonald's teach us an important management lesson. Strategies and plans, no matter how well conceived, are no guarantee of organizational success. Those strategies and plans need to be updated and carried out by skilled and motivated employees amid changing circumstances and an occasional crisis. Adjustments and corrective action are inevitable. This final chapter helps present and future managers put this lesson to work by introducing fundamentals of organizational control, discussing crisis management, and exploring product and service quality.

Fundamentals of Organizational Control

control: *taking preventive or corrective actions to keep things on track*

The word *control* suggests the operations of checking, testing, regulation, verification, or adjustment. As a management function, **control** is the process of taking the necessary preventive or corrective actions to ensure that the organization's mission and objectives are accomplished as effectively and efficiently as possible. Objectives are yardsticks against which actual performance can be measured. If actual performance is consistent with the appropriate objective, things will proceed as planned. If not, changes must be made. Successful managers detect (and even anticipate) deviations from desirable standards and make appropriate adjustments.[2] Those adjustments can range from ordering more raw materials to overhauling a production line; from discarding an unnecessary procedure to hiring additional personnel; from containing an unexpected crisis to firing a defrauder. Although the possible adjustments exercised as part of the control function are countless, the purpose of the control function is always the same: *Get the job done despite environmental, organizational, and behavioral obstacles and uncertainties.* Here is how Michael Dell, founder of the computer powerhouse bearing his name, explains his company's secret to steady growth:

> *We all make mistakes. It's not as though at any given time, Dell doesn't have some part of the business that's not working for us as it should. But we have a culture of continuous improvement. We train employees to constantly ask themselves: "How do we grow faster? How do we lower our cost structure? How do we improve service for customers?"*[3]

Types of Control

1. IDENTIFY three types of control and the components common to all control systems.

Every open system processes inputs from the surrounding environment to produce a unique set of outputs. Natural open systems, such as the human body, are kept in life-sustaining balance through automatic feedback mechanisms. In contrast, artificial open systems, such as organizations, do not have automatic controls. Instead, they require constant monitoring and adjustment to control for deviations from standards. Figure 17.1 illustrates the control function. Notice the three different types of control: feedforward, concurrent, and feedback.

If ever there was a need for feedforward control, this is it! Malden Mills' giant circular knitting machine in Lawrence, Massachusetts, produces tubes of polyester fabric used to make Polartec garments for rugged outdoor wear. Feedforward control, the anticipation and prevention of problems, is required to make sure the automatic equipment is maintained and loaded properly. If not, costly batches of scrap material would pile up quickly.

Figure 17.1 Three Types of Control

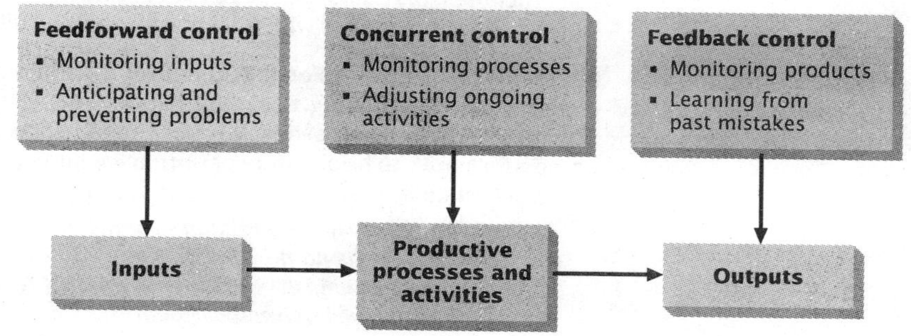

feedforward control: *active anticipation and prevention of problems, rather than passive reaction*

■ **Feedforward Control.** According to two early proponents of feedforward control, "the only way [managers] can exercise control effectively is to see the problems coming in time to do something about them."[4] **Feedforward control** is the active anticipation of problems and their timely prevention, rather than after-the-fact reaction. Carpenters have their own instructive version of feedforward control: "Measure twice, cut once." It is important to note that planning and feedforward control are two related but different processes. Planning answers the question "Where are we going and how will we get there?" Feedforward control addresses the issue "What can we do ahead of time to help our plan succeed?" For many industries—including agriculture, insurance, and transportation—feedforward control involves keeping a close eye on the weather:

> *As typhoon Nanmadol spun across the South pacific . . . [in late 2004], few people monitored it as closely as FedEx's meteorologists in Memphis. The company runs its Asian flights out of a single-runway airport nestled on a narrow strip between a mountainside and the Philippines' Subic Bay. When a bad storm rolls through, it can shut the place down. On December 1, just 24 hours before the storm hit, managing director of global operations John Dunavant set his contingency plan in motion: Fourteen wide-body MD-11 airplanes and roughly 50 employees scrambled to Taipei [Taiwan], where FedEx could operate its hub without delays until the weather cleared. "Most of the time weather is forecasted," Dunavant says, calling weather the single greatest challenge in operating his 663 airplanes. "Since it is, we should always be able to proactively implement a solution."*[5]

Product design, preventive maintenance on machinery and equipment, and *due diligence* also qualify as feedforward control. On a personal level, think of due diligence as refusing to go on a blind date without first researching the person's background and reputation.[6]

Of the three types of control, American managers tend to do the poorest job with feedforward control. Longer-term thinking and better cross-functional communication could help this situation.

concurrent control: *monitoring and adjusting ongoing activities and processes*

■ **Concurrent Control.** This second type of controi might well be called real-time control because it deals with the present rather than with the future or past. **Concurrent control** involves monitoring and adjusting ongoing activities and processes to ensure compliance with standards.[7] When you are using an old bread toaster, for instance, you can set the automatic control mechanism and run the risk of ending up with a piece of charcoal. Because old-fashioned toaster control mechanisms often malfunction, they are not a very reliable form of feedforward control. To compensate, you can exercise concurrent control by keeping an eye on the toasting process and ejecting your toast by hand when it reaches just the right shade. So, too, construction supervisors engage in concurrent control when they help electricians, carpenters, and plumbers with difficult tasks at the building site.

feedback control: *checking a completed activity and learning from mistakes*

■ **Feedback Control.** **Feedback control** is gathering information about a completed activity, evaluating that information, and taking steps to improve similar activities in the future. Feedback control permits managers to use information on past performance to bring future performance into line with planned objectives and acceptable standards. For example, consider the famous Aflac duck:

> *After spending nearly $200 million over the last four years on ads featuring a duck that quacks its name, Aflac has gained plenty of name recognition. Too bad name recognition isn't the same as product recognition: 60 percent of the people Aflac surveyed in a recent poll weren't sure what the company actually does (it sells insurance that pays the bills when an accident keeps you off the job). The fix? A new $50 million campaign that subtly lays blame at the feet of its mascot.*[8]

Critics of feedback control say it is like closing the gate after the horse (or duck?) is gone. Because corrective action is taken after the fact, costs tend to pile up quickly, and problems and deviations persist.

On the positive side, feedback control tests the quality and validity of objectives and standards. Objectives found to be impossible to attain should be made more reasonable. Those that prove too easy need to be toughened.

In summary, successful managers exercise all three types of control in today's complex organizations.[9] Feedforward control helps managers avoid mistakes in the first place; concurrent control enables them to catch mistakes as they are being made; feedback control keeps them from repeating past mistakes. Interaction and a workable balance among the three types of control are desirable.

17a Quick Quiz

Based on the Neon compact car, the PT Cruiser was a big hit in the 2000 and 2001 model years; demand quickly exceeded the capacity of the Mexican plant where it was built. But DaimlerChrysler was unable to shift overflow production to its Neon plant in Belvidere, Ill., which had capacity to spare. Why? Planners had neglected to make the Belvidere paint shop tall enough for the PT Cruiser, which is a few inches higher than the neon. The oversight meant the company flushed away $480 million in forgone pretax profits, estimates [an industry analyst].

Source: Stuart F. Brown, "Toyota's Global Body Shop," Fortune *(February 9, 2004): 120[F].*

QUESTION:

What sort of control—feedforward, concurrent, or feedback—was needed here? Explain.

For further information about the interactive annotations in this chapter, visit our Web site (**http://business.college.hmco.com/students/**) and select Kreitner, *Management,* 10e

■ Components of Organizational Control Systems

The owner-manager of a small business such as a dry-cleaning establishment can keep things under control by personally overseeing operations and making necessary adjustments. An electrician can be called in to fix a broken pressing machine, poor workmanship can be improved through coaching, a customer's complaint can be handled immediately, or a shortage of change in the cash register can be remedied. A small organization directed by a single, highly motivated individual with expert knowledge of all aspects of the operation represents the ideal control situation.[10] Unfortunately, the size and complexity of most productive organizations have made firsthand control by a single person obsolete. Consequently, multilevel, multidimensional organizational control systems have evolved.

A study of nine large companies in different industries sheds some light on the mechanics of complex organizational control systems.[11] After interviewing dozens of key managers, the researchers identified six distinct control subsystems (we have added a seventh):

1. ***Strategic plans.*** Qualitative analyses of the company's position within the industry
2. ***Long-range plans.*** Typically, five-year financial projections
3. ***Annual operating budgets.*** Annual estimates of profit, expenses, and financial indicators
4. ***Statistical reports.*** Quarterly, monthly, or weekly nonfinancial statistical summaries of key indicators such as orders received and personnel surpluses or shortages
5. ***Performance appraisals.*** Evaluation of employees through the use of management by objectives (MBO) or rating scales
6. ***Policies and procedures.*** Organizational and departmental standard operating procedures referred to on an as-needed basis
7. ***The organization's culture.*** As discussed in Chapter 9, stories, rituals, and company legends have a profound impact on how things are done in specific organizations.[12] Take Toyota, for example:

   > *An old Toyota proverb goes something like this: To make a better product, get off your rear end and experience the marketplace. Charged with revamping the Sienna minivan for 2004, Toyota chief engineer Yuji Yokoya did just that. To improve on the previous Sienna—small and underpowered—Yokoya embarked on a 53,000–mile North American minivan road trip that included five cross-continent treks. . . . [When asked why, he simply said], "The road will tell us."*
   >
   > *. . . Yokoya had many epiphanies. In Santa Fe, N.M., narrow downtown streets convinced him that the new Sienna should have a tighter turning radius. On the gravel of the Alaskan Highway, he understood the need for all-wheel drive.*[13]

   In more typical circumstances, employees who deviate from cultural norms are promptly straightened out with glances, remarks, or ridicule.

Complex organizational control systems such as these help keep things on the right track because they embrace three basic components that are common to all organizational control systems: objectives, standards, and an evaluation-reward system.[14]

■ **Objectives.** In Chapter 6, we defined an *objective* as a target signifying what should be accomplished and when. Objectives are an indispensable part of any control system because they provide measurable reference points for corrective action. Yearly progress reports let managers know if they are on target or if corrective actions, such as creating a new advertising campaign, are necessary.

■ **Standards.** Whereas objectives serve as measurable targets, standards serve as guideposts on the way to reaching those targets. Standards provide feedforward control by warning people when they are off the track.[15] Golfers use par as a standard for gauging the quality of their game. When the objective is to shoot par, a golfer who exceeds par on a hole is warned that he or she must improve on later holes to achieve the objective. Universities exercise a degree of feedforward control over student performance by establishing and following admission standards for grades and test scores. Businesses rely on many different kinds of standards, including those in purchasing, engineering, time, safety, accounting, and quality.

benchmarking: *identifying, studying, and building upon the best practices of organizational role models*

A proven technique for establishing challenging standards is **benchmarking**—that is, identifying, studying, and imitating the *best practices* of market leaders.[16] The central idea in benchmarking is to be competitive by striving to be as good as or better than the *best* in the business. The search for benchmarks is not restricted to one's own industry. Consider, for example, United Airlines' benchmarking efforts in Marina Del Rey, California:

In a bid to boost the quality of its overseas service, United Airlines is bringing some of its attendants to the best hotels, such as the Ritz-Carlton here, to learn the fine points of catering to the needs of the well-heeled.

"They are very much recognized name-wise for a higher level of service," explains United trainer Christine Swanstrom. "The clientele we're trying to attract in international is the clientele that would stay at a Ritz."[17]

■ **An Evaluation-Reward System.** Because employees do not all achieve equal results, some sort of performance review is required to document individual and/or team contributions to organizational objectives. Extrinsic rewards need to be tied equitably to documented results[18] and improvement. A carefully conceived and clearly communicated evaluation-reward scheme can shape favorable effort-reward expectancies, thus motivating better performance. This is how CEO Paul R. Charron got Liz Claiborne Inc., the large apparel company, back on track:

. . . Charron changed the measure of performance and the trigger for bonuses to one common metric. The yardstick—direct operating profit—is reinforced through quarterly performance reviews and is now imprinted on the Claiborne culture.[19]

When integrated systematically, objectives, standards, and an equitable evaluation-reward system constitute an invaluable control mechanism.

2. DISCUSS organizational control from a strategic perspective.

■ Strategic Control

Managers who fail to complement their strategic planning with strategic control, as recommended in Chapter 7, will find themselves winning some battles but losing the war.[20] The performance pyramid in Figure 17.2 illustrates the necessarily tight linkage between planning and control. It is a strategic model because everything is oriented toward the strategic peak of the pyramid. Objectives based on the corporate vision (or mission) are translated downward during planning. As plans become real-

Figure 17.2 The Performance Pyramid for Strategic Control

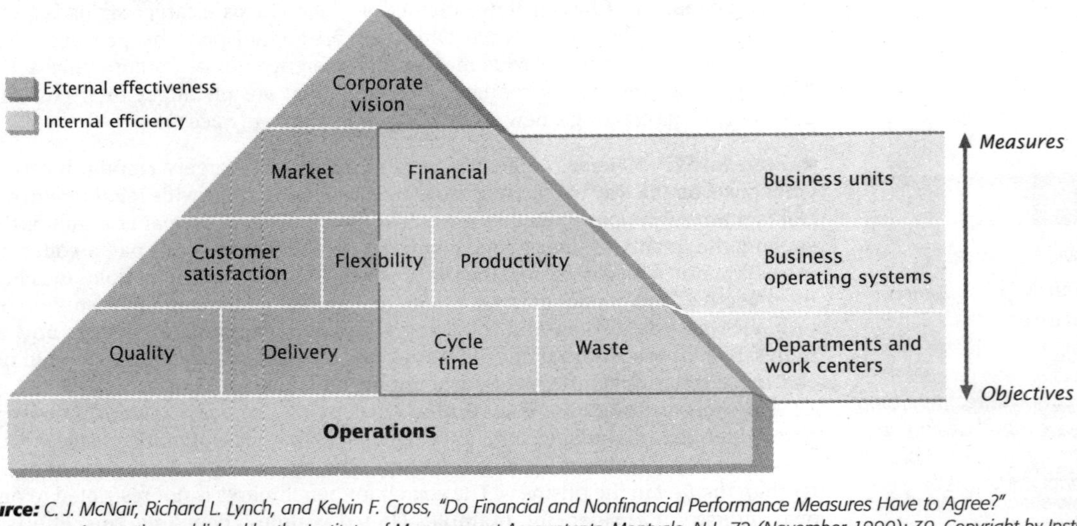

***Source:** C. J. McNair, Richard L. Lynch, and Kelvin F. Cross, "Do Financial and Nonfinancial Performance Measures Have to Agree?"* Management Accounting *published by the Institute of Management Accountants, Montvale, N.J., 72 (November 1990): 30. Copyright by Institute of Management Accountants. Reprinted by permission.*

ity, control measures of activities and results are translated up the pyramid. The flow of objectives and measures requires a good information system.

Criteria related to external effectiveness and those related to internal efficiency are distinguished in Figure 17.2 by color coding. Significantly, all of the external effectiveness areas are focused on the marketplace in general and on the *customer* in particular. According to the performance pyramid, control measures are needed for cycle time, waste, flexibility, productivity, and financial results. *Cycle time* is the time it takes for a product to be transformed from raw materials or parts into a finished good. Note that *flexibility* is related to both effectiveness and efficiency. A garden tractor manufacturer, for example, needs to be externally flexible in adapting to changing customer demands and internally flexible in training employees to handle new technology.

17b Back to the Opening Case

Using Figure 17.2 as a guide, indicate what elements of strategic control are evident in the McDonald's case.

Identifying Control Problems

Control problems have a way of quietly snowballing to overwhelming proportions. Progressive managers can take constructive steps to keep today's complex operations under control.[21] Two very different approaches are executive reality checks and internal auditing.

executive reality check: *top managers periodically working at lower-level jobs to become more aware of operations*

Executive Reality Check. The **executive reality check** occurs when top-level managers periodically work "in the trenches" to increase their awareness of operations. Ingvar Kamprad, the 78-year-old Swedish founder of the Ikea chain of 200 home furnishing superstores worldwide, is an inspiring role model in this regard:

> *On this cold, gray December morning [in Paramus, N.J.], Kamprad begins a store tour here at 6 A.M. Dressed casually in trousers, a sweater and his barnyard-style jacket, he points out the good, bad and ugly of displays, merchandise and selling techniques along the way.*
>
> *When he's pleased, he gets excited and yells in his still-strong Swedish accent, "Congratulations!" He especially likes the display to promote the Stranda line for $875 and the $9.99 Bekväm wooden step stool.*
>
> *When he doesn't like something, he explains with tact and energy how to do it better. . . .*
>
> *He walks the length of a 350,000-square-feet store and critiques each of 50 room settings.*
>
> *By year's end, Kamprad will have walked through 20 stores with managers, associates and company executives who laugh, listen and take notes on his advice throughout the 12-hour tours.*[22]

Executive reality checks not only alert top managers to control problems but also foster empathy for lower-level employees' problems and concerns.[23] In addition to first-hand reality checks, an internal audit can identify weak spots and problems in the organizational control system.

17c A CEO Who Takes Out the Garbage?

David Neeleman, CEO, JetBlue Airways:

This week, I'm flying to Florida for work, and on the way down and back I'll serve drinks and snacks along with the crew and take out the garbage when we're done. It's a chance to serve the customer directly.

Source: As quoted in Daisy Wademan, "Lessons from the Slums of Brazil," Harvard Business Review, *83 (March 2005): 24.*

QUESTION:
How should Neeleman explain to a group of stockholders that he isn't wasting his valuable executive time?

Internal Audits. There are two general types of auditing, external and internal. External auditing, generally performed by certified public accountants (CPAs), is the verification of an organization's financial records and reports. In the United States, the protection of stockholders' interests is the primary rationale for objective external audits. Of course, the Internal Revenue Service (IRS) and the Securities and Exchange Commission (SEC) also have a stake in external auditors' watchdog function. Ideally, external auditors help keep organizations honest by double-checking to see whether reported financial results are derived through generally accepted accounting principles and are based on material fact, not fiction.[24] Thanks to the Enron/Arthur Andersen scandal (among several others), external auditing has been put under the microscope, and needed financial reforms such as the Sarbanes-Oxley Act of 2002 are now in place. Managers who "cook the books" run a greater risk than ever of paying stiff fines and doing jail time.[25] One of Sarbanes-Oxley's most notable requirements forces chief executive officers and chief financial officers to personally sign and certify their company's periodic financial statements and reports.

> *The penalties for non-compliance are staggering. For example, a CEO or CFO who falsely represents company finances may be fined up to $1 million and/or imprisoned for up to 10 years. The penalty for willful violations is up to $5 million and/or 20 years imprisonment.*[26]

On the positive side, auditing is a hot job category these days.[27]

Internal auditing differs from external auditing in a number of ways. First, and most obviously, it is performed by an organization's staff rather than by outsiders. General Electric, for example, employs 500 internal auditors.[28] Second, internal auditing is intended to serve the interests of the organization as a whole. Also, as the following definition illustrates, internal auditing tends to be more encompassing than the external variety: " **Internal auditing** is the independent appraisal of the various operations and systems control within an organization to determine whether acceptable policies and procedures are followed, established standards are met, resources are used efficiently and economically, planned missions are accomplished effectively, and the organization's objectives are being achieved."[29]

internal auditing: *independent appraisal of organizational operations and systems to assess their effectiveness and efficiency*

The product of internal auditing is called a *process audit* by some and a *management audit* by others. Internal audits certainly are necessary, as discovered by a 2004 survey of 203 auditors: 92 percent "identified various gaps in their companies' accounting controls."[30] To strengthen the objectivity of internal auditing, experts recommend that internal auditors report directly to the top person in the organization. In organization development terms, some "unfreezing" needs to be done to quiet the common complaint that internal auditing is a ploy used by top management for snooping and meddling. Timely and valid internal audits are a primary safeguard against organizational decline, as discussed in Chapter 9, as well as against theft and fraud.[31]

■ **Symptoms of Inadequate Control.** When a comprehensive internal audit is not available, a general checklist of symptoms of inadequate control can be a useful diagnostic tool. Although every situation has some unusual problems, certain symptoms are common:

- An unexplained decline in revenues or profits
- A degradation of service (customer complaints)
- Employee dissatisfaction (complaints, grievances, turnover)
- Cash shortages caused by bloated inventories or delinquent accounts receivable
- Idle facilities or personnel

Source: *DILBERT © Scott Adams/Distributed by United Feature Syndicate, Inc.*

- Disorganized operations (workflow bottlenecks, excessive paperwork)
- Excessive costs
- Evidence of waste and inefficiency (scrap, rework)[32]

Problems in one or more of these areas may be a signal that things are getting out of control.

Crisis Management

The September 11, 2001, terrorist attacks on America were a symbolic wake-up call for any managers who had a lax attitude toward organizational crisis management programs.[33] And companies that were already prepared stepped up their preparedness. FedEx, for example, now has "a dedicated security force that is more than 500 employees strong."[34] Beyond terrorism, managers need to be vigilant for a vast array of trouble spots. Here are some examples of crisis-generating events for businesses in recent years:

- The U.S. West Coast port shutdown in 2002 (see The Global Manager)
- McDonald's loss of two CEOs in 2004 (see the chapter-opening case)[35]
- Four hurricanes in 2004 costing Florida grapefruit growers 63 percent of their crop[36]
- Merck's 2004 recall of "Vioxx, its $2.5-billion-a-year arthritis medicine, because the drug has been shown to double the risk of heart attacks and strokes in long-term users."[37]

In short, business-as-usual inevitably involves the occasional crisis that demands skillful crisis management and disaster recovery.[38]

Today, the diversity and scope of organizational crises stretch the imagination. Experts on the subject define an *organizational crisis* this way:

> *An organizational crisis is a low-probability, high-impact event that threatens the viability of the organization and is characterized by ambiguity of cause, effect, and means of resolution, as well as by belief that decisions must be made swiftly.*[39]

crisis management: *anticipating and preparing for events that could damage the organization*

Clearly, managers need to "manage the unthinkable" in a foresighted, systematic, and timely manner.[40] Enter the emerging discipline known as *crisis management.*

Geologically speaking, Japan is a violent country. Devastating earthquakes and tsunamis are constant threats. These highly trained and well-equipped Tokyo firefighters are seen here participating in a drill conducted by the Fire and Disaster Management Agency. Thinking about and preparing for the unthinkable is what crisis management is all about.

■ Crisis Management Defined

Traditionally, crisis management was viewed negatively, as "managerial firefighting"—waiting for things to go wrong and then scurrying to limit the damage. More recently, the term has taken on a more precise and proactive meaning. In fact, a body of theory and practice is evolving around the idea that managers should think about the unthinkable and expect the unexpected.[41] **Crisis management** is the systematic anticipation of and preparation for internal and external problems that could seriously threaten an organization's reputation, profitability, or survival. Crisis management involves much more than an expedient public relations ploy or so-called spin control to make the organization look good amid bad circumstances. This new discipline is intertwined with strategic control.

THE GLOBAL MANAGER

How Dell Survived a Global Supply Chain Crisis

Two years ago, a 10-day labor lockout idled 10,000 union dockworkers, shut down 29 West Coast ports extending from Los Angeles to Seattle, and blocked hundreds of cargo ships from unloading the raw materials and finished goods that fuel U.S. commerce. The port closings paralyzed global supply chains, bloodied retailers and manufacturers, and ultimately cost U.S. consumers and businesses billions. Analysts expected that Dell, with its just-in-time manufacturing model, would be especially hard hit when parts failed to reach its two U.S.-based factories. Without warehouses filled with motherboards and hard drives, they figured, the world's largest PC maker would simply find itself with nothing to sell within a matter of days. And Dell knew all too well that its ultralean, high-speed business model left it vulnerable to just such an intolerable prospect. "When a labor problem or an earthquake or a SARS epidemic breaks out, we've got to react quicker than anyone else," says Dick Hunter, the company's supply-chain czar for the Americas. "There's no other choice. We know these things are going to happen; we must move fast to fix them. We just can't tolerate any kind of delay."

Fortunately, the same ethos of speed and flexibility that seems to put Dell at the mercy of disruptions also helps it deal with them. Dell was in constant, round-the-clock communication with its parts makers in Taiwan, China, and Malaysia, and its U.S.-based shipping partners, who alerted it to the possibility of a lockout some six months before it occurred. Hunter dispatched a "tiger team" of 10 logistics specialists to Long Beach, California, and other ports; they worked hand in hand with Dell's carrying and freight-forwarding networks to assemble a contingency plan.

When the tiger team confirmed that the closings were all but certain, Dell moved into high gear. It chartered 18 747s from UPS, Northwest Airlines, China Airlines, and other carriers. A 747 holds the equivalent of 10 tractor-trailers—enough parts to manufacture 10,000 PCs. The bidding for the planes grew fierce, running as high as $1.1 million for a one-way flight from Asia to the West Coast. But because Dell got in early, it kept its costs to about $500,000 per plane. Moreover, Dell worked with its Asia-based suppliers to ensure that its parts were always at the Shanghai and Taipei airports in time for its returning charters to land, reload, refuel, and take off. The company was consistently able to get its planes to the United States and back within 33 hours, which kept its costs down and its supply chain moving.

Meanwhile, Dell had people on the ground in every major harbor. In Asia, these freight specialists saw to it that Dell's parts were the last to be loaded onto each cargo ship so they'd be unloaded first when the ship hit the West Coast. The biggest test came when the ports reopened and companies scrambled to sort through the mess of thousands of backed-up containers. Hunter's tiger team had anticipated this logistical nightmare. Even though Dell had PC components in hundreds of containers on 50 ships, it knew the exact moment when each would be cycled through the harbor, and it was among the first to unload its parts and speed them to its factories in Austin and Nashville. In the end, Dell did the impossible: It survived a 10-day supply-chain blackout with roughly 72 hours of inventory, and it never delayed a customer order.

Source: From Bill Breen, "Living in Dell Time," Fast Company, *no. 88 (November 2004): 86–88. Reprinted by permission of* Fast Company.

17d Back to the Opening Case

Did anything that occurred in the McDonald's case qualify as a crisis? Explain the implications.

3. IDENTIFY the four key elements of a crisis management program.

■ Developing a Crisis Management Program

As illustrated in Figure 17.3, a crisis management program is made up of four elements. Disasters need to be anticipated, contingency plans need to be formulated, and crisis management teams need to be staffed and trained. Finally, the program needs to be perfected through realistic practice. Let us examine each of these elements.

■ Conducting a Crisis Audit. A crisis audit is a systematic way of seeking out trouble spots and vulnerabilities. Disaster scenarios become the topic of discussion as managers ask a series of "What if?" questions. Lists such as the one in Table 17.1 can be useful during this stage. Some crises, such as the untimely death of a key executive, are universal and hence readily identified. Others are industry-specific. For example, crashes are an all-too-real disaster scenario for passenger airline companies.[42]

Figure 17.3 Key Elements in a Crisis Management Program

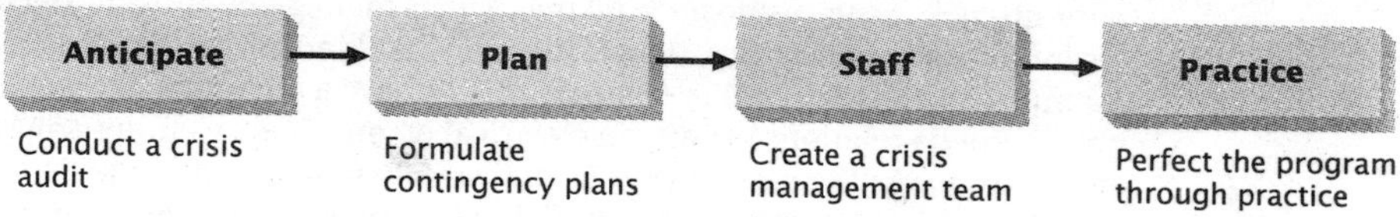

contingency plan: *a backup plan for emergencies*

■ **Formulating Contingency Plans.** A **contingency plan** is a backup plan that can be put into effect when things go wrong.[43] Whenever possible, each contingency plan should specify early warning signals, actions to be taken, and expected consequences of those actions.

> *Attention to detail is a crucial component of most contingency plans. Dow has produced a 20-page program for communicating with the public during a disaster, right down to such particulars as who is going to run the copy machines. Many companies designate a single corporate spokesperson to field all inquiries from the press. A list may be drawn up of those executives to be notified in emergency situations, and the late-night phone numbers of local radio and television stations may be kept posted on office walls.*[44]

Both crisis audits and related contingency plans need to be updated at least annually and, if changing conditions dictate, more often.

Table 17.1 An Organizational Crisis Can Come in Many Different Forms

• Extortion	• Bribery
• Hostile takeover	• Information sabotage
• Product tampering	• Workplace bombing
• Vehicular fatality	• Terrorist attack
• Copyright infringement	• Plant explosion
• Environmental spill	• Sexual harassment
• Computer tampering	• Escape of hazardous materials
• Security breach	• Personnel assault
• Executive kidnapping	• Assault of customers
• Product/service boycott	• Product recall
• Work-related homicide	• Counterfeiting
• Malicious rumor	• Natural disaster that destroys corporate headquarters
• Natural disaster that disrupts a major product or service	• Natural disaster that eliminates key stakeholders
• Natural disaster that destroys organizational information base	

Source: Academy of Management Executive: The Thinking Manager's Source *by Christine Pearson & Judith Clair. Copyright 1998 by ACADEMY OF MANAGEMENT. Reproduced with permission of Academy of Management in the format Textbook via Copyright Clearance Center.*

Creating a Crisis Management Team. Organizational crisis management teams have been likened to SWAT teams that police departments use for extraordinary situations such as hostage takings. Crisis management teams necessarily represent different specialties, depending on what kinds of crises are envisioned. For example, an electrical utility company might have a crisis management team made up of a media relations expert, an electrical engineer, a consumer affairs specialist, and a lawyer. As the case of Dow Chemical Canada illustrates, quick response and effective communication are the hallmarks of an effective crisis management team:

> *Dow Chemical Canada decided to improve its crisis plans after a railroad car carrying a Dow chemical derailed near Toronto in 1979, forcing the evacuation of 250,000 residents. Since then, Dow Canada has prepared information kits on the hazards of its products and [has] trained executives in interview techniques.*
>
> *. . . Another accident [years later] spilled toxic chemicals into a river that supplies water for several towns. Almost immediately, Dow Canada's emergency-response team arrived at the site and set up a press center to distribute information about the chemicals. They also recruited a neutral expert—the regional public health officer—to speak about the hazards and how to deal with them. The result: officials praised Dow's response.*[45]

Although an exact figure is not available, many companies have crisis management teams in place today.

Perfecting the Program Through Practice. Like athletic teams, crisis management teams can gain the necessary teamwork, effectiveness, and speed of response only through diligent practice. Simulations, drills, and mock disasters provide this invaluable practice. Top-management support of such exercises is essential to provide good role models and create a sense of importance. Moreover, reinforcing employee efforts in this area with an effective reward system can encourage serious practice.

Experts say management's two biggest mistakes regarding organizational crises are (1) ignoring early warning signs and (2) denying the existence of a problem when disaster strikes. These mistakes cost Ford Motor Company "about $3 billion to replace 10.6 million Firestone tires. . . . More than 250 people were killed and hundreds more injured in accidents involving Bridgestone/Firestone tires."[46] A good crisis management program effectively eliminates these self-defeating mistakes. Nike, for example, is getting it right after some initial stumbles:

> *When Nike was getting pummeled on the subject [of sweatshop conditions at its 900 or so independent foreign suppliers] in the 1990s, it typically had only two responses: anger and panic. Executives would issue denials, lash out at critics, and then rush someone to the offending supplier to put out the fire. But since 2002, Nike has built an elaborate program to deal with charges of labor exploitation. It allows random factory inspections by the Fair Labor Assn., a monitoring outfit that it founded with human rights groups and other big companies . . . that use overseas contractors. Nike also has an in-house staff of 97 which has inspected 600 factories in the past two years, grading them on labor standards. [Says a company official,] "You haven't heard about us recently because we have had our head down doing it the hard way. Now we have a system to deal with the labor issue, not a crisis mentality."*[47]

17e The Truth, and Nothing But the Truth

Howard Rubenstein, renowned public relations (PR) expert:

> *My first ground rule is always to tell the truth. A client will call and say, "This terrible thing happened to me. What should I say?" I say, "Wait a minute. First ask: What was the right thing to do? Then do it." Some of the people involved in the current corporate scandals thought they could talk their way out of a corner. They should have instead consulted their lawyer, talked to a PR person who would only deal in accurate statements, or say nothing at all.*

Source: As quoted in Adam Haft, "How I Did It: Howard Rubenstein," Inc., *26 (March 2004): 88–90.*

QUESTIONS:

Why do people in crisis situations consistently ignore this simple advice? How would you respond to a cynic who said, "Good PR people are just professional liars." How do you tend to respond to a crisis in your life?

The Quality Challenge

Not too many years ago, North American industry was roundly criticized for paying inadequate attention to the quality of goods and services. Today, many organizations have achieved a dramatic turnaround.[48] There is even a national trophy for quality in the United States that means prestige and lots of free media exposure for winners: the Malcolm Baldrige National Quality Award. Named for a former U.S. secretary of commerce, it was launched by Congress in 1987 to encourage and reward world-class quality.[49] Some observers claim the drive for quality was a passing fad. Tom Peters, the well-known management writer and consultant, offered this instructive perspective in a question-and-answer session:

> *Q: Do you think the bloom is off the quality movement?*
> *A: I think it's in the genes. The quality movement has gone from hype to something people do. The average American manager, whether she or he is in accounting or purchasing or engineering, takes for granted that quality is a major thing you think about in life. You can't compete with shabby products.*[50]

Anyone tempted to dismiss quality as a once-hot topic past its prime should ponder this situation:

> *It was a moment execs at Medtronic Inc. had always dreaded. In . . . [2004], the medical-products maker had to recall thousands of defibrillators after learning that the devices, implanted in the chests of patients with heart disease, were taking too long to discharge a shock as their batteries aged and lost power. At least four people may have died and another may have been seriously hurt as a result.*[51]

Quality is not always a life-or-death matter, but it certainly is a major *quality-of-life* factor for each of us.

The balance of this chapter builds a foundation of understanding about quality. The following questions will be answered: How are product and service quality defined? What does total quality management (TQM) involve? What is Deming management?

Defining Quality

quality: *conformance to requirements*

According to quality expert Philip Crosby, the basic definition of **quality** is "conformance to requirements."[52] But whose requirements? The sound quality of a CD player may seem flawless to its new owner, adequate to the engineer who helped design it, and terrible to an accomplished musician. In regard to *service* quality, being put on hold for 30 seconds when calling a computer company's hot line may be acceptable for one person but very irritating for another. Because quality is much more than a simple either/or proposition, both product and service quality need to be analyzed. To do this, we will explore five types of product quality, the unique challenges faced by service organizations, and the ways in which consumers judge service quality.

Five Types of Product Quality

4. IDENTIFY five types of product quality.

Other specialists in the field have refined Crosby's general perspective by identifying at least five different types of product quality: transcendent, product-based, user-based, manufacturing-based, and value-based.[53] Each represents a unique and useful perspective on product quality.

Transcendent Quality. Inherent value or innate excellence is apparent to the individual. Observing people's varied reactions to pieces of art in a museum is a good way to appreciate the subjectiveness of this type of quality. Beauty, as they say, is in the eye of the beholder.

This Brown Cow yogurt advertisement is trying to "moooove" the customer by appealing to a combination of product quality types. Brown Cow makes great-tasting yogurt (user-based quality) in small batches (manufacturing-based quality) from fresh whole Jersey cow milk (product-based quality).

■ **Product-Based Quality.** The presence or absence of a given product attribute is the primary determinant of this type of quality. Soft tissues, rough sandpaper, flawless glass, sweet candy, and crunchy granola exemplify product-based quality in very different ways. This is where the quality of key ingredients comes to the fore:

> *"Cashmere" sweaters, for example, that cost significantly less than . . . [$100] may be only partly cashmere, the unltrafine wool from the undercoat of the cashmere goat. . . .*
>
> *Raw cashmere costs about $90 a kilogram (2.2 lbs.) and a woman's sweater takes about 12 ounces.*
>
> Consumer Reports *magazine recently became suspicious when $50 "cashmere" sweaters were spotted in food markets. Its tests of the fabric showed the sweaters had been blended with cheaper treated wool that appeared to be cashmere—except under a microscope.*[54]

■ **User-Based Quality.** Here, the quality of a product is determined by its ability to meet the user's expectations, preferences, and tastes. Does it get the job done? Is it reliable? Does it taste good? Customer satisfaction surveys conducted by *Consumer Reports* magazine[55] give smart shoppers valuable input about user-based quality.[56]

■ **Manufacturing-Based Quality.** How well does the product conform to its design specifications or blueprint? The closer the match between the intended product and the actual one, the higher the quality. Car doors designed to close easily, quietly, and snugly exhibit high quality if they do so. This category corresponds to Crosby's "conformance to requirements" definition of quality.

■ **Value-Based Quality.** When you hear someone say, "I got a lot for my money," the speaker is describing value-based quality. Cost-benefit relationships are very subjective because they derive from human perception and personal preferences. About value, *Fortune* magazine observed that "[t]he concept can be nebulous because each buyer assesses value individually. In the end, value is simply giving customers what they want at a price they consider fair."[57] Wal-Mart's "everyday low price" strategy very successfully exploits this important type of product quality.

■ Unique Challenges for Service Providers

Services are a rapidly growing and increasingly important part of today's global economy. Convincing evidence of this can be found in the annual *Fortune* 500 list of the largest U.S. companies by sales revenue. Among the top ten in 2005 were Wal-Mart (retailing), Citigroup (banking), and American International Group (insurance).

17f Has American Beer Gone Flat?

European visitors have grumbled for years about the dominance of generic, bland-tasting beer in America. Despite a proliferation of microbreweries in the U.S. during the last decade, over 85% of the American beer market consists of relatively homogeneous products that most consumers could not differentiate in taste tests. . . . Could it be that the American beer consumers' market is stuck in a bad, sub-optimal equilibrium . . .?

Source: David Y. Choi and Martin H. Stack, "The All-American Beer: A Case of Inferior Standard (Taste) Prevailing?" Business Horizons, *48 (January-February 2005): 80.*

QUESTIONS:

Which of the five types of product quality is at issue here? What other products have suffered from this sort of decline in popular standards? From a business standpoint, why does the erosion of traditional standards of quality occur?

Wal-Mart, a pure service business, topped the list which has long been dominated by petroleum refiners and automobile companies. Wal-Mart, with annual revenues approaching $300 billion, has 1,400,000 employees.[58] (If Wal-Mart were a city, it would rank among the 10 largest in the United States.) Indeed, the vast majority of the U.S. labor force now works in the service sector.

Because services are customer-driven, pleasing the customer is more important than ever.[59] Experts say it costs five times more to win a new customer than it does to keep an existing one.[60] Still, U.S. companies lose an average of about 20 percent of their customers each year.[61] Service-quality strategists emphasize that it is no longer enough simply to satisfy the customer. The strategic service challenge today is to *anticipate* and *exceed* the customer's expectations. Many managers of service operations, following the lead of Leon Leonwood Bean, the legendary founder of L.L. Bean Inc., regard customer satisfaction as an ethical responsibility.

> *The first product Leon Bean ever sold was a disaster. It was 1912, and Bean, a 40–year-old hunter and fisherman, had concocted for his own use a hybrid hunting boot with a leather top and a rubber bottom. He liked his invention so much he started selling the boots through the mail to fellow sportsmen, promising refunds if customers weren't satisfied. They weren't—90 of his first 100 pairs fell apart and were returned.*
>
> *. . . he kept his word and refunded the full price, but then what? Did he stop promising refunds? No. Bean went in the other direction: He borrowed $400—a lot of money for a partner in a small town clothing store in Maine—and used it to perfect the boot. Then he perfected the guarantee. His credo: "No sale is really complete until the product is worn out, and the customer is satisfied."*[62]

Leon Leonwood Bean surely would be proud that in a 2004 study of telephone service representatives (nearly 100 years after he founded the company), L.L. Bean's reps rated tops in friendliness.[63]

5. EXPLAIN how providing a service differs from manufacturing a product, and **IDENTIFY** the five service-quality dimensions.

To varying extents, virtually every organization is a service organization. Pure service organizations (such as day-care centers) and manufacturers that provide not only products but also delivery and installation services face similar challenges. Specifically, they need to understand and manage five distinctive service characteristics:[64]

1. ***Customers participate directly in the production process.*** Although people do not go to the factory to help build the cars and refrigerators that they eventually buy, they do need to be present when their hair is styled or a broken bone is set.
2. ***Services are consumed immediately and cannot be stored.*** Hairstylists cannot store up a supply of haircuts in the same way that electronics manufacturer Intel can amass an inventory of computer chips.
3. ***Services are provided where and when the customer desires.*** McDonald's does more business by building thousands of restaurants in convenient locations around the world than it would if everyone had to travel to its Oakbrook, Illinois, headquarters to get a Big Mac and fries. Accommodating customers' sometimes odd schedules is a fact of life for service providers. Insurance salespersons generally work evenings and weekends during their clients' leisure periods.

Source: *Steve Kelley*

4. ***Services tend to be labor-intensive.*** Although skilled labor has been replaced by machines such as automatic bank tellers in some service jobs, most services are provided by people to customers face to face. Consequently, the morale and social skills of service employees are vitally important. In fact, customer service has been called a *performing art* requiring a good deal of "emotional labor."[65] It isn't easy to look happy and work hard for an angry customer when you're having a bad day, but good customer service demands it.
5. ***Services are intangible.*** Objectively measuring an intangible service is more difficult than measuring a tangible good, but nonetheless it is necessary. For example, this is how a Pennsylvania electrical parts maker measures key services. During one observation period, the company reportedly shipped 93 percent of its orders on time and averaged a delay of 3.5 seconds in answering phone calls from customers.[66]

Because customers are more intimately involved in the service-delivery process than in the manufacturing process, we need to go directly to the customer for service-quality criteria. As service-quality experts tell us,

> *Quality control of a service entails watching a process unfold and evaluating it against the consumer's judgment. The only completely valid standard of comparison is the customer's level of satisfaction. That's a perception—something appreciably more slippery to measure than the physical dimensions of a product.*[67]

How, then, do consumers judge service quality?

■ Defining Service Quality

Researchers at Texas A&M University uncovered valuable insights about customer perceptions of service quality.[68] They surveyed hundreds of customers of various types of service organizations. The following five service-quality dimensions emerged: *reliabil-*

17g I've Got Just One Question for You

Consumer behavior researchers studied the correlation between survey responses for 4,000 consumers and their loyalty to companies and products, as demonstrated by their actual purchases or recommendations to others. The best predictor across all industries was "How likely is it that you would recommend [company X] to a friend or colleague?"

Source: Frederick F. Reichheld, "The One Number You Need to Grow," Harvard Business Review, *81 (December 2003): 50.*

QUESTIONS:

As a customer, is the answer to this question a key indicator of your satisfaction? Explain why or why not. What other considerations affect whether or not you are a satisfied customer?

ity, assurance, tangibles, empathy, and *responsiveness.* (You may find it helpful to remember these with the acronym RATER.)[69] Customers apparently judge the quality of each service transaction in terms of these five dimensions. (To better understand each dimension and to gauge your own service-quality satisfaction, take a moment now to complete the Hands-On Exercise at the end of this chapter.)

Which of the five RATER dimensions is most important to you? In the Texas A&M study, *reliability* was the most important dimension of service quality, regardless of the type of service involved. Anyone who has waited impatiently for an overdue airplane knows firsthand the central importance of service reliability.[70]

Specific ways to improve product and service quality are presented throughout the rest of this chapter.

An Introduction to Total Quality Management (TQM)

total quality management (TQM): *creating an organizational culture committed to continuous improvement in every regard*

6. DEFINE *total quality management (TQM),* and **SPECIFY** the four basic TQM principles.

Definitions of TQM are many and varied, which is not surprising for an area that has been subject to intense discussion and debate in recent years.[71] For our present purposes, **total quality management (TQM)** is defined as creating an organizational culture committed to the continuous improvement of skills, teamwork, processes, product and service quality, and customer satisfaction.[72] Consultant Richard Schonberger's shorthand definition calls TQM "continuous, customer-centered, employee-driven improvement."[73]

Our definition of TQM is anchored to *organizational culture* because successful TQM is deeply embedded in virtually every aspect of organizational life. As discussed in detail in Chapter 9, an organization's culture encompasses all the assumptions its employees take for granted about how people should think and act. In other words, personal commitment to systematic continuous improvement needs to become an everyday matter of "that's just the way we do things here." For example, Dr. Frank P. Carrubba, chief technical officer at Philips, the huge Dutch electronics firm, believes it is never too early to get people thinking about quality:

> *"It is not good enough to invent something new," he says. "An elegant result that is not strategic or reproducible in a reliable, high-quality way is not worth much to the customer. Quality has to begin in research. We have to invent in an environment that reflects the same quality we want to achieve throughout the company."*[74]

As might be expected with a topic that received so much attention in a relatively short period of time, some unrealistic expectations were created. Unrealistic expectations inevitably led to disappointment and the need for a new quick fix.[75] However, managers with realistic expectations about the deep and long-term commitment necessary for successful TQM can make it work. TQM can have a positive impact if managers understand and enact these four principles of TQM:

1. Do it right the first time.
2. Be customer-centered.
3. Make continuous improvement a way of life.
4. Build teamwork and empowerment.[76]

Let us examine each of these TQM principles.

1. Do It Right the First Time

As noted in Chapter 1, the trend in recent practice has been toward designing and building quality into the product. This approach is much less costly than fixing or throwing away substandard parts and finished products. Ford Motor Company learned the first lesson of TQM the hard way, not only in the Firestone tire situation, but in this more recent case as well: "Ford Motor must replace defective ignition devices on 2 million California vehicles prone to stalling, a judge ruled. . . . The order could cost Ford $300 million."[77] Schonberger, who has studied many Japanese and U.S. factories firsthand, contends that "errors, if any, should be caught and corrected at the source, i.e., where the work is performed."[78] Consider, for example, the work of a pastry chef. This is what Kimberly Davis Cuthbert, owner of Sweet Jazmines, a Berwyn, Pennsylvania, made-to-order bakery, says:

> *"If the recipe is cream the butter for three minutes, cream the butter and the cream cheese for another three minutes, add the sugar four times for 2 1/2 [minutes], then that's what you have to do. It's very scientific, and that's the only way I found out that I could do this and train other people to do it and have it come out the same way every time."*
>
> *For the pastry chef, there is no room for error, unlike the culinary chef who can usually salvage something.*
>
> *"If we overcook a flank steak, we can cut it into strips and make fajitas. Spinach can always be made into cream of spinach," says Sylvia Smith, a culinary chef and caterer in Metropolitan Washington. "But baking is an exact art. Once you mess up, you have to throw it out.*[79]

A great many jobs in today's economy are like baking. Generally, comprehensive training in TQM tools and statistical process control is essential if employees are to accept personal responsibility for quality improvement.

2. Be Customer-Centered

internal customers: *anyone in your organization who cannot do a good job unless you do a good job*

customer-centered: *satisfying the customer's needs by anticipating, listening, and responding*

Everyone has one or more customers in a TQM organization. They may be internal or external customers. **Internal customers** are other members of the organization who rely on *your* work to get *their* job done.[80] For example, a corporate lawyer employed by Marriott does not directly serve the hotel chain's customers by changing beds, serving meals, or carrying luggage. But that lawyer has an internal customer when a Marriott manager needs to be defended in court.

Regarding external customers, TQM requires all employees who deal directly with outsiders to be customer-centered. Being **customer-centered** means (1) anticipating the customer's needs, (2) listening to the customer, (3) learning how to satisfy the customer, and (4) responding appropriately to the customer.[81] Listening to the customer is a major stumbling block for many companies. But at Coach, known for its trendy women's handbags, listening to the customer is practically a religion.

> *Today Coach annually interviews at least 10,000 customers individually (primarily by telephone) to keep tabs on how the brand is faring in their minds. During the company's transformation, clerks intercepted shoppers to ask about specific products, whether they preferred chrome or nickel, or if they thought the length of the strap was right.*
>
> *Coach also tests its products carefully in a limited number of its 174 stores in North America six months before a product comes out. . . . "It's street-level information, multiple angles, not just surveys and focus groups," says [a marketing consultant].*[82]

Appropriate responses to customers depend upon the specific nature of the business.[83] For example, Table 17.2 (on p. 520) lists good and bad customer service behaviors at a U.S. supermarket chain. Notice how service-quality training led to very different patterns of behavior for the different jobs.

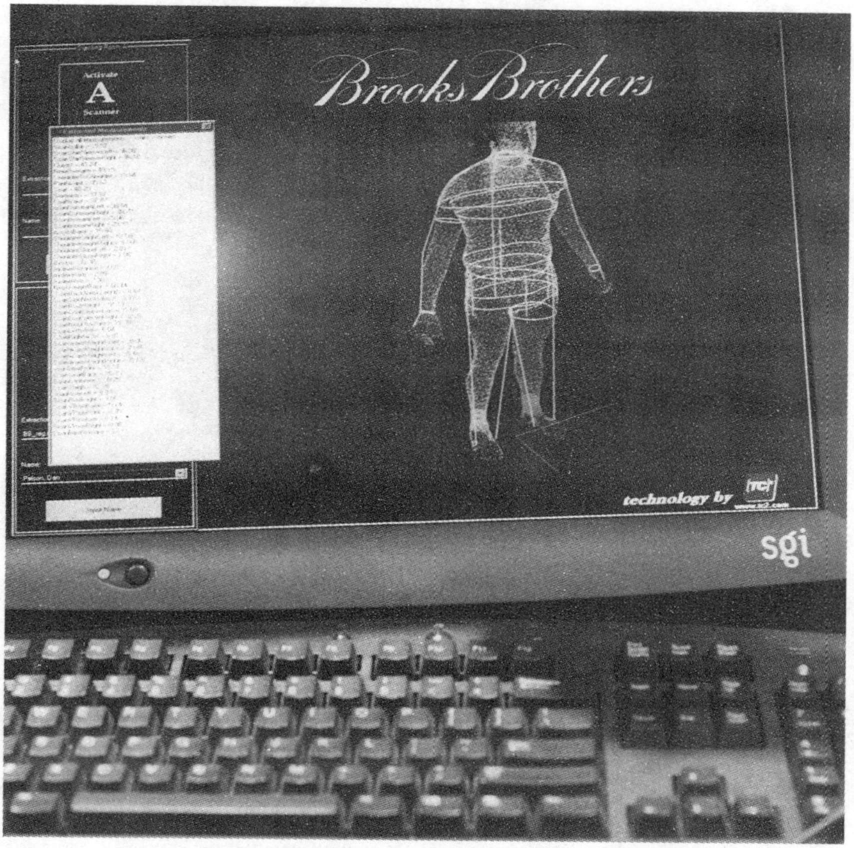

TQM principles urge all of us to get close to the customer. At Brooks Brothers' flagship store in New York City, that advice has been taken literally. A full body scan by a $75,000 machine ensures that the customer's new suit fits like a glove.

17h Is the Customer Always Right?

Jack Welch; retired CEO of General Electric:

> *We used to give speeches to our people: "No one can guarantee you a job other than satisfied customers." That's the only thing that works. Nothing creates work other than products and services you provide that create satisfied customers.*

Source: As quoted in Stephen B. Shepard, "Life After GE? And How," Business Week *(March 8, 2004): 77.*

QUESTIONS:

Anyone who has worked serving the public knows that "customers" can be impatient, rude, dishonest, and shoplifters. So how can the customer *always* be right? Explain how this needs to be sorted out.

Vague requests to "be nice to the customer" are useless in TQM organizations. *Behavior,* not good intentions, is what really matters. As discussed in Chapter 15 in relation to behavior modification, desirable behavior needs to be strengthened with *positive reinforcement.* A good role model in this regard is Motorola's new CEO, Edward J. Zander:

> *Zander has been relentless in trying to get the most out of his staff. A new bonus plan bases 25% on three key areas: customer satisfaction, product reliability, and the cost of poor quality. When the heads of each business unit first laid out their targets, Zander's no-nonsense roots showed. "You're sandbagging," he barked. Before long, the targets were more difficult. "We're driving for improvement year over year," says Michael J. Fenger, a vet Zander picked to improve corporate quality.*[84]

Table 17.2 Turning a Supermarket into a Customer-Centered Organization

Employees	Behaviors before the change	Behaviors after the change
Bag packers	Ignore customers Lack of packing standards	Greet customers Respond to customers Ask for customers' preference
Cashiers	Ignore customers Lack of eye contact	Greet customers Respond to customers Assist customers Speak clearly Call customers by name
Shelf stockers	Ignore customers Don't know store	Respond to customers Help customers with correct product location information Knowledgeable about product location
Department workers	Ignore customers Limited knowledge	Respond to customers Know products Know store
Department managers	Ignore customers Ignore workers	Respond to customers Reward employees for responding to customers
Store managers	Ignore customers Stay in booth	Respond to customers Reward employees for service Appraise employees on customer service

Source: *Reprinted from* Organizational Dynamics, *Summer 1992, Randall S. Schuler, "Strategic Human Resource Management: Linking the People with the Strategic Needs of the Business," exhibit 4. Copyright 1992, with permission from Elsevier Science.*

■ 3. Make Continuous Improvement a Way of Life

kaizen: *a Japanese word meaning "continuous improvement"*

The Japanese word for "continuous improvement" is ***kaizen***, which means improving the overall system by constantly improving the little details. TQM managers dedicated to *kaizen* are never totally happy with things. *Kaizen* practitioners view quality as an endless journey, not a final destination. They are always experimenting, measuring, adjusting, and improving. Rather than naïvely assuming that zero defects necessarily means perfection has been achieved, they search for potential and actual trouble spots. *Fortune* magazine recently explained how *kaizen* is a comprehensive concept at Toyota:

> *The soul of the Toyota production system is . . .* kaizen. *The word is often translated as "continuous improvement," but its essence is the notion that engineers, managers, and line workers collaborate continually to systematize production tasks and identify incremental changes to make work go more smoothly. Toyota strives to keep inventories as close to zero as possible, not only to minimize costs but also to ferret out inefficiencies the moment*

they occur. Toyota deliberately runs production lines at full tilt. And workers are given authority to stop the process and summon assistance at the first sign of trouble.[85]

There are four general avenues for continuous improvement:

- Improved and more consistent product and service *quality*
- Faster *cycle times* (in cycles ranging from product development to order processing to payroll processing)
- Greater *flexibility* (for example, faster response to changing customer demands and new technology)
- Lower *costs* and less *waste* (for example, eliminating needless steps, scrap, rework, and non–value-adding activities)[86]

Significantly, these are not tradeoffs, as traditionally believed. In other words, TQM advocates reject the notion that a gain on one front must mean a loss on another. Greater quality, speed, and flexibility have to be achieved at lower cost and with less waste. This is an "all things are possible" approach to management. It requires diligent effort and creativity.[87]

■ 4. Build Teamwork and Empowerment

Earlier, we referred to TQM as employee-driven. In other words, it empowers employees at all levels in order to tap their full creativity, motivation, and commitment. *Empowerment,* as defined in Chapter 15, occurs when employees are adequately trained, provided with all relevant information and the best possible tools, fully involved in key decisions, and fairly rewarded for results.[88] TQM advocates prefer to reorganize the typical hierarchy into teams of people from different specialties. For a prime example, consider how Chrysler Corporation reinvented itself prior to becoming part of DaimlerChrysler:

Gone are the days when the development of a new vehicle plodded through a rigid set of sequential "chimneys"—from design to engineering to procurement and supply to manufacturing to marketing and sales—until, seven or eight years later, the new model turned up in the customer's driveway. Today Chrysler is organized into four streamlined platform teams: large car, small car, minivan, and Jeep/truck. Each team is composed of product and manufacturing engineers, planners and buyers, marketers, designers, financial analysts, and outside suppliers, and each is responsible for getting their vehicles to market.

"It's not the old way: an engineer finishing his piece of the car and tossing the plan over the fence to the next guy up the line," says [retired] chairman Lee A. Iacocca. "Platform teams are about everybody working together. The result is better quality, lower cost, and a reduction in the time it takes to get a product to market."[89]

In earlier chapters you encountered many ways to promote teamwork and employee involvement: suggestion systems (Chapter 12), quality control circles, and self-managed teams (Chapter 13), teamwork and cross-functional teams (Chapter 14), and participative leadership (Chapter 15). Each can be a valuable component of TQM.

7. DESCRIBE at least three of the seven TQM process improvement tools.

■ The Seven Basic TQM Process Improvement Tools

Continuous improvement of productive processes in factories, offices, stores, hospitals, hotels, and banks requires lots of measurement. Skilled TQM managers have a large repertoire of graphical and statistical tools at their disposal. The beginner's set consists of the seven tools displayed in Figure 17.4. A brief overview of each will help promote awareness and establish a foundation for further study.

Figure 17.4 Seven Basic TQM Tools

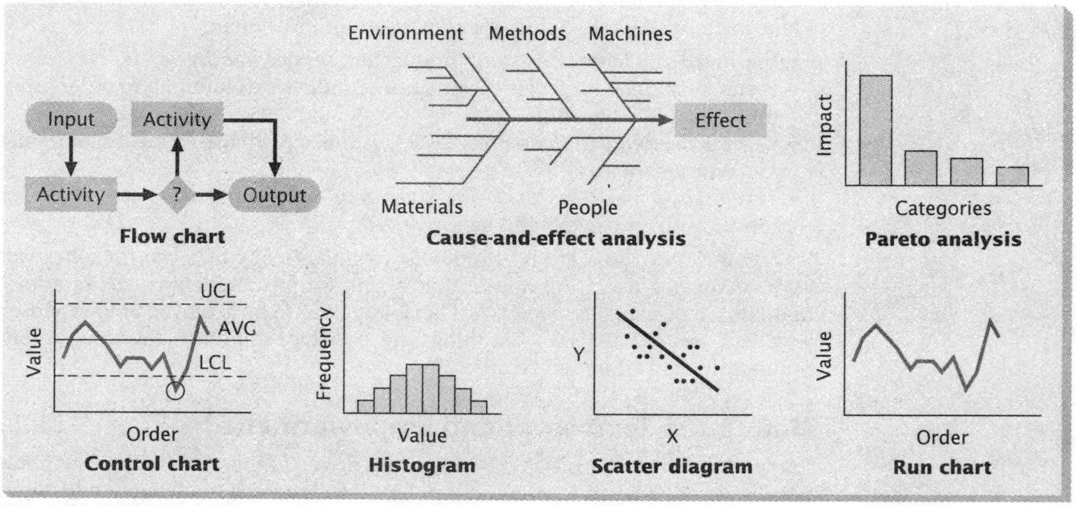

Source: *Arthur R. Tenner and Irving J. DeToro,* Total Quality Management: Three Steps to Continuous Improvement *(Figure 9.2, p. 113). © 1992 by Addison-Wesley Publishing Company, Inc. Reprinted by permission of Pearson Education, Inc. Publishing as Pearson Addison Welsey.*

flow chart: *graphical display of a sequence of activities and decisions*

■ **Flow Chart.** A **flow chart** is a graphical representation of a sequence of activities and decisions. Standard flow-charting symbols include boxes for events or activities, diamonds for key decisions, and ovals for start and stop points. Flow charts show, for instance, how a property damage claim moves through an insurance company. Armed with knowledge of who does what to the claim, and in which sequence, management can streamline the process by eliminating unnecessary steps or delays. Chapter 6 shows a sample flow chart as a planning and control tool. TQM teams have found flowcharting to be a valuable tool for increasing efficiency, reducing costs, and eliminating waste.

fishbone diagram: *a cause-and-effect diagram*

■ **Cause-and-Effect Analysis.** The **fishbone diagram**, named for its rough resemblance to a fish skeleton, helps TQM teams visualize important cause-and-effect relationships. (Some refer to fishbone diagrams as Ishikawa diagrams, in tribute to the Japanese quality pioneer mentioned in Chapter 2.) For example, did a computer crash because of an operator error, an equipment failure, a power surge, or a software problem? A TQM team can systematically track down a likely cause by constructing a fishbone diagram. An illustrative fishbone diagram is presented in Skills & Tools at the end of Chapter 8.

Pareto analysis: *bar chart indicating which problem needs the most attention*

■ **Pareto Analysis.** This technique, popularized by quality expert Joseph M. Juran and discussed in Chapter 6, is named for the Italian economist Vilfredo Pareto (1848–1923). Pareto detected the so-called 80/20 pattern in many real-world situations: relatively few people or events (about 20 percent) account for most of the results or impacts (about 80 percent). It is thus most efficient to focus on the few things (or people) that make the biggest difference. The next time you are in class, for example, notice how relatively few students offer the great majority of the comments in class. Likewise, a few students account for most of the absenteeism during the semester. In TQM, conducting a **Pareto analysis** involves constructing a bar chart by counting and tallying the number of times significant quality problems occur. The tallest bar on the chart, representing the most common problem, demands prompt attention. In a newspaper printing operation, for example, the most common cause of printing press stoppages for the week might turn out to be poor-quality paper. A quick glance at a Pareto chart would alert management of the need to demand better quality from the paper supplier.

control chart: *visual aid showing acceptable and unacceptable variations from the norm for repetitive operations*

■ **Control Chart.** *Statistical process control* of repetitive operations helps employees keep key quality measurements within an acceptable range. A **control chart** is used to monitor actual versus desired quality measurements during repetitive operations. Consider the job of drilling a 2-centimeter hole in 1,000 pieces of metal. According to design specifications, the hole should have an inside diameter no larger than 2.1 centimeters and no smaller than 1.9 centimeters. These measurements are the upper control limit (UCL) and the lower control limit (LCL). Any hole diameters within these limits are acceptable quality. Random measurements of the hole diameters need to be taken during the drilling operation to monitor quality. When these random measurements are plotted on a control chart, like the one in Figure 17.4, the operator has a handy visual aid that flags violations of the control limits and signals the need for corrective action. Perhaps the drill needs to be cleaned, sharpened, or replaced. This sort of statistical process control is considerably less expensive than having to redrill or scrap 1,000 pieces of metal with wrong-sized holes.

histogram: *bar chart indicating deviations from a standard bell-shaped curve*

■ **Histogram.** A **histogram** is a bar chart showing whether repeated measurements of a given quality characteristic conform to a standard bell-shaped curve. Deviations from the standard signal the need for corrective action. The controversial practice of teachers "curving" grades when there is an abnormally high or low grade distribution can be implemented with a histogram.

scatter diagram: *diagram that plots the relationship between two variables*

■ **Scatter Diagram.** A **scatter diagram** is used to plot the correlation between two variables. The one illustrated in Figure 17.4 indicates a negative correlation. In other words, as the value of variable X increases, the value of variable Y tends to decrease. A design engineer for a sporting goods company would find this particular type of correlation while testing the relationship between various thicknesses of fishing rods and flexibility. The thicker the rod, the lower the flexibility.

run chart: *a trend chart for tracking a variable over time*

■ **Run Chart.** Also called a time series or trend chart, a **run chart** tracks the frequency or amount of a given variable over time. Significant deviations from the norm signal the need for corrective action. Hospitals monitor vital body signs such as temperature and blood pressure with daily logs, which are actually run charts. TQM teams can use them to spot "bad days." For example, automobiles made in U.S. factories on a Friday or Monday historically have had more quality defects than those assembled on a Tuesday, Wednesday, or Thursday.

Before we move on to Deming management, an important point needs to be made. As experts on the subject remind us, "Tools are necessary but not sufficient for TQM."[90] Successful TQM requires a long-term, organizationwide drive for continuous improvement. The appropriate time frame is *years*, not days or months. Tools such as benchmarking and control charts are just one visible feature of that process. Invisible factors—such as values, learning, attitudes, motivation, and personal commitment—dictate the ultimate success of TQM.

17i Quick Quiz

Situation: A mutual fund company raised its minimum initial investment from zero to $2,500. Why? Smaller accounts are just too expensive. "About 41 percent of all our phone calls were from people with account balances of less than $1,000," said a company official.

Source: John Waggoner, "Twentieth Century Plans for Millennium," USA Today *(August 11, 1994): 8B.*

QUESTION:
This line of thinking best reflects an application of which of the seven basic TQM tools? Explain your reasoning.

Deming Management

It is hard to overstate the worldwide impact of W. Edwards Deming's revolutionary ideas about management. His ideas have directly and indirectly created better and more productive work environments for countless millions of people. This section builds upon the historical sketch in Chapter 2 by examining basic principles of Deming management and Deming's famous 14 points.

■ Principles of Deming Management

Deming management: *application of W. Edwards Deming's ideas for more responsive, more democratic, and less wasteful organizations*

Deming management is the application of W. Edwards Deming's ideas to revitalize productive systems by making them more responsive to the customer, more democratic, and more efficient. This approach qualifies as a revolution because, when first proposed by Deming in the 1950s, it directly challenged the legacy of Taylor's scientific management.[91] Scientific management led to rigid and autocratic organizations unresponsive to customers and employees alike. Deming management proposed essentially the opposite approach. Some of the principles discussed below may not seem revolutionary today because Deming management has become ingrained in everyday *good* management.

■ Quality Improvement Drives the Entire Economy. Higher quality eventually means more jobs. Deming's simple yet convincing logic is presented in Figure 17.5. Quality improvement is a powerful engine driving out waste and inefficiency. Quality also generates higher productivity, greater market share, and new business and employment opportunities. In short, everybody wins when quality improves.[92]

■ The Customer Always Comes First. In his influential 1986 text *Out of the Crisis*, Deming wrote, "The consumer is the most important part of the production line. Quality should be aimed at the needs of the consumer, present and future."[93] Of course, these are just inspirational words until they are enacted faithfully by individuals on the job.

■ Don't Blame the Person, Fix the System. Deming management chides U.S. managers for being preoccupied with finding someone to blame rather than fixing problems. His research convinced him that "the system"—meaning management, work rules, technology, and the organization's structure and culture—typically is responsible for upwards of 85 percent of substandard quality. People can and will turn out superior quality, *if* the system is redesigned to permit them to do so. Deming

Figure 17.5 Everyone Benefits from Improved Quality

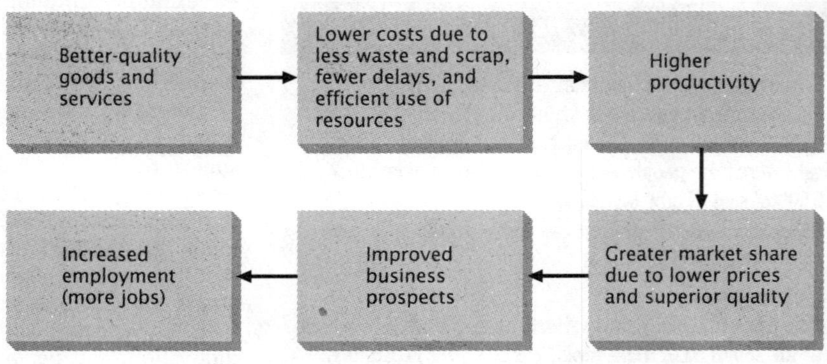

Source: *Adapted from W. Edwards Deming,* Out of the Crisis *(Cambridge, Mass.: MIT Press, 1986), p. 3.*

management urges managers to treat employees as internal customers, listening and responding to their ideas and suggestions for improvement. After all, who knows more about a particular job—the person who performs it for 2,000 hours a year or a manager who stops by now and again?

PDCA cycle: *Deming's plan-do-check-act cycle that relies on observed data for continuous improvement of operations*

■ **Plan-Do-Check-Act.** Deming's approach calls for making informed decisions on the basis of hard data. His recommended tool for this process is what is popularly known as the **PDCA cycle** (plan-do-check-act cycle). Deming preferred the term *Shewhart cycle*,[94] in recognition of the father of statistical quality control, Walter A. Shewhart, mentioned in Chapter 2. (Japanese managers call it the Deming cycle.) Whatever the label, the PDCA cycle reminds managers to focus on what is really important, use observed data, start small and build upon accumulated knowledge, and be research-oriented in observing changes and results (see Figure 17.6). The

Figure 17.6 Deming's PDCA Cycle

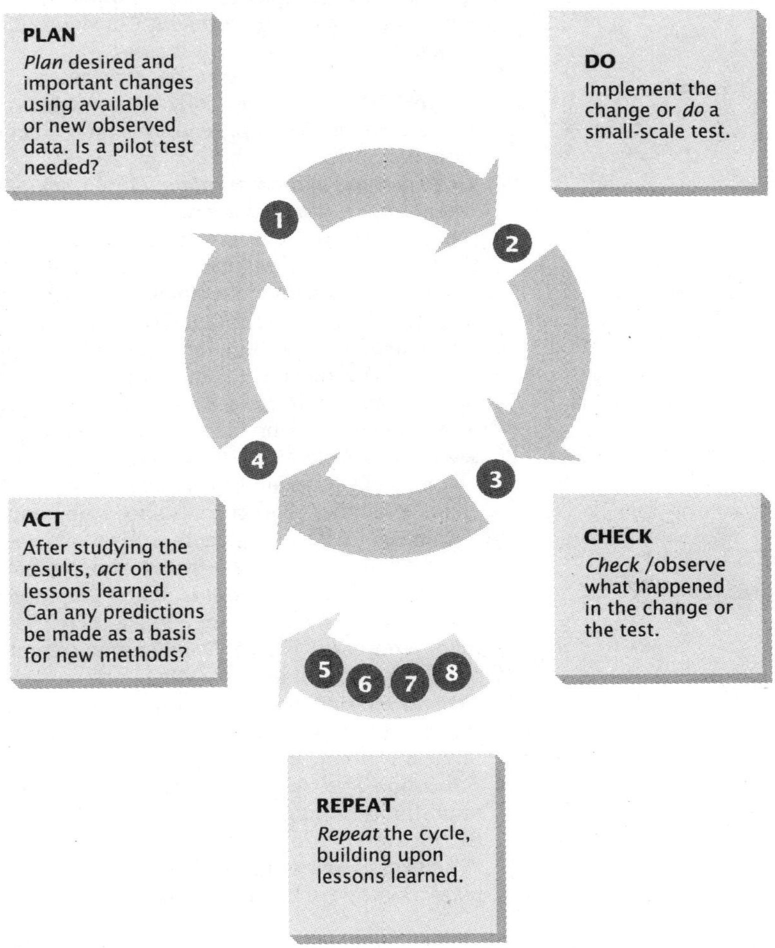

Source: *Adapted from W. Edwards Deming,* Out of the Crisis *(Cambridge, Mass.: MIT Press, 1986), p. 88.*

8. EXPLAIN how Deming's PDCA cycle can improve the overall management process.

influence of Deming management was obvious at Intel when then-CEO Craig Barrett gave his employees a pep talk in a 2004 Webcast:

> *"There is nothing new in anything I'm saying," said Barrett, adding that the principles of quality—planning, doing, checking, and acting—were first elucidated some 70 years ago. "I expect everyone to adopt this system."*[95]

■ Deming's 14 Points

9. SPECIFY and **DISCUSS** at least four of Deming's famous 14 points.

Deming formulated his 14 points to transform U.S. industry from what he considered to be its backward ways. Here is a summary of the 14 points constituting the heart and soul of Deming management:[96]

1. ***Constant purpose.*** Strive for continuous improvement in products and services to remain competitive.
2. ***New philosophy.*** Western management needs to awaken to the realities of a new economic age by demanding wiser use of all resources.
3. ***Give up on quality by inspection.*** Inspecting for faulty products is unnecessary if quality is built in from the very beginning.
4. ***Avoid the constant search for lowest-cost suppliers.*** Build long-term, loyal, and trusting relationships with single suppliers.
5. ***Seek continuous improvement.*** Constantly improve production processes for greater productivity and lower costs.
6. ***Train everyone.*** Make sure people have a clear idea of how to do their job. Informally learning a new job from coworkers entrenches bad work habits.
7. ***Provide real leadership.*** Leading is more than telling. It involves providing individualized help.
8. ***Drive fear out of the workplace.*** Employees continue to do things the wrong way when they are afraid to ask questions about why and how. According to Deming, "No one can put in his best performance unless he feels secure. *Se* comes from the Latin, meaning without, *cure* means fear or care. *Secure* means without fear, not afraid to express ideas, not afraid to ask questions."[97] Lack of job security is a major stumbling block for quality improvement in America.
9. ***Promote teamwork.*** Bureaucratic barriers between departments and functional specialists need to be broken down. Customer satisfaction is the common goal.
10. ***Avoid slogans and targets.*** Because the *system* is largely responsible for product quality, putting pressure on individuals who feel they do not control the system breeds resentment. Posters with slogans such as "zero defects" and "take pride in quality" do nothing to help the individual measure and improve productive processes. Control charts and other process-control tools, in contrast, give employees direction and encouragement. Deming's approach tells managers that if they provide leadership and continually improve the system, the scoreboard will take care of itself.
11. ***Get rid of numerical quotas.*** When employees aggressively pursue numerical goals or quotas, they too often take their eyes off quality, continuous improvement, and costs. Hence, Deming management strongly rejects the practice of management by objectives (MBO),[98] discussed in Chapter 6.
12. ***Remove barriers that stifle pride in workmanship.*** Poor management, inadequate instruction, faulty equipment, and pressure to achieve a numerical goal get in the way of continuous improvement.
13. ***Education and self-improvement are key.*** Greater knowledge means greater opportunity. Continuous improvement should be the number one career objective for everyone in the organization.
14. ***"The transformation is everyone's job."***[99] Virtually *everyone* in the organization plays a key role in implementing Deming management.

SUMMARY

1. Feedforward control is preventive in nature, whereas feedback control is based on the evaluation of past performance. Managers engage in concurrent control when they monitor and adjust ongoing operations to keep them performing up to standard. The three basic components of organizational control systems are objectives, standards, and an evaluation-reward system.
2. According to the performance pyramid, strategic control involves the downward translation of objectives and the upward translation of performance measures. Both external effectiveness and internal efficiency criteria need to be achieved.
3. The four elements of a crisis management program are (1) *anticipate* (conduct a crisis audit), (2) *plan* (formulate contingency plans), (3) *staff* (create a crisis management team), and (4) *practice* (perfect the program through practice).
4. Product quality involves much more than the basic idea of "conformance to requirements." Five types of product quality are transcendent, product-based, user-based, manufacturing-based, and value-based.
5. Service providers face a unique set of challenges that distinguish them from manufacturers. Because we live in a predominantly service economy, it is important to recognize these challenges: (1) direct customer participation, (2) immediate consumption of services, (3) provision of services at customers' convenience, (4) the tendency of services to be more labor-intensive than manufacturing, and (5) the intangibility of services, making them harder to measure. Consumer research uncovered five service-quality dimensions: reliability, assurance, tangibles, empathy, and responsiveness (RATER). Consumers consistently rank *reliability* number one.
6. Total quality management (TQM) involves creating a culture dedicated to customer-centered, employee-driven continuous improvement. The four TQM principles are
   - Do it right the first time.
   - Be customer-centered.
   - Make continuous improvement a way of life.
   - Build teamwork and empowerment.
7. Seven basic TQM process improvement tools are flow charts, fishbone diagrams, Pareto analysis, control charts, histograms, scatter diagrams, and run charts.
8. Deming's plan-do-check-act (PDCA) cycle forces managers to make decisions and take actions on the basis of observed and carefully measured data. This procedure removes quality-threatening guesswork. The PDCA cycle also helps managers focus on what is really important. PDCA work never ends, because lessons learned from one cycle are incorporated into the next.
9. Deming formulated his famous 14 points in an effort to revolutionize Western management practices. In summary, they urge managers to seek continuous improvement through extensive training, leadership, teamwork, and self-improvement. The points call for *doing away with* mass quality inspections, with selecting suppliers only on the basis of low cost, fear, slogans and numerical quotas, and with barriers to pride in workmanship. This transformation, according to Deming, is *everyone's* job.

TERMS TO UNDERSTAND

- Control, p. 501
- Feedforward control, p. 503
- Concurrent control, p. 503
- Feedback control, p. 504
- Benchmarking, p. 505
- Executive reality check, p. 507
- Internal auditing, p. 508
- Crisis management, p. 509
- Contingency plan, p. 511
- Quality, p. 513
- Total Quality Management (TQM), p. 517
- Internal customers, p. 518
- Customer-centered, p. 518
- *kaizen*, p. 520
- Flow chart, p. 522
- Fishbone diagram, p. 522
- Pareto analysis, p. 522
- Control chart, p. 523
- Histogram, p. 523
- Scatter diagram, p. 523
- Run chart, p. 523
- Deming management, p. 524
- PDCA cycle, p. 525

SKILLS & TOOLS

How to Avoid a Public Relations Nightmare in a Crisis

1. **Prepare written organizational policies,** including:
   - an employee handbook
   - policies for screening potential employees (including volunteers)
   - anti-discrimination and -harassment policies
   - financial control systems
   - an ethics policy
2. **Be sure all employees** (including volunteers) understand the organization's policies.
3. **Create a written crisis plan,** clearly stating what will be done and who will do it in case of a crisis. Make sure your plan includes:
   - names and contact numbers of people to contact in an emergency
   - a list of questions you're likely to be asked by the media and other stakeholders in a crisis
   - forms to record the details of what happens in a crisis
   - details on who will communicate what to whom
   - your goals for effective crisis communications—the outcomes you hope for and how you will measure success.
4. **Build trust and respect** with local media representatives.
5. **Appoint someone to communicate** with the media and someone to meet with victims' families in case of an emergency. Choose these people *before* a crisis occurs. They should know what's expected and be ready to swing into action at the first hint of a problem.
6. **Keep communication lines open** between your organization and its stakeholders at all times.
7. **Hold frequent brainstorming and roleplaying sessions.** Encourage all staff to participate, and be open to all their ideas.
8. **Accept the blame** when your organization makes an error. Let the public know what you're doing to be sure the problem isn't repeated.
9. **Always tell the truth.**
10. **Don't wait until a crisis occurs** before implementing these ideas. Begin today to prevent the preventable and prepare for the inevitable.

Source: *Lolita Hendrix, "Will You Be Ready When Disaster Strikes,"* Nonprofit World, *18 (May-June 2000): 37. Reprinted by permission.*

HANDS-ON EXERCISE

Measuring Service Quality

Think of the kind of treatment you have received in service establishments recently. Pick a specific restaurant, hair-styling salon, bank, airline, hospital, government agency, auto repair shop, department store, bookstore, or other service organization, and rate the kind of customer service you received, using the following five RATER factors. Circle one response for each factor and total them.

1. ***Reliability:*** ability to perform the desired service dependably, accurately, and consistently.

Very poor 1 2 3 4 5 6 7 8 9 10 Very good

2. ***Assurance:*** employees' knowledge, courtesy, and ability to convey trust and confidence.

Very poor 1 2 3 4 5 6 7 8 9 10 Very good

3. ***Tangibles:*** physical facilities, equipment, appearance of personnel.

Very poor 1 2 3 4 5 6 7 8 9 10 Very good

4. ***Empathy:*** provision of caring, individualized attention to customers.

Very poor 1 2 3 4 5 6 7 8 9 10 Very good

5. ***Responsiveness:*** willingness to provide prompt service and help customers.

Very poor 1 2 3 4 5 6 7 8 9 10 Very good

Total score = _____

Scoring Key

1. 5–10 Cruel and unusual punishment.
2. 11–20 You call this service?
3. 21–30 Average, but who wants average service?
4. 31–40 Close only counts in horseshoes.
5. 41–50 Service hall-of-fame candidate.

For Consideration/Discussion

1. If your service encounter was good (or bad), how many other people have you told about it? Why do people tend to pass along more stories about bad service than about good service?
2. Which of the five service-quality criteria was a major problem in the specific service situation you chose? What corrective actions should management take?
3. In the service situation you selected, which of the five criteria was most important to you? Why? Did you walk away satisfied? Why or why not?
4. If your present (or most recent) job involves rendering a service, how would you score yourself on the RATER factors? What needs to be done to improve your total score?
5. Does the most important RATER factor change for various types of service (for instance, a visit to the doctor versus flying on a commercial airliner)? Explain, with specific examples.
6. Generally speaking, which of the RATER factors is the weak link for today's service organizations? What remedies do you recommend?

INTERNET EXERCISES

1. **An Internet search for higher-quality customer service:** For the vast majority of today's employees who work in the service sector, service quality has two faces: *providing* services and *paying for and receiving* services. Hence, learning more about service quality can have a double benefit as we become better both as service providers and as consumers. Customer service expert John Tschohl's Web site (**www.customer-service.com**) for the Service Quality Institute that he founded and heads is an excellent resource. At the home page, click on "Media Articles." Under the heading "Review Past Articles," select and read at least three of the brief tutorials. Recommended ones include "8 Steps to Pleasing the Customer" and "The Customer Is Boss."

   Learning Points: 1. What was the most useful thing you learned about customer service? Explain. 2. If you presently have a service job, what did Tschohl teach you about providing better service? 3. What did Tschohl teach you about demanding and getting better customer service?

2. **Check it out:** Product recalls are concrete evidence that product quality needs improvement. For a comprehensive listing of product recalls in the United States, go to **www.recalls.gov**. Browse the various categories for useful and possibly injury-avoiding or life-saving information on products you own or are thinking of buying. Everything from vehicle crash test data to food recalls can be found at this Web site. You can even use this site to report product defects you have experienced.

For updates to these exercises, visit our Web site (**http://business.college.hmco.com/students/**) and select Kreitner, *Management*, 10e.

CLOSING CASE

Pristine International

Pristine International Limited which represented the international business arm of the Pristine Group of Industries, one of the largest business houses, was established in the year 1971 at Pune. The Group had a sound international business reputation for its technological prowess, quality commitment, and its reliability. The Group had aggregate assets of nearly Rs 4,500 crores with a turnover of Rs 3,300 crores. It had employee strength of 2,50,000. Pristine International Limited was India's largest international trading company in the private sector and its annual turnover touched 1,450 crores. It was engaged in the manufacturing and trading of the textiles, execution of turnkey projects and the project related management services abroad. The company had a network of international offices in the globally significant commercial places. It was assisted in its global networking by the associate Pristine Group's offices in other countries. Pristine International had the total employee strength of 1,500 people working in India and abroad. It had 3 divisions of dyeing, cutting and stitching. The total strength of the workforce in these 3 divisions was 1,010 with 25 managers, 125 officers, 200 staff supervisors and 660 workers (which included 12 female workers). The average worker was in his late thirties and had done his basic education.

One of the Pristine consultants, Ramesh Sharma, while on a business trip to Japan, picked up the concept of quality improvement. The concept was concretized back home in the form of Quality Improvement Project (QIP). It was actively supported by the top management through facilitation and technical support to the QIP groups and was coordinated by Ramachandran, the CEO. QIP was essentially implemented through groups of people, who voluntarily meet at regular intervals to identify, analyze and solve the problems related to the work improvement and the cost-reduction. The underlying belief that led to QIP groups is that group decisions were likely to be superior to the individual decisions. The composition of QIP groups took the form of groups of people drawn from similar as well as cross-functional areas. The leadership norm for QIP overruled seniority. The leadership happened by rotation and the group leader had to be active and absorbing. The qualifying traits expected of a leader were good interpersonal skills and an ability to shoulder additional responsibility. The group had a facilitator who was responsible for coordination and direction of the group activities within the organization. The three divisions of dyeing, cutting and stitching had 8, 7 and 4 QIP groups respectively. The membership of these QIP groups was purely voluntary but the participation of the members was ensured through follow-up and an erratic member was replaced if need arose. The QIP was not linked to any incentive scheme, it was conceived with the intention of greater worker participation and involvement in the company's work processes as well as to improve organizational climate, to promote effective communication and achieve cost reduction.

It was also aimed at promoting leadership qualities and personal development of the workers coupled with the business objective of enhancing quality and reducing rejection and reworking. The process was also initiated to inspire greater team spirit and harmonious superior-subordinate relationships. The idea was to promote the culture of problem prevention at Pristine International Limited.

While reviewing its business operations, the company's top management felt that there was an urgent need to cut down operating costs and during one such review they found that heavy costs were incurred due to high wastage. One of the QIP groups in the stitching unit decided to address this problem. This QIP group comprised of Sudhir Bhandarkar, a manager aged 36, Kailash Chandra, a supervisor aged 38, P Shewale, a worker aged 35, B L Shirke, a worker aged 39, Madhusudan Das, a worker aged 36 and P S Tiwari, a worker aged 37. This QIP group met every week for 2 hours during working hours with the venue, day and time communicated to them well in advance. They had a series of meetings to address the problem of wastage. The preliminary meetings focused on listing down the causes leading to wastage. After this, the group used Ishikawa Diagram for analysis of the causes and effects. The Ishikawa Diagram or a Fish-bone diagram is the visual representation of various factors of a problem or phenomenon. This helps in arriving at concrete action for a specific problem. So after attempting the Ishikawa Diagram, in a subsequent meeting, through brain storming, techniques for wastage reduction were generated by the group. Brain storming helped them in generating creative ideas for wastage reduction. Each idea was discussed extensively. Finally, BL Shirke's idea for wastage reduction was unanimously chosen for implementation. This idea simply suggested the use of left-over pieces of cloth to be used in stitching new garments with the help of the fashion designing unit of the company. The idea's practical feasibility, based on an elaborate discussion and subsequent analysis, led to the unanimous decision that this technique be used hereafter for reducing wastage. The leader of the group, Madhusudan Das recapitulated the action plan with specific responsibilities lined out for each group member for necessary action. Though, generally employees are not rewarded for their suggestions, BL Shirke was rewarded monetarily. Pristine International's problem of high wastage was effectively addressed, which subsequently led to the enhanced productivity and greater employee motivation. Though Pristine International Limited saw an inherent risk of managing higher employee aspirations while implementing QIP, it successfully used QIP for operational efficiency and employee motivation for healthier organizational climate.

For Discussion

1. Pristine International used QIP as a group process to resolve the problems, if you were to advise the top management on resolving their problems, what solution would you offer and why?
2. As a member of the QIP at Pristine International, what alternative method would you suggest for the wastage reduction?
3. Do you believe that QIP is an effective tool for addressing organizational problems? Give reasons for your answer.

Source: *Case Method in Management Education, Upinder Dhar & Santosh Dhar, Excel Books, New Delhi, 2002, pp. 320-322.*

TEST PREPPER

True/False Questions

______ **1.** Objectives are yardsticks against which actual performance can be measured.

______ **2.** Two components of the performance pyramid for strategic control are flexibility and cycle times.

______ **3.** A high-probability, low-impact event with a clear cause-and-effect relationship is an organizational crisis.

______ **4.** "Beauty is in the eye of the beholder" describes transcendent quality.

______ **5.** Services cannot be measured because they are intangible.

______ **6.** Calling TQM customer-centered and employee-driven is appropriate.

______ **7.** A French word meaning "put the customer first" is *kaizen.*

______ **8.** Constructing a statistical process control chart is part of Pareto analysis.

______ **9.** In Deming's PDCA cycle, the "C" stands for "control."

______ **10.** One of Deming's 14 points is a recommendation to get rid of numerical quotas.

Multiple-Choice Questions

1. What type of control involves monitoring and adjusting ongoing activities and processes?
A. Benchmarking
B. Feedback control
C. Quality control
D. Concurrent control
E. Feedforward control

2. ______ involves identifying, studying, and building upon the best practices of organizational role models.
A. Benchmarking
B. *Kaizen*
C. Pareto analysis
D. The PDCA cycle
E. TQM

3. According to experts, to whom should internal auditors report their findings?
A. The corporate treasurer
B. The Internal Revenue Service
C. All employees
D. The head of accounting
E. The organization's top manager

4. A back-up plan for emergencies is called a ______ plan.
A. fall-back
B. contingency
C. reserve
D. benchmark
E. crisis

5. Which of the following is *not* one of the five types of product quality?
A. Value-based quality
B. User-based quality
C. Technology-based quality
D. Manufacturing-based quality
E. Product-based quality

6. The RATER service-quality dimension related to the provision of caring and individualized attention to customers is
A. assurance.
B. reliability.
C. responsiveness.
D. professionalism.
E. empathy.

7. Which of the following terms refers to anyone within the organization who relies on your work to get their work done?
A. Quality partner
B. Lateral associate
C. *Kaizen*
D. Internal customer
E. Downstream coworker

8. Which of the following do TQM advocates prefer, rather than the typical hierarchy?
A. No middle managers
B. Inverted organizations
C. Leaderless three-person teams
D. Teams of different specialists
E. Circular organizations

9. An acceptable quality measurement, on a TQM control chart, should fall
A. between the upper and lower control limits.
B. below the lower control limit.
C. outside the upper and lower control limits.
D. above the upper control limit.
E. on the median line.

10. According to Deming, ______ is the most important part of the production line.
A. technology
B. the employee
C. the supervisor
D. engineering
E. the consumer

ACE self-test

Want more questions? Visit the student Web site at http://business.college.hmco.com/students/ (select Kreitner, ***Management,*** **10e) and take the ACE quizzes for more practice.**

Managers-in-Action Videos

5A Finagle A Bagel's Management, Organization, and Production Finesse

A skilled management team, headed by husband-and-wife managing partners Alan Litchman and Laura B. Trust, helps this Boston-area chain of bagel cafes succeed in a competitive marketplace. We see the complex inner workings of a combination wholesale and retail food operation. A hands-on corporate culture keeps things humming and product quality first-rate. For more background, see **www.finagleabagel.com.**

Learning Objective: To demonstrate how to organize and control all the working parts of a complex growing business to achieve high product/service quality and customer satisfaction.

Links to Textual Material: **Chapter 8:** Decision making **Chapter 9:** Organizational structure and effectiveness **Chapter 17:** Organizational control; product and service quality; total quality management (TQM)

Discussion Questions:

1. Using Figure 8.1 as a guide, how many sources of decision complexity can you detect in this video case?
2. How important is feedforward control, as described in Chapter 17, at Finagle A Bagel?
3. Which one of the five types of product quality, discussed in Chapter 17, reigns supreme at Finagle A Bagel?
4. Which of the four principles of total quality management (TQM) can you find evidence of in this video case? Explain.
5. Which of Deming's 14 points are evident at Finagle A Bagel?

5B Training a Sales Employee at REI

Store manager Bob Voltz introduces us to REI, a consumer cooperative outdoor sporting goods store started in 1938 in Seattle. REI has become one of the biggest stores in the sporting goods business in the United States. "REI is more than a store, it's a lifestyle," says director of training Steve Kittel. We follow the progress of new employee Susan Lee as she explains life at REI. A five-step customer service program is detailed. For more background, see the Closing Case in Chapter 7 and **www.rei.com.**

Learning Objective: To illustrate how a well-run retail company achieves good customer service and high customer satisfaction.

Links to Textual Material: **Chapter 9:** Organizational culture **Chapter 11:** Training **Chapter 13:** Motivation **Chapter 17:** Organizational control; Product/service quality; Total quality management; Deming management

Discussion Questions:

1. Judging on the basis of everything you have read in this textbook, how would you rate the management of REI? Explain.
2. What is the connection between training new employees about company values and service quality?
3. Which components of organizational control, discussed in Chapter 17, are evident in this video case?
4. Using the Hands-On Exercise for Chapter 17, what score would you give the customer service quality at REI?
5. Which total quality management (TQM) principles covered in Chapter 17 are most evident at REI? Explain their practical significance.

Test Prepper Answers

CHAPTER 1

True/False: 1. False 2. False 3. False 4. True 5. True 6. False 7. True 8. True 9. False 10. False
Multiple-Choice: 1. E 2. C 3. B 4. C 5. E 6. A 7. E 8. D 9. E 10. D

CHAPTER 2

True/False: 1. True 2. True 3. False 4. False 5. False 6. True 7. False 8. False 9. False 10. True
Multiple-Choice: 1. B 2. B 3. E 4. B 5. C 6. A 7. C 8. D 9. E 10. E

CHAPTER 3

True/False: 1. True 2. False 3. True 4. False 5. False 6. False 7. False 8. False 9. False 10. True
Multiple-Choice: 1. E 2. A 3. D 4. C 5. B 6. B 7. B 8. D 9. E 10. E

CHAPTER 4

True/False: 1. False 2. True 3. False 4. True 5. False 6. False 7. True 8. False 9. True 10. True
Multiple-Choice: 1. A 2. B 3. C 4. C 5. B 6. D 7. A 8. A 9. B 10. C

CHAPTER 5

True/False: 1. False 2. True 3. False 4. True 5. True 6. True 7. False 8. True 9. True 10. False
Multiple-Choice: 1. E 2. E 3. B 4. C 5. E 6. C 7. B 8. C 9. A 10. B

CHAPTER 6

True/False: 1. True 2. False 3. False 4. False 5. True 6. False 7. True 8. True 9. False 10. True
Multiple-Choice: 1. C 2. C 3. A 4. B 5. B 6. E 7. D 8. D 9. C 10. C

CHAPTER 7

True/False: 1. True 2. False 3. False 4. True 5. False 6. False 7. False 8. False 9. True 10. True
Multiple-Choice: 1. D 2. D 3. D 4. D 5. E 6. A 7. B 8. E 9. A 10. D

CHAPTER 8

True/False: 1. False 2. False 3. True 4. True 5. True 6. False 7. True 8. False 9. False 10. True
Multiple-Choice: 1. D 2. D 3. E 4. C 5. C 6. B 7. A 8. E 9. B 10. A

CHAPTER 9

True/False: 1. False 2. False 3. True 4. False 5. True 6. True 7. True 8. False 9. False 10. True
Multiple-Choice: 1. D 2. B 3. C 4. B 5. E 6. B 7. C 8. A 9. A 10. D

CHAPTER 10

True/False: 1. False 2. False 3. True 4. True 5. True 6. True 7. False 8. False 9. True 10. True
Multiple-Choice: 1. D 2. A 3. B 4. B 5. C 6. B 7. A 8. D 9. E 10. C

CHAPTER 11

True/False: 1. True 2. True 3. True 4. True 5. False 6. False 7. False 8. True 9. False 10. True
Multiple-Choice: 1. B 2. E 3. A 4. C 5. C 6. A 7. D 8. C 9. A 10. B

CHAPTER 12

True/False: 1. True 2. False 3. True 4. True 5. False 6. False 7. True 8. False 9. False 10. True
Multiple-Choice: 1. A 2. D 3. B 4. C 5. A 6. D 7. B 8. D 9. D 10. E

CHAPTER 13

True/False: 1. False 2. True 3. True 4. False 5. False 6. True 7. True 8. False 9. False 10. True
Multiple-Choice: 1. E 2. B 3. E 4. C 5. A 6. E 7. C 8. E 9. A 10. E

CHAPTER 14

True/False: 1. True 2. True 3. False 4. False 5. False 6. False 7. True 8. False 9. True 10. True
Multiple-Choice: 1. A 2. E 3. B 4. A 5. E 6. D 7. A 8. C 9. E 10. E

CHAPTER 15

True/False: 1. True 2. False 3. True 4. True 5. False 6. False 7. False 8. True 9. True 10. True
Multiple-Choice: 1. D 2. C 3. A 4. C 5. B 6. A 7. C 8. E 9. A 10. B

CHAPTER 16

True/False: 1. False 2. True 3. False 4. True 5. False 6. False 7. True 8. False 9. True 10. False
Multiple-Choice: 1. C 2. D 3. D 4. E 5. D 6. E 7. A 8. E 9. B 10. A

CHAPTER 17

True/False: 1. True 2. True 3. False 4. True 5. False 6. True 7. False 8. False 9. False 10. True
Multiple-Choice: 1. D 2. A 3. E 4. B 5. C 6. E 7. D 8. D 9. A 10. E

References

CHAPTER 1

1. **Opening Quote** Henry Mintzberg, "Third-Generation Management Development," *Training & Development,* (March 2004): 30. (emphasis added.)
2. Joan Magretta, *What Management Is: How It Works and Why It's Everyone's Business* (New York: The Free Press, 2002), p. 7.
3. As quoted in Kathryn Tyler, "The Boss Makes the Weather," *HR Magazine,* 49 (May 2004): 93. Also see Kerry J. Sulkowicz, "The Corporate Shrink," *Fast Company,* no. 83 (June 2004): 48; and Marshall Goldsmith, "Nice Guys Finish First," *Fast Company,* no. 88 (November 2004): 123.
4. Ellen Van Velsor and Jean Brittain Leslie, "Why Executives Derail: Perspectives Across Time and Cultures," *Academy of Management Executive,* 9 (November 1995): 63. For related studies, see Frank Shipper and John E. Dillard Jr., "A Study of Impending Derailment and Recovery of Middle Managers Across Career Stages," *Human Resource Management,* 39 (Winter 2000): 331–345; and Heather Johnson, "Heat Wave," *Training,* 41 (March 2004): 14.
5. Jon Swartz, "Conway's Ethics Led to Firing," *USA Today* (October 5, 2004): 1B. For related research, see Bennett J. Tepper, "Consequences of Abusive Supervision," *Academy of Management Journal,* 43 (April 2000): 178–190.
6. Data from David Welch, "GM: Gunning It in China," *Business Week* (June 21, 2004): 112–115.
7. See Gary S. Becker, "How the Skeptics Missed the Power of Productivity," *Business Week* (January 12, 2004: 26; Michael J. Mandel, "Productivity: Who Wins, Who Loses," *Business Week* (March 22, 2004): 44–46; Del Jones and Barbara Hansen, "Productivity Gains Roll at Their Fastest Clip in 31 Years," *USA Today* (June 14, 2004): 1B– 2B; Michael J. Mandel, "Productivity: Will the Miracle Last?" *Business Week* (July 12, 2004): 32–35; and Rich Miller, "Raising Red Flags About Productivity," *Business Week* (November 22, 2004): 46.
8. Stanley Holmes, "A Plane That Could Change the Game," *Business Week* (August 9, 2004): 33.
9. Data from Evelyn L. Wright, "Cracks in the Greenhouse?" *Business Week* (July 26, 1999): 74, 76; and Jon Talton, "Real Price of Crude Oil Adds Up to More Than Dollars on the Barrel," *The Arizona Republic* (January 1, 2002): D1. Also see "Clearing the Air: Greenhouse Gas," *Business Week* (March 8, 2004): 11
10. For example, see Nicholas Varchaver, "How to Kick the Oil Habit," *Fortune* (August 23, 2004): 100–114; Otis Port, "Another Dawn for Solar Power," *Business Week* (September 6, 2004): 94–95; Jeffrey Ball, "Efforts to Reduce U.S. Addiction to Oil Are Few," *Wall Street Journal* (September 28, 2004): A8; Nicholas Stein, "Water, Water: But There's Not Enough to Go Around," *Fortune* (October 4, 2004): 115, 124; and Scott Kirsner, "Green Power," *Fast Company,* no. 89 (December 2004): 81–88.
11. Data from "How Much the Global Population Grows," *USA Today* (April 14, 2004): 1A. U.S. population data and projections are reported in Haya El Nasser, "U.S. Population Tops 290M, Could Reach 300M by 2007," *USA Today* (December 19, 2003): 3A; and "Growing Bigger by the Decade," *USA Today* (April 7, 2004): 1A.
12. Data from Margie Mason, "World Populace Will Max Out, Study Finds," *USA Today* (August 2, 2001): 8D.
13. See Elizabeth Weise, "Global Hunger Is Increasing, Report Says," *USA Today* (November 25, 2003): 13A.
14. Diane Brady, "Wanted: Eclectic Visionary with a Sense of Humor," *Business Week* (August 28, 2000): 143.
15. Even the legal definition of a manager/supervisor is being revamped by the U.S. government. See Margaret M. Clark, "NLRB Still Unsure How to Define 'Supervisor,'" *HR Magazine,* 48 (September 2003): 23–24; and Margaret M. Clark, "NLRB General Counsel's Office Issues Liberal Criteria for Defining 'Supervisor,'" *HR Magazine,* 49 (February 2004): 30.
16. Bruce Horovitz, "10 Things McDonald's Must Do to Get Its House in Order," *USA Today* (December 12, 2002): 3B.
17. Data from Robert Barker, "Why Things May Go Better with Coke," *Business Week* (February 10, 2003): 89.
18. Data from Lou Dobbs, "Dangerously Dependent," *U.S. News & World Report* (February 9, 2004): 40.
19. Data from Elizabeth Weise, "Seafood Sellers Stuck with a New Label? *USA Today* (September 30, 2004): 8D.
20. Data from Monica Gagnier, "3M's Sticky Situation," *Business Week* (November 1, 2004): 48.
21. For good overviews of the offshoring controversy, see Peter Coy, "The Future of Work," *Business Week* (March 22, 2004): 50–52; and Daniel Altman, "A More Productive Outsourcing Debate," *Business 2.0,* 5 (May 2004): 39.
22. See Pamela Babcock, "America's Newest Export: White-Collar Jobs," *HR Magazine,* 49 (April 2004): 50–57.
23. Diane E. Lewis, "Jobs Offshoring Here to Stay," *Arizona Republic* (October 17, 2004): D1.
24. James Sloan Allen, "Capitalism Globe Trots with Jordan," *USA Today* (August 16, 1999): 6B. Also see Sara Terry, "Free Trade Isn't Fair," *Fast Company,* no. 38 (September 2000): 250–258; and James Cox, "Think Tank Study Assails Globalization," *USA Today* (December 4, 2000): 5B.
25. A good historical overview of the quality movement can be found in R. Ray Gehani, "Quality Value-Chain: A Meta-Synthesis of Frontiers of Quality Movement," *Academy of Management Executive,* 7 (May 1993): 29–42.
26. See, for example, Michelle Kessler, "Rash of Recalls Dogs Tech Companies," *USA Today* (July 6, 2004): 1B; and Jena McGregor, "It's All About the Shoes," *Fast Company,* no. 86 (September 2004): 85–86.
27. See Kenneth R. Thompson, "Confronting the Paradoxes in a Total Quality Environment," *Organizational Dynamics,* 26 (Winter 1998): 62–74; and Thomas J. Douglas and William Q. Judge Jr., "Total Quality Management Implementation and Competitive Advantage: The Role of Structural Control and Exploration," *Academy of Management Journal,* 44 (February 2001): 158–169.
28. See, for example, David Stipp, "The Pentagon's Weather Nightmare," *Fortune* (February 9, 2004): 100–108; and John Carey, "Global Warming," *Business Week* (August 16, 2004): 60–69.
29. Drawn from Alex Lash, "Toyota's Green Giant," *Business 2.0,* 5 (May 2004): 72. Also see Patricia Sellers, "Hank Paulson's Secret Life," *Fortune* (January 12, 2004): 121–128; and John Ritter, "Buildings Designed in Cool Shades of 'Green,'" *USA Today* (March 31, 2004): 15A.
30. See Rogene A. Buchholz, "The Natural Environment: Does It Count?" *Academy of Management Executive,* 18 (May 2004): 130–133.
31. See Pratima Bansal and Kendall Roth, "Why Companies Go Green: A Model of Ecological Responsiveness," *Academy of Management Journal,* 43 (August 2000): 717–736; and Abby Schultz, "Can This Copy Shop Go Green?" *Fast Company,* no. 80 (March 2004): 33.
32. William McDonough and Michael Braungart, *Cradle to Grave: Remaking the Way We Make Things* (New York: North Point Press, 2002), pp. 15–16. For a brief overview, see Brian Dumaine, "Mr. Natural," *Fortune* (October 29, 2002): 184, 186.
33. Data from Gene Koretz, "On Wall Street, Green Is Golden," *Business Week* (January 8, 2001): 30.
34. Keith Naughton, "The CEO Party Is Over," *Newsweek* (January 6, 2003): 55. Also see Geoffrey Colvin, "The Verdict on Business: Presumed Guilty," *Fortune*

(November 15, 2004): 78.

35. Del Jones, "CEOs of the Future Get Formal Training to Take Giant Leap," *USA Today* (December 1, 2003): 2B. Also see Dale Buss, "Corporate Compasses," *HR Magazine*, 49 (June 2004): 127–132.
36. Julie Amparano, "As Ethics Crisis Grows, Businesses Take Action," *Arizona Republic* (November 24, 1996): D9.
37. See Janet Kornblum, "First U.S. Web Page Went Up 10 Years Ago," *USA Today* (December 11, 2001): 3D; Otis Port, "He Made the Net Work," *Business Week* (September 27, 2004): 20; and Otis Port, "Spinning the World's Web," *Business Week* (November 8, 2004): 16.
38. Data from a September 3, 2004 press release in **www.c-i-a.com**.
39. Data from Patricia Sellers, "Meg Whitman, eBay," *Fortune* (August 9, 2004): 106.
40. See Charles C. Mann, "Taming the Web," *Technology Review*, 104 (September 2001): 44–51; Jon Swartz, "Experts Fear Cyberspace Could Be Terrorists' Next Target," *USA Today* (October 9, 2001): 1B–2B; and Jennifer Reingold, "What We Learned in the New Economy," *Fast Company*, no. 80 (March 2004): 56–68.
41. Data from Eric Hellweg, "Excite.com—99.85% Off!!!" *Business 2.0*, 3 (January 2002): 18. More dot-com wreckage is reported in Jon Swartz, "Dot-Commers Buy Back Start-Ups at Bargain Prices," *USA Today* (January 22, 2002): 1B.
42. See Timothy J. Mullaney, "E-Biz Strikes Again!" *Business Week* (May 10, 2004): 80–82; and Timothy J. Mullaney, "The Net," *Business Week* (June 28, 2004): 116–117.
43. Quoted in Cheryl Dahle,"Putting Its Chips on the Net," *Fast Company*, no. 48 (July 2001): 154; Also see Peter J. Brews and Christopher L. Tucci, "Internetworking: Building Internet-Generation Companies," *Academy of Management Executive*, 17 (November 2003): 8–22; and Varun Grover and Pradipkumar Ramanlal, "Digital Economics and the E-business Dilemma," *Business Horizons*, 47 (July-August 2004): 71–80.
44. For example, see Nigel Andrews and Laura D'Andrea Tyson, "The Upwardly Global MBA," *Strategy + Business*, 36 (Fall 2004): 60–69.
45. For related research, see Frank Shipper, "A Study of the Psychometric Properties of the Managerial Skill Scales of the Survey of Management Practices," *Educational and Psychological Measurement*, 55 (June 1995): 468–479; Frank Shipper and Charles S. White, "Mastery, Frequency, and Interaction of Managerial Behaviors Relative to Subunit Effectiveness," *Human Relations*, 52 (January 1999): 49–66; and Frank Shipper and Jeanette Davy, "A Model and Investigation of Managerial Skills, Employees'Attitudes, and Managerial Performance," *The Leadership Quarterly*, 13, no. 2 (2002): 95–120.
46. See Henri Fayol, *General and Industrial Management*, trans. Constance Storrs (London: Isaac Pitman & Sons, 1949).
47. Clark L. Wilson, *How and Why Effective Managers Balance Their Skills: Technical, Teambuilding, Drive* (Columbia, Md.: Rockatech Multimedia Publishing, 2003), pp. 13, 18–20.
48. See Henry Mintzberg, "Managerial Work: Analysis from Observation," *Management Science*, 18 (October 1971): B97–B110.
49. See Scott Adams, *The Dilbert Principle* (New York: HarperBusiness, 1996); and Lisa A. Burke and Jo Ellen Moore, "Contemporary Satire of Corporate Managers: Time to Cut the Boss Some Slack?" *Business Horizons*, 42 (July-August 1999): 63–67.
50. "AMA Research," *Management Review*, 85 (July 1996): 10.
51. Henry Mintzberg, "The Manager's Job: Folklore and Fact," *Harvard Business Review*, 53 (July-August 1975): 54. For Mintzberg's recent thoughts about managing, see Jonathan Gosling and Henry Mintzberg,"The Five Minds of a Manager," *Harvard Business Review*, 81 (November 2003): 54–63.
52. As quoted in Alan Deutschman, "The CEO's Secret of Managing Time," *Fortune* (June 1, 1992): 136.
53. Jonathan Gosling and Henry Mintzberg, "Reflect Yourself," *HR Magazine*, 49 (September 2004): 151–152.
54. See Martin M. Broadwell and Carol Broadwell Dietrich, "Culture Clash: How to Turn Blue-Collar Workers into Good Supervisors," *Training*, 37 (March 2000): 34–36.
55. Adapted from Earnest R. Archer, "Things You Lose the Right to Do When You Become a Manager," *Supervisory Management*, 35 (July 1990): 8–9. Also see "Do I Have To?" *Business Week* (July 7, 2003): 14; and Nadine Heintz, "Why Can't We Be Friends?" *Inc.*, 26 (January 2004): 31–32.
56. See Henry Mintzberg, "The MBA Menace," *Fast Company*, no. 83 (June 2004): 31–32; Jennifer Merritt, "Masters of Barely Anything," *Business Week* (July 12, 2004): 22; and Diana Middleton, "Is the Focus Too Fine?" *Business Week* (October 18, 2004): 92.
57. See Ron Zemke, "The Honeywell Studies: How Managers Learn to Manage," *Training*, 22 (August 1985): 46–51.
58. Adapted from Robin Snell, "Graduating from the School of Hard Knocks?" *Journal of Management Development*, 8, no. 5 (1989): 23–30. Also see Sidney Finkelstein, *Why Smart Executives Fail* (New York: Portfolio, 2003); Michael E. Porter, Jay W. Lorsch, and Nitin Nohria, "Seven Surprises for New CEOs," *Harvard Business Review*, 82 (October 2004): 62–72; and David Welch, "Toughest Job Yet for This Mr. Fixit," *Business Week* (November 15, 2004): 72, 74.
59. Brad Stone, "Nike's Short Game," *Newsweek* (January 26, 2004): 40–41.
60. See Craig C. Lundberg, "Is There Really Nothing So Practical as a Good Theory?" *Business Horizons*, 47 (September-October 2004): 7–14.
61. See Paul Falcone, "The Business Partner Model," *HR Magazine*, 49 (August 2004): 121–125.
62. Drawn from Jim Hopkins, "PCs, Immigrants Help Launch Millions of Little Firms," *USA Today* (October 30, 2002): 1B.
63. Data from "Global 500: World's Largest Corporations," *Fortune* (July 26, 2004): 163, 182. For more, see Charles Fishman, "The Wal-Mart You Don't Know," *Fast Company*, no. 77 (December 2003): 68–80; and Jerry Useem, "Should We Admire Wal-Mart?" *Fortune* (March 8, 2004): 118, 120.
64. Data from Jim Hopkins, "Small Businesses Not Making Full Use of the Web," *USA Today* (August 28, 2001): 1B.
65. Data from Jim Hopkins, "Small Businesses Hold Off on Big Purchases," *USA Today* (October 16, 2001): 1B.
66. Data from Jim Hopkins, "New Bosses Should Develop Management Skills," *USA Today* (September 12, 2001): 9B; and Jim Hopkins, "Micro-Businesses Targeted as Source of Sales Revenue," *USA Today* (April 3, 2001); 1B.
67. Data from Jim Hopkins, "More Self-Employed Bet on Not Getting Sick, Hurt," *USA Today* (August 23, 2004): 1B.
68. See George Gendron, "The Failure Myth," *Inc.* (January 2001): 13.
69. See David R. Francis, "Spiking Stereotypes About Small Firms," *Christian Science Monitor* (May 7, 1993): 9; Gene Koretz, "A Surprising Finding on New-Business Mortality Rates," *Business Week* (June 14, 1993): 22; and James Aley, "Debunking the Failure Fallacy," *Fortune* (September 6, 1993): 21. For related reading, see Sydney Finkelstein, "The Myth of Managerial Superiority in Internet Startups: An Autopsy," *Organizational Dynamics*, 30 (Fall 2001): 172–185.
70. Data from Larry Light, "Small Business: The Job Engine Needs Fuel," *Business Week* (March 1, 1993): 78.
71. Data from Charles Burck, "Where Good Jobs Grow," *Fortune* (June 14, 1993): 22. Also see Gene Koretz, "Where the New Jobs Are," *Business Week* (March 20, 1995): 24.
72. For more on Birch's research, see Alan Webber, "Business Race Isn't Always to the Swift, but Bet That Way," *USA Today* (February 3, 1998): 15A. Also see "The Gazelle Theory," *Inc.*, 23 (May 29, 2001): 28–29; and Magnus Aronsson, "Education Matters—But Does Entrepreneurship Education? An Interview with David Birch," *Academy of Management Learning and Education*, 3 (September 2004): 289–292.
73. For data on pay in big companies versus small companies, see Michael Mandel, "Big Players Offer Better Pay," *Business Week* (August 30, 1999): 30. For small busi-

ness health insurance data, see Howard Gleckman, "Whose Plan Is Healthier?" *Business Week* (May 24, 2004): 90, 92; and Jim Hopkins, "Rising Benefit Costs Hurt Small Businesses' Financial Health," *USA Today* (June 4, 2004): 1B–2B.

74. For interesting reading on partnerships, see Patrick J. Sauer, "How to Work with a Partner (Year After Year After Year)," *Inc.*, 26 (October 2004): 88–89; and Michael S. Hopkins, "How to Work (If You Must) with Your Spouse," *Inc.*, 26 (October 2004): 91. Consulting is discussed in Suzanne McGee, "Getting Started: Brains for Hire," *Inc.*, 26 (April 2004): 61, 63.
75. See Susan J. Wells, "Franshisors Walk a Fine Line," *HR Magazine*, 49 (August 2004): 48–53.
76. See recent issues of *Inc.* and *Fast Company* magazines for inspiring small-business success stories.
77. Howard H. Stevenson and J. Carlos Jarillo, "A Paradigm of Entrepreneurship: Entrepreneurial Management," *Strategic Management Journal*, 11 (Summer 1990): 23 (emphasis added).
78. As quoted in Rob Walker, "Because Optimism Is Essential," *Inc.*, 26 (April 2004): 150.
79. Ibid. Also see John Case, "Why 20 Million of You Can't Be Wrong," *Inc.*, 26 (April 2004): 100–105.
80. As quoted in Bruce Rosenstein, "Inspiration for Entrepreneur Wannabes," *USA Today* (October 11, 2004): 9B. Also see Jim Hopkins, "Venture Capital 101: Entrepreneur Courses Increase," *USA Today* (January 5, 2004): 1B; Jim Hopkins, "Entrepreneurs Are Born, But Can They Be Taught?" *USA Today* (April 7, 2004): 1B–2B ; and Dean A. Shepherd, "Educating Entrepreneurship Students About Emotion and Learning from Failure," *Academy of Management Learning and Education*, 3 (September 2004): 274–287.
81. Stephanie Armour, "UBUBU Boldly Launches Start-Up in Cyberspace," *USA Today* (June 19, 2000): 3B. Also see Marc Malone, "The Small Business Ego Trap," *Business Horizons*, 47 (July-August 2004): 17–22.
82. Steven Berglas, "GIs for Guts," *Inc.*, 22 (May 2000): 45.
83. Joshua Hyatt, "The Real Secrets of Entrepreneurs," *Fortune* (November 15, 2004): 186. Also see Andrew Park, "Thinking Out of the Box," *Business Week* (November 22, 2004): 22.

CHAPTER 2

1. **Opening Quote** John W. Gardner, *Self-Renewal: The Individual and the Innovative Society* (New York: Harper & Row, 1964), chap. 11.
2. For an interesting historical perspective, see David Strutton, "The Courtly Path to Managerial Leadership," *Business Horizons*, 47 (January-February 2004): 7–18.
3. Alonzo L. McDonald, as quoted in Alan M. Kantrow, ed., "Why History Matters to Managers," *Harvard Business Review*, 64 (January-February 1986): 82. Also see Arthur G. Bedeian, "The Gift of Professional Maturity," *Academy of Management Learning and Education*, 3 (March 2004): 92–98.
4. Barbara S. Lawrence, "Historical Perspective: Using the Past to Study the Present," *Academy of Management Review*, 9 (April 1984): 307.
5. See Morgan Witzel, *Fifty Key Figures in Management* (London: Routledge, 2003). A review of this book by W. Jack Duncan can be found in "Book Reviews," *Academy of Management Review*, 29 (October 2004): 687–689.
6. For a discussion in this area, see "How Business Schools Began," *Business Week* (October 19, 1963): 114–116. Also see John Trinkaus, "Urwick on the Business Academy," *Business Horizons*, 35 (September-October 1992): 25–29.
7. The top ten most influential management thinkers of the twentieth century, as selected by the readers of *Business Horizons* magazine, are discussed in Dennis W. Organ, "And the Winners Are. . . ," *Business Horizons*, 43 (March-April 2000): 1–3.
8. See Marian M. Extejt and Jonathan E. Smith, "The Behavioral Sciences and Management: An Evaluation of Relevant Journals," *Journal of Management*, 16 (September 1990): 539–551. For a list of 40 management-oriented periodicals, see Jonathan L. Johnson and Philip M. Podsakoff, "Journal Influence in the Field of Management: An Analysis Using Salancik's Index in a Dependency Network," *Academy of Management Journal*, 37 (October 1994): 1392–1407.
9. For advice on dealing with information overload, see Suzy Wetlaufer, "Thanks for Asking," *Harvard Business Review*, 80 (February 2002): 10.
10. See the instructive timeline in "Management Ideas Through Time," *Management Review*, 87 (January 1998): 16–19. Also see Daniel A. Wren and Ronald G. Greenwood, *Management Innovators: The People and Ideas That Shaped Modern Business* (New York: Oxford University Press, 1998).
11. For ideas about the related area of management as a profession, see Rakesh Khurana, "You Got a License to Run That Company?" *Harvard Business Review*, 82 (February 2004): 14.
12. Craig C. Lundberg, "Is There Really Nothing So Practical as a Good Theory?" *Business Horizons*, 47 (September-October 2004): 10.
13. Based on Jennifer Alsever Beauprez, "Retired CEO Takes Expertise to Iraq," *Arizona Republic* (December 13, 2003): A26.
14. See Henri Fayol, *General and Industrial Management*, trans. Constance Storrs (London: Isaac Pitman & Sons, 1949). An interesting review by Nancy M. Carter of Fayol's book can be found in Allen C. Bluedorn, ed., "Special Book Review Section on the Classics of Management," *Academy of Management Review*, 11 (April 1986): 454–456.
15. Stephen J. Carroll and Dennis J. Gillen, "Are the Classical Management Functions Useful in Describing Managerial Work?" *Academy of Management Review*, 12 (January 1987): 48.
16. Frank B. Copley, *Frederick W. Taylor: Father of Scientific Management* (New York: Harper & Brothers, 1923), I: 3. Also see the brief profile of Taylor in "Taylorism," *Business Week*: 100 Years of Innovation (Summer 1999): 16.
17. For expanded treatment, see Frank B. Copley, *Frederick W. Taylor: The Principles of Scientific Management* (New York: Harper & Brothers, 1911). A good retrospective review of Taylor's classic writings may be found in Bluedorn, ed., "Special Book Review Section on the Classics of Management," pp. 443–447. Robert Kanigel's *One Best Way*, a modern biography of Taylor, is reviewed in Alan Farnham, "The Man Who Changed Work Forever," *Fortune* (July 21, 1997): 114.
18. For an interesting update on Taylor, see Christopher Farrell, "Micromanaging from the Grave," *Business Week* (May 15, 1995): 34.
19. George D. Babcock, *The Taylor System in Franklin Management*, 2nd ed. (New York: Engineering Magazine Company, 1917), p. 31.
20. Taylor's seminal 1911 book *The Principles of Scientific Management* was recently selected by a panel of management experts as the most influential management book of the twentieth century: See Arthur G. Bedeian and Daniel A. Wren, "Most Influential Management Books of the 20th Century," *Organizational Dynamics*, 29 (Winter 2001): 221–225. Also see Oswald Jones, "Scientific Management, Culture and Control: A First-Hand Account of Taylorism in Practice," *Human Relations*, 53 (May 2000): 631–653.
21. For an alternative perspective and detailed critique of Taylor's experiments with pig iron handlers, see Charles D. Wrege and Richard M. Hodgetts, "Frederick W. Taylor's 1899 Pig Iron Observations: Examining Fact, Fiction, and Lessons for the New Millennium," *Academy of Management Journal*, 43 (December 2000): 1283–1291.
22. Frederick W. Taylor, *Shop Management* (New York: Harper & Brothers, 1911), p. 22.
23. Frank B. Gilbreth and Lillian M. Gilbreth, *Applied Motion Study* (New York: Sturgis & Walton, 1917), p. 42. A retrospective review of the Gilbreths' writings, by Daniel J. Brass, can be found in Bluedorn, ed., "Special Book Review Section on the Classics of Management," pp. 448–451.

24. See Frank B. Gilbreth Jr., and Ernestine Gilbreth Carey, *Cheaper by the Dozen* (New York: Thomas Y. Crowell, 1948).
25. For example, see the Gantt chart on p. 64 of Tom D. Conkright, "So You're Going to Manage a Project," *Training*, 35 (January 1998): 62–67.
26. For detailed coverage of Gantt's contributions, see H. L. Gantt, *Work, Wages, and Profits*, 2nd ed. (New York: Engineering Magazine Company, 1913). An interesting update on Gantt's contributions can be found in Peter B. Peterson, "Training and Development: The Views of Henry L. Gantt (1861–1919)," *SAM Advanced Management Journal*, 52 (Winter 1987): 20–23.
27. Good historical overviews of the quality movement include Ron Zemke, "A Bluffer's Guide to TQM," *Training*, 30 (April 1993): 48–55; R. Ray Gehani, "Quality Value-Chain: A Meta-Synthesis of Frontiers of Quality Movement," *Academy of Management Executive*, 7 (May 1993): 29–42; and Sangit Chatterjee and Mustafa Yilmaz, "Quality Confusion: Too Many Gurus, Not Enough Disciples," *Business Horizons*, 36 (May-June 1993): 15–18. A look back at the roots of the quality movement can be found in Geoffrey Colvin, "A Concise History of Management Hooey," *Fortune* (June 28, 2004): 166–176.
28. Mary Walton, *Deming Management at Work* (New York: Putnam, 1990), p. 13. See John Hillkirk, "World-Famous Quality Expert Dead at 93," *USA Today* (December 21, 1993): 1B–2B; Peter Nulty, "The National Business Hall of Fame: W. Edwards Deming," *Fortune* (April 4, 1994): 124; Keki R. Bhote, " Dr. W. Edwards Deming—A Prophet with Belated Honor in His Own Country," *National Productivity Review*, 13 (Spring 1994): 153–159; Anne Willette, "Deming Legacy Gives Firms Quality Challenge," *USA Today* (October 19, 1994): 2B; and M. R. Yilmaz and Sangit Chatterjee, "Deming and the Quality of Software Development," *Business Horizons*, 40 (November-December 1997): 51–58.
29. See Jack Gordon, "An Interview with Joseph M. Juran," *Training*, 31 (May 1994): 35–41. Deming and Juran are saluted in Otis Port, "The Kings of Quality," *Business Week* (August 30, 2004): 20.
30. Zemke, "A Bluffer's Guide to TQM," p. 51. Also see Joseph M. Juran, "Made in U.S.A.: A Renaissance in Quality," *Harvard Business Review*, 71 (July-August 1993): 42–50.
31. See Armand V. Feigenbaum, "How Total Quality Counters Three Forces of International Competitiveness," *National Productivity Review*, 13 (Summer 1994): 327–330. More of Feigenbaum's ideas can be found in Del Jones, "Employers Going for Quality Hires, Not Quantity," *USA Today* (December 11, 1997): 1B.
32. Crosby's more recent ideas may be found in Philip B. Crosby, *Completeness: Quality for the 21st Century* (New York: Dutton, 1992).
33. Edwin A. Locke, "The Ideas of Frederick W. Taylor: An Evaluation," *Academy of Management Review*, 7 (January 1982): 22–23. Also see David H. Freedman, "Is Management Still a Science?" *Harvard Business Review*, 70 (November-December 1992): 26–38.
34. See Donald W. Fogarty, Thomas R. Hoffman, and Peter W. Stonebraker, *Production and Operations Management* (Cincinnati, Ohio: South-Western Publishing Co., 1989), pp. 7–8; and Vincent A. Mabert, "Operations in the American Economy: Liability or Asset?" *Business Horizons*, 35 (July-August 1992): 3–5.
35. The Hawthorne studies are discussed in detail in F. J. Roethlisberger and William J. Dickson, *Management and the Worker* (Cambridge, Mass.: Harvard University Press, 1939). Dennis W. Organ's review of this classic book, in which he criticizes the usual textbook treatment of it, can be found in Bluedorn, ed., "Special Book Review Section on the Classics of Management," pp. 459–463.
36. See Ellen S. O'Connor, "The Politics of Management Thought: A Case Study of the Harvard Business School and the Human Relations School," *Academy of Management Review*, 24 (January 1999): 117–131.
37. See Henry C. Metcalf and L. Urwick, *Dynamic Administration: The Collected Papers of Mary Parker Follett* (New York: Harper & Brothers, 1942); Mary Parker Follett, *Freedom and Coordination* (London: Management Publications Trust, 1949). A review by Diane L. Ferry of *Dynamic Administration* can be found in Bluedorn, ed., "Special Book Review Section on the Classics of Management," pp. 451–454.
38. See L. D. Parker, "Control in Organizational Life: The Contribution of Mary Parker Follett," *Academy of Management Review*, 9 (October 1984): 736–745; Albie M. Davis, "An Interview with Mary Parker Follett," *Negotiation Journal*, 5 (July 1989): 223–225; and Dana Wechsler Linden, "The Mother of Them All," *Forbes* (January 16, 1995): 75–76.
39. See David Jacobs, "Book Review Essay: Douglas McGregor—The Human Side of Enterprise in Peril," *Academy of Management Review*, 29 (April 2004): 293–296.
40. For a case study of a military leader's transition from a Theory X style to a Theory Y style, see D. Michael Abrashoff, "Retention Through Redemption," *Harvard Business Review*, 79 (February 2001): 136–141.
41. John B. Miner, "The Rated Importance, Scientific Validity, and Usefulness of Organizational Behavior Theories: A Quantitative Review," *Academy of Management Learning and Education*, 2 (September 2003): 250–268.
42. For example, the new field of positive psychology has evolved into positive organizational behavior. See Martin E.P. Seligman and Mihaly Csikszentmihalyi, "Positive Psychology: An Introduction, *American Psychologist*, 55 (January 2000): 5–14; and Thomas A. Wright, "Positive Organizational Behavior: An Idea Whose Time Has Truly Come," *Journal of Organizational Behavior*, 24 (June 2003): 437–442.
43. The founders of Hewlett-Packard Co. are recognized for their pioneering efforts to put people first in Peter Burrows, "Architects of the Info Age," *Business Week* (March 29, 2004): 22.
44. An interesting and instructive timeline of human resource milestones can be found in "Training and Development in the 20th Century," *Training*, 35 (September 1998): 49–56.
45. For a statistical interpretation of the Hawthorne studies, see Richard Herbert Franke and James D. Kaul, "The Hawthorne Experiments: First Statistical Interpretation," *American Sociological Review*, 43 (October 1978): 623–643. Also see Stephen R. G. Jones, "Worker Interdependence and Output: The Hawthorne Studies Reevaluated," *American Sociological Review*, 55 (April 1990): 176–190.
46. Russell L. Ackoff, "Science in the Systems Age: Beyond IE, OR, and MS," *Operations Research*, 21 (May-June 1973): 664.
47. Charles J. Coleman and David D. Palmer, "Organizational Application of System Theory," *Business Horizons*, 16 (December 1973): 77.
48. Chester I. Barnard, *The Functions of the Executive* (Cambridge, Mass.: Harvard University Press, 1938), p. 65.
49. Ibid., p. 82. A retrospective review, by Thomas L. Keon, of Barnard's *The Functions of the Executive* can be found in Bluedorn, ed., "Special Book Review Section on the Classics of Management," pp. 456–459.
50. For details, see Lori Verstegen Ryan and William G. Scott, "Ethics and Organizational Reflection: The Rockefeller Foundation and Postwar 'Moral Deficits,' 1942–1954," *Academy of Management Review*, 20 (April 1995): 438–461.
51. Ludwig von Bertalanffy, "The History and Status of General Systems Theory," *Academy of Management Journal*, 15 (December 1972): 411.
52. For an example of an economic/industrial hierarchy of organizations, see Figure 2 (p. 774) in Philip Rich, "The Organizational Taxonomy: Definition and Design," *Academy of Management Review*, 17 (October 1992): 758–781.
53. Susan Albers Mohrman and Allan M. Mohrman Jr., "Organizational Change and Learning," in *Organizing for the Future: The New Logic for Managing Complex Organizations*, eds. Jay R. Galbraith, Edward E. Lawler III, and Associates (San Francisco: Jossey-

Bass, 1993), p. 89. For an excellent overview of organizational learning, see David A. Garvin, "Building a Learning Organization," *Harvard Business Review*, 71 (July-August 1993): 78–91. Also see Robert Aubrey and Paul M. Cohen, *Working Wisdom: Timeless Skills and Vanguard Strategies for Learning Organizations* (San Francisco: Jossey-Bass, 1995); and Timothy T. Baldwin and Camden C. Danielson, "Building a Learning Strategy at the Top: Interviews with Ten of America's CLOs," *Business Horizons*, 43 (November-December 2000): 5–14.

54. For an excellent collection of readings, see *Harvard Business Review on Knowledge Management* (Boston: Harvard Business School Publishing, 1998).
55. For example, see Gary Weiss, "Chaos Hits Wall Street—The Theory, That Is," *Business Week* (November 2, 1992): 138–140.
56. See Benyamin Bergmann Lichtenstein, "Self-Organized Transitions: A Pattern amid the Chaos of Transformative Change," *Academy of Management Executive*, 14 (November 2000): 128–141; and Polly LaBarre, "Organize Yourself," *Fast Company*, no. 50 (September 2001): 60.
57. Fred Luthans, *Introduction to Management: A Contingency Approach* (New York: McGraw-Hill, 1976), p. 28. Also see Henry L. Tosi Jr. and John W. Slocum Jr., "Contingency Theory: Some Suggested Directions," *Journal of Management*, 10 (Spring 1984): 9–26.
58. Y. K. Shetty, "Contingency Management: Current Perspective for Managing Organizations," *Management International Review*, 14, no. 6 (1974): 27.
59. See Joseph W. McGuire, "Management Theory: Retreat to the Academy," *Business Horizons*, 25 (July-August 1982): 37.
60. See Laurence Prusak and Thomas H. Davenport, "Who Are the Gurus' Gurus?" *Harvard Business Review*, 81 (December 2003): 14–16; Bruce Rosenstein, "Pipe Dream Leads to Memoir," *USA Today* (August 9, 2004): 5B; and Peter F. Drucker, *The Daily Drucker: 366 Days of Insight and Motivation for Getting the Right Things Done* (New York : HarperBusiness, 2004).
61. Data from John A. Byrne, "How the Best Get Better," *Business Week* (September 14, 1987): 98–99.
62. Data from Ryan Underwood, "A *Field Guide* to the Gurus," *Fast Company*, no. 88 (November 2004): 104.
63. See Del Jones, "It's Nothing Personal? On 'Apprentice,' It's All Personal," *USA Today* (March 26, 2004): 6B; and Del Jones and Bill Keveney, "10 Lessons of 'The Apprentice,'" *USA Today* (April 15, 2004): 1A, 5A.
64. For a variety of perspectives, see Kevin Maney, "True Believers Ignite Super Sales Rate for 'Good to Great,'" *USA Today* (May 18, 2004): 1B–2B; Ryan Underwood, "The Fable," *Fast Company*, no. 84 (July 2004): 82–85; Martin Kihn, "In Search of Dwarfs," *Fast Company*, no. 87 (October 2004): 40; Jennifer Reingold and Ryan Underwood, "Was *Built to Last* Built to Last?" *Fast Company*, no. 88 (November 2004): 102–111; and Daniel McGinn, "Re-engineering 2.0," *Newsweek* (November 22, 2004): 59.
65. Craig M. McAllaster, "The 5 P's of Change: Leading Change by Effectively Utilizing Leverage Points Within an Organization," *Organizational Dynamics*, 33, no. 3 (2004): 321.
66. See Michael A. Hitt and R. Duane Ireland, "Peters and Waterman Revisited: The Unended Quest for Excellence," *Academy of Management Executive*, 1 (May 1987): 91–98.
67. Regarding management fads, see Adam Hanft, "What I Learned from *The Sopranos*," *Inc.*, 26 (May 2004): 130; Danny Miller, Jon Hartwick, and Isabelle Le Breton-Miller, "How to Detect a Management Fad—and Distinguish It from a Classic," *Business Horizons*, 47 (July-August 2004): 7–16; and Stanley Bing, "Remembrance of Fads Past," *Fortune* (November 15, 2004): 244.
68. Excerpted from Amy Cortese, "Weapons of Mass Disruption," *Business 2.0* (January 2002): 44.

CHAPTER 3

1. **Opening Quote** As quoted in R. Stanley Williams, "You Ain't Seen Nothin' Yet," *Business 2.0* (September 26, 2000): 168.
2. For general trends and implications, see Karen Colteryahn and Patty Davis, "8 Trends You Need to Know Now," *T + D*, 58 (January 2004): 28–36; and Holly Dolezalek and Tammy Galvin, "Future Scan," *Training*, 41 (September 2004): 30–36.
3. For example, see Jenny S.Y. Lee et al., "Changing Roles and Values of Female Consumers in China," *Business Horizons*, 47 (May-June 2004): 17–22; Clay Chandler, "Little Emperors," *Fortune* (October 4, 2004): 138–150; and "Population Grows Older," *USA Today* (October 5, 2004): 1B.
4. Janet Kornblum, "'A Nation of Caregivers,'" *USA Today* (April 6, 2004): 6D.
5. Data from Robert J. Samuelson, "Protecting the Welfare State," *Newsweek* (March 8, 2004): 37.
6. For instructive reading, see Walter Updegrave, "Real-World Retirement Guide," *Money*, 33 (November 2004): 95–98; Phillip Longman, "Fixing Social Security," *Fortune* (November 1, 2004): 78; Christopher Farrell, "The Worry Years," *Business Week* (November 29, 2004): 144; and Walter Updegrave, "When to Take Social Security," *Money*, 33 (December 2004): 69–70.
7. Mark Yost, "GE Focuses of Fridges from Bottom Freezer Up," *USA Today* (November 29, 2002): 10B.
8. Data from Dean Foust, "For Banks, Money Also Talks in Spanish," *Business Week* (January 13, 2003): 111; and Nick Pachetti, "Media *gigante*," *Money*, 33 (October 2004): 68, 71.
9. See Jennifer Schramm, "A Worker Gap Ahead?" *HR Magazine*, 48 (June 2003): 240; and Steve Bates, "Labor Shortage? What Labor Shortage?" *HR Magazine*, 48 (October 2003): 12.
10. See Jeff Barbian, "Get 'Em While They're Young," *Training*, 41 (January 2004): 44–46; and Ann Pomeroy, "Global Competition Increases," *HR Magazine*, 49 (August 2004): 16.
11. Data from Barbara Hagenbaugh, "Good Help Hard to Find for Manufacturers," *USA Today* (April 16, 2004): 1B. Also see Craig R. Taylor, "Retention Leadership," *T+D*, 58 (March 2004): 41–45; Gail Johnson, "The Tomorrow Team," *Training*, 41 (August 2004): 16; and Susan Meisinger, "Shortage of Skilled Workers Threatens Economy," *HR Magazine*, 49 (November 2004): 12.
12. Data from Troy Segal, "When Johnny's Whole Family Can't Read," *Business Week* (July 20, 1992): 68–70. Also see Lindsey Tanner, "Perhaps Johnny Really Can't Read as Well as Jane," *USA Today* (April 28, 2004): 9D.
13. "Illiteracy Still a Problem," *USA Today* (November 29, 2000): 1A.
14. Data from Tammy Galvin, "2001 Industry Report," *Training*, 38 (October 2001): 40–75.
15. Russell Wild, "Great Jobs," *AARP: The Magazine*, 46 (November-December 2003): 52. Also see Steven Dahlberg, "The New Elderhood," *Training*, 41 (February 2004): 46–47; and Ron Schoolmeester, "Retirement Isn't Just a Date—It's a New Life," *USA Today* (November 23, 2004): 1A, 8A.
16. Mark Clements, "What We Say About Aging," *Parade Magazine* (December 12, 1993): 4. Also see Sharon Jayson, "It's Time to Grow Up—Later," *USA Today* (September 30, 2004): 1D–2D.
17. See Kimberly A. Wrenn and Todd J. Maurer, "Beliefs About Older Workers' Learning and Development Behavior in Relation to Beliefs About Malleability of Skills, Age-Related Decline, and Control," *Journal of Applied Social Psychology*, 34 (February 2004): 223–242; and Ruth Kanfer and Phillip L. Ackerman, "Aging, Adult Development, and Work Motivation," *Academy of Management Review*, 29 (July 2004): 440–458.
18. Excerpted from Paul Mayrand, "Older Workers: A Problem or the Solution?" *Proceedings: Textbook Authors Conference* (AARP: Washington, D.C., October 21, 1992), pp. 28–29. © Reprinted by permission of AARP.
19. See Martin M. Greller and Linda K. Stroh, "Making the Most of 'Late-Career' for Employers and Workers Themselves: Becoming Elders Not Relics," *Organizational Dynamics*, 33, no. 2

(2004): 202–214; and Jann Freed, "The Next Opportunity," *Training*, 41 (March 2004): 74.
20. Data from "Mass Layoffs in USA Idle 2.5 Million in 2001," *USA Today* (January 30, 2002): 1B.
21. Data compiled from "Employment & Unemployment (Mass layoffs)," **www.bls.gov**.
22. Robert Aubrey and Paul M. Cohen, *Working Wisdom: Timeless Skills and Vanguard Strategies for Learning Organizations* (San Francisco: Jossey-Bass, 1995), p. 29.
23. See Michelle Conlin, "And Now, the Just-in-Time Employee," *Business Week* (August 28, 2000): 168–170.
24. John Huey, "Where Managers Will Go," *Fortune* (January 27, 1992): 51.
25. See Sue Kirchhoff, "Minorities Haven't Felt Economic Growth," *USA Today* (June 17, 2004): 4B.
26. Data from **www.bls.gov**.
27. Barbara Hagenbaugh, "Women's Pay Suffers Setback vs. Men's," *USA Today* (August 27, 2004): 4B.
28. Data from Aaron Bernstein, "Women's Pay: Why the Gap Remains a Chasm," *Business Week* (June 14, 2004): 58–59.
29. For specific data, see Kimberly Blanton, "More Women in Top-Tier Jobs Earn 6 Figures," *Arizona Republic* (April 11, 2004): D1, D5; Emily Thornton, "Fed Up—and Fighting Back," *Business Week* (September 20, 2004): 100–101.
30. Data from "Female Managers Still Earn Less, GAO Says," *USA Today* (January 24, 2002): 1B.
31. See Linda Tischler, "Where Are the Women? So What Happened? *Fast Company*, no. 79 (February 2004): 52–60; Brian Hindo, "Women's Pace: Steady But Slow," *Business Week* (April 12, 2004): 14; Karyn-Siobhan Robinson, "For Working Women, Job Equality Elusive," *HR Magazine*, 49 (May 2004): 36; and Nancy Lockwood, "The Glass Ceiling: Domestic and International Perspectives," 2004 Research Quarterly, *HR Magazine*, 49 (June 2004): 1–11.
32. Ann M. Morrison and Mary Ann Von Glinow, "Women and Minorities in Management," *American Psychologist*, 45 (February 1990): 200 (emphasis added).
33. Data from Del Jones, "2003: Year of the Woman Among the 'Fortune' 500," *USA Today* (December 30, 2003): 1B–2B; and Kimberly L. Allers, "The New Black Power on Wall Street," *Fortune* (June 28, 2004): 126–134.
34. Data from Del Jones, "Women Make Gains on Boards, But Room to Grow," *USA Today* (December 4, 2003): 4B.
35. As quoted in Rhonda Richards, "More Women Poised for Role as CEO," *USA Today* (March 26, 1996): 2B. Also see Anna Fels, "Do Women Lack Ambition?" *Harvard Business Review*, 82 (April 2004): 50–60; and Matt Krantz, "More Women Take CFO Roles," *USA Today* (October 13, 2004): 3B.
36. Richard McGill Murphy, "The New Soccer Moms," *Fortune* (July 26, 2004): 156D.
37. For specifics, see Stephanie Armour, "Minority Job Losses Shrink Gains Made in '90s," *USA Today* (January 14, 2002): 1B.
38. See Michelle Conlin and Aaron Bernstein, "Working. . . and Poor," *Business Week* (May 31, 2004): 58–68.
39. Data from Kathryn Tyler, "Making the Transition," *HR Magazine*, 49 (October 2004): 97–102.
40. Gene Koretz, "Taking Stock of the Flexible Work Force," *Business Week* (July 24, 1989): 12.
41. Abrahm Lustgarten, "A Hot, Steaming Cup of Customer Awareness," *Fortune* (November 15, 2004): 192. For more, see Andy Serwer, "Hot Starbucks to Go," *Fortune* (January 26, 2004): 60–74.
42. Data from Todd J. Thorsteinson, "Job Attitudes of Part-Time vs. Full-Time Workers: A Meta-Analytic Review," *Journal of Occupational and Organizational Psychology*, 76 (June 2003): 151–177.
43. See Martha Frase-Blunt, "Short-Term Executives," *HR Magazine*, 49 (June 2004): 110–114.
44. Sue Kirchhoff and Barbara Hagenbaugh, "Immigration: A Fiscal Boon or Financial Strain?" *USA Today* (January 22, 2004): 2B.
45. Sue Kirchhoff, "Immigrants Chase American Dream," *USA Today* (August 5, 2004): 1B–2B.
46. Tamara Henry, "Societal Shifts Could Alter Education by Midcentury," *USA Today* (February 26, 2001): 6D. Also see "Celebrating Hispanic People, Culture," *USA Today* (September 15, 2004): 1A.
47. Data from Kate Bonamici, "Going Long on Latinos," *Fortune* (February 23, 2004): 153; and Brian Grow, "Hispanic Nation," *Business Week* (March 15, 2004): 58–70. Also see Robert Rodriguez, "Tapping the Hispanic Labor Pool," *HR Magazine*, 49 (April 2004): 72–79.
48. Data from Del Jones, "Setting Diversity's Foundation in the Bottom Line," *USA Today* (October 15, 1996): 4B.
49. See Gary Becker, "The Wise Way to Stem Illegal Immigration," *Business Week* (April 26, 2004): 28.
50. For more, see Martha Frase-Blunt, "Selecting a Diversity Consultant," *HR Magazine*, 49 (June 2004): 147–155; David A. Thomas, "Diversity as Strategy," *Harvard Business Review*, 82 (September 2004): 98–108; and Gail Johnson, "Time to Broaden Diversity," *Training*, 41 (September 2004): 16.
51. For example, see Cora Daniels, "50 Best Companies for Minorities," *Fortune* (June 28, 2004): 136–146.
52. Jack McDevitt, "Are We Becoming a Country of Haters?" *USA Today* (September 2, 1992): 9A.
53. Adapted from Sheryl Hilliard Tucker and Kevin D. Thompson, "Will Diversity = Opportunity + Advancement for Blacks?" *Black Enterprise*, 21 (November 1990): 50–60; and Lee Gardenswartz and Anita Rowe, "Important Steps for Implementing Diversity Training," *Mosaics*, 8 (July-August 2002): 5.
54. Research support can be found in Joseph J. Martocchio, "Age-Related Differences in Employee Absenteeism: A Meta-Analysis," *Psychology and Aging*, 4 (December 1989): 409–414.
55. Douglas T. Hall and Victoria A. Parker, "The Role of Workplace Flexibility in Managing Diversity," *Organizational Dynamics*, 22 (Summer 1993): 8.
56. Martin Kasindorf, "Slim-Fast Drops Goldberg over Bush Puns," *USA Today* (July 15, 2004): 1B.
57. Steven L. Wartick and Robert E. Rude, "Issues Management: Corporate Fad or Corporate Function?" *California Management Review*, 29 (Fall 1986): 124–140. Also see Andrew J. Hoffman, "Institutional Evolution and Change: Environmentalism and the U.S. Chemical Industry," *Academy of Management Journal*, 42 (August 1999): 351–371.
58. See, for example, John Ritter, "California Tries to Slam Lid on Big Boxed Wal-Mart," *USA Today* (March 2, 2004): 1B–2B; Stephanie Armour, "'Rife with Discrimination,'" *USA Today* (June 24, 2004): 3B; and Cora Daniels, "Wal-Mart's Women Problem," *Fortune* (July 12, 2004): 28.
59. Emily Kaiser, "Wal-Mart Looks to Reputation," *USA Today* (September 9, 2004): 5B.
60. Based on Jim Hopkins, "Wal-Mart Widens Political Reach, Giving Primarily to GOP," *USA Today* (February 3, 2004): 1B.
61. David B. Yoffie and Mary Kwak, "Playing by the Rules," *Harvard Business Review*, 79 (June 2001): 119–120.
62. Drawn from S. Prakash Sethi, "Serving the Public Interest: Corporate Political Action for the 1980s," *Management Review*, 70 (March 1981): 8–11. Also see David J. Dent, "Hands On: Playing Politics," *Inc.*, 26 (September 2004): 29–30.
63. Based on James Mehring, "Soft Money's Flabby Return," *Business Week* (April 26, 2004): 30.
64. Michelle Kessler, "Techies Plug In to Capitol Hill Power," *USA Today* (June 23, 2004): 1B.
65. Christopher Palmeri, "E-Advocacy: How to Make a Corporate Cause Click," *Business Week* (January 12, 2004): 14.
66. Sandra Sobiera, "Bush Signs Corporate Fraud Crackdown Bill," **www.azcentral.com** (July 31, 2002): 1. Also see Howard Fineman and Michael Isikoff, "Laying Down the Law," *Newsweek* (August 5, 2002): 20–23; and Michael Arndt, "A Boon for Bean Counters," *Business Week* (November 22, 2004): 13.
67. Edward Iwata, "Ex-Dynegy Exec Gets 24 Years in Prison," *USA Today* (March 26, 2004): 1B.
68. Michelle Conlin, "If the Pardon Doesn't Come Through. . . ," *Business Week* (April

2, 2001): 64–65. Also see Geoffrey Colvin, "White-Collar Crooks Have No Idea What They're in For," *Fortune* (July 26, 2004): 60.

69. Lawyer and survey data from Del Jones, "Lawyers, Wannabes on the Rise," *USA Today* (December 26, 2003): 5B.
70. Roger Parloff, "Is Fat the Next Tobacco?" *Fortune* (February 3, 2003): 52.
71. Marianne M. Jennings and Frank Shipper, *Avoiding and Surviving Lawsuits* (San Francisco: Jossey-Bass, 1989), p. 118 (emphasis added).
72. John R. Allison, "Easing the Pain of Legal Disputes: The Evolution and Future of Reform," *Business Horizons*, 33 (September-October 1990): 15. For more, see Margaret M. Clark, "A Jury of Their Peers," *HR Magazine*, 49 (January 2004): 54–59; Gary Weiss, "Walled Off from Justice?" *Business Week* (March 22, 2004): 90–92; F. Peter Phillips, "Ten Ways to Sabotage Dispute Management," *HR Magazine*, 49 (September 2004): 163–168; and John Parauda and Jathan Janove, "Settle for Less," *HR Magazine*, 49 (November 2004): 135–139.
73. Jeannine Aversa, "Financing Isn't Their Strong Subject," *Arizona Republic* (April 4, 2004): D7.
74. Dave Patel, "Location, Location, Location," *HR Magazine*, 46 (November 2001): 168. Also see Jess McCuan, "Guard Your Exits!" *Inc.*, 26 (April 2004): 44, 46; and Uday Karmarkar, "Will You Survive the Services Revolution?" *Harvard Business Review*, 82 (June 2004): 100–107.
75. Based on Peter Svensson, "Outsource-Proof Jobs," *Arizona Republic* (July 17, 2004): D3. Also see Alison Overholt, "The Labor-Shortage Myth," *Fast Company*, no. 85 (August 2004): 23–24.
76. Data from 1998–1999 *Occupational Outlook Handbook*, September 1999 (**stats.bls.gov/oco/oco2003.htm**). Also see Kristine Ellis, "Mind the Gap" *Training*, 39 (January 2002): 30–35.
77. Paul A. Samuelson, *Economics*, 10th ed. (New York: McGraw-Hill, 1976), p. 253. Also see Geoffrey Colvin, "China Brings the Old Economy Roaring Back," *Fortune* (June 28, 2004): 60; and Thor Valdmanis, "Tuck's MBAs Are Hot Property Again," *USA Today* (July 1, 2004): 5B.
78. Darrell Rigby, "Moving Upward in a Downturn," *Harvard Business Review*, 79 (June 2001): 100. Also see Amitabh S. Raturi and Eric P. Jack, "Creating a Volume-Flexible Firm," *Business Horizons*, 47 (November-December 2004): 69–78.
79. "Fast Talk," *Fast Company*, no. 82 (May 2004): 64.
80. See Robert J. Samuelson, "Optimists—Or Just Dreamers?" *Newsweek* (January 14, 2002): 39; and Margaret Popper, "No Confidence in These Indexes," *Business Week* (January 28, 2002): 26.
81. Daniel Gross, "The Revenge of the Business Cycle," *Fortune* (July 26, 2004): 58.
82. For an informative discussion of the value of economic forecasting, see Peter L. Bernstein and Theodore H. Silbert, "Are Economic Forecasters Worth Listening To?" *Harvard Business Review*, 62 (September-October 1984): 32–40. Also see Geoffrey Colvin, "Listen to the People Who Got the Election Right," *Fortune* (November 29, 2004): 82.
83. Lawrence S. Davidson, "Knowing the Unknowable," *Business Horizons*, 32 (September-October 1989): 7.
84. David Fairlamb, "Hurting in Lockstep," *Business Week* (October 22, 2001): 30.
85. Data from Brian Bremner, "Why Debt Could Drag Japan Back Down," *Business Week* (July 5, 2004): 57.
86. Sue Kirchhoff, "Fed Imposes Fine of $100M on Swiss Bank," *USA Today* (May 11, 2004): 2B.
87. James Cox, "Tensions Rise as Economic Power Tilts," *USA Today* (August 11, 2004): 2B.
88. John Naisbitt and Patricia Aburdene, *Megatrends 2000* (New York: William Morrow, 1990), p. 21. Also see John Heilemann, "Gearing Ourselves for Globalization," *Business 2.0*, 5 (August 2004): 34, 36.
89. See William Underhill, "EU *Parlez-Vous* Maltese?" *Newsweek* (March 22, 2004): 12; Noelle Knox, "EU Expansion Brings USA Opportunities," *USA Today* (April 27, 2004): 1B–2B; and Elliott Blair Smith, "WTO Makes Deal on Agriculture Subsidies," *USA Today* (August 2, 2004): 1B.
90. Thomas A. Stewart, "Welcome to the Revolution," *Fortune* (December 13, 1993): 67. Also see Jeffrey D. Sachs, "Welcome to the Asian Century," *Fortune* (January 12, 2004): 53–54.
91. Michael J. Mandel, "From America: Boom—and Bust," *Business Week* (January 28, 2002): 26. Also see Peter Coy, "The Trade Gap: How Long Can It Go On?" *Business Week* (November 22, 2004): 134, 136.
92. Data from Tom Martin and Deborah Greenwood, "The World Economy in Charts," *Fortune* (July 26, 1993): 88–94.
93. Data from "Global 500 Notes," *Fortune* (July 26, 2004): 182; Toyota advertisement, *Business Week* (August 30, 2004): 144; and **www.toyota.com/usa**. Also see Alex Taylor III, "Toyota's Secret Weapon," *Fortune* (August 23, 2004): 60–66; and Christine Tierney, "Huge Risk of Building U.S. Factories Paid Off for Both Honda, Ohio," *USA Today* (September 7, 2004): 4B.
94. Del Jones, "Foreign Firms Snap Up U.S. Rivals," *USA Today* (March 7, 2001): 6B.
95. For more, see Jeffrey E. Garten, "Offshoring: You Ain't Seen Nothin' Yet," *Business Week* (June 21, 2004): 28; Karyn-Siobhan Robinson, "'Offshoring' Crisis Is a Myth, Foundation Says," *HR Magazine*, 49 (July 2004): 30; and Alan Deutschman, "Offshoring Creativity," *Fast Company*, no. 89 (December 2004): 29–30.
96. Jerome B. Wiesner, "Technology and Innovation," in *Technological Innovation and Society*, ed. Dean Morse and Aaron W. Warner (New York: Columbia University Press, 1966), p. 11.
97. Walter Kiechel III, "How We Will Work in the Year 2000," *Fortune* (May 17, 1993): 39. Also see Tammy Galvin, "A Social Time Bomb," *Training*, 41 (July 2004): 4.
98. For good reading on innovation, see Bhaskar Chakravorti, "The New Rules for Bringing Innovation to Market," *Harvard Business Review*, 82 (March 2004): 58–67; Seth Godin, "The Best Things in Life Are Free," *Fast Company*, no. 83 (June 2004): 88–93; Gary Hamel and Gary Getz, "Funding Growth in an Age of Austerity," *Harvard Business Review*, 82 (July-August 2004): 76–83; Bob Parks, "Technology Map of the World," *Business 2.0*, 5 (August 2004): 111–116; Michael J. Mandel, "This Way to the Future," *Business Week* (October 11, 2004): 92–98; Harold Evans, "What Drives America's Great Innovators?" *Fortune* (October 18, 2004): 84, 86; Brad Stone, "Factory of the Future?" *Newsweek* (November 22, 2004): 60–61; and Michael A. Prospero, "Innovation Scorecard," *Fast Company*, no. 89 (December 2004): 65–67.
99. Pete Engardio, "Scouring the Planet for Brainiacs," *Business Week* (October 11, 2004): 102.
100. Brian Dumaine, "Closing the Innovation Gap," *Fortune* (December 2, 1991): 57.
101. Bill Breen, "The Thrill of Defeat," *Fast Company*, no. 83 (June 2004): 77 (emphasis added).
102. Based on Stratford Sherman, "When Laws of Physics Meet Laws of the Jungle," *Fortune* (May 15, 1995): 193–194.
103. Joseph Weber, "Quick, Save the Ozone," *Business Week* (May 17, 1993): 78. For a graphic snapshot of how long it takes consumers to adopt new electronic technologies, see "New Technologies Take Time," *Business Week* (April 19, 1999): 8.
104. David Whitford, "A Human Place to Work," *Fortune* (January 8, 2001): 110. Also see Michael Arndt, "3M: A Lab for Growth?" *Business Week* (January 21, 2002): 50–51.
105. Robert J. Herbold, "Inside Microsoft: Balancing Creativity and Discipline," *Harvard Business Review*, 80 (January 2002): 73–74.
106. See Morgan L. Swink, J. Christopher Sandvig, and Vincent A. Mabert, "Adding 'Zip' to Product Development: Concurrent Engineering Methods and Tools," *Business Horizons*, 39 (March-April 1996): 41–49; and Bob Filipczak, "Concurrent Engineering: A Team by Any Other Name?" *Training*, 33 (August 1996): 54–59.
107. See Bill Joy, "Large Problem: How Big Companies Can Innovate," *Fortune* (November 15, 2004): 214.
108. See Gifford Pinchot III, *Intrapreneuring* (New York: Harper & Row, 1985), p. xvii.
109. Tim Smart, "Kathleen Synnott: Shaping the Mailrooms of Tomorrow," *Business Week* (November 16, 1992): 66.
110. Vince Luchsinger and D. Ray Bagby, "Entrepreneurship and Intrapreneur-

ship: Behaviors, Comparisons, and Contrasts," *SAM Advanced Management Journal*, 52 (Summer 1987): 12. Also see related articles on intrapreneurship in the same issue. For intrapreneurs in action, see Christine Canabou, "Free to Innovate," *Fast Company*, no. 52 (November 2001): 60–62.

CHAPTER 4

1. **Opening Quote** As quoted in Saren Starbridge, "Anita Roddick: Fair Trade," *Living Planet*, 3 (Spring 2001): 92.
2. Data from James Cox, "As Economy Expands, India on 'Verge of Something Big,'" *USA Today* (February 9, 2004): 1B–2B. For more on doing business in India, see Manjeet Kripalani and Pete Engardio, "The Rise of India," *Business Week* (December 8, 2003): 66–76; and Om Malik, "The New Land of Opportunity," *Business 2.0*, 5 (July 2004): 72–79.
3. *Wall Street Journal*, from Marcus W. Brauchli, "Echoes of the Past," (September 26, 1996): R24.Wall Street Journal. Eastern Edition [only staff-produced materials may be used] by Marcus Brauchli. Copyright 1996 by Dow Jones & Co Inc. Reproduced with permission of Dow Jones & Co. Inc in the format Textbook via Copyright Clearance Center. For another good historical perspective, see Michael J. Mandel, "Does It Matter If China Catches Up to the U.S.?" *Business Week* (December 6, 2004): 122, 124.
4. Greg Barrett, "Made in America? Not Likely," *USA Today* (December 15, 2003): 11B.
5. Nick Olivari, "Citigroup Private Banking Unit in Japan Suspended," *USA Today* (September 20, 2004): 2B.
6. Data from Lauren Young, "One Way to Get New Investors," *Business Week* (May 31, 2004): 100; and Geri Smith, "Made in the *Maquilas*—Again," *Business Week* (August 16, 2004): 45.
7. Drawn from Billy House, "'Made in Mexico' Uniforms Chafe Border Patrol Agents," *Arizona Republic* (June 11, 2004): A1–A2.
8. Data from "Snapshots of the Next Century," *Business Week : 21st Century Capitalism* (Special Issue, 1994): 194. Also see Paul Magnusson, "Globalization Is Great—Sort Of," *Business Week* (April 25, 2005): 25.
9. Nancy J. Adler, *International Dimensions of Organizational Behavior*, 4th ed. (Cincinnati: Thomson Learning, 2002), p. 3.
10. See Sandra Mottner and James P. Johnson, "Motivations and Risks in International Licensing: A Review and Implications for Licensing to Transitional and Emerging Economies," *Journal of World Business*, 35 (Summer 2000): 171–188; and Thomas Y. Choi, Jaroslaw Budny, and Norbert Wank, "Intellectual Property Management: A Knowledge Supply Chain Perspective," *Business Horizons*, 47 (January-February 2004): 37–44.
11. Data from "Chip Licensing Deal," *USA Today* (November 27, 1996): 1B. *Note:* This six-step sequence is based on Alan M. Rugman, "A New Theory of the Multinational Enterprise: Internationalization versus Internalization," *Columbia Journal of World Business*, 15 (Spring 1980): 23–29. Also see Walter Kuemmerle, "Go Global—or No?" *Harvard Business Review*, 79 (June 2001): 37–49; and Jane W. Lu and Paul W. Beamish, "International Diversification and Firm Performance: The S-Curve Hypothesis," *Academy of Management Journal*, 47 (August 2004): 598–609.
12. See William McCarty, Mark Kasoff, and Doug Smith, "The Importance of International Business at the Local Level," *Business Horizons*, 43 (May-June 2000): 35–42.
13. For related discussion, see James Bamford, David Ernst, and David G. Fubini, "Launching a World-Class Joint Venture," *Harvard Business Review*, 82 (February 2004): 90–100; and Donald Gerwin, "Coordinating New Product Development in Strategic Alliances," *Academy of Management Review*, 29 (April 2004): 241–257.
14. Chris Woodyard, "Honda, GE Build New Jet Engine," *USA Today* (February 17, 2004): 1B.
15. Jeremy Main, "Making Global Alliances Work," *Fortune* (December 17, 1990): 121–126.
16. Adapted from Ibid. and David Lei and John W. Slocum Jr., "Global Strategic Alliances: Payoffs and Pitfalls," *Organizational Dynamics*, 19 (Winter 1991): 44–62. Also see Mihir A. Desai, C. Fritz Foley, and James R. Hines Jr., "Venture Out Alone," *Harvard Business Review*, 82 (March 2004): 22.
17. See Brian Bremner, "Japan: A Tale of Two Mergers," *Business Week* (May 10, 2004): 42; and Jeffrey H. Dyer, Prashant Kale, and Harbir Singh, "When to Ally and When to Acquire," *Harvard Business Review*, 82 (July-August 2004): 108–115.
18. Joan Warner, "The World Is Not Always Your Oyster," *Business Week* (October 30, 1995): 132. Also see Ping Deng, "Outward Investment by Chinese MNCs: Motivations and Implications," *Business Horizons*, 47 (May-June 2004): 8–16.
19. For example, see Bruce Kogut, "What Makes a Company Global?" *Harvard Business Review*, 77 (January-February 1999): 165–170; and Thomas A. Stewart, "Getting Real About Going Global," *Fortune* (February 15, 1999): 170, 172.
20. For an interesting twist, see Diane Brady and Kerry Capell, "GE Breaks the Mold to Spur Innovation," *Business Week* (April 26, 2004): 88–89.
21. Based on Fons Trompenaars and Charles Hampden-Turner, *Riding the Waves of Culture: Understanding Cultural Diversity in Global Business*, 2nd ed. (New York: McGraw-Hill, 1998), pp. 191–192; Marie-Claude Boudreau, Karen D. Loch, Daniel Robey, and Detmar Straud, "Going Global: Using Information Technology to Advance the Competitiveness of the Virtual Transnational Organization," *Academy of Management Executive*, 12 (November 1998): 120–128; and Anil K. Gupta and Vijay Govindarajan, "Converting Global Presence into Global Competitive Advantage," *Academy of Management Executive*, 15 (May 2001): 45–56.
22. Stanley Reed, "Busting Up Sweden Inc.," *Business Week* (February 22, 1999): 52, 54. For another example, see Sophie Hares, "'Unmistakably Australian' News Corp. Moves to NYC," *USA Today* (April 7, 2004): 6B.
23. For example, see Tatiana Kostova and Srilata Zaheer, "Organizational Legitimacy Under Conditions of Complexity: The Case of the Multinational Enterprise," *Academy of Management Review*, 24 (January 1999): 64–81. Transnationalism in terrorist organizations is discussed in Fareed Zakaria, "Terrorists Don't Need States," *Newsweek* (April 5, 2004): 37.
24. "Amidst Stiffer International Competition, U.S. Managers Need a Broader Perspective," *Management Review*, 69 (March 1980): 34.
25. C. Bremmer, "The Global Manager—Insights in Succeeding the Challenge," unpublished paper, 1994, as quoted in Philip R. Harris and Robert T. Moran, *Managing Cultural Differences*, 4th ed. (Houston: Gulf Publishing, 1996), pp. 4–5.
26. P. Christopher Earley and Elaine Mosakowski, "Toward Culture Intelligence: Turning Cultural Differences into a Workplace Advantage," *Academy of Management Executive*, 18 (August 2004): 155. Also see the cultural intelligence exercise on p. 143 of P. Christopher Earley and Elaine Mosakowski, "Cultural Intelligence," *Harvard Business Review*, 82 (October 2004): 139–146.
27. Howard V. Perlmutter, "The Tortuous Evolution of the Multinational Corporation," *Columbia Journal of World Business*, 4 (January-February 1969): 11. Also see Malika Richards and Michael Y. Hu, "U.S. Subsidiary Control in Malaysia and Singapore," *Business Horizons*, 46 (November-December 2003): 71–76.
28. Perlmutter and a colleague later added "regiocentric attitude" to their typology. Such an attitude centers on a regional identification (North America, Europe, and Asia, for example). See David A. Heenan and Howard V. Perlmutter, *Multinational Organization Development* (Reading, Mass.: Addison-Wesley, 1979).
29. Drawn from Brian Dumaine, "The New Turnaround Champs," *Fortune* (July 16, 1990): 36–44.
30. See Amy Borrus, "Can Japan's Giants Cut the Apron Strings?" *Business Week* (May

14, 1990): 105–106.
31. See Brian Grow, "Hispanic Nation," *Business Week* (March 15, 2004): 58–70.
32. Data from Andrea Coombes, "Fluency in Foreign Language Called Plus for Workers," *Arizona Republic* (January 18, 2004): D1.
33. Julia Lieblich, "If You Want a Big, New Market . . ." *Fortune* (November 21, 1988): 181. Population update from Grow, "Hispanic Nation."
34. Perlmutter, "The Tortuous Evolution of the Multinational Corporation," p. 16.
35. Gail Dutton, "Building a Global Brain," *Management Review*, 88 (May 1999): 34–38.
36. Rahul Jacob, "Trust the Locals, Win Worldwide," *Fortune* (May 4, 1992): 76.
37. Ibid.
38. Arvind V. Phatak and Mohammed M. Habib, "The Dynamics of International Business Negotiations," *Business Horizons*, 39 (May-June 1996): 34.
39. For more, see Adler, *International Dimensions of Organizational Behavior*, pp. 16–34.
40. As quoted in "How Cultures Collide," *Psychology Today*, 10 (July 1976): 69.
41. Trompenaars and Hampden-Turner, *Riding the Waves of Culture*, p. 3.
42. Ronald Inglehart and Wayne E. Baker, "Modernization's Challenge to Traditional Values: Who's Afraid of Ronald McDonald?" *The Futurist*, 35 (March-April 2001): 18, 21. Also see Stanley Holmes, "Starbucks: An American in Paris," *Business Week* (December 8, 2003): 11.
43. Drawn from "Maine Hospital Open to Gown Redesign," *USA Today* (August 18, 2004): 12B. For other examples, see Julie Rawe, "Vegas Plays to the World," *Time* (July 26, 2004): 34–35; and Sue Kirchhoff, "Different Cultures Value Different Features," *USA Today* (August 5, 2004): 2B.
44. See "How Cultures Collide," pp. 66–74, 97; Edward T. Hall, *The Hidden Dimension* (Garden City, N.Y.: Doubleday, 1996); and Mary Munter, "Cross-Cultural Communication for Managers," *Business Horizons*, 36 (May-June 1993): 69–78.
45. Ronald E. Dulek, John S. Fielden, and John S. Hill, "International Communication: An Executive Primer," *Business Horizons*, 34 (January-February 1991): 21.
46. For example, see Robert House, Mansour Javidan, Paul Hanges, and Peter Dorfman, "Understanding Cultures and Implicit Leadership Theories Across the Globe: An Introduction to Project GLOBE," *Journal of World Business*, 37 (Spring 2002): 3–10; and Robert J. House, Paul J. Hanges, Mansour Javidan, Peter W. Dorfman, and Vipin Gupta, eds., *Culture, Leadership, and Organizations: The GLOBE Study of 62 Societies* (Thousand Oaks, Calif.: Sage, 2004).
47. For more, see Mansour Javidan and Robert J. House, "Cultural Acumen for the Global Manager: Lessons from Project GLOBE," *Organizational Dynamics*, 29 (Spring 2001): 289–305.
48. This list is based on Edward T. Hall, "The Silent Language in Overseas Business," *Harvard Business Review*, 38 (May-June 1960): 87–96; Rose Knotts, "Cross-Cultural Management: Transformations and Adaptations," *Business Horizons*, 32 (January-February 1989): 29–33; and Adler, *International Dimensions of Organizational Behavior*, pp. 27–28.
49. For related research, see Markus Kemmelmeier et al., "Individualism, Collectivism, and Authoritarianism in Seven Societies," *Journal of Cross-Cultural Psychology*, 34 (May 2003): 304–322; Shuyuan Wang and Catherine S. Tamis-LeMonda, "Do Child-Rearing Values in Taiwan and the United States Reflect Cultural Values of Collectivism and Individualism?" *Journal of Cross-Cultural Psychology*, 34 (November 2003): 629–642; and Juri Allik and Anu Realo, "Individualism-Collectivism and Social Capital," *Journal of Cross-Cultural Psychology*, 35 (January 2004): 29–49.
50. For detailed discussion, see Allen C. Bluedorn, Carol Felker Kaufman, and Paul M. Lane, "How Many Things Do You Like to Do at Once? An Introduction to Monochronic and Polychronic Time," *Academy of Management Executive*, 6 (November 1992): 17–26.
51. Tom Weir, "Four Days Out, Athens Confident It'll Be Ready," *USA Today* (August 9, 2004): 2A.
52. See Carol Saunders, Craig Van Slyke, and Douglas R. Vogel, "My Time or Yours? Managing Time Visions in Global Virtual Teams," *Academy of Management Executive*, 18 (February 2004): 19–31.
53. See Karl Albrecht, "Lost in the Translation," *Training*, 33 (June 1996): 66–70; Daniel Pianko, "Smooth Translations," *Management Review*, 85 (July 1996): 10; and Rebecca Ganzel, "Universal Translator? Not Quite," *Training*, 36 (April 1999): 22, 24.
54. Jerry Shine, "More US Students Tackle Japanese," *Christian Science Monitor* (November 25, 1991): 14. Also see Mary Ann von Glinow, Debra L. Shapiro, and Jeanne M. Brett, "Can We *Talk*, and Should We? Managing Emotional Conflict in Multicultural Teams," *Academy of Management Review*, 29 (October 2004): 578–592; and Mary Yoko Brannen, "When Mickey Loses Face: Recontextualization, Semantic Fit, and the Semiotics of Foreignness," *Academy of Management Review*, 29 (October 2004): 593–616.
55. Kathryn Tyler, "I Say Potato, You Say *Patata*," *HR Magazine*, 49 (January 2004): 87.
56. Data from Greg Toppo, "Chinese Makes Advances in High Schools," *USA Today* (December 10, 2003): 12D.
57. See Nalini Tarakeshwar, Jeffrey Stanton, and Kenneth I. Pargament, "Religion: An Overlooked Dimension in Cross-Cultural Psychology," *Journal of Cross-Cultural Psychology*, 34 (July 2003): 377–394; and Heather Johnson, "Taboo No More," *Training*, 41 (April 2004): 22–26.
58. Based on Figure 2 in Gary Bonvillian and William A. Nowlin, "Cultural Awareness: An Essential Element of Doing Business Abroad," *Business Horizons*, 37 (November-December 1994): 44–50.
59. "Burger Boost," *USA Today* (October 11, 1995): 1B. Also see Michael Arndt, "A Misguided Beef with McDonald's," *Business Week* (May 21, 2001): 14.
60. See Peter B. Smith, "Nations, Cultures, and Individuals: New Perspectives and Old Dilemmas," *Journal of Cross-Cultural Psychology*, 35 (January 2004): 6–12.
61. Del Jones, "American CEO in Europe Blends Leadership Styles," *USA Today* (June 21, 2004): 4B.
62. See Geert Hofstede, *Culture's Consequences: Comparing Values, Behaviors, Institutions, and Organizations Across Nations*, 2nd ed. (Thousand Oaks, Calif.: Sage, 2001); Michael H. Hoppe, "An Interview with Geert Hofstede," *Academy of Management Executive*, 18 (February 2004): 75–79; John W. Bing, "Hofstede's Consequences: The Impact of His Work on Consulting and Business Practices," *Academy of Management Executive*, 18 (February 2004): 80–87; and Harry C. Triandis, "The Many Dimensions of Culture," *Academy of Management Executive*, 18 (February 2004): 88–93.
63. An extension of Hofstede's original work can be found in Geert Hofstede and Michael Harris Bond, "The Confucius Connection: From Cultural Roots to Economic Growth," *Organizational Dynamics*, 16 (Spring 1988): 4–21. Also see Geert Hofstede, "Problems Remain, but Theories Will Change: The Universal and the Specific in 21st-Century Global Management," *Organizational Dynamics*, 28 (Summer 1999): 34–44; Sang M. Lee and Suzanne J. Peterson, "Culture, Entrepreneurial Orientation, and Global Competitiveness," *Journal of World Business*," 35 (Winter 2000): 401–416; and Ashleigh Merritt, "Culture in the Cockpit: Do Hofstede's Dimensions Replicate?" *Journal of Cross-Cultural Psychology*, 31 (May 2000): 283–301.
64. See Itzhak Harpaz, "The Importance of Work Goals: An International Perspective," *Journal of International Business Studies*, 21 (First Quarter 1990): 75–93. Also see David A. Ralston, David J. Gustafson, Priscilla M. Elsass, Fanny Cheung, and Robert H. Terpstra, "Eastern Values: A Comparison of Managers in the United States, Hong Kong, and the People's Republic of China," *Journal of Applied Psychology*, 77 (October 1992): 664–671.
65. See Bodil Jones, "What Future European Recruits Want," *Management Review*, 87 (January 1998): 6; Bill Leonard, "Workers' Attitudes Similar Worldwide," *HR Magazine*, 43 (December 1998): 28, 30; and

Cheryl Comeau Kirschner, "It's a Small World," *Management Review*, 88 (March 1999): 8.

66. Based on discussion in Peter W. Dorfman, Paul J. Hanges, and Felix C. Brodbeck, "Leadership and Cultural Variation: The Identification of Culturally Endorsed Leadership Profiles," in Robert J. House, Paul J. Hanges, Mansour Javidan, Peter W. Dorfman, and Vipin Gupta, eds., *Culture, Leadership, and Organizations: The GLOBE Study of 62 Societies* (Thousand Oaks, Calif.: Sage, 2004), pp. 669–719.
67. Data from Dianne H. B. Welsh, Fred Luthans, and Steven M. Sommer, "Managing Russian Factory Workers: The Impact of U.S.-Based Behavioral and Participative Techniques," *Academy of Management Journal*, 36 (February 1993): 58–79. For related reading, see Dong I. Jung and Bruce J. Avolio, "Effects of Leadership Style and Followers' Cultural Orientation on Performance in Group and Individual Task Conditions," *Academy of Management Journal*, 42 (April 1999): 208–218.
68. Kristin Dunlap Godsey, "Thread by Thread," *Success*, 43 (April 1996): 8.
69. See Anne S. Tsui, Hui Wang, Katherine Xin, Lihua Zhang, and P.P. Fu, "'Let a Thousand Flowers Bloom': Variation of Leadership Styles Among Chinese CEOs," *Organizational Dynamics*, 33, no. 1 (2004): 5–20; and Juan Antonio Fernandez, "The Gentleman's Code of Confucius: Leadership by Values," *Organizational Dynamics*, 33, no. 1 (2004): 21–31.
70. Marshall Loeb, "The Real Fast Track Is Overseas," *Fortune* (August 21, 1995): 129. For more, see Mason A. Carpenter, Wm. Gerard Sanders, and Hal B. Gregersen, "Building Human Capital with Organizational Content: The Impact of International Assignment Experience on Multicultural Firm Performance and CEO Pay," *Academy of Management Journal*, 44 (June 2001): 493–511; and "International Experience Aids Career," *USA Today* (January 28, 2002): 1B.
71. Data from J. Stewart Black and Hal B. Gregersen, "The Right Way to Manage Expats," *Harvard Business Review*, 77 (March-April 1999): 52–63; and Gary S. Insch and John D. Daniels, "Causes and Consequences of Declining Early Departures from Foreign Assignments," *Business Horizons*, 45 (November-December 2002): 39–48.
72. Data from Robert O'Connor, "Plug the Expat Knowledge Drain," *HR Magazine*, 47 (October 2002): 101–107; and Carla Joinson, "No Returns," *HR Magazine*, 47 (November 2002): 70–77.
73. Elisabeth Marx, *Breaking Through Culture Shock: What You Need to Succeed in International Business* (London: Nicholas Brealey Publishing, 2001), p. 7.
74. Based on Insch and Daniels, "Causes and Consequences of Declining Early Departures from Foreign Assignments."
75. *Academy of Management Learning & Education* by Yoshitaka Yamazaki and Christopher Kayes. Copyright 2004 by *Academy of Management Learning & Education*. Reproduced with permission of *Academy of Management Learning & Education* in the format Textbook via Copyright Clearance Center.
76. List based on Rosalie L. Tung, "Selection and Training of Personnel for Overseas Assignments," *Columbia Journal of World Business*, 16 (Spring 1981): 68–78; and Mark E. Mendenhall, Gunter K. Stahl, Ina Ehnert, Gary Oddou, Joyce S. Osland, and Torsten M. Kuhlmann, "Evaluation Studies of Cross-Cultural Training Programs: A Review of the Literature from 1988 to 2000," in Dan Landis, Janet M. Bennett, and Milton J. Bennett, eds., *Handbook of Intercultural Training*, 3rd ed. (Thousand Oaks, Calif.: Sage, 2004), pp. 129–143.
77. Oliver Teves, "Filipinos Embrace the 'In' Job," *Arizona Republic* (December 6, 2003): D5.
78. See P. Christopher Earley and Randall S. Peterson, "The Elusive Cultural Chameleon: Cultural Intelligence as a New Approach to Intercultural Training for the Global Manager," *Academy of Management Learning and Education*, 3 (March 2004): 100–115.
79. Robert Moran, "Children of Bilingualism," *International Management*, 45 (November 1990): 93. Also see "Online Conversations Build Language Skills," *Training*, 42 (April 2005): 9; and Tom Price, "Talk Is Cheap," *Business 2.0*. 6 (March 2005): 110, 112.
80. Based on Joann S. Lublin, "An Overseas Stint Can Be a Ticket to the Top," *Wall Street Journal* (January 29, 1996): B1, B5.
81. See Phyllis Tharenou, "The Initial Development of Receptivity to Working Abroad: Self-Initiated International Work Opportunities in Young Graduate Employees," *Journal of Occupational and Organizational Psychology*, 76 (December 2003): 489–515.
82. Jessi Hempel, "It Takes a Village—And a Consultant," *Business Week* (September 6, 2004): 76.
83. See P. Christopher Earley, "Intercultural Training for Managers: A Comparison of Documentary and Interpersonal Methods," *Academy of Management Journal*, 30 (December 1987): 685–698. A comprehensive overview of 18 different cross-cultural training methods can be found in Table 3.3 on page 79 of Sandra M. Fowler and Judith M. Bloom, "An Analysis of Methods for Intercultural Training," in Dan Landis, Janet M. Bennett, and Milton J. Bennett, eds., *Handbook of Intercultural Training* (Thousand Oaks, Calif.: Sage, 2004), pp. 37–84.
84. An excellent resource book is J. Stewart Black, Hal B. Gregersen, and Mark E. Mendenhall, *Global Assignments: Successfully Expatriating and Repatriating International Managers* (San Francisco: Jossey-Bass, 1992). Also see Juan I. Sanchez, Paul E. Spector, and Cary L. Cooper, "Adapting to a Boundaryless World: A Developmental Expatriate Model," *Academy of Management Executive*, 14 (May 2000): 96–106; and Susan Meisinger, "Going Global: A Smart Move for HR Professionals," *HR Magazine*, 49 (March 2004): 6.
85. See Elisabeth Marx, *Breaking Through Culture Shock: What You Need to Succeed in International Business* (London: Nicholas Brealey Publishing, 2001); and Annelies E.M. van Vianen, Irene E. De Pater, Amy L. Kristof-Brown, and Erin C. Johnson, "Fitting in: Surface- and Deep-Level Cultural Differences and Expatriates' Adjustment," *Academy of Management Journal*, 47 (October 2004): 697–709.
86. See Stephenie Overman, "Mentors Without Borders," *HR Magazine*, 49 (March 2004): 83–85.
87. See Andrea C. Poe, "Welcome Back," *HR Magazine*, 45 (March 2000): 94–105; and Jeff Barbian, "Return to Sender," *Training*, 39 (January 2002): 40–43; and Annette B. Bossard and Richard B. Peterson, "The Repatriate Experience as Seen by American Expatriates," *Journal of World Business*, 40 (February 2005): 9–28.
88. Data from Rosalie L. Tung, "American Expatriates Abroad: From Neophytes to Cosmopolitans," *Journal of World Business*, 33 (Summer 1998): 125–144.
89. See Rosalie L. Tung, "Female Expatriates: The Model Global Manager?" *Organizational Dynamics*, 33, no. 3 (2004): 243–253.
90. David Stauffer, "No Need for Inter-American Culture Clash," *Management Review*, 87 (January 1998): 8. Also see Arup Varma, Linda K. Stroh, and Lisa B. Schmitt, "Women and International Assignments: The Impact of Supervisor-Subordinate Relationships," *Journal of World Business*, 36 (Winter 2001): 380–388.
91. See Louisa Wah, "Surfing the Rough Sea," *Management Review*, 87 (September 1998): 25–29; and Paula M. Caligiuri and Wayne F. Cascio, "Can We Send Her There? Maximizing the Success of Western Women on Global Assignments," *Journal of World Business*, 33 (Winter 1998): 394–416.
92. See Lynette Clemetson, "Soul and Sushi," *Newsweek* (May 4, 1998): 38–41.
93. For helpful tips, see Linda K. Stroh, Arup Varma, and Stacey J. Valy-Durbin, "Why Are Women Left Home: Are They Unwilling to Go on International Assignments?" *Journal of World Business*, 35 (Fall 2000): 241–255.
94. For more, see David Ahlstrom, Garry Bruton, and Eunice S. Chan, "HRM of Foreign Firms in China: The Challenge of Managing Host Country Personnel," *Business Horizons*, 44 (May-June 2001): 59–68; Yaping Gong, "Subsidiary Staffing

in Multinational Enterprises: Agency, Resources, and Performance," *Academy of Management Journal*, 46 (December 2003): 728–739; and Timothy Dwyer, "Localization's Hidden Costs," *HR Magazine*, 49 (June 2004): 135–144.

CHAPTER 5

1. **Opening Quote** Stephen R. Covey, *Principle-Centered Leadership* (New York: Simon & Schuster, 1991), p. 95.
2. For an interesting look back at Rockefeller, see Jerry Useem, "Entrepreneur of the Century," *Inc.* Twentieth anniversary issue, 21 (May 18, 1999): 159–173.
3. Thomas M. Jones, "Corporate Social Responsibility Revisited, Redefined," *California Management Review*, 22 (Spring 1980): 59–60. Also see Abagail McWilliams and Donald Siegel, "Corporate Social Responsibility: A Theory of the Firm Perspective." *Academy of Management Rewiew*, 26 (January 2001): 117–127; and Homer H. Johnson, "Corporate Social Audits—This Time Around," *Business Horizons*, 44 (May-June 2001): 29–36.
4. For example, see W.M. Greenfield, "In the Name of Corporate Social Responsibility," *Business Horizons*, 47 (January-February 2004): 19–28.
5. Nancy R. Lockwood, "Corporate Social Responsibility: HR's Leadership Role," 2004 Research Quarterly insert, *HR Magazine*, 49 (December 2004): 2.
6. Archie B. Carroll, "Managing Ethically with Global Stakeholders: A Present and Future Challenge," *Academy of Management Executive*, 18 (May 2004): 118.
7. Ibid., pp. 117–118.
8. See Petra Christmann, "Multinational Companies and the Natural Environment: Determinants of Global Environmental Policy Standardization," *Academy of Management Journal*, 47 (October 2004): 747–760.
9. Tachi Kiuchi, "Fast Talk," *Fast Company*, no. 78 (January 2004): 64.
10. Alison Overholt, "The Good Earth," *Fast Company*, no. 77 (December 2003): 86.
11. This distinction between the economic and the socioeconomic models is based partly on discussion in Courtney C. Brown, *Beyond the Bottom Line* (New York: Macmillan, 1979), pp. 82–83.
12. See the discussion in Art Wolfe, "We've Had Enough Business Ethics," *Business Horizons*, 36 (May-June 1993): 1–3. Also see Robert J. Samuelson, "The Spirit of Adam Smith," *Newsweek* (December 2, 1996): 63; Geoffrey Colvin, "Capitalists: Savor This Moment," *Fortune* (July 24, 2000): 64; and Anthony Bianco, "The Enduring Corporation," *Business Week* (August 28, 2000): 198–204.
13. As quoted in Keith H. Hammonds, "Writing a New Social Contract," *Business Week* (March 11, 1996): 60.
14. Data from "Fortune 5 Hundred Largest U.S. Corporations," *Fortune* (April 16, 2001): F1.
15. Robert Kuttner, "Enron: A Powerful Blow to Market Fundamentals," *Business Week* (February 4, 2002): 20.
16. For more, see Daniel McGinn, "The Ripple Effect," *Newsweek* (February 18, 2002): 29–32; Jayne O'Donnell and Gary Strauss, "Enron Investigator Blasts Senior Managers," *USA Today* (February 5, 2002): 1B; and John Ellis, "Life After Enron's Death," *Fast Company*, no. 56 (March 2002): 118, 120.
17. See Stuart L. Hart and Sanjay Sharma, "Engaging Fringe Stakeholders for Competitive Imagination," *Academy of Management Executive*, 18 (February 2004): 7–18; Terry Leap and Misty L. Loughry, "The Stakeholder-Friendly Firm," *Business Horizons*, 47 (March-April 2004): 27–32; O.C. Ferrell, "Business Ethics and Customer Stakeholders," *Academy of Management Executive*, 18 (May 2004): 126–129; Rogene A. Buchholz, "The Natural Environment: Does It Count?" *Academy of Management Executive*, 18 (May 2004): 130–133; and Richard J. Martinez and Patricia M. Norman, "Whither Reputation? The Effects of Different Stakeholders," *Business Horizons*, 47 (September-October 2004): 25–32.
18. For an interesting example, see Michelle Conlin, "From Plunderer to Protector," *Business Week* (July 19, 2004): 60–61.
19. "Fast Talk," *Fast Company*, no. 78 (January 2004): 62.
20. These arguments have been adapted in part from Jones, "Corporate Social Responsibility Revisited," p. 61; and Keith Davis and William C. Frederick, *Business and Society: Management, Public Policy, and Ethics*, 5th ed. (New York: McGraw-Hill, 1984), pp. 28–41.
21. Davis and Frederick, *Business and Society*, p. 34.
22. Ron Zemke, "The Confidence Crisis," *Training*, 41 (June 2004): 22. Also see Sajnicole A. Joni, "The Geography of Trust," *Harvard Business Review*, 82 (March 2004): 82–88.
23. Drawn from Ian Wilson, "What One Company Is Doing About Today's Demands on Business," in *Changing Business-Society Interrelationships*, ed. George A. Steiner (Los Angeles: UCLA Graduate School of Management, 1975). Other models are presented in Homer H. Johnson, "Does It Pay to Be Good? Social Responsibility and Financial Performance," *Business Horizons*, 46 (November-December 2003): 34–40; and Simon Zadek, "The Path to Corporate Responsibility," *Harvard Business Review*, 82 (December 2004): 125–132.
24. Mike France, "The World War on Tobacco," *Business Week* (November 11, 1996): 100. Also see John Carey, "Big Tobacco Blows Some Smoke," *Business Week* (August 14, 2000): 8; and Paul Raeburn, "Blowing Smoke over Ventilation," *Business Week* (May 7, 2001): 72–73.
25. Monica Gagnier, "As Detroit Fight Back," *Business Week* (December 20, 2004): 46.
26. Betsy Carpenter, "Fighting for a Forgotten Forest," *U.S. News & World Report* (February 9, 2004): 60.
27. As quoted in Abrahm Lustgarten, "Warm, Fuzzy, and Highly Profitable," *Fortune* (November 15, 2004): 194.
28. For more, see Nelson D. Schwartz, "Inside the Head of BP," *Fortune* (July 26, 2004): 68–76; and Peter Lorenzi, "Managing for the Common Good: Prosocial Leadership," *Organizational Dynamics*, 33, no. 3 (2004): 282–291.
29. See Thomas S. Bateman and J. Michael Crant, "Proactive Behavior: Meaning, Impact, Recommendations," *Business Horizons*, 42 (May-June 1999): 63–70.
30. See Vincent Jeffries, "Virtue and the Altruistic Personality," *Sociological Perspectives*, 41, no. 1 (1998): 151–166. The case against altruism is presented in Edwin A. Locke and Terry W. Noel, "Right Problem, Wrong Solution: A Rejoinder to Mitroff's & Swanson's Call to Action," *The Academy of Management News*, 35 (October 2004): 4.
31. Based on Joseph Weber, "3M's Big Cleanup," *Business Week* (June 5, 2000): 96–98.
32. Data from Michael V. Russo and Paul A. Fouts, "A Resource-Based Perspective on Corporate Environmental Performance and Profitability," *Academy of Management Journal*, 40 (June 1997): 534–559.
33. Based on Daniel B. Turban and Daniel W. Greening, "Corporate Social Performance and Organizational Attractiveness to Prospective Employees," *Academy of Management Journal*, 40 (June 1996): 658–672. Also see Johnson, "Does It Pay to Be Good? Social Responsibility and Financial Performance"; Louis Lavelle, "Playing Fair Pays Off," *Business Week* (February 23, 2004): 14; and Abrahm Lustgarten, "Lean, Mean—and Green? *Fortune* (July 26, 2004): 210.
34. Data from Robert L. Gnaizda, "A Closer Look at Corporate Giving," *Business Week* (December 22, 2003): 18.
35. Louis W. Fry, Gerald D. Keim, and Roger E. Meiners, "Corporate Contributions: Altruistic or For-Profit?" *Academy of Management Journal*, 25 (March 1982): 105.
36. For complete details, see Richard E. Wokutch and Barbara A. Spencer, "Corporate Saints and Sinners: The Effects of Philanthropic and Illegal Activity on Organizational Performance," *California Management Review*, 29 (Winter 1987): 62–77. Also see Mike France, "How Ken Lay's Charity Could Pay Off," *Business Week* (July 19, 2004): 13.
37. Jessi Hempel and Lauren Gard, "The Corporate Givers," *Business Week* (November 29, 2004): 100. For more examples, see Del Jones, "Hasbro, Pfizer Get Award for Charity Efforts," *USA Today* (February 23, 2004): 9B; Christine Dugas, "Citigroup Invests in Financial Literacy," *USA Today* (April 7, 2004): 2B;

Kerry Capell, "Vaccinating the World's Poor," *Business Week* (April 26, 2004): 65–69; and Catherine Arnst, "Why Business Should Make AIDS Its Business," *Business Week* (August 2, 2004): 78, 80.
38. As quoted in Heather Johnson, "The ROI of ROPI," *Training*, 41 (February 2004): 18.
39. Data from Thor Valdmanis, "Final 2 Banks Settle for $100 Million," *USA Today* (August 27, 2004): 1B; "Jury Slaps Tyson Foods with $1.3B Verdict," *USA Today* (February 18, 2004): 1B; Greg Farrell, "SEC Hits Bristol-Myers with $150 Million Fine," *USA Today* (August 5, 2004): 1B; John Waggoner and Christine Dugas, "Painful Year for Funds in Scandal," *USA Today* (September 3, 2004): 1B; and Jayne O'Donnell and Michelle Kessler, "Infineon Accepts $160M Fine for Fixing Prices on Chips," *USA Today* (September 16, 2004): 1B.
40. Shoshana Zuboff, "From Subject to Citizen," *Fast Company*, no. 82 (May 2004): 104.
41. Data from Karen Colteryahn and Patty Davis, "8 Trends You Need to Know Now," *Training and Development*, 58 (January 2004): 28–36.
42. An excellent resource book is LaRue Tone Hosmer, *Moral Leadership in Business* (Burr Ridge, Ill.: Irwin, 1994). Also see Ryan Underwood, "God Bless Our Corrupt Leaders," *Fast Company*, no. 86 (September 2004): 42.
43. See Rushworth M. Kidder, "Tough Choices: Why It's Getting Harder to Be Ethical," *The Futurist*, 29 (September-October 1995): 29–32.
44. See the five–article series on business ethics in the May 2004 issue of *Academy of Management Executive*; Terry Thomas, John R. Schermerhorn, Jr., and John W. Dienhart, "Strategic Leadership of Ethical Behavior in Business," *Academy of Management Executive*, 18 (May 2004): 56–66; Dale Buss, "Corporate Compasses," *HR Magazine*, 49 (June 2004): 127–134; and Jennifer Schramm, "Perceptions on Ethics," *HR Magazine*, 49 (November 2004): 176.
45. O. C. Ferrell and John Fraedrich, *Business Ethics: Ethical Decision Making and Cases* (Boston: Houghton Mifflin, 1991), pp. 10–11.
46. Business ethics research findings are reviewed in Phillip V. Lewis, "Defining 'Business Ethics': Like Nailing Jell-O to a Wall," *Journal of Business Ethics*, 4 (October 1985): 377–383. Also see Lawrence J. Walker and Karl H. Hennig, "Differing Conceptions of Moral Exemplarity: Just, Brave, and Caring," *Journal of Personality and Social Psychology*, 86 (April 2004): 629–647; and John B. Cullen, K. Praveen Parboteeah, and Martin Hoegl, "Cross-National Differences in Managers' Willingness to Justify Ethically Suspect Behaviors: A Test of Institutional Anomie Theory," *Academy of Management Journal*, 47 (June 2004): 411–421.
47. Del Jones, "48% of Workers Admit to Unethical or Illegal Acts," *USA Today* (April 4, 1997): 1A.
48. Ibid., p. 2A.
49. Robert J. Grossman, "The Five-Finger Bonus: The Fraud Triangle at Work," *HR Magazine*, 48 (October 2003): 41. For an update on MCI, see Joseph McCafferty, "Extreme Makeover," *CFO* (July 2004): 47–52.
50. For related research, see Maurice E. Schweitzer, Lisa Ordonez, and Bambi Douma, "Goal Setting as a Motivator of Unethical Behavior," *Academy of Management Journal*, 47 (June 2004): 422–432.
51. Data from John F. Veiga, Timothy D. Golden, and Kathleen Dechant, "Why Managers Bend Company Rules," *Academy of Management Executive*, 18 (May 2004): 84–90.
52. William Rudelius and Rogene A. Buchholz, "Ethical Problems of Purchasing Managers," *Harvard Business Review*, 57 (March-April 1979): 12. Also see Alan J. Dubinsky, Eric N. Berkowitz, and William Rudelius, "Ethical Problems of Field Sales Personnel," *MSU Business Topics*, 28 (Summer 1980): 11–16; James R. Davis, "Ambiguity, Ethics, and the Bottom Line," *Business Horizons*, 32 (May-June 1989): 65–70; and "Cheating Hearts," *USA Today* (February 15, 2001): 1B.
53. Vikas Anand, Blake E. Ashforth, and Mahendra Joshi, "Business as Usual: The Acceptance and Perpetuation of Corruption in Organizations," *Academy of Management Executive*, 18 (May 2004): 51. Also see Oliver Ryan, "By the Numbers," *Fortune* (November 15, 2004): 40; and Mark A. Barnett, Fred W. Sanborn, and Andrea C. Shane, "Factors Associated with Individuals' Likelihood of Engaging in Various Minor Moral and Legal Violations," *Basic and Applied Social Psychology*, 27 (March 2005): 77–84.
54. As quoted in Del Jones, "Military a Model for Execs," *USA Today* (June 9, 2004): 4B.
55. For inspiring reading, see John McCain, "In Search of Courage," *Fast Company*, no. 86 (September 2004): 53–56.
56. See Kevin Gibson, "Excuses, Excuses: Moral Slippage in the Workplace," *Business Horizons*, 43 (November-December 2000): 65–72.
57. For a good management-oriented discussion of values, see Barry Z. Posner and Warren H. Schmidt, "Values and the American Manager: An Update Updated," *California Management Review*, 34 (Spring 1992): 80–94.
58. Joseph Weber, "Keeping Out of a Jam," *Business Week* (October 4, 2004): 104.
59. Michael Schrage, "I Wasn't Fired," *Fortune* (January 21, 2002): 128.
60. For a landmark treatment of values, see Milton Rokeach, *Beliefs, Attitudes, and Values* (San Francisco: Jossey-Bass, 1968), p. 124; and Milton Rokeach and Sandra J. Ball-Rokeach, "Stability and Change in American Value Priorities, 1968–1981," *American Psychologist*, 44 (May 1989): 775–784. Also see Gregory R. Maio and James M. Olson, "Values as Truisms: Evidence and Implications," *Journal of Personality and Social Psychology*, 74 (February 1998): 294–311.
61. Rokeach, *Beliefs, Attitudes, and Values*, p. 124.
62. See Rick Wartzman, "Nature or Nurture? Study Blames Ethical Lapses on Corporate Goals," *Wall Street Journal* (October 9, 1987): 27. Two other Rokeach scale studies are reported in Maris G. Martinsons and Aelita Brivins Martinsons, "Conquering Cultural Constraints to Cultivate Chinese Management Creativity and Innovation," *Journal of Management Development*, 15, no. 9 (1996): 18–35; and Ralph A. Rodriguez, "Challenging Demographic Reductionism: A Pilot Study Investigating Diversity in Group Composition," *Small Group Research*, 29 (December 1998): 744–759. Also see Shalom H. Schwartz and Galit Sagie, "Value Consensus and Importance: A Cross-National Study," *Journal of Cross-Cultural Psychology*, 31 (July 2000): 465–497.
63. Marc Gunther, "God & Business," *Fortune* (July 9, 2001): 58–80; and Gary R. Weaver and Bradley R. Agle, "Religiosity and Ethical Behavior in Organizations: A Symbolic Interactionist Perspective," *Academy of Management Review*, 27 (January 2002): 77–97.
64. See Edward Soule, "Managerial Moral Strategies—In Search of a Few Good Principles," *Academy of Management Review*, 27 (January 2002): 114–124.
65. Excerpted from Hosmer, *Moral Leadership in Business*, pp. 39–41. © 1994, McGraw-Hill. Reproduced with permission of The McGraw-Hill Companies.
66. See Archie B. Carroll, "In Search of the Moral Manager," *Business Horizons*, 30 (March-April 1987): 7–15. Also see Gary R. Weaver, "Ethics and Employees: Making the Connection," *Academy of Management Executive*, 18 (May 2004): 121–125.
67. Data from "The Stat," *Business Week* (December 29, 2003): 16.
68. Data from "Ethics Training a Low Priority," *USA Today* (January 29, 2004): 1B.
69. Peter Navarro, "Why Johnny Can't Lead," *Harvard Business Review*, 82 (December 2004): 17. Also see Fara Warner, "Ethics? Ask a First Grader," *Fast Company*, no. 83 (June 2004): 45; Mica Schneider, "Poor Marks for Ethics Teaching," *Business Week* (June 14, 2004): 16; and Jennifer Merritt, "Welcome to Ethics 101," *Business Week* (October 18, 2004): 90.
70. For example, see Dawn Blalock, "Study Shows Many Execs Are Quick to Write Off Ethics," *Wall Street Journal* (March 26, 1996): C1, C22; and Liz Simpson, "Taking

the High Road," *Training*, 39 (January 2002): 36–38.

71. For details, see John A. Byrne, "The Best-Laid Ethics Programs . . . " *Business Week* (March 9, 1992): 67–69.
72. See Holly Dolezalek, "Eye on Ethics," *Training*, 40 (November 2003): 42–45.
73. Based on discussion in Brad Lee Thompson, "Ethics Training Enters the Real World," *Training*, 27 (October 1990): 82–94. For reasons why ethics programs fail, see Paul C. Judge, "Ethics for Hire," *Business Week* (July 15, 1996): 26–28.
74. For ground-breaking material on ethical advocates, see Theodore V. Purcell, "Electing an 'Angel's Advocate' to the Board," *Management Review*, 65 (May 1976): 4–11; Theodore V. Purcell, "Institutionalizing Ethics into Top Management Decisions," *Public Relations Quarterly*, 22 (Summer 1977): 15–20. Also see Dov Seidman, "The Case for Ethical Leadership," *Academy of Management Executive*, 18 (May 2004): 134–138; and Robert M. Fulmer, "The Challenge of Ethical Leadership," *Organizational Dynamics*, 33, no. 3 (2004): 307–317.
75. See Linda Klebe Trevino and Michael E. Brown, "Managing to Be Ethical: Debunking Five Business Ethics Myths," *Academy of Management Executive*, 18 (May 2004): 69–81.
76. "Business's Big Morality Play," *Dun's Review* (August 1980): 56.
77. See Margaret M. Clark, "New Sentencing Guidelines to Reward Ethical Culture, Compliance Commitment," *HR Magazine*, 49 (September 2004): 28.
78. See Richard P. Nielsen, "Changing Unethical Organizational Behavior," *Academy of Management Executive*, 3 (May 1989): 123–130. Relative to the Enron case, see Wendy Zellner, "A Hero—and a Smoking-Gun Letter," *Business Week* (January 28, 2002): 34–35; and Greg Farrell and Jayne O'Donnell, "Watkins Testifies Skilling, Fastow Duped Lay, Board," *USA Today* (February 15, 2002): 1B–2B.
79. See "Former Enron Vice President Sherron Watkins on the Enron Collapse," *Academy of Management Executive*, 17 (November 2003): 119–125; Amanda Ripley and Maggie Sieger, "The Special Agent," *Time* (January 6, 2003): 34–40; Christine Dugas, "Spotlight Hits Whistle-Blower," *USA Today* (December 10, 2003): 3B; and Alan Levin, "Pa. Hometown Proud of MP Who Blew Whistle on Scandal," *USA Today* (May 10, 2004): 4A.
80. Ralph Nader, "An Anatomy of Whistle Blowing," in *Whistle Blowing*, ed. Ralph Nader, Peter Petkas, and Kate Blackwell (New York: Bantam, 1972), p. 7. For interesting case studies of whistle-blowers, see William McGowan, "The Whistleblowers Hall of Fame," *Business and Society Review*, 52 (Winter 1985): 31–36.
81. The federal Whistleblowers Protection Act of 1989 is discussed in David Israel and Anita Lechner, "Protection for Whistleblowers," *Personnel Administrator*, 34 (July 1989): 106. Also see Jayne O'Donnell, "It's Tough to Get a Lawsuit Heard," *USA Today* (July 29, 2004): 2B; and Maria Greco Danaher, "Internal Complaints May Support Whistle-Blower Claim," *HR Magazine*, 49 (December 2004): 108.
82. Data from Jayne O'Donnell, "$26.6M Won't Change Me, Whistle-Blower Says," *USA Today* (May 14, 2004): 2B. Also see Neil Weinberg, "The Dark Side of Whistleblowing," *Forbes* (March 14, 2005): 90–98.
83. Jayne O'Donnell, "Complainants Take Risks Unfathomable to Most," *USA Today* (July 29, 2004): 1B.
84. Adapted from Kenneth D. Walters, "Your Employees' Right to Blow the Whistle," *Harvard Business Review*, 53 (July-August 1975): 26–34, 161–162. Also see Janet P. Near and Marcia P. Miceli, "Effective Whistle-Blowing," *Academy of Management Review*, 20 (July 1995): 679–708; and Kate Walter, "Ethics Hot Lines Tap into More Than Wrongdoing," *HR Magazine*, 40 (September 1995): 79–85.

CHAPTER 6

1. **Opening Quote** As quoted in Brent Schlender, "Peter Drucker Takes the Long View," *Fortune* (September 28, 1998): 170.
2. Herb Greenberg, "Prescription for Recovery," *Fortune* (July 23, 2001): 252.
3. See Andrew Campbell, "Tailored, Not Benchmarked: A Fresh Look at Corporate Planning," *Harvard Business Review*, 77 (March-April 1999): 41–50.
4. For example, see John Carey, "Shell: The Case of the Missing Oil," *Business Week* (January 26, 2004): 45–46; and Sarah Bartlett, "What We Didn't Plan For," *Inc.*, 27 (January 2005): 74–81.
5. Based on discussion in Frances J. Milliken, "Three Types of Perceived Uncertainty About the Environment: State, Effect, and Response Uncertainty," *Academy of Management Review*, 12 (January 1987): 133–143. Also see Hugh Courtney, *20/20 Foresight: Crafting Strategy in an Uncertain World* (Boston: Harvard Business School Press, 2001): ch. 2.
6. For example, see Michelle Kessler, "Brain Drain Signals Trouble at Technology Companies," *USA Today* (November 2, 2004): 1B–2B.
7. See Raymond E. Miles and Charles C. Snow, *Organizational Strategy, Structure, and Process* (New York: McGraw-Hill, 1978), p. 29. A validation of the Miles and Snow model can be found in Stephen M. Shortell and Edward J. Zajak, "Perceptual and Archival Measures of Miles and Snow's Strategic Types: A Comprehensive Assessment of Reliability and Validity," *Academy of Management Journal*, 33 (December 1990): 817–832. Also see the four articles accompanying David J. Ketchen, Jr., "Introduction: Raymond E. Miles and Charles C. Snow's *Organizational Strategy, Structure, and Process*," *Academy of Management Executive*, 17 (November 2003): 95–96.
8. Data from Joseph Weber, "Harley Investors May Get a Wobbly Ride," *Business Week* (February 11, 2002): 65.
9. Ellen Florian, "Six Lessons from the Fast Lane," *Fortune* (September 6, 2004): 150. For related reading on prospectors, see Cliff Edwards, "Intel," *Business Week* (March 8, 2004): 56–64; Geoffrey A. Moore, "Darwin and the Demon: Innovating Within Established Enterprises," *Harvard Business Review*, Special Issue: Top-Line Growth, 82 (July-August 2004): 86–92; Kathleen Kerwin, "How to Market a Groundbreaker," *Business Week* (October 18, 2004): 104, 106; and David H. Freedman, "Freeing Your Inner Think Tank," *Inc.*, 27 (May 2005): 65–66.
10. William Boulding and Markus Christen, "First-Mover Disadvantage," *Harvard Business Review*, 79 (October 2001): 20–21 (emphasis added). Also see Jim Collins, "Best Beats First," *Inc.*, 22 (August 2000): 48–52; and Kevin Maney, "Impregnable 'First Mover Advantage' Philosophy Suddenly Isn't," *USA Today* (July 18, 2001): 3B.
11. See David H. Freedman, "Burt Rutan: Entrepreneur of the Year," *Inc.*, 27 (January 2005): 58–66.
12. David Stires, "Rx for Investors," *Fortune* (May 3, 2004): 170. For more on analyzers, see Eric Bonabeau, "The Perils of the Imitation Age," *Harvard Business Review*, 82 (June 2004): 45–54; and Owen Thomas, "The 800-Lb. Copycat," *Business 2.0*, 5 (September 2004): 100.
13. Kevin Maney, "Kodak to Lay Off 15,000, Cut Manufacturing Capacity," *USA Today* (January 23, 2004): 4B. Another reactor, Motorola, is profiled in Michelle Kessler, "Parts Shortages Mean Some Hot Gifts Missing in Action," *USA Today* (December 17, 2003): 6B.
14. Based on data in Ben Dobbin, "Kodak Cutting More Workers," *Arizona Republic* (January 23, 2004): D1–D2.
15. For details, see Jeffrey S. Conant, Michael P. Mokwa, and P. Rajan Varadarajan, "Strategic Types, Distinctive Marketing Competencies and Organizational Performance: A Multiple Measures Based Study," *Strategic Management Journal*, 11 (September 1990): 365–383. Also see Shaker A. Zahra and John A. Pearce II, "Research Evidence on the Miles-Snow Typology," *Journal of Management*, 16 (December 1990): 751–768.
16. Based on Mary M. Crossan, Henry W. Lane, Roderick E. White, and Leo Klus, "The Improvising Organization: Where Planning Meets Opportunity," *Organizational Dynamics*, 24 (Spring 1996): 20–35. Also see Constantinos

Markides and Constantinos D. Charitou, "Competing with Dual Business Models: A Contingency Approach," *Academy of Management Executive*, 18 (August 2004): 22–36; and Benson Honig, "Entrepreneurship Education: Toward a Model of Contingency-Based Business Planning," *Academy of Management Learning and Education*, 3 (September 2004): 258–273.

17. See Michael Arndt, "3M's Rising Star," *Business Week* (April 12, 2004): 62–74.
18. "$1.4B Authorized to Restore Everglades," *USA Today* (December 12, 2000): 15A. A company with a redefined mission is discussed in Andrew Park, "Can EMC Find Growth Beyond Hardware?" *Business Week* (November 1, 2004): 62–63.
19. Scott Adams, "Dilbert's Management Handbook," *Fortune* (May 13, 1996): 104.
20. Based on R. Duane Ireland and Michael A. Hitt, "Mission Statements: Importance, Challenge, and Recommendations for Development," *Business Horizons*, 35 (May-June 1992): 34–42. Also see V. Kasturi Rangan, "Lofty Missions, Down-to-Earth Plans," *Harvard Business Review*, 82 (March 2004): 112–119; Jennifer Reingold, "The Liberator," *Fast Company*, no. 83 (June 2004): 82–85; and Marshall Goldsmith, "Goal 1, Mission 0," *Fast Company*, no. 85 (August 2004): 91.
21. Bill Saporito, "PPG: Shiny, Not Dull," *Fortune* (July 17, 1989): 107.
22. Dan Sullivan, "The Reality Gap," *Inc.*, 21 (March 1999): 119.
23. Anthony P. Raia, *Managing by Objectives* (Glenview, Ill.: Scott, Foresman, 1974), p. 24.
24. For an excellent and comprehensive treatment of goal setting, see Edwin A. Locke and Gary P. Latham, *Goal Setting: A Motivational Technique That Works!* (Englewood Cliffs, N.J.: Prentice-Hall, 1984). Also see Robert D. Pritchard, Philip L. Roth, Steven D. Jones, Patricia J. Galgay, and Margaret D. Watson, "Designing a Goal-Setting System to Enhance Performance: A Practical Guide," *Organizational Dynamics*, 17 (Summer 1988): 69–78.
25. John A. Byrne and Heather Timmons, "Tough Times for a New CEO," *Business Week* (October 29, 2001): 66.
26. For example, see Edward C. Baig, "Secretaries for the Rest of Us," *Business Week* (November 16, 1998): 146; Ed Brown, "Stephen Covey's New One-Day Seminar," *Fortune* (February 1, 1999): 138, 140; and Donna J. Abernathy, "A Get-Real Guide to Time Management," *Training & Development*, 53 (June 1999): 22–26.
27. Raia, *Managing by Objectives*, p. 54.
28. Brian Grow, "Thinking Outside the Big Box," *Business Week* (October 25, 2004): 70.
29. Richard Koch, *The 80/20 Principle: The Secret of Achieving More with Less* (New York: Currency Doubleday, 1998), p. 4. Also see Gail Johnson, "Squeaky Wheels," *Training*, 41 (June 2004): 20.
30. Diane Brady, "Why Service Stinks," *Business Week* (October 23, 2000): 126.
31. Elizabeth Esfahani, "How to Get Tough with Bad Customers," *Business 2.0*, 5 (October 2004): 52.
32. See Barbara Moses, "The Busyness Trap," *Training*, 35 (November 1998): 38–42; Sumantra Ghoshal and Heike Bruch, "Reclaim Your Job," *Harvard Business Review*, 82 (March 2004): 41–45; Seth Godin, "If It's Urgent, Ignore It," *Fast Company*, no. 81 (April 2004): 101; Stanley Bing, "Diagnosis: Executive ADD," *Fortune* (May 31, 2004): 216; Alison Stein Wellner, "The Time Trap," *Inc.*, 26 (June 2004): 42–43; and Nanci Hellmich, "Most People Multitask, So Most People Don't Sit Down to Eat," *USA Today* (September 30, 2004): 8D.
33. See Steven Berglas, "Chronic Time Abuse," *Harvard Business Review*, 82 (June 2004): 90–97; and Michael C. Mankins, "Stop Wasting Valuable Time," *Harvard Business Review*, 82 (September 2004): 58–65.
34. See Peter F. Drucker, *The Practice of Management* (New York: Harper & Row, 1954). For a short update on Drucker, see Thomas A. Stewart, "Effective Immediately," *Harvard Business Review*, 82 (June 2004): 10.
35. As an indication of the widespread interest in MBO, more than 700 books, articles, and technical papers had been written on the subject by the late 1970s. For a brief history of MBO, see George S. Odiorne, "MBO: A Backward Glance," *Business Horizons*, 21 (October 1978): 14–24. An excellent collection of readings on MBO may be found in George Odiorne, Heinz Weihrich, and Jack Mendieson, *Executive Skills: A Management by Objectives Approach* (Dubuque, Iowa: Wm. C. Brown, 1980). Also see Henry H. Beam, "George Odiorne," *Business Horizons*, 39 (November-December 1996): 73–76.
36. T. J. Rodgers, "No Excuses Management," *Harvard Business Review*, 68 (July-August 1990): 87, 89.
37. For related reading, see Philippe Haspeslagh, Tomo Noda, and Fares Boulos, "It's Not Just About the Numbers," *Harvard Business Review*, 79 (July-August 2001): 65–73.
38. For example, see Jan P. Muczyk and Bernard C. Reimann, "MBO as a Complement to Effective Leadership," *Academy of Management Executive*, 3 (May 1989): 131–139.
39. An interesting study of the positive and negative aspects of MBO may be found in Robert C. Ford and Frank S. McLaughlin, "Avoiding Disappointment in MBO Programs," *Human Resource Management*, 21 (Summer 1982): 44–49. Positive research evidence is summarized in Robert Rodgers and John E. Hunter, "Impact of Management by Objectives on Organizational Productivity," *Human Resource Management*, 76 (April 1991): 322–336.
40. For a critical appraisal of MBO core assumptions, see David Halpern and Stephen Osofsky, "A Dissenting View of MBO," *Public Personnel Management*, 19 (Fall 1990): 321–330. Deming's critical comments may be found in W. Edwards Deming, *Out of the Crisis* (Cambridge, Mass.: MIT Press, 1986), pp. 23–96; and Dennis W. Organ, "The Editor's Chair," *Business Horizons*, 39 (November-December 1996): 1.
41. See Richard Babcock and Peter F. Sorensen Jr., "An MBO Check-List: Are Conditions Right for Implementation?" *Management Review*, 68 (June 1979): 59–62.
42. Robert Rodgers and John E. Hunter, "Impact of Management by Objectives on Organizational Productivity," *Journal of Applied Psychology*, 76 (April 1991): 322.
43. See Robert Rodgers, John E. Hunter, and Deborah L. Rogers, "Influence of Top Management Commitment on Management Program Success," *Journal of Applied Psychology*, 78 (February 1993): 151–155.
44. See Jeffrey K. Pinto and Om P. Kharbanda, "Lessons for an Accidental Profession," *Business Horizons*, 38 (March-April 1995): 41–50. For an excellent resource book, see Jeffrey K. Pinto and O. P. Kharbanda, *Successful Project Managers: Leading Your Team to Success* (New York: Van Nostrand Reinhold, 1995).
45. Project Management Institute, "What Is a Project?" **www.pmi.org**, p. 1.
46. April Umminger, "Gala Runs on Flower Power," *USA Today* (February 27, 2004): 3E.
47. Louisa Wah, "Most IT Projects Prove Inefficient," *Management Review*, 88 (January 1999): 7. Also see Nadim Matta and Sandy Krieger, "From IT Solutions to Business Results," *Business Horizons*, 44 (November-December 2001): 45–50.
48. See Jennifer E. Jenkins, "Moving Beyond a Project's Implementation Phase," *Nursing Management*, 27 (January 1996): 48B, 48D.
49. See recent issues of *Project Management Journal*.
50. Excerpted from a list of 26 attributes in "4.1 Software Attributes," **www.project-manager.com**.
51. Based on Sheila Simsarian Webber and Maria T. Torti, "Project Managers Doubling as Client Account Executives," *Academy of Management Executive*, 18 (February 2004): 60–71. Also see Sheila Simsarian Webber and Richard J. Klimoski, "Client-Project Manager Engagements, Trust, and Loyalty," *Journal of Organizational Behavior*, 25 (December 2004): 997–1013.
52. Jimmie West, "Show Me the Value," *Training*, 40 (September 2003): 62.
53. Based partly on discussion in Pinto and Kharbanda, *Successful Project Managers*,

p. 147.

54. See Dan Carrison, "Fueling Deadline Urgency," *HR Magazine*, 48 (December 2003): 111–115; Tammy Galvin, "Managing Projects," *Training*, 41 (January 2004): 12; and Yukika Awazu, Kevin C. Desouza, and J. Roberto Evaristo, "Stopping Runaway IT Projects," *Business Horizons*, 47 (January-February 2004): 73–80.
55. One example of the application of a flow chart is Sharon M. McKinnon, "How Important Are Those Foreign Operations? A Flow-Chart Approach to Loan Analysis," *Financial Analysts Journal*, 41 (January-February 1985): 75–78.
56. For examples of early Gantt charts, see H. L. Gantt, *Organizing for Work* (New York: Harcourt, Brace and Howe, 1919), ch. 8.
57. Gantt chart applications can be found in Conkright, "So You're Going to Manage a Project," p. 64; and Andrew Raskin, "Task Masters," *Inc.* Tech 1999, no. 1 (1999): 62–72.
58. Ivars Avots, "The Management Side of PERT," *California Management Review*, 4 (Winter 1962): 16–27.
59. Additional information on PERT can be found in Nancy Madlin, "Streamlining the PERT Chart," *Management Review*, 75 (September 1986): 67–68; Eric C. Silverberg, "Predicting Project Completion," *Research Technology Review*, 34 (May-June 1991): 46–49; Robert L. Armacost and Rohne L. Jauernig, "Planning and Managing a Major Recruiting Project," *Public Personnel Management*, 20 (Summer 1991): 115–126; T. M. Williams, "Practical Use of Distributions in Network Analysis," *Journal of the Operational Research Society*, 43 (March 1992): 265–270; and Hooshang Kuklan, "Effective Project Management: An Expanded Network Approach," *Journal of Systems Management*, 44 (March 1993): 12–16.
60. Adapted in part from John Fertakis and John Moss, "An Introduction to PERT and PERT/Cost Systems," *Managerial Planning*, 19 (January-February 1971): 24–31.

CHAPTER 7

1. **Opening Quote** Laurel Cutler is vice chair of FCB/Leber Katz Partners, an advertising agency in New York City. Quoted in Susan Caminiti, "The Payoff from a Good Reputation," *Fortune* (February 10, 1992): 74.
2. Data from "Fortune 1,000 Ranked Within Industries," *Fortune* (April 5, 2004): F–51.
3. For good background reading on strategic management, see George Stalk, Jr., and Rob Lachenauer, "Hard Ball: Five Killer Strategies for Trouncing the Competition," *Harvard Business Review*, 82 (April 2004): 62–71; Stephen Cummings and Duncan Angwin, "The Future Shape of Strategy: Lemmings or Chimeras?" *Academy of Management Executive*, 18 (May 2004): 21–36; Ranjay Gulati, "How CEOs Manage Growth Agendas," *Harvard Business Review*, Special Issue: Top-Line Growth, 82 (July-August 2004): 124–132; and W. Chan Kim and Renee Mauborgne, "Blue Ocean Strategy," *Harvard Business Review*, 82 (October 2004): 76–84.
4. Data from C. Chet Miller and Laura B. Cardinal, "Strategic Planning and Firm Performance: A Synthesis of More Than Two Decades of Research," *Academy of Management Journal*, 37 (December 1994): 1649–1665.
5. Data from "U.S. Executives Cite Main Issues," *USA Today* (October 8, 2004): 1A.
6. As quoted in Ron Insana, "Dell Knows His Niche and He'll Stick with It," *USA Today* (April 5, 2004): 3B.
7. See Michael C. Mankins, "Stop Wasting Valuable Time," *Harvard Business Review*, 82 (September 2004): 58–65.
8. Steve Bates, "Murky Corporate Goals Can Undermine Recovery," *HR Magazine*, 47 (November 2002): 14.
9. Strategy making is discussed in Michael Beer and Russell A. Eisenstat, "How to Have an Honest Conversation About Your Business Strategy," *Harvard Business Review*, 82 (February 2004): 82–89; and Kwaku Atuahene-Gima and Haiyang Li, "Strategic Decision Comprehensiveness and New Product Development Outcomes in New Technology Ventures," *Academy of Management Journal*, 47 (August 2004): 583–597.
10. John A. Byrne, "Strategic Planning," *Business Week* (August 26, 1996): 52.
11. Data from Joseph Weber, "Keeping Out of a Jam," *Business Week* (October 4, 2004): 104–106. Also see Ellen Florian, "Six Lessons from the Fast Lane," *Fortune* (September 6, 2004): 156.
12. Based on a definitional framework found in David J. Teece, "Economic Analysis and Strategic Management," *California Management Review*, 26 (Spring 1984): 87. An alternative view calls for supplementing the notion of "fit" with the concept of "stretch," thus better accommodating situations in which a company's aspirations exceed its present resource capabilities. See Gary Hamel and C. K. Prahalad, "Strategy as Stretch and Leverage," *Harvard Business Review*, 71 (March-April 1993): 75–84.
13. Based on discussion in Donald C. Hambrick and James W. Fredrickson, "Are You Sure You Have a Strategy?" *Academy of Management Executive*, 15 (November 2001): 48–59. For related research, see Mason A. Carpenter and James D. Westphal, "The Strategic Context of External Network Ties: Examining the Impact of Director Appointments on Board Involvement in Strategic Decision Making," *Academy of Management Journal*, 44 (August 2001): 639–660.
14. See Michael A. Hitt, Barbara W. Keats, and Samuel M. DeMarie, "Navigating in the New Competitive Landscape: Building Strategic Flexibility and Competitive Advantage in the 21st Century," *Academy of Management Executive*, 12 (November 1998): 22–42. For related reading, see Richard T. Watson, Pierre Berthon, Leyland F. Pitt, and George M. Zinkhan, "Marketing in the Age of the Network: From Marketplace to U-Space," *Business Horizons*, 47 (November-December 2004): 33–40.
15. Ronald Henkoff, "How to Plan for 1995," *Fortune* (December 31, 1990): 70.
16. Heather Johnson, "Learn or Burn," *Training*, 41 (April 2004): 19.
17. See William R. King and David I. Cleland, *Strategic Planning and Policy* (New York: Van Nostrand Reinhold, 1978), pp. 180–183; Laura Landro, "Giants Talk Synergy But Few Make It Work," *Wall Street Journal* (September 25, 1995): B1–B2; and Thomas Osegowitsch, "The Art and Science of Synergy: The Case of the Auto Industry," *Business Horizons*, 44 (March-April 2001): 17–24.
18. Patricia Sellers, "P&G: Teaching an Old Dog New Tricks," *Fortune* (May 31, 2004): 168.
19. Chris Woodyard, "FedEx Ponies Up $2.4B for Kinko's," *USA Today* (December 31, 2003): 1B.
20. "Hotels Developing Multiple Personalities," *USA Today* (September 10, 1996): 4B.
21. Marc Gunther, "Stampp Corbin: Recycling Electronic Waste," *Fortune* (August 23, 2004): 121.
22. Catherine Yang, "Easy Broadband—And Smarter Power," *Business Week* (November 22, 2004): 132.
23. Drawn from Fred Vogelstein, "How Intel Got Inside," *Fortune* (October 4, 2004): 127–136.
24. See Don Moyer, "The Sin in Synergy," *Harvard Business Review*, 82 (March 2004): 131.
25. See Michael E. Porter, *Competitive Strategy* (New York: Free Press, 1980), p. 35; and Michael E. Porter, *The Competitive Advantage of Nations* (New York: Free Press, 1990), p. 39. For updates on Michael Porter, see James Surowiecki, "The Return of Michael Porter," *Fortune* (February 1, 1999): 135–138; Richard M. Hodgetts, "A Conversation with Michael E. Porter: A 'Significant Extension' Toward Operational Improvement and Positioning," *Organizational Dynamics*, 28 (Summer 1999): 24–33; and Jessi Hempel, "Inner Cities Are Where the Money Is," *Business Week* (December 27, 2004): 16.
26. Porter, *The Competitive Advantage of Nations*, p. 37. Also see Keith H. Hammonds, "Michael Porter's Big Ideas," *Fast Company*, no. 44 (March 2001): 150–156.
27. For more on branding, see Linda Tischler, "The *Good* Brand," *Fast Company*, no. 85 (August 2004): 47–49; Douglas B. Holt, John A. Quelch, and Earl L. Taylor, "How Global Brands Compete,"

Harvard Business Review, 82 (September 2004): 68–75; and Roland T. Rust, Valarie A. Zeithaml, and Katherine N. Lemon, "Customer-Centered Brand Management," *Harvard Business Review*, 82 (September 2004): 110–118.

28. Ron Zemke and Dick Schaaf, *The Service Edge* (New York: New American Library, 1989), p. 360.
29. As quoted in Bruce Horovitz and Theresa Howard, "With Image Crumbling, Kmart Files Chapter 11," *USA Today* (January 23, 2002): 1B. Also see Jerry Useem, "Should We Admire Wal-Mart?" *Fortune* (March 8, 2004): 118, 120; and Jack Ewing, "The Next Wal-Mart?" *Business Week* (April 26, 2004): 60–62.
30. For related reading, see Cliff Edwards, "The EU's Hard Look Inside Intel," *Business Week* (June 21, 2004): 13; and Robert Levine, "Dummies for Dummies," *Business 2.0*, 5 (December 2004): 76–77.
31. Adrienne Carter, "Foot Locker," *Money*, 31 (January 2002): 69.
32. Another example of this strategy is discussed in Curtis Rist, "The Sultan of Stitch," *Business 2.0*, 5 (September 2004): 56.
33. For details, see Luis Ma. R. Calingo, "Environmental Determinants of Generic Competitive Strategies: Preliminary Evidence from Structured Content Analysis of *Fortune* and *Business Week* Articles (1983–1984)," *Human Relations*, 42 (April 1989): 353–369. For related research, see Praveen R. Nayyar, "Performance Effects of Three Foci in Service Firms," *Academy of Management Journal*, 35 (December 1992): 985–1009.
34. James F. Moore, *The Death of Competition: Leadership and Strategy in the Age of Business Ecosystems* (New York: HarperBusiness, 1996), p. 25. For relevant background material, see Warren Boeker, "Organizational Strategy: An Ecological Perspective," *Academy of Management Journal*, 34 (September 1991): 613–635; and James F. Moore, "Predators and Prey: A New Ecology of Competition," *Harvard Business Review*, 71 (May-June 1993): 75–86. Also see Marco Iansiti and Roy Levien, "Strategy as Ecology," *Harvard Business Review*, 82 (March 2004): 68–78.
35. See Courtney Shelton Hunt and Howard E. Aldrich, "The Second Ecology: Creation and Evolution of Organizational Communities," in *Research in Organizational Behavior*, vol. 20, ed. Barry M. Staw and L. L. Cummings (Greenwich, Conn.: JAI Press, 1998), pp. 267–301.
36. For more, see Cliff Edwards, "Intel," *Business Week* (March 8, 2004): 56–64; and Cliff Edwards, "Getting Intel Back on the Inside Track," *Business Week* (November 29, 2004): 39.
37. "Companies Find Niche with Online Programs," *USA Today* (December 11, 2003): 2B.
38. For example, see Patrick J. Sauer, "Are You Ready for Some Football Cliches?" *Inc.*, 25 (October 2003): 96–100.
39. Moore, *The Death of Competition*, p. 61.
40. "OnStar: Competitors Can Be Partners," *Fast Company*, no. 81 (April 2004): 68.
41. See Jennifer Reingold, "What We Learned in the New Economy," *Fast Company*, no. 80 (March 2004): 56–68; Timothy J. Mullaney, "The Net," *Business Week* (June 28, 2004): 116–117; and Robert D. Hof, "The Web for the People," *Business Week* (December 6, 2004): 18.
42. As quoted in Bill Breen, "Banker's Hours," *Fast Company*, no. 52 (November 2001): 200, 202.
43. For more, see "The New Technology Crib Sheet: Basic Training," *Inc.* Technology, 23 (September 2001): 194–202; Varun Grover and Pradipkumar Ramanlal, "Digital Economics and the E-Business Dilemma," *Business Horizons*, 47 (July-August 2004): 71–80; Otis Port, "He Made the Net Work," *Business Week* (September 27, 2004): 20; and Otis Port, "Spinning the World's Web," *Business Week* (November 8, 2004): 16.
44. Robert D. Hof, "The Wizard of Web Retailing," *Business Week* (December 20, 2004): 18.
45. See Timothy J. Mullaney, "E-Biz Strikes Again," *Business Week* (May 10, 2004): 80–82; Alison Overholt, "Search for Tomorrow," *Fast Company*, no. 85 (August 2004): 69–71; Andy Reinhardt, "Net Phone Calls, Free—and Clear," *Business Week* (November 1, 2004): 60–61; Stephen Baker, "The Online Ad Surge," *Business Week* (November 22, 2004): 76–82; Stephen Baker, "Where the Real Internet Money Is Made," *Business Week* (December 27, 2004): 98–100; and Bob Buderi, "Conquering the Digital Haystack," *Inc.*, 27 (January 2005): 34–35.
46. Based on G.T. Lumpkin and Gregory G. Dess, "E-Business Strategies and Internet Business Models: How the Internet Adds Value," *Organizational Dynamics*, 33, no. 2 (2004): 161–173.
47. See Erick Schonfeld, "How to Manage Growth: Meg Whitman, CEO, eBay," *Business 2.0*, 5 (December 2004): 99.
48. See Andrew Tilin, "Jon Gales: The Blogger Who Makes $55K Working 3 Hours a Day," *Business 2.0*, 5 (November 2004): 112; and Ben Elgin, "Information at Warp Speed," *Business Week* (December 27, 2004): 18.
49. Michael E. Porter, "Strategy and the Internet," *Harvard Business Review*, 79 (March 2001): 76.
50. Based on Leyland Pitt, Pierre Berthon, and Richard T. Watson, "Cyberservice: Taming Service Marketing Problems with the World Wide Web," *Business Horizons*, 42 (January-February 1999): 11–18; Chris Charuhas, "How to Train Web-Site Builders," *Training*, 36 (August 1999): 48–53; and John R. Graham, "How Can We Get More Visitors to Our Web Site?" *Canadian Manager*, 25 (Fall 2000): 16–17.
51. Data from Jon Swartz, "E-Tailers Ring Up a Record Holiday Week," *USA Today* (December 27, 2001): 3B. Also see Jeanette Brown, "Shoppers Are Beating a Path to the Web," *Business Week* (December 24, 2001): 41.
52. Based on Jon Swartz, "Retailers Discover Leap to Web's a Doozy," *USA Today* (December 18, 2001): 3B.
53. Based on discussion in Lorrie Grant, "Lands' End Is an Ultimate Online Model," *USA Today* (December 3, 2004): 1B–2B.
54. See Jennifer Reingold, "Into Thin Air," *Fast Company*, no. 81 (April 2004): 78–82.
55. For an alternative perspective, see Mahesh Gupta, Lynn Boyd, and Lyle Sussman, "To Better Maps: A TOC Primer for Strategic Planning," *Business Horizons*, 47 (March-April 2004): 15–26.
56. Henry Mintzberg, "The Design School: Reconsidering the Basic Premises of Strategic Management," *Strategic Management Journal*, 11 (March-April 1990): 192.
57. See "Mission Statement Myopia," *Training*, 41 (December 2004): 16.
58. Richard F. Vancil, "Strategy Formulation in Complex Organizations," *Sloan Management Review*, 17 (Winter 1976): 18. Also see Brian J. Huffman, "Why Environmental Scanning Works Except When You Need It," *Business Horizons*, 47 (May-June 2004): 39–48; and Norm Brodsky, "The Myths About Niches," *Inc.*, 26 (August 2004): 53–54..
59. As quoted in Fred Vogelstein, "It's Not Just Business, It's Personal," *Fortune* (November 15, 2004). 200.
60. See Michael Yaziji, "Turning Gadflies into Allies," *Harvard Business Review*, 82 (February 2004): 110–115; Brian Caulfield, "Know Your Enemy," *Business 2.0*, 5 (June 2004): 89–90; and Ellen Florian, "Find the Right Path: Symantec," *Fortune* (September 6, 2004): 154, 156.
61. "Is Your Company an Extrovert?" *Management Review*, 85 (March 1996): 7.
62. Duff McDonald, "Meet eBay's New Postman," *Business 2.0*, 5 (September 2004): 52.
63. See Dave Ulrich and Norm Smallwood, "Capitalizing on Capabilities," *Harvard Business Review*, 82 (June 2004): 119–127.
64. Adapted from Andrew Bartmess and Keith Cerny, "Building Competitive Advantage Through a Global Network of Capabilities," *California Management Review*, 35 (Winter 1993): 78–103.
65. See David A. Thomas, "Diversity as Strategy," *Harvard Business Review*, 82 (September 2004): 98–108.
66. As quoted in Alan Webber, "The Old Economy Meets the New Economy," *Fast Company*, no. 51 (October 2001): 74. For more on strategic speed, see "Is Your Company Up to Speed?" *Fast Company*, no. 71 (June 2003): 81–86; Kathleen Kerwin, "How Would You Like Your

Ford?" *Business Week* (August 9, 2004): 34; and Hau L. Lee, "The Triple-A Supply Chain," *Harvard Business Review*, 82 (October 2004): 102–112.

67. For essential reading in this area, see Michael and James Champy, *Reengineering the Corporation: A Manifesto for Business Revolution* (New York: HarperBusiness, 1993); and James Champy, *Reengineering Management: The New Mandate for Leadership* (New York: HarperBusiness, 1995). Also see Gail L. Rein, "FEEL IT—A Method for Achieving Sustainable Process Changes," *Business Horizons*, 47 (May-June 2004): 75–81; and Daniel McGinn, "Re-engineering 2.0," *Newsweek* (November 22, 2004): 59.
68. According to Henry Mintzberg, there are four reasons why organizations need strategies: (1) to set direction, (2) to focus effort of contributors, (3) to define the organization, and (4) to provide consistency. For more, see Henry Mintzberg, "The Strategy Concept II: Another Look at Why Organizations Need Strategies," *California Management Review*, 30 (Fall 1987): 25–32.
69. Waldron Berry, "Beyond Strategic Planning," *Managerial Planning*, 29 (March-April 1981): 14.
70. See Eric Beaudan, "The Failure of Strategy," *Ivey Business Journal*, 65 (January-February 2001): 64–86.
71. Charles H. Roush Jr. and Ben C. Ball Jr., "Controlling the Implementation of Strategy," *Managerial Planning*, 29 (November-December 1980): 4.
72. Donald C. Hambrick and Albert A. Cannella Jr., "Strategy Implementation as Substance and Selling," *Academy of Management Executive*, 3 (November 1989): 282–283. Another good discussion of strategic implementation may be found in Orit Gadiesh and James L. Gilbert, "Transforming Corner-Office Strategy into Frontline Action," *Harvard Business Review*, 79 (May 2001): 72–79.
73. As quoted in "How to Keep Your Company's Edge," *Business 2.0*, 4 (December 2003): 93.
74. William D. Guth and Ian C. Macmillian, "Strategy Implementation versus Middle Management Self-Interest," *Strategic Management Journal*, 7 (July-August 1986): 321.
75. See Gail Johnson, "Brain Drain," *Training*, 40 (December 2003): 16.
76. See Gary Meyer, "eWorkbench: Real-Time Tracking of Synchronized Goals," *HR Magazine* (April 2001): 115–118 (**www.workscape.com**).
77. See F.C. "Ted" Weston, Jr., "ERP II: The Extended Enterprise System," *Business Horizons*, 46 (November-December 2003): 49–55.
78. See Vasudevan Ramanujan and N. Venkatraman, "Planning and Performance: A New Look at an Old Question," *Business Horizons*, 30 (May-June 1987): 19–25.
79. See Ken McGee, "Give Me That Real-Time Information," *Harvard Business Review*, 82 (April 2004): 26.
80. See Andy Hines, "A Checklist for Evaluating Forecasts," *The Futurist*, 29 (November-December 1995): 20–24.
81. See Laura Rich, "The Follies of Holiday Forecasting," *Business 2.0*, 5 (November 2004): 90, 92; and Geoffrey Colvin, "Listen to the People Who Got the Election Right," *Fortune* (November 29, 2004): 82.
82. An excellent overview of forecasting techniques may be found in David M. Georgoff and Robert G. Murdick, "Manager's Guide to Forecasting," *Harvard Business Review*, 64 (January-February 1986): 110–120.
83. Based on C. W. J. Granger, *Forecasting in Business and Economics* (New York: Academic Press, 1980), pp. 6–10.
84. Paul Kaihla, "Inside Cisco's $2 Billion Blunder," *Business 2.0*, 3 (March 2002): 88–89.
85. See Louis Lavelle, "The Case of the Corporate Spy," *Business Week* (November 26, 2001): 56, 58.
86. Duncan Martell, "Rumors Fly About iPod Upgrade," *USA Today* (October 12, 2004): 2B.
87. See Chiquan Guo, "Marketing Research: *Cui bono?*" *Business Horizons*, 47 (September-October 2004): 33–38.
88. See Steven Schnaars and Paschalina (Lilia) Ziamou, "The Essentials of Scenario Writing," *Business Horizons*, 44 (July- August 2001): 25–31; and Hugh Courtney, "Scenario Planning," *20-20 Foresight: Crafting Strategy in an Uncertain World* (Boston: Harvard Business School Press, 2001), pp. 160–165.
89. Steven P. Schnaars, "How to Develop and Use Scenarios," *Long Range Planning*, 20 (February 1987): 106.
90. For sample scenarios, see David Stipp, "The Pentagon's Weather Nightmare," *Fortune* (February 9, 2004): 100–108; Bob Parks, "The World of Business in 2020," *Business 2.0*, 5 (April 2004): 119–124; and Peter Schwartz, "Future Shock," *Fortune* (April 5, 2004): 260–266. Interesting scenarios for the U.S. Social Security system are presented in Peter Coy, "Social Security: The Long View," *Business Week* (January 14, 2002): 24.
91. Leonard Fuld, "Be Prepared," *Harvard Business Review*, 81 (November 2003): 20.
92. Ibid.
93. Peter Coy and Neil Gross, "21 Ideas for the 21st Century," *Business Week* (August 30, 1999): 82. Also see Jeffrey Pfeffer, "The Whole Truth and Nothing But," *Business 2.0*, 5 (October 2004): 78.
94. See "Slipping into the Future," *Fast Company*, no. 89 (December 2004): 88.
95. See Nancy Chambers, "The Really Long View," *Management Review*, 87 (January 1998): 10–15; Karen Thomas, "Fashion Understatement: That's So 5 Minutes Ago," *USA Today* (March 23, 1999): 1D–2D; and H. Donald Hopkins, "Using History for Strategic Problem-Solving: The Harley-Davidson Effect," *Business Horizons*, 42 (March-April 1999): 52–60.
96. See Wendy Zellner, "Chrysler's Next Generation," *Business Week* (December 19, 1988): 52–57.

CHAPTER 8

1. **Opening Quote** Norm Brodsky, "The Thin Red Line," *Inc.*, 26 (January 2004): 49.
2. See R. Duane Ireland and C. Chet Miller, "Decision-Making and Firm Success," *Academy of Management Executive*, 18 (November 2004): 8–12.
3. Data from "Hurry Up and Decide!" *Business Week* (May 14, 2001): 16.
4. Andrew Backover and Elliot Blair Smith, "AT&T Wireless Gambit Places Cingular at Top," *USA Today* (February 18, 2004): 1B.
5. Morgan W. McCall, Jr. and Robert E. Kaplan, *Whatever It Takes: The Realities of Managerial Decision Making*, 2nd ed. (Englewood Cliffs, N.J.: Prentice-Hall, 1990), p. 5.
6. Paul Hoversten, "Backers Hope Amenities Will Quiet Critics," *USA Today* (February 22, 1995): 2A.
7. Michael Parrish, "Former Arco Chief Still Gambling on Oil Strikes," *Los Angeles Times* (September 21, 1993): D1.
8. Matthew L. Ward, "Airports Must Make Way for Airbus' Gigantic A380," *The Arizona Republic* (February 11, 2001): D1. Also see Carol Matlock, "Airbus Has a Weight Problem," *Business Week* (June 28, 2004): 63.
9. Eric W. K. Tsang, "Superstition and Decision-Making: Contradiction or Complement?" *Academy of Management Executive*, 18 (November 2004): 92.
10. Justin Martin, "Tomorrow's CEOs," *Fortune* (June 24, 1996): 90.
11. Steven M. Gillon, "Unintended Consequences: Why Our Plans Don't Go According to Plan," *The Futurist*, 35 (March-April 2001): 49.
12. See Edward Tenner, *Why Things Bite Back: Technology and the Revenge of Unintended Consequences* (New York: Vintage Books, 1996), ch. 1; and Peter Eisler, "Fallout Likely Caused 15,000 Deaths," *USA Today* (February 28, 2002): 1A.
13. For an interesting example, see Ivan Amato, "Tin Whiskers: The Next Y2K Problem?" *Fortune* (January 10, 2005): 27–28.
14. Abrahm Lustgarten, "Pick Industry. Dive in. Repeat," *Fortune* (November 15, 2004): 202.
15. For related reading, see Eric Bonabeau, "Predicting the Unpredictable," *Harvard Business Review*, 80 (March 2002): 109–116; Darren Dahl, "Conduct Due Diligence," *Inc.*, 26 (October 2004): 98; and Karen Hopkins, "The Risk Agenda," Special Advertising Section, *Business Week* (November 22, 2004).
16. See Kent D. Miller and Wei-Ru Chen, "Variable Organizational Risk Preferences: Tests of the March-Shapira

Model," *Academy of Management Journal*, 47 (February 2004): 105–115.

17. See Bill Treasurer, "How Risk-Taking Really Works," *Training*, 37 (January 2000): 40–44.
18. Paul Raeburn, "A Biotech Boom with a Difference," *Business Week* (December 31, 2001): 52. Also see Faith Arner, "The High Cost of Drugs Hits a Drugmaker," *Business Week* (December 29, 2003): 14; and Julie Schmit, "Drugmakers Gamble Big on Generics," *USA Today* (August 24, 2004): 1B.
19. See Jerry Adler, "Mind Reading," *Newsweek* (July 5, 2004): 42–47.
20. For related reading, see Alison Overholt, "Are You a Polyolefin Optimizer? Take This Quiz," *Fast Company*, no. 81 (April 2004): 37.
21. See Kerry J. Sulkowicz, "The Corporate Shrink," *Fast Company*, no. 88 (November 2004): 52; and Eugene Sadler-Smith and Erella Shefy, "The Intuitive Executive: Understanding and Applying 'Gut Feel' in Decision-Making," *Academy of Management Executive*, 18 (November 2004): 76–91.
22. Abrahm Lustgarten, "From Art House to Mouse House to. . .?" *Fortune* (November 15, 2004): 198. For a profile of another intuitive executive, see "Arthur Levinson: Genentech," *Business Week* (January 12, 2004): 59.
23. As quoted in Keith H. Hammonds, "Continental's Turnaround Pilot," *Fast Company*, no. 53 (December 2001): 100. Also see Jonathan Alter, "Your Gut Only Gets You So Far," *Newsweek* (October 11, 2004): 29.
24. For research on decision styles, see Susanne G. Scott and Reginald A. Bruce, "Decision-Making Style: The Development and Assessment of a New Measure," *Educational and Psychological Measurement*, 55 (October 1995): 818–831; and Stacey M. Whitecotton, D. Elaine Sanders, and Kathleen B. Norris, "Improving Predictive Accuracy with a Combination of Human Intuition and Mechanical Decision Aids," *Organizational Behavior and Human Decision Processes*, 76 (December 1998): 325–348.
25. See Beverly Geber, "A Quick Course in Decision Science," *Training*, 25 (April 1988): 54–55; Alan E. Singer, Steven Lysonski, Ming Singer, and David Hayes, "Ethical Myopia: The Case of 'Framing' by Framing," *Journal of Business Ethics*, 10 (January 1991): 29–36; and Glen Whyte, "Decision Failures: Why They Occur and How to Prevent Them," *Academy of Management Executive*, 5 (August 1991): 23–31.
26. Irwin P. Levin, Sara K. Schnittjer, and Shannon L. Thee, "Information Framing Effects in Social and Personal Decisions," *Journal of Experimental Social Psychology*, 24 (November 1988): 527. For additional research evidence, see Michael J. Zickar and Scott Highhouse, "Looking Closer at the Effects of Framing on Risky Choice: An Item Response Theory Analysis," *Organizational Behavior and Human Decision Processes*, 75 (July 1998): 75–91; and Vikas Mittal and William T. Ross Jr., "The Impact of Positive and Negative Affect and Issue Framing on Issue Interpretation and Risk Taking," *Organizational Behavior and Human Decision Processes*, 76 (December 1998): 298–324.
27. For good background reading, see Barry M. Staw and Jerry Ross, "Knowing When to Pull the Plug," *Harvard Business Review*, 65 (March-April 1987): 68–74; and Barry M. Staw and Jerry Ross, "Understanding Behavior in Escalation Situations," *Science*, 246 (October 13, 1989): 216–220. Also see William S. Silver and Terence R. Mitchell, "The Status Quo Tendency in Decision Making," *Organizational Dynamics*, 18 (Spring 1990): 34–46.
28. See Joel Brockner, "The Escalation of Commitment to a Failing Course of Action: Toward Theoretical Progress," *Academy of Management Review*, 17 (January 1992): 39–61; Beth Dietz-Uhler, "The Escalation of Commitment in Political Decision-Making Groups: A Social Identity Approach," *European Journal of Social Psychology*, 26 (July-August 1996): 611–629; Jennifer L. DeNicolis and Donald A. Hantula, "Sinking Shots and Sinking Costs? Or, How Long Can I Play in the NBA?" *Academy of Management Executive*, 10 (August 1996): 66–67; Marc D. Street and William P. Anthony, "A Conceptual Framework Establishing the Relationship Between Groupthink and Escalating Commitment Behavior," *Small Group Research*, 28 (May 1997): 267–293; and Asghar Zardkoohi, "Do Real Options Lead to Escalation of Commitment?" *Academy of Management Review*, 29 (January 2004): 111–119.
29. For related research evidence, see Itamar Simonson and Barry M. Staw, "Deescalation Strategies: A Comparison of Techniques for Reducing Commitment to Losing Courses of Action," *Journal of Applied Psychology*, 77 (August 1992): 419–426.
30. As quoted in "Navy Cancels Contract for Attack Planes," *Christian Science Monitor* (January 9, 1991): 3. Also see Russell Mitchell, "Desperately Seeking an Attack Bomber," *Business Week* (January 21, 1991): 35. Another good case study of escalation can be found in Jerry Ross and Barry M. Staw, "Organizational Escalation and Exit: Lessons from the Shoreham Nuclear Power Plant," *Academy of Management Journal*, 36 (August 1993): 701–732.
31. Sidney Finkelstein, *Why Smart Executives Fail—and What You Can Learn from Their Mistakes* (New York : Portfolio, 2003), pp. 223–224.
32. For an interesting exercise, see J. Edward Russo and Paul J. H. Schoemaker, "The Overconfidence Quiz," *Harvard Business Review*, 68 (September-October 1990): 236–237.
33. See Mark Simon, "Man, I'm Smart About How Stupid I Am!" *Business Horizons*, 44 (July-August 2001): 21–24.
34. Decision traps and personal investing are instructively covered in Gary Belsky and Thomas Gilovich, *Why Smart People Make Big Money Mistakes—and How to Correct Them: Lessons from the New Science of Behavioral Economics* (New York : Fireside, 1999), ch. 6; and Jason Zweig, "Do You Sabotage Yourself?" *Money*, 30 (May 2001): 74–78.
35. An excellent resource book is James G. March, *A Primer on Decision Making: How Decisions Happen* (New York: Free Press, 1994). Also see Catherine A. Maritan, "Capital Investment as Investing in Organizational Capabilities: An Empirically Grounded Process Model," *Academy of Management Journal*, 44 (June 2001): 513–531.
36. Drawn from Gardiner Morse, "By Any Other Name," *Harvard Business Review*, 82 (November 2004): 30.
37. Belsky and Gilovich, *Why Smart People Make Big Money Mistakes—and How to Correct Them*, pp. 100–101.
38. For example, see Herbert A. Simon, *The New Science of Management Decision*, rev. ed. (Englewood Cliffs, N.J.: Prentice-Hall, 1977), p. 40. Also see James W. Dean Jr. and Mark P. Sharfman, "Does Decision Process Matter? A Study of Strategic Decision-Making Effectiveness," *Academy of Management Journal*, 39 (April 1996): 368–396; Jerre L. Stead, "Whose Decision Is It, Anyway?" *Management Review*, 88 (January 1999): 13; Anna Muoio, "All the Right Moves," *Fast Company*, no. 24 (May 1999): 192–200; and Brian Palmer, "Click Here for Decisions," *Fortune* (May 10, 1999): 153–156.
39. Andrew S. Grove, *High Output Management* (New York: Random House, 1983), p. 98.
40. Simon, *The New Science of Management Decision*, p. 46.
41. See David R. A. Skidd, "Revisiting Bounded Rationality," *Journal of Management Inquiry*, 1 (December 1992): 343–347; and March, *A Primer on Decision Making*, pp. 8–9.
42. See Charles R. Schwenk, "The Use of Participant Recollection in the Modeling of Organizational Decision Processes," *Academy of Management Review*, 10 (July 1985): 496–503. Also see the discussion of "adaptive decision making" in Amitai Etzioni, "Humble Decision Making," *Harvard Business Review*, 67 (July-August 1989): 122–126; and Janet Barnard, "Successful CEOs Talk About Decision Making," *Business Horizons*, 35 (September-October 1992): 70–74.
43. For more on strategic decision making, see Paul C. Nutt, "Expanding the Search for Alternatives During Strategic Decision-Making," *Academy of Manage-

ment Executive, 18 (November 2004): 13–28; and Jay J. Janney and Gregory G. Dess, "Can Real-Options Analysis Improve Decision-Making? Promises and Pitfalls," *Academy of Management Executive*, 18 (November 2004): 60–75.

44. Chester I. Barnard, *The Functions of the Executive* (Cambridge, Mass.: Harvard University Press, 1938), p. 190. Also see Susan S. Kirschenbaum, "Influence of Experience on Information-Gathering Strategies," *Journal of Applied Psychology*, 77 (June 1992): 343–352.
45. See Stuart F. Brown, "Making Decisions in a Flood of Data," *Fortune* (August 13, 2001): 148[B]–148[H].
46. For good background reading, see *Harvard Business Review on Knowledge Management* (Boston: Harvard Business School Publishing, 1998); Thomas A. Stewart, "The Case Against Knowledge Management," *Business 2.0*, 3 (February 2002): 80–83; Brandon Hall, "Are You Ready for the Future?" *Training*, 41 (January 2004): 14; and Michael Weeks, "Knowledge Management in the Wild," *Business Horizons*, 47 (November-December 2004): 15–24..
47. David W. De Long and Patricia Seemann, "Confronting Conceptual Confusion and Conflict in Knowledge Management," *Organizational Dynamics*, 29 (Summer 2000): 33.
48. Dorothy Leonard and Walter Swap, "Deep Smarts," *Harvard Business Review*, 82 (September 2004): 92.
49. For more on tacit knowledge, see Roy Lubit, "Tacit Knowledge and Knowledge Management: The Keys to Sustainable Competitive Advantage," *Organizational Dynamics*, 29 (Winter 2001): 164–178; and Paul Davidson, "Tacit Finds Matches in Company E-mail," *USA Today* (June 14, 2004): 3B.
50. See Rob Cross, Andrew Parker Laurence Prusak, and Stephen P. Borgatti, "Knowing What We Know: Supporting Knowledge Creation and Sharing in Social Networks," *Organizational Dynamics*, 30 (Fall 2001): 100–120; and Rob Cross and Jonathon N. Cummings, "Tie and Network Correlates of Individual Performance in Knowledge-Intensive Work," *Academy of Management Journal*, 47 (December 2004): 928–937.
51. See Kevin C. Desouza and Yukika Awazu, "Knowledge Management," *HR Magazine*, 48 (November 2003): 107–112.
52. Paul Kaihla, "The Matchmaker in the Machine," *Business 2.0*, 5 (January-February 2004): 52, 54.
53. Information flows between people from different organizations is covered in Lee Fleming and Adam Juda, "A Network of Invention," *Harvard Business Review*, 82 (April 2004): 22; and Stephen Tallman, Mark Jenkins, Nick Henry, and Steven Pinch, "Knowledge, Clusters, and Competitive Advantage," *Academy of Management Review*, 29 (April 2004): 258–271.
54. Jeffrey Hsu and Tony Lockwood, "Collaborative Computing," *Byte*, 18 (March 1993): 113. Also see Anthony M. Townsend, Michael E. Whitman, and Anthony R. Hendrickson, "Computer Support System Adds Power to Group Processes," *HR Magazine*, 40 (September 1995): 87–91.
55. Catherine Romano, "The Power of Collaboration: Untapped," *Management Review*, 86 (January 1997): 7. See Jennifer Hedlund, Daniel R. Ilgen, and John R. Hollenbeck, "Decision Accuracy in Computer-Mediated versus Face-to-Face Decision-Making Teams," *Organizational Behavior and Human Decision Processes*, 76 (October 1998): 30–47; Kevin Maney, "Software Genius Gets into Groove," *USA Today* (February 12, 2001): 1B–2B; and Alison Overholt, "Virtually There?" *Fast Company*, no. 56 (March 2002): 108–114.
56. George P. Huber, *Managerial Decision Making* (Glenview, Ill.: Scott, Foresman, 1980), pp. 141–142. Also see Michael Pacanowsky, "Team Tools for Wicked Problems," *Organizational Dynamics*, 23 (Winter 1995): 36–51.
57. As quoted in Ronald Henkoff, "A Whole New Set of Glitches for Digital's Robert Palmer," *Fortune* (August 19, 1996): 193.
58. See Steven G. Rogelberg, Janet L. Barnes-Farrell, and Charles A. Lowe, "The Stepladder Technique: An Alternative Group Structure Facilitating Effective Group Decision Making," *Journal of Applied Psychology*, 77 (October 1992): 730–737; Steven W. Floyd and Bill Wooldridge, "Managing Strategic Consensus: The Foundation of Effective Implementation," *Academy of Management Executive*, 6 (November 1992): 27–39; James R. Larson Jr., Caryn Christensen, Timothy M. Franz, and Ann S. Abbott, "Diagnosing Groups: The Pooling, Management, and Impact of Shared and Unshared Case Information in Team-Based Medical Decision Making," *Journal of Personality and Social Psychology*, 75 (July 1998): 93–108; and Daniel P. Forbes and Francis J. Milliken, "Cognition and Corporate Governance: Understanding Boards of Directors as Strategic Decision-Making Groups," *Academy of Management Review*, 24 (July 1999): 489–505.
59. See Priscilla M. Elsass and Laura M. Graves, "Demographic Diversity in Decision-Making Groups: The Experiences of Women and People of Color," *Academy of Management Review*, 22 (October 1997): 946–973; and Katherine Hawkins and Christopher B. Power, "Gender Differences in Questions Asked During Small Decision-Making Group Discussions," *Small Group Research*, (April 1999): 235–256.
60. See Gayle W. Hill, "Group versus Individual Performance: Are N + 1 Heads Better Than One?" *Psychological Bulletin*, 91 (May 1982): 517–539. Also see John P. Wanous and Margaret A. Youtz, "Solution Diversity and the Quality of Group Decisions," *Academy of Management Journal*, 29 (March 1986): 149–158; and Warren Watson, Larry K. Michaelsen, and Walt Sharp, "Member Competence, Group Interaction, and Group Decision Making: A Longitudinal Study," *Journal of Applied Psychology*, 76 (December 1991): 803–809.
61. See John Grossmann, "Thinking Small," *Inc.*, 26 (August 2004): 34; and Richard Florida, "America's Looming Creativity Crisis," *Harvard Business Review*, 82 (October 2004): 122–136.
62. A good historical perspective on creativity can be found in Michael Michalko, "Thinking Like a Genius," *The Futurist*, 32 (May 1998): 21–25.
63. Based on discussion in N. R. F. Maier, Mara Julius, and James Thurber, "Studies in Creativity: Individual Differences in the Storing and Utilization of Information," *The American Journal of Psychology*, 80 (December 1967): 492–519.
64. Sidney J. Parnes, "Learning Creative Behavior," *The Futurist*, 18 (August 1984): 30–31. Also see Liz Simpson, "Fostering Creativity," *Training*, 38 (December 2001): 54–57; and Polly LaBarre, "Weird Ideas That Work," *Fast Company*, no. 54 (January 2002): 68–73.
65. As quoted in Ryan Underwood, "Fast Talk: Question Assumptions," *Fast Company*, no. 89 (December 2004): 44.
66. See Arthur Koestler, *The Act of Creation* (London: Hutchinson, 1969), p. 27.
67. See James L. Adams, *Conceptual Blockbusting* (San Francisco: Freeman, 1974), p. 35. Also see Bruce Nussbaum, "This Is the IDEO Way," *Business Week* (May 17, 2004): 89.
68. See Charles R. Day Jr., "What a Dumb Idea," *Industry Week* (January 2, 1989): 27–28; and "In Search of Oink," *Management Review*, 88 (January 1999): 32–36.
69. Minda Zetlin, "Nurturing Nonconformists," *Management Review*, 88 (October 1999): 30. Similar results were found in a parallel study reported in Bill Breen, "The 6 Myths of Creativity," *Fast Company*, no. 89 (December 2004): 75–78.
70. See Anne Fisher, "How to Encourage Bright Ideas," *Fortune* (May 3, 2004): 70; Sylvia Nasar, "What Makes Beautiful Minds," *Fast Company*, no. 89 (December 2004): 50–52; and Linda Tischler, "The Care and Feeding of the Creative Class," *Fast Company*, no. 89 (December 2004): 93–95.
71. As quoted in Abrahm Lustgarten, "A Hot, Steaming Cup of Customer Awareness," *Fortune* (November 15, 2004): 192.
72. See Ian Wylie, "Failure Is Glorious," *Fast Company*, no. 51 (October 2001): 35–38.
73. List adapted from Roger von Oech, *A Whack on the Side of the Head* (New York:

Warner Books, 1983). Reprinted by permission.
74. Huber, *Managerial Decision Making*, p. 12. Also see Brent Roper, "Sizing Up Business Problems," *HR Magazine*, 46 (November 2001): 50–56.
75. As quoted in Thomas Mucha, "How to Ask the Right Questions," *Business 2.0*, 5 (December 2004): 118.
76. A good typology of business problems is discussed in Tom Kramlinger, "A Trainer's Guide to Business Problems," *Training*, 30 (March 1993): 47–50.
77. Louis S. Richman, "How to Get Ahead in America," *Fortune* (May 16, 1994): 48.
78. For an empirical classification of organizational problems, see David A. Cowan, "Developing a Classification Structure of Organizational Problems: An Empirical Investigation," *Academy of Management Journal*, 33 (June 1990): 366–390.
79. Adapted from Huber, *Managerial Decision Making*, pp. 13–15. Also see Norm Brodsky, "Problems, Problems: Are You Getting to the Root Causes? *Inc.*, 26 (February 2004): 43–44.
80. Marshall Sashkin and Kenneth J. Kiser, *Total Quality Management* (Seabrook, Md.: Ducochon Press, 1991), p. 153.
81. Adams, *Conceptual Blockbusting*, p. 7.
82. See Michael Schrage, "Playing Around with Brainstorming," *Harvard Business Review*, 79 (March 2001): 149–154.
83. For related research, see John J. Sosik, Bruce J. Avolio, and Surinder S. Kahai, "Inspiring Group Creativity: Comparing Anonymous and Identified Electronic Brainstorming," *Small Group Research*, 29 (February 1998): 3–31.
84. Jerry Useem, "Another Boss Another Revolution," *Fortune* (April 5, 2004): 112.
85. See Russell L. Ackoff, "The Art and Science of Mess Management," *Interfaces*, 11 (February 1981): 20–26. Also see Russell L. Ackoff, *Management in Small Doses* (New York: Wiley, 1986), pp. 102–103.
86. See March, *A Primer on Decision Making*, p. 18; and Gina Imperato, "When Is 'Good Enough' Good Enough?" *Fast Company*, no. 26 (July-August 1999): 52.
87. Ackoff, "The Art and Science of Mess Management," p. 22.
88. As quoted in James B. Treece, "Shaking Up Detroit," *Business Week* (August 14, 1989): 78.
89. Paul Hawken, "Problems, Problems," *Inc.*, 9 (September 1987): 24.

CHAPTER 9

1. **Opening Quote** Kevin Freiberg and Jackie Freiberg, *Nuts! Southwest Airlines' Crazy Recipe for Business and Personal Success* (Austin, Texas: Bard Press, 1996), p. 155.
2. Data from **www.southwest.com**.
3. As quoted in Keith H. Hammonds, "We, Incorporated," *Fast Company*, no. 84 (July 2004): 87.
4. See B. J. Hodge, William P. Anthony, and Lawrence M. Gales, *Organization Theory: A Strategic Approach*, 5th ed. (Upper Saddle River, N.J.: Prentice-Hall, 1996), p. 10.
5. Adapted from Edgar H. Schein, *Organizational Psychology*, 3rd ed. (Englewood Cliffs, N.J.: Prentice-Hall, 1980), pp. 12–15.
6. See Adam Smith, *The Wealth of Nations* (New York: Modern Library, 1937), p. 7.
7. For example, see Tom Peters's opinions in "Author: More Women Should Be in Charge," *USA Today* (December 8, 2003): 13B.
8. Elliot Jaques, "In Praise of Hierarchy," *Harvard Business Review*, 68 (January-February 1990): 127. Also see Harold J. Leavitt, "Why Hierarchies Thrive," *Harvard Business Review*, 81 (March 2003): 96–102.
9. For an interesting biography of Henry Ford, see Ann Jardim, *The First Henry Ford: A Study in Personality and Business Leadership* (Cambridge, Mass.: MIT Press, 1970), p. 40.
10. This classification scheme is adapted from Peter M. Blau and William R. Scott, *Formal Organizations* (San Francisco: Chandler, 1962).
11. For more on nonprofits, see John A Quelch, James E. Austin, and Nathalie Laidler-Kylander, "Mining Gold in Not-for-Profit Brands," *Harvard Business Review*, 82 (April 2004): 24; Anne Fisher, "The Realities of Joining a Nonprofit," *Fortune* (August 9, 2004): 54; Julie Appleby, "Scales Tipping Against Tax-Exempt Hospitals," *USA Today* (August 24, 2004): 1B–2B; and "Not-for-Profits: Training for the Future," *Training*, 41 (December 2004): 13.
12. Data from Barrington Salmon, "How Charity Should Work," *USA Today* (March 22, 2004): 11B; "The Stat," *Business Week* (August 9, 2004): 10; and Jessi Hempel, "When Charity Begins at Home," *Business Week* (November 8, 2004): 76.
13. See Jonathan Turley, "Non-Profits' Executives Avoid Scrutiny, Valid Reforms," *USA Today* (February 12, 2004): 15A; Jessi Hempel and Amy Borrus, "Now the Nonprofits Need Cleaning Up," *Business Week* (June 21, 2004): 107–108; Jessi Hempel, "Nonprofits Under the Microscope," *Business Week* (August 30, 2004): 13; and Julie Appleby, "IRS Looking Closely at What Non-Profits Pay," *USA Today* (September 30, 2004): 2B.
14. Data from "Working for the Federal Government," *USA Today* (January 22, 2002): 1B. Also see Mahlon Apgar, IV, and John M. Keane, "New Business with the New Military," *Harvard Business Review*, 82 (September 2004): 45–56.
15. For related reading about crisis management, see James Lardner, "Be Prepared!" *Business 2.0*, 3 (January 2002): 41–52; and Joseph M. Grant and David A. Mack, "Preparing for the Battle: Healthy Leadership During Organizational Crisis," *Organizational Dynamics*, 33, no. 4 (2004): 409–425.
16. See Marc Cecere, "Drawing the Lines," *Harvard Business Review*, 79 (November 2001): 24.
17. For real-life versions of this story, see Lynn Henning, "Catau Still Enjoys Tying One On," *Detroit News* (July 4, 1999): 8D; Alan R. Kamuda, "Local Manufacturer's Lures Catch On with Fishermen," *Detroit Free Press* (March 30, 2000: 6D; and Dimitra Kessenides, "Getting Started: Buyer Beware," *Inc.*, 26 (December 2004): 48, 51.
18. James G. March, *Handbook of Organizations* (Chicago: Rand McNally, 1965), p. ix.
19. For more recent research, see Sydney Finkelstein and Richard A. D'Aveni, "CEO Duality as a Double-Edged Sword: How Boards of Directors Balance Entrenchment Avoidance and Unity of Command," *Academy of Management Journal*, 37 (October 1994): 1079–1108.
20. Drawn from Max Weber, *The Theory of Social and Economic Organization*, trans. A. M. Henderson and Talcott Parsons (New York: Oxford University Press, 1947). A critique based on the claim that Weber's work was mistranslated can be found in Richard M. Weiss, "Weber on Bureaucracy: Management Consultant or Political Theorist?" *Academy of Management Review*, 8 (April 1983): 242–248.
21. For a more detailed discussion, consult Warren G. Bennis, *Changing Organizations* (New York: McGraw-Hill, 1966), pp. 4–5.
22. For an excellent critique of modern bureaucracies, see Ralph P. Hummel, *The Bureaucratic Experience*, 3rd ed. (New York: St. Martin's Press, 1987).
23. Del Jones, "Welch: Nurture Best Workers, Lose Bottom 10%," *USA Today* (February 27, 2001): 2B.
24. See Paul Jarley, Jack Fiorito, and John Thomas Delaney, "A Structural Contingency Approach to Bureaucracy and Democracy in U.S. National Unions," *Academy of Management Journal*, 40 (August 1997): 831–861.
25. See, for example, Brian Dumaine, "The Bureaucracy Busters," *Fortune* (June 17, 1991): 36–50. Also see Craig J. Cantoni, "Eliminating Bureaucracy—Roots and All," *Management Review*, 82 (December 1993): 30–33; Gifford Pinchot and Elizabeth Pinchot, "Beyond Bureaucracy," *Business Ethics*, 8 (March–April 1994): 26–29; Oren Harari, "Let the Computers Be the Bureaucrats," *Management Review*, 85 (September 1996): 57–60; and David Welch, "Reinventing the Company," *Business Week* (March 22, 2004): 24.
26. Chester I. Barnard, *The Functions of the Executive* (Cambridge, Mass.: Harvard University Press, 1938), p. 165.
27. Charles Perrow, "The Short and Glorious History of Organizational Theory," *Organizational Dynamics*, 2 (Summer

1973): 4. Also see Joseph Ofori-Dankwa and Scott D. Julian, "Complexifying Organizational Theory: Illustrations Using Time Research," *Academy of Management Review*, 26 (July 2001): 415–430.

28. See Alan P. Brache and Geary A. Rummler, "Managing an Organization as a System," *Training*, 34 (February 1997): 68–74; Toby J. Tetenbaum, "Shifting Paradigms: From Newton to Chaos," *Organizational Dynamics*, 26 (Spring 1998): 21–32; and Rosabeth Moss Kanter, "Managing for Long-Term Success," *The Futurist*, 32 (August-September 1998): 43–45.
29. Stratford Sherman, "Andy Grove: How Intel Makes Spending Pay Off," *Fortune* (February 22, 1993): 58. Also see Alan M. Webber, "How Business Is a Lot Like Life," *Fast Company*, no. 45 (April 2001): 130–136; and John Child and Rita Gunther McGrath, "Organizations Unfettered: Organizational Form in an Information-Intensive Economy," *Academy of Management Journal*, 44 (December 2001): 1135–1148.
30. For related reading, see Marianne W. Lewis, "Exploring Paradox: Toward a More Comprehensive Guide," *Academy of Management Review*, 25 (October 2000): 760–776.
31. Fremont E. Kast and James E. Rosenzweig, *Organization and Management: A Systems and Contingency Approach*, 3rd ed. (New York: McGraw-Hill, 1979), p. 103. An excellent glossary of open-system terms can be found on page 102 of this source.
32. See Stephen Baker, "The Minimill That Acts Like a Biggie," *Business Week* (September 30, 1996): 100, 104; and Dean Foust, "Nucor: Meltdown in the Corner Office," *Business Week* (June 21, 1999): 37.
33. See V. Daniel R. Guide Jr. and Luk N. Van Wassenhove, "The Reverse Supply Chain," *Harvard Business Review*, 80 (February 2002): 25–26; and David Ticoll, "Get Self-Organized," *Harvard Business Review*, 82 (September 2004): 18–19.
34. See Chris Argyris, "The Executive Mind and Double-Loop Learning," *Organizational Dynamics*, 11 (Autumn 1982): 4–22; and Chris Argyris, "Teaching Smart People How to Learn," *Harvard Business Review*, 69 (May-June 1991): 99–109.
35. See Peter M. Senge, *The Fifth Discipline: The Art and Practice of the Learning Organization* (New York: Doubleday, 1990); Dusya Vera and Mary Crossan, "Strategic Leadership and Organizational Learning," *Academy of Management Review*, 29 (April 2004): 222–240; and G. Tomas M. Hult, David J. Ketchen Jr., and Stanley F. Slater, "Information Processing, Knowledge Development, and Strategic Supply Chain Performance," *Academy of Management Journal*, 47 (April 2004): 241–253.
36. David A. Garvin, "Building a Learning Organization, *Harvard Business Review*, 71 (July-August 1993): 78–91. For an extension, see Rob Cross, Andrew Parker, Laurence Prusak, and Stephen P. Borgatti, "Knowing What We Know: Supporting Knowledge Creation and Sharing in Social Networks," *Organizational Dynamics*, 30 (Fall 2001): 100–120. Also see Hans Berends, Kees Boersma, and Mathieu Weggeman, "The Structuration of Organizational Learning, *Human Relations*, 56 (September 2003): 1035–1056; and Thomas B. Lawrence, Michael K. Mauws, Bruno Dyck, and Robert F. Kleysen, "The Politics of Organizational Learning: Integrating Power into the 4I Framework," *Academy of Management Review*, 30 (January 2005): 180–191.
37. David Lei, John W. Slocum, and Robert A. Pitts, "Designing Organizations for Competitive Advantage: The Power of Unlearning and Learning," *Organizational Dynamics*, 27 (Winter 1999): 30. For a different perspective, see "Dee W. Hock," *Fast Company*, no. 26 (July-August 1999): 90.
38. For learning organizations in action, see Jack Welch, *Straight from the Gut* (New York: Warner Books, 2001), pp. 181–184; Robert Buderi, "Intel Revamps R&D," *Technology Review*, 104 (October 2001): 24–25; and "Grow or Die," *Training*, 39 (January 2002): 17.
39. Kim Cameron, "Critical Questions in Assessing Organizational Effectiveness," *Organizational Dynamics*, 9 (Autumn 1980): 70.
40. See Raj Aggarwal, "Using Economic Profit to Assess Performance: A Metric for Modern Firms," *Business Horizons*, 44 (January-February 2001): 55–60.
41. Winslow Buxton, "Growth from Top to Bottom," *Management Review*, 88 (July-August 1999): 11.
42. Detailed discussions of alternative models of organizational effectiveness may be found in Kishore Gawande and Timothy Wheeler, "Measures of Effectiveness for Governmental Organizations," *Management Science*, 45 (January 1999): 42–58; Edward V. McIntyre, "Accounting Choices and EVA," *Business Horizons*, 42 (January-February 1999): 66–72; and Toby D. Wall, Jonathan Michie, Malcolm Patterson, Stephen J. Wood, Maura Sheehan, Chris W. Clegg, and Michael West, "On the Validity of Subjective Measures of Company Performance," *Personnel Psychology*, 57 (Spring 2004): 95–118.
43. See Jeffrey Pfeffer, "When It Comes to 'Best Practices'—Why Do Smart Organizations Occasionally Do Dumb Things?" *Organizational Dynamics*, 25 (Summer 1996): 33–44; and Michael Beer, "How to Develop an Organization Capable of Sustained High Performance: Embrace the Drive for Results-Capability Development Paradox," *Organizational Dynamics*, 29 (Spring 2001): 233–247.
44. It is instructive to ponder why companies fall from grace over the years. One tracking device is *Fortune* magazine's annual list of "America's Most Admired Corporations." For example, see Ann Harrington, "America's Most Admired Companies," *Fortune* (March 8, 2004): 80–82.
45. Data from Ellen Simon, "AT&T to Stop Marketing Its Long-Distance Service," *Juneau Empire* (July 23, 2004): A7; Marilyn Adams, "More Jobs Could Be Cut at United," *USA Today* (September 2, 2004): 3B; and "Nortel Networks to Eliminate 3,250 Jobs," *USA Today* (October 1, 2004): 1B.
46. Peter Lorange and Robert T. Nelson, "How to Recognize—and Avoid—Organizational Decline," *Sloan Management Review*, 28 (Spring 1987): 41. For turnaround stories, see Colette A. Frayne and Robert E. Callahan, "Safeco CEO Mike McGavick on Leading a Turnaround," *Academy of Management Executive*, 18 (August 2004): 143–150; and Brian Grow, "Can Wonder Bread Rise Again?" *Business Week* (October 18, 2004): 108, 110.A
47. As quoted in Thor Valdmanis, "Researcher: Success Calls for Constant Reinvention," *USA Today* (August 6, 2004): 5B. Complacency at Nokia is discussed in Kevin Maney, "CEO Ollila Says Nokia's 'Sisu' Will See It Past Tough Times," *USA Today* (July 21, 2004): 1B–2B.
48. Drawn from Valdmanis, "Researcher: Success Calls for Constant Reinvention."
49. Data from "*Fortune* 500 Largest U.S. Corporations," *Fortune* (April 16, 2001): F1; "The 100 Best Companies," *Fortune* (January 8, 2001): 152; and Greg Farrell, "Accounting Firm Destroyed Enron Records," *USA Today* (January 11, 2002): 1B. Also see Wendy Zellner and Stephanie Anderson Forest, "The Fall of Enron," *Business Week* (December 17, 2001): 30–36; Bethany McLean, "Why Enron Went Bust," *Fortune* (December 24, 2001): 58–68; and Greg Farrell and Del Jones, "How Did Enron Come Unplugged?" *USA Today* (January 14, 2002): 1B–2B.
50. See Robert I. Sutton and Thomas D'Aunno, "Decreasing Organizational Size: Untangling the Effects of Money and People," *Academy of Management Review*, 14 (April 1989): 194–212.
51. See Kim S. Cameron, David A. Whetten, and Myung U. Kim, "Organizational Dysfunctions of Decline," *Academy of Management Journal*, 30 (March 1987): 126–138.
52. See Stephanie N. Mehta, "Lessons from the Lucent Debacle," *Fortune* (February 5, 2001): 143–148.
53. Michelle Kessler, "Brain Drain Signals Trouble at Technology Companies," *USA Today* (November 2, 2004): 1B.
54. Jim Kerstetter and Peter Burrows, "A CEO's Last Stand," *Business Week* (July

26, 2004): 64, 66.

55. Symptoms of organizational decline at Bethlehem Steel, Coca-Cola, Nokia, Fannie Mae, and Delta Air Lines are discussed in Carol J. Loomis, "The Sinking of Bethlehem Steel," *Fortune* (April 5, 2004): 174–187; Betsy Morris, "The Real Story," *Fortune* (May 31, 2004): 84–98; Nelson D. Schwartz, "Has Nokia Lost It?" *Fortune* (January 24, 2005): 98–106; Bethany McLean, "The Fall of Fannie Mae," *Fortune* (January 24, 2005): 122–140; and Dan Reed, "Delta Posts Record Losses for Quarter, '04," *USA Today* (January 21, 2005): 1B.
56. See Mark A. Mone, William McKinley, and Vincent L. Barker III, "Organizational Decline and Innovation: A Contingency Framework," *Academy of Management Review*, 23 (January 1998): 115–132; Arthur G. Bedeian and Achilles A. Armenakis, "The Cesspool Syndrome: How Dreck Floats to the Top of Declining Organizations," *Academy of Management Executive*, 12 (February 1998): 58–63; Donald N. Sull, "Why Good Companies Go Bad," *Harvard Business Review*, 77 (July-August 1999): 42–52; and Walter J. Ferrier, Ken G. Smith, and Curtis M. Grimm, "The Role of Competitive Action in Market Share Erosion and Industry Dethronement: A Study of Industry Leaders and Challengers," *Academy of Management Journal*, 42 (August 1999): 372–388.
57. Peter F. Drucker, *Managing the Non-Profit Organization* (New York: HarperCollins, 1990), p. 66.
58. The battle against complacency is discussed in Tim Smart, "GE's Welch: 'Fighting Like Hell to Be No. 1,'" *Business Week* (July 8, 1996): 48; and John P. Kotter, "Kill Complacency," *Fortune* (August 5, 1996): 168–170. Also see Ronald Henkoff, "Growing Your Company: Five Ways to Do It Right!" *Fortune* (November 25, 1996): 78–88.
59. As quoted in Dori Jones Yang and Andrea Rothman, "Reinventing Boeing," *Business Week* (March 1, 1993): 61.
60. Wayne F. Cascio, "Downsizing: What Do We Know? What Have We Learned?" *Academy of Management Executive*, 7 (February 1993): 95. Three downsizing strategies are discussed in Kim S. Cameron, Sarah J. Freeman, and Aneil K. Mishra, "Best Practices in White-Collar Downsizing: Managing Contradictions," *Academy of Management Executive*, 5 (August 1991): 57–73. Also see Charles R. Eitel, "The Ten Disciplines of Business Turnaround," *Management Review*, 87 (December 1998): 13; James R. Morris, Wayne F. Cascio, and Clifford E. Young, "Downsizing After All These Years: Questions and Answers About Who Did It, How Many Did It, and Who Benefited from It," *Organizational Dynamics*, 27 (Winter 1999): 78–87; and Bo Burlingham, "The Downsizer's Dilemma," *Inc.*, 23 (December 2001): 106–107.
61. See Michael Arndt, "How Companies Can Marry Well: European–U.S. Mergers Pay Off," *Business Week* (March 4, 2002): 28.
62. Gene Koretz, ". . . And How It Is Paying Off," *Business Week* (November 25, 1996): 30. For an alternative view, see Gene Koretz, "Big Payoffs from Layoffs," *Business Week* (February 24, 1997): 30.
63. Based on Elizabeth Lesly and Larry Light, "When Layoffs Alone Don't Turn the Tide," *Business Week* (December 7, 1992): 100–101. Also see Stephanie Armour, "Morale, Performance Slump After Layoffs," *USA Today* (July 30, 2001): 1B; Louis Lavelle, "Swing That Ax with Care," *Business Week* (February 11, 2002): 78; and William J. Baumol, Alan S. Blinder, and Edward N. Wolff, *Downsizing in America: Reality, Causes, and Consequences* (New York : Russell Sage Foundation, 2003).
64. See Janina C. Latack, Angelo J. Kinicki, and Gregory E. Prussia, "An Integrative Process Model of Coping with Job Loss," *Academy of Management Review*, 20 (April 1995): 311–342; Kay Devine, Trish Reay, Linda Stainton, and Ruth Collins-Nakai, "Downsizing Outcomes: Better a Victim Than a Survivor?" *Human Resource Management*, 42 (Summer 2003): 109–124; S. Douglas Pugh, Daniel P. Skarlicki, and Brian S. Passell, "After the Fall: Layoff Victims' Trust and Cynicism in Re-employment," *Journal of Occupational and Organizational Psychology*, 76 (June 2003): 201–212; and Barbara Hagenbaugh, "Lives Unraveled," *USA Today* (July 30, 2004): 1B–2B.
65. For example, see Paul Falcone, "A Scripted Layoff," *HR Magazine*, 47 (February 2002): 89–91; Daniel Roth, "How to Cut Pay, Lay Off 8,000 People, and Still Have Workers Who Love You," *Fortune* (February 4, 2002): 62–68; and Sandra Block, "Survival Guide for Workers on the Edge," *USA Today* (October 22, 2004): 3B.
66. See Stephanie Armour, "Employers Reassign Workers to Save Jobs," *USA Today* (December 26, 2001): 1B.
67. See, for example, Stephanie Armour, "Workers Take Pay Cuts over Pink Slips," *USA Today* (April 13, 2001): 1B; and "Take the Road Less Traveled," *HR Magazine*, 46 (July 2001): 46–51.
68. Michelle Neely Martinez, "To Have and to Hold," *HR Magazine*, 43 (September 1998): 130–139.
69. Stephanie Armour, "Companies Get Creative to Avoid Layoffs," *USA Today* (September 5, 2001): 1B.
70. "Southwest Offers Buyouts to Most Workers," *USA Today* (May 28, 2004): 1B.
71. Eric Schine, "Take the Money and Run—Or Take Your Chances," *Business Week* (August 16, 1993): 28. Also see Pat Wechsler, "AT&T Managers Rush Out the Door," *Business Week* (June 15, 1998): 53.
72. Plant-closing legislation and programs are discussed in Angelo Kinicki, Jeffrey Bracker, Robert Kreitner, Chris Lockwood, and David Lemak, "Socially Responsible Plant Closings," *Personnel Administrator*, 32 (June 1987): 116–128.
73. For a good overview, see "Closing Law's Key Provisions," *Nation's Business* (January 1989): 58, 60. Also see Richard A. Starkweather and Cheryl L. Steinbacher, "Job Satisfaction Affects the Bottom Line," *HR Magazine*, 43 (September 1998): 110–112.
74. See Nancy Hatch Woodward, "Spousal Support," *HR Magazine*, 46 (December 2001): 79–83.
75. "HR Executives Embrace Outplacement Assistance Efforts," *HR Magazine*, 49 (March 2004): 12.
76. See Shari Caudron, "Teach Downsizing Survivors How to Thrive," *Personnel Journal*, 75 (January 1996): 38–48; Marc Adams, "Training Employees as Partners," *HR Magazine*, 44 (February 1999): 64–70; and Kerry J. Sulkowicz, "The Corporate Shrink," *Fast Company*, no. 89 (December 2004): 40. For a positive discussion of layoff survivors, see Stephanie Armour, "Layoff Survivors Climb Ladder Faster," *USA Today* (September 10, 2001): 1B:
77. See David M. Slipy, "Anthropologist Uncovers Real Workplace Attitudes," *HR Magazine*, 35 (October 1990): 76–79; and David A. Kaplan, "Studying the Gearheads," *Newsweek* (August 3, 1998): 62.
78. This definition is based in part on Linda Smircich, "Concepts of Culture and Organizational Analysis," *Administrative Science Quarterly*, 28 (September 1983): 339–358. Also see Patrick M. Lencioni, "Make Your Values Mean Something," *Harvard Business Review*, 80 (July 2002): 113–117; and James M. Higgins and Craig McAllaster, "Want Innovation? Then Use Cultural Artifacts That Support It," *Organizational Dynamics*, 31 (August 2002): 74–84.
79. Data from John E. Sheridan, "Organizational Culture and Employee Retention," *Academy of Management Journal*, 35 (December 1992): 1036–1056. For parallel findings, see Shelly Branch, "The 100 Best Companies to Work for in America," *Fortune* (January 11, 1999): 118–144. Also see Daniel R. Denison, Stephanie Haaland, and Paulo Goelzer, "Corporate Culture and Organizational Effectiveness: Is Asia Different from the Rest of the World?" *Organizational Dynamics*, 33, no. 1 (2004): 98–109.
80. For more, see Jerry Want, "When Worlds Collide: Culture Clash," *Journal of Business Strategy*, 24 (September 2003): 14–21; Pamela Babcock, "Is Your Company Two-Faced?" *HR Magazine*, 49 (January 2004): 42–47; and Richard O. Mason, "Lessons in Organizational Ethics from the *Columbia* Disaster: Can a Culture Be Lethal?" *Organizational Dynamics*, 33, no. 2 (2004): 128–142.
81. Peter C. Reynolds, "Imposing a Corporate Culture," *Psychology Today*, 21 (March 1987): 38.

82. Based on Harrison M. Trice and Janice M. Beyer, *The Cultures of Work Organizations* (Englewood Cliffs, N.J.: Prentice-Hall, 1993), pp. 5–8.
83. As quoted in Stephen B. Shepard, "A Talk with Jeff Immelt," *Business Week* (January 28, 2002): 103.
84. See, for example, Beverly Geber, "100 Days of Training," *Training*, 36 (January 1999): 62–66; Peter Troiano, "Post-Merger Challenges," *Management Review*, 88 (January 1999): 6; and Robert J. Grossman, "Irreconcilable Differences," *HR Magazine*, 44 (April 1999): 42–48.
85. "A. G. Lafley: Procter & Gamble," *Business Week* (January 13, 2003): 67.
86. See David Dorsey, "The New Spirit of Work," *Fast Company*, no. 16 (August 1998): 125–134; and Jim Collins, "When Good Managers Manage Too Much," *Inc.*, 21 (April 1999): 31–32.
87. As quoted in Sandra Block, "Bridgeway Founder Wins with Integrity," *USA Today* (December 17, 2003): 5B.
88. For related research, see Elizabeth Wolfe Morrison, "Newcomers' Relationships: The Role of Social Network Ties During Socialization," *Academy of Management Journal*, 45 (December 2002): 1149–1160; and Julia Balogun and Gerry Johnson, "Organizational Restructuring and Middle Manager Sensemaking," *Academy of Management Journal*, 47 (August 2004): 523–549.
89. Alan L. Wilkins, "The Culture Audit: A Tool for Understanding Organizations," *Organizational Dynamics*, 12 (Autumn 1983): 34–35. Also see Gene J. Koprowski, "Rude Awakening," *HR Magazine*, 49 (September 2004): 50–55.
90. Rebecca Ganzel, "Putting Out the Welcome Mat," *Training*, 35 (March 1998): 54. Also see Noel M. Tichy, "No Ordinary Boot Camp," *Harvard Business Review*, 79 (April 2001): 63–70; and "Executive Orientation Gets Poor Marks in Survey," *HR Magazine*, 49 (March 2004): 12.
91. For the full *story*, see Douglas A. Ready, "How Storytelling Builds Next-Generation Leaders," *MIT Sloan Management Review*, 43 (Summer 2002): 63–69; Stephen Denning, "Telling Tales," *Harvard Business Review*, 82 (May 2004): 122–129; and Camille H. James and William C. Minnis, "Organizational Storytelling: It Makes Sense," *Business Horizons*, 47 (July-August 2004): 23–32.
92. Alan L. Wilkins, "The Creation of Company Cultures: The Role of Stories and Human Resource Systems," *Human Resource Management*, 23 (Spring 1984): 43.
93. Adapted from Terrence E. Deal and Allan A. Kennedy, *Corporate Cultures: The Rites and Rituals of Corporate Life* (Reading, Mass.: Addison-Wesley, 1982), pp. 136–139.
94. Eight tips for maintaining the strength of an organization's culture are presented in Trice and Beyer, *Cultures of Work Organizations*, pp. 378–391. Companies with strong cultures are profiled in Ira Sager, "Phil Knight Kicks Off His CEO Shoes," *Business Week* (December 20, 2004): 13; and Matthew Boyle, The Wegmans Way," *Fortune* (January 24, 2005): 62–68.

CHAPTER 10

1. **Opening Quote** "Sam Walton in His Own Words," *Fortune* (June 29, 1992): 104.
2. For more, go to **www.gore.com** and click on "About Us."
3. See Ann Harrington, "Hall of Fame," *Fortune* (January 24, 2005): 94.
4. For research support, see Terry L. Amburgey and Tina Dacin, "As the Left Foot Follows the Right? The Dynamics of Strategic and Structural Change," *Academy of Management Journal*, 37 (December 1994): 1427–1452.
5. Michael Goold and Andrew Campbell, "Do You Have a Well-Designed Organization?" *Harvard Business Review*, 80 (March 2002): 117.
6. Based on Cristina B. Gibson and Julian Birkinshaw, "The Antecedents, Consequences, and Mediating Role of Organizational Ambidexterity," *Academy of Management Journal*, 47 (April 2004): 209–226. Also see Charles A. O'Reilly III and Michael L. Tushman, "The Ambidextrous Organization," *Harvard Business Review*, 82 (April 2004): 74–81.
7. An interesting overview is Robert W. Keidel, "Rethinking Organizational Design," *Academy of Management Executive*, 8 (November 1994): 12–30. Also see D. Harold Doty, William H. Glick, and George P. Huber, "Fit, Equifinality, and Organizational Effectiveness: A Test of Two Configurational Theories," *Academy of Management Journal*, 36 (December 1993): 1196–1250. For discussion of the interplay between language and organization, see Daniel Robichaud, Helene Giroux, and James R. Taylor, "The Metaconversation: The Recursive Property of Language as a Key to Organizing," *Academy of Management Review*, 29 (October 2004): 617–634.
8. See Tom Burns and G. M. Stalker, *The Management of Innovation* (London: Tavistock, 1961), ch. 5.
9. See John A. Courtright, Gail T. Fairhurst, and L. Edna Rogers, "Interaction Patterns in Organic and Mechanistic Systems," *Academy of Management Journal*, 32 (December 1989): 773–802.
10. Ben Elgin, "Running the Tightest Ship on the Net," *Business Week* (January 29, 2001): 126.
11. Robert Levering and Milton Moskowitz, "The 100 Best Companies to Work For," *Fortune* (January 24, 2005): 90.
12. Jenny C. McCune, "The Change Makers," *Management Review*, 88 (May 1999): 17. Also see Peter F. Drucker, "Change Leaders," *Inc.*, 21 (June 1999): 65–72.
13. For a complete summary of Woodward's findings, see Joan Woodward, *Industrial Organization: Theory and Practice* (London: Oxford University Press, 1965), ch. 4.
14. Adapted from Paul R. Lawrence and Jay W. Lorsch, *Organization and Environment* (Homewood, Ill.: Irwin, 1967), p. 11. One new approach to organizational integration is presented in Eileen M. Van Aken, Dominic J. Monetta, and D. Scott Sink, "Affinity Groups: The Missing Link in Employee Involvement," *Organizational Dynamics*, 22 (Spring 1994): 38–54. Also see Anthony Lee Patti and James Patrick Gilbert, "Collocating New Product Development Teams: Why, When, Where, and How?" *Business Horizons*, 40 (November-December 1997): 59–64; and Gail Edmondson, "Where Science Is More Than Skin Deep," *Business Week* (June 28, 1999): 75.
15. Lawrence and Lorsch, *Organization and Environment*, p. 157.
16. A good update on integration is Susan Albers Mohrman, "Integrating Roles and Structure in the Lateral Organization," in *Organizing for the Future: The New Logic for Managing Complex Organizations*, ed. Jay R. Galbraith, Edward E. Lawler III, et al. (San Francisco: Jossey-Bass, 1993), pp. 109–141.
17. Cheryl Comeau-Kirschner, "The Push for Profits," *Management Review*, 88 (February 1999): 7.
18. For details, see John E. Ettlie and Ernesto M. Reza, "Organizational Integration and Process Innovation," *Academy of Management Journal* (October 1992): 759–827.
19. "Best Managers: Terry Semel; Yahoo," *Business Week* (January 12, 2004): 64.
20. See Marco Iansiti, "Shooting the Rapids: Managing Product Development in Turbulent Environments," *California Management Review*, 38 (Fall 1995): 37–58; and David A. Morand, "The Role of Behavioral Formality and Informality in the Enactment of Bureaucratic versus Organic Organizations," *Academy of Management Review*, 20 (October 1995): 831–872.
21. James D. Thompson, *Organizations in Action* (New York: McGraw-Hill, 1967), p. 59.
22. Based in part on Jay R. Galbraith, *Designing Organizations: An Executive Briefing on Strategy, Structure, and Process* (San Francisco: Jossey-Bass, 1995): pp. 24–37.
23. Catherine Arnst, "A Freewheeling Youngster Named IBM," *Business Week* (May 3, 1993): 136.
24. See Michelle Kessler, "It's Official: IBM Sells PC Unit to Chinese Company," *USA Today* (December 8, 2004): 1B; and Kevin Maney, "Pioneer IBM Finally Finds Its Way Out of the PC Wilderness," *USA Today* (December 8, 2004): 3B.
25. Based on "General Electric Reorganizes Some Businesses for Growth," *East Valley/Scottsdale Tribune* (December 5, 2003): B3.
26. For related research, see Arturs Kalnins, "Divisional Multimarket Contact Within

and Between Multiunit Organizations," *Academy of Management Journal*, 47 (February 2004): 117–128.

27. Adapted from "Dial 800, Talk to Omaha," *Fortune* (January 29, 1990): 16; Rhonda Richards, "Technology Makes Omaha Hotel-Booking Capital," *USA Today* (April 7, 1994): 4B; and Robert D. Kaplan, *An Empire Wilderness: Travels into America's Future* (New York: Random House, 1998), p. 59.
28. Cliff Edwards, "Shaking Up Intel's Insides," *Business Week* (January 31, 2005): 35. For another example of product-service, see Kevin Maney, "CEO Ollila Says Nokia's 'Sisu' Will See It Past Tough Times," *USA Today* (July 21, 2004): 1B–2B.
29. For more, see Michael Hammer and James Champy, *Reengineering the Corporation: A Manifesto for Business Revolution* (New York: HarperCollins, 1993); James Champy, *Reengineering Management: The Mandate for New Leadership* (New York: HarperBusiness, 1995); Dutch Holland and Sanjiv Kumar, "Getting Past the Obstacles to Successful Reengineering," *Business Horizons*, 38 (May-June 1995): 79–85; and Rob Duboff and Craig Carter, "Reengineering from the Outside In," *Management Review*, 84 (November 1995): 42–46.
30. See John A. Byrne, "The Horizontal Corporation," *Business Week* (December 20, 1993): 76–81; and Susan Sonnesyn Brooks, "Managing a Horizontal Revolution," *HR Magazine*, 40 (June 1995): 52–58.
31. Rahul Jacob, "The Struggle to Create an Organization for the 21st Century," *Fortune* (April 3, 1995): 91. For related reading, see Michael H. Martin, "Smart Managing," *Fortune* (February 2, 1998): 149–151; and David Stamps, "Enterprise Training: This Changes *Everything*," *Training*, 36 (January 1999): 40–48.
32. David Kiley, "Coke Reorganizes; President Resigns," *USA Today* (March 5, 2001): 2B.
33. A sample of contingency design research is Richard A. D'Aveni and Anne Y. Ilinitch, "Complex Patterns of Vertical Integration in the Forest Products Industry: Systematic and Bankruptcy Risks," *Academy of Management Journal*, 35 (August 1992): 596–625.
34. For an extensive bibliography on this subject, see David D. Van Fleet and Arthur G. Bedeian, "A History of the Span of Management," *Academy of Management Review*, 2 (July 1977): 356–372.
35. L. Urwick, *The Elements of Administration* (New York: Harper & Row, 1944), pp. 52–53.
36. For details of this study, see James C. Worthy, "Organizational Structure and Employee Morale," *American Sociological Review*, 15 (April 1950): 169–179.
37. Drawn from C. W. Barkdull, "Span of Control—A Method of Evaluation," *Michigan Business Review*, 15 (May 1963): 25–32.
38. William H. Wagel, "Keeping the Organization Lean at Federal Express," *Personnel*, 64 (March 1987): 4–12.
39. Paul Kaestle, "A New Rationale for Organizational Structure," *Planning Review*, 18 (July-August 1990): 22. Also see Robert W. Keidel, "Triangular Design: A New Organizational Geometry," *Academy of Management Executive*, 4 (November 1990): 21–37.
40. For example, see Jeffrey Schmidt, "Breaking Down Fiefdoms," *Management Review*, 86 (January 1997): 45–49; and Michael E. Raynor and Joseph L. Bower, "Lead from the Center: How to Manage Divisions Dynamically," *Harvard Business Review*, 79 (May 2001): 92–100.
41. For a comprehensive research summary on centralization and organizational effectiveness, see George P. Huber, C. Chet Miller, and William H. Glick, "Developing More Encompassing Theories About Organizations: The Centralization-Effectiveness Relationship as an Example," *Organization Science*, 1 (1990): 11–40.
42. Decentralization in the U.S. Marines is discussed in Nicole Gull, "Managing on the Front Lines," *Inc.*, 26 (May 2004): 24.
43. Based on William E. Rothschild, "How to Ensure the Continued Growth of Strategic Planning," *Journal of Business Strategy*, 1 (Summer 1980): 11–18.
44. Louise Lee, "Nordstrom Cleans Out Its Closets," *Business Week* (May 22, 2000): 105. Microsoft's SBU-type structure is discussed in Kevin Maney, "CEO Helps Microsoft Enter Its 30s Gracefully," *USA Today* (January 25, 2005): 1B–2B.
45. For complete details, see Anil K. Gupta, "SBU Strategies, Corporate-SBU Relations, and SBU Effectiveness in Strategy Implementation," *Academy of Management Journal*, 30 (September 1987): 477–500. Also see V. Govindarajan and Joseph Fisher, "Strategy, Control Systems, and Resource Sharing: Effects on Business-Unit Performance," *Academy of Management Journal*, 33 (June 1990): 259–285.
46. For details, see Meni Koslowsky, "Staff/Line Distinctions in Job and Organizational Commitment," *Journal of Occupational Psychology*, 63 (June 1990): 167–173. Also see Hillel Schmid, "Staff and Line Relationships Revisited: The Case of Community Service Agencies," *Public Personnel Management*, 19 (Spring 1990): 71–83.
47. Jay R. Galbraith and Edward E. Lawler III, "Challenges to the Established Order," in Galbraith, Lawler, et al., *Organizing for the Future*, p. 6. Also see Thomas A. Stewart, "Yikes! Deadwood Is Creeping Back," *Fortune* (August 18, 1997): 221–222; and "Are You a Partner with Line Management?" *Training*, 36 (January 1999): 26–27.
48. See Louis A. Allen, "The Line-Staff Relationship," *Management Record*, 17 (September 1955): 346–349, 374–376.
49. Ibid., p. 348.
50. See David I. Cleland, "Why Project Management?" *Business Horizons*, 7 (Winter 1964): 81–88. For a discussion of how project management has evolved into matrix management, see David I. Cleland, "The Cultural Ambience of the Matrix Organization," *Management Review*, 70 (November 1981): 24–28, 37–39; and David I. Cleland, "Matrix Management (Part II): A Kaleidoscope of Organizational Systems," *Management Review*, 70 (December 1981): 48–56.
51. See Thomas A. Stewart, "The Corporate Jungle Spawns a New Species: The Project Manager," *Fortune*, (July 10, 1995): 179–180.
52. For a good overview, see Christopher A. Bartlett and Sumantra Ghoshal, "Matrix Management: Not a Structure, a Frame of Mind," *Harvard Business Review*, 68 (July-August 1990): 138–145.
53. An informative description of a successful matrix organization may be found in Ellen Kolton, "Team Players," *Inc.* (September 1984): 140–144.
54. See William F. Joyce, "Matrix Organization: A Social Experiment," *Academy of Management Journal*, 29 (September 1986): 536–561.
55. Drawn from Richard M. Hodgetts, "Leadership Techniques in the Project Organization," *Academy of Management Journal*, 11 (June 1968): 211–219. Also see Jeffrey K. Pinto and O. P. Kharbanda, *Successful Project Management: Leading Your Team to Success* (New York: Van Nostrand Reinhold, 1995).
56. Drawn from Susan G. Turner, Dawn R. Utley, and Jerry D. Westbrook, "Project Managers and Functional Managers: A Case Study of Job Satisfaction in a Matrix Organization," *Project Management Journal*, 29 (September 1998): 11–19.
57. See "An About-Face in TI's Culture," *Business Week* (July 5, 1982): 77.
58. Data from Erik W. Larson and David H. Gobeli, "Matrix Management: Contradictions and Insights," *California Management Review*, 29 (Summer 1987): 126–138. Also see Lawton R. Burns and Douglas R. Wholey, "Adoption and Abandonment of Matrix Management Programs: Effects of Organizational Characteristics and Interorganizational Networks," *Academy of Management Journal*, 36 (February 1993): 106–138; and Richard E. Anderson, "Matrix Redux," *Business Horizons*, 37 (November-December 1994): 6–10.
59. See Larry Bossidy, "The Job No CEO Should Delegate," *Harvard Business Review*, 79 (March 2001): 46–49; and Sharon Gazda, "The Art of Delegating," *HR Magazine*, 47 (January 2002): 75–78.
60. Adapted from Marion E. Haynes, "Delegation: There's More to It Than Letting Someone Else Do It!" *Supervisory Management*, 25 (January 1980): 9–15. Three types of delegation—incremental, sequential, and functional—are discussed in William R. Tracey, "Deft

Delegation: Multiplying Your Effectiveness," *Personnel*, 65 (February 1988): 36–42. Also see Pinto and Kharbanda, *Successful Project Management*, pp. 103–107.
61. Delegation styles of selected U.S. presidents are examined in Edward J. Mayo and Lance P. Jarvis, "Delegation 101: Lessons from the White House," *Business Horizons*, 31 (September-October 1988): 2–12.
62. Alex Taylor III, "Iacocca's Time of Trouble," *Fortune* (March 14, 1988): 79, 81.
63. Andrew S. Grove, *High Output Management* (New York: Random House, 1983), p. 60. Also see Wilson Harrell, "Your Biggest Mistake," *Success*, 43 (March 1996): 88.
64. For interesting facts about delegating, see "Top Dogs," *Fortune* (September 30, 1996): 189; and Bill Leonard, "Good Assistants Make Managers More Efficient," *HR Magazine*, 44 (February 1999): 12.
65. "How Conservatism Wins in the Hottest Market," *Business Week* (January 17, 1977): 43.
66. Adapted from William H. Newman, "Overcoming Obstacles to Effective Delegation," *Management Review*, 45 (January 1956): 36–41; and from Eugene Raudsepp, "Why Supervisors Don't Delegate," *Supervision*, 41 (May 1979): 12–15. Also see Francie Dalton, "Delegation Pitfalls," *Association Management*, 57 (February 2005): 65–72; and Tora Estep, "Devilish Delegation at the Department of Ominous Mechanical Mishaps," *Training and Development*, 59 (March 2005): 68–70.
67. Humorous practical tips on delegation can be found in Julie Rozetta Tuinstra, "Work Like a Toddler," *Training and Development*, 58 (September 2004): 25.
68. For more on initiative, see Michael Frese, Wolfgang Kring, Andrea Soose, and Jeanette Zempel, "Personal Initiative at Work: Differences Between East and West Germany," *Academy of Management Journal*, 39 (February 1996): 37–63; and Alan L. Frohman, "Igniting Organizational Change from Below: The Power of Personal Initiative," *Organizational Dynamics*, 25 (Winter 1997): 39–53.
69. Peter F. Drucker, *Managing the Non-Profit Organization* (New York: HarperCollins, 1990), p. 117. Also see Jim Holt, "Management Master," *Management Review*, 88 (November 1999): 15.
70. See, for example, Warren G. Bennis, *Changing Organizations* (New York: McGraw-Hill, 1966).
71. As quoted in Noel M. Tichy and Stratford Sherman, *Control Your Destiny or Someone Else Will: How Jack Welch Is Making General Electric the World's Most Competitive Corporation* (New York: Doubleday, 1993), p. 21. Also see Peter Coy, "The 21st Century Corporation: The Creative Economy," *Business Week* (August 28, 2000): 76–82; and Sheila M. Puffer, "Changing Organizational Structures: An Interview with Rosabeth Moss Kanter," *Academy of Management Executive*, 18 (May 2004): 96–105.
72. Brian Dumaine, "The New Non-Manager Managers," *Fortune* (February 22, 1993): 80. Also see Leonard R. Sayles, "Doing Things Right: A New Imperative for Middle Managers," *Organizational Dynamics*, 21 (Spring 1993): 5–14.
73. Data from Joseph Weber, "Farewell, Fast Track," *Business Week* (December 10, 1990): 192–200.
74. Data from Ricardo Sookdeo, "Why to Buy Big in Bad Times," *Fortune* (July 27, 1992): 96.
75. Edward E. Lawler III, "Substitutes for Hierarchy," *Organizational Dynamics*, 17 (Summer 1988): 15. For a good critique of hierarchy and teams, see "The Team Troubles That Won't Go Away," *Training*, 31 (August 1994): 25–34.
76. Data from David Woodruff, "Ford Has a Better Idea: Let Someone Else Have the Idea," *Business Week* (April 30, 1990): 116–117. Also see Wendy Zellner, "Go-Go Goliaths," *Business Week* (February 13, 1995): 64–70.
77. See Peter F. Drucker, "The Coming of the New Organization," *Harvard Business Review*, 66 (January-February 1988): 45–53. See Carol A. Beatty and Brenda A. Barker Scott, *Building Smart Teams: A Roadmap to High Performance* (Thousand Oaks, Calif.; Sage, 2004).
78. See Donald D. Davis, "The Tao of Leadership in Virtual Teams," *Organizational Dynamics*, 33, no. 1 (2004): 47–62; Ann Majchrzak, Arvind Malhotra, Jeffrey Stamps, and Jessica Lipnack, "Can Absence Make a Team Grow Stronger?" *Harvard Business Review*, 82 (May 2004): 131–137; and Claus W. Langfred, "Too Much of a Good Thing? Negative Effects of High Trust and Individual Autonomy in Self-Managing Teams," *Academy of Management Journal*, 47 (June 2004): 385–399.
79. See Richard Z. Gooding and John A. Wagner III, "A Meta-Analytic Review of the Relationship Between Size and Performance: The Productivity and Efficiency of Organizations and Their Subunits," *Administrative Science Quarterly*, 30 (December 1985): 462–481; Edward E. Lawler III, "Rethinking Organization Size," *Organizational Dynamics*, 26 (Autumn 1997): 24–35; Charles Handy, *The Hungry Spirit* (New York: Broadway Books, 1998), pp. 107–108; and Oren Harari, "Too Big for Your Own Good?" *Management Review*, 87 (November 1998): 30–32.
80. John A. Byrne, "Is Your Company Too Big?" *Business Week* (March 27, 1989): 92. For more on Parker Hannifin, see Christopher Palmeri, "A Process That Never Ends," *Forbes* (December 21, 1992): 52–55. Small units with Dell Computer Corp. are discussed in Carla Joinson, "Moving at the Speed of Dell," *HR Magazine*, 44 (April 1999): 50–56.
81. As quoted in Marshall Loeb, "Jack Welch Lets Fly on Budgets, Bonuses, and Buddy Boards," *Fortune* (May 29, 1995): 145.
82. See Gregory G. Dess, Abdul M. A. Rasheed, Kevin J. McLaughlin, and Richard L. Priem, "The New Corporate Architecture," *Academy of Management Executive*, 9 (August 1995): 7–20; Alan Hurwitz, "Organizational Structures for the 'New World Order,'" *Business Horizons*, 39 (May-June 1996): 5–14; and James Brian Quinn, Philip Anderson, and Sydney Finkelstein, "Leveraging Intellect," *Academy of Management Executive*, 10 (August 1996): 7–27.
83. See Robert J. Trent, "Becoming an Effective Teaming Organization," *Business Horizons*, 47 (March-April 2004): 33–40; and Nadine Heintz, "Smells Like Team Spirit," *Inc.*, 26 (May 2004): 58.
84. Toby Tetenbaum and Hilary Tetenbaum, "Office 2000: Tear Down the Walls," *Training*, 37 (February 2000): 60.
85. A good resource book is William G. Dyer, *Team Building: Current Issues and New Alternatives*, 3rd ed. (Reading, Mass.: Addison-Wesley, 1995).
86. See Melissa A. Schilling and H. Kevin Steensma, "The Use of Modular Organizational Forms: An Industry-Level Analysis," *Academy of Management Journal*, 44 (December 2001): 1149–1168; and Jathan W. Janove, "Management by Remote Control," *HR Magazine*, 49 (April 2004): 119–124.
87. Steve Hamm, "Linux Inc.," *Business Week* (January 31, 2005): 62.
88. Another interesting global virtual organization is profiled in Kevin Maney, "Kazaa Creators' Latest Invention, Skype, Could Turn Telcom on Its Ear," *USA Today* (April 14, 2004): 3B.
89. For example, see Michael V. Copeland, "These Boots Really Were Made for Walking," *Business 2.0*, 5 (October 2004): 72, 74.
90. Research on the behavioral implications of virtual organizations is reported in Deondra S. Conner, "Social Comparison in Virtual Work Environments: An Examination of Contemporary Referent Selection," *Journal of Occupational and Organizational Psychology*, 76 (March 2003): 133–147.

CHAPTER 11

1. **Opening Quote** As quoted in Paul B. Brown, "What I Know Now," *Fast Company*, no. 91 (February 2005): 96.
2. Drawn from "Peterson Thrives on HR Challenges," *HR Magazine*, 43 (September 1998): 98, 100.
3. See Fred Luthans, Paul A. Marsnik, and Kyle W. Luthans, "A Contingency Matrix Approach to IHRM," *Human Resource Management*, 36 (Summer 1997): 183–199; and Johngseok Bae and John J. Lawler, "Organizational and HRM Strategies in Korea: Impact on Firm

Performance in an Emerging Economy," *Academy of Management Journal*, 43 (June 2000): 502–517.

4. Leon Rubis, "Analytical Graphics Works for Its Workers," *HR Magazine*, 49 (July 2004): 47.
5. Jeffrey B. Arthur, "Effects of Human Resource Systems on Manufacturing Performance and Turnover," *Academy of Management Journal*, 37 (June 1994): 670. Similar findings are reported in Heather Johnson, "Super HR," *Training*, 41 (August 2004): 18. Also see David E. Bowen and Cheri Ostroff, "Understanding HRM-Firm Performance Linkages: The Role of the 'Strength' of the HRM System," *Academy of Management Review*, 29 (April 2004): 203–221.
6. For example, see Bill Roberts, "Side by Side," *HR Magazine*, 49 (March 2004): 52–57; Robert C. Ford, "David Neeleman, CEO of JetBlue Airways, on People + Strategy = Growth," *Academy of Management Executive*, 18 (May 2004): 139–143; and Robert J. Grossman, "HR on the Board," *HR Magazine*, 49 (June 2004): 56–63.
7. See Pamela Babcock, "Slicing Off Pieces of HR," *HR Magazine*, 49 (July 2004): 70–76; Robert J. Grossman, "Sticker Shock," *HR Magazine*, 49 (July 2004): 78–86; Susan Meisinger, "Outsourcing: A Challenge and an Opportunity," *HR Magazine*, 49 (September 2004): 8; and Jennifer Schramm, "Top Trends Facing HR," *HR Magazine*, 49 (October 2004): 152.
8. See Carl E. Fey, Antonina Pavlovskaya, and Ningyu Tang, "Does One Shoe Fit Everyone? A Comparison of Human Resource Management in Russia, China, and Finland," *Organizational Dynamics*, 33, no. 1 (2004): 79–97; Bill Leonard, "The Art of HR Diplomacy," *HR Magazine*, 49 (June 2004): 82–86; and Jennifer Schramm, "Global Challenges," *HR Magazine*, 49 (December 2004): 128.
9. Bill Leonard, "Straight Talk," *HR Magazine*, 47 (January 2002): 46–51. Also see Patrick Mirza, "Future Workplaces Will Require Greater HR Adaptability," *HR Magazine*, 49 (May 2004): 12; and Susan Meisinger, "HR Leadership Is Key to Creating Better Workplaces," *HR Magazine*, 49 (August 2004): 12.
10. Brian E. Becker, Mark A. Huselid, and Dave Ulrich, *The HR Scorecard: Linking People, Strategy, and Performance* (Boston: Harvard Business School Press, 2001): p. 4.
11. For more see Robert S. Kaplan and David P. Norton, "Measuring the Strategic Readiness of Intangible Assets," *Harvard Business Review*," 82 (February 2004): 52–63; Brandon Hall, "Here Comes Human Capital Management," *Training*, 41 (March 2004): 16–17; and Robert J. Grossman, "Blind Investment," *HR Magazine*, 50 (January 2005): 40–47.
12. "The 100 Best Companies to Work For," *Fortune* (February 4, 2002): 84. Also see Jane Larson, "Competing Is Key, Says Intel CEO," *Arizona Republic* (June 5, 2004): D1–D2. For more stories about companies helping schools, see George Anders, "The *Re*education of Silicon Valley," *Fast Company*, no. 57 (April 2002): 100–108.
13. Scott Adams, "Dilbert's Management Handbook," *Fortune* (May 13, 1996): 99, 108.
14. As quoted in John Huey, "Outlaw Flyboy CEOs," *Fortune* (November 13, 2000): 246. For a profile of Southwest's new CEO, Gary Kelly, see "Southwest CEO Puts Emphasis on Character," *USA Today* (September 27, 2004): 3B.
15. Data from Jeffrey Pfeffer, *The Human Equation: Building Profits by Putting People First* (Boston: Harvard Business School Press, 1998); and Jeffrey Pfeffer and John F. Veiga, "Putting People First for Organizational Success," *Academy of Management Executive*, 13 (May 1999): 37–48. Also see R. Brayton Bowen, "Today's Workforce Requires New Age Currency," *HR Magazine*, 49 (March 2004): 101–106; Haig R. Nalbantian and Anne Szostak, "How Fleet Bank Fought Employee Flight," *Harvard Business Review*, 82 (April 2004): 116–125; Timothy Butler and James Waldroop, "Understanding 'People' People," *Harvard Business Review*, 82 (June 2004): 78–86; and "50 Best Small & Medium Places to Work," *HR Magazine*, 49 (July 2004): 44–63.
16. See Jim Collins, *Good to Great: Why Some Companies Make the Leap... and Others Don't* (New York : HarperCollins, 2001); and Jim Collins, "Good to Great," *Fast Company*, no. 51 (October 2001): 90–104.
17. See Boris Groysberg, Ashish Nanda, and Nitin Nohria, "The Risky Business of Hiring Stars," *Harvard Business Review*, 82 (May 2004): 92–100; Ryan Underwood, "How to Spot A-Players," *Fast Company*, no. 84 (July 2004): 87–89; and Charlotte Garvey, "The Next Generation of Hiring Metrics," *HR Magazine*, 50 (April 2005): 71–76.
18. Based on "What Are CEOs Thinking?" *USA Today* (May 3, 2001): 1B. Also see Tammy Galvin, "The Tip of the Iceberg," *Training*, 41 (January 2004): 6; and Arie C. Glebbeek and Erik H. Bax, "Is High Employee Turnover Really Harmful? An Empirical Test Using Company Records." *Academy of Management Journal*, 47 (April 2004): 277–286.
19. As quoted in Tim Talevich, "Carly Unplugged," *The Costco Connection*, 19 (June 2004): 19. For an update on Carly Fiorina, see "Why Carly's Big Bet Is Failing," *Fortune* (February 7, 2005): 50–64.
20. For related research, see Derek R. Avery, Morela Hernandez, and Michelle R. Hebl, "Who's Watching the Race? Racial Salience in Recruitment Advertising," *Journal of Applied Social Psychology*, 34 (January 2004): 146–161.
21. See Cora Daniels, "50 Best Companies for Minorities," *Fortune* (June 28, 2004): 136–146. The business case for diversity at PepsiCo is stated in "The Best Managers: Steven Reinemund, PepsiCo," *Business Week* (January 10, 2005): 56–57. Also see the series of articles on Diversity and the Workplace in the *Journal of Organizational Behavior*, 25 (September 2004).
22. See Martha Frase-Blunt, "Make a Good First Impression," *HR Magazine*, 49 (April 2004): 80–86.
23. Ann Harrington, "Make That Switch," *Fortune* (February 4, 2002): 1 at **www.fortune.com/careers**. Also see Anne Fisher, "How to Ruin an Online Job Hunt," *Fortune* (June 28, 2004): 43.
24. For more, see Timothy S. Bland and Sue S. Stalcup, "Build a Legal Employment Application," *HR Magazine*, 44 (March 1999): 129–133. Also see Robert Rodriguez, "Tapping the Hispanic Labor Pool," *HR Magazine*, 49 (April 2004): 72–79; and Barbara Kantrowitz and Julie Scelfo, "American Masala," *Newsweek* (March 22, 2004): 50–57.
25. Pamela Babcock, "Spotting Lies," *HR Magazine*, 48 (October 2003): 47. Also see Drew Robb, "Screening for Speedier Selection," *HR Magazine*, 49 (September 2004): 143–148.
26. Merry Mayer, "Background Checks in Focus," *HR Magazine*, 47 (January 2002): 59. Also see Ann Davis, "Employers Dig Deep into Workers' Pasts, Citing Terrorism Fears," *Wall Street Journal* (March 12, 2002): A1, A12; Bill Leonard, "Crime-Data Software for Police May Benefit Employers," *HR Magazine*, 48 (January 2003): 27; and Maria Greco Danaher, "Lack of Background Check Leads to Liability," *HR Magazine*, 50 (January 2005): 94.
27. Based on "Wal-Mart to Run Background Checks," *USA Today* (August 13, 2004): 1B.
28. Fred Vogelstein, "Google @ $165: Are These Guys for Real?" *Fortune* (December 13, 2004): 106, 108.
29. See Sharon Fears, "The Demise of Job Descriptions," *HR Magazine*, 45 (August 2000): 184; and Carla Joinson, "Refocusing Job Descriptions," *HR Magazine*, 46 (January 2001): 66–72.
30. David A. Brookmire and Amy A. Burton, "A Format for Packaging Your Affirmative Action Program," *Personnel Journal*, 57 (June 1978): 294. Also see Marc A. Mandelman, "Title VII Protects Welfare-to-Work Participants," *HR Magazine*, 49 (May 2004): 111–112..
31. See Cliff Edwards, "Coming Out in Corporate America," *Business Week* (December 15, 2003): 64–72; Stephanie Armour, "Gay Marriage Debate Moves into Workplace," *USA Today* (April 14, 2004): 1B–2B; Karyn-Siobhan Robinson, "HR Begins to Confront Workplace Implications of Same-Sex Marriages," *HR Magazine*, 49 (May 2004): 28; and John Simons, "Gay Marriage: Corporate America Blazed the Trail," *Fortune* (June

14, 2004): 42, 44.

32. Data from Theresa Howard, "Coke Settles Bias Lawsuit for $192.5M," *USA Today* (November 17, 2000): 1B; and Stephanie Armour, "Bias Suits Put Spotlight on Workplace Diversity," *USA Today* (January 10, 2001): 1B–2B.
33. Data from "Boeing Settles Bias Case, Will Pay Up to $72.5 Mil.," *Arizona Republic* (July 17, 2004): D7.
34. See Charlene Marmer Solomon, "Frequently Asked Questions About Affirmative Action," *Personnel Journal*, 74 (August 1995): 61. For historical perspectives, see Janet Kornblum, "Integration Makes Gains, But Perceptions Slower to Change," *USA Today* (April 6, 2004): 7D; and Roger O. Crockett, "Putting Words to the Dream," *Business Week* (July 12, 2004): 16.
35. See Jennifer Schramm, "Acting Affirmatively," *HR Magazine*, 48 (September 2003): 192; and Fred L. Fry and Jennifer R. D. Burgess, "The End of the Need for Affirmative Action" Are We There Yet?" *Business Horizons*, 46 (November-December 2003): 7–16.
36. For related discussion, see Robert J. Grossman, "Constant Inconsistency," *HR Magazine*, 48 (December 2003): 68–74; Margaret M. Clark, "While Some Employers See No Incentive for EEOC Mediation, Others Find Benefits," *HR Magazine*, 49 (January 2004): 36; and Paul Oyer and Scott Schaefer, "The Bias Backfire," *Harvard Business Review*, 82 (November 2004): 26.
37. Julia Lawlor, "Study: Affirmative-Action Hires' Abilities Doubted," *USA Today* (August 31, 1992): 3B. The complete study is reported in Madeline E. Heilman, Caryn J. Block, and Jonathan A. Lucas, "Presumed Incompetent? Stigmatization and Affirmative Action Efforts," *Journal of Applied Psychology*, 77 (August 1992): 536–554. Also see Beverly L. Little, William D. Murry, and James C. Wimbush, "Perceptions of Workplace Affirmative Action Plans," *Group & Organization Management*, 23 (March 1998): 27–47.
38. Yehouda Shenhav, "Entrance of Blacks and Women into Managerial Positions in Scientific and Engineering Occupations: A Longitudinal Analysis," *Academy of Management Journal*, 35 (October 1992): 897. Also see Mike McNamee, "The Proof Is in Performance," *Business Week* (July 15, 1996): 22. A female executive's view can be found in "Helayne Spivak," *Fast Company*, no. 27 (September 1999): 113.
39. For example, see Jonathan Kaufman, "White Men Shake Off That Losing Feeling on Affirmative Action," *Wall Street Journal* (September 5, 1996): A1, A4.
40. R. Roosevelt Thomas Jr., "From Affirmative Action to Affirming Diversity," *Harvard Business Review*, 68 (March-April 1990): 114. For an interview with R. Roosevelt Thomas, see Ellen Neuborne, "Diversity Challenges Many Companies," *USA Today* (November 18, 1996): 10B. Also see William Atkinson, "Bringing Diversity to White Men," *HR Magazine*, 46 (September 2001): 76–83.
41. For more on diversity, see Martha Frase-Blunt, "Selecting a Diversity Consultant," *HR Magazine*, 49 (June 2004): 147–155; David A. Thomas, "Diversity as Strategy," *Harvard Business Review*, 82 (September 2004): 98–108; and Gail Johnson, "Time to Broaden Diversity," *Training*, 41 (September 2004): 16.
42. As quoted in Ryan Underwood, "No Brakes," *Fast Company*, no. 86 (September 2004): 112.
43. Joel Schettler, "Equal Access to All," *Training*, 39 (January 2002): 44. Also see Jim Barthold, "Waiting in the Wings," *HR Magazine*, 49 (April 2004): 88–95.
44. For inspiring stories, see Kim Painter, "Miracles Keep Happening," *USA Today* (May 13, 2004): 9D; and Linda Tischler, "A Design for Living," *Fast Company*, no. 85 (August 2004): 76–79.
45. For more, see Cheryl Comeau-Kirschner, "New ADA Guidelines," *Management Review*, 88 (April 1999): 6; Robert H. Schwartz, Frederick R. Post, and Jack L. Simonetti, "The ADA and the Mentally Disabled: What Must Firms Do?" *Business Horizons*, 43 (July-August 2000): 52–58; and Eric V. Neumann and Brian H. Kleiner, "How to Accommodate Disabilities Under ADA," *Nonprofit World*, 18 (September-October 2000): 29–33.
46. Gene Koretz, "Dubious Aid for the Disabled," *Business Week* (November 9, 1998): 30..
47. Jack Gillum, "Disabled Are Losing Optimism, Survey Shows," *USA Today* (June 28, 2004): 6D.
48. Susan B. Garland, "Protecting the Disabled Won't Cripple Business," *Business Week* (April 26, 1999): 73. For related reading, see Margaret M. Clark, "High Court's ADA Ruling Leaves Some Accommodations Questions Unanswered," *HR Magazine*, 49 (January 2004): 30; Saundra Jackson, "Disabled Workers, Salary Talk, State Taxes," *HR Magazine*, 49 (March 2004): 39; and Adrienne Colella, Ramona L. Paetzold, and Maura A. Belliveau, "Factors Affecting Coworkers' Procedural Justice Inferences of the Workplace Accommodations of Employees with Disabilities," *Personnel Psychology*, 57 (Spring 2004): 1–23.
49. See John Williams, "Enabling Technologies," *Business Week* (March 20, 2000): 68, 70; and Otis Port, "Artificial Eyes, Turbine Hearts," *Business Week* (March 20, 2000): 72–73. Also see Kathryn Tyler, "Ready to Be Heard," *HR Magazine*, 49 (September 2004): 70–76.
50. See Jonathan A. Segal, "Throw Supervisors a Lifeline and Save Yourself: Having ADA Compliance Knowledge Is Useless Unless You Share It," *HR Magazine*, 48 (June 2003): 167–179; and Mary E. McLaughlin, Myrtle P. Bell, and Donna Y. Stringer, "Stigma and Acceptance of Persons with Disabilities," *Group and Organization Management*, 29 (June 2004): 302–333.
51. See Dave Patel, "Testing, Testing, Testing," *HR Magazine*, 47 (February 2002): 112.
52. See Scott B. Parry, "How to Validate an Assessment Tool," *Training*, 30 (April 1993): 37–42.
53. See John Bacon, "Polygraphs Can Lie, Researchers Say," *USA Today* (October 9, 2002): 3A; James E. Wanek, Paul R. Sackett, and Deniz S. Ones, "Towards an Understanding of Integrity Test Similarities and Differences: An Item-Level Analysis of Seven Tests," *Personnel Psychology*, 56 (Winter 2003): 873–894; Jared Sandberg, "How I Survived Tests That Introduced Me to My Inner Executive," *Wall Street Journal* (March 10, 2004): B1; Del Jones, "Was the Writing on the Wall, . . . or Their Annual Reports?" *USA Today* (March 29, 2004): 3B; Kerry J. Sulkowicz, "The Corporate Shrink," *Fast Company*, no. 87 (October 2004): 48; "Measuring Character," *Training*, 41 (October 2004): 16; and Holly Dolezalek, "Tests on Trial," *Training*, 42 (April 2005): 32–34.
54. Rod Kurtz, "Testing, Testing . . .," *Inc.*, 26 (June 2004): 36.
55. See Kerry J. Sulkowicz, "The Corporate Shrink," *Fast Company*, no. 90 (January 2005): 38.
56. "Structured Interviewing: Avoiding Selection Problems," by Elliott D. Pursell, Michael A. Campion, and Sarah R. Gaylord, copyright November 1980. Reprinted with permission of *Personnel Journal*, Costa Mesa, Calif.; all rights reserved.
57. Barbara Whitaker Shimko, "New Breed Workers Need New Yardsticks," *Business Horizons*, 33 (November-December 1990): 35–36. For related research, see Allen I. Huffcutt and Philip L. Roth, "Racial Group Differences in Employment Interview Evaluations," *Journal of Applied Psychology*, 83 (April 1998): 179–189.
58. Practical tips on interviewing can be found in Tahl Raz, "How Would You Design Bill Gates's Bathroom?" *Inc.*, 25 (May 2003): 35; Anne Fisher, "How Can I Survive a Phone Interview?" *Fortune* (April 19, 2004): 54; Anne Fisher, "Truly Puzzling Interview Questions," *Fortune* (September 20, 2004): 70; John Kador, *How to Ace the Brainteaser Interview* (New York : McGraw-Hill, 2005); "12 Ways to Keep Good People," *Training*, 36 (April 1999): 19; Claudio Fernandez-Araoz, "Hiring Without Firing," *Harvard Business Review*, 77 (July-August 1999): 109–120; and Jim Kennedy, "What to Do When Job Applicants Tell Tales of Invented Lives," *Training*, 36 (October 1999): 110–114.
59. Based on Pursell et al., "Structured

Interviewing."
60. Based on Bruce Bloom, "Behavioral Interviewing: The Future Direction and Focus of the Employment Interview." Paper presented to the Midwest Business Administration Association, Chicago (March 27, 1998). Also see Andrea C. Poe, "Graduate Work," *HR Magazine*, 48 (October 2003): 95–100; and Joey George and Kent Marett, "The Truth About Lies," *HR Magazine*, 49 (May 2004): 87–91.
61. Del J. Still, *High Impact Hiring: How to Interview and Select Outstanding Employees*, 2nd ed., rev. (Dana Point, Calif.: Management Development Systems, 2001), pp. 53–54 (emphasis added).
62. As quoted in Kathryn Tyler, "One Bad Apple," *HR Magazine*, 49 (December 2004): 85.
63. Data from David Stamps, "Performance Appraisals: Out of Sync and as Unpopular as Ever," *Training*, 32 (August 1995): 16. Also see Tom Coens and Mary Jenkins, *Abolishing Performance Appraisals: Why They Backfire and What to Do Instead* (San Francisco: Berrett-Koehler, 2000); Anne Fisher, "Help! My Performance Review Was Grossly Unfair," *Fortune* (September 20, 2004): 70; and Drew Robb, "Building a Better Workforce," *HR Magazine*, 49 (October 2004): 86–94.
64. Tammy Galvin, "The Weakest Link," *Training*, 38 (December 2001): 8. Also see Lin Grensing-Pophal, "Motivate Managers to Review Performance," *HR Magazine*, 46 (March 2001): 44–48.
65. Data from "What to Do with an Egg-Sucking Dog?" *Training*, 33 (October 1996): 17–21.
66. See Karen McKirchy, *Powerful Performance Appraisals: How to Set Expectations and Work Together to Improve Performance* (Franklin Lakes, N.J.: Career Press, 1998); Carla Joinson, "Making Sure Employees Measure Up," *HR Magazine*, 46 (March 2001): 36–41; and Gail Johnson, "Room for Improvement," *Training*, 40 (December 2003): 18–19.
67. For EEOC guidelines during performance appraisal, see William S. Swan and Philip Margulies, *How to Do a Superior Performance Appraisal* (New York: Wiley, 1991).
68. Adapted from Hubert S. Field and William H. Holley, "The Relationship of Performance Appraisal System Characteristics to Verdicts in Selected Employment Discrimination Cases," *Academy of Management Journal*, 25 (June 1982): 392–406. A more recent analysis of 51 cases that derived similar criteria can be found in Gerald V. Barrett and Mary C. Kernan, "Performance Appraisal and Terminations: A Review of Court Decisions Since *Brito* v. *Zia* with Implications for Personnel Practices," *Personnel Psychology*, 40 (Autumn 1987): 489–503.
69. For more, see Dick Grote, "Painless Performance Appraisals Focus on Results, Behaviors," *HR Magazine*, 43 (October 1998): 52–58.
70. See Paul Falcone, "Watch What You Write," *HR Magazine*, 49 (November 2004): 125–128.
71. For related research, see Todd J. Maurer, Jerry K. Palmer, and Donna K. Ashe, "Diaries, Checklists, Evaluations, and Contrast Effects in Measurement of Behavior," *Journal of Applied Psychology*, 78 (April 1993): 226–231.
72. Alan M. Webber, "How Business Is a Lot Like Life," *Fast Company*, no. 45 (April 2001): 135.
73. Matthew Boyle, "Performance Reviews: Perilous Curves Ahead," *Fortune* (May 28, 2001): 187. Also see Steve Bates, "Forced Ranking," *HR Magazine*, 48 (June 2003): 62–68; and Gail Johnson, "Forced Ranking: The Good, the Bad, and the Alternative," *Training*, 41 (May 2004): 24–34.
74. See David Kiley and Del Jones, "Ford Alters Worker Evaluation Process," *USA Today* (July 11, 2001): 1B; and Earle Eldridge, "Ford Settles 2 Lawsuits by White Male Workers," *USA Today* (December 19, 2001): 3B.
75. See Jai Ghorpade, "Managing Five Paradoxes of 360-Degree Feedback," *Academy of Management Executive*, 14 (February 2000): 140–150; Angelo S. DeNisi and Avraham N. Kluger, "Feedback Effectiveness: Can 360-Degree Appraisals Be Improved?" *Academy of Management Executive*, 14 (February 2000): 129–139; and William C. Byham, "Fixing the Instrument," *Training*, 41 (July 2004): 50.
76. See David A. Waldman, Leanne E. Atwater, and David Antonioni, "Has 360 Degree Feedback Gone Amok?" *Academy of Management Executive*, 12 (May 1998): 86–94; and Dennis E. Coates, "Don't Tie 360 Feedback to Pay," *Training*, 35 (September 1998): 68–78.
77. Based on Fred Luthans and Suzanne J. Peterson, "360–Degree Feedback with Systematic Coaching: Empirical Analysis Suggests a Winning Combination," *Human Resource Management*, 42 (Fall 2003): 243–256. Also see Angelo J. Kinicki, Gregory E. Prussia, Bin (Joshua) Wu, and Frances M. McKee-Ryan, "A Covariance Structure Analysis of Employees' Response to Performance Feedback," *Journal of Applied Psychology*, 89 (December 2004): 1057–1069.
78. "Best Practices: Executive Coaching, Wachovia," *Training*, 41 (March 2004): 61. For related reading, see Kristine Ellis, "Individual Development Plans: The Building Blocks of Development," *Training*, 41 (December 2004): 20–25.
79. Data from Holly Dolezalek, "Industry Report 2004," *Training*, 41 (October 2004): 20–37. Also see Laurie Bassi and Daniel McMurrer, "How's Your Return on People?" *Harvard Business Review*, 82 (March 2004): 18; Brandon Hall, "Time to Execute," *Training*, 41 (December 2004): 12; and Brad Cooper, "Training as an Operational Necessity," *Training*, 42 (April 2005): 42.
80. As quoted in Edward E. Gordon, "The 2010 Crossroad," *Training*, 42 (January 2005): 34.
81. See Catherine Arnst, "Getting Girls to the Lab Bench," *Business Week* (February 7, 2005): 42.
82. Gordon, "The 2010 Crossroad," p. 35
83. Robert Levering and Milton Moskowitz, "The 100 Best Companies to Work For," *Fortune* (January 24, 2005): 86.
84. Dolezalek, "Industry Report 2004," p. 20.
85. See Holly Dolezalek, "Dose of Reality," *Training*, 41 (April 2004): 28–34; Holly Dolezalek, "The State of the E-Learning Market," *Training*, 41 (September 2004): 20–28; Sarah Boehle, "Simulations: The Next Generation of E-Learning," *Training*, 42 (January 2005): 22–31; Anne Fisher, "Find Online Training That Pays Off," *Fortune* (February 7, 2005): 34; and "Update on Corporate Universities," *Training*, 42 (April 2005): 8.
86. Kenneth N. Wexley and Gary P. Latham, *Developing and Training Human Resources in Organizations* (Glenview, Ill.: Scott, Foresman, 1981): 75–77. Also see Karl Albrecht, "Take Time for Effective Learning," *Training*, 41 (July 2004): 38–42; and Brandon Hall, "Ready, Set, Innovate," *Training*, 42 (January 2005): 36.
87. Wexley and Latham, *Developing and Training Human Resources in Organizations*, p. 77. Also see Diana Hird, "What Makes a Training Program Good?" *Training*, 37 (June 2000): 48–52.
88. Training program assessment/evaluation is covered in Heather Johnson, "The Whole Picture?" *Training*, 41 (July 2004): 30–34; and Kristine Ellis, "What's the ROI of ROI?" *Training*, 42 (January 2005): 16–21.
89. See Kimberly Eretzian Smirles, "Attributions of Responsibility in Cases of Sexual Harassment: The Person and the Situation," *Journal of Applied Social Psychology*, 34 (February 2004): 342–365.
90. Ruhal Dooley, "Parental Leave, Behavior at Work, Camera Use," *HR Magazine*, 49 (July 2004): 42.
91. See Adam Shell, "Morgan Stanley Settles Sex-Bias Case," *USA Today* (July 13, 2004): 1B; Robert K. Robinson, Geralyn McClure Franklin, and Walter J. Davis, "Sexual Harassment Redux," *Business Horizons*, 47 (July-August 2004): 3–5; Linda Wasmer Andrews, "Hard-Core Offenders," *HR Magazine*, 49 (December 2004): 42–48; and Thomas O. McCarthy, "Sexual Conduct: Equal Abuse Unequal Harm," *HR Magazine*, 50 (January 2005): 93–94.
92. Data from Stephanie Armour, "More Men Say They Are Sexually Harassed at Work," *USA Today* (September 17, 2004):

1B. Also see "Daily Downer," *Training*, 42 (April 2005): 12.
93. "Dow Chemical Fires 50 for Porno E-Mail," *USA Today* (July 28, 2000): 1B.
94. Data from Tamara Henry, "Sexual Harassment Pervades Schools, Study Says," *USA Today* (July 23, 1996): 8B. Also see John Tuohy, "Sex Discrimination Infects Med Schools," *USA Today* (June 7, 2000): 8D.
95. For a list of verbal and nonverbal forms of general harassment, see R. Bruce McAfee and Diana L. Deadrick, "Teach Employees to Just Say 'No!'" *HR Magazine*, 41 (February 1996): 86–89.
96. For details, see David E. Terpstra and Douglas D. Baker, "Outcomes of Federal Court Decisions on Sexual Harassment," *Academy of Management Journal*, 35 (March 1992): 181–190. Also see Jonathan A. Segal, "HR as Judge, Jury, Prosecutor and Defender," *HR Magazine*, 46 (October 2001): 141–154.
97. See Sue K. Willman, "The New Law of Training," *HR Magazine*, 49 (May 2004): 115–118; Jathan W. Janove, "Private 101," *HR Magazine*, 49 (July 2004): 127–131; and Jathan W. Janove, "Conclude and Communicate," *HR Magazine*, 49 (August 2004): 131–134.
98. Data from Brian O'Reilly, "In a Dry Era You Can Still Be Trapped by Drinking," *Fortune* (March 6, 1995): 167–177; and Marilyn Chase, "Finding Ways to Reach an Alcoholic Who Has Elaborate Defenses," *Wall Street Journal* (October 23, 1995): B1.
99. "Volunteers to Test Alcoholism Treatments," *USA Today* (April 11, 2001): 7D. Also see Lauren M. Bernardi, "Alcohol and Employees: Risks and Responsibilities," *Canadian Manager*, 26 (Summer 2001): 17–18.
100. Data from "Almost 50% Have Used Illicit Drugs," *USA Today* (August 12, 2004): 1A.
101. Matthew Boyle, "The New E-Workplace," *Fortune* (October 1, 2001): 176.
102. Data from Robert Davis, "Demands, Isolation of Dentistry Open Gates to Drug Addiction," *USA Today* (April 15, 1999): 1A–2A; and "Recovery Gets Going," *Training*, 41 (December 2004): 14.
103. Based on Janice Castro, "Battling the Enemy Within," *Time* (March 17, 1986): 52–61; and Peter Corbett, "Bush on Drug War: 'Failure Not Option,'" *Arizona Republic* (April 9, 1999): E1, E3.
104. Data from Aja Whitaker, "Tight Labor Market Could Mean More Drug Abuse," *Management Review*, 88 (October 1999): 8. Also see Donna Leinwand, "Study: Drugs Cost U.S. $400B," *USA Today* (March 9, 2001): 10A.
105. See Jonathan A. Segal, "Drugs, Alcohol and the ADA," *HR Magazine*, 37 (December 1992): 73–76. Also see Jess McCuan, "When an Addict Seeks a Job," *Inc.*, 26 (March 2004): 30.
106. Janet Deming, "Drug-Free Workplace Is Good Business," *HR Magazine*, 35 (April 1990): 61. For more, see **http://said.dol.gov.**
107. See Louisa Wah, "Treatment vs. Termination," *Management Review*, 87 (April 1998): 8.; and Norm Brodsky, "Just Say Yes: How a Policy That Sounds Tough Can Turn into a Lifeline for Some," *Inc.*, 26 (November 2004): 67–68.
108. Ruby M. Yandrick, "The EAP Struggle: Counselors or Referrers?" *HR Magazine*, 43 (August 1998): 90–96; Jane Easter Bahls, "Handle with Care," *HR Magazine*, 44 (March 1999): 60–66; and Bill Leonard, "EAPs Pushed to the Limit Following the Terrorist Attacks," *HR Magazine*, 46 (December 2001): 25.
109. Stuart Feldman, "Today's EAPs Make the Grade," *Personnel*, 68 (February 1991): 3.

CHAPTER 12

1. **Opening Quote** Laurence J. Peter, *Peter's Quotations* (New York: Bantam, 1977), p. 100.
2. For example, see Mary Young and James E. Post, "Managing to Communicate, Communicating to Manage: How Leading Companies Communicate with Employees," *Organizational Dynamics*, 22 (Summer 1993): 31–43; and Ale Smidts, Ad Th. H. Pruyn, and Cees B. M. van Riel, "The Impact of Employee Communication and Perceived External Prestige on Organizational Identification," *Academy of Management Journal*, 49 (October 2001): 1051–1062.
3. "Wanted: Management Skills," *Training*, 41 (November 2004): 19.
4. Data from **www.nbr.com**, November 18, 2004. Also see Stanley Bing, "Bye-bye, BlackBerry," *Fortune* (January 10, 2005): 102.
5. Stephanie Armour, "Failure to Communicate Costly for Companies," *USA Today* (September 30, 1998): 1B.
6. Keith Davis, *Human Behavior at Work: Organizational Behavior*, 6th ed. (New York: McGraw-Hill, 1981), p. 399.
7. For an instructive distinction between one-way (the arrow model) and two-way (the circuit model) communication, see Phillip G. Clampitt, *Communicating for Managerial Effectiveness* (Newbury Park, Calif.: Sage, 1991), pp. 1–24.
8. For interesting reading, see Harriet Rubin, "The Power of Words," *Fast Company*, no. 21 (January 1999): 142–151.
9. See Thomas H. Davenport and John C. Beck, *The Attention Economy: Understanding the New Currency of Business* (Boston: Harvard Business School Press, 2001).
10. Trudy Milburn, "Bridging Cultural Gaps," *Management Review*, 86 (January 1997): 27. Also see Linda Kathryn Larkey, "Toward a Theory of Communicative Interactions in Culturally Diverse Workgroups," *Academy of Management Review*, 21 (April 1996): 463–491; and Jack L. Mendleson and C. Dianne Mendleson, "An Action Plan to Improve Difficult Communication," *HR Magazine*, 41 (October 1996): 118–126.
11. Ernest Gundling, "How to Communicate Globally," *Training & Development*, 53 (June 1999): 30. Also see Ernest Gundling, *Working GlobeSmart: 12 People Skills for Doing Business Across Borders* (Palo Alto, Calif.: Davies-Black, 2003); and Dan Landis, Janet M. Bennett, and Milton J. Bennett, eds., *Handbook of Intercultural Training*, 3rd ed. (Thousand Oaks, Calif.: Sage, 2004).
12. See Robert H. Lengel and Richard L. Daft, "The Selection of Communication Media as an Executive Skill," *Academy of Management Executive*, 2 (August 1988): 225–232. For a research update, see John R. Carlson and Robert W. Zmud, "Channel Expansion Theory and the Experiential Nature of Media Richness Perceptions," *Academy of Management Journal*, 42 (April 1999): 153–170. Also see Bruce Barry and Ingrid Smithey Fulmer, "The Medium and the Message: The Adaptive Use of Communication Media in Dyadic Influence," *Academy of Management Review*, 29 (April 2004): 272–292.
13. See Pamela Babcock, "Sending the Message," *HR Magazine*, 48 (November 2003): 66–70.
14. See Karl Albrecht, "Lost in the Translation," *Training*, 33 (June 1996): 66–70; and Jean-Anne Jordon, "Clear Speaking Improves Career Prospects," *HR Magazine*, 41 (June 1996): 75–82.
15. Drawn from Manjeet Kripalani, "Investing in India: Not for the Fainthearted," *Business Week* (August 11, 1997): 46–47.
16. Don Moyer, "You Say Po-Tay-Toes, I Hear To-Mah-Toes," *Harvard Business Review*, 82 (September 2004): 140.
17. Data from Louisa Wah, "An Ounce of Prevention," *Management Review*, 87 (October 1998): 9. Feedback on performance is covered in Sherry E. Moss and Juan I. Sanchez, "Are Your Employees Avoiding You? Managerial Strategies for Closing the Feedback Gap," *Academy of Management Executive*, 18 (February 2004): 32–44; and Gardiner Morse, "Feedback Backlash," *Harvard Business Review*, 82 (October 2004): 28. Research on feedback recipients is reported in Angelo J. Kinicki, Gregory E. Prussia, Bin (Joshua) Wu, and Frances M. McKee-Ryan, "A Covariance Structure Analysis of Employees' Response to Performance Feedback," *Journal of Applied Psychology*, 89 (December 2004): 1057–1069.
18. See Bella M. DePaulo, Deborah A. Kashy, Susan E. Kirkendol, Melissa M. Wyer, and Jennifer A. Epstein, "Lying in Everyday Life," *Journal of Personality and Social Psychology*, 70 (May 1996): 979–995; and Deborah A. Kashy and Bella M. DePaulo, "Who Lies?" *Journal of Personality and Social Psychology*, 70 (May 1996): 1037–1051.
19. Frank Snowden Hopkins, "Communication: The Civilizing Force,"

The Futurist, 15 (April 1981): 39.

20. See Paul A. Argenti, Robert A. Howell, and Karen A. Beck, "The Strategic Communication Imperative," *MIT Sloan Management Review*, 46 (Spring 2005): 83–89.
21. Phillip G. Clampitt, Robert J. DeKoch, and Thomas Cashman, "A Strategy for Communicating About Uncertainty," *Academy of Management Executive*, 14 (November 2000): 48.
22. Ibid.
23. Ibid.
24. "Reining In Office Rumors," *Inc.*, 26 (November 2004): 60.
25. Lisa A. Burke and Jessica Morris Wise, "The Effective Care, Handling, and Pruning of the Office Grapevine," *Business Horizons*, 46 (May-June 2003): 73–74.
26. See "The Stat," *Business Week* (January 31, 2005): 14.
27. David Kirkpatrick, "It's Hard to Manage If You Don't Blog," *Fortune* (October 4, 2004): 46. Also see Michelle Conlin and Andrew Park, "Blogging with the Boss's Blessing," *Business Week* (June 28, 2004): 100, 102; David Kirkpatrick and Daniel Roth, "Why There's No Escaping the Blog," *Fortune* (January 10, 2005): 44–50; David Welch, "The Blog from the Rust Belt," *Business Week* (February 7, 2005): 12; and Stephen Baker and Heather Green, "Blogs Will Change Your Business," *Business Week* (May 2, 2005): 56–67.
28. John W. Newstrom, Robert E. Monczka, and William E. Reif, "Perceptions of the Grapevine: Its Value and Influence," *Journal of Business Communication*, 11 (Spring 1974): 12–20.
29. See Roy Rowan, "Where Did *That* Rumor Come From?" *Fortune* (August 13, 1979): 130–137.
30. See Nicholas Difonzo, Prashant Bordia, and Ralph L. Rosnow, "Reining in Rumors," *Organizational Dynamics*, 23 (Summer 1994): 47–62; and Nancy B. Kurland and Lisa Hope Pelled, "Passing the Word: Toward a Model of Gossip and Power in the Workplace," *Academy of Management Review*, 25 (April 2000): 428–438.
31. Patricia Sellers, "Lessons from TV's New Bosses," *Fortune* (March 14, 1988): 115, 118. For an update on Tisch, see Kimberly Weisul, "One Bear Doesn't Make It a Picnic," *Business Week* (March 25, 2002): 8.
32. See Alan Zaremba, "Working with the Organizational Grapevine," *Personnel Journal*, 67 (July 1988): 38–41.
33. See "Patrolling the Online Rumor Mill," *Training*, 37 (June 2000): 29; and Chris Woodyard, "Lurker Prowls Web to Clarify Issues, Answer Questions," *USA Today* (February 6, 2001): 6B.
34. "Executives Favor Plucking the Fruits from Employee Grapevine," *Association Management*, 36 (April 1984): 105.
35. A comprehensive discussion of rumors and rumor control can be found in Ralph L. Rosnow, "Inside Rumor: A Personal Journey," *American Psychologist*, 46 (May 1991): 484–496. Also see Lin Grensing-Pophal, "Got the Message?" *HR Magazine*, 46 (April 2001): 74–79.
36. Tammy Galvin, "Nothing Ventured," *Training*, 41 (February 2004): 4.
37. See Jack Griffin, "The Body's Language," in *How to Say It from the Heart* (Paramus, N.J.: Prentice- Hall Press, 2001), pp. 13–25; and Ronald E. Riggio and Robert S. Feldman, *Applications of Nonverbal Communication* (Mahwah, N.J.: Erlbaum, 2004).
38. See Albert Mehrabian, "Communication Without Words," *Psychology Today*, 2 (September 1968): 53–55. For a discussion of the nonverbal origins of language, see Sharon Begley, "Talking from Hand to Mouth," *Newsweek* (March 15, 1999): 56–58. Nonverbal cues are discussed in Thomas K. Connellan, "Great Expectations, Great Results," *HR Magazine*, 48 (June 2003): 155–150.
39. Pierre Mornell, "The Sounds of Silence," *Inc.*, 23 (February 2001): 117.
40. See Maria Puente, "How NOT to Dress for Work," *USA Today* (December 1, 2004): 1D–2D.
41. Excerpt from Brian Hickey, "People Packaging," *America West Airlines Magazine*, 5 (September 1990): 61. Reprinted by permission of the author. Also see Bill Leonard, "Casual Dress Policies Can Trip Up Job Applicants," *HR Magazine*, 46 (June 2001): 33, 35.
42. This three-way breakdown comes from Dale G. Leathers, *Nonverbal Communication Systems* (Boston: Allyn & Bacon, 1976), ch. 2. Also see James M. Carroll and James A. Russell, "Facial Expressions in Hollywood's Portrayal of Emotion," *Journal of Personality and Social Psychology*, 72 (January 1997): 164–176.
43. For details see Mac Fulfer, "Nonverbal Communication: How to Read What's Plain as the Nose. . .or Eyelid. . .or Chin . . .on Their Faces," *Journal of Organization Excellence*, 20 (Spring 2001): 19–27. Also see Bobbie Gossage, "What a Smile Means," *Inc.*, 25 (October 2003): 20; Andy Raskin, "A Face Any Business Can Trust," *Business 2.0*, 4 (December 2003): 58–60; Stephanie Clifford, "It's Official: MBAs Are a Bunch of Clowns," *Inc.*, 27 (February 2005): 23.
44. Paul C. Judge, "High Tech Star," *Business Week* (March 15, 1999): 75.
45. Based on A. Keenan, "Effects of the Non-Verbal Behaviour of Interviewers on Candidates' Performance," *Journal of Occupational Psychology*, 49, no. 3 (1976): 171–175. Also see Stanford W. Gregory Jr. and Stephen Webster, "Nonverbal Signal in Voices of Interview Partners Effectively Predicts Communication Accommodation and Social Status Perceptions," *Journal of Personality and Social Psychology*, 70 (June 1996): 1231–1240; Jeff Mowatt, "Making Connections: How to Create Rapport with Anyone in Under 30 Seconds," *Canadian Manager*, 25 (Fall 2000): 26, 29; and Nick Morgan, "The Kinesthetic Speaker: Putting Action into Words," *Harvard Business Review*, 79 (April 2001): 112–120.
46. See Linda L. Carli, Suzanne J. LaFleur, and Christopher C. Loeber, "Nonverbal Behavior, Gender, and Influence," *Journal of Personality and Social Psychology*, 68 (June 1995): 1030–1041.
47. For details, see Dore Butler and Florence L. Geis, "Nonverbal Affect Responses to Male and Female Leaders: Implications for Leadership Evaluations," *Journal of Personality and Social Psychology*, 58 (January 1990): 48–59.
48. Based on Ben Brown, "Atlanta Out to Mind Its Manners," *USA Today* (March 14, 1996): 7C. Also see Andrew L. Molinsky, Mary Anne Krabbenhoft, Nalini Ambady, and Y. Susan Choi, "Cracking the Nonverbal Code: Intercultural Competence and Gesture Recognition Across Cultures," *Journal of Cross-Cultural Psychology*, 36 (May 2005): 380–395.
49. See Andrea C. Poe, "Mind Their Manners," *HR Magazine*, 46 (May 2001): 75–80; Noelle Knox, "Expert: Mind Your Manners, It's Good Business," *USA Today* (June 28, 2001): 7B; and Rod Kurtz, "Is Etiquette a Core Value?" *Inc.*, 26 (May 2004): 22.
50. "Workers Are Surveyed on Communication," *Arizona Republic* (December 26, 2004): D6. Also see Jeffrey Pfeffer, "The Whole Truth and Nothing But," *Business 2.0*, 5 (October 2004): 78.
51. David Kirkpatrick, "Sam Palmisano: IBM," *Fortune* (August 9, 2004): 96. IBM employee data from "Fortune 1,000 Ranked Within Industries," *Fortune* (April 5, 2004): F-48.
52. For related research, see Wendy R. Boswell and Julie B. Olson-Buchanan, "Experiencing Mistreatment at Work: The Role of Grievance Filing, Nature of Mistreatment, and Employee Withdrawal," *Academy of Management Journal*, 47 (February 2004): 129–139.
53. For details, see Dick Grote and Jim Wimberly, "Peer Review," *Training*, 30 (March 1993): 51–55.
54. See Jack Welch, *Jack: Straight from the Gut* (New York: Warner Business Books, 2001), pp. 393–394; and Palmer Morrel-Samuels, "Getting the Truth into Workplace Surveys," *Harvard Business Review*, 80 (February 2002): 111–118.
55. Charlotte Garvey, "Connecting the Organizational Pulse to the Bottom Line," *HR Magazine*, 49 (June 2004): 71.
56. See Gail Johnson, "What Matters Most," *Training*, 41 (May 2004): 19; Adrienne Fox, "Who Needs Attitude?" *HR Magazine*, 49 (June 2004): 18; and Gail Johnson, "Time to Take Action," *Training*, 41 (September 2004): 18..
57. See Robert J. Aiello, "Employee Attitude Surveys: Impact on Corporate

Decisions," *Public Relations Journal* (March 1983): 21.
58. Robert Levering and Milton Moskowitz, "The 100 Best Companies to Work For," *Fortune* (January 12, 2004): 78. Also see Barry Nalebuff and Ian Ayres, "Encouraging Suggestive Behavior," *Harvard Business Review*, 82 (December 2004): 18.
59. Paul Keegan, "Please, Just Don't Call Us Cheap," *Business 2.0*, 3 (February 2002): 51.
60. Data from Robert Levering and Milton Moskowitz, "The 100 Best Companies to Work For," *Fortune* (January 24, 2005): 84.
61. See James S. Larson, "Employee Participation in Federal Management," *Public Personnel Management*, 18 (Winter 1989): 404–414. Also see John Tschohl, "Be Bad," *Canadian Manager*, 23 (Winter 1998): 23–24; Stephanie Armour, "Firms Tap Employees for Cost-Saving Suggestions," *USA Today* (January 26, 1999): 1B; and Dale K. DuPont, "Eureka! Tools for Encouraging Employee Suggestions," *HR Magazine*, 44 (September 1999): 134–143.
62. Alison Stein Wellner, "Everyone's a Critic," *Inc.*, 26 (July 2004): 38, 41.
63. See Cheryl Dahle, "What Are You Complaining About?" *Fast Company*, no. 46 (May 2001): 66, 68; John Weeks, "Whining Away the Hours," *Harvard Business Review*, 82 (May 2004): 20–21.
64. Martha Frase-Blunt, "Meeting with the Boss," *HR Magazine*, 48 (June 2003): 95.
65. Curtis Sittenfeld, "Here's How GSA Changed Its Ways," *Fast Company*, no. 25 (June 1999): 88.
66. For more, see Bill Leonard, "Cyberventing," *HR Magazine*, 44 (November 1999): 34–39; and John Simons, "Stop Moaning About Gripe Sites and Log On," *Fortune* (April 2, 2001): 181–182.
67. For more, see Martha Frase-Blunt, "Making Exit Interviews Work," *HR Magazine*, 49 (August 2004); 109–113.
68. "Exit Interviews Used Irregularly," *Arizona Republic* (February 25, 2001): D2.
69. Paul Kaihla, "Acing the Exit Interview," *Business 2.0*, 5 (May 2004): 77.
70. Charles F. Knight, "Emerson Electric: Consistent Profits, Consistently," *Harvard Business Review*, 70 (January-February 1992): 60.
71. Catherine Yang, "Low-Wage Lessons," *Business Week* (November 11, 1996): 114.
72. Ron Lieber, "Timex Resets Its Watch," *Fast Company*, no. 52 (November 2001): 48.
73. Based on Rachel Sauer, "Jawing the Jargon," *Arizona Republic* (November 6, 2004): D3.
74. See Bob Filipczak, "Obfuscation Resounding: Corporate Communication in America," *Training*, 32 (July 1995): 29–36.
75. For discussion of male versus female communication styles, see Dayle M. Smith, *Women at Work: Leadership for the Next Century* (Upper Saddle River, N.J.: Prentice- Hall, 2000), pp. 26–32.
76. Wendy Martyna, "What Does 'He' Mean? Use of the Generic Masculine," *Journal of Communication*, 28 (Winter 1978): 138. A later study with similar results is Janet A. Sniezek and Christine H. Jazwinski, "Gender Bias in English: In Search of Fair Language," *Journal of Applied Social Psychology*, 16, no. 7 (1986): 642–662. Also see Patricia C. Kelley, "Can Feminist Language Change Organizational Behavior? Some Research Questions," *Business & Society*, 35 (March 1996): 84–88.
77. Del Jones, "'Code Words' Cloud Issue of Discrimination at Work," *USA Today* (October 1, 1996): 1B–2B.
78. See Deirdre Donahue, "Explosive, 'Troublesome' N-Word Gets an Airing," *USA Today* (January 10, 2002): 6D.
79. See Cliff Edwards, "Lighten Up, Road Warriors," *Business Week* (October 25, 2004): 110–111; Matthew Maier, "Cutting the Wires at Work," *Business 2.0*, 5 (November 2004): 97–98; Glenn Fleishman, "The Road Warrior's Wi-Fi Survival Guide," *Business 2.0*, 5 (December 2004): 161–166; and Ian Mount, "Icebreaking for Geeks—and More," *Fast Company*, no. 90 (January 2005): 33.
80. Del Jones, "E-Mail Avalanche Even Buries CEOs," *USA Today* (January 4, 2002): 1A.
81. Jon Swartz, "E-Mail Overload Taxes Workers and Companies," *USA Today* (June 26, 2001): 1A.
82. See Stepanie Armour, "More Companies Keep Track of Workers' Email," *USA Today*, June 13, 2005, p. 48.
83. See Ann Pomeroy, "Business 'Fast and Loose' with E-mail, IMs—Study," *HR Magazine*, 49 (November 2004): 32, 34.
84. See Jon Swartz, "Companies Step Up Monitoring of Internal Networks," *USA Today* (December 14, 2004): 1B.
85. Stephanie Armour, "You Have (Too Much) E-Mail," *USA Today* (March 2, 1999): 3B.
86. Data from Jon Swartz, "Is the Future of E-Mail Under Cyberattack?" *USA Today* (June 15, 2004): 4B; Jon Swartz, "Spammers Have Ignored Federal Law," *USA Today* (January 3, 2005): 1B. Also see Jon Swartz, "Spammers Convicted; First Felony Case," *USA Today* (November 4, 2004): 1B; and Erin Chambers, "The Lid on Spam Is Still Loose," *Business Week* (February 7, 2005): 10.
87. See Brad Stone, "Invasion of the PC Snatchers," *Newsweek* (December 13, 2004): 47.
88. This list is based on Eryn Brown, "You've Got Mail. :-o," *Fortune* (December 7, 1998): 36, 40; Joan Tunstall, *Better, Faster Email: Getting the Most Out of Email* (St. Leonards, Australia: Allen & Unwin, 1999); Donna J. Abernathy, "You've Got Email," *Training & Development*, 53 (April 1999): 18; and Andrea C. Poe, "Don't Touch That 'Send' Button!" *HR Magazine*, 46 (July 2001): 74–80. For additional useful e-mail tips, see Tammy Galvin, "E-Mail Madness," *Training*, 41 (April 2004): 16.
89. Based on Swartz, "E-Mail Overload Taxes Workers and Companies." Also see Jon Swartz, "Spam's Irritating Cousin, Spim, on the Loose," *USA Today* (March 1, 2004): 1B; Brian Braiker, "Instant Security," *Newsweek* (August 30, 2004): 55; and Brian Barker, "Noted: Instant Messaging," *Training*, 41 (November 2004): 18.
90. Heather Johnson, "Instant Lawsuit?" *Training*, 41 (September 2004): 16.
91. Data from **www.ctia.org**.
92. For a historical perspective on cell phones, see Stephanie N. Mehta, "Cellular Evolution," *Fortune* (August 23, 2004): 80–86. Also see Kevin Maney, "Cellphones, Net Could Have Saved Thousands from Waves," *USA Today* (January 5, 2005): 3B.
93. Data from Chris Woodyard, "Some Offices Opt for Cellphones Only," *USA Today* (January 25, 2005): 1B.
94. See Charisse Jones, "New Jersey and D.C. Are Telling Drivers to Hang Up," *USA Today* (June 29, 2004): 3A; Dan Reed, "In-Flight Cellphones 'Worked Great' in Test," *USA Today* (July 20, 2004): 8B; and Robert J. Samuelson, "A Cell Phone? Never For Me," *Newsweek* (August 23, 2004): 63.
95. See Deborah Sharp, "Be Polite, Be Discreet, Be Quiet," *USA Today* (September 4, 2001): 4A.
96. Drawn from Stephanie Armour, "Camera Phones Don't Click at Work," *USA Today* (January 12, 2004): 1B.
97. See Andrea Bennett, "Beam Yourself into a Meeting," *Fortune* (January 21, 2002): 128; and Barbara De Lollis, "Talking Heads Are Catching On As Web Meetings Take Off," *USA Today* (September 7, 2004): 7B.
98. Bill Breen, "Hidden Asset," *Fast Company*, no. 80 (March 2004): 95.
99. Data from Stephanie Armour, "Videoconferencing Takes Off As Job Interviews Go Remote," *USA Today* (January 22, 2002): 3B.
100. "Video Conferencing Gains New Appeal," *Arizona Republic* (September 23, 2001): D1.
101. Tips adapted in part from Michael Emery and Margaret Schubert, "A Trainer's Guide to Videoconferencing," *Training*, 30 (June 1993): 59–63. Also see "Tips for the Photophobic," *Training*, 35 (October 1998): 26.
102. Data from Karyn-Siobhan Robinson, "Where Did Everybody Go? *HR Magazine*, 49 (May 2004): 38.
103. Data from Robert Levering and Milton Moskowitz, "The 100 Best Companies to Work For," *Fortune* (January 12, 2004): 72.
104. Stephanie Armour, "More Bosses Getting into the Telecommuting Biz," *USA Today* (November 3, 2004): 2B.
105. See Jon Swartz, "Inmates vs.

Outsourcing," *USA Today* (July 7, 2004): 1B–2B; and Timothy D. Golden and John F. Veiga, "The Impact of Extent of Telecommuting on Job Satisfaction: Resolving Inconsistent Findings," *Journal of Management,* 31, no. 2 (2005): 301–318.

106. Joelle Jay, "On Communicating Well," *HR Magazine,* 50 (January 2005): 87–90.

107. Data from Judi Brownell, "Perceptions of Effective Listeners: A Management Study," *Journal of Business Communication,* 27 (Fall 1990): 401–415.

108. Data from Cynthia Hamilton and Brian H. Kleiner, "Steps to Better Listening," *Personnel Journal,* 66 (February 1987): 20–21. Also see Roger R. Pearman, "Want to Lead Others? Listen First," *Training,* 41 (October 2004): 54.

109. This list has been adapted from John F. Kikoski, "Communication: Understanding It, Improving It," *Personnel Journal,* 59 (February 1980): 126–131; John L. DiGaetani, "The Business of Listening," *Business Horizons,* 23 (October 1980): 40–46; P. Slizewski, "Tips for Active Listening," *HR Focus* (May 1995): 7; and Griffin, "10 Ways to Become a Better Listener," in *How to Say It from the Heart,* pp. 39–42.

110. "Listen Up, Leaders: Let Workers Do the Talking," *HR Magazine,* 48 (October 2003): 14.

111. See Wendy Zellner, "O.K., So He's Not Sam Walton," *Business Week* (March 16, 1992): 56–58.

112. Barbara Hagenbaugh, "Good Help Hard to Find for Manufacturers," *USA Today* (April 16, 2004): 1B. For tips, see Anita Bruzzese, "Avoid Resume Pitfalls," *Arizona Republic* (November 14, 2004): EC 1.

113. See Laura Vanderkam, "Writing a Wrong," *USA Today* (December 1, 2004): 21A.

114. Robert F. DeGise, "Writing: Don't Let the Mechanics Obscure the Message," *Supervisory Management,* 21 (April 1976): 26–28. Also see Deborah Dumaine, "Leadership in Writing," *Training and Development,* 58 (December 2004): 52–54.

115. See "Give the Boot to Hackneyed Phrases," *Training,* 27 (August 1990): 10. Also see Herschell Gordon Lewis, "100 of the Easiest Ways to Begin an Effective Sales Letter," *Direct Marketing,* 56 (February 1994): 32–34.

116. Data from "How Workers Communicate," *USA Today* (January 3, 2001): 1B. Also see Michael A. Prospero, "Two Words You Never Hear Together: 'Great Meeting,'" *Fast Company,* no. 83 (June 2004): 38.

117. "Meeting 'Mania' Squanders Time and Money," *HR Magazine,* 43 (August 1998): 24, 26.

118. As summarized in Michelle Archer, "Inject Some Drama, Structure in Office Meetings," *USA Today* (June 7, 2004): 11B. See Patrick M. Lencioni, *Death by Meeting: A Leadership Fable About Solving the Most Painful Problem in Business* (San Francisco: Jossey-Bass, 2004).

119. Data from Anne Fisher, "How Much PowerPoint Is Enough?" *Fortune* (May 31, 2004): 56. Also see Kevin Ferguson, "Reinventing the Powerpoint," *Inc.,* 26 (March 2004): 42.

120. This list is based in part on discussions in Stephanie Armour, "Team Efforts, Technology Add New Reasons to Meet," *USA Today* (December 8, 1997): 2A; and John E. Tropman, *Making Meetings Work: Achieving High Quality Group Decisions,* 2nd ed. (Thousand Oaks, Calif.: Sage, 2003).

CHAPTER 13

1. **Opening Quote** Keith Davis, *Human Behavior at Work: Organizational Behavior,* 6th ed. (New York: McGraw-Hill, 1981), p. 2.

2. For an excellent historical and conceptual treatment of basic motivation theory, see the collection of readings in Chapter 2 of Richard M. Steers, Lyman W. Porter, and Gregory A. Bigley, *Motivation and Leadership at Work,* 6th ed. (New York: McGraw-Hill, 1996).

3. For recent perspectives on motivation, see Leigh Buchanan, "Let Me Take You Down," *Harvard Business Review,* 82 (March 2004): 20–21; William Roiter and Margaret Butteriss, "Managing the Falling MVP," *HR Magazine,* 49 (July 2004): 117–120; Richard M. Steers, Richard T. Mowday, and Debra L. Shapiro, "The Future of Work Motivation Theory," *Academy of Management Review,* 29 (July 2004): 379–387; Edwin A. Locke and Gary P. Latham, "What Should We Do About Motivation Theory? Six Recommendations for the Twenty-First Century," *Academy of Managmeent Review,* 29 (July 2004): 388–403; and Anne Fisher, "Turn Star Employees into Superstars," *Fortune* (December 13, 2004): 70.

4. See A. H. Maslow, "A Theory of Human Motivation," *Psychological Review,* 50 (July 1943): 370–396; Ron Zemke, "Maslow for a New Millennium," *Training,* 35 (December 1998): 54–58; Robin Marantz Henig, "Basic Needs Met? Next Comes Happiness," *USA Today* (January 2, 2001): 11A; and Bill Cooke, Albert J. Mills, and Elizabeth S. Kelley, "Situating Maslow in Cold War America: A Recontextualization of Management Theory," *Group and Organization Management,* 30 (April 2005): 129–152.

5. Maslow, "A Theory of Human Motivation," p. 375.

6. Jennifer Schramm, "Feeling Safe," *HR Magazine,* 49 (May 2004): 152.

7. Dean Foust, "Man on the Spot," *Business Week* (May 3, 1999): 142–143.

8. For more, see Gene Koretz, "The Vital Role of Self-Esteem," *Business Week* (February 2, 1998): 26; Donald G. Gardner and Jon L. Pierce, "Self-Esteem and Self-Efficacy Within the Organizational Context: An Empirical Investigation," *Group & Organization Management,* 23 (March 1998): 48–70; and Perry Pascarella, "It All Begins with Self-Esteem," *Management Review,* 88 (February 1999): 60–61.

9. Maslow, "A Theory of Human Motivation," p. 382.

10. As quoted in Steve Jones, "Keys' Next Chapter Is Her Soulful 'Diary,'" *USA Today* (December 1, 2003): 5D. Also see Edna Gundersen, "At 80, 'Gatemouth' Has Grown Beyond Blues," *USA Today* (November 29, 2004): 4D.

11. George W. Cherry, "The Serendipity of the Fully Functioning Manager," *Sloan Management Review,* 17 (Spring 1976): 73.

12. Vance F. Mitchell and Pravin Moudgill, "Measurement of Maslow's Need Hierarchy," *Organizational Behavior and Human Performance,* 16 (August 1976): 348.

13. For example, see Ellen L. Betz, "Two Tests of Maslow's Theory of Need Fulfillment," *Journal of Vocational Behavior,* 24 (April 1984): 204–220.

14. Edward E. Lawler, *Motivation in Work Organizations* (Monterey, Calif.: Brooks/Cole, 1973), p. 34.

15. See Frederick Herzberg, Bernard Mausner, and Barbara Bloch Snyderman, *The Motivation to Work,* 2nd ed. (New York: Wiley, 1959). For a marketing application of Herzberg's theory, see Earl Naumann and Donald W. Jackson Jr., "One More Time: How Do You Satisfy Customers?" *Business Horizons,* 42 (May-June 1999): 71–76. Also see Jamie Malanowski, "Soul Assassins," *Fast Company,* no. 94 (May 2005): 85–89.

16. Frederick Herzberg, "One More Time: How Do You Motivate Employees?" *Harvard Business Review,* 46 (January-February 1968): 56. For another view, see Dennis W. Organ, "The Happy Curve," *Business Horizons,* 38 (May-June 1995): 1–3. Herzberg's methodology is replicated in Susan G. Turner, Dawn R. Utley, and Jerry D. Westbrook, "Project Managers and Functional Managers: A Case Study of Job Satisfaction in a Matrix Organization," *Project Management Journal,* 29 (September 1998): 11–19.

17. James K. Harter, Frank L. Schmidt, and Theodore L. Hayes, "Business-Unit-Level Relationship Between Employee Satisfaction, Employee Engagement, and Business Outcomes: A Meta-Analysis," *Journal of Applied Psychology,* 87 (April 2002): 268. Also see Thomas A. Wright and Russell Cropanzano, "The Role of Psychological Well-Being in Job Performance: A Fresh Look at an Age-Old Quest," *Organizational Dynamics,* 33, no. 4 (2004): 338–351; and Margaret Heffernan, "The Morale of the Story," *Fast Company,* no. 92 (March 2005): 79–81.

18. See Robert J. House and Lawrence A. Wigdor, "Herzberg's Dual-Factor Theory

of Job Satisfaction and Motivation: A Review of the Evidence and a Criticism," *Personnel Psychology*, 20 (1967): 369–389.

19. For example, see Peter W. Hom, "Expectancy Prediction of Reenlistment in the National Guard," *Journal of Vocational Behavior*, 16 (April 1980): 235–248; John P. Wanous, Thomas L. Keon, and Janina C. Latack, "Expectancy Theory and Occupational/Organizational Choices: A Review and Test," *Organizational Behavior and Human Performance*, 32 (August 1983): 66–86; Alan W. Stacy, Keith F. Widaman, and G. Alan Marlatt, "Expectancy Models of Alcohol Use," *Journal of Personality and Social Psychology*, 58 (May 1990): 918–928; and Anne S. Tsui, Susan J. Ashford, Lynda St. Clair, and Katherine R. Xin, "Dealing with Discrepant Expectations: Response Strategies and Managerial Effectiveness," *Academy of Management Journal*, 38 (December 1995): 1515–1543.
20. See Bill Leonard, "College Students Confident They Will Reach Career Goals Quickly," *HR Magazine*, 46 (April 2001): 27.
21. "Noël Forgeard," *Business Week* (January 8, 2001): 76.
22. For example, see Jim Collins, "Turning Goals into Results: The Power of Catalytic Mechanisms," *Harvard Business Review*, 77 (July–August 1999): 71–82.
23. See, for example, Edwin A. Locke and Gary P. Latham, *Goal Setting: A Motivational Technique That Works!* (Englewood Cliffs, N.J.: Prentice-Hall, 1984). Also see Yitzhak Fried and Linda Haynes Slowik, "Enriching Goal-Setting Theory with Time: An Integrated Approach," *Academy of Management Review*, 29 (July 2004): 404–422; Edwin A. Locke, "Guest Editor's Introduction: Goal-Setting Theory and Its Applications to the World of Business," *Academy of Management Executive*, 18 (November 2004): 124–125; Gary P. Latham, "The Motivational Benefits of Goal-Setting," *Academy of Management Executive*, 18 (November 2004): 126–129; and Gerard H. Seijts and Gary P. Latham, "Learning Versus Performance Goals: When Should Each Be Used?" *Academy of Management Executive*, 19 (February 2005): 124–131.
24. See, for example, Edwin A. Locke, Keryll N. Shaw, Lise M. Saari, and Gary P. Latham, "Goal Setting and Task Performance: 1969–1980," *Psychological Bulletin*, 90 (July 1981): 125–152; Anthony J. Mento, Robert P. Steel, and Ronald J. Karren, "A Meta-Analytic Study of the Effects of Goal Setting on Task Performance: 1966–1984," *Organizational Behavior and Human Decision Processes*, 39 (February 1987): 52–83; Don VandeWalle, Steven P. Brown, William L. Cron, and John W. Slocum Jr., "The Influence of Goal Orientation and Self-Regulation Tactics on Sales Performance: A Longitudinal Field Test," *Journal of Applied Psychology*, 84 (April 1999): 249–259; and Gerard H. Seijts, Gary P. Latham, Kevin Tasa, and Brandon W. Latham, "Goal Setting and Goal Orientation: An Integration of Two Different Yet Related Literatures," *Academy of Management Journal*, 47 (April 2004): 227–239.
25. "ThermoSTAT," *Training*, 40 (July-August 2003): 16.
26. See Steven Kerr and Steffen Landauer, "Using Stretch Goals to Promote Organizational Effectiveness and Personal Growth: General Electric and Goldman Sachs," *Academy of Management Executive*, 18 (November 2004): 134–138; and Karyll N. Shaw, "Changing the Goal-Setting Process at Microsoft," *Academy of Management Executive*, 18 (November 2004): 139–142.
27. See Christopher Earley, Gregory B. Northcraft, Cynthia Lee, and Terri R. Lituchy, "Impact of Process and Outcome Feedback on the Relation of Goal Setting to Task Performance," *Academy of Management Journal*, 33 (March 1990): 87–105.
28. John Huey, "America's Most Successful Merchant," *Fortune* (September 23, 1991): 50. For an update, see Hank Gilman, "The Most Underrated CEO Ever," *Fortune* (April 5, 2004): 242–248.
29. Stephen Phillips and Amy Dunkin, "King Customer," *Business Week* (March 12, 1990): 91.
30. See Edwin A. Locke, "Linking Goals to Monetary Incentives," *Academy of Management Executive*, 18 (November 2004): 130–133.
31. Lewis Carroll, *Alice's Adventures in Wonderland* (Philadelphia: The John C. Winston Company, 1923), p. 57.
32. See Marilyn Elias, "Routine Job May Take Toll on Heart," *USA Today* (September 25, 1995): 1D; Jia Lin Xie and Gary Johns, "Job Scope and Stress: Can Job Scope Be Too High?" *Academy of Management Journal*, 38 (October 1995): 1288–1309; and "Stranger in Blue-Collar Land," *Training*, 36 (August 1999): 20.
33. Adapted from J. Richard Hackman, "The Design of Work in the 1980s," *Organizational Dynamics*, 7 (Summer 1978): 3–17. An instructive four-way analysis of job design may be found in Michael A. Campion and Paul W. Thayer, "Job Design: Approaches, Outcomes, and Trade-Offs," *Organizational Dynamics*, 15 (Winter 1987): 66–79.
34. Rick Wartzman, "Houston Turns Out to Be the Capital of the Egg Roll," *Wall Street Journal* (December 7, 1995): A1.
35. For an interesting discussion of people who do society's "dirty work," see Blake E. Ashforth and Glen E. Kreiner, "'How Can You Do It?' Dirty Work and the Challenge of Constructing a Positive Identity," *Academy of Management Review*, 24 (July 1999): 413–434.
36. Jean M. Phillips, "Effects of Realistic Job Previews on Multiple Organizational Outcomes: A Meta-Analysis," *Academy of Management Journal*, 41 (December 1998): 686. Also see Peter W. Hom, Roger W. Griffeth, Leslie E. Palich, and Jeffrey S. Bracker, "Revisiting Met Expectations as a Reason Why Realistic Job Previews Work," *Personnel Psychology*, 52 (Spring 1999): 97–112.
37. See James M. Mehring, "Flexibility Is No Key to Stability," *Business Week* (March 5, 2001): 30; and Martha Frase-Blunt, "Ready, Set, Rotate!" *HR Magazine*, 46 (October 2001): 46–53.
38. David Welch, "How Nissan Laps Detroit," *Business Week* (December 22, 2003): 60.
39. See Lee Smith, "The FBI Is a Tough Outfit to Run," *Fortune* (October 9, 1989): 133–140. Also see Michael A. Campion, Lisa Cheraskin, and Michael J. Stevens, "Career-Related Antecedents and Outcomes of Job Rotation," *Academy of Management Journal*, 37 (December 1994): 1518–1542. For a condensed version of the foregoing study, see Susan Stites-Doe, "The New Story About Job Rotation," *Academy of Management Executive*, 10 (February 1996): 86–87.
40. See M. A. Howell, "Time Off as a Reward for Productivity," *Personnel Administration*, 34 (November-December 1971): 48–51.
41. Fred Luthans and Robert Kreitner, *Organizational Behavior Modification and Beyond: An Operant and Social Learning Approach* (Glenview, Ill.: Scott, Foresman, 1985), p. 192. Also see Diane L. Lockwood and Fred Luthans, "Contingent Time Off: A Nonfinancial Incentive for Improving Productivity," *Management Review*, 73 (July 1984): 48–52. The case for a six-hour work day is presented in "That's Why They Call It 'Work,'" *Fast Company*, no. 29 (November 1999): 194.
42. Data from Carla O'Dell and Jerry McAdams, "The Revolution in Employee Rewards," *Management Review*, 76 (March 1987): 30–33. For a recent example of CTO in action, see Thomas Petzinger Jr., "They Keep Workers Motivated to Make Annoying Phone Calls," *Wall Street Journal* (September 20, 1996): B1.
43. J. Richard Hackman and Greg R. Oldham, *Work Redesign* (Reading, Mass.: Addison-Wesley, 1980), p. 20. Also see Michael A. Campion and Michael J. Stevens, "Neglected Questions in Job Design: How People Design Jobs, Task-Job Predictability, and Influence of Training," *Journal of Business and Psychology*, 6 (Winter 1991): 169–191; and Gary Johns, Jia Lin Xie, and Yongqing Fang, "Mediating and Moderating Effects in Job Design," *Journal of Management*, 18 (December 1992): 657–676.
44. David Kirkpatrick, "How Safe Are Video Terminals?" *Fortune* (August 29, 1988):

71. For related research, see Michael A. Campion and Carol L. McClelland, "Interdisciplinary Examination of the Costs and Benefits of Enlarged Jobs: A Job Design Quasi-Experiment," *Journal of Applied Psychology*, 76 (April 1991): 186–198.
45. See J. Barton Cunningham and Ted Eberle, "A Guide to Job Enrichment and Redesign," *Personnel*, 67 (February 1990): 56–61; Roger E. Herman and Joyce L. Gioia, "Making Work Meaningful: Secrets of the Future-Focused Corporation," *The Futurist*, 32 (December 1998): 24–38; and Donna Fenn, "Redesign Work," *Inc.*, 21 (June 1999): 74–84.
46. As quoted in John Bowe, Marisa Bowe, and Sabin Streeter, eds., *Gig: Americans Talk About Their Jobs at the Turn of the Millennium* (New York: Crown Publishers, 2000), p. 30.
47. Hackman and Oldham, *Work Redesign*, pp. 78–80. Also see John W. Medcof, "The Job Characteristics of Computing and Non-Computing Work Activities," *Journal of Occupational and Organizational Psychology*, 69 (June 1996): 199–212; and Joan R. Rentsch and Robert P. Steel, "Testing the Durability of Job Characteristics as Predictors of Absenteeism over a Six-Year Period," *Personnel Psychology*, 51 (Spring 1998): 165–190.
48. See Deborah J. Dwyer and Marilyn L. Fox, "The Moderating Role of Hostility in the Relationship Between Enriched Jobs and Health," *Academy of Management Journal*, 43 (December 2000): 1086–1096; and Amy Wrzesniewskiand Jane E. Dutton, "Crafting a Job: Revisioning Employees as Active Crafters of Their Work," *Academy of Management Review*, 26 (April 2001): 179–201.
49. See Bob Nelson and Dean R. Spitzer,, *The 1001 Rewards & Recognition Fieldbook* (New York: Workman, 2002).
50. See Sheena S. Iyengar and Mark R. Lepper, "Rethinking the Value of Choice: A Cultural Perspective on Intrinsic Motivation," *Journal of Personality and Social Psychology*, 76 (March 1999): 349–366; and Bob Urichuck, "Employee Recognition and Praise," *Canadian Manager*, 24 (Summer 1999): 27–29.
51. As quoted in Roundtable, "All in a Day's Work," *Harvard Business Review* (Special Issue: Breakthrough Leadership), 79 (December 2001): 62. Also see Leigh Buchanan, The Things They Do for Love," *Harvard Business Review*, 82 (December 2004): 19–20.
52. See Joy E. Beatty, "Grades as Money and the Role of the Market Metaphor in Management Education," *Academy of Management Learning and Education*, 3 (June 2004): 187–196; Charlotte Garvey, "Meaningful Tokens of Appreciation," *HR Magazine*, 49 (August 2004): 101–106; Lin Grensing-Pophal, "Money Talks," *HR Magazine*, 49 (September 2004): 125–132; and Nicole Gull, "Taking the Pain Out of Payday," *Inc.*, 27 (January 2005): 36.
53. James C. Cooper and Kathleen Madigan, "The Second Half Should Be Healthier," *Business Week* (August 13, 2001): 26.
54. See Jennifer Schramm, "Living Wages," *HR Magazine*, 49 (March 2004): 152; and Margaret M. Clark, "Step by Step," *HR Magazine*, 50 (February 2005): 60–64.
55. See Susan J. Wells, "Merging Compensation Strategies," *HR Magazine*, 49 (May 2004): 66–78; Karen Renk, "The Power of Incentive Programs," *HR Magazine*, 49 (September 2004): 91–96; Anne Fisher, "A Strategic Way to Calculate Pay," *Fortune* (November 1, 2004): 62; Charlotte Garvey, "Philosophizing Compensation," *HR Magazine*, 50 (January 2005): 73–76 ; and Jason D. Shaw, Nina Gupta, Atul Mitra, and Gerald E. Ledford, Jr., Success and Survival of Skill-Based Pay Plans," *Journal of Management*, no. 1 (2005): 28–49.
56. See Pamela Babcock, "Find Out What Workers Want," *HR Magazine*, 50 (April 2005): 50–56.
57. See Bill Leonard, "Perks Give Way to Life-Cycle Benefits Plans," *HR Magazine*, 40 (March 1995): 45–48.
58. "Companies Offer Benefits Cafeteria-Style," *Business Week* (November 13, 1978): 116. Also see Anand Natarajan, "The Roll-Your-Own Health Plan," *Business Week* (January 26, 2004): 16.
59. For complete details, see Alison E. Barber, Randall B. Dunham, and Roger A. Formisano, "The Impact of Flexible Benefits on Employee Satisfaction: A Field Study," *Personnel Psychology*, 45 (Spring 1992): 55–75.
60. See David Fiedler, "Should You Adjust Your Sales Compensation?" *HR Magazine*, 47 (February 2002): 79–82.
61. For more, see Kelly Mollica, "Perceptions of Fairness," *HR Magazine*, 49 (June 2004): 169–178; and Jerald Greenberg, "Stress Fairness to Fare No Stress: Managing Workplace Stress by Promoting Organizational Justice," *Organizational Dynamics*, 33, no. 4 (2004): 352–365.
62. A good overview of equity theory can be found in Robert P. Vecchio, "Models of Psychological Inequity," *Organizational Behavior and Human Performance*, 34 (October 1984): 266–282.
63. See J. Stacy Adams and Patricia R. Jacobsen, "Effects of Wage Inequities on Work Quality," *Journal of Abnormal and Social Psychology*, 69 (1964): 19–25; Jerald Greenberg and Suzyn Ornstein, "High Status Job Title as Compensation for Underpayment: A Test of Equity Theory," *Journal of Applied Psychology*, 68 (May 1983): 285–297.
64. For examples, see Gary Strauss, "Why Are These CEOs Smiling? Must Be Payday," *USA Today* (March 25, 2002): 1B–2B; Jerry Useem, "Have They No Shame?" *Fortune* (April 28, 2003): 56–64; Jeffrey Pfeffer, "Stop Picking Workers' Pockets," *Business 2.0.* 5 (July 2004): 64; and Louis Lavelle, "Another Stellar Year for Honchos," *Business Week* (December 27, 2004): 14.
65. "What Has Undermined Your Trust in Companies?" *USA Today* (February 10, 2004): 1B.
66. Pablo Galarza and Stephen Gandel, "Invest Like a Legend," *Money*, 33 (October 2004): 118. Also see Peter Burrows, "Cisco's Disconnect," *Business Week* (August 30, 2004): 56.
67. See Jeffrey Pfeffer, "Sins of Commission," *Business 2.0*, 5 (May 2004): 56; "Performance-Based Pay Plans," *HR Magazine*, 49 (June 2004): 22; Ann Pomeroy, "Stock Option 'Golden Age' May Be Over," *HR Magazine*, 49 (August 2004): 18; and Louis Lavelle, "They're Opting Out of Options," *Business Week* (February 28, 2005): 13.
68. Chris Taylor, "On-the-Spot Incentives," *HR Magazine*, 49 (May 2004): 82. Also see Karen Kroll, "Paying for Performance," *Inc.*, 26 (November 2004): 46.
69. See Peter V. LeBlanc and Paul W. Mulvey, "How American Workers See the Rewards of Work," *Compensation & Benefits Review*, 30 (January-February 1998): 24–28; and Louisa Wah, "Rewarding Efficient Teamwork," *Management Review*, 88 (February 1999): 7.
70. George Gendron, "Steel Man: Ken Iverson," *Inc.* (April 1986): 47–48.
71. The case *against* incentives is presented in Alfie Kohn, "Why Incentive Plans Cannot Work," *Harvard Business Review*, 71 (September-October 1993): 54–63. Also see Peter Nulty, "Incentive Pay Can Be Crippling," *Fortune* (November 13, 1995): 23; Robert Eisenberger and Judy Cameron, "Detrimental Effects of Reward," *American Psychologist*, 51 (November 1996): 1153–1166; and Alfie Kohn, "Challenging Behaviorist Dogma: Myths About Money and Motivation," *Compensation & Benefits Review*, 30 (March-April 1998): 27, 33–37.
72. Employee involvement is thoughtfully discussed in Jay R. Galbraith, Edward E. Lawler III, et al., *Organizing for the Future: The New Logic for Managing Complex Organizations* (San Francisco: Jossey-Bass, 1993), chs. 6 and 7. Also see Richard L. Daft, "*Theory Z*: Opening the Corporate Door for Participative Management," *Academy of Management Executive*, 18 (November 2004): 117–121.
73. See W. Alan Randolph, "Navigating the Journey to Empowerment," *Organizational Dynamics*, 23 (Spring 1995): 19–32; Robert C. Ford and Myron D. Fottler, "Empowerment: A Matter of Degree," *Academy of Management Executive*, 9 (August 1995): 21–31; Jeffrey S. Harrison and R. Edward Freeman, "Special Topic: Democracy In and Around Organizations: Is Organizational

Democracy Worth the Effort?" *Academy of Management Executive*, 18 (August 2004): 49–53; and Jeffrey L. Kerr, "The Limits of Organizational Democracy," *Academy of Management Executive*, 18 (August 2004): 81–97.

74. For details see James P. Guthrie, "High-Involvement Work Practices, Turnover, and Productivity: Evidence from New Zealand," *Academy of Management Journal*, 44 (February 2001): 180–190. Also see Abraham Sagie and Zeynep Aycan, "A Cross-Cultural Analysis of Participative Decision-Making in Organizations," *Human Relations*, 56 (April 2003): 453–473.
75. See Edward E. Lawler III and Susan A. Mohrman, "Quality Circles: After the Honeymoon," *Organizational Dynamics*, 15 (Spring 1987): 42–54; and Gerald E. Ledford Jr., Edward E. Lawler III, and Susan A. Mohrman, "The Quality Circle and Its Variations," in *Productivity in Organizations*, ed. John P. Campbell, Richard J. Campbell, et al. (San Francisco: Jossey-Bass, 1988), pp. 255–294.
76. Evidence of a positive long-term impact on productivity may be found in Mitchell L. Marks, Philip H. Mirvis, Edward J. Hackett, and James F. Grady Jr., "Employee Participation in a Quality Circle Program: Impact on Quality of Work Life, Productivity, and Absenteeism," *Journal of Applied Psychology*, 71 (February 1986): 61–69. Also see Everett E. Adam Jr., "Quality Circle Performance," *Journal of Management*, 17 (March 1991): 25–39.
77. Frank Shipper, "Tapping Creativity," *Quality Circles Journal*, 4 (August 1981): 12. Also see Amal Kumar Naj, "Some Manufacturers Drop Effort to Adopt Japanese Techniques," *Wall Street Journal* (May 7, 1993): A1.
78. Raj Aggarwal and Betty J. Simkins, "Open Book Management—Optimizing Human Capital," *Business Horizons*, 44 (September-October 2001): 5.
79. For more on OEM, see Tim R. V. Davis, "Open-Book Management: Its Promise and Pitfalls," *Organizational Dynamics*, 25 (Winter 1997): 7–20. Also see John Case, "HR Learns How to Open the Books," *HR Magazine*, 43 (May 1998): 70–76; Perry Pascarella, "Open the Books to Unleash Your People," *Management Review*, 87 (May 1998): 58–60; and "July Poll Results: Open-Book Management," *HR Magazine*, 43 (September 1998): 18.
80. See W. Alan Randolph, "Rethinking Empowerment: Why Is It So Hard to Achieve?" *Organizational Dynamics*, 29 (Fall 2000): 94–107; Laurence Prusak and Don Cohen, "How to Invest in Social Capital," *Harvard Business Review*, 79 (June 2001): 86–93; Christopher A. Bartlett and Sumantra Ghoshal, "Building Competitive Advantage Through People," *MIT Sloan Management Review*, 43 (Winter 2002): 34–41; and Ginger L. Graham, "If You Want Honesty, Break Some Rules," *Harvard Business Review*, 80 (April 2002): 42–47.
81. As quoted in Hank Gilman, "The Most Underrated CEO Ever," *Fortune* (April 5, 2004): 244.
82. Heather Johnson, "Out with the Belly Flops," *Training*, 38 (December 2001): 22.
83. For related reading, see Noel M. Tichy, "No Ordinary Boot Camp," *Harvard Business Review*, 79 (April 2001): 63–70; Philippe Haspeslagh, Tomo Noda, and Fares Boulos, "It's Not Just About the Numbers," *Harvard Business Review*, 79 (July-August 2001): 65–73; and Bo Burlingham, "Jack Stack, SRC Holdings: For Going Naked," *Inc.*, 26 (April 2004): 134–135.
84. For more, see Ruth Wageman, "Critical Success Factors for Creating Superb Self-Managing Teams," *Organizational Dynamics*, 26 (Summer 1997): 49–61; Bradley L. Kirkman and Debra L. Shapiro, "The Impact of Cultural Values on Job Satisfaction and Organizational Commitment in Self-Managing Work Teams: The Mediating Role of Employee Resistance," *Academy of Management Journal*, 44 (June 2001): 557–569; and Carol A. Beatty and Brenda A. Barker Scott, *Building Smart Teams: A Roadmap to High Performance* (Thousand Oaks, Calif.: Sage, 2004).
85. Data from "1996 Industry Report: What Self-Managing Teams Manage," *Training*, 33 (October 1996): 69.
86. Keith H. Hammonds, "Growth Search," *Fast Company*, no. 69 (April 2003): 79–80.
87. Brian Dumaine, "Who Needs a Boss?" *Fortune* (May 7, 1990): 52. Also see Claus W. Langfred, "Too Much of a Good Thing? Negative Effects of High Trust and Individual Autonomy in Self-Managing Teams," *Academy of Management Journal*, 47 (June 2004): 385–399.
88. John Hoerr, "The Payoff from Teamwork," *Business Week* (July 10, 1989): 57. For related research evidence, see Rosemary Batt, "Who Benefits from Teams? Comparing Workers, Supervisors, and Managers," *Industrial Relations*, 43 (January 2004): 183–209.
89. See John Hoerr, "Work Teams Can Rev Up Paper-Pushers, Too," *Business Week* (November 28, 1988): 64–72; and Beverly Geber, "Can TQM Cure Health Care?" *Training*, 29 (August 1992): 25–34.
90. Adapted from David I. Levine, "Participation, Productivity, and the Firm's Environment," *California Management Review*, 32 (Summer 1990): 86–100.
91. For good advice, see Robert C. Liden, Sandy J. Wayne, and Lisa Bradway, "Connections Make the Difference," *HR Magazine*, 41 (February 1996): 73–79; and Michael Donovan, "The First Step to Self-Direction is NOT Empowerment," *Journal for Quality and Participation*, 19 (June 1996): 64–66.
92. Katherine I. Miller and Peter R. Monge, "Participation, Satisfaction, and Productivity: A Meta-Analytic Review," *Academy of Management Journal*, 29 (December 1986): 748.
93. For example, see Adolph Haasen, "Opel Eisenach GMBH—Creating a High-Productivity Workplace," *Organizational Dynamics*, 24 (Spring 1996): 80–85.
94. As quoted in Paul B. Brown, "What I Know Now," *Fast Company*, no. 91 (February 2005): 96. Also see Marshall Goldsmith, "Do You Love What You Do?" *Fast Company*, no. 92 (March 2005): 88.
95. Judith Warner, "Mommy Madness," *Newsweek* (February 21, 2005): 49.
96. As quoted in Sheila M. Puffer, "Changing Organizational Structures: An Intrerview with Rosabeth Moss Kanter," *Academy of Management Executive*, 18 (May 2004): 101.
97. See Jeffrey Pfeffer, "All Work, No Play? It Doesn't Pay," *Business 2.0*, 5 (August 2004): 50; Jonathan D. Quick, Amy B. Henley, and James Campbell Quick, "The Balancing Act: At Work and at Home," *Organizational Dynamics*, 33, no. 4 (2004): 426–438; Marilyn Elias, "The Family-First Generation," *USA Today* (December 13, 2004): 5D; Andrew Park, "Between a Rocker And a High Chair," *Business Week* (February 21, 2005): 86, 88; and Jennifer Merritt, "MBA Family Values," *Business Week* (March 14, 2005): 104–106.
98. See Karen S. Kush and Linda K. Stroh, "Flextime: Myth or Reality?" *Business Horizons*, 37 (September-October 1994): 51–55; David Stamps, "Taming Time with Flexible Work," *Training*, 32 (May 1995): 60–66; Elizabeth Sheley, "Flexible Work Options: Beyond 9 to 5," *HR Magazine*, 41 (February 1996): 52–58; and Genevieve Capowski, "The Joy of Flex," *Management Review*, 85 (March 1996): 12–18.
99. Robert Levering and Milton Moskowitz, "The 100 Best Companies to Work For," *Fortune* (January 12, 2004): 66.
100. Data from "More Women Value Flex Time," *USA Today* (August 1, 2000): 1B.
101. Data from Heather Johnson, "Roll Call," *Training*, 39 (March 2002): 16.
102. See Kimberlianne Podlas, "Reasonable Accommodation or Special Privilege? Flextime, Telecommuting, and the ADA," *Business Horizons*, 44 (September-October 2001): 61–65.
103. Data from V. K. Narayanan and Raghu Nath, "A Field Test of Some Attitudinal and Behavioral Consequences of Flextime," *Journal of Applied Psychology*, 67 (April 1982): 214–218; David A. Ralston, William P. Anthony, and David J. Gustafson, "Employees May Love Flextime, But What Does It Do to the Organization's Productivity?" *Journal of Applied Psychology*, 70 (May 1985): 272–279; and Charles S. Rodgers, "The Flexible Workplace: What Have We Learned?" *Human Resources Management*, 31 (Fall 1992): 183–199.
104. Mark Henricks, "Flextime Revisited," *Southwest Airlines Spirit*, 13 (August

2004): 52–56.

105. Based on Del Jones, "Sara Lee Biggest (for Now) with Female CEO," *USA Today* (February 11, 2005): 4B.
106. See Jon L. Pierce and Randall B. Dunham, "The 12-Hour Work Day: A 48-Hour, Eight-Day Week," *Academy of Management Journal*, 35 (December 1992): 1086–1098; and Dominic Bencivenga, "Compressed Weeks Fill an HR Niche," *HR Magazine*, 40 (June 1995): 71–74.
107. See Elizabeth Sheley, "Job Sharing Offers Unique Challenges," *HR Magazine*, 41 (January 1996): 46–49; Carla Joinson, "Time Share," *HR Magazine*, 43 (December 1998): 104–112; Rosalind Chait Barnett and Douglas T. Hall, "How to Use Reduced Hours to Win the War for Talent," *Organizational Dynamics*, 29 (Winter 2001): 192–210; and Cynthia R. Cunningham and Shelley S. Murray, "Two Executives, One Career," *Harvard Business Review*, 83 (February 2005): 125–131.
108. Data from M. F. J. Martens, F. J. N. Nijhuis, M. P. J. Van Boxtel, and J. A. Knottnerus, "Flexible Work Schedules and Mental and Physical Health. A Study of a Working Population with Non-Traditional Working Hours," *Journal of Organizational Behavior*, 20 (January 1999): 35–46.
109. Quoted material and data from Nancy R. Lockwood, "Work/Life Balance: Challenges and Solutions," 2003 Research Quarterly, *HR Magazine*, 48 (June 2003): 7.
110. For more, see Eric Paltell, "FMLA: After Six Years, a Bit More Clarity," *HR Magazine*, 44 (September 1999): 144–150; Gene Koretz, "Did Maternity Leave Law Help?" *Business Week* (April 17, 2000): 36; Steve Bates, "Whirlwind of Change," *HR Magazine*, 46 (August 2001): 62–66; and Kathryn Tyler, "All Present and Accounted For?" *HR Magazine*, 46 (October 2001): 101–109.
111. Robert Levering and Milton Moskowitz, "The 100 Best Companies to Work For," *Fortune* (January 24, 2005): 74–86.
112. See Terence F. Shea, "Help with Elder Care," *HR Magazine*, 48 (September 2003): 113–118; Karyn-Siobhan Robinson, "Employers Increase Work/Life Programs," *HR Magazine*, 49 (March 2004): 32; Jena McGregor, "Balance & Balance Sheets," *Fast Company*, no. 82 (May 2004): 96–97; and Nadine Heintz, "Can I Bring the Kids?" *Inc.*, 26 (June 2004): 40.
113. See Elayne Robertson Demby, "Do Your Family-Friendly Programs Make Cents?" *HR Magazine*, 49 (January 2004): 74–78.
114. Ibid., p. 76.
115. See Sora Song, "The Price of Pressure," *Time* (July 19, 2004): 68–69; Michele Orecklin, "Stress and the Superdad," *Time* (August 23, 2004): 38–39; and Del Jones, "Some Employees Find Stress Provides Spark for Innovation," *USA Today* (February 21, 2005): 3B.
116. See James Campbell Quick and Jonathan D. Quick, "Healthy, Happy, Productive Work: A Leadership Challenge," *Organizational Dynamics*, 33, no. 4 (2004): 329–337; Dawn S. Onley, "Doc in a Box," *HR Magazine*, 50 (January 2005): 83–85; Society for Human Resource Management, "Preventive Health Care," *Workplace Visions*, no. 1 (2005): 1–8; and Stephanie Clifford, "Fit for the Executive Suite," *Inc.*, 27 (May 2005): 76.
117. Daniel Yee, "Fit Workers Keep Insurance Costs Low," *Arizona Republic* (October 17, 2004): D3. Also see Christopher P. Neck and Kenneth H. Cooper, "The Fit Executive: Exercise and Diet Guidelines for Enhancing Performance," *Academy of Management Executive*, 14 (May 2000): 72–83; Catherine Arnst, "How to Weigh the Competing Claims of All Those Weight-Loss Plans," *Business Week* (August 30, 2004): 139–141; and Anne Underwood, "For a Happy Heart," *Newsweek* (September 27, 2004): 54–56.
118. Drawn from Robert Levering and Milton Moskowitz, "The 100 Best Companies to Work For," *Fortune* (January 20, 2003): 127–152; and Robert Levering and Milton Moskowitz, "The 100 Best Companies to Work For," *Fortune* (January 12, 2004): 56–76.
119. Robert Levering and Milton Moskowitz, "The 100 Best Companies to Work For," *Fortune* (January 24, 2005): 88.
120. For more, see Joel Schettler, "Successful Sabbaticals," *Training*, 39 (June 2002): 26; and Nadine Heintz, "Breaking Away," *Inc.*, 26 (October 2004): 44.
121. "Heart Disease Claims a Million Lives," *USA Today* (January 2, 2002): 6D.

CHAPTER 14

1. **Opening Quote** As quoted in Brian Grow, "Fat's in the Fire for This Burger King," *Business Week* (November 8, 2004): 70.
2. James P. Masciarelli, "Are You Managing Your Relationships?" *Management Review*, 87 (April 1998): 41. Also see David Lidsky, "Winning the Relationship Game," *Fast Company*, no. 87 (October 2004): 113–115.
3. Robert Kreitner and Angelo Kinicki, *Organizational Behavior*, 6th ed. (Burr Ridge, Ill.: McGraw-Hill/Irwin, 2004), pp. 9–10. For more, see Harald M. Fischer and Timothy G. Pollock, "Effects of Social Capital and Power on Surviving Transformational Change: The Case of Initial Public Offerings," *Academy Of Management Journal*, 47 (August 2004): 463–481; M. Ann McFadyen and Albert A. Cannella Jr., "Social Capital and Knowledge Creation: Diminishing Returns of the Number and Strength of Exchange Relationships," *Academy of Management Journal*, 47 (October 2004): 735–746; and Andrew C. Inkpen and Eric W. K. Tsang, "Social Capital, Networks, and Knowledge Transfer," *Academy of Management Review*, 30 (January 2005): 146–165.
4. Joseph A. Litterer, *The Analysis of Organizations*, 2nd ed. (New York: Wiley, 1973), p. 231.
5. For an excellent elaboration of this definition, see David Horton Smith, "A Parsimonious Definition of 'Group': Toward Conceptual Clarity and Scientific Utility," *Sociological Inquiry*, 37 (Spring 1967): 141–167. Also see Daniel J. Brass, Joseph Galaskiewicz, Henrich R. Greve, and Wenpin Tsai, "Taking Stock of Networks and Organizations: A Multilevel Perspective," *Academy of Management Journal*, 47 (December 2004): 795–817.
6. For related research, see Prithviraj Chattopadhyay, Malgorzata Tluchowska, and Elizabeth George, "Identifying the Ingroup: A Closer Look at the Influence of Demographic Dissimilarity on Employee Social Identity," *Academy of Management Review*, 29 (April 2004): 180–202; and Hongseok Oh, Myung-Ho Chung, and Giuseppe Labianca, "Group Social Capital and Group Effectiveness: The Role of Informal Socializing Ties," *Academy of Management Journal*, 47 (December 2004): 860–875.
7. For example, see Joe Labianca, "The Ties That Bind," *Harvard Business Review*, 82 (October 2004): 19; and Rob Cross and Sally Colella, "Building Vibrant Employee Networks," *HR Magazine*, 49 (December 2004): 101–104.
8. David Krackhardt and Jeffrey R. Hanson, "Informal Networks: The Company Behind the Chart," *Harvard Business Review*, 71 (July-August 1993): 104.
9. See Cathy Olofson, "Let Outsiders In, Turn Your Insiders Out," *Fast Company*, no. 22 (February-March 1999): 46.
10. For related research, see Jennifer A. Chatman and Charles A. O'Reilly, "Asymmetric Reactions to Work Group Sex Diversity Among Men and Women," *Academy of Management Journal*, 47 (April 2004): 193–208; and Mark Van Vugt and Claire M. Hart, "Social Identity as Social Glue: The Origin of Group Loyalty," *Journal of Personality and Social Psychology*, 86 (April 2004): 585–598.
11. Peter Nulty, "Cool Heads Are Trying to Keep Commodore Hot," *Fortune* (July 23, 1984): 38, 40.
12. Albert A. Harrison, *Individuals and Groups: Understanding Social Behavior* (Monterey, Calif.: Brooks/Cole, 1976), p. 16. Also see Elizabeth Wolfe Morrison, "Role Definitions and Organizational Citizenship Behavior: The Importance of the Employee's Perspective," *Academy of Management Journal*, 37 (December 1994): 1543–1567; and Richard G. Netemeyer, Scott Burton, and Mark W. Johnston, "A Nested Comparison of Four Models of the Consequences of Role Perception Variables," *Organizational Behavior and Human Decision Processes*, 61 (January 1995): 77–93.

13. See, for instance, Jo Ellen Moore, "Are You Burning Out Valuable Resources?" *HR Magazine*, 44 (January 1999): 93–97. Also see Blake E. Ashforth, Glen E. Kreiner, and Mel Fugate, "All in a Day's Work: Boundaries and Micro Role Transitions," *Academy of Management Review*, 25 (July 2000): 472–491; and Peter W. Hom and Angelo J. Kinicki, "Toward a Greater Understanding of How Dissatisfaction Drives Employee Turnover," *Academy of Management Journal*, 44 (October 2001): 975–987.
14. Harrison, *Individuals and Groups*, p. 401.
15. For example, see Gary Blau, "Influence of Group Lateness on Individual Lateness: A Cross-Level Examination," *Academy of Management Journal*, 38 (October 1995): 1483–1496; Jeffrey A. LePine and Linn Van Dyne, "Peer Responses to Low Performers: An Attributional Model of Helping in the Context of Groups," *Academy of Management Review*, 26 (January 2001): 67–84; and Jennifer A. Chatman and Francis J. Flynn, "The Influence of Demographic Heterogeneity on the Emergence and Consequences of Cooperative Norms in Work Teams," *Academy of Management Journal*, 44 (October 2001): 956–974.
16. Adapted from Daniel C. Feldman, "The Development and Enforcement of Group Norms," *Academy of Management Review*, 9 (January 1984): 47–53. Also see Jose M. Marques, Dominic Abrams, Dario Paez, and Cristina Martinez-Taboada, "The Role of Categorization and In-Group Norms in Judgments of Groups and Their Members," *Journal of Personality and Social Psychology*, 75 (October 1998): 976–988.
17. See Kenneth J. Bettenhausen and Keith J. Murnigham, "The Development of an Intragroup Norm and the Effects of Interpersonal and Structural Challenges," *Administrative Science Quarterly*, 36 (March 1991): 20–35.
18. Gwendolyn Kelly, "Why This Med Student Is Sticking with Primary Care," *Business Week* (November 2, 1992): 125.
19. For related research, see Linda Klebe Trevino and Bart Victor, "Peer Reporting of Unethical Behavior: A Social Context Perspective," *Academy of Management Journal*, 35 (March 1992): 38–64; and Andrew Spicer, Thomas W. Dunfee, and Wendy J. Bailey, "Does National Context Matter in Ethical Decision Making? An Empirical Test of Integrative Social Contracts Theory," *Academy of Management Journal*, 47 (August 2004): 610–620.
20. From *Group Effectiveness in Organizations* by L. N. Jewell and H. J. Reitz (Scott, Foresman, 1981). Reprinted by permission of the authors. Also see Lynn R. Offermann and Rebecca K. Spiros, "The Science and Practice of Team Development: Improving the Link," *Academy of Management Journal*, 44 (April 2001): 376–392.
21. Susan A. Wheelan and Felice Tilin, "The Relationship Between Faculty Group Development and School Productivity," *Small Group Research*, 30 (February 1999): 59.
22. For more, see Chao C. Chen, Xiao-Ping Chen, and James R. Meindl, "How Can Cooperation Be Fostered? The Cultural Effects of Individualism-Collectivism," *Academy of Management Review*, 23 (April 1998): 285–304. Also see Katherine J. Klein, Beng-Chong Lim, Jessica L. Saltz, and David M. Mayer, "How Do They Get There? An Examination of the Antecedents of Centrality in Team Networks," *Academy of Management Journal*, 47 (December 2004): 952–963.
23. See Vanessa Urch Druskat and Steven B. Wolff, "Building the Emotional Intelligence of Groups," *Harvard Business Review*, 79 (March 2001): 81–90.
24. The following discussion of the six stages of group development is adapted from *Group Effectiveness in Organizations* by Linda N. Jewell and H. Joseph Reitz. Copyright 1981, Scott, Foresman and Company, pp. 15–20. Reprinted by permission. For ground-breaking research in this area, see Warren G. Bennis and Herbert A. Shepard, "A Theory of Group Development," *Human Relations*, 9 (1956); 415–437; Bruce W. Tuckman and Mary Ann C. Jensen, "Stages of Small-Group Development Revisited," *Group & Organization Studies*, 2 (December 1977): 419–427; and John F. McGrew, John G. Bilotta, and Janet M. Deeney, "Software Team Formation and Decay: Extending the Standard Model for Small Groups," *Small Group Research*, 30 (April 1999): 209–234.
25. For practical advice, see John E. Tropman, *Making Meetings Work: Achieving High Quality Decisions* (Thousand Oaks, Calif.: Sage, 2003); and Tim Ursiny, *The Cowards Guide to Conflict: Empowering Solutions for Those Who Would Rather Run Than Fight* (Naperville, Ill.: Sourcebooks, 2003).
26. For a cross-cultural perspective, see Cristina B. Gibson, "Do They Do What They Believe They Can? Group Efficacy and Group Effectiveness Across Tasks and Cultures," *Academy of Management Journal*, 42 (April 1999): 138–152.
27. For example, see Pamela L. Perrewé, Kelly L. Zellars, Gerald R. Ferris, Ana Maria Rossi, Charles J. Kacmar, and David A. Ralston, "Neutralizing Job Stressors: Political Skill as an Antidote to the Dysfunctional Consequences of Role Conflict," *Academy of Management Journal*, 47 (February 2004): 141–152; Pamela L. Perrewé and Debra L. Nelson, "Gender and Career Success: The Facilitative Role of Political Skill," *Organizational Dynamics*, 33, no. 4 (2004): 366–378; Judith A. Clair, Joy E. Beatty, and Tammy L. Maclean, "Out of Sight But Not Out of Mind: Managing Invisible Social Identities in the Workplace," *Academy of Management Review*, 30 (January 2005): 78–95; Thomas B. Lawrence, Michael K. Mauws, Bruno Dyck, and Robert F. Kleysen, "The Politics of Organizational Learning: Integrating Power into the 4I Framework," *Academy of Management Review*, 30 (January 2005): 180–191; and Gerald R. Ferris, Darren C. Treadway, Robert W. Kolodinsky, Wayne A. Hochwarter, Charles J. Kacmar, Ceasar Douglas, and Dwight D. Frink, "Development and Validation of the Political Skill Inventory," *Journal of Management*, 31, no. 1 (2005): 126–152.
28. See Del Jones and Bill Keveney, "10 Lessons of 'The Apprentice,'" *USA Today* (April 15, 2004): 1A, 5A; Del Jones, "America Loves to Hate Dastardly CEOs," *USA Today* (September 15, 2004): 1B–2B; and Ann Pomeroy, "Business Reality TV?" *HR Magazine*, 50 (January 2005): 14.
29. As quoted in Anne Fisher, "Putting Your Mouth Where the Money Is," *Fortune* (September 3, 2001): 238. Also see Jared Sandberg, "Sabotage 101: The Sinister Art of Back-Stabbing," *Wall Street Journal* (February 11, 2004): B1; Jared Sandberg, "From the Front Lines: Bosses Muster Staffs for Border Skirmishes," *Wall Street Journal* (February 18, 2004): B1; Samuel B. Bacharach, "Politically Proactive," *Fast Company*, no. 94 (May 2005): 93; Kerry J. Sulkowicz, "The Corporate Shrink," *Fast Company*, no. 94 (May 2005): 96; and Patricia Sellers, "Fast Eddie Roughs Up Sears' Staff," *Fortune* (May 2, 2005): 20.
30. Marcia Stepanek, "How Fast Is Net Fast?" *Business Week* E.BIZ (November 1, 1999): EB 54.
31. Data from "9-to-5 Not for Everyone," *USA Today* (October 13, 1999): 1B.
32. See Gerald R. Ferris, Pamela L. Perrewé, William P. Anthony, and David C. Gilmore, "Political Skill at Work," *Organizational Dynamics*, 28 (Spring 2000): 25–37; Jennifer Reingold, "Suck Up and Move Up," *Fast Company*, no. 90 (January 2005): 34; and Alison Stein Wellner, "Playing Well with Others," *Inc.*, 27 (January 2005): 29–31.
33. Ethical implications are discussed in Erik W. Larson and Jonathan B. King, "The Systematic Distortion of Information: An Ongoing Challenge to Management," *Organizational Dynamics*, 24 (Winter 1996): 49–61; and Peter Troiano, "Nice Guys Finish First," *Management Review*, 87 (December 1998): 8.
34. Victor Murray and Jeffrey Gandz, "Games Executives Play: Politics at Work," *Business Horizons*, 23 (December 1980): 16.
35. Andrew J. DuBrin, *Fundamentals of Organizational Behavior: An Applied Perspective*, 2nd ed. (Elmsford, N.Y.: Pergamon Press, 1978): p. 154.
36. Jared Sandberg, "Better Than Great—and Other Tall Tales of Self-Evaluations," *Wall Street Journal* (March 12, 2003): B1. Also see Herminia Ibarra and Kent Lineback,

"What's Your Story?" *Harvard Business Review*, 83 (January 2005): 64–71.

37. Dan Farrell and James C. Petersen, "Patterns of Political Behavior in Organizations," *Academy of Management Review*, 7 (July 1982): 407. Also see Jeff Barbian, "It's Who You Know," *Training*, 38 (December 2001): 22; and Stanley Bing, "Throwing the Elephant: Zen and the Art of Managing Up," *Fortune* (March 18, 2002): 115–116.
38. See "Blowing the Whistle on Billing Abuse," *Money*, 34 (January 2005): 81; and John Simons, "Blowing the Whistle at the FDA," *Fortune* (January 24, 2005): 32.
39. James R. Healey, "Covert Activity Saved Sports Car," *USA Today* (March 19, 1997): 1B. Also see Denis Collins, "Case Study: 15 Lessons Learned from the Death of a Gainsharing Plan," *Compensation & Benefits Review*, 28 (March-April 1996): 31–40.
40. Adapted from Dan L. Madison, Robert W. Allen, Lyman W. Porter, Patricia A. Renwick, and Bronston T. Mayes, "Organizational Politics: An Exploration of Managers' Perceptions," *Human Relations*, 33 (February 1980): 79–100. Also see Andrew J. DuBrin, "Career Maturity, Organizational Rank, and Political Behavioral Tendencies: A Correlational Analysis of Organizational Politics and Career Experience," *Psychological Reports*, 63 (October 1988): 531–537.
41. Madison et al., "Organizational Politics," p. 97.
42. These six political tactics have been adapted from a more extensive list found in DuBrin, *Fundamentals of Organizational Behavior*, pp. 158–170. Also see Roos Vonk, "The Slime Effect: Suspicion and Dislike of Likeable Behavior Toward Superiors," *Journal of Personality and Social Psychology*, 74 (April 1998): 849–864; Carol Memmott, "How to Play Cutthroat Office Politics and Win," *USA Today* (July 13, 1998): 2B; and David G. Baldwin, "How to Win the Blame Game," *Harvard Business Review*, 79 (July-August 2001): 55–62.
43. Adapted from DuBrin, *Fundamentals of Organizational Behavior*, pp. 179–182.
44. Kevin Maney, "CEO Ollila Says Nokia's 'Sisu' Will See It Past Tough Times," *USA Today* (July 21, 2004): 2B. Also see Brian Dumaine, "I'd Rather Be Inventing," *Fortune* (November 15, 2004): 194.
45. Blind conformity at Enron is discussed in Greg Farrell and Jayne O'Donnell, "Watkins Testifies Skilling, Fastow Duped Lay, Board," *USA Today* (February 15, 2002): 1B–2B. Also see Shoshana Zuboff, "A Starter Kit for Business Ethics," *Fast Company*, no. 90 (January 2005): 91.
46. See Solomon E. Asch, *Social Psychology* (Englewood Cliffs, N.J.: Prentice-Hall, 1952), ch. 16.
47. For details, see Taha Amir, "The Asch Conformity Effect: A Study in Kuwait," *Social Behavior and Personality*, 12, no. 2 (1984): 187–190; Timothy P. Williams and Shunya Sogon, "Group Composition and Conforming Behavior in Japanese Students," *Japanese Psychological Research*, 26, no. 4 (1984): 231–234.
48. Data from Rod Bond and Peter B. Smith, "Culture and Conformity: A Meta-Analysis of Studies Using Asch's (1952b, 1956) Line Judgment Task," *Psychological Bulletin*, 119 (January 1996): 111–137. Also see Sandra L. Robinson and Anne M. O'Leary-Kelly, "Monkey See, Monkey Do: The Influence of Work Groups on the Antisocial Behavior of Employees," *Academy of Management Journal*, 41 (December 1998): 658–672.
49. Irving L. Janis, *Groupthink*, 2nd ed. (Boston: Houghton Mifflin, 1982), p. 9. See also A. Amin Mohamed and Frank A. Wiebe, "Toward a Process Theory of Groupthink," *Small Group Research*, 27 (August 1996): 416–430; Kjell Granstrom and Dan Stiwne, "A Bipolar Model of Groupthink: An Expansion of Janis's Concept," *Small Group Research*, 29 (February 1998): 32–56; the entire February-March 1998 issue of *Organizational Behavior and Human Decision Processes*; Annette R. Flippen, "Understanding Groupthink from a Self-Regulatory Perspective," *Small Group Research*, 30 (April 1999): 139–165; Jin Nam Choi and Myung Un Kim, "The Organizational Application of Groupthink and Its Limitations in Organizations," *Journal of Applied Psychology*, 84 (April 1999): 297–306; and Walter Shapiro, "Groupthink a Danger for White House War Planners," *USA Today* (October 3, 2001): 7A.
50. Adapted from a list in Janis, *Groupthink*, pp. 174–175.
51. Ibid., p. 275.
52. For excellent discussions of the devil's advocate role, see Charles R. Schwenk, "Devil's Advocacy in Managerial Decision Making," *Journal of Management Studies*, 21 (April 1984): 153–168; and Richard A. Cosier and Charles R. Schwenk, "Agreement and Thinking Alike: Ingredients for Poor Decisions," *Academy of Management Executive*, 4 (February 1990): 69–74.
53. Adapted from a list in Janis, *Groupthink*, pp. 262–271.
54. See Rafe Needleman, "Building the Perfect Board," *Business 2.0*, 4 (May 2003): 58–59; Kerry J. Sulkowicz, "The Corporate Shrink," *Fast Company*, no. 82 (May 2004): 54; David A. Nadler, "Building Better Boards," *Harvard Business Review*, 82 (May 2004): 102–111; and Brent Schlender, "Inside Andy Grove's Latest Crusade," *Fortune* (August 23, 2004): 68–78.
55. Barbara Kellerman, *Bad Leadership: What It Is, How It Happens, Why It Matters* (Boston: Harvard Business School Press, 2004), pp. 139–140.
56. Other problems related in part to groupthink are discussed in Paul F. Levy, "The Nut Island Effect: When Good Teams Go Wrong," *Harvard Business Review*, 79 (March 2001): 51–59; and Michael Harvey, Milorad M. Novicevic, M. Ronald Buckley, and Jonathon R.B. Halbesleben, "The Abilene Paradox After Thirty Years: A Global Perspective," *Organizational Dynamics*, 33, no. 2 (2004): 215–226.
57. Ronald Grover, "The Heavyweight on Latin Airwaves," *Business Week* (August 9, 2004): 62–63.
58. See Robert J. Trent, "Becoming an Effective Teaming Organization," *Business Horizons*, 47 (March-April 2004): 33–40; and Paul B. Brown, "What I Know Now," *Fast Company*, no. 90 (January 2005): 96.
59. An instructive distinction between work groups and teams is presented in Jon R. Katzenbach and Douglas K. Smith, "The Discipline of Teams," *Harvard Business Review*, 71 (March-April 1993): 111–120. Also see Jon R. Katzenbach and Douglas K. Smith, *The Wisdom of Teams: Creating the High-Performance Organization* (New York: HarperCollins, 1999); Carol A. Beatty and Brenda A. Barker Scott, *Building Smart Teams: A Roadmap to High Performance* (Thousand Oaks, Calif.: Sage, 2004); and Gilad Chen, Lisa M. Donahue, and Richard J. Klimoski, "Training Undergraduates to Work in Organizational Teams," *Academy of Management Learning and Education*, 3 (March 2004): 27–40.
60. See Amy E. Randel and Kimberly S. Jaussi, "Functional Background Identity, Diversity, and Individual Performance in Cross-Functional Teams," *Academy of Management Journal*, 46 (December 2003): 763–774; and Lee Fleming, "Perfecting Cross-Pollination," *Harvard Business Review*, 82 (September 2004): 22–24.
61. Dori Jones Yang, "Grace Robertson: Piloting a Superfast Rollout at Boeing," *Business Week* (August 30, 1993): 77.
62. See Ann Majchrzak, Arvind Malhotra, Jeffrey Stamps, and Jessica Lipnack, "Can Absence Make a Team Grow Stronger?" *Harvard Business Review*, 82 (May 2004): 131–137.
63. For a virtual team manager in action, see Riza Cruz, "At the Desk of Herman Miller's Greg Parsons," *Business 2.0*, 3 (April 2002): 114–115. Also see Faith Keenan and Spencer E. Ante, "The New Teamwork," *Business Week e.biz* (February 18, 2002): EB 12–EB 16.
64. See Kim Kiser, "Working on World Time," *Training*, 36 (March 1999): 28–34.
65. See Donald D. Davis, "The Tao of Leadership in Virtual Teams," *Organizational Dynamics*, 33, no. 1 (2004): 47–62; Jathan W. Janove, "Management by Remote Control," *HR Magazine*, 49 (April 2004): 119–124; Bradley L. Kirkman, Benson Rosen, Paul E. Tesluk, and Cristina B. Gibson, "The Impact of Team Empowerment on

Virtual Team Performance: The Moderating Role of Face-to-Face Interaction," *Academy of Management Journal*, 47 (April 2004): 175–192; and Jill E. Nemiro, *Creativity in Virtual Teams: Key Components for Success* (New York : Pfeiffer, 2004).

66. See Bianca Beersma, John R. Hollenbeck, Stephen E. Humphrey, Henry Moon, Donald E. Conlon, and Daniel R. Ilgen, "Cooperation, Competition, and Team Performance: Toward a Contingency Approach," *Academy of Management Journal*, 46 (October 2003): 572–590.
67. See Hans J. Thamhain, "Managing Technologically Innovative Team Efforts Toward New Product Success," *Journal of Product Innovation Management*, 7 (March 1990): 5–18. Also see the following study of team effectiveness: Richard J. Magjuka and Timothy T. Baldwin, "Team-Based Employee Involvement Programs: Effects of Design and Administration," *Personnel Psychology*, 44 (Winter 1991): 793–812.
68. See Nancy Katz, "Sports Teams as a Model for Workplace Teams: Lessons and Liabilities," *Academy of Management Executive*, 15 (August 2001): 56–67; Geoffrey Colvin, "Think You Can Bobsled? Ha!" *Fortune* (March 18, 2002): 50; and Rosabeth Moss Kanter, *Confidence: How Winning Streaks & Losing Streaks Begin and End* (New York : Crown Business, 2004).
69. See Don Knight, Cathy C. Durham, and Edwin A. Locke, "The Relationship of Team Goals, Incentives, and Efficacy to Strategic Risk, Tactical Implementation, and Performance," *Academy of Management Journal*, 44 (April 2001): 326–338.
70. Three kinds of trust are discussed in Douglas A. Houston, "Trust in the Networked Economy: Doing Business on Web Time," *Business Horizons*, 44 (March-April 2001): 38–44. Also see Saj-nicole A. Joni, "The Geography of Trust," *Harvard Business Review*, 82 (March 2004): 82–88.
71. See Chris Huxham and Siv Vangen, "Doing Things Collaboratively: Realizing the Advantage or Succumbing to Inertia?" *Organizational Dynamics*, 33, no. 2 (2004): 190–201; and Heather Johnson, "Trust Falls," *Training*, 41 (June 2004): 15.
72. Jeffrey Pfeffer, "More Mr. Nice Guy," *Business 2.0*, 4 (December 2003): 78.
73. Data from "Little Faith in Executives," *USA Today* (April 5, 2004): 1B. Also see Ron Zemke, "The Confidence Crisis," *Training*, 41 (June 2004): 22–30.
74. Laurence Prusak and Don Cohen, "How to Invest in Social Capital," *Harvard Business Review*, 79 (June 2001): 90.
75. See Dale E. Zand, "Trust and Managerial Problem Solving," *Administrative Science Quarterly*, 17 (June 1972): 229–239.
76. Trustworthiness is discussed in Thomas A. Stewart, "Whom Can You Trust? It's Not So Easy to Tell," *Fortune* (June 12, 2000): 331–334; Cam Caldwell and Stephen E. Clapham, "Organizational Trustworthiness: An International Perspective," *Journal of Business Ethics*, 47 (November 2003): 349–364; and Alison Stein Wellner, "Who Can You Trust?" *Inc.*, 26 (October 2004): 39–40.
77. Adapted from Fernando Bartolomé, "Nobody Trusts the Boss Completely—Now What?" *Harvard Business Review*, 67 (March-April 1989): 137–139. Also see Ron Zemke, "Can You Manage Trust?" *Training*, 37 (February 2000): 76–83; and James Lardner, "Why Should Anyone Believe You?" *Business 2.0*, 3 (March 2002): 40–48.
78. See Kimberly D. Elsbach and Greg Elofson, "How the Packaging of Decision Explanations Affects Perceptions of Trustworthiness," *Academy of Management Journal*, 43 (February 2000): 80–89; and Michele Williams, "In Whom We Trust: Group Membership as an Affective Context for Trust Development," *Academy of Management Review*, 26 (July 2001): 377–396.

CHAPTER 15

1. **Opening Quote** As quoted in Zena Olijnyk, "The Home Depot Boss on Small Wins," *Canadian Business* (November 8, 2004); **www.canadianbusiness.com**.
2. Ramin Setoodeh, "Calling Avon's Lady," *Newsweek* (January 3, 2005): 100–101.
3. See Gary Yukl and Cecilia M. Falbe, "Influence Tactics and Objectives in Upward, Downward, and Lateral Influence Attempts," *Journal of Applied Psychology*, 75 (April 1990); 132–140. For a comprehensive collection of readings on influence, see Lyman W. Porter, Harold L. Angle, and Robert W. Allen, *Organizational Influence Processes*, 2nd ed. (Armonk, N.Y.: M.E. Sharpe, 2003).
4. Adapted from Yukl and Falbe, "Influence Tactics and Objectives in Upward, Downward, and Lateral Influence Attempts." Also see Gary Yukl, Cecilia M. Falbe, and Joo Young Youn, "Patterns of Influence Behavior for Managers," *Group & Organization Management*, 18 (March 1993): 5–28; Randall A. Gordon, "Impact of Ingratiation on Judgments and Evaluations: A Meta-Analytic Investigation," *Journal of Personality and Social Psychology*, 71 (July 1996): 54–70; and P. P. Fu, T. K. Peng, Jeffrey C. Kennedy, and Gary Yukl, "Examining the Preferences of Influence Tactics in Chinese Societies: A Comparison of Chinese Managers in Hong Kong, Taiwan and Mainland China," *Organizational Dynamics*, 33, no. 1 (2004): 32–46.
5. See Robert B. Miller, Gary A. Williams, and Alden M. Hayashi, *The 5 Paths to Persuasion: The Art of Selling Your Message* (New York: Warner Business, 2004): and Del Jones, "Debating Skills Come in Handy in Business," *USA Today* (September 30, 2004): 3B.
6. See Jeffrey Pfeffer, "How to Turn on the Charm," *Business 2.0*, 5 (June 2004): 76; and Jennifer Reingold, "Suck Up and Move Up," *Fast Company*, no. 90 (January 2005): 34.
7. Linda Tischler, "IBM's Management Makeover," *Fast Company*, no. 88 (November 2004): 113.
8. See George F. Dreher, Thomas W. Dougherty, and William Whitely, "Influence Tactics and Salary Attainment: A Gender-Specific Analysis," *Sex Roles*, 20 (May 1989): 535–550; and Herman Aguinis and Susan K. R. Adams, "Social-Role versus Structural Models of Gender and Influence Use in Organizations," *Group & Organization Studies*, 23 (December 1998): 414–446.
9. See Mahfooz A. Ansari and Alka Kapoor, "Organizational Context and Upward Influence Tactics," *Organizational Behavior and Human Decision Processes*, 40 (August 1987): 39–49.
10. Dean Tjosvold, "The Dynamics of Positive Power," *Training and Development Journal*, 38 (June 1984): 72.
11. See Toddi Gutner, "A 12-Step Program to Gaining Power," *Business Week* (December 24, 2001): 88. Also see Janet O. Hagberg, *Real Power: Stages of Personal Power in Organizations*, 3rd ed. (Salem, Wis.: Sheffield Publishing, 2003); and Thomas B. Lawrence, Michael K. Mauws, Bruno Dyck, and Robert F. Kleysen, "The Politics of Organizational Learning: Integrating Power into the 4I Framework," *Academy of Management Review*, 30 (January 2005): 180–191.
12. Morgan McCall Jr., "Power, Influence, and Authority: The Hazards of Carrying a Sword," *Technical Report*, 10 (Greensboro, N.C.: Center for Creative Leadership, 1978), p. 5.
13. For more on these three effects of power, see Anthony T. Cobb, "An Episodic Model of Power: Toward an Integration of Theory and Research," *Academy of Management Review*, 9 (July 1984): 482–493. Also see C. Marlene Fiol, Edward J. O'Connor, and Herman Aguinis, "All for One and One for All? The Development and Transfer of Power Across Organizational Levels," *Academy of Management Review*, 26 (April 2001): 224–242.
14. Based on Edwin P. Hollander and Lynn R. Offermann, "Power and Leadership in Organizations: Relationships in Transition," *American Psychologist*, 45 (February 1990): 179–189.
15. See William A. Kahn and Kathy E. Kram, "Authority at Work: Internal Models and Their Organizational Consequences," *Academy of Management Review*, 19 (January 1994): 17–50.
16. "There Is No State Here Anymore," *Newsweek* (February 24, 1997): 42.
17. For related discussion, see Allan R. Cohen and David L. Bradford, "Influence Without Authority: The Use of Alliances,

Reciprocity, and Exchange to Accomplish Work," *Organizational Dynamics*, 17 (Winter 1989): 4–17; and Allan R. Cohen and David L. Bradford, *Influence Without Authority* (New York: Wiley, 1990).

18. For case studies in managerial power, see Geoffrey Colvin, "Power 25: The Most Powerful People in Business," *Fortune* (August 9, 2004): 90–106; and Johnnie L. Roberts, "Striking a Hot Match," *Newsweek* (January 24, 2005): 54–55.
19. See John R. P. French Jr. and Bertram Raven, "The Bases of Social Power," *Studies in Social Power*, ed. Dorwin Cartwright (Ann Arbor: University of Michigan Press, 1959), pp. 150–167. Eight different sources of power are discussed in Hugh R. Taylor, "Power at Work," *Personnel Journal*, 65 (April 1986): 42–49. Also see H. Eugene Baker III, "'Wax On—Wax Off': French and Raven at the Movies," *Journal of Management Education*, 17 (November 1993): 517–519.
20. John P. Kotter, "Power, Dependence, and Effective Management," *Harvard Business Review*, 55 (July-August 1977): 128. Also see Marshall Goldsmith, "It's Not a Fair Fight If You're the CEO," *Fast Company*, no. 89 (December 2004): 99.
21. For revealing case studies, see Barbara Kellerman, *Bad Leadership: What It Is, How It Happens, Why It Matters* (Boston: Harvard Business School Press, 2004); and Devin Leonard, "Greenberg & Sons," *Fortune* (February 21, 2005): 104–114.
22. Ann Pomeroy, "Thanks, But No Thanks," *HR Magazine*, 49 (December 2004): 18.
23. Patricia Sellers, "What Exactly Is Charisma?" *Fortune* (January 15, 1996): 68. Also see Daniel Sankowsky, "The Charismatic Leader as Narcissist: Understanding the Abuse of Power," *Organizational Dynamics*, 23 (Spring 1995): 57–71.
24. See Scott E. Seibert, Seth R. Silver, and W. Alan Randolph, "Taking Empowerment to the Next Level: A Multiple-Level Model of Empowerment, Performance, and Satisfaction," *Academy of Management Journal*, 47 (June 2004): 332–349; and Bill Roberts, "Empowerment or Imposition?" *HR Magazine*, 49 (June 2004): 157–166.
25. As quoted in Laurel Shaper Walters, "A Leader Redefines Management," *Christian Science Monitor* (September 22, 1992): 14. For Frances Hesselbein's ideas about leadership, see Roundtable Discussion, "All in a Day's Work," *Harvard Business Review* (Special Issue: Breakthrough Leadership), 79 (December 2001): 54–66.
26. Based on discussion in Stephen R. Covey, *Principle-Centered Leadership* (New York: Simon & Schuster, 1991), pp. 214–216. Also see W. Alan Randolph, "Navigating the Journey to Empowerment," *Organizational Dynamics*, 23 (Spring 1995): 19–32; Peter T. Coleman, "Implicit Theories of Organizational Power and Priming Effects on Managerial Power-Sharing Decisions: An Experimental Study," *Journal of Applied Social Psychology*, 34 (February 2004): 297–321; and Bradley L. Kirkman, Benson Rosen, Paul E. Tesluk, and Cristina B. Gibson, "The Impact of Team Empowerment on Virtual Team Performance: The Moderating Role of Face-to-Face Interaction," *Academy of Management Journal*, 47 (April 2004): 175–192.
27. John A. Byrne, "The Environment Was Ripe for Abuse," *Business Week* (February 25, 2002): 119.
28. See Warren G. Bennis, "The Seven Ages of the Leader," *Harvard Business Review* (Special Issue: Inside the Mind of the Leader), 82 (January 2004): 46–53; David Halberstam, "The Greatness That Cannot Be Taught," *Fast Company*, no. 86 (September 2004): 62–66; Scott Kirsner, "4 Leaders You Should Know," *Fast Company*, no. 91 (February 2005): 68–72; and Manfred F. R. Kets de Vries, "Leadership Group Coaching in Action: The Zen of Creating High Performance Teams," *Academy of Management Executive*, 19 (February 2005): 61–76.
29. See Harper W. Moulton, "Leadership Through Executive Education," *Business Horizons*, 47 (March-April 2004): 7–14; the series of five articles on "How Can Organizations Best Prepare People to Lead and Manage Others?" in *Academy of Management Executive*, 18 (August 2004): 118–142; Douglas A. Ready, "How to Grow Great Leaders," *Harvard Business Review*, 82 (December 2004): 92–100; Dan Ciampa, "Almost Ready: How Leaders Move Up," *Harvard Business Review*, 83 (January 2005): 46–53; and Ryan Underwood, "Are You Being Coached?" *Fast Company*, no. 91 (February 2005): 83–85.
30. Peter F. Drucker, "What Makes an Effective Executive," *Harvard Business Review*, 82 (June 2004): 59.
31. See Hao Ma, Ranjan Karri, Kumar Chittipeddi, "The Paradox of Managerial Tyranny," *Business Horizons*, 47 (July-August 2004): 33–40.
32. Inspired by the definition in Andrew J. DuBrin, *Leadership: Research Findings, Practice and Skills*, 2nd ed. (Boston: Houghton Mifflin, 1998), p. 2. Also see Francis J. Yammarino, Fred Dansereau, and Christina J. Kennedy, "A Multiple-Level Multidimensional Approach to Leadership: Viewing Leadership Through an Elephant's Eye," *Organizational Dynamics*, 29 (Winter 2001): 149–163.
33. Catherine M. Dalton, "The Changing Identity of Corporate America: Opportunity, Duty, Leadership," *Business Horizons*, 48 (January-February 2005): 2–3.
34. As quoted in Oren Harari, *The Leadership Secrets of Colin Powell* (New York: McGraw-Hill, 2002): p. 13.
35. See John J. Sosik, Don I. Jung, Yair Berson, Shelley D. Dionne, and Kimberly S. Jaussi, "Making All the Right Connections: The Strategic Leadership of Top Executives in High-Tech Organizations," *Organizational Dynamics*, 34, no. 1 (2005): 47–61; and Ellen Florian Kratz, "Get Me a CEO From GE!" *Fortune* (April 18, 2005): 147–152.
36. As quoted in Bridget Finn, "How to Turn Managers into Leaders," *Business 2.0*, 5 (September 2004): 70.
37. See Gary A. Yukl, *Leadership in Organizations*, 5th ed. (Upper Saddle River, N.J.: Prentice-Hall, 2001).
38. See David L. Cawthon, "Leadership: The Great Man Theory Revisited," *Business Horizons*, 39 (May-June 1996): 1–4; Richard S. Tedlow, "What Titans Can Teach Us," *Harvard Business Review* (Special Issue: Breakthrough Leadership), 79 (December 2001): 70–79; Ron Zemke, "End of the Heroic Leader," *Training*, 41 (January 2004): 10; Catherine M. Dalton, "Of Heroes and Leaders," *Business Horizons*, 47 (November-December 2004): 1–2; and Jon Meacham, "A Road Map to Making History," *Newsweek* (January 24, 2005): 42–43.
39. Fred Luthans, *Organizational Behavior*, 3rd ed. (New York: McGraw-Hill, 1981), p. 419. Also see Gail Dutton, "Leadership in a Post-Heroic Age," *Management Review*, 85 (October 1996): 7.
40. Ralph M. Stogdill, "Personal Factors Associated with Leadership: A Survey of the Literature," *Journal of Psychology*, 25 (1948): 63.
41. See Daniel Goleman, *Emotional Intelligence* (New York: Bantam Books, 1995); Michaela Davies, Lazar Stankov, and Richard D. Roberts, "Emotional Intelligence: In Search of an Elusive Construct," *Journal of Personality and Social Psychology*, 75 (October 1998): 989–1015; and Daniel Goleman, "Never Stop Learning," *Harvard Business Review* (Special Issue: Inside the Mind of the Leader), 82 (January 2004): 28–29.
42. Michelle Neely Martinez, "The Smarts That Count," *HR Magazine*, 42 (November 1997): 72.
43. Based on and adapted from Daniel Goleman, Richard Boyatzis, and Annie McKee, "Primal Leadership," *Harvard Business Review* (Special Issue: Breakthrough Leadership), 79 (December 2001): 49. Also see Daniel Goleman, Richard Boyatzis, and Annie McKee, *Primal Leadership: Realizing the Power of Emotional Intelligence* (Boston: Harvard Business School Press, 2002); and Robert B. McKenna and Paul R. Yost, "The Differentiated Leader: Specific Strategies for Handling Today's Adverse Situations," *Organizational Dynamics*, 33, no. 3 (2004): 292–306.
44. See Susan Meisinger, "Courage: An

Essential Leadership Trait," *HR Magazine*, 49 (February 2004): 8; Gail Johnson, "5 Ways to Sabotage Your Leadership Ability," *Training*, 41 (April 2004): 17; Laura Morgan Roberts, Gretchen Spreitzer, Jane Dutton, Robert Quinn, Emily Heaphy, and Brianna Barker, "How to Play to Your Strengths," *Harvard Business Review*, 83 (January 2005): 74–80; and Kerry J. Sulkowicz, "The Corporate Shrink," *Fast Company*, no. 95 (June 2005): 96.

45. Data from Judy B. Rosener, "Ways Women Lead," *Harvard Business Review*, 68 (November-December 1990): 119–125. Also see Rochelle Sharpe, "As Leaders, Women Rule," *Business Week* (November 20, 2000): 74–84; and Kate Ludeman and Eddie Erlandson, "Coaching the Alpha Male," *Harvard Business Review*, 82 (May 2004): 58–67.
46. See "Ways Women and Men Lead," *Harvard Business Review*, 69 (January-February 1991): 150–160.
47. Data from Alice H. Eagly and Blair T. Johnson, "Gender and Leadership Style: A Meta-Analysis," *Psychological Bulletin*, 108 (September 1990): 233–256. A similar finding is reported in Robert P. Vecchio, "Leadership and Gender Advantage," *The Leadership Quarterly*, 13 (December 2002): 643–671.
48. Kurt Lewin, Ronald Lippitt, and Ralph K. White, "Patterns of Aggressive Behavior in Experimentally Created 'Social Climates,'" *Journal of Social Psychology*, 10 (May 1939): 271–299.
49. Dexter Roberts, "China Goes Shopping," *Business Week* (December 20, 2004): 34.
50. For an informative summary of this research, see Edwin A. Fleishman, "Twenty Years of Consideration and Structure," in *Current Developments in the Study of Leadership*, ed. Edwin A. Fleishman and James G. Hunt (Carbondale, Ill.: Southern Illinois University Press, 1973), pp. 1–40. Also see Vishwanath V. Baba and Merle E. Ace, "Serendipity in Leadership: Initiating Structure and Consideration in the Classroom," *Human Relations*, 42 (June 1989): 509–525.
51. Three popular extensions of the Ohio State leadership studies may be found in Robert R. Blake and Anne McCanse, *Leadership Dilemmas—Grid Solutions* (Houston: Gulf Publishing, 1990); William J. Reddin, *Managerial Effectiveness* (New York: McGraw-Hill, 1970); and Paul Hersey and Kenneth H. Blanchard, *Management of Organizational Behavior: Utilizing Human Resources*, 5th ed. (Englewood Cliffs, N.J.: Prentice-Hall, 1988), p. 171. Empirical lack of support for Hersey and Blanchard's situational leadership theory is reported in Jane R. Goodson, Gail W. McGee, and James F. Cashman, "Situational Leadership Theory: A Test of Leadership Prescriptions," *Group & Organization Studies*, 14 (December 1989): 446–461.
52. See Abraham K. Korman, "Consideration, 'Initiating Structure,' and Organizational Criteria—A Review," *Personnel Psychology*, 19 (Winter 1966): 349–361.
53. See Blake and McCanse, *Leadership Dilemmas—Grid Solutions*.
54. See Tom Lester, "Taking Guard on the Grid," *Management Today* (March 1991): 93–94.
55. For details of this study, see Robert R. Blake and Jane Srygley Mouton, "Management by Grid® Principles or Situationalism: Which?" *Group & Organization Studies*, 6 (December 1981): 439–455. Also see Robert R. Blake and Jane Srygley Mouton, "A Comparative Analysis of Situationalism and 9,9 Management by Principle," *Organizational Dynamics*, 10 (Spring 1982): 20–43. For another view of leader behavior, see Susan A. Tynan, "Best Behaviors," *Management Review*, 88 (November 1999): 58–61.
56. Stanley Holmes, "The Jack Welch of the Meat Aisle," *Business Week* (January 24, 2005): 61.
57. Fred E. Fiedler, "Job Engineering for Effective Leadership: A New Approach," *Management Review*, 66 (September 1977): 29.
58. For an excellent comprehensive validation study, see Michael J. Strube and Joseph E. Garcia, "A Meta-Analytic Investigation of Fiedler's Contingency Model of Leadership Effectiveness," *Psychological Bulletin*, 90 (September 1981): 307–321.
59. Fred E. Fiedler and Martin M. Chemers, *Leadership and Effective Management* (Glenview, Ill.: Scott, Foresman, 1974), p. 91.
60. Robert J. House and Terence R. Mitchell, "Path-Goal Theory of Leadership," *Journal of Contemporary Business*, 3 (Autumn 1974): 85. The entire Autumn 1974 issue is devoted to an instructive review of contrasting theories of leadership.
61. As quoted in Michael Kelley, "The Clear Leader," *Fast Company*, no. 92 (March 2005): 66. Also see Marcus Buckingham, *The One Thing You Need to Know . . . About Great Managing, Great Leading, and Sustained Individual Success* (N.Y.: Free Press, 2005).
62. Adapted from Robert J. House, "Path-Goal Theory of Leadership: Lessons, Legacy, and a Reformulated Theory," *The Leadership Quarterly*, 7 (Autumn 1996): 323–352.
63. For path-goal research, see Abduhl-Rahim A. Al-Gattan, "Test of the Path-Goal Theory of Leadership in the Multinational Domain," *Group & Organization Studies*, 10 (December 1985): 429–445; Robert T. Keller, "A Test of the Path-Goal Theory of Leadership with Need for Clarity as a Moderator in Research and Development Organizations," *Journal of Applied Psychology*, 74 (April 1989): 208–212; John E. Mathieu, "A Test of Subordinates' Achievement and Affiliation Needs as Moderators of Leader Path-Goal Relationships," *Basic and Applied Social Psychology*, 11 (June 1990): 179–189; and Retha A. Price, "An Investigation of Path-Goal Leadership Theory in Marketing Channels," *Journal of Retailing*, 67 (Fall 1991): 339–361.
64. See J. McGregor Burns, *Leadership* (New York: HarperCollins, 1978). Also see Frederick F. Reichheld, "Lead for Loyalty," *Harvard Business Review*, 79 (July-August 2001): 76–84.
65. See Michael Frese, Susanne Beimel, and Sandra Schoenborn, "Action Training for Charismatic Leadership: Two Evaluations of Studies of a Commercial Training Module on Inspirational Communication of a Vision," *Personnel Psychology*, 56 (Autumn 2003): 671–697; Joyce E. Bono and Timothy A. Judge, "Self-Concordance at Work: Toward Understanding the Motivational Effects of Transformational Leaders," *Academy of Management Journal*, 46 (October 2003): 554–571; Michael Maccoby, "Why People Follow the Leader: The Power of Transference," *Harvard Business Review*, 82 (September 2004): 76–85; and Jane M. Howell and Boas Shamir, "The Role of Followers in the Charismatic Leadership Process: Relationships and Their Consequences," *Academy of Management Review*, 30 (January 2005): 96–112.
66. A critique of charismatic leadership can be found in Joshua Macht, "Jim Collins to CEOs: Lose the Charisma," *Business 2.0*, 2 (October 2001): 121–122. Also see Jack Welch, *Jack: Straight from the Gut* (New York: Warner Business Books, 2001); and Bruce Horovitz and Theresa Howard, "Wendy's Loses Its Legend," *USA Today* (January 9, 2002): 1B–2B.
67. See Joseph Seltzer and Bernard M. Bass, "Transformational Leadership: Beyond Initiation and Consideration," *Journal of Management*, 16 (December 1990): 693–703.
68. For research support, see David A. Waldman, Gabriel G. Ramírez, Robert J. House, and Phanish Puranam, "Does Leadership Matter? CEO Leadership Attributes and Profitability Under Conditions of Perceived Environmental Uncertainty," *Academy of Management Journal*, 44 (February 2001): 134–143.
69. For example, see Jane M. Howell and Peter J. Frost, "A Laboratory Study of Charismatic Leadership," *Organizational Behavior and Human Decision Processes*, 43 (April 1989): 243–269; Bernard M. Bass, "From Transactional to Transformational Leadership: Learning to Share the Vision," *Organizational Dynamics*, 18 (Winter 1990): 19–31; Ronald J. Deluga, "The Effects of Transformational, Transactional, and Laissez-Faire Leadership Characteristics

on Subordinate-Influencing Behavior," *Basic and Applied Social Psychology*, 11 (June 1990): 191–203; Robert T. Keller, "Transformational Leadership and the Performance of Research and Development Project Groups," *Journal of Management*, 18 (September 1992): 489–501; Philip M. Podsakoff, Scott B. MacKenzie, and William H. Bommer, "Transformational Leader Behaviors and Substitutes for Leadership as Determinants of Employee Satisfaction, Commitment, Trust, and Organizational Citizenship Behaviors," *Journal of Management*, 22, no. 2 (1996): 259–298; J. Bruce Tracey and Timothy R. Hinkin, "Transformational Leadership or Effective Managerial Practices?" *Group & Organization Management*, 23 (September 1998): 220–236; David A. Waldman and Francis J. Yammarino, "CEO Charismatic Leadership: Levels-of-Management and Levels-of-Analysis Effects," *Academy of Management Review*, 24 (April 1999): 266–285; and Warren Bennis, "The End of Leadership: Exemplary Leadership Is Impossible Without Full Inclusion, Initiatives, and Cooperation of Followers," *Organizational Dynamics*, 28 (Summer 1999): 71–80.

70. Robert J. Sternberg, "WICS: A Model of Leadership in Organizations," *Academy of Management Learning and Education*, 2 (December 2003): 388.
71. For related reading, see Dov Seidman, "The Case for Ethical Leadership," *Academy of Management Executive*, 18 (May 2004): 134–138; and Robert M. Fulmer, "The Challenge of Ethical Leadership," *Organizational Dynamics*, 33, no. 3 (2004): 307–317.
72. For more on the servant leader philosophy, see Robert K. Greenleaf, *Servant Leadership: A Journey into the Nature of Legitimate Power and Greatness* (New York: Paulist Press, 1977); Walter Kiechel III, "The Leader as Servant," *Fortune* (May 4, 1992): 121–122; Larry C. Spears, *Reflections on Leadership: How Robert K. Greenleaf's Theory of Servant-Leadership Influenced Today's Top Management Thinkers* (New York: Wiley, 1995); Don M. Frick, *Robert K. Greenleaf: A Life of Servant Leadership* (San Francisco: Berrett-Koehler, 2004); and Joanne H. Gavin and Richard O. Mason, "The Virtuous Organization: The Value of Happiness in the Workplace," *Organizational Dynamics*, 33, no. 4 (2004): 379–392. Also see Peter Cairo, David L. Dotlich, and Stephen H. Rhinesmith, "The Unnatural Leader," *Training and Development*, 59 (March 2005): 26–31.
73. David Leon Moore, "Wooden's Wizardry Wears Well," *USA Today* (March 29, 1995): 1C–2C. Also see "The 'Wizard' Turns 90," *USA Today* (October 11, 2000): 10C.
74. See Barbara Kellerman, *Bad Leadership: What It Is, How It Happens, Why It Matters* (Boston: Harvard Business School Press, 2004).
75. Andrew Park, "Thinking Out of the Box," *Business Week* (November 22, 2004): 22.
76. For more, see Andrea C. Poe, "Establishing Positive Mentor Relationships," *HR Magazine*, 47 (February 2002): 62–69; Harriet Rubin, "The Trouble with Mentors," *Fast Company*, no. 56 (March 2002): 44–46; Steve Bates, "Mentors Help Meld Cultures in Mergers," *HR Magazine*, 47 (March 2002): 10, 12; Fara Warner, "Inside Intel's Mentoring Movement," *Fast Company*, no. 57 (April 2002): 116–120; Stephanie Overman, "Mentors Without Borders," *HR Magazine*, 49 (March 2004): 83–85; and Michael Shenkman, "Born to Be Recognized," *Training*, 42 (January 2005): 42.
77. Abraham Zaleznik, "Managers and Leaders: Are They Different?" *Harvard Business Review*, 55 (May-June 1977): 76. Also see Heather Johnson, "The Ins and Outs of Executive Coaching," *Training*, 41 (May 2004): 36–41; and Stratford Sherman and Alyssa Freas, "The Wild West of Executive Coaching," *Harvard Business Review*, 82 (November 2004): 82–90.
78. For details, see Ellen A. Fagenson, "The Mentor Advantage: Perceived Career/Job Experiences of Protégés versus Non-Protégés," *Journal of Organizational Behavior*, 10 (October 1989): 309–320. More mentoring research findings are reported in Belle Rose Ragins, John L. Cotton, and Janice S. Miller, "Marginal Mentoring: The Effects of Type of Mentor, Quality of Relationship, and Program Design on Work and Career Attitudes," *Academy of Management Journal*, 43 (December 2000): 1177–1194; Melenie J. Lankau and Terri A. Scandura, "An Investigation of Personal Learning in Mentoring Relationships: Content, Antecedents, and Consequences," *Academy of Management Journal*, 45 (August 2002): 779–790; and Shana A. Simon and Lillian T. Eby, "A Typology of Negative Mentoring Experiences: A Multidimensional Scaling Study," *Human Relations*, 56, no. 9 (2003): 1083–1106.
79. See Erik Gunn, "Mentoring: The Democratic Version," *Training*, 32 (August 1995): 64–67.; Also see Kathryn Tyler, "Find Your Mentor," *HR Magazine*, 49 (March 2004): 89–93.
80. Jeremy Kahn, "The World's Most Admired Companies," *Fortune* (October 11, 1999): 275.
81. "Executive Orientations Get Poor Marks in Survey," *HR Magazine*, 49 (March 2004): 12.
82. For more, see Kathy E. Kram, "Phases of the Mentor Relationship," *Academy of Management Journal*, 26 (December 1983): 608–625.
83. Suzanne C. de Janasz, Sherry E. Sullivan, and Vicki Whiting, "Mentor Networks and Career Success: Lessons for Turbulent Times," *Academy of Management Executive*, 17 (November 2003): 79.
84. Good discussions of women and mentoring can be found in Belle Rose Ragins and John L. Cotton, "Easier Said Than Done: Gender Differences in Perceived Barriers to Gaining a Mentor," *Academy of Management Journal*, 34 (December 1991): 939–951; Victoria A. Parker and Kathy E. Kram, "Women Mentoring Women: Creating Conditions for Connection," *Business Horizons*, 36 (March–April 1993): 42–51; and Susan J. Wells, "Smoothing the Way," *HR Magazine*, 46 (June 2001): 52–58.
85. For more, see George F. Dreher and Josephine A. Chargois, "Gender, Mentoring Experiences, and Salary Attainment Among Graduates of an Historically Black University," *Journal of Vocational Behavior*, 53 (December 1998): 401–416; David A. Thomas, "The Truth About Mentoring Minorities: Race Matters," *Harvard Business Review*, 79 (April 2001): 99–107; Robert J. Grossman, "Mentors in Demand," *HR Magazine*, 45 (March 2000): 42–43; and Jonathan A. Segal, "Mirror-Image Mentoring," *HR Magazine*, 45 (March 2000): 157–166.
86. For a contemporary perspective on behaviorism, see Richard J. DeGrandpre, "A Science of Meaning: Can Behaviorism Bring Meaning to Psychological Science?" *American Psychologist*, 55 (July 2000): 721–738.
87. See Edward L. Thorndike, *Educational Psychology: The Psychology of Learning* (New York: Columbia University Press, 1913), II, 4.
88. For an instructive account of operant conditioning applied to human behavior, see B. F. Skinner, *Science and Human Behavior* (New York: Free Press, 1953), pp. 62–66. A good update is B. F. Skinner, "What Is Wrong with Daily Life in the Western World," *American Psychologist*, 41 (May 1986): 568–574. Also see Marilyn B. Gilbert and Thomas F. Gilbert, "What Skinner Gave Us," *Training*, 28 (September 1991): 42–48.
89. For example, see Tom Kramlinger and Tom Huberty, "Behaviorism versus Humanism," *Training & Development Journal*, 44 (December 1990): 41–45; and Alfie Kohn, "Challenging Behaviorist Dogma: Myths About Money and Motivation," *Compensation & Benefits Review*, 30 (March-April 1998): 27, 33–37.
90. For example, see Bob Filipczak, "Why No One Likes Your Incentive Program," *Training*, 30 (August 1993): 19–25; and Alfie Kohn, "Why Incentive Plans Cannot Work," *Harvard Business Review*, 71 (September-October 1993): 54–63.
91. For positive evidence and background, see Alexander D. Stajkovic and Fred Luthans, "A Meta-Analysis of the Effects of Organizational Behavior Modification on Task Performance, 1975–95," *Academy of Management Journal*, 40 (October 1997): 1122–1149; Fred Luthans

and Alexander D. Stajkovic, "Reinforce for Performance: The Need to Go Beyond Pay and Even Rewards," *Academy of Management Executive*, 13 (May 1999): 49–57; Cheryl Comeau-Kirschner, "Improving Productivity Doesn't Cost a Dime," *Management Review*, 88 (January 1999): 7; and Alexander D. Stajkovic and Fred Luthans, "Differential Effects of Incentive Motivators on Work Performance," *Academy of Management Journal*, 44 (June 2001): 580–590.

92. Dale Feuer, "Training for Fast Times," *Training*, 24 (July 1987): 28.
93. See Robert Kegan and Lisa Laskow Lahey, "More Powerful Communication: From the Language of Prizes and Praising to the Language of Ongoing Regard," *Journal of Organizational Excellence*, 20 (Summer 2001): 11–17; and Leigh Buchanan, "Managing One-to-One," *Inc.*, 23 (October 2001): 82–88. For an example of a punishment that backfired, see Steve Powers, "What Economists Aren't Telling You," *Business 2.0*, 6 (May 2005): 32.
94. Alan Farnham, "The Trust Gap," *Fortune* (December 4, 1989): 74. Another example of positive reinforcement in business can be found in Jess McCuan, "The Ultimate Sales Incentive," *Inc.*, 26 (May 2004): 32.
95. Kenneth Blanchard and Spencer Johnson, *The One Minute Manager* (New York: Berkley, 1982), p. 45 (emphasis added). Also see Kenneth Blanchard and Robert Lorber, *Putting the One Minute Manager to Work* (New York: Berkley, 1984).
96. Tom Rath and Donald O. Clifton, *How Full Is Your Bucket? Positive Strategies for Work and Life* (New York: Gallup Press, 2004), p. 57. Also see Kerry Hannon, "Praise Cranks Up Productivity," *USA Today* (August 30, 2004): 6B.
97. For detailed treatment of B. Mod. in the workplace, see Fred Luthans and Robert Kreitner, *Organizational Behavior Modification and Beyond: An Operant and Social Learning Approach* (Glenview, Ill.: Scott, Foresman, 1985).Also see Ahmad Diba, "If Pat Sajak Were Your CEO . . .," *Fortune* (December 18, 2000): 330; and Bobbie Gossage, "Lose Weight, Get a Toaster," *Inc.*, 27 (January 2005): 24.
98. Robert Levering and Milton Moskowitz, "The 100 Best Companies to Work For," *Fortune* (January 24, 2005): 76.
99. Ibid., p. 88.
100. Ibid., p. 82.
101. Ibid., p. 90.
102. Ten items excerpted from a 25-item survey in Anne Fisher, "Success Secret: A High Emotional IQ," *Fortune* (October 26, 1998): 293–298.
103. See Janet O. Hagberg, *Real Power: Stages of Personal Power in Organizations, 3rd edition* (Salem, Wis.: Sheffield Publishing, 2003). I would like to sincerely thank Carlton F. Harvey, Ph.D., for introducing me to this fascinating book.

CHAPTER 16

1. **Opening Quote** Dean Tjosvold, *Learning to Manage Conflict: Getting People to Work Together Productively* (New York: Lexington, 1993), p. xi.
2. Ann Pomeroy, "CEO Challenges in 2004," *HR Magazine*, 49 (October 2004): 18.
3. "The Best Managers: Steven Reinemund, PepsiCo," *Business Week* (January 10, 2005): 56.
4. See Gary Hamel, "Revolution vs. Evolution," *Harvard Business Review*, 79 (May 2001): 150–154; Seth Godin, "Slowly I Turned . . . Step by Step . . . Inch by Inch," *Fast Company*, no. 70 (May 2003): 72; and Jerry Useem, "Another Boss Another Revolution," *Fortune* (April 5, 2004): 112–124.
5. As quoted in Del Jones, "Xerox CEO: Customers, Employees Come First," *USA Today* (December 15, 2003): 3B.
6. See Carrie R. Leana and Bruce Barry, "Stability and Change as Simultaneous Experiences in Organizational Life," *Academy of Management Review*, 25 (October 2000): 753–759; Eric Abrahamson, *Change Without Pain: How Managers Can Overcome Initiative Overload, Organizational Chaos, and Employee Burnout* (Boston: Harvard Business School Press, 2004), pp. 6–7; and Alan Deutschman, "Making Change: Why Is It So Darn Hard to Change Our Ways?" *Fast Company*, no.94 (May 2005): 52–62.
7. Adapted from discussion in David A. Nadler and Michael L. Tushman, "Organizational Frame Bending: Principles for Managing Reorientation," *Academy of Management Executive*, 3 (August 1989): 194–204. Also see Robert H. Schaffer and Matthew K. McCreight, "Build Your Own Change Model," *Business Horizons*, 47 (May-June 2004): 33–38.
8. *Kaizen* at Toyota is discussed in Clay Chandler, "Full Speed Ahead," *Fortune* (February 7, 2005): 78–84.
9. See Brian Dumaine, "Creating a New Company Culture," *Fortune* (January 15, 1990): 127–131.
10. See Tom Duening, "Our Turbulent Times? The Case for Evolutionary Organizational Change," *Business Horizons*, 40 (January-February 1997): 2–8.
11. Theresa Howard, "Big-Box Stores Squeeze into Big Apple," *USA Today* (October 19, 2004): 3B.
12. Based on "'Wall Street Journal' to Start Sat. Edition," *USA Today* (September 16, 2004): 1B.
13. Kathy Rebello, "Inside Microsoft," *Business Week* (July 15, 1996): 57. For an update, see Jim Frederick, "Microsoft's $40 Billion Bet," *Money*, 31 (May 2002): 66–80. Also see John Amis, Trevor Slack, and C. R. Hinings, "The Pace, Sequence, and Linearity of Radical Change," *Academy of Management Journal*, 47 (February 2004): 15–39; and Michael Hammer, "Deep Change: How Operational Innovation Can Transform Your Company," *Harvard Business Review*, 82 (April 2004): 84–93.
14. See Russ Vince and Michael Broussine, "Paradox, Defense and Attachment: Accessing and Working with Emotions and Relations Underlying Organizational Change," *Organization Studies*, 17, no. 1 (1996): 1–21.
15. See Robert H. Miles, "Beyond the Age of Dilbert: Accelerating Corporate Transformations by Rapidly Engaging All Employees," *Organizational Dynamics*, 29 (Spring 2001): 313– 321.
16. See Timothy A. Judge, Carl J. Thoresen, Vladimir Pucik, and Theresa M. Welbourne, "Managerial Coping with Organizational Change: A Dispositional Perspective," *Journal of Applied Psychology*, 84 (February 1999): 107–122; Quy Nguyen Huy, "Emotional Capability, Emotional Intelligence, and Radical Change," *Academy of Management Review*, 24 (April 1999): 325–345; and Cheryl Dahle, "Big Learning, Fast Futures," *Fast Company*, no. 25 (June 1999): 46, 48.
17. For example, see Roundtable Discussion, "Fast Talk: The Old Economy Meets the New Economy," *Fast Company*, no. 51 (October 2001): 70–80.
18. Ichak Adizes, *Mastering Change: The Power of Mutual Trust and Respect in Personal Life, Family Life, Business and Society* (Santa Monica, Calif.: Adizes Institute, 1991), p. 6.
19. See "The 3G Economy," *Business 2.0*, 6 (March 2005): 82.
20. See Peter de Jager, "Resistance to Change: A New View of an Old Problem," *The Futurist*, 35 (May-June 2001): 24–27; Seth Godin, "What Did You Do During the 2000s?" *Fast Company*, no. 71 (June 2003): 70; Seth Godin, "The Threat of Pigeons and Other Fundamentalists," *Fast Company*, no. 56 (July 2003): 56; and Jeffrey Pfeffer, "Breaking Through Excuses," *Business 2.0*, 6 (May 2005): 76.
21. J. Alan Ofner, "Managing Change," *Personnel Administrator*, 29 (September 1984): 20.
22. Peter Coy, "The Perils of Picking the Wrong Standard," *Business Week* (October 8, 1990): 145.
23. Diane Brady, "Act II," *Business Week* (March 29, 2004): 76.
24. This list is based in part on John P. Kotter and Leonard A. Schlesinger, "Choosing Strategies for Change," *Harvard Business Review*, 57 (March-April 1979): 106–114; and Joseph Stanislao and Bettie C. Stanislao, "Dealing with Resistance to Change," *Business Horizons*, 26 (July-August 1983): 74–78.
25. Del Jones, "When You're Smiling, Are You Seething Inside?" *USA Today* (April 12, 2004): 2B.
26. Robert Kegan and Lisa Laskow Lahey, "The Real Reason People Won't Change," *Harvard Business Review*, 79 (November 2001): 86.
27. For example, see Kristine Ellis, "Straight

from the Top," *Training*, 41 (February 2004): 42–44; Bill Roberts, "Empowerment or Imposition?" *HR Magazine*, 49 (June 2004): 157–166; and David A. Garvin and Michael A. Roberto, "Change Through Persuasion," *Harvard Business Review*, 83 (February 2005): 104–112.
28. As quoted in Del Jones, "Product Development Can Fill Prescription for Success," *USA Today* (May 30, 2000): 7B.
29. See Paul S. Goodman and Denise M. Rousseau, "Organizational Change That Produces Results: The Linkage Approach," *Academy of Management Executive*, 18 (August 2004): 7–19; and Craig M. McAllaster, "The 5 P's of Change: Leading Change by Effectively Utilizing Leverage Points Within an Organization," *Organizational Dynamics*, 33, no. 3 (2004): 318–328.
30. See Allison Rossett, "Training & Organization Development: Separated at Birth?" *Training*, 33 (April 1996): 53–59; Joseph A. Raelin, "Action Learning and Action Science: Are They Different?" *Organizational Dynamics*, 26 (Summer 1997): 21–34; Robert N. Llewellyn, "When to Call the Organization Doctor," *HR Magazine*, 47 (March 2002): 79–83; and Darin E. Hartley, "OD Wired," *Training and Development*, 58 (August 2004): 20–22.
31. Philip G. Hanson and Bernard Lubin, "Answers to Questions Frequently Asked About Organization Development," in *The Emerging Practice of Organization Development*, ed. Walter Sikes, Allan Drexler, and Jack Grant (Alexandria, Va.: NTL Institute, 1989), p. 16 (emphasis added). For good background information on current OD practices, see W. Warner Burke, "The New Agenda for Organization Development," *Organizational Dynamics*, 26 (Summer 1997): 7–20; Chuck McVinney, "Dream Weaver," *Training & Development* 53 (April 1999): 39–42; and Ron Zemke, "Don't Fix That Company!" *Training*, 36 (June 1999): 26–33.
32. W. Warner Burke, *Organization Development: A Normative View* (Reading, Mass.: Addison-Wesley, 1987), p. 9. Also see Benjamin Schneider, Arthur P. Brief, and Richard A. Guzzo, "Creating a Climate and Culture for Sustainable Organizational Change," *Organizational Dynamics*, 24 (Spring 1996): 7–19.
33. See Julia Boorstin, "The Making of a Model Consultant," *Fortune* (January 22, 2001): 158, 160.
34. For example, see Joel Schettler, "Bruce Kestelman," *Training*, 38 (November 2001): 36–39.
35. This list is based on Wendell French, "Organization Development Objectives, Assumptions, and Strategies," *California Management Review*, 12 (Winter 1969): 23–34; and Charles Kiefer and Peter Stroh, "A New Paradigm for Organization Development," *Training and Development Journal*, 37 (April 1983): 26–35.
36. See Robert J. Marshak, "Managing the Metaphors of Change," *Organizational Dynamics*, 22 (Summer 1993): 44–56; Craig L. Pearce and Charles P. Osmond, "Metaphors for Change: The ALPs Model of Change Management," *Organizational Dynamics*, 24 (Winter 1996): 23–35; and Ian Palmer and Richard Dunford, "Conflicting Uses of Metaphors: Reconceptualizing Their Use in the Field of Organizational Change," *Academy of Management Review*, 21 (July 1996): 691–717.
37. A successful application of Lewin's model at British Airways is discussed in Leonard D. Goodstein and W. Warner Burke, "Creating Successful Organization Change," *Organizational Dynamics*, 19 (Spring 1991): 4–17. Also see Gib Akin and Ian Palmer, "Putting Metaphors to Work for Change in Organizations," *Organizational Dynamics*, 28 (Winter 2000): 67–79; Richard S. Allen and Kendyl A. Montgomery, "Applying an Organizational Development Approach to Creating Diversity," *Organizational Dynamics*, 30 (Fall 2001): 149–161; and Mark Herron, "Training Alone Is Not Enough," *Training*, 39 (February 2002): 72.
38. For details on how poor "unfreezing" threatened the Hewlett-Packard/Compaq Computer merger plan, see Peter Burrows, "Carly's Last Stand?" *Business Week* (December 24, 2001): 62–70.
39. As quoted in Linda Tischler, "Kenny Moore Held a Funeral and Everyone Came," *Fast Company*, no. 79 (February 2004): 30.
40. For example, see Anita Lienart, "Drawing on the Pioneer Spirit," *Management Review*, 87 (December 1998): 19.
41. Bill Breen and Cheryl Dahl, "Field Guide for Change," *Fast Company*, no. 30 (December 1999): 384. Also see Oren Harari, "Leading Change from the Middle," *Management Review*, 88 (February 1999): 29–32; David Butcher and Sally Atkinson, "The Bottom-Up Principle," *Management Review*, 89 (January 2000): 48–53; and Keith H. Hammonds, "A Lever Long Enough to Move the World," *Fast Company*, no. 90 (January 2005): 60–63.
42. Debra E. Meyerson, *Tempered Radicals: How People Use Difference to Inspire Change at Work* (Boston: Harvard Business School Press, 2001), p. xi. Also see Debra E. Meyerson, "Radical Change, the Quiet Way," *Harvard Business Review*, 79 (October 2001): 92–100.
43. Adapted from "Tips for Tempered Radicals" in Keith H. Hammonds, "Practical Radicals," *Fast Company*, no. 38 (September 2000): 162–174.
44. For practical insights on organizational change, see Scott Kirsner, "How to Stay on the Move . . . When the World Is Slowing Down," *Fast Company*, no. 48 (July 2001): 113–121; Shaul Fox and Yair Amichai-Hamburger, "The Power of Emotional Appeals in Promoting Organizational Change Programs," *Academy of Management Executive*, 15 (November 2001): 84–94; Robert A. F. Reisner, "When a Turnaround Stalls," *Harvard Business Review*, 80 (February 2002): 45–51; and Seth Godin, "Rules for Off-Roading at Work," *Fast Company*, no. 84 (July 2004): 95.
45. Abraham Zaleznik, "Real Work," *Harvard Business Review*, 67 (January-February 1989): 59–60.
46. For example, see Stephanie Armour, "The Mind of a Killer: Death in the Workplace," *USA Today* (July 15, 2004): 1A–2A; John Putzier, "Weirdos in the Workplace," *Training*, 42 (January 2005): 14; and Anne Fisher, "How to Prevent Violence at Work," *Fortune* (February 21, 2005): 42.
47. Dean Tjosvold, *Learning to Manage Conflict: Getting People to Work Together Productively* (New York: Lexington, 1993), p. 8.
48. Ibid. Also see Allen C. Amason, "Distinguishing the Effects of Functional and Dysfunctional Conflict on Strategic Decision Making: Resolving a Paradox for Top Management Teams," *Academy of Management Journal*, 39 (February 1996): 123–148; and Samuel S. Corl, "Agreeing to Disagree," *Purchasing Today*, 7 (February 1996): 10–11.
49. For case studies of problems associated with competitive conflict, see Ben Elgin, "Inside Yahoo!" *Business Week* (May 21, 2001): 114–123; Stanley Holmes, "Pulp Friction at Weyerhauser," *Business Week* (March 11, 2002): 66, 68; and Peter Burrows, "What Price Victory at Hewlett-Packard?" *Business Week* (April 1, 2002): 36–37. Also see "When Bosses Attack," *Training*, 42 (May 2005): 10; and Amy Cortese, "Where Fight Club Meets the Office," *Business 2.0*, 6 (May 2005): 129.
50. Walter Kiechel III, "How to Escape the Echo Chamber," *Fortune* (June 18, 1990): 130. For other good material on constructive conflict, see Dean Tjosvold, Chun Hui, and Kenneth S. Law, "Constructive Conflict in China: Cooperative Conflict as a Bridge Between East and West," *Journal of World Business*, 36 (Summer 2001): 166–183.
51. Cliff Edwards, "Supercharging Silicon Valley," *Business Week* (October 4, 2004): 18. Also see Abrahm Lustgarten, "Warm, Fuzzy, and Highly Profitable: Patagonia," *Fortune* (November 15, 2004): 194.
52. For a good overview of managing conflict, see Kenneth Cloke and Joan Goldsmith, *Resolving Conflicts at Work: A Complete Guide for Everyone on the Job* (San Francisco: Jossey-Bass, 2000). Also see Jeff Weiss and Jonathan Hughes, "What Collaboration? Accept—and Actively Manage—Conflict," *Harvard Business Review*, 83 (March 2005): 92–101; and Kelley Mollica, "Stay Above the Fray," *HR Magazine*, 50 (April 2005): 111–115.
53. See Christine M. Pearson and Christine L. Porath, "On the Nature, Consequences and Remedies of Workplace Incivility: No

Time for 'Nice'? Think Again," *Academy of Management Executive*, 19 (February 2005): 7–18; and Jeff Weiss and Jonathan Hughes, "Want Collaboration? Accept—and Actively Manage—Conflict," *Harvard Business Review*, 83 (March 2005): 92–101.

54. See Dean Tjosvold and Margaret Poon, "Dealing with Scarce Resources," *Group & Organization Management*, 23 (September 1998): 237–255.
55. See "Defanging the Drainers," *Training*, 42 (January 2005): 12.
56. See Bronwyn Fryer, "The Micromanager," *Harvard Business Review*, 82 (September 2004): 31–40.
57. See Tim Ursiny, *The Coward's Guide to Conflict: Empowering Solutions for Those Who Would Rather Run Than Fight* (Naperville, Ill.: Sourcebooks, 2003), ch. 2.
58. Stephen P. Robbins, *Managing Organizational Conflict: A Nontraditional Approach* (Englewood Cliffs, N.J.: Prentice-Hall, 1974), p. 62.
59. See William H. Ross and Donald E. Conlon, "Hybrid Forms of Third-Party Dispute Resolution: Theoretical Implications of Combining Mediation and Arbitration," *Academy of Management Review*, 25 (April 2000): 416–427; and Stephanie Armour, "Arbitration's Rise Raises Fairness Issue," *USA Today* (June 12, 2001): 1B–2B.
60. Brian Grow, "Fat's in the Fire for This Burger King," *Business Week* (November 8, 2004): 70.
61. See M. Afzalur Rahim, "A Measure of Styles of Handling Conflict," *Academy of Management Journal*, 26 (June 1983): 368–376; Erich Brockmann, "Removing the Paradox of Conflict from Group Decisions," *Academy of Management Executive*, 10 (May 1996): 61–62; and Donald E. Conlon and Daniel P. Sullivan, "Examining the Actions of Organizations in Conflict: Evidence from the Delaware Court of Chancery," *Academy of Management Journal*, 42 (June 1999): 319–329.
62. See Kathryn Tyler, "The Art of Give-and-Take," *HR Magazine*, 49 (November 2004): 107–116; Donna Rosato, "How to Ask Your Boss for More," *Money*, 33 (November 2004): 124–133; Anne Fisher, "How to Ask For—and Get—a Raise Now," *Fortune* (December 27, 2004): 47; Kathryn Tyler, "Good-Faith Bargaining," *HR Magazine*, 50 (January 2005): 48–53; Peter Barron Stark and Jane Flaherty, "How to Negotiate," *Training and Development*, 58 (June 2004): 52–54; and Michael Kaplan, "How to Negotiate Anything: Seven Rules for Getting What You Want on Your Own Terms," *Money*, 34 (May 2005): 117–119.
63. Data from Laurie R. Weingart, Elaine B. Hyder, and Michael J. Prietula, "Knowledge Matters: The Effects of Tactical Descriptions on Negotiation Behavior and Outcome," *Journal of Personality and Social Psychology*, 70 (June 1996): 1205–1217. Also see Gerben A. van Kleef, Carsten K. W. De Dreu, and Antony S. R. Manstead, "The Interpersonal Effects of Anger and Happiness in Negotiations," *Journal of Personality and Social Psychology*, 86 (January 2004): 57–76; and Leigh Thompson and Geoffrey J. Leonardelli, "The Big Bang: The Evolution of Negotiation Research," *Academy of Management Executive*, 18 (August 2004): 113–117.
64. Margaret A. Neale and Max H. Bazerman, "Negotiating Rationally: The Power and Impact of the Negotiator's Frame," *Academy of Management Executive*, 6 (August 1992): 42–51.
65. See Ian Mount, "How to Deliver an Ultimatum," *Inc.*, 26 (October 2004): 101.
66. See Danny Ertel, "Getting Past Yes: Negotiating As If Implementation Mattered," *Harvard Business Review*, 82 (November 2004): 60–68.
67. Cross-cultural negotiation is discussed in Élise Campbell and Jeffrey J. Reuer, "International Alliance Negotiations: Legal Issues for General Managers," *Business Horizons*, 44 (January-February 2001): 19–26; Pervez Ghauri and Tony Fang, "Negotiating with the Chinese: A Socio-Cultural Analysis," *Journal of World Business*, 36 (Fall 2001): 303–325; and James K. Sebenius, "The Hidden Challenge of Cross-Border Negotiations," *Harvard Business Review*, 80 (March 2002): 76–85.
68. Stephen R. Covey, *The Seven Habits of Highly Effective People* (New York: Simon & Schuster, 1989), p. 207. Also see Stephen R. Covey, *The 8th Habit: From Effectiveness to Greatness* (New York : Free Press, 2004).
69. A good resource book is Roger Fisher and Danny Ertel, *Getting Ready to Negotiate: The Getting to Yes Workbook* (New York: Penguin, 1995). Also see Deborah M. Kolb and Judith Williams, "Breakthrough Bargaining," *Harvard Business Review*, 79 (February 2001): 88–97.
70. Sean Donahue, "Tom's of Mainstream," *Business 2.0*, 5 (December 2004): 73.
71. Roger Fisher and William Ury, *Getting to Yes: Negotiating Agreement Without Giving In* (Boston: Houghton Mifflin, 1981), p. 104. Also see Bert Spector, "An Interview with Roger Fisher and William Ury," *Academy of Management Executive*, 18 (August 2004): 101–108; Bridget Booth and Matt McCredie, "Taking Steps Toward 'Getting to Yes' at Blue Cross and Blue Shield of Florida," *Academy of Management Executive*, 18 (August 2004): 109–112; and Peter H. Kim and Alison R. Fragale, "Choosing the Path to Bargaining Power: An Empirical Comparison of BATNAs and Contributions in Negotiation," *Journal of Applied Psychology*, 90 (March 2005): 373–381.
72. See Chapter 9 in Max H. Bazerman and Margaret A. Neale, *Negotiating Rationally* (New York: Free Press, 1992), pp. 67–76. Also see Joan F. Brett, Gregory B. Northcraft, and Robin L. Pinkley, "Stairways to Heaven: An Interlocking Self-Regulation Model of Negotiation," *Academy of Management Review*, 24 (July 1999): 435–451; Geoffrey Cullinan, Jean-Marc Le Roux, and Rolf-Magnus Weddigen, "When to Walk Away from a Deal," *Harvard Business Review*, 82 (April 2004): 96–104; and Elliott Yama, "Purchasing Hardball, Playing Price," *Business Horizons*, 47 (September-October 2004): 62–66.
73. An informative and entertaining introduction to a four-step win-win model can be found in Ross R. Reck and Brian G. Long, *The Win-Win Negotiator: How to Negotiate Favorable Agreements That Last* (New York: Pocket Books, 1987).
74. Based on discussion in Karl Albrecht and Steve Albrecht, "Added Value Negotiating," *Training*, 30 (April 1993): 26–29.
75. Ibid., p. 29.
76. Excerpted from Cloke and Goldsmith, *Resolving Conflicts at Work*, pp. 114–116.

CHAPTER 17

1. **Opening Quote** As quoted in David Lidsky, "Fast Talk: Share Best Practices," *Fast Company*, no. 91 (February 2005): 42.
2. Carol Hymowitz, "How CEOs Can Keep Informed Even as Work Stretches Across Globe," *Wall Street Journal* (March 12, 2002): B1.
3. As quoted in Thomas A. Stewart and Louise O'Brien, "Execution Without Excuses," *Harvard Business Review*, 83 (March 2005): 106.
4. For example, see Harold Koontz and Robert W. Bradspies, "Managing Through Feedforward Control," *Business Horizons*, 15 (June 1972): 27.
5. Abrahm Lustgarten, "Getting Ahead of the Weather," *Fortune* (February 7, 2005): 87–88.
6. For material related to the need for feedforward control, see Bharat Anand and Alexander Galetovic, "How Market Smarts Can Protect Property Rights," *Harvard Business Review*, 82 (December 2004): 72–79; Christian Rossetti and Thomas Y. Choi, "On the Dark Side of Strategic Sourcing: Experiences from the Aerospace Industry," *Academy of Management Executive*, 19 (February 2005): 46–60; and Lora Kolodny, "The Art of the Press Release," *Inc.*, 27 (March 2005): 36.
7. See Ken McGee, "Give Me That Real-Time Information," *Harvard Business Review*, 82 (April 2004): 26.
8. Michael V. Copeland and Owen Thomas, "Hits & Misses," *Business 2.0*, 6 (January-February 2005): 130.
9. For more examples, see "Windows XP Update to Be Completed 'in the Coming Days.'" *USA Today* (August 6, 2004): 5B; and Andy Serwer, "Toyota Rolls Out a

New Economy-Class Drug Plan," *Fortune* (January 24, 2005): 47.

10. For discussion of a small business that got out of control, see D. M. Osborne, "Fast-Paced Rivals Silence Talking-Beeper Service," *Inc.*, 21 (December 1999): 40. Also see Anne Stuart, "The Pita Principle," *Inc.*, 23 (August 2001): 58–64.
11. See Richard L. Daft and Norman B. Macintosh, "The Nature and Use of Formal Control Systems for Management Control and Strategy Implementation," *Journal of Management*, 10 (Spring 1984): 43–66.
12. See Harrison M. Trice and Janice M. Beyer, *The Cultures of Work Organizations* (Englewood Cliffs, N.J.: Prentice-Hall, 1993).
13. Andrew Tilin, "The Smartest Company of the Year," *Business 2.0*, 6 (January-February 2005): 67–68.
14. Based on Eric Flamholtz, "Organizational Control Systems as a Managerial Tool," *California Management Review*, 22 (Winter 1979): 50–59.
15. For related reading, see Stephanie Clifford, "So Many Standards to Follow, So Little Payoff," *Inc.*, 27 (May 2005): 25–27.
16. For more, see "Benchmarking for the Future," *Purchasing Today*, 12 (January 2001): 40–49; Ilan Mochari, "Steal This Strategy," *Inc.*, 23 (July 2001): 62–68; Gabriel Szulanski and Sidney Winter, "Getting It Right the Second Time," *Harvard Business Review*, 80 (January 2002): 62–69; and Heather Johnson, "All in Favor Say 'Benchmark!'" *Training*, 41 (August 2004): 30–34. For contrary views, see Jeffrey Pfeffer, "Dare to Be Different," *Business 2.0*, 5 (September 2004): 58; and Lynda Gratton and Sumantra Ghoshal, "Beyond Best Practice," *MIT Sloan Management Review*, 46 (Spring 2005): 49–57.
17. Chris Woodyard, "United Polishes Its First-Class Act," *USA Today* (March 2, 1999): 10B. Also see Faith Keenan, "The Marines Learn New Tactics—From Wal-Mart," *Business Week* (December 24, 2001): 74.
18. See Christopher D. Ittner and David F. Larcker, "Coming Up Short," *Harvard Business Review*, 81 (November 2003): 88–95.
19. Nanette Byrnes, "No Nonsense at Liz Claiborne," *Business Week* (July 5, 2004): 74.
20. For more on strategic control, see John H. Lingle and William A. Schiemann, "From Balanced Scorecard to Strategic Gauges: Is Measurement Worth It?" *Management Review*, 85 (March 1996): 56–61; Joseph C. Picken and Gregory G. Dess, "Out of (Strategic) Control," *Organizational Dynamics*, 26 (Summer 1997): 35–48; and Michael Treacy and Jim Sims, "Take Command of Your Growth," *Harvard Business Review*, 82 (April 2004): 127–133.
21. For a brief case study of financial control problems in the Catholic Church, see William C. Symonds, "The Economic Strain on the Church," *Business Week* (April 15, 2002): 34–40.
22. Theresa Howard, "Ikea Builds on Furnishings Success," *USA Today* (December 29, 2004): 3B.
23. See Del Jones, "CEOs of the Future Get Formal Training to Take Giant Leap," *USA Today* (December 1, 2003): 1B–2B; Diane Brady, "The CEO Really Cleaned Up," *Business Week* (March 8, 2004): 14; Kate Bonamici, "You Do the Dishes, I'll Mind the Store," *Fortune* (November 15, 2004): 200; and Jeffrey Pfeffer, "A Field Day for Executives," *Business 2.0*, 5 (December 2004): 88.
24. See David Henry, "How Clean Are the Books?" *Business Week* (March 7, 2005): 108–110.
25. See David Henry, "Fuzzy Numbers," *Business Week* (October 4, 2004): 78–88; Gail Johnson, "The Perfect Storm," *Training*, 41 (October 2004): 38–49; and David Henry and Amy Borrus, "Death, Taxes & Sarbanes-Oxley?" *Business Week* (January 17, 2005): 28–31.
26. Jonathan A. Segal, "The Joy of Uncooking," *HR Magazine*, 47 (November 2002): 53.
27. See Michael Arndt, "A Boon for the Bean Counters," *Business Week* (November 22, 2004): 13; and Nanette Byrnes, "Green Eyeshades Never Looked So Sexy," *Business Week* (January 10, 2005): 44.
28. Data from Justin Fox, "What's So Great About GE?" *Fortune* (March 4, 2002): 64–67.
29. Lawrence B. Sawyer, "Internal Auditing: Yesterday, Today, and Tomorrow," *The Internal Auditor*, 36 (December 1979): 26 (emphasis added).
30. "The Stat," *Business Week* (July 19, 2004): 16.
31. See Thomas Mucha, "The Fraud Cop," *Business 2.0*, 3 (April 2002): 90–91; and Robert J. Grossman, "The Five-Finger Bonus," *HR Magazine*, 48 (October 2003): 38–44.
32. This list is based in part on Donald W. Murr, Harry B. Bracey Jr., and William K. Hill, "How to Improve Your Organization's Management Controls," *Management Review*, 69 (October 1980): 56–63.
33. See Mimi Hall, "Officials Trying to Reduce Holes in Security Net," *USA Today* (September 14, 2004): 9A.
34. CEO Fred Smith, as quoted in Matthew Boyle, "Fred Smith Delivers the Goods," *Fortune* (August 23, 2004): 32.
35. See Robin Ajello, "No Clean Bill of Health Yet," *Business Week* (October 11, 2004): 58; and Michael Arndt, "Now It's His Shift," *Business Week* (December 6, 2004): 52.
36. Data from Barbara Hagenbaugh, "Citrus Production Down, But Stockpiles Will Pick Up Slack," *USA Today* (October 13, 2004): 3B.
37. John Simons and David Stipp, "Will Merck Survive Vioxx?" *Fortune* (November 1, 2004): 91–92. Also see Rita Rubin, "Merck Repeats: We Didn't Know of Vioxx Threat," *USA Today* (October 14, 2004): 2B.
38. See Joseph M. Grant and David A. Mack, "Preparing for the Battle: Healthy Leadership During Organizational Crisis," *Organizational Dynamics*, 33, no. 4 (2004): 409–425.
39. Christine M. Pearson and Judith A. Clair, "Reframing Crisis Management," *Academy of Management Review*, 23 (January 1998): 60. Also see Gilbert Probst and Sebastian Raisch, "Organizational Crisis: The Logic of Failure," *Academy of Management Executive*, 19 (February 2005): 90–105.
40. See Jeffrey Pfeffer, "Only You Can Prevent Corporate Fires," *Business 2.0*, 5 (April 2004): 76; Holly Dolezalek, "Building in Safety," *Training*, 41 (July 2004): 20; Peter Lewis, "Companies Turn to Private Spies," *Fortune* (August 23, 2004): 24, 26; and Susan Ladika, "Executive Protection," *HR Magazine*, 49 (October 2004): 105–109.
41. See Simon Moore, "Disaster's Future: The Prospects for Corporate Crisis Management and Communication," *Business Horizons*, 47 (January-February 2004): 29–36; Steven R. Ash and Douglas K. Ross, "Crisis Management Through the Lens of Epidemiology," *Business Horizons*, 47 (May-June 2004): 49–57; and John C. Hale, Timothy D. Landry, and Charles M. Wood, "Susceptibility Audits: A Tool for Safeguarding Information Assets," *Business Horizons*, 47 (May-June 2004): 59–66.
42. See Marilyn Adams, "Southwest Manages a Crisis," *USA Today* (March 20, 2000): 6B.
43. See Dale D. McConkey, "Planning for Uncertainty," *Business Horizons*, 30 (January-February 1987): 40–45; Brahim Herbane, Dominic Elliot, and Ethne Swartz, "Contingency and Continua: Achieving Excellence Through Business Continuity Planning," *Business Horizons*, 40 (November- December 1997): 19–25; and Gardiner Morse, "What's the Plan?" *Harvard Business Review*, 82 (June 2004): 21–22.
44. Barbara Rudolph, "Coping with Catastrophe," *Time* (February 24, 1986): 53.
45. William C. Symonds, "How Companies Are Learning to Prepare for the Worst," *Business Week* (December 23, 1985): 76.
46. "Ford Ends Tire-Replacement Program," *USA Today* (April 1, 2002): 2B. Also see David Kiley and James R. Healey, "Ford CEO Takes Recall Reins as More Questions Arise," *USA Today* (August 17, 2000): 1B–2B.
47. Stanley Holmes, "The New Nike," *Business Week* (September 20, 2004): 84.
48. See Woodruff Imberman, "The American Quest for Quality," *Business Horizons*, 42 (September-October 1999): 11–16; "Hundai: Chung Mong Koo," *Business Week* (January 10, 2005): 65; and Dean B. McFarlin and Robert F. Chelle, "Quality Research and Practical Relevance: Can We Find the 'Sweet Spot'?" *Academy of*

Management Executive, 19 (February 2005): 158–160. Maytag, an organization with quality problems, is profiled in Michael V. Copeland, "Stuck in the Spin Cycle," *Business 2.0*, 6 (May 2005): 74–75.
49. See John R. Dew, "Learning from Baldrige Winners at the University of Alabama," *Journal of Organizational Excellence*, 20 (Spring 2001): 49–56; and Del Jones, "Baldrige Award Honors Record 7 Quality Winners," *USA Today* (November 26, 2003): 6B.
50. Chris Woodyard, Bruce Horovitz, Gary Strauss, and Anne Willette, "Quality Guru Now Plugs Innovation," *USA Today* (February 27, 1998): 8B.
51. Michael Arndt, "High-Tech—And Handcrafted," *Business Week* (July 5, 2004): 86.
52. Philip B. Crosby, *Quality Without Tears: The Art of Hassle-Free Management* (New York: Plume, 1984), p. 64. Also see Philip B. Crosby, *Completeness: Quality for the 21st Century* (New York: Dutton, 1992), p. 116.
53. Adapted in part from Ron Zemke, "A Bluffer's Guide to TQM," *Training*, 30 (April 1993): 48–55.
54. See Lorrie Grant, "Don't Let Bargain 'Cashmere' Pull the Wool Over Your Eyes," *USA Today* (December 10, 2004): 6B.
55. For subscription information, see **www.consumerreports.org**.
56. See David Y. Choi and Martin H. Stack, "The All-American Beer: A Case of Inferior Standard (Taste) Prevailing?" *Business Horizons*, 48 (January-February 2005): 79–86.
57. Stratford Sherman, "How to Prosper in the Value Decade," *Fortune* (November 30, 1992): 91. Also see Gerald E. Smith and Thomas T. Nagle, "Frames of Reference and Buyers' Perception of Price and Value," *California Management Review*, 38 (Fall 1995): 98–116.
58. Data from "Fortune 500 Largest U.S. Corporations," *Fortune* (April 5,2004): F1, F52.
59. See Benjamin Schneider, "Welcome to the World of Services Management," *Academy of Management Executive*, 18 (May 2004): 144–150; Uday Karmarker, "Will You Survive the Services Revolution?" *Harvard Business Review*, 82 (June 2004): 100–107; Tim R.V. Davis, "Different Service Firms, Different International Strategies," *Business Horizons*, 47 (November-December 2004): 51–59; and Jeffrey F. Rayport and Bernard J. Jaworski, "Best Face Forward," *Harvard Business Review*, 82 (December 2004): 47–58.
60. Data from Patricia Sellers, "Getting Customers to Love You," *Fortune* (March 13, 1989): 38–49.
61. Data from Patricia Sellers, "What Customers Really Want," *Fortune* (June 4, 1990): 58–68.
62. Excerpted from Peter Nulty, "The National Business Hall of Fame," *Fortune* (April 5, 1993): 112, 114.
63. Data from Toddi Gutner, "Where Phone Service Is Warm and Fuzzy," *Business Week* (July 5, 2004): 103.
64. Based on discussions in M. Jill Austin, "Planning in Service Organizations," *SAM Advanced Management Journal*, 55 (Summer 1990): 7–12; Everett E. Adam Jr. and Paul M. Swamidass, "Assessing Operations Management from a Strategic Perspective," *Journal of Management*, 15 (June 1989): 181–203; and Ron Zemke, "The Emerging Art of Service Management," *Training*, 29 (January 1992): 37–42.
65. See, for example, Richard B. Chase and Sriram Dasu, "Want to Perfect Your Company's Service? Use Behavioral Science," *Harvard Business Review*, 79 (June 2001): 79–84; Anne Fisher, "A Happy Staff Equals Happy Customers," *Fortune* (July 12, 2004): 52; and Lorna Doucet, "Service Provider Hostility and Service Quality," *Academy of Management Journal*, 47 (October 2004): 761–771.
66. Data from Andrew Erdman, "Staying Ahead of 800 Competitors," *Fortune* (June 1, 1992): 111–112.
67. Ron Zemke and Dick Schaaf, *The Service Edge: 101 Companies That Profit from Customer Care* (New York: New American Library, 1989), p. 14. Also see Linda H. Heuring, "Patients First," *HR Magazine*, 48 (July 2003): 64–69; and Jena McGregor, "2004 Fast Company Customer First Awards," *Fast Company*, no. 87 (October 2004): 79–88.
68. See Leonard L. Berry, A. Parasuraman, and Valarie A. Zeithaml, "The Service-Quality Puzzle," *Business Horizons*, 31 (September-October 1988): 35–43; Leonard L. Berry, A. Parasuraman, and Valarie A. Zeithaml, "Improving Service Quality in America: Lessons Learned," *Academy of Management Executive*, 8 (May 1994): 32–45; Leonard L. Berry, Kathleen Seiders, and Larry G. Gresham, "For Love and Money: The Common Traits of Successful Retailers," *Organizational Dynamics*, 26 (Autumn 1997): 7–23; and Kathleen Seiders and Leonard L. Berry, "Service Fairness: What It Is and Why It Matters," *Academy of Management Executive*, 12 (May 1998): 8–20.
69. Based on Paul Hellman, "Rating Your Dentist," *Management Review*, 87 (July-August 1998): 64.
70. See Christopher Meyer, "While Customers Wait, Add Value," *Harvard Business Review*, 79 (July-August 2001): 24–26. Service quality problems are identified in Monica Gagnier, "Where Are Time's Tapes?" *Business Week* (May 16, 2005): 42; and Elizabeth Weise, "Medical Errors Still Claiming Many Lives," *USA Today* (May 18, 2005): 1A.
71. For example, see Steven N. Silverman and Lori L. Silverman, "TOM: The Story of How the Q Lost Its Tail," *Nonprofit World*, 18 (November-December 2000): 25–26; Thomas J. Douglas and William Q. Judge Jr., "Total Quality Management Implementation and Competitive Advantage: The Role of Structural Control and Exploration," *Academy of Management Journal*, 44 (February 2001): 158–169; William Roth and Terry Capuano, "Systemic versus Nonsystemic Approaches to Quality Improvement," *Journal of Organizational Excellence*, 20 (Spring 2001): 57–64; and Richard S. Allen and Ralph H. Kilmann, "Aligning Reward Practices in Support of Total Quality Management," *Business Horizons*, 44 (May-June 2001): 77–84.
72. Inspired by a more lengthy definition in Marshall Sashkin and Kenneth J. Kiser, *Total Quality Management* (Seabrook, Md.: Ducochon Press, 1991), p. 25. Another good introduction to TQM is Arthur R. Tenner and Irving J. DeToro, *Total Quality Management: Three Steps to Continuous Improvement* (Reading, Mass.: Addison-Wesley, 1992). Also see the entire July 1994 issue of *Academy of Management Review*.
73. Richard J. Schonberger, "Total Quality Management Cuts a Broad Swath—Through Manufacturing and Beyond," *Organizational Dynamics*, 20 (Spring 1992): 18.
74. "Aiming for the Stars at Philips," Special Advertising Section, Quality '92: Leading the World-Class Company, *Time* (September 21, 1992): 26.
75. See John Shea and David Gobeli, "TQM: The Experiences of Ten Small Businesses," *Business Horizons*, 38 (January-February 1995): 71–77; Loyd Eskildson, "TQM's Role in Corporate Success: Analyzing the Evidence," *National Productivity Review*, 14 (Autumn 1995): 25–38; Richard Reed, David J. Lemak, and Joseph C. Montgomery, "Beyond Process: TQM Content and Firm Performance," *Academy of Management Review*, 21 (January 1996): 173–202; and William A. Hubiak and Susan Jones O'Donnell, "Do Americans Have Their Minds Set Against TQM?" *National Productivity Review*, 15 (Summer 1996): 19–32.
76. Adapted and condensed from David E. Bowen and Edward E. Lawler III, "Total Quality–Oriented Human Resources Management," *Organizational Dynamics*, 20 (Spring 1992): Exhibit 1, 29–41.
77. "Judge Orders Ford to Replace Faulty Device," *USA Today* (April 15, 2001): 1B. Also see Michelle Kessler, "Rash of Recalls Dogs Tech Companies," *USA Today* (July 6, 2004): 1B.
78. Richard J. Schonberger, *Japanese Manufacturing Techniques: Nine Hidden Lessons in Simplicity* (New York: Free Press, 1982), p. 35. Also see Barry Berman, "Planning for the Inevitable Product Recall," *Business Horizons*, 42 (March-April 1999): 69–78.
79. Lorrie Grant, "Pastry Chef's Surprising Flavors Spell Sweet Success," *USA Today* (May 10, 2004): 3B.
80. For contrasting views, see Christopher W. L. Hart, "The Power of Internal Guarantees," *Harvard Business Review*, 73 (January-February 1995): 64–73; and

Thomas A. Stewart, "Another Fad Worth Killing," *Fortune* (February 3, 1997): 119–120.

81. See Danielle Sacks, "Getting to 'Very Satisfied,'" *Fast Company*, no. 79 (February 2004): 32; Brian Caulfield, "How to Win Customer Loyalty," *Business 2.0*, 5 (March 2004): 77–78; Stephen Brown, "O Customer, Where Art Thou?" *Business Horizons*, 47 (July-August 2004): 61–70; and Roland T. Rust, Valarie A. Zeithaml, and Katherine N. Lemon, "Customer-Centered Brand Management," *Harvard Business Review*, 82 (September 2004): 110–118.
82. Ellen Florian, "Six Lessons from the Fast Lane," *Fortune* (September 6, 2004): 150.
83. See Om Malik, "The 22-Karat PC," *Business 2.0*, 5 (May 2004): 78; Alison Overholt, "Cuckoo for Customers," *Fast Company*, no. 83 (June 2004): 86–87; and Gail J. McGovern, David Court, John A. Quelch, and Blair Crawford, "Bringing Customers into the Boardroom," *Harvard Business Review*, 82 (November 2004): 70–80.
84. Roger O. Crockett, "Reinventing Motorola," *Business Week* (August 2, 2004): 83.
85. Clay Chandler, "Full Speed Ahead," *Fortune* (February 7, 2005): 82. Also see Paul Migliorato, "Toyota Retools Japan," *Business 2.0*. 5 (August 2004): 39–41; and Jeffrey Pfeffer, "How Companies Get Smart," *Business 2.0*, 6 (January-February 2005): 74.
86. Based on discussion in Richard J. Schonberger, "Is Strategy Strategic? Impact of Total Quality Management on Strategy," *Academy of Management Executive*, 6 (August 1992): 80–87.
87. See D. Keith Denton, "Creating a System for Continuous Improvement," *Business Horizons*, 38 (January-February 1995): 16–21; and Thomas Y. Choi, Manus Rungtusanatham, and Ji-Sung Kim, "Continuous Improvement on the Shop Floor: Lessons from Small to Midsize Firms," *Business Horizons*, 40 (November- December 1997): 45–50.
88. Edward E. Lawler III, "Total Quality Management and Employee Involvement: Are They Compatible?" *Academy of Management Executive*, 8 (February 1994): 68–76.
89. "Reinventing Chrysler," Special Advertising Section, Quality '92: Leading the World-Class Company, *Time* (September 21, 1992): 20.
90. Sashkin and Kiser, *Total Quality Management*, p. 42. Six Sigma, another set of quality improvement tools, is discussed in Lee Clifford, "Why You Can Safely Ignore Six Sigma," *Fortune* (January 22, 2001): 140; Kristine Ellis, "Mastering Six Sigma," *Training*, 38 (December 2001): 30–35; and Michael Hammer, "Process Management and the Future of Six Sigma," *MIT Sloan Management Review*, 43 (Winter 2002): 26–32.
91. Based on discussion in Mary Walton, *Deming Management at Work* (New York: Perigee, 1990), p. 16.
92. See Marta Mooney, "Deming's Real Legacy: An Easier Way to Manage Knowledge," *National Productivity Review*, 15 (Summer 1996): 1–8; and Pamela J. Kidder and Bobbie Ryan, "How the Deming Philosophy Transformed the Department of the Navy," *National Productivity Review*, 15 (Summer 1996): 55–63.
93. W. Edwards Deming, *Out of the Crisis* (Cambridge, Mass.: MIT Press, 1986): p. 5. Also see Oren Harari, "Beyond Zero Defects," *Management Review*, 88 (October 1999): 34–36.
94. See Figure 5 in Deming, *Out of the Crisis*, p. 88.
95. Gary D. Fackler, "Barrett Calls for Rededication to Intel Values," **circuit.intel.com**, July 14, 2004, p. 3.
96. Adapted from discussion in Deming, *Out of the Crisis*, pp. 23–96; and Howard S. Gitlow and Shelly J. Gitlow, *The Deming Guide to Quality and Competitive Position* (Englewood Cliffs, N.J.: Prentice-Hall, 1987). Also see M. R. Yilmaz and Sangit Chatterjee, "Deming and the Quality of Software Development," *Business Horizons*, 40 (November-December 1997): 51–58.
97. Deming, *Out of the Crisis*, p. 59.
98. The debate is framed in Paula Phillips Carson and Kerry D. Carson, "Deming versus Traditional Management Theorists on Goal Setting: Can Both Be Right?" *Business Horizons*, 36 (September-October 1993): 79–84.
99. Deming, *Out of the Crisis*, p. 24.